Engage—Inspire—Activate

Child Development: An Active Learning Approach is . . .

*A*pplied

Within each chapter, the authors demonstrate the wide range of real-world applications of psychological research to child development. Students learn to appreciate how research relates to the everyday realities of development—for example, how attachment theory affects development across the life span and how evolutionary developmental psychology helps explain early puberty in girls.

*C*urrent

Students engage in the most up-to-the-minute topics shaping the field of child development—including a focus on neuroscience, diversity, and culture.

*T*opical

Students learn about child development in a streamlined manner without repetition of each concept for each age group. This approach allows students to engage with each topic in depth and to clearly see the continuities and discontinuities in development.

*I*nnovative

The distinctive Active Learning features incorporated throughout the book foster a dynamic and personal learning process for students.

*V*irtual

Instructors and students alike gain more from this course with the free, open-access, robust ancillaries featuring PowerPoint slides, chapter-specific videos, self-quizzes, and "Learning From SAGE Journal Articles" available at **www.sagepub.com/levine**.

*E*ngaging

The text includes evidence-based teaching and learning strategies that involve inquiry into learning. The topical coverage and pedagogical features in this book help students discover the excitement of studying child development, enhance their learning, and equip them with tools they can use long after the class ends.

Students gain a solid basis in both foundational and current child development topics to help them succeed in their course—and beyond.

Reflecting the increasing importance of the study of **neuroscience** in child development, the authors have devoted a separate section in the book to brain development and behavior. They have also incorporated such information where relevant throughout the book in an accessible manner appropriate for students with a limited background in biology.

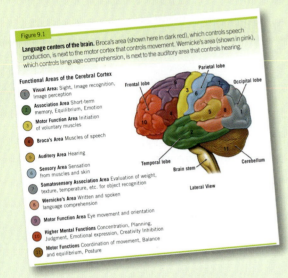

Figure 9.1

Language centers of the brain. Broca's area (shown here in dark red), which controls speech production, is next to the motor cortex that controls movement. Wernicke's area (shown in pink), which controls language comprehension, is next to the auditory area that controls hearing.

Functional Areas of the Cerebral Cortex

1. **Visual Area:** Sight, Image recognition, Image perception
2. **Association Area** Short-term memory, Equilibrium, Emotion
3. **Motor Function Area** Initiation of voluntary muscles
4. **Broca's Area** Muscles of speech
5. **Auditory Area** Hearing
6. **Sensory Area** Sensation from muscles and skin
7. **Somatosensory Association Area** Evaluation of weight, texture, temperature, etc. for object recognition
8. **Wernicke's Area** Written and spoken language comprehension
9. **Motor Function Area** Eye movement and orientation
10. **Higher Mental Functions** Concentration, Planning, Judgment, Emotional expression, Creativity Inhibition
11. **Motor Functions** Coordination of movement, Balance and equilibrium, Posture

Frontal lobe · Parietal lobe · Occipital lobe · Temporal lobe · Cerebellum · Brain stem · Lateral View

"The focus on neuroscience and culture ensures the textbook teaches the students about the most current findings and thinking in the field, and the focus on psychopathology provides students with information that is useful for practitioners and others who care for and work with children."

—Jessica Dennis, *California State University, Los Angeles*

The authors introduce issues of **diversity and culture** at the beginning of the book and then integrate these concepts into each topical area to give the broader picture of how the many different circumstances of children's lives around the world influence each aspect of development.

Bilingualism and Bilingual Education

TRUE/FALSE

9. When a young child learns two languages at the same time, the extra effort it takes to learn the second language slows down the child's general cognitive development.

False. Young children actually can learn two languages simultaneously without great difficulty. Contrary to the belief that doing this might hurt the child's cognitive

Learning to speak a language is a complex cognitive task, so learning to speak two different languages is even more cognitively complex. For this reason, parents sometimes wonder whether being bilingual is so demanding that it will hurt a child's overall cognitive development. Fortunately this does not appear to be the case. Many people around the world speak more than one language, and a growing body of research on bilingualism indicates that parents do *not* need to worry about having their children learn two languages at the same time at an early age (Bialystok & Viswanathan, 2009; Hakuta & Garcia, 1989; Kovács & Mehler, 2009; Sorace, 2006). Children who simultaneously learn two languages reach language milestones at approximately the same age as children who are monolingual (Petitto et al., 2001). However, there is *not* strong research support for the idea that bilingualism gives children an across-the-board advantage in cognitive performance. Ellen Bialystok (2001), an expert in bilingualism and second-language acquisition, has said that "broadly based statements about intellectual superiority are probably excessive and unsupportable" (p. 188), although there is evidence to support the idea that bilingual children have some advantages over monolingual children in some specific cognitive processes.

Learning a second language at a young age makes it more likely that the child will speak it without a detectable accent (Asher & Garcia, 1969) and will be proficient at using the language

Learning Disabilities

As you learned in Chapter 8, *learning disabilities* is a broad term that encompasses a number of different types of learning problems. Here we will focus on learning disabilities that include the ability to understand or use spoken or written language (NINDS, 2007). These problems often co-occur, so it is not unusual, for instance, for a child with delayed speech development to have more difficulty than other children learning how to read. These disabilities may be very frustrating for children. Think for a moment about that uncomfortable feeling that goes along with having a word you are searching for on the tip of your tongue, and you will be able to relate to the frustration that a child with a language disorder can experience on a regular basis (American Speech-Language-Hearing Association [ASHA], 1997–2009).

Reading and writing involve complex sets of skills that need to work together perfectly. When you read, you need to simultaneously "focus attention on the printed marks and control eye movements across the page, recognize the sounds associated with letters, understand words and grammar, build ideas and images, compare new ideas to what you already know, [and] store ideas in memory" (NIMH, 1993, p. 4). This process requires the interaction and coordination of the visual, language, and memory portions of the brain. Children with **dyslexia** have particular difficulty distinguishing or separating the sounds in spoken words, which creates problems when they are learning to spell and read written words (Council for Exceptional Children, 2009; NIMH, 1993). As children move through the grades, the reading that they are expected to do shifts from recognition of letters and words to much more complex tasks that involve concept formation and reading comprehension. Some children with dyslexia may not be identified until the reading demands reach this level. The writing disorder **dysgraphia** includes trouble with spelling, handwriting, or expressing thoughts on paper. Writing also is a complex skill because it involves the complex coordination of vocabulary, grammar, hand movements, and memory (NIMH, 1993).

by difficulties with writing, including trouble with spelling, handwriting, or expressing thoughts on paper.

The integrated coverage of **psychopathology** and developmental differences provides students with a better understanding of the wide spectrum of human behavior.

Classroom-tested pedagogy encourages critical thinking and makes learning about child development a meaningful experience.

Test Your Knowledge

Test your knowledge of child development by deciding whether each of the following statements is *true or false*, and then check your answers as you read the chapter.

1. **True/False:** Infants are born with a preference for listening to their native language.
2. **True/False:** A sensitive parent should be able to tell the difference between a baby who is crying because he is hungry and one who is crying because he is in pain or is lonely.
3. **True/False:** It is perfectly fine to use baby talk with infants.
4. **True/False:** Teaching babies to use sign language will delay development of spoken language.
5. **True/False:** If a young child says, "I goed outside," the child's parent will be most likely to say, "No, you meant to say, 'I went outside.'"
6. **True/False:** Using flash cards, repetition, and word drills is a good way to ensure that a child develops early literacy skills.
7. **True/False:** By the time they reach eighth grade, fewer than one third of students in the United States are reading at or above their grade level.
8. **True/False:** When young children use spelling that they have "invented" (rather than conventional spelling), it slows down their ability to learn how to spell correctly.
9. **True/False:** When a young child learns two languages at the same time, the extra effort it takes to learn the second language slows down the child's general cognitive development.
10. **True/False:** Most children who are learning disabled have average or above-average intelligence.

Correct answers: (1) True, (2) False, (3) True, (4) False, (5) False, (6) False, (7) True, (8) False, (9) False, (10) True

Test Your Knowledge true/false prereading assessments compel students to consider their beliefs about child development—especially in terms of what they may think is "right." This plants a seed that is reinforced as they read about each topic in a given chapter.

> "The advantages and points of distinction are the Active Learning features, the Journey of Research features, the web links, the great pictures, and the wonderful examples the authors have provided. All of these features illustrate the course material and make it easier for students to understand."
>
> —Amanda R. Lipko,
> *The College at Brockport, State University of New York*

Observing Conversation Skills

ACTIVE LEARNING

You may not have thought about how many social skills we use when we engage in a conversation. All of these skills work together to give meaning to what we are saying and to ensure that we are actually communicating by exchanging information when we talk to each other.

Find some place where you can watch people who know each other engage in conversation. A cafeteria on your campus or a student study lounge would be a good place to do this. If you do this activity in class, you can have some students be partners for this exercise by engaging in a conversation while other students conduct the observations. To reduce some of the awkwardness, give the students a topic for their conversation. It can be something as simple as discussing the weather last week, something that has happened on your campus recently, or their opinion about whether we should ask for paper or plastic when we shop for our groceries (the topic doesn't matter very much, as long as it is not too controversial because we want to observe a conversation, not an argument).

As they talk, for 3 to 5 minutes try to carefully observe all the things that they do to sustain that conversation and to communicate effectively. When you have a list, compare it to the description of conversational clues that follow in the text. How many of them did you notice and include in your notes?

The authors have designed each distinctive **Active Learning** activity to solidify students' knowledge by connecting their personal experiences to the materials presented in the book. Individual and small-group activities range from students reflecting on and sharing their own experiences while growing up to seeking out additional information through the use of library resources or the Internet.

> "I really like the Active Learning exercises. I think this is one of the major ways the text is superior to other texts I have used."
>
> —Claire Novosad,
> *Southern Connecticut State University*

Bilingual Education—Sink or Swim?

JOURNEY of RESEARCH

Research on bilingual education is embedded in political, philosophical, and social contexts. At times our educational system has accommodated bilingualism, at times there has been opposition to it, and at still other times it has been largely ignored (Crawford, 1995). This laissez-faire attitude resulted at least in part from the assumption that non-English speakers would want to be assimilated into the great American "melting pot" and would strive on their own to quickly learn English so that the educational system wouldn't need to do anything special to facilitate this.

In the 18th and 19th centuries, immigrants often lived in their own communities and ran their own schools in which instruction was given in their native language (Public Broadcasting Service [PBS], 2001). At this time, several states had laws that allowed children to be taught in schools in the language of their parents at the parents' request. However, by the end of the 1800s, the tide had 2001). This trend was amplified when entry into World War I raised concerns in the United States about the loyalty of non-English speakers and provoked hostility against people who spoke German (PBS, 2001). Eventually this hostility became hostility against the use of any minority language in schools. By the mid-1920s, virtually all bilingual education in public schools had been eliminated (PBS, 2001).

The tide changed again in the 1960s against a backdrop of desegregation in public schools and the civil rights movement (Crawford, 1995). Another important factor in this shift in attitude toward bilingualism was the sharp increase in the number of immigrants arriving in the country. By the mid-1960s, immigrant populations comprised a substantial part of the school-age population in some parts of the country. These immigrant populations—Chinese families in San Francisco, Cuban families in Miami, and Chicano families

The **Journey of Research** features provide students with the historical context for important topics in development. This helps students understand that our ideas in developmental science change as our knowledge grows.

This book also . . .

- **Focuses on what constitutes evidence:** In keeping with current best practices throughout the social and behavioral sciences, the authors explain and then reinforce the importance of convincing evidence within an agreed-upon framework.
- **Encourages critical thinking and analysis:** Along with the pedagogy integrated throughout to make students think deeply about the material, this text encourages students to become good consumers of information on development (as seen in Chapter 1; in Chapter 3 the authors specifically address how to evaluate information found on the web).
- **Emphasizes *how* to learn:** The authors ensure that learning and engagement continue far beyond the classroom. They include guidelines, tools, and resources throughout the book and online (such as the use of databases including PsycINFO and Medline as well as the Internet) to inspire students to delve further into studying and understanding child development.

Comprehensive online resources at **www.sagepub.com/levine** support and enhance instructors' and students' experiences.

⑨SAGE

Home | ⓘ Contact us | ⑦ Help

Child Development
An Active Learning Approach
Laura E. Levine and Joyce Munsch

Home | Instructor resources | Student resources

About the Book

Within each chapter of this innovative topical text, the authors engage students by demonstrating the wide range of real-world applications of psychological research connected to child development. In particular, the distinctive Active Learning features incorporated throughout the book foster a dynamic and personal learning process for students. The authors cover the latest topics shaping the field of child development—including a focus on neuroscience, diversity, and culture—without losing the interest of undergraduate students. The pedagogical features in this text and the accompanying ancillaries package help students discover the excitement of studying child development, enhance their learning, and equip them with tools they can use long after the class ends.

Authors: Laura E. Levine and Joyce Munsch

Pub Date: September 2010

Pages: 656

Learn more about this book

Instructor Resources

This site is password protected 🔒

Please read the information to your right. To access the site, click on the sign in button on the right hand side below.

This site is designed to help create a significant learning opportunity for your students by encouraging active participation, experience and reflection.

Student Resources

This open-access website is intended to enhance your use of *Child Development: An Active Learning Approach* by Laura E. Levine and Joyce Munsch with a variety of study materials and additional resources.

First-time Users

Many of the materials on the instructor site, are only available to Faculty and Administrative Staff at Higher Education Institutions who have been approved to request Review Copies by SAGE.

To create an account, please click here. In order to be approved, you must provide your institution and the course that you are or will be teaching. Once you have created an account and you have been validated as a faculty member, you will be able to access the instructor site.

Please note: Validation usually takes approximately 24-48 hours to be completed.

If you have any questions, please contact SAGE Customer Service at 1.800.818.7243 from 6:00 am to 5:00 pm PST.

Returning Users

If you already have an account with SAGE, log in using the email address and password created when registering with SAGE.

Sign In ▶

SAGE Publications, Inc. | ©2010

- Instructors benefit from access to the password-protected Instructor Teaching Site, which includes a test bank; PowerPoint slides; video resources; chapter lecture notes and teaching tips; long- and short-term course projects; classroom activities and discussion questions; tables, figures, and illustrative materials from the text; and sample course syllabi for quarter and semester programs.
- Students maximize their understanding of child development through the free, open-access Student Study Site. Valuable resources such as eFlashcards; self-quizzes, including multiple-choice and true/false questions; Internet exercises; video resources correlated to each chapter; and full-text SAGE journal articles help promote critical thinking and active learning.

child
development

AN ACTIVE LEARNING APPROACH

Laura E. Levine
Central Connecticut State University

Joyce Munsch
California State University, Northridge

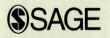

SAGE

Los Angeles | London | New Delhi
Singapore | Washington DC

For information:

SAGE Publications, Inc.
2455 Teller Road
Thousand Oaks, California 91320
E-mail: order@sagepub.com

SAGE Publications Ltd.
1 Oliver's Yard
55 City Road
London, EC1Y 1SP
United Kingdom

SAGE Publications India Pvt. Ltd.
B 1/I 1 Mohan Cooperative Industrial Area
Mathura Road, New Delhi 110 044
India

SAGE Publications Asia-Pacific Pte. Ltd.
33 Pekin Street #02-01
Far East Square
Singapore 048763

Printed in Canada

Library of Congress Cataloging-in-Publication Data

Levine, Laura E.
Child development : an active learning approach / Laura E. Levine, Joyce Munsch.
    p. cm.
Includes bibliographical references and index.
ISBN 978-1-4129-8918-3 (miscellaneous)
ISBN 978-1-4129-6850-8 (pbk.)
    1. Child psychology. 2. Child development. I. Munsch, Joyce. II. Title.

BF721.L5225 2011
155.4—dc22   2010023924

This book is printed on acid-free paper.

10 11 12 13 14   10 9 8 7 6 5 4 3 2 1

Acquisitions Editor:	Christine Cardone
Associate Editor:	Julie Nemer
Assistant Editor:	Eve Oettinger
Editorial Assistant:	Sarita Sarak
Production Editor:	Laureen Gleason
Copy Editor:	Melinda Masson
Typesetter:	C&M Digitals (P) Ltd.
Proofreader:	Jenifer Kooiman
Indexer:	William Ragsdale
Cover Designer:	Gail Buschman
Marketing Manager:	Stephanie Adams

Brief Contents

Detailed Contents

About the Authors

Laura E. Levine received her PhD in developmental and clinical psychology from the University of Michigan. After working with children and families at the Children's Psychiatric Hospital and in private practice in Ann Arbor for 10 years, she moved to Connecticut and was a stay-at-home mother of her two children for 6 years. She returned to academia in 1994 and has been teaching child psychology and life span human development for over 15 years at Central Connecticut State University, where she is currently a professor in the Department of Psychology. She has received two teaching awards, and her research on the social development of young children and on the relation of media use to attention difficulties has appeared in journals such as *Developmental Psychology*, the *Journal of Applied Developmental Psychology, Infant Mental Health Journal, Infant and Child Development, Computers and Education*, and *CyberPsychology, Behavior, and Social Networking*.

Dr. Levine has been very active in promoting excellence in college teaching. She was involved in the creation of the Center for Teaching Excellence and Leadership Development at Central Connecticut State University and served on the board of the Connecticut Consortium to Enhance Learning and Teaching. She created numerous programs for faculty both at her university and at regional and national conferences. Her work on the scholarship of teaching and learning can be found in *New Directions for Teaching and Learning, College Teaching,* and the *International Journal for the Scholarship of Teaching and Learning*.

Joyce Munsch received her PhD in human development and family studies from Cornell University. She was a faculty member in human development and family studies at Texas Tech University for 14 years, where she also served as associate dean for research in the College of Human Sciences for 2 years. In 2002, Dr. Munsch came to California State University at Northridge as the founding chair and professor in the Department of Child and Adolescent Development.

Dr. Munsch's research has focused on adolescent stress and coping and social network research. Her work has been published in the *Journal of School Psychology, Adolescence, The Journal of Early Adolescence,* the *Journal of Research on Adolescence,* and the *American Journal of Orthopsychiatry.* Throughout her career, Dr. Munsch has administered grants that support community-based programs. She was the codirector of the Early Head Start program at Texas Tech University and co–principal investigator for three Texas Youth Commission (Department of Juvenile Justice) grants. At Cal State Northridge, she has administered the Jumpstart program for over 7 years. Her commitment to community service learning was recognized in 2005 when she was awarded the CSUN Visionary Community Service Learning Award. At Texas Tech, she was the College of Human Sciences nominee for the Hemphill-Wells New Professor Excellence in Teaching Award, the Barnie E. Rushing Jr. Faculty Distinguished Research Award, the El Paso Energy Foundation Faculty Achievement Award, and the President's Excellence in Teaching Award, and she received the Kathryn Burleson Faculty Service Award and the College of Human Sciences Outstanding Researcher Award.

Preface

The inspiration for this book grew out of an experience that I, Laura Levine, had several years ago on my campus at Central Connecticut State University. I led a faculty discussion group that focused on a book by Dee Fink called *Creating Significant Learning Experiences.* That discussion inspired me and the other participants to revise our courses in ways that would create long-lasting experiences for our students. I chose to change my child development course using ideas from that discussion. As I used these ideas with my students, I realized that my new approach could be incorporated into a textbook that would make learning about children and adolescents a more active and personal process for students. Fortunately, SAGE shared my excitement and introduced me to Joyce Munsch, at California State University at Northridge, whose expertise in adolescent development and passion for teaching were a perfect match. Both of us are strongly committed to enhancing student learning in our courses by creating significant learning experiences.

Child Development: An Active Learning Approach is the result of our efforts to make this happen. In this book, we take a *topical approach* to child development that allows students to clearly see the continuities and discontinuities in development without the necessity of reintroducing each topical area with each new age group studied. Throughout the book, we encourage students to take part in activities that will help them connect to the content in a relevant way so that they are engaged in an active journey to discover the principles and understand the findings from the field of child development. The topical coverage and pedagogical features in this book have been conceived and carefully executed to help students discover the excitement of studying child development and to equip them with tools they can use long after they take this class.

Philosophical Approach

Challenging Misconceptions

One of the challenges in teaching this course is to help students give up some of the intuitive ideas or simplistic thinking that they have about child development. Many students enter courses on child and adolescent development confident that they already know most of what they need to know about development and that this is "all just common sense," but experienced instructors know that some of the most important information in their courses is, in fact, counterintuitive. Unfortunately, students' original ideas are often quite difficult to change, and many students complete courses in child development with their misconceptions intact. We ask students to begin each chapter by testing their knowledge of child development. Unexpected or surprising answers to these questions draw the students into the chapter to find information related to their misconceptions. In addition, the activities throughout the book encourage students to seek out further information and to learn to evaluate that information rather than accepting what they hear without question. Finally, we provide opportunities throughout the book for students to better understand how our understanding of child development has evolved through the scientific process to reach our current state of knowledge.

Active Learning

This book actively engages students to provide them with a solid foundation in theories, research, and the application of information related to child and adolescent development. Features that engage students are often included in textbooks as "add-ons," but our active learning philosophy is at the heart of all of the pedagogy provided throughout this book. As educators, we know that students must *act* on the material presented in a course to make it their own. We all try to do this in a number of ways in our classrooms, but for the student, reading a textbook is a solitary and often passive process. To combat this tendency, we use the key pedagogical features described below to capture students' interest and turn reading into an active process.

Focus on What Constitutes Evidence

We help students realize that although there is a place for "what I think" and for individual examples, the strength of social science rests on marshaling convincing evidence within an agreed-upon framework. Basic concepts about research are introduced in a separate chapter, but these ideas are also reinforced and developed throughout the book.

Emphasis on Learning How to Learn

Long after they leave the classroom, students who interact with children and adolescents will need to find information to answer questions that arise. We want to encourage students' independent pursuit of knowledge about child development, so we provide them with tools that will help them do that. They are introduced to the use of databases including PsycINFO and Medline, as well as the Internet, as research tools, and activities in the text and in the Online Instructor's Manual suggest ways in which they can conduct their own research and find information on topics that interest them.

Critical Thinking Skills

When students look for information on their own, they need to critically evaluate the content of the information they find. In Chapter 1 we talk about how to be a good consumer of information on development, and in Chapter 3 we talk about how to evaluate information found on the web. In addition, the true/false questions continuously challenge students to thoughtfully consider what they believe about child development and to evaluate the sources of those beliefs. The Online Instructor's Manual and student webpage provide access to research articles that students can explore independently to add to their understanding of topics. The ability to evaluate ideas about children and their development will be beneficial to students who plan to go on for graduate study, those who will work directly with children and families in professional careers, and those who will use these ideas when caring for their own children.

Neuroscience

To reflect the burgeoning interest in the field of neuroscience and its implications for child development, we have devoted a separate section in the book to brain development and behavior. In addition, we have included information on brain function where it is relevant throughout the book. This information is presented in clear language that makes it appropriate for the student of child development who may not have a strong background in biology.

Diversity and Culture

Issues of diversity and culture are introduced at the beginning of the text, but these concepts are then integrated into each topic area in order to give the broader picture of how each aspect of development is influenced by the many different circumstances that constitute children's lives around the world.

Psychopathology

Coverage of topics related to psychopathology or developmental differences gives students a better understanding of the continuum of human behavior. Rather than confine information on psychopathology to a single chapter, we have integrated these topics where they give students a deeper understanding of how they relate to the development of all children.

Active Learning

A variety of active learning activities in the text complement and enhance the ideas presented in each chapter. Activities might involve asking students (a) to reflect on their own experiences while growing up (and perhaps compare those experiences to the experiences of classmates), (b) to immediately test their understanding of a concept, (c) to conduct an observation or interview related to text material, (d) to carry out a simple activity and reflect on what they've learned, or (e) to seek out information that goes beyond the text through the use of library resources or the Internet. Each of these activities is designed to consolidate student learning through personal experiences that illustrate the ideas presented in the book.

Test Your Knowledge

To challenge misconceptions that students often bring with them to a course in child development, each chapter begins with a true/false quiz that contains interesting and provocative questions related to the material in that chapter. The quizzes are designed to tap into commonly held beliefs or ideas that have a strong intuitive sense of what should be "right." Students can immediately check whether their answers are correct. When they get a question wrong, they can satisfy their own curiosity about the topic by finding that question with a brief answer in the margins of the relevant section in the text. Their interest is piqued when their assumptions are challenged. This plants a seed that is reinforced when they again read about the topic in the context of the chapter.

Journey of Research

It is not unusual for students of child and adolescent development to expect that by the end of the semester, they will have simple answers to a number of very complex questions. Of course we can seldom provide these simple answers. Instead we need to help students understand that the science of child development is an ongoing endeavor and that we continue to build and add to our understanding each day. Although it is important that students learn about our current best knowledge, this information is more meaningful when students understand it in the context of our evolving ideas about development. To help students better understand this material, we keep the focus of the text on the current state of knowledge and use the Journey of Research feature to provide the historical contextual information on the topic. This helps students understand that what they learn today in their class may be information that changes—sometimes substantially—in the future as our body of knowledge grows. This is, after all, how the scientific process works.

Ancillaries

For the Instructor

The password-protected Instructor Site at **www.sagepub.com/levine** gives instructors access to an Online Instructor's Manual with a full complement of resources to support and enhance their child development course. The following assets are available on the teaching site:

- A **test bank** with more than 1,500 author-created multiple-choice, true/false, short-answer, and essay questions. The test bank is provided on the site in Word format as well as in our Diploma computerized testing software. Diploma is a question authoring and management tool that enables instructors to edit the existing test bank questions, add their own questions, and create customizable quizzes and exams. After tests have been created, they can be printed, exported into Word, or exported into popular course management systems such as Blackboard or WebCT.
- **PowerPoint slides** for each chapter, for use in lecture and review. Slides are integrated with the book's distinctive features and incorporate key tables, figures, and photos.
- **Video resources** that enhance the information in each chapter. Video icons are strategically placed within the textbook to indicate where a video resource is available on both the Instructor and Student Sites. The Instructor Teaching Site also has an expanded set of additional video links.
- **Chapter lecture notes** that summarize content and provide key teaching points.
- **Chapter teaching tips** that offer strategies to promote active learning in the classroom.
- Long- and short-term **course projects**, **classroom activities**, and **discussion questions** to stimulate creative and interactive approaches to the material.
- **Tables, figures, and illustrative materials** in PDF form for use in PowerPoint slides or online teaching demonstration.
- Sample **course syllabi** for quarter and semester systems.

For the Student

To maximize students' understanding of child development and promote critical thinking and active learning, we have provided the following chapter-specific student resources on the open-access portion of **www.sagepub.com/levine**:

- eFlashcards that reiterate key chapter terms and concepts.
- Self-quizzes, including multiple-choice and true/false questions.
- Internet activities designed to encourage student exploration of child development.
- Video resources related to each chapter.
- Full-text SAGE journal articles with critical thinking questions.

Acknowledgments

We want to thank our wonderful team at SAGE Publications who have helped us bring this book into being. Cheri Delello brought us together and started us on the path. Erik Evans guided us and cheered us along through a first draft of the manuscript. Chris Cardone brought us through the home stretch to make this book a reality. We also want to thank our developmental editors Deya Saoud and Julie Nemer for their help in our writing process. Jerry Westby and Lisa Shaw offered their support at crucial times. We appreciate the help of Stephanie Adams for promoting and marketing the book, Eve Oettinger for helping us through the ancillary process, and Laureen Gleason and Melinda Masson for their invaluable help with bringing the book through the production process. Finally, thanks go to editorial assistants Lara Grambling and Sarita Sarak for all their help.

We also are grateful to our students who helped us as we prepared the book, including Johanna Correll, Alissa Giacona, Amanda Johnson, Sajel Lala, Sarah Newton, Renee Ortiz, and Elizabeth Torres. We also received helpful feedback from the students who took our child development courses and used earlier versions of the book manuscript. They provided us with invaluable feedback on what worked well and what didn't. We thank them for their thoughtful comments and their patience.

It goes without saying that much appreciation must go to our families and friends who supported us throughout this lengthy and intensive process.

We would like to thank the following individuals who assisted in the development of the manuscript through their careful and thoughtful reviews:

P. Gnanaolivu Aaron, *Indiana State University*

Maria Carla Chiarella, *Wingate University*

Youngon Choi, *Skidmore College*

Joanne Curran, *State University of New York–Oneonta*

Jessica Dennis, *California State University–Los Angeles*

Tina Du Rocher Schudlich, *Western Washington University*

Nancy Dye, *Humboldt State University*

Christine E. Fullmer Delgado, *University of Miami*

Hema Ganapathy Coleman, *Indiana State University*

Kee Jeong Kim, *Virginia Tech University*

Mary R. Langenbrunner, *Eastern Tennessee State University*

Amanda R. Lipko, *State University of New York–Brockport*

Ashley Maynard, *University of Hawaii*

Simone Nguyen, *University of North Carolina–Wilmington*

Claire Novosad, *Southern Connecticut State University*

Sarah Pierce, *Louisiana State University*

Lisa Rosen, *University of Texas at Dallas*

Elizabeth Short, *Case Western Reserve University*

Tami Sullivan, *State University of New York–Brockport*

Dana Van Abbema, *St. Mary's College of Maryland*

Paige Ware, *Southern Methodist University*

Sheri D. Young, *John Carroll University*

Finally, we want to thank our family, friends, students, and others whose stories have become a part of this book.

part I

Understanding Development

Why and How We Study Children and Adolescents

chapter 1

Introduction

Issues in Child Development

1

Why We Study the Development of Children and Adolescents

Childhood—The *First* Step in the Process of Development

Take a moment to think about why you want to learn about children, adolescents, and their development. Students are interested in child development for a number of different reasons. Your career goal may involve working with children or adolescents through teaching, being a child psychologist, or practicing pediatric medicine. Perhaps you want to better understand yourself or those you know by exploring how childhood has affected who you have become. You may enjoy the interactions you have with children and want to understand them better, or your interest may be more scientific, with a focus on understanding the research that explains the processes of development.

Your particular goal will influence how you approach the information in this book. If your goal is to understand the scientific research on the nature of child and adolescent development, you will be asking what new understanding each piece of research provides and what new questions it opens up. If your goal is to help children, you will be trying to figure out how to use and apply this information when working directly with children. You may also want to use the information to make changes that will help children develop in an optimum way, such as advocating for children through the passage of new laws and policies that can affect the nature of foster care or family leave from work. If your goal is to teach children, you will want to take information about how children learn and grow from this course in order to maximize how much your students can benefit from your classes.

In this book, our goal is to provide you with information and activities that will stimulate your thinking in all of these ways. We want to share with you the excitement that we feel about the topic of child and adolescent development and to pique your curiosity so that you will want to learn even more about it. By the time you have finished reading this book, you will have a solid foundation in a number of important topics related to development. It is our hope that this will motivate you to take additional courses about children and their development.

To reach these goals, we have incorporated a number of special features into this book that are intended to enhance your learning. We begin Chapters 2 through 15 by inviting you to **Test Your Knowledge** with 10 true/false questions. People often think that they know a great deal about child and adolescent development because, after all, we've all gone through it! But many of the findings in the field of child development are not as intuitive as you might think. These questions are designed to make you aware of some common misconceptions about child development. We hope that if you are surprised by the answers, it will stimulate your curiosity about the information contained in the chapter. You will find the questions and the answers to these questions in the margin near the relevant information.

We have attempted to write each chapter in a way that creates a clear story about what we know about children's development. This story is based on a body of information that has changed over time because it is the nature of a science that as we learn more, new questions come to mind. New techniques for answering these questions develop as well, and the body of knowledge continues to grow and to change. For this reason we have included features called **Journey of Research** to show you how important ideas about children have changed over time as our understanding has grown. Our current understanding will make more sense to you when you understand the context from which it comes.

We all learn best when we can relate new ideas to our own experiences. To this end, we provide our **Active Learning** features. Throughout this book you will find activities that help you feel or think the way a child feels or thinks or remember how you felt as you had different experiences while growing up. Other activities allow you to carry out simple experiments or observations with children and adolescents to see for yourself examples of the behaviors we are describing. You also will find some activities that are designed to help you learn how to find the kind of information you will need when you are working with children, while others involve interviewing parents about their experiences. All of these activities are designed to help you become engaged with the material so you can relate it to your own life and gain new insight into various aspects of development. Each of us constructs our understanding of any new information in a unique way. We want to provide you with experiences that will help you see the material in many different ways. We hope that all of these experiences help you develop a deep understanding of the material so that your new knowledge will stay with you far beyond the end of the course you are taking and will influence how you understand and interact with children and adolescents in the future.

In this first chapter, we introduce some of the basic concepts of child and adolescent development. We will first look at *why* people study children. We will discuss why the early years of life are so important but also why later childhood and adolescence are important in establishing who we become as adults. We will then discuss some of the basic issues about how development occurs. In this section of the chapter, you will learn that even people working in the field of child development sometimes do not agree on the best way to look at or interpret what they see going on in development. In the second section, we will look briefly at *how* we study the behavior of children and adolescents and why they do the things they do. Finally, we will present some ways that people *use* knowledge about children to promote positive development. We also will introduce you to some careers that require a solid understanding of child and adolescent development and provide you with ideas about how you can learn more about careers that interest you.

The Impact of Early Experience on Later Development

One important reason to study children is the belief that experiences in childhood shape who we become in adulthood. Sigmund Freud, the father of psychoanalysis, believed that a person's character and mental life were determined by 6 years of age. Although we now know that this is an overstatement, we continue to learn more and more about how important early

Video Link 1.1
Early development.

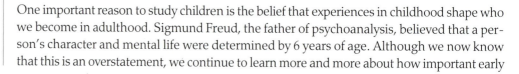

What lies ahead. This book will look at the experiences that influence development from infancy through adolescence. Each age makes a unique contribution to this process.

experiences are for later development. For example, new research findings about the brain demonstrate that the connections formed between nerve cells are shaped in significant ways by early experience. You will learn more about this process in Chapter 6. We have also discovered that early social experiences, such as the formation of a secure attachment to caregivers, are linked to the types of chemicals that the brain tends to produce when we are in stressful situations later in life. These chemicals affect how we respond emotionally, determining whether we are overwhelmed with fear or experience a stimulating challenge when we are under stress. Chapter 10 gives more information about this topic.

One way in which we learn about how early development affects us throughout life is by means of longitudinal studies. As you will learn in Chapter 3, in longitudinal research, scientists study a group of children over time; for example, the children may be tested, observed, or interviewed at age 3 and then again at ages 6, 9, 12, and 15. Researchers who do this type of study can then get some idea of how early development is related to later outcomes.

Longitudinal studies have provided ample evidence that early traits, behaviors, and experiences are related to many adult outcomes. For example, Lewis Terman began a longitudinal study of gifted children that has lasted over 80 years (Leslie, 2000). Although Terman himself died many years ago, others are now mining his data to answer many questions about life span development. One finding is that those children who were rated high in the quality Terman called conscientiousness or social dependability (including the qualities of "prudence, conscientiousness, freedom from vanity/egotism, and truthfulness"; Friedman et al., 1995, p. 698) had many positive outcomes in adulthood, including a reduction of 30% in the likelihood that they would die in any particular year. Conscientious children were also less likely to commit suicide than children who were less socially dependable (Lester, 2001). It appears that even the likelihood of death can be predicted, at least to some extent, from personality characteristics in childhood!

Longitudinal studies. Longitudinal research has found that conscientious children, perhaps like this helpful girl, live longer lives than those who are less conscientious.

How does earlier conscientiousness link with these later outcomes? This connection is partially explained by the fact that conscientious individuals were less likely to smoke and drink alcohol to excess, both of which are predictive of a shorter life span. There is more to the connection than this, but the rest is still open to speculation. Some have hypothesized that conscientious people have better marriages, while others think they may be more prepared to handle the emotional difficulties that they encounter (Friedman et al., 1995). Ongoing research is needed to address the full complexity of these connections.

Walter Mischel and his colleagues have carried out longitudinal studies that demonstrate that self-control in 4-year-olds is predictive of the ability to delay gratification in adolescence (Shoda, Mischel, & Peake, 1990). Four-year-olds were told that they could have something desirable like a marshmallow right away, or they could have two marshmallows if they waited until the researcher returned awhile later. The length of time that they could wait at this age was related to later judgments by parents about how well they could control themselves as adolescents. In addition, children who were able to wait because they distracted themselves so they wouldn't think about the marshmallow were more successful at age 18 at a task that required that they exercise self-control. Although it is tempting to think that this means that learning to have more self-control results in better outcomes later in life, we need to be careful about the conclusions we draw from such research.

Video Link 1.2
Early child care.

This consistency from childhood to late adolescence may indicate inborn individual differences in brain functioning that are present even at an early age (Eigsti et al., 2006). However, there also is evidence that early *experiences* may have a profound effect on later functioning; that is, what *happens* to us may be as important as the characteristics with which we are born. A large national study undertaken by the National Institute of Child Health and Human Development has given us a look at how early child care is related to children's functioning (Belsky et al., 2007). Major findings include that the quality of early care, regardless of who provided it, is related to vocabulary development in fifth grade. Vocabulary is a major predictor of reading ability. A second finding is that children who spent more time in child care centers before they reached school age were somewhat more likely to have behavior problems in sixth grade. This was not found for children in other forms of care. However, the strongest finding is that the quality of parenting during infancy and preschool predicts later achievement and well-being more strongly than any other aspects of care. Children with positive, warm relationships with their parents were more likely to do well later in life.

The Impact of Later Experience

Although the early stages of development are clearly important for later development and functioning, Charles Nelson (1999), neuroscientist and developmental psychologist, has argued that the first 3 years of life are no more important than later periods of development. He likens early development to building the foundation of a house. A solid foundation is essential, but the ultimate shape and function of the house depends on adding the walls, the roof, the pipes, and all the rest. Nelson's focus is on the development of the brain, but his comments could apply to many other areas of child development. He states that the basic form of the brain is set down within the first years of life but it is continually affected by the experiences we have later in life. For example, although the cognitive abilities of orphans who were severely deprived in infancy remain below those of children who were raised at home, orphans who are adopted into well-functioning, warm families usually show great improvement in their cognitive functioning, and the earlier they are adopted and the less time they spend in the orphanage, the better their cognitive outcomes (Morison & Ellwood, 2000). Therefore, very early experience has an impact, but the ongoing circumstances of children's lives also affect how they grow and develop.

For another example of the role of both early and later development, see **Journey of Research: Attachment and Its Consequences**.

Attachment and Its Consequences

This shift in our thinking—from a focus on early experiences to an understanding that later experiences continue to build upon and modify those early experiences—is illustrated by research done on the topic of attachment. Attachment is the emotional bond that develops between an infant and caregivers during the first year of life. You will learn much more about attachment in Chapter 10. Alan Sroufe has made it his life's work to follow children from infancy through adolescence and beyond to see how early attachment is related to later emotional, social, and cognitive functioning.

In 1974–1975, he recruited 267 pregnant women from a poor, urban setting to take part in the Minnesota Parent-Child Project. He and his colleagues assessed attachment and many other facets of development through the first year of each child's life and continued to assess the children at least once a year through Grade 7. In the early '90s, he reported on the development of the children he had studied through the age of 14 (Sroufe, Carlson, & Shulman, 1993). At that point, he concluded that children who had secure attachment in infancy were significantly different from those who had insecure attachments at each age level that had been studied. In preschool, the children who had initially been securely attached were more self-confident, better able to control impulses, and more popular with peers. In middle childhood, the securely attached children were found to excel in everything from physical coordination to

independence to persistence in completing tasks. In adolescence, secure children were more capable of expressing and experiencing their feelings and made more friendships in a camp setting. At this point in his thinking, Sroufe appeared to find a straight line of development, starting from early attachment and going straight through to adolescent competence.

However, in a book chapter published in 2005, Sroufe, Egeland, Carlson, and Collins reported new results from the same longitudinal study, based on data that were then available for the participants through 26 years of age. At this point the outcome became much more complex. Sroufe and his colleagues stated, "Attachment variations represent 'initial conditions' in the unfolding of . . . [the peer relationship] system, but they do not completely specify the outcome" (p. 55). As new evidence came in from the study, they changed their thinking to accommodate the finding that experiences other than attachment also played an important role in determining how these children developed. For example, the nature of their adult relationships was related not only to attachment but also to the nature of their earlier peer relationships. The initial conclusion that experiences early in life have consequences for functioning later in life had to be tempered to acknowledge that experiences all along the path to adulthood contribute to an adult's psychological functioning. Early attachment may lay a foundation, and a very important one, but events throughout our lives affect how we change and grow.

JOURNEY *of* **RESEARCH**

Video Link 1.3
Alan Sroufe.

Understanding How Development Happens

Domains of Development

Child development involves the systematic changes that occur as we move from birth to young adulthood. Some of these changes occur as the result of physical maturation that is guided primarily by our genetic programming. Other changes occur as the result of the experiences we have. We often also distinguish between the physical, cognitive, and social-emotional domains of development. **Physical development** includes the biological changes that occur in the body, including changes in size and strength, as well as the integration of sensory and motor

Physical development Biological changes that occur in the body and brain, including changes in size and strength, integration of sensory and motor activities, and development of fine and gross motor skills.

Cognitive development Changes in the way we think, understand, and reason about the world.

Social-emotional development The ways we connect to other individuals and understand emotions.

activities. It involves the development of both fine motor skills (such as writing) and gross motor skills (such as running and jumping). Neurological, or brain, development has become a major area for research about development. **Cognitive development** includes changes in the way we think, understand, and reason about the world. It includes the accumulation of knowledge as well as the way we use that information for problem solving and decision making. **Social-emotional development** includes all the ways that we connect to other individuals, as well as the ways we understand our emotions and the emotions of others. It includes learning how to interact effectively with others and how to regulate our emotions.

While it is useful to make distinctions between these domains, you should understand that they continually interact with each other. Development in one domain often impacts development in the others. For instance, adolescents undergo dramatic physical changes over a short period of time when they go through puberty. Although these are physical changes, they also have a dramatic impact on adolescents' social development. As these children look more like adults and less like children, adults give them more responsibility, and greater maturity is expected of them. These opportunities, in turn, contribute to the cognitive development of adolescents as they learn from their new experiences. In a similar way, when infants learn to walk and can get around on their own, the acquisition of this physical skill impacts their relationship with caregivers. The word *no* is heard much more frequently now, and infants need more careful supervision by adults because they now can get themselves into dangerous situations. And, of course, infants' enhanced ability to explore the environment gives them many new opportunities to learn about the world in ways that advance their cognitive development.

Issues in the Field of Development

There are some ideas that are woven throughout the history of the study of child development. These ideas reflect various ways we can think about and understand the nature of childhood and the process of development. These issues have been vigorously debated over the years by experts in the field, but all of us have our own ideas about children. You brought some of your own thoughts on these important topics with you when you first entered this class. Stop for a few minutes and think of a couple of sentences or phrases that capture what you believe to be true about how child development occurs.

Domains of development. When we study development, we look at changes in the physical, cognitive, and social-emotional development of children and adolescents.

Do you believe that if you spare the rod you will spoil the child? Or that as the twig is bent, so grows the tree? Do you think that children are like little sponges? Or that they grow in leaps and bounds? Each of these bits of folk wisdom touches on one of the issues that have been debated within the field of child development. We will briefly discuss several of those issues here but will return to these same issues at various points throughout the book.

Nature The influence of genetic inheritance on children's development.

Nurture The influence of learning and the environment on children's development.

The Relative Influence of Nature and Nurture. When we talk about **nature** in child development, we are talking about what comes to children through the genetic makeup they receive from their parents. When we talk about **nurture**, we are referring to the influence of the environment, including the experiences that occur and the learning that takes place. The field of child development recognizes that both nature and nurture play a role in shaping the course of development, but how we have viewed the relative influence of each has changed over time. It also differs from one theoretical perspective to another and from one aspect of development to another.

For example, some aspects of physical development are strongly influenced by your genes. Tall parents tend to have tall children because of the strong impact of genetics on this characteristic, but this doesn't mean that the environment doesn't have some influence on the process of physical development. A child who is quite ill throughout childhood or who has an extremely inadequate diet while growing up will not reach his or her full genetic potential and will be shorter than we would expect solely based upon the child's genetic potential. Other aspects of development are influenced more by the environment and learning than by genetics. All neurologically intact human infants learn to use language. The potential to learn language comes to us through the genetic "hardwiring" of our brain. However, as you know, the way that people use language varies greatly. Some people have huge vocabularies and express themselves eloquently both in their speech and in their writing, while others seem to get along with a limited vocabulary and minimal communication skills. What accounts for this difference? In many cases it is the richness and complexity of the language environment in which the child lives. What children hear and how they are engaged in talk with parents and others are environmental influences on their language development. Chapter 4 will give you a great deal more information on the topic of nature and nature.

Continuous Versus Stagelike Development. Another issue has centered on the way that change occurs during development. Is development a series of small steps that modify behavior bit by bit, or does it proceed in leaps and bounds? In Chapter 2 and throughout the rest of the book, you will learn about some theories in the field of child development that describe development as a series of stages that children move through, similar to the "leaps" described above. Each stage has characteristics that make it distinct from the stages that come before it or after it. Other theories, however, describe processes that change development in small increments.

Another way to think about this issue is by distinguishing between **quantitative changes** and **qualitative changes**. A quantitative change is a change in the amount or quantity of what you are measuring. As children grow they get taller (that is, they add inches to their height), they learn more new words (that is, the size of their vocabulary grows), and they acquire more factual knowledge (that is, the amount of information in their knowledge base grows). All of these are quantitative changes. However, there are some aspects of development that are not just the accumulation of more inches or words. For some aspects of development, the overall

Qualitative changes Changes in the overall nature of what you are examining.

Quantitative changes Changes in the amount or quantity of what you are measuring.

Quantitative change and qualitative change. As children grow, there are quantitative changes that are evident in this photo (for example, they grow taller and weigh more), but there are also qualitative changes that are less easy to see (for example, movement from one cognitive stage to the next).

Stage theories Theories of development in which each stage in life is seen as qualitatively different from the ones that come before and after.

quality changes, and the result is something that is not just more or less but altogether different. Walking is qualitatively different from crawling, and thinking about abstract concepts such as justice or fairness is qualitatively different from knowing something more concrete, such as the capitals of all 50 states. **Stage theories** typically describe qualitative changes in development, but incremental theories describe quantitative changes. Both types of change occur, and that is why we don't have a single theory that describes all aspects of development. Some theories are more appropriate for describing certain types of changes than others.

The issue of how to best describe the changes that occur in development has been highly debated by theorists and researchers who see development differently. For example, you will learn that Jean Piaget described stages of cognitive development based on qualitative changes in the way children think that occur between infancy, preschool, school age, and adolescence. Other researchers have argued that these changes are not sudden jumps but instead happen in a slow, gradual way; that is, they are quantitative in nature, not qualitative.

Stability Versus Change. As we described earlier, researchers have looked at the impact of early experiences on later development. Related to this idea is the question of how much we change during the process of development. As we grow, develop, and mature, are we basically the same people we were at earlier ages, or do we reinvent ourselves along the way? We find evidence of both stability and change as we look at development. For instance, characteristics such as anxiety (Weems, 2008), shyness (Dennissen, Asendorpf, & van Aken, 2008; Schmidt & Tasker, 2000), and aggressiveness (Dennissen et al., 2008; Kokko & Pulkkinen, 2005) tend to be relatively stable over time. However, the specific way in which these characteristics are expressed changes with a child's age. Anxiety in young children is caused by separation from caregivers or fear of physical danger, for school-age children it is social phobia or fear of achievement evaluation, and for adolescents it is fear of failure and criticism (Weems, 2008). The form that aggression takes also changes as a function of the child's age. Young children hit, kick, or throw things when they are angry, but school-age children express their aggression through teasing, taunting, and name-calling (Kokko & Pulkkinen, 2005; Loeber & Hay, 1997) and adolescents attack each other through social means (for example, spreading rumors, excluding people from social activities).

However, the fact that there is a fair amount of stability in some personality characteristics or the fact that there are predictable age-related changes does not mean that development is on a fixed or immutable course. To the contrary, some of the most interesting research that is done in child development looks at the variety of paths that children take as they move through development. When we look at these variations in development, rather than just at the average for all children, we are able to describe individuals more accurately.

Figure 1.1 shows the results of a longitudinal study of oppositional behavior in children from the ages of 6 to 15 (Nagin & Tremblay, 1999). Oppositional behavior includes refusing to share and being irritable, disobedient, and inconsiderate. Nagin and Tremblay (1999) identified four different patterns of stability or change in this behavior, shown by the four different lines in the graph: (a) The "low" group starts at a low level and remains at a low level through the period of time studied; (b) the "moderate desisters" group starts at a moderately high level at age 6 but largely desists, or stops, these behaviors over the period studied; (c) the "high-level desisters" group starts at a relatively high level but ends at a considerably lower level; and (d) the "chronic" group starts at a high level and persists at that level throughout the study. As you look at Figure 1.1, do you wonder what factors contributed to change in a pathway or to its stability? That would be a logical next thing to think about because such information could help us develop interventions to change pathways that lead to problem behavior.

Developmental psychopathology An approach to understanding mental and behavioral problems based on the idea that biological, psychological, and social influences affect development to produce adaptive or maladaptive outcomes.

Adaptive and Maladaptive Development. As we saw in the example above, some children develop in a way that is optimally adapted to the environment, and some children develop maladaptive accommodations to the environment. The field of **developmental psychopathology**

Figure 1.1

Patterns of stability and change. By looking at individual differences in patterns of change over time, the researchers who carried out this study were able to see that some children showed stability in their level of oppositional behavior while others changed over time.

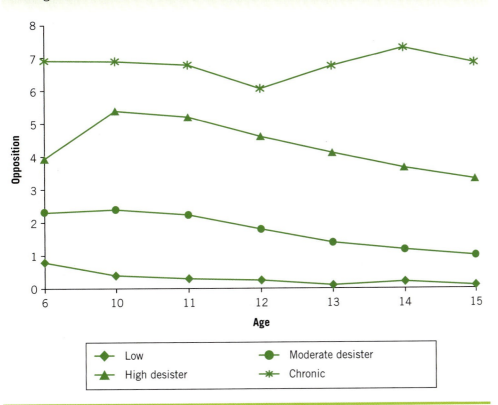

approaches behavioral and emotional disorders as distortions of normal development (Cicchetti & Toth, 2009). Rather than looking at a problem such as depression separately, this approach ties the development of depression to normal processes that have gone awry. In order to understand atypical development, it is important to understand normal development. This approach focuses equally on children's resilience and their disorders. You will see in this book that there is no chapter specifically on psychopathology. Instead, language disorders appear in the chapter on normal language development, and attachment disorders appear in the chapter on emotional development. Thinking about atypical development this way may help reduce the stigma associated with mental disorders because they are seen as variations in development rather than as illnesses.

Developmental pathways may progress in a number of ways. Different pathways may result in the same outcome, a process known as **equifinality** (*equi* = equal, *finality* = ends). For example, depression may result from biological and genetic processes, but it also can result from early traumatic experiences. The same pathways may also lead to different outcomes, known as **multifinality** (Cicchetti & Toth, 2009). For example, child abuse may result in many different long-term outcomes for children that can include depression but also can include resiliency and healing. You will see that development is a complex process affected by many biological, environmental, and internal processes unfolding over time.

Equifinality Different developmental pathways may result in the same outcome.

Multifinality The same pathways may lead to different developmental outcomes.

Individual Differences and Diversity. Scientific research strives to identify general principles that describe average or typical patterns. We want to be able to make general statements about what usually happens. But you cannot spend much time observing children or adolescents without recognizing how different each one is from all the others. Our study of children needs to deal with both aspects of development—those aspects that are universal and shared by all or almost all individuals and those in which we are different from each other. Throughout this book you will learn about general conclusions that are drawn from research. For example, adolescents who do well in school generally have high self-esteem. Children who are raised by harsh, punitive parents are often aggressive. Children who are actively rejected by their peers are at risk for a number of social and emotional problems.

Yes, these are true as general statements, but there also are numerous exceptions to them. Exceptions to the general rule are particularly interesting to us because they often give us insight into the developmental process that we would not have otherwise. For example, children who grow up in poverty and who have parents who cannot effectively care for them are at risk for a number of developmental and mental health problems, but among such children, there is a small group that manages to thrive in the face of great difficulty. By looking at these children, we can identify factors that help protect a child from some developmental risks.

We have learned that the outcomes from general findings can be modified by the individual characteristics of a child or an adolescent. The child's gender, age, ethnic or racial background, and socioeconomic status are just some of the characteristics that may influence the specific outcome in any given situation. For instance, maternal depression when a child is 2 years old has a stronger effect on sons' acting out (for example, being aggressive, breaking rules) than it has on daughters', but by first grade the effect has become stronger for daughters than for sons (Blatt-Eisengart, Drabick, Monahan, & Steinberg, 2009). The maternal characteristic of depression appears to have a different effect on boys than it has on girls. In another study, researchers found that having a mother return to paid employment in the year following the birth of her child was associated with lower scores on a test of vocabulary for White children but not for Black or Hispanic children. They also found that maternal employment in the baby's first year was associated with higher levels of behavioral problems in Hispanic children than in White or Black children (Berger, Brooks-Gunn, Paxson, & Waldfogel, 2008). What is particularly interesting in this study is that the researchers controlled for a number of factors besides ethnicity or race that might account for these differences, including the type of child care the child received, whether there were older siblings in the family, whether the parents were married or not, the family's financial status, and the mother's level of education. Even with all those factors taken into account, the ethnic and racial differences remained. Clearly when we look for general explanations for what affects a child's development, we also need to remember that the same or similar experiences might influence a child differently depending on the child's characteristics or the circumstances in which the child lives.

Individual differences. Characteristics of individual children, such as age, gender, or ethnic background, can affect the developmental process. Outcomes that apply to one particular group of children will not necessarily apply to another group.

It is not just individual differences that may affect general findings; group differences, such as those between different cultures, also have an impact on children's experiences. As you read this book, it is important that you keep in mind which populations have been studied in the research we describe. Some of the findings may be universal and apply to everyone, but some may apply only to a particular population. Throughout the book we draw upon cross-cultural research to illustrate both of these points: research that finds similarities across cultures and suggests that there is a universal process at work and research that illustrates important differences between cultures. We will introduce the topic of culture and its effects on child development in Chapter 4, but you should watch for examples that show the diversity of the lives of children embedded throughout the text. Much of what you will read is based on research carried out in Western, developed countries, but increasingly the study of child development seeks to understand children within the context of their own cultures. One of the important changes in the field of child development in recent years has been a deeper, richer appreciation of diversity.

The Role of the Child in Development. Some of the most influential theories in child development describe ways in which the circumstances of children's lives shape their development. The clearest example of this type of theory is called learning theory or behaviorism. As you will learn in Chapter 2, this approach explores how the systematic use of rewards and punishment affects the likelihood that a child will—or won't—behave in certain ways. The theory of behaviorism was originally based on the idea that children are passive recipients of forces outside of their control. You may agree with this point of view if you think that children are little sponges that absorb whatever they are exposed to or that they are like lumps of clay that parents shape into the type of children they want. If you believe that we are purely the product of our genes, you also endorse this view of the child as passive.

However, other theories in child development have given children a much more active role in shaping their own development. We have already mentioned Jean Piaget, a Swiss psychologist who developed a theory of cognitive development that has changed our way of thinking about how children learn about the world. Rather than seeing children as passive recipients of knowledge dispensed by others, he proposed that children actively explore their environment and in the process create their own theories about the world and how it works. Another influential theorist, Lev Vygotsky, a Russian psychologist, proposed that learning is a collaborative process in which the child seeks to solve problems but more experienced people engage in what he called scaffolding to provide just enough help to allow the child to continue learning independently. More recently, behavioral genetics has described a process of **active niche picking** (Scarr & McCartney, 1983) in which people express their genetic tendencies by "seek[ing] out environments they find compatible and stimulating" (p. 427).

Richard Lerner (1982) provided a concise summary of the developmental process when he said that children are both the products *and* the producers of their own development. According to Lerner, we all develop in multiple contexts that include our family, schools, neighborhood, peer groups, communities, and cultures. Characteristics of the child evoke different reactions from the people with whom the child interacts, and these reactions provide feedback to the child in a way that can change the child. For example, peers react to an adolescent who is physically attractive in a way that is different from the way they react to an adolescent who isn't. Also, the peer response to socially skilled children is different from the response to socially awkward ones. These reactions feed back to adolescents and children and affect their level of self-esteem, which, in turn, will affect their future interactions with peers.

The goal for development, in this view, is to have a good fit between the characteristics of the child or adolescent and the demands of the environment. For example, a child who is easily distracted may have a great deal of difficulty in a classroom, a context that demands that children control their impulses and focus on the work at hand while screening out the other activities going on in the room. However, the same child may flourish in a family in which everyone is always very physically active. Are you an early bird or a night owl? An early bird growing up in a

Active niche picking A process in which people express their genetic tendencies by finding environments that match and enhance those tendencies.

family of night owls has some difficulty fitting in. So does a night owl who is assigned to share a dorm room with an early bird. That is just a small example, but you can think of others.

In conclusion, as you continue to read this book, think about how you conceptualize development and how it happens. You should expect that your ideas will undergo some significant changes as your understanding of this process grows.

How We Study the Development of Children and Adolescents

How do we begin to answer some of the questions we have raised? The field of child development has drawn upon knowledge taken from many different disciplines in its search for answers. Psychology, education, sociology, medicine, nutrition, family studies, and fields such as history and economics all have added to our understanding of how children grow and develop. For this reason, child development is considered an interdisciplinary field (Lerner, 1982).

Research Methods

We also have developed a wide range of methods and techniques to aid us in our study of children. Chapter 3 provides detailed information on methods that are widely used in the field of child development, so we simply want to introduce you to some basic concepts here. The methods widely used when studying children and adolescents include observation, self-reports, case studies of individuals, standardized tests, and biological measures, as well as experimental methods.

Numerous tests have been developed by psychologists over the years to measure a wide variety of human traits, abilities, and attitudes. **Achievement tests** and **ability tests** measure intellectual ability and cognitive functioning. These tests allow the performance of an individual to be compared to the performance of similar individuals so that you can make a relative judgment on the individual's performance (that is, whether he or she is performing at an average level or above or below average). **Personality tests** "evaluate the thoughts, emotions, attitudes, and behavioral traits that comprise personality" (Ford-Martin, 2006, p. 1531) and can be used to identify strengths, weaknesses, and disorders. A particular type of personality assessment is a **projective test** in which people are given an ambiguous stimulus and asked to interpret what they see or what they think is going on. This type of test is based on the idea that people will project aspects of their own personality onto external stimuli, such as an amorphous inkblot (the Rorschach test), so that their responses can be interpreted by the examiner (Lilienfeld, Wood, & Garb, 2000).

Neuropsychological tests are used to assess neurological functioning to identify problems or disorders, such as developmental delays. Medical advances have made techniques such as

Achievement tests   Standardized measures of learning connected with academic subjects.

Ability tests   Standardized measures of intellectual ability.

Personality tests   Tests that evaluate the thoughts, emotions, attitudes, and behavioral traits that comprise personality.

Projective tests   Assessments based on an individual's projections of aspects of his or her personality onto ambiguous external stimuli, such as an inkblot.

Neuropsychological tests   Tests used to assess brain function.

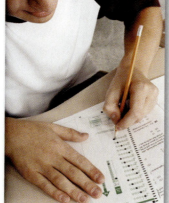

Types of tests. These are an example of an achievement test and a projective test. What is each test designed to assess?

MRI (magnetic resonance imaging), which produces a 3-D map of the different types of tissue in the body, and fMRI (functional magnetic resonance imaging), which measures changes in blood flow to different areas in the brain, available to research scientists (Almli, Rivkin, McKinstry, & Brain Development Cooperative Group, 2007; Conkle, 2009). With these tools, we have continued to greatly expand our understanding of brain functioning. You will learn more about these tests in Chapter 3.

Sometimes we use interviews or surveys to gather information. Interviews can be structured (every person interviewed is asked the same questions in the same way), semistructured (every person interviewed is asked the same set of basic questions, but the interviewer asks additional questions to follow up on the answers the interviewee provides), or unstructured (the questions asked are open, and the interviewer can be very flexible in choosing those questions).

Each of these methods has a different set of advantages and disadvantages. The goal of a researcher is always to choose the method that is most appropriate for studying whatever he or she is interested in. **Journey of Research: From Baby Diaries to Structural Equation Modeling** gives you a sense of how methods used to study development have changed over time and specifically how our use of statistics has evolved over the last hundred years or so to help us answer complex questions about development.

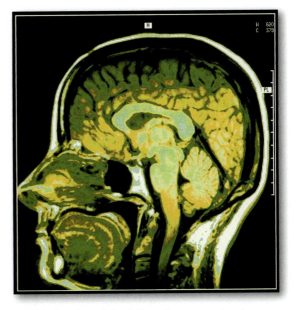

MRI side view of a man's head. Magnetic resonance imaging (MRI) can be used to diagnose diseases of the brain or nervous system, but it can also be used in research to study brain structure.

From Baby Diaries to Structural Equation Modeling

Early studies of children relied upon one of the simplest scientific methods: careful observation. A number of people who have influenced the field of child development learned a great deal about children and development by carefully observing their own children, using what was known as a **baby diary**. Charles Darwin in the 19th century, and Arnold Gesell and Jean Piaget in the early 20th century, used this technique. Darwin (1877) documented the changes in emotional development in his own son, and Piaget (1962) used observations of his own children to develop and test some important ideas about cognitive development. Arnold Gesell and Frances Ilg (1943) used photography to document their observations of the physical milestones that young children pass through.

Observation continues to be essential to understanding children's behavior; however, the way that we are able to analyze these observations has changed radically. As our understanding of child development has grown, so has the complexity of the questions we ask and, consequently, so have the analytic techniques we use to answer those questions. We have very sophisticated statistical techniques today that, with the aid of computers, allow us to examine intricate patterns of relationships. These new techniques allow us to ask new types of questions, and this, too, helps us develop a deeper understanding of children's development. Today psychologists use techniques called path analysis and structural equation modeling to examine how multiple aspects of children's lives and experiences are interrelated across time. Figure 1.2 illustrates how complex such an analysis can be (Dubow, Boxer, & Huesmann, 2008).

JOURNEY *of* RESEARCH

Baby diary A careful recording of the development of one's own children.

(Continued)

(Continued)

Figure 1.2

No simple answers. The researchers who carried out this study used path analysis to examine how characteristics of a child and the child's family situation at age 8 were related to problem drinking in adulthood four decades later.

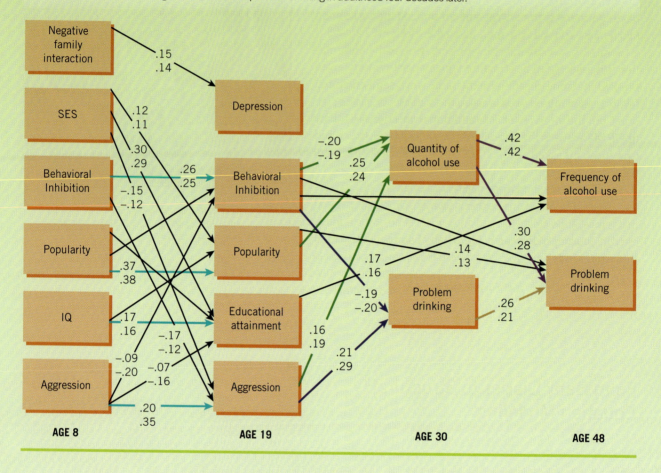

Don't be intimidated by the complexity of this diagram. In this book we will interpret research findings for you wherever necessary, and if you continue to take courses in child development, you will begin to develop the ability to do this on your own. Although the diagram is complex, the findings are fairly straightforward if you break them down.

First, child characteristics were pretty stable from age 8 to age 19 (shown in light blue in Figure 1.2). For example, aggressive children tended to remain aggressive; popular ones remained popular. Second, adolescents who were more shy, quiet, and cautious (what this research calls "behavioral inhibition") at age 19 reported lower levels of consumption of alcohol at age 30, but those who were popular and/ or aggressive reported higher levels. These different

pathways are shown in green. Likewise, adolescents who were behaviorally inhibited at age 19 report less problem drinking at age 30, and those who were aggressive reported more problem drinking (shown in dark blue). Finally, the quantity of alcohol consumed at age 30 predicted both the frequency of alcohol use and problem drinking at age 48 (shown in purple), and problem drinking at age 30 was related to problem drinking later at age 48 (shown in tan). Note that when the correlation coefficient (the number appearing on an arrow) is negative, it indicates a negative relationship, so as the value of a variable goes up, the value of the related variable goes down. Taken together, these findings are not too surprising, but they do illustrate the pathways that link these behaviors together.

Being a Good Consumer of Developmental Information

Information about children and child development is everywhere. Books, magazines, television programs, and the Internet have an almost endless amount of information. As a result, you are bringing your own understanding of child development with you into this class. Those ideas are based on what you have heard, what you have read, and what you have experienced or witnessed in your own journey through development to this point in time. We said at the beginning of the chapter that we want to challenge you to examine these preconceived ideas and to test them against the research we have included in this textbook. We believe that a great deal of what you encounter in this book is going to become a part of your understanding of how children and adolescents develop after you complete this course. However, long after this course is done, you will still be getting information from all those same sources—books, magazines, television, and personal experiences—and we want you to be able to sift through all this information in a way that helps you stay well informed about those topics that interest you.

To become a good consumer of this information now and in the future, these are some of the things that you should consider:

Know the Source of Your Information

In the 1970s, "Question authority!" was a popular saying. This is not a bad idea when you are evaluating the legitimacy of supposedly scientific information that you hear on the topic of child development. On a regular basis, we see experts on television who comment on recent news events or new research findings. Some of them even have television shows of their own. Undoubtedly some of these experts have excellent qualifications, but before accepting everything you hear as a complete and frank assessment of the information being reported, you should have some idea of what those qualifications are.

Articles published in professional journals go through a process in which other people who are knowledgeable about the topic of an article critique it and make suggestions for improvement before it is published. This is called a **peer review**. Articles also usually identify the authors' professional affiliation. They may be faculty members at a university or be employed by a research institute or a government agency. There also may be information about where the authors received their education and professional training. By using the electronic databases at your campus library, you can do a search by an author's name to see his or her body of published work. Most researchers build their expertise in a few specific areas over a period of years, but remember that just because someone with experience and expertise says something, it does not necessarily mean that it is true.

Peer review A process in which professionals critique an article and make suggestions for improvement before it is published.

Video Link 1.4
Peer review.

Something Old, Something New

A science is an organized body of knowledge that is accumulated over time, so that body of knowledge changes and grows. New ideas come into existence, and old ideas fall out of favor as they are replaced with newer and better information. As we mentioned earlier, the **Journey of Research** features will give you a sense of how our thinking on particular topics has changed over time. For instance, autism was once attributed to (or perhaps we should say "was blamed on") mothers who were cold and rejecting toward their children, but today research on autism focuses on differences in the structure and functioning of the brain in autistic children as an underlying cause. The fact that an idea has been around for a long time—or that many people endorse an idea—does not necessarily mean that the idea is true. Remember that for a very long time, everyone believed that the earth was flat. Likewise, just because something represents our newest insights or ideas, it doesn't necessarily mean that this idea is better than what we had previously thought. All new ideas that enter a science are subjected to review and critique by people in the field, and research findings need to be tested and **replicated** by others before we can gain confidence that they are accurate and reliable. The best suggestion is to be open to new ideas but to

Replicate To find the same results as in a previous research study.

be cautious about jumping on a bandwagon until there is good evidence that the bandwagon is going in the right direction. If new ideas cannot be replicated, they are not a fact—they are a fluke!

On this point, Kenneth S. Pope (1996) said:

> Science works best when claims and hypotheses can be continually questioned. That which tends to disallow doubt and discredit anyone who disagrees is unlikely to foster the scientific venture or promote public policies and clinical practices based on scientific principles. Each scientific claim should prevail or fall on its research validation and logic. (p. 971)

Become a Critical Thinker

As you learn about child development, don't hesitate to look for answers to your own questions. No single book can contain all the information you need on any topic. There is a wealth of information available to us today, so seek out divergent opinions on topics that intrigue you. Expose yourself to a wide range of ideas. You will probably find some ideas that make sense to you and some that are harder for you to accept, but keep an open mind and don't stop asking questions and learning more about what interests you. Just be sure that you turn to credible sources of information as you go through this process.

Beware Generalizations

Did you hear the story about the friend of a friend who had something amazing happen? Another thing that you need to guard against when thinking about child development is taking one particular instance or example—no matter how amazing it is—and generalizing it to other people. It is easy to think about things that we have experienced ourselves and to assume that others have had the same or similar experiences with the same or similar consequences. As we noted above, exceptions to the rule can always be interesting and we can learn from them, but saying that is different from thinking that those exceptions *are* the rule.

Your own experiences are meaningful and real. They all become part of what has made you the person you are today and help shape the person you will be tomorrow. That fact is never in question. We are not denying the validity of your experiences, but you need to realize that they may not represent the average or typical experience of other people. Trying to generalize from one particular experience to general statements is always dangerous. When samples are chosen for research, we try to make them representative of the people we are interested in studying so we can generalize the results from the research sample to that general population. It is not always possible to put together large samples for research, but when generalizing from small samples, we need to be cautious.

The converse of this is also true. When you read about conclusions drawn from research, they may not describe what your personal experiences were. That does not mean that the research is invalid. Rather it means that the research describes the outcome for groups, not every individual within a group. When the topic of spanking (and the problems associated with it) is discussed in class, there often will be a student or two who want to say that they were spanked as children and they turned out just fine. They are probably right, because spanking doesn't affect all children in the same way. One child may have her feelings hurt and withdraw when she is spanked, while another child may feel angry and aggressive in the same circumstance. Or a young child may accept a spanking as a legitimate punishment by a parent, but an older child or teenagers might not feel the same way. These individual differences can lead to different outcomes. However, across many children, the relationship between physical punishment and increased aggressiveness in the child is a reliable finding. Likewise, saying that men are more aggressive than women does not mean that every man is more aggressive than any woman. This means that *on average* there is a difference between the groups but within those groups there is a good deal of individual variability.

Perceptual Bias

It is easier to spot something you are looking for—or to overlook or disregard something that you weren't expecting—rather than the other way around. This **perceptual bias** can have an effect on your learning. It will be easier for you to remember the facts you encounter that fit well with your expectations and to forget or ignore those that don't. That is one reason why we are using misconceptions to identify ideas that you may have in your mind before you begin reading each of the following chapters in this book. This can help you pay more attention to those ideas so you can look at the evidence presented in the book and then decide whether you still believe what you previously thought was true.

Perceptual bias The tendency to see and understand something in the way you expected.

"It's All Common Sense"

Finally, students sometimes think that child development is just common sense. Unfortunately it isn't that simple. Some findings sound like common sense, but others are counterintuitive. Sometimes we fall back on what is called **folk wisdom** to describe our beliefs about development. As we mentioned at the beginning of this chapter, we need to be careful not to confuse folk wisdom or popular beliefs with scientific evidence. Folk wisdom may have a grain of truth in it, but it usually does not help us understand the reasons for what we see. Sometimes folk wisdom is simply wrong. Do you believe that sticks and stones may break your bones but names will never hurt you? That "wisdom" may not be true for children who are victims of verbal bullying. And other times folk wisdom is contradictory. Do you believe that opposites attract . . . or that birds of a feather flock together?

Folk wisdom Knowledge that is widely accepted but has not been scientifically tested.

Throughout this book we will challenge you to examine your own beliefs about child development. **Active Learning: Testing Your Knowledge of Child Development** provides a selection of questions that appear in the chapters that follow. Test your current knowledge about these topics.

Testing Your Knowledge of Child Development

ACTIVE LEARNING

1	True	False	Genes have been found to play a role in the development of almost all behaviors that have been studied.
2	True	False	Infants who are born to women with HIV are almost certain to have the disease themselves.
3	True	False	Humans use only 10% of their brain.
4	True	False	Results from intelligence testing indicate that people are getting smarter and smarter.
5	True	False	It is perfectly fine to use baby talk with infants.
6	True	False	People all over the world understand each other's emotional expressions.
7	True	False	A good deal of parent-adolescent conflict is normal in families with adolescents.
8	True	False	Many children and teens these days are "overscheduled," spending most of their time after school in multiple organized activities, such as sports and music lessons.
9	True	False	The incidence of stepfamilies in the United States has not changed much from 1900 to today.
10	True	False	Adults who were abused as children are very likely to become abusive parents themselves.

(Continued)

(Continued)

Answers:

1. **True.** Behavioral genetics has shown that almost all behaviors studied have some genetic component. However, different traits and behaviors are more or less heritable (Chapter 4).

2. **False.** Infants born to mothers with HIV who are receiving no treatment have a 1-in-4 chance of having the disease. Infants born to mothers with HIV who *are* receiving treatment (such as AZT) have only a 2% chance of having the disease themselves (Chapter 5).

3. **False.** Neurologist Barry Gordon, who studies the brain, finds the notion that we use only 10% of our brain ridiculous. He says, "It turns out . . . that we use virtually every part of the brain, and that [most of] the brain is active almost all the time" (Boyd, 2008, para. 5) (Chapter 6).

4. **True.** In the past century, people have scored higher and higher on standardized tests of intelligence. As a result, the test scores have had to be readjusted to reset what level of performance is considered "average" (Chapter 8).

5. **True.** The way that adults often talk to babies—in a high-pitched voice, with a great deal of exaggeration, and in a singsong rhythm—is actually well suited to the hearing capabilities and preferences of a baby. Babies pay attention to us when we talk this way, and doing it will not delay their language development (Chapter 9).

6. **False.** Although some aspects of emotional expression appear to be universal, there are cultural differences in how we understand others' emotions (Chapter 10).

7. **False.** A good deal of parent-adolescent conflict occurs in *some* families, but conflict is not overwhelming or pervasive in most families. And, when conflict occurs, it is usually about everyday issues like homework or messy rooms rather than about explosive issues like sexual behavior or substance use (Chapter 12).

8. **False.** A small minority of children and teens could be described as "overscheduled," but 40% are not involved in any after-school activities (Chapter 13).

9. **True.** The incidence (or likelihood of occurrence) of stepfamilies is similar in these two periods of time, but the reason for the creation of stepfamilies has changed. Today they are primarily due to divorce, but in the past they were due to death of one of the parents or marital desertion (Chapter 14).

10. **False.** This is one of the most serious misunderstandings about child abuse. About 30% of abused children perpetuate the cycle by repeating abuse in the next generation, but the majority of abused children do not. They successfully break that vicious cycle when they reach adulthood (Chapter 15).

How did you do? Many of these questions represent common beliefs; therefore, it wouldn't be surprising if you got a number of the questions wrong. We hope that seeing discrepancies between what you think is true and what research evidence has shown will make you eager to learn more about these topics. The explanations you will find in the chapters are more extensive than the brief ones we provide here, so you will learn a great deal more about each of these topics.

How We Apply Child Development Knowledge to Support Optimal Development

In this section we will show that what you will learn from this book about children and adolescents can be used in many ways to improve their lives. An understanding of how children think, feel, learn, and grow, as well as how they change and stay the same, is essential to the ability to foster positive development. This understanding can help parents and family members; professionals who work with children and families such as psychologists, social workers, counselors, and child development specialists; and people who create and carry out policies and programs that affect children and their families.

Parents and Family Members

A solid understanding of child development can help all parents. Many parents read books, search websites, and browse magazines designed to help them understand their children so they can become better parents. The shelves of bookstores are filled with books on parenting, some based on solid research and some based on untested ideas. How useful any of these sources of information will be to an interested parent depends largely upon how solidly the information in them is grounded in scientific research. Parents' understanding of their children's needs and abilities at each stage of development helps them respond empathically as well as provide the appropriate type of stimulation to support their children's growth and development.

For some parents, knowledge about child development is even more crucial. Parents who are at higher risk for child abuse and neglect can benefit from intervention programs that help them understand their children better and provide support for their efforts at positive parenting. Teen parents are more likely than older parents to lack knowledge about what to expect about their child's development, so they may underestimate what children understand and can do. As a result, they may not provide the kind of stimulation that will help their child's mind grow. On the other hand, they may expect their children to be able to do things they cannot yet do and become impatient or punitive when their child does not live up to these unrealistic expectations (Culp, Culp, Blankemeyer, & Passmark, 1998). When teen parents are provided with information about child development, along with other types of support from a trained home visitor, their ability to empathize with their child increases, and they understand more about how to discipline their child without

Programs to support parents. Incarcerated parents have been helped by programs such as The Family Nurturing Program. Such programs help parents maintain a relationship with their children while they are physically separated from them and also help the parents learn how to promote positive development in their children.

resorting to physical punishment. Teens also are more likely than older mothers to have children in order to have "someone who loves me," not realizing that children do not make up for the lack of parenting they may have experienced as they were growing up. Home visitation programs can result in an increased understanding that parents comfort their children and not the other way around (Culp et al., 1998). Another high-risk group that can benefit from parenting interventions is incarcerated parents. When one group of incarcerated parents took part in a program called The Family Nurturing Program, many showed the same kind of gains as those found with the teenagers. They became more empathic and less punitive and developed more realistic expectations for their children (Palusci, Crum, Bliss, & Bavolek, 2008).

Child Development Professionals

An understanding of child development is essential to the work that many professionals do with children and families. The role that it plays in careers such as being a child psychologist or teacher might be obvious, but one of the most exciting things about this field is its relevance to a wide range of careers. We recognize that students today are interested in knowing where their education can eventually lead them and are hungry for information about future careers. It's important that you know where you can find good information to answer your questions. If you are taking this course because you are considering a career related to child development, how much do you know about the career you are thinking about entering? You will have a chance to assess your current knowledge about a career related to child development a bit later in this chapter when you complete **Active Learning: How Much Do You Know About Careers in Child Development?**

Video Link 1.5
Career: psychologist.

Video Link 1.6
Career: child care.

Careers in child development. Knowledge about child development is essential to people working in many different careers (including pediatricians, teachers, social workers, counselors, therapists, lawyers, and nurses). If you are interested in a career working with children, there are many opportunities available to you.

The Bureau of Labor Statistics (2010) has assembled current information on a large number of careers. Go to its website at www.bls.gov and type "Occupational Outlook Handbook" into the search box. There also is likely to be a copy of the Bureau of Labor Statistics *Occupational Outlook Handbook* in your campus library. The *Handbook* is revised every 2 years, so it always contains up-to-date information.

Click on the first letter of the career you are interested in exploring to bring up a list of all the careers starting with that letter and search down the list for the one you are interested in, or type the name of your career in the search box on the page. For each career, you will find information on the following:

- The nature of the work—This section provides information on job conditions and responsibilities, including the work environments in which people in this career work.
- Training, other qualifications, and advancement—This describes the education and training that are required both for entry into the field and for advancement within this career. You will also find information on any certifications or licenses that are required to work in this profession. Certification and licensure usually require taking some sort of test to assess your competency in the field.
- Employment—This section describes where these professionals are employed (in government agencies, private employment, schools or medical settings, etc.).
- Job outlook—Here you will find current information on the job prospects for this career. You'll learn how many people are currently employed in it and whether the demand for professionals in this career is increasing or decreasing (and at what rate).
- Projections data—This section shows you the projection for how demand for this career will change over the next 10 years.
- Earnings—This section has information on average salaries earned in this career (by setting, if that is applicable). Under "For the Latest Wage Information," with one click you can learn about the average and hourly salaries in this career (again, by employment setting, if relevant), and you can even find some information about variations in salary depending on geographical location.
- Related occupations—Some of the most helpful information at this site appears in this section. You will find a list of careers related to the one that you are researching. Maybe you are thinking that you would like to be a child psychologist, but you realize that you actually know relatively little about what that means. Here you can find out that related careers include being a counselor, social worker, special education teacher, or recreation worker. If you click on any of these links, it will take you to the page in the *Occupational Outlook Handbook* that provides all the information on that alternative career.
- Sources of additional information—This section provides links to professional organizations that support and advocate for people working in that field. The organization webpages are rich sources of information about each career, and you should look at one or two of them before you finish exploring this page.

How Much Do You Know About Careers in Child Development?

ACTIVE LEARNING

If you are interested in a career that involves working with children, complete this table with what you currently know about the career you would like to enter when you finish your education. If you haven't settled on a career yet, simply choose one that currently holds some interest for you. Even if you feel you have very little information on a particular topic, take your best guess at an answer. When you have completed the table, go to the Bureau of Labor Statistics *Occupational Outlook Handbook* and find the information available there.

Although the *Handbook* lists hundreds of occupations, you won't find every conceivable job title. For instance, *child life specialist* and *early interventionist* are not yet in the *Handbook*, but you can find information on a related career (for example, child life specialists do work similar to what a counselor does, but they work in the specialized setting of a hospital and their clients are sick children and their families) to begin your search.

Name the career you researched: _____

Does it appear in the *Occupational Outlook Handbook* (OOH)?   Yes   No

(If "no," name the related career you researched): _____

Topic	Your Current Knowledge	Information From the OOH
Educational level required for entry into this career (for example, high school diploma, associate's degree, bachelor's degree, master's degree, PhD, or other advanced degree)		
Educational level required for advancement in this career		
Important day-to-day work responsibilities (that is, what you will do each day in this career)		
Work setting (for example, office, school, hospital) and how much travel is required (if any)		
Median annual earnings		
Demand (for example, is the demand for this career expected to increase or decrease over the next 10 years, and by how much?)		

In different ways and at different levels, people in all the helping professions are involved in prevention, intervention, and promoting positive development. Throughout this book you will learn about research that has identified ways to help prevent developmental problems. You will learn about **protective factors** or ones that, when they are present, "increase the health and well-being of children and families" (U.S. Department of Health and Human Services, 2008c, para. 1). Protective factors buffer the effect of negative conditions in the child's environment. For example, children growing up in an environment in which illegal drugs are readily available and where many people in the children's social world abuse drugs would be at high risk of becoming drug abusers themselves. However, in these circumstances, having parents who do a good job of

Protective factors Aspects of life that increase the health and well-being of children and families.

monitoring and supervising their children (that is, they know *where* their children are, *whom* their children are with, and *what* they are doing) acts as a protective factor that lowers this risk.

Protective factors can exist at the level of the individual (for example, a child who has positive self-esteem or who is academically skilled), at the level of the family (for example, a family that has warm, nurturing relationships among its members), or at the level of the community (for example, economic stability). Many different professionals are involved in prevention programs to enhance the protective factors that support children's growth. Some professionals, such as community organizers, community psychologists, outreach workers, and community health educators, work in communities.

Early identification of potential problems is another way in which professionals attempt to eliminate or reduce the threats to healthy development. Closely related to prevention is the process of **intervention**. When we become aware of a problem, we have a variety of ways in which we can intervene to try to correct it. Child therapy and family therapy are two ways to address problems. In child therapy, the therapist meets individually with the child, while family therapy involves the whole, or part, of the family. Social workers, psychologists, marriage and family therapists, and child psychiatrists are some of the professionals who may provide these types of intervention. Sometimes problems are identified in school, and intervention can come from an array of professionals within the school system. These may include school psychologists, school social workers, guidance counselors, and others whose training is specifically geared toward issues related to children's functioning within schools.

Finally, professionals and nonprofessionals alike work to promote the optimal development of children and adolescents. This is a primary goal of professionals who work in the field of education (especially classroom teachers, resource teachers, administrators, and counselors), and mental health professionals, youth service workers, and representatives of faith-based organizations who run community programs or after-school programs for children share this goal. In a multitude of ways parents, other relatives, and friends also do many things to support optimal development. A strong foundation in child development helps each of them recognize ways to support and encourage children and adolescents to reach their full potential.

Intervention   Treatment of a problem after it has been identified.

Social policy
Government or private policies for dealing with social issues.

Making social policy. Social policy that affects children and families is made at the highest levels of the federal government down to local school boards and neighborhood councils. Interested citizens also take part when they write letters to elected officials, sign petitions, work for causes they support, and vote.

Government, Organizations, and Citizens—Creating Social Policy

Most often we think about applying our understanding of child development directly to the children with whom we work. However, the well-being of children and families is also affected by the laws and programs that make up **social policy**. Research on child development informs the people who make these policies. For example, Walter Gilliam, director of the Edward Zigler Center in Child Development and Social Policy at Yale University, found that preschool children in Connecticut were more than 3 times as likely to be expelled as children in Grades K–12 (Gilliam, 2005). His research also showed that when a mental health consultant was available to help teachers develop ways to handle problem behaviors, far fewer children were expelled (Bell, 2008). He took his findings to legislators to advocate for a solution. His research and advocacy led to changes in five states, which have increased the number of mental health consultants they provide to preschools. Consider how many young children are being better served because of the research and advocacy of Dr. Gilliam.

Another example is an organization called Child Trends that sponsors research on children and adolescents and then uses its findings to advocate for programs and policies that will help with the issues it's examined. For instance, the organization presented evidence that teen pregnancy was starting to increase in 2006 and 2007, after a number of years of declining teenage birthrates. They were able to present lawmakers with hard facts about both the human and the monetary costs ($9.2 billion a year) of teen childbearing (Holcombe, Peterson, & Manlove, 2009). This type of presentation is far more convincing to those who must provide the funds for programs to prevent teen pregnancy than simple statements of need, unsupported by research evidence. **Active Learning: Social Policy Affecting Children and Adolescents** provides some additional information on the type of issues that social policy organizations have focused on in recent years.

Social Policy Affecting Children and Adolescents

ACTIVE LEARNING

There are a number of organizations in the United States that devote a great deal of their resources to developing social policy that informs legislators and private citizens about topics of importance to the country. We have included here information about a few of these organizations. After reading about the recent research reports and policy briefs prepared by these organizations, you will want to visit their websites to retrieve the reports that interest you or to further explore the information available from the organizations.

The RAND Corporation (2009) is a nonprofit institution with a mission to "help improve policy and decision making through research and analysis." Although it conducts research on a wide range of topics, topics related to children include a study of the effect of charter schools on student achievement, an evaluation of a community-based support group for adolescent substance abusers, a study of the effectiveness of virginity pledges taken by adolescents, and a study of group home placements for adjudicated adolescents. You will find its home page at www.rand.org; then click on "Research Areas" to find a complete list of social policy topics.

The Annie E. Casey Foundation (2009) has a primary mission to "foster public policies, human-service reforms, and community supports that more effectively meet the needs of today's vulnerable children and families." From its home page at http://www.aecf.org, click on "Publications/Multimedia" and then choose a topic from the menu of publication areas. Topic areas include child welfare, community change, economic security, education, health, and juvenile justice. Under each topic, you can select from a number of subtopics. For instance, under the topic "Education," you will find research reports and policy briefs on early education and school readiness, family and community involvement, policy reform, and school choice.

The Future of Children is a collaboration of the Woodrow Wilson School of Public and International Affairs at Princeton University and the Brookings Institution. The organization's website, http://futureofchildren.org, states, "The mission of The Future of Children is to translate the best social science research about children and youth into information that is useful to policymakers, practitioners, grant-makers, advocates, the media, and students of public policy" (The Future of Children, 2010). This organization publishes two issues of its journal each year, with each issue devoted to a single topic. Issues in 2008 and 2009 included such topics as America's high schools, juvenile justice, and children and electronic media. This organization is dedicated to making scientifically based information available to the widest possible audience. From its home page, you can click on webcasts to see presentations on subjects such as the role of high schools in preparing disadvantaged students for college and preventing child maltreatment. In addition, this organization can be found on Facebook and Twitter, and it maintains a blog.

The Society for Research in Child Development is a professional organization with close to 6,000 members in the United States and around the world. It periodically produces policy briefs on a variety of topics related to child development. Go to its home page at http://www.srcd.org and select "Social Policy Report" from the drop-down menu of publications. Finally, select "Social Policy Report Briefs" to access the individual reports.

Remember these organizations when you need to find current research on children and adolescents as you write papers for your courses. There is a wealth of information at each site.

Finally, as citizens, it is our responsibility to vote and to speak out for the well-being of our children—and the more we understand about their needs, the more effective we will be in doing so.

Conclusion

We hope that this chapter has made you eager to explore child development through the topics presented in this book. In this chapter we have introduced you to some of the basic concepts in the field of child development. The rest of the book will elaborate on these concepts in many ways. You will study the theories and methods that are the basis for research about children. You will then learn about how both nature and nurture work together to influence growth and development. After reading about the beginnings of life, you will learn about the basic areas of development: physical, cognitive, language, emotional, identity, and social. You will then take a look at the contexts in which children live their lives: family, play, media, and leisure activities. Finally, you will study those factors that influence the health and well-being of children, including issues such as poverty, mental illness, and racial discrimination, and you will learn how children may thrive even in difficult circumstances. Studying how children develop has serious consequences for our ability to understand children and to foster their positive growth. We hope that reading this book and taking an active role in your own learning process through the use of the activities we have provided will help you examine your current beliefs about children and adolescents and move to a new level of understanding that you will take with you and build upon as you interact with children and adolescents long after this course is over.

CHAPTER SUMMARY

1. In what ways is early development important?
    Longitudinal studies that follow people from childhood through adulthood have given us some ideas about how to predict later outcomes from early development and have also shown effects of early experiences on later development.

2. In what ways is later development important?
    Later experiences and physical maturation build upon earlier development to create outcomes that may not be predictable from aspects of early development alone.

3. What are the central domains of development?
    Physical development is the biologically based changes that occur as children grow. **Cognitive development** is the changes that take place in children's thinking and learning. **Social-emotional development** is the changes that occur in children's understanding and expression of emotions as well as their ability to interact with other people.

4. What issues have been central to the study of children and adolescents?
    a. The **nature-nurture** debate focuses on the role of genetics and the role of experience in development.

    b. Development can be continuous, or **quantitative** in nature, focusing on small, quantifiable changes indicating more or less of something; or, it can be stagelike, or **qualitative** in nature, focusing on overall changes in the nature of something—not just more or less, but different.

    c. Some aspects of development change, and some show stability over time and do not show much change.

    d. Children's development may result in adaptive behaviors or in maladaptive behaviors. Different developmental pathways may result in the same outcome (**equifinality**), and the same developmental pathways may result in different outcomes (**multifinality**).

    e. Although research often results in generalizations about groups of people, individual differences are also central to the study of child development. In addition, diversity between different groups of people must be taken into account when examining the results of research.

    f. Children play an active role in their own development, actively constructing their own understanding of their experiences and seeking out settings that fit their genetic endowment. Their own characteristics influence how others will respond to them. Finding a good fit within their environment is important for optimal development.

5. How have the ways that we study children changed over the last 100 years?

We continue to study children through observations, tests, and experiments, but the complexity of the questions we can ask and answer has increased and continues to do so as we build on earlier findings by researchers of child development and statistical analyses become more sophisticated.

6. What is important to examine when evaluating information about child development?

You must know that the source of your information is based on scientific evidence that has been **replicated** in studies done by more than one researcher. Look for many different sources of information and think critically about them. Don't generalize from a single example, but also don't reject the results of research because your individual experiences don't seem to correspond to the research findings. Try to be objective so that you don't fall prey to **perceptual bias** that just confirms what you already expected. Finally, examine your preconceptions carefully to determine what is scientifically based fact and what is unproven **folk wisdom**.

7. How can parents and other family members use information about child development?

Informed parents and family members are better able to understand their children's needs and abilities at each stage of development, which helps them respond empathically as well as provide the appropriate type of stimulation to support their children's growth and development. Certain groups of parents who are at high risk for inadequate parenting, such as teenage parents and incarcerated parents, are helped by parent education programs to promote their understanding of their children.

8. How can professionals who work with children use information about child development?

An understanding of children, adolescents, and their development is important in a wide range of careers. In addition to pediatricians and teachers, social workers, counselors, therapists, lawyers, nurses, and people in many other careers all draw upon this knowledge in the work that they do. People in all the helping professions are involved with prevention, **intervention**, and promoting positive development.

9. How can government, organizations, and citizens use information about child development?

The well-being of children and families is affected by the laws and programs that make up **social policy**. Lawmakers and program developers must understand how policies will affect children and their families. They can develop programs that will enhance the chances for optimal development of many children. Citizens armed with child development knowledge can advocate and/or vote for policies that will promote positive child development.

Go to **www.sagepub.com/levine** for additional exercises and video resources. Select **Chapter 1, Introduction,** for chapter-specific activities.

Chapter Outline

chapter 2

Theories of Development

2

When we study and work with children and adolescents, we want to make sense out of what we observe. The explanations that we and others develop about why children behave in certain ways become theories. Throughout the history of the study of child development, many different, and often opposing, theories have developed. In this chapter we describe some of the basic characteristics of different developmental theories, such as whether children change over time in small incremental steps or in large leaps. We then discuss some of the major theories that have influenced how we understand child development today. Some of these theories have their origins in the early 20th, or even late 19th, century, but each has modern applications that we have included in this chapter. No theory is a static "truth" that never changes. We will see how ideas about children and adolescents have developed over time in reaction to society's changes and in response to new research that provides evidence for which theories have merit and which will be laid aside.

Test Your Knowledge

Test your knowledge of child development by deciding whether each of the following statements is *true* or *false,* and then check your answers as you read the chapter.

1. **True/False:** If you pick a baby up every time she cries, she will cry more.
2. **True/False:** Research tells us whether a theory is true or false.
3. **True/False:** The bulk of your personality is fixed and established by the time you enter adolescence.
4. **True/False:** Children can learn to fear objects such as white rats and pieces of toast.
5. **True/False:** The best way to establish and maintain a behavior is to reward people every time they do the behavior that you are interested in.
6. **True/False:** The best way to get rid of an undesirable behavior in a child is to punish a child for doing it.
7. **True/False:** When young children are selfish and self-centered it is because their parents overindulge them.
8. **True/False:** Darwin's concept of the "survival of the fittest" means that the strongest animal is most likely to survive.
9. **True/False:** If a child is experiencing a lot of stress at home, the child will show behavior problems in the classroom.
10. **True/False:** Babies lose the stepping reflex they have at birth because their legs become too heavy for them to lift.

Correct answers: (1) False, (2) False, (3) False, (4) True, (5) False, (6) False, (7) False, (8) False, (9) False, (10) True

Basic Principles and Applications

Why Are Theories Important?

The study of child and adolescent development, as with all scientific study, is driven by theories. Developmental theories are basic principles or formulations that help us *organize* our observations in order to *understand* and *predict* human development. For example, a parent might react to an infant's excessive crying very differently depending on his understanding of what this crying means. If he subscribes to the theory of behaviorism, he might believe that picking up the crying baby will reward that behavior and make the baby cry more. However, if he subscribes to the theory of ethology, he might believe the crying is a behavior that signals that the baby needs comfort. If that need is met, it will help the baby develop a secure attachment that will eventually help the baby cry less (Bell & Ainsworth, 1972).

Although we all have our own personal "theories" about various aspects of human behavior, the theories that we use to build a scientific understanding about child and adolescent development must be public and testable. In the scientific process, which we will describe in detail in Chapter 3, these theories are the basis from which we generate specific, testable hypotheses. From the example above, we might generate a specific hypothesis that babies whose parents pick them up when they cry in the first 3 months of life will cry less over time. If the hypothesis turns out to be correct, it will provide support for ethological theory. If we find the opposite, that babies who are picked up cry more, this will provide support for behaviorist theory. In fact, as is often the case, recent research has shown a combination of these two effects.

St. James-Roberts (2007) studied two types of parenting: "demand parenting," in which babies were reliably picked up when they cried, and "structured parenting," in which standard bedtimes and routines were put in place and some crying was acceptable. (Note that no one simply left babies to cry!) Demand parenting resulted in babies crying less during the first 3 months of life but continuing to cry at night after that age. Structured parenting resulted in more crying during the first 3 months but reduced crying at night thereafter.

Most theories can never be proven beyond a shadow of any doubt, but the scientific process allows us to provide evidence that supports or opposes the truth of these ideas. An example of how this process works is Darwin's theory of evolution. Some say that evolution is not a proven fact, and technically this is true. However, the enormous body of evidence that supports its ideas outweighs the evidence against it. Consequently, evolutionary theory is widely accepted in scientific circles today. On the other hand, other theories have come and gone as evidence piled up that did not fit with the predictions that emerged from them. For example, one hypothesis that emerged from psychoanalytic theory was that early mothering is the cause of the development of the severe mental illness known as schizophrenia (Ambert, 1997). As research continued, it became clear that the more likely culprit in the development of schizophrenia is a combination of genetic endowment and environmental influence, which might even include prenatal events, such as a mother's illness (Boksa, 2008). The concept of mothers as the cause for this disease has thankfully disappeared.

How Do Developmental Theories Differ?

As you will remember from Chapter 1, development has to do with both stability and change over time, so each developmental theory must address the issues of how and why change happens and why some aspects of behavior remain the same.

How Does Change Happen?

The "how" part of this question has been addressed in two ways: *qualitative change* and *quantitative change*. If you change the quantity of something, you just add to or take away from the

TRUE/FALSE

1. If you pick a baby up every time she cries, she will cry more.

    False. Parents who reliably pick up their babies when they cry have babies who cry less in the first 3 months of life. However, their babies also continue to cry at night longer than babies who are allowed to cry a bit when they are upset.

TRUE/FALSE

2. Research tells us whether a theory is true or false.

    False. Research provides evidence that supports or fails to support ideas from a particular theory, but by itself it does not tell us whether the theory is true or false. As we accumulate more information, we can decide whether that theory is helpful or not and whether it needs to be modified.

original amount or number. However, if you change the quality of something, you make that thing substantially different from the way it was before. For example, you can change a bowl of water quantitatively by adding more water. However, you can change the *quality* of water by changing the temperature. At room temperature, water is a liquid, but if you put it in the freezer, it becomes ice—a solid—and if you boil it, it becomes steam—a gas. In like manner, there are developmental theories that describe change as happening little by little, smoothly over time (like adding small amounts of water to a glass). These are quantitative approaches to understanding development. For instance, we grow physically inch by inch, and we can recognize words more quickly as we learn to read. In other theories, big changes occur at certain ages that alter the nature of the child or adolescent in significant ways (like the change of water to ice or steam). These qualitative theories are called stage theories, as each stage in life is seen as different from the ones that come before and after. For example, puberty triggers large changes in many areas of development. One way to think about these two kinds of change is to consider the development of memory. Children can remember more and more as they get older (quantitative change), but they may *suddenly* increase their memory capacity when they develop a new way of encoding information into memory (qualitative change) (Siegler & Crowley, 1991).

Why Does Change Happen?

Developmental change may be driven by biological processes inside each person, by environmental events that affect each person, or by an interaction of the two. Developmental theories can fall anywhere along this continuum of explanations. For psychoanalysts, our behavior is primarily driven by our sex drive. For behaviorists, we develop because of the effects of the environment. Several theories see behavior resulting from evolutionary processes based on adaptation of the organism to the environment. Some cognitive theories are based on the need of humans to master and understand their world. You will read more in detail about each of these theories later in this chapter.

No theory develops in a vacuum. It never happens that a person, no matter how brilliant, reaches a new idea without developing that idea from theories and observations that came before. Therefore, in this chapter we give some background to explain the historical origins of the theories we describe. We present some of the basic concepts that formed the basis for the original theory. We then look at how the theory has changed over time and how the theory is currently being applied. As you read about each theory, keep two questions in mind:

1. How does the theory describe development? Does change occur (a) quantitatively, in small steps, or (b) qualitatively, in distinct stages?

2. What drives development? Is development the product of (a) biological processes, (b) environmental processes, or (c) a combination of both biology and environment?

Theories of Child and Adolescent Development

Psychoanalytic Theory

We begin our discussion of theories with psychoanalytic theory. Although psychoanalytic theory has been very controversial throughout its existence, many of its concepts have become part of our assumptions about how the mind works. As we entered the 21st century, the impact of this theory in our culture was acknowledged by *Time* magazine, which chose Sigmund Freud, the father of psychoanalysis, as one of the 100 most influential people of the 20th century (Gay, 1999).

Video Link 2.1
Sigmund Freud.

Unconscious mind The thoughts and feelings about which we are unaware.

Free association The process used by psychoanalysis in which one thinks of anything that comes to mind in relation to a dream or another thought in order to discover the contents of the unconscious mind.

Sigmund Freud (1856–1939) was a physician in Vienna who created the theory of psycho-analysis (*psyche* = the mind; *analysis* implies looking at the parts of the mind individually to see how they relate). Freud believed that we are aware of some of our thoughts, which are in our conscious mind, and we are unaware of other thoughts, which are in our **unconscious mind**. Often we have thoughts, memories, and feelings that would be unacceptable to us, so we repress them; that is, we hide them from ourselves in our unconscious mind (Freud, 1953c). Many of these thoughts are linked with events from our childhood. Freud believed that the key to healthy psychological functioning lies in discovering the unconscious thoughts or memories associated with these symptoms. He believed that **free association**, in which a person allows thoughts to float freely without censorship, and dream analysis are ways of gaining insight into the working of the unconscious mind (Freud, 1950). When a person who is suffering from anxieties and maladaptive behaviors comes to understand his underlying thoughts and feelings, his psychological well-being will improve. This is the basis for psycho-analytic psychotherapy. To experience the technique of free association, try **Active Learning: Free Association**.

ACTIVE LEARNING

Free Association

Free association starts with a stimulus, which could be a dream or a word. The person who is free associating tries to let her mind float free and says the first thing that comes to her mind. For example, if someone is told to free associate to the word *blue,* her first association might be to say the word *green.* She might then say what *green* brings to mind and come up with a list like this: *blue, green, sea, ocean, fish, swim, water, drink, lemonade, lunch.* This example might come from a person in an 11 a.m. class who is hungry!

Now you try it. When you read the word at the end of this sentence, write down a series of 10 words that spontaneously come to mind: *child* _____ _____ _____ _____

_____ _____ _____ _____ _____ _____

Freud would say that this type of free association gives a clue as to the unconscious contents of your mind. Did the words you wrote reflect particular concerns, interests, or issues on your mind recently?

When one professor carried out this experiment shortly after the attacks on the World Trade Center on September 11, 2001, students' responses to a simple color word, such as *blue* or *green*, were different from those she had received in other years, when the stimulus word had led students to issues of school or money. In 2001, the same words resulted in content reflecting violence, fear, and anxiety, revealing the underlying thoughts and emotions that were just below the surface of the students' everyday experiences. If you were in psychoanalytic psychotherapy, the process would be designed to lead you ever deeper into your unknown thoughts and feelings. You might find it interesting to compare the last word on your list of free associations with that of other students in your class to see how many different directions the word *child* can take you.

Id According to psychoanalytic theory, the basic drives, such as sex and hunger.

Pleasure principle The idea that the id seeks immediate gratification for all of its urges to feel pleasure.

Ego The part of the personality that contends with the reality of the world and controls the basic drives.

Freud theorized that our personality is made up of three parts: the id, the ego, and the super-ego. According to Freud, we are all born with an **id**, which consists of our basic drives. Infants have no way to control their drives: They want *what* they want *when* they want it! An infant is not going to wait politely for you to get off the phone when she is feeling very hungry. She is going to cry and demand food, expressing her need to satisfy this basic drive. The id operates on what Freud called the **pleasure principle** because it seeks immediate gratification for all of its urges.

As children grow older they begin to become aware of the reality of the world around them and begin to develop the ability to think and control their emotions. This ability to negotiate between basic drives and the real world is the province of the **ego**. As the ego develops, the child is still motivated by her basic drives, but she now is able to interact in the real world to get her needs met. Even though she is hungry, she might now realize that if she waits until you are off the phone and asks politely, she may be more likely to get her cookie. This way of dealing with our wants and desires is known as the **reality principle**.

Finally, sometime between the ages of 5 and 7, the child begins to incorporate moral principles that work against the drive-motivated functioning of the id. These moral principles are maintained by the **superego**. Freud believed that until this time children do not have any internal sense of guilt that guides their actions. Whereas a younger child might simply take a cookie when hungry, an older child will be able to control herself and resist the temptation because she knows that taking a cookie when she isn't supposed to is wrong.

Sigmund Freud's Psychosexual Stages

Freud believed our most basic drive is the sex drive. If you believe that biologically speaking the goal of our lives is to pass on our genes, then you might agree with Freud that the sex drive is central to everything else. He outlined five stages in child and adolescent development, which he called **psychosexual stages**. At each of these stages, sexual energy is invested in a different part of the body, and gratification of the urges associated with those areas of the body is particularly pleasurable. He labeled these stages the oral, anal, phallic, latency, and genital stages. He believed that the way in which gratification of urges is handled during each of these stages determines the nature of an adult's personality and character. Disturbances in any of the stages can result in psychological disturbance in adulthood. We will describe these stages and Freud's ideas about the effects later in life if development during these stages does not go well.

The **oral stage** lasts from birth to about 18 months of age. The zone of pleasure is the mouth. A baby for whom taking in food is not pleasurable might not survive. If you give a 6-month-old baby a toy, what is the first thing she is likely to do? Toy makers are aware that children are likely to put anything in their mouths and warn us against giving them toys with small parts that can cause choking. Freud developed the idea that someone can get "stuck" or fixated in one of the first three psychosexual stages of early childhood. That person will then exhibit characteristics of that stage later in life (Freud, 1953c). For example, an individual who is fixated in the oral stage may want to continue to try to satisfy his oral urges by overeating or smoking. Many of us have some remnants of this stage as we chew on our fingers or pencils; however, a fixation is really only a concern when it interferes with adaptive functioning in some critical way.

The **anal stage** lasts from 18 months to 3 years. At this age the pleasure center moves to the anus, and issues of toilet training become central. Although many of us squirm to think of the anus as a pleasure center, we have only to listen to the "poopy talk" of young children to see the hilarity it brings about. The task of the child at this age is to learn to control his bodily urges to conform to society's expectations. A person who is fixated at this stage may become overcontrolled (referred to as "anal compulsive") as an adult (Freud, 1959). Everything must be in its proper place to an extreme degree. Conversely, someone might become "anal explosive," creating "messes" wherever he goes.

The **phallic stage** lasts from 3 to 6 years of age. At this stage Freud believed that the paths followed by boys and girls diverge in ways that have been extremely controversial. We will first look at the path for boys. A boy's pleasure becomes focused on the penis. Many parents must patiently explain to their little boy that he cannot keep his hand in his pants while out in company. Later during this stage the boy develops what Freud called the **Oedipus complex**, named after the character from Greek mythology who unknowingly killed his own father and married his mother. The boy focuses all his affections on his mother (you may have heard a small boy claiming that he is going to marry his mommy when he grows up) and becomes angry at his father, who stands in the way of the child's sole possession of her (Freud, 1953c). However, in the normal course of events, the boy becomes uncomfortable with this anger at his father. Rather than experiencing the anger, he projects the feeling onto his father and fears that his father is angry at

Reality principle The psychoanalytic concept that the ego has the ability to deal with the real world and not just drives and fantasy.

Superego Freud's concept of the conscience or sense of right and wrong.

Psychosexual stages Freud's stages that are based on the idea that at each stage sexual energy is invested in a different part of the body.

Oral stage Freud's first stage in which the sexual drive is located in the mouth for infants.

Anal stage Freud's second stage of development during which toddlers' sexual energy is focused on the anus. Toilet training and control are major issues.

Phallic stage Freud's third stage, involving children 3–6 years of age, in which boys experience the Oedipus complex and girls experience the Electra complex.

Oedipus complex In Freudian theory, young boys want to marry their mothers and kill their fathers. They fear castration at the hands of their fathers in retaliation for their wish to possess their mother.

him. In this stage when he is focused on his own penis, the retribution he imagines from his father is that he will cut off the boy's penis. Consequently, the boy develops what Freud called castration anxiety. In order to avoid this fate, the boy gives up his dream of marrying his mother and decides to become like or *identify* with his father (Freud, 1953b). A man who does not resolve the Oedipus complex may become fixated in this stage. He may find rivalry or competition with other men overwhelming, as he doubts his ability to measure up to others. He may also find it difficult to have intimate relations with women, as they remind him of forbidden impulses toward his mother.

For girls, the picture is much more complicated and controversial, even for therapists who practice psychoanalysis. In the phallic stage, Freud (1953a) believed that girls come to believe that they once had a penis and that it was cut off, leaving them with penis envy. Girls go through a similar complex, called the **Electra complex**, in which they want to marry their fathers and do away with their mothers. (For example, one little girl was heard to say, "I want to give my father a golden ring and my mother a poison apple.") Freud believed that girls must learn to identify with their mothers, whom they see as damaged in the same way that they themselves are. The only way in which they will achieve a sense of wholeness is when they produce a penis by having a baby boy. Freud (1953a) believed that girls must accept their passive, receptive nature and those who do not adequately resolve the Electra complex might try to overcome their feelings of inferiority by being too assertive and masculine.

The critique of Freud's view of female development has been fierce, even from the early days of the development of psychoanalytic theory. Female psychoanalysts have argued that this explanation of female development has more to do with a little boy's view of girls than the girl's view of herself (Gay, 1988). They also have argued that boys and men are just as jealous of women's ability to give birth as girls are of a boy's penis (Lips, 2008). Feminist Gloria Steinem (1995) satirized Freud's treatment of women by proposing a version of psychoanalytic theory developed by a fictional "Phyllis Freud," based on womb and breast envy rather than penis envy.

The **latency stage** occurs between 6 and 12 years of age. *Latent* means inactive, and Freud believed that during this time the sex drive goes underground (Freud, 1953c). Children move from their fantasies in the phallic period of marrying their parent to a new realization that they must take the long road toward learning to become a grown-up. The sex drive provides energy for the learning that must take place but is not expressed overtly. Children transfer their interest from parents to peers (Freud, 1965). At this age children who had cross-sex friendships often relinquish them as boys and girls learn the meaning of "cooties" and each sex professes disgust for the other.

This separation of the sexes begins to change at age 12, when young adolescents enter the **genital stage**. At this point, sexual energy is focused on the genital area, and true sexual interest occurs between peers.

Electra complex
According to Freud, the desire of the young girl to marry her father and kill her mother.

Latency stage   Freud's fourth stage, involving children ages 6–12, when the sex drive goes underground.

Genital stage   Freud's fifth and final stage in which people 12 and older develop adult sexuality.

Psychosocial stages   Erikson's stages that are based on a central conflict to be resolved involving the social world and the development of identity.

Freud's latency stage. Does this picture of girls interacting with girls and boys interacting with boys remind you of your own experience in elementary school?

Erik Erikson's Psychosocial Stages

Many of the people who initially studied and worked with Freud have gone on to change psychoanalytic theory in significant ways. Erik Homburger Erikson (1902–1994) is one of the most influential. Erikson focused more on issues of the ego rather than the id. *Ego* means "I" or "self," and Erikson's major focus was on the development of identity. He described a series of stages based on issues that arise during the process of psychosocial development (Erikson, 1963). Erikson describes **psychosocial stages** (as opposed to Freud's psycho*sexual* stages) because these issues are rooted in social experiences that are typical of each stage of development rather than in sexual urges. At each age he believed that there is a central

Table 2.1

A comparison of Freud's and Erikson's stages of development

Ages	Freud's Psychosexual Stages		Erikson's Psychosocial Stages	
Infancy	Oral	Pleasure is focused on the mouth and "taking in"	Trust vs. mistrust	Development of trust in maternal care and in one's own ability to cope vs. hopelessness
Toddlerhood	Anal	Pleasure is focused on the anal region and control of one's own body and its products	Autonomy vs. shame and doubt	Independence and self-control vs. lack of confidence
Preschool	Phallic	Pleasure is focused on the genital area; development of the "family romance": Oedipus and Electra complexes	Initiative vs. guilt	Exuberant activity vs. overcontrol
School age	Latency	Sexual energy goes underground as child focuses on peers and learning	Industry vs. inferiority	Learning the tasks of one's society vs. a sense of inadequacy
Adolescence	Genital	Sexual energy reaches adult level, with focus on intimate relationships	Identity vs. role confusion	Integration of previous experiences to form an identity vs. confusion about one's role in society
Early adulthood	"	"	Intimacy vs. isolation	Ability to form close relationships vs. fear of losing the self
Middle adulthood	"	"	Generativity vs. stagnation	Guiding the next generation vs. preoccupation with one's own needs
Later adulthood	"	"	Integrity vs. despair	Achievement of a sense of meaning in life vs. focus on fear of death

conflict to be resolved and the way in which we resolve that conflict lays the groundwork for the next stages of our development. For example, Erikson believed that infants have to establish trust in the world around them (he called the central conflict for infants *trust vs. mistrust*), while toddlers have to struggle with developing autonomy, or a level of independence from their parents (*autonomy vs. shame and doubt*). These stages, as well as the rest of Erikson's eight stages, are described briefly in comparison to Freud's psychosexual stages in Table 2.1. As individuals deal with each of these conflicts, at each stage they can achieve a more positive (for example, trust and autonomy) or a more negative (for example, mistrust and shame and doubt) sense of themselves and the world around them. None of us have a purely positive or purely negative set of experiences on these issues; therefore, we can think of the two possible outcomes of each stage as two sides of a teeter-totter, with one higher than the other but both actively in play.

The other important aspect of Erikson's theory is that he believed that development does not stop in adolescence. He went beyond Freud's stages to add three stages of adulthood. He was the first theorist to acknowledge that we continue to grow and develop throughout our lives.

Modern Applications of Psychoanalytic Theory

Although psychoanalytic theory has been controversial, ideas that come from psychoanalytic theory are still very influential, particularly in relation to the study of the development of mental and emotional disorders, a field known as developmental psychopathology (Fonagy, Target, & Gergely, 2006). Many psychotherapists continue to use therapy that is designed to uncover

3. The bulk of your personality is fixed and established by the time you enter adolescence. **TRUE/FALSE**

False. Theorists such as Erik Erikson have described developmental challenges that shape our personality beyond adolescence and throughout the life span.

inner conflicts from earlier life experiences, especially early trauma, as the basis for current psychological symptoms. A number of modern theories and therapeutic approaches (including ego psychology, conflict theory, object relations theory, and self psychology) also have their roots in concepts taken from psychoanalytic theory. If you take advanced courses in psychology, you are likely to learn more about some of these approaches. Evidence from other types of research that follow the scientific method (see Chapter 3) has yielded mixed results. Some ideas have been supported by research, and others have not.

Erikson's ideas about the effect of social experiences on the development of personality throughout the life span have remained an important influence in the field of child development. A number of his ideas have influenced contemporary child care practices and our understanding of how development occurs as a series of interrelated experiences. For instance, we urge new parents to be sensitive and responsive to their infants as a way to establish a sense of trust, as Erikson described. We better understand the challenge of adolescence when we see it as a struggle to establish a coherent sense of individual identity. Erikson's concept of identity formation in adolescence has spawned extensive research on this topic that will be discussed further in Chapter 11. These concepts have also been used to help in the treatment of children with emotional disturbances by providing a framework for understanding the central issues to be dealt with at different ages.

Erikson's ideas also have remained influential because they are a good reflection of how we think about development today, as we outlined these issues in Chapter 1. We are interested in understanding the contexts in which development occurs, so the central role that Erikson gives to the influence of culture, the environment, and social experiences on development fits well with this modern perspective. Today we see the child as an active participant in shaping his or her own development, as did Erikson. Also in line with Erikson's theoretical ideas, we see both change (as reflected in different crises identified in each of the stages he described) and stability (as seen in the idea that later stages continue to be influenced by the resolution of issues at earlier stages) as related aspects of development.

Behaviorism and Social Cognitive Theory

A very different school of thought about how children develop is offered by the learning theories. Whereas psychoanalytic theory focuses on internal processes of the mind, the learning theories focus on observable behavior. These theories are based on the interaction of the stimulus of events in the external environment with the response of the child. We will describe the learning theories known as **behaviorism** (which is based on principles of classical conditioning and operant conditioning) and **social cognitive theory** (which is based on principles of modeling and imitation).

John B. Watson and Classical Conditioning

John B. Watson (1878–1958) is the father of the theory known as behaviorism. Unlike other psychologists in the early 1900s, he was not interested in studying the impact of internal factors such as genetic influences and the workings of the mind on human development (Buckley, 1989). Instead, he concentrated on what he could see: behavior, or what people *do*. The field of psychology was just emerging, and psychologists in America were trying hard to establish the field as an experimental science, with testable hypotheses based on observable phenomena rather than unseen concepts such as Freud's unconscious mind.

Watson believed that the environment is the most important factor in determining our personality, our abilities, and all our other qualities. He subscribed to a notion put forth by great philosophers including Aristotle and John Locke that we are born a "blank slate" or tabula rasa, ready to be drawn upon by environmental experiences. He felt so strongly about this that he made the following statement:

Behaviorism The theory developed by John B. Watson that focuses on environmental control of observable behavior.

Social cognitive theory The theory that individuals learn by observing others and imitating their behavior.

Give me a dozen healthy infants, well-formed, and my own specified world to bring them up in and I'll guarantee to take any one at random and train him to become any type of specialist I might select—doctor, lawyer, artist, merchant-chief and, yes, even beggar-man and thief, regardless of his talents, penchants, tendencies, abilities, vocations, and race of his ancestors. I am going beyond my facts and I admit it, but so have the advocates of the contrary and they have been doing it for many thousands of years. (Watson, 1928, p. 104)

One way in which we learn from our environment, according to Watson, is through a process called **classical conditioning**, illustrated in Figure 2.1. In this process, a particular stimulus, or event in the environment, is paired with another stimulus over and over again. The first stimulus, known as the *unconditioned stimulus*, provokes a natural response, known as the *unconditioned response*. For example, Ivan Pavlov (1849–1936), a Russian physiologist who was studying reflexes and the processes of digestion, presented food to hungry dogs in his lab. In response, the dogs salivated, just as you would if you were hungry and walked by a bakery. The food is called the unconditioned stimulus because it elicits a natural, or unconditioned, response. Then Pavlov preceded the presentation of the food with a distinctive noise, such as a bell ringing, each time he presented the food. The bell did not at first provoke salivation from the dogs, so initially it was considered a neutral stimulus. However, over time the dogs began to associate the sound of the bell with the food, so the animals had *learned* something about the bell and it now became a *conditioned stimulus*. Finally, Pavlov presented only the bell and found that the dogs continued to salivate just as if the food had been presented. Salivation to an unnatural stimulus, such as a bell, is known as a *conditioned response* (Pavlov, 1927). (If you have pets, do they show evidence of classical conditioning? Do they get excited at the sound of the can opener, even if you are opening a can of crushed pineapple for yourself and not a can of pet food for them?)

Classical conditioning The process by which a stimulus (the unconditioned stimulus) that naturally evokes a certain response (the unconditioned response) is paired repeatedly with a neutral stimulus. Eventually the neutral stimulus becomes the conditioned stimulus and evokes the same response, now called the conditioned response.

Figure 2.1

Classical conditioning. This figure shows the steps in the process of classical conditioning.

BEFORE CONDITIONING

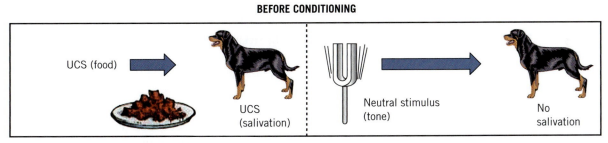

An unconditioned stimulus (UCS) produces an unconditioned response (UCR).

A neutral stimulus produces no salivation response.

DURING CONDITIONING

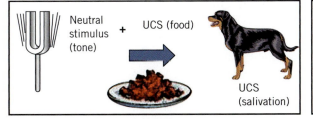

The unconditioned stimulus is repeatedly presented just after the neutral stimulus. The unconditioned stimulus continues to produce an unconditioned response.

AFTER CONDITIONING

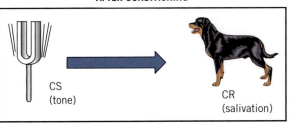

The neutral stimulus alone now produces a conditioned response (CR), thereby becoming a conditioned stimulus (CS).

TRUE/FALSE

4. Children can learn to fear objects such as white rats and pieces of toast.

True. Through the process of classical conditioning, objects that initially do not produce fear can be paired with things that do, until we learn to fear the object that started out neutral.

Video Link 2.2
Watson and Little Albert.

In a famous experiment involving Little Albert, a 9-month-old infant, Watson applied the idea of classical conditioning to humans (Watson & Rayner, 1920). He carried out an experiment designed to demonstrate that he could use classical conditioning to create fear in a human infant where none had existed before. When Little Albert was first shown a white rat, he was curious and unafraid (so the rat was initially a neutral stimulus because it did not produce a fear response). Watson then made a loud clanging sound (the unconditioned stimulus), which startled Little Albert, who began to cry with fear (the unconditioned response). Watson then made the loud clanging noise at the same time that he presented the white rat to the infant. He did this numerous times over a number of days. Eventually he stopped making the loud sound, and yet every time he showed Little Albert the white rat (which by now had become a conditioned stimulus), the infant continued to show fear (which now was a conditioned, or learned, response). This process of association of stimuli (rat and sound) is called classical conditioning. Watson also claimed that this fear generalized to other furry creatures and objects like a Santa Claus mask.

Aside from the obvious ethical questions there are about carrying out research like this with an infant, there are also many questions about the scientific quality and meaning of the research that Watson carried out with Little Albert. Other people who subsequently carried out this type of classical conditioning with other infants were unable to replicate the results that Watson had described (Harris, 1979). Even in Watson and Rayner's (1920) own description, there were times when Little Albert did not show much fear of the rat or of the other stimuli to which he supposedly had generalized his fear, such as a rabbit and a dog.

Watson never attempted to decondition Little Albert's fear before he was removed by his mother, a wet nurse at the hospital in which the experiments were done. According to a biography of Watson, he was so focused on debunking psychoanalytic theory and so disinterested in the welfare of his little subject that he even "speculated with some amusement that if little Albert developed a phobia to fur coats later in life, some psychiatrist would be sure to attempt to find some sexual basis for the fear" (Buckley, 1989, p. 122). In recent years a group of researchers assembled evidence about who Albert was, traced his history, and found that sadly he likely died at age 6 of a brain disease, so we can only speculate about any long-term effects of Watson's research (Beck, Levinson, & Irons, 2009).

A common experience of classical conditioning is when someone gets sick from eating something specific, like a particular candy bar. This person may find that seeing that candy bar subsequently makes him feel queasy. The sick feeling has become classically conditioned to the sight of that candy. Another example with more serious consequences is that some cancer patients receiving chemotherapy that makes them sick to their stomach will develop anticipatory nausea before they receive their treatment (Stockhorst, Klosterhalfen, Klosterhalfen, Winkelmann, & Steingrueber, 1993).

To check whether you understand the steps of the classical conditioning process, try **Active Learning: Understanding the Process of Classical Conditioning**.

ACTIVE LEARNING   Understanding the Process of Classical Conditioning

Read the following paragraph and then answer the questions below.

Imagine that you have a defective toaster that gives you an electric shock every time you take a piece of toast out of it. Time after time, when you reach for the toast, you get a slight electric shock. That electric shock hurts enough that it makes a little tingle run down your spine. You go to a friend's house for lunch, and she places a tuna-on-toast sandwich in front of you, and as you reach for your sandwich, a little tingle runs down your spine. Can you identify all of the elements in this classical conditioning paradigm listed below?

Unconditioned stimulus (the stimulus that naturally is tied to a response that you can't control):

_____

Unconditioned response (the response that is automatic):

_____

Conditioned stimulus (the stimulus that is paired with the unconditioned stimulus):

_____

Conditioned response (the response you have learned):

_____

Answer: Originally, the unconditioned stimulus always produces the unconditioned response. In this case, a mild electric shock will always produce a tingle down your spine, so the *shock from the toaster is the unconditioned stimulus* and *the tingle is the unconditioned response*. However, over time the shock has been paired with the sight of a piece of toast. You didn't originally feel a tingle every time you saw a piece of toast, so for the sake of this example, the *toast was originally a neutral stimulus*. But with repeated experiences with your defective toaster you have learned something about it and now associate the toast with the shock from the toaster. The toast has *become a conditioned stimulus*. After many experiences, the sight of the toast at your friend's house (far away from your defective toaster) produces the response that you have learned *(the conditioned response)*, and you *feel a tingle even when you don't get an electric shock*.

One of the dangers of this type of learning is that once the conditioned (or learned) response is established, people understandably avoid the stimulus that produces the unpleasant unconditioned response so they don't have the opportunity to find out that they really have nothing to fear. You might think for a minute about whether you have any unreasonable fears that might have their roots in classical conditioning. Does the sight of spiders make your heart race and your stomach churn? Maybe when you were a toddler, you saw a spider and thought you would make friends with it, but as you reached out to pet it, some adult snatched you up and screamed as he stomped on that poor, helpless spider. That would scare a toddler very badly and could lay the groundwork for a lifelong fear of spiders. Sometimes these types of fears begin to limit what people who experience them are able to do. This type of unreasonable fear is called a **phobia**.

Modern Applications of Classical Conditioning

Modern-day psychologists have built upon the ideas of Watson's classical conditioning to develop effective treatments for phobias. As we said, people who experience phobias avoid the object of their fears. The treatment of phobias involves exposing them to these fearful situations in a controlled way. For example, following Watson's experiment with Little Albert, psychologist Mary Cover Jones (1924) studied a 2-year-old boy she referred to as Peter who seemed to have the exact phobias of rats, rabbits, and such that Watson had conditioned into Little Albert. She set out to undo these fears. The most effective methods she used involved "deconditioning" Peter by presenting him with candy at the same time as the rabbit was brought to him or by encouraging imitation when he saw another child holding the rabbit. It has also been found that exposure to a feared stimulus, even without a new positive association, can be an effective treatment for many phobias, from fear of flying to fear of snakes (Foa & Kozak, 1986). Exposure through the use of virtual reality has also been found to be as effective in many cases as real-life experience with the stimulus (Choy, Fyer, & Lipsitz, 2007).

Virtual reality has recently been used in the treatment of posttraumatic stress disorder (PTSD) in soldiers returning from Iraq (Mitchell, 2007). Exposure to a virtual image of an Iraqi

Phobia An irrational fear of something specific that is so severe that it interferes with day-to-day functioning.

Virtual reality treatment for fear of flying. Virtual exposure to the feared experience helps many overcome phobias. How would a behaviorist explain why this procedure works?

View of virtual reality. This is what someone who is afraid of flying might see when wearing a virtual reality helmet.

Operant conditioning
The process that happens when the response that follows a behavior causes that behavior to happen more.

Reinforcement   A response to a behavior that causes that behavior to happen more.

Schedules of reinforcement
Schedules (ratio or interval) on which reinforcement can be delivered based upon a fixed or variable number of responses or fixed or variable lengths of time.

TRUE/FALSE

5.   The best way to establish and maintain a behavior is to reward people every time they do the behavior that you are interested in.

   False. While rewarding someone all the time helps establish a behavior quickly, when the reward stops, the behavior will also disappear quickly. Behavior is maintained longer if you reward it on a random basis. Doing this takes longer to establish the behavior, but it makes the behavior much more resistant to disappearing.

village helped the soldiers overcome the debilitating fear reactions that resulted from experiences they had during their tour of duty in Iraq.

B. F. Skinner and Operant Conditioning

B. F. Skinner (1904–1990) further developed the theory of behaviorism by introducing the idea of **operant conditioning**. While studying rat behavior at Harvard, he noticed that the rats were affected not by what came before their behavior, as was true of classical conditioning, but by what came *after* (Vargas, 2005). He developed the idea that spontaneous behaviors are controlled by the environment's response to them. When this response is something pleasant or positive, it acts as a **reinforcement** (or reward), which increases the likelihood that the behavior will continue or happen again. Reinforcement can be planned, like the candies we give to toddlers when they use the potty, or unplanned, like nodding and smiling when someone is talking to you. As long as you smile and nod, the person is likely to continue to talk with you because he finds the way you are responding to him pleasant and rewarding. However, if you turn away or look bored, he will be likely to stop.

Schedules of Reinforcement. Skinner found that some ways of giving reinforcement are more effective in controlling behavior than others. He compared two types of such **schedules of reinforcement**: interval schedules and ratio schedules. With an interval schedule, a reinforcement is given after a particular *period of time*. The interval can be fixed, meaning that it is always the same amount of time. Think about how you would study if you knew you were going to have a quiz every 2 weeks. Alternatively the interval can be variable, meaning that it may come after different time periods. Think now about how your study habits would change if you knew you would have quizzes but didn't know when they would be given (Steiner & Smith, 1999). Which schedule would result in more consistent study habits? When the interval is fixed, the behavior tends to drop to a low level immediately after the reinforcement (for example, a great grade on your quiz) and to stay low until around the time of the next reinforcement, when the behavior picks up sharply (for example, cramming). If your reinforcement of getting a good grade depends on "pop quizzes" that are unpredictable, your best strategy is to study at a steady pace so you are always ready.

With a ratio schedule, the reinforcement comes after a certain *number of behaviors*, and again, this schedule can be fixed, meaning it occurs after the same number of behaviors each time, or variable, meaning it occurs after differing numbers of behaviors (Skinner, 1953). Your favorite frequent-buyer's card would be a good example of a fixed-ratio schedule. After you buy 10 cups of coffee (or order five pizzas), you get the next one free. On the other hand, gambling casinos use a variable-ratio schedule in the design of their slot machines (Steiner & Smith, 1999). What would happen if you knew that the machine paid off after every 25 games? Chances are, you'd let someone else play the first 24 games! With a variable ratio, you would want to be playing (and paying for) *every* game, in case that was the one that paid off. The intense concentration of the players glued to these machines is testimony to the effectiveness of a variable-ratio schedule in maintaining behavior at a high level. You can test the effects of reinforcement (with a better goal than gambling) by trying **Active Learning: Reward Yourself!**

The effects of reinforcement. Many people spend hours at casino slot machines. Do you think that the schedule of reinforcement (how often and when they win) has anything to do with this?

Reward Yourself!

ACTIVE
LEARNING

Of course you already know that reading your textbook helps boost your grades (and presumably increases your learning). Although grades themselves are a form of reinforcement, they are quite long-term, and many people might need a more immediate reinforcer to do what is needed to achieve them. If you are someone who does not stay current with your class readings, set up a reinforcement program for yourself. First, keep track of how many pages of reading you are currently doing in a week. Next, choose a reward you know to be effective for you and keep track of your progress. For example, see how many pages you should be reading during a given week. For every 5 or 10 pages that you read, give yourself a treat, such as listening to one or two of your favorite songs. Again, keep track of the number of pages you are reading during 1 week. Did you end up reading more when you gave yourself a reinforcement?

What type of schedule of reinforcement would you be using if you rewarded yourself after every 10 pages of reading? At the end of 15 minutes of reading?

Did you recognize the first example as a fixed-ratio schedule and the second as a fixed-interval schedule?

Shaping Behaviors. Reinforcement of a behavior cannot occur if that behavior doesn't occur. For example, you cannot reinforce positive peer interaction with a child who does not interact with his peers. However, Skinner developed the idea, based on his work with pigeons, that behavior could slowly be "shaped," through reinforcement of behaviors that

Video Link 2.3
Skinner's pigeons.

progressively get more and more like the behaviors desired. In this way he was able to train pigeons not only to play Ping-Pong but to play with the reward coming only when they won a point!

To use shaping with a child who does not interact with peers, you could use a series of rewards that begin when the child is simply near another child. The next step might be that the child is reinforced only when he looks at the other child, and finally the reinforcement might only be provided when he speaks while looking at the child. Eventually, the reward would be contingent only on true interaction with a peer.

Negative reinforcement   In operant conditioning, the removal of an unpleasant stimulus makes a behavior more likely to happen again.

Punishment   Administering a negative consequence or taking away a positive reinforcement to reduce the likelihood of an undesirable behavior occurring.

Extinction   In operant conditioning, the process by which a behavior stops when it receives no response from the environment.

Negative Reinforcement. So far we have looked at how reinforcement is used to make someone act a certain way. What happens when we want someone to *stop* a certain behavior? A common misconception is that we use something called **negative reinforcement**. To keep yourself from making this mistake, remember that *any kind* of reinforcement makes a behavior happen *more*. The term *negative* in this phrase means that a behavior is reinforced and therefore occurs more often, not because you are given something you like (such as a candy or a smile) as in positive reinforcement, but because something you *don't* like is taken away. For example, a parent is reinforced for picking up a crying baby because the baby stops crying. This is a good example of how children shape their parents' behavior. The parent will continue to pick the baby up because the crying stops. Do you wear your seat belt when you drive? You should simply because it helps keep you safe, but car manufacturers weren't sure that was enough of an incentive, so they installed an obnoxious buzzer that won't turn off until you buckle your belt. Getting away from that annoying sound is another example of negative reinforcement because it makes it more likely that you will put on your belt as soon as you get in the car in the future.

TRUE/FALSE

6.   The best way to get rid of an undesirable behavior in a child is to punish a child for doing it.

False. Punishment might temporarily stop the behavior from appearing, but when the punishment stops, the undesirable behavior often returns. Ignoring the behavior (a process called *extinction*) is a more reliable way to get rid of an undesirable behavior because we seldom continue to do things that don't "pay off" for us in some way.

Punishment and Extinction. So how do we stop an undesirable behavior? **Punishment** is one means to this end. Punishment consists of administering a negative consequence (such as a spanking) or taking away a positive reinforcement (such as "no dessert because you didn't eat your dinner!") in response to an unwanted behavior. However, Skinner (1953) believed that punishment is not as reliably effective as an alternative, which he called **extinction**. Behaviors are extinguished when they receive *no* response from the environment. A child may be looking for *any* response from a parent; therefore, even yelling or spanking may unintentionally reinforce the undesirable behavior because the child wants parental attention. Skinner believed that the most effective way to control behavior is to ignore undesirable behavior while reinforcing desirable behavior. For example, a teacher might ignore a squabble between two children (thereby denying them attention from the teacher) but later compliment them on their positive play behaviors. As the time spent in positive play increases, there should be less and less opportunity for squabbling. You will read more about the problems associated with the use of punishment in Chapters 12 and 14.

Figure 2.2 illustrates the differences among reinforcement, negative reinforcement, and punishment.

Modern Applications of Operant Conditioning

Operant conditioning has been used as a classroom management strategy for many years. Students may be given tokens, stickers, or check marks on a classroom chart to reward good behavior. At some point these tokens can be redeemed for gifts, privileges, or special activities.

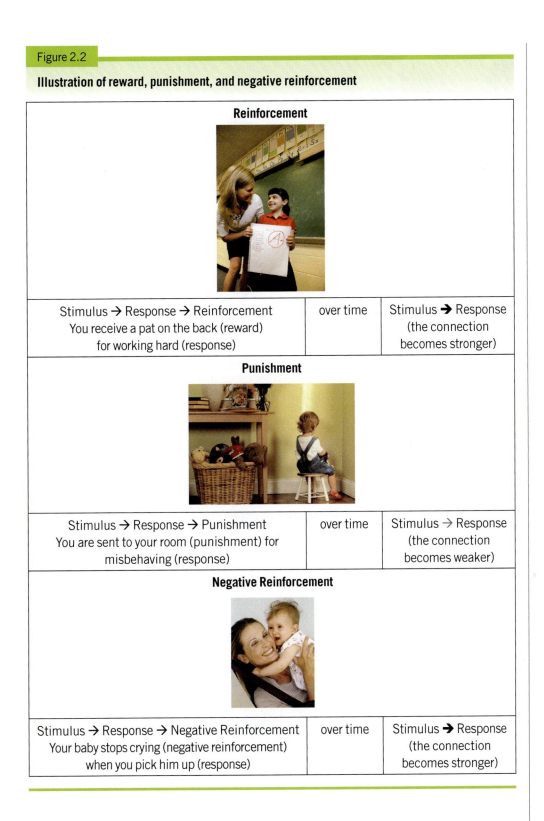

Figure 2.2

Illustration of reward, punishment, and negative reinforcement

Reinforcement

Stimulus → Response → Reinforcement You receive a pat on the back (reward) for working hard (response)	over time	Stimulus → Response (the connection becomes stronger)

Punishment

Stimulus → Response → Punishment You are sent to your room (punishment) for misbehaving (response)	over time	Stimulus → Response (the connection becomes weaker)

Negative Reinforcement

Stimulus → Response → Negative Reinforcement Your baby stops crying (negative reinforcement) when you pick him up (response)	over time	Stimulus → Response (the connection becomes stronger)

In 1997, officials in the town of Tepoztlán in Mexico decided to try to change self-defeating behaviors of the poor, such as absence from school, by directly reinforcing the behavior they wanted to see. *Progresa/Oportunidades* is a program that *pays* poor women for keeping their children in school, going for medical appointments, and a variety of other behaviors. The results

Rewarding school attendance. Under Mexico's *Progresa/Oportunidades* initiative, families of students who have good attendance records receive financial aid from the government to reinforce their attendance.

have been so encouraging that in 2007, Mayor Michael Bloomberg brought the program to New York City (Rivera, 2007). Part of the program, which is being developed at 15 schools by Roland Fryer of the American Inequality Lab at Harvard University's Department of Economics, may include paying children for high test scores on standardized tests (Bosman, 2007). A similar program, called Earning by Learning, in the Dallas, Texas, school system pays children for every book they read (Morris-Lindsey, 2006). These programs are very controversial. Do you think they would be effective at getting students to earn better grades? What problems might there be with this type of program?

Albert Bandura and Social Cognitive Theory

Albert Bandura, a psychology professor at Stanford University who was originally trained as a behaviorist (Pajares & Schunk, 2002), became discontented with the idea that all behavior develops because of the environment's direct response to it. It is difficult or impossible to identify either unconditioned stimuli or reinforcements for the entire range of human behavior that we see. For Bandura, a third learning principle beyond classical and operant conditioning became central. That principle was learning through imitation. He believed that people learn new behaviors simply from watching others rather than by direct reinforcement of their own behaviors from the environment (Bandura, 1986). As he studied imitation of a model, he returned to the view, rejected by both Watson and Skinner, that internal mental processes (cognition) play an important role in human behavior and development. For this reason, he called his theory of learning a *social cognitive learning theory* because the learning occurs from watching other people (social) but is also processed in one's mind (cognitive). For Bandura, imitation has four parts: attention to a model, mental representation or memory of that model's actions, motoric ability to reproduce the action, and the motivation to imitate the action (Grusec, 1992). Let's rephrase that to help you better understand the process: You need to notice what someone else is doing (attention) and then be able to remember what you saw (mental representation) and actually be able to do the same thing yourself (motoric response) if or when you want to (motivation). If all these conditions are in place, you will be able to repeat the behavior (imitate) that you saw modeled by someone else.

Bandura's earliest work was designed to show how children learn by direct observation. In his classic experiment, one group of children observed an adult on television act aggressively to a "Bobo doll" (a large inflated figure of a clown that is weighted on the bottom), hitting it, kicking it, throwing it, and hitting it with a toy hammer (Bandura, Ross, & Ross, 1963). These children and other children who had not seen the video were then brought individually into a room containing both aggressive and nonaggressive toys, including the Bobo doll. The children who had seen the adult attacking the Bobo doll were much more likely to hit, kick, or throw the doll or hit it with a hammer. This should not be surprising to anyone who has watched children on a playground doing karate chops like Teenage Mutant Ninja Turtles or other characters they have seen on TV and in movies. Furthermore, he found that the children exposed to the adult model were also aggressive to the doll in ways they had not seen, such as shooting it with a toy gun. In contrast, the children in this study who hadn't seen the adult model attacking the Bobo doll never carried out these aggressive acts. Bandura concluded that observation of a model may provoke a more generalized response based on the

Bandura's experiment on modeling. What did this boy and girl learn by watching the adult in the film at the top?

children's cognitive understanding of what was happening. In this case, they may have specifically seen the adult hit the Bobo doll, but they also understood that the generalized idea was to be aggressive to the doll.

Bandura's later development of his theory placed greater emphasis on the cognitive, or thinking, aspects of behavior development and specifically on thinking about one's own ability to have control in one's life. Over time the name of his theory changed to eliminate *learning*, because this term was connected with the idea of conditioning, over which we have little or no control because the environment is controlling us. Bandura renamed his theory *social cognitive theory* to emphasize that thought has social origins but is then processed through our own individual cognitive interpretations. His research has focused on **self-efficacy** or "the core belief that one has the power to influence one's own functioning and life circumstances" (Bandura, Caprara, Barbaranelli, Pastorelli, & Regalia, 2001, p. 125). These beliefs play a crucial role in understanding motivation because they are powerful predictors of which goals we will pursue (Pajares, 2005). We tend to pursue tasks at which we believe we can succeed and to avoid ones at which we believe we will fail.

Modern Applications of Social Cognitive Theory

Social cognitive theory has found wide applications in a variety of situations that involve a personal decision to make changes in one's life. According to Pajares (2005), "Empirical evidence supports Bandura's contention that self-efficacy beliefs touch virtually every aspect of people's lives—whether they think productively, self-debilitatingly, pessimistically or optimistically; how much effort they expend on an activity; how well they motivate themselves and persevere in the face of adversities; how they regulate their thinking and behavior; and their vulnerability

Video Link 2.4
Bandura's experiments.

Self-efficacy Bandura's concept of a belief in our power to influence our own functioning and life circumstances.

to stress and depression"(p. 341). Health self-efficacy (the belief that you can make decisions or change behaviors that impact your health and well-being) has been associated with positive lifestyle changes in adolescents with HIV, patients in cardiac rehabilitation, and adults suffering from osteoporosis (Jones, Renger, & Kang, 2007). Coping self-efficacy has been associated with recovery from posttraumatic stress disorder in victims of natural disasters, military combatants, and victims of sexual or criminal assault (Benight & Bandura, 2004).

But perhaps the most important application of the idea of self-efficacy has been in the area of education. Students with a sense of self-efficacy work harder and longer at academic tasks, tackle more difficult tasks, and have a greater sense of optimism that they will succeed (Pajares, 2002). These findings, in turn, have effected change in aspects of the school environment. Educational practices such as grouping students by ability level or placing emphasis on performance on standardized tests can be damaging to students who do not have a strong sense of self-efficacy in the classroom, but authentic praise that is tied to mastery experiences improves confidence and builds a sense of competence (Pajares, 2002). We will return to this idea in Chapter 11 when we discuss how it has become distorted by the self-esteem movement in schools that has often promoted the idea of offering praise as a way to raise self-esteem without linking that praise to meaningful mastery experiences.

Theories of Cognitive Development

The following theories take the area of cognitive development, which focuses on the processes of the mind, including thinking and learning, as their major focus. We will introduce these ideas in this chapter and then examine them further in Chapter 7, where we will discuss cognitive development.

Jean Piaget's Cognitive Developmental Theory

Jean Piaget (1896–1980) was a Swiss scientist whose theory has been very influential in the way we think about child development. Like Freud, Piaget was honored by *Time* magazine as one of the 100 most influential people of the 20th century (Papert, 1999). Piaget studied children's thinking through what he called the "clinical method." He encouraged children to talk freely and learned about their thoughts from a detailed analysis of what they said (Piaget, 1955).

Video Link 2.5
Jean Piaget.

Schema A cognitive framework that places concepts, objects, or experiences into categories or groups of associations.

What Is a Schema? Piaget believed that we are constantly adapting to our environment. In order to do so, we use our minds to organize the world in ways that we can understand. This organization is based on the development of "schemas." A **schema** is a cognitive framework that places a concept into categories and associations. For example, we all have a schema for gender, which contains all the expectations and associations that we activate when we see women and men. In one interesting study, children looked at either pictures that would be consistent with gender expectations (for example, a woman washing dishes and a man working under a car) or pictures that might not be consistent with gender expectations (for example, a man washing dishes and a woman working under a car). When they later tried to remember what they had seen, those children who had a very stereotyped schema for gender were more likely to change the gender of the people in the gender-inconsistent pictures; that is, they remembered a man working under a car and a woman washing dishes (Carter & Levy, 1988). The stereotypical nature of these children's schemas even affected their memory, so they believed that what they had seen conformed to their expectations.

Assimilation Fitting new experiences into existing mental schemas.

How Do We Use Schemas? Piaget set out two processes of adaptation: assimilation and accommodation. In **assimilation**, we take new information and fit it into a schema, whether

Table 2.2

Piaget's stage theory. Piaget believed that children's thinking changes in qualitative ways as they move through the four stages of cognitive development.

Stage	Age	Description	
Sensorimotor	Birth–2 years	Infants take in information through their senses and their action upon the world.	
Preoperational	2–7 years	Young children do not yet think logically, and their thinking is egocentric.	
Concrete operations	7–12 years	Children now think logically, but their thinking is concrete and not abstract.	
Formal operations	12 years and older	Adolescents can think both logically and abstractly.	

it really fits there or not. Take the example of a little boy who goes to the zoo and sees an elephant for the first time. He turns to his mother and says, "Look, it's a big doggy with two tails!" In this case, the child has a schema for *doggy* but not one for *elephant*, so he does his best to make sense out of seeing an animal with both a trunk and a tail by trying to fit this new experience into what he already knows. Will he always think the elephant is a strange dog? Of course not, and this is where the process of **accommodation** comes in. As his mother explains to him about elephants, pointing out their unique features, he accommodates this new information by creating a new schema, one for elephants. Piaget described a process he called **equilibration** as a constant seesaw between assimilation and accommodation. We are constantly experiencing and learning more about our world, and we must make sense out of what we see as best we can, using concepts we understand. We assimilate new information into existing schemas if we can make that work. If the new information cannot be assimilated, that throws us into a state of disequilibrium. By creating a new schema to accommodate the new information, we are returned to a steady state of equilibration. If you have ever worked very hard to understand something you found difficult and finally had a "breakthrough" or "aha" experience, then you know the sensation of opening up your mind in a new way, which is indicative of accommodation. The frustration you felt when you didn't understand gives way to a sense of resolution, or equilibrium.

Stages of Development. Like Freud and Erikson, Piaget believed that children change in qualitative ways from one age period to the next. The stages that he described were based on how he believed the mind works at each age level. (Remember that Freud's stages are based on the progression of the sex drive and Erikson's on the social development of the self.) In this chapter we will give a brief overview of Piaget's stages (see Table 2.2), but they will be described in more depth in Chapter 7.

The first stage is the **sensorimotor stage**, which begins at birth and ends at about 2 years. As the name of this stage implies, Piaget believed that infants organize their world by means of their senses and their physical action upon it. Therefore, action schemas determine their understanding. For infants, objects do not exist in and of themselves but exist only in relation to the infant's action on them. He termed this a lack of **object permanence**. For an infant, out of sight is literally out of mind. By the end of this stage, infants have learned that objects continue to exist, and they have begun to represent objects, people, and events in their minds.

Accommodation Changing your mental schemas so they fit new experiences.

Equilibration An attempt to resolve uncertainty to return to a comfortable cognitive state.

Sensorimotor stage Piaget's first stage in which infants learn through their senses and their actions upon the world.

Object permanence The understanding that objects still exist when an infant does not see them.

Preoperational stage
Piaget's second stage of development, in which children ages 2–7 do not yet have logical thought, instead thinking magically and egocentrically.

TRUE/FALSE

7. When young children are selfish and self-centered it is because their parents overindulge them.

False. According to Piaget, children may appear to be selfish and self-centered because they are incapable of seeing things from another person's point of view. He called this characteristic *egocentrism*.

Egocentrism   The inability to see or understand things from someone else's perspective.

Concrete operations The third stage in Piaget's theory in which children between 6 and 12 years of age develop logical thinking that is still not abstract.

Formal operations Piaget's fourth stage in which people 12 and older think both logically and abstractly.

Constructivism   The idea that humans actively construct their understanding of the world, rather than passively receiving knowledge.

The second stage is the **preoperational stage**, which lasts from 2 to 7 years of age. For Piaget, the term "operations" refers to logical thought processes. The name of this stage implies that preschool children do not yet have logical thinking (perhaps this is why we do not have them start formal schooling until late in this stage). The major accomplishment of this stage is the ability to think using symbols—that is, a representation of something that is not there. Toddlers can think about and refer to objects that are not in their immediate vicinity because they can represent them in their minds. They can *tell* you about an apple they ate yesterday, unlike the infant who must *show* you the actual apple.

Another important characteristic of preoperational thought is **egocentrism** (remember, *ego* means "I" or "self," and therefore the child's world centers around his own point of view). Be careful in understanding this term. It is *not* the same as selfishness or egotism (thinking *you* are the *greatest*). It really means that children of this age are unable to understand that someone else's perspective could be different from their own. The result may be a "selfish" child who grabs toys from others, but the reason is that the child cannot yet understand that someone else wants the same toy just as much as she does.

The third stage is **concrete operations**, which lasts from 7 to 12 years of age. By 7 years of age, most children have begun to think logically. The limitation of this period is that thinking is concrete rather than abstract. For example, how would you explain the saying "Don't put all your eggs in one basket"? As an abstract thinker, you might say, "Don't count on only one plan to work out. Have some backup plans." Now compare what a concrete thinker might say: "When you go to the store, take two baskets and put half your eggs in one and half in the other." Concrete thought is very much in the here and now. This is probably why we don't start teaching subjects that involve abstract thinking such as political science or philosophy to children until they are at least in middle school.

The fourth and final stage is **formal operations**, which begins at 12 years of age and, according to Piaget, describes cognitive abilities in adulthood as well. As adolescence begins, children develop the ability to think both logically and abstractly.

Modern Applications of Piaget's Theory

Although Piaget's theories have received a good deal of criticism about specifics (such as when exactly children develop different cognitive abilities), his legacy may lie in his concept of **constructivism**. He understood that we do not operate like video cameras, taking in what is around us passively and indiscriminately. Instead, Piaget believed that we are active learners, always working to construct our understanding of the world. Piaget saw children as being like "little scientists," always actively experimenting on the world to increase their understanding of it.

These ideas have had a great impact on educational practices, taking the focus away from rote learning of facts and fostering a teaching style that promotes the child's active approach to constructing his own learning. Many teachers use Piaget's ideas as the basis for their teaching style (Hinde & Perry, 2007), and research in this area is ongoing. For example, Constance Kamii and her colleagues (Kamii, Rummelsburg, & Kari, 2005) examined the efficacy of active, constructive learning. They gave low-socioeconomic status, low-achieving students in first grade active, math-related activities to explore (for example, pick-up sticks and group-based arithmetic games) instead of traditional math assignments (for example, "What is 2 + 2?"). At the end of the year, these students scored higher on tests of mental arithmetic and logical reasoning than did similar students who had received teacher-directed, pencil-and-paper instruction.

Lev Vygotsky's Sociocultural Theory

Lev Semenovich Vygotsky (1896–1934), a Russian psychologist, had somewhat different ideas about cognitive development. Instead of seeing children as "little scientists" who carry out informal experiments to figure out the world around them, Vygotsky (1978b) emphasized the importance of the social world and of culture in promoting cognitive growth. According to Vygotsky, learning first takes place in the interaction between people. The individual then internalizes that learning, and it becomes a part of her own, independent thinking: "First it appears between people as an interpsychological category and then within the child as an intrapsychological category" (Vygotsky, 1986, p. 163).

Vygotsky believed that looking at what the child is capable of learning in interaction with a skilled helper is a better indicator of his level of cognitive development than just testing what he already knows. He was more interested in what the child could become than in how he currently functioned (Wertsch, 1985). Vygotsky (1978a) developed the concept of the **zone of proximal development**, which he defined as "the distance between the actual developmental level as determined by independent problem solving and the level of potential development as determined through problem solving under adult guidance or in collaboration with more capable peers" (p. 86). *Proximal* refers to being near or close. A good teacher stays close to what children already know but then helps them take the next step. Of necessity, this involves a dialogue between the teacher and learners, as the teacher probes what the children know in order to shape the next step. The process by which this learning happens is referred to as **scaffolding**. A scaffold is a structure put around a building to allow people to work on it. In like fashion, adults help the "construction" of the child's understanding by providing guidance and support. Just as the scaffold comes down when a building is completed, so too the adult can step back when the child fully understands. For example, if you have a jack-in-the-box and want to play with a 6-month-old baby, you will likely just turn the handle for him and watch his reaction. When the child is 2 years old, you might hold his hand on the handle so he can learn to turn it. When he is 4, you might just give him the toy and watch: Your input is no longer needed, and your "scaffolding" can come down.

Modern Applications of Vygotsky's Theory

Interest in Vygotsky's ideas has grown over time. While Piaget helped promote the idea of active learning and construction of knowledge in the field of education, Vygotsky's ideas have been used to give more concrete form to how teachers can promote active learning through scaffolding and the zone of proximal development (Miller, 2006).

Information Processing

In the 1950s, experimental psychologist Donald Broadbent (1926–1993) and others were struggling with the issue of how people work with machines. They found that the behaviorist stimulus-response paradigm was not adequate for their study because they had to understand all the steps that came *between* the environmental stimulus and the individual response. In the late '50s, Broadbent published a paper in which he brought together the ideas about these intervening processes, such as attention, memory, and decision making, which became the basis for the theory of information processing (Broadbent, 1958/1987; Massaro & Cowan, 1993).

The information processing approach likens the mind to a computer. Just as a computer has both hardware and software, so does the human mind. The "hardware" is the storage device, such as the hard drive, which is equivalent to human memory storage in the brain. The "software" is the computer program that processes the information that enters the storage device. This is equivalent to cognitive processes such as attention, organization, and retrieval strategies. People take in information through their senses, process this information so that some of it enters into memory, and later try to remember what they have learned when they need it. One characteristic of information processing is breaking down the way we understand and use

Zone of proximal development According to Vygotsky, this is what a child cannot do on her own but can do with a little help from someone more skilled or knowledgeable.

Scaffolding The idea that more knowledgeable adults and children support a child's learning by providing help to move the child just beyond his current level of capability.

Sensory memory The capacity for information that comes in through our senses to be retained for a very brief period of time in its raw form.

Working (or short-term) memory Memory capacity that is limited to only a brief time but that also allows the mind to process information in order to move it into long-term memory.

Long-term memory The capacity for nearly permanent retention of memories.

information into steps, such as the steps in memory described above: acquiring information, storing it, and retrieving it (Robinson-Riegler & Robinson-Riegler, 2008).

Continuing this analogy of human memory as a computer, there are three structures, each of which serves a different function: sensory memory, working (or short-term) memory, and long-term memory. As information comes in through our senses, it is retained for a very brief period of time in its raw form. This is known as **sensory memory**. You can think of this as analogous to input devices such as the keyboard or mouse on your computer. In this fraction of a second the information either moves along to the next step or is lost and does not stay in our mind. Information that moves along then enters **working (or short-term) memory**. Think of this as analogous to a computer's RAM or random-access memory. The capacity of short-term memory is limited, and information can be retained for only a brief time *unless* the information is processed. Working memory takes those short-term memories and processes them in a variety of ways. Rehearsal is one of the important ways that we can do this. Repeating information to ourselves preserves it in its original form until it can be organized (or, in information processing terms, "encoded") and moved along into **long-term memory**, which is thought to be capable of permanent storage. See **Active Learning: Encoding Processes** to examine different ways to encode information into memory.

ACTIVE LEARNING

Encoding Processes

Imagine that you need to memorize the following list of words:

Seashell	Soccer	Beach	Skiing
Baseball	Sand	Basketball	Seagull

How would you try to do it? Some possible strategies you might use include (a) repeating the words over and over, (b) dividing the list into those words that start with *s* and those that start with *b*, (c) dividing the list into sports- and beach-related words, (d) making a sentence or two using the words, and (e) imagining a picture that includes what each word represents.

Repetition	Initial Sound	Concept	Sentence	Imagery
Seashell Baseball Soccer Sand Beach Basketball Skiing Seagull Seashell Baseball Soccer Sand Beach Basketball Skiing Seagull Seashell Baseball Soccer Sand Beach Basketball Skiing Seagull	S *sound* Seashell Soccer Sand Skiing Seagull B *sound* Baseball Beach Basketball	*Sports* Baseball Soccer Basketball Skiing *Beach* Seashell Sand Beach Seagull	I took my *baseball* and my *basketball* to the *beach*. I sat on the *sand* and played with a *seashell* as I watched a *seagull* fly by. It was so hot that I wished I were *skiing* or even playing *soccer* instead.	Create pictures in your mind that include several images in each (a boy on a *beach* holding a *baseball* in one hand and a *basketball* in the other with a *seagull* sitting on his head)

Which of these approaches do you think would work best for you? Choose one and give yourself 30 seconds to memorize this new list of words. Then cover this list and test yourself. How effective was the technique you used?

Classroom	Cardinal	Canary
Pencil	Paper	Computer
Penguin	Parakeet	PowerPoint

All of these ways of trying to remember a list of words are examples of **encoding processes** (and they are also techniques you may want to consider using when memory is required in your studying!).

Encoding processes
The transformation processes through which new information is stored in long-term memory.

It is all well and good to *put* something into our memory, but the real trick is to *retrieve* that information when we need it. If information has not been carefully organized and encoded in this process, it will be difficult to find in our storage when we need to use it. You undoubtedly have had the experience of knowing that you know something (it's on the tip of your tongue!) but not being able to bring it back into your working memory to use it. Similarly you have probably lost a document on your computer when you haven't been careful to store it away in the correct folder. (Wouldn't it be nice if we had a "find" function in our brains like we have on the computer, to help us out in these situations?)

The idea described above, that information is processed through a series of locations (sensory to short-term to long-term memory "stores"), is known as the **stores model** of memory, illustrated in Figure 2.3. A more recent way of thinking about the memory process is known as a **connectionist** or **network model**. Using this model, you can think of memory as a neural network that consists of concept nodes that are interconnected by links. For example, when we see a white duck, different concept nodes may be activated. One node can represent a specific concept (*white*), one can represent a higher-order concept (*duck*), and one can represent a superordinate concept (*bird*) depending on how the neurons are activated (Robinson-Riegler & Robinson-Riegler, 2008). The concept nodes are analogous to nerve cells in the brain, and the links are connections between individual neurons. When information is stored in memory, it becomes a new node that is connected to other nodes in the network. Although each node is connected in some way to other pieces of information in our memory, the strength of these connections can vary, and learning involves modifying the weight of these connections. When

Stores model   The idea that information is processed through a series of mental locations (sensory to short-term to long-term memory "stores").

Connectionist/network model   In this model of memory, the process is envisioned as a neural network that consists of concept nodes that are interconnected by links.

Figure 2.3

The stores model of memory. This early model of information processing showed information moving through a set of locations or "stores" to end up in long-term storage where it could later be retrieved and used by working memory.

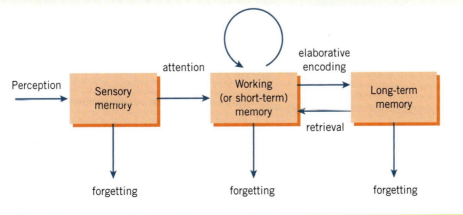

input comes into the system (for example, the sight of a bird in flight), certain nodes are activated. If the links between those nodes are strong enough, the output is a concept (in this case, *bird*). Rather than representing memory or learning as the transfer of information from one storage box to another, this newer way of thinking about information processing more closely reflects our current understanding that neurons in the brain operate through multiple connections with other neurons throughout the brain.

Modern Applications of Information Processing

As we mentioned, one strength of the information processing approach is that it breaks down cognitive processes into their component steps. This approach has been used to design better teaching techniques to help ensure student learning. For example, the process of learning to read has been broken down into its component parts. Two important parts are the ability to name letters accurately and the ability to name letters quickly. Research has shown that the speed with which a child can name letters, even if he makes mistakes, is more important for later reading efficiency than total accuracy of letter naming. Processing of letters must become automatic if a child is going to be able to read fluently (Ritchey & Speece, 2006). With this information, teachers will have a better idea of how to develop skills that will help children learn to read.

Other applications of principles from information processing theory to classroom practice include being sure that you have the learner's attention before you start, connecting new knowledge to other information that is already in the individual's memory, and requiring the learner to actively process new incoming information (Slate & Charlesworth, 1988). You can get a student's attention by presenting information in a novel way, by changing the volume and tone of your voice, or by moving across the room to write information on the board. You can help students make the necessary connections between old and new material by presenting a lot of examples or giving them assignments that require that they integrate new information with previous knowledge. Using discussion groups and classroom activities helps ensure that the students are actively engaged with and using newly acquired knowledge. Completing the Active Learning activities and trying to answer the true/false questions in this book give you the opportunity to remain actively engaged in learning the material.

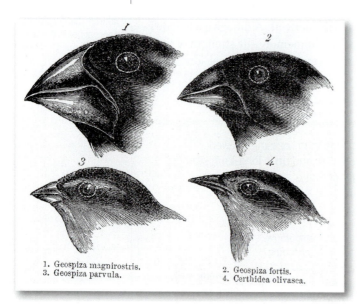

Darwin's finches. These finches came from one evolutionary ancestor but now live on different islands in the Galápagos. Each island has a somewhat different type of food appropriate for birds. Can you see the differences among the beaks of these four types of birds? Imagine what makes each type of beak most adaptive for a particular type of food.

Evolutionary Theories

Charles Darwin and the Theory of Evolution

In 1859, Charles Darwin (1809–1882) published *On the Origin of Species* and introduced the idea of evolution to a wide audience. As he traveled around the world, observing animals and plants in their native settings, Darwin developed the idea that natural selection, or survival of the fittest, accounts for changes in species from one generation to the next. The "fittest" animals or plants are not necessarily the strongest but rather those that *adapt* most successfully to their environment. Those who are successful are most likely to produce offspring and pass on their genes to the next generation. This theory has become a core understanding underlying much of biological science today.

The theory of evolution is illustrated by the differences in the beaks of finches that Darwin found on different Galápagos Islands, off the western coast of South America. The islands have different types of terrain. Some are dry and others are mountainous, and the type of vegetation that grows on each varies accordingly. Although the birds that Darwin found on these islands were similar to each other, each had a different type of beak that enabled the birds to eat the type of food available on their island. It appears that, as the birds migrated from one island to another, only those who could successfully manage the food available were able to survive and pass on their genes. Eventually, the populations became different on each island as they adapted to their environment.

Two theories of development that are based on Darwin's ideas are ethology and sociobiology. **Ethology** is the study of animal behavior (including humans) in the natural environment. **Sociobiology** is a newer theory that proposes that social behavior is determined by genes that evolved to promote adaptation. We will describe each of these approaches here.

Ethology

Konrad Lorenz (1903–1989) is considered to be the father of modern ethology (Tinbergen, 1963). As a zoologist studying animal behavior in Munich, Germany, he observed ducks and geese and found that when these animals are born, they *immediately* follow their mothers. This behavior, which he called **imprinting**, is adaptive because the mother is necessary to provide food and protection from predators. Newborn animals that follow their mothers are more likely to grow up and pass their genes on to their own babies. Babies who don't follow their mothers are more likely to starve or be eaten by predators. Lorenz determined that this behavior results from genetically determined tendencies to respond to very specific stimuli in the environment. He showed that the baby geese's behavior is released in response to any large moving object they see shortly after birth. To test his idea, he removed the mother goose as her eggs were hatching. Then, walking by the newborn goslings himself, he found that the babies would follow him just as they would have followed their mother. He believed that these innate releasing mechanisms allow for an immediate and permanent type of learning (Lorenz, 1988). For this and other research on animal behavior, Lorenz and two colleagues were awarded the Nobel Prize in 1973.

Some researchers attempted to apply the idea of imprinting to human behavior, in the form of "bonding." They claimed that infants must have skin-to-skin contact with their mother within the first few hours after birth for bonding, or love, to develop. As with many direct applications of

8. Darwin's concept of the "survival of the fittest" means that the strongest animal is most likely to survive. **TRUE/FALSE**

False. Fittest in this sense means "best adapted to the environment." The one who is best adapted may have some characteristic other than strength that determines whether he will live to pass on his genes to the next generation.

Ethology The study of animal and human behavior in the natural environment.

Sociobiology A theory that proposes that social behavior is determined by genes that evolved to promote adaptation.

Imprinting In ethology, the automatic process by which animals attach to their mothers.

Konrad Lorenz and imprinting. Konrad Lorenz observed the behavior of geese (left) and demonstrated the presence of imprinting by removing the mother goose and substituting himself (right).

Video Link 2.6
Lorenz and goslings.

animal behavior to humans, this has not turned out to be the case. Although animal behavior can give us some ideas about human behavior, the direct application of one to the other is usually too simplistic. You can read more about this research in Chapter 10 where we talk about the development of attachment. For an example of animal behavior that *does* correspond more clearly to human behavior, see **Active Learning: Rough-and-Tumble Play**.

ACTIVE LEARNING

Rough-and-Tumble Play

One example of a similarity between animal behavior and human behavior is the existence of rough-and-tumble play, which appears in many species. Rough-and-tumble (R&T) play consists of "play" fighting, wrestling, and chasing (Pellegrini, 1987). It is not the same as real aggression as all parties know that the goal is not to hurt anyone. Children often laugh while engaging in R&T play. Children, especially boys, all around the world take part in this type of play (Whiting & Edwards, 1973). If you were an ethologist, how would you explain this behavior? Think about what adaptive value the behavior might have either at the time that it happens or in the future for the participants. Remember your own experiences with rough-and-tumble play to add your own thoughts and feelings to your understanding of the behavior.

Rough-and-tumble play. How would an ethologist explain the presence of rough-and-tumble play in many species and in human societies around the world? How do we know this is play and not real fighting?

Answer: There have been several ethologically based explanations for rough-and-tumble play. One explanation is that it is practice for later aggressive and defensive behavior in adulthood, because this type of activity develops muscles and endurance (Pellegrini, 1987). Another possible explanation, found more with adolescents than younger children, is that R&T play is used to establish dominance (Fry, 2005; Pellegrini, 2003). Just as chickens develop a "pecking order," teens can use R&T play to find out who is stronger and more skilled without needing to have a real fight.

Sociobiology

Biologist Edward O. Wilson published the book *Sociobiology: The New Synthesis* in 1975, introducing a new area of study based on evolutionary theory. Sociobiology examines the role that genes and biology play in the development of social behavior and culture. An example of what sociobiologists study is the impact of kinship on relationships.

The members of your family, unless you are adopted, share some of your genes. Therefore, it is argued that you have a stake in making sure that they survive to pass on the genes that you share. As a result, societies have created titles for relatives, such as *father, daughter, aunt,* and *brother-in-law,* that bestow a special status on those to whom you are related. The theory of sociobiology states that for these reasons people are more likely to protect, help, and give to relatives than to other people. Such behaviors promote the well-being of the kinship group and consequently that gene pool (Pollet, 2007). A second function of kin relationships is to avoid incest. Throughout the world, society has made sexual contact between close relatives taboo. Genetically this makes sense, as incestuous relationships are more likely to produce offspring that carry active forms of destructive genes that otherwise lie dormant. For example, a woman with the recessive gene for Tay-Sachs, an illness that kills infants by the age of 2 years, is more likely to have a child who has this condition if she marries a relative because they share a common genetic inheritance, so her partner may also carry a recessive gene for Tay-Sachs.

David Buss and his colleagues have examined topics such as mate selection in relation to evolutionary theory. They argue that men and women choose partners to optimize the chances that they will be able to pass on their genes to the next generation. Women must invest a large amount of time and energy in bearing and raising one baby. Therefore, they search for a stable mate with the resources (in our culture, that is money!) that will help ensure that each baby survives. Men, on the other hand, use only minimal energy to contribute their genes to the next generation. They can create more than one baby at a time, by mating with many women. Therefore, they are attracted to women whose appearance reflects a high likelihood of fertility, including youth and health (Barker, 2006). These different preferences by men and women are found in many places around the world and do not appear to be influenced by women's income level (Wiederman & Allgeier, 1992).

Modern Applications of Evolutionary Theory

Ideas taken from evolutionary theory have influenced research on several important topics in the field of child development, including aggression, altruism, attachment, and social dominance hierarchies. Understanding the adaptive value of each of these behaviors gives us insight into the mechanisms that contribute to them.

Evolutionary approaches such as ethology and sociobiology have contributed to a newer approach known as evolutionary developmental psychology (Blasi & Bjorklund, 2003; Causey, Gardiner, & Bjorklund, 2008). This new approach applies the principles and ideas of evolutionary theory specifically to questions of how and why children develop as they do. Children's behavior is seen as an adaptation to the environment in two ways: (a) What children do is adaptive because it is a preparation for adult life, and (b) what children do is adaptive at their own stage of development and in their specific life circumstances. This newer approach places greater emphasis on the role of the environment (rather than the role of instinctive behavior) in influencing behavior and links the influence of the environment with the expression of genes, in a process known as epigenesis (Blasi & Bjorklund, 2003). We will discuss epigenesis more thoroughly in Chapter 4.

One example of research based on an evolutionary developmental approach has focused on the onset of puberty in girls. Age of onset is affected by many factors but is largely controlled by our genes. The age at which a girl's mother began puberty is a good predictor of when her daughter will begin puberty. However, research has shown that girls enter puberty at earlier ages when their parents have a high level of conflict with little support or satisfaction in their marriage or when their father is absent or severely dysfunctional (Saxbe & Repetti, 2009; Tither & Ellis, 2008). Evolutionary developmental psychologists explain this finding by pointing to built-in genetic adaptations that are set to respond to particular environmental circumstances in childhood because they have led to success in passing on one's genes to the next generation. In the case of early puberty, Bruce Ellis has explained the association with parental characteristics this way: "In the world in which humans evolved, dangerous or unstable home environments meant a shorter lifespan, and going into puberty earlier in this context increased chances of surviving, reproducing and passing on your genes" (Harrison, 2008, para. 10).

Evolutionary developmental psychology often has been used in conjunction with other theoretical approaches, providing us with new hypotheses to test and drawing our attention to the need to understand the evolutionary functions that are served by different types of human behavior if we hope to fully understand them (Blasi & Bjorklund, 2003).

Ecological Theory

We tend to think of the study of ecology as focusing on plants and animals and their relationships to the environment. For example, on a large scale, we are learning more and more about how human impact on the earth's atmosphere is creating global climate change, which is affecting even the survival of polar bears and penguins. These creatures have adapted to specific environments, called ecological niches. When these environments change, the whole system of interrelationships of plants and animals changes, and some organisms will disappear.

In the 1970s, Urie Bronfenbrenner (1917–2005) applied these ideas to the field of developmental psychology to create a theory of human ecology, in which he defined development as a function of the "interaction between the developing organism and the enduring environments or contexts in which it lives out its life" (Bronfenbrenner, 1975, p. 439). Bronfenbrenner believed that you cannot understand the life course of an individual without understanding how that person interacts with all the different facets of his environment. He also believed that this is a dynamic process: All aspects of the environment affect the individual, and the individual affects all aspects of his environment.

Bronfenbrenner (1977) proposed that individuals grow and develop within a nested set of influences that he divided into four systems, the microsystem, mesosystem, exosystem, and macrosystem, as shown in Figure 2.4. He subsequently added a dimension of time, called the chronosystem (Bronfenbrenner, 1986). These systems are embedded one within the other, each influencing the other in a back-and-forth fashion, and the relationship between systems changes as the child grows and develops. Within each system, if you change one thing it affects everything else in the system.

The **microsystem** includes the interaction of the person in her immediate settings, such as home, school, or friendship groups. The microsystem contains all the face-to-face interactions that include the developing person. The **mesosystem** consists of the interaction among these various settings. For example, a child's experiences at home influence her progress at school, and her experiences at school influence her interactions at home. The **exosystem** consists of settings that the child never enters (*external* to the child) but that affect the child's development nevertheless (Bronfenbrenner, 1986). For example, even if the child never goes to the parents' workplace, what happens in that setting can have an effect on the child. A job that is so demanding that it leaves a parent exhausted at the end of the day affects how the parents

Microsystem In ecological theory, the interaction of the person in her immediate settings, such as home, school, or friendship groups.

Mesosystem The interaction among the various settings in the microsystem, such as a child's school and home.

Exosystem Settings that the child never enters (*external* to the child) but that affect the child's development nevertheless, such as the parents' place of work.

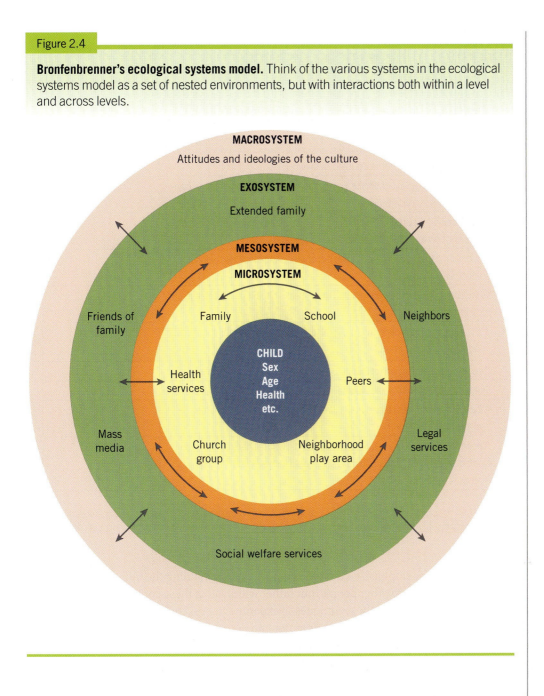

Figure 2.4

Bronfenbrenner's ecological systems model. Think of the various systems in the ecological systems model as a set of nested environments, but with interactions both within a level and across levels.

will interact with their children when they come home. The **macrosystem** consists of cultural norms that guide the nature of the organizations and places that make up one's everyday life. For example, the macrosystem in the United States includes the ideology of democracy, as well as the value that is placed on individual achievement. The **chronosystem** consists of the "changes (and continuities) over time in the environments in which the person is living" (Bronfenbrenner, 1986, p. 724).

It will be easier for you to remember the various "systems" that make up ecological theory if you are able to recognize examples of each of them. **Active Learning: Examples of Ecological Systems** gives you a chance to do this.

Macrosystem Cultural norms that guide the nature of the organizations and places that make up one's everyday life.

Chronosystem The dimension of time, including one's age and the time in history in which one lives.

ACTIVE LEARNING

Examples of Ecological Systems

Match each description below with the correct level of the ecological system that it represents. The levels are the microsystem, mesosystem, macrosystem, exosystem, and chronosystem.

Example	System Level
1. The number of mothers with children under the age of 5 who were employed outside the home doubled between 1970 and 1990.	
2. A child's parents go to school for a parent-teacher conference so they can find out how their child is doing.	
3. Native American parents raise their children to avoid interpersonal conflicts and to cooperate with others to work for the greater good.	
4. The child's preschool teacher shows the child how to stack two blocks upon each other.	
5. New parents in Germany are entitled to 47 weeks of paid parental leave after the birth of their baby.	
6. A parent gets a promotion and a big raise, but that also means that he will need to work longer hours.	
7. Parents invite a teen's group of friends to their house to watch some movies.	
8. Fathers today take a more active role in parenting than fathers in the past did.	
9. A teenager and his best friend make plans for how they will spend time together on the weekend.	
10. A new mother spends some time with her friends, who tell her that she is too worried about caring for her baby and she should just relax and enjoy being a mother.	

Answers: (1) chronosystem, (2) mesosystem, (3) macrosystem, (4) microsystem, (5) macrosystem, (6) exosystem, (7) mesosystem, (8) chronosystem, (9) microsystem, (10) exosystem

TRUE/FALSE

9. If a child is experiencing a lot of stress at home, the child will show behavior problems in the classroom.

False. Although there is likely to be some carryover from home to classroom, research based on ecological theory has shown that both stress at home *and* the quality of the classroom environment (including whether or not there are other children with behavior problems in the classroom) play a role in determining whether a child will have behavior problems at school.

Bronfenbrenner emphasized the importance of understanding the individual, not on her own or with one or two other people, but rather within all of these contexts. His theory is, in part, a criticism of some of the techniques of experimental psychology, in which children are tested in the laboratory with an experimenter and perhaps a parent, and the results are then assumed to be true in the child's natural setting. He developed the idea of "ecological validity," meaning that research and its interpretation must take the environment into account, whether the environment is a laboratory or a natural setting. For example, a laboratory may be an excellent place to look at reactions to strange situations, but it is not necessarily a good way to look at the everyday interactions of parent and child (Bronfenbrenner, 1977).

Modern Applications of Ecological Theory

In a recent study, Brophy-Herb, Lee, Nievar, and Stollak (2006) used ecological theory as a basis for understanding the development of social competence in preschoolers. Instead of looking at single variables like socioeconomic status or family stress as predictors of children's social competence, they examined an intersecting and nested array of variables that they believed would have an influence on social competence. These variables were individual characteristics (age, sex, and level of stress of the child); family characteristics (married or divorced, level of stress, socioeconomic status); teacher behavior (authoritative style); and classroom climate (warmth, organization, and number of children with behavior problems). One finding illustrates the complexity of the findings. Although they found that children with more stress in their lives were rated as having lower social competence, the nature of the child's classroom modified this relationship. In a classroom in which many children had behavior problems, a child experiencing high stress was more likely to have those problems than a stressed child in a classroom with few other children with behavior problems.

Another legacy of human ecology is the application of theory to policy, action research, and making change happen. A human ecologist believes that all levels of society impact human development. The logical extension of this belief is involvement in the creation of social policy, including legislation and programs at all levels of government. Bronfenbrenner himself was involved with the creation of Head Start, a program that was designed to help disadvantaged children by providing interventions at several different levels. Head Start provides an excellent educational program for children but also helps their families' well-being by providing help with financial, social, educational, and psychological difficulties they might be experiencing. It also works hard to create links between the classroom setting and the child's home.

We have now presented a number of different theories designed to explain aspects of child development. In order to have a broader historical understanding of how these theories developed, read **Journey of Research: Theories in Historical Context**.

Theories in Historical Context

JOURNEY *of* **RESEARCH**

As you have seen throughout this chapter, theories have a central role in our understanding of child development. They shape the type of questions we ask, the type of research we conduct, and often the interpretation we place on our findings. However, it is important to understand that theoretical ideas do not appear in a vacuum. The influential theorists in our field all have developed their ideas in a particular culture and at a particular point in historical time, and their ideas about child development reflect these influences. If you stop and think for a moment about how the world you live in today influences the way you think about children and how they develop, you will realize that our culture and our experiences so color our worldview that we might not even be aware of those influences unless we make a conscious effort to think about them.

This is not a complete review of the history of developmental theories, but these examples will illustrate this point.

Freud's psychoanalytic theory. Some aspects of Freud's theory may seem quaint or even a bit strange to us today because they are based on beliefs about human sexuality that reflect the culture at the time in which Freud lived—the Victorian era of the late 19th century. This was a time in history when sexuality was treated as something private or even shameful. Sex was seen as a necessary evil for procreation within a marriage, and sex for pleasure was more likely to be relegated to a man's encounters with prostitutes, rather than with his wife (Goodwin, 2005).

In this context, Freud interpreted the mental disorders that he was seeing in his patients as the product of some sexual trauma—real or imagined— in their early experiences. He reasoned that if you cannot accept sexual feelings or thoughts, they will be pushed down into the unconscious, only to resurface from time to time in ways that disrupt your functioning (Goodwin, 2005). While this explanation may have made sense in the context of the Victorian era, it may have little relevance in cultures where sexual impulses are seen as a normal expression of our humanity. The fact that biological instincts played a central role in Freud's theory also is not surprising given that Freud was trained as a medical doctor.

John B. Watson and behaviorism. Behaviorism came to prominence in America in the early part of the 20th century, at a time when psychology was moving away from Freud's focus on what was going on inside a person's mind (either the conscious or

(Continued)

(Continued)

the unconscious part of it) and toward a focus on what was observable—the person's behavior (Crain, 2005; Goodwin, 2005). In 1913, Watson published an article titled "Psychology as the Behaviorist Views It" in which he described psychology as a "purely objective experimental branch of natural science" (Watson, 1994, p. 248) with a goal of predicting and controlling behavior.

Over the years, his writings attracted the attention of both the scientific community and the general public. Watson had been trained as a comparative psychologist (a psychologist who studies the behavior of humans and other animals and makes cross-species comparisons), so his thinking was influenced by the work of a contemporary Russian physiologist, Ivan Pavlov. Watson came to believe that all one needed to do to understand development was to understand the stimulus-response relations that controlled it (Lerner, 2002). In his 1928 book, *Psychological Care of Infant and Child,* Watson applied the principles of classical and operant conditioning to child rearing. For instance, he warned parents that being too affectionate toward their children would make the children irresponsible, dependent, and unsuccessful in later life. The book found a ready audience because at this point in history, parents wanted to benefit from this new, more scientific approach to understanding behavior. Behaviorism also fit well with American ideals of uniqueness, independence, and individual achievement.

Although behaviorist psychology dominated American psychology until the middle of the 20th century, it was *not* widely influential in Europe (Goodwin, 2005). Ideas from cognitive theorists such as Piaget and Vygotsky were more influential in European psychology.

Jean Piaget and cognitive developmental theory. Today Jean Piaget is recognized as one of the most influential theorists in the field of development, but when his work initially was published in the 1920s and 1930s, it received a cool reception in America (Whitman, 1980). Piaget's ideas and methodology were just out of step with American psychology. While American psychology was moving in a more rigorous scientific direction, Piaget was conducting research using open-ended clinical interviews with children. In the middle of an interview, he might suddenly change the questions he was asking in order to pursue something that the child had said that caught his interest (Piaget, 1969). He also spent a great deal of time observing the spontaneous behavior of children, including his own three children. His research did not contain statistics to back up his conclusions, did not provide detailed reports of the methodology he used, and used abstract concepts as explanations (Lerner, 2002). While American psychologists were busy measuring

what children knew through the use of standardized tests, Piaget was interested in understanding *how* they arrived at this knowledge (Newman & Newman, 2007).

By the 1960s, however, a reaction was developing to strict behaviorist approaches and their reduction of human behavior to a set of stimulus-response connections. American psychologists had become more open to new ideas like *humanistic psychology,* which emphasizes a person's conscious ability to make choices, and *ecological psychology,* which examines behavior within multiple contexts. In this new climate, Piaget's ideas were now embraced for the richness with which they described children's ways of understanding their world.

Urie Bronfenbrenner and ecological systems theory. Another strong statement of growing dissatisfaction with the direction in which psychology was going came from Urie Bronfenbrenner in an article written in 1977 for the journal *American Psychologist.* In it Bronfenbrenner decries what he saw as a narrow focus on collecting data for data's sake and a reliance on experimental designs that were so carefully controlled that they resulted in highly artificial situations that bore little resemblance to the real life of children. His appraisal of the state of American developmental psychology was captured in his statement that "it can be said that much of contemporary developmental psychology is the science of the strange behavior of children in strange situations with strange adults for the briefest possible periods of time" (Bronfenbrenner, 1977, p. 513). Rather than seeing the environment as something that needs to be controlled, Bronfenbrenner believed that we must study behavior as it occurs embedded within a nest of environments and settings because each of these has its own impact on the process.

The 1960s and 1970s were a time of great societal change in America, and part of this change was a new appreciation of the pluralism and diversity of experiences that people had. Bronfenbrenner's ecological systems theory used a more holistic approach to draw attention to the immediate, as well as the distant, influences on development (Lerner, 2002). The challenge for researchers today is to find ways to study the incredible complexity of multiple, interacting influences on development. The result of doing this, however, is a richer, more complete understanding of the process of human development.

Each of these theories continues to exert some influence on our study of child and adolescent development to this day, although they are not equally influential. As you continue to read this book, you will see frequent references to these theorists and will be introduced to other more recent theoretical approaches to understanding development that have not been included in this chapter.

Biological Approaches to Understanding Child Development

The following theories and approaches concentrate on the physical aspects of children's growth and how these aspects interact with psychological development.

Maturational Theory

One of the early approaches to the study of children was based on biological maturation. Gesell and Ilg (1943, 1946) wrote several books describing an orderly unfolding of both physical and psychological changes that could be generally expected in all children. According to this viewpoint, all children go through the same stages of development based on the maturation of their brain and body. This includes everything from the changing ability to grasp objects in infancy to the changing way in which children acquire or collect objects (at age 6 they collect "odds and ends rather sporadically," while at 7 they collect "with purpose and specific and sustained interest") (Gesell & Ilg, 1946, p. 24). This approach provides little room for cultural or individual differences.

Dynamic Systems Theory

The idea that all of psychological development is due to biological maturation is no longer accepted because biological maturation itself may vary for individual children in different circumstances. Esther Thelen's theory, called **dynamic systems theory**, provides evidence that biological maturation operates in interaction with environmental influences (Spencer et al., 2006). Thelen found that the nature of physical development was flexible, not absolute. For example, newborn babies have a stepping reflex in which they appear to be walking when held upright, even though they cannot support their own weight. This reflex typically disappears at about 2 to 3 months of age, and it was initially thought that this was a product of brain maturation. However, Thelen found that babies who seem to have lost their initial stepping reflex will begin stepping again if placed up to their chests in water so that their legs are not so heavy, which means that the disappearance of this reflex is not driven solely by brain development (Thelen, 1989). Infants stop "stepping" reflexively when their legs become too heavy for them to lift. Thelen posited that the development of real walking is not just a matter of biological maturation but a coming together of many different experiences, bodily growth, and motivation. She showed that infants develop these abilities in different ways, depending on such characteristics as weight and activity level. They experiment with how to do things, such as reaching and grabbing, and each action influences what the next action will be. In Chapter 6 we will show how early walking develops differently in cultures that motivate their infants in ways that fit with their society's needs and expectations.

Neuropsychology and Behavioral Genomics

New technologies have allowed us to study both **neuropsychology** (the interaction of the *brain* and behavior) and **behavioral genomics** (the interaction of *genes* and behavior). These new approaches are on the cutting edge of research in the field of child development today because of new technology that has allowed researchers to investigate both the brain and genes in much more detail. We will be discussing them in some depth in Chapters 4 and 6, so we will only introduce them briefly here.

Researchers can now use technology to see the structure and functioning of our brains and to identify specific genes to try to understand their role in development. The earliest

Gesell's research. Arnold Gesell used the scientific methodology of his time to study the physical development of children.

Video Link 2.7
Arnold Gesell.

10. Babies lose the stepping reflex they have at birth because their legs become too heavy for them to lift.

TRUE/FALSE

True. It was assumed that the loss of the stepping reflex is a product of brain maturation. However, Esther Thelen showed that babies regain the reflex when their legs are easier to raise while held upright in water.

Dynamic systems theory Esther Thelen's theory that biological maturation is not independent of the environmental influences that surround the developing child.

Neuropsychology The study of the interaction of the brain and behavior.

Behavioral genomics Research that links behaviors with specific genes.

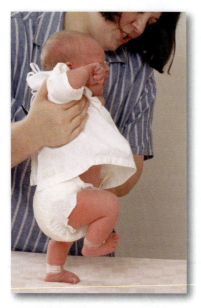

The stepping reflex. The stepping reflex is present in young infants. If you support their weight and allow their feet to touch a flat surface, they will raise and lower their legs as though they are walking.

approach to the study of both genes and the brain was very deterministic. The belief was that biology determines behavior. However, the more we learn about the functioning of both the brain and genes, the clearer it becomes that the effects go in both directions. These findings have produced an avalanche of new research. Biology has an impact on behavior, but the environment also affects our biological functioning. As we shall see in Chapter 6, the brain's development is to some extent dependent upon an individual's experiences. The development of connections between nerve cells, the coating of the nervous system, and the neurochemistry of the brain are all shaped in part by what a person does. The expression of genes is also affected by environmental events. These interactions will be discussed in Chapter 4.

Culture and Developmental Theory

It should be clear to you that all of the theories we have presented in this chapter were developed by European or American theorists, yet the course of child development is linked with the particular culture in which children are living. Western psychology has been exported to many countries around the world, with a variety of positive and negative results. However, it is important to take into account the indigenous theories of child development that guide how children are raised in a variety of cultures. When we assume that all societies must conform to Western values, we overlook the realities that have created differing ideas that are adaptive within their particular context and environment.

As an example of the differences that may be found, many of the theories we've described focus on the development of the individual. Erik Erikson sees the basic conflict of adolescence as *identity versus identity confusion*. However, this focus on individual identity and individual needs and achievements is largely a Western value. Developmental theory in many non-Western cultures focuses instead on the role of the individual in the context of the social group. For example, Nsamenang and Lo-oh (2010) explain that in sub-Saharan Africa, the overarching theory of development "positions the child not in his or her sovereignty but as socially integrated in a human community" (p. 386). We will learn more about these cultural comparisons in Chapter 4 and throughout the book. For now it is important to keep in mind the context in which these basic theories were developed within the Western world.

Conclusion

Studying these theories should help you understand the source of most of the rest of the ideas presented in this book. By exploring the big questions of why and how we develop from childhood through adolescence, we gain a deeper understanding of our observations and interactions. Although you might be tempted to say "I agree" or "I don't agree" with any particular theory, it is important to base our opinions on reasoned arguments that can be tested. Whether we accept one theory or another should ultimately depend on the evidence that supports or refutes each one. In the next chapter we will examine how psychologists carry out research to help us approach a more accurate understanding of human development.

In this chapter we have discussed many different theoretical approaches to child development. Many of these ideas will be applied to issues presented in future chapters. In order to see the bigger picture of when these theorists developed their ideas, see the timeline presented in Figure 2.5.

Figure 2.5

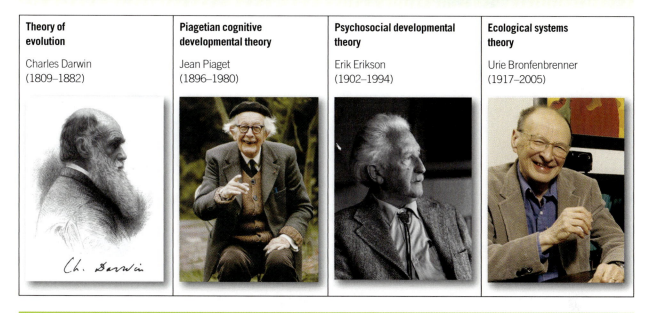

A timeline of developmental theories. This timeline helps put into historical perspective a few of the theories we have discussed in this chapter. Think about the influence that each theorist may have had on those who followed and how each one had innovative ideas that changed the direction of the study of children.

Theory of evolution	Piagetian cognitive developmental theory	Psychosocial developmental theory	Ecological systems theory
Charles Darwin (1809–1882)	Jean Piaget (1896–1980)	Erik Erikson (1902–1994)	Urie Bronfenbrenner (1917–2005)

We know that remembering the details of the theories can be a challenge. **Active Learning: Mnemonics (Memory Devices)** gives you some ideas that may help you remember stages and basic concepts within the different theories. These approaches to studying can be applied throughout the book.

Mnemonics (Memory Devices)

ACTIVE LEARNING

The material in this chapter is challenging because you must understand, remember, and keep separate in your mind many different theories. The best things you can do to *understand* this material are to (a) take an active approach toward reading the chapter (take notes, try out the Active Learning exercises, ask yourself questions, discuss your reading with others), (b) take part in your class discussions, and (c) ask your instructor questions about what you don't understand. In this activity, we offer some ideas about ways to help yourself *remember* the material. Memory devices such as these are referred to as mnemonics (neh-MON-ics; Bloom & Lamkin, 2006).

1. To help yourself remember Freud's stages of psychosexual development, you can think:
   Freud's on a Plane, Let's Go!
   Each letter of the phrase corresponds to one of the stages in the order Freud described:

   Freud's
   on—Oral
   a—Anal
   Plane—Phallic
   Let's—Latency
   Go!—Genital

(Continued)

(Continued)

You can associate this with the picture of Freud on a plane shown in Figure 2.6 and say the words out loud to reinforce your memory using as many different sensory modes as possible.

Figure 2.6

Mnemonic for Freud's theory. Use this picture of Freud on an airplane to help you remember the mnemonic "Freud's on a Plane, Let's Go!"

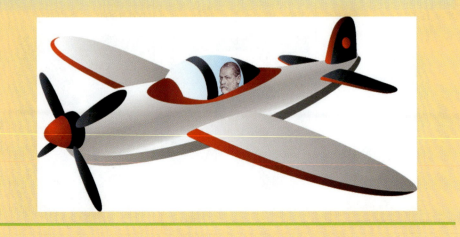

2. To remember the two basic learning principles of behaviorism, you might remember that behaviorism has to do with *control* of behavior by the environment. In the same way, police might control behavior of people in a crowd. A possible mnemonic to remember the two learning principles is to think of a "behaviorism C-OP," where *C* is for classical conditioning and *OP* is for operant conditioning. The picture below should be unique enough to help!

Mnemonic for classical and operant conditioning. Keep this unusual image in mind to remember the mnemonic "C-OP."

3. You can remember Piaget's stages of cognitive development by thinking:

Piaget's SPaCeForce

S = sensorimotor
P = preoperational
C = concrete operations
F = formal operations

Again, saying it out loud and remembering a picture that fits with it can also help aid memory.

Mnemonics have been found to be most successful when the person who is trying to remember something makes them up himself or herself (Bloom & Lamkin, 2006). We provide our ideas for mnemonics but encourage you to make up your own that will be personally meaningful to you. For example, if music is your interest, you might remember the two basic learning principles of behaviorism by thinking of classical (*C*) and pop (*OP*) music to remember classical and operant conditioning. You might even try to think of each type of music to cement the memory in your mind.

There are many ways that may be effective in helping you remember. Music is a great way to remember, as you know when you hear a song from your youth and can immediately sing the words. We have been learning using music all our lives. How hard is it to say the alphabet without singing it? If you could make up a song that would include what you are trying to remember, so much the better!

To complete this Active Learning activity, take a concept from this chapter that you would like to remember. Make up a mnemonic and practice it. You can use one of the items listed above, but make up your own mnemonic to personalize it so that it will stay in your memory. Test yourself on your memory for this concept after 3 days and after 6 days. Did it help you?

CHAPTER SUMMARY

1. How would you answer the two questions posed at the beginning of the chapter for each theory that has been presented?
   a. How does each theory describe development? Does change occur (a) quantitatively, in small steps, or (b) qualitatively, in distinct stages?
   b. What drives development: (a) biological processes, (b) environmental processes, or (c) a combination of both biology and environment?

Theory	Quantitative or qualitative change	Biology and/or environment
Psychoanalytic theory	Qualitative: Freud has 5 stages Erikson has 8 stages	Biology drives development and is affected by environmental experiences.
Behaviorism	Quantitative	Environment.
Piaget's cognitive theory	Qualitative: Piaget has 4 stages	Biology drives development, and environment shapes it.
Vygotsky's cognitive theory	Quantitative	Environment, in the form of culture and social influence, drives development.
Information processing	Quantitative	Biology and environment interact.
Evolutionary theories	N/A	Biology underlies adaptation to the environment.
Ecological theory	Quantitative	A nesting of environmental influences are also affected by a child's biology.
Biological theories	Quantitative	Biology is the focus of these theories, but environment influences biological development.

2. What are Freud's stages, and why are they called psychosexual?

Freud believed that sexuality is the driving force for development. He further believed that the focus of the sexual drive shifts from one area of the body to another as the child develops. This formed the basis for his stages: **oral**, **anal**, **phallic**, **latency**, and **genital**.

3. What are Erikson's stages of development, and how does his theory differ from Freud's?

Erik Erikson followed the psychoanalytic tradition, but he thought that the social world and the development of identity were more important forces for development than

sexuality. That is why his stages are called psychosocial. He developed eight stages based on the issues that he felt must be dealt with at each age period of life, such as trust versus mistrust in infancy and industry versus inferiority in school-age children. He also differed from Freud in his idea that development continues throughout life so his stages continue through later adulthood.

4. What is classical conditioning?

Classical conditioning is a process first described by Pavlov based on his work with dogs and further developed by John B. Watson, in which an unconditioned stimulus (one that naturally causes a unconditioned response) is paired with a neutral stimulus, which does not ordinarily provoke the unconditioned response (for example, dogs salivate when they smell meat, but not when they hear a bell). After repeated pairings of the two stimuli, the neutral stimulus then elicits the unconditioned response as well (for example, the dog salivates when it hears the bell). When this happens, the neutral stimulus has become the conditioned stimulus, and the learned response is called the conditioned response.

5. What is operant conditioning?

B. F. Skinner developed the concept of **operant conditioning**, which happens when something that follows a behavior causes that behavior to happen more. This **reinforcement** can be applied in different schedules: fixed or random interval (time), and fixed or random ratio (number of behaviors).

6. What is the basic learning process of social cognitive theory?

Albert Bandura developed social cognitive theory, which emphasizes the importance of imitation as a learning process. We see other people modeling certain behaviors, and if we admire those people or see them rewarded for what they do, we are likely to imitate them.

7. How does Piaget describe the learning process?

Piaget's theory of cognitive development states that we organize the world according to our past experiences into **schemas**. We **assimilate** new information to fit into our schemas, and we must **accommodate** new information by changing our schemas when we encounter information that does not fit well into existing schemas.

8. How does Vygotsky's theory of cognitive development differ from Piaget's?

While Piaget saw children as "little scientists" experimenting on their own, Vygotsky emphasized the role of social interaction in creating our understanding of the world. Through a process he called **scaffolding**, Vygotsky believed that adults or older children build up children's knowledge by helping them go just beyond what they can do themselves. Learning occurs in what Vygotsky called the **zone of proximal development**.

9. What model for mental functioning does information processing use?

Information processing compares the way we think to the way that a computer operates. The "hardware" of a computer (for example, the hard drive) is equivalent to the human brain and sensory system. The "software" of a computer (for example, the particular program that processes incoming information) is equivalent to human cognitive processes such as attention, organization, and retrieval strategies.

10. What are the two models of memory developed by information processing theory?

The **stores model** of human memory showed information moving through a set of locations or "stores" to end up in long-term storage where it could later be retrieved and used by working memory. The **connectionist** or **network model** describes memory as a neural network that consists of concept nodes that are interconnected by links.

11. How has Darwin's theory of evolution been applied to the study of child development?

Two theories of human behavior have emerged from evolutionary theory. **Ethology** is the study of animal and human behavior in relation to their adaptation to the natural environment. **Sociobiology** is a newer theory that proposes that human social behavior is determined by genes that evolved to promote adaptation.

12. What are the five levels of "ecology" that influence child development according to Bronfenbrenner?

Urie Bronfenbrenner proposed that individuals grow and develop within a nested set of influences that he divided into five systems: **microsystem** (immediate environment), **mesosystem** (interactions among the elements of the microsystem), **exosystem** (settings that the child never enters but that influence development), **macrosystem** (cultural norms), and **chronosystem** (changes that occur in the environment over time).

13. How do maturational theory and dynamic systems theory differ in their explanations of physical development?

Maturational theory, developed by Arnold Gesell, emphasizes the role of biological factors to explain physical development. **Dynamic systems theory**, developed by Esther Thelen, emphasizes the interaction of biological maturation with environmental influences in physical development.

14. What are neuropsychology and behavioral genomics?

Neuropsychology is the study of the brain and behavior. **Behavioral genomics** is the study of genes and behavior. Both have benefited from recent technological advances that allow researchers to see specific brain functions and specific genes. The surprising finding is that both the brain and genes are influenced and shaped by environment and experiences, rather than operating independently to determine behavior.

15. What role does culture play in child development?

All cultures have their own theories about how children develop. We must always keep in mind the realities of children's lives in different settings to understand what is most adaptive within their particular context and environment.

Go to **www.sagepub.com/levine** for additional exercises and video resources. Select **Chapter 2, Theories of Development,** for chapter-specific activities.

c h a p t e r   3

How We Study Children and Adolescents

3

In this chapter we will look at how researchers study children and adolescents in order to add to our understanding of growth and development. We all have some intuitive beliefs about development, often based upon our own life experiences, but social scientists subject their ideas to rigorous scientific testing in order to determine whether or not their ideas are valid. This can be done in a number of ways, each of which has its own advantages and disadvantages. That means that there isn't one best way to study development. Rather we look for the most appropriate method to investigate the particular topic we want to examine.

Test Your Knowledge

Test your knowledge of child development by deciding whether each of the following statements is *true* or *false*, and then check your answers as you read the chapter.

1. **True/False:** If we conduct research on students at a large high school, we can assume that our findings will apply to any adolescent who is the same age as the ones we have studied.
2. **True/False:** The best way to do research on development is to conduct experiments.
3. **True/False:** When conducting research by doing an observation, it is important that the person who is doing the observation does not know the purpose of the research.
4. **True/False:** If observations are carefully done, you will be able to determine the causes of the behavior you are observing.
5. **True/False:** Children's memories are good enough to allow them to give reliable eyewitness testimony.
6. **True/False:** Studying a single individual intensively is a valid scientific methodology.
7. **True/False:** An experiment always consists of an experimental situation set up by researchers to test specific hypotheses.
8. **True/False:** Even if research consistently finds that mothers who talk to their children a great deal have children with high self-esteem, we should not conclude that frequent conversations with parents build self-esteem in children.
9. **True/False:** Research has shown that boys who watch a lot of violence on TV are more aggressive, but if you know someone who watches a lot of violence and you see that he is not at all aggressive, this disproves the research.
10. **True/False:** Once we have established that the results of our research are statistically significant, we can be confident they will have an impact on real-world situations.

Correct answers: (1) False, (2) False, (3) True, (4) False, (5) True, (6) True, (7) False, (8) True, (9) False, (10) False

We will look at how the scientific method is used in both basic and applied research on child and adolescent development. We have organized the first part of this chapter to follow the basic outline used in most research articles in child development: First we discuss the development and operationalization of hypotheses. Next we describe the methods used to test the hypotheses, including *who* is studied and *how* they are studied, and review the advantages and disadvantages of each method we might use. We also look at how these methods fit into different research designs. Then we discuss how to interpret the results that emerge from the research.

After this overall description of research, we will consider the special challenges that come along with conducting research with children and adolescents. Finally, we will provide a guide to help you search for and evaluate research-based information that will help your understanding of the development of children and adolescents.

The Scientific Method

Basic and Applied Research

Basic research
Research that has the primary goal of adding to our body of knowledge rather than having immediate direct application.

The primary goal of much research is to add to our understanding of development and to help us refine our theories. This type of research is called **basic research** because whether or not the results have any direct application is not the primary concern. Basic research helps satisfy our curiosity and increases our understanding of the world we live in, rather than necessarily solving problems or creating new products. For example, on its website the National Institute of Child Health and Human Development (2008) states that its research program "emphasizes the importance of fundamental investigations into the physics, chemistry, and biology of cells, their component parts, and the processes that govern and regulate their function" (para. 2). It might not be clear from this description that this basic research is ultimately aimed at promoting the health of children and their parents. On the other hand, there is research that clearly is intended from its conception to help us make changes that will affect children's lives. This is called **applied research** because its goal is to solve immediate problems or improve the human condition. Applied research might look at the effect of different parenting styles, classroom practices, or health care policies with the goal of improving what we do with children.

Applied research
Research that has the primary goal of solving problems or improving the human condition.

Of course this is not a black-or-white situation. Dr. Ashok Gadgil (n.d.) of the Lawrence Berkeley National Laboratory has offered some guidelines for distinguishing between basic and applied research. He suggests that if we can find a practical use for knowledge within a couple of years, it is applied research. If the knowledge finds a use in 20 to 50 years, it is somewhat applied and somewhat basic. But if we cannot foresee an application of the knowledge that comes from the research, it is basic research.

Developing Hypotheses

Scientific method The process of formulating and testing hypotheses in a rigorous and objective manner.

Hypothesis
A prediction, often based upon theoretical ideas or observations, that is tested by the scientific method.

Because the field of child development is grounded in science, we rely upon the **scientific method** to build our understanding of it. This process often starts with our observations. If you spend any amount of time watching children, whether you are looking at their moment-to-moment behavior or at how they grow, change, and develop over time, you probably will have some questions about what you see. And if you have questions, it is also likely that you will have at least some speculation about possible answers to those questions. In the scientific method, theories, such as those you read about in the last chapter, are developed to answer the questions that arise from our observations. From these theories we develop predictions about what children will think, feel, and do in certain situations. These predictions are called **hypotheses**.

However, no matter how much a particular hypothesis seems to make good sense, it still needs to be put to a test. Research that is done using the methods described in this chapter is designed to test hypotheses. If we cannot find a way to subject a hypothesis to a test, it has little or no scientific value, and it remains in the realm of speculation. For example, you may believe that watching too much television can cause children to have a short attention span, but until this belief is tested and supported by research, it remains just a hypothesis. We will use an example of research that was designed to test this hypothesis in the **Active Learning: The Scientific Method** activities (beginning with **Forming a Hypothesis**) that will continue throughout this chapter.

Testing a hypothesis. Does watching television affect children's ability to stay on task and to stay focused when they need to? Research by Levine and Waite (2000) has tried to answer this question.

The Scientific Method—Forming a Hypothesis

ACTIVE LEARNING

Research articles most often begin with an abstract that briefly summarizes the entire article.

1. First read the following abstract of an article by Levine and Waite published in 2000:

Abstract

To evaluate the common assumption that television viewing is related to attentional difficulties in school, 70 fourth and fifth grade students recorded a "television diary" for one week and reported their preferred television shows. Parents estimated their child's television viewing time and reported their child's preferred shows. Assessment of attentional difficulties included teacher ratings, parent ratings, standardized tests, and classroom observations. It was found that the amount of television a child viewed was significantly related to teacher ratings of attentional difficulties, but not to parent ratings, classroom observations or a standardized test. Type of shows viewed did not relate to any attentional outcome variable. There was a clear relationship between fourth and fifth grade children's ability to pay attention in school, as assessed by their teacher, and the amount of time they spent watching television.

2. After reading this abstract, look again at the first sentence. Write down what you believe to be the major hypothesis, or prediction, of this study.

    Hypothesis: _____

Answer:
In the first section of their paper, in which the authors review what other researchers have found that leads to their own hypothesis, they state: "The major hypothesis of this study is that for children in later elementary school the amount of television viewed will be related to 'ADHD behaviors,' especially as shown in the classroom" (Levine & Waite, 2000, p. 667). This means that the authors predict that the more television children watch, the more difficulty they will have maintaining their attention and not being disturbed by distractions. Note for now that the hypothesis says "will be related to" and not "will cause." We will return to this point when we discuss experimental and correlational research designs later in the chapter.

Types of aggression. Aggression can take different forms. It can involve a struggle over a toy or being harassed by a bully, but gossip is another way that children and adolescents hurt each other.

Operationalizing Concepts

Operationalize To define a concept in a way that allows it to be measured.

In order to test a hypothesis, we need to **operationalize** the concepts we want to study. When we do this, we find some way to turn the concept into something we can see and measure. However, this process isn't as simple as it may sound. For example, suppose you are interested in studying aggression. You probably think that aggression is one of those things that you would recognize if you saw it, but would you? It might be fairly straightforward if we restricted ourselves to considering hitting, kicking, or pinching someone as our operationalization of aggression, but measuring these behaviors only taps into *physical aggression*. Maybe we should add calling names, swearing, and screaming to our list. These are all types of *verbal aggression*. But isn't it also pretty hurtful when someone spreads rumors about you or tries to turn other people against you? These are examples of a type of indirect aggression called *relational aggression*. Have you ever been in a situation where someone has intentionally undermined your best efforts? For instance, if your friend really doesn't want to go to a party with you, she might agree to go but on the night of the party have one problem after another until finally it is just too late to even think about going. Although she appears to have agreed to do what you wanted to do, she effectively sabotaged the effort. This kind of undermining of effort is called *passive aggression*.

Measures of any or all of these types of aggression might be included in our operationalization of the concept. The important point is that you must make it clear what you are including in your definition of aggression and what you are not including. **Active Learning: The Scientific Method—Operationalizing Concepts** gives you a chance to see for yourself how difficult this step of the scientific process can be.

Operationalizing "inattention." This child is daydreaming and not paying attention to what is happening in her classroom. What other behaviors could you measure that would indicate "inattention"?

The Scientific Method—Operationalizing Concepts

ACTIVE LEARNING

Continuing with our example, Levine and Waite (2000) were interested in looking at the effect of television viewing on children's attentional behavior. To operationalize "television viewing," they had the children keep diaries of their television viewing for 1 week and asked the children's parents to estimate how much television their children watched. This is a pretty straightforward way to operationalize "television viewing," but it is more difficult to decide how you would operationalize "attentional behavior." These authors operationalized this concept as behavior that indicated that a child was paying attention during a task in the classroom. They assessed this behavior by observing children in their classrooms for 15-minute periods during which they recorded each child's behavior in the following categories: "being off task, fidgeting, inappropriate vocalizations, playing with an object, and being out of seat" (Levine & Waite, 2000, p. 672, adapted from Barkley, 1991).

Think about ways you could operationalize each of the following concepts if you wanted to measure them as a part of your research. Be very clear in your descriptions of each type of behavior you include so someone else who is looking at the same behaviors that you are looking at could place the behaviors into the same categories. For example, if you wanted to observe aggression, you might first choose a specific aspect of aggression (for example, physical aggression). You would then need to define this in behavioral terms (for example, physical aggression is any action that causes physical pain to another child). Then you would need to describe the specific behaviors you would record (for example, hitting, biting, pinching) during your observation.

Try operationalizing the following concepts, as you might observe them in adolescents. Define the concept and then describe specifically how you would assess it:

- Self-esteem
- Stress
- Affection

Compare your list with those of other students in your class and discuss the following:

- How much overlap there is in the behaviors each student identified as part of the operationalization of the concept
- Whether the description of each behavior is clear and unambiguous
- Whether the categories of behavior described cover the entire range of the concept or only a portion of that range
- How you would measure each of your indicators (for example, by observation, self-report of the participants, reports of others, physiological measurement)

Reliability and Validity

Two essential characteristics of any measure used in scientific research are **reliability** and **validity**. A measure is reliable when it produces the same or similar results each time it is used. For example, if we use a measure of self-esteem, we would expect a given child or adolescent to score at about the same level if we administered the measure on several occasions. There would, of course, be *some* variation from one occasion to another. Poor performance on a classroom test or an argument with a best friend might lower self-esteem on one occasion, while an extraordinary achievement might elevate it on another, but a measure would not be very useful in research if it assessed a child's self-esteem as very high on one occasion, very low on another, and somewhere in between on a third occasion when circumstances hadn't changed substantially. Think of it this way: If you wanted to get an accurate measure of a child's height, would you use a metal ruler or a ruler made out of a rubber band? If you wanted your measure to be

Reliability The ability of a measure to produce consistent results.

Validity A measure that accurately measures what it purports to measure.

Interrater reliability
A measure of consistency in the data gathered by multiple observers.

Generalize To draw inferences from the findings of research on a specific sample about a larger group or population.

Population A set that includes everyone in a category of individuals that we are interested in studying (for example, all toddlers, all teenagers with learning disabilities).

Representative sample A group of participants in a research study who have individual characteristics in the same distribution that exists in the population.

TRUE/FALSE

1. If we conduct research on students at a large high school, we can assume that our findings will apply to any adolescent who is the same age as the ones we have studied.

   False. The conclusions from research should only be extended to groups similar to the original group of subjects. We would need to know more about the socioeconomic and demographic characteristics of the students at the original high school before determining how far we could generalize these results.

reliable, you would opt for the metal ruler because it is most likely to give you the same estimate each time that you use it to measure the child's height.

We also need to be sure that our measures accurately reflect the construct or characteristic in which we are interested. A measure is considered *valid* if it measures what it purports to measure. For example, in **Active Learning: The Scientific Method—Operationalizing Concepts**, you might have defined self-esteem for an adolescent as a feeling of being proud of one's self for one's achievements. You might then have tried to measure this concept by asking questions such as "Are you proud of your accomplishments?" and "Do you ever feel bad about yourself when you are not able to do something well?" It certainly *appears* that these questions would be a valid measure of the concept you are trying to assess, so this is called *face validity*. However, there are many other ways to see whether your questionnaire is a valid measure of self-esteem. One way is to give your participants your questionnaire and another measure of self-esteem that has already been widely used. If the results from your measure are similar to the results from the other measure, this is another indication that your measure may be a valid assessment of self-esteem.

Another type of reliability (there are several) is called **interrater reliability**. This means that if different people (called the "raters") use a given measure, they should get very similar results. In the study by Levine and Waite (2000), the authors statistically assessed the interrater reliability of their measure of "attention." They reported that when two raters observed the same child but independently scored the child's behavior using their measure of attention, the raters' scores agreed with each other at a very high level. The reported agreement ranged from .88 to .98. A perfect reliability coefficient would be 1.0, so this is strong evidence that the measure of attentiveness they used has very good interrater reliability.

Sampling and Representative Samples

We want our research to do more than say something about the particular children or adolescents who take part in our research. We want to be able to **generalize** our results to larger populations, but this step must be taken with great caution. For example, if we conducted research at kindergartens in suburban schools, we would need to be careful not to mistakenly assume that our findings would apply equally to children from social, economic, or ethnic backgrounds that are very different from those of the children we studied. We might not find the same results if our research involved children from low-income families enrolled in a Head Start program or children from higher-income families enrolled in an expensive private school.

To understand the process of sampling, we need to distinguish between a **population** and a sample. A population includes everyone in the category we are interested in studying or learning more about. All toddlers, all elementary school children with dyslexia, or all adolescent females—each represents a population. But, thinking about these groups, it is clear that including an entire population in any research study is impossible, so we need to select a sample from that population. Because we want to be able to generalize the findings from a particular study to the population, samples are constructed to reflect the characteristics of the population of interest, so they are called **representative samples**. If we want to generalize our findings to all toddlers, for instance, we need to include boys and girls in the age range we are interested in and to include demographic characteristics (for example, socioeconomic characteristics, ethnic and racial diversity, types of family structure) in proportions that are similar to the general population. If our sample is more limited than that (for example, if it primarily includes Anglo children from middle-class two-parent families), we need to be careful to generalize our results only to children with these characteristics. If you read research that is published in professional journals, you'll see how careful researchers are to specify how broadly their conclusions can be applied, and they often call for additional research that will extend their work to a broader cross section of participants. Representative sampling is used in all types of research, whether the researchers carry out surveys, questionnaires, observations, or experiments.

An example of what can happen when this is *not* done correctly comes from research on air bags in automobiles. Air bags save lives. Research clearly shows that, but it also shows that air bags are not equally effective for all drivers and passengers. Although air bags can help prevent crash fatalities, they also can cause a range of injuries that include corneal abrasions, aortic ruptures, abdominal injuries, and fractures of the forearms (Segui-Gomez, 2000), and women are more likely than men to suffer these air bag–induced injuries. Women are at greater risk because they tend to sit closer to the air bag and an injury is more likely in the first few inches after the air bag deploys. The problem comes from the fact that the force of deployment was initially determined using crash test dummies that were built to reflect the size of the average American male. Generalizing from a set of findings of what made air bags most effective for the average man to the population as a whole actually ended up placing women and children at greater risk for nonfatal injuries. Fortunately, research is now being conducted with female-size and child-size crash dummies to collect new data that will help manufacturers develop air bags that are more effective for everyone (Nikkel, 2009). **Active Learning: The Scientific Method—Sampling** allows you to look closely at the sample used by Levine and Waite (2000), think about the characteristics of the sample used in this research, and decide to which groups of children the results of this study can be generalized.

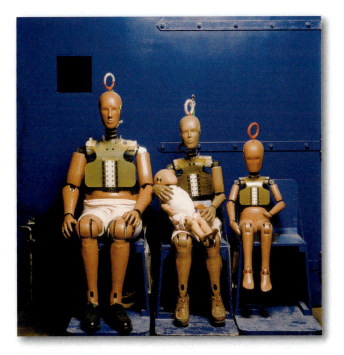

One size does not fit all. Automotive engineers originally designed air bags to protect the "average" American man. Today they realize that passengers come in all shapes and sizes and what works for an average-size man doesn't work well for others.

The Scientific Method—Sampling

Returning again to the research on television and attention, we can look at how these authors (Levine & Waite, 2000) selected the sample for their research. Read the following description of the children who took part in the study:

> Seventy fourth and fifth grade students participated in the study. There were 33 girls and 37 boys. Children's ages ranged from 8 years 6 months to 11 years 9 months. . . . The children came from four public schools: two schools were urban, one was suburban, and one was rural. Fifty children were white, non-Hispanic; three were Hispanic, two were African American, one was Asian, one was reported as "other" and not specified. Thirteen parents chose not to report the child's ethnicity. The sample was primarily middle and working class. (Levine & Waite, 2000, p. 670)

From this description of the sample, describe the population to which the results of this study might apply. Which populations would not necessarily follow the same pattern as found in this sample?

Answer: The research results can apply to both boys and girls who are about 8–12 years old. The children can be from urban, suburban, or rural settings. The results will apply primarily to White middle- and working-class children but not to minority children, who were not represented in numbers large enough to allow conclusions to be drawn about them.

TRUE/FALSE

2. The best way to do research on development is to conduct experiments.

False. As you see throughout this chapter, excellent research on development is conducted using a variety of methods. There isn't a single "right" or "best" method. Some methods simply are more appropriate for answering certain types of questions than others.

Methods and Measures

Once researchers have developed their hypothesis, operationalized the concepts within it, and chosen their sample, they must decide how they will gather the data for their study. There are many methods that are used to gather scientific information, and each method has both advantages and disadvantages (see Table 3.1). We can be most confident about our results if researchers find the same outcomes using several different types of methods. We will describe six of the ways most commonly used to study children and adolescents: observations, self-report measures, standardized tests, physiological measures, archival records, and case studies.

Observations

We can learn a great deal about anything we are interested in—including development—by making careful observations. Scientific observations differ from our casual, everyday observations of the world because they need to be both systematic and objective.

Table 3.1

A comparison of research methods

Method	Advantages	Disadvantages
Observations	Rich source of information Can observe behavior as it naturally occurs Can be conducted in a laboratory to gain control in the situation Can lead to new hypotheses	Can be confused with interpretation Potential observer bias Can produce large amounts of raw data that must be coded and analyzed The presence of an observer may change the behavior being observed Cannot identify the causes of behavior
Surveys, questionnaires	Gathers information quickly and efficiently Can be used to gather information on many different topics	Questions must be precisely worded Questions can be misleading or biased Respondent may not answer honestly Respondent may not be able to accurately recall or report on behavior Respondent may provide a socially desirable answer rather than a truthful answer
Interviews (structured and clinical)	Can be a first-person or a third-person account	No second observer to verify the information
Standardized tests	Can assess many qualities or characteristics Allow an individual to be compared to the average performance of a group	Norms need to be periodically updated Performance tests must be scored and interpreted by trained examiner May be biased against certain groups
Physiological measures	Can gather data that don't require language or an active response from participants	Equipment is expensive and can be difficult to maintain Interpretation of data is not always clear
Case studies	Source of rich information and hypotheses Can utilize multiple methods	Information may have limited generalizability Time intensive Threat from possible observer bias
Experiments	Can determine the causes of behavior	Must ensure groups tested are comparable Cannot be used to study some topics

They require careful planning and careful execution to be valid. To understand more about the difference between objective observation and subjective interpretation, see **Active Learning: Observation or Interpretation?**

Observation or Interpretation?

A narrative description is a complete, step-by-step description of the behaviors a child performs. It is important to learn to separate this objective description from nonobjective interpretations. To better understand this distinction, observe a child for about 15–30 minutes (you can really observe anyone if a child is not readily available). Divide the pages you use into two columns. In the left column, write down what you see the child do. For example:

Observation: Annie stands in the doorway and looks into the room. She buries her head in her father's leg and holds on.

Later, in the right column, give your interpretation of the behaviors. For example:

Interpretation: Annie seemed shy about entering the room and turned to her father for comfort.

Your interpretations should be about the child's behavior and *not* a summary statement about what the child "is like," because the child may appear to be different at another time. For example, don't write that Annie is a shy child. Maybe she doesn't feel well that day but usually bounces into the room with no fear. It takes many observations to make any kind of general statement about a child.

Observer bias The tendency for an observer to notice and report events that he is expecting to see.

If the researchers who are conducting the observations are testing their own hypotheses, there is a risk that they might see or pay more attention to things that tend to support those hypotheses and overlook things that don't. This tendency is called **observer bias**. We have already described one way to avoid observational bias. Having more than one observer code the observations helps to assure us that the observations are objective, rather than subjective. Another safeguard is to use observers who are "blind" to the hypothesis they are testing. That means that they don't know the specific hypothesis that is being tested, so it cannot affect their perception of the events they are observing.

Observations can be made in a setting where the behavior of interest naturally occurs, or they can be made in a setting that offers more control over circumstances, such as a research laboratory. Advantages of doing observations in naturally occurring settings include the fact that we get to see children behaving as they normally do within the social relationships that shape their development every day of their lives and we see them in situations that have real emotional significance for the children (Dunn, 2005b). However, moving observations into a laboratory gives researchers greater control over the situation and allows researchers to create a specific set of conditions in which to conduct their observations. You will read about some of the early influential work in the field of child development that used observation as its methodology in **Journey of Research: Doing Observational Research**.

3. When conducting research by doing an observation, it is important that the person who is doing the observation does not know the purpose of the research.

TRUE/FALSE

True. If the observer knows the purpose of the research or the hypothesis that is being tested by it, it may subtly influence what he sees and pays attention to, so it is preferable if he doesn't have this information.

JOURNEY of RESEARCH

Doing Observational Research

The study of child development as a scientific effort is a relatively recent occurrence, but parents have been watching their children's growth and development for a very long time and keeping records of these events for their own enjoyment. In the 1800s, educated parents often kept what were called *baby biographies* of their children, but in 1877 Charles Darwin, a renowned scientist of the day, took the notable step of publishing some observations he had made of his own son in the scientific journal *Mind*. In this article, Darwin described what he had observed regarding early reflexive behaviors in the infant, as well as the emergence of later voluntary movement. He also noted incidents of anger, fear, pleasure, and affection in his son. The fact that a noted scientist found these observations worthy of publication in a journal gave the study of children's development a legitimacy that it hadn't had before.

Years later, one of the most influential developmental theorists, Jean Piaget, made extensive, detailed observations of his three children, and these observations formed the basis of a number of his writings on cognitive development (see, for example, Piaget, 1952). Piaget's first book, *The Language and Thought of the Child* (1926), was based upon an analysis of the naturally occurring speech of two 6-year-old children over a period of an entire month as observed and recorded by a team of three investigators.

At about this same time, Roger G. Barker and Herbert F. Wright were conducting research at the Midwest Psychological Field Station. It was their intent to study the 119 children living in a Midwestern town using a methodology they called "ecological psychology." As they explained, "Our research plans differed from those of most other psychologists in that we forsook the laboratory and clinic for the 'natural' habitats of our subjects" (Barker & Associates, 1978, p. 2). In just one of the publications that resulted from their work, it took the authors 435 pages to record and interpret a single 14-hour observation of one 7-year-old boy (Barker & Wright, 1951). It took a team of eight observers, each making 1-minute observations, to record this information—a very labor-intensive process, to say the least!

Thanks to the advent of newer technologies, we no longer need to send teams of researchers into the field to collect data, but in her 1990 presidential address to the Society for Research on Adolescence, E. Mavis Hetherington (1991) described research on the effects of divorce and remarriage on children's adjustment and family functioning that was based upon hundreds of hours of videotapes taken at family dinners and during family problem-solving sessions. Although the videotape recorded the behavior, someone still had to view all those tapes and code the behavior recorded on them before Dr. Hetherington and her colleagues had the data they needed for their analysis.

Whether observations are done on a playground with paper and pencil or in a high-tech research laboratory filled with digital cameras, the goal remains one of capturing the full, rich range of behavior as it naturally occurs.

Making a detailed record of everything that happens in a stream of behavior can make researchers aware of aspects of behavior that they haven't noticed before and can be a good source of new hypotheses for future research. Both of these are advantages of doing observational studies. However, recording everything that happens even in a fairly short period of time produces a tremendous amount of raw data that need to be analyzed and reduced before useful information emerges.

For this reason, researchers often structure their observations in ways that allow them to focus on specific behaviors. If the researchers are interested in a specific type of behavior, they might use an **event sample** in which they only record information about all occurrences of that particular behavior during their observation. This technique works best for behavior that represents a cohesive sequence of behavior (that is, an episode that has a beginning, a middle, and an end). For instance, episodes of fantasy play or episodes of bullying lend themselves well to this technique.

Event sample A data collection technique in which a researcher records information about all occurrences of a coherent set of behaviors being investigated.

A different way to structure an observation is known as a **time sample**. This technique works better for observing behaviors that occur relatively frequently. The researchers start by developing a checklist of the behaviors that are of interest to their study. They observe each child within specific time intervals. For example, if the observer has been watching to see whether a child is out of her seat, he might report that the child was out of her seat during 10 out of 15 one-minute intervals. Did you recognize this as a description of what Levine and Waite (2000) did for the classroom observation of the children in their study? For an example of the type of time sample chart that could be used to assess inattentiveness, see Figure 3.1. Using this technique, a researcher can gather data from a large number of children in a relatively brief period of time.

Time sample A data collection technique in which a researcher observes an individual for a predetermined period of time and records the occurrence of specific behaviors of interest to the research during that period.

Figure 3.1

Time sample chart. This chart, developed by Barkley (1991), was used by Levine and Waite (2000) in their research on television viewing and attention in school-age children. While observers watched a particular child in a classroom, they listened to a tape that played a tone at the end of each minute. If they saw any of the behaviors on the chart occur before the next tone, they checked the box for that minute.

RESTRICTED ACADEMIC SITUATION CODING SHEET

Interval #:	1	2	3	4	5	6	7	8	9	10	11	12	13	14	15
Off task															
Fidgeting															
Vocalizing															
Plays w/obj.															
Out of seat															

Interval #:	16	17	18	19	20	21	22	23	24	25	26	27	28	29	30
Off task															
Fidgeting															
Vocalizing															
Plays w/obj.															
Out of seat															

Interval #:	31	32	33	34	35	36	37	38	39	40		Total
Off task												/40
Fidgeting												/40
Vocalizing												/40
Plays w/obj.												/40
Out of seat												/40
									Total:			/200

Child's Name: _____

Code Initials: _____

Date: _____

| Week # | Initial | Wk.1 | Wk.2 | Wk.3 | Wk.4 |

Comments:

Although observations are very useful sources of information about behavior, there are some limitations when using this method. First, our goal is to capture behavior as it naturally occurs, but the mere presence of an observer might change the way that people behave. Fortunately children usually adapt to the presence of an observer without too much difficulty. Although they are initially curious and might ask questions about what the observer is doing, the lure of getting back to what they were doing (such as playing with their friends) is usually far stronger.

Another limitation of observational research is that it doesn't tell us directly about the causes of behavior. If you observe a child who stays on the sidelines when other children are playing and refuses to interact with the other children, there are many possible explanations for this behavior. From the observation alone, it is impossible to tell whether this is the behavior of a child who simply is not very social, a temporary reaction to something that occurred earlier in the day, or an indication of an adjustment problem for the child. Based upon these observations, the researcher might formulate a hypothesis to explain the child's behavior, but additional research would need to be conducted to determine the specific cause of the observed behavior.

Self-Report Measures

Another way to gather information relatively quickly and efficiently is to use self-report measures such as **surveys** or **questionnaires**. However, in order for these methods to be effective, the survey or questionnaire needs to be carefully designed.

You may have had the experience of trying to complete a survey in which the questions were unclear or difficult to answer. For instance, if your professor asked you to respond to the question "How long has Child Development been your favorite course?" you might not find it easy to give a completely accurate answer (perhaps because you haven't decided that Child Development *is* your favorite course—at least, not yet!). It wouldn't matter how much you wanted to give accurate information; a poorly designed questionnaire might not allow you to do so. Of course another possibility is that the person taking the survey is unwilling or unable to give complete or accurate responses. And sometimes people give the answer they think the researcher is looking for or give answers that they think make them look good in the eyes of the researcher (a problem that is called *social desirability*). For example, students being surveyed about their drug and alcohol use may downplay the amount they use so they will not look deviant to the researcher. You can see how social desirability becomes a challenge for researchers who are investigating a topic that is a sensitive one, such as sexuality, drugs, or prejudice.

The usefulness of the conclusion you can draw from survey, interview, or questionnaire data is largely dependent on the accuracy and validity of the responses received, so having questions that are precise, well written, and understandable is essential to the validity of the research. Typically each survey participant responds to the same questions, presented in the same order. These questions might be open ended (for example, "What do you do when you are spending time with your friends?" or "What is your favorite subject in school?") or may use a forced-choice format (for example, "How many hours a week do you watch television: (a) less than 1 hour, (b) between 1 and 3 hours, (c) between 3 and 6 hours, or (d) 6 hours or more?"). An important illustration of how the way a question is asked can affect the response you get appears in **Journey of Research: Children's Eyewitness Testimony**.

TRUE/FALSE

4. If observations are carefully done, you will be able to determine the causes of the behavior you are observing.

False. Observations are important sources of information and can be used to test hypotheses, but the observer does not have enough control over the situation to be able to determine what causes the behaviors that are observed.

Surveys A data collection technique that asks respondents to answer questions.

Questionnaires A written form of a survey.

Children's Eyewitness Testimony

JOURNEY *of* **RESEARCH**

Prior to the 1990s there was relatively little research on children's ability to accurately recall events so that they could serve as eyewitnesses. Until that time research on children's memories had focused on things like their memory capacity, speed of processing, and the strategies they use to aid their recall, but in the 1990s there were some high-profile cases of alleged child abuse that placed children in the witness seat. Under relentless and often suggestive questioning, the children described horrific abuse at the hands of adults who were caring for them. Based on this testimony, a number of defendants received jail sentences. However, in all these cases, the charges were dismissed or the plaintiffs were eventually released after serving years in prison because of the improper way that evidence had been gathered.

One of the most notorious cases involved the McMartin Preschool. The following example shows how the children were questioned in this case, in which seven teachers were accused of sexually abusing several hundred young children:

Interviewer: Can you remember the naked pictures?

Child: (Shakes head "no")

Interviewer: Can't remember that part?

Child: (Shakes head "no")

Interviewer: Why don't you think about that for a while, okay? Your memory might come back to you.

(Interview Number 111, p. 29 as cited in Garven, Wood, Malpass, & Shaw, 1998)

It is clear from this example that the interviewer had a particular answer in mind and wanted the child to give that answer. The questioning is not at all unbiased.

Even young children are able to accurately recall events (there is more information on children's memory capabilities in Chapter 7), but here we are looking specifically at how the nature of the questions themselves affects children's recall. Some research has looked at interviewing techniques that are extremely misleading. In some cases, children have been subjected to repeated questioning, as well as overt suggestions from the interviewer about what has happened to them. There has even been pressure placed on child witnesses suggesting that their peers have already provided certain information to the interviewer (Ceci & Bruck, 1995).

However, Goodman and Schaaf (1997) suggest that instead of thinking of questions as being misleading or not, we should think about *degrees* of suggestion. Children are limited in their ability to understand and interpret language, and how we use language can be both subtle and powerful at the same time. To make this point, think for a minute about the subtle difference between asking someone "Did you see that?" and asking her "Didn't you see that?" The first alternative suggests that there can be one of two legitimate answers ("Yes, I saw that" or "No, I didn't see that"), but the second alternative implies that you may have missed something that someone else saw. The pressure is to respond to the second question by saying "Of course I saw that." While you may feel that you would respond to such a question by simply saying what you did or didn't see, regardless of how the question was phrased, a child is more likely to be swayed by the question itself.

Finally, remember that when we are talking about children as eyewitnesses, we often are dealing with sensitive legal matters such as child abuse or family violence. The challenge then becomes twofold: One is to avoid eliciting erroneous information with misleading questions or poor interviewing technique, but the other is to be sure that all necessary information is, in fact, disclosed (Goodman & Schaaf, 1997). There is still a great deal of research to be done on children's testimony before we will know how to best strike that balance so that we are able to gather the information we need to protect the child's best interest.

5. Children's memories are good enough to allow them to give reliable eyewitness testimony.   ✓✗ **TRUE/FALSE**

True. Children's memories are good enough to give reliable testimony, but they are more easily influenced than adults and older children by the nature of the questions they are asked.

Video Link 3.1
Interview on sexual abuse.

Video Link 3.2
Testifying in court.

Conducting an interview is another type of self-report measure. Usually an interviewer asks everyone who is interviewed the same set of questions, but sometimes the interviewer might want to ask additional follow-up questions or ask the respondent to expand upon his or her original answers or provide examples. In this case, the researcher uses a **clinical interview** as the research method. This method allows the researcher greater flexibility.

As we mentioned earlier in this chapter, Piaget used clinical interviews extensively. In the following example of his technique, Piaget told stories to children to examine their sense of morality. In one pair of stories he asked the children he was interviewing to compare the actions of two girls. The first girl, Marie, wants to surprise her mother by sewing her a nice present. She doesn't really know how to use the scissors and ends up cutting a big hole in her own dress. The second girl, Margaret, takes her mother's scissors while her mother is out. She doesn't really know how to use them and makes a little hole in her own dress. Piaget would then ask a series of questions to determine which girl the children considered to be naughtier. Here is one example:

P: Which one is the naughtiest?

C: The one who made the big hole.

P: Why did she make this hole?

C: She wanted to give her mother a surprise.

P: That's right. Then which of the little girls was nicest?

C: (hesitation)

P: Say what you think.

C: The one who made the little hole is the nicest.

P: If you were the mother . . . which would you have punished most?

C: The one who made a big hole.

(Statements are quoted from Piaget, 1965, p. 127)

Clinical interview
An interview strategy in which the interviewer can deviate from a standard set of questions to gather additional information.

How naughty is this? Piaget asked children who is naughtier: a child who makes a big hole in her dress while trying to make her mother a present or a child who makes a small hole in her dress while playing with scissors she shouldn't have. What would you say?

Although this interview has some standard questions like "Which one is the naughtiest?", many of the other questions are unique, based on a particular child's responses.

A variation on the self-report approach is to rely upon a second party to provide the information you are looking for. This is a particularly important way to collect data on infants and children who are too young to respond to an interviewer's questions. The more time the people being interviewed spend with the child and the more familiar they are with the child's behavior, the more likely it is that they will be able to provide high-quality information. Because parents, child care providers, and teachers all spend a great deal of time with young children, they are frequently used as sources of information. For example, parents have been asked to describe behavior of their toddlers that might place the child at risk (Scarborough, Hebbeler, Spiker, & Simeonsson, 2007), and preschool teachers have been asked to rate children's social competence, internalizing behaviors, and externalizing behaviors (Anthony et al., 2005).

Standardized Tests

Tests can provide information on a wide range of topics relevant to understanding development. You are probably familiar with standardized tests such as IQ tests and achievement tests. The process of standardizing a test involves administering the test to large groups of children to establish norms for the test. A **norm** represents the average or typical performance of a child of a given age on the test. When the test is later used with other children, an individual child's performance on the test can be compared to the child's age norms to determine whether that child is performing at the same level as the average child of the same age or is performing above or below average.

Let's say that during the norming of a new test of mathematical ability, the 8-year-old children in the norming sample answered an average of 34 questions correctly. An 8-year-old child who later takes the test and answers 39 questions correctly would be performing beyond the level expected of a child of this age, and one who answers 28 questions correctly would be performing below the norm or expected level for this age. Many of these tests are paper-and-pencil tests that can be administered to groups of children all at the same time, but some of them are called *performance tests* because they require the child to do something (for example, assemble a puzzle, build a tower of blocks). Someone who has been trained to administer and interpret the test, such as a school psychologist, works one-on-one with the child to administer a performance test. Read about some of the controversies surrounding the use of standardized tests, including the SAT and ACT, in **Journey of Research: Standardized Testing**.

Norms The average or typical performance of an individual of a given age on a test.

Standardized Testing

S tandardized testing has been a controversial topic for many years. Much of this controversy has centered on the question of what it is that these tests are actually measuring (that is, people have questioned the *validity* of the tests). Do they measure what they say they are measuring?

Intelligence tests were the first standardized tests to be used on a large-scale basis. You will read more about the history of intelligence testing in Chapter 8, but it is enough for now to say that the tests were originally developed to compare an individual child to others of the same age to determine whether the child could benefit from a public school education. However, one of their early wide-scale applications was during World War I and World War II when the military used intelligence tests to determine what duties a new recruit would be assigned (Glaser, 1993). Controversy arose because the tests found that native-born Americans scored better on the tests than immigrants, immigrants from Northern and Western Europe scored better than ones from Southern and Eastern Europe, and Black Americans received the lowest scores of all (Glaser, 1993).

The controversy revolved around the interpretation of the test results (you'll read more about this topic later in the chapter). Did the group differences in test scores reflect inherent differences in mental abilities between these groups, or were the tests biased in some way that put certain groups at more of a disadvantage than other groups?

Several historical events and societal changes contributed to the dramatic increase in the use

JOURNEY *of* **RESEARCH**

(Continued)

(Continued)

of standardized tests (especially IQ tests) in public schools. In the 1950s Russia was the first country to launch a satellite into outer space, and America felt that its students were falling behind those in other countries (Glaser, 1993). Intelligence testing became a way to assess how well our students were doing in school. In the 1960s, the federal government made a considerable amount of money and resources available to schools to help them improve education, especially in science and math. Standardized tests again were seen as a quick and easy way to determine where there was the greatest need for these resources and to assess the effectiveness of how the money was being spent (Perrone, 1991). This trend toward increasing reliance on standardized testing in schools has continued. In 1994 the Elementary and Secondary Education Act required standardized testing in U.S. public schools, and in 2001 the No Child Left Behind Act tied federal funding for public schools to student results on standardized tests (Wenning, Herdman, & Smith, 2003).

Now, in addition to the concerns about possible bias in standardized test scores, the increasing emphasis on the results from standardized tests has fueled other concerns, such as the concern that teachers (whose evaluations often heavily depend on their students' test scores) will "teach to the test." Critics say that this focus on making certain that children do well on a standardized set of questions narrows the scope of the curriculum. It also places more of an emphasis on rote memorization of facts, rather than a deep understanding of the material.

Another type of standardized test that you are probably familiar with is college entrance tests such as the SAT (Scholastic Assessment Test, formerly known as the Scholastic Aptitude Test) or the ACT (American College Testing program). These tests have received the same types of criticisms that intelligence tests have, including the claim that they are biased or discriminate against certain groups of students and that they do not accurately predict success in college (that is, they are not valid).

This has spurred a debate about why colleges continue to use them (Dowling, 1999), and in recent years some colleges have stopped using them or have made them optional. Typically high school grade point average and SAT/ACT scores are moderately strong predictors of college grade point average, and when taken together, they predict college GPA slightly better than either one on their own (Schmitt et al., 2009). However, the relationship between SAT/ACT scores and college grade point average is slightly weaker for minority students. The concern that this has raised about the possibility that the SAT and ACT may discriminate against certain groups is ironic because these tests were initially used as a way to level the playing field so that intellectually promising students from humble backgrounds would have a chance to gain entrance to elite educational institutions.

If the fact is that SAT or ACT scores add little to admissions decisions beyond other measures (such as high school grade point average) but do no harm, this question probably would not generate much controversy, but the fact is that men score higher than women, Asians/Asian Americans/Pacific Islanders and Whites score higher than Mexican Americans/Latinos or African Americans, and students from families with higher incomes score higher than students from families with lower incomes (College Board, 2008; FairTest.org, 2008; see Table 3.2), and these test score differences could be enough to prevent a student from being admitted to college, especially to highly competitive schools.

We are left with the issue of how we interpret these findings: Do the differences in SAT scores reflect inherent differences in ability or aptitude, or do they reflect differences in educational opportunity, motivation, being good at taking tests, or something else? Continue to think about this when you read the section of this chapter on interpreting results.

500 (–2)

Table 3.2

2008 College-bound seniors' average SAT scores. This table shows average SAT scores for males and females, different ethnic groups, and different socioeconomic statuses.

2008 COLLEGE-BOUND SENIORS' AVERAGE SAT SCORES With Score Changes From 2007 (Approximately 1.51 million test takers, of whom 53.5% were female)				
	Critical Reading	**Math**	**Writing**	**Total**
Gender				
Female	500 (–2)	500 (+1)	501 (+1)	1,501 (0)
Male	504 (0)	533 (0)	488 (–1)	1,525 (–1)
Ethnicity				
Amer. Indian or Alaskan Native	485 (–2)	491 (–3)	470 (–3)	1,446 (–8)
Asian, Asian Amer. or Pacific Islander	513 (–1)	581 (+3)	516 (+3)	1,610 (+5)
African American or Black	430 (–3)	426 (–3)	424 (–1)	1,280 (–7)
Mexican or Mexican American	454 (–1)	463 (–3)	447 (–3)	1,364 (–7)
Puerto Rican	456 (–3)	453 (–1)	445 (–2)	1,354 (–6)
Other Hispanic or Latino	455 (–4)	461 (–2)	448 (–2)	1,364 (–8)
White	528 (+1)	537 (+3)	518 (0)	1,583 (+4)
Other	496 (–1)	512 (0)	494 (+1)	1,502 (0)
No Response (6%)	471 (–9)	492 (–5)	467 (–7)	1,430 (–21)
Family Income (in $20,000 bands in 2008; previously in $10,000 bands up to $100K)				
Less than $20,000/year	434	456	430	1,320
$ 20,000–$40,000/year	462	473	453	1,388
$ 40,000–$60,000/year	488	496	477	1,461
$ 60,000–$80,000/year	502	510	490	1,502
$ 80,000–$100,000/year	514	525	504	1,543
$100,000–$120,000/year	522	534	512	1,568
$120,000–$140,000/year	526	537	517	1,580
$140,000–$160,000/year	533	546	525	1,604
$160,000–$180,000	535	548	529	1,612
More than $200,000/year	554	570	552	1,676
No Response (37%) (scores not reported)				
All Test Takers	**502 (0)**	**515 (0)**	**494 (0)**	**1,511 (0)**

In addition to using standardized tests to determine whether children are "on track" in terms of their timetable of development, tests are also useful for assessing the effectiveness of programs and interventions. For example, the effectiveness of a summer enrichment program that paired talented young adolescents from limited-opportunity backgrounds with high school students or college-aged students was assessed using standardized tests of mathematics and reading skills (Laird & Feldman, 2004). In another program evaluation, a standardized test of math ability was used to assess the effectiveness of a 6-week classroom intervention conducted in Head Start classrooms that was designed to promote emergent math skills in preschool children (Arnold, Fisher, & Doctoroff, 2002).

Physiological Measures

Gathering valid and reliable data from infants and young children presents a special challenge to researchers for a number of reasons (de Haan, 2007). They can't answer questions because either they are not speaking at all yet or their language ability is so limited that they can't understand and follow complex instructions or provide complex verbal responses to questions. They also have limited control over many motor responses that are used in some tests designed for use with older children, adolescents, or adults. Finally, their attention spans are notoriously short, so keeping them on task is another challenge.

However, researchers now have an arsenal of devices that allow them to measure and interpret what is going on inside the infant without needing to rely on the infant's communication. Such tests provide important information on the functioning of the central nervous system and are frequently used in research that looks at emotions because different emotions produce different physiological effects on the body. By using electroencephalograms (EEGs, which measure electrical activity in the brain) and event-related potentials (ERPs, which measure the brain's electrical response to meaningful sensory stimuli), researchers can measure neural activity during a number of brain states, even when an infant is asleep (Banaschewski & Brandeis, 2007). In a recent study, researchers studied how 12-month-old infants reacted to stimuli in the environment when their caregivers reacted to an event in a positive, negative, or neutral way (de Haan, 2007). By measuring event-related potentials, they found that the infants paid more attention to the stimuli when their caregivers reacted in a negative way than when the caregivers reacted in a neutral or positive way. In an evolutionary sense, it makes sense that infants would pay more attention to things that their caregivers found unpleasant or distressing.

Look at the photo that shows a type of cortical cap that is used to record brain activity in an infant. To make the necessary measurements, a cap with electrodes embedded in it is placed snugly on the child's head. Note that this technique is noninvasive and it is not painful for the child.

Both magnetic resonance imaging (MRI) and functional magnetic resonance imaging (fMRI) are biophysiological measures that have been used in developmental research. The MRI gives us a picture of the structures of the brain, while the fMRI measures changes in the flow of blood in different parts of the brain and produces a computerized image of this activity.

Cortical measurement. This infant's brain activity is being measured by means of a specially designed "electrode hat."

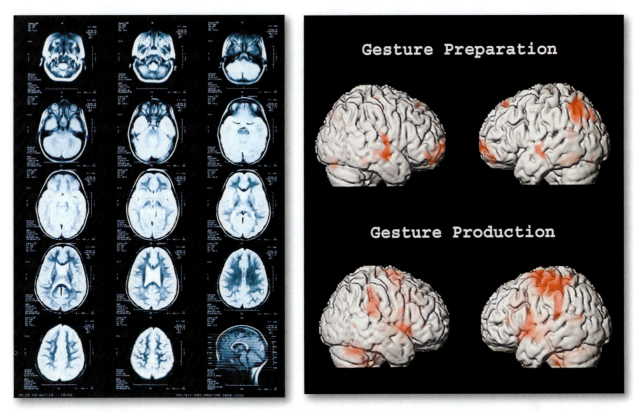

MRIs and fMRIs. The MRI image (left) shows pictures of successive sections through the brain from the back to the front. The fMRI image (right) shows where the blood is flowing through the brain when the person thinks about an activity and actually does that activity.

Although these techniques require expensive and sophisticated equipment, they are helping us get a new understanding of things we would not be able to study without them. For example, studies that have compared cortical functions in adults and adolescents have found that these two groups process information differently, with adolescents often using different brain regions than adults (Yurgelun-Todd, 2007). Research that has used MRIs to scan the brains of children diagnosed as autistic has found that the part of the brain that controls face recognition is underactive in these children (Kalb, 2005). As you may know, children with autism often do not make eye contact with others and show little or no interest in social relationships.

Archival Records

Researchers don't always collect their own data. They may use **archival records**, or data that were collected by others, sometimes for a different reason. For instance, a researcher might use historical diaries, letters, or photographs to gain insight into what childhood was like in the past. Reports and statistics collected by the U.S. government provide a historical snapshot of many topics relevant for a developmental researcher, as do medical records or school records.

One of the most ambitious sources of archival data related to child development is the Panel Study of Income Dynamics (PSID; Hill, 1992). Data collection from a nationally representative sample of over 18,000 individuals began in 1967 and has continued on a yearly basis since then. In 1997 a cohort of children from birth to age 12 was added to the data collection. Through in-person interviews with parents and children younger than age 18 and telephone interviews with children over the age of 18, information was gathered on a

Archival records Data collected at an earlier date that are used for research purposes.

number of family, school, and neighborhood characteristics that are linked to cognitive and behavioral development of the children (U.S. Department of Health and Human Services, n.d.b). Because data collection of this scope requires a great deal of time, money, and effort, making archival data available to many researchers is more cost-effective than having each researcher collect data individually. According to Shultz, Hoffman, and Reiter-Polman (2005), more than 1,600 books, chapters, articles, reports, and dissertations have used the data archives of the PSID.

Case Studies

A case study takes a comprehensive and intensive look at a single individual or a small group of individuals. Case studies have been used to investigate widely different research questions, ranging from the role that a man's perception of his own father has in whether the man becomes a successful entrepreneur (Strenger & Burak, 2005), to the perception of children, parents, and professionals on how to best manage childhood asthma (Lyte, Milnes, & Keating, 2007), to understanding how an adolescent deals with having HIV-positive parents (Lowe, 2007).

Video Link 3.3
Genie.

Video Link 3.4
Genie Part I.

Individuals who are subjects of case studies are often exceptional in some way, which is what makes them interesting subjects for this type of examination. One well-known case study involved Genie, a young girl who had been raised in conditions of horrible deprivation. Throughout her childhood, she spent most of her time strapped to a chair in a back bedroom of her family home where she had little social contact or interaction with others. In 1970, the girl's situation came to the attention of welfare authorities in Los Angeles, and Genie was removed from her home. At that point her overall development was severely retarded, and she had little functional language. As horrific as these circumstances were, Genie provided a unique opportunity for scientists to examine the idea that there is a critical period for language development. Genie was already past the age when children normally develop language, and helping her develop language would be a task that took a great deal of effort over the next several years. During that time, developmentalists used a variety of methods to document her progress (Rymer, 1993), and the results of these efforts have become part of the videotapes, books, and articles that have been produced on Genie's story.

Video Link 3.5
Genie Part II.

Earlier in this chapter we talked about the need to guard against observer bias when doing observational research. Because of the nature of the close relationship that can develop between the researcher and the subject of a case study, it is particularly important that the researcher strive to remain objective in his or her observations and interpretation of data. Because of the intense nature of a case study, it is difficult to have a second person who can independently confirm what is seen and recorded. In the case of Genie, even though she had multiple caregivers and researchers who worked with her over the years, all of them knew of her circumstances prior to her coming into their care, and all were aware of the efforts being made to rehabilitate her, so it was difficult for them to be impartial observers.

TRUE/FALSE

6. Studying a single individual intensively is a valid scientific methodology.

True. This type of research is called a *case study*, and case studies can provide valuable information to a researcher. We do, however, have to be careful about generalizing from the study of one individual to larger groups of people.

Despite these challenges, case studies offer us a rich and deep picture of development because they can bring together information from multiple sources using multiple methods, including interviews, observations, tests, and documents. Although the findings from case studies may have limited generalizability, they can be a rich source of new hypotheses that can be explored by future research with other more typical or representative groups of individuals.

Active Learning: The Scientific Method—Measures will help you review some of the types of measures we have just discussed by asking you to recognize examples of them.

The Scientific Method—Measures

ACTIVE LEARNING

Now let's examine the types of measures used in the study on television viewing and attention problems by Levine and Waite (2000). In the abstract of the article, the authors state that "70 fourth and fifth grade students recorded a 'television diary' for one week and reported their preferred television shows. Parents estimated their child's television viewing time and reported their child's preferred shows. The assessment of attentional difficulties included teacher ratings [the ADD-H Comprehensive Teachers Rating Scale], parent ratings [the Distractibility/Hyperactivity scale (DI) of the Parenting Stress Index], standardized tests [the Stroop color and word test], and classroom observations" (Levine & Waite, 2000, p. 667).

For each type of measure listed below, put an X in front of the measure if it was used in this research (leave blank if it wasn't used). If a method was used, describe what type of data was collected using this measure.

____ observations _____

____ self-report measures _____

____ standardized tests _____

____ physiological measures _____

____ archival records _____

____ case studies _____

____ other types of measures _____

Answers:

X observations: classroom observations of attention difficulties

X self-report measures: child's television diary and parent's report of the child's preferred shows

X standardized tests: the Stroop color and word test, the ADD-H Comprehensive Teachers Rating Scale, and the Distractibility/Hyperactivity scale (DI) of the Parenting Stress Index

____ physiological measures

____ archival records

____ case studies

____ other types of measures

How Research Is Designed

Experimental Designs: Identifying the Causes of Behavior

As useful as observations, surveys, and case studies are, conducting experiments still occupies a central place in our repertoire of research methods. One reason is that experiments allow us to do something that the other methods can't—they can *identify the causes* of behavior. With other methods, such as observations or tests, we cannot be certain what underlies the behavior we see. Although we can speculate about the causes, we do not have enough control over the situation to make a firm determination. However, when a researcher designs an experiment, the goal is to control as many aspects of the experimental situation as possible so that the researcher can draw conclusions about the causes of the outcome observed in the experiment.

How Experiments Are Done. Experiments can take different forms and can contain one, two, or more groups. However, these are the essential components that you will find in most experiments:

Experimental group The group in an experiment that gets the special treatment that is of interest to the researcher.

Control group The group in an experiment that does not get the special treatment and provides a baseline against which the experimental group can be compared.

Random assignment Assigning participants to the experimental and control groups by chance so that the groups will not systematically differ from each other.

Variable A characteristic that can be measured and that can have different values.

Independent variable The variable in an experiment that the researcher manipulates.

Dependent variable The outcome of interest to the researcher that is measured at the end of an experiment.

- The **experimental group** is the group that gets the special treatment that is of interest to the researcher.
- The **control group** does not get the special treatment and provides a baseline against which the experimental group can be compared.
- The participants are **randomly assigned** either to the experimental group or to the control group. Because this assignment is made by chance, it is likely that the two groups will start out being very similar to each other, without any systematic differences that could affect the outcome of the experiment. To get a random assignment to groups, you could simply flip a coin for each participant, with all "heads" going into one group and all "tails" going into the other; or you could put the names of all participants in a hat and pull them out, alternately assigning the names to one of the groups or the other.
- The **independent variable** is what the researcher hypothesizes will make a difference between the experimental and control groups (a **variable** is simply something that can be measured and have different values—that is, it can vary). The assumption is that the independent variable is the cause of any change that occurs following the experiment.
- The **dependent variable** is the outcome of interest to the researcher. It is measured at the end of the experiment to see whether manipulating the independent variable has produced the expected effect.

If we look at an example of experimental research, this terminology will have more meaning for you. In one study, researchers wanted to know whether changing the way in which parents read to their preschoolers would affect the child's later language development (Whitehurst et al., 1988). The participants in this experiment were recruited by placing an advertisement in suburban newspapers, and the final sample included 30 middle-class, intact families. Families were randomly assigned to the experimental group or the control group, with the restriction that there be an equal number of boys and girls in each group. The children in both groups were tested at the start of the study to be sure that they did not differ on several measures of development, including a measure of language milestones. Such a pretest comparison gives us confidence that the two groups are similar before we begin any experimental intervention.

The control group was asked to keep reading to their children in the same way they had been doing. (Remember, the control group provides the baseline for detecting any changes that result from the experimental manipulation during the research.) The parents in the experimental group took part in two 25- to 30-minute training sessions. (Remember, the experimental group is the group that gets the treatment that the researchers are interested in studying.) In those sessions the parents were taught not to ask their children questions that could be answered by simply pointing to things, to increase their use of open-ended questions, and to expand upon their children's answers. (This is what was different between the experimental group and the control group, so whether the parents received this training or not is the independent variable.) All parents audiotaped the time they spent reading to their children.

At the end of 4 weeks, the children's language was again tested. The children in the experimental group used longer sentences and used more phrases and fewer single words during these tests than children in the control group. The dependent variable is the outcome of interest to the researcher and what is measured at the end of the experiment and compared between the experimental group and the control group. In this study, the children's language ability was the dependent variable. Figure 3.2 shows the steps in this process and can help you understand how they relate to each other.

Because the two groups of children were similar at the start of the experiment on the measure the researchers were interested in, and because the only relevant difference between the groups during the 4 weeks of the reading intervention appeared to be how the parents read to their children, the researchers concluded that the intervention was the *cause* of the difference they observed at the end of the experiment. **Active Learning: The Experimental Method** gives you an opportunity to review the terminology used in experiments and to check that you can recognize each element when you see it in the description of an experiment.

Figure 3.2

The experimental process. This figure shows you how an experiment (in this case an experiment to promote language development) is conducted, starting with a sample of the population of interest to the researcher and ending with results that can be interpreted.

Step 1	Step 2	Step 3: Pretest	Step 4: Treatment	Step 5: Posttest	Step 6: Compare Results
A representative group of children is chosen to be in the study	Children are randomly assigned to groups	Pretest establishes groups are the same	Independent variable is administered to the experimental group	Dependent variable is measured	Supports hypothesis
Sample	Experimental Group	Score on test of language development	Training sessions on reading to children	Score on test of language development	Exp'l group score > Control group score
	Control Group	Score on test of language development	No training sessions	Score on test of language development	

The Experimental Method

ACTIVE **LEARNING**

Now you can test your understanding of the experimental method by identifying the components of an experiment in this example taken from a study by Beth Hennessey (2007) that was designed to build social competence in a sample of school-age children.

A total of 154 fourth graders in eight classrooms participated in the study. Half of the classrooms were in schools located in an upper-middle-class suburban area, and half were from schools that served more diverse populations. Half of the classrooms had teachers who were very familiar with the Open Circle Program, a social skills training program that "encourages students, teachers and administrators to learn and practice communication, self-control and social problem-solving skills" (Hennessey, 2007, p. 349). All of the students and their teachers completed the Social Skills Rating System in the fall, before the program began, and again in the spring after the program ended. The classroom teachers also were asked to rate their students' social competence at both times. Based on the teachers' reports, Hennessey concluded that the students who were in the classrooms that used the Open Circle Program training showed greater improvement in their social skills and problem-solving behavior than students who didn't receive this training.

From the description of this experiment, identify the following:

Experimental group _____

Control group _____

Independent variable _____

Dependent variable _____

Answers:
Experimental group: the group that received the Open Circle Program training
Control group: the group that did not receive the Open Circle Program training
Independent variable: whether the group received the social skills training or not
Dependent variable: the measure of social competence and problem solving

A type of "natural experiment." When children are adopted from a foreign country, they must learn a new language. This creates a natural experiment that lets us study how children learn language once they are past the sensitive period for language development.

Although doing experimental research lets us control many aspects of a situation that might affect an outcome (and, therefore, allows us to presume that we understand the cause of any changes that we find in the results), there is still the possibility that some other variable or condition that we haven't taken into account is responsible for the outcome. For this reason, it is essential that experiments be carefully planned and carefully executed. It also may have occurred to you by now that, as appealing as using the experimental method might be to researchers, it cannot be used to answer many of the questions that are of great interest to us as developmentalists. There are many situations that we could never ethically create as an experiment. For example, we couldn't deny a child a vaccination, an education, or social contact with peers just to see what effect this deprivation would have on the child's development.

Natural or "Quasi" Experiments. Sometimes, however, a situation occurs without our intervention, and we can use that situation as a **natural or "quasi" experiment** to test hypotheses. We would not intentionally deprive a child of an opportunity to learn language during the sensitive period for language development in infancy, but Snedeker, Geren, and Shafto (2007) were able to use a sample of children who were adopted from foreign countries as preschoolers to study whether they went through the same stages of language development as native English-speaking children go through while they learned English. The researchers wanted to know whether the more advanced level of cognitive development of the adopted children at the time that they were learning English would affect how they acquired English as a second language.

In another natural experiment, Brouwers, Mishra, and Van de Vijver (2006) studied children in the province of Karwar in India to disentangle the effects of cognitive maturation, experiential learning, and formal schooling on the development of cognitive skills. In Karwar, children can enter formal schooling at any time, so children who are the same age can differ in the number of years of schooling they have. However, the process of cognitive maturation would be the same for all the children in the sample because this is a biological process, and all of them would have had the same learning experiences in their natural environment (that is, their home and their community). For example, all of these children had cared for animals, gathered food for the family, and made small purchases at local stores.

In a culture such as ours in which all children begin formal schooling at about the same age, it is difficult to determine how much (or what aspects) of their cognitive development is attributable to their formal education and how much is the result of cognitive maturation or the experiences of everyday living. This naturally occurring situation in India could answer these questions without withholding an educational opportunity from any of the children.

Although the children who attended school scored higher than those who didn't on both the tests that were based upon the everyday experiences of children in that culture and the tests of more formal knowledge, Brouwers et al. (2006) concluded that there were no major qualitative differences in cognitive functioning between the children who attended school and those who didn't. They also concluded that "school attendance has a substantially smaller impact on competence than has the natural stimulation provided by everyday life" (p. 566). They interpret their results as supporting the ideas of Piaget and Vygotsky regarding the importance of everyday experiences for children's cognitive development.

TRUE/FALSE

7. An experiment always consists of an experimental situation set up by researchers to test specific hypotheses.

False. There are *natural experiments* in which a researcher takes advantage of a situation that has occurred naturally but that then can be studied in a rigorous, scientific way.

Natural or "quasi" experiment Research in which the members of the groups are selected because they represent different "treatment" conditions.

A natural experiment on the effect of schooling. Children in India who attended school were not substantially different in their cognitive functioning from those who didn't. Brouwers, Mishra, and Van de Vijver (2006) concluded that this finding highlights the important role of everyday experiences for cognitive development.

This type of research is considered experimental because, similar to research conducted in a laboratory or other controlled settings, researchers attempt to control as many variables as possible with the exception of the independent variable they are interested in studying. In the study by Brouwers et al. (2006), the children came from families who had similar social and economic status, and all the children had similar life experiences in terms of what they were expected to do to help their families. The only variable that differed between them was the number of years they had attended school. That is why, when there was a difference between groups, it could be attributed to number of years of schooling.

Correlational Designs

Correlational research examines the relationship between two or more variables. When we look at **correlations**, we are interested in two things: the *strength* of the relationship and the *direction* of the relationship. Figure 3.3 will help you visualize these aspects of correlations as we describe them. We'll talk first about the direction of the relationship. Correlations can be *positive* or *negative*. In a **positive correlation**, the value of one variable increases as the value of the second variable increases. For example, lifetime earnings are positively correlated with the number of years in school. As years completed in school go up, so do your lifetime earnings. We hope you find that to be good news! In a **negative correlation**, as the value of one variable increases, the value of the second variable decreases. For example, the more often people brush their teeth, the lower their rate of tooth decay.

Correlations
A measure of the strength and direction of the relationship between two variables.

Positive correlation
A correlation in which increases in one variable are associated with increases in another variable.

Negative correlation
A correlation in which increases in one variable are associated with decreases in another variable.

Figure 3.3

Examples of correlations. In these graphs, each dot represents an individual's scores on Variables 1 and 2. Lines that slope upward indicate a positive correlation, and ones that slope downward indicate a negative correlation. The "spread" of the data points around the line shows how strong the correlation is. The closer the points are to falling on a straight line, the stronger the correlation.

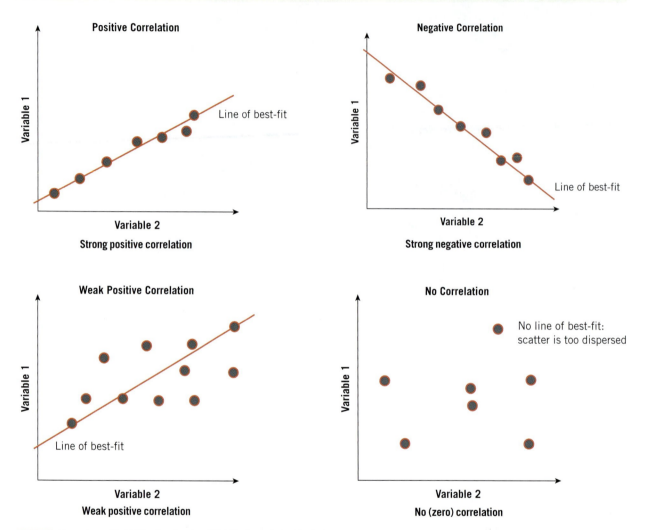

The second characteristic of correlations is the strength of the relationship between two variables. This can range from a correlation of +1.0 (a perfect positive correlation) to a correlation of −1.0 (a perfect negative correlation). At either of these extremes, a change of one unit of measurement in one of the variables is accompanied by a change in one unit of measurement in the second variable. If we were to plot this relationship, it would form a straight line, indicating that the two variables are very tightly tied together. As a correlation moves from +1 or −1 toward 0, the relationship between the variables gets weaker and weaker. An increase in the value of one of the variables is now associated with a range of values for the second variable. For instance, the correlation between people's shoe size and their IQ would probably be close to zero because there is no reason to think that these characteristics are related to each other in any systematic way. Many correlations in development research are in the moderate range of +.15 to +.40. You can test your understanding of the direction and magnitude of correlations by completing **Active Learning: Positive and Negative Correlations**.

Positive and Negative Correlations

A school counselor uses three different tests to assess children's aptitude for math so she can advise the school about the best placement for each child. After testing 400 children, she measures each child's actual performance in math classes and correlates it with the results of the three tests. She finds the following correlations:

Test 1: −.85

Test 2: +.35

Test 3: +.65

Which test should she keep as the best predictor of how a child is going to do in math, and why is that test the best predictor?

SOURCE: Adapted from Chew, 2006.

Answer: The correct answer is Test 1. Although the correlation is negative, it is the *strongest* relationship between the test and math performance because the number (.85) is the one closest to 1.0. To use this information correctly, however, the counselor needs to remember that students with high scores on this aptitude test are likely to perform *poorly* in math classes because this is a negative correlation.

We can get a good understanding of the meaning of the strength of a correlation by looking at the research that has compared the correlation of IQ scores between individuals with different genetic relationships to each other. The reasoning behind this research is that if genetics makes an important contribution to intelligence, we would expect that people with a close genetic relationship (such as a parent and a child, or siblings) would have IQ scores that are more similar than people with a more distant genetic relationship (such as cousins). This is exactly the pattern that has been found. In a study that reviewed 111 studies on familial resemblance in cognitive abilities, it was found that the correlation of IQ scores for monozygotic (identical) twins was +.86, whereas the correlation between cousins was +.15 (Bouchard & McGue, 1981). If a "perfect" correlation is +1.0, a correlation of +.86 is quite high. It means that if we know the IQ score for one of the identical twins, we can make a very good prediction of the IQ score of the second twin. On the other hand, a correlation of +.15 means that a specific IQ score for one cousin could be associated with a wide range of possible IQ scores for the second cousin. This makes it much more difficult to make an accurate prediction.

If you read an article in your local newspaper that said, "Study finds that drinking soda causes obesity," would you tend to believe it? What if the article went on to say that there is a strong positive correlation between the number of sodas that an individual consumes in a given week and how overweight that person is? Would you be convinced now? You shouldn't be.

Stop for a moment and think about what we *don't* know based on this information. We know nothing about the other diet choices made by the people in this study, what other sweetened beverages they may consume on a regular basis, how much or little exercise they get, and many, many other things that affect a person's weight. There are a great number of correlational studies in the developmental literature, and we do know a good deal about a topic when we understand the relationship between two variables, but we must use caution when interpreting correlational findings because the fact that two things occur together does *not* mean that one of them caused the other.

Correlational research is nonexperimental research. Although it tells us the relationship between two variables (in this case, soda consumption and weight), we do not know what (if anything) was controlled in the study. A third variable that wasn't even measured by the correlational research might be responsible for changes in the variables that were measured. For instance, people who are poorer tend to have diets that contain more carbohydrates (such as sugar) because these foods are both cheap and filling. In this case, it may be socioeconomic status that contributes both to increased soda consumption and to weight gain.

8. Even if research consistently finds that mothers who talk to their children a great deal have children with high self-esteem, we should not conclude that frequent conversations with parents build self-esteem in children.

TRUE/FALSE

True. You *cannot* assume that two things that go together necessarily cause each other. There may be some other factor at work that is responsible for both the mother's talkativeness and the child's self-esteem.

Direction of effects. Who is driving the process of development in these pictures? The parent? The child? Or are they mutually influencing each other?

To illustrate this point further, we might find that there is a fairly strong positive correlation between the amount of stress that children report having in their lives and the number of days they miss from school because they are ill. However, it would be dangerous for us to conclude from this finding that high levels of stress *cause* illness. Please understand that this *might* be the case, but we do not have enough information from this correlational study to draw that conclusion because both of our variables (stressful life conditions and poor health) might be affected by a third variable that was not included in our study. In this case, impoverished living conditions could be that third variable. Children who come from poorer families probably have more stress in their lives, but these same children also may have less healthy lifestyles and less access to medical care when they need it. It is the family's financial status that is responsible for both of these things.

Does this mean that we can never answer the question of whether it is stress or economic circumstances that cause poor health in children? Not exactly. We could conduct a natural experiment in which we only include children from the same economic background. Thus their families' economic circumstances would be "controlled" in this research because we would make them the same across all of our participants. Another approach that helps clarify the direction of effects is to statistically control for economic status. There are statistical techniques that allow us to take this effect out of our equation. Either of these approaches would allow us to see whether stressful life circumstances are related to health outcomes over and above the effect of the family's economic situation. **Journey of Research: Direction of Effects** talks more about how our understanding of cause and effect has changed in developmental research.

Direction of Effects

The simplest way to try to understand cause and effect is to look for **unidirectional effects**, or those that run in only one direction. In early scientific research done on parenting, the presumption was that effects run only one way: from the parent to the child. A different point of view was introduced in 1974 by Lewis and Rosenblum in a book titled *The Effect of the Infant on Its Caregiver,* in which the authors argue that the effect runs in both directions. This would be a **bidirectional effect**. While it is true that parents influence and to some extent shape their children, it also is true that children have an effect upon and try to shape their parents. In fact, this is probably true in any relationship you can think of. Husbands have an effect on the behavior of their wives, but wives also shape the behavior of their husbands. Siblings mutually affect each other's behavior. Teachers try to shape their students' behavior, but students often very effectively shape their teacher's behavior. If you notice that people in your class squirm in their seats and begin gathering up their possessions as your class nears its end, it might be that they are hoping they will shape your professor's "wrapping up the class for today" behavior. And if your professor announces, "We have one more important thing to discuss today," the direction of the effect has just shifted back in the other direction as people settle back into their seats.

Beyond the realization that children play a role in the bidirectional relationship with their parents, we also came to realize that patterns of interaction occur across time. When we add the dimension of time to our thinking, the effect is now a **transactional effect**. Gerald Patterson and his colleagues (Patterson, 1982; Patterson, Reid, & Dishion, 1992) coined the term *coercive parenting* to describe what happens over time in families with difficult children. When a child does not comply with his parents' requests, the parents escalate their demands and become more insistent that their child listen to them and obey. As their parenting becomes more harsh and punitive, the child becomes resentful and is more obstinate and disobedient. The parents, in turn, may react (or overreact) by further escalating their demands for obedience and compliance. As parents and child continue to try to mutually shape each other's behavior, the interactions become more hostile over time.

JOURNEY *of* RESEARCH

Unidirectional effect Influence that runs in only one direction (for example, from a parent to his or her child).

Bidirectional effect Mutual influence between two individuals.

Transactional effect A bidirectional effect in which there are changes over time as a result of the ongoing interaction between the individuals.

Before moving on to our next topic, check your understanding of the different types of methods that are used in child development research by completing **Active Learning: The Scientific Method—Research Methods**.

The Scientific Method—Research Methods

ACTIVE LEARNING

Look again at the abstract of the article by Levine and Waite (2000) near the beginning of this chapter. In it you have enough information to answer these questions:

1. Does this study use an experiment or a correlational research design? Here is a hint: Did the experimenters randomly assign children to different groups who then received different treatments?
2. Can the researchers conclude that television viewing causes children to have attention problems? Why or why not?

Answers:

1. The children were not randomly assigned to groups. The researchers looked at the relationship between the amount of television they watched and their attentional difficulties (that is, they correlated these two measures). They did not directly manipulate the amount of television that the children watched, so this research is a correlational research design.
2. The answer again is no. Because this is a correlational design, the researchers cannot conclude anything about causation. They can only state that television viewing is related to attention difficulties. Just as we described above, it is possible (and some have argued for this point of view) that children who have attention difficulties are more likely to watch a lot of television, which may hold their attention more effectively than other activities, so we can't be sure which variable is the cause and which is the effect. It is also possible that a third variable, such as parental depression or neglect, might cause both increased television viewing and attention problems.

Developmental Designs

We have been talking about methods that are used to test scientific hypotheses, but each of these methods can be used within different research designs that look at development. If we define development as "change with age," there are several ways to examine the changes that occur as children grow and develop. As we look at these designs, we will find that each has its own advantages and disadvantages, but that each also has a place in looking at the complex questions we have about development.

Longitudinal design
A research design that follows one group of individuals over time and looks at the same or similar measures at each point of testing.

Longitudinal Research. A **longitudinal design** follows one group of individuals across time and looks at the same or similar measures at each point of testing. The biggest advantage that comes with doing a longitudinal study is that it gives us the clearest picture of how the variables we are interested in change as a function of age.

For example, all children show some aggressive behavior, but the way that aggression is expressed changes as children get older. In a recent study of 23,000 Canadian children from birth to age 11, researchers examined age-related changes in one specific type of aggression: indirect aggression (Vaillancourt, Miller, Fagbemi, Cote, & Tremblay, 2007). Indirect aggression is a type of socially manipulative aggression, such as saying things behind a person's back to hurt her or betraying someone else's secrets. The researchers interviewed the children's mothers every 2 years for 8 years, when the children were 2, 4, 6, 8, and 10 years old. Through this longitudinal approach, the researchers found that indirect aggression increased between the ages of 4 and 6, but they did not find an increase between the ages of 6 and 10.

In a recent study of depression, Tram and Cole (2006) conducted a longitudinal study of 1,269 children and adolescents from the fall of fifth grade to the spring of eighth grade. The participants (and their parents and peers) provided data once every 6 months over this period. The results from this longitudinal study found that the stability of depressive symptoms was very high, although that stability did decline at the time of the transition from elementary school to middle school. Figure 3.4 shows the results from this study.

Figure 3.4

Longitudinal study of depression. The level of depression in this sample of adolescents remained relatively stable from the start of fifth grade until the end of eighth grade, except during early adolescence when they were dealing with a lot of change and stress in their lives.

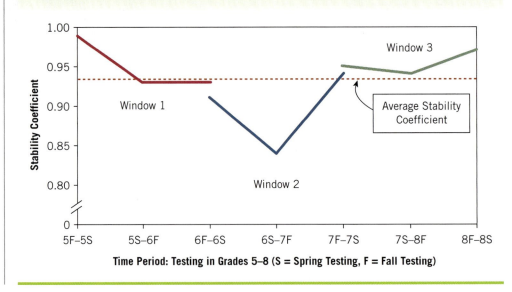

Time Period: Testing in Grades 5–8 (S = Spring Testing, F = Fall Testing)

Although longitudinal research provides unique and valuable information, it can be a difficult method to use. Before we go any further with this topic, stop for a moment and decide for yourself what would be some of the challenges of following 23,000 children for 8 years while testing them every other year, or following over 1,200 students for 4 years while testing them every 6 months. In either case, it should be clear to you that these are very ambitious research efforts.

Because you need to track your study participants across a period of time, it is inevitable that some of the participants who begin a longitudinal study will not complete all the waves of data collection. The loss of participants from a sample over the course of a longitudinal study is called **attrition**. If all participants had an equal risk of dropping out of the study before its completion, this would reduce the size of your sample and reduce your ability to detect differences among the participants, but it might not otherwise jeopardize the validity of your research. However, all students are *not* at an equal risk of dropping out (Miller & Wright, 1995). Some children and adolescents are more likely than others to move, to be unavailable when one or more of the data collections occur, or simply to decide to withdraw from the study. Which children do you think are at greater risk of not remaining in a longitudinal study until it ends? For instance, we might expect that it would be more difficult to retain children who are poorer, less healthy, or more trouble prone because these children may be absent from school more often or may move more frequently and change schools.

Attrition The loss of participants over the course of a longitudinal study.

To the extent that it is children with these characteristics who drop out more frequently, they change the composition of the sample and make it less representative than it was when the study began. So, although we may have started with a representative sample, over time **sample bias** will creep into our study. If the most trouble-prone children are the ones most likely to drop out, how will this affect the final results of the study and the conclusions we draw from them? It means that the children who remain in the study may be functioning at a higher level in any number of ways compared to the children who were lost from the sample, and this would inflate our estimate of the children's abilities.

Sample bias Changes in the makeup of the sample in a longitudinal or cross-sequential study that make the sample less representative over time.

Think of it this way. If you have ever watched the national college basketball play-offs (the NCAA "March Madness"), you have an idea of what happens in longitudinal research. You could measure the average basketball skill level across all the players in the 64 teams that begin the competition. However, during the play-offs, teams are defeated and drop out of the competition. If you based your final estimate of basketball skills on the teams that made it through to the Final Four, your estimate would be considerably higher than your original estimate because the teams with the weaker players have been eliminated. The same thing happens as more problematic children drop out of our longitudinal research, and the longer the period of time covered by the study, the greater this risk becomes.

To answer the question that we asked you earlier about the challenges of doing longitudinal studies such as the ones conducted by Tram and Cole (2006) and by Vaillancourt et al. (2007), you probably realize that it takes a good deal of time and money and a large number

Sample bias. Just as the weakest players and teams are eliminated early during the NCAA basketball play-offs, the research participants with the most problems in their lives are more likely to drop out of a longitudinal study over time. This creates bias in the sample.

of research personnel to conduct a study of a large group of individuals across multiple waves of data collection. Many researchers do not have the resources they would need to conduct this type of research.

Other challenges of doing longitudinal studies include the fact that researchers become locked into using one set of measures, even if better alternatives come along during the course of the study. In addition, if the same or similar measures are used repeatedly, it is possible that there is a practice effect and a participant's response will be influenced by how that individual answered questions at an earlier point in the study. Why are researchers in this difficult position? Because if they change measures during the study and find changes in the level of the outcomes they are measuring, they cannot be sure whether the change was attributable to the fact that the participants were older or whether the new measure was actually measuring something slightly different than the original measure. Despite these concerns, however, longitudinal research still provides a very powerful way to look at developmental change, and that is why it is still used.

Cross-Sectional Research. A **cross-sectional design** is an approach that uses multiple groups of participants who represent the age span of interest to the researcher. If you were interested in developmental changes between elementary and middle school, you could use groups of participants who were 8 years old, 10 years old, and 12 years old and collect data from all the groups of participants at about the same time. Then, by comparing the results between groups, you could construct a picture of the changes that occur over that period of development. Because all of the data collection occurs at the same time, you can efficiently collect data from a large number of participants in a relatively quick, cost-effective manner. Obviously participant dropout is not an issue because there is only a single data collection. Based on cross-sectional research, you will know that children of different ages show differences on the outcome you measured, but you won't know *why*. We presume that it is age changes that are responsible, but we need to be careful when making these presumptions.

One of the big issues for researchers to deal with when doing cross-sectional research is that the different age groups in the study must be as similar as possible on any variable that might affect the study's outcome. Here is an extreme example to make this point clear. Imagine you are interested in how self-esteem changes during the transition from elementary to middle school. To examine these changes, you used a group of 8-year-old students who attended a public elementary school in a disadvantaged neighborhood, a group of 10-year-old students from a private school with a religious affiliation, and a group of 12-year-old students from a suburban public school. Even if you found differences in self-esteem between the groups, could you correctly interpret them as age-related changes or changes associated with school transitions? Clearly you couldn't. Because the groups came from such widely different school settings (and, therefore, it is likely that they differ from each other in a variety of ways), you could not make any valid interpretation of these data. The differences that may exist between groups used in actual cross-sectional research would be much more subtle than those in our example, but any difference between the groups that is not recognized and accounted for by the research can be a threat to the validity of the conclusions drawn from this type of research.

Finally, cross-sectional research can be affected by what is known as the **cohort effect**. A cohort is a group of people born at about the same point in historical time. A cohort effect becomes a concern in cross-sectional research when the range of ages represented by the different groups is large enough that the participants in them come from different birth cohorts or when some aspect of the environment has changed significantly between the groups in the study. The "baby boom" generation describes people born between the mid-1940s and the mid-1960s; "Gen Xers" were born between the early 1960s and the late 1970s; and "millennials" were born between the late 1970s and about 1995. You can easily see how members of these different cohorts would have different experiences while growing up that make them different in a number of ways. For example, millennials grew up with computers, but baby boomers

Cross-sectional design
A research design that uses multiple groups of participants who represent the age span of interest to the researcher.

Cohort effect
Differences between groups in a cross section or cross-sequential study that are attributable to the fact that the participants have had different life experiences.

Cohort effects. When groups in cross-sectional research come from different cohorts (or birth groups), it is important not to interpret differences we observe as due to age if they may actually represent differences in cohort life experiences. This child may know more about computers than her grandfather, but it is because she has had more experience using them, not because young people are smarter than older people.

never saw a personal computer until they were adults, which is one reason why your parents might turn to you for your expertise when their computer doesn't work. If we were to measure competence in computer use, we would likely find that the millennials are more skilled than the baby boomers. However, we could not conclude that as people get older they become less skilled at using a computer! The difference we see is due to a different set of life experiences, *not* to a loss of computer skills with increasing age. This is an important point to keep in mind because researchers want to conclude that differences seen between age groups in cross-sectional research are due to developmental changes, but it is possible that they are due to historical changes instead.

Cross-Sequential Research. Finally, the **cross-sequential design** brings together elements of cross-sectional research and longitudinal research. This design uses several groups of people of different ages who begin their participation in the study at the same time (just as cross-sectional research does) and follows the groups over a period of time (just as longitudinal research does). What makes this method unique is that there is overlap between the groups on their ages at one point in the testing. For example, if we were interested in looking at children's health over the age range from birth until age 20, we could assess four different groups: infants, 5-year-olds, 10-year-olds, and 15-year-olds. If we repeated our assessment 5 years later (when the infants were 5 years old, the 5-year-olds were 10, etc.), we then would have two different groups that had been assessed at age 5. Because we only needed to follow the groups for 5 years, we would have reduced the risk of participants dropping out of the research study to below what it would have been in a 20-year study (and therefore reduced sample bias). We also would have reduced the time, money, and personnel needed to conduct the study compared to a 20-year-long study of children's health. Finally, if there were any cohort differences between the groups, those effects would have become apparent in the results.

Even though some advantages are gained through the use of cross-sequential research, you still need to construct the cohort groups so that they are as much alike as possible at the start of the study, and you still need to be able to track and reassess the groups at regular intervals, so sample attrition and practice effects are still potential problems. Test your understanding of these three different developmental research designs by trying **Active Learning: Developmental Research Designs**.

Cross-sequential design A research design that uses multiple groups of participants and follows them over a period of time, with the beginning age of each group being the ending age of another group.

Developmental Research Designs

ACTIVE LEARNING

Look at the chart below and answer the following questions:

1. If only Group A was tested, what type of developmental research design would this be?
2. If only Testing Year 2010 was carried out, what type of developmental research design would this be?
3. If all the groups were tested in years 2010 and 2015, what type of developmental research design would this be?

Testing Year 2010	Testing Year 2015
Group A age 10	Group A age 15
Group B age 5	Group B age 10
Group C newborn	Group C age 5

Answers:

1. Longitudinal research design because the same group of participants is followed and retested after 5 years.
2. Cross-sectional research design because different age groups are tested and compared at the same time.
3. Cross-sequential research design because different age groups are compared and the groups also are followed and retested after 5 years.

TRUE/FALSE

9. Research has shown that boys who watch a lot of violence on TV are more aggressive, but if you know someone who watches a lot of violence and you see that he is not at all aggressive, this disproves the research.

False. Research tells us about what is average or typical for a group of people. The fact that some individuals fall outside of that range does *not* invalidate the research. It simply illustrates the great diversity we see in the behavior of children, adolescents, and adults.

Null hypothesis The hypothesis tested by an experiment that there will be no difference in the outcome for the groups in an experiment.

TRUE/FALSE

10. Once we have established that the results of our research are statistically significant, we can be confident they will have an impact on real-world situations.

False. There is a difference between statistical significance and practical significance. Results that are statistically significant do not always translate into something that has consequences in the real world.

Interpreting the Results of a Study

This step in the scientific method reminds us that after we conduct research, the results still must be interpreted. Two people may look at the results of a study and interpret them in a different way. The accuracy of our final understanding of what the study showed is greatly affected by how the data are interpreted. The following list shows some important ways to make a realistic interpretation of a study's results:

1. We have already discussed the fact that we need to be careful not to generalize our results beyond the characteristics of the sample that participated in the research.

2. We also need to guard against reaching conclusions that go beyond the scope of the research. For instance, you wouldn't use the results from one small-scale study as the basis for recommending wholesale changes to the nation's educational system.

3. We need to remember that conclusions drawn from research—even very carefully conducted research—are generalizations that apply to groups of individuals. As you learned in Chapter 1, there is a great deal of diversity among individuals within any group. Therefore our conclusions will not apply to every single child, and the fact that there are children who do *not* fit the general pattern does not invalidate the general conclusion. There are always exceptions, and that is not necessarily bad. Understanding what sets some individuals apart from the group or what makes an individual child or adolescent the exception to a general rule is an important goal of developmental research in and of itself.

4. When interpreting the results of research we also need to distinguish between *statistical significance* and *practical significance*. Even though a researcher might find results that are statistically significant, the results may not be very important. We describe this difference more fully in the next paragraphs.

The results of research are tested using various statistical methods to determine whether the outcomes that were observed may have happened by chance. If you were evaluating the effectiveness of a new program intended to improve social problem-solving skills, you would hypothesize that the students who participate in the program will have better social problem-solving skills than a similar group of students who don't participate in the program. The statistical test you use would test the **null hypothesis** that there will be *no difference* between the groups on your measure of problem-solving skills at the end of the research. If you found a difference in the group scores, the statistical test would tell you how likely it is that the difference you observed had occurred by chance. For instance, the statistical test might determine that the results that were observed would occur only once in a hundred times by chance. This probability would be reported in a research article as $p < .01$. Probability levels are typically set at .05, .01, .001, or .0001. The smaller the probability, the smaller the likelihood that this is a chance finding. Tests of statistical significance give us confidence that results from research are not accidents or flukes.

However, even if the results of a research study are statistically significant, you still might wonder whether the findings make any difference in the real world. A study might find that differences between two groups are statistically significant (that is, they did not happen by chance), but this does not mean that the difference is large or important. For instance, in the example above, let's imagine that the scores on the test of social problem solving could range from 0 to 50, and the group that received the problem-solving skills training scored an average of 42 on this test, while the group that did not have the intervention scored 38. Does a 4-point difference on this test make any difference in the quality of the social relationships that these children have? Does it make them any happier or better adjusted? This is a difficult question to answer. Longitudinal research that follows these children over time could begin to draw a picture of the long-term effect of this intervention so that we could assess the program's practical significance.

Students from the University of Michigan (Benson, n.d.) have provided a nice illustration of the difference between statistical and practical significance. In the first case, 5 out of 100 people taking part in a study die before the study ends. In the second case, 5 out of 100 people taking part in a study are less happy at the end of the study than they were at the beginning. In both of these cases, the outcome may be statistically significant, indicating that this is not a chance finding, but in terms of practical significance, these are two very different outcomes that affect people's lives in very different ways.

Replication of Results

Our confidence that our conclusions are valid is strengthened if we are able to replicate or repeat our findings. We can do this by repeating the research using other groups that are the same or similar to the group we originally studied or by extending the research to new groups to determine whether the conclusions can be generalized to new situations (Shaughnessy & Zechmeister, 1994). We also expect that other researchers will be able to replicate our results by conducting their own independent research and coming to the same or similar conclusions.

When findings are published in research journals or presented at professional meetings, it gives others the opportunity to independently verify what we have found and further increases our confidence in the validity of our findings. Presenting findings publicly also allows other researchers to critique the way that the research was conducted and identify any possible flaws in the logic or problems with the methodology, analysis, or interpretation of the findings. Sometimes a statistical procedure called **meta-analysis** is used to combine the data from different studies to determine whether there is a consistent pattern of findings across studies. We described a meta-analysis earlier in this chapter when we described the relationship between genetic similarity and IQ. That research pulled together results from 111 studies before reaching its conclusions (Bouchard & McGue, 1981), so we can have a great deal of confidence in the conclusion drawn from it.

Meta-analysis A statistical procedure that combines data from different studies to determine whether there is a consistent pattern of findings across studies.

Ethics in Research With Children and Adolescents

Any research that involves human participants must ensure the safety and well-being of those participants. The U.S. Department of Health and Human Services (2005a) has issued a set of regulations that describe the specific protections that must be in place. According to these regulations, participants should be exposed to minimum risks during their participation in the research, and any potential risk must be weighed against the anticipated benefits from the research. All participants must give **informed consent** for their participation. That means that they have been informed of the purpose of the research and its risks and benefits and have freely agreed—without coercion—to participate. They also have the right to withdraw their consent and discontinue participation at any point, if they want to. Finally, the privacy of participants is protected, and the data that are collected must be treated as confidential. However, these regulations also recognize that there are some groups of research participants that require special consideration, and these groups include animals that are used in scientific research, mentally disabled persons, and children.

Informed consent Informing research participants of the risks and benefits of participating in the research and guaranteeing them the right to withdraw from participation if they wish.

The Society for Research in Child Development (SRCD, 2007), a professional organization for researchers, practitioners, and human development professionals, has developed guidelines specifically for research with children. These guidelines include the expectation that no physical or psychological harm will be done to children who participate in research and that the researcher will use the least stressful research procedures possible. The researcher also must seek consent both from the children and their parents. If children are not old enough to give consent because they do not necessarily understand the full significance of the research, they still must assent if they are old enough to do that. That means that the children freely choose to participate and are able to terminate participation at any point if they want to. If, during the course of the research, the researcher becomes aware of any threat to the child's well-being, it is the responsibility of the researcher to inform the parents and arrange for assistance for the child. Researchers also are advised that "because the investigator's words may carry unintended weight with parents and children, caution should be exercised in reporting results, making evaluative statements, or giving advice" to families who take part in the research (SRCD, 2007).

Finding and Assessing Information About Development

Scientific information about development can be found from many sources. There are hundreds of professional journals devoted to publishing the results of research on various topics in development. There also are numerous professional newsletters and magazines that are published on a regular basis, as well as popular press publications, such as parenting magazines, that help disseminate new information in the field. Of course, the Internet is filled with information and advice on topics related to development, and television programs regularly feature information on children and their development. With so much information out there, how can you judge the quality of the information that you see? It is important that you become an informed consumer of developmental information.

Your campus library owns many journals in the field of child development, as well as many books and professional publications, and you can trust that these are reliable sources of information. All of the books and journals that you will find there were evaluated by the library staff for accuracy before being added to the library's collection. Libraries today have made the job of locating research information easier than ever because they also subscribe to a number of electronic databases that give you almost immediate access to numerous journals in an electronic format. By logging on to your library's website, you can search by key words or by subject to locate information from journals, books, presentations at professional meetings, and government publications. If you haven't used these electronic databases, you should ask the reference librarian at your campus library to tell you where you can learn how to use these campus resources.

Video Link 3.6
Using PsycINFO.

When you log on to your library's list of databases, you will find that most of them are specialized. Each is devoted primarily to a particular discipline or field of study. Among the ones of greatest interest to students in child and adolescent development are PsycINFO and ERIC (Education Resources Information Center). PsycINFO allows you to search over 2,400 journals, as well as books and book chapters, published from the 1800s to the present (American Psychological Association, 2009). ERIC is sponsored by the U.S. Department of Education and has more than 1.3 million bibliographic records of journal articles and other education-related materials (Education Resources Information Center, n.d.). In these databases, you can find abstracts (brief summaries of the research done and the conclusions drawn from it) and information about which journal contains the complete article. You may be able to find these articles in journals on the shelves of your library or through electronic databases, which offer access to articles electronically so they can be read online or downloaded to your computer. Many campus libraries will also get articles from other libraries for you if your campus library doesn't own the journal in which the article appears.

As we described earlier, many journals use a peer review process to determine which articles they will print. After researchers submit articles that they want to publish in the journal, the journal editors send the article out to a group of professionals who are knowledgeable about the topic of the research. These research peers, in turn, tell the editors whether they think the article should be published and often ask for clarification or for additional information from the author to improve the manuscript before it is published. The editor makes the final determination about if—or when—the article is ready to be published. This means that when you take information from a peer-reviewed journal, you can be sure that the information passed professional scrutiny before it ever got into print.

However, when you turn to the Internet to find information and use a search engine such as Yahoo!, Google, or AltaVista, you need to provide your own scrutiny and use good judgment. Remember that anyone can post information on the web, so the authors of some webpages do not necessarily have any particular expertise. Although the Wikipedia website is popular with college students, you should realize that you know little or nothing about the qualifications of the authors of articles that appear on this site. Did you know that anyone can edit an existing posting on Wikipedia and change the information in it? For these reasons, this is not considered a reliable source of information for most purposes. If you do use a site like this, use it as a starting point only, and be sure to expand your search to include other professional sources of information. Many Wikipedia entries include a bibliography of professional books and articles that may help send you in the right direction to find scientific information on the topic you are researching.

There are criteria that can be used to evaluate webpages that you want to use for research. You might use different criteria if you are just searching for information for entertainment purposes, but Jim Kapoun (1998) prepared the guidelines shown in Table 3.3 for academic web searches. You can use these guidelines to evaluate a webpage that interests you by completing **Active Learning: Evaluating Information on the Web.**

Table 3.3

Five criteria for evaluating webpages

Evaluation of Web Documents	How to Interpret the Basics
1. Accuracy of Web Documents • Who wrote the page and can you contact him or her? • What is the purpose of the document and why was it produced? • Is this person qualified to write this document?	**Accuracy** • Make sure the author provides e-mail or a contact address/phone number. • Know the distinction between author and Webmaster.
2. Authority of Web Documents • Who published the document and is it separate from the "Webmaster"? • Check the domain of the document, [and ask] what institution publishes this document? • Does the publisher list his or her qualifications?	**Authority** • What credentials are listed for the author(s)? • Where is the document published? Check URL domain.
3. Objectivity of Web Documents • What goals/objectives does this page meet? • How detailed is the information? • What opinions (if any) are expressed by the author?	**Objectivity** • Determine if page is a mask for advertising; if so information might be biased. • View any Web page as you would an infomercial on television. Ask yourself why was this written and for whom?
4. Currency of Web Documents • When was it produced? • When was it updated? • How up-to-date are the links (if any)?	**Currency** • How many dead links are on the page? • Are the links current or updated regularly? • Is the information on the page outdated?
5. Coverage of the Web Documents • Are the links (if any) evaluated and do they complement the documents' theme? • Is it all images or a balance of text and images? • Is the information presented cited correctly?	**Coverage** • If page requires special software to view the information, how much are you missing if you don't have the software? • Is it free, or is there a fee, to obtain the information? • Is there an option for text only, or frames, or a suggested browser for better viewing?

Putting It All Together
- **Accuracy.** If your page lists the author and institution that published the page and provides a way of contacting him/her, and . . .
- **Authority.** If your page lists the author credentials and its domain is preferred (.edu, .gov, .org, or .net), and . . .
- **Objectivity.** If your page provides accurate information with limited advertising and it is objective in presenting the information, and . . .
- **Currency.** If your page is current and updated regularly (as stated on the page) and the links (if any) are also up-to-date, and . . .
- **Coverage.** If you can view the information properly—not limited by fees, browser technology, or software requirement, then . . .
- **You may have a Web page that could be of value to your research!**

ACTIVE
LEARNING

Evaluating Information on the Web

Pick a topic related to child development that you would like to know more about. For example, what is the effect of violent video games on children's level of aggression, or how does parental divorce affect teens' romantic relationships? Find research on a website devoted to this topic through the use of a search engine such as Google. Evaluate what you found on the website using the criteria provided by Kapoun (1998).

Name of the site you found: _____

URL: _____

1. Accuracy of Web Documents • Who wrote the page and can you contact him or her? • What is the purpose of the document and why was it produced? • Is this person qualified to write this document?	
2. Authority of Web Documents • Who published the document and is it separate from the "Webmaster"? • Check the domain of the document, [and ask] what institution publishes this document? • Does the publisher list his or her qualifications?	
3. Objectivity of Web Documents • What goals/objectives does this page meet? • How detailed is the information? • What opinions (if any) are expressed by the author?	
4. Currency of Web Documents • When was it produced? • When was it updated? • How up-to-date are the links (if any)?	
5. Coverage of the Web Documents • Are the links (if any) evaluated and do they complement the documents' theme? • Is it all images or a balance of text and images? • Is the information presented/cited correctly?	

What is your overall evaluation of the accuracy and helpfulness of this site?

_____

_____

Next, log on to PsycINFO through your campus library website and search for the same research topic. Be sure to enter the topic you've chosen, not a full sentence or phrase; for example, enter *video games* on one line and *aggression* on the next, rather than entering *effect of video games on aggression* on one line. Chances are that your search will return many, many published articles. If it doesn't, try changing one or more of your search terms. For instance, if you searched for *teenagers*, you could try searching for the term *adolescents*. Choose one or two of the articles that you find that give you electronic access to the full text of the articles and look over the information.

What are advantages and disadvantages of using each of these sources (the Internet and PsycINFO) for finding information on child development? How much do you trust the information in each? What gives you confidence in the results you found? To see how easily someone might be tricked by false websites, go to the student exercises on the study site at www.sagepub.com/levine. How convincing are the websites that you see? What these examples show you is that even when you are being mindful of the guidelines for evaluating a website, you can still be fooled by a tricky site, so you also need to use your own good common sense.

Conclusion

In this chapter you received a broad introduction to the various ways that researchers add to our knowledge base in child and adolescent development. Each approach has advantages and disadvantages, but no one approach is the best choice in all situations. Instead we strive to find an approach or method that is appropriate for the type of research we are conducting. Beyond that, as information accumulates over time, we build our confidence in our findings and conclusions. This is particularly true when different methods have been used by different researchers but the information they find fits together into a coherent picture. You also have learned about strategies you can use in this class to find reliable and valid information to answer your own questions. You will use all of this information to understand and evaluate what you read in the rest of this book and in your ongoing study of child development.

CHAPTER SUMMARY

1. **What is the scientific method?**

   The **scientific method** is the way we add knowledge to our understanding of child development. It begins with observations, which generate **hypotheses**. After we **operationalize** the concepts in our hypotheses, we select a **representative sample** that participates in the research. Any measures that we use must be **reliable** and **valid**.

2. **What methods are used to test hypotheses?**

   Research can be conducted using naturalistic observation or by asking children (or people who know them well) to report on behaviors. Self-report measures include **surveys**, **questionnaires**, and interviews (including **clinical interviews**). We also gather data by using standardized tests, physiological measures, or **archival records**. Sometimes a case study is conducted to intensively study a single individual who is of interest.

3. **How are experiments done?**

   We begin with a sample that is representative of the **population** we are interested in. Participants are **randomly assigned** to either the **experimental group** or the **control group**. The experimental group receives the **independent variable** (the **variable** that is being studied), and the control group does not (it acts as the baseline against which the experimental group is compared). At the conclusion of the experiment, the **dependent variable** is measured for both groups and compared. If there is a difference, we can conclude that the independent variable caused the change.

4. **What is a correlation?**

   A **correlation** is a measure of the strength and direction of the relationship between two variables. The strongest correlation is +1.0, and the weakest is 0. Although a correlation indicates that two variables are related, it cannot tell us what causes the relationship.

5. **What are "direction of effects" models?**

   We can assume that the influence between two people flows from one of them to the other (a **unidirectional** model, such as "parents influence children" or "children influence their parents") or that the influence is mutual with each party influencing the other (a **bidirectional** model). When we look at mutual influence across time, it is called a **transactional** model.

6. **What types of research designs are used?**

   In a **longitudinal design**, a single group of study participants is followed for a period of time and is tested or assessed repeatedly. In a **cross-sectional design**, several groups of participants of different ages are assessed at the same time and compared to get a picture of how changes occur as a function of age. The groups in a cross-sectional design must be comparable to each other in as many ways as possible. In a **cross-sequential design**, several groups are followed for a period of time, with an overlap in the age at which one group begins the study and another group finishes it.

7. **How do we interpret the results of a study?**

   In interpreting the results of a study, we must be careful not to **generalize** the results beyond the characteristics of the sample used in the research or to draw conclusions that go beyond the scope of the study. We also need to remember that the results apply to groups, not individuals, so we can expect to find individuals who are exceptions to the study results. Finally, we need to assess the practical significance of the findings. Tests of probability help us determine how much confidence we can have that our results are not a chance occurrence.

8. **What special measures do we need to take when conducting research on children?**

   All research must protect the physical and psychological safety and well-being of participants and minimize any risk to them. If children are old enough to understand the nature of the research, they are asked to provide **informed consent**. Children (or their parents) have the right to withdraw from participation in the study at any point.

9. **How do we become good consumers of scientific research?**

   It is important to use reliable sources of information, such as articles published in peer-reviewed journals. When using information from the Internet, you should consider the accuracy of the information and the qualifications of the author of the information, as well as its objectivity, currency, and coverage.

 Go to **www.sagepub.com/levine** for additional exercises and video resources. Select **Chapter 3, How We Study Children and Adolescents,** for chapter-specific activities.

part II

Beginnings

Chapter Outline

chapter 4

How Children Develop

Nature Through Nurture

4

Throughout the history of the study of human development, the question of whether our behavior, thoughts, and feelings result from nature (our **genes**) or nurture (our environment) has been a central concern. The controversy was originally described as nature *versus* nurture. To look at an example of how scientists approached this issue, let's say you are an aggressive (or shy, or outgoing . . .) person. Researchers wanted to find out whether you became aggressive because you were "born that way," with genes from your parents determining the outcome, or whether you learned to be aggressive because of what you saw or experienced in your environment. People initially argued for one side or the other, but it became clear that the outcome was a mixture of both. (For a historical view of this argument, see **Journey of Research: Genes and Environment**.) At that point the argument shifted to describing

Gene The basic unit of inheritance, genes are made of DNA and they give the messages to the body to create proteins that are the basis for the body's development and functioning.

Test Your Knowledge

Test your knowledge of child development by deciding whether each of the following statements is *true* or *false,* and then check your answers as you read the chapter.

1. **True/False:** A central question in psychology today is whether we act the way we do because of our genes or because of environmental influences.
2. **True/False:** Each human being has hundreds of thousands of genes that make him or her a unique individual.
3. **True/False:** When a child is conceived, it is the mother's genetic material that determines the gender of the child.
4. **True/False:** Women who give birth when they are 35 to 40 years old are twice as likely to have twins compared to younger women.
5. **True/False:** The tendency to have identical twins runs in families.
6. **True/False:** Two parents with brown eyes can still have a child with blue eyes.
7. **True/False:** Females are more likely to have a genetic disorder than males.
8. **True/False:** The experiences you have in your life can change the structure of your genes.
9. **True/False:** At age 17, Mike is already a heavy drinker. Both of his parents have struggled with alcoholism for a long time. Therefore, genes must have determined that Mike would also become an alcoholic.
10. **True/False:** Genes have been found to play a role in the development of almost all behaviors that have been studied.

Correct answers: (1) False, (2) False, (3) False, (4) True, (5) False, (6) True, (7) False, (8) False, (9) False, (10) True

1. A central question in psychology today is whether we act the way we do because of our genes or because of environmental influences.

False. Most psychologists now agree that an interaction of both genes and environment occurs in most behaviors. The idea that we will find that one or the other is the cause of certain behaviors is not the central focus of research today.

the proportion of each part in the mix. It is only now, with our ability to localize specific genes, that we have been able to see that it is not just "a mixture of both" but that genes and environment interact in complex and even surprising ways. What is clear is that each is essential for the functioning of the other.

D. O. Hebb said that asking whether behavior is due to nature or to nurture is similar to asking whether the area of a rectangle is due to its length or its width (Meaney, 2004). Just as both length and width are necessary to determine area, so, too, both genes and environment are necessary to determine behavioral development. According to physician and researcher David Reiss (2001), "Current advances in genetic research suggest that the old dichotomy between 'genes' and 'environment' is dead" (para. 1). We have left behind the era of "nature *versus* nurture" and entered the era of "nature *through* nurture," in which many genes, particularly those related to traits and behaviors, are expressed only through their interaction with the environment. In this chapter, we examine what we know about the effects of genes and the environment. We will first examine how genes work and how they impact development. We will then describe what we now know about how genes and environment interact. Finally, we examine some environmental effects on development, specifically the all-important role that culture plays in child and adolescent development.

Genes and Environment

JOURNEY *of* RESEARCH

Eugenics The concept that desirable traits can be bred into human beings, while undesirable ones can be bred out.

The nature/nurture controversy was first mentioned by Francis Galton in the 1860s. Following certain principles of evolutionary theory developed by his cousin Charles Darwin, Galton concluded that desirable traits could be bred into human beings, while undesirable ones could be bred out, a concept he called **eugenics**. This process would involve reproduction by superior human beings and sterilization of inferior ones. This idea became so influential that, beginning in 1907, 30 states in the United States passed laws allowing for the forced sterilization of about 60,000 people considered to be "criminals, idiots, rapists, and imbeciles" (Watson, 2003, p. 27). The terms *idiot* and *imbecile* in those days were not just name-calling. They indicated levels of performance on IQ tests. As the Nazis came to power in Germany in the 1930s, they also enthusiastically adopted a policy that embraced eugenics. They began with sterilization but then moved to mass murder of all those deemed unfit to reproduce for a multitude of reasons. This came to include annihilation of entire ethnic groups, specifically Jews and Gypsies, in the service of creating a pure "Aryan race" (Watson, 2003).

As a result of eugenics and its excesses, genetics research came to be seen as suspect. This provided an opportunity for behaviorism, with its emphasis on the role of the environment, to dominate the study of psychology for many years. The search for the biological underpinnings of behavior was set aside, and the pendulum moved to the side of nurture as the explanation for human behavior. Freud's psychoanalytic theory also became a force in this direction because psychiatric illnesses were seen as the result of early childhood experiences. For example, the severe mental disorder schizophrenia, which is marked by extreme difficulty with thinking (including possibly hallucinations) and language, was thought to be caused by a mother who gave her child such contradictory signals that the child had to split from reality to deal with the stress. We now know that this approach, too, was an overly simplistic explanation with little scientific merit.

At this point in history, it is clear that both genes and environment make a contribution to complex outcomes. The goal now is to understand the complex interaction between these factors.

The Study of Genetics and Behavior

How We Study Genes and Behavior

The modern study of genetics began in 1866 when Gregor Mendel published a paper outlining a number of the principles that guide the transmission of genetic information from one generation to another. However, it took until 1900 before the significance of his work was recognized (Lane, 1994). The basic principles of inheritance that he described came to be known as Mendelian inheritance. We will discuss these principles shortly. Mendel studied the way in which characteristics of pea plants were passed on from one generation to the next. However, he did not know about genes and how they work. It was not until the 1950s that James Watson and Francis Crick discovered the basic secrets of genetic structure and function. Their finding allowed scientists to understand the exact process that underlies the genetic transmission first described by Mendel. In 1990, with James Watson as its first director, the Human Genome Project undertook the ambitious goal of mapping all of the human genes (National Human Genome Research Institute, 2009). In 2003, exactly 50 years after Watson and Crick's discovery, a mapping of the entire sequence of DNA that makes up the human genome was completed (Human Genome Project Information, 2008c). Figure 4.1 represents the mapping of genes found by the Human Genome Project on chromosome 12.

Genes are linked to our most basic physical characteristics. However, in the study of children and adolescents we are most interested in how they relate to behavior and its development. There are three ways in which genetic effects on behavior have been investigated: (a) Molecular genetics is focused at the level of the cell, (b) behavioral genetics is focused at the level of behavior, and (c) behavioral genomics connects the behavioral and the cellular levels. We will now describe each of these in more detail.

Molecular Genetics

Molecular genetics focuses on the identification of particular genes to understand how these genes work within the cell. A gene carries a chemical set of instructions that tells the cell how to produce specific proteins (Jorde, Carey, Bamshad, & White, 2006). For example, a particular gene contains the instructions to produce a protein called phenylalanine hydroxylase (PAH), which breaks down a common protein in the human diet. Through the study of molecular genetics, scientists discovered that when this gene has a certain defect, it does not give the correct information to produce PAH. When a child inherits a gene with this defective information from both parents, the child will have a potentially deadly condition known as phenylketonuria or PKU (Scriver, 2007). You will learn more about this condition later in the chapter. With the molecular genetics approach, scientists begin at the molecular level and eventually attempt to link these biochemical processes to observable behavior.

> **Molecular genetics** Research focused on the identification of particular genes to identify how these genes work within the cell.

Behavioral Genetics

Behavioral genetics begins with behavior and attempts to define the role genes play in producing that behavior in comparison to environmental effects. As we will see, these studies take advantage of "natural experiments," such as adoption. Children who are adopted share genes with their birth parents, but they share their environment with their adoptive parents. As an example, if we look at large numbers of adopted children and find that they are generally more similar to their birth parents than their adoptive parents on a trait such as fearfulness, we can conclude that genes play a primary role in determining who is more fearful. Until recently, this was the end point of this research because there was no way to know which specific genes were involved in the behaviors that were studied, but with our current knowledge of the human genome, these findings now are a first step

> **Behavioral genetics** Research to determine the degree of genetic basis for a behavior, a trait, or an ability through means including twin studies and adoption studies.

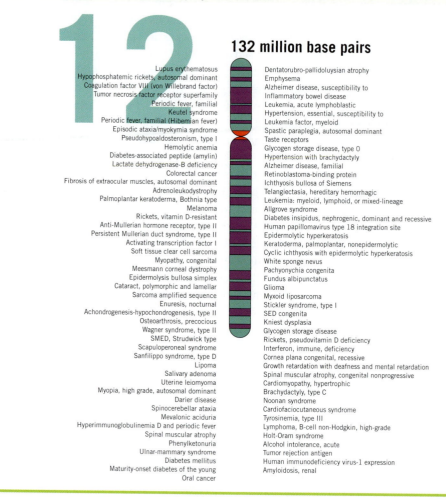

Figure 4.1

Chromosome 12. The Human Genome Project found that chromosome 12 contains 132 million base pairs that are linked with the variety of body functions, diseases, and behaviors shown in this figure. This is just a partial list of all the gene functions found for this chromosome. A list of the traits and disorders associated so far with all 23 human chromosomes can be found at the project's website.

132 million base pairs

Lupus erythematosus
Hypophosphatemic rickets, autosomal dominant
Coagulation factor VIII (von Willebrand factor)
Tumor necrosis factor receptor superfamily
Periodic fever, familial
Keutel syndrome
Periodic fever, familial (Hibemian fever)
Episodic ataxia/myokymia syndrome
Pseudohypoaldosteronism, type I
Hemolytic anemia
Diabetes-associated peptide (amylin)
Lactate dehydrogenase-B deficiency
Colorectal cancer
Fibrosis of extraocular muscles, autosomal dominant
Adrenoleukodystrophy
Palmoplantar keratoderma, Bothnia type
Melanoma
Rickets, vitamin D-resistant
Anti-Mullerian hormone receptor, type II
Persistent Mullerian duct syndrome, type II
Activating transcription factor I
Soft tissue clear cell sarcoma
Myopathy, congenital
Meesmann corneal dystrophy
Epidermolysis bullosa simplex
Cataract, polymorphic and lamellar
Sarcoma amplified sequence
Enuresis, nocturnal
Achondrogenesis-hypochondrogenesis, type II
Osteoarthrosis, precocious
Wagner syndrome, type II
SMED, Strudwick type
Scapuloperoneal syndrome
Sanfilippo syndrome, type D
Lipoma
Salivary adenoma
Uterine leiomyoma
Myopia, high grade, autosomal dominant
Darier disease
Spinocerebellar ataxia
Mevalonic aciduria
Hyperimmunoglobulinemia D and periodic fever
Spinal muscular atrophy
Phenylketonuria
Ulnar-mammary syndrome
Diabetes mellitus
Maturity-onset diabetes of the young
Oral cancer

Dentatorubro-pallidoluysian atrophy
Emphysema
Alzheimer disease, susceptibility to
Inflammatory bowel disease
Leukemia, acute lymphoblastic
Hypertension, essential, susceptibility to
Leukemia factor, myeloid
Spastic paraplegia, autosomal dominant
Taste receptors
Glycogen storage disease, type 0
Hypertension with brachydactyly
Alzheimer disease, familial
Retinoblastoma-binding protein
Ichthyosis bullosa of Siemens
Telangiectasia, hereditary hemorrhagic
Leukemia: myeloid, lymphoid, or mixed-lineage
Allgrove syndrome
Diabetes insipidus, nephrogenic, dominant and recessive
Human papillomavirus type 18 integration site
Epidermolytic hyperkeratosis
Keratoderma, palmoplantar, nonepidermolytic
Cyclic ichthyosis with epidermolytic hyperkeratosis
White sponge nevus
Pachyonychia congenita
Fundus albipunctatus
Glioma
Myxoid liposarcoma
Stickler syndrome, type I
SED congenita
Kniest dysplasia
Glycogen storage disease
Rickets, pseudovitamin D deficiency
Interferon, immune, deficiency
Cornea plana congenital, recessive
Growth retardation with deafness and mental retardation
Spinal muscular atrophy, congenital nonprogressive
Cardiomyopathy, hypertrophic
Brachydactyly, type C
Noonan syndrome
Cardiofaciocutaneous syndrome
Tyrosinemia, type III
Lymphoma, B-cell non-Hodgkin, high-grade
Holt-Oram syndrome
Alcohol intolerance, acute
Tumor rejection antigen
Human immunodeficiency virus-1 expression
Amyloidosis, renal

toward determining which genes are linked with particular behaviors. We will describe the behavioral genetics approach in more detail later in this chapter.

Behavioral Genomics

Behavioral genomics

Research that links behaviors with specific genes.

Behavioral genomics is a new field that has emerged to bridge molecular genetics, which focuses on activity at the level of the cell, and behavioral genetics, which focuses on activity at the level of human behavior (Plomin, DeFries, Craig, & McGuffin, 2003a). As new techniques for gene identification have proliferated in recent years, behavioral genomics has given us an approach that links behaviors with specific genes. When scientists find a genetic association for a particular behavior, using the approaches of behavioral genetics described above, they can then use molecular genetics to identify the specific genes that may be involved in producing that behavior.

How Do Genes Work?

When the Human Genome Project completed mapping all of the genes that make a human being, one of the biggest surprises was that the total came to only about 25,000–30,000 genes, not the 100,000 or more that researchers had expected to find (Human Genome Project Information, 2008b). If the number of genes alone determined how complex and sophisticated we are as a species, then it would appear that we are only a little more complicated than plants, mice, or fruit flies. Other differences in how genes work must account for the large differences we see between species. Also, 99.9% of the bases that make up the human genome are identical for all human beings. Our differences account for only one tenth of 1% of our genetic inheritance (U.S. Department of Energy Genome Programs, 2003). Although most of the genes have been identified, we know what fewer than 50% of those genes actually do (Human Genome Project Information, 2009; U.S. Department of Energy Genome Programs, 2003). We will review below the basic functioning of genes.

Our Genetic Beginnings

We all begin our lives when our mother's egg joins with our father's sperm to form a **zygote**. Eggs and sperm each contain half of our genetic material, which is organized into 23 strands of genes, called **chromosomes**. When fertilization of a human egg occurs, the genetic material from the sperm pairs up with the genetic material from the egg to form 23 matched pairs of chromosomes. Within each chromosome pair, genes with the same function pair up. As you can see in Figure 4.2, in 22 of these pairs of chromosomes (called

2. Each human being has hundreds of thousands of genes that make him or her a unique individual. **TRUE/FALSE**

    False. The Human Genome Project has discovered that humans only have about 25,000–30,000 genes, approximately the same number as mice or fruit flies.

3. When a child is conceived, it is the mother's genetic material that determines the gender of the child. **TRUE/FALSE**

    False. It is the type of chromosomal material contained in a male's sperm that is responsible for determining the gender of the newly conceived child.

Figure 4.2

Human chromosomes. This image shows a full set of 23 pairs of chromosomes for a female and for a male. Note the difference between the 23rd chromosome pairs. XX is a genetic female, and XY is a genetic male.

Female Chromosomes

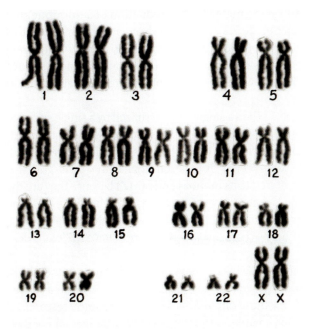

Male Chromosomes

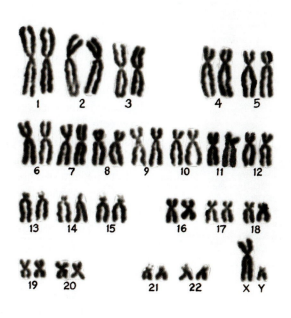

Zygote The fertilized egg that begins to divide into the cells that will develop into the embryo.

Chromosomes The strands of genes that constitute the human genetic endowment.

Dizygotic (DZ) twins Formed when a woman produces two ova or eggs, which are fertilized by two sperm; genetically DZ twins are as similar as any siblings.

Monozygotic (MZ) twins Formed when a woman produces one egg that is fertilized by one sperm and then splits to form two individuals with the same genes.

autosomes) the two chromosomes look very similar. Note, however, that the chromosomes in the 23rd pair may look different because it is this pair that determines the sex of the child. These two chromosomes have been named the X chromosome and the Y chromosome. Because women have two X chromosomes, the eggs they produce can only contain X chromosomes in the 23rd position. Because men have an X and a Y chromosome, the sperm they produce can contain either an X or a Y chromosome in this position. When the egg and the sperm unite, it is the father's contribution of either an X or a Y chromosome that determines the sex of the child. A conception with an X chromosome from both parents is a female. One with an X chromosome from the mother and a Y chromosome from the father is a male.

Sometimes fertilization can result in the conception of more than one child. The occurrence of twins has been important in the study of behavioral genetics, as we will see later in this chapter. Twins can be conceived in two ways. In the first way, a mother's ovary can release two eggs during a menstrual cycle, and each of these eggs can be fertilized by a different sperm (there are thousands of sperm released during a single male ejaculation). The resulting twins are referred to as **dizygotic (DZ)**, because they came from two (di-) fertilized eggs (zygotes). They are as genetically similar to each other as any pair of siblings, which is why this type of twins is often referred to as fraternal twins. The word *fraternal* has to do with brothers, just like "fraternity brothers," but fraternal twins can also be sisters or a sister and a brother. Because each egg is fertilized by a different sperm, one sperm can be carrying an X chromosome while the other is carrying a Y chromosome, so fraternal twins don't have to be the same sex.

The tendency to have dizygotic twins is genetically related: Some families are more likely to have them than others. Also, in spite of the fact that overall fertility declines as women get older, women over age 35 are more likely to have DZ twins (Fletcher, Zach, Pramanik, & Ford, 2009). The rate of twinning for women ages 35 to 40 is double the rate for women who are younger, and women who become pregnant after the age of 45 have a 1-in-3 chance of having a multiple birth (Bortolus et al., 1999). Some part of this increase is due to the greater likelihood in recent years that older mothers will have used fertility drugs or in vitro fertilization to get pregnant, but it is normal changes in the woman's reproductive system that account for most of the increase. After the age of 35, a woman's ovaries decline in their ability to release eggs, so the woman's body increases its production of a hormone that can counter this decline (Beemsterboer et al., 2006). If the body creates too much of this hormone, multiple eggs are released. This provides another explanation for why the rate of multiple births has increased in recent years. Women have been waiting longer to have their babies, and the older they are when they become pregnant, the greater their chance of a multiple pregnancy.

The second way that twins are formed is when a single egg is fertilized by a single sperm to form a zygote. The zygote begins replicating and producing additional cells, but early in this process, for reasons that we don't really understand, the ball of cells splits into two (Gilbert, 2000). Each ball of cells continues to develop prenatally to become one of the twins. This process results in identical twins who are referred to as **monozygotic (MZ)** because they are the product of a single (mono) fertilized egg (zygote). Because monozygotic twins share the same set of genetic material (including the information on chromosome pair 23), they are always the same gender. This type of twinning occurs by chance, so the tendency to have MZ twins does not run in families.

It has always been a puzzle why identical twins can have small differences in their basic appearance or develop different genetically based disorders. Scientists had previously assumed that the environment was responsible for these differences. However, recently researchers have discovered that even identical twins have small differences in the arrangement of their

TRUE/FALSE

4. Women who give birth when they are 35 to 40 years old are twice as likely to have twins compared to younger women.

   True. Although the fertility of women declines as they age, other changes in their bodies can result in the release of more than one egg during a menstrual cycle, making the conception of twins more likely than when they were younger.

TRUE/FALSE

5. The tendency to have identical twins runs in families.

   False. There are two types of twins: identical and fraternal. Although fraternal twins run in families, identical twins do not.

Twins and triplets. Identical twins are always the same gender, but fraternal twins can be the same gender or different. Triplets can be identical or fraternal or a set of identical twins with a fraternal sibling!

Video Link 4.1
Differences in identical twins.

genes, and these differences may result in observable and sometimes significant differences (Bruder et al., 2008).

Chromosomes, Genes, DNA, and Bases (GATC)

Chromosomes are made up of genes, and genes are made up of *DNA* (deoxyribonucleic acid). DNA consists of two chains of *nucleotides* (the basic unit of DNA that consists of a chemical base, a phosphate group, and a sugar molecule) that twirl around each other in a "double helix" that looks much like a winding staircase with a banister, as illustrated in Figure 4.3. There are four nitrogen-containing bases that make up the alphabet of genetic inheritance: guanine (G), adenine (A), thymine (T), and cytosine (C) (Alberts et al., 2002). One way to help remember this is to think of a science fiction film called *Gattaca*, which is about a time in the future when all human beings are genetically manufactured (DeVito & Niccol, 1997). The name *Gattaca* will remind you of the four bases: G, A, T, and C. The arrangement of many millions of these four nucleotides determines how the basic proteins used by the body will be created. These proteins determine both the form and the function of our bodies.

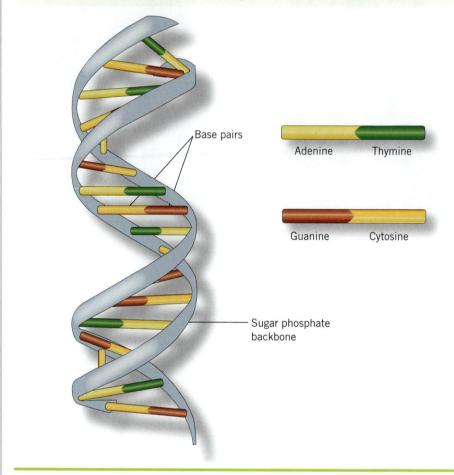

Figure 4.3

A human DNA molecule. In the double helix molecule that makes up DNA, the base adenine always pairs with the base thymine, and the base guanine always pairs with the base cytosine. This "alphabet" of only four letters produces strings of bases that write the instructions for all the cells in our body.

Base pairs

Adenine   Thymine

Guanine   Cytosine

Sugar phosphate backbone

A gene is made up of these bases as a sentence is made up of words. A sentence can contain all kinds of information and instructions. A gene contains information and instructions for the body to make a protein (Jorde et al., 2006). The trick to identifying a particular gene is finding the combination of G, A, T, and C that functions to give the body directions to create a certain protein. To better understand this process, look at the following:

Gotothegrocerystorepickupmilkcomehome

One way to divide this would be as follows:

Got oth egro

Ceryst orepick upm

ilk comeho me

We all know this is wrong and makes no sense. You would really divide this sequence of letters into three meaningful instructions:

Go to the grocery store.

Pick up milk.

Come home.

In the same way, scientists have taken sequences of bases such as ATCATCTTTGGTGTT and determined how to divide them into units that give clear instructions. In this case, the sequence shown above is just part of a gene called CFTR that is actually 250,000 base pairs long. Changes, or mutations, in this gene are linked to the development of cystic fibrosis, a disorder that affects the functioning of the lungs (Human Genome Project Information, 2003). With this very basic understanding of how genes operate within the cell, we will now discuss how genes are translated into our physical appearance and our behaviors.

Gene dominance. Do you look as similar to one of your parents as this girl does to her mother? Inheritance of dominant genes from one parent or the other can result in striking resemblances.

Mendelian Inheritance: Dominant and Recessive Genes

You may be told that you look very much like your father or exactly like your mother. How can this be, when you receive an equal number of chromosomes from each parent? When eggs and sperm are formed, the genes of each parent "unzip" along the double helix so that these cells each contain half the genetic material usually found in the cell. At conception, when egg and sperm combine, the genes from one parent are zipped up to similar genes from the other parent. Each gene from the father is paired with a gene from the mother. Traditional Mendelian genetics (named for Gregor Mendel, whose work was introduced at the beginning of this chapter) tells us that each pair of genes is made up of some combination of dominant and recessive genes. A person's **genotype** or **genome** includes both dominant and recessive genes, but the person's **phenotype** is what is actually expressed in the body, and this is usually the information contained in the dominant genes. It is possible for the expression of genes in the phenotype to be affected by many other variables, but the typical pattern we observe is that the information from the dominant gene partner is expressed in the phenotype while the recessive gene is not, unless it is paired with another recessive gene. For example, brown (B) eye color is dominant over blue (b) eye color (it is not really as simple as this, but we'll tell you more about what makes this process more complex after we work through this example). If your mother has brown eyes because she has two genes for brown eyes in her genotype and your father has blue eyes, which *must* come from two recessive genes for blue eyes, you will have brown eyes because you have received at least one dominant gene for brown eyes in your genotype. Your mother can only pass along the dominant brown eye genes to her children (because that is the only genetic information she has for this trait), and your father can only pass on genetic information for blue eyes (because that is all he has for this trait). The only possible genetic combination in the children from this couple is one dominant gene for brown eyes and one recessive gene for blue eyes. Therefore, brown eyes will be expressed in the phenotype of all the children in this family.

However, you still will carry in your genome the one recessive gene for blue eyes that you received from your father. And if you have a child with someone who has brown eyes but who also carries one recessive gene for blue eyes, you will have a blue-eyed child if those two recessive genes are paired in the child. See Figure 4.4 to better understand how this might happen.

Although eye color is frequently used to illustrate the idea of dominant and recessive genes, you may have already realized that it isn't that simple. People also have green eyes, gray eyes, and hazel eyes. Although brown as an eye color is dominant over any of these alternatives, green, gray, and hazel eyes have their own dominance hierarchies. Also, the color of some people's eyes is bright and clear, and the color of other people's eyes is soft and

Genotype or genome   All of a person's genes, including those that are active and those that are silent.

Phenotype   The genetically based characteristics that are actually shown in one's body.

6. Two parents with brown eyes can still have a child with blue eyes.   **TRUE/FALSE**

   True. The gene for blue eyes is recessive, so a parent can carry that gene without it showing up in the parent's physical appearance. If each parent has a recessive gene for blue eyes, a child could end up with two recessive genes (one from each brown-eyed parent) and have blue eyes.

Genetic transmission of eye color (dominant and recessive genes).

Figure 4.4.a Both parents have only dominant genes for brown eyes, so that is the only genetic information they can pass to their children. All their children will have brown eyes.

Figure 4.4.b The father only has recessive genes for blue eyes, so that is all he can pass along to his child. The mother only has dominant genes for brown eyes, so that is all she can pass along. Each child will have one gene for blue eyes and one gene for brown eyes, so all the children will have brown eyes.

Figure 4.4.c Both parents only have recessive genes for blue eyes. They both have blue eyes and can only pass genes for blue eyes to their children, so all their children will have blue eyes.

Figure 4.4.d Each parent has both a dominant gene for brown eyes and a recessive gene for blue eyes (so both have brown eyes). However, if each passes along a recessive gene for blue eyes, the child will have blue eyes, but if either parent passes along a gene for brown eyes, the child will have brown eyes.

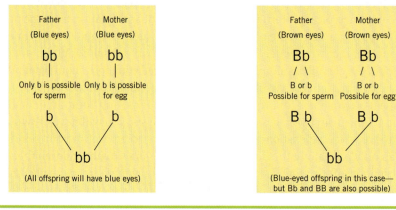

washed out. And you may even know someone who has one blue eye and one brown eye. Suffice it to say that the genetic process is more complicated than our example because there are genes for eye colors other than brown and blue that can be arranged in a dominance hierarchy, there are modifier genes that can influence the intensity of eye color, and there are mutation and genetic accidents that can negate the effects of one of the genes in a pair. Despite these variations, however, an understanding of the how dominant and recessive genes work is still central to an understanding of genetic inheritance. You can use Table 4.1 to estimate the likelihood that you will have a child with a certain eye color.

Table 4.1

Baby eye color predictor. This table allows you to estimate the likelihood of a baby's eye color when you know the eye color of the parents. Because you don't know the genotype of the parents, there are two parts to the chart. The first part shows the likelihood if the parents are heterogeneous, meaning they have genes for different color eyes; for example, a parent with brown eyes has one gene for brown eyes and one for blue eyes. The second part shows the likelihood if the parents are homogeneous, meaning their gene pair is the same; for example, a parent with brown eyes has two genes for brown eyes. Pick a color for Parent A and one for Parent B and see what happens when the two parents meet. Note that 50/50 means there is an even chance that the baby could have the eye color of either parent.

Heterogeneous Inheritance (More Likely)				
	Parent A			
Parent B	**Brown**	**Blue**	**Green**	**Hazel**
Brown	75% brown	50/50	50/50	50/50
Blue	50/50	> 99% blue	50/50	50/50
Green	50/50	50/50	> 99% green	50/50
Hazel	50/50	50/50	50/50	> 99% hazel

Homogeneous Inheritance (Less Likely)				
	Parent A			
Parent B	**Brown**	**Blue**	**Green**	**Hazel**
Brown	> 99% brown	> 99% brown	> 99% brown	> 99% brown
Blue	> 99% brown	> 99% blue	50/50	50/50
Green	> 99% brown	50/50	> 99% green	50/50
Hazel	> 99% brown	50/50	50/50	> 99% hazel

Whether you have blue eyes or brown eyes is not crucial to your future development. Other types of gene pairings, however, are quite crucial because some genetic disorders are caused by two recessive genes pairing up with each other. This is true of the disease sickle-cell anemia, which is found in 1 of every 500 African Americans. Sickle-cell anemia is a painful and destructive disease in which the shape of red blood cells is distorted. Normal red blood cells are smooth and round, but sickle cells look like the letter *C* (National Heart, Lung and Blood Institute [NHLBI], 2007). Normal red blood cells contain a lot of surface area, which enables them to transport oxygen throughout the body, but sickle cells are not able to do this effectively. Further, while normal cells are soft and easily fit through even small blood vessels, sickle cells are hard and tend to clump together and block the flow of an adequate amount of blood into these parts of the body, as shown in Figure 4.5. This failure to transport oxygen to where it is needed results in pain and can eventually cause damage to the organs (NHLBI, 2007). We will discuss genetic disorders more fully later in this chapter.

Figure 4.5

Sickle-cell anemia. Normal red blood cells move freely through the blood vessels (A). Sickle-shaped red blood cells stick together and block the normal flow of blood, depriving the organs of needed oxygen (B).

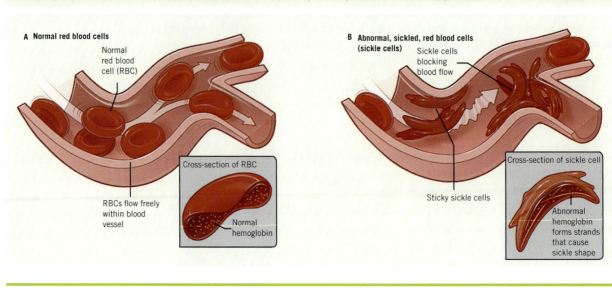

Video Link 4.2
Sickle cell anemia.

You may wonder why such maladaptive genes would not have disappeared from the human gene pool, but there is a good evolutionary reason why they haven't. It turns out that, although having two such recessive genes is harmful, having *one* of these recessive genes may be protective in certain environments. The recessive gene for sickle-cell anemia, which is carried in the genotype of about 1 in 10 African Americans, appears to protect people from malaria (Wolters Kluwer Health, 2009). The first hint that this might be true came from the observation that the areas in Africa in which this gene is found in the population are almost identical to the areas in which malaria is a major problem. With these protective advantages, individuals with these recessive genes are more likely to survive to pass them on to the next generation (Ringelhann, Hathorn, Jilly, Grant, & Parniczky, 1976). However, if two people who carry the recessive gene have children, there is a 1-in-4 chance that their children will inherit two recessive genes and suffer from sickle-cell anemia. For a better idea about how disorders can result from recessive genes, try to answer the questions in **Active Learning: Understanding the Inheritance of Tay-Sachs Disease**.

Understanding the Inheritance of Tay-Sachs Disease

Tay-Sachs is a terrible genetic disease that results in progressive neurological deterioration and death of an infant, usually by age 5. The highest occurrence of this illness happens among Ashkenazi Jews, whose ancestors came from Eastern Europe (Wolter Kluwer Health, 2009), and elevated levels are also found in French Canadians living in Quebec (Hechtman et al., 1990). There is a recessive gene that is responsible for Tay-Sachs, and there is a simple blood test that can locate that gene. Answer the questions below to enhance your understanding of how a recessive gene works:

1. A woman decides to be tested for the Tay-Sachs gene and finds that she is a "carrier" of Tay-Sachs. That means that she has the gene for the disease. Does this mean she has to worry that she will get Tay-Sachs herself? What, if anything, does she have to worry about?

2. Can you determine the likelihood that any child she has will inherit Tay-Sachs disease, or do you need other information to do this?

3. Her husband decides also to be tested and finds that he does not carry the Tay-Sachs gene. What is the likelihood now that this couple will have a child who has this disease?

4. What if her husband finds that he, too, is a carrier? Now what is the likelihood that a child of theirs will have Tay-Sachs?

Answers:

1. The woman will not get the disease herself. Because the gene is recessive, for a carrier the dominant partner in this gene pair will determine the outcome, or phenotype, of the person. In the case of a carrier, she "carries" the gene but does not experience its effects.

2. We cannot know what the likelihood is of her child developing Tay-Sachs without knowing the genotype of the father of the baby. If he is a carrier, he could pass a recessive gene for the condition on to his children. A baby must inherit the recessive Tay-Sachs gene from both the mother and the father to get the disease.

3. If the husband is not a carrier, there is *no* chance that the child will have Tay-Sachs because the baby must have two Tay-Sachs genes, one from the mother and one from the father. Any children from this couple will inherit one dominant gene from the father that will protect them from inheriting Tay-Sachs.

4. Look at the chart below (referred to as a Punnett square) that shows the possible pairings of a mother's and a father's genes to see what the likelihood is of a child having the Tay-Sachs disease when both parents are carriers:

Father	Mother	
	Tay-Sachs (ts) gene (recessive)	Normal (N) gene (dominant)
Tay-Sachs (ts) gene (recessive)	ts/ts*	ts/N
Normal (N) gene (dominant)	N/ts	N/N

*This is the only combination that will result in the child having Tay-Sachs because both parents are contributing a recessive gene for the disease. Therefore, there is a 1-in-4 (or 25%) chance that the child will get the disease. Furthermore, each time this couple conceives a child, there will always be a 25% chance that the child will have the disease.

As we've shown, a single gene pair can be responsible for deadly disorders. At least with animals, one single gene pair also can be linked with behaviors that appear to be quite complex. For example, in a small animal called a vole, one particular gene determines whether an animal is monogamous or "plays the field." There are many types of voles in the wild. While the prairie vole chooses a partner for life, the meadow vole mates with whomever is available. Scientists discovered that the gene that produces the hormone vasopressin differs in these two types of voles. When they switched that gene between the two types of voles, the monogamous prairie vole became a wanderer, and the wandering meadow vole immediately began to direct his mating energies toward one female only and gave up his wandering ways (Lim et al., 2004). It is unlikely that we will find a single gene that determines such complex behavior in human beings. However, in recent research

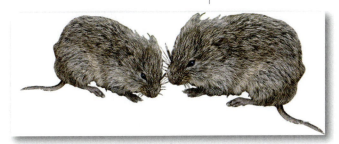

Pair-bonding. This type of vole mates for life. How could you turn them into animals that have no special mate?

in Sweden, it was found that men with a certain form of the vasopressin gene are more likely than other men to have trouble with long-term, committed relationships (Walum et al., 2008). Clearly, human genes will interact with cultural expectations to determine practices such as monogamy or polygamy. However, it is interesting to begin to uncover in the animal world the role of some genes that are similar to those found in humans.

One Behavior, Many Genes; One Gene, Many Effects

Polygenic inheritance
Numerous genes may interact together to promote any particular trait or behavior.

Most human behaviors are unlikely to be the result of one and only one gene. **Polygenic inheritance** means that tens or even hundreds of different genes may interact together to promote any particular trait or behavior (McGuffin, Riley, & Plomin, 2001). In addition, they may interact with our environmental experiences in ways we will describe below. Therefore, the determination of any trait or ability is likely to be multifactorial; that is, it depends on many factors, including a number of genes interacting with one another and with various aspects of the environment. In addition, any one gene may have many different influences. This is referred to as **pleiotropic effects**. For example, one gene might be implicated in aggression but might also be involved in regulation of heart rate (Rowe, 2003). Therefore, although scientists have identified the functions of some individual genes, we will have to be careful not to oversimplify the findings that emerge as research continues.

Pleiotropic effects Any single gene may have many different influences.

Genetic Disorders

Up to this point we have discussed the range of outcomes in various aspects of human functioning in which genes play a role. Now we will focus on situations in which genes contribute to disorders that interfere with healthy functioning of the human mind and body. There are three types of genetic disorders that we will describe: **single gene disorders**, **chromosome disorders**, and **multifactorial inheritance disorders** (Wolters Kluwer Health, 2009).

Single gene disorders
Genetic disorders caused by recessive genes or mutations.

Chromosome disorders
Disorders that result when too many or too few chromosomes are formed or when there is a change in the structure of the chromosome caused by breakage.

Multifactorial inheritance disorders Disorders result from the interaction of many genes and also environmental influences.

Mutations Changes in the formation of genes that occur as cells divide.

Single Gene Disorders

As we previously described, a gene is like a sentence that is made up of the bases G, A, T, and C instead of words (Jorde et al., 2006). Just as a sentence must have all the words in order to make sense, so too the bases must be in a certain order to work correctly to create a necessary protein. Genetically based disorders can occur in two ways: (a) An individual inherits a pair of recessive genes that code for that disorder, or (b) mistakes in the formation of genes, known as **mutations**, occur as cells divide so that some of the bases that give the instructions to create proteins are out of order or missing. Mutations are very common, and most do not cause problems for individuals and their development. In fact, evolution of the species depends on the occurrence of mutations that turn out to be adaptive and are therefore handed down from generation to generation. However, some mutations do cause genetic disorders (Wolters Kluwer Health, 2009).

There are a number of diseases that are caused by a single gene. If you completed **Active Learning: Understanding the Inheritance of Tay-Sachs Disease**, you saw that Tay-Sachs is one of them. Others include phenylketonuria (PKU) and cystic fibrosis. Phenylketonuria is a condition in which the child cannot digest a common protein in the human diet. This condition can result in mental retardation (de Groot, Hoeksma, Blau, Reijngoud, & van Spronsen, 2010). Cystic fibrosis is a condition in which the child's body produces a thick, sticky mucus that clogs the lungs, making the child vulnerable to pulmonary infections. It is also associated with nutritional deficiencies (Ratjen & Döring, 2003). As we noted earlier in the chapter, scientists have identified the cause of cystic fibrosis as a missing sequence in a specific gene called the CFTR gene. The normal sequence is ATCAT**CTT**TGGTGTT, but some children inherit a version of this gene in which the three bases that are highlighted here are missing. As a result, a critical part of the protein that the gene creates is missing (Human Genome Project Information, 2003).

Problems Associated With the Y Chromosome

Most genetic disorders are coded on recessive genes, but most of the time the recessive gene is paired with a dominant gene, which protects the individual from developing the disorder. One student put it succinctly: "If one gene is screwed up, you have a backup." As long as the dominant gene is doing its job, the dysfunctional gene will likely not be noticed. However, there is one situation in which recessive genes will be expressed because there is no second gene to create a pair. As you can see in the photo on this page, the Y chromosome is much smaller than the X chromosome and contains the lowest number of genes of all of the chromosomes: 231. By comparison, chromosome 1, an autosome, contains the most genes: 2,968. In addition, only some of the 231 genes on the Y chromosome are active. When an X chromosome pairs with a Y chromosome to create a boy, only 54 of the X chromosome's 1,098 active genes find a partner in the Y chromosome (Spencer, 2005). The problem that results is that any genes on the

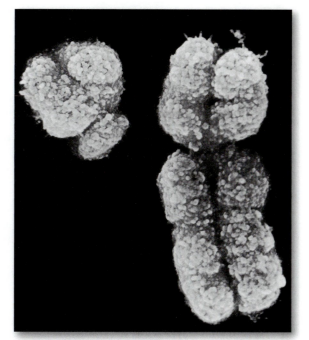

X and Y chromosomes. Do you see the potential problem when the X chromosome and the Y chromosome pair up? Large portions of the X chromosome (the one on the right) do not have a partner on the Y chromosome (the one on the left), and therefore any recessive gene on the X chromosome without a partner will appear in the male's phenotype. If the recessive gene is the source of a genetic problem, the man is vulnerable to it.

X chromosome that do not have a partner will be expressed, whether they are normally recessive or dominant. The outcome is an increased vulnerability of boys to the effects of recessive genes that are carried on the X chromosome that cause such problems as red-green color blindness, hemophilia, or Duchenne muscular dystrophy (Jorde et al., 2006).

Chromosome Disorders

Genetic disorders may occur at the level of the gene or at the level of the chromosome. Chromosomal disorders occur (a) when one of the 23 pairs of chromosomes contains either one or three chromosomes rather than two (see the configuration that causes Down syndrome in Figure 4.6) or (b) when there is a change in the structure of the chromosome caused by breakage (National Human Genome Research Institute, 2007a). When sections of chromosomes break apart, they may not come back together in their original form. Some sections may be turned around backward or may even link to a different chromosome. Both of these types of abnormality may occur by chance, but the second type also can be passed along to a child by a parent who has this type of chromosomal pattern. Table 4.2 describes a number of conditions that are caused by chromosomal abnormalities.

Multifactorial Inheritance Disorders

Many disorders, including depression, alcoholism, schizophrenia, and autism, appear to have some genetic input. However, it is likely that these disorders result from the interaction

7. Females are more likely to have a genetic disorder than males. **TRUE/FALSE**

False. A number of genetic disorders are equally likely to affect males and females, but there is an additional group of conditions that are related to the chromosome that determines the gender of the child. Because the male's Y chromosome is smaller than the X chromosome with which it is paired, males are more vulnerable to this group of recessive gene disorders.

Video Link 4.3
Down syndrome.

Figure 4.6

Chromosomes for Down syndrome. Compare these chromosomes from someone with Down syndrome with those in Figure 4.2. Did you notice the extra copy of the 21st chromosome? This is referred to as *trisomy* because there are 3 chromosomes instead of 2.

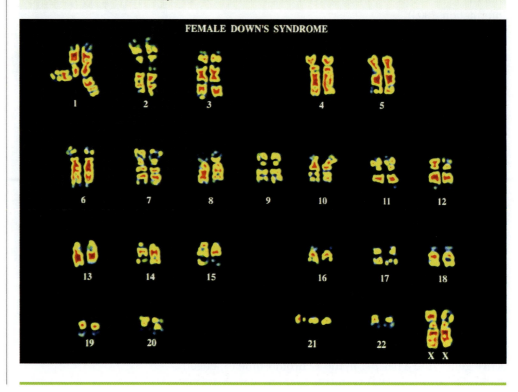

Table 4.2

Chromosomal abnormalities

Disorder	Chromosomal description	Symptom description	Treatments
Down syndrome	One extra chromosome 21	Mental retardation; typical facial features; poor muscle tone; possible problems with heart, digestion, and hearing	Physical, occupational, speech and educational therapy; medical intervention as needed
Klinefelter syndrome	An extra X chromosome in men (XXY in the 23rd position)	Infertility; small genitals; enlarged breasts; reduced facial, armpit, and pubic hair; possible autoimmune disorders	Testosterone therapy, medical intervention as needed
Turner syndrome	A missing X chromosome in women (XO in the 23rd position)	Short stature, webbing of the neck, lack of development of ovaries resulting in lack of sexual maturation at puberty	Estrogen replacement therapy, growth hormone administration is possible
Fragile X syndrome	One gene segment on the X chromosome (CGG) is repeated 200 times, rather than 5–40 times	Mental retardation and learning disabilities; distractibility and impulsivity; twice as likely in males, who have typical facial features and possible autism	Early intervention, special education, treatment for ADHD

of many genes that also interact with environmental influences. There are no genetic tests for this type of multifactorial problem at this time (National Human Genome Research Institute, 2007b), but we are able to counsel and advise potential parents about a number of other conditions that have a genetic basis.

Genetic Counseling and Testing

In each pregnancy, any couple statistically has a 3% chance of having a child with a genetically based disorder. Based on these odds, there is usually no reason for genetic counseling. However, in some cases individual risk is higher, and such individuals may want to seek out a genetic counselor to help them assess the type and amount of risk. See Table 4.3 for additional information about couples who are at an increased risk of having a child born with a birth defect who might consider having genetic counseling.

Genetic counseling and testing may occur before or during a pregnancy. When you meet with a genetic counselor, he or she will ask you about your own medical history and also your family's history of diseases and genetic disorders. The counselor may then recommend certain tests. Blood tests can be used at any time to determine the presence of single recessive genes that are more common in certain populations, such as the genes for Tay-Sachs disease (Ashkenazi Jews), sickle-cell anemia (African-Americans or Africans), and thalassemia (Southeast Asians, Taiwanese, Chinese, Filipinos, Italians, Greeks, or Middle Easterners), a blood disorder associated with reduced production of hemoglobin (American Medical Association, 2008). As we saw before in **Active Learning: Understanding the Inheritance of Tay-Sachs Disease**, you would only be concerned about these possible disorders if both partners were found to carry the recessive gene for the condition.

During pregnancy, there are several tests that can be done to identify some possible genetic abnormalities in the developing fetus. Tests of the mother's blood, such as the *alpha-fetoprotein test,* may uncover abnormalities in hormone levels that signal the possibility of neural tube defects (such as spina bifida) or Down syndrome (Larson, 2002). Subsequently, **amniocentesis** and **chorionic villus sampling (CVS)** can be carried out to identify chromosome disorders as well as some single gene disorders, such as sickle-cell anemia. However, there are many other

Down syndrome. This boy shows the facial features that are typically associated with Down syndrome, including almond-shaped eyes.

Amniocentesis A test to look for genetic abnormalities prenatally, in which a physician uses a long, thin needle to extract amniotic fluid, which is then tested.

Chorionic villus sampling (CVS) A test to look for genetic abnormalities prenatally, in which a small tube is inserted either through the vagina and cervix or through a needle inserted in the abdomen, and a sample of cells from the chorion is retrieved for testing.

Table 4.3

Who should receive genetic counseling?

The March of Dimes organization (2008) recommends that the following individuals consult with a genetic counselor:

- Those who have, or are concerned that they might have, an inherited disorder or birth defect.
- Women who are pregnant or planning to be after age 35.
- Couples who already have a child with mental retardation, an inherited disorder, or a birth defect.
- Couples whose infant has a genetic disease diagnosed by routine newborn screening.
- Women who have had babies who died in infancy or three or more miscarriages.
- People concerned that their jobs, lifestyles, or medical history may pose a risk to outcome of pregnancy. Common causes of concern include exposure to radiation, medications, illegal drugs, chemicals, or infections.
- Couples who would like testing or more information about genetic conditions that occur frequently in their ethnic group.
- Couples who are first cousins or other close blood relatives.
- Pregnant women whose ultrasound examinations or blood testing indicate that their pregnancy may be at increased risk for certain complications or birth defects.

Figure 4.7

Genetic testing. During amniocentesis, a physician uses an ultrasound to locate the fetus and then uses a long, thin needle to extract about 4 teaspoons of amniotic fluid. Fetal cells floating in the fluid can be tested for genetic problems. In chorionic villus sampling, a small tube, or catheter, is inserted either through the vagina and cervix or through a needle inserted in the abdomen, and a sample of cells from the chorion (which has the same genetic makeup as the fetus) is retrieved for testing.

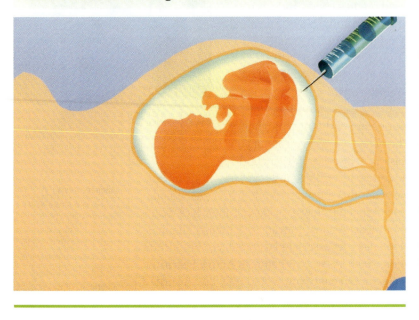

Video Link 4.4
Genetic tests.

Gene therapy
Treatment of genetic disorders through implanting or disabling specific genes.

genetic and nongenetic factors that may cause birth defects that are not assessed by these tests. As noted above, most women will *not* receive these tests.

As shown in Figure 4.7, in amniocentesis, a long, thin needle is inserted through the mother's abdomen and into the amniotic sac, which surrounds the fetus. Cells from the skin surface of the developing embryo are routinely shed into the amniotic fluid that surrounds the embryo. When fluid from the sac is withdrawn, it contains fetal cells that can be analyzed for genetic abnormalities. In CVS, cells are obtained from microscopic projections called villi found on the outside layer of the embryonic sac, called the chorion. These may be obtained either through the abdomen or through the vagina and cervix, and the sample is then analyzed (Jorde et al., 2006). Because all of the structures that support the pregnancy (including the placenta, the amnion, and the chorion) are the result of the conception, the cells they contain have the same genetic makeup as the embryo, and that is why they can be tested for genetic problems. CVS is performed at 10–11 weeks of gestation, while amniocentesis cannot be performed until 15–17 weeks. The risk of miscarriage resulting from the procedure itself is slightly higher for CVS than for amniocentesis, but the parents receive information on any possible genetic problems earlier in the pregnancy (Jorde et al., 2006).

Gene Therapy

Although **gene therapy** for humans is not yet available, scientists are working on several ways to use all of our new knowledge about genes to prevent and treat human disorders. We've all experienced the unpleasant effects when a virus infects our cells, but researchers are using viruses that have been genetically altered to "infect" cells with healthy genes to replace disordered ones (Human Genome Project Information, 2008a). Using a different technique, scientists have also been able to localize and then disable certain problematic genes. For example, researchers at Leiden University Medical Center in the Netherlands were recently able to block the action of a gene implicated in the development of Duchenne muscular dystrophy (Grady, 2007). Although the results were modest, the idea that we may intervene at the level of genes is intriguing. At present this type of work is being done only on an experimental basis (National Cancer Institute Fact Sheet, 2006), but it is one of the exciting avenues of research in the field of behavioral genetics.

One positive outcome of a better understanding of the interaction of genes and environment is that we now know that the solution to genetically based problems will not necessarily involve interventions at the microscopic level of the gene. Some genes can be turned on or off by environmental interventions. For example, we have long known that the effects of the genetic disorder phenylketonuria (PKU) can be prevented by removing phenylalanine from the diet of those newborns found to carry the recessive gene (Plomin, DeFries, Craig, & McGuffin, 2003b). Remember that a child who has PKU has inherited recessive genes that cannot produce an enzyme that is essential in the digestion of phenylalanine, a common protein that is found in foods such as beef, poultry, fish, eggs, milk products such as yogurt and cheese, and wheat products (de Baulny, Abadie, Feillet, & de Parscau, 2007). When phenylalanine is taken in as part of the child's diet, it can only be partially digested because of the missing enzyme. This produces harmful substances that can damage the child's brain and central nervous system, resulting in mental retardation (de Groot et al., 2010). Once again, it is not the gene itself that causes the problem, but rather the interaction of the gene with the newborn's intake of food containing phenylalanine. By eliminating the phenylalanine from the diet of an infant through the use of a special formula, the harmful effects are eliminated (Wappner, Cho, Kronmal, Schuett, & Seashore, 1999). Because the brain is growing so rapidly during the early years, it is particularly vulnerable to these damaging toxic effects. The National Institute of Child Health and Human Development (2006) recommends that people with PKU maintain a diet low in phenylalanine throughout their lives to prevent the appearance of symptoms. A diet that primarily includes fruits, vegetables, and low-protein grain products helps maintain a safe level of phenylalanine in the person's system.

In the future, perhaps we will be able to provide early intervention for babies with other identifiable genes that cause behavioral disorders. In the next section we will examine more about the interaction of genes and environment. It may surprise you to see that some genes are only activated by environmental experiences. As we find out more about these interactions, we may be able to intervene early to change the environments that switch on genes that support destructive behavior.

The Interaction of Genes and Environment

Canalization

There is considerable variability in how strongly genes affect different traits or characteristics. Although some characteristics seem to be relatively impervious to environmental influences, others are much more easily influenced. This observation is captured by the concept of **canalization** proposed by Conrad Hal Waddington (1942). Imagine yourself standing on the top of a steep hill and looking down from that vantage point. You would see that water and weather had carved gullies (or canals) into the hillside. Some of them would be deep and narrow, and others would be shallow and wide. If you began rolling large balls down that hillside, some would travel down the deep, narrow pathways and end up in about the same place every time, but others would travel down the shallow, wide pathways and might or might not stay within the gully and end up on one side or the other of the gully by the time they reached the bottom of the hill.

In a similar way we can think of some traits as being deeply canalized. Under all but the most extreme environmental conditions, genes for highly canalized traits have a self-righting tendency that produces the expected developmental outcome (Black, Hess, & Berenson-Howard, 2000; Gottlieb, 1991). For example, across a wide spectrum of environmental conditions, almost all infants reach the early motor milestones, like sitting up and walking. Likewise almost all infants go through the early stages of language development and coo and babble in a predictable sequence. After this early period of canalization, as infants become toddlers, the quality of their language environment becomes increasingly important (Black et al., 2000). In contrast, a trait such as intelligence has much more variability in its outcome. This genetic

Canalization The degree to which the expression of a gene is influenced by the environment.

pathway is less constrained or less deeply canalized so it is more influenced by the landscape of the child's environment. The concept of canalization gives us insight into the complex interaction between our genetic endowment and the influence of the environment.

How the Environment Shapes Gene Expression

Our understanding of genetic inheritance has become much more complex since the time of Mendel. We now know that the same genes can act differently in a variety of circumstances. When the Human Genome Project mapped all of the genes that make up a human being, the researchers discovered vast areas that appeared to be "junk," in that they did not code for proteins and often repeated themselves over and over and over again (Watson, 2003).

Another very important finding is that we have many genes that have the capacity to create proteins but do not necessarily do so because they are "silent." The term **epigenetics**, literally "over the genes," has been used to describe a system, called the epigenome, by which genes are activated or silenced (Zhang & Meaney, 2010). It turns out that all living things have chemical tags that can turn the gene's activity on or off. While the genome doesn't change (that is, the structure of the gene remains the same), the way that each gene is expressed may be very different depending on these chemical tags. What is most important is that the tags can be influenced by events or circumstances in the individual's environment. One way to think about it is that the genome is the "hard drive," while the epigenome is the "software" that puts genes into play. Just as software on a computer can be changed to run the hardware in different ways, so, too, the epigenome can be changed by environmental experiences to activate genes in different ways.

Epigenetics has been described as the bridge between nature and nurture (Zhang & Meaney, 2010). One example of how epigenetics works has been demonstrated by Michael Meaney, a researcher at McGill University, who studied rat mothers and their offspring. He and his colleagues found that rat babies reared by mothers who ignored them and did not touch them were more fearful and stressed by environmental events later in their lives. This was shown both by the babies' behavior and by the levels of stress hormones produced by their bodies. These researchers were able to link this behavior with a particular gene that was active in babies reared by nurturing mothers but had been "turned off" in these neglected babies. In order to be sure that this effect was due to the behavior of the mother and not to her genes, the researchers switched babies between nurturing and non-nurturing mothers, and the results were the same: In those babies who had been reared by non-nurturing mothers the gene had been "turned off" even though their biological mothers were very nurturing (Diorio & Meaney, 2007). In an evolutionary sense, it appears that baby rats who do not experience adequate mothering "reprogram" their genes. The result of this reprogramming is that the babies respond more quickly to stress. The evolutionary advantage is an increased responsiveness that allows them to respond quickly to danger, rather than waiting for unresponsive mothers to protect them.

Although there are obviously large differences between rats and humans, biologically there also are some similarities. Research has shown that when human mothers are highly unresponsive to their infants, the babies respond to stressful situations with higher levels of stress hormones, just like the baby rats whose mothers ignored them (Gunnar & Cheatham, 2003; Gunnar & Quevedo, 2007). Increased levels of stress hormones have also been found in children who suffered severe neglect in orphanages during their first 8 months of life, even when they were subsequently adopted into well-functioning families (Gunnar & Cheatham, 2003). At present there have not been specific genes identified that are turned on or off to explain these changes. We can only speculate that the mechanism in humans may be similar to that found in rats.

Another example of the impact of epigenetics is found in research on the development of high levels of aggression. Researchers have found that humans have one of two versions of a

Epigenetics A system by which genes are activated or silenced in response to events or circumstances in the individual's environment.

Video Link 4.5
Epigenetics.

8. The experiences you have in your life can change the structure of your genes.

TRUE/FALSE

False. Your genes are permanently arranged when you are conceived. However, the *expression* of these genes can be affected by your experiences; that is, the activity of some genes may be triggered or silenced by your environment.

Table 4.4

Interaction of genes and environment. This table shows the outcome when boys have different versions of the gene that produces MAO-A in relation to their early life experiences. When they have the predisposing gene *and* they experience child abuse, they are more likely to be highly aggressive as adults.

| | | Version of gene that produces MAO-A | |
		Gene producing low levels of MAO-A	Gene producing average levels of MAO-A
Experience of child abuse	Yes	Higher average levels of aggression	Typical levels of aggression
	No	Typical levels of aggression	Typical levels of aggression

gene on the X chromosome that determines how much of an enzyme called MAO-A (monoamine oxidase-A) is produced in their bodies. There is some evidence that individuals who have less MAO-A tend to be more aggressive. You might think that this is evidence that some forms of aggression may be genetically determined, and you would be partially right. However, in a longitudinal study in New Zealand, not all boys with the version of the gene that produces lower levels of MAO-A turned out to be aggressive. (Only boys were studied because it is more complicated to study girls, who have *two* X chromosomes.) The boys with this version of the gene who *also* experienced abuse during their childhood were much more likely to become aggressive adults. The environmental trigger of abuse early in life "turned on" the negative effects of the lower level of MAO-A (Caspi et al., 2002). Those boys with the other version of the gene were much less likely to become aggressive, whether they experienced child abuse or not. See Table 4.4 for a visual representation of the relationship between the genetic inheritance and environmental experiences in producing higher levels of aggression. This finding has been confirmed in several subsequent studies (Kim-Cohen et al., 2006; Reif et al., 2007), and similar results have been found for different genes relating to depression and posttraumatic stress disorder (Binder et al., 2008; Caspi et al., 2003).

Aggression is also addressed in a study of adults who had been adopted at birth. Cadoret, Yates, Troughton, Woodworth, and Steward (1995) found that these adults were more likely to be aggressive if their biological parents had shown antisocial behavior problems *and* their experience with their adoptive parents had been difficult (for example, there was divorce or substance abuse in their adopted family). Again, a specific combination of genes and environmental experiences was necessary to produce the behavior. Based upon studies such as these, it appears that certain genes can make individuals more or less susceptible to environmental effects (Dick & Rose, 2004).

Uncertainties in the Study of Gene-Environment Interaction

Another example of the type of recent research designed to show the interaction of genes and environment is the research on the timing of the onset of puberty, especially for girls. Puberty is "turned on" by the action of certain genes. The individual timing of the onset of puberty (that is, whether you enter puberty before, after, or at the same time as your peers) is in part inherited. If your mother entered puberty at an early age, you are also more likely to experience puberty early (Belsky et al., 2007; Ellis & Essex, 2007). However, there are a variety of environmental factors that also appear to turn on the genes for puberty.

Greater weight, including obesity, is associated with earlier puberty, but there also is evidence that girls are more likely to experience earlier puberty when they experience difficult early family life and when their fathers are absent (Ellis & Essex, 2007; Posner, 2006). We do

Like father, like son. Is it genes or environment that creates the similarity? Evel Knievel attempted to jump the Caesars Palace fountains in Las Vegas on his motorcycle in 1967. The attempt landed him in a coma for a month. His son Robbie took up the challenge and completed it successfully in 1989.

not yet know how this interaction occurs, and it is possible that a purely genetic explanation may be adequate. For example, one particular gene that is associated with aggression in men (the X-linked AR gene) also can be inherited by a daughter. However, in girls, this gene is not associated with aggression but instead acts to trigger early puberty. Therefore, a difficult family life, created by an aggressive father, may simply be an expression of a paternal gene that is also inherited by the daughter. It would not be the father's aggression that turned on the gene for puberty, but rather inheritance of the gene itself that both promotes the father's aggression and turns on early puberty (Posner, 2006). This is another example of the complexity that awaits us as we try to fully understand the interaction of genes and the environment.

How Genes Shape the Environment

So far we have described how genes affect physical and biological processes and how the environment influences the expression of genes to produce various developmental outcomes. A third developmental mechanism involves the ways in which genes influence the nature of the environment in which they exist.

Sandra Scarr (1992) proposed that one way to think about how genes shape the environment is to think of them as passive, active, or evocative. When genes are **passive**, they don't have to do much to be expressed, because children are born into a family that provides them with both their genes and their environment. For example, Robbie Knievel probably inherited genes for risk-taking from his famous father Evel. However, it is also likely that his father encouraged and trained him in motorcycle jumping as he grew up. In the end, Robbie outdistanced his dad. He jumped 150 feet over the fountains at Caesars Palace in Las Vegas, a trick that Evel had paid for with a month in the hospital (BBC News, 1998). Robbie may have been born with genes that promote risk-taking, but his environment also promoted the expression of the genes he inherited. Think of people you know, or famous people, who have successfully followed in their parents' footsteps, sometimes even topping their achievements. Children who have a genetic predisposition to be talented musicians often grow up in homes that are filled with music. Children who have the genetic predisposition to be gifted athletes often grow up in homes where physical activity is encouraged and supported. Within these supportive environments, genetic tendencies are expressed freely.

Genes are **active** when they become a driving force for children to seek out experiences that fit their genetic endowments (Rowe, 2003). A child with genes that promote risk-taking may be drawn like a magnet to snowboarding, bungee jumping, or whatever is offered that provides

Passive gene-environment interaction When a child's family shares his own genetically determined abilities and interests.

Active gene-environment interaction When one's genetic endowment becomes a driving force for children to seek out experiences that fit their genetic endowments.

a physical and risky challenge. On the other hand, a child with a genetic predisposition to be timid will seek out activities that are solitary and not overly stimulating or exciting. This type of gene effect is also called **niche-picking** or niche-building. In your environment you find the part of it (the niche) in which you feel most comfortable, and you actively make this choice (Feinberg, Reiss, Neiderhiser, & Hetherington, 2005).

Finally, genes are **evocative** when they cause the children to act in a way that draws out or "evokes" certain responses from those around them. In research by Cadoret et al. (1995), the hostile behavior of an adopted child, which may have its origins in the genes inherited from the child's birth parents, evoked harsh discipline from the child's adoptive mother. This harsh discipline further promoted the hostility and aggression of the child. On the other hand, an infant with an easy temperament may evoke more positive social interaction from others just because it is such a pleasure to interact with an infant who smiles and coos at everything you do. In this way, we can think of children as shaping the environment in which they live and have their experiences.

Behavioral Genetics

In spite of the fact that scientists have identified the genes that make up the human genome, we are still a long way from knowing what most of our genes actually do and how our behaviors relate to gene functioning. Although molecular genetics, which focuses on identifiable individual genes, has become the major area of research in recent years, the more traditional approach called behavioral genetics, described earlier in the chapter, continues to provide important information.

Behavioral genetics begins with the study of a particular behavior. Historically researchers have used several approaches to try to distinguish the relative influence of genes and environment on individual differences in that behavior. You might think that you could just see how similar children are to their parents and that would tell you how much of a particular behavior is genetic, but as we described above, genetic influences and environmental setting are often intertwined in complex ways. For example, imagine walking into the home of a new friend. You discover that this friend is a very talented pianist. You then find out that both parents in this family perform with a local choir and their youngest child is a gifted violinist. What would you conclude about the source of this musical talent? Did the children in this family inherit genes for their musical ability, or did they learn about music from the experiences that their parents have provided for them? In this situation, there is no way to know which has happened. In fact, it's likely that both genes and environment have had an effect; however, scientifically it is impossible to sort out which factor had what effect.

In theory you might solve this problem by taking children from musical families and placing them in families that are not musical to see what happens. If musical ability is determined by genes, these children will still develop this talent. If it is determined by environmental influences, they will not necessarily be musical. Earlier in this chapter we described research such as this in which rats were switched from nurturing to non-nurturing mothers and vice versa. Obviously it would be highly unethical to do anything like this with human beings, so psychologists have had to look for natural situations that might provide the same information. Three types of studies have been carried out that take advantage of such natural situations: studies of adopted children, comparisons of identical (monozygotic, or MZ) and fraternal (dizygotic, or DZ) twins, and studies of MZ twins who were adopted in infancy and reared by different families.

Studies of Adopted Children

Children who are adopted have birth parents from whom they inherited their genes and adoptive parents who provide the environment in which they grow up. In order to look at

Niche-picking
Individuals choose the part of their environment (the "niche") in which they feel comfortable, based on their genetic predispositions.

Evocative gene-environment interaction
When children's genetic endowment causes them to act in a way that draws out or "evokes" certain responses from those around them.

9. At age 17, Mike is already a heavy drinker. Both of his parents have struggled with alcoholism for a long time. Therefore, genes must have determined that Mike would also become an alcoholic.

TRUE/FALSE

False. The effect of genes on complex behaviors such as alcoholism is not that straightforward. A variety of factors, including many factors in the person's environment, also play an important role.

Concordance rate The degree to which a trait or an ability of one individual is similar to that of another; used to examine similarities between twins and among adopted children and their biological and adoptive parents.

the relative contribution of genes and environment on whatever developmental outcome the researchers are studying, they must have information on both the adoptive parents and the biological parents. They then look at the **concordance rate**, a measure of similarity, between the children and each of their two sets of parents. One example of this type of research has been carried out to determine the heritability of alcoholism. Cadoret, Troughton, and O'Gorman (1987) found that adoptees who had one or more birth parents and/or grandparents who had alcoholism were 4.6 times as likely as others to develop alcoholism themselves. By comparison, if the adoptive parents were alcoholic, the risk of the child developing alcoholism was raised 2.7 times. This indicates that both genes and environment played a role, but in this instance the stronger influence appeared to be genetic.

Examine for yourself the evidence for genetic and environmental input into the development of alcoholism by trying **Active Learning: Alcoholism, Genes, and Environment**. You can also carry out this activity with any behavior, trait, or disorder for which you would like to learn more about the genetic and environmental contributions.

ACTIVE LEARNING

Alcoholism, Genes, and Environment

If someone develops alcoholism and it is found that both his parents are also alcoholic, does that mean that he inherited the addiction from his parents? Maybe he *learned* the behavior of drinking to excess from his parents. This activity is a chance to practice the skills you learned in Chapter 3 in regard to the use of databases to search for reliable information. In order to examine the possible causes of alcoholism, use the database PsycINFO and use the following words in separate searches (remember to put only one word in each line of the search box): (a) *alcoholism* and *genes*, (b) *alcoholism* and *urban environment* (or *alcoholism* and *rural environment*), (c) *alcoholism* and *family environment*. For each one, examine the abstract of several articles to see what evidence there is that alcoholism has a genetic cause, an environmental cause, or a combination of the two. Compare your findings with those of other classmates. You may also search in a database such as Medline that is more focused on biological factors, or one that is more focused on environmental factors such as Sociological Abstracts.

Research Comparing Identical and Fraternal Twins

Another approach that has been used to try to determine the relative influence of genes and environment has capitalized on the fact that there are two types of twins. As you'll remember, identical or monozygotic twins are more likely to share all their genes in common (even though recent research has shown there may be small differences), while fraternal or dizygotic twins share about half of their genes in common, just as any two siblings would. However, both types of twins usually grow up in the same environment. After all, they are born to the same parents in the same family at the same point in time. Therefore, scientists have tried to determine which behaviors or traits of personality are linked with genetic inheritance by looking at how similar the twins are to each other on those behaviors or traits. If identical twins, who are more likely to have all of their genes in common, are more similar to each other on a trait such as shyness than are fraternal twins, who have only half of their genes in common, the researchers conclude that genes play a role in determining whether someone is shy.

Using this type of study to look at the causes of alcoholism, Pagan et al. (2006) followed twins from adolescence through early adulthood. They found that the age of initiating use of alcohol was no more similar for identical twins than for fraternal twins. However, there were more similarities between identical twins in the amount they drank and in who became problem drinkers in late adolescence and early adulthood. This study provides additional evidence that genes do play a role in the development of problem drinking.

Identical Twins Reared Apart

The third type of research is a combination of twin and adoption research. Scientists such as Thomas Bouchard at the University of Minnesota have located identical and fraternal twins who were adopted into separate families to determine how similar they are to each other (Bouchard, Lykken, McGue, & Segal, 1990). These researchers have argued that their findings show that identical twins reared apart are about as similar to each other on aspects of their personality, interests, and social attitudes as identical twins reared together, and are more similar than fraternal twins reared apart. Despite widespread media reports that these twins were eerily similar—marrying women with the same name, wearing the same clothes, giving their dog the same name—there has been much criticism of how this research was done. Joseph (2001) makes the case that many of these "separated" twins actually knew each other. For instance, they may have been adopted by relatives who lived in the same area, and this could account for many of their similarities. Also, the children were not always adopted at birth, so some were raised together for a number of years before they were separated. Finally, he argues that these twins should be compared to people unknown to each other who are the same age, sex, race, and ethnicity, and who have a similar level of attractiveness, as each of these characteristics is also likely to make people similar to each other. Only if the identical twins were truly separated at birth and really didn't know each other as they were growing up but still turned out to be significantly more similar to each other than the strangers would there be evidence for a strong genetic influence. **Active Learning: Twins Separated at Birth** may give you some sense of the role that coincidence might play in similarities found between identical twins reared apart.

Twins Separated at Birth

The research on twins separated at birth has reported some similarities among reunited twins that are very surprising (Lykken, McGue, Tellegen, & Bouchard, 1992). Information published from the Minnesota Study of Twins Reared Apart reports stories about a pair of reunited twins who were habitual gigglers, another pair who used the same brand of toothpaste and shaving lotion, and even one pair who had both been married to women named Linda whom they later divorced only to subsequently marry women named Betty. The challenge with this type of report is to separate out characteristics and behaviors that have genetic or environmental underpinnings from those that are merely coincidences.

Would you be surprised to find out that you were sitting in class next to someone who had your same birthday? You should be because that is not highly likely. However, if your class has only 23 students in it, there is a 50-50 chance that there is at least one shared birthday among your classmates (Mathematical Association of America, 1998). The likelihood of a shared birthday increases as the size of the group increases, so in a large class, you are almost certain to find some "birthday buddies" among your classmates.

The point is that the odds of finding a similarity between people who don't know each other are sometimes surprisingly high. Your professor may give you the opportunity to complete the following activity during one of your classes, but you can do it on your own outside class. Take a few minutes to talk to someone you don't know. Introduce yourself and tell each other a little about yourselves. In your conversation include some discussion about where you grew up and went to school, the number of brothers or sisters you have, what you like to do with your time, some personal preferences (such as your favorite brand of clothes, favorite foods, or favorite recording artists), and how you would describe yourself (for example, outgoing, friendly, kind, or thoughtful), and finally describe some of the things you are good at (for example, sports, academics, or arts). Keep track of any similarities that you discover. At any point, did you begin to wonder if you were twins separated at birth? Probably not, but in all likelihood some interesting—if not eerie—consequences emerged from your conversation. Did you remember to ask the person you were talking to when his or her birthday is?

ACTIVE LEARNING

Video Link 4.6
Identical twins reared apart.

10. Genes have been found to play a role in the development of almost all behaviors that have been studied.

True. Behavioral genetics has shown that almost all behaviors studied have some genetic input. However, different traits and behaviors are more or less heritable.

More Recent Research Approaches

Until recently, research based on behavioral genetics has focused on determining "heritability"; that is, to what extent do genes create behaviors? The specific effect of the environment was not examined. Newer studies, however, have included a focus on particular aspects of the environment and have attempted to measure their impact on human behavior. The three paradigms of behavioral genetic research that we described above (adoption studies, studies comparing identical and fraternal twins, and studies of identical twins reared apart) have been expanded. For example, Dick and Rose (2004) studied twins but also included one close friend of each twin in the study. All of these children had neighborhood, school, and community in common, but only the twins also had some genes and their family setting in common. This approach allowed the researchers to determine that the age at which children began to smoke and drink was more related to neighborhood, school, and community characteristics than it was to genes or family upbringing. In other words, the twins were no more similar to each other in these behaviors than they were to their friends. Although behavioral genetics has shown that almost all behaviors studied have some genetic input (Dick & Rose, 2004), it is still useful to determine which traits and behaviors are highly likely to involve genetic input because this will aid in the search for the specific genes involved. On the other hand, it is also important to figure out which aspects of the environment are influential in the development of behavior so that we can promote those environments that are associated with positive outcomes.

The Study of Culture and Behavior

In this chapter on the nature-nurture debate, we focused first on nature (in the form of genes) and on how genes relate to development. We then examined research that ties nature and nurture together, through concepts such as canalization and epigenesis. We will now focus on the nurture side of this debate. Studies of human growth and development have yet to come up with any behavior, personality trait, or ability that is due entirely to our genetic inheritance. Studies on the heritability of any trait or ability inevitably show that environment also plays a role in the development of that trait or ability. If a trait is found to be 50% determined by genes, this necessarily means that 50% is not the result of gene activity and is likely due to the effects of the environment. In the long run, examining the impact of genes on development may be a simple task in comparison to finding the impact of "the environment." There are so many aspects of the environment that we certainly cannot cover in this chapter more than a fraction of the ones that affect us. However, throughout the rest of this book we will continue to discuss specific aspects of the environment that affect child development. For example, poverty plays an important role in how children grow and develop, so we will talk about the effects of poverty on cognitive development in Chapter 8 and on health and well-being in Chapter 15.

One theory in particular has attempted to systematize how we examine the effects of the environment on development. In Chapter 2, we described how Urie Bronfenbrenner's ecological theory attempts to classify the different levels of environmental effects, from the microsystem through the macrosystem, with each level interacting with the others and with the individual. In this section we focus on the outermost layer, the macrosystem, which is made up of the larger culture. We will show how the broad values and norms of our culture filter down through the layers until they affect parents' interactions with their children within the microsystem and finally affect the children themselves, as they internalize cultural values. Eventually children come to see the world differently depending on the culture in which they live.

What Is Culture?

There have been many different definitions of **culture** because culture is an abstract concept, not something we can touch or put under a microscope. Culture emerges from a particular group's "environmental niche"; for example, a desert society is going to have different rules and traditions than a society located on rich farmland. The niche could also be described as urban versus rural, or wealth versus poverty. Even the technological landscape of a particular group, such as availability of television or cell phones, shapes the environmental niche. Culture forms to promote the survival of the group that lives in this niche. Matsumoto and Juang (2004) point out that culture is a way of describing similarities within one group of people and differences between groups of people. The similarities and differences may consist of behavioral expectations, such as whether you shake hands or bow when introduced to someone, or the types of foods you eat, the kinds of clothes you wear, or the things you celebrate.

Culturally based behaviors, beliefs, and institutions are handed down from generation to generation, just as genes are. In an attempt to compare these inheritances to those of genes, some have referred to these "unit[s] of cultural evolution and selection" as **memes** (Wilkins, 1998, para. 1). Both culture and genes change over time; they are part of a dynamic process of development across the generations. But we should not make the mistake of assuming that *all* the people of any culture (especially cultures other than our own) accept and enact all aspects of the culture in which they live. For instance, while American culture has certain general characteristics, such as an emphasis on individualism and competition, we know that there are many individual differences; for example, one person may be much more competitive than another. This same fact holds true in other cultural groups as well. Even in a culture where the expectation is that adolescents will accept what their parents say, some adolescents will be more deferential to their parents than others, and some will be more rebellious. While it is important to understand and acknowledge the influence of a person's culture, we must not forget to see that person as an individual with opinions and ideas that may differ from the strict expectations of culture.

Stereotyping

It seems to be a very common human practice to identify oneself with a particular group of people (our *in-group*). This, in turn, has consequences for our feelings and understanding about others who are not in our group (the *out-group*). Whereas people tend to see the people in their own group as individuals, with differences in personality, talents, and opinions, they tend to see people in the out-group as all the same; for example, an individual of one race might think that people of a different race all look the same (Bartsch, Judd, Louw, Park, & Ryan, 1997).

Instead of looking at all of the complexity of an individual, we often use shortcuts to draw conclusions about someone based on the group with which we identify him or her (for example, the Japanese culture emphasizes hard work, so when meeting someone we may think: "You're Japanese; therefore you must be very hardworking"). This generalizing of characteristics leads to **stereotyping** of individuals. We may then prejudge other people before we have even met them. Once we have a stereotype of a particular group, we tend to notice those people who fit that stereotype in some way, and not the people who do not, so that our observations simply reconfirm our initial ideas. In research conducted in Canada, Euro Canadian and Native Canadian children were shown pictures of children from these two cultural backgrounds (Corenblum, 2003). For each picture of a child, the participants were read a list of behaviors that applied to the person in that picture. Some behaviors were considered positive or negative stereotypes of each ethnic group. Later the children were asked to recall as many behaviors as they could about each picture they had seen. Both Euro Canadian and Native

Culture Culture is the system of behaviors, norms, beliefs, and traditions that form in order to promote the survival of a group that lives in a particular environmental niche. It is a way of describing similarities within one group of people and differences between groups of people.

Memes Units of culture that are handed down from one generation to the next.

Stereotyping Conclusions made about someone based solely on the group with which he or she is identified.

Cultural differences. Which of these photos fits your idea of how to raise a child? Culture affects what we expect parents to do. In Western society, young children generally do not take care of infants. In some African societies, talking directly to young children is seen as ridiculous.

Canadian children remembered more positive stereotypes applied to the Euro Canadian children in the pictures and more negative stereotypes about the Native Canadian children. In effect, both groups of children tended to forget the positive behaviors that were associated with the Native Canadians and the negative behaviors that were associated with the Euro Canadians, thus reinforcing their preexisting stereotypes. This is one reason why stereotypes are so difficult to change. Even when we encounter information that is contrary to a stereotype, we are less likely to remember it or to remember it accurately.

Difference Versus Deficit

Researchers have been guilty at times of this same type of cultural insensitivity. In examining a culture other than their own, their tendency was to use their own culture as the standard, and to see any deviation from that standard as a weakness or deficit in the other culture (Wargo, 2007). As scientists have become more aware of the problems in this approach, they have become more adept at looking at the differences between cultures in their own context, rather than making value judgments about another culture.

We often assume that the way we do things is the right way and that other ways are wrong. For example, Robert LeVine et al. (1994) showed American mothers videos of mothers from the Gusii people in Kenya. The Americans were appalled that 5- and 6-year-old children were put in charge of their infant siblings and that mothers did not praise their children. On the other hand, when he showed tapes of the American mothers to the Gusii mothers, they were appalled that mothers did not nurse their babies immediately when they cried and could not understand why they talked to their babies when the babies clearly could not understand them.

In order to understand a culture other than our own, we must understand its environmental context and its values. The goals of child rearing may be somewhat different depending on these factors. For example, infant mortality is a major problem for the Gusii. Therefore, the protection and health of their infants is the primary concern. For Americans, health is also an issue but can usually take a backseat to an emphasis on engaging and teaching infants. As a result, the Gusiis' main emphasis is on soothing and calming their babies to keep an equilibrium that is most conducive to the baby's healthy development, so they nurse their babies often to prevent the stress of crying. Americans' main emphasis is on talking to their babies, offering toys, and interacting to create a strong emotional bond and stimulate the infant's cognitive development. Evidence of this is found in the huge infant toy industry, with many companies offering educational, age-appropriate toys for every stage of infancy. Neither of these approaches is right or wrong. Both are responsive to the realities of their environment, usually in a way to best promote the well-being of the children. For an example of how we may misinterpret the actions and intentions of people whose culture is different from our own, see **Active Learning: Cultural Competence and Grief**.

Cultural Competence and Grief

ACTIVE LEARNING

Joanne Cacciatore (2009) recounts an experience she had with a family that had just experienced the unexpected death of an 18-month-old son. Although two sets of grandparents and the young child's parents were present, no one except one of the grandfathers would talk with a representative of the medical examiner's office. When the grandfather did talk with her, he did not make eye contact and stayed at least 4 feet away from her while they talked. He steadfastly insisted that no autopsy be performed on the child's body, even though the law required one in cases of sudden child deaths in his state. The family sat in the medical examiner's office for almost 2 hours in silence and with little or no show of emotion. When they finally were asked if they wanted to have some time with the dead child to say their good-byes, they did not want to do it. In fact, they adamantly refused.

How would you interpret this family's behavior? What circumstances could account for it? How does this behavior fit with your cultural beliefs regarding how a family grieves the death of a young child? Does the behavior seem typical, atypical, or pathological to you?

Answer: These behaviors are completely expected and normal for some Native American families. It was the proper role of the grandfather in these circumstances to be the spokesman for the family. Native Americans may not make sustained eye contact when talking to others and may not display emotion, even when they are dealing with personal grief. Because this culture values listening, it is not unusual for its members to remain silent even while sitting together. Autopsies are usually prohibited, as is postmortem contact with the deceased. In the cultural context of this family, their behavior was appropriate, respectful, and in keeping with their traditions and beliefs (Cacciatore, 2009). Remember, however, that within any culture there is a range of individual differences. Other Native American families that are more acculturated might not adhere to all these cultural traditions. In fact, in the situation described by Cacciatore (2009), after the family members were allowed enough time to grieve in their way, they decided to spend some time with their child and were at peace with their decision to do so.

Individualism and Collectivism

One way in which cultures vary is along the continuum from **individualistic** to **collectivist**. U.S. culture is based on values of rugged individualism. Our heroes often are those who are self-made and managed to rise from deprived circumstances to become successful. In other cultures, the emphasis is more on an obligation to those around you: your family or your group, however you define it. The questionnaire in **Active Learning: What Are Your**

Individualism The cultural value that emphasizes the importance of the individual with emphasis on independence and reliance on one's own abilities.

Collectivism The cultural value that emphasizes obligations to others within your group.

Culturally Based Beliefs? will give you some idea of how individualistic or collectivistic your own values are. Because there is great diversity within every culture (including the United States), even people who have grown up in this country have beliefs that differ from one person to another.

Video Link 4.7
Cultural differences.

What Are Your Culturally Based Beliefs?

It is very difficult for us to be aware of how culture affects us in our beliefs and in our everyday life. Culture pervades every aspect of our lives. As a result, we often take it for granted and assume that everyone else is having the same experience that we are having. As someone said, "Fish don't notice the water they swim in." In the same way we don't notice our culture unless we come up against cultural expectations that are quite different from our own.

You can get some idea of where your own beliefs fall on the continuum between individualism and collectivism by completing the following questionnaire. Remember that there are no right or wrong answers in a questionnaire such as this. Be honest with yourself about your answers.

Consider whether you would *agree* or *disagree* with the following statements:

1. I tend to do my own thing, and others in my family do the same.
2. To understand who I am, you must see me with members of my group.
3. I take great pride in accomplishing what no one else can accomplish.
4. To me, pleasure is spending time with others.
5. It is important to me that I perform better than others on a task.
6. I would help, within my means, if a relative were in financial difficulty.
7. I am unique—different from others in many respects.
8. I make an effort to avoid disagreements with my group members.
9. I like my privacy.
10. How I behave depends on whom I am with, where I am, or both.
11. I know my weaknesses and strengths.
12. I have respect for the authority figures with whom I interact.
13. I always state my opinions very clearly.
14. I would rather do a group paper or lab than do one alone.

SOURCE: Oyserman, Coon, & Kemmelmeier (2002, p. 9).

Answers: If you agreed with more of the odd-numbered questions, your value system tends to be more individualistic. If you agreed with more of the even-numbered questions, your value system tends to be more collectivistic. Although the culture in the United States tends to value individualism, that does not mean that every person in this country subscribes to this value. What did your scores indicate about your values? Do you think that the culture in which you live or grew up plays a role in why you have these values?

The difference between people from individualistic and collectivistic cultural backgrounds can become apparent when people from those cultures interact. Cathy Small, an anthropology professor at a university in Arizona, "went underground" as a student at her own university to study student culture (Nathan, 2005). She found that many foreign students were surprised that there was much less sense of obligation to help friends in this country. Although Americans are friendly, this does not necessarily lead to active help or support, as it would in another culture. One student from Mexico said,

> I was living in a new country and I needed help. Like with setting up a bank account and doing the lease. It was new for me. . . . And when I tell my friends that I had a hard day trying to figure out all the things they say, 'Oh, I'm so sorry for you.' . . . In Mexico, when someone is a friend, then regardless of the situation, even if I would get in trouble, I would help them. . . . 'So sorry for you' doesn't help!" (Nathan, 2005, p. 75)

The sense of responsibility to one's group is not expressed in the same way in our individualistic society as it would be in societies with more collectivistic values.

Culture is expressed in behaviors such as how we greet others and in the types of social obligations described above. There are also much more subtle ways in which culture becomes a part of us, guiding not only our behaviors but the way in which we think or experience our feelings. Even the way we physically see the world around us may be affected by our cultural experience. Less individualistic cultures from East Asia, such as Japan and China, tend to emphasize the importance of how people interact with each other and their environment. For example, one focus of the ancient study of feng shui is on how living space should relate to the overall environment, such as natural wind and light patterns. As we have seen, American culture is much more concerned with the autonomous individual.

Masuda and Nisbett (2001) demonstrated how cultural differences can affect our perceptions. (Before you read any further, look at the photo on this page. Write down a description of what you see.) They showed Americans and Japanese a film of an underwater scene, including fish and other small animals surrounded by seaweed and rocks. When asked what they had seen, Americans were more likely to describe the large, moving fish, while Japanese participants were more likely to describe the context and the relationships between all the objects in the scene. (What did you focus on?) One interesting outcome of this difference in focus was that the Japanese participants remembered more of what they had seen than the Americans. On the other hand, Japanese participants' memory for what they had seen in the video was affected by the background in which it was placed. They were less likely to remember having seen a particular fish if it was shown with a different background than with the original background. American participants were not affected by the background because their focus was on individual fish, and less on the fish's relationship to its surroundings.

What do you see here? On a piece of paper, write down what you see in this picture. Does your description begin with the fish in the foreground or with the overall scene? Do you describe one fish in detail or the relationship between the fish, the rocks, and the seaweed? Japanese and American students differ in their emphasis on the individual objects or on the objects within their context.

Recent research has even shown cultural differences in brain function based on whether the individual was told to pay attention to context or not. The frontal regions of the brain, associated with control of attention, were more active when Americans were told to focus on context and East Asians were told *not* to focus on context (Hedden, Ketay, Aron, Markus, & Gabrieli, 2008). This means that it took more concentration to perform in a way that was not culturally preferred. You might argue that these groups are genetically different and that is the cause of these physical differences, but the researchers found that the degree to which each individual agreed with his or her cultural values was related to the degree of activation of the brain when faced with the nonpreferred or less familiar task. This finding indicates that it is not the genetic background of an individual, but rather the cultural background, that is influencing his or her attentional style.

The Transmission of Culture

How is such subtle cultural information taught to children? Certainly there are some cultural expectations that are taught explicitly to children—for example, "Look at me when

Cultural differences in feeding. How do these different approaches to feeding babies reflect cultural values?

I'm speaking to you" versus "Be careful to show respect and look down when addressing your elders." However, much cultural information is conveyed in much more subtle forms. Robin Harwood, a researcher at Ruhr University in Bochum, Germany, studied middle-class mothers in Connecticut and in Puerto Rico. She was interested in how the individualistic values of American society and the more collectivist values of Puerto Rican society might be taught even to infants through the way that their mothers interacted with them. With this in mind, Harwood and her colleagues set out to see whether the feeding practices of mothers in the two cultures would reflect these different value systems (Miller & Harwood, 2002). Think about the scene you expect to see when a mother feeds her 1-year-old baby. If you were born in the United States, most likely you have an image of the baby sitting in a high chair. The mother spoon-feeds the baby but often lets the baby take the spoon to begin learning to feed herself (usually with messy and somewhat hilarious results, as shown in the leftmost photo on this page). She may also put some "finger food," like dry cereal, on the tray for the baby to take on her own. Contrast this picture with that of the typical Puerto Rican mother and baby. This mother spoon-feeds the baby to make sure that the baby eats well, the feeding remaining under her control and not the baby's, as shown in the photo at the right. What is the message that each mother is giving to her baby from her earliest days of life? The American mother is saying, "Be independent. Learn to do things on your own separately from me. We will watch and praise you." The Puerto Rican mother is saying, "Be close to family. Listen to and cooperate with your parents. Enjoy your food in the context of family love and expectations for proper behavior." Thus, cultural values are translated directly into parenting techniques. Babies are learning the values of their culture even with their first bites of food.

Conclusion

All human beings are originally created through the combination of the genes of their two parents. However, we are born into a cultural environment that shapes the way that those genes will be expressed. As we have seen, our genetic inheritance also shapes the environment we will experience. We are a long way from understanding all of the complex interaction between our genetic inheritance and our cultural and environmental experiences. As we continue in our study of child development, we will examine how our physical, cognitive, language, emotional, and social development are shaped both by our genetic inheritance and by the environmental context of our lives.

CHAPTER SUMMARY

1. **What are three ways in which scientists study the interaction of genes and human behavior?**

   Scientists have examined behaviors of twins and adopted children to try to figure out whether there is any genetic involvement in producing specific behaviors. This approach is called **behavioral genetics**. More basic research, called **molecular genetics**, focuses on particular genes and how they function within the cells. A combination of these two approaches, known as **behavioral genomics**, links specific behaviors with specific genes.

2. **What are genes, and how do they work?**

   Chromosomes are made of chains of **genes**, which consist of chains of nucleotide bases, guanine, adenine, thymine, and cytosine. The order of these bases gives a cell the instructions for producing different proteins. The **genotype** includes all the pairs of genes a person has. The **phenotype** is the way those genes are expressed. Dominant genes are expressed regardless of the gene they are paired with on a particular chromosome pair. Recessive genes are expressed only if they are paired with another recessive gene or if they are carried on the X chromosome of a male child. Each trait or behavior can be produced by the interaction of many genes, a process called **polygenic inheritance**. In addition, any one gene may have many different influences. This is referred to as **pleiotropic effects**.

3. **How do genes and chromosomes result in disorders?**

   Disorders can be **single gene disorders, chromosome disorders**, or the result of **multifactorial inheritance disorders**. Disorders such as sickle-cell anemia and Tay-Sachs disease result when an individual inherits a pair of recessive genes that code for that disorder. Disorders such as cystic fibrosis result when **mutations** occur as cells divide. Chromosomal disorders such as Down syndrome occur when a child receives the wrong number of chromosomes or when there is a change in the structure of the chromosome caused by breakage. Multifactorial inheritance disorders, such as depression or alcoholism, result from the interaction of many genes that interact with environmental influences.

4. **How does the environment affect the functioning of genes, and how do genes affect an individual's environment?**

   Canalization is the degree to which genes are affected by environmental variations. Genes that are expressed regardless of environmental influences are deeply canalized, while those whose influence varies in relation to the environment are less deeply canalized. Specific genes may be activated or silenced as a result of experiences from the environment in a process called **epigenetics**. Genes can also affect the nature of an individual's environment. In **passive gene-environment interaction**, children are born into a family that shares and promotes its own genetically determined abilities and interests. In **active gene-environment interaction**, children seek out experiences on their own that fit their genetic endowments. In **evocative gene-environment interaction**, children act in a way that draws out or "evokes" certain responses from those around them.

5. **How do researchers examine the contribution of genes and the contribution of environmental influences on children's behavior?**

   Three types of research studies have looked at the relative contribution of genes and environment on children's behavior. They include adoption studies, twin studies, and studies of identical twins reared apart.

6. **What is culture?**

   Culture includes the characteristics (including behaviors, rituals, and beliefs) that a particular group has developed as it has adapted to its environment. These characteristics are similar within a group, often different from those of other groups, and handed down from generation to generation.

7. **How do we understand the effect that the culture has on the individual?**

   While learning about other people's cultures, we must guard against **stereotyping** individuals, which is often linked to prejudices against the people of a certain culture. It is important to understand differences between cultures as adaptations to different life circumstances rather than seeing them as deficits.

8. **What are individualism and collectivism, and how do they affect individual development?**

   Cultures are described as **individualistic** if they emphasize the importance of the individual person's welfare over that of the group in which he or she lives. Cultures are **collectivistic** if they emphasize the importance of the group's welfare over that of the individuals that make up the group. These different values can influence our beliefs, our interactions with others, and even the way in which we perceive the world around us.

9. **How do parents hand their culture down to their children?**

   Cultural attitudes and behaviors may be taught explicitly to young children, but parents teach young children to conform to cultural values even from the very first interactions with infants. The way that parents hold, feed, and talk to their infants reflects their cultural values, which are transmitted in this indirect way.

Go to **www.sagepub.com/levine** for additional exercises and video resources. Select **Chapter 4, How Children Develop,** for chapter-specific activities.

chapter 5

Prenatal Development, Birth, and the Newborn

5

From the moment a sperm unites with an egg in the process of **fertilization**, the complicated and miraculous process of development begins. As you learned in Chapter 4, that moment determines the genetic makeup of the new individual, but from that very moment the fertilized egg, or zygote, also begins interacting with the environment. What happens in the prenatal environment of a woman's womb over the next 9 months can have a tremendous effect on the course of development. As you'll see in this chapter, the process has some safeguards built in to it that help ensure that the newborn is healthy and fully ready to enter the world, but the system is not perfect and the number of potential threats is substantial. Fortunately we know a great deal today about ways to help a mother get through her pregnancy without complications and how to help the newborn get off to the best possible start in life.

Fertilization The process by which a sperm penetrates an egg.

Test Your Knowledge

Test your knowledge of child development by deciding whether each of the following statements is *true* or *false,* and then check your answers as you read the chapter.

1. **True/False:** When a child is conceived, there is a 50-50 chance the child will be a male.
2. **True/False:** More than half of all conceptions never implant in the woman's uterus.
3. **True/False:** Using techniques that are available today, parents can choose the gender of their baby with 100% accuracy.
4. **True/False:** Research has shown that exposing a fetus to extra stimulation (for example, playing music near the woman's stomach) can stimulate advanced cognitive development.
5. **True/False:** Excessive drinking while a woman is pregnant can cause Down syndrome.
6. **True/False:** Smoking marijuana while pregnant can make the child more susceptible to marijuana addiction when the child is an adult.
7. **True/False:** Infants who are born to women with HIV are almost certain to have the disease themselves.
8. **True/False:** If a couple loses an infant to sudden infant death syndrome, the best thing you can do is to tell them that it isn't their fault and help them look to the future by reminding them that they still can have other children.
9. **True/False:** An infant who is born prematurely will have developmental problems and lag behind other children of the same age.
10. **True/False:** Following the birth of a baby, modern couples pretty much share household and child care responsibilities.

Correct answers: (1) False, (2) True, (3) False, (4) False, (5) False, (6) True, (7) False, (8) False, (9) False, (10) False

Video Link 5.1
Prenatal development.

In this chapter we describe the process of prenatal development. We also look at the experience of birth from the perspective of the mother, the father, and the infant and look at how the couple handles the transition to becoming a family. Finally we look at some of the amazing capabilities of the newborn.

Prenatal Development

Ovum An unfertilized egg.

Ovulation The release of a mature egg from an ovary.

TRUE/FALSE

1. When a child is conceived, there is a 50-50 chance the child will be a male.

   False. Sperm that contain a Y chromosome are lighter than sperm that contain an X chromosome, so they can swim faster and are more likely to reach the egg first. Consequently there are about 107 to 170 male conceptions for every 100 female conceptions.

Gestational age The length of time since the conception of a developing organism.

Germinal stage The prenatal stage that lasts from conception to 2 weeks postconception.

TRUE/FALSE

2. More than half of all conceptions never implant in the woman's uterus.

   True. About 60% of all conceptions fail to implant in the uterus. They simply pass out of the woman's body without her even realizing there had been a conception.

The Three Stages of Prenatal Development

The prenatal journey begins when a follicle in a woman's ovary matures and releases an **ovum** (or egg) during her monthly menstrual cycle in the process called **ovulation**. The ovum begins to travel down the fallopian tube toward the uterus. This is where fertilization occurs when the egg is penetrated by one of the approximately 300 million sperm that are released into the woman's reproductive system during an act of intercourse. You'll remember from Chapter 4 that this is when the child's biological sex is determined. If the sperm that unites with the egg is carrying a Y chromosome in the 23rd pair of chromosomes, the conception is a male, but if it is carrying an X chromosome, the conception is a female.

It may surprise you to learn that there is quite a substantial difference in the rate of conception for males and females. Between 107 and 170 males are conceived for every 100 females (Kalben, 2002). If you think back to what you learned about chromosomes in the previous chapter, is the reason for this gender disparity clear to you? Because the Y chromosome is much smaller than the X chromosome, sperm that have a Y chromosome are lighter than those with an X chromosome, so they can swim faster and are more likely to reach the egg first. However, males also are more vulnerable during prenatal development, so fewer male conceptions survive. By the time they are born, the ratio of males to females has dropped to 106 live male births for every 100 live female births (Cunningham et al., 2005; Kalben, 2002).

Prenatal development is divided into three stages of very different lengths. The germinal stage lasts from conception to 2 weeks, the embryonic stage lasts from 2 weeks to 2 months, and the last stage, called the fetal stage, is the longest, lasting from 2 months until birth at about 9 months or 38 weeks after conception. The length of time since conception is called the **gestational age** of the developing organism. We'll describe what happens in each of these stages in detail.

The Germinal Stage (Conception to 2 Weeks)

The first stage of prenatal development is called the **germinal stage**, and it begins when the sperm penetrates the egg. Once fertilization occurs and a zygote (or fertilized egg) has been created, the outside of the egg thickens so that no other sperm will be able to enter the egg. The newly created zygote continues its journey through the fallopian tube, and the process of cell division begins (see Figure 5.1). It takes about 15 hours for that single cell to become 2 cells, and then the process continues with 2 cells becoming 4, the 4 becoming 8, and so on, until there is a ball of 32 cells. At this point (about 5 days after conception), the mass of cells is ready to implant into the lining of the uterus. During the woman's menstrual cycle, her hormones have prepared the lining for just this purpose. If the ball of cells fails to implant for any reason, it passes out of the woman's body without her even realizing there had been a conception. This is not at all uncommon. In fact, it is estimated that about 60% of conceptions fail to implant and do not survive (Moore & Persaud, 2003). If it does successfully implant, the process of establishing the connection between mother and embryo has begun.

Figure 5.1

The germinal stage. In the week following the fertilization of the ovum, the newly formed zygote travels down the fallopian tube, and the developing blastocyst implants in the lining of the uterus.

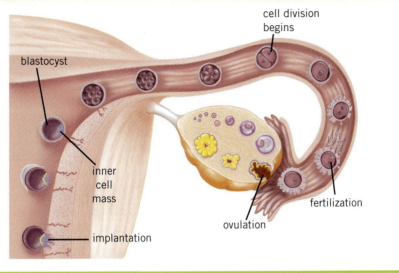

As the number of cells continues to proliferate, the solid ball of cells becomes a hollow ball called a **blastocyst**, which now has a solid group of cells at one end (the **inner cell mass**) and an outer ring of cells (the **trophoblast**) (see Figure 5.2). The inner cell mass will go on to become the embryo and part of the amnion that surrounds the embryo, and the outer ring of cells will become the support system for the pregnancy, which includes the placenta and the chorion. We will describe these structures and their functions when we discuss the next stage of prenatal development.

Cells in the trophoblast secrete an enzyme that digests some of the lining in the uterus so that the blastocyst can securely embed itself there. After implantation, fingerlike extensions from the outer layer of the trophoblast grow into the uterus, and a connection between the embryo and the mother is established (Galan & Hobbins, 2003). Now, for the first time, the embryo begins to draw nourishment from the mother. Up to this point, its only source of nourishment has come from material contained in the original egg cell, but once an outside source of nourishment is available, the blastocyst can really begin to grow in size.

Infertility. Couples who engage in frequent, unprotected sex can expect to conceive a child within 1 year, so failure to conceive within that length of time may mean that **infertility** is a

Figure 5.2

Development of the blastocyst. As the zygote continues to replicate and divide, a solid ball of cells forms. The cells fold over themselves and form a hollow ball of cells called the blastocyst, which contains the inner cell mass (which becomes the embryo) and an outer ring of cells called the trophoblast (which becomes the support system for the pregnancy).

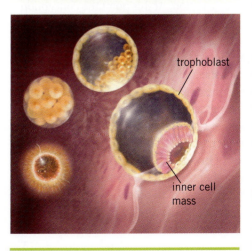

Blastocyst A hollow ball of cells that consists of the inner cell mass (which becomes the embryo) and an outer ring of cells (which becomes the placenta and chorion).

Inner cell mass A solid clump of cells in the blastocyst, which later develops into the embryo.

Trophoblast The outer ring of cells in the blastocyst that later develops into the support system for the pregnancy.

Infertility The inability to conceive within 1 year of frequent, unprotected sex.

Video Link 5.2
In vitro fertilization.

TRUE/FALSE

3. Using techniques that are available today, parents can choose the gender of their baby with 100% accuracy.

True. Gender selection is possible by using the medical technique known as *preimplantation genetic diagnosis (PGD)*. Embryos are created outside the woman's body, and only embryos of the chosen sex are implanted in the mother's womb.

Embryonic stage The prenatal stage that lasts from 2 weeks to 2 months postconception.

Embryo The developing organism from conception to the beginning of the third month of a pregnancy.

Chorion The outer fetal membrane that surrounds the fetus and gives rise to the placenta.

Amnion The inner fetal membrane that surrounds the fetus and is filled with amniotic fluid.

Placenta The organ that supports a pregnancy by bringing oxygen and nutrients to the embryo from the mother through the umbilical cord and carrying away fetal waste products.

Fetus The developing organism from the end of the eighth week after conception until birth.

Table 5.1

Infertility treatment and interventions

Female fertility drugs	Drugs can stimulate the production and release of eggs from a woman's uterus.
Artificial insemination	Sperm (from the woman's partner or from a donor) is placed in the womb at the time of ovulation. Can be used in conjunction with fertility drugs to increase the chance of success.
Gamete intrafallopian transfer	The egg and sperm are collected and placed directly in the woman's fallopian tubes so that fertilization takes place in her body, rather than in a laboratory.
In vitro fertilization	Eggs are surgically removed from a woman and mixed with a sample of sperm (from the woman's partner or a donor) to create one or more embryos, which are then placed in the uterus.
Intracytoplasmic sperm injection	If sperm count is low, the sperm are damaged, or they show poor motility, a single sperm cell that is viable can be injected directly into an egg to create an embryo.
Preimplantation genetic diagnosis	Embryos are created and tested before they are implanted in the woman's womb. Originally developed to help families at risk of having children with gender-related genetic disorders, this technique can be used to select the embryos by gender. Use solely for gender selection is highly controversial and is even against the law in some European countries.

problem for the couple. By this definition, an estimated 10% to 15% of couples in the United States are infertile (Jose-Miller, Boyden, & Frey, 2007). In about 40% of the cases the cause has something to do with female factors, in another 40% it is attributable to male factors, and in the remaining cases the cause is mutual or cannot be determined (Gordon, Rydfors, Druzin, & Tadir, 2001). Medical science today can offer infertile couples a wide range of interventions, and several of them are described in Table 5.1.

The Embryonic Stage (2 Weeks to 2 Months)

The **embryonic stage** begins at about 2 weeks postconception. At this point the conception is called an **embryo**.

The support system for the pregnancy includes two fetal membranes as well as the placenta and umbilical cord. You can think of the membranes as two sacs, one inside the other. The **chorion** is the outer one, and the connection that it establishes with the uterus gives rise to the placenta. The inner one, called the **amnion**, surrounds the developing embryo and is filled with amniotic fluid to cushion and protect the fetus during development. Early in development, before the embryo is capable of spontaneous movement, smooth muscle fibers in the amnion spontaneously contract and gently rock the embryo (Schaeberle, 2007).

The **placenta** performs the essential functions of bringing oxygen and nutrients to the developing embryo (later called a **fetus**) from the mother through the umbilical cord and carrying away fetal waste products. As shown in Figure 5.3, this transfer between the mother and the embryo occurs *without* any intermingling of the blood of the mother and the embryo (Cunningham et al., 2005). Maternal blood (which has a high concentration of oxygen and nutrients) flows into the placenta, where it fills up empty spaces. If you look carefully at Figure 5.3,

Figure 5.3

Functions of the placenta. It is within the placenta that oxygen and nutrients in the maternal blood are picked up by the fetal blood, and waste products carried in the fetal blood are released into the maternal blood to be disposed of by the mother's body.

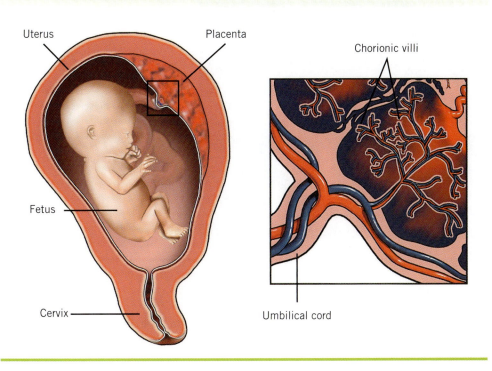

you'll see that the fetal arteries occupy these spaces, but also note that they spiral around within the spaces and then return to the fetus as a closed loop. They do *not* directly connect to the maternal arteries or veins. This is why a mother and her child can have different blood types. The two blood systems remain separate throughout the pregnancy.

Because the concentration of oxygen and nutrients in the fetal blood is low, these substances are absorbed by the fetal blood and carried back to the developing fetus. In a similar way, the waste products that are in high concentration in the fetal blood move into the spaces, where the maternal blood picks them up to transport back to the mother for disposal through her organ systems. As we will discuss later in the chapter, this "transport system" can prevent some substances from moving from the mother to the fetus because the substances are too large to pass through the walls of the arteries, but there are many substances that are potentially damaging to the developing embryo that unfortunately can move across the placenta and enter the fetal blood system.

During the embryonic stage, the inner cell mass differentiates into three layers, each of which goes on to become different organs and structures. This differentiation is shown in Figure 5.4. The outermost layer, which is called the **ectoderm** (*ecto* means "outside" or "external"), becomes the skin, the sense organs, and the brain and spinal cord. The innermost layer called the **endoderm** (*endo* means "within" or "inner") goes on to become the respiratory system, the digestive system, the liver, and the pancreas. The layer between these two other layers, the **mesoderm** (*meso* means "middle"), becomes the muscles, bones, blood, heart, kidneys, and gonads (Gilbert, 2006).

During this stage, all of the major organ systems of the body are laid down in a process called **organogenesis** (the *genesis* or beginning of the organs). By the end of this stage—which only lasts from Week 2 until Week 8 of the pregnancy—the brain and nervous system develop, a primitive heart forms and begins to beat, and limbs appear. At this point in development,

Ectoderm The outermost layer of the inner cell mass that later becomes the skin, sense organs, brain, and spinal cord.

Endoderm The innermost layer of the inner cell mass that later becomes the respiratory system, digestive system, liver, and pancreas.

Mesoderm The middle layer of the inner cell mass that later becomes the muscles, bones, blood, heart, kidney, and gonads.

Organogenesis The process in prenatal development by which all of the major organ systems of the body are laid down.

Figure 5.4

Differentiation of the inner cell mass. The cells in the inner cell mass differentiate into three different types of cell, each of which goes on to have a different function.

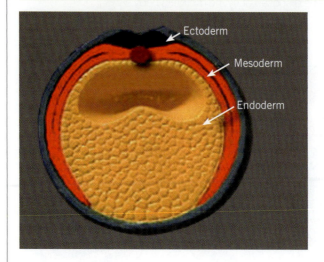

Ectoderm → skin, sense organs, brain, and spinal cord.

Mesoderm → muscles, blood, bones, and circulatory system.

Endoderm → respiratory system, digestive system, liver, and pancreas.

Cephalocaudal development
A principle whereby development proceeds from the head region down through the body.

Critical period   A period of time during which development is occurring rapidly and the organism is especially sensitive to damage, which often is severe and irreversible.

however, the sex organs are undifferentiated. Although the biological sex of the embryo is determined at conception by the chromosomal information carried in the sperm, up until this point in the pregnancy, the internal and external appearance of male and female embryos is the same (McClure & Fitch, 2005). These organs do not differentiate in their appearance until later in the pregnancy, so we'll return to them later in this chapter.

Throughout the prenatal period, development is from the head region down through the body. This is called **cephalocaudal development** (*cephalus* means "head," and *caudal* means "tail"). Throughout the pregnancy, but especially in the early months, the upper half of the embryo (and later the fetus) is more advanced than the lower half. At 9 weeks of age, the head represents about half of the entire length of the fetus because the brain is developing so rapidly that it outpaces the rest of the body.

At 4 weeks a primitive heart begins beating, and at about 5 to 6 weeks spontaneous movement begins, although the mother cannot yet feel this movement. By 8 weeks, the end of this stage of prenatal development, all of the major organs and structures of the body have been laid down and are in place. Because all the initial structures and systems undergo very rapid development within a very short period of time, it is a **critical period** for development. Anything in the prenatal environment that disrupts the process at this point can cause damage that is both severe and irreversible. That is why it is particularly important that the mother do all that she can to provide a safe and healthy prenatal environment. Unfortunately, at this point the woman may not even realize that she is pregnant. If genetic abnormalities are present in the embryo, they may result in an early miscarriage that ends the pregnancy. It is estimated that 50% to 80% of miscarriages that occur in the first trimester of a pregnancy are caused by chromosomal abnormalities and not by anything the woman has done (Simpson, 2007).

The embryo now is just over 1 inch in length and weighs less than one thirtieth of an ounce, but it is already an amazingly complex organism. Although the organ systems are formed, they will need quite a bit more time before they are developed enough to become functional and can do the work they are intended to do.

The Fetal Stage (2 Months to Birth)

From the beginning of the third month until the baby is born is the third stage of prenatal development, the **fetal stage**. This stage is characterized by the continued growth of the fetus and a remarkable increase in size and weight. All of the organ systems need to complete their development and become functional so that the newborn will be capable of surviving independently of the mother after birth.

Fetal stage The prenatal stage that lasts from 2 months postconception until birth.

One particularly significant event during this period is the transformation of the genitalia of the fetus into male or female genitalia. Remember that up to this point, the development of males and females has followed the same pathway, but at 9 weeks the testes of a male fetus begin to produce the male hormone *androgen*, and that hormone alters the development of the genitalia from that point on (McClure & Fitch, 2005). Without the production of androgen, the genitalia of female fetuses continue along their developmental pathway, and a female reproductive system is laid down. Hormones produced prenatally not only shape the physical development of the fetus; they also influence the development of the brain. At 26 weeks, differences between male and female brains already can be seen in an ultrasound scan (Achiron, Lipitz, & Achiron, 2001), but we should remember that there are many more similarities than differences between male and female brains, and many other factors, such as experiences later in life, affect the formation of boys' and girls' brains. It is not clear to us yet what the differences in prenatal brain formation mean for later development (Lips, 2006).

At about 10 weeks, fetal breathing movements begin, although there is no air in the amniotic sac to breathe. Instead fetuses breathe in and then expel amniotic fluid. Fetuses that are 24 to 28 weeks old breathe about 14% of the time, and this rate increases to about 30% of the time in 32- to 40-week-old fetuses (Kisilevsky & Low, 1998). However, there is a decrease in this activity during the 3 days prior to the beginning of labor, and the activity ceases during the active phase of labor and doesn't resume until the newborn takes a first breath of air.

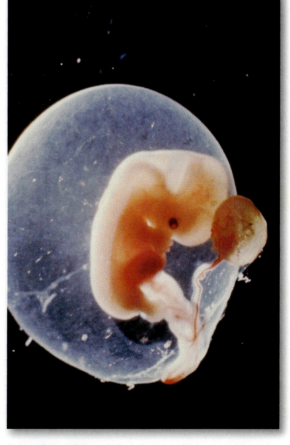

Between Week 12 and Week 16, most women will begin to feel the movement of the fetus. At first it feels like a light fluttering, and first-time mothers may mistake it for digestive functioning. However, as time goes on, the movement becomes more and more marked. By a gestational age of 20 weeks, fetuses have been recorded moving more than 50 times in a single 50-minute session (DiPietro et al., 2004). Fetal movement continues to decline from this point until the baby is born, and rest-activity cycles appear midway through the pregnancy (de Medina, Visser, Huizink, Buitelaar, & Mulder, 2003). In research, the level of fetal activity at a gestational age of 36 weeks was found to predict activity level of boys at 1 year of age (DiPietro et al., 2002; Groome et al., 1999). It appears that an active fetus is likely to become an active baby, at least for boys.

At 32 weeks, the fetus spends between 90% and 95% of its time sleeping (Hopson, 1998), but it still develops quite a repertoire of activities prior to birth. We have learned a great deal in recent years about behavioral competencies that develop prenatally so that the newborn enters the world ready to begin interacting with the world.

Embryonic development. At 6 weeks postconception, you can see that a primitive heart has formed in this embryo. You also can see how the cephalocaudal principle affects prenatal development. The head and arms are considerably more developed than the lower parts of the body.

Although the fetus is protected from extreme stimulation within its uterine environment, it is not isolated from the sensory world. In fact, it interacts with a complex intrauterine environment (Smotherman & Robinson, 1996), and by the time the baby is born, all of the senses are functional to some extent (Hopkins & Johnson, 2005). The cutaneous senses (or "skin senses" such as touch and pain) and the proprioceptive senses (the ones that detect motion or the position of the body) are the first to develop. Dr. Heidelise Als, a developmental psychologist at Harvard Medical School, has commented on the amount of tactile stimulation the fetus gives itself. She has said, "It touches a hand to the face, one hand to the other hand, clasps its foot, touches its foot to its legs, its hand to its umbilical cord" (Hopson, 1998, p. 45). The cutaneous senses are followed by the chemical senses such as smell and taste and the vestibular senses (your sense of equilibrium and balance). The last to develop are the auditory and visual senses (Lecanuet, Graniere-Deferre, & DeCasper, 2005). The intrauterine environment provides at least some stimulation for all these senses. For instance, acoustic stimuli can be transmitted through the mother's abdomen to provide auditory stimulation (Smotherman & Robinson, 1996). Amniotic fluid carries chemosensory molecules that stimulate the smell and taste receptors, and movement of the fetus stimulates the vestibular senses (Lecanuet et al., 2005).

What we see throughout the prenatal period is a great deal of continuity as systems develop and later become functional. This prepares the newborn to begin interacting with—and responding to—the environment almost immediately after birth. We'll return to this point and look further at the capabilities of newborns in Chapter 6, but before we leave this topic, there is a word of caution. We have learned a great deal about the fetus's prenatal sensory experiences and now even have evidence that some simple forms of learning can occur before birth. These are all positive signs of an intact and functional central nervous system, but Lecanuet et al. (2005) caution that we should not presume that prenatal differences in stimulation are related to later differences in cognitive functioning. The research on prenatal sensory capabilities has led to the development and marketing of a variety of gadgets that purport to stimulate neural growth or to facilitate learning, memory, thinking, and even social interaction. However, these respected researchers say that this shows a lack of understanding of the meaning of the research. In their view, stimulation that goes beyond what is normally provided to the developing fetus is *not* necessarily better and could, in fact, even be harmful. The sounds of a mother's everyday conversation and the internal sounds of her body are enough stimulation for now.

There are many other common beliefs about pregnancy that have been handed down from generation to generation. Test yourself by answering the questions in **Active Learning: Old Wives' Tale or Scientific Fact?** to see which of these ideas have a scientific basis and which do not.

TRUE/FALSE

4. Research has shown that exposing a fetus to extra stimulation (for example, playing music near the woman's stomach) can stimulate advanced cognitive development.

False. Although a fetus is able to hear and even respond to sounds prior to birth, there is no evidence that stimulation beyond the level provided by the natural prenatal environment has any extra cognitive benefits.

ACTIVE LEARNING

Old Wives' Tale or Scientific Fact?

Throughout this book we are asking you to test your commonsense or intuitive knowledge of development against what we know about it scientifically. There are probably more old wives' tales about pregnancy than about any other period in development. Which of the following statements about pregnancy are *true*, and which are *false*?

1. True/False: A fast fetal heart rate means you are having a girl.
2. True/False: When you are pregnant, you are eating for two.
3. True/False: You shouldn't dye your hair while you are pregnant.
4. True/False: Don't jog while you are pregnant.
5. True/False: For each baby, you will lose a tooth.

6. True/False: Having sex while you are pregnant will hurt the baby.
7. True/False: Women may have difficulty concentrating in the first 3 months of a pregnancy.
8. True/False: Pregnant women have a special glow.
9. True/False: Your hair will fall out after your pregnancy.

SOURCES: Gardephe & Ettlinger (1993); KidsHealth (2008).

Answers:

1. False. Fetal heart rate changes with the amount of fetal activity but does not differ by gender.
2. True. But you need to remember that the second person you are "eating for" probably weighs 8 pounds or less! That means that an additional 300 calories a day on average is all the extra calories that you need to consume.
3. True. Chemicals that are used in hair dyes can penetrate the scalp and enter the mother's bloodstream, so they can cross the placenta. For that reason it is probably best to not use hair coloring during a pregnancy (especially in the early months) or to use only natural coloring such as henna.
4. Probably true. We say "probably true" because a woman who was an avid runner before becoming pregnant can probably safely continue the activity, but the ligaments and tendons in a woman's body become softer, her breasts enlarge, and her center of gravity shifts during her pregnancy, so there is increased risk for the pregnant casual runner. These women should consult their physicians about whether they can continue running. For these women, other physical activity, like swimming or walking, might be a better choice.
5. False. You need 50% more calcium in your diet while you are pregnant, but it will come from your bones, not your teeth, if your dietary intake is not adequate.
6. False. The baby is protected within the amniotic sac, so sexual activity should not affect it. However, because membranes can rupture later in a pregnancy, using a condom near the end of a pregnancy to guard against infection is a good precaution.
7. True. Fatigue, morning sickness, and preoccupation with the pregnancy itself can make a woman forgetful early in her pregnancy.
8. True. The woman's body produces a great volume of blood to support the pregnancy, which results in more blood flow in the vessels and an increase in oil gland secretions. This could be responsible for the "glow" that we associate with pregnancy.
9. True. Hormones secreted during a pregnancy cause hair to grow faster and fall out less, but the hormonal changes that follow the birth of the baby can cause a significant amount of hair to fall out as the body readjusts.

Health and Risks in Pregnancy

Three Trimesters of Pregnancy

We have described the three stages of prenatal development: germinal, embryonic, and fetal. However, from the point of view of the pregnant woman, the 9 months of pregnancy are divided in a different way. Each 3-month period is called a trimester, and each has its own characteristics. During the first trimester it may not be apparent to other people that the woman is pregnant, but changes in the level of her hormones may cause certain effects, including fatigue, breast tenderness, and "morning sickness," which is nausea that often subsides as the day progresses. In the second trimester, the pregnancy begins to become apparent as the fetus grows larger. The woman now is able to feel the fetus moving inside of her (called the *quickening*). By the third trimester the fetus is growing larger, and the woman becomes more tired and uncomfortable (Chye, Teng, Hao, & Seng, 2008). At the end of this time she will experience the fetus dropping lower within her, as it begins to get into position to begin the birth process.

You can learn much about pregnancy from a woman who has gone through it. Use the guidelines in **Active Learning: An Interview With a Mother** to talk with your own mother or with another woman who has gone through pregnancy.

An Interview With a Mother

If possible, interview your mother about her experiences when she was pregnant with you. Jog her memory by finding old photos or baby books. Ask about her experiences during each of the three trimesters. If your mother is not available, you can interview another woman about her experiences. If you yourself have given birth, write a journal of your prenatal experiences or allow yourself to be interviewed by someone else in your class.

One note of warning: Interviewing your mother can become a very emotional experience for you and your mother. Often people share a new feeling of closeness; however, occasionally people might find out about something that is disturbing. If this does happen to you, be sure that you are comfortable talking with someone close to you or a counselor at your college's health services to help you cope with your feelings. Remember also that although the process of prenatal development is universal, individuals experience each pregnancy in unique ways, so in this activity you are looking at the experiences of a single individual.

The Expectant Father

Many changes also occur for a man when he learns that he is about to become a father, although these are primarily psychological and emotional changes rather than physical ones. Throughout the pregnancy there is much that he can do to help his partner. He can help her to choose a healthy diet, encourage her to get enough rest and appropriate amounts of exercise, and support her as she deals with the emotional and physical changes of pregnancy. If a man takes the time to learn about the physical changes of pregnancy, he can better understand the mood swings, nausea, fatigue, and breast tenderness that often occur early in a woman's pregnancy or the fatigue, indigestion, and physical discomfort that occur in late pregnancy. Many men accompany their partners to doctor's appointments or childbirth classes and actively prepare for the birth process. By nurturing and caring for his partner during her pregnancy, he shows that he is preparing to be nurturing with his newborn child.

Anthropologists have observed a phenomenon called **couvade** (from the French word *couver*, meaning "to hatch") in men from different cultures around the world (Brennan, Marshall-Lucette, Ayers, & Ahmed, 2007; Chernella, 1991). In ritualistic *couvade*, a man experiences a sympathetic pregnancy while his partner is pregnant. In some cases this involves the man feigning contractions and labor pains at the same time that the mother is in labor. In the modern world, a type of psychosomatic couvade occurs in which men experience a variety of symptoms associated with pregnancy, including weight gain, nausea, indigestion, backaches, mood swings, and food cravings. These are actually fairly common occurrences. Between 11% and 65% of husbands of pregnant women report such symptoms (Bartlett, 2004; Masoni, Trimarchi, dePunzio, & Fioretti, 1994). Anxiety about the impending birth, empathy or sympathy with the man's partner, guilt for having impregnated the woman, and even jealousy of the woman's capability of giving birth have all been suggested as possible explanations for this phenomenon.

Miscarriage

Unfortunately it is not an uncommon occurrence for a pregnancy to result in **miscarriage**, which is the natural loss of a pregnancy before 20 weeks gestational age of the fetus (Branch

Couvade A sympathetic pregnancy in which a man experiences a variety of symptoms associated with pregnancy or childbirth while his partner is pregnant.

Miscarriage The natural loss of a pregnancy before the fetus reaches a gestational age of 20 weeks.

& Scott, 2003). Most miscarriages occur during the early weeks of a pregnancy, before the woman even knows that she is pregnant. On the other hand, women who know they are pregnant and miscarry a wanted pregnancy experience a real sense of loss that should be acknowledged.

As we mentioned earlier, genetic abnormalities are the most common cause of miscarriage. Errors in the genes or chromosomes may not allow the fetus to develop normally, so growth stops and a miscarriage results. However, in many cases the cause of miscarriage is unknown. In most cases, women who have a miscarriage are able to have children through a future pregnancy. However, there are some factors that make miscarriage more likely, and we will discuss some of these factors in the following sections as we discuss threats to a full-term pregnancy.

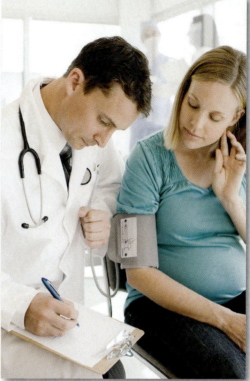

Prenatal care. Regular visits to a doctor throughout a woman's pregnancy are an essential part of prenatal care. The doctor will monitor that the pregnancy is progressing normally and that the woman remains in good health.

Maternal Health and Well-Being

Seeing a physician on a regular basis, beginning early in the pregnancy, is one of the best things that a woman can do to avoid problems later on. In fact, starting to take good care of yourself even before you become pregnant is a very good idea. According to the Maternal and Child Health Bureau of the U.S. Department of Health and Human Services (n.d.a), babies who are born to mothers who have not received prenatal care are 3 times more likely to be born at a low birth weight and 5 times more likely to die in the first year of life compared to babies born to mothers who have received prenatal care.

Most women see their doctor for the first time between 2 and 4 weeks after they have missed a period. Typically in the United States women see their doctors about every 4 weeks through their second trimester, and then see them every 2 weeks until they are a month away from their due date, when they move to having weekly visits. Women who have chronic conditions, such as diabetes, asthma, or allergies, may need to see their health care provider more frequently or may be referred to a physician who specializes in high-risk pregnancies. They also may need to eliminate or change the dosage of any medication they are taking, especially in the early months of their pregnancy, but these changes should only be made in careful consultation with a physician. There is more information on the use of medication while pregnant later in this chapter.

Although the United States spends about twice as much per person on health care as any other country, Americans' maternal health and infant health are *not* the best in the world (Kaiser Family Foundation, 2007). As you can see in Figure 5.5, the percentage of women receiving what is considered by the National Center for Health Statistics to be adequate prenatal care or better differs from one state to another, and even in the top-ranked states it is not 100% of women who are receiving good prenatal care.

In 2005, the lifetime risk of a woman's death from pregnancy-related problems was 1 out of 2,500 for the United States. If you think those are good odds, you should know that they are worse than those of 26 other industrialized countries, including Switzerland, Lithuania, Japan, Ireland, and Portugal (UNICEF, 2007). In addition, there is a significant racial disparity in the rates of maternal death in the United States. In 2004, White women averaged 9.3 maternal deaths per 100,000 while Black women averaged 34.7, more than 3 times the rate of White women (Miniño, Heron, Murphy, & Kochanek, 2007).

Video Link 5.3
Early prenatal visit.

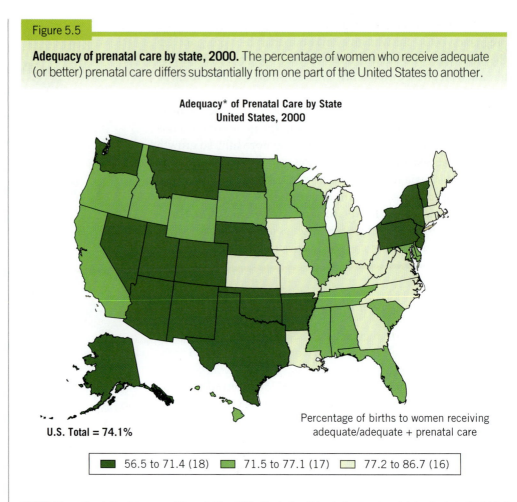

Figure 5.5

Adequacy of prenatal care by state, 2000. The percentage of women who receive adequate (or better) prenatal care differs substantially from one part of the United States to another.

Adequacy* of Prenatal Care by State
United States, 2000

U.S. Total = 74.1%

Percentage of births to women receiving adequate/adequate + prenatal care

| ■ 56.5 to 71.4 (18) | ■ 71.5 to 77.1 (17) | □ 77.2 to 86.7 (16) |

NOTES: *According to the Adequacy of Prenatal Care Utilization Index. Value in () = number of states (includes District of Columbia). Value ranges are based on an equal number of items in each range

Maternal Diet

Adequate nutrition and a well-balanced diet are essential for both a mother and her baby during a pregnancy. However, the developing baby is so small relative to the size of the mother that an average of 300 extra calories a day is all that is needed to support prenatal growth (Katz, 2003), with fewer calories required early in the pregnancy and more calories required nearer to the time for delivery. The recommended weight gain for women who begin their pregnancy at a normal weight is 25 to 35 pounds (Katz, 2003). Women who are underweight at the beginning of their pregnancy can safely gain a bit more, and women who are overweight should gain less, although this is *not* a good time to severely restrict your calories. The goal is a newborn that weighs between 7 and 8 pounds for Caucasian babies and slightly less for newborns of African or Asian descent (Olds, London, & Ladewig, 2002). Infants who are born smaller than average for their gestational age are more vulnerable to infections, and those who are much larger than average increase the length of the labor and difficulties in the delivery itself. In cases where a mother is malnourished—and by that we mean that she has a severely restricted diet, not just a less-than-optimal one—the negative consequences are severe and long-lasting, affecting both the structure of the infant's brain (its size and the number of neurons and connections in it) and its functions (including varying degrees of retardation and learning disabilities) (Morgane et al., 1993).

The nutritional recommendations for pregnant women look very much like any well-balanced diet. Eating four to six smaller meals, rather than three larger ones, can help the woman avoid morning sickness early in her pregnancy or heartburn later on. The diet should include food from the five food groups and six to eight glasses of water, juice, or milk each day, with only a limited amount of fatty food, empty calories, and caffeine (U.S. Department of Agriculture, 2009b). Pregnant women are advised to limit their caffeine intake to 200 milligrams a day (Katz, 2003). This is the amount of caffeine found in one 12-ounce cup of coffee, although the caffeine content of coffee can differ quite a bit depending on the brand of coffee and how it is prepared. Although moderate caffeine intake is usually considered safe, some studies have reported a relationship between 3 cups of coffee daily and miscarriage, so restricting caffeine consumption is a good precaution (Katz, 2003). Caffeine also can come from tea, chocolate, soda, and any other foods containing chocolate, so their consumption also should be limited or eliminated from the diet.

Because pregnant women need to be sure that their diet has an adequate amount of vitamins and minerals, doctors usually prescribe a multivitamin or prenatal vitamin. Folic acid, which is one of the B vitamins, plays an important role in preventing defects of the brain and spinal cord, so it is a good idea for women who are planning on becoming pregnant to be sure their diet contains an adequate amount of this essential vitamin even before they become pregnant (Chye et al., 2008). Folate, the form of folic acid that occurs naturally in foods, is found in fortified breakfast cereals, enriched grain products, beans and leafy green vegetables, and orange juice, but it also is available as a food supplement. Doctors also may recommend iron or calcium supplements (Katz, 2003).

Healthy eating while pregnant. Healthy eating is always important, but it is particularly important while you are pregnant. The mother's diet provides all of the nutrients that her developing child needs. Avoiding foods that can be harmful is equally essential.

What makes the topic of prenatal diet a bit trickier is that while there are specific things that should be included in the woman's diet, there also are things that must be avoided because of risks associated with them. For instance, soft cheeses such as Brie or feta or uncooked hot dogs and luncheon meats can contain bacteria, and certain fish including shark and swordfish may have high levels of mercury or industrial pollutants (Chye et al., 2008). Most books written for pregnant women contain detailed information on how to have a safe and healthy diet while pregnant.

Recent research on prenatal development in primates has shown that a subtle type of prenatal programming can occur in the womb, which leaves the infant vulnerable to experiences that occur after birth (Coe & Lubach, 2008). For example, when a mother's diet is inadequate for a sustained portion of the pregnancy, infants who are later raised in an environment where there is abundant food are more prone to obesity. Starvation lowers your basal metabolic rate (the rate at which you use energy when you are resting), so having a lower basal metabolic rate means that you will burn calories more slowly. Infants who are "starved" prenatally are programmed to burn calories more slowly after they are born, placing them at greater risk of obesity and potentially of diabetes later in development.

Teratogens Agents that can disrupt prenatal development and cause malformations or termination of the pregnancy.

Teratogens

Unfortunately there are a number of things that can have a negative impact on prenatal development. They are broadly referred to as **teratogens**, or agents that can cause malformations in an embryo or a fetus. They include diseases that a mother has or contracts during her pregnancy (such as rubella, syphilis, or HIV), things that the mother ingests (such as alcohol, medication, or drugs), and toxins in the environment (such as mercury in the foods she eats or exposure to X-rays or environmental pollution).

There seems to be an almost endless list of potential teratogens, so we can only talk briefly about some of the most common ones in this chapter. However, before we turn our attention to the details, this is a good time to remind you again that early and continuous prenatal care is the best preventative strategy. A pregnant woman should regularly see a physician who can answer her questions and provide her with sound medical advice throughout her pregnancy. In addition to avoiding substances that can be harmful to the baby (which is *essential*), a woman can also do many proactive things that help ensure her good health throughout the pregnancy, like eating well, getting an appropriate amount of exercise, and getting enough rest.

Each teratogen has a specific effect on the developing embryo or fetus and can result in a structural abnormality, such as missing or malformed limbs, or a functional deficit, such as hearing loss or mental retardation. The level of the impairment also can range from mild to severe. The nature and magnitude of the effect depends upon *when* in the prenatal period the fetus or embryo is exposed to the teratogen, the *amount* or dosage of the exposure, and the *length of time* the exposure continues. For example, an exposure that could end a pregnancy if it occurred early in the germinal period might produce serious physical defects if it occurred during the embryonic period but result in much less severe defects if it occurred late in the fetal period.

The effect of a woman contracting rubella (or German measles) at different points in her pregnancy provides a good illustration of this point. The effect of rubella on an adult woman is rather mild, but its effects on a pregnancy can be devastating. Exposure to rubella in the first 11 weeks of the pregnancy results in birth defects that include significant problems with vision, hearing, and the functioning of the heart in 90% of the cases, but exposure later in the pregnancy results in 20% of infants born with congenital defects (Reef & Redd, 2008). Fortunately rubella rarely occurs in the United States because children are routinely vaccinated for the disease (Zimmerman & Reef, 2001). However, this is not the case in other parts of the world. For instance, in Europe over 300,000 cases of rubella were reported in 2003 (Pandolfi, Chiaradia, Moncada, Rava, & Tozzi, 2009), so most of the cases of maternal rubella in the United States occur among foreign-born residents who came to the United States from countries that do not have vaccination programs (Zimmerman & Reef, 2001). Rubella continues to be a threat to fetal development in other parts of the world.

TRUE/FALSE

5. Excessive drinking while a woman is pregnant can cause Down syndrome.

False. Excessive drinking is associated with *fetal alcohol syndrome*, not Down syndrome. Down syndrome is the result of a chromosomal abnormality.

Fetal alcohol syndrome (FAS) A condition in the child resulting from heavy or binge consumption of alcohol during a pregnancy; associated with characteristic facial features, small stature, and a small head, as well as cognitive deficits and trouble controlling behavior and regulating emotions.

Alcohol and Smoking. Alcohol should not be a part of a pregnant woman's diet, and smoking is never a good idea. When you drink an alcoholic beverage—whether it is beer, wine, or hard liquor—the alcohol in it enters your bloodstream and circulates through your system until your liver can break it down over the next couple of hours and it can pass from your system. During that time, because the concentration of alcohol in a pregnant woman's bloodstream is higher than the concentration in the fetal blood, the alcohol crosses the placenta and does damage to the developing embryo or fetus. The relatively small size of the embryo, together with the fact that vital organ systems may be in critical stages of development, helps explain why even a small amount of alcohol can be a problem. The effect of alcohol on a 120-pound woman is different from the effect on a 1- or 2-pound fetus.

The most clear-cut effect of alcohol on a pregnancy is seen in children born to women who have consumed large quantities of alcohol (usually defined as 4 to 5 drinks a day or 7 to 14 drinks a week) throughout their pregnancy or who have had occasional bouts of binge drinking (defined as having 5 or more drinks at one time). In this case, the result can be **fetal alcohol syndrome (FAS)**. Physical characteristics associated with fetal alcohol syndrome include

Facial characteristics of children with fetal alcohol syndrome. These photos show some of the facial features that are characteristic in children with fetal alcohol syndrome, including a smooth ridge between the nose and upper lip, a thin upper lip, wide-spaced eyes, underdeveloped ears, and an upturned nose with a flat bridge.

SOURCE: © Susan Astley, PhD, University of Washington.

abnormal facial features, small stature, and a small head. These children also have a number of cognitive deficits that include problems with learning, memory, and attention span (Centers for Disease Control and Prevention [CDC], 2006), as well as trouble controlling their behavior and regulating their emotions. FAS represents the extreme end of a continuum of problems known as **fetal alcohol spectrum disorders (FASDs)**, which can include any subset of characteristics of FAS at varying levels of severity and other more subtle or functional deficits that include difficulty with abstract thinking, poor problem-solving skills, mood swings, or being defensive or stubborn (CDC, 2006). According to the Centers for Disease Control and Prevention (2006), fetal alcohol syndrome is the leading preventable cause of mental retardation and birth defects. Our understanding of how alcohol affects a pregnancy is described in **Journey of Research: Understanding the Effects of Alcohol on a Pregnancy**.

The effects of prenatal exposure to alcohol are permanent and irreversible. Although stopping drinking at any point in a pregnancy prevents further damage, it does *not* reverse the harm that has already been done. Although the estimated incidence of FAS differs depending upon the population studied and the way the condition is identified and assessed, the Centers for Disease Control and Prevention (2006) estimate the incidence at 0.2 to 1.5 per 1,000 live births, with FASDs occurring at 3 times that rate. There are intervention programs that can help improve the functioning of children born with FAS and FASDs, but this is a completely preventable condition and, in this case, an ounce of prevention is worth more than a pound of cure.

Fetal alcohol spectrum disorders (FASDs) A range of impairments in a child resulting from consumption of alcohol during a pregnancy; associated with any subset of characteristics of fetal alcohol syndrome at varying levels of severity and other more subtle or functional deficits.

Video Link 5.4
Child with FAS.

Understanding the Effects of Alcohol on a Pregnancy

People have suspected that alcohol has a negative impact on pregnancies for a very long time. Even the ancient Greeks and Romans suspected there was a link and warned couples against being intoxicated at the time a child was conceived (Calhoun & Warren, 2006). However, they believed that it was intoxication at the time of conception, rather than during the pregnancy itself, that was a problem and thought that the father's intoxication could have as much, if not more, of an effect than the mother's intoxication.

One of the first mentions of concern in the medical literature appeared in the 1700s, when a group of physicians in England described women alcoholics giving birth to children who were "weak, feeble, and distempered" (Calhoun & Warren, 2006, p. 169). In 1899 an English deputy medical examiner noted that alcoholic mothers had an increased risk of having a child who was stillborn. Based on his observations, he concluded that alcohol had a direct toxic effect on the embryo.

These early observations linking alcohol and birth defects were largely ignored by the medical

JOURNEY *of*
RESEARCH

(Continued)

(Continued)

community until a group of French researchers published a paper in the 1960s describing some commonly occurring problems noted in the offspring of a group of 100 women who drank heavily during their pregnancy (Calhoun & Warren, 2006). This was followed by a series of papers published in the 1970s by British researchers who identified the shared anomalies among children born to chronic alcoholic mothers. They concluded that alcohol was the cause of these anomalies and coined the term *fetal alcohol syndrome* (Calhoun & Warren, 2006). As interest in this topic took hold, research examined other factors that contributed to the problems seen in children born to alcoholic mothers. In addition to drinking, these women likely were doing a number of things that negatively affected their pregnancy. They may have smoked, been malnourished, received no prenatal care, or had untreated medical conditions.

As public concern continued to grow, the U.S. Food and Drug Administration issued a bulletin in 1977 that discouraged "binge" or "chronic, excessive" drinking during pregnancy (Bobo, Klepinger, & Dong, 2006, p. 1062). A decade later the federal Alcoholic Beverage Labeling Act was passed. The act required that alcoholic beverages carry a warning that they should not be consumed during a pregnancy because of the risk of birth defects. Several health initiatives since then have tried to inform women of this danger. In 2005, the Surgeon General updated an advisory originally issued in 1981 that suggested that pregnant women "*limit* [emphasis added] the amount of alcohol they drink" by saying that "*no amount* [emphasis added] of alcohol consumption can be considered safe during a pregnancy" and warning women that alcohol can damage the fetus at any stage in a pregnancy (U.S. Department of Health and Human Services [USDHHS], 2005b).

Because so much development occurs in the weeks before a woman realizes she is pregnant and because nearly one half of all pregnancies in the United States are unplanned (Centers for Disease Control and Prevention, 2005a), abstaining from alcohol if you are sexually active even before you become pregnant is a good idea.

The good news is that a great deal has been done in recent years to inform women about these risks and the healthy choices they can make. How successful have these efforts been? If you look at Figure 5.6, you will see the results from a study that followed 6,283 females from 1979 to 1995 (Bobo et al., 2006). Although drinking while pregnant has declined among all groups studied since the early 1980s, 23% of the sample in 1994–1995 still reported drinking while pregnant. A more recent report from the National Survey on Drug Use and Health (USDHHS, 2008b) found that almost 16% of the pregnant women surveyed said that they had consumed alcohol during the previous month. Although there has been progress and we clearly are on the right path, we still have a way to go on this journey.

Figure 5.6

Incidence of alcohol use during pregnancy (1982–1995). The percentage of pregnant women who report drinking during their pregnancy has changed from 1982 to 1995. Although there has been a significant decline, 1 in 8 pregnant women in 2007 reported that they had consumed alcohol during the previous month. How could we do a better job of informing pregnant women about the dangers of consuming alcohol during their pregnancies?

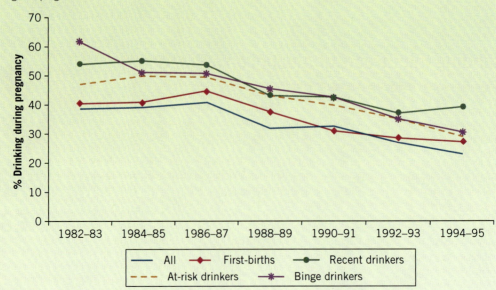

Drinking during pregnancy among all births, first births, and births among recent, binge, and at-risk drinkers, National Longitudinal Survey of Labor Market Experiences in Youth (NLSY) cohort. Percentages based on weighted data, Cochran-Armitage trend test (2-tailed) for all comparisons: $p < 0.0001$.

Another source of developmental risk that is totally preventable is maternal smoking, as well as exposure to secondhand smoke during a pregnancy (CDC, 2000, 2007c; Rogers, 2009). Cigarette smoke contains over 4,000 chemicals, including formaldehyde, arsenic, and lead, and the more a woman smokes, the greater her risk of having a low-birth-weight baby (Rogers, 2009). As a woman smokes, the level of carbon monoxide in her blood increases, and this reduces the capacity of her blood to carry oxygen. Because the nicotine in the smoke constricts the blood vessels, this further limits the flow of oxygen and nutrients to the fetus through the placenta. Also, nicotine is an addictive substance that tends to suppress appetite, so pregnant smokers eat less. All of these factors contribute to the growth retardation that is so strongly associated with babies born to smokers.

Smoking also has been associated with an increased risk of miscarriage, premature birth, low birth weight, and sudden infant death (Shea & Steiner, 2008). The effects are so pervasive that Jauniaux and Greenough (2007) recently made the claim that in many countries smoking has replaced poverty as the most important risk factor for all these negative pregnancy-related outcomes. In their estimation, smoking while pregnant costs the United States $250 million in direct medical costs each year, and they predict that a reduction of just 1% in smoking prevalence would lower the incidence of babies born at low birth weight by 1,300 infants each year. A report compiled by the Surgeon General of the United States echoes this claim by estimating that eliminating maternal smoking could result in "a 10% reduction in all infant deaths and a 12% reduction in deaths from **perinatal** [that is, 'at the time of birth'] conditions" (CDC, 2000, para. 10).

Perinatal   At the time of birth.

The negative effects are not restricted to the prenatal period. Maternal smoking while pregnant has been identified as a major contributor to later developmental problems including attention deficit hyperactivity disorder, conduct disorders, and learning disabilities (Rogers, 2009; Shea & Steiner, 2008; Slotkin, 2008). Exposure to prenatal nicotine alters the trajectory of brain development in ways that contribute to functional deficits throughout a child's life span, with the effects being more pronounced in male brains than in female brains (Slotkin, 2008) and in children from low-income families (Rauh et al., 2004).

The situation as it now stands is a mixture of good news and bad news. While smoking has decreased among the general population over the last couple of decades, it has decreased at a slower rate among young women ages 19 to 29 than among other groups, and according to the Centers for Disease Control and Prevention (2000), between 12% and 22% of women still smoke while they are pregnant. That's the bad news. The good news is that when women stop smoking, even as late as the second trimester of their pregnancy, the weight and body measurements of their infants are comparable to those of infants whose mothers were nonsmokers (American Congress of Obstetricians and Gynecologists [ACOG], 2005; CDC, 2000). Just a little more bad news before we leave this topic: Babies born to mothers who smoke during their pregnancy appear to undergo withdrawal symptoms similar to those seen in babies born to mothers addicted to illicit drugs (Law et al., 2003), and maternal smoking during a pregnancy is a strong predictor of whether or not adolescents begin smoking and become addicted themselves, regardless of whether their parents smoked during their childhood (Abreu-Villac, Seidler, Tate, Cousins, & Slotkin, 2004).

Prescription and Over-the-Counter Drugs. It is difficult to make general statements about the use of drugs (either prescription medications or over-the-counter drugs) except to say that nothing should be used while a woman is pregnant unless it is necessary and the woman has consulted her physician about the usage. This is a complex decision because the potential effect of drugs on a pregnancy depends upon the specific type of medication that is used, when in the pregnancy it is taken, for how long it is used, and its dosage. A woman and her doctor need to weigh the potential benefits from using the drugs against the possible risks for the fetus. To see how safe your own medications would be for a pregnant woman, try **Active Learning: Safety of Medications During Pregnancy**.

ACTIVE LEARNING

Safety of Medications During Pregnancy

Do you know whether the medications that are in your medicine cabinet right now are safe for use during pregnancy? Make a list of all of your medications (both prescription and over-the-counter medications), vitamins, and herbal supplements, and check their safety.

You can start by visiting your campus library where there are reference books that will help you. The *Physicians' Desk Reference* (PDR Staff, 2010a) is a book that contains the information that you usually get from the insert that comes with your prescription when you pick it up at a pharmacy, including any warnings or contraindications for the drug's use. There also is a separate volume of the *Physicians' Desk Reference* (PDR Staff, 2010b) that deals specifically with nonprescription drugs, dietary supplements, and herbal medicines. Some of these volumes may be available to you electronically through the PDR Network website (PDR Network, 2009a, 2009b, 2010).

You also can search the Internet by typing the name of a specific drug and the word *pregnancy* to see if there are any advisories against its use. If you do this, however, please be sure that you pay attention to the credentials of the site you are using. Sites maintained by the Centers for Disease Control and Prevention, the National Institutes of Health, or the American Congress of Obstetricians and Gynecologists will give you information you can trust.

After you complete your search, take some time to think about what a pregnant woman would need to consider when weighing the benefits resulting from the use of these medications and supplements against the potential risk to her pregnancy and developing fetus.

If a medication is going to be harmful, it is most likely to be harmful in the early weeks of the pregnancy during that critical period in development, but there are some medications that should never be used during a pregnancy. They include the drug Accutane that is used to treat acne (Honein, Paulozzi, & Erickson, 2001), Soriatane that is used to treat the skin condition of psoriasis (Stiefel Laboratories, 2008), and thalidomide (Ito et al., 2010). Soriatane can be harmful if used up to 3 years before the woman becomes pregnant. In recent years, the drug thalidomide has been used to treat multiple myeloma, complications of AIDS, and leprosy, but if used during a pregnancy, it can have devastating effects on a developing fetus, including missing or malformed arms and legs.

When a woman has an infection or a chronic condition such as asthma, diabetes, or high blood pressure, continuing to take her medication may be necessary during her pregnancy. For example, women who are diabetic have an increased risk of miscarriage, stillbirths, and some birth defects if they do not effectively control their glucose level while they are pregnant (Cunningham et al., 2005). For women living with AIDS, the Centers for Disease Control and Prevention (1994) recommends continuing to use zidovudine (also known as AZT) during pregnancy because it lowers the risk that she will pass HIV to her unborn child. Although there also is a large body of research on the use of antidepressants during pregnancy, the findings about the effects of these drugs on the fetus have been mixed (Field, 2007).

Pregnancy normally brings with it some discomforts, such as backaches, nausea, or heartburn. Pregnant women also catch colds and get the flu. It is best if the woman avoids using over-the-counter medications to relieve these symptoms. Because most herbal remedies and food supplements have not been tested by the U.S. Food and Drug Administration for safety, it is best to avoid them completely during a pregnancy. Again, if a woman wants to use any of these products, she should discuss this decision with her physician first.

Illegal Drugs. It is difficult to conduct research on the effect of illegal drugs on a human pregnancy because it is difficult to get accurate information from mothers who are using illegal

Video Link 5.5
Thalidomide.

substances about the amount or type of drugs they use, or the length of time they have used them. It also is difficult to disentangle the effect of the drugs themselves from the effect of other things that might be going on that negatively affect the pregnancy. A woman who is using illegal drugs may be less likely to see a doctor during her pregnancy or may not see a doctor early in her pregnancy, and she may be less likely to take good care of herself in other ways.

Despite these difficulties, there has been a good deal of research on the effect of marijuana and cocaine on pregnancies in recent years. Newborns who have been exposed to cocaine prenatally show signs of withdrawal several weeks after they are born (Field, 2007). They also are at an increased risk for problems with motor development as newborns. In infancy they are more likely to have problems with information processing and language development and to have other neurological and cognitive deficits (Field, 2007). Prenatal exposure can also affect how the infant interacts with his or her parents after birth. Infants rely upon crying to signal distress. However, infants who were prenatally exposed to cocaine are less clear in the signals they send (Field, 2007). When mothers who currently were or were not using cocaine listened to a recording of infant cries, the mothers using cocaine rated the cries as less aversive and less urgent sounding. These mothers also said they would be less likely to pick up or feed the infant in response to the cries and more likely to just "wait and see" before responding (Schuetze, Zeskind, & Eiden, 2003). Providing adequate care to an infant obviously is more difficult for women who continue their use of cocaine after their babies are born.

Marijuana is the most commonly used illicit drug in the United States among women in their childbearing years, with 2.9% of women in a national sample of 2,613 women self-reporting this behavior (National Institute on Drug Abuse, 1997). The psychoactive ingredient in marijuana is cannabis, and cannabis crosses the placenta barrier (Huizink & Mulder, 2006). Most of the studies on the effect of marijuana have been done with mothers who are heavy users, and these studies have found a pattern of neurological and behavioral effects. Increased tremors and startle responses (Fried & Makin, 1987) and altered sleep patterns (Huizink & Mulder, 2006) have been reported for infants who were prenatally exposed to cannabis. Research on the effect of marijuana on cognitive development on young children has been mixed, but research with older children has more consistently found a negative effect on cognitive executive functioning (which includes the ability to organize and integrate information), cognitive flexibility in problem solving, sustained and focused attention, and abstract reasoning (Huizink & Mulder, 2006). There also are a number of studies that report more impulsivity and hyperactivity in children who have been exposed prenatally. A possible explanation for this finding is that cannabis alters the neurology in the prefrontal cortex, the site in the brain that is responsible for higher cognitive functioning.

Studies that have exposed animals to cannabis prenatally have found evidence that there are changes in the sensitivity of the specific brain circuits that are involved in the reward system of the brain, potentially making this substance even more reinforcing for adult animals with this prenatal history (Malanga & Kosofsky, 2003). Unfortunately, even women who stop using marijuana while they are pregnant are likely to return to using after they have their babies (Bailey, Hill, Hawkins, Catalano, & Abbott, 2008), creating an environment in which children with a possible neurological sensitivity to marijuana also have role models who are engaging in this behavior. Although the effects of marijuana use may be subtle, "even subtle effects can have both short-term and long-term implications" for the child's development (Huizink & Mulder, 2006, p. 36), so women need to think carefully about these implications before using recreational drugs.

Diseases. If a woman has a sexually transmitted infection (STI) while she is pregnant, it can affect her pregnancy and possibly affect her unborn child. Some sexually transmitted infections, such as syphilis and HIV, can cross the placenta and infect the baby prenatally, while others, such as gonorrhea, genital herpes, and chlamydia, are present in the birth canal and can infect the baby during the birth process (USDHHS, 2009). Women should be screened for STIs

6. Smoking marijuana while pregnant can make the child more susceptible to marijuana addiction when the child is an adult.

TRUE/FALSE

True. Prenatal exposure to cannabis (the active ingredient in marijuana) can affect the brain In a way that makes smoking marijuana more rewarding later in adolescence or adulthood.

early in their pregnancy. Bacterial infections such as chlamydia, gonorrhea, and syphilis can be treated and cured with antibiotics during the pregnancy (CDC, 2008c). Although viral STIs such as genital herpes and HIV cannot be cured, antiviral medication can reduce the symptoms and their effect on the developing fetus (CDC, 2008c).

We mentioned earlier in this chapter that the Centers for Disease Control and Prevention recommends that women with HIV/AIDS continue taking their antiviral medication (such as AZT) during their pregnancy. This is because treatment can dramatically reduce the risk of the mother transmitting the disease to her child. The virus that causes HIV can be passed from mother to baby during the pregnancy because the virus can cross the placenta, but it also can be passed along when the baby is being delivered or after the baby is born through the mother's breast milk (so it is recommended that HIV-positive mothers not breast-feed their infants). If the woman takes antiviral medication while pregnant and if the baby is treated with the same medication after birth, the infection risk for the infant drops to less than 2% (CDC, 2007b). This risk is probably lower than many people believe. Currently there are between 100 and 200 cases of infants born in the United States with the virus annually. For infants with less than the median level of the virus in their blood, only 15% progress to having AIDS or dying from the disease, and at even lower levels of the virus, researchers have seen no progression to disease or death (Shearer et al., 1997). Figure 5.7 illustrates the decline that has occurred in perinatally acquired pediatric AIDS in the United States.

Neonatal herpes is another maternal infection that can have devastating consequences for an infant. Infants who are born with the disease and do not respond to treatment are at risk for neurological damage, mental retardation, or death (American Social Health Association [ASHA], 1996). Fortunately the risk of an infant contracting herpes appears to be low.

TRUE/FALSE

7. Infants who are born to women with HIV are almost certain to have the disease themselves.

False. Infants born to HIV-positive mothers who are receiving no treatment have a 1-in-4 chance of having the disease. Infants born to mothers with HIV who *are* receiving treatment (such as AZT) and who receive antiviral medication after they are born have about a 2% chance of developing the disease themselves.

Figure 5.7

Number of pediatric AIDS cases in the United States, 1985–2007. "Perinatal transmission" includes the transmission of HIV from mother to child during pregnancy, labor and delivery, or breastfeeding. With the use of antiretroviral medications during pregnancy, the rate of transmission has decreased dramatically in recent years. Continued treatment of infected infants after birth further reduces the number who go on to develop AIDS.

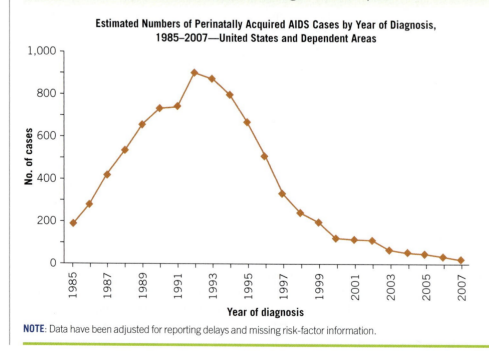

Estimated Numbers of Perinatally Acquired AIDS Cases by Year of Diagnosis, 1985–2007—United States and Dependent Areas

NOTE: Data have been adjusted for reporting delays and missing risk-factor information.

According to the American Social Health Association (1996), an estimated 20% to 25% of pregnant women have genital herpes, but the infection rate for their babies is 0.1% (that is, one tenth of one percent). Contrary to what you might expect, the risk of transmitting herpes prenatally to an infant is lowest in women who have had the disease for quite a while and who do not have symptoms of an outbreak when their baby is born and greatest for women who contract the disease late in their pregnancy (ASHA, 1996). This is because the woman's own body develops antibodies against the disease over time, and these maternal antibodies can cross the placenta to the fetus beginning at about the 28th week of the pregnancy to offer some degree of immunity to the infant. Ninety percent of the cases of herpes in infants are transmitted to the infant as the infant passes through the birth canal. Consequently, if a mother has active genital herpes at the time she goes into labor, the infant is usually delivered by cesarean section (CDC, 2008c). Neonatal herpes also can be transmitted after the baby is born often through kissing by an adult with an active oral herpes infection (ASHA, 1996), so it is just good common sense to avoid that kind of contact.

Maternal Stress. Whenever we are under stress, our body produces stress hormones, and one of those hormones, cortisol, can pass through the placenta. High levels of maternal stress hormones during a pregnancy have been associated with lower birth weight and a slower growth rate in the fetus and with temperamental difficulties in infants (Wadhwa, 2005). As we have seen for other conditions that affect a pregnancy, the exact effect of prenatal stress depends upon the nature, timing, and duration of it, but Wadhwa (2005) concluded that stress early in the prenatal period has a greater impact on fetal growth and length of gestation than stress later in prenatal development. Everyone experiences varying levels of stress from time to time throughout the day and from one day to another. The danger is not from this type of short-lived everyday stress but from chronic stress that is experienced at a very high level.

We can conclude this section of the chapter by saying that there are a number of factors that can adversely affect prenatal development, but there is much that a pregnant woman can do to help ensure the health and well-being of her baby by being careful. The goal of any pregnancy is to have a healthy baby, and fortunately this is exactly what happens in most cases. Although the risks are real and we need to guard against them whenever possible, there also is a great resiliency in the developing child. And, as we point out throughout this book, what happens to the child after the baby is born has a huge impact on the eventual developmental outcome. Children who are born with birth defects or developmental deficits can benefit greatly from growing up in a nurturing, supportive environment. Early intervention can do a great deal to help these children develop to their fullest potential.

Maternal stress. Pregnancy brings with it some unique stresses, but excessive stress from any source can affect the fetus because stress hormones cross through the placenta. What are some of the things a pregnant woman could do to manage her level of stress?

The Birth Experience

Labor and Delivery

After months of waiting, the parents-to-be are understandably excited—and perhaps a bit apprehensive—when labor finally begins. How long the process will take and the woman's subjective experience of the birth can be quite variable from one woman to the next.

Earlier in the pregnancy the woman may have felt some contractions called Braxton Hicks contractions. These are uterine contractions that can begin as early as the sixth week of pregnancy but aren't noticeable until midpregnancy. They usually are infrequent, painless, and sporadic (Cunningham et al., 2005). However, as the woman gets closer to her due date, the contractions begin to soften and thin out the cervix, preparing it for true labor. We'll look at each of the three stages of labor in detail.

Video Link 5.6
Stages of labor.

Early labor The first phase in the first stage of labor in which contractions are usually not painful but the cervix begins to thin out and dilate.

Active labor The second phase in the first stage of labor in which contractions become longer, stronger, and more frequent and a woman may require pain medication; begins when the cervix has dilated to 4 centimeters and lasts on average 3 to 8 hours.

Transition The third phase in the first stage of labor in which contractions come in rapid succession and last up to 90 seconds each, with little or no pause between them; lasts on average between 15 minutes and 3 hours and ends when cervix has dilated 10 centimeters.

Doula A trained, knowledgeable companion who is present at a birth to support the woman through her labor and delivery.

For first-time mothers, the first stage of labor usually lasts between 10 and 20 hours, although it could go on for days. So much happens during this stage that it is divided into three phases. During **early labor**, true contractions begin. At first they last about 30 to 60 seconds and come every 5 to 20 minutes. At this point, the contractions themselves are usually not very painful, and most women can safely remain at home, taking part in light activities or using the time to get some rest, if possible. The contractions now begin to thin out (or *efface*) and open up (or *dilate*) the cervix. As the cervix opens, a mucus plug is discharged from the vagina.

When the cervix has dilated to 4 centimeters, the second phase called **active labor** begins, and the contractions become longer, stronger, and more frequent (Cunningham et al., 2005). The cervix continues dilating, but now at a more rapid pace. When contractions last 1 minute and are coming about every 5 minutes, it is time for the woman to get to the hospital or birthing center (ACOG, 2007). It is during this phase of active labor that women may feel they need some pain medication or will want to use the breathing and relaxation strategies they learned during childbirth classes. About half of American women use an epidural during their labor. An epidural is a regional anesthesia that blocks the nerve impulses from the lower spine and decreases sensation in the lower half of the body to give some pain relief (American Pregnancy Association, 2007). On average, this second phase of labor lasts between 3 and 8 hours.

Once the dilation of the cervix reaches 7 centimeters, the woman enters the third phase called **transition** (Cunningham et al., 2005). It is the shortest, but also the most difficult, phase of labor, lasting on average between 15 minutes and 3 hours. Contractions are now coming in very rapid succession and last up to 90 seconds each, with little or no pause between them. For about three quarters of women, the amniotic sac ruptures (that is, her *water breaks*) near the end of this phase. The woman's partner, her labor coach, or a member of the health care team can provide support and encouragement and help make her comfortable as she moves through this stage.

When the cervix has dilated 10 centimeters, the second stage of labor begins. The uterine contractions now begin to push the baby down through the birth canal. Many women feel a strong urge to push with each contraction. This can help the progress of the birth, although at some point the woman may be told to try to resist the urge to push so that the vaginal area can stretch more slowly, rather than tear. In nearly 40% of vaginal deliveries in the United States, the doctor or midwife makes a surgical incision called an episiotomy from the back of the vagina to the anus to allow the baby to exit the birth canal without creating more of a tear in the tissue (Allen & Hanson, 2005). Once the baby's head emerges from the birth canal, the health care provider will clear the baby's airways and check the position of the umbilical cord. Fairly rapidly one shoulder and then the other are delivered, and the rest of the baby's body quickly follows. If everything is going normally, the baby may be placed on his mother's stomach while the umbilical cord is clamped and cut.

Now the third stage of labor begins. The uterus begins to contract again to expel the placenta. This generally occurs without any pain or discomfort to the mother, and this stage lasts only 5 to 10 minutes (ACOG, 2007). The contraction of the uterus helps close off the blood vessels where the placenta separated from the uterus to prevent further bleeding. If an episiotomy has been performed, the doctor will close that incision at this time.

Birthing Options

Today there is a wide range of birthing options available to women, including giving birth in a hospital, at a birthing center (which can be part of a hospital or a freestanding facility), or at home. A small percentage of births that take place at home or at a birthing center are *water births*, in which the delivery takes place in a tub of warm water that is intended to relax the mother during labor and ease the transition for the newborn from the womb to the outside world.

Births can be attended by a physician, a midwife, or a doula. In the United States, midwives attend 6% of all births, and 98% of those births occur in a hospital or a birth center (Mendola, 1999), but midwives are used much more extensively in other parts of the world. **Doulas** are

Birthing options. Women have some choice about where and how they give birth. The birth can take place in a hospital, in a tub of water (either at a birthing center or at home), or at home. The birth can be assisted by a physician, midwife, or doula. What do you think are advantages or disadvantages of each of these alternatives?

another alternative. Unlike a physician or midwife, a doula does not assist directly in the birth process but rather is a trained, knowledgeable companion who is present at the birth to support the woman through her labor and delivery. Some doulas also have specialized training to help the family adjust to the new birth. With so many birthing options available, determining which alternative is the best one for an individual woman depends on her personal preferences and her medical condition, but she also needs to consider both the risks and the benefits of each alternative to make the best decision.

When a woman decides to give birth in a hospital, she has access to a full range of medical professionals and medical technology in case there is an emergency and to pain medications and medical procedures. However, hospitals are sometimes seen as impersonal settings in which the woman gives up much control over the circumstances of the birth (Williams & Umberson, 1999). There also has been concern that medical interventions are overused in hospital settings.

Although there are medical rationales for each procedure, each type of intervention carries with it some type of cost. For instance, labor can be initiated through the use of medications or by rupturing the amniotic sac if the woman has passed her due date and the baby is becoming too large or if other medical conditions are threatening the health of the baby. However, it is also sometimes done as an elective procedure for the convenience of the family or a physician (Dublin, Lydon-Rochelle, Kaplan, Watts, & Critchlow, 2000). Labor is induced for 20% to 34% of the births in the United States (Lydon-Rochelle et al., 2007). Although the risks associated with induced labor are small, it can trigger contractions that are too frequent or that are abnormally long and strong. This can physically exhaust the woman and make her feel unprepared and out of control during her labor.

In hospitals, women most commonly lie on their backs to give birth. This position was adopted because it is most convenient for medical personnel, who want to be able to check the progress of delivery, but it is often not the most comfortable position for the laboring woman. A birth center or home birth gives women more options. They have greater freedom to move around during labor and can get into different positions, such as squatting, that may help alleviate their discomfort and assist the birth process. They also usually can eat or drink if they want to. Home births are typically reserved for low-risk pregnancies. Midwives can attend women during hospital births or home births.

The Birth Experience of the Baby

You probably have heard stories about labor and delivery from the perspective of the mother, but have you ever wondered how this is experienced by the baby? It can seem pretty traumatic. The baby is pushed through the birth canal, with uterine contractions intermittently causing oxygen deprivation (Langercrantz & Slotkin, 1986), and the newborn rapidly goes from a warm, quiet, and dark prenatal environment into a bright, noisy, and cold postnatal environment. Fortunately babies are physiologically well prepared to handle the stress of being born. For one thing, the skull of a baby is composed of separate plates that can overlap and compress during the birth process, allowing the head to elongate so it can fit through the birth canal. For another, the compression of the baby's head and the oxygen deprivation that accompanies the contractions trigger the release of stress hormones that actually prepare the baby to survive on its own. These hormones help clear the lungs after birth and promote normal breathing, and they ensure that there is a rich supply of blood to the heart and brain (Langercrantz & Slotkin, 1986).

As soon as the baby's head is delivered, the doctor or midwife will wipe the baby's face and mouth and use a rubber syringe to clear away any material in the mouth and air passages. Most babies begin breathing spontaneously at this point, but as many as 10% of newborns need some form of resuscitation to help them start breathing (Cunningham et al., 2005). After the baby emerges, the umbilical cord is clamped and cut after it stops pulsing. A few drops of an antibiotic such as a silver nitrate solution, tetracycline, or erythromycin are placed in the baby's eyes. This procedure is required in most states as a way to prevent infection that could be caused by any organisms that were present in the birth canal (Cunningham et al., 2005).

The baby's overall condition is assessed using the **Apgar Scale** at 1 minute and again at 5 minutes after birth. The newborn receives 0, 1, or 2 points for its *Activity* level, *Pulse*, *Grimace* (reflex irritability), *Appearance*, and *Respiration*. A total score of 7 to 10 points is the normal range, and for newborns who are in this range, routine care will continue, with a reassessment of their status at 5 minutes. The baby will be kept warm and placed on the mother's stomach for some skin-to-skin contact or placed in her arms so mother and baby can meet each other for the first time. An Apgar score in the range of 4 to 6 indicates that some intervention is needed. This might be some additional suction to help the baby breathe, massaging, or administering oxygen. A score of 3 or less means that some immediate lifesaving intervention is needed (Bregman, 2005).

The Birth Experience of the Mother

The woman's experience of childbirth is affected by many factors, including whether her pregnancy was planned, how easy or difficult her pregnancy was, how much support she has received from loved ones and the professionals who were caring for her, if or when she received medication during labor, and how well she understands the process her body is going through. Since the 1970s and 1980s, when even normal births were treated as medical events to be handled solely by doctors and nurses (Williams & Umberson, 1999), women have become more active participants in the birth process. Today they have access to a great deal of information on labor and delivery through books, magazines, the Internet, and conversations with their care providers and other women who have gone through the experience. What most first-time mothers in Western societies do *not* have is personal experience witnessing a birth (something that is not the case in cultures where birth is a more communal event). Because individual birth experiences are so different, talking to a few mothers may not be particularly helpful for the mother-to-be, so many women take some form of childbirth preparation, such

Apgar Scale
An assessment of a newborn's overall condition at 1 minute and 5 minutes after birth that is based upon the newborn's activity level, pulse, grimace, appearance, and respiration.

Video Link 5.7
Apgar assessment.

as a Lamaze class. Lamaze childbirth preparation is so popular that one quarter of American women who give birth each year have attended classes (Lamaze International, n.d.).

According to Lamaze International (n.d.), prepared childbirth involves more than learning a few breathing techniques. It has evolved into a complete philosophy of childbirth that includes the tenets that birth is normal, natural, and healthy; that a woman's inner wisdom will guide her through the process; and that she has the right to give birth free of medical interventions (Lamaze International, 2010). To empower women to do this, Lamaze classes provide a great deal of information about the process of labor and delivery because knowing what is happening—and understanding that it is a normal part of the process—helps relieve stress and anxiety (Mackey, 1990). This also enables the woman to work with what is happening to her body, rather than fight against it. In addition to breathing techniques, women learn relaxation methods and techniques for pushing during contractions as a part of this preparation (Lamaze International, n.d.).

Attending Lamaze childbirth classes. Many couples take some type of class to prepare them for childbirth. With this training, a husband, a partner, or another trusted person can act as a labor coach and support and assist the woman while she is in labor.

Having a labor coach can provide invaluable support for the woman. A personal labor coach usually is a husband, partner, relative, or close friend who has attended childbirth preparation classes with the woman and who is committed to being supportive of her through the delivery process. A coach may do specific things that help the woman relax, such as tracking and reporting her progress through each contraction, providing some distraction to get her mind off the contractions, or doing physical things to make her more comfortable like providing a massage or helping her change her position. By contrast, a doula is a professional labor coach. Doulas usually are paid for their services and typically meet with the mother before she is ready to deliver her baby. They are present through the labor and even come to the home to meet with the mother and infant after the birth. Either type of support can be very beneficial, but doulas have the advantage of having professional training and the experience of having participated in a number of deliveries that can run the gamut from simple to quite complicated.

Video Link 5.8
Natural childbirth.

In one controlled study, women who were randomly assigned to receive continuous support from a doula during labor had lower rates of cesarean section deliveries and fewer forceps deliveries, needed less epidural anesthesia, and had shorter labors than women in the control group who were simply observed during their labor (Kennell, Klaus, McGrath, Robertson, & Hinkley, 1991). Because women find it comforting to have someone who can assure them that what they are experiencing is normal and to be expected, one possible explanation for why doulas are so beneficial is that their presence reduces the amount of stress hormones that the woman produces during her labor.

In non-Western cultures, the birth process may be quite different from what we have just described. For example, an Ifaluk woman, who lives in Micronesia on one of two tiny islands in the Pacific Ocean, gives birth in a birth house, accompanied by a midwife and her female relatives (Le, 2000). When the baby is ready to be born, the woman kneels on a mat and helps the baby out by herself. She must try not to show distress or pain, in accord with the Ifaluk value of remaining calm at all times. If there are complications, the other women will help. After the baby is born, the woman's mother helps by holding the baby and then bathes the baby in the ocean. By contrast, in Westernized hospitals, as we described earlier, the care of the newborn is turned over to medical professionals.

It is a common misunderstanding to think that after a baby is born, a new mother automatically follows her instincts and knows just what to do. In fact, many first-time mothers are not necessarily comfortable with breastfeeding, changing diapers, or soothing a crying baby. Women around the world must learn how to be mothers, and there is a myriad of ways in which this happens. For most women, the way they themselves were mothered as a child often provides an unconscious model of what a mother should be like. In addition, many women turn to their own mothers for support and guidance when their first child is born. New mothers also frequently turn to other sources of advice, including other new mothers, relatives, child care professionals, and books or websites on child care (Walker, 2005). However, when a woman receives conflicting advice from different sources, it adds to her stress rather than relieving it. Mothers report that when this happens, they fall back upon relying on their own instincts or experiences, or they use the baby's cues to guide their decision (Walker, 2005).

In many cultures, the pressure to be a "perfect mother" can be intense, and all the complex emotions that occur with the birth of a child are often overlooked. However, in the right circumstances, having a child can be a truly amazing experience. Women are happiest about their new babies when they have had a choice about whether to have a child; have support from a partner, family, and others; and have adequate resources to support the child (Lips, 2006). However, pregnancy, childbirth, and child rearing are all experiences that will touch on the full range of human emotion. In a society that idealizes mothers as being totally self-sacrificing, all-giving nurturers, women who struggle with the normal array of mixed feelings may have an added burden of feeling guilty that they are not living up to the ideal when they feel sadness or anxiety following the birth of their baby.

New mothers do get some help from their biology. Nurturing behavior gets a boost from hormones such as oxytocin and prolactin, which are at elevated levels in expectant and new mothers (Bower, 2005; Brunton & Russell, 2008; Lim & Young, 2006). Interestingly, there also is some evidence to suggest that hormonal changes in males may be linked with fathering behavior. In research on experimental animals, levels of progesterone, normally considered to be important in female behavior, were found to play a role in determining levels of paternal responsiveness, which was also linked with decreased levels of aggression (Schneider et al., 2003). In humans, Storey, Walsh, Quinton, and Wynne-Edwards (2000) studied expectant couples who were living together and found that immediately before their baby's birth both men and women had higher than normal levels of certain hormones, specifically prolactin and cortisol. Following the birth both also showed lowered levels of testosterone, the hormone that is often linked with aggressive behavior. The pattern of increasing and decreasing hormones of the father was similar to that of his partner in each couple. For men, this pattern of hormone change was strongest in those who experienced the pregnancy-like symptoms of couvade that we described earlier.

The rapid hormonal changes that occur following a birth, along with the other stresses that new mothers experience, frequently result in the "baby blues" or sometimes even postpartum depression (Cunningham et al., 2005). The symptoms of the "baby blues" include mood swings, sadness, loss of appetite, trouble sleeping, and irritability. Often a little time, together with some rest and help with caring for the newborn, is enough to alleviate the symptoms. **Postpartum depression** is more severe, lasts for more than 2 weeks, and begins within the first 3 months following a delivery (Cunningham et al., 2005). Symptoms include sadness, lack of energy, trouble concentrating, and feelings of guilt or worthlessness, and are severe enough that they interfere with the woman's ability to function. Women who have sad feelings that persist should consult with their doctors because there are effective treatments that can help restore their well-being. The most common approaches to treating postpartum depression include antidepressant medications and counseling or therapy (Logsdon, Wisner, & Shanahan, 2007).

Just as there are cultural differences in the birth process, there are some differences in what happens after birth. To continue our cross-cultural comparison with the Ifaluk mother's experience, one big difference is that the new Ifaluk mother will never be left alone in the first 10 days

Postpartum depression
A severe depression anytime in the first year after childbirth that lasts for more than 2 weeks; symptoms are severe enough that they interfere with the woman's ability to function.

of the baby's life. When the mother leaves the birth house after 10 days, she is not expected to do any work for the first 3 months of the baby's life. Other women, usually relatives, will cook and take care of household tasks while the mother rests (Le, 2000). By contrast, women in Western society have few rituals to mark this big event in their lives. There is little recognition by society that their new role is valued, and there may be limited social support (Munhall, 2007). Many new mothers spend a good deal of time alone with their baby, and this can be stressful if they are uncertain about how to care for their newborns. They often receive some help from the baby's father and from their own mother or other relatives, but much of the day may be spent alone. Other new mothers feel pressure to quickly return to work and may be torn between their desire to devote themselves completely to the care of their infant and the need or desire to spend the majority of their day at work. Women in American society have many choices, but having many choices means that they can second-guess their decisions, whatever they are.

The Birth Experience of the Father

For many men today, choosing to actively participate in the birth of their babies by being present during labor and in the delivery room is one of the ways they express their empathy for their partners. However, this is not a universal experience. Some men—who are no less loving or concerned about their partner and their child than other men—for their own reasons do not want to put themselves this close to the birth. Fortunately, infants can bond with fathers the same way they can bond with mothers without having immediate contact at birth.

For men who choose to actively participate, the actual experience may fall short of their expectations (Bartlett, 2004; Reed, 2005). In a review of the literature, Bartlett (2004) concluded that many men feel coerced to participate in the process and that their most outstanding memory of the birth is the pain that their partner was experiencing. They also report feeling unprepared for their role as labor coach (especially younger men and first-time fathers) and feeling that they were not needed or even were in the way during the delivery. Despite these feelings, many men are overcome with a powerful and perhaps unexpected rush of emotions following the birth of their baby (Reed, 2005). Those early moments and the opportunity to see and hold their newborn become rich rewards for the new father.

However, it is still true in many cultures that fathers and other men are strictly prohibited from taking part in the birth experience and early care of the baby. Ifaluk men are only allowed to see their newborn from a distance while the mother and baby stay in the birth house for the first 10 days. During this time, the father has two responsibilities: to provide the mother with fish to eat and to make a cradle for the baby. On the other hand, the Ifaluk mother hands over responsibility for care of the child to the father when the child is 2 years old, and he becomes the major caretaker for the next 2 to 3 years (Le, 2000). Clearly, the role of the father can differ enormously from one culture to another.

A new father is born. The transition to becoming a new father can be a powerful experience for men. A father's role today involves much more than being the breadwinner for the family. Fathers can be sensitive and nurturant caregivers for their newborn infants.

The Couple's Experience

A number of years ago, a sociologist named Jessie Bernard (1972) suggested that how men and women experience their marriage is so different that rather than "their marriage," we could talk about "his marriage" and "her marriage." Perhaps the same can be said of the couple's experience of the birth of their child. An interesting study conducted in 1999 by

Williams and Umberson illustrated how mothers and fathers can experience the medical technologies that are routinely used during labor in a very different way.

Most of the couples in their sample had a routine sonogram during the pregnancy. A sonogram uses sound waves to produce a picture of the developing fetus. For many of the men, seeing the image of their baby was what first brought home to them the reality of the pregnancy, but it was less important to the women who already had experienced the physical changes that accompany an early pregnancy, such as nausea and weight gain. This is not to say that the sonogram was unimportant to them, but the pregnancy had become "real" for them long before this event.

As we've said, most men who participate in the birth of their child attend childbirth classes along with their partner to prepare for their role as their partner's labor coach. The men in this sample saw providing support and encouragement to their wives as a critical aspect of their involvement in labor and delivery. In some cases a medical device called a fetal monitor is used to monitor the mother's contractions and fetal heart rate during labor. Fathers in this study felt that the monitor enabled them to provide vital information to their wives. They saw providing this information as even more important than simply providing support and encouragement because they felt empowered to take action in case a complication arose. In sharp contrast to the men's perception, however, in almost all cases the women perceived the fetal monitor as being of little value—and even being a bit annoying. Williams and Umberson (1999) quote one of the participants in the study as saying,

> It was just irritating for people to say, "Oh, a contraction is starting." I'm like, "It started a few seconds ago and I'm aware." And then they say, "Oh, now it's over." I'm like, "No, that may be what it looks like on the screen but, believe me, it's not over." (p. 159)

Finally, the use of an epidural injection to reduce the mother's pain had relatively little effect on fathers. Although they were happy that it made their wives more comfortable, they had attended childbirth classes to prepare for their role as a labor coach with the goal of helping control their partner's pain, but now medication had taken over most of that function. For the women, the use of medication evoked mixed reactions. While it enabled them to control their pain, they felt it made them relinquish control over their bodies. For one thing, it restrained their movement. They had been told in childbirth classes that moving around and walking would assist their labor, but they now were immobilized and often even were tethered to an intravenous drip.

Williams and Umberson (1999) concluded that most of the women in their study had adopted a *goal-oriented* rather than *experience-oriented* approach to childbirth. The goal was to minimize pain while having a healthy baby, and medical interventions were seen as essential to reaching that goal. A woman who is more focused on the *experience* of childbirth, including experiencing the pain that comes with it, would likely make different choices when planning for her birth experience.

The Newborn

Babies enter the world equipped in many ways to begin their journey of development and to interact with the people who will love and care for them along the way. The journey is easier for some newborns than others, but in this section we'll examine the capabilities that the newborn possesses from birth, some of the challenges that newborns face in those early months of life, and the ways that the birth of a baby impacts the parents and their relationship.

Newborn Capabilities

In the early days of the field of psychology, William James (1890/1990) described the world of the infant as "one great blooming, buzzing confusion" (p. 462), and the idea that

Infant states. Infants continually move through a series of states that allow them to regulate the amount of stimulation that they receive. Can you see how this is an adaptive way for an infant to meet his or her needs for rest, stimulation, and physical care?

newborns were unable to make sense out of their world persisted for a number of years. Today we know that this statement seriously underestimates the capabilities of newborns to receive information about the world through all of their senses in an organized way and to respond to that information. As we said earlier in this chapter, all of the senses begin developing during the prenatal period and become functional before birth. Some senses are more advanced in their development than others when the infant is born, but there is no doubt that the newborn can hear, see, taste, smell, and respond to touch. You will learn more about the continuity in the development of the senses in Chapter 6.

Infant States

Newborns have a limited capacity to process information from the environment, so they have a set of **infant states** that represent different levels of consciousness. Moving through these states helps the infants regulate the level of stimulation they receive so that they can keep the input at a level they can process. At one end of the continuum is crying, and at the other is deep sleep. Let's start at the quiet end of this continuum.

Newborns spend most of their day asleep, and it is normal for them to sleep 16 to 18 hours out of each day (Hanrahan, 2006). About half of this time is spent in REM (rapid eye movement) sleep, which is the light sleep where dreams occur, and half is spent in regular sleep, which ranges from drowsiness where the eyes open and close to a deep sleep in which the

Infant states Different levels of consciousness used to regulate the amount of stimulation an infant receives; states range from crying to deep sleep.

Video Link 5.9
Infant sleeping.

infant is quiet and doesn't move. Because infants' stomachs are so small, they will wake up to eat about every 3 or 4 hours throughout the day and the night. By 6 months of age, most babies will sleep through the night for 12 hours or more and continue to take daytime naps (Hanrahan, 2006).

A topic related to infant sleeping that has been controversial is cosleeping (Sobralske & Gruber, 2009). Although sharing a family bed is a common practice in many cultures around the world, the American Academy of Pediatrics (AAP) has been critical of this practice. A report issued by the organization's Task Force on Sudden Infant Death Syndrome in 2005 (and reaffirmed by the organization in 2009) concluded that "the evidence is growing that bed sharing, as practiced in the United States and other Western countries, is more hazardous than the infant sleeping on a separate sleep surface and, therefore, recommends that infants not bed share during sleep. Infants may be brought into bed for nursing or comforting but should be returned to their own crib or bassinet when the parent is ready to return to sleep" (AAP, 2005, p. 1252). While the Task Force acknowledged that bed sharing facilitates breastfeeding (which it strongly supports) and enhances bonding, it was the organization's recommendation that infants sleep close to their parents (perhaps in a crib in the parents' room), but not in the same bed.

When infants are awake, they can be in a stage of *quiet alertness* in which their eyes are open and they are attentive to what is going on around them but they are very still, or in a stage of *active alertness* in which they are still alert to what is going on in their environment but they are moving around. Young infants are quiet and awake for only about 1 hour out of each day, and this state comes in episodes that only last 5 to 10 minutes at a time (Maurer & Maurer, 1988). The last state on the continuum is crying, which is the way infants signal that they need something. Sensitively responding to infants' needs can help this state pass.

Even at this young age, there are individual differences in how regular infants are in their behavior. Some infants have regular and predictable schedules and are easy to calm down when they are upset, but others are much more variable in their schedule and much more difficult to soothe. Some infants smoothly transition from one state to another, and others move rapidly or unexpectedly from one state to another. Some infants signal what they need in a way that is clear and easy for parents to interpret so they can promptly respond, and others are much more difficult for new parents to "read." You will learn more about these differences in temperament in Chapter 10. Over those early weeks, parents come to know the unique characteristics of their infants, and in most cases, parents and infant are able to get in sync with each other so things go relatively smoothly. That doesn't mean, however, that there won't be plenty of nights with too little sleep for the new parents and times when they worry about how well they are doing.

Risks to Infants' Health and Well-Being

Infant Mortality

Infant mortality The rate of infant death within the first year of life.

In general, developed countries have far lower rates of **infant mortality** (deaths within the first year of life) than less developed countries. However, even within the more developed world, there is variation in how effective each country is at preventing infant death. Figure 5.8 shows the infant mortality rates for a number of developed countries. Note where the United States ranks in this figure. Despite its wealth and the availability of (but not always access to) world-class medical facilities, the United States has the same or worse infant mortality rates compared with 37 other industrialized countries (Hoover Institution, 2007). In the United States, an average of 6.4 babies out of 1,000 live births die within the first year. In 2005, the United States was the same as or worse than 38 other countries in the number of deaths of children under age 5 (UNICEF, 2007). As with maternal mortality, rates of infant mortality vary by race. In 2004, the statistics were 5.66 deaths per 1,000 live births for White infants and 13.79 for Black infants (Miniño et al., 2007).

Video Link 5.10
Infant mortality.

Figure 5.8

Comparison of international infant mortality rates: 2000. In a comparison of infant mortality rates in a number of industrialized countries, the United States ranks near the bottom of the list. What do you think accounts for this low ranking?

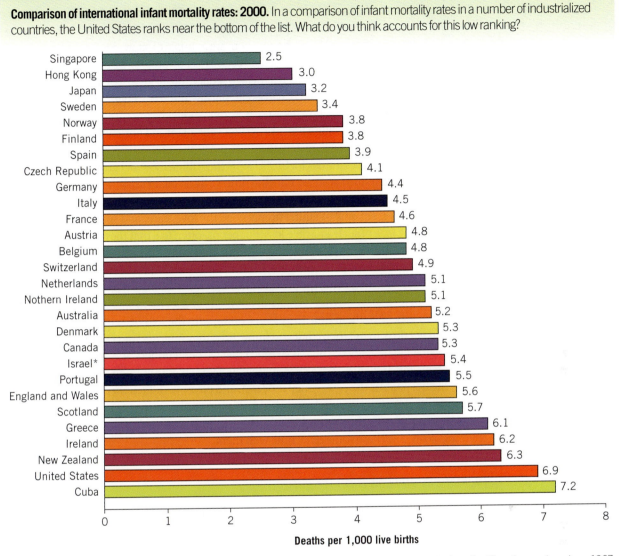

Country	Deaths per 1,000 live births
Singapore	2.5
Hong Kong	3.0
Japan	3.2
Sweden	3.4
Norway	3.8
Finland	3.8
Spain	3.9
Czech Republic	4.1
Germany	4.4
Italy	4.5
France	4.6
Austria	4.8
Belgium	4.8
Switzerland	4.9
Netherlands	5.1
Nothern Ireland	5.1
Australia	5.2
Denmark	5.3
Canada	5.3
Israel*	5.4
Portugal	5.5
England and Wales	5.6
Scotland	5.7
Greece	6.1
Ireland	6.2
New Zealand	6.3
United States	6.9
Cuba	7.2

Deaths per 1,000 live births

* Includes data for East Jerusalem and Israeli residents in certain other territories under occupation by Israeli military forces since June 1967.

Sudden Infant Death Syndrome (SIDS)

Having an infant die unexpectedly is a parent's worst nightmare. Sadly, **sudden infant death syndrome (SIDS)**, or the unexpected death of an apparently healthy infant, is the leading cause of death for children between the ages of 1 month and 1 year (AAP, 2005). Deaths from SIDS peak between the ages of 2 months and 4 months and only rarely occur before 1 month of age (AAP, 2005).

Unfortunately we do not understand the cause of SIDS. There probably never will be a simple explanation because, in all likelihood, there is not a single cause of all cases of SIDS. The cause likely is a combination of factors including some physical vulnerability in the infant (for example, some abnormality in the part of the brain that controls breathing, a brain chemical imbalance, a bacterial infection), some stressor in the environment (for example, secondhand smoke, overheating the infant with too much clothing or an overheated room), and a

Sudden infant death syndrome (SIDS) The unexpected death of an apparently healthy infant; the rate of SIDS peaks between the ages of 2 months and 4 months.

critical period in early development (Mayo Clinic, 2009b). When several of these factors come together, it is the combination that places the infant at greater risk.

Because the list of risk factors that have been identified for SIDS is quite long and because some of them are not under the control of the parent, it may seem that there is little that a concerned parent can do. That conclusion would be wrong. There are a couple of strategies that are both simple and effective. You might have heard about the "back to sleep" program. Putting an infant down to sleep on his or her back has done a great deal to reduce the incidence of SIDS (Task Force on Sudden Infant Death Syndrome, 2005). Babies can still have "tummy time" when they are awake and someone is watching them, but this is not how they should be put to sleep. Other simple but effective things to do include using a firm mattress for your infant and not smoking in the home. As we described earlier in the chapter, maternal smoking while the mother is pregnant or after the baby is born significantly increases the risk for SIDS. Doing these things does not guarantee that an infant will be safe, but they are smart and easy things to do to lower an infant's risk.

When parents lose an infant to SIDS, it is natural that they not only feel overwhelming grief but also may feel a great deal of guilt. Parents need the love, care, and support of their family and friends in the face of such a terrible loss, but people often feel that they don't know what to do or what to say to offer the grieving parents any comfort. First Candle (n.d.), a national non-profit organization that supports infant health and survival issues, makes some helpful suggestions: Even if it is difficult for you, get in touch with the family members, let them know that you are sorry about their loss and that you care about them, and let them share whatever they want to share with you. Give them time to grieve. Coping with the loss of a child takes time. What you should *not* do is to tell them that you know how they feel, and never press the family for details about what happened. There is so much that we don't understand about SIDS that they may not have much that they can share with you. Don't blame anyone (not the parents, the doctor, the hospital, or the emergency services), and please don't tell them that they can have another child. Babies are not replaceable, and it is insensitive to suggest that they are. Even if you feel awkward and a bit uncomfortable, reach out to the parents and, if you can't think of anything to say, just share some quiet time with them.

Prematurity and Low Birth Weight

A number of factors can place a newborn at risk, but being born prematurely or being born at a low birth weight is a significant risk factor. **Prematurity** is defined as a birth that occurs before a gestational age of 37 weeks. Determining that a baby has a **low birth weight** is a function of the gestational age of the infant. For babies born at full term (37–42 weeks of gestation), a weight of less than 5 pounds, 4 ounces, is considered a low birth weight. Babies who are born small for their gestational age are particularly at risk.

Birth data compiled by the Centers for Disease Control and Prevention (2007a) for 2005 found that the rate of premature births in the United States is 12.7% or 525,000 babies annually. Premature infants are at risk of suffering from a number of neurological and development problems. Beyond the human cost, prematurity carries a large financial cost as well. An estimate made in 2005 claimed that preterm births in the United States cost more than $26.2 billion for medical care, lost labor productivity, and early intervention services (Williamson et al., 2008). The direct health costs for the first year of life of a premature baby average $41,610, or *15 times* the cost of a healthy, full-term delivery. That is more than the $33,696 it cost for a year's tuition at Harvard in 2009–2010 (Mitchell, 2009).

We have made great strides in recent years in being able to care for newborns who are born prematurely. Medical technology today helps ensure not only their survival but also their healthy development. The modern neonatal intensive care unit (NICU) has roots that reach back over 100 years. Read **Journey of Research: From Child Hatchery to Modern NICU** to understand the progress that has been made.

TRUE/FALSE

8. If a couple loses an infant to sudden infant death syndrome, the best thing you can do is to tell them that it isn't their fault and help them look to the future by reminding them that they still can have other children.

False. Parents (or others) should never be blamed for an infant's unexpected death, so reassuring them of this is important, but children are not replaceable so it would not be a good idea to say otherwise.

Prematurity A birth that occurs before a gestational age of 37 weeks.

Low birth weight A full-term infant who weighs less than 5 pounds, 4 ounces.

From Child Hatchery to Modern NICU

The first incubators. Early incubators were relatively primitive devices, but they provided essential care for premature infants by maintaining the heat and humidity at levels necessary for them.

One of the first incubators was developed by obstetrician Étienne Stéphane Tarnier in the 1880s (Sammons & Lewis, 1985). It consisted of a wooden box that was divided into two compartments. Half of the bottom compartment was left open to allow for circulation of air, and the other half held stone bottles filled with hot water to control the temperature. As the air circulated into the upper compartment, which contained the infant, it passed over a wet sponge to pick up moisture. A chimney in the top compartment allowed the air to pass over the infant and exit into the room (Neonatology on the Web, 2007). In addition to controlling heat and humidity and isolating sick infants from healthy ones (Sammons & Lewis, 1985), the "incubator is so simple that any village carpenter can make it, and cheap enough to be within the means of all but the most destitute" (Neonatology on the Web, 2007, para. 3).

In 1896, Martin A. Couney supervised a display of incubators with six premature infants in them at the Berlin World's Fair in an exhibit named "Kinderbrutanstalt" or "child hatchery." This exhibit was such a commercial success (yes, people were willing to pay admission to see these wonders) that he

repeated it at other expositions around the world (Snow, 1981). In 1903, Couney set up an exhibition at Coney Island, where he exhibited premature babies in incubators until the 1940s, when the public's interest seemed to wane. He did provide excellent care to the infants in his charge and claimed that 6,500 of the 8,000 infants in his care survived, including an infant as small as 1.5 pounds (Snow, 1981).

A number of physicians adopted these techniques (Sammons & Lewis, 1985), but as the care of premature infants moved into the hands of medical specialists, parents were routinely excluded from the nursery. Professionals were then surprised that parents had difficulty when the baby was returned to their care. This practice continued until the 1970s (Sammons & Lewis, 1985), but today parents are an important part of the team that cares for a premature infant. They are encouraged to participate in the care and feeding of their infant, to ask questions so they understand the complicated medical interventions that may be sustaining their infant, and to get close to their infant to begin building a bond.

In the past, premature infants were not handled to prevent overstimulating them and to reduce the risk of infection, but research has shown that touch and stimulation at a level that is appropriate for the capacity of the premature infant is beneficial. Parents might even be encouraged to provide **kangaroo care** (a practice where the baby is placed in skin-to-skin contact with the parent's bare chest or breasts and draped with a blanket), or the infant may receive infant massage (Field, Diego, & Hernandez-Reif, 2007). Tiffany Field, a leading researcher from the Touch Research Institute at Miami University, has extensively studied the effect of systematic massage on premature infants. Her research has shown that three 15-minute sessions provided for a period of 10 days can result in a 47% greater weight gain compared to infants who don't receive massage (Field et al., 2007). Take a look at the picture of a modern NICU on the next page to see how far we have come from that first sawdust-filled box.

JOURNEY *of* RESEARCH

Kangaroo care
A practice where the baby is placed in skin-to-skin contact with the parent's bare chest or breasts and draped with a blanket.

Video Link 5.11
Infant massage.

A modern neonatal intensive care unit (NICU). Modern hospitals can provide intensive medical care for premature infants. Their environment is carefully controlled, and their bodily functions are continually monitored. Even very small premature infants are now able to survive, but what are the costs of this care?

Video Link 5.12
Modern NICU operation.

Because of their prematurity, these infants are not yet able to regulate their bodily functions in the same way that a full-term infant can. The neonatal intensive care unit (NICU) has been specifically designed to monitor the functioning of the infant (for example, temperature, heart function, breathing, blood pressure) and to compensate for things that the infants cannot yet do for themselves. Premature infants do not have a layer of body fat that helps them regulate body temperature and fluid loss, so incubators provide constant levels of heat and moisture. They may not yet have a sucking reflex or gag reflex, so they need special feeding procedures. Their immature central nervous system means that they easily can be overwhelmed by stimuli, so the light level is kept low, noise is minimized, and the infants are handled slowly and gently (VanderBerg, 2007). Overall the personnel in the NICU need to be particularly sensitive toward an infant who cannot signal what he needs (Smotherman & Robinson, 1996; VanderBerg, 2007).

Medical technology continues to advance the care of premature infants, and modern NICUs are very successful at saving even very small, fragile babies. The survival rate for premature babies weighing less than 2 pounds (800 grams) is now more than 90%, and even babies weighing just over a pound (500 grams) have a 40% to 50% chance of surviving (Smotherman & Robinson, 1996). However, as birth weight goes down, the risk of complications gets greater. This has created a dilemma for medical professionals who work with these tiny patients. Most NICUs provide intensive care to infants born at a gestational age of 25 weeks or more, but may provide it to infants at a gestational age of 23 or 24 weeks only with the agreement of the parents (Tyson, Nehal, Langer, Green, & Higgins, 2008; see also Cunningham et al., 2005). The question is whether there is a point at which a premature infant is so small and the chance of survival is so little that the humane thing to do is to provide comfort care rather than trying to save the life of the infant. Comfort care involves providing for the basic needs of the infant but not using heroic measures that might cause additional pain and suffering without being likely to prolong the life of the infant. In making a difficult decision like this, other factors than gestational age need to be considered because we do not have a precise way to measure gestational age (Tyson et al., 2008).

Despite our best efforts, a number of premature infants do not survive, and prematurity accounts for more than 70% of neonatal deaths (Williamson et al., 2008). However, there is a wide range of developmental outcomes among the infants who do survive. Some premature infants go on to have few, if any, developmental problems while other premature infants experience lifelong disabilities that can range from mild to very severe (Tyson et al., 2008). Many factors—prenatal conditions, birth circumstances, number and quality of medical services utilized by the family, availability and access to intervention services, and many more—come together to determine the quality of the final outcome.

The causes of prematurity are not well understood. The increase in the number of multiple births is one factor because multiples are more likely to be

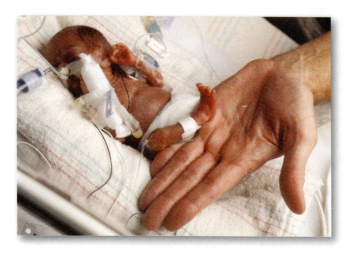

The smallest surviving premature infant. This is the smallest premature infant known to survive. Her name is Rumaisa Rahman, and she was born in December 2004 in Maywood, Illinois, weighing 8.6 ounces at birth (or a little over one-half pound). As technology improves, we are able to help smaller and smaller infants survive.

born prematurely. Unhealthy maternal behaviors during pregnancy, such as smoking, drinking, or using drugs, also are responsible for some premature and low-birth-weight births (Browne, 2005). In some cases there is an abnormality in the woman's reproductive system, such as a placenta that prematurely separates from the uterus or a cervix that opens too soon, but in many cases the underlying cause of premature births is unknown (Edgren, 2002).

When infants finally are large enough to leave the NICU, their parents need to turn their attention to what they can do to help their children reach their fullest potential. Numerous studies have looked at the outcomes for premature infants, and a consistent finding from that body of research is that low-birth-weight and premature infants are at an increased risk for cognitive impairment and academic failure as they grow up (Hill, Brooks-Gunn, & Waldfogel, 2003; Jepsen & Martin, 2006). They also can have sensory or motor impairments or be medically fragile. The risk for developmental problems increases as a function of the gestational age of the infant, so those who are born the earliest are also those who are at greatest risk (Cunningham et al., 2005; Dombrowski, Noonan, & Martin, 2007), but even in the case of very premature infants born at 24 to 26 weeks, 20% of the children were "totally free of impairment at 5 years of age or more" (Cunningham et al., 2005, p. 857).

To have good developmental outcomes, premature infants and their parents need access to comprehensive services that start early in development and are delivered consistently over a period of time (Hill et al., 2003). Even under the best of circumstances, caring for a premature infant places extraordinary demands upon a parent. That means that parents need to stay motivated to use the services and to follow through on the recommendations made by the professionals who work with their child. For this reason, how the parents view their infants and their expectations for the infants' outcomes is crucial.

If parents see their infant in a negative way and have low expectations for their child, they may unconsciously treat their infant in ways that actually hinder the child's development. This is called a *prematurity stereotype*, and both mothers of premature infants and mothers of full-term infants may see premature infants in a stereotypically negative way. When parents watched videotapes of premature infants and full-term infants, the premature infants were rated as being less physically mature in appearance, less sociable, less cognitively competent, and less behaviorally mature (Stern, Karraker, McIntosh, Moritzen, & Olexa, 2006). This was a negative stereotype, however, because all the videotapes actually showed full-term infants. When the researchers labeled the infant in the video as "premature," the behavior of a full-term infant was seen in a less favorable way simply because of the label and the preconceptions that came with it. For this reason it is important that we help parents of premature infants understand that their infants can have good developmental outcomes so that they can see and appreciate the progress that their children make.

The Transition to Parenthood

Becoming a parent is one of life's most important transitions. At the moment a baby is born, so is a new parent. Think for a moment about some of the major transitions you've had in your life. Whether it is moving from elementary school to middle school, getting your first paying job, moving out of your parents' home to live on your own, or coming to college, any major transition brings with it some amount of stress and requires coping and adjustment for you to handle it successfully. Becoming a parent affects all aspects of your life including your sense of identity, your relationships with your partner and others, and your career, so it is not surprising that becoming a parent involves a good deal of stress.

As a part of the Child and Family Development Project conducted at The Pennsylvania State University, researchers identified a number of issues that surface for new parents (Belsky & Kelly, 1994). These issues include fatigue and exhaustion (especially in the early weeks after the birth and especially for the mother), as well as feelings of anxiety, depression, and self-doubt about parental competence. Women worry about changes in their physical appearance and their figure,

9. An infant who is born prematurely will have developmental problems and lag behind other children of the same age.

TRUE/FALSE

False. Some premature infants (especially ones who were born very early) have lifelong developmental problems, but in many cases the development of premature infants does *not* differ substantially from that of full-term infants.

and men worry about providing for their family financially (Halle et al., 2008). Both worry about the increase in household responsibilities and changed relationships with in-laws (who also have an adjustment to make as they become grandparents, aunts, and uncles). And, of course, they both find sources of gratification, including the fact that they find the new baby to be irresistible and may become totally preoccupied with thoughts about the baby. If you have spent time with new parents, you have probably noticed that it is difficult to get them to talk about anything else!

How to divide the additional work that comes from having a baby in the household often becomes a sore point for the couple. One reason is that men and women often use a different yardstick to measure their contribution to this workload. If men compare what they do around the house and their direct contribution to caring for the newborn (that is, changing diapers, feeding the infant, getting up during the night) against what their fathers did, their contribution is significant in comparison. Between 1965 and 2003, the amount of time that men spent in child care tripled (Bianchi, Robinson, & Milkie, 2006). However, in most cases men's contribution still is only about 30% of what their partners are doing. Women's workload contribution to household chores increases by about 20% following the birth of a new baby (Belsky & Kelly, 1994), and between 1965 and 2003, the amount of time that women spent in child care and interacting with children doubled (Sullivan & Coltrane, 2008). Using that yardstick to measure the parents' relative contribution to child care, new mothers can end up feeling unhappy and disgruntled. Another change in the nature of the marital relationship that has been found in a number of studies is that the partners assume a more traditional division of household labor following the birth of a baby (Cowan & Cowan, 1992; Fox, 2001; Gjerdingen & Center, 2005). Fox (2001) has summarized this difference in roles by saying that as mothers assume more responsibility for child care, fathers "typically become mothers' helpers, babies' playmates and family providers" (p. 375).

We mentioned earlier that Jessie Bernard (1972) said that every marriage really consists of "his marriage" and "her marriage." Perhaps nowhere is this truer than when a couple becomes parents. In their book *The Transition to Parenthood* (1994), Jay Belsky and John Kelly say that while men and women become parents at the *same time*, they don't become parents in the *same way*. You can see some of these differences if you interview a couple who have recently become parents using the material in **Active Learning: When Partners Become Parents**.

TRUE/FALSE

10. Following the birth of a baby, modern couples pretty much share household and child care responsibilities.

False. Despite the fact that many new fathers today contribute more to household and child care responsibilities than their fathers probably did, it still is likely to be only about 30% of what their partners are doing.

ACTIVE LEARNING

When Partners Become Parents

If you know a couple who became first-time parents within the last few months, ask them to complete this quiz, which is adapted from research by Sean E. Brotherson (2004, 2007).

1. Make two copies of this list of transition issues, one for each partner.

Lack of sleep and tiredness	Anxiety about child illnesses
Changing diapers	Increased chores and housework
Expensive baby clothes	Decline in sexual interest
Financially providing for the family	Nutritional needs of the child
Lack of time for watching television	Doubts about parental competence/skill
Dissatisfaction with personal appearance	Recovery from labor and delivery
Concern about spouse's needs	Intrusive in-laws
Unpredictable shifts in mood and anxiety	Marital communication
Cost of child care	Changes in body figure
Time together as a couple	Financial preparation for child's schooling
Loss of free time for self and social activities	Individual stress about roles and responsibilities
Change in work situation	Couple disagreement about roles
Overstimulation of the child	Decisions about child care

2. Ask the partners on their own to look over the list and choose *their* own personal top 5 issues.

3. Next ask them to pick what they think are the top 5 issues for their partner.

4. Have the partners compare their lists to see what issues they share in common and where there are differences. Also look at how well the partners understand what are the top concerns for their partner.

5. Explain to your interviewees that mothers and fathers often differ on these concerns. Understanding what concerns they share and which ones differ gives them an opportunity to be more supportive and understanding toward their partner during this transition to parenthood.

In light of the amount of stress and the significant change in roles that occurs, the transition to becoming parents can have a negative impact on how satisfied the partners are with their marriage (Belsky & Kelly, 1994; Cowan & Cowan, 1995; Doss, Rhoades, Stanley, & Markman, 2009; Lawrence, Rothman, Cobb, Rothman, & Bradbury, 2008; Twenge, Campbell, & Foster, 2003). In a carefully controlled study, new parents were matched with a group of married couples who were childless by choice. Marital satisfaction was measured in the first 6 months of marriage, 1 month prior to the birth of the first child, and again at 6 and 12 months after the birth, with marital satisfaction measured at comparable times for the childless couples (Lawrence et al., 2008). The couples who became parents had a steeper drop in marital satisfaction from the time of the birth of the baby to the end of the first year postpartum than the childless couples who were married the same length of time. The authors conclude that the transition to parenthood has an adverse effect on martial satisfaction for at least that period of time. However, couples that were more satisfied with their marriages were more likely to have planned for their pregnancy, and couples that had planned pregnancies showed less of a decline during the transition to parenthood than couples that hadn't. The authors summarize their findings by saying that "parenthood hastens marital decline—even among relatively satisfied couples who select themselves into this transition—but planning status and pre-pregnancy marital satisfaction generally protect marriages from these declines" (Lawrence et al., 2008, p. 41).

When looking at the research on marital satisfaction, it is important to remember that a family is a system, and for most couples it is likely that any decline in satisfaction with their marriage is offset by other satisfactions that the couple gets from taking on its new role as parents. For instance, becoming a parent adds a new dimension to one's sense of personal identity (Lee, MacDermid, Dohring, & Kossek, 2005; Nomaguchi & Milkie, 2003; Reeves, 2006). In this new role, parents also have an opportunity to expand their network of social relationships (Gallagher & Gerstel, 2001; Nomaguchi & Milkie, 2003) and feeling competent as a parent contributes to a general sense of self-efficacy or control over what happens in one's life (Gallagher & Gerstel, 2001; Nomaguchi & Milkie, 2003; Wenger & Fowers, 2008). In fact, according to one recent study, most parents feel very good about the job they are doing as a parent and feel very good about how their child is developing (Wenger & Fowers, 2008). In a nationally representative sample of parents (Sweet & Bumpass, 1987), only 8% of the parents agreed with the statement that they wish they could be free from the responsibility of being a parent, and over three quarters of the parents in another national sample agreed that children are "the main satisfaction" in their life (Mellman, Lazarus, & Rivlin, 1990).

Conclusion

In this chapter we have described the incredible journey that is prenatal development. This journey took us from a single fertilized cell to a newborn ready to begin interacting with the environment and the people in it. In spite of all the risks we have outlined here, the vast majority of pregnancies end with the birth of a healthy, well-functioning baby, and, in spite of the difficulties parents encounter along the way, most would, and do, choose to do it all over again. In the chapters that follow, we will look at the basic developmental processes that occur as the newborn eventually becomes an adolescent. In the next chapter, we will focus on the processes of physical development as they begin in infancy and continue through childhood and adolescence.

CHAPTER SUMMARY

1. **What happens at the beginning of prenatal development?**
During **ovulation**, a woman's ovary releases an egg (or **ovum**). If it is fertilized by a sperm, the resulting zygote begins the process of prenatal development. That single cell multiplies until it becomes a hollow ball of cells called a **blastocyst**, which implants in the lining of the uterus. This is the **germinal stage** of prenatal development.

2. **What happens after the blastocyst implants in the uterus?**
In the **embryonic stage**, the number of cells in the blastocyst continues to increase until they form an **inner cell mass** (which becomes the **embryo**) and a ring of cells called the **trophoblast** (which becomes the support system for the pregnancy, including the **placenta**). The layers of the inner cell mass (the **endoderm**, **mesoderm**, and **ectoderm**) go on to become different organ systems in the body in a process called **organogenesis**. This is a **critical period** in development, and the developing embryo is very vulnerable to **teratogens**, which can disrupt the developmental process. The placenta brings oxygen and nutrients to the embryo by transfer from maternal blood through the placenta and carries away fetal waste. In the third stage of prenatal development, the **fetal stage**, the fetus grows in size and weight, and all the organ systems become functional prior to birth.

3. **What can a woman do to try to ensure a healthy pregnancy?**
Seeing a physician for early and regular prenatal visits will help ensure that a pregnancy progresses normally. A pregnant woman also needs to eat a healthy diet and avoid foods that can be dangerous while pregnant. She should limit her intake of caffeine and avoid drinking alcohol (which could result in **fetal alcohol syndrome** or **fetal alcohol spectrum disorders** in her unborn baby) and smoking (which is associated with low-birth-weight babies and premature deliveries, as well as developmental problems later in childhood). The use of illegal drugs threatens a pregnancy directly and is associated with a number of other harmful behaviors. Animal studies suggest that prenatal exposure to illegal drugs may alter the sensitivity of the developing brain to the active substances in those drugs. Prescription and over-the-counter drugs should only be used in consultation with the woman's physician. Any preexisting illnesses (such as a sexually transmitted infection) should be treated to protect the unborn baby, and pregnant women should try to reduce their stress level as much as possible since stress hormones can cross the placenta.

4. **What happens when a pregnant woman finally goes into labor?**
Labor occurs in three stages: In the first stage (which consists of **early labor**, **active labor**, and **transition**), contractions dilate and efface the cervix. Contractions become longer, stronger, and more frequent until the cervix is dilated to 10 centimeters. In the second stage of labor, the infant is born, and the condition of the newborn is assessed using the **Apgar Scale**. In the third stage of labor, the placenta is delivered.

5. **What birthing options do expectant parents have?**
Expectant parents can plan to have their baby in a hospital, at a birthing center, or at home. Some even choose to have water births. The woman can be assisted by a physician, a midwife, or a **doula**, and many fathers take childbirth classes so they can be present and assist with the birth of their child. Couples who take Lamaze childbirth preparation classes receive information on labor and delivery and learn techniques that can help control the pain of childbirth. However, many women in the United States also use analgesic medication (such as an epidural) to do this. Although this is a typical pattern in the United States and many other Western cultures, the experience of childbirth varies greatly from one culture to another.

6. **What do new mothers face following the birth of their babies?**
Many women experience a good deal of pressure (both perceived and real) to be "perfect mothers," but it takes time for a new mother to learn how to care for her newborn. Hormonal changes, both in the mother and in the new father, help prepare them to do this. Some new mothers suffer from the "baby blues," which are relatively mild and short-term, but others experience **postpartum depression**, which is more severe and long-lasting and requires medical intervention.

7. What are some capabilities of the newborn?

All of the newborn's senses are functional by the time of a full-term birth. The infant has different **infant states** that help keep sensory stimulation at a level that the newborn can process. A newborn spends most of the day asleep. Infants differ in how regular their schedules are and how easy they are to soothe.

8. What are threats to the well-being of infants?

Rates of **infant mortality** in the United States are higher than they are in many other industrialized countries. When a seemingly healthy infant dies unexpectedly, it is called **sudden infant death syndrome (SIDS)**. Not smoking while pregnant and after the birth of the baby and placing the infant on his back to sleep on a firm mattress are two simple things that help reduce this risk. Although there are some benefits of infants cosleeping with parents, the American Academy of Pediatrics recommends against it in order to reduce the possibility of SIDS.

When infants are born **prematurely** or at **low birth weight** they are at an increased risk for problems with physical and cognitive development. Premature infants usually receive special care following their birth in a neonatal intensive care unit, and they can have good developmental outcomes if they receive early intervention services.

9. How do new parents respond to the birth of their baby?

New parents often become totally enthralled with their new baby. However, exhaustion, anxiety, depression, and self-doubt about parental competence may cause problems for them. Women worry about changes in their physical appearance, men worry about providing financially for their family, and both worry about the increase in household responsibilities and changed relationships with in-laws. Marital relations must go through a period of readjustment, with some dissatisfaction as a common outcome. On the other hand, for many parents, having a new baby adds new feelings of competence, new social connections, and a sense of satisfaction in their parenting role.

Go to **www.sagepub.com/levine** for additional exercises and video resources. Select **Chapter 5, Prenatal Development, Birth, and the Newborn,** for chapter-specific activities.

part III

Building Blocks of Development

How Children Grow

Chapter Outline

chapter 6

Physical Development

The Body and the Brain

6

I n Chapter 1 we introduced you to the idea that there are different domains of development. In this section of the book, we look at each of these domains in more detail. We will describe physical, cognitive, social, and emotional development, as well as language and identity development. Although we have divided development into these separate aspects, in some respects it is an artificial division. Increasingly, research on children's development has attempted to integrate these areas to understand how they interact and influence each other. An example of this approach is found in a special section of the journal *Child Development*, published during the summer of 2009, which is

Test Your Knowledge

Test your knowledge of child development by deciding whether each of the following statements is *true* or *false,* and then check your answers as you read the chapter.

1. **True/False:** Humans use only 10% of their brains.
2. **True/False:** Newborn babies form synapses (connections between nerve cells) in their brains at the rate of a hundred new connections each second.
3. **True/False:** Children who practice the violin every day for many years become better at playing the violin in part because their activity makes physical changes in the structure of their brains.
4. **True/False:** There has been an alarming increase in the incidence of autism in recent years, and this is good cause for alarm.
5. **True/False:** It is important that infants crawl before they walk. If they go directly to walking they are more likely to develop learning disabilities later in life.
6. **True/False:** Infants are born with a taste for the foods common in their culture.
7. **True/False:** Adolescent girls who go through puberty earlier than their peers are happier and healthier than girls who go through puberty later.
8. **True/False:** In the United States, 90% of adolescents between the ages of 15 and 19 have had sex at least once.
9. **True/False:** Children who were breast-fed have higher IQ scores than those who were not.
10. **True/False:** The most effective way to prevent eating disorders is to give adolescents information about how harmful these behaviors can be to the adolescent's body.

Correct answers: (1) False, (2) False, (3) True, (4) False, (5) False, (6) True, (7) False, (8) False, (9) False, (10) False devoted to *developmental social cognitive neuroscience*. The articles in this issue look specifically at how development occurs through the interaction of social development, cognitive development, and brain development.

Even as we study one particular domain, such as physical development, we must keep in mind that each aspect of development affects and is affected by the others. For example, infants who experience a high level of stress (emotional) because of abuse or neglect are found to have higher levels of stress hormones later in life (physical), which may result in hyper-vigilance, the tendency to watch for and anticipate danger in the environment (cognitive) (Gunnar, 2007). Keeping in mind the fact that human beings are not just the sum of their parts, we approach our presentation of the basic building blocks of development with the awareness that we cannot really separate the effects of one "building block" from those of the others.

In this chapter, we will present some of the central issues in regard to the physical development of infants, children, and adolescents. We will begin by looking at how the brain develops (including some information on disabilities associated with brain development). We then will examine how we move from the physical helplessness of newborns to the incredible motor skills we see in children and adolescents. In the third section, we will discuss how our senses develop as we grow. In the last two sections, we will show how the body grows from infancy through the sexual maturation of adolescence and describe the critical role that nutrition plays in healthy growth.

Brain Development

1. Humans use only 10% of their brains.

TRUE/FALSE

False. Neurologist Barry Gordon, who studies the brain, says, "It turns out . . . that we use virtually every part of the brain, and that [most of] the brain is active almost all the time." (Boyd, 2008, para. 5)

We begin our study of brain development by addressing two common misconceptions. The first is the well-known myth that humans use only 10% of their brains. As we describe the parts and the functions of the brain in the following sections, it should become clear to you that we use *all* of our brains (Boyd, 2008). The second misconception is that brain and body are two separate entities—that what we *think* has little to do with how our bodies function and that our body's functioning has little to do with our thoughts. We will emphasize the ways in which the brain and the body are connected. What affects the brain affects the body, and what affects the body affects the brain (Diamond, 2009). To begin to see the surprising ways in which the brain and the body interact, try **Active Learning: Brain and Body**.

ACTIVE LEARNING

Brain and Body

Sit comfortably in a chair. Cross your right leg over your left (at the knee or ankle). Circle your right foot to the right (in a clockwise direction). Now, using your right hand, draw a number 6 in the air. Were you able to keep your foot circling to the right? A few people can, but most people cannot. This is easy to do using your right foot and your *left* hand, so the problem lies in the fact that the left side of your brain controls the right side of your body and seems to be able to go in only one direction at a time! You know that your body is physically capable of doing both actions, but your brain may not let you do both at the same time. Children too are limited in their physical abilities in part because of their brain development. We will be learning about the impact of the brain on the body's activities, but we will also learn about the impact the body has on the brain and the effect that experience has on the development of *both* body and brain.

Structures of the Brain

The brain is an organ of the body made up of a number of different parts. We can examine the brain from two perspectives: from side to side and from back to front. If you could see into a person's head as you looked down at that person, you would see that the brain is divided down the middle into two halves, or **hemispheres**. Some parts of the brain are the same on both sides, and some are different. For example, the motor cortex that controls the body's movements is similar on both sides, but the control crosses over: The right side of the brain controls the left side of the body, and vice versa. However, the language centers of the brain appear largely on the left side, at least for right-handed people. Lefties may have their language centers on either or both sides. The two sides of the brain communicate with each other through the structure that joins them, called the **corpus callosum**. Although the two sides have distinct functions, there is no such thing as being totally "right-brained" or "left-brained." Both halves of our brains are involved in complex ways in almost everything we do. For example, although much of language is processed on the left side, specific aspects of language, such as humor and the emotional tone of what you say, are found in the right hemisphere (Kinsbourne, 2009).

We get a different view of the brain when we look at it from the side. The parts, or lobes, of the brain have some distinct functions, which we describe below. However, as we saw with the two hemispheres, it is important to realize that most aspects of human functioning involve many parts of the brain in coordination with one another. For example, the occipital lobe is known to control vision; however, the parietal, temporal, and frontal lobes also play a role in vision (Merck Manual, 2008).

Look at Figure 6.1, along with Table 6.1, to identify the parts of the brain in this image, working from the back of the head (on the right side) toward the front (on the left side). Starting at the lower back of the head, the brain stem (in blue) includes the spinal cord, which controls our basic functions such as breathing. Next, the cerebellum (in green) controls balance and movement. Above the cerebellum, the cerebrum or cortex controls the higher functions of thought and action. The cerebrum includes many different parts, including the occipital lobe (in yellow), which processes vision; the temporal lobe (in pink), which processes hearing; the parietal lobe (in orange), which processes sensory input and spatial awareness; and the frontal lobe (in red), which processes complex thoughts, movement, language, and self-control. The very front of the cerebrum is called the prefrontal cortex, which controls judgment and the ability to plan. Within the cerebrum, but not visible in Figure 6.1, are the amygdala and the hippocampus, which are important in the experience and expression of emotions, memories, and sensations (Bear, Connors, & Paradiso, 2007). Although this is a good description of some of the functions that we currently know are associated with different areas of the brain, brain research is one of the most active areas in the field of child development, so our understanding of brain functions will undoubtedly change as research continues.

As we continue our discussion of the brain, this overview should help you think about how different aspects of physical development are linked back to the different parts of the brain and the functions they control. In future chapters you will learn more about the cognitive, language, and emotion centers of the brain and their functions.

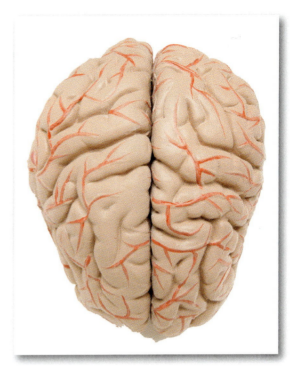

The two hemispheres of the human brain. Although the two hemispheres of the brain may look similar, some brain functions are handled mainly by one side, other functions are handled mainly by the other side, and some are handled by both. The corpus callosum (not shown in this picture) connects the two hemispheres so they can communicate with each other.

Hemispheres   The two halves of the cerebellum.

Corpus callosum   The band of fibers that connects the two hemispheres of the brain.

Figure 6.1

Side view of the human brain. Use the color code in Table 6.1 to locate the different areas of the brain in this photo. Pay attention to the different functions controlled by each brain structure.

Table 6.1

Brain structures and functions

Name of structure	Color in figure	Some functions of each structure
Brain stem	Blue	Includes the spinal cord, which controls our basic functions such as breathing
Cerebellum	Green	Controls balance and movement
Occipital lobe	Yellow	Processes visual information
Temporal lobe	Pink	Involved in hearing, language, memory for facts, visual memory, emotion
Parietal lobe	Orange	Processes sensory input and spatial awareness
Frontal lobe	Red	Processes complex thoughts, movement, language, working memory, and self-control

Developmental Processes

Neurons and Synaptic Connections

The brain is made of 100 billion nerve cells, called **neurons** (Pakkenberg & Gundersen, 1997). Each nerve cell sends messages via special chemicals called **neurotransmitters** (*neuro* refers to the neurons of the brain; *transmit* is to send) to other nerve cells through extensions of the cell called **axons**. Each cell receives messages through receptors called **dendrites**. The place where the axon from one neuron meets the dendrite of another neuron is called the **synapse** as illustrated in Figure 6.2. Just about everything we do depends on communication between nerve cells. Neurotransmitters are released from one cell and bring their "message" to the second cell. Adults have approximately 1 quadrillion (!) of these synaptic connections. Infants' brains are more active than adults' brains because they are so busy forming connections (Gopnik, Meltzoff, & Kuhl, 1999).

Infants are born with almost all the neurons they will ever have; however, they have relatively few synapses or connections between them. As a result, babies have fewer inborn behavior patterns than other animals, and they are more open to learning from their environment. The experiences they have actually shape the development of synaptic connections and the formation of their brains (Rosenzweig, Breedlove, & Watson, 2005). The development of new synapses is referred to as **synaptogenesis**. After a baby is born, new synapses may be formed at the rate of more than a *million* connections *per second* (Greenough, Black, & Wallace, 1987).

Plasticity of the Brain: Experience-Expectant Versus Experience-Dependent Brain Development

The ability of the infant brain to change in form and function is referred to as **plasticity**. If you, as an adult, had half of your brain (one hemisphere) removed, the result would be catastrophic. You would lose movement in the opposite side of your body, and you would lose the functions handled in that hemisphere. For example, people who have damage to the language centers in the left hemisphere may be unable to speak. However, until about age 4 or 5, children who have had one hemisphere removed as a result of an otherwise untreatable condition, such as severe epilepsy, can recover almost full function (Eliot, 1999). This occurs because the brain at this young age has enough plasticity that brain cells that were originally intended to serve one function (for example, controlling movement) can turn into cells that control another function instead (for example, language).

At various times within the first years of life, babies' brains produce many more synaptic connections than are found in the adult brain (Gopnik et al., 1999; Huttenlocher & Dabholkar, 1997). However, many of these connections do not survive. In a process called **pruning**, synaptic connections that are used remain, and those that are not used deteriorate and disappear. Just as you prune away dead branches on a tree to strengthen it, this process strengthens the brain. Rather than being a terrible loss, this process produces a brain that is much more efficient (Huttenlocher, 1999). In fact, we will see later in this chapter that some researchers connect a lack of pruning to the development of the disorder known as autism. The normal pruning process is completed in some areas of the brain by age 12. In others, especially the prefrontal cortex, which controls judgment and impulse control, the process is not completed until well into adolescence or early adulthood (Giedd, 2004; Gogtay et al., 2004; Huttenlocher & Dabholkar, 1997).

What determines which synaptic connections will remain? The process of pruning follows a "use it or lose it" principle. Greenough et al. (1987) described two ways that this happens: experience-expectant mechanisms and experience-dependent mechanisms. **Experience-expectant brain development** occurs because our brain *expects* certain

---

Neurons The cells that make up the nervous system of the body.

Neurotransmitters Chemicals that transmit nerve impulses across a synapse from one nerve cell to another.

Axons The parts of a nerve cell that conduct impulses away from the cell body.

Dendrites The portions of a neuron that receive impulses from other neurons.

Synapse The place where the axon from one neuron meets the dendrite of another neuron.

Synaptogenesis The development of new synapses.

2. Newborn babies form synapses (connections between nerve cells) in their brains at the rate of a hundred new connections each second. **TRUE/FALSE**

False. New synapses form *much* faster than that. Newborns form over a million new connections between neurons every second.

Plasticity The ability of an immature brain to change in form and function.

Pruning The deterioration and disappearance of synapses that are not used.

Video Link 6.1
Removed right hemisphere.

Experience-expectant brain development Development that occurs when we encounter experiences that our brain *expects* as a normal event.

Neurons and synapses. Two nerve cells (neurons) are connected to each other as the axon of one reaches the dendrite of the other at the synapse (shown at the left). At the synapse, chemicals called neurotransmitters are released from one cell and bring their "message" to the second cell (shown at the right).

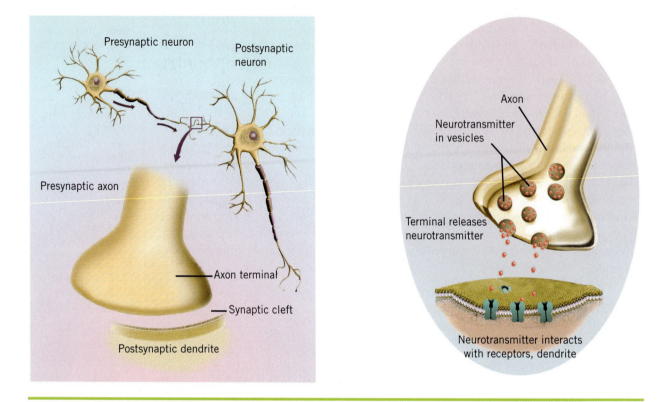

Video Link 6.2
A baby's brain.

Experience-dependent brain development
Development that occurs in response to specific learning experiences.

events to happen. For example, in the normal course of events our eyes will be exposed to light. When these expected events occur, the pathways that are used are retained. In experiments with kittens, Hubel and Wiesel (1965) showed that if this does not happen, the eye still develops normally, but the part of the brain that processes visual information does not function. Kittens with one eye closed for a period of time after birth were never able to develop vision in that eye, even when the eye was later open. This is why children who have one eye that has considerably less vision or doesn't coordinate with the other eye (a condition called amblyopia or "lazy eye") must have intervention early in their lives, or they may lose effective vision in that eye.

Experience-dependent brain development is much more individual and depends on each person's particular experiences. In addition to unused synapses being pruned away, it appears that new synapses develop in response to stimulation. For example, Elbert, Pantev, Wienbruch, Rockstroh, and Taub (1995) studied the brains of violinists. If you pretend to play the violin, on which hand are the fingers more active? If you imagine playing the violin you will see that the fingers of your left hand move all around, pressing on the strings to produce different notes, while the fingers of your right hand usually stay in one position, holding the bow. Elbert found that the area of the right side of the brain that controls the left hand has many more synaptic connections than the same area of the left side of the brain in violinists. It is unlikely that these people are born this way, making them more likely to become violinists.

Instead, the constant use of the fingers of the left hand to move and hold the appropriate strings on the violin further develops that part of the right side of the brain.

Myelination of Neurons in the Brain

So far we have discussed the development of synapses through the process of synaptogenesis, but in order for messages to be sent successfully, another necessary process in the development of the nervous system is **myelination**. In order for neurons to work efficiently, they need to be coated with a fatty substance known as myelin, as shown in Figure 6.3.

Picture an electrical cord between the wall socket and your lamp. How does the message travel from your light switch to turn on the lamp on your desk? Within the electrical cord is a metal wire that carries the electrical current. If bare wire were used with no insulation, not only would you get a shock when you touched it, but your light would not work very well. Only some of the current, not all of it, would be likely to arrive at its goal. For that reason, an electrical cord is always insulated with some material that cannot carry an electric current. As a result the electrical message turns your light on. In a similar fashion, the neurons in the nervous system are insulated with myelin so that the message sent by the neurotransmitters will be received most effectively.

3. Children who practice the violin every day for many years become better at playing the violin in part because their activity makes physical changes in the structure of their brains. **TRUE/FALSE**

True. Research has shown that for children who play violin, the part of the brain that controls motor activity on the left side of the body is more developed than that same part of the brain that controls the right side of the body. Violinists use the fingers on their left hand to move along the length of the strings, but the fingers of the right hand only hold the bow.

Myelination The process of laying down a fatty sheath of myelin on the neurons.

Figure 6.3

The myelin sheath. The myelin sheath is a fatty coating that wraps around the nerves to ensure that the chemical messages sent between neurons are delivered efficiently. In this figure, the axon is shown in blue with the myelin sheath wrapped around it. A cross section is shown here so you can see how the coating wraps around the axon.

When babies are born, just as the synaptic connections are not complete, so too the myelin sheath does not yet cover all of the nerves in the nervous system. The process of producing synaptic connections, pruning away those that are not being used, and myelinating the connections that are left will continue throughout childhood and adolescence (Paus et al., 1999). These processes improve the efficiency of the signals sent from the brain to the body and result in greater organization of the brain (Society for Neuroscience, 2008). We have already learned that synaptogenesis is affected by our experiences through the process of experience-dependent brain development. There is also evidence that myelination is affected by our experiences. Bengtsson et al. (2005) compared brain development in children who spent long hours practicing piano to that in children who did not play piano. Their evidence indicates that the extra stimulation that certain neurons experience when children are practicing results in more myelination of those neurons, including those in the corpus callosum, which connect the two hemispheres of the brain. The corpus callosum is involved in the ability to coordinate movements of your two hands at the same time. In this study, children who played piano had increased brain efficiency, and this increased ability continued into adolescence. This finding may help explain the musical abilities of Mozart, an extraordinary composer and pianist. Although Mozart was clearly a genius in the creation of music, it appears that the long hours that his overbearing father forced him to practice may actually have helped his talent develop by further developing this area of his brain.

Video Link 6.3
Adolescent brain development.

The adolescent brain continues to develop in many ways, including the continued myelination of speech centers and motor centers, particularly the centers involved in the coordination and movement of the fingers, which allows for greater ability in drawing, weaving, and other fine motor skills (Paus et al., 1999). Of great interest is the finding that development is still occurring in the prefrontal cortex, that part of the brain that has to do with judgment and impulse control. There is a growth spurt in the development of new synapses in this area of the brain at age 9 or 10, and then another round of pruning begins in early adolescence. In addition, the connections between these centers for reasoning and those for emotions, such as the amygdala, are still developing, so emotional responses in adolescents are less tempered by reasoning than will be the case in adults (Society for Neuroscience, 2007b). The tendency of some adolescents to act on their emotions without thinking through a situation may be related to the immaturity of this system in their brain. In **Active Learning: Teenage Brain Development** you will see how this information has even played a role in judgments made by the legal system.

ACTIVE LEARNING

Teenage Brain Development

Imagine that you are serving on a jury deciding the following case: At age 17, Christopher Simmons brutally murdered an elderly woman, Mrs. Shirley Crook, as he robbed her house. Simmons was convicted of this crime. It is now your job to assign punishment: life in prison or the death penalty. What factors would you take into account in making your decision? Would the defendant's age be one of them? Give your decision and the reasons for it, and then see below to find out what the Supreme Court decided and why.

Answer: In fact, Christopher Simmons was initially sentenced to death by a lower court. The case eventually went to the Supreme Court, which overturned this penalty in favor of life in prison. During the Supreme Court considerations, the American Society for Adolescent Psychiatry (supported by the American Psychological Association, among other organizations) entered into evidence an argument that adolescents may have impaired impulse control and judgment because of the immaturity of their brain development. In particular, the prefrontal cortex, which controls these functions, is not fully developed (Lehmann, 2004). In the final decision, Justice Anthony Kennedy stated, "The adolescent's brain works differently from ours. Parents know it" (Anderson, 2005, para. 25). This is still a very controversial issue. Would you agree that adolescent brain development should be an argument to limit the harshness of punishment for crimes committed? Why or why not?

Disabilities Related to Brain Development

When brain development does not occur as expected, or when there is damage to the brain at any point, a number of disabilities may result. We discuss here two very different types of outcome: cerebral palsy and autism. We discuss cerebral palsy because specific brain abnormalities are known to cause this disability. We include autism in this section on the brain because, although the precise cause (or causes) of autism remains elusive, there now is almost universal agreement that there is an underlying biological explanation connected with brain development.

Cerebral Palsy

The term **cerebral palsy** can be used to describe a number of chronic conditions that appear early in development and primarily involve body movement, muscle tone, and muscle coordination (de Paula Careta & Louro, 2005). The cause is faulty development or damage to one or more of the parts of the brain that control motor functioning and posture. While some children are profoundly affected and need total care, others show only mild impairment and require little or no special assistance.

Infants born prematurely or at low birth weight, or whose mothers had an infection during their pregnancies, are at an increased risk of developing cerebral palsy (MacLennan, 1999; United Cerebral Palsy, 2007). About 70% of the cases of cerebral palsy result from brain injury during prenatal development, most often with no known cause, and an additional 10%–20% are due to brain injury during the birth process itself (United Cerebral Palsy, 2007). The remaining 10% occur after the infant is born but early in development, when an infection or injury causes damage to the brain. This is just one of the many good reasons why parents need to be sure that their infants are protected from falls and always securely buckled into an approved safety seat when riding in the car. Each year in the United States, about 3,000 babies and an additional 1,500 preschoolers are diagnosed with the condition (de Paula Careta & Louro, 2005). Although this condition does not get progressively worse, early intervention and therapy can be beneficial to the child by preventing or delaying the onset of secondary problems.

Cerebral palsy is not a disease, it is not communicable, and (unfortunately) it cannot be cured. Because there is a wide range of symptoms and degree of severity, the goal of any intervention is to create an individual treatment plan that meets each child's unique needs. Today medications can help control seizures and muscle spasms, surgery can lengthen muscles and tendons that are too short to function, and physical therapy can help the child build necessary skills. You also may have seen new technologies that let a child with cerebral palsy use even limited head movements to operate a computer with a voice synthesizer to communicate. With the menu of treatments available, early identification and intervention remain the best chance for children with cerebral palsy to maximize their potential.

Cerebral palsy
A chronic condition that appears early in development and primarily involves problems with body movement and muscle coordination.

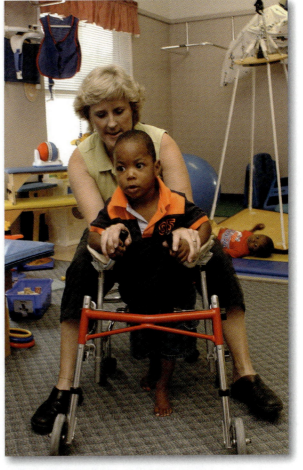

Physical therapy session for a child with cerebral palsy. When cerebral palsy affects a child's motor abilities, therapy such as this can help the child improve his movement, flexibility, and balance.

Autism

Autism A pervasive developmental disorder that is characterized by difficulties with social interaction, problems with verbal and nonverbal communication, and deficits in symbolic and imaginative play.

Autism is a pervasive developmental disorder that is linked with brain function. It is characterized by three distinctive behaviors: difficulties with social interaction, problems with verbal and nonverbal communication, and deficits in symbolic and imaginative play (Bishop, Luyster, Richler, & Lord, 2008). (You will find more information about autism and language development in Chapter 9.) Autism is one of several conditions that are part of what is called the autism spectrum, which can range from relatively mild to very debilitating. The number and specific types of developmental delay interact with the child's overall intellectual ability to produce a range of outcomes for the child (Coplan, 2000). For some children, the severity of the condition lessens over time and they can function well with just a little guidance and support, but others need ongoing close supervision and care throughout their lives. In a few rare cases, the child can even show extraordinary abilities in a limited area of expertise—what is called being a *savant*. If you have seen the movie *Rain Man*, you may remember that the main character suffers from autism, but he also has an extraordinary mathematical ability (Cheatham, Rucker, & Polloway, 1995).

Over the years, a number of possible causes of autism have been proposed and investigated. See **Journey of Research: Searching for the Cause of Autism** for more information and to see how our understanding of possible causes of autism has changed over time.

Searching for the Cause of Autism

JOURNEY *of* RESEARCH

In an early description of autism, the psychiatrist Leo Kanner (1949) identified the cause as parental coldness marked by a mechanical attention to the child's needs, without any genuine warmth or enjoyment. The infant's aloofness and withdrawal were seen as an adaptive response to an almost intolerable situation. As a result of Kanner's description, the psychological literature from the 1940s through the early 1970s was filled with references to what were called "refrigerator mothers" (Frith, 2003).

More contemporary research has focused on possible biological causes. Evidence for a genetic cause comes from the observation that autism runs in families (Bailey, LeCourteur, Gottesman, & Bolton, 1995) and the fact that boys are 4.3 times more likely than girls to be diagnosed as autistic (Fombonne, 2005). Other lines of research have identified structural differences in the brains of autistic children, such as a massive overgrowth of brain synapses and a lack of synaptic pruning (Carper & Courchesne, 2005). Remember our earlier discussion of the importance of synaptic

pruning for efficient brain function? Still other research has found functional differences, such as reduced activity in the dorsal medial-frontal cortex, the portion of the brain that mediates emotional and social responsiveness (Mundy, 2003). These differences in the brains of autistic children may contribute to the difficulty they have in understanding what other people are thinking, which has been referred to as "mindblindness" (Baron-Cohen, 2001). You will learn more about this aspect of autism in Chapter 12.

A third line of research has examined possible environmental causes (or triggers) of autism. The one that you may have heard of is the research that has looked at the role of mercury used as a preservative in the measles-mumps-rubella (MMR) vaccine given to infants as a possible trigger for the disorder. In 1998 the British medical journal *Lancet* published a study that appeared to find a link between the vaccine and autism (Wakefield et al., 1998). In response to this report and other similar research (California Department of Developmental

Services, 1999), public concern about the safety of the vaccine grew. However, in 2004, 10 of the 12 original authors of the *Lancet* article issued a retraction of their research that said, in part: "We wish to make it clear that in [the 1998] paper no causal link was established between MMR vaccine and autism as the data were insufficient. . . . We consider now is the appropriate time that we should [get] together formally to retract the interpretation placed upon findings in the [1998] paper" (Murch et al., 2004, p. 750).

The scientific consensus at this time is that clinical evidence does not support the contention that immunizations are a cause for autism (Centers for Disease Control and Prevention [CDC], 2009b; Dales, Hammer, & Smith, 2001). For instance, Fombonne, Zakarian, Bennett, Meng, and McLean-Heywood (2005) found that there was no difference in the incidence of autism in a cohort of children in Montreal, Quebec, Canada, who had received one MMR vaccination versus those who had received two. Further, when the mercury compound in the vaccine was eventually removed from the vaccine, there was no parallel decrease in the incidence of autism. In fact, the incidence in the group of children who had not received the vaccine was slightly higher (Fombonne et al., 2005). The far stronger research evidence for a genetic component and/or neurological involvement makes it unlikely that some event after the child has been born (such as an immunization) is the cause (Taylor, 2006). Because understanding the cause of autism is of such great importance, research on this topic will need to continue.

Accurately estimating the prevalence of autism spectrum disorders is not easy. In December 2009, the Centers for Disease Control and Prevention (2009b) released statistics estimating that 1 out of every 110 children in the United States has an autism spectrum disorder. This estimate represented a 57% increase in diagnosed cases of autism between 2000 and 2009. Understandably information such as this has led to concern about a possible epidemic or a baffling explosion of autism (Gernsbacher, Dawson, & Goldsmith, 2005).

It is obvious that genetics cannot explain such a sudden increase, so as described in the **Journey of Research: Searching for the Cause of Autism**, the fear has been that there is something in the environment that is responsible for the upsurge. However, a far simpler explanation has been offered by Gernsbacher and colleagues (2005), who suggested that changes in how we identify autism spectrum disorders have led to improved case finding. When autism first appeared in the *Diagnostic and Statistical Manual of Mental Disorders* (DSM) in 1980, a diagnosis of autism included six criteria that all had to be present. However, in 1994 the updated DSM-IV added 16 criteria to the list, and only half of them need to be present to satisfy this diagnosis. The description of the criteria also was broadened. For instance, "gross deficits in language" became "difficulty sustaining a conversation" (Gernsbacher et al., 2005, p. 56). The definition, which had previously described autism, now included three separate but related diagnostic categories referred to as autism spectrum disorders (CDC, 2009b).

The Centers for Disease Control and Prevention acknowledges that there has been a dramatic increase in the number of diagnosed cases of autism spectrum disorders (ASDs) in the previous decade but concludes that whether it is the broader definition of ASDs, a true increase in the risk for a child developing an ASD, or an increased community awareness of the disorder that brings more children in for assessment cannot be determined at this time (CDC, 2009b; see also Fombonne, 2005). Each of these factors probably has made some contribution to the increase.

Although any increase in the true incidence of ASDs would be a cause for concern, the identification of a greater number of children with an autism spectrum disorder is not, in and of itself, necessarily a bad thing. The children who are now being identified represent a group of children who otherwise might have been overlooked but who can benefit from early and comprehensive intervention. **Active Learning: Community Resources** guides you in finding resources in your own community for children with autism and cerebral palsy.

4. There has been an alarming increase in the incidence of autism in recent years, and this is good cause for alarm.

TRUE/FALSE

False. While it is true that there has been an increase in the number of children diagnosed as autistic, this may not be a cause for alarm. We have broadened the criteria used to diagnose autism, so we now may be identifying more children with an autism spectrum disorder who can benefit from intervention, and that would be a good thing.

Community Resources

Use an online search engine to locate resources for children and adolescents with cerebral palsy or autism within your community. If you were a parent or teacher of a child with either of these conditions, what sources of support would be available to you? Volunteering with these agencies is a good way to find out more about what life is like for children and adults with these disorders and also about possible careers in the helping professions.

Motor Development

In the following section we will examine the development of motor skills. We begin with a description of babies' first movements: the reflexes. We then describe how the myelination of the nervous system plays a large role in determining the sequence in which motor milestones are achieved. Finally, we discuss other factors, such as physical activity, that influence the development of motor skills.

Infant Reflexes

Reflexes Patterned, involuntary motor responses that are controlled by the lower brain centers.

Newborns can't move around on their own and they don't have much control over their limbs, but from the time they are born they have a set of involuntary, patterned motor responses called **reflexes** that are controlled by the lower brain centers and that help them respond to some of the stimuli in the environment. These reflexes are hardwired into the newborn's nervous system, so they don't need to be learned. Within the first few months of life, the higher centers of the brain develop and take over from the lower centers. As this happens, most of these reflexes disappear on a predictable timetable (see Table 6.2) and are replaced by voluntary and intentional actions. For instance, if you gently touch a newborn's cheek, she will reflexively turn in the direction of the touch to find a source of food. It doesn't take very long, however, for even a young infant to learn signals indicating that she is about to be fed. At that point, she will begin to turn in the direction of her caregiver as soon as she senses that it is mealtime.

It is not as though reflexes and voluntary behavior are two distinct types of response. There is a continuum that represents different mixes of reflexive and voluntary behavior that we see as motor development proceeds (Anderson, Roth, & Campos, 2005). However, if a reflex is missing or fails to disappear when it should, this can be an indication there is a neurological problem, and the infant should be assessed by a doctor.

Infants begin moving even before birth, exercising their developing muscles and giving feedback to the motor cortex of the brain that helps develop voluntary movements after birth (Eliot, 1999). Although the fetus cannot voluntarily control its movements, it is possible to see prenatal ultrasound pictures of babies sucking their thumb. It appears that some kind of reflexive behavior may result in

Prenatal thumb sucking. Reflex activities may result in thumb sucking as early as 12–14 weeks of gestational age.

Table 6.2

Newborn reflexes

Reflex	Description	When this reflex disappears
Sucking reflex	When something touches the roof of the baby's mouth, her lips close and she will suck reflexively.	About 2 months
Crawling reflex	When the baby is placed on his tummy, his legs will make crawling motions even though he is not able to move forward.	About 2 months
Moro reflex (or startle reflex)	When a baby loses support and feels like she is falling or hears a loud sound, she will flail her arms and legs outward. Most babies will cry when startled and then will pull their limbs back in.	About 3 months
Stepping reflex	If you support the baby's weight but let his feet touch the ground, he will lift and set his feet in a "walking" motion.	About 3 months
Galant reflex	When the baby is lying on her stomach and you stroke her middle or lower back near the spine, she will curve her body toward the side that is being stroked.	About 4 months
Tonic neck reflex	When a baby is placed on his back, he will stretch out the arm and leg in the direction he is facing and pull inward the opposite arm and leg.	About 4 months
Babinski reflex	When you stroke the side of a baby's foot, her toes will fan out and her foot will turn inward.	About 4 months
Rooting reflex	If you gently stroke the baby's cheek, he will turn in the direction of the touch.	About 4 months
Palmar grasp	When you touch the baby's palm with your index finger, she will clench your finger.	About 6 months
Gag reflex	This reflexive gag helps prevent choking.	This reflex does not disappear.
Righting reflex	When a baby is placed on her tummy, she will lift her head to clear her nose and mouth.	This reflex does not disappear.

SOURCE: National Institutes of Health (2009); The Free Dictionary (2009).

the fetus "finding" its thumb (Becher, 2006). Interestingly, the preference for one thumb or the other is predictive of whether the child will be right-handed or left-handed (Hepper, Wells, & Lynch, 2005).

Development of Motor Skills

Two basic forms of motor skills are gross motor and fine motor. **Gross motor skills** involve the large muscle groups of the body (for example, the legs and arms). **Fine motor skills** involve small movements, mostly of the hands and fingers, but also of the lips and tongue. The development of these skills is linked with the development of the brain and the entire nervous system.

The motor cortex is the strip at the top of the brain that goes from "ear to ear" and controls the conscious motor movements of the body (Bower, 2004). If you were to guess, which parts of the body do you think take up most of the area in the motor cortex? If you guessed the legs, because they are large and have so much movement, you will be surprised. The majority of

Video Link 6.4
Newborn reflexes.

Gross motor skills Skills that involve the large muscle groups of the body—for example, the legs and arms.

Fine motor skills Skills that involve small movements, mostly of the hands and fingers, but also of the lips and tongue.

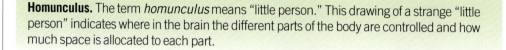

Figure 6.4

Homunculus. The term *homunculus* means "little person." This drawing of a strange "little person" indicates where in the brain the different parts of the body are controlled and how much space is allocated to each part.

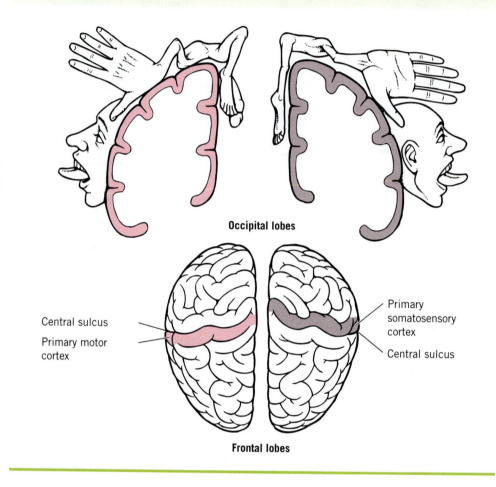

Occipital lobes

Central sulcus

Primary motor cortex

Primary somatosensory cortex

Central sulcus

Frontal lobes

the motor cortex is used to control the mouth and the hands, which contain many more muscles than the legs. Look at Figure 6.4 to see how the body is represented in the brain, both for motor activities and for sensory input. A recent finding about the motor cortex has added to our understanding of how complex the function of the brain truly is. Neuroscientists in England found that the motor cortex is activated not just when we actually act, for example when we kick something, but also when we read action words, such as *kick* (Bower, 2004).

Myelination of Motor Neurons

The brain connects through the spinal cord to all of the neurons in the body. As we discussed previously, the nervous system works more efficiently when it has been coated with the fatty substance known as myelin. This is true for the neurons in the brain but is also true for the motor neurons in the body. The myelin sheath is set down in the nervous system in the body in two directions: from the head downward (in a *cephalocaudal* direction, from head to tail) and from the torso out to the extremities of the fingers and toes (in a **proximodistal** direction, from the center of the body out toward the extremities). The cephalocaudal direction of myelination results in infants gaining control of their bodies in the following sequence.

Proximodistal
Development that proceeds from the central axis of the body toward the extremities.

Milestones in motor development. As myelination moves downward through the body from the head to the lower limbs, infants gain control over each part of their body in succession. You may have noticed that this sequence helps explain the motor milestones that most babies go through and that parents joyfully record in their baby books.

1. Head and neck: Parents of newborn infants must be careful to support the baby's head, but as myelination proceeds downward, babies become able to hold up their head independently.

2. Shoulders: A newborn placed on his stomach will remain in that position, but as myelination moves down the neck, the baby will be able to raise his head to see the world.

3. Shoulders: As the shoulders come under control, the baby will reach the next milestone: rolling over (from stomach to back and from back to stomach).

4. Arms and chest: With control of this region, the baby will be able to use his arms to push up from his stomach to be able to survey a larger area around him. However, his legs are still flat to the floor.

5. Hips: When the hips and back come under the baby's control, she can now begin to sit up, at first with support and then independently.

6. Thighs: With control of the legs, babies can pull their legs underneath them and begin to crawl. Often babies will initially crawl backward, in part because their control of their arms is greater than their control of their legs (Greene, 2004).

7. Lower legs: With control traveling down the thighs to the lower part of the legs, babies begin to pull up on furniture to a standing position.

8. Feet: Control of the feet is needed in order to walk independently. At first babies walk with feet wide apart and hands raised to help with balance. As they gain more control of their feet and toes and better balance, their gait becomes more like that of an adult.

Proximodistal development of motor skills. Look at how you hold your pen or pencil. Which fingers do you use, and how do you use them? Compare how your hand works to how these children are able to use their hands. Why do you think that preschoolers are often given "fat crayons" to use instead of pens?

The proximodistal direction of myelination, from the central axis of the body out to the extremities, has the following results:

1. Torso: Babies will roll over, using control of their chest and shoulders.

2. Arms: Control of the arms begins with the ability to swipe at objects infants see. They become able to use their arms to push up from the ground, which eventually develops into crawling.

3. Hands: When infants begin to purposefully grasp objects, they scoop objects with all their fingers up against their palms, in what is called the palmar grasp.

4. Fingers: As they gain control of their fingers, they can use thumb and forefinger to pick up things as small as Cheerios. This is called the pincer grasp. Only later can they control the rest of their fingers to be able to use a tripod grasp, using thumb, forefinger, and middle finger to hold a pencil.

To understand the important functions of the myelin sheath, we can look at a disease called Guillain-Barré (GHEE-yan bah-RAY). This illness occurs when the white cells in the body that usually fight off disease attack the myelin sheath instead. The myelin is stripped off in the direction opposite from how it was put down—that is, from the feet up and from the fingers inward toward the middle of the body. Consequently people with Guillain-Barré first lose control of their feet and then are unable to move their legs as the disease moves up their body in the reverse order of the cephalocaudal principle. Likewise in their extremities they first lose control of their fingers, then their hands, and then their arms in the reverse order of the proximodistal principle (Bear et al., 2007; Simmons, 2010).

Variability in Motor Milestones

Although brain development is necessary for motor skill development, it is not the only factor involved. The development of motor milestones happens in the same way for most babies around the world. This fact indicates that motor development is strongly controlled by our genes, which dictate the expected sequence of development. Thus, motor development can be described as strongly canalized, as we described in Chapter 4; that is, genes only allow for a few possibilities in response to the environment. However, there is some variation in the timing of motor milestones. For example, although most infants in the United States walk by 12–14 months, some walk as early as 9 months and some not until 18 months. Development may be uneven with some areas forging ahead while others are slower to develop. A pediatrician would be able to discuss with parents whether or not a later onset of walking is of concern for their child or whether it is just a normal variation in development of motor skills.

In addition to individual differences, there are cultural differences in the age at which children begin to walk. These differences result from child care practices that are linked to cultural practices and beliefs. For example, Super (1976) found that Kenyan parents "practiced" walking and sitting skills with their babies, and as a result their babies reached these particular milestones sooner than American babies. As we described earlier, the stepping reflex typically disappears at about 3 months of age as babies become chunkier and they cannot support their heavy bodies with their small legs (Thelen, Fisher, & Ridley-Johnson, 2002). In contrast, the Kenyan babies did not lose their reflex before they developed real walking. Other activities that they did not practice, such as rolling over, did not develop more quickly. Clearly, specific skills developed earlier because these babies practiced them, with the help of their parents. To test this hypothesis, Zelazo, Zelazo, Cohen, and Zelazo (1993) had Canadian parents practice walking skills or sitting skills with their 6-week-old babies. They found that skill development was quite specific: Those trained in walking were able to walk at an earlier age, while those trained in sitting performed this action at an earlier age. Therefore, even though genes are responsible for the general development of these skills, the environment can affect their fine-tuning. Although this research supports the idea that these motor skills can be advanced by practice, we also want you to remember that it is not necessary to do this. Even when a culture's child-rearing practices do not include "practice walking," all infants learn to walk.

We have seen that the development of motor skills results from input from genes, maturation, and the environment. However, researcher Esther Thelen, whose dynamic systems theory we described in Chapter 2, has shown that development of motor skills is even more complex. For example, newborns are unable to control the movement of their arms to reach for something. It was assumed that the development of eye-hand control is the necessary factor in determining when infants will be able to control their movements. However, Thelen and her colleagues were able to show that activity level is another major factor. Infants had to control the speed with which they moved their arm to successfully grasp a desired object, so infants who were more active had to learn to slow down and control their reach, while those who were less active had to increase the velocity of their reach to be successful (Thelen et al., 1993). The infant needed to find the best fit between her physical style and the demands of the task. In the human dynamic system, many factors, including physical, cognitive, and social factors, must come together to determine all behaviors.

Another example of the effects of experience on the development of motor skills involves the Back to Sleep program instituted by the American Academy of Pediatrics. In 1992, this group began to recommend that infants be put to sleep on their backs to reduce the risk of sudden infant death syndrome (SIDS). As you learned in Chapter 5, since that time the incidence

5. It is important that infants crawl before they walk. If they go directly to walking they are more likely to develop learning disabilities later in life.

TRUE/FALSE

False. Babies may or may not crawl in a typical "bear walk" fashion, but this has no implications for the development of their cognitive (or physical) abilities later in life.

of SIDS has decreased by more than 50% (National Institute of Child Health and Human Development, 2010). However, there is some evidence that an unintended consequence of this policy is that infants are starting to crawl at later ages (Davis, Moon, Sachs, & Ottolini, 1998). When babies sleep on their stomachs they reflexively move their arms and legs, strengthening those muscles, but when they sleep on their backs they do not get this stimulation. As a result, pediatricians and others are now recommending that parents be sure to give their infants "tummy time" every day under the watchful eye of an adult. On the other hand, going directly from sitting to walking does not indicate that there are motor problems, and infants who sleep on their backs walk at the same age as other infants (Davis et al., 1998).

Although research is showing the complexity of motor development, the real-world approach to fostering young children's motor skills remains simple. Parents can promote normal development of motor skills by providing a safe, "baby-proofed" space that is large enough for infants and toddlers to explore and by enthusiastically encouraging the development of each motor milestone in its turn.

You can learn more about the development of children's motor skills by carrying out **Active Learning: Checklist of Motor Skill Development** with a child.

ACTIVE LEARNING

Checklist of Motor Skill Development

Using books or online resources, create a checklist of different behaviors that a child or an adolescent could perform at different ages for one aspect of motor development (for example, fine motor skills, gross motor skills, balance). For instance, for gross motor skills, you might ask the child to play "Simon Says" with you. You can demonstrate motor skills ranging from standing on one foot to doing cartwheels (if you can do them!), depending on the age of the child. Ask the child to perform them after you.

You might work with others who are observing children of different ages to create the checklist so that you use it to compare the changes that occur with age. If you do this, you will need to find actions appropriate for children younger than the youngest child and older than the oldest child. Begin testing a little below your child's age level and continue until the child is unable to perform several actions. Always respond positively to the child's attempts and don't let the child become frustrated by asking him to perform actions that are much too difficult for him.

Were you surprised by any of the actions your child could or could not perform? How would you explain the upper limits of the child's abilities—lack of practice, level of brain maturation, development of motor coordination, or other reasons? If you were able to compare your observations with other people's, did you find trends of physical development across ages, and did you find individual differences between children of the same age?

The Importance of Physical Activity

In spite of the fact that Kenyans seem to win marathons more than would be expected (BBC News, 2005), there is no evidence that their early proficiency in walking, described above, relates to any greater physical skills later in life. Rather, many attribute Kenyans' success to the result of *ongoing* practice. Elijah Maanzo (2005), a young Kenyan runner, wrote, "As young Kenyans, we ran five kilometres to school every morning. And as children, we saw our parents run to work. We ran to church, to the river, everywhere. To a Kenyan, running is part of our daily lifestyle. Our victories at international events are just proof of this" (para. 10).

Physical activity is important for children and teens at all ages. As schools are cutting recess time, it becomes even more important for families to ensure that their children are running, biking, and playing actively for their long-term health and the development of their muscles. The Centers for Disease Control and Prevention (2008b) recommends that children take part in 60 minutes of exercise per day, including aerobic, muscle-strengthening, and bone-strengthening activities. These activities do not need to include intensive involvement in sports, unless your child loves sports. Walking to school, riding a bike, or raking leaves can all be sources of healthful exercise. The physical benefit of exercise continues throughout your life. What you may not realize is that physical activity is related not just to optimal functioning of your muscles but also to optimal functioning of your brain. In children as well as in older adults, the level and nature of brain activity has been found to be related to the level of physical activity in which the individuals engage (Bear et al., 2007; Hillman, Buck, Themanson, Pontifex, & Castelli, 2009; Society for Neuroscience, 2007a; van Gelder et al., 2004). The message is to back away from the TV, computer, and video games and go outside to play! We will discuss more about physical activities in relation to play and the media in Chapter 13.

Sensation and Perception

In the next section we will describe how the development of the brain and the senses predisposes babies to form the all-important attachments to their caregivers. We know that having a baby reach the physical developmental milestones we've described above is a source of joy and pride for the parents, but babies have other capabilities that draw parents into a bond with them. Infants also use the information that comes to them through their senses to learn about the world in which they live.

When we talk about **sensations**, we are referring to the information from the environment that is picked up by our sense organs. For instance, light from the environment stimulates the retina of the eye, sound waves stimulate the auditory nerves in the inner ear, and chemical compounds in the food we eat stimulate the taste receptors on our tongue. However, it is the brain that puts the sensory information that it receives together so that it can attach meaning to that information and interpret what is happening in the world. This is the process of **perception**. For example, light within a certain range of wavelengths is the color red and within another range of wavelengths is the color blue. But, when the retina of your eye is stimulated with the wavelength for red, how do you know whether you are seeing an apple or a fire truck? Your brain takes this visual information for color; puts it together with other information about shape, size, and position; and draws upon previous experience to interpret this pattern of sensations as an apple.

Video Link 6.5
Sensations and perceptions.

Sensations The information from the environment that is picked up by our sense organs.

Perception The process of interpreting and attaching meaning to sensory information.

Mirror neurons Neurons that fire both when an individual acts and when the individual observes the same action performed by another.

Mirror Neurons

Newborn babies are capable of imitating adults' simple facial expressions (Meltzoff & Moore, 1997). If you stick out your tongue at a baby, the baby may stick her tongue out at you. Until recently, scientists had little idea how infants were capable of manipulating parts of their body they can't even see, but in the 1990s a team of Italian researchers was studying the brains of macaque monkeys when they discovered what are now called **mirror neurons** (Winerman, 2005). They found that the same neurons fired if the monkey put something to the monkey's own mouth, or if the monkey saw the researcher put something to

Mirror neurons. Mirror neurons may give infants the ability to imitate simple actions that they see others do. This baby is responding to her mother sticking out her tongue. Try this for yourself with a young infant. How do you feel when the infant responds to you by doing what you just did?

the researcher's mouth. Results from brain imaging studies indicate that for humans the same regions are activated for both experienced and observed motor movement and emotional expression. For newborns, this built-in system may activate an automatic imitative response. Just as we automatically cringe when we see a baby cry in response to an injection, or open our mouths as we feed babies, or laugh when we hear others laugh (which is why laugh tracks are added to television shows!), babies also imitate automatically. This is a powerful way in which babies are brought into the social world. They learn from us, and we enjoy seeing ourselves reflected in our babies.

Development of the Five Senses

Vision

Visual acuity The ability to see things in sharp detail.

Although newborns are capable of focusing their eyes, their vision is much worse than normal adult vision. The **visual acuity** of young infants (or the ability to see things in sharp detail) is about 20/400, which means that an infant can clearly see at 20 feet what an adult with normal vision can see at 400 feet (Balaban & Reisenauer, 2005). They will not develop adult levels of visual acuity until sometime between 6 months and 3 years (Slater, Field, & Hernandez-Reif, 2007).

However, infants can see faces, and from birth they are attracted to looking at the faces of people around them, especially their mother (Farroni, Menon, & Johnson, 2006). In addition, they tend to concentrate on areas of high contrast—that is, where darkest dark meets lightest light. At first this may mean that they scan the parent's hairline, but if you think about what area on the human face has the highest contrast, you may agree that it is the eyes, where the white of the eye surrounds a darker center. At 2 months of age, infants concentrate attention on the eyes (Ramsey-Rennels & Langlois, 2007). Think about how you would feel when holding a baby who looks you directly in the eye. Many parents respond with the feeling that "this baby *knows* me." Haith, Bergman, and Moore (1977) have argued that babies are responding to social stimuli, not just high contrast, because their research showed that babies focused more on their mothers' eyes when their mothers were talking than when they were silent. If high contrast was the only factor, the child would pay equal attention to the eyes whether the mother was talking or not. More recently, Farroni and her colleagues (2006) found that newborns look more at the face of a person who is gazing directly at them rather than looking away. However, regardless of whether this is a "trick of nature" or a true social response, the fact that babies tend to "look you in the eye" is surely an adaptive way they attract others to interact with them. In fact, research has shown that mothers are more likely to continue to interact warmly with their infants when they are looking their mothers in the eye (Haith et al., 1977).

Hearing

Hearing becomes functional while the fetus is still in the womb, and one sound fetuses hear loudly is their mother's voice. Subsequently, babies show a preference for their mother's voice within the first 3 days of life (DeCasper & Fifer, 1987). In a famous experiment that used a preference paradigm, mothers read *The Cat in the Hat* (or two other stories) aloud twice a day to their unborn baby during the last 6 weeks of their pregnancy (DeCasper & Spence, 1986). Within hours of their birth, the newborns were given a special pacifier. If the infants sucked on the pacifier in a certain way, they heard a recording of their mother reading *The Cat in the Hat*, but if they sucked in a different way they could hear a recording of her reading something else. The researchers concluded that babies showed memory for what they had heard prenatally because they were more likely to suck the pacifier in the way that would produce the recording of *The Cat in the Hat*. Try **Active Learning: Prenatal Hearing** to get a sense of what sounds a fetus might hear before birth.

Prenatal Hearing

What do babies hear prenatally? To get a little bit of an idea, press your ear against another person's stomach (choose someone you know well!). What sounds do you hear? Babies hear all this and more: the mother's heartbeat and sounds of digestion, as well as talking and outside sounds. In fact, many babies seem to need a certain level of noise in their first few months after birth in order to sleep. Many parents resort to leaving a vacuum cleaner running or putting the baby near a running clothes dryer to provide a level of background sound. Teddy bears that have built-in "heart sounds" also can help soothe babies.

Smell

Babies know their mother's smell from very early in their lives. Within the first 6 days of life, they will turn toward their mother's smell more often than toward another mother's scent (MacFarlane, 1975), and research has shown that babies who are being breast-fed recognize their mother's scent within the first 2 weeks of life (Cernoch & Porter, 1985). This may be linked to a similarity between the smell of the amniotic fluid they experienced before birth and the smell of the mother's breast milk (Marlier, Schaal, & Soussignan, 1998). Babies are even soothed by the scent of clothes that their mother has been wearing (Sullivan & Toubas, 1998).

Taste

Infants prefer sweet taste and react negatively to salty, sour, and bitter tastes (Rosenstein & Oster, 2005). Mother's milk is sweet, so this draws the baby to the food and to the mother. This taste preference has been used to help infants who must undergo a painful procedure. Baby boys sucking a sweet pacifier while undergoing circumcision cried less than those who used an unflavored pacifier (Blass & Hoffmeyer, 1991). In addition, mother's milk, as well as amniotic fluid, takes on some of the flavor of the foods the mother eats (Fifer, Monk, & Grose-Fifer, 2004). Therefore, babies are introduced to the tastes of their local foods even before birth, and there is evidence that early experience with particular tastes becomes acceptance or preference for such tastes later in life (Mennella, Griffin, & Beauchamp, 2004).

Touch

Touch is very soothing. In one study, babies who were held in skin-to-skin contact with their mothers cried less when given a slightly painful medical procedure (in this case, it was a heel stick to extract a small amount of blood) (Gray, Watt, & Blass, 2000). As we discussed in Chapter 5, Tiffany Field and her colleagues at the Touch Research Institute at the University of Miami have found that infant massage improves growth and effectively soothes babies of all ages, even premature babies (Dieter, Field, Hernandez-Reif, Emory, & Redzepi, 2003; Field et al., 2004). Many adults who have had a massage know how relaxing it can be. Massage with children can be helpful in improving conditions that range from anxiety (Field et al., 1992) to HIV (Diego, Hernandez-Reif, Field, Friedman, & Shaw, 2001). The research by Field and her colleagues appears to show that not only can massage make you feel better; it also can raise the level of your body's ability to fight off the effects of disease.

6. Infants are born with a taste for the foods common in their culture. **TRUE/FALSE**

True. Because a mother's amniotic fluid takes on some of the flavor of the food she eats while she is pregnant, infants have some experience with these tastes even before they are born.

Taste preferences. A mother's amniotic fluid can carry chemosensory molecules from food that she eats. These molecules, in turn, can stimulate the fetus's smell and taste receptors before birth. After an infant is born, the infant's food environment continues to reinforce those cultural tastes and smells.

Cross-Modal Transfer of Perception

Infants perceive the world through their senses as we've described for each sense individually. However, the senses also have to work together. For example, if you closed your eyes and touched an apple, when you opened your eyes and someone showed you an apple and an orange, you would know you had just touched the apple by looking at it. In other words, your perception of "apple" crosses from the tactile mode to the visual mode.

Infants, even from birth, show some aspects of cross-modal transfer of perception, but their abilities are limited in a number of ways. They can visually recognize something they have only touched and not seen (as in the apple example above), but they cannot recognize by touch something they have just seen but not previously touched (Sann & Streri, 2007). These abilities are strengthened as infants grow older and have more experience with seeing, touching, hearing, smelling, and tasting many things in their world. Many toys designed for young children incorporate features that let them use their senses to explore the world. **Active Learning: How Toys Stimulate Babies' Senses** lets you identify some of these features for yourself in a popular infant's toy.

ACTIVE LEARNING

How Toys Stimulate Babies' Senses

This toy can be held by any of the handles, all of which have different textures. When a baby shakes it, it makes a soft chiming sound. The cube gives off a pleasant smell. Find at least five different ways in which this toy provides appropriate sensory stimulation for a baby.

Possible answers:

1. High-contrast eyes on the birds attract the baby's eye to develop vision.
2. Different textures develop the sense of touch.
3. The sound it makes stimulates hearing.
4. Babies are attracted to faces, so they will be drawn to the birds' faces.
5. It is entirely soft and therefore safe for a baby to use.
6. Babies can hold the cube with two hands, helping with coordination.

Sensory Preferences and Connection to Caregivers

To review, we have seen that infants prefer to look at faces, naturally "look you in the eye," know their mother's voice, and prefer her scent and the taste of her milk. In addition, infants are able to naturally imitate people from their first days of life. Clearly from the minute we are born, we are well equipped to enter a social world, and we are prepared to form relationships with those who take care of us. Although true attachment will not develop until later in the first year of life, as we will discuss in Chapter 10, infants prefer the special people who care for them and draw them into relationships.

Body Growth and Changes

Our bodies change in many ways as we grow. In this section we will discuss how bodily proportions change, from the large head and small body of the infant to adult proportions. One part of the body that does not grow is the teeth. We will talk about development of baby teeth and then about how they must be lost to make way for larger adult teeth. Finally, we will discuss the major changes that happen to the body during puberty as children move into sexual maturity.

Infant Proportions

Of course all babies are beautiful, but beyond that they share some physical characteristics that draw us to them. When they are born, the comparative proportions of their heads and bodies are very different from those of older children and adults. A baby's head is very large in comparison to his small, helpless-looking body. If you do the activity described in **Active Learning: Head-to-Body Proportions** with a young child, you will see for yourself how short the child's arms are in comparison to the size of her head.

Head-to-Body Proportions

Take your right hand and reach over your head to touch your left ear. No problem, right? Now ask a toddler or preschooler to do the same thing, helping her if necessary. How far does the child's hand get over her head? Most likely the child's arm will not reach the opposite ear because her head is much larger in relation to the rest of her body than the head of an adult is to his body.

As children mature, their arms and legs lengthen, and the rest of the body catches up in size to the head. This fact has been used in some countries as a rough test of the child's readiness to attend school. In one area of Tanzania, where there were inadequate birth records to document children's ages, this test was used to determine the level of children's physical maturation and therefore their readiness to start school (Beasley et al., 2000).

In addition to their large head, infants also have large eyes, a small nose and mouth, and relatively fat cheeks. There may be an evolutionary reason for this appearance: It makes babies appear cute, and we are attracted to taking care of them (Vance, 2007). According to Volk, Lukjanczuk, and Quinsey (2005), adults are less likely to say they want to adopt a baby they don't find to be "cute." A secret that few parents will reveal is that some aspects of baby care can be very unpleasant because they must deal with all kinds of bodily fluids, smells, and being up half the night, but as a new mother once wrote: "It's a good thing God made babies so cute, otherwise you would send them right back to the hospital!" Anyone who has seen the movie *E.T.* (Spielberg, 1982) knows that in spite of how frightening this "extraterrestrial" looked, with his large head, large eyes, and helpless-looking body, we loved him and wanted to help him get home again! In the same way, we protect and nurture our babies in spite of the difficulties of caring for them, and this is in part because of the effect that their bodily proportions have on us.

Changing Bodily Proportions

Growth during infancy and until age 2 is very rapid. The average infant doubles her birth weight by about 5 months of age, and triples it by her first birthday. During this same time, the infant will add about 10 inches or 50% to her length at birth. If the same rate of growth applied to the average 11- or 12-year-old, it would be terrifying, but after their second birthday, growth

Infant facial features. Can you see how the facial features we find so endearing in infants were used by the makers of the movie *E.T.* to make us care about E.T.'s welfare?

slows down and children then continue adding about 2 inches a year until they hit the adolescent growth spurt, when the rate of growth again increases (Nemours Foundation, 2004). Two-year-olds are approximately half the height they will be in adulthood, so to get an estimate of a child's adult height, you could double the height of a 2-year-old. However, a better indicator would be to look at the height of family members. Assuming adequate nutrition, height is highly genetic, so it is very likely that a child's eventual height will fall somewhere within the range of the height of her close relatives. As the long bones of the arms and legs lengthen, children begin to look more like adults and less like babies. A person's "skeletal age" can be determined by examining the active growth centers at the ends of growing bones known as the epiphyses (eh-PIF-i-sees) as shown in Figure 6.5. Bones continue to grow until sometime, usually during adolescence, when the soft spongy ends of the bone harden off and growth is complete.

Changes in the production of hormones in late childhood trigger the onset of puberty. Growth hormones work together with sex hormones (particularly estrogen for adolescent females and testosterone for adolescent males) to produce the rapid increase in height in both girls and boys that is known as the **adolescent growth spurt**. Girls, on average, begin their growth spurt at about 9 to 10 years of age. The onset of **menarche** (the first menstrual flow, or "period," which is usually experienced between the ages of 10 and 16 by girls in the United States) is related to the closure of the epiphyses. In the next few years after the onset of menarche, bone growth will decrease for girls (Porcu et al., 1994). Boys typically start their growth spurt about 2 years later than girls (Krabbe, Christiansen, Rødbro, & Transbol, 1979; Malina, Bouchard, & Oded, 2004). At the peak of the adolescent growth spurt, a young person can add 4 inches in height in a single year. This pubertal growth spurt ends by about age 15 for girls and age 16 or 17 for boys. At this point the soft spongy ends of the bone harden off, and growth is complete. **Active Learning: Your Growth in Childhood** guides you in looking back at your own physical development during your childhood.

Adolescent growth spurt The period of rapid increase in height and weight that occurs in early adolescence.

Menarche A girl's first menstrual period.

Figure 6.5

Epiphysis of the bones. Growth centers are found at ends of bones. The ends remain soft until children reach their adult size, when the ends will harden and growth will stop. This image shows how the bone develops from cartilage (in blue) to hard bone with the soft tissue at the ends.

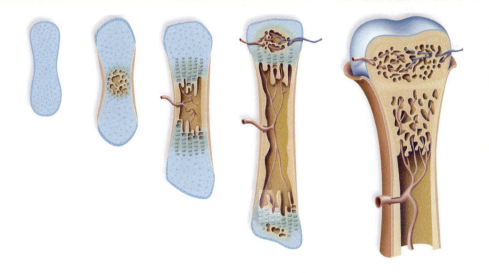

Your Growth in Childhood

ACTIVE LEARNING

Families often keep track of their children's growth. See whether your family kept a "baby book" detailing your growth in the early years. If your parents later marked your growth on a wall, look at the rate of change over time. Were there some periods of more rapid growth compared to other times in your life? If possible, compare these changes to those of your siblings or of your friends or classmates. At what points were girls taller than boys? When did this change?

Teething and the "Tooth Fairy"

As the body grows and proportions change, the face changes as well. One factor in this change is the development of teeth. Babies are usually born toothless (a fact that most nursing mothers appreciate), but within the first year, teething occurs and baby teeth emerge. However, these baby teeth will not last very long. A very exciting development for children at about age 6 is the loss of their first baby tooth. Parents often celebrate this event as an early rite of passage from infancy to childhood by giving gifts. In the United States, often the "tooth fairy" exchanges money for a tooth left under the child's pillow. In Costa Rica, parents plate baby teeth with gold and make them into earrings. In Eastern Europe, the ritual includes children throwing their tooth onto their roof and telling the mice to bring them a better tooth (Beeler & Karas, 2001).

Why do we lose our first teeth? Unlike bones, teeth do not grow. As our jaws grow, the teeth look smaller and smaller by comparison (Churchill, 2006). Meanwhile our bodies have been developing much larger teeth under the gums that will push out the smaller ones. Children

Losing baby teeth. Do you remember feeling as excited about losing your baby teeth as this girl appears to be? Notice that her two bottom teeth are new ones coming in and are larger than the others.

Puberty The physical changes that occur in adolescence that make an individual capable of sexual reproduction.

Primary sex characteristics Changes that occur in the organs necessary for reproduction.

Spermarche The beginning of production of viable sperm.

Secondary sex characteristics Characteristics that are associated with gender but do not directly involve the sex organs.

who have just gotten their adult-size teeth may take awhile to "grow into their teeth," which initially look very large in relation to the size of their faces.

Sexual Development

Puberty

Some of the most dramatic physical changes that occur at any time in development are seen as children enter adolescence. The rapid growth that we recognize as the adolescent growth spurt is one outward sign of a number of changes that are occurring as children move through **puberty**. The pubertal process moves the young person toward sexual maturity, but it actually begins earlier than many people realize. At some point between the ages of 5 and 9, the adrenal gland increases its production of androgens in both boys and girls. This will later be linked to the growth of facial hair (in boys) and pubic and armpit hair (in both boys and girls). A few years later, estrogen produced by the girl's ovaries will trigger changes in the growth of her uterus, vagina, and breasts and will cause fat to accumulate in the distribution pattern that is typical of females. Estrogen is also necessary to support the girl's menstrual cycles. Androgens (especially testosterone) produced by the boy's testes increase muscle mass and stimulate the growth of facial and pubic hair (Salkind, 2005b).

The entire process, which takes about 4 years, begins (and therefore also ends) earlier for girls than for boys. During puberty, primary and secondary sex characteristics develop. **Primary sex characteristics** involve changes that occur in the organs necessary for reproduction. For example, changes in the vagina, ovaries, and uterus of the female, and in the testes and penis of the male, are primary sex characteristics. For females, this process culminates in menarche and the beginning of ovulation. For males, it culminates in **spermarche**, or the ability to produce viable sperm. Changes that are associated with gender but do not directly involve the sex organs are **secondary sex characteristics**. Breast development in females, deepening of the voice in males, and growth of pubic and underarm hair in both genders are examples of secondary sex characteristics. Secondary sex characteristics are important outward signs to others that a child is becoming physically mature. The way that both peers and adults interact with a young person often is affected by these changes. As young people look less like children and more like adults, they tend to be treated more like adults.

As we already discussed, the long bones of the body grow rapidly during puberty and produce the adolescent growth spurt. However, the adolescent body also adds muscle and fat. Gender differences in fat and lean body mass are small in infancy and childhood, when girls have only slightly more fat than boys. However, these differences increase in adolescence. Although the adolescent growth spurt is accompanied by increases in lean body mass and body fat for both genders, girls accumulate a greater percentage of body fat, while boys accumulate a greater percentage of lean muscle mass (Forbes, 1989). By the end of adolescence, boys have a higher lean body mass to height ratio than girls. There is a critical level of body fat that is necessary for girls to maintain regular menstrual periods. That is why women who are anorexic, or who exercise so strenuously that their reserves of body fat drop to extremely low levels (for example, athletes or dancers), may have irregular periods or their periods may stop altogether.

The Timing of Puberty. Although the *sequence* of events that occur during puberty is fixed, the *timing* is variable. The age at which girls experience menarche has declined in industrialized countries since the mid-1800s, a change that is known as the **secular trend** (Roche, 1979). Improvements in nutrition, sanitation, and health care have all contributed to this pattern of decline. This also explains why the age of menarche today remains higher in undeveloped countries than in developed ones.

Factors like quality of diet and living conditions help us understand the differences we see from one country to another, but what helps explain the variations we see *within* a single country? Diet and health can play a role within a country, but so does body type, heredity, and ethnic background. Girls from families with more social and economic resources reach menarche 3 months to 3 years before girls from disadvantaged families (Parent et al., 2003), perhaps because of better diet and better overall health in more well-to-do families. The fat cells in a girl's body release a protein called leptin, which tells the brain that fat stores are adequate to sustain puberty. As a result, girls who are heavier than average are likely to go through puberty at a younger age than girls who are average in weight or thinner. Heredity plays a role because daughters go through puberty at an age that is similar to that of their mothers (Ersoy, Balkan, Gunay, & Egemen, 2005). Finally, there are ethnic differences. In the United States, Black adolescents reach menarche on average at a younger age than White girls of similar age and body weight (Malina et al., 2004).

Because the physical changes of puberty have such a profound effect on how the young person is seen by others, undergoing these changes relatively earlier—or considerably later—than age-mates can have a significantly different impact on development. Research on pubertal timing goes back to the 1950s, but there has been a consistent set of conclusions reached by research conducted since then. Early maturation appears to have a number of advantages for adolescent boys, and late maturation has a number of disadvantages. For girls, the picture isn't quite as clear. Early maturation can put the girl at some risk, but maturing at the same time as or slightly later than peers has some advantages.

Early-maturing boys tend to have positive self-images and feel good about themselves in a number of ways, including being more self-confident and seeing themselves as independent. Late-maturing boys, on the other hand, have more negative self-concepts and are more likely to feel inadequate and rejected (Mussen & Jones, 1957). Consequently, they may suffer from depression (Kaltiala-Heino, Kosunen, & Rimpela, 2003). Because boys who mature earlier are taller and heavier than their peers, they are likely to be the athletes in the group, and this gives them a lot of status in the peer group. However, early-maturing boys tend to spend their time with older peers because their physical development is a better match with that of older adolescents (Caspi, Lynam, Moffitt, & Silva, 1993; Stattin & Magnusson, 1990), and this can expose them to behaviors they are not yet ready to handle. For instance, they are more likely to begin using drugs and alcohol (Tschann et al., 1994; Westling, Andrews, Hampson, & Peterson, 2008; Wiesner & Ittel, 2002). These risks are even greater for adolescents growing up in disadvantaged neighborhoods or who have parents who are harsh or inconsistent in their discipline (Ge, Brody, Conger, Simons, & Murry, 2002).

Every day the media bombards us with images of attractive, sexy young women who seem to have anything good that life can offer, so it might seem that maturing early would be an advantage for girls, but that is hardly the case. When a girl physically matures earlier than the other girls her age, it tends to set her apart and isolates her from them. In fact, it might even inspire a bit of jealousy or envy (Caspi et al., 1993). And, because girls on average physically mature about 2 years before boys do, most boys her age are not interested

Secular trend The downward movement of the age at which girls experience menarche in industrialized countries since the mid-1800s.

7. Adolescent girls who go through puberty earlier than their peers are happier and healthier than girls who go through puberty later.

TRUE/FALSE

False. Early-maturing girls may feel socially isolated from their less mature peers. This sometimes pushes them toward relationships with older adolescents, which exposes them to behaviors that can place them at risk.

in this girl who is becoming a woman right in front of their eyes and might even be a bit intimidated by her.

Similar to what we saw with early-maturing boys, this social isolation from age-mates might drive the girl to spend time with older adolescents (Caspi et al., 1993; Stattin & Magnusson, 1990). A physically mature but chronologically young adolescent girl might be particularly susceptible to peer pressure to drink, smoke, or be sexually active because she does not yet have the cognitive maturity to know if, when, and how to say no—and to stick to it (Stattin & Magnusson, 1990).

Girls who mature on a timetable that is similar to (or even slightly behind) that of most of their age-mates are the ones who have an advantage (Tobin-Richards, Boxer, McNeill-Kavrell, & Petersen, 1984). They fit in comfortably with the girls their own age but also with most of the boys. This means that they have support from a peer group that is dealing with the same issues and concerns that they have. And, of course, being a female who remains relatively thin fits well with the cultural stereotype of what an attractive young woman should look like. Consequently, these girls tend to have positive body images (Tobin-Richards et al., 1984).

Precocious puberty
A condition in which pubertal changes begin at an extraordinarily early age (as young as 6 or 7 years of age).

In a small percentage of girls, the earliest events in the pubertal sequence (such as the beginning of breast buds and appearance of pubic hair) have been reported as early as 6 or 7 years of age (Nield, Cakan, & Kamat, 2007). This occurrence, known as **precocious puberty**, has received increasing attention (Parent et al., 2003). There are rare medical conditions, such as hormonal disorders or brain tumors, that can be the cause of these early changes, but other cases probably represent girls who are simply the earliest-maturing girls among their peers. It is clear that girls who experience these changes in their bodies at such a young age need extra support and good information to help them deal with the situation. They lack one important thing that helps make puberty seem like a normal change for most girls. They don't have a group of peers who are going through the same experience with them.

The good news is that by the end of high school, almost all adolescents have undergone the physical changes of puberty, and a distinction between "early" and "late" maturers no longer has much meaning (Natsuaki, Biehl, & Ge, 2009). Unless the differences in timing of physical maturation have been responsible for other risky behaviors that become problematic in and of themselves (van Jaarsveld, Fidler, Simon, & Wardle, 2007), adolescents are again on a pretty level playing field in this regard. **Active Learning: Timing of Puberty** helps you reflect on your own experiences as you went through puberty.

ACTIVE LEARNING

Timing of Puberty

Think back to when you went through puberty. (Some of you, especially boys, may still be experiencing some of these changes such as growth in height and increase in facial hair.) Do you remember your changes occurring before, after, or at the same time as those of your peers? When you compared yourself with others, were those comparisons favorable or not, and why? You might want to discuss your experiences with others to find out more about the range of ways in which adolescents experience puberty and variations in its timing and the possible impact of these differences on adolescent development.

Rites of passage   Rituals that publicly mark a change in status from child to adult.

Rites of Passage From Childhood to Adolescence. The stage of adolescence is marked in cultures around the world by rituals called **rites of passage** that publicly mark a change in status from child to adult. Many rituals are based on religious beliefs, and some are explicitly linked to the sexual maturation of the adolescent.

Rites of passage. The tooth-filing ceremony in the Balinese tradition, the quinceañera in the Latin American tradition, and the Bar Mitzvah in the Jewish tradition are all cultural ceremonies intended to do the same thing: acknowledge the transition of a young person from the status of child to that of adult.

In the United States, several traditional rites of passage may be familiar to you. In the Jewish tradition, boys at age 13 and girls at age 12 celebrate the Bar Mitzvah or Bat Mitzvah (which means "son, or daughter, of the commandment" in Hebrew). In this ceremony the boy or girl may lead a religious service in order to display all he or she has learned in his or her religious education. This is followed by a party celebrating the child's acceptance as an adult member of the community, with the responsibility to carry out the religious commandments. A rite of passage that has come to the United States from Latin America is called the quinceañera. In this tradition girls are given a special party to mark their 15th birthday (Alomar & Zwolinski, 2002). The party is almost like a wedding, with the girl dressed in an elaborate dress, possibly white, and a number of her friends to attend her. The high point of the event is a religious ceremony, a Mass of thanksgiving. Traditionally, the quinceañera announces that the girl is of marriageable age; in other words, she is no longer a child but has become a young woman.

Around the world, other rites of passage take a variety of forms that may not be familiar to you. Spiritual beliefs in Bali are reflected in a tooth-filing ceremony for adolescents. In this culture, it is believed that teeth are symbols of bad impulses, such as greed and jealousy. Therefore, filing them makes a person more beautiful, both physically and spiritually (Bali Travel Guidebook, 2002). Young people are considered to be adults following this ceremony.

In some cultures, the rites of passage are explicitly linked to the sexual maturation of adolescence. For example, the Apache Sunrise Ceremony is held the summer after a girl has her first menstrual period. In southern Africa, traditional Zulu and Xhosa boys undergo circumcision during a ritual to mark their movement into manhood. The boys are supposed to perform an act of bravery, following which they are taken to a seclusion lodge where a circumcision ceremony takes place. They must show their manhood by not reacting to the pain. After the ceremony the boys are painted with white chalk to show their purity. They are instructed by an elder on their adult responsibilities, including sexual responsibility. When the wounds are finally healed, they wash off the white chalk. Finally, a great ceremony marks the end of their childhood and the beginning of their manhood (Mandela, 1994).

Reflect on the importance of any ritual that may have marked your movement from childhood to adulthood as you were growing up by answering the questions posed in **Active Learning: Rites of Passage**.

Video Link 6.6
Bali tooth-filling ceremony.

Video Link 6.7
Quinceañera.

Video Link 6.8
Bar Mitzvah.

Rites of Passage

Have you experienced anything you might consider a ritual that marked your movement to adulthood? In your religion there may be rituals that happen in adolescence that mark a new level of responsibility and understanding. Although the United States has few formal rituals, you can probably think of important events that translate into the concept "I am an adult now." A common and meaningful one is receiving a driver's license. In our mobile society, being able to get from place to place on one's own is central to adulthood. What other events can you think of that are linked to public acknowledgement of a new maturity? Could you create a new rite of passage that would be meaningful to you and would symbolize the movement from childhood to adolescence in your society?

TRUE/FALSE

8. In the United States, 90% of adolescents between the ages of 15 and 19 have had sex at least once.

False. Although some adolescents think that "everyone is doing it," only half of the adolescents between ages 15 and 19 report that they have had sex at least once.

Risks of Sexual Maturation

After adolescents go through puberty, males can produce viable sperm, and females can become pregnant. For most adolescents, their growing interest in the opposite sex eventually leads to having romantic relationships, and for some of those adolescents, it also leads to the decision to become sexually active. Culture has a strong influence on if or when an adolescent makes this transition, but in the United States, about half of all teenagers between the ages of 15 and 19 report that they have had sex at least once (Abma, Martinez, Mosher, & Dawson, 2004). Not surprisingly, the percentage of adolescents who have had intercourse at least once increases with age (see Figure 6.6).

The decision to become sexually active carries with it some potential risks. Females are at risk of becoming pregnant, and both sexes are at risk of contracting a sexually transmitted infection. We will look at the consequences of both of these possibilities on adolescent development and describe ways in which adolescents can protect themselves from these risks.

Figure 6.6

Percentage of adolescents who have had intercourse by age. Not surprisingly, the percentage of adolescents who report being sexually active increases as the adolescents get older. The rate of increase is fairly steady across adolescence, and males and females are similar in the age at which they make this transition.

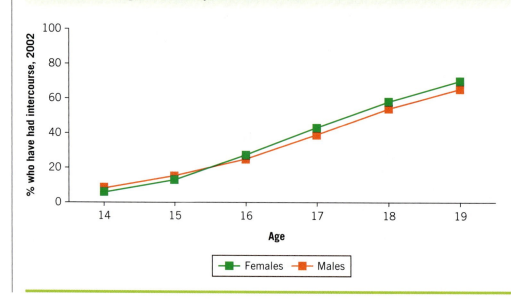

Adolescent Pregnancies. The rate of adolescent pregnancies in the United States decreased substantially between 1991 and 2005. This decline was attributed to several factors. One important factor was the fact that adolescents were abstaining from sex longer and were not becoming sexually active until they were older (CDC, 2010b; Mohn, Tingle, & Finger, 2002). In addition, the percentage of adolescents who reported having initiated sexual intercourse before the age of 13 dropped from 10.2% in 1991 to 5.9% in 2009 (CDC, 2010b).

But these findings still leave us with the question of *why* adolescents might be waiting longer to have intercourse. Some adolescents have voluntarily taken a **virginity pledge** (that is, a pledge to abstain from having sex). Although taking the pledge does not necessarily prevent adolescents from *ever* becoming sexually active, it can affect the age at which they make this transition (Bearman & Brucker, 2001; Martino, Elliott, Collins, Kanouse, & Berry, 2008). Virginity pledges appear to be most effective among the youngest study participants (Bearman & Brucker, 2001). We already know that the percentage of adolescents who are sexually active increases with age, so taking the pledge may delay intercourse within the youngest group, even if they eventually make the transition at some point in adolescence.

Another explanation for the decline in the teenage birthrate is that adolescents who *are* sexually active are making better use of contraception (Darroch & Singh, 1999). According to the Youth Risk Behavior Survey, the percentage of sexually active adolescents who reported using a condom during their last intercourse increased from 46.2% in 1991 to 54.4% in 2001 (Sexuality Information and Education Council of the United States, 2005).

We certainly hope that the efforts to educate adolescents about the consequences of their decisions regarding sexual activity also played a role in the decrease in the number of adolescent pregnancies. Despite these efforts, however, adolescents growing up in economically disadvantaged circumstances continue to be at an elevated risk. Although low-income adolescents are 38% of the population of women between the ages of 15 and 19, they account for 73% of all pregnancies in that age group.

Unfortunately the decades-long reduction in the number of adolescent pregnancies may be reversing itself. Preliminary data for 2007 (the most current national statistics available at this time) show that the teenage birthrate increased by 5% between 2005 and 2007 (CDC, 2009c; see Figure 6.7 on page 220). The increase occurred across all groups, with the exception of Asian American teenagers and teen mothers under the age of 14. Some possible explanations for the increase include the fact that (a) the proportion of Hispanic teens in the population has increased, and this group has the highest teen pregnancy rate; (b) economic changes have resulted in more families being economically disadvantaged; and (c) perhaps policymakers and service providers have become complacent after years of steady decline in the teen pregnancy rate, so there is a need for them to renew their efforts (Moore, 2009). We will need to wait to see whether this recent increase is the start of a new trend or just a temporary aberration.

The United States continues to have one of the highest rates of births to adolescents among industrialized countries (Lara-Torre, 2009). As you can see from Figure 6.8 on page 221, the adolescent pregnancy rate in the United States is more than 6 times the rate in the Netherlands, almost 4 times the rate in Germany, and almost 3 times the rate in France (Alford & Hauser, 2009). According to a report from the American Academy of Pediatrics Committee on Adolescence (2001), approximately 9% of sexually active 14-year-olds become pregnant each year,

Virginity pledge A promise made by children or adolescents to abstain from becoming sexually active before marriage.

Balancing motherhood and homework. For a teen mother, one of the biggest challenges is being able to stay in school. This young mother is attending a school in Albuquerque, New Mexico, that provides special support to pregnant teens and teen mothers to help them do this.

Figure 6.7

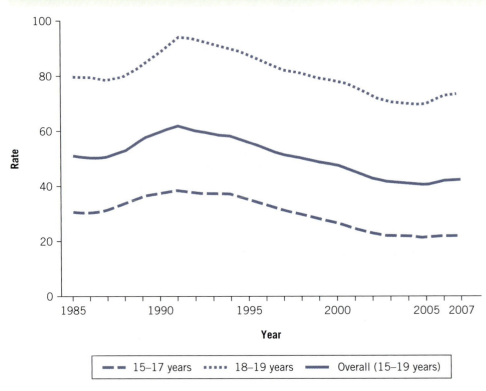

Changes in the adolescent birthrate for teens aged 15–19 in the United States (1985–2007).
After decades of decline in the adolescent birthrate, there has been a recent reversal of this trend. What do you think might account for this change?

Legend: - - - 15–17 years   ····· 18–19 years   ——— Overall (15–19 years)

*Per 1,000 women for specified age group.

and this percentage climbs to 18% among 15- to 17-year-olds and to 22% among 18- to 19-year-olds. The birthrate to adolescent mothers in the United States is 9 times higher than the rate in the Netherlands (Alford & Hauser, 2009), and adolescents in the Netherlands are far less likely to contract a sexually transmitted infection than adolescents in the United States (Schalet, 2007).

Schalet (2007) attributed the lower rates of adolescent pregnancy, births, abortions, and sexually transmitted infections among adolescents in the Netherlands to the fact that poverty is more widespread and more intense in the United States than it is in the Netherlands. Adolescents in the Netherlands also have easier access to comprehensive sex education and reproductive health services than many adolescents in the United States, and there is generally a less fearful attitude toward adolescent sexuality in the Netherlands. Schalet illustrates the difference in attitude between the two countries with this quote from a government-funded youth initiative in the Netherlands:

> Parents, educators, and other professionals rarely tell young people to stay away from sex, or to say no to sex. Dutch policy is aimed at assisting young people to behave responsibly in this respect. The Dutch approach means spending less time and effort trying to prevent young people from becoming sexually active, and more time and effort in educating and empowering young people to behave responsibly when they do become sexually active. (p. 4)

This approach seems to be working for Dutch teenagers. When they become sexually active, they use contraception at a substantially higher rate than do American teens. Because almost

Figure 6.8

International comparison of teen pregnancy rate and teen birthrate. Both the adolescent pregnancy rate and the adolescent birthrate in the United States continue to be much higher than in other industrialized countries. What accounts for this large difference?

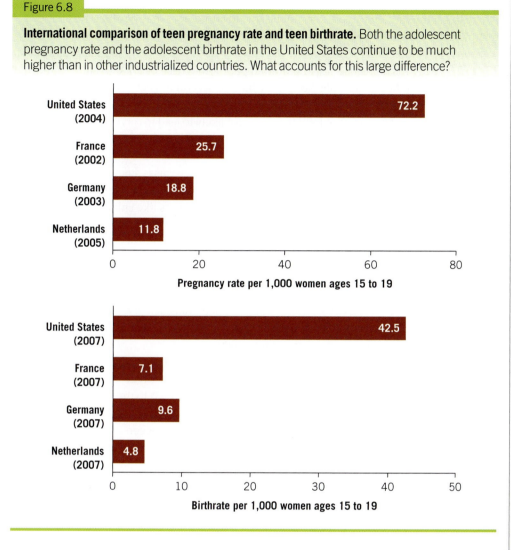

Pregnancy rate per 1,000 women ages 15 to 19

Birthrate per 1,000 women ages 15 to 19

900,000 infants are born to teenage mothers in the United States each year, we continue to search for effective pregnancy prevention programs. Allen, Seitz, and Apfel (2007) have suggested that the only effective approach will be one that targets the "whole person" rather than one that tries to deal with adolescents as a "bundle of sexual urges to be controlled" (p. 197). They suggest that to do this we will need to find ways to build competencies that protect the adolescent not just from sexual activity but from a whole range of risky behaviors. We will return to a discussion of risky behaviors during adolescence in Chapter 15.

Sexually Transmitted Infections. A second serious risk that goes along with being sexually active is the risk of contracting a **sexually transmitted infection (STI)**. The Centers for Disease Control and Prevention (2005c) estimates that there are about 19 million *new* infections each year, and almost half of them occur in young people between the ages of 15 and 24. Of course many more cases go undiagnosed and are never reported, and several of the most common infections (such as the human papillomavirus or genital herpes) are not even counted for statistical purposes.

Many STIs can be treated, but adolescents don't always get the treatment they need. Many STIs do not produce any symptoms that make the individual aware that he or she should seek

Sexually transmitted infection (STI) A disease or infection that is transmitted by direct sexual contact.

medical treatment. And even when adolescents are aware of a problem, they may not know where to get the care they need, may not be able to afford it, or may be afraid that if they get treatment, their treatment will not remain confidential.

Each type of infection carries its own set of risks. About half of all the STIs diagnosed in 15- to 24-year-olds are caused by the human papillomavirus, or HPV (Alan Guttmacher Institute, 2009). Although this infection can be harmless, certain types of HPV can lead to cervical cancer (Dailard, 2006). In June 2006, the Food and Drug Administration approved a vaccine that can prevent the types of HPV that are most likely to lead to cervical cancer, but there is debate in the United States about whether the vaccine should be required for young girls. Opponents worry that the unintended message will be that people are expecting these young girls to become sexually active in the near future. Also, since this is a new vaccine, there are concerns about its possible long-term safety and overall effectiveness (Dailard, 2006).

Other commonly occurring STIs include bacterial infections like chlamydia, gonorrhea, and syphilis. There are an estimated 2.8 million new cases of chlamydia each year, and females between the ages of 15 and 19 have the highest infection rate (Weinstock, Berman, & Cates, 2004). The rate of reported cases of chlamydia is 7 times higher among Black females than among White females and is twice as high among Blacks as among Hispanic females (CDC, 2005c). Distressingly, after reaching an all-time low in 2000, cases of primary and secondary syphilis are again increasing (CDC, 2005c). It is fortunate that each of these infections can be treated and cured, but if left untreated, each can lead to serious complications, including death in the case of syphilis (Alan Guttmacher Institute, 2009).

It is a different story with viral infections, such as HIV/AIDS, hepatitis B, and herpes, which are treatable but *not* curable (Alan Guttmacher Institute, 2009). In 2003, young adults and adolescents represented 12.2% of the cases of HIV/AIDS reported to the Centers for Disease Control and Prevention. HIV/AIDS was among the top 10 causes of death for young people between the ages of 20 and 24, and Black males and females between the ages of 15 and 24 (Rangel, Gavin, Reed, Fowler, & Lee, 2006). However, when we talk about the number of cases of AIDS identified among adolescents, we need to remember that this infection takes about 10 years to develop. That means that even if an individual is infected in his or her teens, we may not see the symptoms from the infection until the young person is in his or her 20s. It is no exaggeration to continue to describe AIDS as an epidemic, despite the progress we have made in developing antiviral drugs that help extend the life of infected individuals.

One of the things that contribute to the high rates of STIs among adolescents is the fact that they are still dating and have not yet entered into monogamous relationships. Not surprisingly, as your number of partners goes up, so does your risk of contracting an STI. Condoms offer the best protection from STIs for sexually active adolescents. However, although both male and female adolescents ages 15 to 19 reported substantial increases in the use of condoms between 1988 and 1995, condoms still are not used consistently (Murphy & Boggess, 1998). Hispanic males have a lower level of consistent condom use than other males, but there is plenty of room for improvement across all ethnic and racial groups. In the words of Lescano, Vazquez, Brown, Litvin, and Pugatch (2006), the number of acts of unprotected sex between adolescents remains "substantial" (p. 443).

Nutrition

The growth and development we have been describing relies to a large extent upon healthy nutrition for infants, children, and adolescents. In this section we will discuss how to get babies off to a healthy start and describe how to continue to provide a healthy diet for children. We will also describe difficulties with nutrition, from malnourishment to obesity to eating disorders.

Breastfeeding

In 2000, the Surgeon General of the United States, David Satcher, issued a statement that identified breastfeeding "as the 'ideal method of feeding and nurturing infants' and a national health priority" (Philipp, Merewood, & O'Brien, 2001, p. 584). The American Academy of Pediatrics and the American Dietetic Association recommend that babies be exclusively breast-fed until 6 months of age. Other foods can be added between 6 months and 1 year. In spite of these recommendations, in 2004, only about a third of infants were exclusively breast-fed for 3 months, and about 41% were breast-fed, possibly with supplementary foods, for 6 months. The lowest rates were among Black or African American mothers. Women who were more likely to breast-feed were older, had more education, were married, and lived in metropolitan areas (Li, Darling, Maurice, Barker, & Grummer-Strawn, 2005).

Breastfeeding at work. Places of employment can support the decision of their female employees to breast-feed their infants by providing a space that the employees can use for nursing breaks or to pump breast milk that can be stored and used later by their infants while their mothers are away from them.

Why are rates of breastfeeding so low in the United States? Many women choose not to breast-feed or are unable to overcome difficulty they experience while trying to do so, but the rate of breastfeeding is also affected by the attitudes of society. One example of negative societal attitudes toward breastfeeding is the case of Emily Gillette. In November 2006, Ms. Gillette was breast-feeding her baby on a plane while waiting for takeoff. She was sitting in the second to last row, between her husband and the window. A flight attendant handed her a blanket and asked her to cover up. Claiming she was being discreet and that she had a right to nurse her child, she refused. She was then made to leave the plane (Associated Press, 2006). Ms. Gillette filed a lawsuit against the airline, and women around the country demonstrated through "nurse-ins" at airports around the country.

Video Link 6.9
Breastfeeding.

There have been serious questions about how well hospitals, places of work, and other institutions support a woman's decision to breast-feed her infant. For example, the rate of breastfeeding might be improved if workplaces provided private settings for mothers to pump milk for their babies or if hospitals did not give free samples of formula provided by the companies that produce them to new mothers when they leave the hospital.

Breastfeeding offers benefits to both the baby and the mother. Around the world, in both underdeveloped and developed countries, babies who are breast-fed are less likely to suffer and die from diarrhea and acute lower respiratory infections (Arifeen et al., 2001; Bahl et al., 2005; Clemens et al., 1999; Quigley, Kelly, & Sacker, 2007). Breast milk provides the baby with antibodies that come from the mother's body and help fight off infection. There is some evidence that breastfeeding promotes earlier development of the infant's own immune system (Jackson & Nazar, 2006). Other benefits include fewer colds, fewer ear infections, lower rates of type 2 diabetes, and lower rates of SIDS (CDC, 2007). There is even some indication that it may help prevent childhood and adolescent obesity, although more evidence is needed to prove this conclusively (CDC, 2007; Dewey, 2003; von Kries et al., 1999). However, there is no clear evidence that breastfeeding is linked to intelligence or cognitive abilities later in life (Ip et al., 2007).

For the mother, production of breast milk is related to production of the chemical oxytocin, which helps the uterus return to shape. Although this chemical also delays the return of fertility, women are advised not to rely exclusively on breastfeeding to prevent another pregnancy. In addition, lactation appears to make mothers more relaxed and less reactive to stress, possibly by reducing blood pressure (Light et al., 2000; Tu, Lupien, & Walker, 2005). In the long term, it

9. Children who were breast-fed have higher IQ scores than those who were not. **TRUE/FALSE**

False. Although breastfeeding has many positive effects, early research showing higher IQ scores for breast-fed infants has not been confirmed by subsequent findings.

has also been found that women who breast-feed have a reduced risk of some breast and ovarian cancers and type 2 diabetes (Ip et al., 2007).

Breastfeeding may also benefit both the individual family and society as a whole. It has been calculated that increasing the rate of breastfeeding to the level recommended by the Surgeon General would save a minimum of $3.6 billion through lowered health care costs and less loss of wages because of caring for a sick child (Weimer, 2001). An additional benefit for an individual family is that it does not have to pay for formula.

There are certain rare circumstances under which breastfeeding is not recommended. You learned in Chapter 5 that HIV can be transmitted from an infected mother to her infant through breast milk, so HIV-positive mothers should not breast-feed. Most drugs that are prescribed by a physician are not likely to be harmful to the infant, but when a woman is undergoing chemotherapy or using antibiotics, antianxiety medications, or antidepressants (American Academy of Pediatrics Committee on Drugs, 2001), these substances enter the woman's breast milk. For this reason, the safest course of action is not to use medications while breast-feeding unless they are medically necessary, and even then they should be used only in consultation with the woman's doctor. Also, nursing women who smoke have nicotine in their milk, so this is another good reason to give up smoking.

Healthy Eating

Food preferences and eating habits are established early in life. Children who get off to a good start with a diet that contains a variety of healthy foods benefit not only in childhood but throughout adolescence and into adulthood. However, for many families, providing a healthy diet is not an easy thing to do. A recent study of 5,000 children, ages 6 to 18, found that the children had too much dietary fat and sodium in their diet and that too much of their food energy came from added sugars, such as those found in sugary soft drinks (Gleason & Suitor, 2001). A healthful diet is particularly necessary to support the periods of rapid growth that occur in infancy and again at the start of adolescence. Remember that when we talk about "diet," we are *not* talking about "dieting." We are interested in the amount, quality, and diversity of the food that a child or an adolescent eats, not the restriction of calories with the goal of losing weight.

The U.S. Department of Agriculture (USDA, 2009a) has developed the *Healthy Eating Index* to measure dietary quality. The index assesses the degree to which a diet conforms to the USDA food pyramid, as well as the amount of fat, cholesterol, and sodium it contains. As you can see in Figure 6.9, only about a quarter of diets for young children are classified as "good" using this index, and the percentage of diets classified as "good" decreases with age. By adolescence, slightly more than 20% of diets are considered "poor" and fewer than 5% are considered "good." The rest (by far the majority) are classified as "in need of improvement" (Federal Interagency Forum on Child and Family Statistics, 2008).

In addition to the foods that are included in a healthy diet, there are some foods that should be avoided because they pose a type of risk for young children. Unpasteurized milk or food juices (such as fresh juice made at home from unwashed fruits or juice bought from a roadside stand) can contain harmful bacteria. Honey can contain the botulinum organism, and raw eggs can contain salmonella. Adults need to be particularly careful about giving young children firm, round foods such as popcorn, whole grapes, or hot dogs because these foods are approximately the size of a child's airway and can lodge in the child's throat and cause choking (American Academy of Pediatrics, 2006b).

Malnourishment

When children are malnourished they do not receive the right amount or mix of nutrients necessary to sustain their growth and good health. We often associate malnourishment with

Figure 6.9

Percentage of children ages 2–18 by age and diet quality as measured by the Healthy Eating Index, 1994–1996, 1999–2000, and 2001–2002.

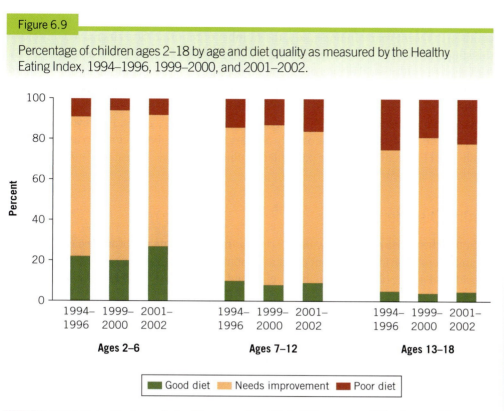

NOTE: The maximum combined score for the 10 components is 100. An HEI score above 80 implies a good diet, an HEI score between 51 and 80 implies a diet that needs improvement, and an HEI score less than 51 implies a poor diet. Data for the three time periods are not necessarily comparable because of methodological differences in data collection.

children who live in third world countries or countries being torn apart by war, but it exists to some extent in every country, including the United States. However, a much greater threat in the United States than malnutrition is **undernutrition**, a deficiency of calories or of one or more essential nutrients.

A paradoxical situation called **food insecurity** exists for people who do not always have the economic resources to purchase an adequate amount of food to meet their basic needs (Kaiser et al., 2003). For these people, hunger and obesity can exist side by side (Wickrama, Wickrama, & Bryant, 2006). For instance, a family might consume lower-cost foods that are relatively high in calories to keep family members from feeling hungry. Also, when food is not consistently available, adults and children may adopt the strategy of overeating when it *is*. This pattern of feast and famine can result in weight gain over time. Beyond that, parents from all socioeconomic classes may not understand nutrition well enough to make the best dietary choices for their families.

Obesity

Obesity among both adults and children has become an increasing concern in America. **Obesity** is defined as being 20% or more over an individual's ideal body weight. For children, what constitutes an ideal weight will vary by age. Surveys done in 1976–1980 and in 2003–2004 showed a tripling in the percentage of children considered obese in only 20 years. According to the National Institute of Child Health and Human Development (2007), almost 1 in 5 American children now is overweight. Because overweight children are likely to become overweight adolescents who in turn become overweight adults, this is a serious and ongoing health concern (Malina et al., 2004).

Undernutrition A deficiency of calories or of one or more essential nutrients.

Food insecurity A situation in which food is often scarce or unavailable, causing people to overeat when they do have access to food.

Obesity Being 20% or more over an individual's ideal body weight.

Being overweight has been linked to the dramatic increase in type 2 diabetes among children in recent years. In one study, the number of reported cases increased tenfold in the single 12-year period between 1982 and 1994 (Koplan, Liverman, & Kraak, 2005). Although the full clinical effects of childhood obesity may not become apparent for years, they include elevated blood pressure, increased serum lipid levels, and even some cancers (Malina et al., 2004). The cost of these problems to society—in addition to the tremendous personal cost to the individual—is staggering (Koplan et al., 2005). However, the social and emotional consequences of obesity also are very real. Obese adolescents, especially White and Hispanic females, are particularly vulnerable to low self-esteem and depression (Koplan et al., 2005).

Eating Disorders

Anorexia nervosa
A condition in which individuals become obsessed with their weight and intentionally restrict food intake to a point that it may become life threatening.

Although there are a number of eating disorders, the dramatic nature of anorexia nervosa and bulimia keeps them in the forefront of our attention. **Anorexia nervosa** is a condition in which individuals become obsessed with their weight and intentionally restrict their intake of food to a point that it may become life threatening. Anorexics lose 15% or more of their body weight, yet they still see themselves as grossly overweight and remain fearful of gaining weight. This condition takes a terrible toll on the young person's overall health. As the level of body fat falls, young women either fail to begin menstruating, or their menstrual periods become erratic or cease altogether. There are a number of changes that can easily be seen, including thinning hair, brittle nails, a yellowing of the skin, and the growth of a fine downy hair on the face, arms, and back. Many anorexics experience more serious changes, including gastrointestinal problems, cardiovascular problems (such as a slow heart rate, low blood pressure, irregular heartbeats, and EKG abnormalities), and osteoporosis. They also may experience lethargy and cold intolerance (Costin, 1999).

Because anorexia can be life threatening, hospitalization may be required, but the prognosis is not encouraging. Hospitalization often occurs late in the process after a great deal of physical damage has already been done. Although some programs have had success with helping the anorexic regain weight, relapses following treatment are common, and mortality from anorexia is higher than for other psychiatric disorders, as high as 15% in some studies (Gowers & Doherty, 2007).

Who is susceptible to this condition? Anorexics have been described as high-achieving, goal-oriented, and highly controlled individuals (National Institutes of Health, 2007). Psychological factors such as depression and low body esteem also are predictive of later eating disorders in both boys and girls (Gardner, Stark, Friedman, & Jackson, 2000). Another possibility is that conflict related to autonomy and control may set up a dysfunctional family dynamic that contributes to this disorder. If parents are seen as demanding, overprotective, or overcontrolling, the adolescent can reassert his or her autonomy by controlling what and when he or she eats. Likewise, if the adolescent wants parental attention, this behavior is one way to get it.

Bulimia   An eating disorder characterized by eating binges, followed by purging (for example, self-induced vomiting or the excessive use of laxatives) to get rid of the food.

Bulimia is an eating disorder that is characterized by eating binges in which enormous amounts of food are consumed, followed by self-induced vomiting or the excessive use of laxatives to get rid of the food. Individuals suffering from bulimia differ from those suffering from anorexia in several ways. First, in contrast with the anorexic whose goal is weight loss, the goal of most bulimics is to prevent weight gain. Second, while anorexics try to have complete control over their behavior, the eating behavior of bulimics is impulsive and out of control, and they often feel guilt and shame after an episode of binging. Third, the causes of bulimia are less well understood than the causes of anorexia. This may be because many cases of bulimia go undetected because bulimics are maintaining their weight, not losing a great deal of weight. Research involving clinical samples of bulimics has found that their families tend to be stressed and chaotic (Kent & Clopton, 1992). A combination of treatments appears to be what works the best for bulimics (Mitchell, Peterson, Myers, & Wonderlich, 2001). Interventions might involve a combination of individual and family therapy, nutrition counseling, peer support groups, and even medication, if warranted. The fact that bulimics often experience shame, guilt, or embarrassment about their condition can actually aid in their eventual recovery.

It is difficult to estimate the prevalence of eating disorders because much of the behavior associated with them is secret behavior, but we believe that about 0.5%–1% of adolescents and college-age women suffer from anorexia and about 1%–3% have bulimia (Carlson, Eisenstat, & Ziporyn, 2004). However, one study that followed almost 500 adolescents for 8 years found that 12% of the sample experienced some form of eating disorder during that time (Stice, Marti, Shaw, & Jaconis, 2009). A large number of the adolescents in this study who did not reach the level of having a diagnosis of an eating disorder were able to recover, but relapses were also very common. Between 13% and 17% of the adolescents who were at a subclinical level during the study went on to develop a full-blown eating disorder (Stice et al., 2009). Although we tend to think of eating disorders as conditions that affect female adolescents or young adult women, about 10% of the sufferers are men, and men may account for as much as 25% of all binge disorders (Weltzin et al., 2005). Participating in activities where weight is a continuing issue (such as gymnastics or dance for females and wrestling for males) can put both girls and boys at risk.

There are no simple explanations for what causes eating disorders. Both anorexia and bulimia can begin with normal dieting and concerns about weight that reflect the emphasis placed on thinness in our culture. In Chapter 13, we will talk more about the impact of exposure to the "thin ideal" in media on eating disorders in the United States and as far away as Fiji. The possibility that there are underlying genetic causes comes from family and twin studies (Klump, Kaye, & Strober, 2001). Another factor is that girls who mature earlier than other girls are at risk because their early physical maturation is associated with being heavier than their peers (Tyrka, Graber, & Brooks-Gunn, 2000). Finally, psychological factors such as depression and low body esteem also are predictive of developing eating disorders in both boys and girls (Gardner et al., 2000).

In a review of programs designed to *prevent* eating disorders (rather than to treat them once they occur), Stice and Shaw (2004) found that the most effective programs were ones that target high-risk groups of adolescents, rather than the general population of adolescents. They also found that older adolescents benefited more than younger ones, perhaps because the risk of developing an eating disorder increases after age 15. It may surprise you to learn that programs that focus on providing information to adolescents about the harmful effects of disordered eating were ineffective at producing a change in the adolescent's behavior. Rather, it was programs that focused on changing maladaptive attitudes (such as seeing a thin body as the ideal body type or feeling very dissatisfied with your own body) and maladaptive behaviors (such as fasting or overeating) that were the most effective.

There are many other sources of risk to the health of children and adolescents, such as smoking, alcohol, and drugs. We discuss these further in Chapter 15 where we discuss health, well-being, and resilience.

The pressure to be thin. The cultural ideal of thinness makes an impact on even very young girls. In a 2007 study, 40% of 9- and 10-year-olds claimed they were on some kind of a diet to help them lose weight (Agras, Bryson, Hammer, & Kraemer, 2007).

10. The most effective way to prevent eating disorders is to give adolescents information about how harmful these behaviors can be to the adolescent's body.

TRUE/FALSE

False. Teaching adolescents about the harmful effects of eating disorders is less effective in preventing these disorders than changing teens' attitudes about what their bodies should look like.

Conclusion

The healthy development and functioning of the human body is central to all aspects of human experience. We have seen in this chapter that physical development relates to many aspects of emotional, social, and cognitive development. In the next chapters we will look at these areas, with the clear understanding that all of these aspects of development are linked to what we have studied in this chapter: brain function, sensory development, physical changes such as those in puberty, and the health of the body.

CHAPTER SUMMARY

1. How are the brains of children and adolescents similar to and different from the brains of adults?

   All brains have a similar structure. They are divided into two **hemispheres**, which are connected by the **corpus callosum**. Each area of the brain handles some specialized functions. The brain is made up of **neurons**. Although infants have billions of neurons, they have relatively few **synapses** that connect them. In early brain development, **synaptogenesis** forms connections between neurons, and **myelination** improves the efficiency of the neural impulses. Unused synapses are **pruned**, but when an individual encounters typical experiences, **experience-expectant brain development** occurs and those synaptic connections are retained. When an individual encounters unique experiences, **experience-dependent brain development** occurs and new synapses are formed. Brain development continues through adolescence, especially the development of the prefrontal cortex.

2. What types of disabilities are related to brain development?

   Cerebral palsy is a condition that involves problems with body movement and muscle coordination. **Autism** is a pervasive developmental disorder that involves difficulties with social interaction, communication, and play. Cerebral palsy results from damage to some part of the brain prenatally, at birth, or shortly thereafter, and autism may be caused by different patterns of brain development (for example, failure to prune unnecessary synapses). There is no empirical support for the idea that vaccinations are a cause of autism.

3. How does early motor development proceed?

   Infants are born with a set of **reflexes**, but reflexes are fairly quickly replaced with voluntary movement as the nervous system matures. Children gain control over both **fine motor skills** and **gross motor skills**, and these skills develop following the *cephalocaudal* and **proximodistal** principles (moving from the head to the tail, and from the center of the body to the extremities).

4. What factors influence and shape motor development?

   Motor development is shaped by a complex interaction of genes, maturation, and environmental experiences. Parenting practices (such as letting an infant "practice walk" or putting an infant "back to sleep") can influence how quickly infants develop specific motor skills. Throughout development, children and adolescents benefit from physical activity.

5. How do infants' senses help them understand the world?

   Infants are born with a fully functional set of sense organs. The information registered by the sense organs (called **sensations**) is transmitted to the brain where it is integrated into a coherent picture of the external world (in the process of **perception**). Infants also may automatically imitate simple behaviors that they see because **mirror neurons** in the brain fire in the same way when the infant sees a behavior as when the infant actually performs the behavior.

6. How do the senses develop during infancy?

   Although an infant's **visual acuity** is initially poor, it develops to adult levels by 6 months to 3 years after birth. Hearing is well developed at birth, and infants have shown a preference for their mothers' voices, which they heard while still in the womb. The infant's sense of smell also is highly developed at birth, and infants prefer sweet tastes to other tastes and are sensitive to touch.

7. How do children's bodies change from infancy through adolescence?

   Infants grow very rapidly in the first few years of life, and then the rate of growth slows substantially until the child enters adolescence and experiences the **adolescent growth spurt**. When adolescents go through **puberty**, they become capable of reproducing. Girls experience **menarche**, and boys experience **spermarche**. Both **primary sex characteristics** and **secondary sex characteristics** develop. The timing of puberty has an impact on an individual's social, emotional, and cognitive development. Maturing early has some advantages for boys and disadvantages for girls, but both early-maturing boys and early-maturing girls can be at risk of being drawn into risky behavior if they associate with older peers. Children who go through pubertal changes at very early ages experience **precocious puberty**. The transition from childhood to adulthood is marked in different cultures through a variety of **rites of passage**.

8. What risks come along with sexual maturation?
Sexually mature adolescents may become sexually active, and sexually active female adolescents are at risk of becoming pregnant. After years of decline, the adolescent pregnancy rate in the United States may be starting to increase. The United States already has one of the highest rates of adolescent pregnancies in the industrialized world. Taking a **virginity pledge** may delay initiation into sexual activity, and sexually active adolescents are also making better use of contraception. However, unprotected sex can result in a **sexually transmitted infection (STI)** for both males and females.

9. What role does nutrition play in development?
Good nutrition is essential at each stage of development. Breastfeeding helps an infant get off to a good start and has benefits for the nursing mother as well, but levels of breastfeeding in the United States are not as high as they are in other countries. Food preferences and eating habits are established early in life. However, the diets of many children and adolescents in the United States would not be classified as "good." Children in the United States are more likely to suffer from **undernutrition** than malnutrition. When an adequate diet is not always available, people may experience **food insecurity**. **Obesity** is a major health risk because it is associated with diabetes and other health problems. At the other extreme, some children and adolescents experience eating disorders, such as **anorexia nervosa** or **bulimia**, and do not receive adequate nutrition while compromising their health in a number of other ways.

 Go to **www.sagepub.com/levine** for additional exercises and video resources. Select **Chapter 6, Physical Development,** for chapter-specific activities.

chapter 7

Cognitive Development

7

In this chapter you will learn about the theories and research that contribute to current thinking about how children's cognitive abilities develop. You were briefly introduced to the theories of Piaget, Vygotsky, and information processing in Chapter 2. In this chapter we will look into these theories in more depth and examine some of the research that supports or challenges their ideas. We will also introduce you to a new theory called the theory of core knowledge.

What Is Cognitive Development?

Simply stated, cognition is the study of how the mind works. When we study cognitive development, we are acknowledging the fact that changes occur in how we think and learn as we grow. The difference between how children think and how adults think is more than the difference in how much they know. There are differences in the very way that they think about and understand their experiences.

Test Your Knowledge

Test your knowledge of child development by deciding whether each of the following statements is *true* or *false*, and then check your answers as you read the chapter.

1. **True/False:** The primary difference between how young children and adults think about and understand the world is the difference in the amount of information they know.
2. **True/False:** If a young child drops an object from her high chair over and over again, she is probably just asserting herself and testing her parents' patience.
3. **True/False:** We describe preschoolers as egocentric because they are selfish.
4. **True/False:** An infant would be surprised if an object moved over the edge of a table but didn't fall (as though she somehow understood how gravity operates).
5. **True/False:** Infants who quickly grow bored when they are repeatedly shown a simple object turn out to have higher intelligence later in childhood.
6. **True/False:** Adolescents are able to study while listening to a favorite TV show because by this age their attentional processes are so well developed that they can split their attention between multiple activities.
7. **True/False:** Attention deficit hyperactivity disorder is a disorder of childhood, and fortunately children outgrow the symptoms with age.
8. **True/False:** The primary cause of attention deficit hyperactivity disorder is poor parenting.
9. **True/False:** Few people have clear memories of what happened in their lives before the age of 3.
10. **True/False:** Young children may believe that they remember something that never happened if someone repeatedly suggests it to them.

Correct answers: (1) False, (2) False, (3) False, (4) True, (5) True, (6) False, (7) False, (8) False, (9) True, (10) True

The first time that psychologists began to study the nature of children's thought was in the early 1900s when they developed and used intelligence tests to assess children's abilities in order to improve their education. Two theorists, Piaget and Vygotsky, both began their careers by using intelligence tests in their work with children. They used intelligence tests to compare children's abilities in order to identify which children were likely to have more difficulty in school. However, each found problems with how intelligence was conceptualized and measured by these tests. Both Piaget and Vygotsky were inspired by their experiences to formulate new theories to describe how children's cognitive abilities develop. Both were interested in describing normal processes of development, rather than focusing on children's difficulties. In the following **Journey of Research: Binet's Intelligence Test and Its Unintended Consequences**, you can read more about how work in intelligence testing and theoretical work on cognitive development intermingled. We will take up the topic of intelligence in Chapter 8 but focus in this chapter on the theories of cognitive development.

JOURNEY of RESEARCH

Binet's Intelligence Test and Its Unintended Consequences

We will read in Chapter 8 that Alfred Binet was the first psychologist to attempt to assess children's intelligence in a systematic fashion. His work led directly to the development of the IQ test. However, his work also had several indirect effects on the study of cognitive development. Early in his career, developmental theorist Jean Piaget worked in Binet's laboratory, helping standardize intelligence tests by asking children specific questions. However, Piaget was not particularly interested in whether or not children knew the "correct" answers. He was far more intrigued by the incorrect answers that children gave because he saw them as a useful way to begin understanding how children truly think (Wadsworth, 1996).

Russian psychologist Lev Vygotsky also was influenced by Binet's work. He too worked with children to identify their intellectual abilities, and he also began with Binet's ideas about assessing the child's current abilities. However, he came to believe that it was just as important to assess which intellectual abilities were in the process of forming as to assess which ones were already in place. Unlike Binet, Vygotsky did not see intelligence as developing in only one predictable way (Del Rio & Alvarez, 2007). Therefore he believed in testing the child's "readiness" to learn, which he referred to as the zone of proximal development (Vygotsky, 1978a).

In this chapter we will find out how the ideas of Piaget and Vygotsky developed into theories that have been very influential in our understanding of how children think and learn.

Theories of Cognitive Development

Piaget's Theory of Cognitive Development

Jean Piaget (1896–1980) was a student of biology before he studied psychology and child development. By age 10, he had already published his first article in the field of biology on his study of an albino sparrow he had seen in a park (McKeachie & Sims, 2004). He continued his biological interests with research on mollusks, those hard-shelled sea creatures such as oysters, snails, and clams. He had published over 20 articles on the subject by the time he was 21, and he completed his doctoral dissertation on the mollusks of the Valais region in Switzerland (Singer & Revenson, 1996).

If one of your friends was like the young Piaget, you might be concerned that his or her life was too narrowly focused on one thing, and Piaget's godfather also had that concern. He introduced the young man to the study of philosophy, and Piaget then became interested in the philosophical question of how we come to know and understand our world, an area of study referred to as epistemology. His approach to studying the development of the human mind was a synthesis of ideas drawn from biology and philosophy, along with an interest in finding evidence for theories based on experimentation. On the one hand, he looked at human beings as biological organisms, who must adapt successfully to their environment, just as snails and clams do. On the other hand, he looked at the more unique characteristics of the human mind, with its capacity for reflection and understanding, and wondered how it all worked. As we will see, both approaches contributed to the theory of **genetic-epistemology** (*genetic* from biology, *epistemology* from philosophy) that he developed.

Many developmental researchers have claimed that Jean Piaget revolutionized the study of children's cognitive development (Flavell, Miller, & Miller, 2002). Although his theory has received some criticism and has undergone some revision over the years, it provides a set of basic principles to guide our understanding of cognitive development that are found in most current theories. They include the following ideas:

1. Intelligence is an active, constructive, and dynamic process.

2. Mistakes children make in their thinking are usually meaningful because they indicate the nature of their thought processes at their current stage of development.

3. As children develop, the structure of their thinking changes, and these new modes of thought are based on the earlier structures (Flavell et al., 2002).

We introduced Piaget's theory in Chapter 2. In this chapter we will review Piaget's basic ideas about how cognitive development occurs and then describe in more depth his four stages of development. Piaget believed that in order to adapt successfully to our environment and ensure our survival, we are always actively trying to make sense of our experiences. "Making sense" means organizing our experiences so that we can understand them. **Active Learning: Organizing by Cognitive Schema** gives you a chance to explore the different ways that a single set of objects can be organized, depending on which concepts you use to do it.

Genetic-epistemology Piaget's theory that development of knowledge is based on both genetics (from biology) and epistemology (a philosophical understanding of the nature of knowledge).

Organizing by Cognitive Schema

ACTIVE LEARNING

Let's say that it is your task to organize the room shown below so that you will be able to find everything again when you want it. Take a minute to decide how you would organize this room.

You could do this in several different ways: (a) separate items by function: shoes, clothes, and toys; (b) separate them by color: all blue, purple, red, and orange. Would you have a different way of organizing the room? In Piaget's terms, each of these ways of organizing the room might indicate a schema that you have. A **schema** is a cognitive framework that places concepts, objects, or experiences into categories or groups of associations. In the examples above, you might have a schema for "things you wear," "things to play with," or simply color differences. Your own schema might have been quite different, like "things that go in a drawer" versus "things that go in a cupboard." Each person has a unique way of organizing experiences based on the schemas he or she has developed.

Schema A cognitive framework that places concepts, objects, or experiences into categories or groups of associations.

Assimilation Fitting new experiences into existing mental schemas.

Disequilibrium A state of confusion in which your schemas do not fit your experiences.

Equilibration An attempt to resolve uncertainty to return to a comfortable cognitive state.

Accommodation Changing your mental schemas so they fit new experiences.

TRUE/FALSE

1. The primary difference between how young children and adults think about and understand the world is the difference in the amount of information they know.

   False. Although there are differences in the amount of knowledge, the more important differences are qualitative, or differences in the way adults and children think and understand the world.

Circular reaction An infant's repetition of a reflexive action that results in a pleasurable experience.

Often, when we have a new experience, it immediately makes sense to us because we can fit it into a schema we already have. For example, a child may have a new kind of sandwich that she easily understands is a kind of food similar to foods she's had before. When we can fit new experiences easily into our preexisting schemas, Piaget called this process **assimilation**. However, let's say that this child has never seen crab served in its shell. If the child is served something that is this different from the foods she is familiar with, she may not connect it with her schema for food. Piaget would say that she is thrown into a state of confusion, or **disequilibrium**, by the experience. People generally find the uncertainty of disequilibrium uncomfortable, so they try to make sense out of what they are seeing, to return to a comfortable state through a process Piaget referred to as **equilibration**. Changing your schemas to fit new experiences is called **accommodation**, because you are accommodating or changing the way you think about something in order to understand new information. In this case, if a parent can convince the child to try eating the crab, she may discover that it is a delicious food, and she accommodates her existing schema. With this disequilibrium resolved, she now adds crab to her schema for food.

Piaget's Stages of Cognitive Development

As a result of his research and his conversations with children, Piaget believed that children think in a different way than adults do. He not only believed that were there quantitative differences (that is, children simply have less information or less skill in thinking), but what is more important is that he also believed there were qualitative differences, meaning that children think in a particular way that is unique to their developmental level.

Based on detailed observations of his own children as well as experiments with groups of children, he identified four different stages from infancy through adolescence, each representing different qualities of thought. Each stage is built on the abilities acquired during the previous one, but each has features that are new and unique to that new stage. We will describe these stages in some detail, along with activities you can do to understand firsthand how children think at each age level. Piaget set out the ages for each stage as approximations. Some children reach them sooner or later than others. What he felt was most important is that these stages could only occur in the order he described: Children could not jump from sensorimotor thinking to formal operations and then back to concrete operations. The path of development only moves in one direction.

Sensorimotor Stage (Birth–2 Years). The first stage in Piaget's theory is the sensorimotor stage. As the name of this stage implies, Piaget believed that infants organize their world by means of their senses and their physical action upon it. There are four general trends in development within the sensorimotor period: (a) from reflexes to goal-directed activity, (b) from the body to the outside world, (c) development of object permanence, and (d) from action to mental representation.

From reflexes to goal-directed activity. As we learned in Chapter 6, all infants are born with reflexes, which are automatic, patterned behaviors that have some survival value. These behaviors are not learned but are built into the nervous system. However, Piaget said that learning begins even in the first month of life as infants begin to adapt these reflexes to the environment. For example, the sucking reflex is usually evoked when the lips are touched. However, this reflexive behavior can occur during sleep or can be interrupted if the infant is looking for food and instead gets a shirt! In this way, even these automatic behaviors begin to accommodate to the environment (Piaget, 1962).

Between 1 and 4 months, infants begin to use reflexes in different ways. When the reflex results in a pleasurable experience, the infant repeats it over and over again. For example, when the infant somehow gets his thumb in his mouth it begins what Piaget called a **circular reaction**. The action produces a good feeling, which prompts him to continue the action, and the good feeling continues to stimulate the action, in a circular fashion. When the baby's thumb falls out of his mouth, he has to rediscover the action that will place it back where it feels good (Piaget, 1962). The different circular reactions the infant is developing can also be referred to as **motor schemas**. Infants organize their understanding of the world through their action on it. We all know that if you give an 8-month-old any object, the first thing she will do is put it in her mouth. She is using this sucking or mouthing schema as her way of organizing the world: Is this object a "suckable"? How does it taste? How does it feel in my mouth?

Between 8 and 12 months, infants combine the motor schemas they have already developed to begin to solve problems. No longer do they just repeat actions over and over for the pleasure of it. Now they have a goal in mind and use their schemas for grasping, hitting, and mouthing in combinations to reach that goal. At the next stage, usually between the ages of 12 and 18 months, infants develop new behaviors that allow them to achieve their goals. Although the child still repeats actions over and over, now he does it with planned variations designed to "see what happens when I do *this*!" For example, any parent knows the stage babies go through when they continually drop things on purpose. Each time the child does this, the action is a little different as he experiments with "What happens when I drop it this way? What happens when I drop it and Mommy is there? What happens when I drop it and she's not there?" This can be very frustrating for parents, but Piaget saw it as an example of the active experimentation that children engage in at all ages.

From the body to the outside world. When babies are first born, their major interests surround their bodily needs: hunger, sleep, comfort. As they grow, their attention is increasingly focused on the world around them. As their vision and coordination improve, infants begin to apply circular reactions to objects outside of their own bodies. For example, if a baby kicks her legs and sees that the mobile hanging over her crib moves in response, she repeats the kicking over and over until she tires of the "excitement" of the response (Rovee-Collier, 1999).

Development of object permanence. Piaget believed that newborns do not understand that objects (or people for that matter) exist outside of their own action upon them; that is, they lack **object permanence**. An infant grasping a toy experiences "grasping a toy," not "I, a separate entity, am grasping this toy, which also has an existence of its own" (Fast, 1985). While the child is grasping the toy, it is part of his experience, but when he is not, the toy doesn't exist for him. As the infant develops new means of exploration, he learns that he can grasp the toy and also chew on it and also look at it. When he applies *several* motor schemas to an object, the motor schemas become detached from the object itself. The toy is no longer just "something I grasp," but "a thing separate from my actions on it." Finally, by the end of the sensorimotor stage, the child understands that objects exist independently and act according to their own rules (Fast, 1985). You can use Piaget's tests described in **Active Learning: Testing Object Permanence** to determine whether or not a baby has developed object permanence.

Motor schema. This baby is using a motor schema to explore objects. As long as this activity is pleasurable, the baby will continue to repeat it in a pattern called a circular reaction.

Motor schema Infants' understanding of the world through their action on it.

2. If a young child drops an object from her high chair over and over again, she is probably just asserting herself and testing her parents' patience. **TRUE/FALSE**

False. This is the child's way of experimenting to discover how things work in the world. If you watch closely, you'll see that she probably varies how she drops the object from one time to another.

Object permanence The understanding that objects still exist when an infant does not see them.

A-not-B task A test for object permanence in which an object is hidden under cloth A and then moved under cloth B.

Testing Object Permanence

Piaget (1954) devised a series of experiments called the **A-not-B task** to test infants' object permanence. You can carry out this test if you have access to a child between birth and age 2. If others in your class test children of different ages within this 2-year range, you can compare results to see how object permanence changes during this period of time. You will need to have an interesting toy or object that is safe for an infant to have (that is, nothing the child can choke on or that is otherwise unsafe to put in the mouth) and two cloths to cover the objects. There are three steps to the series of experiments Piaget carried out:

1. Show the infant the toy and be sure he is interested in the toy and is watching you. Then hide the toy under one of the cloths, which are set side by side between you and the child. Observe and record whether he searches for the toy.

The development of object permanence. How does the concept of object permanence explain why this baby loses interest in the toy dog when it is hidden?

2. If the baby searches for the toy in Step 1, begin Step 2 by hiding the toy under the same cloth. Then, while the baby is still watching, move the toy from under the first cloth to under the second cloth. Observe and record where the baby searches.

3. If the baby finds the toy the second time, carry out the same experiment as above, but try to move the toy from the first cloth to the second without the baby seeing what you are doing.

Follow-up: Do you think the child you are testing shows through his behaviors that he understands that objects continue to exist even if he can't see them? Is he tricked when you move the toy?

In Piaget's experiments, young infants would not search at all when an object was hidden. It was as if they believed that the toy simply disappeared when it was hidden. At an older age they would search under the first cloth hiding the object but give up if the toy was moved under a second cloth, even if they clearly saw the experimenter move the object under the second cloth. This is known as the A-not-B error, because the infant continues to look in the first location, *A,* and does not switch to the second location, *B,* where the object is now hidden. A third step is that the baby will search when she sees the object moved from *A* to *B* but not when it is moved when the baby is not looking. Finally, when the infant has true object permanence she will continue to search regardless of the movement of the object. There is no question in the baby's mind that the toy still exists even though she can no longer see it, and she will search until the toy is recovered.

Video Link 7.1
Object permanence.

In recent years questions have been raised about the validity of Piaget's ideas about the development of object permanence. Read about this ongoing controversy in **Journey of Research: The Debate About Object Permanence**.

The Debate About Object Permanence

JOURNEY *of* **RESEARCH**

Piaget's notion that infants are not born with true object permanence has been very controversial. For instance, Baillargeon (2008) has proposed that infants are born with "persistence"—that is, an understanding that objects persist through time and space. In other words, they are born with object permanence. This idea is part of the approach that has been labeled the theory of core knowledge, which we will discuss a little later in this chapter. While Piaget used active searching as the criterion to determine whether a child had object permanence, modern researchers have used more sophisticated techniques.

For example, researchers are now able to use computer software to track where a baby is looking. Based upon the idea that infants will look longer at events that surprise them, researchers have shown that babies look longer at events that violate an expectation of object permanence. For example, Baillargeon, Spelke, and Wasserman (1985) showed 4-month-old babies a toy. A screen was then placed in front of the toy and tipped slowly backward. In the real world, the screen would hit the toy and stop tipping. Some babies

saw exactly that (the expected outcome). However, some babies saw the screen continue to tip all the way back, as if it was going right through the toy (an unexpected outcome). Babies in the unexpected outcome condition looked significantly longer than those in the expected outcome condition. Therefore, it appeared that babies knew the object should still be there and stop the screen from tipping backward even though they couldn't see it.

However, infants who are this same age seem to have difficulty tracking an object when it goes behind another object. If infants understand that objects persist even when they are out of sight, they should know that they still exist behind the screen and will reappear on the other side. One study made use of new technology to track infant eye movements and found that 4-month-olds did not predict the reappearance of an object after it went behind another object (Bremner et al., 2005). Therefore, the controversy about whether object permanence develops through experience, as Piaget said, or whether it is inborn, as Baillargeon proposed, is ongoing.

Video Link 7.2
Experiment by Baillargeon.

From action to mental representation. As we have seen, Piaget believed that infants understood the world through motor schemas, such as grasping, sucking, and shaking. Motor schemas are quite different from the kinds of schemas that are based on concepts and inner thought that we illustrated in **Active Learning: Organizing by Cognitive Schema**. Piaget theorized that ultimately these motor schemas would become the basis for internal, cognitive representations of the world. He believed that children's first thoughts are mental representations of the actions they have been performing. In other words, the motor schemas are internalized, and the infant can *think* of them instead of actually *doing* them. Piaget (1963) provides the following example of the planning that can now occur: His daughter Jacqueline, at the age of 1 year and 7 months, tried to put a chain necklace into a matchbox. Over and over she tried to put one end of the chain in, then the next part, and then the next. However, each time the first part would fall out as she was trying to put the rest in, and she remained unsuccessful. Piaget reported that his other daughter Lucienne at an older age used her new abilities to think ahead rather than to just act. With the same objective of putting the necklace into the matchbox, she rolled the necklace into a ball and successfully placed it into the box. Instead of the trial-and-error approach of her sister at a younger age, Lucienne was able to think about an effective way to accomplish this goal and then did it.

Preoperational Stage (2–7 Years). Piaget defined his second stage by what it lacks: operations. For Piaget, the term *operations* has a very particular meaning. **Operations** are mental actions

Operations Mental actions that follow systematic, logical rules.

that follow systematic, logical rules. When children are *pre*operational, they do not think in a logical way. We will look at what makes children understand differently from adults, but first we will discuss the new and positive change during this period: the ability to use symbols.

According to Piaget, the major accomplishment of the preoperational stage is the ability to represent actions mentally rather than physically. A symbol is anything that represents something else that is not present. For example, a child may use a banana to represent a telephone, but symbols at this age are still very concrete. Abstract symbols, such as a balance scale representing the concept of justice, are still outside of the comprehension of the preoperational child. Three ways in which children demonstrate their ability to use symbols are fantasy play, language, and drawings.

In fantasy play children use objects or themselves and other people to represent something that is not there. While they may actually be holding a banana, in their mind they are imagining that it is a telephone, and they can pretend to talk to someone at the other end of the line, who is also a figment of their imagination. Another example of the use of symbols in fantasy is the imaginary companion. Some children create an entire person, who is so real to them that their imaginary friend must have a seat at the dinner table and be served his own food. For Piaget, the development of language is important mainly because it also shows that children can use symbols. Whenever we say a word, we are representing something that is not there. Look at this word: **APPLE**. You will notice that it is not round, and if you lick the page in your textbook, you will find that it isn't sweet. It isn't even red, but you knew the object in the real world that it stood for when you first read it. In a similar way, if we say "table," we no longer have to have the table in front of us. Finally, children demonstrate the use of symbols whenever they make a drawing of something, even if that drawing is not recognizable by someone else. To the child, the drawing is still a representation of whatever she had in mind. However, random marking on the page by an infant who just likes to see the colors would certainly not reflect symbolic thinking. Two-year-olds demonstrate that they understand the representative nature of pictures. For example, a toddler shown a picture of a banana does not try to eat it. Instead the child understands that the picture only represents a real banana (Preissler & Bloom, 2007).

While the use of symbols is a major step forward and liberates children from the immediate physical world, Piaget also placed considerable emphasis on the limitations of children's thought at this age. We next describe three limitations that characterize preoperational thought: transductive reasoning, egocentrism, and animism. We will also describe the reasons why children in the preoperational stage cannot solve what are called conservation problems.

Transductive reasoning. Adults and older children usually think logically, using deductive and inductive reasoning to figure out problems. Deductive reasoning starts with a general premise (for example, "All apples have cores") and moves to specific conclusions ("This is an apple; therefore it must have a core"). This is the basis of hypothesis testing, which we described in Chapter 3 as a basis for scientific research. Inductive reasoning starts with individual examples ("I see many apples, and they all have cores") and ends with general principles ("Therefore all apples have cores"). This is similar to the way that we collect observations to develop theories. Piaget found in his interviews with children that their logic was neither deductive nor inductive. Instead, they moved freely from one particular observation to another, creating causal links where none existed. He called this **transductive reasoning**. One example he gives is his daughter Lucienne's statement: "I haven't had my nap, therefore it isn't afternoon," as if her taking a nap caused it to be afternoon (Piaget, 1962, p. 232). Preoperational children may base their conclusions on a set of unrelated facts, or they may assume that things that just happen to occur at about the same time cause each other. For example, an angry child might accuse an innocent bystander of doing him harm by reasoning, "You were there when I fell, so it's your fault that I hurt myself."

Magical explanations may be the best that children can do to understand the world, but this may lead to tricky situations when dealing with children who are convinced of the reality of their thoughts. For instance, a child might become distraught if a brother became sick after they had a fight because the child thinks that it was his angry thoughts that caused his brother's illness.

Transductive reasoning Thought that connects one particular observation to another by creating causal links where none exist.

Even adults may keep some vestiges of magical thinking when there are situations that they don't understand or can't control. Many people who are involved in sports, theater performance, or other situations in which circumstances outside their control may influence how well they perform have special pieces of clothing they must wear or rituals they feel they must do to ensure that they will do well. Just watch professional baseball players. How many do something like undoing and redoing their wristbands every time they come up to the plate? You yourself may believe that your favorite team will not win unless you are wearing a certain shirt. These are holdovers of magical thinking.

Egocentrism. Piaget believed that young children find it difficult to see the world from another person's point of view, especially if that point of view differs from their own. Piaget called this **egocentrism** (*ego* means "I" or "self"; therefore the child's world centers around his own point of view). Be careful in understanding this term. It is *not* the same as selfishness or egotism (thinking *you* are the *greatest*), although young children have plenty of each of those characteristics as well. It really means that the child's mind is insufficiently developed to allow her to understand that someone else's perspective could be different from her own. The result may be a "selfish" child who grabs toys from others, but the reason is that the child cannot yet understand that someone else wants the same toy just as much as she does. It is important to set appropriate limits on behavior, but it is equally important to help the child become aware of the thoughts and feelings of others to overcome behavior that appears to be willfully selfish.

Childhood fears. Preschool children's magical thinking, typical of Piaget's stage of preoperational thought, makes them vulnerable to fears such as these. What are some ways to help children cope with such fears?

3. We describe preschoolers as egocentric because they are selfish. **TRUE/FALSE**

False. Preschoolers have trouble seeing and understanding the world from someone else's perspective. This may make them appear to be selfish, but it is because of this cognitive limitation.

Egocentrism The inability to see or understand things from someone else's perspective.

Figure 7.1

Piaget's three mountains task. In Piaget's three mountains task, a child who is egocentric believes that the doll sees the same view that she herself sees.

In the youngest preoperational children, egocentrism can be found even in terms of what they think someone else sees. For example, if someone on the phone asks a child how old she is, the child may hold up two fingers to indicate 2 years old, thinking that if she can see her fingers, then the person at the other end of the line can too. Piaget's famous "three mountains task," illustrated in Figure 7.1, showed children a large model of three mountains (remember they lived in Switzerland where mountains were very familiar to them!) on a table (Piaget & Inhelder, 1956). With the child standing on one side of the table, she was shown pictures of the mountains that showed what they looked like from all four sides of the table. She was asked what a doll would see from each side of the table. Regardless of where the doll was, 4-year-old children reported that the dolls saw the same

Animism　Giving human characteristics, such as thought and intention, to inanimate or natural things.

Video Link 7.3
Piaget's conservation experiment.

Conservation　The understanding that a basic quantity of something (amount, volume, mass) remains the same regardless of changes in appearance.

Video Link 7.4
Piaget's conservation experiment (additional clip).

Centration　Focusing on only one aspect of a situation.

Decentration　The ability to think about more than one aspect of a situation at a time.

view that they themselves saw. In other words, they did not differentiate between their own point of view and that of others. Egocentrism may be expressed in other ways. For example, if you ask a 3-year-old what to get Mommy for her birthday, he may reply "a toy truck!" If he likes it, he believes that she must like it as well. Egocentrism makes it difficult for children to understand that other people see, feel, think, and understand things differently than they do.

Animism. Egocentrism leads to the child's belief in **animism**; that is, children give human characteristics, such as thought and intention, to inanimate or natural things. Piaget (1962) gave the following examples: A child asked about a swirl of dead leaves, "Do they like dancing?" and another stated when she missed a train, "Doesn't the train know we aren't in it?" (pp. 251–252). Be careful in your understanding of the concept of animism. It is not the same as pretending. A child who knows she is pretending to have her doll play a game with her is not engaging in animism. If she truly believes that the doll can be angry about losing a game, then she is using animism.

Conservation. There is another important cognitive skill that preoperational children have not yet acquired: **conservation**. Piaget believed that preschool children do not understand that a basic quantity of something (amount, volume, mass) remains the same regardless of changes in its appearance. For example, you still have the same amount of clay whether you flatten it into a pancake, make a ball, or roll it into a tube. The only way you have a different amount of clay is if you add some or remove some of it.

Piaget believed that one reason why preschool children are fooled when the shape of the clay changes is because they can only focus on one aspect of a problem at a time, a cognitive limitation he called **centration**. For instance, when preoperational children see water in several glasses, they only notice the height of the water and decide that the glass with the higher level has more water in it. When children are in the stage of concrete operations, they begin to **decenter** and are able to think about more than one aspect of this situation at a time. In this stage, the child will see that the level is higher in one glass but the glass is thinner, while the level of water in the other is lower but that glass is wider. Once the child has this understanding, he will be able to come to the correct solution more easily. See **Active Learning: Conservation** for tests you can carry out with preschool and school-age children to understand more about conservation.

ACTIVE
LEARNING

Conservation

To see the development of conservation, have a preschool child (age 3–5) and/or a school-age child (age 6–10) carry out the following tasks. Be sure to ask the preschooler the questions first if you are testing two children at the same time.

1. **Conservation of volume** (see Figure 7.2a). Equipment: two identical transparent containers and a third container that is a different shape. Fill the two identical containers with the same amount of water. Show these to the child and ask, "Do these containers have the same

Figure 7.2

Piaget's conservation of volume, mass, and number tasks. These illustrations show you the types of transformations that occur when you are testing a child's ability to use reversibility and decentration to solve conservation problems.

Piaget's Conservation Tasks

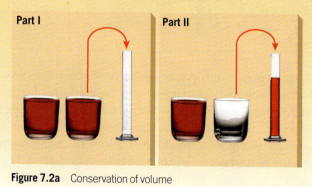

Figure 7.2a　Conservation of volume

amount of water, or does one container have more than the other?" Be sure to adjust the amount of water until the child agrees that the containers have the same amount. Then tell the child to watch while you pour the water from one of the identical containers into the third container. Ask the child, "Now do these two containers have the same amount of water, or does one container have more than the other?" If the child answers that one has more, ask which one. For each child, be sure to ask *why* he or she thinks that they are the same (if that's what the child said) or why he or she thinks that one has more than the other (if that was the child's response).

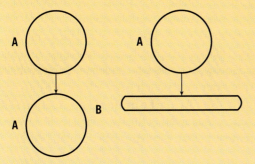
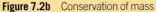

Figure 7.2b   Conservation of mass

2. **Conservation of mass** (see Figure 7.2b). Equipment: play dough or clay. Make two identical balls of clay. Show them to the child and ask, "Do these two pieces of clay have the same amount of clay [play dough], or does one have more than the other?" Be sure to adjust the amount of clay until the child agrees that the two pieces have the same amount. Then take one ball and roll it into a long tube. Ask the child, "Now, do these two pieces of clay have the same amount of clay, or does one have more than the other?" Be sure to ask each child *why* he or she thinks the two pieces of clay have the same amount or why one has more than the other, depending on how the child answered.

Figure 7.2c   Conservation of number

3. **Conservation of number** (see Figure 7.2c). Equipment: eight identical items, such as pennies or cookies. Make two rows of four items parallel to each other. Ask the child, "Does this row have the same number of pennies [or cookies] as this other row?" If the child does not agree they are the same, show the child by counting that each has four, and then ask again. Once the child has agreed that the rows are the same, move the pennies or cookies in one row so that they are much farther apart. Then ask the child, "Now, are there the same number of pennies [or cookies] in these two rows, or does one have more than the other?" Again, be sure to ask the child to explain his or her answer.

If the child you have tested is fooled by the change in the appearance of the liquid, the clay, or the row of objects, that child is still in the preoperational stage and cannot yet conserve volume, mass, or number. If the child is not fooled, he or she has developed the ability to conserve and is in concrete operations. Some children may show conservation for some of the tests but not for all. These children are in a transitional state, moving from preoperational to concrete operational thinking.

To conclude, the preoperational stage is marked by an advance to symbolic thinking, but children's thinking at this stage is tied to what they see rather than what they reason out with the use of logic. Their perception is still tied to their own point of view, although they gradually begin to realize that others may see and understand the world differently than they do. Many of the limitations found in preoperational children are overcome in the next stage of concrete operations.

Stage of Concrete Operations (7–12 Years).

The third stage in Piaget's theory is concrete operations. Children in the stage of concrete operations can think logically, rather than magically, but they are still unable to understand abstract concepts. We will talk about two cognitive advances in concrete operational thinking: reversibility and classification. Once children develop these cognitive skills, they are able to solve conservation problems.

Reversibility. **Reversibility** is the ability to reverse mental operations. This ability allows a child to overcome the pull toward perceptual bias when making certain judgments about conservation tasks. For example, if the contents of a short, wide glass are poured into a tall, thin glass, the water level will be higher in the second glass. Perceptually, this may cause the child to think the second glass contains more water. However, a child who understands reversibility can think about the fact that if you reverse the procedure and pour the water back into the short glass, the amount will still be the same. If you carried out **Active Learning: Conservation** with a child in concrete operations, the child may have explained that the two glasses still have the same amount of water because "you can pour the water back into the other container and see that they are the same."

This same ability is necessary for a child to understand that if 1 + 1 = 2, then necessarily 2 − 1 = 1, a basic foundation for understanding arithmetic. In the concrete operational stage, children are now paying attention to *how* something changes, not just the beginning and end states. Children in the preoperational stage look only at the first level of the water and the second level, not at the action that occurs between the two levels, and therefore reach the wrong conclusion and think the volume of the water has changed.

Classification. Piaget saw the ability to classify objects into larger categories as central to concrete operations. The game of "20 Questions," in which a child must ask a series of questions that can be answered "yes" or "no" to figure out what the other person has chosen to think about, provides a good opportunity to see the difference in **classification** skills between preoperational and concrete operational stages. When playing 20 Questions, the first question an adult or older child is likely to ask is something like "Is it alive?" This is a highly efficient question because this eliminates a very large number of potential items: everything that is or is not alive. Children in the concrete operational stage will continue to work their way down from larger to smaller categories (for example, "Is it an animal?" or "Is it a plant?"), but children in the preoperational stage may start with very specific questions like "Is it a cat?" or "Is it my chair?" These children do not yet understand that individual objects can fit into larger categories. (Remember that children at that age are egocentric, so whatever is in their head must also be in yours!) For Piaget, logical operations allow the child to understand that everything fits into larger and larger categories.

Stage of Formal Operations (12 Years and Older).

The stage of formal operations is marked by the development of abstract thinking. Piaget (1999) stated that by the age of about 12 children begin to reason using hypotheses, and he called this **hypothetico-deductive reasoning**. Hypothetico-deductive reasoning allows individuals to generate new possibilities and form hypotheses in order to answer questions. See **Active Learning: Formal Operations** for one example of Piaget's research. In the formal operational stage, teens can think about broad abstract concepts such as democracy, rather than just concrete concepts, such as counting votes in an election. Teens may become idealistic at this stage, because they can imagine what *could be,* rather than what *is.* This idealism may motivate them to become involved in activities in which they are committed to a larger goal.

Reversibility The ability to reverse mental operations.

Classification The ability to organize objects into hierarchical conceptual categories.

Hypothetico-deductive reasoning The ability to form hypotheses about how the world works and to reason logically about these hypotheses.

Video Link 7.5
Concrete and formal operational thinking.

Formal Operations

Piaget tested children of various ages on what he called the "pendulum problem." He provided each child with a pendulum, consisting of an object hanging from a string, and asked the child to figure out what determines how fast the string swings back and forth: the weight at the end of the string, the length of the string, the strength of the initial push, or the height from which the weight is dropped.

Set this experiment up for yourself. Find a length of string and attach an object to the end of it. Suspend the object so it can swing freely. Write down the process by which you would test which of the four possibilities is the answer to what determines how fast the string swings.

A young child would simply try different things in any way and could possibly stumble upon the right answer. However, formal operations would allow you to approach this problem in a systematic, scientific way. The issues are the same as those we described in Chapter 3 in regard to testing hypotheses. In effect, we must think of all the possible answers to the problem and then test our specific hypotheses by controlling all the variables other than the one we are testing. If you want to know the effect of the weight at the end of the string, you must vary the weight while keeping the length of the string, the strength of the initial push, and the height from which the weight is dropped the same. If varying the weight did not make a difference, you might then move on to testing the strength of the initial push and so on through all the possibilities.

Have you figured out the answer to the pendulum problem? It is the length of the string that determines how fast it goes back and forth.

Adolescent egocentrism. David Elkind has proposed that there is a resurgence of egocentrism in early adolescence. This means that young teens are unable to see the world from others' perspectives. However, this egocentrism is different from that of the preoperational child. Elkind stated that adolescent egocentrism is expressed through what he has called the imaginary audience and the personal fable (Alberts, Elkind, & Ginsberg, 2007).

Imaginary audience
The belief that one is the center of other people's attention much of the time.

When Elkind refers to an **imaginary audience**, he means that young teens believe that they are the center of other people's attention in the same way that they are the center of their own attention. Teens may refuse to go to school because their hair looks bad, or they may become self-conscious about the way their body looks. In the young teen's mind, everyone at school will also be very aware of his or her perceived flaws. Although it is true that teens can be very cruel to one another, the chances are that most other teens are more concerned about how they themselves look than they are about how other people look.

Although the "audience" can be seen as harsh and judgmental, it can also be positive: "Sometimes when I see a good-looking girl/boy, I think that they are looking at me in a very admiring way" (Alberts et al., 2007, p. 75). Or a teen may

The imaginary audience. This girl likely assumes that others are looking as closely at her appearance as she is. Is her "audience" real or imaginary?

be dancing at a party and think everyone is looking at her because of how cool she looks. She is sure that all the other people around her are spending tremendous energy noticing and thinking about her. In these ways the teen, like the preschooler, has difficulty seeing the world from someone else's point of view and realizing that she is not the center of the other person's world. Elkind has developed the Imaginary Audience Scale to measure this aspect of adolescent egocentrism (Elkind & Bowen, 1979). The following is an example from that scale:

> Instructions: Please read the following stories carefully and assume that the events actually happened to you. Place a check next to the answer that best describes what you would do or feel in the real situation.
>
> You are sitting in class and have discovered that your jeans have a small but noticeable split along the side seam. Your teacher has offered extra credit toward his/her course grade to anyone who can write the correct answer to a question on the blackboard. Would you get up in front of the class and go to the blackboard, or would you remain seated?
>
> _____Go to the blackboard as though nothing had happened.
> _____Go to the blackboard and try to hide the split.
> _____Remain seated.
> (Elkind & Bowen, 1979)

The first answer reflects a willingness to be exposed to the imaginary audience. The second reflects more discomfort, and the third reflects the most discomfort with exposing yourself to an imaginary audience. Elkind and Bowen (1979) found that the highest scores on this scale, indicating acute awareness of an imaginary audience, were found in eighth graders, a time when adolescents are particularly sensitive about their appearance.

A **personal fable** is a belief held by teenagers that their experiences are unique and different from those of all other people. For example, a girl whose boyfriend has broken up with her may think, "My mother could never understand what I am going through. She could never have felt a love like I felt!" Unfortunately the personal fable can be the basis of risky behaviors. A teen may understand the effect of alcohol on reaction time but still believe that he is such a good driver that "I can drive drunk and nothing will happen to me!" Or a teen might understand the risks of unprotected sex but still feel that "I won't get pregnant—that only happens to other people." In one study designed to assess the presence of personal fables, middle schoolers were given a series of statements such as this: "When my parents or friends tell me that they know how I feel, I don't believe that they really do." This research showed that those young teens whose ideas reflected the presence of a personal fable were more likely to report an attraction to risky behavior such as a willingness to try cigarettes for the first time (Alberts et al., 2007).

Piaget's studies led him to the conclusion that the stage of formal operations was the final, highest stage of mental development. However, some theorists who have come after Piaget believe that cognitive development continues beyond this level to another stage called **postformal or dialectical thinking**. In this stage there is a movement away from pure logic. The individual comes to understand that rather than knowledge being absolute (that is, rather than there being one right answer and one answer only), knowledge is relative. Postformal thinkers understand that knowledge can be complex, even contradictory, and filled with paradoxes, but they can analyze and bring together contradictory thoughts and emotions (Labouvie-Vief, 2006).

Critique of Piaget's Work

Although Piaget's experiments demonstrate aspects of children's behaviors that have been replicated many times, some researchers later argued that Piaget drew incorrect conclusions from the results he found. Two of the criticisms focus on the age at which Piaget says each of the cognitive abilities emerge and on the critical issue of whether cognitive abilities develop together in qualitative stages or separately in small steps. The third major criticism has centered on whether the stages Piaget described are universal or culturally determined.

Ages and Stages. As researchers have examined concepts like egocentrism and classification, they have found that some of the procedures that Piaget used were so complicated that they

---

Personal fable The belief (often held by teenagers) that you are in some way unique and different from all other people.

Postformal or dialectical thinking The ability to analyze and bring together contradictory thoughts and emotions.

were difficult for children to understand, or that there were aspects of the tests that were not related to the underlying ability Piaget claimed to be testing. For example, one ability that he believed appears only in concrete operations is seriation, or putting objects in order by height, weight, or some other quality. If you give a young child many sticks of different lengths to put in order by height, he is unlikely to be able to do so accurately. However, if you give this same child three sticks to put in order, he may be able to do so with no difficulty. Therefore, young children are capable of seriating but are unable to do so when their abilities are overwhelmed by the complexity of the task. There have been many studies that have demonstrated capabilities in younger children than Piaget found by using procedures that have been simplified in this way.

Are There Really Stages of Cognitive Development? You'll remember from Chapter 1 that the issue of whether development proceeds through a series of small steps or in leaps and bounds is a central issue for all developmental theories. Piaget's theory organized development into stages that reflect qualitatively new ways of thinking, but some critics have claimed that more recent evidence indicates that these stages do not really exist as distinct entities. For instance, Mareschal and Shultz (1999) describe development of the ability to seriate as a series of small steps: "Seriation development is essentially due to an increase in the precision of processing rather than to any fundamental reorganization of knowledge" (p. 177). That would be a quantitative change, rather than a qualitative one. However, others have argued that infants' early abilities that look like the abilities Piaget has described in older children are not necessarily the same thing. For example, an infant's smile, which is directed at any smiling face, has a very different meaning from a teenager's smile directed at a close friend. In the same way, similarities in cognitive abilities may have different meanings at different stages (Kagan, 2008).

Seriation. This child demonstrates seriation: the ability to order the sticks by size. A younger child might be unable to handle this same task with this many sticks. Does this mean the younger child is unable to seriate? Under what conditions might the younger child show this ability?

How Universal Is Cognitive Change? Much of the research inspired by Piaget's theory has been cross-cultural. Researchers were interested in exploring whether the changes that Piaget described occurred in the same way for children all over the world (Maynard, 2008). In the first wave of cross-cultural research, researchers simply took Piaget's ideas and methods and used them in different cultures (Maynard, 2008). In an early review of these studies, Dasen (1972) concluded that most of the descriptive research in non-Western culture confirmed Piaget's idea that there is a series of stages that occur in the order that he described. More recent research in North Africa and the Middle East has confirmed that the same order of stages is found in Saudi Arabian Bedouin children and Egyptian children (Ahmed, 2010). However, cultural factors appear to influence the rate at which a child moves through the stages, and much of the early research described the progress of children in non-Western cultures in negative ways, such as "lagging," "slow," or "retarded" (Maynard, 2008, p. 58; see also Lavallee & Dasen, 1980).

Cross-cultural researchers responded to these conclusions by attempting to adapt Piagetian tasks in ways that made them more culturally relevant for use in non-Western cultures. For example, Saxe and Moylan (1982) adapted Piaget's conservation of length task for use with children from Papua New Guinea. To assess the children's understanding of conservation of length, the researchers used both bamboo sticks of different lengths (material that is similar to the way this task is done in Western settings) and string bags (which are common items in the everyday life of the children in New Guinea). Among children who did not attend Westernized

Culture and cognitive abilities. This girl from Zinacantán, Chiapas (Mexico), will learn to weave extremely intricate patterns that require concrete operations to understand. Researchers have not always looked at culturally defined abilities such as these to determine the level of children's understanding.

Violation of expectation Research based on the finding that babies look longer at unexpected or surprising events.

TRUE/FALSE

4. An infant would be surprised if an object moved over the edge of a table but didn't fall (as though she somehow understood how gravity operates).

True. Research from the core knowledge perspective has found that there appear to be some innate cognitive systems for understanding some aspects of the world.

schools, there was no developmental change in their understanding of the stick task with increasing age, but there clearly was a developmental trend for the string bag task that showed evidence of a growing understanding of conservation. Other research done from this contextual perspective found that children reached the Piagetian cognitive milestones at about the age his theory predicted, if culturally relevant methods of testing were used (Dasen, 1977).

The third phase of this research moved away from comparisons between cultures and began to identify concepts and skills that were adaptive in a particular culture (Maynard, 2008). For instance, Maynard and Greenfield (2003) reported that the tools that are used to teach young girls to weave in the Zinacantec Mayan culture are adapted to the girls' level of cognitive development. Young girls use a tool where "what you see is what you get" (p. 494), but older girls (who are in the stage of concrete operations) use a tool that requires transformation between what the girl sees and what the finished weave looks like, a skill that is not available until they reach this stage of cognitive development. There needs to be a certain level of maturational readiness for this cultural learning to occur.

Controversy continues to surround Piaget's work, and there are many modern theorists who see him only as a "historical figure" with little relevance to modern research (Desrochers, 2008, p. 11). However, there are many others who see his work as the foundation for much of our current understanding of children's cognitive development.

We will next describe an approach to understanding cognitive development that emerged out of research that was critical of Piaget's ideas, called the theory of core knowledge. This approach presents evidence that early cognitive abilities are determined biologically, rather than through interaction with the environment as Piaget had claimed.

Theory of Core Knowledge

Would you be surprised by any of the following?

1. A ball that was buried in the sand in one location is pulled out of the sand in a different location (Newcombe, Sluzenski, & Huttenlocher, 2005).

2. You see one doll in a case. Someone then hides the case, and you see that person add one other doll. When the case is later opened, there are three dolls in it; in other words, $1 + 1 = 3$ (Wynn, 1992).

3. You see a block pushed to the end of a small platform and then beyond the edge so that most of it is not supported, and yet it does not fall (Baillargeon, Needham, & DeVos, 1992).

These are just a few of the scenarios that have been presented to babies within the first year of life to determine their understanding about the nature of objects and how they function. As we described earlier, babies look longer at unexpected or surprising events. Using looking time as a measure of surprise or **violation of expectation**, researchers have found that babies are surprised, just as you would be, at the events described above, even before their first birthday. Clearly the infant's world is not a magical place; nor is it the "blooming, buzzing confusion" described long ago by William James (1890/1990, p. 462). From the three experiments mentioned above, it appears that (a) infants understand that objects remain in the same place unless moved, an indication that they have a form of object permanence; (b) they appear to have a basic concept of number, at least up to three; and (c) they have a basic understanding of the effects of gravity. There are many other competencies that have been explored, and many are found so early that researchers claim that they are innate abilities.

The **theory of core knowledge** is a modern theory based on the idea that humans are born with innate cognitive systems for understanding the world (Spelke & Kinzler, 2007). These basic systems are not developed from experience. Rather they represent areas of core knowledge that appear to be built into the human brain. This theory is a direct challenge to Piaget's ideas that children construct even very basic knowledge about the nature of objects and people through experience. Although researchers who subscribe to the theory of core knowledge claim that infants are born with certain basic knowledge, there are some differing ideas about what comprises that set of knowledge. Spelke and Kinzler (2007) present evidence for four areas of core knowledge:

1. Knowledge that an object moves as a cohesive unit, it does not contact another object unless they are close to each other, and it moves on a continuous path.

2. Knowledge that agents (people) act purposefully toward a goal. Infants also know that objects are not acting with a goal "in mind" in the same way that people do.

3. Knowledge (within limits) of number, as experienced in all modalities—for example, *hearing* a number of tones or *seeing* a number of objects. This understanding is not exact and gets less precise as the number gets larger. The knowledge of number also includes a basic understanding of addition and subtraction.

4. Knowledge of spatial relationships, including how to use the shape of one's environment to find out where one is when one becomes disoriented.

Spelke (2000) argues that later learning is largely based upon these earliest core understandings of the world.

The heart of this controversy has been whether these basic forms of knowledge are innate, as these researchers contend, or whether they are constructed, as Piaget would have said. For example, although Spelke and Kinzler (2007) argued that infants know from birth that people and not objects act with intention, other researchers have provided some evidence that these abilities are learned very early but are not innate. For example, Woodward (2009) found that infants are more likely to understand other people's intentions in reaching for objects after they themselves have learned to intentionally reach for an object. She argues that they learn from their own actions about how to interpret the actions of other people.

The ongoing research in this area is a wonderful example of the scientific process, as evidence and counter-evidence help us refine our understanding of the beginning stages of cognitive development. The findings will help us understand how children and even adults develop more sophisticated understandings based on these early concepts. They may also help us understand some of the difficulties children may have when they move from their primitive core knowledge to a higher level of understanding of the same concept (Spelke, 2000).

It is important to note, however, that some have concluded that this approach is "woefully inadequate to fully explain adult human functioning" (Cole & Cagigas, 2010, p. 131). They argue that culture plays a central role in shaping the nature of cognition, as it develops from its earliest beginnings to its adult form. In the next section we will look at one theory of cognitive development that presents the idea that culture shapes how our thoughts develop.

Theory of core knowledge The theory that basic areas of knowledge are innate and built into the human brain.

Video Link 7.6
Elizabeth Spelke.

Vygotsky's Sociocultural Theory of Cognitive Development

Like Piaget, Vygotsky (1896–1934) did not start out to be a theorist of cognitive development. Although he did take courses in psychology at university, his first jobs were teaching literature and history. Vygotsky lived in Russia during the time of the revolution, when the tsarist government was brought down and a new government based on communist principles was established. These principles had an important role in shaping Vygotsky's thinking about human behavior and the study of the human mind. One basic concept in his theory is that the way we think is most influenced by the social world in which we live. Unlike Piaget, who lived to be 84 years old, Vygotsky's life was cut short when he died at age 37 from tuberculosis (McKeachie & Sims, 2004). His significant contributions to the field came from only 10 years of work.

Although Vygotsky had supported much of the ideology of the communist government, when Joseph Stalin, the powerful new leader of Russia, came into power, he accused Vygotsky of being anti-Marxist and in 1933 had him interrogated (Gredler & Shields, 2008). The following year Vygotsky died of his illness, and 2 years later Stalin banned Vygotsky's work, instead favoring the "reflexology" of Pavlov, which denied the importance of the mind and its inner processes (Trevarthen, 1991). (Remember the research of Pavlov with dogs that was discussed in Chapter 2.) Only after Stalin died was Vygotsky's work again made available for study, and in 1962, his book *Thought and Language* was published in English. Since then his ideas have become very influential in the study and application of cognitive theory.

Vygotsky's theory of cognitive development begins with the social world, and in that way it is very different from Piaget's theory. In contrast to Piaget, who saw the child as an active but largely independent learner, for Vygotsky all learning and ideas begin in the interaction between a child and those with whom he has contact. As a result, all learning is culturally based because all people are situated within their own culture. Each culture has its own adaptations that have survived through generations. The tools, language, and actions of a particular culture are transmitted to the children and serve to shape their cognitive abilities (Gauvain & Parke, 2010). You will remember from Chapter 4 that recent research has shown that culture serves to shape whether we focus on one central object or the whole context of a scene we are viewing (Masuda & Nisbett, 2001).

Vygotsky introduced three ways in which ideas are transmitted from a more experienced person to a child: the zone of proximal development, scaffolding, and private speech. We will describe the first two in detail here. The concept of private speech will be discussed in more detail in Chapter 9 in the context of language development, so we describe it only briefly here.

The zone of proximal development. How is the adult in this picture fostering the child's growing ability to use scissors? How would you define or describe this child's zone of proximal development?

The Zone of Proximal Development (ZPD)

Vygotsky began his work as a psychologist by working with children who had physical and mental impairments. In this work he found it necessary to test the children's mental abilities in order to know how best to teach them. As we described in **Journey of Research: Binet's Intelligence Test and Its Unintended Consequences**, Vygotsky started his work by testing mental abilities as Binet and others did. However, he soon developed the idea that children should be tested twice: the first time performing on their own and the second time performing with a little help from an adult. He believed that the second testing showed which intellectual abilities the children were in the *process* of forming. Unlike Binet, Vygotsky did not see intelligence as developing in only one predictable way (Del Rio & Alvarez, 2007). Therefore he believed in testing the child's "readiness" to learn, as well as his actual level of achievement. He called the abilities that were in the process of forming and that the child would demonstrate with just a little help the zone of proximal development, or ZPD (Gredler & Shields, 2008).

Scaffolding

Scaffolding is what an adult does to move the child through the ZPD to full independent achievement. A scaffold, as we learned in Chapter 2, is the structure that goes up around a building so that workers can stand on it to create or improve the building. In like fashion, Vygotsky saw adults and older children forming a cognitive structure around a child that they could use to move the child to fuller understanding. When that is achieved, the scaffolding is no longer needed and comes down; in other words, the child can now carry out the task independently.

To better understand the ZPD, think about teaching a child to tie her shoes. For an infant, you would simply do it for her. For a 2-year-old, you might hold her hands and do it with her. For a preschooler, you might teach her the "bunny ears" approach, in which the child forms two loops and circles one around the other, maybe with a song or rhyme that goes with the process. By age 6 or 7, you can teach the child the correct way to wrap one string around and through the other. The amount and type of help you provide at each of these steps is the scaffold that supports the child's learning. Finally, no scaffolding is necessary when the child can perform this task on her own. Teaching in this way is a sensitive process of helping the child achieve what is just out of reach and then stepping back when the child can do it alone. When we present learning opportunities that are far beyond the child's current level, the child cannot benefit from our instruction. If we continue to present opportunities that the child has already mastered, this also fails to advance the child's understanding. It is when we get it just right—in the zone that is just a little beyond the child's current level—that our instruction is effective and learning occurs.

Private Speech

Private speech is an essential component of this learning process for Vygotsky. He stated that the child hears what others say to him and then he says it in some form to himself. Scaffolding is what the *adult* does, but private speech is what the *child* does to change external interactions into internal thoughts. For example, an adult might scaffold a child's attempts to put together a jigsaw puzzle by saying, "First try to find the pieces with one flat side to put on the outside edge of the puzzle." You may then hear the child saying to himself, "Flat pieces, find flat pieces." The child is talking to himself in order to guide his own actions. Vygotsky and others have shown that the more difficult the task, the more children talk to themselves in this way (Duncan & Cheyne, 2002; Fernyhough & Fradley, 2005; Kohlberg, Yaeger, & Hjertholm, 1968). Gradually this private (or self-directed) speech becomes inner, unvocalized speech, and finally it becomes thought. Research has shown that young children who talk to themselves in this way use private speech to guide themselves through difficult tasks and are able to carry out these tasks more successfully than those who do not talk to themselves as they work (Berk, Mann, & Ogan, 2006).

Private speech Talking to oneself, often out loud, in order to guide one's own actions.

Information Processing

Information processing has become one of the major contemporary approaches to the study of cognitive development. One problem with presenting information processing theory concisely is that there are many different approaches and the evidence from thousands of research studies does not fit into a single neat framework that explains it all (Fogel, 2002). In Chapter 2, we introduced you to two different models developed by information processing theorists: the *stores model* and the *connectionist or network model.* Each of these is designed to show how information is selected, stored, and retrieved (Meadows, 2006) by drawing an analogy between how computers (in the stores model) or neural networks (in the connectionist model) process information and how humans think. Each approach must explain how we take in information, how we remember it, how we think about it, and what controls and coordinates all those activities.

In order to process information, we must first pay attention to it. We must also remember what we have noticed. We think about what we have learned in a number of different ways, and we think about our thinking. In this section, we will first talk about the processes of attention, then memory, executive function, and finally metacognition.

Attention

When someone is told to "Pay attention!" it means that person should focus her mental processes on one thing (maybe a teacher's words) and not on another (maybe her friends' conversation). Paying attention means tuning in to certain things while tuning out others (**selective attention**) and maintaining focus over time (**sustained attention**) (Fan et al., 2009; Parasuraman, 1998). In this section we will examine how these aspects of attention develop in infancy, childhood, and adolescence. We will then look at what happens when attention does not function as it should in children who have an attention deficit hyperactivity disorder.

Attention in Infancy. What attracts infants' attention? We know that infants will look longer at something they haven't seen before. This inborn preference for novelty makes it highly likely that infants will learn as much as they can about the world by focusing their attention on what is new. The other side of this attraction to novelty is that infants pay less attention to what they have seen before, a process known as **habituation**. For example, if you entered a room that had a noisy air conditioner, you would probably be very aware of the sound at first. After a while, however, you would habituate to the sound, and you would no longer pay any attention to it. In the laboratory, habituation has been used to assess many aspects of cognition that infants obviously cannot tell us about in words. An infant will be shown an object many times, and observers will record how long he looks each time. The rate of habituation is how quickly the infant decreases the length of time spent looking with repeated showings.

As they get older, infants habituate to familiar things more quickly as their ability to process information becomes more efficient (Courage, Reynolds, & Richards, 2006). The rate at which babies habituate is somewhat predictive of later intelligence. However, Colombo and Mitchell (2009) conclude that habituation "does not appear to represent a fundamental or primary component of intelligence, but rather represents a building block for learning and cognition upon which higher-order functions are constructed across early childhood" (p. 230).

You may wonder whether this means that children with short attention spans turn out to have higher IQs than those with longer attention spans, which certainly seems counterintuitive. Courage et al. (2006) also wondered about this question. They showed infants the simple type of stimuli used in most of the research on habituation—for example, black dots on a white background, or a picture of a woman's face. They also showed much more complex stimuli, such as a picture and a video of *Sesame Street.* Although older infants looked less at the simple stimuli, they looked longer at the more complex stimuli. The increasing ability to pay attention to complex and interesting stimuli may be due to the brain's developing ability to voluntarily control attention.

Selective attention Tuning in to certain things while tuning out others.

Sustained attention Maintaining focus over time.

Habituation The reduction in the response to a stimulus that is repeated.

TRUE/FALSE

5. Infants who quickly grow bored when they are repeatedly shown a simple object turn out to have higher intelligence later in childhood.

True. The rate at which infants become bored with, or habituate to, *simple* objects shown repeatedly does predict intelligence later on. However, with more *complex* objects, as infants get older they pay attention for longer periods of time.

Attention in Childhood. As children grow they are increasingly capable of directing and sustaining their attention (López, Menes, & Hernández-Guzmán, 2005). As anyone who has worked in a preschool can tell you, there are some children who can sit in circle time and pay attention, and there are those who have great trouble doing so. Individual differences in the ability to focus and sustain attention may in part be genetic (Posner, Rothbart, & Sheese, 2007), but they are also related to the child's experiences. Attention in preschool children has been linked to differences in parenting that are related to the economic circumstances of families. Low-income mothers are likely to experience more parenting stress and tend to provide less stimulation and support to their children. These differences in parenting are related to more impulsivity and less sustained attention in 5-year-olds, and this, in turn, is related to lower cognitive, academic, and social competence (Dilworth-Bart, Khurshid, & Vandell, 2007). Selective attention continues to develop at least through middle childhood, paralleling growth in the brain throughout this period (Wassenberg et al., 2008).

One aspect of cognitive functioning that affects attention is **processing efficiency** or the speed and accuracy with which we can handle information (Demetriou, Christou, Spanoudis, & Platsidou, 2002; Dempster, 1981; Kail & Ferrer, 2007). To understand this concept better, think of a time when you were learning a complex skill like driving a car with a standard transmission. When you were first learning this skill, you needed to focus all of your attention on what you were supposed to do and when you were supposed to do it. However, as you became more skilled, these actions became more automatic (Diamond, 2006). **Automaticity** describes the process by which skills become so well practiced that you can do them without much conscious thought, which frees up processing capacity for other tasks. When you no longer need to think, "First I step on both the clutch and the brake, then I shift the car into first gear and let up on the clutch slowly," and so on, you free up processing capacity for other things. In children, we see this process at work in the way they learn to count or to recognize words. At first, these cognitive tasks take a good deal of effort on the child's part, but over time they become so automatic that it no longer takes as much processing capacity. For example, children move from the laborious process of sounding out letters to reading words and entire sentences for comprehension (Case, 1985).

Attention in Adolescence. When you sit down to read this book or do other academic work, do you have music on, answer text messages, and/or have TV running in the background? If so, you are like many adolescents who have become so confident in their ability to control their attention that they believe that they can pay attention to several things at the same time. We will discuss more about multitasking when we discuss adolescents' use of media in Chapter 13. Here we will discuss some of the research on how well teens and even older people can divide their attention.

In one experimental study, adolescents were assigned to one of two groups: One group did their homework with soap operas on TV in the background, and the other group did their homework without background TV. Those with the TV on in the background took longer to do the homework because they were distracted by the TV. Also, even though the two groups of students spent the same amount of time actually looking at their homework, the students with TV remembered and understood less when they were tested on the homework (Pool, Koolstra, & van der Voort, 2003). Pool et al. (2003) argue that the distraction of TV interfered with the

Inattention. Not being able to focus and sustain attention on what is happening in the classroom puts a child at a significant disadvantage.

Processing efficiency The speed and accuracy with which one can process information.

Automaticity The process by which skills become so well practiced that you can do them without much conscious thought.

6. Adolescents are able to study while listening to a favorite TV show because by this age their attentional processes are so well developed that they can split their attention between multiple activities.

TRUE/FALSE

False. Although teens may think they can study while listening to TV, research has shown that they remember less and their understanding is more superficial than if they focus all their attention on the task of studying.

The limits of attention. Teens believe that they can do homework effectively and do many other activities at the same time. However, the evidence from research shows this is not true.

Attention deficit hyperactivity disorder (ADHD) A disorder marked by extreme difficulty with inattention, impulsivity, or a combination of both.

TRUE/FALSE

7. Attention deficit hyperactivity disorder is a disorder of childhood, and fortunately children outgrow the symptoms with age.

   False. The symptoms of ADHD may lessen in severity as the child gets older, but ADHD cannot be cured and continues into adolescence and adulthood.

Video Link 7.7
Children with ADHD.

students' ability to integrate all the information from the homework. They ended up with a much more superficial understanding of the material and remembered less. This has been confirmed in neurological research. It appears that when we try to do two things at once we do not use the part of the brain designed for deep processing of information. Instead we use a different part designed for more superficial, rapid processing of information (Foerde, Knowlton, & Poldrack, 2006). Finally, research on study habits has shown that the students who do the worst on their exams are those who study with many distractions: music, television, using e-mail, and/or talking with friends (Gurung, 2005).

Attention Deficit Hyperactivity Disorder. About 3% to 7% of children and teens have extreme difficulty controlling their attention and are diagnosed with **attention deficit hyperactivity disorder**, or **ADHD** (American Psychiatric Association [APA], 2000). This condition is diagnosed much more often in boys than it is in girls.

There are several types of ADHD, so a specific diagnosis depends on the particular characteristics and behaviors seen in the child (APA, 2000). Children are diagnosed with ADHD (primarily inattentive type) when problems with attention are the predominant characteristic of their behavior. These children may have trouble sustaining attention when working on a task, may have difficulty following instructions or organizing their work, are easily distracted, and don't pay careful attention to details or make careless mistakes. By contrast, a diagnosis of ADHD (primarily hyperactive/impulsive type) centers on the child's inability to inhibit and control impulses. These children have difficulty controlling their physical behavior, so they squirm or fidget, have trouble staying in their seats, and may talk excessively. They also seem to act before thinking and blurt out answers or don't wait to take their turn. Finally, children diagnosed with ADHD (combined type) show both types of behavioral cluster (Nolan & Carr, 2000).

Some of this might sound to you like a description of fairly typical behavior seen in an elementary classroom, but the behavior must be much more extreme than that before a child is diagnosed with this condition. A diagnosis requires that the symptoms appear before the age of 7 and continue for at least 6 months, and they must be severe enough that they interfere with the child's ability to function in more than one setting, such as at home and in school, or in school and with peers (APA, 2000). Although the symptoms can change or lessen in severity as the child gets older, ADHD cannot be cured and can continue into adulthood. If it is not diagnosed and treated, it can continue to cause problems in many aspects of the adult's life (Barkley, 2008).

The most effective treatment approach to help children with ADHD is one that brings together several different types of intervention into a comprehensive treatment plan (Nolan & Carr, 2000). Parts of this plan can include work with the parents that helps them learn how to use behavioral intervention strategies in a consistent way to manage the child's behavior, work with the school to develop an educational plan to help the child succeed, and medication to control the symptoms, when necessary. A variety of medications have been used to treat ADHD, but stimulants such as Ritalin are most frequently prescribed. Although the exact way that the medications help regulate behavior is not clear, it appears that they alter the neural activity in the frontal-striatal area of the brain, which ordinarily inhibits behavior (Barkley, 2006). Because this therapeutic approach has been effective in increasing attention, improving

Figure 7.3

Incidence of ADHD. This graph shows the percentage of children in different age groups who have been diagnosed as having ADHD. It also shows the percentage who are on medication to treat the symptoms of this condition.

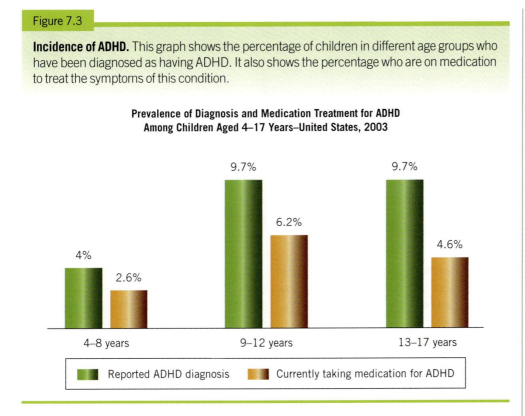

Prevalence of Diagnosis and Medication Treatment for ADHD
Among Children Aged 4–17 Years–United States, 2003

- Reported ADHD diagnosis
- Currently taking medication for ADHD

impulse control, reducing task-irrelevant behavior, and reducing disruptive behavior, it is widely used in school-age populations (Barkley, 2006). Figure 7.3 shows recent statistics on the number of children, from preschoolers through adolescents, who are currently diagnosed with ADHD and who are on some form of medication for the condition.

Some critics have charged that we rely too heavily on medication and that ADHD is being overdiagnosed, but other professionals attribute the increase in the number of children with this diagnosis to better identification of children who otherwise would have gone unrecognized and, therefore, untreated. There is far less research on the use of medication to treat ADHD symptoms in teens and adults than in children, but the existing research appears to support the continued effectiveness of the medications (Barkley, 2006).

It is important to point out here that there is little or no scientific evidence for a variety of other treatment approaches that have been tried over the years (Barkley, 2006). Such alternative treatments have included biofeedback, relaxation training, traditional psychotherapy, play therapy, and a number of dietary modifications (eliminating food additives, dyes, sugar, and other common food ingredients from the diet, or adding vitamins, minerals, or other food supplements to it). Although each of these approaches has its supporters (some of whom are quite vocal about the purported improvements seen in children treated with these approaches), there are no large-scale, rigorous, controlled studies to support their effectiveness.

It is also important to note that we have dispelled the idea that it is poor parenting that causes ADHD (Kutscher, 2008). There is no doubt that the challenging behavior exhibited by children with ADHD can disrupt effective parenting and parents of children with ADHD need to learn how to effectively deal with the child's behavior, but, in this case, the parenting behavior is a response to the characteristics of the child, not a cause of them. One study that looked at the contribution of genetics, child management techniques, and parental characteristics

Video Link 7.8
ADHD and the brain.

Video Link 7.9
Treatment for ADHD.

Video Link 7.10
Myths and facts on ADHD.

8. The primary cause of attention deficit hyperactivity disorder is poor parenting. **TRUE/FALSE**

False. Parenting quality may suffer when a parent is dealing with a child whose behavior is very challenging, but it is a response to the child's characteristics, not a cause of it.

concluded that about half of the explainable variance in ADHD symptoms was attributable to genetic factors, while the effects of adverse family factors including low parental warmth, criticism, and malaise were weak (Goodman & Stevenson, 1989).

Memory

After we have paid attention to something, we must move it into memory if we want to use that information in the future. In Chapter 2 you were introduced to the stores model of memory in which information is first taken in very briefly to the sensory memory store. Some of this information then moves to the short-term, or working, memory where the information is acted upon in a way that can move it to long-term memory. You were also introduced to the connectionist or network model of memory in which new information is associated with already existing information in a complex pattern that does not conform to the simple movement from one store to the next.

Memory in Infancy. How do we know if infants can remember things? Carolyn Rovee-Collier (1999) came up with a unique way to find out. She had infants lie in a crib under a mobile with attractive toys hanging on it. She then tied a ribbon from the baby's ankle to the mobile so that when the baby kicked it would make the mobile shake in a pleasing way. Each baby learned to kick to move the mobile. The babies were then brought back into this situation, some after a day, and some after a week or longer. If the baby remembered the mobile, she would kick right away. If not, she would learn all over again how to make the mobile move. Using this and another paradigm appropriate for somewhat older babies, Rovee-Collier found that 3-month-olds could remember what they needed to do for 1 week and 18-month-olds could remember for 13 weeks.

Infantile Amnesia. Close your eyes for a minute and try to think of the earliest memory you can call to mind. Most people cannot recall memories before age 3 because of what has been called **infantile amnesia**. This term does not mean that infants themselves cannot remember what has happened because we have already seen that they can. Rather it appears that later in life it becomes difficult to remember what happened in that earlier period of time, and there have been different explanations proposed for why infantile amnesia occurs. Howe and Courage (1993) have argued that before infants have a clear sense of self (as we will discuss in Chapter 11), their memories are not organized into a coherent story. Others have argued that developmental changes in the brain may change the way we remember (Bauer, 2007). Rovee-Collier (1999) has argued against this idea, and her research on infants has shown that they have a remarkable ability to remember for lengthy periods of time. However, she argues that memory requires the ability to use the same **encoding processes** that were used when the first experience happened. Infants encode nonverbally (because they have not yet developed language), so when older children and adults try to use their usual verbal encoding methods, they are not able to recall the earlier nonverbally encoded events.

In one interesting study, toddlers were shown a demonstration of how a Magic Shrinking Machine could turn large toys into smaller ones (Simcock & Hayne, 2002). The toddlers were allowed to turn the crank themselves to make this happen. Most of the toddlers who were originally tested this way did not have enough language to describe what had happened. When they were brought back either 6 months or 1 year later, they had adequate vocabulary to describe the event, but they could not, even when shown the device and toys again. However, when they were allowed to use the Magic Shrinking Machine, they remembered just what to do and how it worked. Their nonverbal memory remained, but since the events had never been coded into verbal memory, they were unable to remember them with words to tell others. It appears that we can remember things from infancy nonverbally through our emotions

Video Link 7.11
Experimental paradigm by Rovee-Collier.

✔ ✗
TRUE/FALSE

9. Few people have clear memories of what happened in their lives before the age of 3.

    True. This phenomenon is called infantile amnesia and may result from development of the brain, or the lack of language or a sense of self in young children.

Infantile amnesia The inability to remember experiences that happened to us before we were about 3 years of age.

Encoding processes The transformation processes through which new information is stored in long-term memory.

and actions, but we can't talk about them with others. It has been argued that only when we can talk about events do we remember them in conscious thought (Fogel, 2002). In fact, when mothers talk with young children about their past experiences, their children are more likely to retain memories from early life when they enter adolescence (Jack, MacDonald, Reese, & Hayne, 2009).

Memory in Childhood. As children get older their working memory becomes increasingly effective in storing information that they can later use. Children develop a number of strategies that help them store and retrieve information from their memory, and these strategies improve in complexity and efficiency as children get older. Encoding is one of the ways that information is prepared for memory storage. The more carefully information is encoded and stored away, the greater the likelihood that you will later be able to find and retrieve that information when you need it. We look here at some of the encoding strategies children use as they become increasingly sophisticated at doing this.

Even young children create **scripts** that help them remember what to do in a familiar situation. A script is a document with all the instructions about what to say and do in a dramatic play. The term *script* as we are using it here is memory for what to say and do in particular situations. Children as young as 2 might have a script for going out to lunch at a fast-food restaurant (and may act out that scenario in play with friends), but older children, adolescents, and adults also use scripts. A school-age child might have a script for going to a friend's house for a sleepover, a teenager might have one for how to behave the first time he meets a friend's parents, and college students might have one for what to do during a job interview. You can see how having a script in place helps you remember how to handle different situations.

Simply repeating information (the process of **rehearsal**) is another strategy that children, adolescents, and adults all use. However, younger children tend to simply repeat the information they are trying to learn, whereas older children will repeat the information while also connecting it to other related information they need to remember (Kunzinger, 1985). If you can group information together while you learn it, you are more likely to be able to retrieve and use it later. If you are trying to remember words from a list that contains the words *horse, rose, hammer, bus, pig, cow, tulip, saw, airplane, cow, lily,* and *train,* you can group items into conceptual categories. Horses, pigs, and cows are animals; hammers, saws, and wrenches are tools; roses, tulips, and lilies are flowers; and buses, airplanes, and trains are modes of transportation. Another way to encode them would be by the setting in which you find these items: a farm for the animals, a workshop for the tools, a garden for the flowers, and an airport for the vehicles. Using strategies such as these improves children's recall, but younger children may not recognize which aspects of the information available to them are important features to code in this way (Ackerman, 1997).

Another memory strategy you can use for organizing information that you need to remember is called **elaboration**. The idea here is to create extra connections that can tie information together. You can do this through the use of images or sentences. For instance, if you needed to remember to buy lemons on the way home, you could picture yourself walking to the parking lot wearing lemons on your feet instead of shoes. As you walked to the parking lot after your classes, hopefully this picture would easily come to mind. If you were taking a course on anatomy and you needed to remember that *arteries are thick and elastic and carry blood that is rich in oxygen from the heart,* you could make up a sentence such as "*Art*(ery) was so *thick* around his middle so he had to wear trousers with an *elastic* waistband" (McPherson, 2001).

Knowledge Base. As children and adolescents learn more about the world, they build their knowledge base. This has implications for memory because it becomes easier to store away and recall information when you can make many connections between the new information and previously learned information. Several research studies have found that children who

Scripts Memory for the way a common occurrence in one's life, such as grocery shopping, takes place.

Rehearsal Repeating information in order to remember it.

Elaboration A memory strategy that involves creating extra connections, like images or sentences, that can tie information together.

Building a knowledge base. As children learn more and more about topics that they are interested in, they build their knowledge base. As their knowledge base grows, it becomes easier to learn new information on that same topic.

are already experts in a subject are able to remember more information related to the subject of their expertise than children who are not experts (Chi, 1978; Schneider & Bjorklund, 1992), and older children who are experts also are more likely to organize their recall into meaningful categories (Schneider & Bjorklund, 1992).

You have seen this effect in action if you know a child or an adolescent who has a strong interest in a particular topic and has become an expert in that subject. Children who become fascinated with dinosaurs or baseball statistics, or who know everything imaginable about Harry Potter, quickly digest any new information they encounter on their favorite subject and can begin using that new information immediately with little effort. You can also see this process at work in the course on child development that you are currently taking. Your professor for this course will be able to integrate new information about child development into his or her knowledge base more quickly and with less effort than you are likely to be able to do. By the end of the course, however, your expanding knowledge base will allow you to understand and integrate any new information you encounter on child development more effectively than you could have before you had studied this topic.

False Memories. We all create the story of our lives from our autobiographical memories. However, have you ever been told that a memory you thought had happened to you actually happened to your sister or friend? How easy is it to distort our memories? Research has shown that young children can fairly easily be influenced to think that they have experienced something that never happened. In one study children were told to imagine that they were taking a hot-air balloon ride and to think in detail all about what it was like (Ceci, Bruck, & Loftus, 1998). They were then asked whether this had really happened to them. They were given similar instructions to remember in detail other events, some of which had really happened to them and some of which had not, like the imaginary hot-air balloon ride. The researchers repeated this for 11 weeks, and gradually children began to agree that they had in fact gone on a hot-air balloon ride. On the 12th week, another researcher interviewed each child, telling her that the previous researcher had said some things that were not true. When the child was asked which things had really happened, many still agreed to the false memory of a balloon ride. Younger preschoolers were more likely to make these mistakes than older preschoolers. As we mentioned in Chapter 3, these problems with young children's memories make it especially important that interviewers are trained when dealing with cases of eyewitness testimony involving children. Repeated suggestions that sexual abuse or other events happened may result in false memories for the child.

Executive Function

Executive function is that aspect of brain organization that coordinates attention and memory and controls behavioral responses for the purpose of attaining a certain goal (Blair, Zelazo, & Greenberg, 2005). Executive function includes the ability to stay on task and ignore distractions (called **inhibition**) (Diamond, 2006). It also includes your ability to switch your focus as needed in order to complete the task (called **cognitive flexibility**) (Diamond, 2006). We see these functions change as children develop cognitively. For instance, between the ages of 3 and 5 years, children show a marked improvement in their ability to inhibit extraneous responses, and they also show greater cognitive flexibility that allows them to understand different perspectives (Diamond, 2006). Try **Active Learning: Executive Function** to see how executive function helps or hinders the ability to switch from one task to another.

TRUE/FALSE

10. Young children may believe that they remember something that never happened if someone repeatedly suggests it to them.

True. If someone suggests that something happened, young children may become confused about what they really remember because their memories are influenced by such suggestions.

Executive function The aspect of brain organization that coordinates attention and memory and controls behavioral responses for the purpose of attaining a certain goal.

Inhibition The ability to stay on task and ignore distractions.

Cognitive flexibility The ability to switch focus as needed in order to complete a task.

Executive Function

You can carry out the following test with a child between 3 and 8 years of age to see whether the executive function of her brain enables her to switch from one set of instructions to another.

Materials: Eight Cards

- Three cards with a picture of a blue rabbit and one card with a picture of a red rabbit
- Three cards with a picture of a red boat and one with a picture of a blue boat

Instructions:

1. Face the child across a table. Place one picture of a blue rabbit to your left and one picture of a red boat to your right. Ask the child to "play the shape game." Tell the child that in the shape game, the rabbits go here (in front of the rabbit picture) and the boats go here (in front of the boat picture). Hand the child each of the remaining six cards one at a time and ask for each one, "Where does this one go in the shape game?" Have the child put the picture face down. Don't either praise or correct the child. Record where the child puts the cards.

2. Pick up all of the cards. Now place one picture of the blue boat on your left and one picture of the red rabbit on your right. Tell the child, "We are not going to play the shape game anymore, no way. Now we are going to play the color game. In the color game, blue ones go here (in front of the blue picture) and red ones go here (in front of the red picture)." Hand the child each of the six cards one at a time and ask for each one, "Where does this go in the color game?" Record where the child puts the cards.

What did your child do on the second task? Children tend to continue to do whatever they were told to do first. If the child was able to make the switch to sorting by color rather than by shape, this indicates that her executive function has worked at a high level to inhibit her tendency to repeat the first way she learned to sort the cards—by shape rather than color. In one study, 61% of 3- to 4-year-olds and 29% of 4- to 5-year-olds could not carry out this task correctly (Müller, Dick, Gela, Overton, & Zelazo, 2006). Can you see how both inhibition and cognitive flexibility would be required to carry out this task?

Metacognition

As children move toward adolescence, they become increasingly able to think about and monitor their own thoughts and cognitive activities. This process is called **metacognition**. **Metamemory** specifically refers to the understanding of memory, how it works, and how to use it effectively. To understand metacognition, think about what happens when you are studying for an exam in one of your courses. You might start by assessing how much you already know about a subject. That helps you determine how much time it will take you to prepare. You don't want to make a mistake at this step by underestimating how much work you need to do. Next you can consider which strategies you will use to prepare for your exam. You would most likely choose a different approach when studying for an English lit exam than when studying for a chemistry final. You continue to evaluate your level of understanding as your studying progresses to gauge how much more you need to do or to reevaluate the strategies you are using. After you get your grade on the exam, you can evaluate the effectiveness of the strategies that you used so that you can use this information the next time you need to prepare for an exam to do it more effectively or more efficiently. Each of these "executive decisions" that you make when directing your own learning is an indication of your level of understanding of how cognition and memory work (Winn, 2004). Studies with students from elementary schools (Margosein, Pascarella, & Pflaum, 1982), middle schools (Gaskins & Pressley, 2007),

Metacognition The ability to think about and monitor one's own thoughts and cognitive activities.

Metamemory The understanding of memory, how it works, and how to use it effectively.

Table 7.1

A comparison of four cognitive theories

	Piaget's genetic epistemology theory	**Core knowledge theory**	**Vygotsky's sociocultural theory**	**Information processing theory**
Stages or continuous development	Stages are central to this theory	Development is continuous	Development is continuous	Development is continuous
Role of innate knowledge	Genetic development interacts with environmental experiences	Many aspects of knowledge are innate	Very little role	Brain function is central, but innate knowledge is not
Role of environmental influence	Environment interacts with genetic unfolding	Core aspects of knowledge are built upon by experiences in the environment	The environment and culture are central to cognitive development	Brain function interacts with environmental experiences to produce cognitive development

and college (Cano & Cardelle-Elawar, 2004) have all shown that students' performance can be improved when they better understand how their cognitive processes work.

Comparing Theories of Cognitive Development

In this chapter we have presented four theories of cognitive development that may seem quite different from one another. In fact there are major differences, but there are also some important similarities. See Table 7.1 for a brief summary of some of the basic aspects of each theory.

All of these approaches describe children's cognitive abilities and limitations as they move through development, and all want to understand how more advanced understanding emerges from earlier, less adequate understanding (Meadows, 2006).

One of the ways that Piagetian theory and information processing differ is that Piaget proposed stages based on qualitative changes in the way children think, while information processing focuses on the step-by-step, quantitative changes that occur. However, Robbie Case (1998) brought together Piagetian theory with information processing in a neo-Piagetian theory that starts with the notion of stages but says that movement from one stage to another is the result of increases in the capacity of the child's working memory (the amount of information you can actively deal with at one time). Information processing approaches assume that our capacity to process information is limited, but there are developmental changes that increase the upper limits of that capacity (Kail & Ferrer, 2007). Think of your **processing capacity** as the amount of information that you can think about at one time. The younger the child, the less information she can process at one time. The difficulty that young children have with keeping more than a few items in mind at the same time is related to what Piaget called centration. You'll remember that children in the preoperational stage have difficulty with conservation problems because they center their attention on one aspect of the problem (for example, the height of the liquid in a glass) and seem to ignore others. Their limited processing capacity may account for this difficulty. Because they cannot keep multiple aspects of the situation (for example, both the height of the liquid in a container *and* the width of the container) in mind at the same time, they can only deal with one aspect of this situation, and this misleads them into thinking there are different amounts of liquid in the two containers. As the processing capacity of older children increases, this is no longer a limitation, and they can focus on both the height and the width of the container and solve the problem easily. This example demonstrates how information processing principles may work to flesh out more fully the general ideas that

Processing capacity
The amount of information that you can think about at one time.

Piaget had proposed by examining the underlying mechanisms that lead to the changes he described.

Piaget and Vygotsky wrote to each other, and their ideas changed in response to their correspondence (Pass, 2007). Both theories subscribe to the constructivist point of view. That means that both believe that children are not passive recipients of knowledge but rather construct their understanding, building upon what they already know. The differences arise in the source of the child's construction of knowledge. Piaget saw knowledge as coming from the child's own actions on the environment, but Vygotsky argued that knowledge is embedded in one's social, cultural, and historical surroundings. Language is central to Vygotsky's theory in a way that it is not in Piaget's. For Vygotsky, language shapes thought. For Piaget, although language is important, it is more an expression of the development of thought, specifically the ability to use symbols. In his view, language does not create thought; it expresses it.

The theory of core knowledge differs from all three of the other theories because it argues that basic information and understanding are built into the human brain. Piaget, Vygotsky, and information processing theories all argue that knowledge is built from the interaction of the mind with life experience and that infants do not have certain types of basic information already present at birth (Cohen, Chaput, & Cashon, 2002).

Ongoing research will continue to help determine which aspects of each of these theories describe the different processes of cognitive development most accurately.

Conclusion

We have examined four different approaches to understanding how children's and adolescents' ability to think and to learn changes as they grow. Brain maturation and life experiences influence each other, and both contribute to how cognitive development occurs. In this chapter we have focused on the processes of development that are found in all children. In the next chapter we will look at a specific aspect of cognition: intelligence. The study of intelligence is focused much less on normal development than these four theories. Instead, the focus is on individual differences and what they mean for children's performance in school and in life.

CHAPTER SUMMARY

1. **What is cognitive development?**
   The study of cognition is the study of how the mind works. When we study **cognitive development**, we study how changes occur in how we think and learn as we grow. Children know less than adults, but they also think in different ways.

2. **Describe Piaget's stages of cognitive development.**
   Piaget said that children go through qualitative changes in the way they think, with a specific order to these stages, although the ages at which they occur may vary. The sensorimotor stage comes first, followed by the preoperational stage, the stage of concrete operations, and the stage of formal operations. Infants see the world through their actions on it, but preschoolers develop the ability to represent the world symbolically through mental representation. Children in the preoperational stage have a number of limitations in their thinking, including **egocentrism, transductive reasoning, animism**, and lack of **conservation**. School-age children in concrete operations overcome the limitations of the preoperational stage, and their thought becomes more logical. However, it is not until adolescence and the stage of formal operations that thinking becomes both logical and abstract.

3. What criticisms are there of Piaget's theory?

Research has questioned the ages at which Piaget said that children develop certain abilities. By and large, researchers have found that children are capable of understanding more at a younger age than Piaget gave them credit for. Others have criticized Piaget's idea that different stages mark a major reorganization in the way children think rather than a series of small incremental changes. Finally, cross-cultural research has raised questions about how universal Piaget's stages are, but there is some evidence supporting the contention that they are universal.

4. What is the theory of core knowledge?

The **theory of core knowledge** states that humans are born with areas of knowledge that are innate and built into the human brain. There are some differing ideas about what that knowledge is, but it may include basic understanding of how objects and agents move, the nature of number, and spatial relationships.

5. What are the basic processes described by Vygotsky's sociocultural theory?

Vygotsky saw all learning as based on cultural adaptations that have survived through generations. The tools, language, and actions of a particular culture are transmitted to its children and serve to shape their cognitive abilities. Children have certain capabilities, but to learn they must be helped to move just beyond their current level of understanding, the area called the zone of proximal development (ZPD). Scaffolding is what an adult does to move the child through the ZPD to full independent achievement.

6. What is the theory of information processing?

This theory is designed to show how we take in information, how we remember it, how we think about it, and what controls and coordinates all those activities. This process has been modeled on how computers work or how neural networks process information.

7. How do attention processes change from infancy through adolescence?

Attention means tuning in to certain things while tuning out others (**selective attention**) and maintaining focus over time (**sustained attention**). Infants pay more attention to something that is novel and will spend more time paying attention to complex stimuli than simple stimuli. Both maturation and the influence of environment influence the increases in ability to pay attention in children. **Processing efficiency**, or the speed and accuracy with which we can handle information, increases, and **automaticity** make us able to do certain familiar tasks

without having to pay much attention to them. Although teens think they can pay attention to many things at the same time, research indicates that they will need more time to do something when distracted and will process the information more superficially.

8. What is attention deficit hyperactivity disorder (ADHD), and how can it be treated?

A child or an adolescent with extreme difficulties sustaining attention and/or impulsive behavior may be diagnosed with **ADHD**. Treatment may involve intervention with the family and school as well as medication.

9. How does memory develop from infancy through childhood?

Infants cannot use language in order to encode and remember events as older children do. However, they do remember experiences they have had nonverbally. Three-month-olds can remember experiences over a 1-week period, and 18-month-olds can remember for 13 weeks. Infant memory is nonverbal, so older children and adults have difficulty recalling experiences that happened before the age of 3, which is referred to as **infantile amnesia**. When children develop language they begin to use **encoding** processes within working memory to bring information into long-term memory where it can later be retrieved. These include **scripts**, **rehearsal**, and **elaboration**. When children develop a large enough **knowledge base** on a subject, new information on that topic is more easily remembered, but young children are suggestible and can develop **false memories** of events that never happened to them.

10. What is executive function?

Executive function is that aspect of brain organization that coordinates attention and memory and controls behavioral responses for the purpose of attaining a certain goal.

11. What are metacognition and metamemory?

Metacognition is the ability to think about and monitor one's own thoughts and cognitive activities—in other words, to think about one's own thinking and monitor one's learning. **Metamemory** specifically refers to the understanding of memory, how it works, and how to use it effectively. Adolescents become much more proficient in using metacognition than do younger children.

12. How do the four theories of cognitive development differ, and how are they similar?

Information processing theory describes quantitative changes while Piaget's theory describes qualitative changes. However, cognitive processes described by information processing theory can be used to explain the changes that occur when children move from one Piagetian stage to the next. Piaget and Vygotsky differ in their emphasis on individual or social origins of cognitive development, but both theories take a constructionist point of view. The theory of core knowledge states that basic aspects of knowledge are innate and built into the human brain, while the other three theories describe development as an interaction of brain maturation and environmental experience.

Go to **www.sagepub.com/levine** for additional exercises and video resources. Select **Chapter 7, Cognitive Development,** for chapter-specific activities.

Chapter Outline

chapter 8

Intelligence and Academic Achievement

8

Many of the theories we discussed in Chapter 7 focus on the universal processes of cognitive development—that is, those areas that all children experience and the abilities they all have. There is another tradition in the study of cognitive development that focuses more on individual differences in cognitive abilities (that is, what makes us different from one another rather than what makes us similar). This is the perspective that has guided the study of intelligence. In this chapter, we first will look at how intelligence has been defined and measured. We then will look at variations in intellectual development that include mental retardation and giftedness. Finally, we will examine characteristics of schools that have an impact on student achievement and some of the issues surrounding these characteristics.

Test Your Knowledge

Test your knowledge of child development by deciding whether each of the following statements is *true* or *false,* and then check your answers as you read the chapter.

1. **True/False:** The best way to measure intelligence is to measure how much information someone knows.
2. **True/False:** Results from intelligence testing indicate that people are getting smarter and smarter.
3. **True/False:** Children who are gifted or talented often pay a price for their giftedness because they are likely to be socially or emotionally maladjusted.
4. **True/False:** Creativity and high intelligence often go hand-in-hand.
5. **True/False:** Many children who grow up in poverty go on to become adults who contribute positively to society.
6. **True/False:** Reducing class size should be the first priority in education today.
7. **True/False:** The best way to improve a child's academic performance is to believe in the child and let him know that you have faith in his ability to succeed.
8. **True/False:** Placing high-, average-, and low-performing students together in groups to collaborate on a project is beneficial to all the children in the group.
9. **True/False:** Throughout the elementary school years and into high school, girls do more poorly in math than boys.
10. **True/False:** Most students who drop out of high school go on to eventually complete their high school education.

Correct answers: (1) False, (2) True, (3) False, (4) False, (5) True, (6) False, (7) False, (8) False, (9) False, (10) True

Intelligence

Definition and Assessment

How do we define intelligence? Is there one factor that underlies all intelligence, or is intelligence made up of numerous independent abilities? How do these questions affect why and how we *measure* intelligence? Before reading further, try **Active Learning: Defining Intelligence** to see how *you* would define intelligence.

ACTIVE LEARNING

Defining Intelligence

How do you know when people are intelligent? Is it based on things they are able to do? Is it the amount of information they can remember? Or is it the way they manage their life in the world? Write down three of your ideas about what makes someone intelligent.

How would you measure the kind of abilities you included in your definition of intelligence? Design a test to measure just one of the abilities you described. If possible, discuss these ideas with others in your class who have also written down their ideas. Did you find that you have similar concepts of intelligence, or were there large differences? If there were differences, you are in good company. When 24 prominent experts in the field were asked to define intelligence, they too came up with a number of different definitions (Sternberg & Detterman, 1986).

TRUE/FALSE

1. The best way to measure intelligence is to measure how much information someone knows.

False. It has been difficult for psychologists to agree upon just what constitutes "intelligence," but all the definitions that we use involve much more than the amount of knowledge a person has as the criteria for being intelligent.

Intelligence Those qualities that help us adapt successfully so that we achieve our goals in life.

Fluid intelligence Intelligence that allows us to solve novel problems for which we have little training quickly and effectively.

Crystallized intelligence What we already know and can draw upon to solve problems.

Defining intelligence is the first challenge in trying to understand the nature and application of this concept. Definitions as circular as "intelligence, by definition, is what intelligence tests measure" have been proposed (Jensen, 1972, p. 76). James Flynn (2007), a political scientist who has studied trends in intelligence testing over time, defines intelligence by trying to answer the question "What traits affect our ability to solve problems with cognitive content?" (pp. 53–54). His list includes mental acuity, habits of mind, attitudes, knowledge and information, speed of information processing, and memory. As a third alternative, Robert Sternberg (2002a) defines **intelligence** as those qualities that help us adapt successfully to our environment so that we achieve our goals in life, not just in school.

The second challenge when discussing intelligence is deciding whether it is one ability or many. The idea of a single general intelligence, which has been called "g," has a history that goes back to the very early days of intelligence testing (Gould, 1996). There have been researchers who accept the idea of a general intelligence factor but believe that different abilities lie within that general ability. For example, the Wechsler Intelligence Scale for Children, a widely used intelligence test, gives three scores: a total IQ, a verbal IQ, and a performance IQ. Another way in which "g" has been subdivided is into fluid intelligence and crystallized intelligence. **Fluid intelligence** allows us to solve novel problems for which we have little training and is measured both by how effectively we solve the problems and by how quickly we solve them. **Crystallized intelligence**, on the other hand, is a measure of what we already know that we can draw upon to solve problems (Cattell, 1963). However, there are other psychologists who believe that there is no such generalized intelligence that underlies all mental abilities. In the 1950s, J. P. Guilford proposed a theory of intelligence that encompassed 120 distinct abilities (Cianciolo & Sternberg, 2004). More recently, researchers such as Howard Gardner and Robert Sternberg have described intelligence as a much smaller collection of separate and independent abilities. Thinking of abilities in this way suggests that someone could be strong in one area and weak in another because each type of intellectual ability operates somewhat independently.

To understand more about how intelligence has been conceptualized and measured, read **Journey of Research: The History of Intelligence Tests**.

Intelligence testing. Intelligence tests are very challenging for the test taker because they are designed to determine the limits of one's ability.

The History of Intelligence Tests

Individual differences in mental abilities have long been recognized. In ancient China, civil service exams were given to select the most able candidates, and the philosopher and teacher Confucius himself described three groups of people: (a) people of "great wisdom," (b) people of "average intelligence," and (c) people of "little intelligence" (Zhang, 1988). However, the modern history of intelligence testing begins in the early 1900s when an attempt was made to standardize tests to measure intellectual ability. In 1904 Alfred Binet and Theodore Simon were asked by the Minister of Public Instruction in Paris to develop a test that would help them identify students with mental difficulties in order to develop alternative teaching strategies to help these students do well in school (Sternberg, 2002b). Before this time, students who were judged to be mentally deficient were simply kicked out of school. For example, Thomas Edison's teacher thought he was "addled," so he was not allowed to continue in the classroom and was taught at home (Detterman & Thompson, 1997, p. 1082).

Binet made modest claims for his test: It was designed to reflect a child's level of performance on tasks similar to those required in school

(van der Veer, 2007). His goal was to compare an individual child's mental achievements with those of other children of the same age who were performing well in school. The result was considered the child's **mental age**. For instance, if a 10-year-old child could do all the things 10-year-olds generally do, her mental age (MA) would be 10, but another 10-year-old might only perform at the level of a typical 8-year-old (MA = 8), and another might achieve at the level of a typical 12-year-old (MA = 12). Those who perform below the expected level for their age would be identified as needing an alternative form of instruction in order to be successful in school. In 1908 this test was translated into English, and in 1910 it was published for use in the United States (Biasini, Grupe, Huffman, & Bray, 1999).

It was in the United States that the IQ test was transformed from the simple guide that Binet developed into a measure of an inherited, single quality called "intelligence." At one time in history, this idea led to using the test in the United States to identify individuals with "subnormal intelligence" in order to keep them from passing on their "defective" genes (Gould, 1996). A condition then known as feeble-mindedness was identified by relating scores on these early tests to mental age levels.

JOURNEY *of* **RESEARCH**

Mental age In early intelligence tests, the ability of a child to successfully pass measures designed to assess intelligence at particular ages.

(Continued)

(Continued)

In 1914, William Stern, an influential German psychologist, transformed mental age into what we now know as an **intelligence quotient** (or an IQ score). An intelligence quotient is based on the ratio of mental age to chronological age. An IQ score is calculated by dividing a child's mental age by the child's chronological age and then multiplying by 100. For example, if a 10-year-old scored at the 10-year-old level, her IQ score would be 10 (mental age)/10 (chronological age) x 100 = 100. However, if another 10-year-old scored at the 12-year-old level, her IQ would be 12/10 x 100 = 120.

Eventually researchers became concerned about using mental age as the basis for the IQ score. For one thing, it implied a steady growth from one year to the next, which many felt did not reflect reality (Sternberg, 2002b). So, in place of the ratio IQ, David Wechsler developed IQ tests for adults and children that were based on a **deviation IQ** (Sternberg, 2002b). To determine a deviation IQ, an intelligence test is first administered to a very large sample of individuals of all ages to establish the norms for the test, or expected scores for that population. For each specific age, the expected mean score is arbitrarily set to 100, with a standard deviation from the average score of 15 points. That ensures that most people will fall between 100 – 15 = 85 and 100 + 15 = 115 (see Figure 8.1). Note that as you move farther away from the average (that is, the greater the deviation from average), fewer and fewer people score at those more extreme levels.

When individuals take the Wechsler Intelligence Scale for Children (WISC) or the Wechsler Adult Intelligence Scale (WAIS), their score is compared only to those scores found for other people of their same age. For example, Joe scored higher than the majority

Intelligence quotient
Originally a measure of intelligence calculated based on the ratio of a child's mental age to chronological age, largely replaced now by the deviation IQ.

Deviation IQ A measure of intelligence that is based upon the individual's deviation from the norms for a given test.

Figure 8.1

Normal curve (distribution of IQ scores). IQ tests are designed so that the scores of most people fall near the midpoint (an IQ score of 100). As you move farther away from the center, there are fewer and fewer people at extremely high or extremely low scores.

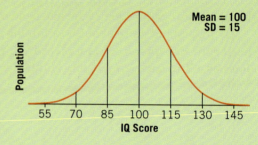

of 10-year-olds. This gave him an IQ score of 120. However, it is no longer said that he scored at the level of a 12-year-old (that is, that he had a mental age of 12). Instead, the deviation IQ score means that he has scored higher than many other children who are 10 by a certain amount.

The WISC measures four factors that contribute to the total IQ: verbal comprehension, perceptual reasoning, working memory, and processing speed (Wechsler, 2003). Each of these measures derives from a child's performance on subtests that assess different abilities. It would not be appropriate for us to provide actual items from the Wechsler tests, but the following examples are similar to ones that are used today or that are from previous versions of the test that are no longer used (see Table 8.1). These will give you an idea of the nature of these tests.

Table 8.1

Wechsler Intelligence Scale for Children (WISC). These are examples of subtests within the WISC and questions similar to those found on the actual test.

Arithmetic	If 4 toys cost 6 dollars, how much do 7 cost?
Vocabulary	What does "debilitating" mean?
Comprehension	Why are streets usually numbered in order?
Block Design	Use blocks to replicate a two-color design.
Similarities	In what way are "dogs" and "rabbits" alike?
Digit Span	Remember progressively longer lists of numbers

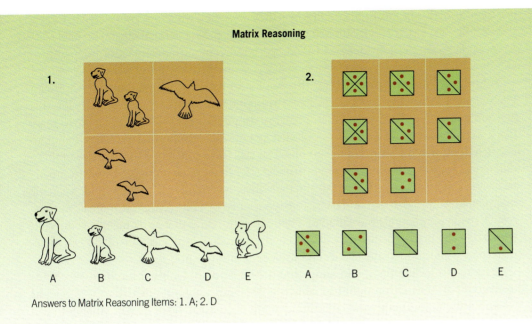

Matrix Reasoning

Answers to Matrix Reasoning Items: 1. A; 2. D

The Nature-Nurture Controversy and Intelligence

You will remember that in Chapter 4 we looked at the relative contribution of nature and nurture to intelligence by describing research that has compared identical twins (who have all or almost all of their genes in common) to fraternal twins (who have about 50% of their genes in common). That research has consistently found that the closer the genetic relationship between two individuals, the more similar their measured intelligence. Across a number of studies, the correlation in IQ scores between identical twins is about +.86 while the correlation between cousins is only +.15 (Bouchard & McGue, 1981).

Over the years, views on the relative influence of genes and environment on intelligence have swung back and forth (Plomin & Petrill, 1997). The first large-scale use of intelligence tests was during World War I, when a large number of soldiers were given tests to determine who would qualify for officer training (Gould, 1996). The biggest impact of this large-scale use of an IQ test came from the finding that the average mental age of the soldiers was about 13, close to the level that had been designated, in the diagnostic terminology of the time, as "moron." A deeply flawed analysis of the scores of army recruits who were immigrants led to the conclusion that immigrants from Northern Europe were more intelligent than those from Southern Europe. This misinterpretation later contributed to the passage of a law in 1924 that severely limited immigration from a number of countries in which people had been found by these tests to have a lower IQ (Gould, 1996).

Using intelligence tests in these ways eventually led to the eugenics movement as described in Chapter 4. The movement was based on the idea that intelligence is linked with certain genes and people with those genes should be encouraged to have children so they can pass on their genes, while those whose genes are linked to lower levels of intelligence should not. In other words, just as farmers can breed animals to promote desirable characteristics, the eugenics movement was based on the idea that humans could be "bred" to be more intelligent. The horrors perpetrated by the Nazis in World War II in the name of eugenics brought an end to the influence of the eugenics movement in the United States.

More recently, the controversy over whether intelligence is due to nature or nurture resurfaced in 1994 when Herrnstein and Murray published their book *The Bell Curve: Intelligence*

Video Link 8.1
History of IQ testing.

and Class Structure in American Life, in which they presented what they considered to be evidence of (in the words of critic Stephen Jay Gould, 1996, p. 34) "permanent and heritable differences" in IQ among individuals and, more specifically, among different racial groups. Much of the controversy arose from the declaration that any inherited differences were *permanent*.

There was such an uproar about this book and its conclusions that the American Psychological Association set up a task force to respond to its claims (Neisser et al., 1996). This task force concluded that racial differences do exist on IQ scores (for example, on average, Black students score lower than White students), but what is important to note is that there is much overlap in the scores of the groups. The task force concluded that the size of these differences were "well within the range of effect sizes that can be produced by environmental factors" (Neisser et al., 1996, p. 94) and that "there is certainly no . . . support for a genetic interpretation" (p. 97). In short, the task force concluded that differences are more likely to be related to environmental issues than to inborn, genetic issues that are somehow connected with race. Later in this chapter we will look at poverty, a significant factor in a child's environment, and its effects upon intelligence and academic achievement.

After reading Chapter 4, you know that the question of whether intelligence comes from genes *or* the environment probably is not the most helpful one to ask. Given what we know about how genes and environment interact, we can be pretty sure that both will have an influence on something as complex as intelligence. A number of research designs have been used to examine the relative influence of genetics and environment on general cognitive abilities. Some have looked at the correlation of IQ scores within families (either between parents and children or between siblings). Others have compared the IQ scores of adopted children to those of their biological and adoptive parents. Still others have compared IQ scores between identical and fraternal twins. In each of these situations, there is a different degree of genetic relationship and a different balance between a shared and a nonshared environment. For example, identical (or monozygotic) twins share almost 100% of their genes in common and share a good deal of the environment in common (although each twin has some novel experiences both within the family and outside of the family that constitute the nonshared environment). By comparison, an adopted child shares about 50% of his genes with his biological parents but almost all of his environment with his adoptive parents. Figure 8.2 shows the different strength of correlations found across different types of comparisons. Remember that the closer a correlation is to +1.0, the more closely the two IQ scores match each other. After examining a wide range of relationships, Plomin and Petrill (1997) came to the conclusion that the influence of genes on general intelligence is "significant and substantial" (p. 56), but they also pointed out that although this is *what is*, it does not have to be *what could be*.

One argument against the idea of an innate, unchangeable IQ comes from the fact that the scoring of IQ tests needs to be readjusted at regular intervals because performance has been going up since the beginning of the 20th century. The norms for IQ tests have been adjusted at a rate of about one third of an IQ point per year in order to make sure that 100 remains the average score (Loehlin, Horn, & Willerman, 1997). This means that if you performed exactly the same way on the second and third versions of the WAIS, you might receive an IQ score of 110 on the second version but only a score of 105 on the third version because the norms had been adjusted upward (Kanaya, Ceci, & Scullin, 2003).

There has been a debate about what these changes, known as the **Flynn effect** after Dr. Robert Flynn who first described it, really mean (Flynn, 1984). As intelligence tests are administered over time, there is a gradual increase in the scores on the tests (Kanaya et al., 2003). Do these increases in scores mean that we are all more intelligent than previous generations? Flynn himself argues that certain abilities *have* increased over time as society has developed an increasing need for them. Doesn't this remind you of Vygotsky's idea that cognitive development is a reflection of the societal and cultural context in which it is embedded? For example, abstract thinking is required for success in modern society, but for farmers

TRUE/FALSE

2. Results from intelligence testing indicate that people are getting smarter and smarter.

True. In the past century, people have scored higher and higher on standardized tests of intelligence. As a result, the test scores have had to be readjusted to reset what level of performance is considered "average."

Flynn effect The increase in intelligence test scores that has occurred over time, necessitating the renorming of the tests.

Figure 8.2

Average correlation for IQ scores across relationships. This figure shows the average correlation from a number of studies that look at the IQ scores across a number of relationship pairs. Note that both the amount of genetic information shared by each pair and the amount of shared environment differ for each group.

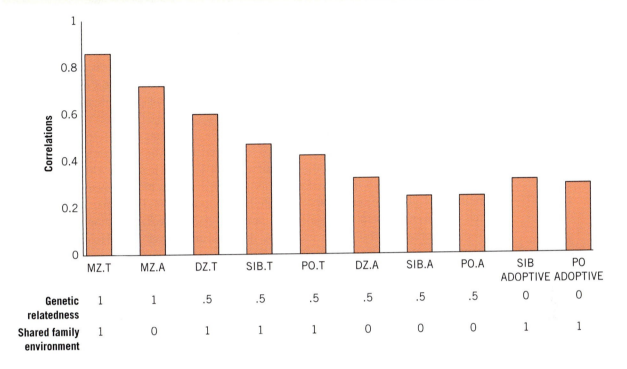

	MZ.T	MZ.A	DZ.T	SIB.T	PO.T	DZ.A	SIB.A	PO.A	SIB ADOPTIVE	PO ADOPTIVE
Genetic relatedness	1	1	.5	.5	.5	.5	.5	.5	0	0
Shared family environment	1	0	1	1	1	0	0	0	1	1

MZ = monozygotic (identical) twins
DZ = dizygotic (fraternal) twins
SIB = siblings
T = reared together
A = reared apart
PO = parent/offspring

in the early part of the 1900s, it may not have been essential. For these farmers, it was only important to know that the similarity between a cow and a goat is that they both needed to be fed, not that they both belonged to a conceptual category of "animal," which would be the correct answer on an IQ test.

Although it is likely that there are differences in genetic potential among individuals or groups of individuals, intelligence is one of those characteristics that we described in Chapter 4 as not very deeply canalized. You'll remember that this means that whatever the genetic starting point, the environment has a substantial impact on the eventual outcome or end point for this characteristic. In Chapter 4, we also said that many important traits are polygenic because many genes work together in combination to produce the trait. Intelligence is one of those polygenic traits. When you have many traits working in concert there is a wide range of potential outcomes (or what we call a **range of reaction**). Where any individual ends up within that range is determined by the quality of the environment and her experience in it, as well as other characteristics of the individual, such as her level of motivation or how hard she is willing to work to attain her goals (Hunt, 1988). Although genes may roughly set an upper and lower limit, experience, especially educational experiences, influences how much of that potential is fulfilled.

Range of reaction The range of potential outcomes for any given genotype.

IQ Scores and Academic Achievement

If we return to Binet's initial goals in developing his test of mental age, the true "test of the test" is whether it can help us identify children who can benefit from appropriate interventions. An intelligence test gives us an estimate of an individual child's performance relative to other children of the same age, but for a child who is performing below expectations, it tells us very little about what kind of help a child needs. The President's Commission on Excellence in Special Education concluded in 2002 that we have not used IQ testing effectively to help us develop individualized programs based on children's strengths and weaknesses and even recommended that we discontinue their use (Benson, 2003). Consequently, other tests have been developed to more specifically identify what is interfering with a child's learning. It takes more than an IQ score to identify a child who has a learning disability or attention deficit hyperactivity disorder. An intelligence test may be part of the assessment, but we do not rely upon it solely for a diagnosis.

It is not surprising to learn that research has shown that scores on IQ tests do predict academic achievement, at least for some groups of children. However, when we say "predict," we mean that IQ scores tell us something about who will do better in school. Although IQ scores help us do this, the prediction is far from perfect. In fact, there may be other factors that are better predictors of academic performance. In a study by Duckworth and Seligman (2005), 164 children were given IQ tests at the beginning of the eighth grade, as well as questionnaires and a very simple test of self-control. They were given a dollar bill in an envelope and told that they could either keep it or return it and, if they returned it, they would receive $2 at the end of the week. For these children, evidence of self-control was twice as predictive of grades in school as their IQ scores. The standardized tests used to assess intelligence don't typically measure factors like self-control. Any student who has ever believed that "I'm just not a good test taker" should be able to think of several other factors that might affect performance on this type of test. That is why children are never identified as having a special educational need based only on a test score. We use the results from multiple tests, along with observations of the child and consultation with people who know the child well (such as parents and teachers), before coming to a conclusion. Later in the chapter we will discuss many other factors related to academic success.

Alternative Views of Intelligence

Many critics of intelligence testing have argued that the kinds of abilities tested by most IQ tests are not the only ones that are related to success in modern society and that there is no one type of intelligence that underlies all others (that is, there is no "g" factor). Two of the most influential contemporary theories have their origins in information processing theory. They are the theory of multiple intelligences and triarchic theory.

Gardner's Theory of Multiple Intelligences

Theory of multiple intelligences The idea that there are a number of different types of intelligence that are all relatively independent of each other.

Howard Gardner proposed a **theory of multiple intelligences**, making the case that there are many different ways to express intelligence. He originally named seven types of intelligence but now includes two more, for a total of nine. However, he states "there is not, and there never can be, a single irrefutable and universally accepted list of human intelligences" (Gardner, 1993, p. 60), so presumably his list may change and/or continue to grow. To support the idea of separate intelligences, Gardner looked for evidence that each specific type of intelligence resides largely in a different part of the brain that has a distinct way of processing information (Torff & Gardner, 1999). For example, a brain injury can impair one type while leaving others virtually unaffected. This means that following an injury to a specific part of the brain, a musician might lose the ability to speak but retain the ability to play music. Gardner argues that this supports the idea that the two intelligences (linguistic and musical) are relatively autonomous. As another example, we often can see significant disparities of ability within a single individual. Gardner specifically points to special populations, such as savants or prodigies. Savants have low overall levels of attainment but have exceptional ability in a very specific domain (like knowledge of the calendar or memorizing the phone book). Likewise prodigies may be rather unremarkable in most areas, while being extremely gifted in one specific area (like playing piano or learning foreign languages).

Some critics do not agree that there is strong evidence for nine different types of intelligence because there is some degree of correlation between them (Klein, 1997). If they were truly independent, ability in one area would not correlate with ability in the others. Although we said in Chapter 6 that certain functions are localized in different areas of the brain, critics point to the fact that few human activities rely upon a single type of ability. As one example, a game of chess requires logical thought to plan your moves, spatial skills to help you visualize the board, and interpersonal skills to determine the strategies that your opponent is likely to use (Torff, 1996). Although these may be separate abilities, they need to work together in the process of completing the game. Further, although Gardner (1999) has claimed that "accumulating neurological evidence is amazingly supportive of the general thrust of MI [multiple intelligences] theory" (p. 88), the neurological evidence that we have to date shows the processing pathways in the brain are shared, not functionally isolated from each other (Waterhouse, 2006). In a critical review of the research on multiple intelligences, Waterhouse (2006) concludes that "to date there have been no published studies that offer evidence of the validity of the MI" (p. 208). A similar conclusion has been expressed by Allix (2000), and even by Gardner and Connell (2000). Proponents of the theory of multiple intelligences say that it takes time for a new approach such as this to develop the methods that can be used to assess and validate a theory.

Despite the concerns that have been expressed by critics of multiple intelligences, Gardner's ideas have been widely accepted and implemented within the field of education (Waterhouse, 2006). Ordinarily we expect new theories to be subjected to rigorous scientific examination, but these ideas appear to have entered the field without that level of testing. One explanation for this is the fact that this theory simply makes sense to many people. Waterhouse (2006) attributes part of the appeal to the fact that the theory of multiple intelligences seems to be more democratic than standard psychometric testing. Traditional intelligence tests appear to give a single estimate of a child's ability, whereas multiple intelligences offer the hope that every child will find some strength and distinctive talent.

We have included in Table 8.2 a brief definition of each of the nine types of intelligence on Gardner's list, together with examples of careers that would be based on each of these strengths. After looking at this table, try **Active Learning: Applying Multiple Intelligences** to see how you would apply Gardner's ideas in an educational setting.

Table 8.2

Gardner's multiple intelligences theory. These are brief descriptions of the nine types of intelligence described by Howard Gardner and some possible careers associated with each type.

Type of intelligence	Description	Possible careers
Linguistic	The ability to use language	Public speakers and writers
Musical	The ability to make music	Composers and musicians
Logical-mathematical	The ability to reason about abstract concepts	Mathematicians and scientists
Spatial	The ability to see the world and then mentally manipulate or recreate what is seen	Engineers and artists
Bodily-kinesthetic	The ability to use one's body effectively	Dancers and athletes
Interpersonal	Skill in interacting with other people	Sales representatives and politicians
Intrapersonal	The ability to understand one's own emotions and thoughts and express them	Actors and poets
Naturalist	The ability to distinguish and categorize natural phenomena	Weather forecasters and park rangers
Existential	The tendency to think about the ultimate questions of life and death	Philosophers and religious leaders

ACTIVE LEARNING

Video Link 8.2
Multiple intelligences in the classroom.

Applying Multiple Intelligences

Imagine you are trying to teach a classroom of second graders about arithmetic. You know that within this class there are children with each type of intelligence that Gardner has described. Design plans for how you would teach to each one so they would best understand. For example, a child with high musical intelligence might learn best from a song about addition. Of course, in the real world, teachers cannot teach everything in nine different ways, but they can vary the ways they teach so that all children will have a chance to learn using their own mental strengths.

Triarchic theory
Sternberg's idea that intelligence represents a balance of analytical, creative, and practical abilities.

Analytical intelligence The type of intelligence that is the one closest to "g" or general intelligence and the one prized highly in most schools.

Creative intelligence The ability to generate ideas and to deal successfully with novelty (sometimes referred to as divergent thinking).

Divergent thinking The ability to find as many possible solutions to a problem as possible, rather than the one "correct" solution.

Practical intelligence The ability to solve everyday problems by changing yourself or your behavior to fit the environment better, changing the environment, or moving to a different environment in which you can be more successful.

Sternberg's Triarchic Theory

Robert Sternberg has also moved away from the idea that there is one underlying determinant of intelligence, "g." He believes that intelligence is related not just to success in school but to success in life. He has said that "one's ability to achieve success depends on capitalizing on one's strengths and correcting or compensating for one's weaknesses through a balance of analytical, creative and practical abilities in order to adapt to, shape and select environments" (Sternberg, 2002a, p. 448). According to Sternberg's **triarchic theory**, living a successful life entails using these three types of intelligence (analytical, creative, and practical) to interact in the best possible way with one's particular environment.

Sternberg describes **analytical intelligence** as the one closest to "g" and the one prized highly in most schools. **Creative intelligence** is the ability to generate ideas and to deal successfully with novelty. This type of intelligence is tested when children are asked to find as many possible solutions to a problem as they can, rather than the one "correct" solution. This is sometimes referred to as **divergent thinking**. **Practical intelligence** relates to the ability "to adapt to, shape and select environments," which includes using abilities to solve everyday problems by changing yourself or your behavior to fit the environment better, changing the environment, or moving to a different environment in which you can be more successful. Although Sternberg's research has provided some support for the existence of these different types of intelligence, he admits that the evidence is limited (Sternberg, Castejón, Prieto, Hautamäki, & Grigorenko, 2001). Yet his research has shown that learning is enhanced when teachers promote all of these different types of intelligence rather than emphasizing memory alone (Sternberg, 2002c). Table 8.3 illustrates differences in teaching and assessment of learning in relation to each of these types of intelligence.

Table 8.3

Prompts used to teach and test memorization versus Sternberg's three types of intelligence.
Schools have traditionally placed an emphasis on memorization, but Sternberg emphasizes intellectual skills beyond memorization. This table shows the kinds of questions used for teaching and assessment of each type of intelligence.

Types of intelligence	Prompts for teaching and testing
Memory (the type of intelligence often emphasized in school)	Recall, recognize, match, verify, repeat
Analytic (Sternberg)	Analyze, evaluate, explain, compare and contrast, judge
Creative (Sternberg)	Create, explore, imagine, suppose, synthesize
Practical (Sternberg)	Put into practice, use, implement, apply

Sternberg's goal is to encourage the educational system to move beyond an emphasis on memory skills to promote and value analytical, creative, and practical abilities. As a child, Sternberg himself felt passed over because his abilities did not fall in the standard areas assessed by schools and IQ tests. He has made it his lifework to bring more understanding to those children whose abilities are different. We will return to a discussion of Sternberg's theory and research later in the chapter when we discuss creativity.

Cognitive Development and Academic Achievement

In this section we will focus on factors and conditions that influence cognitive development and affect children's achievement in school and beyond. We will first look at the influence of individual cognitive abilities, then examine the influence of society (specifically the effect of poverty), and then look at issues within the school environment itself that affect achievement. Finally, we will look at those children who are not succeeding in school to understand the difficulties, realities, and possibilities for them.

Infant Intelligence

Long before children enter school, their intellectual abilities are taking shape. Interest in assessment of infant intelligence has come from two sources: (a) the question of whether infant intelligence is predictive of later intelligence and (b) offering services to infants whose development is not optimal *before* they reach school.

Early tests of infant mental development included the Gesell Developmental Schedules, the Cattell Infant Intelligence Scale, and the Bayley Scales of Infant Development. The Gesell Developmental Schedules

Bayley Scales of Infant Development. This examiner is administering the Bayley Scales of Infant Development to this young child.

assessed gross and fine motor skills, language development, adaptive behavior, and personal-social behaviors from infancy through age 5. You'll remember from Chapter 2 that Arnold Gesell established norms for motor development milestones during infancy and early childhood. Although these schedules did not purport to be tests of intelligence, they could be used to identify young children with neurological impairment or mental retardation, so they have been used to screen for intellectual disabilities. The Cattell Infant Intelligence Scale assesses mental development in infants between 3 and 30 months of age by evaluating motor control while the child manipulates small objects, as well as verbalizations or attempts to communicate (Walsh & Betz, 1995). Finally, the Bayley Scales of Infant Development assess mental, physical, social, and emotional development (Salkind, 2005a). The Mental Scale assesses abilities such as perception, memory, problem solving, and early language development, and the Motor Scale assesses both fine and gross motor skills such as picking up small objects, sitting, and walking. A child's social and emotional development is assessed by the Behavior Rating Scale, which looks at variables such as attention, orientation, and emotional engagement. In 1993 the Scales were revised to include items intended to reduce racial and gender bias in the instrument and to make the activities more appealing to the infants (Salkind, 2005a).

Attempts to link results of these infant intelligence tests with measurements of intelligence and school performance in older children proved to be disappointing. These tests depended upon measures of sensorimotor functioning (Thompson, Fagan, & Fulker, 1991), and infants who did well on measures of sensorimotor functioning were not necessarily children who later performed well on standardized tests of intelligence. This "disconnect" between early measures and later performance initially suggested that there is a qualitative difference in what constitutes intelligence in infancy and what constitutes intelligence in childhood (Thompson et al., 1991).

While tests such as these continue to be used in both clinical and research applications, a newer approach to assessing intelligence in young children draws upon information processing approaches. The techniques that are used were described in Chapter 7. They include measures of infant attention, attraction to novelty, and habituation to a repeated stimulus. Responses to novelty and habituation appear to be particularly important predictive factors for later intelligence (Bornstein et al., 2006; DiLalla et al., 1990; Fagan, Holland, & Wheeler, 2007; Kavšek, 2004). These information processing abilities have been related to both later global intelligence and specific cognitive abilities. For instance, early visual attention has been associated with later language ability (Bornstein & Sigman, 1986). A preference for novelty has been associated with language development, as well as with general intellectual development (Rose, Feldman, Wallace, & Cohen, 1991). Preference for novelty has been associated with both general intelligence and a number of specific cognitive abilities (Rose, Feldman, & Wallace, 1992; Thompson et al., 1991).

This research is increasingly providing evidence for the continuity of intellectual development when measured by these information processing abilities. The explanation for this relationship is based upon the idea that these characteristics are ones that help infants learn from their environment (DiLalla et al., 1990). For instance, an infant who is attracted to novel elements in the environment is better equipped to learn from his experience, and this ability continues to support new learning as the infant moves into childhood and later into adolescence and adulthood.

Cognitive Deficits and Intellectual Gifts

Because of the way that intelligence tests are constructed, most children have cognitive abilities that are near to average; however, some children score considerably above or below average. Look again at Figure 8.1 to remind yourself what the distribution of intelligence scores looks like. At the extreme low end are children who are considered **mentally retarded** or **intellectually disabled** (Hodapp, Maxwell, Sellinger, & Dykens, 2006). At the extreme high end are children who are considered intellectually gifted.

How we identify mental retardation has changed over the years. Usually a score below 70 to 75 on a standard intelligence test is one of the criteria considered when making a determination, but intelligence test scores are *not* the only criteria used to diagnose mental retardation or intellectual disabilities. The second important criterion is the child's ability to function independently, which is called **adaptive functioning** (National Dissemination Center for Children with Disabilities [NDCCD], 2009b). Limitations in adaptive behavior can involve conceptual skills (such as reading, writing, and understanding and using language), social skills (such as handling interpersonal relationships, being responsible, and following rules), and practical skills (such as eating, dressing and taking care of personal hygiene, and preparing meals and handling money) (American Association of Intellectual and Developmental Disabilities, 2008). A professional would use information from a variety of sources including interviews, observations, and informal assessments to compare the child's current level of functioning to that of other children of the same age (Biasini et al., 1999). The third criterion for this diagnosis is that the condition begins before the age of 18. By this comprehensive definition, between 1%

Mentally retarded (or intellectually disabled) A degree of intellectual impairment that includes a low score on a standardized test of intelligence (usually 70 to 75 or lower) and impaired adaptive functioning.

Adaptive functioning A person's ability to function independently.

and 1.5% of the population is considered mentally retarded or intellectually disabled (Hodapp et al., 2006). There is a great deal that can be done to help children with mental retardation reach their full developmental potential through intervention programs and special education. Children who are mentally retarded are able to learn new skills, but they do so more slowly than children with average or above-average abilities (Johnson & Walker, 2006).

We discussed a number of causes of retardation in earlier chapters, including genetic causes such as Down syndrome and Fragile X syndrome, and environmental causes such as fetal alcohol syndrome, extreme malnutrition, and exposure to toxins such as lead or mercury, but professionals are able to identify a specific reason for retardation in only about 25% of cases (U.S. National Library of Medicine, 2007). The more severe the degree of retardation, the more likely it is that the child also will have other disabilities, such as impaired vision, hearing loss, cerebral palsy, or a seizure disorder (CDC, 2005b).

In 1975, federal legislation known as the Individuals with Disabilities Education Act (IDEA) was passed to ensure that children with disabilities received free and appropriate public education. The law has been revised several times since then, but the focus has remained to provide early intervention, special education, and related services to eligible children (U.S. Department of Education, 2007). Infants and toddlers up to the age of 3 are eligible for early intervention services if they are experiencing delays in cognitive development, physical development (including vision and hearing), communication development, social or emotional development, or adaptive development, or if they have a diagnosed condition that is likely to result in a development delay (NDCCD, 2009a). For children and youth between the ages of 3 and 21 years of age, there are 13 disability categories that qualify them for services, and mental retardation is one of those categories (NDCCD, 2009a). Only 1 out of every 10 children who is in special education has some form of mental retardation (NDCCD, 2009b). The criteria for diagnosing mental retardation that are used in IDEA are the same as what we described above, but add an adverse effect of the condition on education as one of the criteria (NDCCD, 2009b).

Another condition related to cognitive ability that is covered by the provisions of IDEA is having a specific **learning disability**. Children with learning disabilities have a "disorder in one or more of the basic psychological processes involved in understanding or in using language, spoken or written, that may manifest itself in an imperfect ability to listen, think, speak, read, write, spell, or to do mathematical calculations" (NDCCD, 2009b, p. 4). A learning disability is *not* the same thing as mental retardation. Rather it is a "neurological condition that interferes with an individual's ability to store, process, or produce information" (Learning Disabilities Association of America [LDAA], 2006, para. 1). If you compare this definition to the one for mental retardation, you will see that the definition for learning disabilities is more specific and limited in scope. Some common specific forms of learning disabilities include the following:

- Dyslexia—difficulties specific to language skills, particularly reading
- Dyscalculia—difficulties in solving math problems and grasping mathematical concepts
- Dysgraphia—difficulties in forming letters and expressing ideas when writing

Learning disabilities often run in families (LDAA, 2006) and cannot be cured, but the effects of a learning disability on a child's development can be reduced significantly with the proper educational support services. With help, children can work with their strengths and learn strategies to help them effectively deal with their disability. That is why the provision of special educational services is so important for these children. Having a learning disability does not mean that children cannot achieve a great deal in their lives. A number of people with

Video Link 8.3
Mental retardation.

Learning disability A disorder in one or more of the basic psychological processes involved in understanding or using language, spoken or written, that may manifest itself in an imperfect ability to listen, think, speak, read, write, spell, or do mathematical calculations.

Video Link 8.4
Learning disabilities.

Gifted (or talented) children   Children and youth who exhibit high performance capability in intellectual, creative, and/or artistic areas; possess an unusual leadership capacity; or excel in specific academic fields.

outstanding accomplishments in their fields have learning disabilities. You may know that the actress Whoopi Goldberg and actors Tom Cruise and Sylvester Stallone are learning disabled, but you may not know that this is also true of the founder of one of the largest financial firms in the United States (Charles Schwab) and some very famous politicians (Nelson Rockefeller and Winston Churchill), athletes (Bruce Jenner and Carl Lewis), and musicians (John Lennon and Cher) (LD OnLine, 2008a, 2008b).

The other end of the continuum of cognitive ability represents children who are functioning at a very high level and have an extraordinary amount of potential for their development. These children are identified as **gifted** or **talented**. It has been difficult to arrive at a single, generally accepted definition of giftedness (Keogh & MacMillan, 1996). Specifically, it has been difficult to move away from relying primarily on measures of intellectual ability as the defining characteristic, even though giftedness includes a wide range of human abilities, talents, and accomplishments (Sternberg, 2004; Sternberg & Zhang, 1995). As part of a recent attempt to provide a definition of giftedness, a federal report titled *National Excellence* said that "these children and youth exhibit high performance capability in intellectual, creative, and/or artistic areas, possess an unusual leadership capacity, or excel in specific academic fields" (Reis, 2004, p. xii).

However, unlike the general consensus we have about the need to provide services to children with intellectual challenges, there has been considerable debate and disagreement about the nature, amount, or type of services that should be provided through the educational system to gifted children. Reis (2004) describes the pattern of support for programs for gifted children as a series of peaks of support followed by valleys of apathy (see also Starko, 1990). When there has been some perceived threat to our country's status or well-being (such as the release of international statistics indicating that American children are lagging behind other nations in their academic achievement or some extraordinary scientific achievement by another nation), there are calls for programs to support the development of our brightest children. When there is no such perceived threat, however, our traditional commitment to egalitarianism in our schools and a fear of possibly creating an aristocratic and elite class of students work against establishing and maintaining programs for gifted and talented students. This tension is heightened in times of tight budgets, when programs for the gifted are seen as a luxury that we can do without (Reis, 2004). In general, the public's opinion seems to support special programs for gifted and talented youngsters as long as these programs do not reduce the opportunities for average or below-average learners (Larsen, Griffin, & Larsen, 1994).

Programs for gifted and talented students can take a variety of forms (Reis, 2004). Classes for gifted children often use an **enrichment approach**, in which the curriculum is covered but in greater depth, breadth, or complexity than is done in a typical classroom. Teachers in these classes usually have a good deal of flexibility in how they structure the students' exploration of the topics covered in the classes. However, many programs for gifted students take place outside of the regular school environment after school, on Saturdays, or during the summer and supplement the instruction the child receives in his or her regular classroom (Brody, 2005; Feldhusen & Dai, 1997).

Offering the child an **accelerated program** in the child's regular school is another approach. This type of program allows the student to move through the standard curriculum but more quickly than is typical. Rather than moving at a pace that suits an entire class of students, the student moves ahead at an individual pace as the student shows mastery of the material. A student who is advanced in a particular subject (for example, mathematics) might take that subject with a class at a higher grade level but remain in his or her regular grade for other subjects, or the student may be allowed to skip an entire grade to accelerate his or her progress in all subjects (Lynch, 1994).

Enrichment approach   An educational approach for gifted children in which the curriculum is covered but in greater depth, breadth, or complexity than is done in a typical classroom.

Accelerated program   A type of program that allows gifted students to move through the standard curriculum but more quickly than is typical.

Accelerated approaches often have encountered resistance based on the presumption that children will complete their secondary schooling early and will not be ready emotionally or socially to move on to a university to complete their education (Southern, Jones, & Fiscus, 1989; Vialle, Ashton, Carlon, & Rankin, 2001). However, the majority of studies that have looked at gifted children enrolled in accelerated programs do not indicate that this is a serious source of concern. In fact, gifted students often report that they were bored, uninterested, and frustrated prior to being accelerated and are more satisfied emotionally and academically after this happens (Kulik & Kulik, 1984; Vialle et al., 2001). Students in accelerated programs continue to perform well academically in their new classrooms (Kulik & Kulik, 1984; Vialle et al., 2001) and say that they do not feel socially isolated from their peers (Feldhusen & Dai, 1997; Sayler & Brookshire, 2004). In fact, contrary to what some people think, gifted children have generally been found to be socially and emotionally well adjusted (Lehman & Erdwins, 2004; Sayler & Brookshire, 2004), to have positive self-esteem (Hoge & Renzulli, 1991), and to not mind being identified as gifted (Feldhusen & Dai, 1997). Carol Dweck (1999), a researcher who has looked extensively at academic motivation, speculated that once children are labeled as gifted, they may avoid challenging tasks at which they might fail because failure would then threaten their special status as gifted. However, Feldhusen and Dai (1997) found that gifted children, in fact, welcome the opportunity to take on challenging tasks, and these authors suggest that a willingness to seek out challenges may be a characteristic of these children.

Outside of the school environment, parents of gifted or talented children can do a great deal to foster and encourage their children's talents. James Alvino (1995) of the National Research Center on the Gifted and Talented at the University of Connecticut suggests that parents provide a rich learning environment for their children that allows for a lot of exploration, but that parents also help their children find a balance between their schoolwork and fun activities so they can manage their stress effectively. One of the things to guard against is adults having such high expectations for their children that they lose sight of the fact that gifted children are, after all, still children.

Creativity and Intelligence

Where does creativity fit into our understanding of intelligence? Is creativity an independent characteristic (that is, can you be creative but not necessarily intelligent)? Or is it closely related to intelligence, so that people who are high (or low) on one are also high (or low) on the other? There has been a substantial amount of research that has examined the relationship between creativity and intelligence.

We need to begin by understanding what we mean when we talk about **creativity**. In the 1950s J. P. Guilford proposed that creativity is based upon an ability to see multiple solutions to a problem (that is, the ability to use divergent thinking), in contrast to what many academic situations require, which is to come up with one correct solution (called **convergent thinking**). According to Guilford (1950), being able to think divergently requires the ability to find multiple solutions relatively quickly (fluency) because the more alternatives you generate, the more likely it is that one or more will be creative; the ability to consider multiple alternatives or shift your mind-set (flexibility); and the ability to come up with solutions that are unique (originality). Most of the tests that are used to measure creativity are based upon these ideas. You can test yourself (or even a few of your friends) by using the examples of items that might be used in a test of creativity in **Active Learning: Creativity Tests**. Robert Sternberg (2003) defines creative thinking as "thinking that is novel and that produces ideas that are of value" (pp. 325–326), and in this sense, we need both divergent thinking to produce new ideas and convergent thinking to narrow the alternative ideas down to the one that is most practical or likely to succeed.

3. Children who are gifted or talented often pay a price for their giftedness because they are likely to be socially or emotionally maladjusted.

TRUE/FALSE

False. Gifted children have generally been found to be socially and emotionally well adjusted and to feel positive about their gifts and abilities.

Creativity Thinking that is novel and that produces ideas that are of value.

Convergent thinking Finding one correct solution for a problem.

ACTIVE LEARNING

Creativity Tests

The following items are similar to items used on various tests of creativity. Give yourself a specific amount of time (perhaps 1 or 2 minutes) and provide as many alternative answers as you can. You might want to do this activity with a small group of friends so you can observe whether there are substantial differences on how individuals perform on these tasks.

Word Fluency	Write as many words beginning with a given letter as you can in a specified amount of time.
Alternate Uses	Give as many possible uses for a given item that you can (for example, a brick, a bicycle tire).
Consequences	Give as many consequences as you can for a hypothetical situation (for example, what if we could live under water? What if animals could talk?).
Making Objects	Draw as many objects as you can using only a specific set of shapes (for example, one circle and two squares).
Decorations	Use as many different designs as possible to outline a common object.

TRUE/FALSE

4. Creativity and high intelligence often go hand-in-hand.

False. There is no relationship between intelligence and creativity. Although a certain amount of intelligence is necessary to be creative, high intelligence is not sufficient by itself.

Threshold theory The theory that intelligence and creativity are related up to approximately an IQ score of 120 but not beyond that.

Much of the research that has been conducted on creativity has examined whether (or to what degree) creativity is a trait independent of intelligence. A number of studies have found that the correlation is positive but moderately low (Kim, 2005; Wallach & Kogan, 1965). However, **threshold theory** has proposed that there are different relationships between intelligence and creativity at different levels of intelligence. Specifically, it says that intelligence and creativity are related up to approximately an IQ score of 120 but not beyond that (Feist & Barron, 2003). This would mean that intelligence is a necessary but not sufficient condition for creativity (Kim, 2005; Runco & Albert, 1986). However, a recent meta-analysis of 21 studies involving over 45,000 participants concluded there was no support for threshold theory (Kim, 2005). The conclusion that Kim draws from this is that even children of relatively low intellect can generate multiple solutions for a problem (that is, they can be creative).

As we discussed earlier, Robert Sternberg believes that there are three types of intelligence—analytical, practical, and creative—and he believes that schools should foster all three. He asserts that classroom teachers may undervalue creativity because they presume that it is the same thing as general intelligence or because they don't know how to teach it. He also maintains that "to a large extent, creativity is not just a matter of thinking in a certain way, but rather it is an attitude toward life" and that "creative people are creative, in large part, because they have *decided* [author's emphasis] to be creative" (Sternberg, 2003, p. 333). Table 8.4 presents 12 decisions that Sternberg says underlie the decision to be a creative thinker. Can you think of ways that a classroom teacher could help children or adolescents develop these attitudes and mind-sets?

As you read through the suggestions in Table 8.4 you will see that many of the characteristics of the environment that support gifted children also apply to supporting creative ones. We need to encourage children to be creative, to experiment and try new things, and to think about situations in fresh ways without being bound to old practices and ideas, and allow them to try and fail without becoming discouraged. As adults, we can also provide a stimulating environment that exposes them to new experiences, and we can urge them to find a passion and follow it.

Table 8.4

How to foster creative thinking. These are suggestions that Robert J. Sternberg makes for how to encourage creative thinking. He believes that classroom teachers can use these suggestions in their classrooms.

Redefine the problem	Don't necessarily accept things just because other people do. Allow yourself to see things differently.
Analyze your own ideas	Critique your own ideas and decide whether they are valuable and worth pursuing or not.
Sell your ideas	Just generating creative ideas is not enough. Because they challenge accepted ways of thinking, they must be "sold" to others.
Knowledge is a double-edged sword	You cannot be creative without being knowledgeable, but previous knowledge also can hamper or hinder creative thinking.
Surmount obstacles	You need to be ready to "defy the crowd" and overcome these obstacles.
Take sensible risks	Rather than providing a safe and conventional answer, be willing to fail by trying new things.
Willingness to grow	Don't become so invested in your own original creative ideas that you are afraid to branch out or explore new ones.
Believe in yourself	Maintain a sense of self-efficacy even when no one else seems to believe in you.
Tolerance of ambiguity	Be willing to tolerate some level of uncertainty while you are waiting to see if your ideas will pan out or not.
Find what you love and do it	You are likely to be most creative when you are doing things you really care about.
Allowing time	Realize that it takes time for incubation, reflection, and selection to develop a creative idea.
Allowing mistakes	Recognize that mistakes will happen, but use them as an opportunity to learn.

Societal Context: The Impact of Poverty on Academic Achievement

Poverty exists around the world and is a threat to healthy growth and development of all children who grow up without adequate resources. In 2007, 18% (or 13.3 million children) were living in poverty in the United States (DeNavas-Walt, Proctor, & Smith, 2008). Many children who grow up in poverty go on to become adults who contribute positively to society, although the percentage is higher for children growing up in more affluent circumstances (Shonkoff & Phillips, 2000). Although childhood poverty has been associated with difficulties for children in all areas of development, the deficits in cognitive functioning and academic achievement have been most clearly documented (McLoyd, 2000).

If you think about all of the problems associated with poverty, you can come up with a very long list, including the following examples:

- Poor health due to unavailability of health care, unsafe living conditions, and poor diet
- Lack of resources in the neighborhood, including structured after-school activities
- High rates of depression and posttraumatic stress disorder in both parents and children

5. Many children who grow up in poverty go on to become adults who contribute positively to society.

TRUE/FALSE

True. Even with the challenges of growing up in poverty, most of these children grow up to contribute positively to society. However, this percentage is less than that for children who grow up in more favorable circumstances.

- Anxiety linked to caring for a family in a dangerous neighborhood where loved ones may be lost to violence or witness frightening events
- High levels of stress that contribute to marital discord and instability
- Safety concerns that limit children's ability to explore their environment
- Poor schools with inadequate facilities
- Racism or other discrimination
- Segregation leading to a lack of opportunities and social exclusion (McLoyd, 2000; Ryan, Fauth, & Brooks-Gunn, 2006)

Affluence and poverty. Compare these two scenes and think about what each setting provides for the children in it and what the consequences might be for the children's academic achievement.

These factors interact with each other in complex ways to decrease academic performance in children. For instance, parents who are struggling with the stresses of poverty are less likely to provide educational stimulation and guidance in the home. They also have lower expectations for their children's achievement. Teachers also are more likely to have low expectations for the achievement of students from impoverished families (McLoyd, 2000). We will discuss the effects of teacher expectancy later in this chapter, but it is clear that children are more likely to respond positively when the adults around them expect that they will be able and motivated to learn.

In the 1960s, the impact of poverty became a national concern in the United States. In 1964, President Lyndon Johnson declared the War on Poverty, a program that included plans to help move families out of poverty. One problem that was identified in this "war" was that children whose families had few resources showed lower levels of cognitive development as early as 18–24 months of age, long before they entered school (Ryan et al., 2006). By the time they entered kindergarten they were already significantly behind their middle-class peers in preacademic skills that would lead to learning basic skills in reading and arithmetic as well as in measured IQ (McLoyd, 2000). When children begin at a low level, it becomes increasingly difficult to catch up, and school can become a source of frustration.

As part of the War on Poverty, the Head Start program was developed in an attempt to help economically disadvantaged children enter school on par with their more economically advantaged peers. Most people think of Head Start as a preschool program, but it is much more than that. Poverty affects families, not just children, and therefore Head Start was designed to help the whole family and the whole child. A caseworker is assigned to each family to help find resources for whatever the family decides are its most pressing needs, including the need for education, employment, health care, or mental health counseling. In addition, children are given two nutritious meals each school day, even if they are only in the classroom in the morning. Dental care and vision screening are provided. Finally, parental involvement is central to children's progress in Head Start and beyond, but because many of the parents whose children are participating in Head Start also grew up in poverty, school may not have been a positive experience for them. In Head Start parents learn skills and attitudes that promote their active involvement in their children's educational experiences both at home and at school. One national study of Head Start outcomes found that when parents were actively involved with Head Start their children's preacademic skills were more likely to improve (Head Start Family and Child Experiences Survey [FACES], 2007).

Research has been conducted on the effectiveness of Head Start from the very beginning of the program. The initial goal of the program was to raise children's IQ scores to the level of middle-class children, and the early findings were very encouraging: Children's IQs rose and remained elevated through second grade. However, as the initial group of children was followed beyond Grade 2, disappointment set in. IQ scores began to decline, eventually looking very similar to the IQ scores of other economically disadvantaged children who had not attended Head Start. At this point there were critics who were ready to discontinue the program, but fortunately there were early intervention programs like the Perry School Program in Ypsilanti, Michigan, that continued their research as the former Head Start children went to high school and beyond. These researchers looked not only at IQ scores but also at the children's future accomplishments. When longitudinal research compared children who had been in Head Start to children from a similar background who had not been in the program, the former Head Start children had higher academic achievement, had fewer grade retentions, had fewer special education placements, and were more likely to graduate from high school. Beyond high school, the young adults who had attended Head Start programs had higher incomes, were less likely to be dependent on welfare, and were less likely to have engaged in criminal behavior (Shonkoff & Phillips, 2000).

A Head Start on school success. A young student is excited after finishing a lesson with the help of a teacher's aide at the Brown E. Moore Head Start Center in Louisiana.

Video Link 8.5
Head Start.

Based upon such research, the argument has been made that the money spent on Head Start (approximately $7,000 per child in 2007) reaps financial benefits that vastly outweigh the initial expense. If you consider the expenses involved when children require special education services or are involved in the criminal justice system, you can begin to see how the initial expenditures that help prevent these placements are justified. Current research has shown that Head Start children significantly increase their early reading and math skills and their vocabulary in 1 year. Some of this change is likely connected to the finding that parents in the program were more likely to read to their children every day (Ryan et al., 2006). While the levels achieved when the children left the program were still below the national average, they continued to improve and look more like average students during kindergarten (Head Start Family and Child Experiences Survey [FACES], 2007). Importantly, on average, Head Start children also showed increases in cooperative behavior in the classroom, and the better their behavior, the higher their cognitive skills were at the end of the year. Many have argued that Head Start must continue to be a program that addresses the whole child, not just cognitive skills, because if a child can't cooperate in the classroom, the child will not be able to learn.

Promoting Learning in School

Learning occurs in many contexts—at a child's home, in school, and in the neighborhood. In this chapter we focus on the school environment and its impact on student learning. There are many issues related to cognitive development that play out within the classroom once the child enters school. We discuss several of these issues and highlight for you some of the complexity surrounding them.

The Role of Class Size

Do you think that it matters how many students there are in a classroom? Will increasing the number from 25 to 30 interfere with the students' ability to learn? Will cutting the number from 25 to 20 improve learning outcomes? In an intuitive sense we might expect that smaller classes would be associated with better student outcomes, but you may be surprised to learn that research has *not* conclusively found this to be the case (Abbeduto & Symons, 2008).

Small class size. Optimal learning occurs when well-trained, enthusiastic teachers can pay close attention to individual students in the early grades. Small class size gives them the opportunity to interact in this way with their students.

When comparing larger classes to smaller classes as they naturally occur within schools, there is evidence from surveys that supports the idea that smaller classes, particularly in the early grades, can benefit students (sometimes substantially) and that these benefits continue into the upper grades (Biddle & Berliner, 2002). There have also been experimental field studies, in which matched groups of children have been assigned to large or small classes, and the differences in outcome favoring small classes remain clear. The gains are similar for boys and girls, but the benefits are strongest for minority students, children from low-income families, and children attending inner-city schools (Biddle & Berliner, 2002), and again the differences are strongest for children in early

TRUE/FALSE

6. Reducing class sizes should be the first priority in education today.

    False. Although small class size in early elementary school is linked to higher academic performance, this is not true for older children, and small class size for children at any age by itself will not make a difference without well-trained and enthusiastic teachers.

elementary school. However, there is no clear evidence that class size in middle or high school promotes better learning (Biddle & Berliner, 2002). In a large national sample of children in Grades 4, 8, and 12, smaller classes were not associated with better test scores on reading. In fact, in eighth grade children in smaller classes had *lower* scores than children in larger classes (Johnson, 2000).

Biddle and Berliner (2002) argue that the most important factors influencing learning for children in the early grades are understanding and managing the expected behavior in a classroom and figuring out whether they are going to be able to handle the challenge of education. Smaller classrooms in these early grades allow teachers to spend more time with individual students to establish effective work habits and positive attitudes toward school. In a smaller classroom less time is spent on classroom management, which frees up more time for academic instruction. However, smaller teacher-to-student ratios by themselves do not ensure that this will happen, and reducing class size is an expensive undertaking. According to Johnson (2000), in fiscal year 2000 alone, Congress allocated $1.3 billion to reduce class size. For this reason, some have questioned whether those resources might be better spent on efforts designed to directly improve teacher preparation and qualifications rather than reducing the number of students they teach in a class. Biddle and Berliner (2002) conclude that smaller classes by themselves will not make a difference if students are not also provided with "well-trained and enthusiastic teachers, appropriate and challenging curriculums, and physical environments in their classrooms and schools that support learning" (p. 21). When teachers are qualified and enthusiastic, then smaller classes do have some benefits for students.

Grade Retention

Social promotion
Promoting a child who has not mastered grade-level material to keep the child in a class with same-age peers.

Another issue related to cognitive achievement in schools is the issue of grade retention. When children have not mastered the material for a grade level, they may be retained in that grade for another year so that they can repeat the material. Sometimes, however, children who have not mastered grade-level material still are promoted to the next grade, a process that is known as **social promotion**. As the term implies, the primary motivation for doing this is to keep the child in a class with same-age peers so that the child is not perceived as a failure and does not become alienated from school (Lorence & Dworkin, 2006). Recently there has been an increase in another type of retention—voluntary grade retention that has been called **academic redshirting** (Frey, 2005). Similar to the practice of "redshirting" an athlete to keep the athlete from playing for a year while he or she matures and develops more skills, in academic redshirting a child is intentionally kept from starting kindergarten for a year to give the child additional time to mature and develop school readiness skills (Frey, 2005). Because there is evidence that middle-class families in suburban communities are more likely to make this choice than other families, some researchers have speculated that for at least some of these families, the intent is to give their children a competitive advantage through delaying their entry to school (Cosden, Zimmer, & Tuss, 1993).

A factor that may play a role in this decision is the type of changes that have occurred in the kindergarten experience. Increasingly kindergarten has moved away from being a place for children to play and develop their social and emotional skills to becoming a place that emphasizes academic skills. Many skills that were previously taught in first grade now are taught in kindergarten (National Association for the Education of Young Children, 2000). With the greater emphasis that is being placed on academic skills, parents who are anxious for their children to be successful academically may think that an additional year before starting school will give their child the chance to develop the skills required to be successful—in kindergarten!

Research that has looked at whether—or when—retention versus social promotion is beneficial to the child has produced mixed findings (Lorence & Dworkin, 2006). There have been methodological flaws in this research that make it difficult to interpret the results and have called into question some of the conclusions drawn from it (Lorence & Dworkin, 2006). There is, however, one set of findings that emerges consistently from this research, and it is that some children are at greater risk than others of being retained. African American students and Hispanic students are more likely to be retained than Anglo students (Frey, 2005; Jacobs & Lefgren, 2004; Meisels & Liaw, 1993), boys are retained at higher rates than girls (Frey, 2005; Karwelt, 1999), and children from low-income families are more likely to be retained than children from more affluent families (Meisels & Liaw, 1993; Southern Regional Education Board, 2001).

Because the research that has looked at whether retention benefits students has not come to a definitive conclusion (Lorence & Dworkin, 2006), maybe we should think instead about the purpose of retention. Students are retained because they have not mastered the material at a certain grade level. If that has not happened on a first attempt, should we think that simply exposing the student to the same information a second time will make the difference (Reynolds, Temple, & McCoy, 1997; Roderick & Nagaoka, 2005; Silberglitt, Appleton, Burns, & Jimerson, 2006)? What works better for students is providing them with extra help and assistance when they repeat a grade (Lorence & Dworkin, 2006; Peterson, DeGracie, & Ayabe, 1987). If you have ever had to retake one of your college courses, you know that if you simply do again what you did the first time, it is likely that you will get the same results. However, if you change what you do or how you do it, you are more likely to have a better outcome. Although this makes sense, it means that schools must be willing to spend the extra money to provide additional help to students who are repeating a grade.

Expectancy Effects

We all can find ourselves living up—or down—to the expectations that other people have for us. The same is true for children in the classroom, but when these **expectancy effects** influence

Academic redshirting
Voluntary grade retention in which a child is kept from starting kindergarten for a year to give additional time to mature and develop school readiness skills.

Expectancy effects The effect that the expectations of others can have on one's self-perception and behavior.

7. The best way to improve a child's academic performance is to believe in the child and let him know that you have faith in his ability to succeed.

False. It *is* important to expect the best that we can from children and that we communicate that to them, but faith in their ability must be accompanied by a strong effort to help them master the material they need to learn.

Self-fulfilling prophecy The process by which expectations or beliefs lead to behaviors that help ensure that you fulfill the initial prophecy or expectation.

the amount of effort that children expend on their schoolwork and that lack of effort lowers a child's academic achievement, there is good reason for concern.

A number of years ago, Robert Rosenthal and Lenore Jacobson (1968) reported the results of an experiment in which they intentionally manipulated teachers' expectation for the academic performance of some of their students. Briefly, the researchers told teachers in six grades that they were able to identify students who would be intellectual "bloomers" over the coming year and that teachers should expect to see significant intellectual growth in these children. The "bloomers" were, in fact, selected randomly from class lists. At the end of the school year, total IQ scores of the "bloomers" were significantly higher than those of the other students who acted as controls for this experiment in some of the grades tested (Snow, 1995). The explanation offered by Rosenthal and Jacobson (1968) was that by changing the expectations that the teachers held for some of the students, it changed the behavior of the teachers in a way that facilitated intellectual growth in the children. Perhaps the teachers spent more time with these children, believing that this additional time was being well used with children who would benefit from it. Perhaps they were more supportive and encouraging toward children who were about to "bloom" or gave them different learning opportunities than they gave the other children.

This research gained a lot of attention both within the fields of education and psychology and by the general public, but it also generated a lot of debate (for example, see Wineburg, 1987a, 1987b). It offered a very optimistic message and suggested an apparently simple way to improve academic performance—believe in the child and communicate that belief to him or her. This idea is behind recent efforts in our schools to boost academic performance by enhancing children's self-esteem. On the other hand, these findings can also be used to blame teachers for children who underperform or perform poorly. Although some attempts to replicate the original findings have been successful, others have not (Cotton, 1989).

Jaime Escalante, the math teacher whose career is portrayed in *Stand and Deliver.*

The mechanism that underlies teacher expectancy effects is called a **self-fulfilling prophecy**. Your expectations cause you to predict (that is, to make a prophecy about) what will happen in the future. Those same expectations or beliefs may lead you to behave in ways that help ensure that you find exactly what you had expected to find (Good, 1987). For instance, if you have low expectations for a child's performance, you may spend little time working with the child or encouraging the child, or you might be overly critical about what the child does. These behaviors deny the child an opportunity to learn and may even make the child dislike school and withdraw from classroom activities. The child also may incorporate how you see him into his own self-concept. He comes to see himself as a failure and gives up trying, so consequently he does poorly—just as you had expected—and your initial prophecy is fulfilled.

How a self-fulfilling prophecy works seems clear enough, but it starts with the assumption that there is an initial faulty perception on the part of the teacher. We assume that a child who *could* succeed is mistakenly seen as someone who is likely to fail. How well does the research support that idea? In fact, research has found that teachers' initial expectations usually are based on accurate information, such as student records of previous achievement (Cotton, 1989; Good, 1987; McKown & Weinstein, 2008; Raudenbush, 1984). Furthermore, most teachers (and particularly those with a good deal of experience in the classroom) are able to adjust their initial expectations and their subsequent instructional approaches as they come to know their students better over the year (Cotton, 1989). Based on a review of the literature, Brophy (1983) estimated that teachers' expectations account for only between 5% and 10% of the variance observed in students' grades. Although teachers' expectations may not have a powerful effect on student outcomes, there still is good reason to make teachers aware of the potential effect of their expectations on their students' performance and to use positive expectations to foster positive performance, rather than having negative expectations that could be harmful. It should be our educational goal to help all children achieve as much of their academic potential as they can.

There have been some very powerful movie portrayals of real teachers who have transformed the lives of their students through their high expectations.

Erin Gruwell, the English teacher whose career is portrayed in *Freedom Writers.*

In *Stand and Deliver* (Menéndez, 1988), a math teacher, Jaime Escalante, challenges a group of predominantly Hispanic students from the Los Angeles barrio to master calculus. The teacher and students work after school, on weekends, and during vacation to overcome cultural deprivation and to rise above the low expectations that everyone else seems to have for these students. By the end of the movie, 18 of the students successfully pass the Advanced Placement test in calculus.

In *Freedom Writers* (LaGravenese, 2007), Erin Gruwell helps a group of gangbangers in a racially divided high school find their voice. Through the reading assignments she gives them and the daily journals that the students keep, they find hope for the future and for their personal educational aspirations. Through the caring and respect that she shows for these teenagers that everyone else had written off, they begin to find meaning and hope for their lives.

In *Lean on Me* (Schiffer & Avildsen, 1989), principal Joe Clark uses "tough love" to get the attention of the students in his school. He fights against city officials who don't agree with his tactics (such as chaining the doors shut to keep troublemakers out), against teachers he considers incompetent, and against parents who don't understand what he is doing to save his school from being closed down. In the process, his high expectations for the students turn the school around and help make it a safe environment in which children can learn.

Joe Clark, the principal whose career is portrayed in *Lean on Me.*

Rafe Esquith, the teacher whose fifth-grade students put on a production of one of Shakespeare's plays each school year.

Video Link 8.6
Rafe Esquith.

The Hobart Shakespeareans (Stuart, 2005) is a documentary film about Rafe Esquith, an extraordinary teacher who teaches fifth-grade students in a large, inner-city school in Los Angeles. His students are primarily from immigrant families whose native language is not English. In addition to a rigorous curriculum that includes English, mathematics, geography, and literature, the students spend the school year studying one of Shakespeare's plays culminating in a full-length, unabridged performance of the play they have studied. In a school environment that is filled with despair, Mr. Esquith is quoted as saying that it is not gangs or drugs that he fears, but rather that "what I fear is that they're ordinary. I don't want my students to be ordinary; I want them to be extraordinary because I know that they are" (Public Broadcasting Service, 2005, para. 4).

All of these teachers have been publicly acknowledged for their inspirational work with students, but there are many such teachers who work with students and make a difference in their lives each day. **Active Learning: Teacher-Heroes in Movies and Real Life** guides you to think about such teachers in your own life.

ACTIVE LEARNING   Teacher-Heroes in Movies and Real Life

Think about the most inspirational teacher you have ever had. What did that person do that was different from what other teachers did that made that person special to you? Was it something she did, something she said, or the way she seemed to feel about you that made a difference? If you have seen any of the inspirational movies about teachers mentioned above, did you see any parallels between your experience and the teachers portrayed in the movies? What downside, if any, is there to these movies creating such high expectations in the mind of the public for what a really great teacher can do for students?

Ability Grouping

Ability grouping   An educational approach that places students of similar ability in learning groups so they can be taught at a level that is most appropriate for their level of understanding.

The positive and negative effects of expectations are one reason why **ability grouping** in schools has become another controversial issue in education. This practice has been called by a variety of names besides ability grouping, including streaming, tracking, and clusters (Trautwein, Ludtke, Marsh, Koller, & Baumert, 2006). The rationale behind this educational approach was that ability groups allowed individual students to be taught at a level that is most appropriate for their current level of understanding. It was intended to allow high-performing students to advance more rapidly (thus avoiding boredom and frustration as they wait for slower students to master the material) and to allow low-performing students to get the material at a slower pace that better matches their ability level. Critics, however, see this stratification as harmful to the low-performing students in several ways, including damaging their self-esteem and creating negative attitudes toward school and schoolwork (Ireson, Hallam, & Plewis, 2001). Other critics have charged that children in lower-ability tracks receive poorer-quality teaching and have a less supportive educational environment, which, in turn, contributes to their lower levels of academic achievement and lower career aspirations (Lucas, 1999).

Cooperative learning   An educational strategy that allows groups of students who are at different ability levels to work together on a common goal, such as a project or an assignment.

Ability tracking has largely been abandoned in the United States (Trautwein et al., 2006) but continues to be used extensively in other countries, such as Germany and Great Britain. In the United States today, cooperative learning has increasingly gained favor. **Cooperative learning** allows groups of students at different ability levels to work together on a common goal, such as a project or an assignment. In cooperative learning, direct instruction comes first, and then the students work on the assignment together. Compared to other instructional approaches, students in cooperative learning groups learn more and retain it longer (Davis, 1993). They also report liking what they are studying more (Davis, 1993). In one study of college-age students, those who participated in collaborative learning groups developed greater critical thinking skills than those who learned individually (although the groups did not differ on a measure of drill-and-practice) (Gokhale, 1995). One explanation for why collaborative learning is beneficial in some cases but not in others is that the complexity of a task is related to how much cognitive processing capacity is required to complete it. When tasks are complex, they make greater demands on cognitive processing, and under these circumstances, dividing the cognitive load among multiple people is beneficial (Kirschner, Paas, & Kirschner, 2009). Of course working in a group, rather than as an individual, requires some additional effort to maintain communication within the group and to integrate individual information into a final group solution, but these efforts are justified for complex tasks. In comparison, this type of collaborative approach would not be particularly beneficial for a simpler task that is within the cognitive processing abilities of any single individual.

While ability grouping creates homogenous groups of students (with students within each track being similar in their ability level), collaborative learning creates heterogeneous groups comprising students of varying ability levels. Proponents of collaborative learning maintain that all students in the group can benefit from this arrangement. In the past you may have heard someone say that the best way to learn something yourself is to teach it to someone else. Likewise, proponents of collaborative learning expect that high-achieving students will benefit from the opportunity to explain concepts to the lower-achieving group members. The low-achieving members of the group benefit by getting assistance, encouragement, and stimulation from the more advanced group members (Marsh et al., 2008). Do you see the Vygotskian principle of scaffolding here when children are learning from their interactions with more skilled peers?

The research on the effectiveness of collaborative learning is mixed (Kirschner et al., 2009). In general, this educational approach seems to be more advantageous for low-performing students than for high-achieving ones (Lou et al., 1996), and there is even some research suggesting that it may lower the accomplishments of high-performing students (see Fuchs, Fuchs, Hamlett, & Karns, 1998). However, a meta-analysis of 21 studies that looked at collaborative learning found that for high-ability students, it simply did not make a difference whether their collaborative group was homogeneous or heterogeneous (Lou et al., 1996). Perhaps it shouldn't surprise us to find that high-ability students can do well under a variety of conditions. A more recent meta-analysis (Neber, Finsterwald, & Urban, 2001) reached the conclusion that although high-achieving students perform better when they are grouped with other high-achieving students, there are benefits other than academic achievement that come along with their participation in a heterogeneous group, including the development of social and leadership skills and enhanced self-esteem.

The Possible "Boy Problem" in Schools

Another fairly recent concern within the school environment has been referred to as the "boy problem." The concern originates in statistics that seem to indicate that it is becoming more difficult for boys than for girls to be successful in school. For instance, a report prepared by the U.S. Department of Education (National Center for Education Statistics, 2004) showed the following:

- Boys are more likely to repeat a grade than girls.
- Boys are more likely to drop out of school than girls.
- Boys are more likely to be diagnosed with a learning disability, emotional disturbance, or a speech impediment than girls.

8. Placing high-, average-, and low-performing students together in groups to collaborate on a project is beneficial to all the children in the group. **TRUE/FALSE**

False. This educational approach is probably most beneficial to low-performing students who have the opportunity to learn from peers who are performing at a higher level. While the highest-performing students may not necessarily benefit from this arrangement, they do not seem to be harmed by this classroom practice.

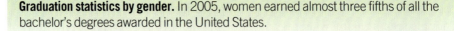

Figure 8.3

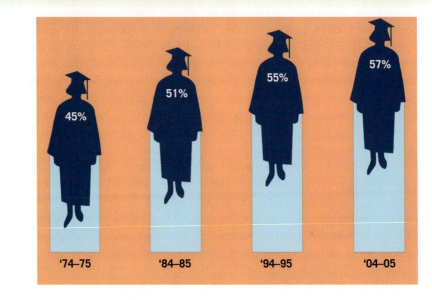

Graduation statistics by gender. In 2005, women earned almost three fifths of all the bachelor's degrees awarded in the United States.

45%   51%   55%   57%

'74–75   '84–85   '94–95   '04–05

- Girls consistently outperform boys in reading and writing.
- More than half of all bachelor's degrees given today are awarded to females (see Figure 8.3).
- More females than males plan to attend graduate school or professional school after completion of their bachelor's degrees.

Supporters of the notion that there is a "boy problem" have placed some of the blame on the curriculum, saying that it emphasizes reading and writing, which are subjects where girls usually outperform boys (Sax, 2007; Von Drehle, 2007); that the books used in school don't interest or appeal to boys as much as they appeal to girls; or that schools are cutting things like science labs, physical education, and recess (activities that favor the experiential learning style of boys) in favor of more of the conventional reading and writing activities (Sax, 2007; Von Drehle, 2007). Consequently there have been calls to create a more "boy-friendly" classroom (Martino & Kehler, 2006). The environment outside of school can also be a factor. Boys spend more time on activities like video games that don't require reading skills, so these skills have less chance to develop outside of the classroom (Rideout, Foehr, Roberts, & Brodie, 1999). Girls, by contrast, are more likely to read for pleasure outside of school (Organisation for Economic Co-operation and Development, 2009).

Others have looked to biological differences between boys and girls for an explanation for their different performance in school classrooms. For example, there is evidence from neurobiology that the developmental trajectory of male and female brains is different, and that the language centers in the brain of an average 5-year-old boy look more like the language centers in the brain of the average 3-year-old girl (Lenroot et al., 2007; Sax, 2007), which makes teaching reading to 5-year-old boys difficult or perhaps even developmentally inappropriate. When boys are not able to succeed at these tasks, it causes frustration, and they tend to avoid these activities in the future.

However, when the issue of boys' school performance was carefully reexamined, the picture became more complicated. Sara Mead (2006) reanalyzed some of the statistics on school performance and came to the conclusion that boys from middle-class or upper-middle-class families are, in fact, performing *better* in school than they have in the past, but the same is not true for minority boys or boys from disadvantaged families (see also Froschl & Sprung, 2008). It appears that the "boy problem" may be narrowed to these particular groups of boys. If we are concerned about differential performance in school, it is not enough to look only at differences between boys and girls. We also need to look at differences *within* groups of boys and *within* groups of girls because there is great diversity within those groups.

The Possible "Girl Problem" in Science and Math

We mentioned above that the concern about a possible "boy problem" in schools was a fairly recent one. By contrast, there is a very long-standing concern about a possible "girl problem" in math and science. Girls are less likely than boys to choose careers in science, technology, engineering, and math, known as STEM. For many years this difference was attributed to lower ability and less interest; however, we now have a very large body of research showing that girls take just as many science and math classes in high school as boys and perform in school at a similar level in both areas (Hill, Corbett, & St. Rose, 2010; Planty, Provasnik, & Daniel, 2007). Studies conducted in recent years have found that mathematical ability as measured by standardized tests was not significantly different in elementary school (Kenney-Benson, Pomerantz, Ryan, & Patrick, 2006; Lachance & Mazzocco, 2006) or middle school (Catsambis, 1994). Furthermore, girls frequently earn better grades in math classes than boys in elementary school and high school (Dwyer & Johnson, 1997; Kenney-Benson et al., 2006). Girls do perform slightly more poorly than boys on "high stakes math tests," including the SAT, the ACT, and the AP test (Hill et al., 2010, p. 5). We will discuss later the concept called stereotype threat that may help explain why girls perform just as well as boys in class but continue to perform more poorly on these tests.

The one area of ability in which there are small but significant differences that favor boys is spatial relationships, and it has been argued that this difference is wired into the brains of boys and girls before birth. Traditionally, boys perform better on several aspects of spatial relationships including mental rotation. The type of test that has been used to assess this ability is shown in Figure 8.4 (Voyer, Voyer, & Bryden, 1995). However, we know from Chapter 6 that our brains continue to develop throughout childhood in response to our experiences. Terlecki, Newcombe, and Little (2008) demonstrated that training girls on spatial skills using computer games based on shapes, such as Tetris, could produce large improvements in their abilities in this area. Although boys may have some genetic advantage in this area, training with girls can improve their performance significantly.

9. Throughout the elementary school years and into high school, girls do more poorly in math than boys. **TRUE/FALSE**

False. This is a very persistent myth, but in fact throughout elementary school and high school there are not significant differences in math grades for boys and girls.

Figure 8.4

Mental rotation tasks. Items such as the one below are one of the few types of tests that consistently show higher performance for boys than girls.

Look at this object:

Two of these four drawings show the same object. Can you find the two? Put a big X across them.

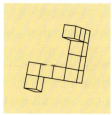

a   b   c   d

Answer: a and c

Despite our understanding that ability level does not clearly differentiate boys and girls, the idea that boys are better than girls at math persists (Else-Quest, Hyde, & Linn, 2010), and the number of girls who enter STEM careers continues to be relatively low. Although 60% of bachelor's degrees are awarded to women, they earn only 20% of the degrees in engineering, computer science, and physics (St. Rose, 2010). Ability may not be the only factor at work here. We also need to consider factors such as attitudes, beliefs, and preferences (Dai, 2006). It is these affective dimensions that often determine where we choose to focus our attention and to place our effort. We again find that in the earlier grades, both boys and girls say that they equally enjoy science (Greenfield, 1997; Slate & Jones, 1998) and both genders have positive attitudes toward math (Fendrich-Salowey, Buchanan, & Drew, 1982; Paulsen & Johnson, 1983), but girls are more likely than boys to be anxious about their ability to perform well in math (Tiedemann, 2000).

There is evidence that with age girls may increasingly buy into the misconception that girls are not as good at math as boys are. Muzzatti and Agnoli (2007) asked elementary school children about their beliefs about boys' ability and girls' ability to do well in math. They report that in second grade boys said that boys' ability was equal to girls' ability, but girls said that girls' ability exceeded boys' ability. In third grade, boys now said that boys' ability exceeded girls' ability, and girls now thought that the ability of boys and girls was equal. However, by fourth grade, boys said that boys' ability exceeded girls' ability, and girls now agreed with them that boys were better at math than girls. Boys and girls both seem to share—and increasingly believe—this common misperception. One outcome is that girls whose math ability is equal to that of boys perceive themselves as less skilled and are less likely to choose a career they believe requires that skill (Correll, 2004; Hill et al., 2010). However, peers also play a role in girls' interest in science and math. Girls who have friends who do well in school are more likely to take advanced math classes (Crosnoe, Riegle-Crumb, Field, Frank, & Muller, 2008).

Where do these ideas come from? In large part, they come from the girls' social environment, including home and school. There is evidence that within the school environment, girls are treated differently than boys, especially in science and math classes, in ways that subtly devalue their ideas and contributions. For instance, in science classes, boys receive more attention than girls, are called on more frequently, and are given more detailed feedback from their teachers (Greenfield, 1997; Jones & Wheatley, 1990; Kahle & Lakes, 1983). Hsiao-Ching She (2000) reported that in a biology class in Taiwan, boys answered 4 times more questions from the teacher than girls, tended to call out answers rather than waiting to be called upon, were called on more frequently by the teacher when they raised their hands, and received 8 times more feedback from the teacher to clarify their answers than girls received. Do you see how this differential treatment over time would discourage girls from participating in class?

Parents' attitudes and beliefs are another important factor. Parents' views of their children's ability are an important influence on how their children assess their own abilities (Tiedemann, 2000). In a way, the parents' stereotyped beliefs become another source of a self-fulfilling prophecy for their children's behavior. They see girls as less capable in math. If their daughters, in turn, begin to see themselves as others see them, they come to believe that they are less capable and may exert less effort or express more dislike for math, and the prophecy is fulfilled when they perform more poorly. Jacquelynne Eccles claims that parents provide many types of messages that undermine their daughters' confidence in their math and science abilities, as well as their interest in pursuing careers in these fields (Jacobs, Davis-Kean, Bleeker, Eccles, & Malanchuk, 2005). When they offer uninvited help with their daughters' math homework, the girls are more likely to perceive their math abilities negatively (Bhanot & Jovanovic, 2005). Even when girls are doing well in these classes, parents tend to attribute their daughters' success to the girls' hard work. By contrast they attribute their sons' success to both talent and effort (Jacobs et al., 2005). Which type of career would you want to pursue? One that you had to work hard at, or one that you were good at? Even when boys and girls are equally successful, they get different messages about *why* they are successful.

The anxiety that results for girls from the prevalent stereotype (which seems to be out of line with girls' actual ability) is linked to the idea of **stereotype threat**. This notion suggests that girls become aware of the stereotyped idea that girls are not good at math or science. When they take a difficult math test, like the SAT, ACT, or AP test, they become anxious because they begin to think that they are proving the stereotype to be correct. Anxiety and high math performance do not go well together, and the girls' performance goes down. However, when girls are specifically told that the test does not reflect anything about girls' and boys' abilities, girls' performance remains equal to that of boys as shown in Figure 8.5 (Spencer, Steele, & Quinn, 1999).

Girls may avoid STEM careers for a number of reasons. They may not want to try careers in which they have to deal with the anxiety of stereotype threat. In order to test the effects of stereotype threat on career choice, college women were shown either commercials that confirmed the stereotype that women are worse at math and science than men or neutral commercials. When they were then asked to choose a career area, women in the first group were more likely than those who saw the neutral commercials to choose careers that did not involve math and science (Davies, Spencer, Quinn, & Gerhardstein, 2002).

Another factor in career choice is that high school girls are more likely than boys to say that their goal in life is to help people and, in general, they don't see science and math as a means to do so (Hill et al., 2010). The one exception is in biology, because many hope to use biology to become doctors or other health professionals (Miller, Slawinski Blessing, & Schwartz, 2006). In general, girls tend to see science as a solitary profession and link it with violence and "blowing

Stereotype threat The anxiety that results when individuals feel they are behaving in ways that confirm stereotyped expectations of a group with which they identify.

Girls and science. Young girls are as interested in science as boys. To sustain this interest, many programs have been developed to encourage girls to enter the fields of math and science.

Figure 8.5

Stereotype threat and math performance. When given a difficult test in math, women who were told that the test reflected gender differences had lower performance relative to men than women who were told that there were no gender differences for this test.

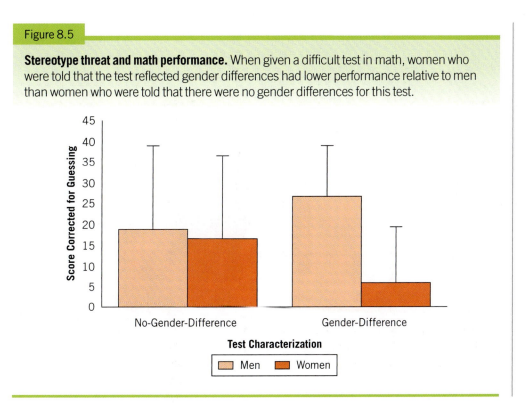

things up" (Miller et al., 2006), and they connect both of these with being male. In addition, as one young woman interested in engineering stated, "It's intimidating being a girl who wants to go into the engineering field when it is definitely a male-dominated career" (Britsch, Callahan, & Peterson, 2010, p. 13). With very few women professionals in these fields, the girls also lack models and mentors to encourage them to pursue careers in the sciences (Blackwell, 2010; Else-Quest et al., 2010).

Video Link 8.7
Promoting girls' interest in science.

There is much being done to encourage girls to enter careers in the STEM fields. Even the Barbie® doll, the standard-bearer for female stereotypes, has begun to take an active role in promoting nonstereotypical roles for girls. Whereas in the past she was programmed to say, "Math class is tough!" more recently the Society of Women Engineers and the National Academy of Engineering helped design a new Computer Engineer Barbie. Commenting on the new Barbie, Rebecca Zook (2010) states that the "false dichotomy—that you have to choose between being feminine and 'looking the part' of a mathematician or scientist—might be part of what turns girls off from math and science in the first place" (para. 6).

Another successful intervention teaches girls that the brain is like a muscle that will grow when it is exercised rather than something that is fixed and unchangeable. When girls receive this intervention, the gender gap on standardized tests in math disappears (Good, Aronson, & Inzlicht, 2003). This new understanding counteracts the stereotype that girls are just not good at these subjects and helps them overcome the effects of stereotype threat.

In the past decade, over 400 intervention projects have been sponsored by the National Science Foundation and the American Association of University Women (AAUW) Educational Foundation and have generally been successful in improving girls' involvement and success in these fields (Darke, Clewell, & Sevo, 2002). Recommendations to improve these interventions include training teachers so that they can incorporate more gender equity projects directly into the school curriculum rather than having these programs outside the regular school day (AAUW Educational Foundation, 2004).

Single-Gender Classrooms

Video Link 8.8
Girls discuss science classes.

Many schools are working at developing alternative classroom environments and activities that equally meet the needs of both boys and girls. In 2006, U.S. Secretary of Education Margaret Spellings announced new regulations that allowed for the development of single-gender

Single-gender classrooms. If girls and boys have different learning styles, they may do better in single-gender classrooms that are tailored to their needs. What do you think children gain—and lose—by being in a single-gender classroom?

classrooms or schools within the public school system (U.S. Department of Education, 2006). Some see this as a possible solution to some of the problems that both boys and girls have because classrooms that are made up only of one sex will be structured to better fit their educational needs. However, critics of this move charge that there are many more similarities between the genders than there are differences between them (Paulson & Teicher, 2006). They fear that this new interpretation of Title IX will roll back gains that have occurred since this landmark legislation that barred sex discrimination in schools (AAUW, 2009). We are still searching for educational solutions that are fair to all: boys and girls, rich and poor, minority and nonminority students.

School Dropouts and the "Forgotten Half"

Since 1988 the National Center for Education Statistics has compiled information on high school completion and dropout rates. In a recent report (Planty et al., 2007), the Center notes that the dropout rate has continued to decline but, as Figure 8.6 shows, students from low-income families are about 6 times more likely to drop out of high school than students from high-income families. Students attending metropolitan urban schools also have an 18% lower graduation rate than the students in surrounding suburban areas (America's Promise Alliance, 2009), and dropout rates are higher for Black and Hispanic students than for White and Asian/ Pacific Islander students. However, according to Child Trends (2010), a nonprofit, nonpartisan research center that studies children and families, the dropout rate for Black students reached a historic low of 9% in 2007, and between 1998 and 2007, the dropout rate for Hispanic students decreased from 30% to 21%. Another bit of good news here is that one study found that 63% of students who drop out of high school go on to eventually pass their GED (General Educational Development test) within 8 years of their original anticipated graduation date (Child Trends,

10. Most students who drop out of high school go on to eventually complete their high school education. **TRUE/FALSE**

True. The chances of a dropout completing high school by completing his or her GED are fairly good. One study found that almost two thirds of students who drop out of high school earn their GED within 8 years of their original anticipated graduation date.

Video Link 8.9
Students at risk for dropping out.

Figure 8.6

High school dropout rates, 1972–2007. Although the high school dropout rate has decreased for all groups of students in the last three decades, students from low-income families continue to be at a substantially higher risk than students from middle-class or upper-class families.

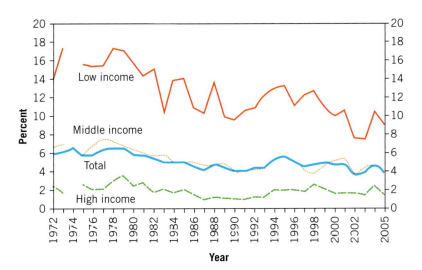

NOTE: The event dropout rate indicates the percentage of youth ages 15–24 who dropped out of Grades 10–12 in the 12 months between one October and the next (for example, October 2004 to October 2005). Dropping out is defined as leaving school without a high school diploma or equivalent credential (for example, a GED).

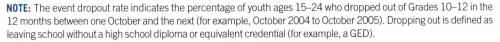

2010). But, of course, it would be in everyone's interest to find ways to keep these students in school so they successfully complete their education sooner rather than later.

In a recent study, a group of researchers examined school records to determine whether there were developmental pathways that distinguished between high school graduates and dropouts (Hickman, Bartholomew, Mathwig, & Heinrich, 2008). The differences they discovered do not seem too surprising. Students who eventually dropped out of high school performed more poorly on standardized tests and received lower course grades than graduates, had higher levels of grade retention and absenteeism, and had more problem behaviors. What was more surprising was the origin of these differences. They began in kindergarten and persisted throughout elementary school, with the gap between future dropouts and their peers who would graduate on time widening as the students moved into middle school and continued into high school. These findings suggest that programs of early intervention, such as Head Start, do *not* start too early because the origins of eventual school dropout arise very early in a child's school career.

Although the dropout rate has been declining, there still is reason to be concerned about it and to look for ways to reduce it further. One student every 26 seconds significantly limits his or her future earnings potential by deciding to drop out (America's Promise Alliance, 2009). Young people who do not complete high school are ill equipped for employment in today's marketplace. They are more likely to be unemployed than high school graduates, and when they are employed, they earn less and hold jobs with less occupational status (Child Trends, 2010).

In 1988, the American Youth Policy Forum drew attention to another group of students who may be at risk in a different way. These students are called the **forgotten half**. They are high school students who *do* graduate from high school but who do not continue their education by going to college. The American Youth Policy Forum felt that these high school students were being shortchanged by the school system because they were not adequately prepared for the transition from school to work (see also America's Promise Alliance, 2009). Consequently there have been calls for our schools to do a better job of preparing students who do not initially intend to continue their education beyond high school.

Because the number of high school students who do continue their education beyond high school has increased since the date of the initial report, the forgotten half has now become the "forgotten third," but the economic prospects for those students are even more bleak than they were for earlier cohorts of students (Jennings & Rentner, 1998) because of the changing nature of the job market.

In a number of European countries, students who do not plan to go to college enter apprentice programs that provide "a multi-year sequence of work-based and school-based learning opportunities providing formal certification of participants' competence" (Hamilton & Hamilton, 1997, p. 1) at the end of their training. There are few programs like this for students in the United States.

The School-to-Work Opportunities Act of 1994 sought to create a school program that would support non-college-bound students by facilitating their transition from school into productive careers (Hamilton & Hamilton, 1999). The intent of the legislation was to provide work-based experiences to *all* students starting in kindergarten and continuing through high school. These experiences fall into three broad categories: (a) visits to workplaces (this includes field trips and **job shadowing** of people who work in various occupations), (b) work-like experiences (this includes service learning, unpaid internships, and youth-run enterprises), and (c) employment (this includes youth jobs that provide employment but not training opportunities, subsidized employment training, cooperative education and paid internships, and youth apprenticeships) (Hamilton & Hamilton, 1997). Such an approach would allow students, regardless of their eventual level of education, to learn about the career options available to them, and this information could better inform their decisions as they move through the educational system.

Forgotten half   High school students who graduate from high school and do not continue their education by going to college but are not well prepared for the transition to work.

Job shadowing   A way to learn about a career by spending time watching a person who is working in that career.

Conclusion

In this chapter we examined how we define and assess intelligence. This included a discussion of the controversy about the relative contributions of genetics and environment. We looked at the full range of intelligence, from children who are intellectually challenged to those who are gifted and talented. In the process, we examined the type of educational opportunities given to these children by our educational system. We also looked at creativity and its relationship to intelligence. Finally, we reviewed the research findings regarding a number of educational policies and practices that are designed to promote learning within the school context and discussed some of the controversies within the field about these topics.

CHAPTER SUMMARY

1. **How do we define intelligence?**

   Intelligence has been a difficult concept to define and operationalize. Definitions usually include the idea that it involves the ability to solve problems and to successfully adapt to our environment so that we can achieve our goals. Debate has centered on whether there is one general underlying factor "g" or whether intelligence comprises a set of relatively independent abilities or skills. The "g" factor is further divided into **fluid intelligence** and **crystallized intelligence**.

2. **What is the relative influence of genetics and environment on intelligence?**

   There has been considerable controversy surrounding this topic. Although both factors make a contribution, their relative contribution appears to change over the course of development with genetic factors being more influential in the early years and environmental factors more influential later on. Genes are thought to set the potential for a range of outcomes (called the **range of reaction**), while it is the environment that determines where within that range the individual falls. Although IQ tests are effective at predicting a child's potential academic achievement, other factors (such as the ability to delay gratification) may predict as well as or even better than IQ tests.

3. **What are the theory of multiple intelligences and triarchic theory?**

   Two theories of intelligence assume that there is a set of abilities or "intelligences" that are relatively independent. The **theory of multiple intelligences** proposes at least nine types of skills or abilities, whereas **triarchic theory** proposes three (analytical, creative, and practical abilities). **Creative intelligence** depends upon **divergent thinking**, rather than **convergent thinking** as required by most standardized tests of intelligence. Although these theories have impacted educational practices, to date there is not strong empirical support for their theoretical constructs or their effectiveness as a teaching approach.

4. **How does poverty affect academic achievement?**

   A number of problems associated with poverty have a negative impact on academic achievement. The Head Start program is an attempt to overcome some of the problems to help young children get off to a good start in school. To do this, Head Start works with the family and the whole child. Initial research found improvement in IQ scores for Head Start participants, but the effects dissipated over a few years. However, more recent longitudinal research has found long-term benefits in terms of academic achievement and fewer school and behavioral problems.

5. **What are some of the issues surrounding the best ways to promote learning in school?**

   One issue has been the role of class size in student achievement. Reduction in class size is more beneficial for low-performing students, but all students can benefit from having a well-qualified teacher who can devote time and attention to individual students. Grade retention is another issue. **Social promotion** moves children along even when they haven't mastered the material, and **academic redshirting** is a voluntary decision to delay entry into school to give a child additional time to mature. The early research on **expectancy effects** found that a teacher's belief about a child's ability could become a **self-fulfilling prophecy**, although the effect is small. However, the expectancies of extraordinary teachers can be a transforming experience for students. There also is a debate about the effect of **ability grouping** in the classroom. **Cooperative learning** appears to be more beneficial for the low-performing students in the group than the high-performing students.

6. Why do some people think our schools have a "boy problem"?

The possible "boy problem" has to do with the fact that in some ways it is more difficult for a boy to be successful in school than it is for a girl. Some attribute the problem to the curriculum, which is a better fit with the skills and interests of girls, but others have attributed it to biological differences. Whatever the cause, the problem is greater for boys from disadvantaged families.

7. Why do some people think we have a "girl problem" in schools?

The "girl problem" involves the fact that, despite grades in math and sciences and a level of interest in these subjects that are similar for boys and girls in the early grades, girls are less likely to continue taking advanced math classes or to prepare for careers in science, technology, engineering, or mathematics. The **stereotype threat** presented by subjects that girls *think* they aren't good at may contribute to these decisions. Other factors, including differential treatment in science and math classes by teachers and low expectations of parents and peers, may also dissuade girls from pursuing math and science in school.

8. Who is most likely to drop out of school, and who are the "forgotten half"?

Although the dropout rate in the United States has continued to decline in recent years, low-income students and Hispanic students are more likely to drop out of high school than other groups of students. Fortunately many dropouts eventually earn a GED. Students who drop out usually have a long history of school-related problems, sometimes beginning as early as kindergarten. The **forgotten half** are those students who graduate from high school but do not go on to college and may not be well prepared for entrance into the workforce. There have been attempts to develop programs similar to the European model of apprenticeships to improve the quality of high school programs.

Go to **www.sagepub.com/levine** for additional exercises and video resources. Select **Chapter 8, Intelligence and Academic Achievement,** for chapter-specific activities.

chapter 9

Language Development

9

From their very first cries, human beings communicate with the world around them. Infants communicate through sounds (crying and cooing) and through body language (pointing and other gestures). However, sometime between 8 and 18 months of age, a major developmental milestone occurs when infants begin to use words to speak. Words are symbolic representations; that is, when a child says "table," we understand that he is referring to a specific thing, and we don't have to see that object. The word represents the object. **Language** can be defined as a system of symbols that is used to communicate. Although language is used to communicate with others, we may also "talk to ourselves" and use words in our thinking. The words we use may influence the way we think about and understand our experiences.

Test Your Knowledge

Test your knowledge of child development by deciding whether each of the following statements is *true* or *false*, and then check your answers as you read the chapter.

1. **True/False:** Infants are born with a preference for listening to their native language.
2. **True/False:** A sensitive parent should be able to tell the difference between a baby who is crying because he is hungry and one who is crying because he is in pain or is lonely.
3. **True/False:** It is perfectly fine to use baby talk with infants.
4. **True/False:** Teaching babies to use sign language will delay development of spoken language.
5. **True/False:** If a young child says, "I goed outside," the child's parent will be most likely to say, "No, you meant to say, 'I *went* outside.'"
6. **True/False:** Using flash cards, repetition, and word drills is a good way to ensure that a child develops early literacy skills.
7. **True/False:** By the time they reach eighth grade, fewer than one third of students in the United States are reading at or above their grade level.
8. **True/False:** When young children use spelling that they have "invented" (rather than conventional spelling), it slows down their ability to learn how to spell correctly.
9. **True/False:** When a young child learns two languages at the same time, the extra effort it takes to learn the second language slows down the child's general cognitive development.
10. **True/False:** Most children who are learning disabled have average or above-average intelligence.

Correct answers: (1) True, (2) False, (3) True, (4) False, (5) False, (6) False, (7) True, (8) False, (9) False, (10) True

Language A system of symbols that is used to communicate with others or in our thinking.

After defining some basic aspects of language that we will use throughout the chapter, we will describe some of the theories that try to explain the amazing process by which we acquire and use language. We will then look at the brain's role in processing and producing language. After a description of the stages of language development—from a baby's first cries through the slang used by teenagers—we will look at the topic of bilingualism. We will examine how learning to speak more than one language affects a child's language development and how our educational system is trying to deal with the increasing number of bilingual children in the classroom. Finally, we will end the chapter with information about disorders that can interfere with children's language development.

Aspects of Language

Phonology The study of the sounds of a language.

Syntax The grammar of a language.

Semantics The study of the meanings of words.

Pragmatics The rules that guide how we use language in social situations.

There are four basic aspects of language that have been studied: phonology, syntax, semantics, and pragmatics. **Phonology** is the study of the sounds of a language. (To remember this term, think of the sounds that come from your tele*phone*, or the word caco*phon*y, meaning a lot of loud, annoying sounds!) **Syntax** is the grammar of a language—that is, how we put words in order and how we change words (for example, *play* becomes *played* when we talk about the past) so they make sense to our listeners. **Semantics** is the meanings of words. **Pragmatics** is how we use language. For example, you probably speak in different ways to your professor, to your friends, and certainly to a 2-year-old. In each case, you are using language in a different way. When children develop the ability to communicate with language, they are developing all four of these areas (Gleason, 2005). They must understand and form the sounds of the language they are learning. They must learn what words mean and how to put them together so they make sense, and they must learn when and how to use language to accommodate to their listeners and to accomplish their goals. We will consider all of these aspects as we describe language development.

Morpheme The smallest unit in a language that has meaning.

Phoneme The smallest distinct sound in a particular language that signals differences between words.

Two basic units are central to the study of language and its development: morphemes and phonemes. A **morpheme** is the smallest unit that has meaning in a language. For example, the word *cats* has two morphemes: *cat* and *s*. *Cat* refers to the animal, and *s* means more than one. A **phoneme** is the smallest distinct sound in a particular language that signals differences between words. For example, *cat* and *bat* are clearly distinct words in English, as indicated by the different beginning sounds. Different languages have types of phonemes that are distinct. For instance, in Japanese, the length of a vowel can indicate a different word. The word *toko* means "bed," while *toko* with a long final *o* means "travel" (Sato, Sogabe, & Mazuka, 2010). In English, no matter how long we draw out the *a* in *cat*, it still means "cat."

Theories of Language Development

There are many different ideas about how children learn to talk and understand language, and many controversies persist to this day. We are still learning about how this amazing process can occur so quickly in the first years of life.

Behaviorism and Social Cognitive Learning Theory

If you were to take a survey of people on the street and ask them how children learn language, the chances are that many would answer "by imitation." Of course imitation must play an important role. After all, children learn the language that they hear, not some other language! The idea that language is learned through imitation is connected with Bandura's theory of social cognitive learning that we read about in Chapter 2. Imitation is the central learning principle of social cognitive theory.

According to B. F. Skinner (1957/1991), language is also shaped through operant conditioning, or reinforcement. When we respond to a baby's babbling with a smile or some vocalization of our own, babies babble even more. If we respond to a request for "cookie" with the desired cookie, it becomes more likely that the child will use that word again the next time she wants a cookie. If we remember that reinforcement is anything that makes a behavior continue, then it is clear that we reinforce the development of a child's language in many ways. Consistent with these ideas, research has shown that the more that mothers respond to their babies' vocalizations, the sooner their babies develop language (Tamis-LeMonda, Bornstein, & Baumwell, 2001).

A mother-infant "conversation." Social cognitive theory emphasizes the importance of social interaction for language learning. As this mother talks to her infant, she models using language to communicate, and the infant wants to imitate her mother to continue the fun.

Nativism

Noam Chomsky (1968) developed a theory that proposes that the human brain is innately wired to learn language. He believes that children could not learn something as complex as human language as quickly as they do unless there is already a grammatical structure for language hardwired in their brains before they ever hear human language. He calls this **universal grammar**. According to this theory, hearing spoken language triggers the activation of this structure and does more than just promote imitation. Chomsky believes that the language that we usually hear is not adequate to explain the construction of all of the rules of language that children quickly learn.

For instance, nativists such as Chomsky point to the evidence that children will say things they have never heard, such as "The cats eated the mouses" rather than "The cats ate the mice." We *hope* that children have never heard adults say something like "eated" or "mouses" and therefore they could not just be imitating language they have heard. However, you can easily see that, although the first sentence is grammatically incorrect, in some respects it *could be* correct. In English we do add -*ed* for the past tense and -*s* for plurals. However, we have exceptions to that rule, called irregular verbs or nouns. When children make this type of grammatical error they are showing that they have learned a pattern, but they are applying it to words that don't follow that pattern. This process of acting as if irregular words follow the regular rules is called **overregularization**. Children are creating these words from their own understanding of grammar, and Chomsky believes that the basic principles of grammar are innate.

Clearly, we do not all speak the same language and the rules for grammar are not the same in all languages, so how can there be a universal grammar? Chomsky believes that there are basic language principles that are hardwired in the brain, similar to the basic principles that underlie the operation of the hard drive of your computer. Just as your computer's hard drive can run many different types of software, the language structures in your brain can process the specific characteristics of many different languages.

Interactionism

A third approach incorporates aspects of both behaviorism and nativism. According to **interactionism**, both children's biological readiness to learn language and their experiences

Nativism A theory of language development that hypothesizes that human brains are innately wired to learn language and that hearing spoken language triggers the activation of a universal grammar.

Universal grammar A hypothesized set of grammatical rules and constraints proposed by Chomsky that is thought to underlie all languages and that is hardwired in the human brain.

Overregularization A type of grammatical error in which children apply a language rule to words that don't follow that rule or pattern (for example, adding an *s* to make the plural of a word like *foot*).

Interactionism A theory of language development that proposes that the child's biological readiness to learn language interacts with the child's experiences with language in the environment to bring about the child's language development.

with language in their environment come together to bring about language development. Just as we learned about how nature is expressed through nurture in Chapter 4, these theorists argue that both are equally necessary for the child to develop language and both must work together.

In addition, interactionism means that language is created socially, in the interaction between infant and adult. For example, adults naturally simplify their speech to young children not because they think "I need to teach this child how to speak!" but because the child then understands and responds to what the adult is saying. The adult is sensitive to the effectiveness of his communication so that when the child does not understand, he simplifies his language until the child does understand (Bohannon & Bonvillian, 2005). Research on mother-infant speech in a variety of cultures has found that mothers make many of the same modifications in their speech to infants, perhaps because these changes produce a good fit between the mother's speech and the infant's perceptual and cognitive capabilities (Fernald & Morikawa, 1993). In addition, adults often repeat what children say but **recast** it into more advanced grammar. For example, a child might say, "More cookie," and the adult might respond, "Oh, do you want more cookies?" In the process, he is modeling a slightly higher level of language proficiency, which the child can then imitate. The child in this example might then say, "Want more cookies."

Cognitive Processing Theory

The question has been raised whether social interaction is enough to explain how children learn language. Another point of view is that learning language is a process of "data crunching," in which children take in and process the language they hear (Hoff & Naigles, 2002, p. 422). These theorists argue that infants are processing language even during the first year of life, before they can speak (Naigles et al., 2009). Therefore, their understanding of language is learned and is not innate as Chomsky's theory asserts. These theorists would say that although the learning may be *motivated* by social interaction, the actual process of learning words and their meanings may rely more on the computational ability of the human brain. Hoff and Naigles (2002) found that toddlers' language learning was not related to the level or nature of social engagement between them and their mothers. Rather, the toddlers they studied learned more words when their mothers exposed them to more language; that is, they talked to them more and used more different words and longer, more complex utterances. Cognitive processing theorists argue that language learning happens independently of mothers' responsiveness to their children's speech and of children's social abilities. They point to the fact that even socially limited children with autism can still develop language as evidence that language development is not dependent on social interaction.

One basic question that this approach has addressed is how infants learn to differentiate words out of the stream of sounds they hear. Although we can see the spaces between words on a written page, these "spaces" are often not evident when we speak. For example, if you heard someone say, "Theelephantisdrinkingwater," how would you figure out that *elephant* is a separate word rather than *antis*? One answer is that infants' brains are constantly "crunching data"; that is, they are figuring out statistically how likely it is that certain sounds will follow each other (Saffran, Johnson, Aslin, & Newport, 1999). For example, when we hear *ele*, it is most often followed by *phant* or *vator*, while the entire word *elephant* can be followed in a sentence by many different sounds. Researchers have used made-up words embedded in random syllables to see whether adults, children, and infants can differentiate the "words" from the rest of the utterance (Saffran et al., 1999; Saffran, Newport, Aslin, Tunick, & Barrueco, 1997). Take a look at the "sentence" below and see if you can figure out what the "word" is:

Bupadapatubitutibubupadadutabapidabupada

Did you discover *bupada?* This is just a brief sample, but when people of all ages hear lengthy readings such as this they are able to pick out what the "words" are even though they have no

Recast To facilitate language learning, adults often repeat what children say but put it into more advanced grammar.

Cognitive processing theory The theory that learning language is a process of "data crunching," in which the actual process of learning words and their meanings relies on the computational ability of the human brain.

real meaning. As infants cannot be asked what a word is, they have been tested by seeing how long they listen to nonsense "words" (such as *bupada*) and how long they listen to random syllables after exposure to a stream of sounds such as that shown above. The consistent result is that they listen longer to the nonwords, which are newer and more interesting to them, than to the more familiar "words" (Aslin, Saffran, & Newport, 1998). Therefore, these researchers argue that our brains are designed like computers to automatically use statistical probability to pick out the words in a stream of speech.

Language and the Brain

As we learned in Chapter 6, there are two halves or hemispheres that comprise the human brain. The left hemisphere contains two areas that are central to language: Broca's area and Wernicke's area. As shown in Figure 9.1, **Broca's area**, which is involved in the production of speech, is located near the motor center of the brain that produces movement of the tongue and lips (Gleason, 2005). A person with damage to this area will have difficulty speaking, leaving out the "little words." For example, when a person with damage in Broca's area was asked about his upcoming weekend plans, he answered, "Boston. College. Football. Saturday" (Gleason, 2005, p. 17).

You can see in Figure 9.1 that **Wernicke's area**, which has to do with understanding and creating the meaning in speech, is located near the auditory center of the brain. Someone with damage to this area of the brain has no trouble producing words, but he has difficulty making

Broca's area The part of the brain that is involved in the physical production of speech.

Wernicke's area The part of the brain that has to do with understanding the meaning in speech.

Figure 9.1

Language centers of the brain. Broca's area (shown here in dark red), which controls speech production, is next to the motor cortex that controls movement. Wernicke's area (shown in pink), which controls language comprehension, is next to the auditory area that controls hearing.

Functional Areas of the Cerebral Cortex

1. **Visual Area:** Sight, Image recognition, Image perception
2. **Association Area** Short-term memory, Equilibrium, Emotion
3. **Motor Function Area** Initiation of voluntary muscles
4. **Broca's Area** Muscles of speech
5. **Auditory Area** Hearing
6. **Sensory Area** Sensation from muscles and skin
7. **Somatosensory Association Area** Evaluation of weight, texture, temperature, etc. for object recognition
8. **Wernicke's Area** Written and spoken language comprehension
9. **Motor Function Area** Eye movement and orientation
10. **Higher Mental Functions** Concentration, Planning, Judgment, Emotional expression, Creativity Inhibition
11. **Motor Functions** Coordination of movement, Balance and equilibrium, Posture

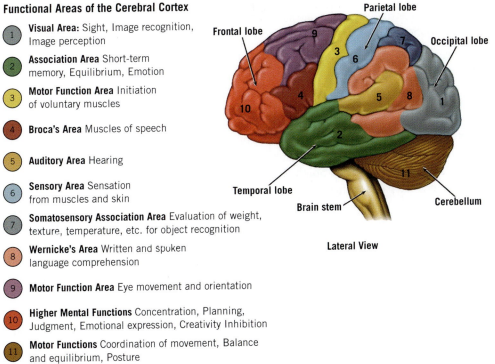

Lateral View

sense. For example, one patient with damage to Wernicke's area responded as follows to the question "What brings you to the hospital?"

> Boy I'm sweating, I'm awful nervous, you know, once in a while I get caught up, I can't mention the tarripoi, a month ago, quite a little, I've done a lot well, I impose a lot, while, on the other hand, you know what I mean, I have to run around, look it over, trebbin and all that sort of stuff. (Gardner, 1976, p. 68)

This patient speaks without any problem but is not making any sense and makes up words, such as *trebbin*.

The capabilities of these two regions do not develop at the same time. Infants *understand* words before they can *say* them. Another way we describe this is to say comprehension of language precedes production of language. When you tell a 1-year-old to put a toy in a box, she will most likely *understand* you and might follow your directions, yet she is not likely to be able to *say* anything close to "put the toy in the box." This differential between **receptive** and **expressive language** continues throughout life (Celce-Murcia & Olshtain, 2001). Even college students can understand a sophisticated or technical lecture in class, while their own speech and writing are likely to be less complex. The brain is not a simple organ, and we continue to learn about its complexity. For instance, although language is primarily handled by the left hemisphere of the brain, some aspects of language, such as recognition of the emotion in someone's words, are found in the right hemisphere (Gleason, 2005). Also, language functions may be distributed differently in women than in men. When researchers watched brain function using an fMRI (functional magnetic resonance imaging), they found that men responded to rhyming tasks with left-hemisphere activity, while women responded with activity from areas in both the left and the right hemispheres (Shaywitz et al., 1995).

Receptive language
The ability to understand words or sentences.

Expressive language The written or spoken language that we use to convey our thoughts, emotions, or needs.

Stages of Language Development

In this section we will describe the development of language, with particular focus on the ability to talk. We purposely de-emphasize the ages at which these developments occur because children differ enormously in the rate at which they develop language. Later in this chapter we will discuss when a caregiver should be concerned about language delays.

Prenatal Development

TRUE/FALSE

1. Infants are born with a preference for listening to their native language.

   True. Infants can hear before they are born, and they develop a preference for the sound patterns of the language they hear prenatally.

Of course babies do not speak before they are born, yet language learning appears to begin before birth. As we described in Chapter 6, during the last trimester of prenatal development the fetus can hear its mother's voice as shown by changes in fetal heart rate and motor activity when the mother is speaking, and this affects its preferences for language after birth in a number of ways (Karmiloff & Karmiloff-Smith, 2001). This was demonstrated in a study in which pregnant women read passages from the Dr. Seuss book *The Cat in the Hat* twice a day when they thought their fetus was awake (DeCasper & Spence, 1986). After the babies were born, those who had heard the story were more likely to try to elicit (by sucking a pacifier in a certain way) the sound of their mother reading *The Cat in the Hat* rather than a new poem they had never heard before. It appears that infants become familiar with and prefer "the rhythms and sounds of language" that they have heard prenatally (Karmiloff & Karmiloff-Smith, 2001, p. 43). As a result, within the first few days of life infants show a preference for the particular language their mother speaks, whether it is English, Arabic, or Chinese. This prenatal awareness of language sets the stage for language learning once the baby is born. In one study it was even shown that babies only 3–5 days old sound like the language they have been hearing when they cry. French babies cried from low pitch to high, while German babies cried from high pitch to low, mimicking the sounds of the language they hear (Mampe, Friederici, Christophe, & Wermke, 2009).

Infants' Preverbal Communication

Crying

Babies cry as soon as they are born. At first this is a reflexive behavior, not intentional communication from the infant. However, crying is not pleasant for adults to hear, so we are motivated to do what it takes to make it stop. The process of communication begins when babies begin to learn that crying can act as a signal that brings relief from hunger, discomfort, and loneliness.

Although babies cry for many reasons, there does not appear to be clear evidence that they have different cries for hunger, pain, or loneliness. Research shows only that parents differentiate the intensity and severity of crying, not the specific reason for the cry (Gustafson, Wood, & Green, 2000). Knowing this should bring relief to parents who have been told that they should recognize *why* their baby is crying but realize that they cannot.

Cooing

Between 2 and 4 months after birth, babies begin to make more pleasant sounds (Menn & Stoel-Gammon, 2005). The sounds they can make are limited because of aspects of their physiology, so they sound a bit like doves "cooing." At this stage they also begin to laugh, which is a great reward to parents! Infants at this stage begin to join in a prelanguage "conversation" with parents (Tamis-LeMonda, Cristofaro, Rodriguez, & Bornstein, 2006). The baby coos; the parent talks back; the baby looks and laughs; the parent smiles and talks. In this way, babies begin to learn how to *use* language even before they can speak.

Babbling

Babies typically begin to make one-syllable sounds, such as *ba* and *da*, when they are 4–6 months old and begin to combine those sounds (*baba, daga*) when they are 6–8 months old (Sachs, 2005). The most common consonant sounds are /b/, /d/, and /m/. At this point, parents get very excited, thinking that the baby means "daddy" when he says "dada" or "mommy" when he says "mama." Although it does not appear that these first vocalizations are meaningful, babies may start to learn their meaning because of the way their parents respond to these sounds (Menn & Stoel-Gammon, 2005). It is interesting to note that in languages from around the world, even among those with no common origins, the words for *father—dada* (English), *abba* (Hebrew), and *baba* (Mandarin Chinese)—and *mother—mama* (English), *ahm* (Arabic), and *manah* (Greek)—start with the earliest sounds babies make.

Bababa changes to *daDAW ee derBEH* as babbling begins to sound more and more like the language the baby is hearing (maybe the second phrase sounds like *the doggie under the bed*) and *not* like other languages. Although babies initially are able to make all the sounds in languages around the world, at this point a baby growing up with English will not produce the type of /r/ sounds used in French or Spanish because the baby is not hearing those sounds in the language environment. Now the feedback from hearing speech plays more of a role in language development than it did earlier. Deaf babies will babble early on, but at the age when hearing babies increase the variety of their sounds, deaf babies do not because they are not receiving this language input from their environment (Menn & Stoel-Gammon, 2005). On the other hand, deaf babies who are learning sign language appear to go through the same stages of language learning as hearing babies, in this case "babbling" with hand gestures instead of sounds.

How Adults Foster Language Development

Before we continue our description of the stages of language development, let's take a focused look at the role that adults play in fostering young children's language development. In many cultures, adults begin to shape infants' developing language ability by talking to them, even when it is clear that the babies do not understand. Adults act as if they do understand and carry

2. A sensitive parent should be able to tell the difference between a baby who is crying because he is hungry and one who is crying because he is in pain or is lonely. **TRUE/FALSE**

False. Infants' crying can differ in intensity and severity, but there does not appear to be a specific cry to signal hunger, pain, or loneliness. Even sensitive parents usually can't make these distinctions.

Video Link 9.1
Cooing.

Video Link 9.2
Babbling.

Video Links 9.3 and 9.4
Babbling and talking.

Laying the foundation for speech. This mother is laying the foundation for her infant's later speech. What is the infant learning about language from this interaction?

Child-directed speech Speech that is tailored to fit the sensory and cognitive capabilities of infants and children so that it holds their attention; includes speaking in a higher pitch with exaggerated intonation and a singsong rhythm and using a simplified vocabulary.

TRUE/FALSE

3. It is perfectly fine to use baby talk with infants.

True. The way that adults often talk to babies—in a high-pitched voice, with a great deal of exaggeration, and in a singsong rhythm—is actually well suited to the hearing capabilities and preferences of a baby. Babies pay attention to us when we talk this way, and doing it will not delay their language development.

on conversations, taking turns with whatever the baby responds. Karmiloff and Karmiloff-Smith (2001) provide the following illustration:

Mother: Oh, so you're HUNgry, are you?
(*Baby kicks.*)

Mother: YES, you ARE hungry. WELL, we'll have to give you some MILK then, won't we?
(*Baby coos.*)

Mother: Ah, so Mommy was RIGHT. It's MILK you want. Shall we change your diaper first?
(*Baby kicks.*)

Mother: RIGHT! A clean diaper. THAT's what you want. GOOD girl. (p. 48)

This type of exchange provides the baby with early experience with the back-and-forth of dialogue that will be important in later speech, but we must be careful about concluding that what adults do is the *most* important factor for children's developing speech. Research with some cultures, such as the Gusii people of Kenya, shows that parents in these cultures speak to their babies much less often than American parents, but their infants still develop language. In fact, when LeVine and his colleagues (1994) instructed Gusii mothers to talk and play with their babies while they were videotaped, they complied but said "it was of course silly to talk to a baby" (p. 210). However, Gusii children become as proficient with their language as American children are with English despite these different early experiences with language. There are many roads to language competence, and we must be careful not to apply one standard to all people.

Child-Directed Speech

The special way that we talk to infants and young children was once referred to as *motherese*. However, since we have found that in most cultures, *all* adults, and children too, change the way they speak to infants and young children, this type of speech is now known as **child-directed speech** (Fernald & Morikawa, 1993). Think about how you talk to babies or how you see others do so. You are unlikely to approach a baby and say in a low, monotone voice, "Hello, baby, how are you today? I hope you are having a fine day."

You would be much more likely to say, "Hel-LO, BAAAA-BEEEE. How are YOU today?" Child- or infant-directed speech is quite different from the way we talk to our friends. Some people believe that these changes are harmful to infants, teaching them the wrong way to speak, but the evidence is that what we naturally do in this way actually fosters language development (Fernald & Morikawa, 1993; Rowe, 2008).

When we talk to babies we generally talk in a higher-pitched voice and exaggerate the ups and downs of our pitch, like a roller coaster. In one study, if 4-month-old babies turned their head in one direction they would hear regular adult speech. If they turned their head in the other direction they would hear child-directed speech. Most infants turned more often in the direction that started the child-directed speech (Fernald, 1985). This finding supports the idea that the reason that we speak in this silly way is because infants pay more attention to us when we do. Although adults in some cultures do not tend to talk to their babies, Fernald (1985) reports that this type of child-directed speech has been found in cultures in America,

Europe, Africa, and Asia. Changing our speech in this way creates a "good fit" with the sensory and cognitive capabilities of the infant and helps hold the infant's attention when we are talking to him (Fernald & Morikawa, 1993). An interesting variation is found among the Kaluli of Papua New Guinea. Although the Kaluli tend not to talk *to* their babies in this way, they hold up the babies to face people and use a similar type of speech to speak *for* the baby (Feld & Shieffelin, 1998). Whether we are talking *with* our baby or talking *for* our baby, either approach shows the infant that speech is a type of interaction between people.

Shared Attention, Gestures, and Sign Language

In the first months after birth, infants are focused mostly on their own bodies and on interaction with the people in their world. At about 6 months they begin to develop more interest in the objects and events around them. At this point, caregivers begin to talk about what the infant sees as both infant and caregiver gaze at objects and events. When babies look or point at what they see, adults tend to label what it is for them (Goldfield & Snow, 2005). In fact, one researcher has referred to pointing as "the royal road," if not the only road, to language development (Butterworth, 2003, p. 9).

Pointing is just one of the gestures that children use to communicate. Infants use many gestures before they can speak, and continue to use them along with speech (Volterra, Caselli, Capirci, & Pizzuto, 2005). In recent years, parents have begun to take advantage of the fact that babies use gestures to communicate before they are capable of speaking by introducing forms of sign language. Nonverbal "signs" are representations that have meaning, just like words. Using signs can reduce frustration for both parent and child when the child can sign what she wants instead of crying. One concern some people have is that babies will rely on these signs and this will delay development of spoken language, but research has shown that this is not true. In fact, babies taught to sign may have a slight advantage in their early spoken language learning (Goodwyn, Acredolo, & Brown, 2000).

Although most parents gesture as they talk to their infants, the amount and type of gesturing differs from parent to parent. Rowe and Goldin-Meadow (2009) found that parents in families of higher socioeconomic status (SES) use gestures with their infants to communicate a broader range of meaning than parents from families of lower SES. In turn, the children from the higher-SES families used more gestures to communicate meaning by 14 months of age, and this difference in gesturing at 14 months predicted differences in the size of the children's vocabulary at 4½ years of age, when they were about to begin kindergarten. Gesturing may enhance language learning in several ways. First, when a child points to an object and a parent "translates" that gesture into a word by naming the object, that word enters the child's vocabulary sooner (Rowe & Goldin-Meadow, 2009). On the other hand, just using gestures without parental naming also enhances vocabulary development. Iverson and Goldin-Meadow (2005) found that when children use a gesture, such as flapping their hands to signify a bird, the actual word *bird* tends to show up about 3 months later. The representation of the idea through gesturing may help the child learn the word meaning and eventually say and use the word.

There also are cultural differences in the use of gestures. For example, Italians tend to use many more gestures than Americans (Iverson, Capirci, Volterra, & Goldin-Meadow, 2008). However, Iverson et al. (2008) found that gesturing seemed to serve the same purpose in both

What is this toddler saying? Toddlers use pointing as a way of communicating before they have words. We don't know what this child is pointing at, but his mother is sure to tell him all about it.

4. Teaching babies to use sign language will delay development of spoken language. **TRUE/FALSE**

False. In fact, there is some evidence that learning to sign actually helps babies' spoken language development.

Video Link 9.5
Sign language.

Baby signing "more." Although babies' ability to say words is limited, this photo shows that they can learn to communicate with signs borrowed from American Sign Language.

populations. For both Italians and Americans, the child's use of gestures together with speech was predictive of the development of the next stage of language development: two-word utterances.

The rate at which children develop language is related to the nature of their interaction with their parents. Children develop language more quickly if their parents talk to them, but more specifically if their parents respond to their interests, for example by naming what they are actually looking at rather than something else. Parents and infants who develop the ability to engage each other in a dynamic way, following each other's leads from one focus of attention to the next, seem to foster language development most effectively (Hoff & Naigles, 2002). Let us now return to our description of the stages of language development as we look at the acquisition of words and sentences.

Toddlers' Development of Words and Sentences

Babbling sometimes leads directly to babies' first words. The sounds they play with while babbling may be the sounds they use for the first words they say (Menn & Stoel-Gammon, 2005). Through their interactions with caregivers, infants begin to associate words with familiar objects and people. When infants as young as 6 months were shown side-by-side videos of their mother and their father but heard either the word *mommy* or the word *daddy*, they spent more time looking at the parent who was being named (Tincoff & Jusczyk, 1999). However, this behavior did *not* transfer to other men and women, so it appears that for the infant the word *mommy* refers to a specific woman, not all women. Remember that comprehension of language precedes the production of language. While infants begin to *understand* words at about 9 months, they do not begin to *say* words, on average, until about 13 months (Tamis-LeMonda et al., 2006). First words may be "made up" by the baby and may not correspond to an adult word. For example, one baby referred to any motorized vehicle as a *gogo*, and *baba* meant water. When the family took him through a car wash, he created a new word combination out of these two made-up words to describe his experience. He called it a *baba-gogo*!

Growth of Vocabulary

At 1 year, babies typically have only a few words, but by 2 years of age they generally have between 200 and 500 words (Fernald, Pinto, Swingley, Weinberg, & McRoberts, 2001). Although they initially learn new words slowly, over this second year of life they begin to learn them more quickly (Ganger & Brent, 2004). For some babies, the learning of new words explodes in what has been called a **vocabulary burst**, but for others the learning is more gradual. This is one of those aspects of development where there is quite a wide range that falls within what would be considered normal. Later in this chapter, we will describe some patterns of language development that fall outside of this normal range and can indicate serious problems, but language delays are not uncommon or necessarily a sign of a disorder.

How do toddlers manage to master their native language so quickly? First, it is during the second year that children begin to understand that words are symbols that stand for objects in the world (Woodward, Markman, & Fitzsimmons, 1994). This provides a strong incentive for children to acquire and use language. Second, researchers have described several assumptions and principles that children use, which seem to facilitate this process. These assumptions

Vocabulary burst
The rapid growth of a child's vocabulary that often occurs in the second year.

are called **constraints** because they limit or constrain the alternatives that the child considers when learning a new word, and this makes the process of acquiring vocabulary easier (Woodward et al., 1994). One of these constraints is the **whole object bias**. When a child sees a giraffe for the first time and someone points to the animal and says "giraffe," the child assumes the word describes the entire animal—not its strange, long neck; not its skinny legs; and not its brown spots. Children make this assumption even when the new object obviously has two parts to it, and even if one of the parts is more prominent than the other (Hollich, Golinkoff, & Hirsh-Pasek, 2007). Another constraint is the **mutual exclusivity constraint**. Children assume that there is one (and only one) name for an object. If they hear a novel word, they assume the new word describes an object that they do not already know the name for because the object wouldn't have two different names (Hansen & Markman, 2009).

The **taxonomic constraint** leads children to assume that two objects that have features in common can have a name in common, but that each object also can have its own individual name (Markman, 1990). For example, both dogs and cats have four legs and a tail and are covered with fur so they are both *animals*, but they each have some unique characteristics that distinguish between them so they also can have their own individual name.

As children apply these principles to their acquisition of new words, they can quickly learn new words, often based on a single exposure, in a process called **fast mapping**. The constraints allow the child to form an initial hypothesis, which can be tested in future situations that provide a basis for rapid acquisition of words (Pan, 2005). The first time a child sees a bus but says "truck," someone will probably point out how a bus and a truck are different. As the child continues to see buses, the use of that particular word will be quickly refined.

English-speaking children typically add nouns to their vocabulary before they add verbs. Nouns are thought to be easier to learn because they refer to objects in the child's world and the child has realized that things should have names (Woodward et al., 1994). However, children learning other languages do not necessarily follow this pattern. In Asian languages such as Korean, nouns can be omitted. In English, nouns often appear at the end of a sentence (for example, "Get the *book*" or "Throw the *ball*"). In Korean and Japanese, verbs often appear at the end of sentences (Fernald & Morikawa, 1993). The end position in a sentence is considered more prominent and therefore easier to learn. This is one explanation for why American infants have larger noun vocabularies than infants from Asian countries at a comparable age, and why Asian infants have larger verb vocabularies.

However, grammatical differences between English and Japanese are not the only factor at work. Fernald and Morikawa (1993) observed several differences in mother-infant interactions that reflect cultural values. While American mothers tended to focus on teaching and naming objects in their speech with their infants, Japanese mothers were more interested in creating a sense of harmony in their interactions. They encouraged empathy by encouraging their infants to express positive feelings and mutual dependence by relying on baby talk more extensively and for longer duration than American mothers. Of course both groups of infants learn to use both nouns and verbs, but they learn them in a different way.

Just as infants can use fast mapping to learn new words, they can use specific types of fast mapping called **syntactic bootstrapping** to use syntax to learn the meaning of new words (Gleitman, 1990) and **semantic bootstrapping** to use conceptual categories (action words or object names) to create grammatical categories (verbs or nouns) (Pinker, 1984). To pull yourself up by your bootstraps is an expression that means to solve a problem using your own resources. In this case, children use knowledge that they have in one domain of language to help them learn another domain (Karmiloff & Karmiloff-Smith, 2001). For example, children might figure out syntax through an understanding of the meanings of words (semantics), or they might figure out word meanings through the placement of the words in a sentence (syntax). Children use their knowledge of the various aspects of their native language as clues (Johnson & de Villiers, 2009).

For instance, there are differences in the forms that words take that help you determine whether a word is a noun or a verb. If you were introduced to two new words—*klumfs* and

Constraints Assumptions that language learners make that limit the alternative meanings that they attribute to new words.

Whole object bias An assumption made by language learners that a word describes an entire object, rather than just some portion of it.

Mutual exclusivity constraint An assumption made by language learners that there is one (and only one) name for an object.

Taxonomic constraint An assumption language learners make that two objects that have features in common can have a name in common, but that each object also can have its own individual name.

Fast mapping A process by which children apply constraints and their knowledge of grammar to learn new words very quickly, often after a single exposure.

Syntactic bootstrapping The use of syntax to learn the meaning of new words (semantics).

Semantic bootstrapping The use of conceptual categories to create grammatical categories.

pribiked—which would you think was a noun and which a verb? You know that we add -*s* to nouns to form a plural in English, so that is a strong clue that *klumfs* is a noun. Likewise, a verb can have a past tense, so the -*ed* at the end of *pribiked* is a strong clue that this is a verb. Second, where a word appears in a sentence (its syntax) provides clues to word meaning. If someone told you that the "thrulm progisted the car," in English the noun usually proceeds the verb, so you could assume that *thrulm* is a noun and *progisted* is a verb. If someone told you that "you have a very *glickle* smile," you might guess that *glickle* is an adjective that modifies or describes your smile.

To see for yourself how constraints can help guide a young child's word learning, try **Active Learning: Using Linguistic Constraints**.

ACTIVE LEARNING

Using Linguistic Constraints

You can use this activity to learn some "novel" words to see how a young child might experience learning them. In each situation, decide what you would say and name the linguistic constraint that you used to guide your decision.

1. You know that a bat is a long, thin object, and you know that a ball is small and round. If I ask you to hand me the glumph, which object do you pick up?

   Which constraint did you use to make your decision?

2. The creature with the pink hair is a lorum. When you have more than one lorum, what do you call them?

   How did you know what more than one lorum is called?

3. These are both floogles, but the green one is a flinger and the purple one is a flagger.

   What constraint helps you understand how these creatures are similar and how they are different?

4. This glumbug is dingling.

   How do you know which of these new words is a noun and which is a verb?

5. If I tell you this is a boblabo, am I naming the creature's beak, its wings, or something else?

   What constraint allows you to determine what the word boblabo *refers to?*

Answers:

1. You know what a bat is and what a ball is, so the *mutual exclusivity constraint* leads you to assume that the new name applies to the object you do not already have a word for.
2. You used your knowledge of the general grammatical rule that you add the letter *s* to nouns to form a plural.
3. The *taxonomic constraint* helps you understand that both creatures can belong to the category of floogles, but because they have unique features, they can also have different names.
4. *Syntactical bootstrapping* helps you identify the form of speech (noun versus verb) by the word's placement in the sentence and the -*ing* at the end of the word that usually indicates an action verb.
5. The *whole object bias* makes it more likely that you assume that a new word applies to the entire object, not just to a portion of it, like a beak or a wing.

Two-Word Phrases

After children have acquired a number of words in their vocabulary, they enter a stage of "rapid syntactic and semantic development" (Waxman & Kosowski, 1990, p. 1463). At around a year and a half, children begin to combine words in phrases such as *Mommy up* or *All gone kitty*. This is the beginning of their use of grammar, and it demonstrates that children create their own grammar, rather than simply making mistakes in using adult grammar (Karmiloff & Karmiloff-Smith, 2001). At this stage, all children around the world use language in the same way, by including only the most basic information in what they say. For example, they may say, "Eat apple," but they cannot say, "I'm eating an apple" or "You ate the apple." For some children, one word, such as *allgone* or *more*, becomes a "pivot" word to which other words are attached, as in *allgone apple* or *allgone mommy*.

Everyday conversation. What might this mother be saying? She might make a statement ("We have lots of blocks here"), ask a question ("Where is the red block?"), or make an evaluation ("Playing with blocks is fun").

Telegraphic Speech

When children begin to put three or more words together, they use the simplest combination of words that convey the meaning they intend. In the days long before instant messaging and texting, people used to send telegrams. When you sent a telegram, you would pay by the word. Therefore, you would not say, "I am going to arrive at 11:00 p.m. at the train station"; instead you might send the message "Arriving station 11 p.m." You would leave out all the little, unnecessary words. When young children begin to put words together, they act as if they have to pay for each word, and they only use the ones necessary to get their point across. This has been referred to as **telegraphic speech**.

Whereas two-word utterances are similar around the world, when children begin to combine three or more words the ordering of the words in these simple sentences reflects the language they are hearing. For example, the order in sentences in English is very likely to be a subject, then a verb, and then the object of the verb: *The dog* (subject) *chased* (verb) *the cat* (object). English-speaking children find it difficult to produce and understand passive sentences in which this order is changed: *The cat was chased by the dog*. However, children who speak Sesotho, a language found in southern Africa, hear passive sentences frequently and can produce these forms as soon as they learn to speak (Demuth, 1990). You can try **Active Learning: The Impact of Word Order** to see whether a child you know understands passive sentences.

Telegraphic speech
A stage in language development in which children only use the words necessary to get their point across and omit small words that are not necessary (for example, *Go up*).

Video Link 9.6
Understanding passive sentences.

The Impact of Word Order

ACTIVE LEARNING

First you will need to take two pieces of paper and draw two pictures. On one piece of paper, draw a dog facing right and running. On the second piece of paper draw a cat facing right and running. Ask a child between 3 and 10 years of age to arrange the pictures to show *The dog is chasing the cat*. Then ask the child to arrange the picture to show *The dog is chased by the cat*. Does the child understand that in the second sentence, which is in the passive form, the cat is actually chasing the dog? If not, this shows that the child still understands language through the grammatical structure of subject-verb-object. Older children understand that this order can be changed. Compare your results with those of others in the class who tested children of different ages.

✓✗

TRUE/FALSE

5. If a young child says, "I goed outside," the child's parent will be most likely to say, "No, you meant to say, 'I *went* outside.'"

False. When children are learning to talk, adults are more likely to respond to the accuracy of what the child says, rather than to correct the child's grammar. In this case, the adult would be more likely to say, "Yes, you did go outside."

One thing parents tend *not* to do with young children is to correct their grammar explicitly. The following story helps show what effect it might have if you were to spend much time correcting young children's grammar. In the 1970s, before the age of the computer, when people still wrote letters to each other, a young man carried on a correspondence with his girlfriend who was at a different college far away. Both of these young people were highly intellectual, as you will see. Each wrote love letters to the other. The recipient would then *correct the grammar* in the letter and send it back to the sender. You probably reacted quite negatively to this scenario, but why? Clearly, dealing with the grammar instead of the content of a love letter took all of the meaning—in this case, the romance—out of the exchange! In the same way, when a child is trying to tell us something, we respond to the content, not the form of what he is saying. When the child says, "Me go store," we answer, "Oh, are you going to the store?" We do not answer, "You should say, 'I am going to the store.'" If we did, the child would be totally confused. Karmiloff and Karmiloff-Smith (2001) provide the following example of what happened when a mother tried to correct her child's grammar:

Child:　Daddy goed to work.

Mother:　Yes, that's right. Daddy went to work.

Child:　Daddy goed to work in car.

Mother:　Yes, Daddy *went* in his car.

Child:　Daddy goed his car very fast.

Mother:　Ah ha, Daddy *went* to work in his car. Say *went* to work, not *goed*. Daddy *went* to work.

Child:　Daddy wented to work. (p. 102)

As this example shows, sometimes even when we directly try to correct grammar, it doesn't work. Also, if you've ever had a parent correct your grammar while you were trying to tell him something important, you can understand a child's frustration when a parent responds to the form of a sentence rather than to the meaning of what is said.

Language Development of Preschoolers

By age 3, most children are putting together multiword sentences. Also, whereas younger children use only the basic forms of words, such as *I go store*, preschoolers begin to add morphemes. At the beginning of the chapter, we defined a morpheme as the smallest unit that has meaning in a language. A morpheme may be a word like *house, car,* or *alligator,* or it may be any part of a word that has meaning, such as *-ed,* which indicates past tense, or *-s,* which indicates a plural. As the preschooler learns to use morphemes appropriately, she no longer says "I walk home" but rather "I walked home" when she means the past tense. As we mentioned in the section on nativist theory above, when children learn to use these added morphemes, they often use them on words for which they don't work. Interestingly, they may use both the correct and the incorrect version, even in the same sentence: *I goed to the store and then went home.* Steven Pinker (1999) has suggested that we have two different mechanisms, one mechanism for learning words that follow regular rules and a different mechanism for learning words that are irregular so that their form must just be memorized rather than figured out. This position is very controversial, because other researchers maintain that only one mechanism is needed to do both tasks (McClelland & Patterson, 2003).

Follow the directions in **Active Learning: Collecting a Language Sample** to look at the nature of a young child's language development.

Collecting a Language Sample

Take a 10- to 15-minute language sample of a child between the ages of 18 months and 4 years by watching the child while he or she is playing with another child or talking with an adult. Try to write down exactly what the child says. How many words does she put together: one, two, three, or more? Look at the stages of development we have described to see where this child fits in. If the child is using just single words, how does she make herself understood (for example, gestures)? If she does put words together, are they in the same order that we would find in adult grammar, or are there words that are left out (for example, *I am going to the store* becomes *I go store*)? Do the words the child uses have appropriate endings (for example, *kicked*, *playing*, *desks*)? Does the child overregularize and put these endings on irregularly formed words (for example, *wented*, *sitted*)? Compare your findings with those of others in your class who observed children older or younger than the child you observed.

There are very large differences in the language environments in which children develop, and these differences have consequences for the children's later development, including their readiness to enter school. In a classic study of children's language environment, Betty Hart and Todd Risley (1995) followed 42 families over a 2½-year period, observing and recording their everyday conversation. Their sample consisted of families who were receiving welfare, working-class families, and families where the parent or parents held professional jobs. The difference in the amount of language that the children were exposed to was striking. On average, parents on welfare used 600 words an hour with their toddlers, working-class parents used 1,300 words, and parents with professional jobs used 2,100 words. Although professional parents did not initiate verbal interactions with their children any more frequently than other parents, they were more likely to respond to what their toddlers said. Parents who were professionals also used more affirmative or encouraging statements and fewer prohibitions (*Stop that* or *Don't*). By the time the children were 3 years old, children in professional families had been exposed to 8 million more words on average than children in welfare families. This cumulative effect is shown in Figure 9.2.

Differences in language development by a family's socioeconomic status continue as children get older. Vasilyeva, Waterfall, and Huttenlocher (2008) looked at the type of early sentences used by children whose parents had different levels of education. One group of parents had high school diplomas as their highest level of education, the second group of parents had college degrees, and the third group of parents had professional degrees (for example, a master's degree, a doctorate, or a professional degree in medicine or law). They found no differences in the children's use of *simple* sentences across groups. The children did not differ in the age at which they started producing simple sentences or in the proportion of simple sentences that they used. However, differences later emerged in the acquisition and use of *complex* sentences. Children from more educated families began producing complex sentences earlier and used them more frequently. Figure 9.3 shows the different paths of development for these two types of sentences. The authors say that children from different educational backgrounds move further apart as they grow older, and other research has shown that the disparity continues beyond the preschool years.

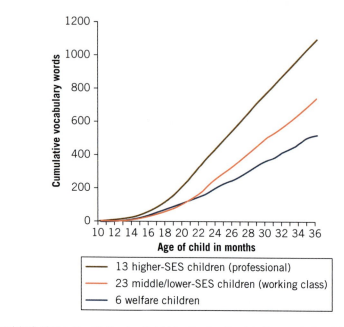

Figure 9.2

Differences in toddlers' vocabulary. The more words toddlers hear in their everyday life, the more they produce when they learn to speak. Children in families in which the parents are professionals hear significantly more words than children in working-class families or families on welfare, and this is reflected in the size of their vocabularies.

13 higher-SES children (professional)
23 middle/lower-SES children (working class)
6 welfare children

Egocentric Versus Private Speech

Although their use of language is rapidly increasing, preschoolers still have some limitations to their ability to communicate with others. Jean Piaget (1973) described the inability of young children to take the role of other people in their conversations as **egocentric speech**. For example, a child may say something like "I went to that place and saw someone going round and round." She does not realize that you have no idea what "that place" is or how someone can go "round and round" because she doesn't understand that you don't know everything that she knows. For Piaget, the explanation for egocentric speech is that children are not born social beings; they must learn to be social and to understand other people's points of view. When they do, their language becomes socialized, and communication is much more effective. Schematically, Piaget described the development of speech as follows:

Presocial speech ⟶ Egocentric speech ⟶ Socialized speech

Lev Vygotsky (1962) had a very different idea about what egocentric speech was. For Vygotsky, children are born social beings, so their speech is never "presocial." Instead, children always intend to communicate, but at some point their speech divides into two types: speech directed at other people and speech directed at oneself. In Chapter 7 we introduced the concept

Egocentric speech
A limitation of young children's communication due to their inability to take the perspective of other people into account.

Figure 9.3

Differences in the complexity of toddlers' sentences. There is little difference in the use of simple sentences among children from families with different levels of education (left). However, there are differences in the number of complex sentences produced by these children (right).

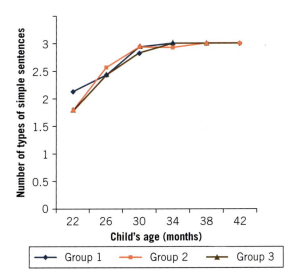

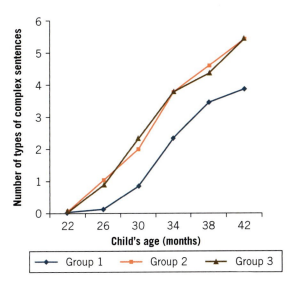

Number of simple sentence types produced by each SES group.

Number of complex sentence types produced by each SES group.

Educational levels of parents: Group 1 (high school graduates), Group 2 (college graduates), Group 3 (professional degrees).

of *private speech*, or talking to oneself. Speech directed at other people continues to be communicative, but private speech becomes increasingly silent. Younger children talk to themselves out loud. Somewhat older children more often whisper or mutter to themselves. Some children may even move their mouths silently. Vygotsky said that this speech becomes internalized eventually as silent speech ("saying it in my head") and then as thought. Schematically, Vygotsky described the development of speech as follows:

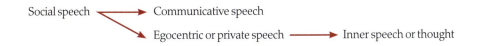

The research on these two points of view has tended to support Vygotsky's point of view. Although children do, at times, engage in egocentric speech that does not take into account the needs of the listener, more often this speech is for the purpose of self-direction, as Vygotsky describes (Berk & Winsler, 1995). Private speech does not end in early childhood. When confronted with a difficult task, about a third of 17-year-olds were found to talk openly (10%) or covertly, such as mumbling or whispering (20%), to themselves (Winsler & Naglieri, 2003). Try **Active Learning: Private Speech** to see how even adults may still engage in private speech.

ACTIVE LEARNING

Private Speech

We sometimes get a glimpse of the use of private speech as adults. If you ever find yourself talking out loud when you are alone, think about what you are most likely to say to yourself. The chances are that what you will say is about tasks that you need to do, like "Oh . . . the psych assignment!" or "Almost forgot that!" These generally have to do with self-direction or organization. As adults, we usually do not vocalize in this way to ourselves, but when we are alone or attempting to do something difficult, we may.

Get a friend to help you with this activity and find a quiet place to do it. Your friend will need a desk or table to work on so he can write. Use a page from a book or a sheet of newspaper that he can write on. Tell him that you are looking at how accurately people can scan written material to find target letters. Tell him that he should "cross out the Ts, circle the Os, and square the Ls" (the latter means that he should draw a box around the letter *L*) on the page you give him. Repeat these instructions a couple of times to be sure he understands (you can say it like a little rhyme) and ask him to repeat it to you a time or two to further confirm his understanding. Tell him that you will later count how many letters he was able to mark up correctly in 3 minutes.

After you are sure your friend understands the instructions, tell him that you will sit out of the way so that you don't distract him and you will tell him when to start and when to stop. After 2 minutes, give him a 1-minute warning (to create a little more pressure on him!). While he is working, listen carefully to hear whether he resorts to using private speech to help him perform the task. Kronk (1994) found that 37 out of 47 participants talked to themselves while working on a difficult cognitive task that she gave them, and that 46 out of 47 talked to themselves if there was someone else who was working on the same task and talking to him- or herself.

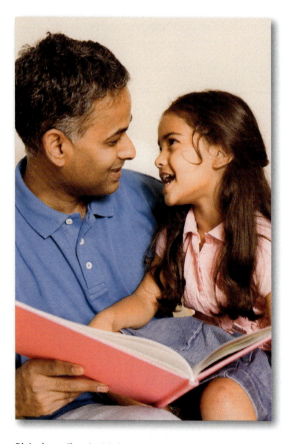

Dialogic reading. As this father reads to his daughter and asks her questions about the story, he actively engages her in the process and lays the groundwork for emergent literacy skills.

Written Language: Early Literacy

Until now, our discussion of language has focused on spoken language. In this section we introduce another very important aspect of language: the ability to understand and use written language. School is the context in which most children learn to read, write, and do arithmetic, but the groundwork for these skills is laid down throughout the preschool years. In recent years we have given increasing attention to **emergent literacy**, the set of skills that develop before children begin formal schooling and that provide the foundation for these academic skills. When a young child picks up a book, holds it right-side-up, and turns the pages, or when the child "reads" a story by looking at the pictures or picks up a pencil and scribbles on a paper, these are all emergent literacy skills.

Research on reading typically has looked at how a child acquires specific skills such as phonetics or decoding letters within the school context, but emergent literacy is a broader concept. It looks at how children learn about reading, writing, and print material either through informal processes, such as parents reading to children before they start school, or through formal instruction they receive in school (Gunn, Simmons, & Kameenui, 1995). This approach looks at the active role the child plays in the process. It also assumes that different aspects of early literacy are developing at the same time and that these aspects are all interrelated.

The process starts in infancy when the child is first exposed to books and to reading. Similar to the way that spoken language develops, the heart of this process is the interaction that takes place between the parent and the child, in this case as the parent reads to a child or tells a story. From these shared experiences the child develops an awareness of print, learns to recognize and name letters, and becomes aware of the sounds associated with different letters (Gunn et al., 1995). As parents tell stories, children also develop listening and comprehension skills, build their vocabulary, and become more comfortable using language themselves (Gunn et al., 1995). However, for this process to work at its best, the child can't just be a passive listener—the child needs to be an active participant in the process (Johnson & Sulzby, 1999).

There is a specific technique that is particularly effective in developing early literacy skills, which is known as **dialogic reading**. As the adult and child look at a picture book together, they actively talk about it. The adult engages the child in the process by asking questions and encouraging a dialogue about what is going on in the story. What is essential to this process, however, is that the partners then switch roles and the child becomes the storyteller and the adult becomes the active listener and questioner (Ghoting & Martin-Díaz, 2006; Institute of Education Sciences, 2007).

In Chapter 7 you learned about Vygotsky's zone of proximal development. This concept helps explain why dialogic reading is such an effective technique. As you know, Vygotsky believed that children learn best when adults (or more skilled peers) expose them to ideas that are just a bit beyond where they are in their own development. Anything too far beyond that is just going to go over the child's head because it is much too advanced, and anything that is below the child's own level of performance won't contribute to his learning because it is what the child already knows. When an adult is successful at keeping the dialogue and questioning during dialogic reading within the child's zone of proximal development, the interactions build upon the child's existing skills and move the child to the next level of understanding. This also helps explain why research has generally found that techniques such as flash cards, workbooks, and repetitive drills do *not* have a beneficial effect on the development of early literacy skills for children with average abilities (Gerard, 2004; Stipek, Milburn, Clements, & Daniels, 1992). Such approaches separate acquiring specific literacy skills from the rich context of reading and do not provide the same sort of sensitive feedback and interaction that dialogic reading can provide.

The basic technique in dialogic reading is the PEER sequence. During the interaction with the child, "the adult **P**rompts the child to say something about the book, **E**valuates the child's response, **E**xpands upon the child's response by rephrasing and adding information to it, and **R**epeats the prompt to make sure the child has learned from the expansion" (Whitehurst, 1992, para. 10). If you are looking at a book with a picture of several animals, you might prompt the child to respond by saying, "Do you see a kitty here?" If the child says, "Here's a kitty," you can say, "Yes [*the evaluation*], and she is sitting next to a doggie [*the expansion*]." And to complete the sequence, repeat, "The doggie is sitting next to the kitty." The goal is to ask questions that encourage the child to think about what she is seeing and to build her language skills in answer to your questions.

Being able to come up with prompts that keep the dialogue going is at the heart of this process. Whitehurst (1992) provides examples of five types of prompts that can be used:

- *Completion prompts* involve leaving a blank at the end of a sentence that the child can fill in. When a child correctly completes the sentence, it helps her understand the structure of language, which will later help her learn to read. If you say, "I think I'll go to the store and buy a _____," you need a noun to correctly complete the sentence, but if you say, "When I ride my bicycle, I go very _____," you need an adverb to correctly complete this one.
- *Recall prompts* ask the child for information about what has already been read. "Where did the little girl want to go?" or "Why was Emma feeling sad?" helps the child pay attention to the plot of the story and how it unfolds. This type of prompt also aids in memory development.
- *Open-ended prompts* ask the child to describe what is happening in a picture. They are different from completion prompts because the child isn't responding to a specific question that

Emergent literacy The set of skills that develop before children begin formal reading instruction, which provide the foundation for later academic skills.

Dialogic reading A technique used to facilitate early literacy, which involves an adult and a child looking at a book together while the adult asks questions and encourages a dialogue, followed by switching roles so the child asks questions of the adult.

6. Using flash cards, repetition, and word drills is a good way to ensure that a child develops early literacy skills. TRUE/FALSE

False. Techniques such as these make the child passive. Children learn literacy skills much more effectively when you use techniques that are interactive and that actively involve the child in the process.

you have posed. The child can describe anything she sees and finds interesting. This gives the child the opportunity to use her expressive language and to pay attention to detail.

- *W- prompts* are the *w* questions that reporters use when gathering information for a story—*what, where, when, why,* and *how* (not a *w* word, but still important for gathering information). If you ask the child *w*hat the character in the story is going to do next, *w*hy the character is excited, or *w*here she thinks the character will go next, you are helping develop her thought processes while building vocabulary.
- *Distancing prompts* take the child out of the storybook to make her think about the real world. If you are reading a story about a dog, you might stop to ask the child about an experience she has recently had with a dog. You might say something like "This dog looks a lot like the dog that we saw at Aunt Cindy's house last week. Do you remember that dog? What did you like about him?"

Video Link 9.7
Dialogic reading.

From this description, you can see how reading becomes an active rather than a passive process for the child when you use these techniques. Many adults love to read to children to expose them to books and new ideas that come from them, but Whitehurst (1992) has pointed out that no one has ever learned to play the piano by simply listening to someone else play. Dialogic reading provides the essential dimension of active involvement and practice, practice, practice that is required in order to develop a complex skill like reading. Follow the directions in **Active Learning: Using Dialogic Reading** to see how you can use this approach when reading with a child.

ACTIVE LEARNING

Using Dialogic Reading

Using the techniques of dialogic reading is a skill and requires practice. Use this as an opportunity to read to a young child (preferably a child who is 3 or 4 years old). If you choose a book you are familiar with (perhaps a favorite book from your own childhood), you will know the story well enough that you can focus your attention on providing prompts for the child. You might want to create a little "cheat sheet" for yourself before you begin because when you are first using dialogic reading, you will probably find yourself stumped from time to time about what kind of prompt to use next. If you practice this technique, however, creating these opportunities for learning will become quite natural to you. Finding that *zone of proximal development* and pitching your comments and questions to a child at just the right level to advance the child's understanding is what many parents, and *all* good teachers, do all the time.

By the age of 3 or 4, children usually can "read" familiar books by retelling stories using the pictures as cues (Johnson & Sulzby, 1999). At around this same age, they begin to experiment with writing in scribbles. As children gain experience with books, they begin to understand the relationship between the words on the page and the content of the story. They learn that it is the words, not the pictures, that tell the story in a book, and they learn the conventions of written language (for example, in English the text is read from the top of the page to the bottom and from left to right) (Gunn et al., 1995). Young children also learn to recognize the letters of the alphabet and the sounds associated with them (which is called **phonological awareness**) (Gunn et al., 1995). Children can pick up this information either through formal instructions or incidentally from being exposed to print information. After children have learned to write the letters of the alphabet and have made connections between letters and their sounds, they often begin to invent their own spelling of words (Johnson & Sulzby, 1999). The results may initially be incomprehensible—for example, a child might write *train* as *chran*—but this first writing is the basis for further learning about spelling and writing, as we will discover in the next section.

Phonological awareness Learning to recognize the letters of the alphabet and the sounds associated with them.

Language Development in School-Age Children

Children gradually come to understand that words are not the same as what they stand for. This understanding is the basis for **metalinguistic abilities**, in which children begin to think about language and how to use it (Pan, 2005). In the following example, 4-year-old Alexander had a specific idea about how words are formed and what they mean:

Alexander:	*I'm* not the cook, I'm the cooker, Mummy. I'm the cooker today.
	Mother explained that the stove was the cooker.
Alexander (furious):	No, no, no, that's the cook, it's me the cooker. (Karmiloff & Karmiloff-Smith, 2001, p. 80)

Alexander was sure that *-er* added to a word indicates that it refers to a living thing, not an object. He was focused on how the words are formed to express the ideas correctly.

Try **Active Learning: Metalinguistic Awareness** to see how older children start to appreciate words as words (for example, "I like the sound of the word *brussels sprouts*, even though I don't like to eat them!").

Metalinguistic abilities The ability to think about and talk about language.

Metalinguistic Awareness

ACTIVE LEARNING

To see whether children at various ages understand that a word is not the same as what it refers to, try the following activity. Ask the child, "What are your favorite things?" and then ask, "What are your favorite words?" For each response to each question, ask why it is her favorite. Compare your child's responses with those of classmates who interviewed children at different ages.

Preschoolers are not likely to differentiate words from the things they refer to. They are likely to say their favorite word is *lollipop* because such candies are delicious. Older children are more likely to know the word is not the same as the thing. They may say they like the same word, *lollipop*, but their reason will be because they like the sounds it makes (Pan, 2005).

These new metalinguistic abilities allow children to use language in new ways. For example, humor takes on a new dimension, as in this example:

KNOCK KNOCK
Who's there?
Lettuce.
Lettuce who?
Lettuce in, we're hungry!

As we can see from this example, many jokes require a fairly sophisticated understanding of language. You won't think the joke is funny unless you understand you have been tricked because the sounds for *lettuce* and *let us* are the same but the meanings are very different. This implies an understanding about words themselves, in this case that words we say can sound alike but indicate very different things.

Table 9.1 describes and illustrates some of the changes in what children find funny as they get older. As you look at these stages, think about what cognitive advances are necessary for a child to move from one stage of humor to another.

School-age children develop the ability to use words to mean something beyond their literal meaning. For example, they can use a metaphor such as *School is a ball!* or *Love is war*. They also begin to use irony or sarcasm, in which the speaker means the opposite of what he is really saying: *Oh my, how* beautiful *that outfit is, with the big tomato stain on the front.* A younger child might believe that you seriously like the design she's made with the tomato sauce.

Table 9.1

Children's humor. What children find funny largely depends on their stage of cognitive development, but the sense that something is inappropriate or incongruous underlies most of what we find funny. Paul McGhee (1979) describes the development of children's humor in these stages.

Stage*	Description	Example
1 (beginning of year 2)	Incongruous juxtaposition of objects, image, or action	Holding a stuffed animal to your ear and talking into it as though it were a telephone
2 (end of year 2 through late preschool years)	Incongruous labeling of objects and events (physical activity is *not* required)	Intentionally naming objects incorrectly (for example, pointing to your nose when someone asks where your ear is)
3 (age 3)	Conceptual incongruity	A violation of the concept of an object (for example, saying that a cat says "moo," calling a boy by a girl's name, or drawing a bicycle with square wheels)
4 (age 7)	Multiple meanings	Using words that have double meanings (for example, "Order in the court!" "I'd like a ham on rye"; "Take a bath." "OK, where should I take it?")
Adolescence and adulthood		Preference for spontaneous wit and amusing anecdotes over memorized jokes and riddles

*Note that the appearance of a new type of humor does not displace the earlier types. For example, although adolescents prefer spontaneous wit to memorized jokes, both adolescents and adults can be amused by a clever pun or play on words. If you found yourself giggling at any of these examples, you realized that even childish humor can still be amusing.

Reading in School-Age Children

With regard to written language, children begin to acquire the skills of conventional literacy as they move from kindergarten to first grade. **Journey of Research: What's the Best Way to Learn to Read?** describes the approaches and debates that have surrounded this question over the years.

What's the Best Way to Learn to Read?

JOURNEY of RESEARCH

Phonics (or basic skills) approach An approach to teaching reading that starts with basic elements like letters and phonemes and teaches children that phonemes can be combined into words before moving on to reading as a whole.

There has been quite a debate over the years about which approach is the best one to use to teach children how to read. The two broad approaches that have been widely used are the **phonics (or basic skills) approach**, which focuses on letter-sound relationships, and **whole language instruction**, which focuses on using reading materials that are inherently interesting to the child (Education Week, 2004).

Children had traditionally learned to read using what today is called authentic literature, such as the Bible or literary classics. They had an inherent interest in being able to read these books. However, in the 1930s, American schools began using basal readers to teach reading. Basal readers relied on nonphonic sight-reading. They contained a limited vocabulary (a

first-grade reader used only 300 words) and a great deal of repetition (Moran, 2000) so that students could easily learn to recognize all of the words. New words were added slowly and repeated frequently after they were introduced.

Perhaps you are familiar with another children's book that uses this same look-say approach. Theodor Seuss Geisel (better known to us as Dr. Seuss) was asked by his publisher to create a children's primer that used only 225 "new reader" vocabulary words. The result was the publication in 1957 of one of the most popular children's books, *The Cat in the Hat* (Dr. Seuss Enterprises, 2002–2004).

However, basal readers fell out of favor in the 1970s as phonics became the dominant approach to teaching reading (Carbo, 1996). The phonics approach is a *bottom-up approach* because it starts with basic elements like letters and phonemes and moves up to words before moving on to reading as a whole (Armbruster, Lehr, & Osborn, 2001). With this approach, children learn that words are composed of separate sounds or phonemes and that phonemes can be combined into words (for example, you would learn the sounds associated with the letters *c* and *a* and *t* before you would combine those sounds into the word *cat*). Children also learn that the process can be reversed and words can be sounded out by breaking them down into their phonemes (Texas Education Agency, 2004). Phonics places the emphasis on building these skills through exercises and practice. The phonics approach has been shown to be effective with at-risk students when they are first learning to read (Moustafa, 2001), and phonological skills are considered by some to be the best predictor of children's success in learning to read (Bingham & Pennington, 2007). You can try some exercises using this approach in **Active Learning: Phonics Can Be Fun**.

In the 1990s, however, the whole language approach gained favor over phonics in the educational community (Pearson, 2004). The whole language approach is a *top-down approach* that emphasizes understanding the meaning of words from the context in which they appear (Armbruster et al., 2001). Advocates for a whole language approach draw a parallel between this way of learning to read and the way that children naturally learn spoken language (Armbruster et al., 2001). In a language-rich environment, children first learn individual words to represent objects, actions, or desires and then learn to put the individual words together into meaningful sentences. In this view, the purpose of reading is to extract meaning from the text rather than to decode individual letters, phonemes, and syllables (Gove, 1983; McCormick, 1988).

The whole language approach returned to an emphasis on authentic literature that had an inherent interest for children, rather than on books built around teaching a set of reading skills. However, this change did not always sit well with teachers who knew that students benefited from instruction and who recognized that it was not enough to immerse students in literature and expect them to figure out the principles of reading on their own. Not only did reading suffer, but so did the students' mastery of subject content because many had difficulty reading textbooks (Pearson, 2004). By the end of the 1990s, the effectiveness of the whole

language approach was being questioned, as much by politicians who were emphasizing accountability in schools as by educators who were critical of the negative effect this approach had on students' performance in subjects other than reading.

In 2001, the National Institute of Child Health and Human Development, together with the U.S. Department of Education, convened a panel of reading experts who were charged to survey the scientific literature on reading. The panel conducted a meta-analysis (see Chapter 3 to review how this research methodology is used) on 38 studies and reached the conclusion that there was "solid support for the conclusion that systematic phonics instruction makes a more significant contribution to children's growth in reading than do alternative programs providing unsystematic or no phonics instruction" (National Reading Panel, 2000, Section 2, p. 45). The report almost immediately came under criticism (see Camilli, Vargas, & Yurecko, 2003; Garan, 2001; Shanahan, 2004; Yatvin, 2002).

Where do we stand today? Although there still is controversy about which approach is "best," there is increasing support for a **balanced reading approach** that combines elements of both the whole language and the phonics approaches (Education Week, 2004; Pearson, 2004; Stoicheva, 1999). Children need to be able to decode words, but they also need to comprehend the meaning of what they read. However, the balance between these two skills might change from one situation to another. For instance, the emphasis might be greater on phonics early in the process of learning to read and might shift gradually to more of a whole language approach as there is a greater need to read for comprehension.

Marie Carbo (1996) has suggested that after 70 years of research we should recognize that no single approach to learning how to read is likely to be most effective for every child. Which approach works best can largely depend on the learning style of the child who is learning to read. She points out that children who have a visual, tactile, and global reading style will enjoy the whole language approach and will be able to learn from it. On the other hand, these children may find phonics both boring and confusing. However, children who are analytic learners and have strong auditory styles can do very well in a phonics program. For these students, a whole language approach may feel too disorganized and haphazard. As with many things in the field of development, finding the right fit is often what works the best for children.

Whole language instruction A way to teach reading that emphasizes understanding the meaning of words from the context in which they appear.

Balanced reading approach An approach to teaching reading that combines elements of the whole language approach (which emphasizes comprehension and meaning) with elements of the phonics approach (which emphasizes decoding of words).

ACTIVE LEARNING

Phonics Can Be Fun

Descriptions of phonics-based reading programs sometimes sound like they are all practice and drill, but activities related to phonics can be fun, as well as educational, for children. The game of "Let's Pretend" helps children focus on the sound of words. You can play this game with an elementary school-age child or group of children. First ask the children to decide on a place where they want to go. Then have them try to name objects that they would take with them that start with the same letter as the place they are going (Texas Education Agency, 2004). For instance, if they want to go to the *beach*, they could say they want to take a *ball*, a *blanket*, and a *bottle* of water.

Another word game adapts the nursery rhyme "Humpty Dumpty" and lets the children fill in words that rhyme at the end of each sentence. This is an example taken from the Texas Education Agency (2004, handout #2):

Teacher: Let's make up our own "Humpty Dumpty." (The teacher then provides the first line of the rhyme.)

Humpty Dumpty sat on a *pear.*

Humpty Dumpty had _____ (a child might say *curly hair*).

Humpty Dumpty rode a _____ (*bear*).

Humpty Dumpty went to _____ (*the fair*).

The children fill in the blanks with any word that rhymes and makes sense in the sentence. This game could be adapted to use with groups. The first group to come up with an appropriate word scores a point.

TRUE/FALSE

7. By the time they reach eighth grade, fewer than one third of students in the United States are reading at or above their grade level.

True. In fact, a recent national assessment of reading proficiency in over 350,000 students found that 29% of eighth-grade students were reading at a level considered to be proficient or above.

Whichever approach—or combination of approaches—schools adopt to teach reading, there is reason for optimism that reading ability is getting better, but there still is a great deal of room for improvement. The most recent report on the results from the National Assessment of Educational Progress showed some modest gains from earlier assessments for both fourth-grade students and eighth-grade students (Lee, Grigg, & Donahue, 2007). In this sample of 350,000 students, 34% of fourth-grade public school students were reading below what is considered a *basic* level (*partial mastery of prerequisite knowledge and skills*), another 34% were reading at the basic level, 24% were reading at a level considered *proficient* (*solid academic performance*), and 7% were at an *advanced* level (*superior performance*) (Lee et al., 2007, p. 16). Among the eighth graders tested, 27% were below the basic level of skills, 43% were at the basic level, 27% were scored as proficient, and only 2% were considered advanced (p. 34). That means that across the two grade levels, about two thirds of the sample was reading at or below the basic level. Although a number of groups showed some gains, there remained a gap between genders (with girls outperforming boys) and between ethnic and racial groups. State-by-state changes from 2005 to 2007 are shown in Figure 9.4.

Writing Skills

Even very young children love to take a crayon or marker and "write" a letter or story. The earliest writing skills (similar to what we saw for the development of reading skills) are basic: Children understand that writing moves from left to right (in English-speaking countries), from the top of the page down, and that it is meant to convey information. As their fine motor skills improve, they can now begin to write recognizable letters. Figure 9.5 is an

Figure 9.4

Changes in reading comprehension scores on the National Assessment of Educational Progress. This map shows a state-by-state comparison of changes in the scores of 350,000 fourth- and eighth-grade students who were assessed in 2005 and 2007. Although there was some improvement, 30 states did not show a change in scores for students in either grade. Compared with 2005,

- 4 states and jurisdictions (District of Columbia, Florida, Hawaii, and Maryland) improved at both grades (shown in teal);

- 13 states (Alabama, Alaska, Georgia, Indiana, Iowa, Kansas, Nevada, New Jersey, New Mexico, Massachusetts, Mississippi, Pennsylvania, and Wyoming) and Department of Defense schools improved at Grade 4 only (shown in red);

- 2 states (Texas and Vermont) improved at Grade 8 only (shown in orange);

- 2 states (North Dakota and Rhode Island) declined at Grade 8 (shown in white); and

- 30 states showed no significant change at either grade (shown in gray).

example of how writing skills develop in young children. Remember from Chapter 6 that children develop their fine motor skills as they develop motor control that moves down their arms to their fingers.

Children love being able to write their own names and often master this skill even before they enter school. Early writing is another skill in which phonological awareness plays an important role. Children will sound out familiar words and "spell" them phonetically. Contrary to what some adults think, using invented spelling does not slow down or prevent a young child from learning conventional spelling. In fact, it can even help them with the task of learning to read (Ouellette & Senschal, 2008). When kindergarten children were trained "to increase the sophistication of their naturally occurring invented spellings" (p. 904), a process that ordinarily occurs as children move toward learning conventional spelling, this group showed more advanced invented spellings and reading of words than children without this training.

8. When young children use spelling that they have "invented" (rather than conventional spelling), it slows down their ability to learn how to spell correctly.

TRUE/FALSE

False. Phonetic (or invented) spelling does not slow down or harm a child's ability to learn to spell correctly.

Figure 9.5

Early writing. This writing sample from a prekindergarten child shows how much progress is made in just a few short months. Children take great pride in learning how to write their names.

This is how I write my name:	This is how I write my name:	This is how I write my name:
September 2007	December 2007	February 2008

In the early elementary grades, children begin to learn and apply conventional spelling rules (such as adding the suffix *-ed* to a word to form the past tense) and to learn more about the typical patterns of occurrence of certain letters in their written language (Kemp & Bryant, 2003). The eventual goal is for the process of spelling to become automatic (Rittle-Johnson & Siegler, 1999) so that the retrieval of information on how to spell a word is very quick and very accurate.

However, writing is more than correctly shaping letters on a piece of paper or stringing words together. We use writing to communicate our ideas, so writing also must include composition skills. Children in the early elementary grades may write about a topic by simply tying together a series of statements that describe the facts (McLane & McNamee, 1990), but there is an important difference between **knowledge telling** (what younger children do) and **knowledge transforming** (what adolescents and adults do). When you rely on knowledge telling, you proceed with little or no evidence of planning or organization of ideas (Bryson & Scardamalia, 1991) with the goal of telling as much as you know about the topic you are writing on. In knowledge transforming, however, the goal becomes to take information and transform it into *ideas* that you can share with your reader so that the reader understands and learns from them. It attempts to convey a deep understanding of the subject. However, the fact that teenagers are capable of doing this does not mean that they necessarily do it.

Knowledge telling
A style of writing (typical of younger children) in which the writer proceeds with little or no evidence of planning or organization of ideas, with the goal of telling as much as he knows about a topic.

Knowledge transforming A style of writing (typical of older children and adolescents) in which the goal is to convey a deeper understanding of a subject by taking information and transforming it into ideas that can be shared with a reader so that the reader understands and learns from those ideas.

The Language of Teenagers

The language of teenagers can sound quite a bit different from that of many adults. In one sense adolescent speech becomes more adult-like in that it becomes increasingly complex. Sentences are longer, and the grammar is more complex. However, adolescents are also more likely to use slang or made-up words, especially with each other. They may do this for fun or to bond with a particular group, or simply to identify with being an adolescent. Teens often change the meaning of a word to its opposite: *That's sick* comes to mean *it's really good* (Karmiloff & Karmiloff-Smith, 2001). Shortcuts may be developed. The very polite *Hello, how do you do?* becomes *'sup?* Adolescent slang sometimes catches on with the wider society and becomes part of how everyone talks (Ely, 2005). We were going to include a list of teen slang words here but realized that they would likely be outdated by the time this book came out. Instead, if you are not far beyond adolescence yourself, think about which words you use with your friends but not with older people, like your parents. Do you have any idea about the origin of those words? Were you using different words when you were in high school or middle school? Is the slang you use particular to the area of the country in which you live or to a particular group to which you belong? Different regions of the country and different subgroups within the country develop their own particular slang. (Teens from Nebraska are less likely than teens from California to use slang pertaining to surfing.)

Teen communication. Many adolescents use their cell phones to text their friends. Although texting uses a lot of abbreviations and special terminology, it fortunately doesn't seem to interfere with adolescents' ability to use standard English.

In recent years, teen language has also been influenced by electronic communication, such as instant messaging and text messaging. As communicators try to make interactions as efficient as possible, they have developed shorthand methods, such as substituting the well-known *LOL* for *laugh out loud* or using *u* instead of *you*. For example, a conversation might proceed as follows (Wikipedia.com):

SUP (what's up?)

NMU (not much, what about you?)

AAS (alive and smiling)

P911 (parents coming into room alert)

G2G (gotta go)

Recent research has found that adolescents are more likely than either older or younger individuals to use text messaging (Drouin & Davis, 2009). Although there has been some concern expressed about whether the continual use of the abbreviations that are typical of text messages would negatively affect a young person's ability to spell or write standard English, this does not appear to be the case. When a group of college students who were regular users of "text speak" were compared to other college students who were not, there was no significant difference between the groups on tests of their literacy level or ability to correctly spell common text speak words (Drouin & Davis, 2009). What is interesting, however, is that both frequent users and those who did not frequently text *thought* that texting would hurt their ability to use standard English. These shortcuts do occasionally sneak into students' written school papers, so it is important for students to learn when it is appropriate to use them and when it is not.

University and business leaders alike are concerned about the number of high school graduates who do not have good writing skills. A survey conducted in 2004 by the National Commission on Writing gathered information from the human resource directors of 120 major American companies. Among the findings that emerged from the survey was the fact that one half of the respondents said that they take writing into consideration when hiring an employee (especially for salaried employees) and that a poorly written application might not be considered for any position. They also reported that two thirds of salaried employees have some responsibility for writing as part of their job and that communicating clearly plays a role in promotion and retention. One respondent to the survey succinctly said, "You can't move up without writing skills" (p. 3). The National Commission on Writing concluded that employees' writing deficiencies cost American businesses as much as $3.3 billion a year. Although teens may have their own ways of talking and writing, when they enter the business world, they need to have a good set of language and writing skills if they expect to be successful.

Bilingualism and Bilingual Education

TRUE/FALSE

9. When a young child learns two languages at the same time, the extra effort it takes to learn the second language slows down the child's general cognitive development.

False. Young children actually can learn two languages simultaneously without great difficulty. Contrary to the belief that doing this might hurt the child's cognitive development, there is some evidence that in some ways it actually enhances it.

Learning to speak a language is a complex cognitive task, so learning to speak two different languages is even more cognitively complex. For this reason, parents sometimes wonder whether being bilingual is so demanding that it will hurt a child's overall cognitive development. Fortunately this does not appear to be the case. Many people around the world speak more than one language, and a growing body of research on bilingualism indicates that parents do *not* need to worry about having their children learn two languages at the same time at an early age (Bialystok & Viswanathan, 2009; Hakuta & Garcia, 1989; Kovács & Mehler, 2009; Sorace, 2006). Children who simultaneously learn two languages reach language milestones at approximately the same age as children who are monolingual (Petitto et al., 2001). However, there is *not* strong research support for the idea that bilingualism gives children an across-the-board advantage in cognitive performance. Ellen Bialystok (2001), an expert in bilingualism and second-language acquisition, has said that "broadly based statements about intellectual superiority are probably excessive and unsupportable" (p. 188), although there is evidence to support the idea that bilingual children have some advantages over monolingual children in some specific cognitive processes.

Learning a second language at a young age makes it more likely that the child will speak it without a detectable accent (Asher & Garcia, 1969) and will be proficient at using the language (Johnson & Newport, 1989). Although not all research indicates that there is an early and critical period for acquiring a second language (Birdsong & Molis, 2001), research on brain function has shown that children who learn two languages from a very young age use the same parts of the brain to process both languages, while children who learn a second language in adolescence use a different part of the brain for that second language (Blakeslee, 1997). There also is growing evidence of enhanced executive control in bilingual children. You will remember from Chapter 7 that executive control functions include an ability to inhibit a response when necessary and the ability to be cognitively flexible and to shift focus from one task to another (Diamond, 2006). Bialystok and Viswanathan (2009) recently reported that bilingual 8-year-old children demonstrated more skill than monolingual children on tasks that required inhibitory control and cognitive flexibility. Interestingly, the bilingual children in this study were children in Canada and India who all spoke English but who spoke a variety of second languages, including Cantonese, French, Hebrew, Mandarin, Punjabi, and Telugu. Differences in executive function even appear in preverbal infants who are from bilingual homes. After infants from monolingual and bilingual homes had learned to anticipate an event based on a verbal clue, when the clue changed the infants from bilingual homes were able to more easily shift to a new response (Kovács & Mehler, 2009).

Research also has found that bilingual children have an advantage in solving problems that require the child to ignore irrelevant or misleading information to solve the problem correctly, have greater mental flexibility and greater creativity, are better at scientific problem solving, and have better concept formation (Andreou & Karapetsas, 2004; Bialystok, 2001; Hakuta, 1987; Hakuta &

Garcia, 1989). In other words, they have metalinguistic skills that allow them to understand and think about language in a more advanced way, including having an understanding of the relative nature of language (that is, that the same object can be called by any of several different names—an object called *table* in English can also be called *mesa* in Spanish). However, on other measures there are no differences between monolingual children and bilingual children, and in some cases monolingual children have the advantage (Bialystok, 2007).

In the United States there are many children for whom English is not their first language, and it is not the language spoken in their home or neighborhood. However, when they get to school, they are generally expected to understand and speak English. There has been much controversy about what is the best way to handle this situation and help ensure that these bilingual learners will be successful in school. See **Journey of Research: Bilingual Education—Sink or Swim?** for a closer look at how our approach to teaching children who are learning English has developed over time.

Bilingual classrooms. Many children in U.S. classrooms speak more than one language. The American educational system has adapted to this diversity through a variety of English-as-a-second-language (ESL) programs.

Bilingual Education—Sink or Swim?

JOURNEY *of* **RESEARCH**

Research on bilingual education is embedded in political, philosophical, and social contexts. At times our educational system has accommodated bilingualism, at times there has been opposition to it, and at still other times it has been largely ignored (Crawford, 1995). This laissez-faire attitude resulted at least in part from the assumption that non-English speakers would want to be assimilated into the great American "melting pot" and would strive on their own to quickly learn English so that the educational system wouldn't need to do anything special to facilitate this.

In the 18th and 19th centuries, immigrants often lived in their own communities and ran their own schools in which instruction was given in their native language (Public Broadcasting Service [PBS], 2001). At this time, several states had laws that allowed children to be taught in schools in the language of their parents at the parents' request. However, by the end of the 1800s, the tide had started to change. For instance, Native Americans were forbidden to be taught in their native language, and laws were passed that required that classes be taught in English (Crawford, 1995; PBS,

2001). This trend was amplified when entry into World War I raised concerns in the United States about the loyalty of non-English speakers and provoked hostility against people who spoke German (PBS, 2001). Eventually this hostility became hostility against the use of any minority language in schools. By the mid-1920s, virtually all bilingual education in public schools had been eliminated (PBS, 2001).

The tide changed again in the 1960s against a backdrop of desegregation in public schools and the civil rights movement (Crawford, 1995). Another important factor in this shift in attitude toward bilingualism was the sharp increase in the number of immigrants arriving in the country. By the mid-1960s, immigrant populations comprised a substantial part of the school-age population in some parts of the country. These immigrant populations—Chinese families in San Francisco, Cuban families in Miami, and Chicano families in Texas—increasingly demanded instruction in their native language and the incorporation of their culture into the curriculum. In response, the federal government passed the Bilingual

(Continued)

(Continued)

Education Act of 1968, which provided supplemental funding for instruction in native languages (PBS, 2001). Under this legislation, children with limited English proficiency were seen as a special needs population that required additional services. The legislation argued that children were being deprived of an education if they were taught in a language they did not understand (Cromwell, 1998a). A second goal of this legislation was to recognize and respect non-native students' cultures and to recognize the cultural pluralism in our society (Cromwell, 1998a).

In the years that followed, the need for language services for children who were not native English speakers continued to grow. By the 1980s, 40% of the U.S. population consisted of minority-language speakers (PBS, 2001), and the 2000 U.S. Census found that one out of every six school-age children spoke a language other than English in the child's home (National Clearinghouse for English Language Acquisition and Language Instruction Educational Programs [NCELALIEP], 2006). Today children with limited English proficiency are the fastest-growing segment of the U.S. school-age population (NCELALIEP, 2006).

This increase in the number of non-native speakers, together with a growing dissatisfaction about the progress that the students were making in learning English in bilingual classes, provoked a backlash that resulted in several pieces of state legislation in the 1980s and 1990s that again eliminated bilingual education or prohibited expenditures for classes in any language other than English (PBS, 2001). It is against this shifting backdrop of social change that research on bilingual education has been conducted.

Video Link 9.8
Immersion program.

Immersion programs
Programs for English language learners in which the students are taught academic subjects in English, with teachers tailoring the language they use to the current language level of their students.

Transitional bilingual education programs Programs for English language learners in which students receive some instruction in their native language while they also receive concentrated instruction in learning English.

Developmental bilingual programs
Programs for English language learners in which students initially receive instruction in core subjects in their native language and receive instruction in art, physical education, and music in English until they have the language skills to be instructed in the core subjects in English.

Programs designed to teach English to children who are not native speakers have taken a variety of forms in the United States. Some of the most common types of programs (Cromwell, 1998a) include the following:

- **Immersion programs** in which the students are taught academic subjects in English, with teachers tailoring the language they use to the current language level of their students.
- **Transitional bilingual education programs** in which the students receive some instruction in their native language while they also receive concentrated instruction in learning English. The goal of transitional programs is to prepare the students to *transition* to regular classes in English as soon as possible so they do not fall behind their peers in content areas such as math, science, and social studies (Ovando & McLaren, 2000).
- **Developmental bilingual programs** that build on students' skills in their native language while they learn English as a second language. Students initially receive instructions in the core subjects in their native language but receive instruction in art, physical education, and music in English. As soon as they have sufficient skills in English, English is then used for instruction in the core subjects as well (Genesee & Cloud, 1998). Students typically remain in these programs longer than in traditional transition programs, but they continue learning English throughout their time in the program.
- Another program model that is used less frequently than other alternatives is a **dual language program** in which children who are native speakers of English and children who are non-native speakers work together in a classroom where *both* majority and minority languages are used (Lindholm-Leary, 2000). This type of program requires highly trained and skilled teachers who can support the development of both languages in their students in a language-integrated classroom. Proponents of this approach emphasize how it promotes bilingualism and academic excellence for both groups of language learners and prepares the students for life in a multicultural world (Lindholm-Leary, 2000).

There has been a great deal of controversy about these various approaches to helping English language learners or children with limited English language proficiency learn English. Consequently it is difficult to determine which approach might be considered best or most effective. Many programs are not pure forms of the approaches we have just described, so it becomes difficult to compare and evaluate programs that are actually hybrids of several approaches (Cromwell, 1998b; Guglielmi, 2008). As noted above in the Journey of Research, the intended goals of the programs have shifted from time to time to reflect changes in the social and political context. For instance, if the goal is to assimilate recent immigrants into the American language and culture, an immersion approach fits well with that goal. On the other hand, if the goal is to promote multiculturalism, a dual language approach fits well with that goal (Ginn, 2008). A committee of the National Research Council (1997) has recommended that rather than trying to find a one-size-fits-all solution, research needs to identify a range of educational approaches that can be tailored to the characteristics of the children in a specific community, while taking into account local needs and the resources available to support the language program.

The debate about how to best educate children who are not native speakers of English will continue within our schools because these children will continue to be a sizeable part of our school-age population. This means that there will be arguments for and against all of the approaches currently used, but Hakuta and Garcia (1989) summed up this debate by saying, "There is hardly any dispute over the ultimate goal of the programs—to 'mainstream' students in monolingual English classrooms with maximal efficiency. The tension has centered on the specific instructional role of the native language: How long, how much, and how intensely should it be used?" (p. 376).

Dual language programs Programs in which children who are native speakers of English and children who are not work together in a classroom where both English and the children's other native languages are used.

Language Disorders

Communication Disorders

We have described the normal or typical pattern of language development in children, but it is also important to remember that there is a good deal of variability in the age at which children reach the various milestones that fall within the normal range. Some children surprise us by racing through the milestones sooner than we might expect (usually to parents' great delight), but others lag behind (no doubt causing their parents some concern). One of the most important things that parents can do is to pay attention to how their child is progressing. If they have questions or concerns, they should talk to their pediatrician and perhaps have the child evaluated by a speech and language specialist. In most cases they will likely get reassurance that their child's language development is in that normal range, but if a problem is identified, early intervention efforts are important and can be very effective.

The *Diagnostic and Statistical Manual of Mental Disorders* (American Psychiatric Association, 2000) identifies several communication disorders that affect children's ability to listen, speak, and use language in their social communications and in school:

- A child with **expressive language disorder** has a more limited vocabulary and has difficulty using tense correctly, recalling words, or producing sentences of the length and complexity that would be expected of a child of that age.
- A child with **phonological disorder** has difficulty producing sounds or using sounds correctly for his age (for example, he substitutes one sound for another).

Expressive language disorder A disorder involving a limited vocabulary and difficulty using tense correctly, recalling words, or producing sentences of the length and complexity that would be expected of a child of that age.

Phonological disorder A language disorder in which the child has difficulty with producing sounds or using sounds correctly.

- **Receptive-expressive language disorder** causes both the child's receptive and the child's expressive language development to be substantially below his performance on a standardized measure of nonverbal intelligence. In addition to the problems described above for an expressive language disorder, a child with receptive-expressive language disorder has difficulty with **receptive language** (that is, with understanding words or sentences).
- *Stuttering* is a disorder in which the child has difficulty with fluency and time patterning of speech (this includes repeating sounds or syllables, pausing within a word, pausing in speech, or repeating whole words).

Again, any child (or adult, for that matter) might show any of these language problems from time to time, but we wouldn't consider this a disorder unless the problems are persistent, the child's language is substantially below what would be expected for a child of the same age, and the problem interferes with other aspects of the child's life, such as her ability to communicate in social interactions with others or her performance in school. Because some studies have found that language disorders are associated with difficulties in parent-child interaction and in social-emotional development, it is important that we identify and treat them as early as possible so that we don't let a whole set of secondary problems develop in addition to the language difficulties (Desmarais, Sylvestre, Meyer, Bairati, & Rouleau, 2008).

Video Link 9.9
Autism.

Autism Spectrum Disorders

Autism was described in Chapter 6 as a pervasive development disorder that is characterized by difficulties with social interaction, problems with verbal and nonverbal communication, and repetitive behaviors with a strong need for sameness in the environment. Language development plays a central role in diagnosing this disorder, so we return to talking about autism in this chapter, with a specific focus on the communication aspects of the disorder.

Remember that autism includes a range of conditions that runs from autism disorder at the severe end to pervasive development disorder (not otherwise specified) and includes a much milder condition called **Asperger's disorder** (American Psychiatric Association, 2000). Autism is not usually diagnosed before age 3, but one of the earliest indications that something may be wrong is that the child does not reach regular milestones in language development, such as using single words by 16 months or combining two words by 2 years of age (National Institute of Mental Health [NIMH], 2009b). The National Institute of Mental Health (2009b) describes a number of ways in which language development or the use of language is different for children along the autism spectrum (see also the National Institute on Deafness and Other Communication Disorders, 2008). As we look at these, you are likely to develop a better understanding of the complexity of this developmental disorder.

Building language skills. This special education teacher is coaching this autistic boy to use sign language to compensate for the problems he has with spoken language.

Some autistic children may not babble or make meaningful gestures, such as pointing to things that they want, or they may not respond to their name, but other children with autism spectrum disorder coo and babble normally although their language doesn't develop from that point forward. Some autistic children remain mute throughout their lives, but others develop some language although they may do it at an unusually late age (between 5 and 9 years) (NIMH, 2009b). The child may know a number of words (in some cases even having an unusually large vocabulary) but may use single words over and over again or be unable to combine the words he does have into meaningful sentences. Some autistic children have **echolalia**, a condition in which they repeat what they hear (like an echo). For example, a parent asks a child, "What do you want, Johnny?" and the child responds, "What do you want, Johnny?" rather than answering the parent's question. Children may do this when they are first learning a language, but the echolalia persists for children on the autism spectrum. Autistic children also may reply to questions in a way that is not responsive. For instance, if you ask a child if he would like something to drink, he might count from one to five for you. Children on the autism spectrum may respond in social situations with "scripts" for what they should say or do. For example, the autistic child may introduce herself by saying, "Hello, my name is Josephine," even though you have met this child many times before and know that her name is Josephine.

Autistic children also have difficulty with many of the skills that are part of what goes on in our typical day-to-day conversations with other people. Try **Active Learning: Observing Conversation Skills** to sharpen your understanding of the skills necessary to carry on an effective conversation.

Echolalia A condition often seen in autistic children in which they repeat what has been said to them instead of responding appropriately.

Nonverbal communication. Communication involves much more than what we say. Our expression, body language, and gestures also convey meaning. What do you understand about these girls' conversation just from seeing them, without hearing what they are saying?

Observing Conversation Skills

ACTIVE LEARNING

You may not have thought about how many social skills we use when we engage in a conversation. All of these skills work together to give meaning to what we are saying and to ensure that we are actually communicating by exchanging information when we talk to each other.

Find some place where you can watch people who know each other engage in conversation. A cafeteria on your campus or a student study lounge would be a good place to do this. If you do this activity in class, you can have some students be partners for this exercise by engaging in a conversation while other students conduct the observations. To reduce some of the awkwardness, give the students a topic for their conversation. It can be something as simple as discussing the weather last week, something that has happened on your campus recently, or their opinion about whether we should ask for paper or plastic when we shop for our groceries (the topic doesn't matter very much, as long as it is not too controversial because we want to observe a conversation, not an argument).

As they talk, for 3 to 5 minutes try to carefully observe all the things that they do to sustain that conversation and to communicate effectively. When you have a list, compare it to the description of conversational clues that follow in the text. How many of them did you notice and include in your notes?

In the United States, conversation is often marked by eye contact between the individuals who are talking. They may smile and nod when they agree with each other or frown if they do not agree. What we say is usually tied to our facial expression and our body language because we are integrated human beings, and all those pieces go together in a way that makes sense. Most of the time, one person waits for the other person to finish talking before adding something to the conversation. They take turns speaking and usually don't interrupt or speak over the other person. They also try to keep the conversation going by adding new information to what has already been said or by asking questions about what the previous speaker has said. They keep an appropriate distance between each other (and "appropriate" depends on the culture you are in and the intimacy of the relationship). Friends often sit closer together than strangers or classmates who are talking to each other. Facial expressions, gestures, and body language fit the topic of the conversation. If the speakers are joking, their faces reflect their amusement, and they may throw their heads back and laugh out loud. If they are discussing something distressing or serious, they may hunch over, bite their nails, or play with their fingers. If someone is sharing a concern or talking about a disappointment, the other person may reach out to touch his arm or back in consolation. If the topic changes from one thing to another, one of the speakers probably indicates that a new topic is being introduced into the conversation by saying something like "By the way . . ." or "I've been meaning to tell you . . ." or "What do you think about . . . ?" We also usually clearly indicate to the person we are speaking to when the conversation is over. We say something like "Well, it was interesting talking to you today" or "I've got to get to class now" or "I'll see you later" to show that the conversation has reached a conclusion.

As you read through the previous paragraph, the content probably seemed very common-sense and familiar. It may have been *so* familiar that you didn't even make note of some of these things if you carried out the observation in the Active Learning feature. Now think for a moment how difficult it would be to have a conversation if the person you were speaking to didn't look you in the eye when you spoke, didn't respond to what you said or responded in a way that didn't relate to what you had just said, didn't show any facial expressions or use any gestures, or used expressions and gestures that were inappropriate for what he was saying (NIMH, 2009b). These are all difficulties with the pragmatics of language that are frequently seen in autistic children.

When autistic children fail to develop language or gestures (such as sign language) to express what they want or need, they may resort to simply grabbing what they want or screaming (NIMH, 2009b). As they grow up and increasingly realize they have difficulty understanding others and making themselves understood, they may become depressed or anxious (NIMH, 2009b). Anger, depression, and anxiety are not symptoms of autism itself. They are secondary consequences of living with this disorder and the challenges it brings with it.

Diagnosing a child as autistic is a conclusion that has great consequences for the child and the family, so we want to make this decision with great caution. Although we typically don't label a child as autistic until he is 3 years or older, there is a growing body of evidence that symptoms of autism are apparent from much younger ages (Kalb, 2005; NIMH, 2009b). While we don't want to rush to judgment in making a diagnosis, there is good reason to identify this condition as soon as we can because the optimal intervention involves at least 2 years of intensive early intervention during the preschool years (Filipek et al., 1999; National Institute of Neurological Disorders and Stroke [NINDS], 2008). Making a diagnosis involves using neurologic assessments as well as cognitive and language testing (NIMH, 2009b). These assessments are typically done by a team of specialists, which can include a psychologist or psychiatrist, a neurologist, a speech therapist, and/or other professionals who work with children with **autism spectrum disorders** (NIMH, 2009b). Based on their evaluation, the child's strengths and weaknesses can be identified, and this information can be used to develop a treatment plan that is tailored to the needs of the individual child. An effective treatment plan will be designed to target the array of symptoms that are associated with autism, including the impaired social interactions, language difficulties, and behavioral problems.

Autism spectrum disorders A group of conditions ranging from severe (autistic disorder) to mild (Asperger's disorder) and characterized by pervasive impairment in thinking, feeling, language, and the ability to relate to others.

Although there is no cure, early and appropriate intervention can bring about substantial improvement in these areas (NINDS, 2008). For instance, highly structured programs that include intensive skill-oriented training can help a child develop social and language skills that she lacks (NINDS, 2008). Under the Individuals with Disabilities Education Act (IDEA) services are provided to families with children under the age of 3 who have special needs. Although each state decides for itself which agency will be responsible for providing these services, all states use specialists who are trained specifically to work with young children (NIMH, 2009b). Together with the family, they develop an Individualized Family Service Plan (IFSP) that describes the services that will be provided (including services to the family, not just the child), and this plan is reviewed at least once every 6 months.

Learning Disabilities

As you learned in Chapter 8, *learning disabilities* is a broad term that encompasses a number of different types of learning problems. Here we will focus on learning disabilities that include the ability to understand or use spoken or written language (NINDS, 2007). These problems often co-occur, so it is not unusual, for instance, for a child with delayed speech development to have more difficulty than other children learning how to read. These disabilities may be very frustrating for children. Think for a moment about that uncomfortable feeling that goes along with having a word you are searching for on the tip of your tongue, and you will be able to relate to the frustration that a child with a language disorder can experience on a regular basis (American Speech-Language-Hearing Association [ASHA], 1997–2009).

Reading and writing involve complex sets of skills that need to work together perfectly. When you read, you need to simultaneously "focus attention on the printed marks and control eye movements across the page, recognize the sounds associated with letters, understand words and grammar, build ideas and images, compare new ideas to what you already know, [and] store ideas in memory" (NIMH, 1993, p. 4). This process requires the interaction and coordination of the visual, language, and memory portions of the brain. Children with **dyslexia** have particular difficulty distinguishing or separating the sounds in spoken words, which creates problems when they are learning to spell and read written words (Council for Exceptional Children, 2009; NIMH, 1993). As children move through the grades, the reading that they are expected to do shifts from recognition of letters and words to much more complex tasks that involve concept formation and reading comprehension. Some children with dyslexia may not be identified until the reading demands reach this level. The writing disorder **dysgraphia** includes trouble with spelling, handwriting, or expressing thoughts on paper. Writing also is a complex skill because it involves the complex coordination of vocabulary, grammar, hand movements, and memory (NIMH, 1993).

Learning disabilities are most often considered to be a result of damage to the brain, which can occur prenatally when the structure of the brain is being laid down, through a lack of oxygen to the brain during the birth process itself, or after birth due to environmental events such as exposure to toxins, severe malnutrition, or even an injury to the head (NIMH, 1993). However, the specific reason for a child's learning disability is often not known. Research

Dyslexia A learning disability in which individuals have difficulty distinguishing or separating the sounds in spoken words, creating problems with spelling and reading.

Dysgraphia A learning disability characterized by difficulties with writing, including trouble with spelling, handwriting, or expressing thoughts on paper.

Reading can be a struggle. Many children take great pleasure in being able to read, but for a child with a learning disability, reading can be a day-to-day struggle. Children with identified learning disabilities can receive special services in their schools.

TRUE/FALSE

10. Most children who are learning disabled have average or above-average intelligence.

True. Learning disabilities are not the same thing as retardation. They involve an inability of the brain to process certain specific types of information, but overall intelligence is not the issue.

on the possible causes of learning disabilities continues because a better understanding of causes will help us do a better job of preventing learning disabilities in the future or develop more effective interventions.

Although learning disabilities have their roots in early development, they usually are not identified until children reach school age and need to begin developing their reading and writing skills. Children develop these abilities at different rates, so we should never jump to the conclusion that a child has a learning disability if she is slower to read and write than other children. The child may need better instructions or more practice and time to develop these skills (National Center for Learning Disabilities [NCLD], 2010). However, if the child's difficulties persist, then it is time to ask the school for an evaluation and assessment. Other causes for the child's difficulty must be ruled out before we make the diagnosis of a learning disability. We have to eliminate sensory impairment (for example, vision loss or hearing impairment), serious emotional disturbance, cultural differences, or insufficient or inappropriate instructions as possible causes of the child's difficulty (NCLD, 2010). We also need to rule out mental impairment. Children who are learning disabled are not mentally retarded, and most children who have a learning disability have average to above-average general intelligence (ASHA, 1997–2009; NCLD, 2010).

The National Center for Learning Disabilities (2010) estimates that 2.8 million children in the United States have a specific learning disability, and the Council for Exceptional Children (2009) reports that more than 50% of the students in special education have a learning disability. Once a child has been diagnosed with a learning disability, the federal IDEA requires that appropriate services be provided. Collaboration among classroom teachers, support specialists, and parents is essential for an optimal outcome for the child.

Children with learning disabilities face more than academic challenges in the classroom, so parents and teachers need to be sensitive to these other sources of stress in the child's life. Because day-to-day expectations in the classroom are difficult for this child, it can have a negative effect on the child's self-esteem (Alexander-Passe, 2006; NCLD, 2010). Children with learning disabilities also may lack interpersonal and social skills that make it difficult for them to make and keep friends, leading to feelings of loneliness (NCLD, 2010). Because children who are different from other children can become a target for bullies, teachers and other school personnel need to be particularly vigilant to protect these children from harm to their physical well-being, self-esteem, and psychological well-being.

Children on their own try to find ways to cope with their challenges. Some underreact by withdrawing from the situation (for example, avoiding school, trying to avoid being called on in class) or by becoming extremely anxious (Thomson, 1996). Others overreact by acting out (for example, becoming the class clown, being aggressive toward other children, engaging in deviant or delinquent behavior) (Alexander-Passe, 2006; Thomson, 1996). Although these are coping mechanisms (and we all use them), they are not productive ones. Withdrawing from a stressful situation may temporarily ease your anxiety, but it doesn't solve your problem. Acting up gets you attention, but it doesn't help you meet your challenges.

Problems that arise in the elementary school years can persist and become worse as children with learning disabilities move into adolescence (Gerber et al., 1990). Recent research that looked at how adolescents with dyslexia coped found some important and interesting gender differences (Alexander-Passe, 2006). This research found that girls were more likely to try to find ways to make themselves feel better about the situation. For instance, they were more likely than boys to try to avoid the tasks at hand or to distract themselves from their problems by socializing with friends rather than studying. In contrast, boys were more likely than girls to attack the situation directly in an attempt to deal with it. They showed persistence and hard work and tried to analyze their past attempts to figure out what went wrong and could be corrected in the future. Similar patterns of gender differences in coping have been found in other research (Greenglass, 2002; Nolen-Hoeksema, 1987; Ptacek, Smith, & Dodge, 1994). In this study, being dyslexic had a greater effect on the academic and general self-esteem of girls than it had on the self-esteem of boys, and girls reported higher levels of depression.

One recommendation, based on these results, is that in addition to the educational needs of students with dyslexia, these students also need special attention to help improve their self-esteem and deal with the emotional fallout from the challenges they face. With appropriate help, many students who have learning disabilities are able to enroll in college and are successful in getting their degree. Many colleges offer support services, such as untimed tests or note-taking services, for students with identified disabilities. You may want to explore the services available on your campus for such students.

A particularly encouraging note comes from another recent study (Seo, Abbott, & Hawkins, 2008) that followed a group of students with learning disabilities from age 10 into young adulthood. Across a number of outcomes, including postsecondary school attainment, rates of employment, amount of earned income, and receiving public assistance, there were no significant differences between students with learning disabilities and their peers except that the former were more likely to be receiving public aid at age 21 (but not at age 24). While not all research on students with learning disabilities has found such positive adult outcomes (for example, Zadok-Levitan & Bronz, 2004), when young people are proactive in dealing with their disability, set goals for themselves, are self-aware and emotionally stable, and have good social support, they can be highly successful (Goldberg, Higgins, Raskind, & Herman, 2003; Raskind, Gerber, Goldberg, Higgins, & Herman, 1998; Seo et al., 2008).

Conclusion

Language is essential to the human experience. We communicate our ideas, feelings, and needs with language, and we use language to understand the world. Infants and toddlers around the world seem to go through the same stages in learning language, and by age 3 or 4, most are able to speak fairly clearly to those around them. Language development does not end in preschool. All four aspects of language (phonology, syntax, semantics, and pragmatics) continue to develop and become more complex and sophisticated through adolescence. Children must also learn to decipher written language if they live in a literate society. When children have difficulty with language development, as in the case of autism or learning disabilities, it is imperative that parents, teachers, and other professionals take all necessary steps to ensure that children achieve the highest level they can attain. As we saw from the description of communication disorders, there are a number of ways in which the language development of an individual child can differ from the typical path that most children follow. However, we also saw that there are approaches that can be used to support the child's language development or communication skills. Language is just one aspect of a child's cognitive development, but it is a central one in most societies around the world.

CHAPTER SUMMARY

1. **What are the four different aspects of language that researchers study?**

Language includes **phonology** (the sounds that make up the language), **syntax** (the grammar of the language), **semantics** (the meanings of words), and **pragmatics** (how we use language in social situations to communicate).

2. **What are the basic theories about how children develop language?**

Behaviorism (B. F. Skinner) emphasizes the role of reinforcement in the environment as a way to motivate and shape children's language development, but social cognitive theory (Albert Bandura) emphasizes the role of imitation of the language that children hear. **Nativism** (Noam Chomsky) emphasizes the role of biology by explaining language development as a result of our brain's inborn capacity to learn language. **Interactionism** brings these ideas together by stating that children's biological readiness to learn language must work together with their experiences with language in their environment to bring about language development. **Cognitive processing theory** is a new approach that emphasizes the "data crunching" capacity of the human mind, suggesting that infants statistically analyze the speech they hear in order to figure out language.

3. **What parts of the brain are specialized for language?**
    Two areas of the brain are particularly important for language development and use: **Broca's area** is important for the production of speech, and **Wernicke's area** is important for understanding and making sense out of speech.

4. **What are the stages of language development from prenatal through preschool?**
    Children move through stages of language development, but there is a good deal of variability from child to child in the age at which each stage appears. Before they can use words, infants communicate by crying, cooing, babbling, and gesturing. Infants and toddlers begin verbalizing by using *one word* at a time (usually nouns in English-speaking cultures) and then create primitive sentences when they put two words together. When children make sentences that contain only the essential words (for example, *Mommy ride car*), this is called **telegraphic speech**.

    Fast mapping allows children to add words rapidly to their vocabulary (often after a single exposure), and **syntactic bootstrapping** and **semantic bootstrapping** help this process. Preschoolers make multiword sentences using grammar that is very close to that of adults, but they continue to make mistakes because they tend to apply rules in cases where they won't work (called **overregularization**).

5. **What are egocentric speech and private speech? How are they similar, and how do they differ?**
    Piaget describes **egocentric speech** as an inability of young children to take the role of the person listening to them. Eventually speech becomes social as the child learns to take into account the listener's point of view. According to Vygotsky, private speech (like egocentric speech) is spoken out loud, but it is not used for social communication. Instead, private speech is used to direct one's own actions, and it eventually is internalized and becomes silent thought.

6. **What is metalinguistic ability, and how is it demonstrated in middle childhood?**
    Metalinguistic ability develops as children begin to think about language in and of itself. With this ability, they can understand that a word is different from what it represents. One outcome is that they are able to understand jokes that are based on changing word meanings.

7. **How is teen language different from language in children and adults?**
    Adolescents' speech is more complex in grammar and in subject matter than children's speech, and it differs from adult speech in the use of slang. Teen language is being affected by the kind of communication used in new technology such as text messaging.

8. **How do children learn to read and write?**
    Development of reading: **Emergent literacy** refers to the set of skills that young children develop before formal instruction in reading. Adults can use **dialogic reading** to talk with young children about the books they are reading together to build a variety of language skills. Once children enter school, they may be taught to read using one of the following approaches: (a) **phonics**, which starts with basic elements like letters and phonemes and teaches children to combine elements into words before moving on to reading as a whole; (b) **whole language instruction**, which emphasizes understanding the meaning of words from the context in which they appear; and (c) **balanced reading**, which combines features of the whole language approach with elements of the phonics approach.

    Development of writing: Young children move from scribbling to forming letters and then words. In school they may move from invented spelling to learning the rules of conventional spelling, until writing becomes an automatic process they don't have to think about. When writing, young children string ideas together with little organization, called **knowledge telling**, but adolescents become capable of writing to convey ideas and deeper understanding of a subject, called **knowledge transforming**.

9. **What are some effects of being bilingual as a child? What types of education programs are used for children who do not speak English?**
    Bilingual children do not generally have any difficulties associated with their use of two languages, and there is some evidence that they may have some advantages over monolingual children, such as showing more advanced executive functioning and self-control.

    The four types of bilingual education programs are (a) **immersion programs**, which teach students only in English; (b) **transitional bilingual education programs**, which teach students in their native language while providing concentrated instruction in learning English; (c) **developmental bilingual programs**, which initially teach core subjects in the students' native language and other instruction in English, and then switch to all English as the students' skills develop; and (d) **dual language programs**, in which children who are native speakers of English and children who are non-native speakers work together in a classroom where *both* languages are used.

10. What are the types of language disorders that children may have?

Disorders specific to language comprehension and production: Types of language disorders include **expressive language disorder** in which the production of language is significantly delayed; **phonological disorder**, which involves difficulty with producing sounds correctly for the child's age; and **receptive-expressive language disorder**, which involves both difficulty with understanding words or sentences and problems with producing and using language. Stuttering is difficulty with fluency and time patterning of speech.

Disorders on the autism spectrum: Children with **autism** often have serious difficulties with speech that can range from a lack of any language to **echolalia** (in which children repeat what is said to them instead of responding).

Learning disabilities related to language: Learning disabilities that specifically involve language include **dyslexia** (difficulty with distinguishing or separating the sounds in spoken words, creating problems when learning to spell and read written words) and **dysgraphia** (difficulty with spelling, handwriting, or expressing thoughts on paper).

Go to **www.sagepub.com/levine** for additional exercises and video resources. Select **Chapter 9, Language Development,** for chapter-specific activities.

chapter 10

Emotional Development and Attachment

10

Emotions: Universality and Difference

What Is Emotion?

When you are sitting in a scary movie, you may experience a rapid heartbeat and a sense of tension, you may grip the arm of your friend next to you, and you may actually jump when the hidden menace jumps out at you. This experience of fear includes your body's physiological reaction, your interpretation of the situation, communication with another person, and your own actions, all parts of what we call **emotion**.

Emotion The body's physiological reaction to a situation, the cognitive interpretation of the situation, communication to another person, and actions.

Test Your Knowledge

Test your knowledge of child development by deciding whether each of the following statements is *true* or *false*, and then check your answers as you read the chapter.

1. **True/False:** People all over the world understand each other's emotional expressions.
2. **True/False:** When babies and young children cry because a parent has left, it is evidence that the children are too attached to their parents.
3. **True/False:** The best indication that an infant has a warm, secure relationship with his or her caregiver is if the infant gets upset when the caregiver leaves the room.
4. **True/False:** Mothers must have immediate contact with their babies after they are born if a secure attachment is to be formed.
5. **True/False:** If a child has developed an insecure attachment to a parent, she can become securely attached later in her life.
6. **True/False:** Teens who are strongly attached to their friends are likely to also be strongly attached to their parents.
7. **True/False:** The average child today reports more anxiety than a child in psychiatric treatment in the 1950s did.
8. **True/False:** School phobias usually are the result of children worrying that they won't do well in school.
9. **True/False:** Throughout childhood and adolescence, girls are more likely to suffer from depression than boys.
10. **True/False:** Hormonal changes at puberty are a likely cause of adolescent depression.

Correct answers: (1) False, (2) False, (3) False, (4) False, (5) True, (6) True, (7) True, (8) False, (9) False, (10) False

Watching scary movies. Scary movies arouse a number of emotional responses. Have you ever thought about why you cover (or partially cover) your eyes when you watch a scary movie? You are trying to control the amount of stimulation that you take in so you can keep it at a level that is arousing and fun but not too overwhelming.

We all experience a range of emotions, from happy to sad, angry to afraid, and embarrassed to disgusted. We will discuss both the biological underpinnings and the environmental influences that shape our expression, experience, and interpretation of emotions.

One way to understand the role of emotions in communication is to look at situations in which they are absent. See **Active Learning: Why We Use Emoticons** to see what problems arise when our electronic communication lacks emotional expression and how people have tried to solve them. You will also learn about some cultural differences in the expression of emotions.

ACTIVE LEARNING

Why We Use Emoticons

Have you ever had an online conversation with someone, only to realize that you had misunderstood what she really meant to say? If someone writes, "I want to see you," how do you interpret that? In 1982, a professor of computer science at Carnegie Mellon University, Scott Fahlman, sent the first emoticon, designed to add emotions to online communication. He wrote, "I propose the following character sequence for joke markers: :-), . . . read it sideways" (Lovering, 2007, p. E2). The joke marker was meant to distinguish sarcastic or silly comments from serious ones, as people were badly misunderstanding each other, going as far as to interpret jokes as real safety warnings (Fahlman, n.d.).

As Internet communication boomed, so did the use of these little characters because people wanted to be sure that the meanings of their words were understood. In the question above, you would read "I want to see you :-)" very differently from "I want to see you >:-(". Emotions are necessary to make sure our meaning is communicated clearly. Of course the emoticons have become much more sophisticated since Fahlman first created them. People have moved away from simple typed emoticons, and there now are entire websites devoted to cartoon emoticons that you can download and use. In fact, if you type *colon–hyphen–close parenthesis,* on many computers this combination of punctuation marks automatically becomes a smiley face.

Emoticons are a "language" that adds emotions to our written conversations, but you may not know that other cultures have their own emoticons that you may not recognize if you are a native speaker of English. Western-style emoticons typically are written so that you need to tip your head to the left to see them. East Asian emoticons are not. Recent research has shown that when trying to interpret photographs of faces expressing different emotions, Westerners tend to scan the whole face, while East Asians focus on the eyes (Jack, Blais, Scheepers, Schyns, & Caldara, 2009). This difference is apparent when we compare emoticons used in these two cultures:

East/West Differences in Emoticons		
Emotion	West	East
Happy	:-)	(^_^)
Sad	:-(	(;_;) or (T_T)
Surprised	:-o	(o.o)

Can you identify the emotions expressed by these emoticons used in East Asia?

(a)	(b)	(c)	(d)
☆⌒(>｡≪)	(￣ω￣)	(>^_^)>(;_;)<(^_^<)	ポッ(*°.°)(°.°*)ポッ

Answers: (a) Getting hurt/experiencing pain; (b) complaint/discontent; (c) offering a hug to a person who is crying; (d) love.

Because there is a physiological component in emotions, we might think that emotions are rooted in our biology and, therefore, they would be similar for all human beings, regardless of their cultural background. Charles Darwin believed there were universal human emotions that evolved as humans developed from animals. In fact, research has found remarkable similarity around the world in the display and understanding of facial expressions that indicate basic emotions: happiness, sadness, fear, anger, surprise/interest, and disgust (Izard, 2007; Oatley, Keltner, & Jenkins, 2006). In addition, there is some evidence for the universality of more complex emotions, such as pride (Tracy & Robins, 2008). The argument has been made that basic emotions are automatic and unlearned, just like our basic taste experiences (sweet, salty, bitter, and sour) (Izard, 2007). Within the first year of life, infants will demonstrate these basic emotions, and research has shown that particular neural systems in the brain are at least "partially dedicated" to the expression of each of these emotions (Izard, 2007, p. 263). Prevalence of these emotions has also been found to change over the course of the first year, with positive affect such as happiness increasing, fear decreasing, and frustration (anger) increasing (Rothbart, Derryberry, & Hershey, 2000).

However, there is also considerable evidence that how we display emotions and how we understand the emotions shown by others are mediated in part by our culture, language, gender, temperament, and personality (Izard, 2007; Matsumoto, 1992, 2006; Matsumoto & Assar, 1992; Russell, 1994; Wierzbicka, 1986). Although our basic emotions appear to be biologically determined, we quickly develop ways of thinking about emotions, called **emotion schemas**, that affect how we experience and show emotions (Izard, 2007). You'll remember that a schema is a cognitive framework that organizes the world into categories and associations. When we experience sadness, we draw upon a wealth of associations and memories to understand what we are feeling. We may label the experience, connect it to our memory of other experiences when

Emotion schemas All the associations and interpretations that an individual connects to a certain emotion.

1. People all over the world understand each other's emotional expressions.   ✓✗ **TRUE/FALSE**

    False. Although some aspects of emotional expression appear to be universal, there also are cultural differences in how we understand others' emotions.

Universal emotions. These girls in Sri Lanka in South Asia (left) and in Benin in West Africa (right) would likely recognize each other's smiles as expressing the same emotion.

we felt sad, and judge whether our expression of sadness is allowable or appropriate, especially in front of other people. For example, the idea that "big boys don't cry" is a powerful control on the expression of sadness that is activated for many boys and may make it difficult for them to get help or even to understand their own sad feelings. A boy in the United States who is hit by a baseball may automatically begin to cry, but his schema for crying includes "big boys don't cry." He decides "I cannot let myself cry," and his facial expression may then reflect anger at himself for experiencing this forbidden emotion. Often sadness is then expressed as anger, which is more acceptable for boys in American culture. These types of connections contribute to our schema of sadness, and these schemas may differ in different cultures.

Cultural differences affect both the display and the interpretation of emotions. Someone may feel a certain way but may change the expression of it in a variety of ways. He may laugh more loudly at his boss's joke, or he may hide his pleasure at someone else's misfortune (Matsumoto, Yoo, Fontaine, & 56 Members of the Multinational Study of Cultural Display Rules, 2009). Matsumoto, Consolacion, and Yamada (2002) reported that people in individualistic cultures, such as the United States, show their feelings more openly than do people from collectivist cultures, such as Japan. Knowing this, a Japanese person interprets someone's small smile as indicating great happiness, while an American interprets a broad grin as moderate happiness. Temperament, the next topic we will discuss, is another one of the "filters" through which we interpret our emotions. The feeling that a shy child might interpret as panic may be what a more adventurous child interprets as excitement.

Temperament

Although most of us will be frightened when we see a horror film, some people will be so terrified that they will never go to see another film like that again, while others will be scared but also excited by it and they will take every opportunity to see more. **Temperament** is the general way in which we respond to experiences in the world, whether they are horror films, doing a class presentation, or being cut off in traffic. Although different experiences evoke different emotional responses, the concept of temperament implies that individuals have a general emotional style that guides their tendency to respond in certain ways to a variety of events in their environment. Some people are usually timid, fearful, and anxious; some are fearless and outgoing; and others are often aggressive and angry.

Temperament. Children's temperament ranges from shy and retiring to outgoing and adventurous, and where a child falls on this continuum influences how that child interprets new experiences. Where would you place yourself? Have you always been that way?

Temperament The general emotional style an individual displays in responding to events.

Some of these differences reflect characteristic ways we have learned to respond to our experiences, but parents report that their children were different from each other from the moment they were born: One was quiet while the other was boisterous; one was demanding while the other was content. There is some evidence that they are right, that we are born with a certain temperament based to some degree on our genetic inheritance (Goldsmith, Lemery, Aksan, & Buss, 2000).

There have been several different approaches to describing and measuring temperament (Strelau, 1998), but one of the most influential ones was developed by Alexander Thomas and Stella Chess (Chess & Thomas, 1999; Thomas & Chess, 1977). Based on their observation of children and families, they identified nine characteristics that contribute to the child's temperament. These characteristics include activity level, adaptability, approach or withdrawal, attention span and persistence, distractibility, intensity of reaction, quality of mood, rhythmicity (or regularity), and threshold of responsiveness. Any individual child can score high, low, or average on each of these characteristics, and combining this information produces three temperament profiles: an easy temperament, a difficult temperament, and a slow-to-warm temperament. Table 10.1 shows where children with each of these temperament profiles fall on each of these dimensions.

Table 10.1

Temperament profiles. This table shows where children who are classified by Thomas and Chess as "easy," "slow to warm," or "difficult" fall on each of the nine dimensions of temperament that they describe. Note that about 35% of children show a mixture of traits that do not fit one of these profiles.

Dimension of Temperament	Easy	Slow to Warm	Difficult
Activity Level	Varies	Low to moderate	Varies
Adaptability	Very adaptable	Slowly adaptable	Slowly adaptable
Approach/Withdrawal	Positive approach	Initial withdrawal	Withdrawal
Attention Span and Persistence	High or low	High or low	High or low
Distractibility	Varies	Varies	Varies
Intensity of Reaction	Low or mild	Mild	Intense
Quality of Mood	Positive	Slightly negative	Negative
Rhythmicity	Very regular	Varies	Irregular
Threshold of Responsiveness	High or low	High or low	High or low

Infants with an **easy temperament** have a generally positive mood, adapt fairly easily to change, and are regular and predictable in their patterns of eating, sleeping, and elimination (Chess & Thomas, 1999). By contrast, infants with a **difficult temperament** have a more negative mood, are easily frustrated and slow to adapt to change, and have irregular patterns of eating, sleeping, and elimination. Children with difficult temperaments also tend to react more intensely to situations than children with easy temperaments. For these children, it is even more important that parents try to keep their environments regular and predictable and that changes be introduced gradually. The third temperament described by Chess and Thomas (1999) is the **slow-to-warm temperament**. The reaction of these children to new experiences is milder than the reaction of a difficult child, and that is true of their reaction both to things that they like and to things that they dislike. However, if they are given some time and are not pressured by adults, with repeated exposure to the new experience they gradually come around on

Easy temperament A child's general responsiveness marked by positive mood, easy adaptation to change, and regularity and predictability in patterns of eating, sleeping, and elimination.

Difficult temperament A child's general responsiveness marked by more negative mood, frustration and intense responses, slow adaptation to change, and irregular patterns of eating, sleeping, and elimination.

Slow-to-warm temperament A general responsiveness marked by a slow adaptation to new experiences and moderate irregularity in eating, sleeping, and elimination.

Goodness of fit   How well a child's temperamental characteristics match with the demands of the environment.

their own. Slow-to-warm children also are less irregular in their eating, sleeping, and elimination patterns than difficult children but are not as regular as easy children.

According to Chess and Thomas (1999), what is most important in determining the consequences of having one type of temperament versus another is the **goodness of fit** between the child's characteristics and the demands of the environment. For instance, if an infant doesn't like a lot of noise and crowds of people, a sensitive parent tries to avoid these situations or plans to take the infant into these situations only when she is well rested, fed, and comfortable (Sturm, 2004).

In their original study on children's temperament, Thomas and Chess (1977) found that easy children made up about 40% of their sample, difficult children made up 10%, and slow-to-warm children made up about 15%. The remainder of the children could not be classified into one of these categories primarily because they displayed these characteristics in a different configuration or were not consistent in the type of behaviors they showed from one occasion to another.

The role that temperament plays in child development will be discussed in many sections throughout this book. For example, later in this chapter we will find that infants' temperament relates to the nature of their attachment to their mother. The question of whether the temperament with which we are born remains the basis for our emotional responses for the rest of our lives is a complicated one. Research shows a tendency for many children to maintain the same temperament over time (Rothbart et al., 2000). However, there are also many children who change. Although children do not tend to change from one extreme to another, smaller changes do occur (Goldsmith et al., 2000). Think about your own temperament. If you are shy now, were you also shy as a child? If you are outgoing now, have you been told that you were very friendly as a child? Were you shy until a certain age and then you changed to become more outgoing? If possible, interview your parent about your temperament as suggested in **Active Learning: Temperament**.

ACTIVE LEARNING

Temperament

Buss, Plomin, and Willerman (1973) developed some different ideas about the dimensions of temperament than those developed by Chess and Thomas. They divided temperament into four dimensions: (a) emotionality or the level of arousal, (b) activity level or the magnitude of the response, (c) sociability or the tendency to approach others, and (d) impulsivity or the quickness of a response. Use these dimensions to interview your parents about what you were like as a newborn, during your first few months of life, and as a toddler. At each stage, how easily were you distressed? How active were you? How much did you enjoy social interaction? How quickly did you respond to situations? Do you feel that your parents' descriptions of you still describe you now in any way? If you feel that your temperament has undergone some significant change, can you identify anything that initiated that change (for instance, becoming more outgoing after you had to move to a new school and make new friends)? These indicators of temperament seem to stay the same for some people and change for others.

So far we have seen that infants are born with the ability to experience and express emotions. Infants are also born with a certain temperament that relates to how intensely they experience emotions. Infants must learn how to deal with these emotional experiences as they grow and develop. There are many tasks that lie ahead. They will need to develop the ability to recognize others' emotions as well as their own. They will learn how to "read" the emotions of others and how to regulate their own emotions through interaction with the people who care for them. We start by describing the nature of those first relationships that shape infants' emotional development. We will return to the development of emotional awareness and self-regulation in Chapter 11 because these are important components of the development of the self.

Attachment

Love is one of the most important and formative of emotions. The first love that we develop is for those who care for us, usually our parents. The nature of love in this relationship consists of an emotional bond, known as **attachment**, and is central to the well-being of infants and children as they grow. In this section we will look at how attachment develops, how it differs from person to person, and what its consequences are. Before continuing, try **Active Learning: Experiencing a Sense of Secure Attachment**.

Attachment An emotional bond to a particular person.

ACTIVE LEARNING

Experiencing a Sense of Secure Attachment

In a quiet place, close your eyes and relax for a brief time. Keeping your eyes closed, try to remember a time in your life when you felt cared for, secure, and loved. If you are able to bring forth a memory, stay with it for a few minutes. Experience that feeling. Whom are you with in this memory? What is happening? Now slowly open your eyes and return to the present. Reflect on your experience. How did you feel? Was there one person in particular who helped you feel that way? This activity is designed to elicit feelings connected with the experience of emotional attachment. These are feeling-memories that we may call on in times of stress. This exercise is not necessarily an easy one to do, so do not be alarmed if you were not able to call forth a memory.

Secure attachment can be defined as a strong, positive emotional bond with a particular person. If you are attached to someone, you are more likely to turn to that person for comfort when you are distressed. You are usually happy to see that person and may be unhappy about separations. This is a person with whom you can feel free to "be yourself" in the fullest sense. Although we talk quite a bit about the development of attachment in infants, attachment remains central to our well-being throughout our lives. In elderly people, it is not uncommon for a husband or wife to die shortly after a spouse dies or is hospitalized (Bower, 2006). It appears that this permanent separation from a loved one may overwhelm the immune system. We can almost think of it as dying of a broken heart.

Secure attachment A strong, positive emotional bond with a person who provides comfort and a sense of security.

Attachment across the life span. Attachment begins in infancy but continues throughout our lives.

Attachment and Adaptation

Both psychoanalytic and behavioral theories originally portrayed attachment as the product of the fact that the mother fed her baby and satisfied the infant's hunger drive. However, current approaches based on ethological theory view attachment as an adaptive behavior, built into us genetically through the process of evolution (See **Journey of Research: The History of the Study of Attachment** for more information about how our thinking about the roots of attachment has changed over the years).

In what ways is attachment adaptive? Alan Sroufe (1997) argues that the goal of attachment is for the infant to feel safe and secure and the baby's behavior is designed to achieve this sense of security. Therefore, when the baby feels threatened, whether it is from a scary noise or from uncomfortable hunger pains, he will act to keep the parent, or caregiver, close. Infant crying, smiling, and following all serve to keep the parent nearby. Because infants are dependent upon an adult caregiver to provide all the things that keep them alive, it makes sense biologically that they would have behaviors built into their repertoire that are designed to keep that parent near.

When babies feel safe and comfortable, they can rely on the parent as a support for exploring the world. Exploration is essential for human learning and is, therefore, also adaptive. When infants feel secure, they are able to explore their environment, checking back from time to time for a hug in a form of "emotional refueling," like a car that runs out of gas and needs to be filled up to continue on its travels (Mahler, Bergman, & Pine, 2000, p. 69). The child uses the parent as a **secure base for exploration**.

Infants also learn to regulate their emotions through the experiences they have with their parents (Sroufe, 1997). Infants initially have difficulty regulating their emotional reactions. For example, when babies begin to cry, they may cry harder and harder, stressing their body's resources. They rely on parents to help control and modulate these feelings. A special relationship forms with the parent as the parent learns to comfort the child effectively. Other people, with whom the infant is not securely attached, may not be able to soothe the infant in the same way. Eventually babies who feel secure learn that they do not have to get out of control in order for their needs to be met.

Secure base for exploration The use of a parent to provide the security that an infant can rely on as she explores the environment.

The History of the Study of Attachment

Drive reduction The idea that human behavior is determined by the motivation to satisfy or reduce the discomfort caused by biological needs or drives.

Cathexis In psychoanalytic theory, the direction of someone's emotional energy to a particular person or object.

In the early- to mid-1900s, both psychoanalytic and behavioral theorists developed ideas about how the bond between child and parent is formed. Both of these theories were based on the idea of **drive reduction**—that is, the idea that human behavior is determined by the motivation to satisfy basic needs. Hunger, for example, is a basic drive. When we feel hungry, we are driven to seek out food, and our drive is reduced when we eat and satisfy that hunger drive. For both theories, the development of a child's attachment to his mother is based upon the mother's ability to satisfy such drives.

You'll remember from Chapter 2 that behavioral theorists based their explanation on the process called classical conditioning. To briefly review, being fed by the mother (originally an unconditioned stimulus) leads to the child's feeling of pleasure (unconditioned response). Because the baby sees the mother each time he is fed, he eventually associates the mother's face (which becomes a conditioned stimulus) with the experience of being fed. He begins to experience the same sense of satisfaction he experiences from feeding when he is in the presence of his mother (a conditioned response) whether she is feeding him or not.

You also will remember that psychoanalysts believed that infants are in the oral stage of psychosexual development, in which the basic drives are centered on the mouth and the experience of "taking in." As the baby satisfies her oral drive, she directs her energy, in a process known as a **cathexis**, first to the mother's breast and subsequently to the mother (Yates, 1991). **Cathexis** became the psychoanalysts' word for attachment. The idea that biological drives are central to human motivation was challenged when Erik Erikson introduced his idea of a psychosocial basis for development, rather than Freud's psychosexual basis. For Erikson, infancy centered on the resolution of the conflict between the development of trust or mistrust in caregivers and in one's own ability to regulate urges (Erikson, 1963).

Harlow's monkeys. In his research, Harry Harlow (1958) found that monkeys preferred a soft cloth "mother," even if it did not provide food, over a wire "mother" who provided food through a bottle. How did this finding challenge the ideas of both psychoanalytic and behavioral theories of attachment?

As Erikson was reshaping the concepts of psychoanalytic theory in the 1950s, the issue of attachment was also being studied by several other groups of researchers. In 1958 Harry Harlow published an article called "The Nature of Love," in which he reported the results of his research with macaque monkeys. In order to examine whether monkeys formed

attachments because of the satisfaction of their hunger drive as some theories proposed or whether there were other reasons behind formation of attachments, Harlow separated infant monkeys from their mothers at birth and raised them with two surrogate mothers. One "mother" was a wire mesh tube, and the other was a wooden tube covered in sponge rubber with terry cloth wrapped around it so that it would be comfortable to touch. Half of the monkeys were fed from a bottle protruding from the wire mother, and half were fed from the cloth mother.

What Harlow found was that infant monkeys spent the majority of their time clinging to the cloth mother regardless of which surrogate mother provided milk. When Harlow frightened the infant monkeys with a loud, moving toy, they were more likely to run to the cloth mother for security. When they were placed in a new, unknown setting, they again preferred to cling to the cloth mother and eventually were able to explore the room, using her as a "safe base" to return to when they became frightened. When she was absent, the babies were distressed and unable to explore the environment or play. Harlow was so impressed with the results of his experiment that he believed the primary function of nursing a baby might actually be to provide contact comfort with the mother and that it was this contact comfort that created the mother-infant attachment, not feeding, as the behaviorists and psychoanalysts believed.

At about the same time, at the Tavistock Clinic in London, John Bowlby, a child psychiatrist trained in psychoanalysis, was exploring his observation that separations from parents had an enormous impact on the psychological well-being of children in the clinic (Ainsworth & Bowlby, 1989). Bowlby believed that psychoanalytic theory could not explain the devastating effect that these experiences had because psychoanalysis focused on internal drives, thoughts, and feelings rather than on experiences in the world. Bowlby felt that Harlow's research confirmed his suspicions that a psychoanalytic explanation for attachment was not adequate.

Bowlby also was intrigued by a new theory that was being proposed, based on observation of natural behavior of animals. Again, from Chapter 2, you will remember that Konrad Lorenz proposed the theory of ethology, based on Darwin's theory of evolution. In

Video Link 10.1
Harlow's monkeys.

(Continued)

(Continued)

this approach, genes are thought to produce certain behaviors. If these behaviors help the animal successfully reproduce, those genes are passed along to the next generation.

One behavior that Lorenz observed was that newborn geese seemed to have an inborn tendency to follow the first large moving object they saw, usually their mother. According to ethological theory, genes that control this behavior would survive because this behavior is adaptive: Baby geese that follow their mothers are less likely to be eaten by predators or die of starvation. You'll also remember that Lorenz called this process imprinting. Lorenz showed that imprinting was an inborn behavior and not a response to behavior by the mother goose by removing a mother immediately after her eggs hatched and substituting himself as the first large moving object the newly hatched goslings saw. The goslings happily followed Dr. Lorenz as their new "mother."

In 1958, Bowlby published an article titled "The Nature of the Child's Tie to His Mother" in which he set forth his new ethological theory of attachment. He argued that attachment is a biologically based, active behavior, equal in importance to the basic drives of hunger and sex, and is related to the infant's need for protection in order to survive. Bowlby believed that behaviors such as crying, smiling, sucking, clinging, and following all help develop attachment between mother and child.

In 1950, Mary Ainsworth joined Bowlby's research team (Ainsworth & Bowlby, 1989). Ainsworth was trained in the scientific method used in psychology and was interested in assessing and classifying different types of emotional security. When she moved from England to Uganda in 1954, she began her research by observing mothers and their infants. Her observations led to her first classification scheme of four categories of attachment, which is now used in research around the world: secure attachment, anxious avoidant attachment, anxious ambivalent/resistant attachment, and disorganized/disoriented attachment.

Research building upon this model of attachment continues and has added to our understanding of the process, but the basic theory outlined by Bowlby and Ainsworth remains the underlying model for most of the work on attachment being done today. In the next sections we will describe first the stages that an infant moves through as he or she develops an attachment to a caregiver, and then the types of attachment relationships that can result from this process.

Video Link 10.2
Lorenz.

Preattachment The stage of development of attachment from birth to 6 weeks, in which infant sensory preferences bring infants into close connection with parents.

Attachment in the making The stage from 6 weeks to 6–8 months in which infants develop stranger anxiety, differentiating those they know from those they don't.

Clear-cut attachment The stage from 6–8 months to 18 months–2 years, when an infant develops separation anxiety when a person he is attached to leaves him.

Goal-corrected partnership The stage of development of attachment from 18 months on, when toddlers create reciprocal relationships with their mothers.

The Development of Attachment: Bowlby's Stages

As John Bowlby (1969) brought new ideas from Harlow's research and from ethological theory into his research on attachment, he described the following four stages in the early development of attachment:

1. **Preattachment** (birth to 6 weeks)

2. **Attachment in the making** (6 weeks to 6–8 months)

3. **Clear-cut attachment** (6–8 months to 18 months–2 years)

4. **Goal-corrected partnership** (also referred to as the formation of reciprocal relationships; 18 months on) (Ainsworth, Blehar, Waters, & Wall, 1978)

We will describe these stages in more detail below.

Preattachment (Birth to 6 Weeks)

As we have already noted, from their earliest days, infants act in ways that attract others to care for them. It is very difficult to sit and do nothing when we hear a baby crying, especially if that baby is our own. Both new mothers and new fathers experience hormonal changes following childbirth that may increase their responsiveness to their baby's distress. Their body responds with more rapid heartbeats and other physiological responses that promote caregiving to their new babies (Berg & Wynne-Edwards, 2001; Fleming, Corter, Stallings, & Sneider, 2002; Frodi & Lamb, 1980; Stallings, Fleming, Corter, Worthman, & Steiner, 2001).

As we discussed in Chapter 6, the sensory preferences of the infant, such as smell and vision, predispose infants to social interactions with the world in general, and with their mothers in particular. For example, infants prefer to see faces, to hear human voices and their mother's voice in particular, to be touched, and to taste sweet things, such as breast milk. They are prewired for social interaction and to begin the process of becoming attached to their parents.

Attachment in the Making (6 Weeks to 6–8 Months)

Babies begin to smile at about 6 weeks of age, but at first these smiles seem almost random—babies seem to smile at specks of dust at the corner of their cribs. However, by about 2 months of age, babies clearly have developed a social smile, which is directed specifically at people (Ellsworth, Muir, & Hains, 1993). Very quickly, smiling that was indiscriminate at first becomes reserved for people the baby recognizes. A 3-month-old baby may look seriously at a stranger but begin to grin when he sees his mother. These early signs of recognition and responsiveness begin to lay a foundation of a special relationship with the familiar and important people in the baby's social world. All new parents will tell you how good it feels when their infants begin to look directly at them and then smile because they recognize that they are looking at someone very special to them.

In many infants, this early discrimination of familiar from unfamiliar intensifies. If you have ever gone to babysit for a 6-month-old infant who has never met you before, you know what **stranger anxiety** means. Sometimes all the baby has to do is see a stranger and he begins wailing. In other cases the baby may interact and smile as long as he is in his mother's arms, but if the stranger tries to hold him, the crying begins.

First smiles. It is a wonderful reward for a new parent when an infant begins to smile at her mother, and fathers feel the same thrill. This is an early step in the process of forming a specific attachment to the infant's caregivers.

Stranger anxiety. Even the nicest stranger may become frightening for a child when the child begins to recognize the difference between people he knows and people he doesn't. This reaction is often seen during the stage of attachment in the making.

Even a parent may temporarily become a "stranger" to his infant by changing his appearance. A father who has always had a beard may appear to be an entirely different person to his infant when he shaves the beard off. As he goes to hold his loving daughter, he may be surprised when she howls with fear. What is the solution? Let the baby see you actually shaving the beard off. Seeing the transformation from one "daddy" to another should help.

Stranger anxiety
Fearfulness that infants develop toward people they do not know.

Attachment and secure base for exploration.
Securely attached children will play away from
the parent, as long as they can go back from
time to time for some "emotional refueling."

Partnership of mother and child. By 18 months children like this boy actively attempt to maintain an interaction with their mother, creating a goal-corrected partnership.

Clear-Cut Attachment (6–8 Months to 18 Months–2 Years)

In this stage, infants begin to move about on their own. Consequently, they are now able to actively maintain contact with their caregiver. To Bowlby, this is the hallmark of true— or "clear-cut"—attachment. Particularly when babies are stressed or afraid, the attachment system with which they are born drives them to seek out their parent (remember Harlow's monkeys who ran to the cloth mother monkey when shown a frightening toy?). During this stage, separation from parents, in and of itself, becomes frightening to infants, and they begin to protest when their parents leave. This distress is referred to as **separation anxiety**. In addition, the parent becomes a secure base for exploration. When a parent is around and the infant can get to the parent, she is comfortable to explore but maintains her sense of security by checking back with the parent from time to time. If the parent is absent, exploration may stop.

If we understand that we feel most comfortable, most "ourselves," when we are with a person we love and trust, then separation anxiety and the need to have a secure base make sense. You may recall a time when you felt homesick, perhaps on a school trip, at summer camp, or even when beginning college. Although you can control your emotions better than an infant, you still may have felt anxiety about being on your own without the people who made you feel most comfortable. If you had access to a phone, did you find that you called your parents or friends back home more frequently? If you think about this situation, you will see a connection to the need for a "secure base" and the "emotional refueling" activities seen in infants.

Goal-Corrected Partnership (18 Months On)

As the baby becomes a toddler, she becomes increasingly aware that her mother has goals and motives that are different from her own. At this point she realizes that she must create a partnership with her mother in their interaction. This partnership is based on the idea of two separate individuals interacting, each with an equal part in keeping the interaction going (Bowlby, 1969).

Separation anxiety
Distress felt when separated from parent.

TRUE/FALSE

2. When babies and young children cry because a parent has left, it is evidence that the children are too attached to their parents.

False. Crying is a normal response to the departure of someone who helps the infant feel secure, and it does not indicate excessive attachment.

At this same age, toddlers begin to represent the world in their minds, and, as you learned in Chapter 7, this representation is referred to as symbolic thinking. Bowlby hypothesized that toddlers now are able to form symbolic representations of the particular attachment relationships they have been experiencing (Bowlby, 1969). This concept, referred to as an **internal working model** of attachment, has helped psychologists understand how early attachment patterns contribute to the close relationships that children—and even adults—develop later in life. Based upon our past experiences, an inner script develops, so in this sense our future interactions are shaped by our past interactions. For example, a child who has been abused may expect aggression from others, and this expectation will shape how the child behaves when the child meets new people. This helps us understand some behavior that otherwise would be quite puzzling. Abused children may respond to new people by provoking them to be angry, possibly re-creating the abuse situation the children previously experienced. If you think about it, this behavior, which at first glance seems strange and even maladaptive, can be an attempt to reduce the uncertainty of the new situation and to control the child's fears by making the new situation one that the child can at least understand based upon previous experiences. In a similar way—but with a very different outcome—children who have been warmly cared for come to expect that others will treat them positively, so these children themselves act in a warm and engaging way. Their own positive interactions then elicit positive responses from others. Observe for yourself how you respond to a person who greets you with a warm, genuine smile in comparison to one who approaches warily, with his eyes down or with an aggressive stare.

Although research supports the idea that internal working models are fairly stable over time, there also is evidence that they can be modified (Pietromonaco & Barrett, 2000). In the case of children with negative working models of attachment, it takes time and patience to overcome the expectations that the child has developed for new relationships, but it can be done.

> **Internal working model** Mental representations of the particular attachment relationships that a child has experienced that become the model for expectations of future relationships.

Ainsworth's Types of Attachment

As you read in **Journey of Research: The History of the Study of Attachment**, Mary Ainsworth was a developmental psychologist who worked with John Bowlby and further developed his ethological theory. Ainsworth was interested in looking at individual differences in the types of attachment that infants and mothers formed together, based on the degree of security the infant felt in that relationship. Security is felt with the person who best understands the infant's signals concerning his needs and desires (Hennighausen & Lyons-Ruth, 2005). Although it is a natural behavior for infants to seek contact with a parent when stressed or frightened, experiences with a particular parent's responses may make it necessary for the infant to find alternative ways of responding in this situation (Bosma & Gerlsma, 2003).

Ainsworth used naturalistic observations of infants and mothers in Uganda and the United States to develop a system to classify types of attachment. Her initial naturalistic observations were later supplemented with a new procedure that she developed for assessing attachment that is known as the **Strange Situation**. The Strange Situation involves a series of events revolving around an infant and his mother that become increasingly stressful for the infant:

> **Strange Situation** Mary Ainsworth's experimental procedure designed to assess security of attachment in infants.

1. Mother and baby enter a comfortable room (equipped with a one-way mirror so they can be observed) with the stranger, who immediately leaves.

2. Baby plays while mother responds naturally.

3. Stranger enters, and at the end of 3 minutes the mother leaves.

4. Baby is in the room with the stranger, who may interact with the baby.

5. Mother returns, stranger leaves, and at the end of 3 minutes the mother again leaves.

3. The best indication that an infant has a warm, secure relationship with his or her caregiver is if the infant gets upset when the caregiver leaves the room.

False. Although securely attached infants may be upset when their mothers leave them, a better indicator of the security of their attachment is how eagerly they respond when their mothers return and how easily they are soothed by their mothers.

Video Link 10.3
Mary Ainsworth and the Strange Situation.

Anxious avoidant attachment An attachment classification in which the infant is not distressed when his mother leaves, is just as comfortable with the stranger as with his mother, and, when his mother returns, does not rush to greet her.

6. Baby is alone for 3 minutes.

7. Stranger enters and may interact with the baby.

8. Mother returns. (Ainsworth & Bell, 1970)

Except for the first episode, each lasts 3 minutes unless the baby is crying, in which case the time period is cut short.

Based on her observations of babies in natural situations and in the Strange Situation, Ainsworth described four types of attachment: secure attachment, anxious avoidant attachment, anxious ambivalent/resistant attachment, and disorganized/disoriented attachment. Initially only the first three categories were included, but Main and Solomon added the fourth in 1990 to describe behaviors seen in the Strange Situation that did not fit into the original three categories. These four types differ on two dimensions: security and organization of behavior.

Ainsworth found two behaviors in her observations that best identified the type of attachment relationship that infants had with their mother. The first was the child's ability to be comfortable and explore a new setting while the mother was in the room, with the mother acting as a secure base for exploration. The second was the child's response to the mother's return to the room, known as reunion behavior—that is, whether the child, who was stressed by the mother's departure, was able to use the mother upon her return to calm down and return to playing. Interestingly, distress at separation itself was *not* a reliable indicator of type of attachment. Table 10.2 relates the type of attachment with the behaviors that typify that category and the type of mothering that has been associated with each type.

Infants with secure attachment rely on their parent to respond to their needs, and turn to their parent when they are stressed. The baby's reliance on a trustworthy parent allows her to explore the environment, knowing that mother is there to help if help is needed. In contrast, infants with insecure attachment have learned that their parent is not as available to them and have adapted in one of two ways: In **anxious avoidant attachment**, the mother has been unresponsive to her infant, and the infant has learned not to rely on her help and support. This infant is not distressed when his mother leaves the room, is just as comfortable with the stranger as with his mother, and, when his mother returns to the room, does not rush to greet

Table 10.2

Types of attachment. This table shows Ainsworth's four types of attachment with their associated behaviors in the Strange Situation and aspects of mothering that have been related to each type.

Type of Attachment	Security/Organization	Safe Base for Exploration	Reunion With Caregiver	Early Mothering
Secure	Secure/organized	Explores freely with caregiver present	Seeks out caregiver and is easily soothed by caregiver	Responsive to infant's needs
Anxious avoidant	Insecure/organized	Explores with or without caregiver's presence	Does not seek out caregiver	Emotionally unavailable, dislikes neediness
Anxious ambivalent/resistant	Insecure/organized	Stays close to caregiver, doesn't explore freely	Both seeks and rejects contact with caregiver	May be attentive, but not in response to baby's cues or needs
Disorganized/disoriented	Insecure/disorganized	May "freeze," explores in a disorganized fashion	May go to caregiver while looking away, shows a dazed expression or fear	Intrusiveness, maltreatment and/or emotional unavailability, confusing or frightening

her. In **anxious ambivalent/resistant attachment**, mothers may interact positively with their infant, but they do not respond to the infant's cues. For example, they may ignore the baby when he is trying to get her attention but may interact when the baby is more interested in sleeping than interacting. In anxious ambivalent/resistant attachment, the infant is reluctant to move away from his mother to explore the room, is very distressed when his mother leaves the room, and will not let the stranger comfort him. When his mother returns, the infant's behavior is described as "ambivalent" because he seems to want to approach his mother but also appears to be angry and resists the mother's attempt to pick him up (Bosma & Gerlsma, 2003).

Although the three types of attachment above differ in level of security, or trust, in their relationships, all three are organized and coherent ways of responding to a particular situation. The fourth category, **disorganized/disoriented attachment**, was identified later to describe infants whose behavior was unpredictable and odd and showed no coherent way of dealing with attachment issues (Hennighausen & Lyons-Ruth, 2010). This category was often linked with parental abuse or neglect and was connected with unmanageable fear. Think about how this pattern would develop: The very person to whom the baby would normally turn when afraid is the same person who is causing the fear. The babies didn't know what to do or where to turn. They could not organize their behavior because they did not have a predictable environment. They never knew what to expect or what was expected of them.

Attachment as a Relationship

Attachment is based upon the relationship between two people, each of whom has an impact on the nature of the relationship. The interaction of a particular child and a particular parent creates a unique relationship that is different from that of any other two people. Many people think, "My sibling and I were raised in the same way, so why are we so different?" There are many answers to this question, but one of them is that the nature of the relationship that each child has with her parents is unique.

The Role of the Mother

Security of attachment has been linked to the nature of parenting in the early months of life. For instance, babies who were securely attached at age 1 had mothers who were responsive to their signals, both soothing the infant when necessary and consistently promoting warm interactions (Hennighausen & Lyons-Ruth, 2005). This connection between warm, responsive parenting and secure attachment has been found in many different cultures around the world (Posada et al., 2002). Mothering was less consistent with infants who had one of the three types of insecure attachment. Specifically, babies with anxious avoidant attachment were more likely to have mothers who were emotionally unavailable and who had rejected their mothering role (Sroufe, 2005). Babies with anxious resistant attachments were more likely to have mothers who were inconsistent in their responsiveness, sometimes responding well and sometimes responding poorly to their babies' needs. Babies with disorganized/disoriented attachment styles were more likely to have mothers who were abusive or neglectful, potentially instilling fear in their babies (Hennighausen & Lyons-Ruth, 2010).

It is too easy to read this information and pass judgment on mothers who have insecurely attached infants, blaming them for not providing an optimal environment for their babies. We need to realize that almost all mothers *want* to be good mothers to their infants, but it isn't as simple as that. What could affect the ability of a mother to be a sensitive, responsive caregiver to her baby? The factors turn out to be remarkably similar to those that help someone through any stressful situation. Remember from Chapter 5 that the transition to becoming a new parent can be a stressful one. Having social, emotional, and material support is important to new mothers because it helps them maintain a positive relationship with their babies

Anxious ambivalent/ resistant attachment An attachment classification in which the infant is reluctant to move away from his mother to explore and is very distressed when his mother leaves, but when his mother returns, he wants to approach her but also angrily resists her attempt to pick him up.

Disorganized/disoriented attachment An attachment classification in which behavior is unpredictable and odd and shows no coherent way of dealing with attachment issues, often linked with parental abuse or neglect.

(Crockenberg, 1981). Mothers are more likely to respond positively to their babies when they have the following:

1. A positive relationship with their partner (Cox, Paley, Payne, & Burchinal, 1999)

2. Adequate economic resources (Crockenberg & Leerkes, 2003)

3. Good psychological health (for example, maternal depression has been linked to insecure attachment) (Martins & Gaffan, 2000)

4. A history of good care in their own childhood (Crockenberg & Leerkes, 2003)

5. An infant who is easy to care for

With regard to this last point, we'll say more about the important role that the characteristics of the infant play in the process in just a little while.

The Role of the Father

Fathers were often neglected in the research on infant attachment. They were seen as secondary to mothers, often with the idea that their primary role was to support the mother. However, it has become clear that infants are capable of forming more than one relationship and that the unique relationship they develop with their fathers plays an important role in their lives (Braungart-Rieker, Courtney, & Garwood, 1999). Some research has shown that fathers are more likely to react sensitively to their sons than their daughters and that baby boys are more likely than baby girls to be securely attached to their fathers (Schoppe-Sullivan et al., 2006). However, both boy and girl infants form attachments to both parents during their first year, and the attachment to the father is as likely to be secure as that to the mother (Schneider-Rosen & Burke, 1999).

Attachment to the father. Fathers as well as mothers can form strong attachments to their infants. The same characteristics—being sensitive and responsive to the infant's needs—are important for father-infant and mother-infant attachment.

The Role of the Infant

Infants, too, play a role in the type of attachment relationship formed with the parent. In Chapter 3 we described relationships as being bidirectional. This means that parents affect children, but children also affect their parents. Any parent of more than one child will tell you that each child seemed to be born with his or her own unique behavioral characteristics. As we discussed earlier in this chapter, these tendencies to react in certain ways to environmental events are known as the child's temperament.

Temperament plays a role in the development of secure attachment, but it is particularly important if the infant is irritable, cries easily and with intensity, and is difficult to soothe. In one study, maternal sensitivity predicted whether the attachment was secure or not, but it was the infant's temperament that predicted the *type* of insecurity the infant exhibited if the infant was insecurely attached (Susman-Stillman, Kalkose, Egeland, & Waldman, 1996). For instance, at 3 months of age, infants who had lower levels of sociability were more likely to have an avoidant attachment at 6 months of age, and infant irritability predicted resistant attachment.

In addition to the role of temperament, there are other factors from the infant that can affect how attachment is first formed, including medical factors such as premature birth and neurological problems (Brisch et al., 2005). Another factor is a condition called infantile colic, in which babies cry inconsolably for long periods of time for no apparent reason. Fortunately this pattern usually ends when the baby is about 3 months old, but infantile colic may have negative effects on the infant's early relationship with his parents. Mothers of colicky infants are more likely to suffer from postpartum depression (Howell, Mora, & Leventhal, 2006), and depressed mothers usually are less sensitive or appropriately responsive to the signals that the infant is sending. In interviews with mothers of colicky infants, it became clear that dealing with babies who cannot be comforted when the mother attempts to soothe them may be interpreted by the mother as a personal rejection, and this can lead to her questioning her efficacy as a parent (Pauli-Pott, Becker, Mertesacker, & Beckmann, 2000). At the very least, infantile colic is exhausting, both emotionally and physically, for all members of the family (Barr, 1995).

All Together Now!

Although we have looked separately at the role of infant and parent in the attachment relationship, researchers are increasingly looking at the complexity of the relationship within the context of the family, society, and culture. An example of this complexity is the finding in one study that whether a child developed a secure or an anxious attachment depended on all of the following variables: infant gender, infant temperament, parental sensitivity, marital conflict, and the dual- or single-earner status of the family. Specifically, boys (but not girls) were found to have less secure attachments to their fathers (but not to their mothers) in dual-earner (but not single-earner) families (Braungart-Rieker et al., 1999).

Another example demonstrates the effects of parent-child interaction over time. In this study, infant negative emotionality (intense and frequent crying) was linked to less sensitive mothering when the babies were 6 months old, and this combination of factors, in turn, led to more insecure attachment at 1 year (Crockenberg, 1981; Sroufe, 2005). In other words, the baby affected the mother, and this interaction influenced development of a secure attachment relationship. To complicate the picture, Crockenberg and Leerkes (2003) found that mothers were likely to be less sensitive to these infants only when they were at risk from poverty, inadequate social support, or a history of parental rejection. Mothers who were *not* at risk were often *more* involved with their fussy babies. The marital relationship has also been found to suffer when a baby has a difficult temperament, with less love and more conflict in the relationship (Crockenberg & Leerkes, 2003).

A way to check your own understanding of the various factors that influence attachment is to see if you can use and apply that information. Try **Active Learning: Educating Parents** to see how you might apply the information you have learned about attachment.

Educating Parents

Imagine that you are a parent educator. Given what you now know about the formation of attachment, plan a class for new parents to explain what attachment is and how they can promote secure attachment in their baby. To help you get started, you will want to think about how you would define attachment for these new parents. What would you tell them about where attachment comes from and how stable it is? What are the best things a parent can do to help ensure their infants will develop a secure attachment? What is something that parents can do for themselves to help them become effective and loving parents?

Before we leave this topic, there is one caveat: Sometimes the literature on attachment makes it sound like infant attachment, or the lack of it, is the fault of the infant's mother because she wasn't sensitive enough or responsive enough. However, by now you know that the quality of an infant's attachment is the product of a number of different factors working together. Parents don't have to be perfect to have a securely attached infant. There is enough resiliency in both infants and parents that most often the outcome is a positive one.

The Biology of Attachment

As we saw in Chapters 4 and 6, researchers are uncovering many links between behavior and biology. In the study of attachment, researchers have looked for neurochemical explanations for development of adaptive and maladaptive behaviors. Pollak and his colleagues studied adopted children who had previously been reared in situations marked by severe neglect in orphanages in Romania and Russia (Fries, Ziegler, Kurian, Jacoris, & Pollak, 2005). Many of these children continued to have problems forming secure attachment relationships with their adoptive parents even though their situation had dramatically improved and they now had parents who wanted and loved them very much.

Fries et al. (2005) found that 3 years after they had been adopted, these children had different hormonal responses to social interaction than other children. The authors studied two neurochemicals (oxytocin and vasopressin) because research with animals has shown that when the level of these chemicals rises, the animals develop more positive social interactions, including attachments between parents and their infants (Fries et al., 2005). They found that children raised by their parents from birth experienced a rise in the chemical oxytocin after interacting with their parents. This chemical may be linked with a positive feeling that arises in connection with warm social interactions (Carter, 2005). However, previously neglected children did not demonstrate a similar rise in oxytocin following interaction with their parents. Additionally, many of these children produced very low levels of vasopressin, a hormone that is linked with the ability to recognize individuals as being familiar. Children reared in deprived situations are sometimes more likely to run to any available adult when distressed rather than to their parents, as we will see below. It is not yet clear whether these chemical responses are set for life or whether they can change with life experience.

Attachment and Culture

Remember that Bowlby (1969) thought that attachment behaviors were adaptive behaviors that helped ensure the survival of infants. This suggests that attachment should be seen in cultures all over the world, and quite a few cross-cultural studies have been conducted to test this premise. Many of these studies have focused on one of two questions: (a) Is the number of secure versus insecure attachments in infants similar from one culture to another? (b) What does a "securely attached" infant look like to mothers in different cultures?

In regard to the first question, cross-cultural research has found that the proportion of infants who are classified by the Strange Situation as having a secure attachment does not differ very much from one country to another (Sagi, van IJzendoorn, & Koren-Karie, 1991; Svanberg, 1998). Secure infants typically account for about two thirds of the infants in a study. What is more likely to differ, however, is the proportion of infants in the different categories of insecure attachment.

In American and North European cultures the most common insecure category is avoidant attachment, but in Israel and Japan, it is an anxious/ambivalent attachment (Svanberg, 1998). Studies conducted in northern Germany in the 1980s found that almost half of the infants were classified as avoidantly attached (which is almost twice the rate typically found in studies with middle-class American infants) (Grossmann, Grossmann, Spangler, Suess, & Unzner, 1985). The authors of this study attributed their finding to the fact that at the time the study was conducted, northern German parents placed a great value on independence and self-reliance. If this type of behavior was encouraged and supported by parents, the child's behavior in the Strange Situation would look like the behavior found in Ainsworth's anxious avoidant classification. Interestingly, when the same researchers later conducted attachment research in southern Germany, the proportions of secure and insecure infants looked quite similar to those typically found in American samples.

Research also has looked at attachment relationships in Japanese culture, but this research has been complicated by the Japanese concept of *amae,* an emotional interdependence between a caregiver and child that is encouraged by the Japanese culture but is not identical to the Western concept of attachment (Vereijken, Riksen-Walraven, & Van Lieshout, 1997). Research by Nakagawa, Lamb, and Miyaki (1992) found that 75% of the Japanese infants in their study were classified as secure (a proportion slightly higher than typically found in Western research), 21% were classified as resistant, and 4% were unclassifiable. However, because *amae* is not the same as attachment, these authors questioned whether a measure such as the Strange Situation, which has been used primarily in research in middle-class Western samples, is valid as a cross-cultural measure.

That leads us to our second question. Rather than asking where children in different cultures fall in Ainsworth's classification scheme, we can ask what parents in different cultures think a securely attached infant looks like. For example, sensitive parenting is found to be related to secure attachment in both the United States and Japan. However, in the United States, mothers are more likely to associate secure attachment in their infants with autonomy and self-determination. In other words, a child is seen as secure if she can move away from her mother and play independently. Mothers in Japan are more likely to see their children as secure if they show behaviors that put them into harmony with others: accommodating to other people, behaving well, and cooperating (Rothbaum, Kakinuma, Nagaoka, & Azuma, 2007). In addition, Japanese mothers are more likely to see their children's unreasonable demands for attention (such as crying every hour through the night while all their needs have already been cared for) as a need for closeness or interdependence, whereas American mothers tend to see this behavior as testing the limits and asserting one's self.

Likewise, although sensitive mothering is related to secure attachment in most cultures, the definition of sensitivity may vary. For example, Carlson and Harwood (2003) found that Puerto Rican mothers were more likely than mothers in Boston to be physically controlling of their infants, and this type of physical control has traditionally been seen as insensitive parenting. However, for Puerto Rican babies, this type of caregiving was associated with a secure attachment pattern in the infants during the Strange Situation. It appears that this type of physical control is seen as a positive value in Puerto Rican culture because it leads to respectful behavior, which is highly valued.

Examining this research reminds us of how difficult it is to search for universal developmental processes when they can take so many forms as we move from one culture to another. We always need to guard against assuming that the way things work in one culture will describe how they work somewhere else.

The Impact of Both Early Attachment and Later Experiences on Development

In Chapter 6, we saw that although infants in Kenya are encouraged to walk at a very early age, it is likely the lifelong practice of running that encourages Kenyans to become marathon winners. In like fashion, although early attachment is very important for later development, lifelong experiences of social interaction, emotional regulation, and opportunities for exploration are also central in forming an individual's personality and capabilities. As research on attachment has grown, it has become increasingly apparent that the type of attachment that an infant forms with his parents, although important, is not the only factor that needs to be considered. In this section we will examine the long-term effects of attachment in infancy and why they are so important. We will also look at other factors that limit or change the impacts of early attachment on later development.

The Myth of Bonding

In 1979, two medical doctors, John Kennell and Marshall H. Klaus, pushed the idea of the importance of early attachment to its extreme. They presented research they believed demonstrated that newborn human infants must experience close physical ("skin-to-skin") contact with their mothers within a few hours after birth for the mothers to be able to form a bond with their infants. In other words, they believed that attachment must start right at birth or there will be negative consequences. Their research received a great deal of attention and transformed the way that hospitals treated new mothers and their infants. Previously newborns had been whisked away by the medical professionals to receive routine neonatal care, while mothers were returned to their rooms to rest and recover. Now parents were given an opportunity to interact with their babies immediately following birth. However, subsequent research failed to confirm the long-term effect of early contact (Eyer, 1992; Myers, 1984). There are many ways in which attachment between parent and child is formed, as you can discover by talking with parents who have adopted a child, and early contact may be desirable but is not essential to the process.

Long-Term Outcomes of Infant Attachment

Research has shown long-term effects of security of attachment in infancy, as Bowlby's concept of internal working models would predict. Securely attached infants have more internal resources with which to cope with difficult events. In their early years, their relationship with their parents serves to soothe and modulate their reactions to frightening or other arousing events. This soothing is then internalized so that at an older age the child or adolescent is able to soothe herself when needed. For example, when a toddler hurts himself, he may turn to his mother who will hold him, put a Band-Aid on his injury, or even take him to the emergency room, if necessary. This toddler develops trust that he can be helped and develops the ability to calm himself and ask for the help he needs. A toddler who is ignored by a parent when he is hurt or whose mother makes the situation worse by yelling at him for hurting himself may not develop the skills needed to deal with his hurts, either physical or emotional, as he grows older. Table 10.3 gives you some examples of what is going on in the minds of children with different types of internal working models.

One reason that security of attachment in infancy can predict later outcomes is because there is a good deal of continuity of attachment styles over time. Several factors contribute to this continuity. For most people, their families do not change drastically, so characteristics of parenting remain stable over time. That means that the patterns of attachment and adaptation developed in

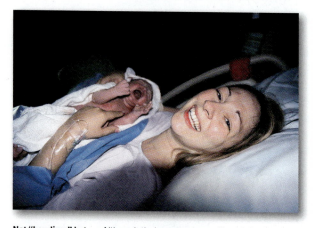

Not "bonding," but . . . Although their research was flawed, the ideas of Kennell and Klaus (1979) about early bonding helped change hospital practices. This mother reflects the joy of being handed her newborn immediately after birth.

TRUE/FALSE

4. Mothers must have immediate contact with their babies after they are born if a secure attachment is to be formed.

False. Although this idea made important changes in hospital practice that allowed mothers to have immediate contact with their infants after birth, the research did not support this idea.

Table 10.3

Internal working models. Think about how having each type of internal working model of attachment would affect a child's approach to and interaction with new people.

Type	Internal Working Model
Secure	I can trust and rely on others. I am lovable, capable, significant, and worthwhile. My world is safe.
Anxious avoidant	Other people are unavailable and rejecting. I have to protect myself. If I deny my needs, I will not be rejected. If I do what is expected of me, I will not be rejected. If I take care of others and deny my own needs, I will be loved.
Anxious ambivalent/resistant	Others are unpredictable, sometimes loving and protective, sometimes hostile and rejecting. I don't know what to expect—I am anxious and angry. I cannot explore—I may miss an opportunity for love and affection. If I can read others and get them to respond, I will get my needs met.
Disorganized/disoriented	My caregiver, at times, seems overwhelmed by me and, at other times, seems very angry with me. Others are abusive—neglectfully, physically, emotionally, and/or sexually. I am unable to get my needs met. I don't know how to protect myself.

infancy continue to be reinforced by later experiences. Also, as we have already described, children usually continue to behave in ways that cause their later relationships to replicate their earlier ones.

Infant attachment is so important to development that it has been associated with a range of developmental outcomes that go beyond ones related to emotional development. We have summarized the results from studies related to long-term outcomes of all kinds in Table 10.4.

Research by Sroufe, Egeland, Carlson, and Collins (2005a) has also shown some evidence that less secure attachment is related to later psychological problems. As shown in Table 10.4, his research team has found that adolescents who had experienced anxious ambivalent/resistant attachment as infants were more likely to have anxiety disorders, such as phobias, posttraumatic stress disorders, or obsessive-compulsive disorders, at age 17. Those who had had anxious avoidant attachment were more likely to have conduct disorders (a pattern of continuous aggression and violation of rules). However, the strongest overall predictor of psychological disorder was disorganized/disoriented attachment in infancy. This type of attachment was most specifically linked with dissociative disorder (a disconnect between the person and her experiences, such as amnesia or what was formerly called multiple personality disorder) (American Psychiatric Association, 2000).

However, what happens when a child's life circumstances *do* change? For instance, what happens when a mother who had developed a secure attachment with her baby becomes preoccupied with a bad marital relationship or becomes depressed? There is ample evidence that shows that changes in life circumstances can change a secure attachment to an insecure one and vice versa (Weinfield, Whaley, & Egeland, 2004). Parents who experience stressful life events often show declines in the quality of their parenting, and the outcome can be a less secure attachment. It is also possible that parents whose lives become more stable as their

5. If a child has developed an insecure attachment to a parent, she can become securely attached later in her life.

 TRUE/FALSE

True. As situations change, attachment can also change. For instance, if a parent was depressed after childbirth and had difficulty creating a secure bond with the baby, when her depression lifts and her interactions change, the child can develop a more secure attachment. Change can also occur in the other direction if parents enter a highly stressful time and have less energy for parenting.

Table 10.4

Long-term outcomes associated with attachment security. The security of an infant's attachment has been associated with a range of developmental outcomes that include social, emotional, and cognitive outcomes.

Attachment Classification	Developmental Outcomes From Longitudinal Studies
Secure	More likely to express distress during separations as 3-year-olds
	Greater concentration in play
	More positive perception of self
	Greater social competence
	Better performance on achievement tests at age 7
	Greater language skills
	Greater conflict resolution skills
	Better school adjustment in general
Anxious avoidant	Lower externalizing behavior
	Less socially competent
	More likely to be rejected by teachers
	More likely to victimize others at school
	Difficulty with emotional closeness
	Conduct disorders, depression
Anxious ambivalent/resistant	Higher levels of externalizing behavior
	More likely to be pampered by teachers
	More likely to be victims at school
	Difficulties with cognitive and social problem solving
	Anxiety disorders, depression
Disorganized/disoriented	Substantial problems at school
	Exhibit substantial aggression
	Problems with integration of identity
	Self-injury
	Dissociative disorders, conduct disorders

children get older are able to develop more secure attachments with their infants (Moss, Cyr, Bureau, Tarabulsy, & Dubois-Comtois, 2005). Moss et al. (2005) studied attachment in children at age 3½ and assessed their attachment again 2 years later. Although the majority of children maintained the same attachment style, they found that children whose attachment style changed from secure to insecure and/or disorganized/disoriented were more likely to have experienced events such as parental hospitalization or death, decreased quality of mother-child interaction, and decreased marital satisfaction of their parents. A child's attachment also can change in a positive direction if the child's parents take part in parenting interventions designed for parents of infants with insecure attachments. These programs can and do change parenting patterns and allow for changes in attachment over time (for example, see Hoffman, Marvin, Cooper, & Powell, 2006). Therefore, it is clear that infants' earliest attachment experiences do not doom infants who begin with insecure attachment and are not a guarantee for those who begin with secure attachment. Even though insecurely attached infants are at an increased risk for psychological problems compared to infants in the other attachment categories, a variety of factors, including having a positive relationship with some other caring adult or the child's own characteristics, can serve as protective factors.

The Importance of Later Experiences

Even if attachment style remains consistent as children grow and develop, there are many other life circumstances that may affect and moderate the effects of those early attachment experiences. As Sroufe and his colleagues have found, later experiences interact with early attachment relationships to help determine adult functioning.

At the University of Minnesota, Alan Sroufe and his colleagues have undertaken a longitudinal study of individuals who were first assessed for attachment style when they were infants. In 1974–1975, 257 low-income pregnant women were recruited for the study. The children of these women were studied from birth through age 26 (Sroufe, Carlson, & Shulman, 1993). An important aspect of Sroufe's work was his focus on patterns of adaptive behavior. He focused on the issues central to adaptation at each age, rather than on particular behaviors (Sroufe, Egeland, Carlson, & Collins, 2005b). In infancy, developing attachment relationships was central. In preschool, the issues included the beginning of peer relationships and the importance of curiosity and self-regulation. In middle childhood, competence and ability to form friendships were important. By adolescence, the development of a sense of identity and the ability to form intimate relationships were key. Note that these issues reflect the developmental crises described by Erik Erikson's theory at these different ages, as described in Chapter 2. In early research reports, Sroufe and his colleagues reported straightforward effects of secure attachment in infancy on later development: Securely attached infants became children who were more competent in their interactions with peers, were more self-reliant, and had better self-control (Sroufe et al., 1993). However, as the children got older, the picture became much more complicated.

For example, the researchers did not find a *direct* link between early attachment and the ability to have intimate, romantic relationships in early adulthood. However, there was an indirect link, mediated through subsequent experiences in the person's life. Although secure attachment in infancy prepares the child for later positive peer relationships, the child's history with peer relationships independently predicted some aspects of adult relationships more clearly than early attachment history, and the combination of early attachment and later experiences with peers was even more predictive of some aspects of later romantic relationships. Each stage provides the foundation for the next stage, but experiences at each successive stage also change the nature and direction of a child's development.

Attachment in Childhood and Adolescence

By the time a child reaches the age of 3, he is able to represent the world and his experiences of it in his mind. At this point Ainsworth's Strange Situation is less effective for assessing attachment because children are more independent and should be less stressed by a situation that involves separations and reunions with a parent. One of the ways in which researchers have examined security of attachment in older children is by having them make up stories based on pictures or words designed to bring out their thoughts about whether the child's world includes a "safe base" through which he can resolve such challenges as falling and hurting his knee or having a "monster" in the bedroom (Waters, Rodrigues, & Ridgeway, 1998). A child who feels he has a secure base might respond to the first dilemma with a story about the child being comforted by the mother and then being told about how to climb safely. A child who is less secure might simply have the child cry and then the mother takes him home. These stories are taken to represent the child's **secure base script**. This script sets out the steps you would follow if you were in distress and needed some help. It includes the idea that if you are in distress, you can approach someone for help who will be available and supportive when you need him, and you will

Secure base script   The expectation that a child develops that distress will or will not be met with care, concern, and support.

experience relief as the result of being close to this person (Waters & Waters, 2006). A securely attached child expects security, while the insecurely attached child does not.

Although most people would not question the continuing importance of attachment relationships for preschoolers and school-age children, the question of adolescent attachment to parents has been more controversial. Contrary to what some people think, parents remain important people in the lives of most adolescents, and the attachment relationship that began in childhood continues to be important to their well-being. Adolescents may not require their parents' physical presence to feel secure, but a sense that their parents are committed to them and their well-being continues to form a secure base that allows the adolescent to explore a widening world of social relationships and experiences. At the same time, as relationships with peers become more intimate and more supportive, peers also can function as a type of attachment relationship (Armsden & Greenberg, 1987).

At one time, we thought of parent and peer relations as being in competition. It was assumed that as the importance of one of these relationships went up, the importance of the other would necessarily need to decrease. However, we now know that adolescents can maintain positive, high-quality relationships with both their parents and their peers, just as the idea of internal working models for relationships would suggest. Raja, McGee, and Stanton (1992) found that attachment to parents and attachment to peers were positively correlated and that it was adolescents with high perceived attachment to *both* parents and peers who reported high levels of perceived strengths (for example, feeling popular, outgoing, or reliable). Further, they found that high attachment to peers could not compensate for low attachment to parents. Adolescents with low reported attachment to parents were the ones who reported the highest levels of conduct problems, inattention, and depression and more frequently experienced negative life events, an indication that insecure attachment continues to be a risk factor even for adolescents.

With adolescents, research has focused on general attachment style, rather than attachment to a specific person. Hazen and Shaver (1987) demonstrated one approach you can examine in **Active Learning: Romantic Attachment Styles**. A secure attachment style has been found to relate not just to romantic relationships but to the way in which teens interact even with strangers. In one study, teens were asked to discuss several topics generally of concern to teens such as appearance and "being respected as an adult" with a peer advisor (Feeney, Cassidy, & Ramos-Marcuse, 2008, p. 1486). Those adolescents who had secure attachment styles were more likely to seek and to accept help. When adolescents have a secure internal working model of attachment, they expect and often succeed in eliciting support from those around them, just as younger children do when they are in distress.

TRUE/FALSE

6. Teens who are strongly attached to their friends are likely to also be strongly attached to their parents.

True. There is a good deal of similarity in the quality of attachment across different relationships even for teenagers who are becoming more independent from their parents.

ACTIVE LEARNING

Romantic Attachment Styles

Internal working models continue to impact significant relationships in late adolescence as people develop committed romantic relationships. Hazen and Shaver (1987) developed a questionnaire that assesses people's romantic attachment styles, using a single response item to classify the participants in their study. Below are the descriptions used in Hazen and Shaver's research to describe romantic relationships. With what you already know about infant attachment, you should be able to recognize which of these descriptions fits the descriptions of the infant attachment categories developed by Ainsworth. Read each description and match it to the correct infant attachment category. Ainsworth's categories are *secure*, *anxious avoidant*, and *anxious ambivalent/resistant*.

Romantic Relationship Descriptions	Attachment Category
I find that others are reluctant to get as close as I would like. I often worry that my partner doesn't really love me or won't want to stay with me. I want to merge completely with another person, and this desire sometimes scares people away.	
I find it relatively easy to get close to others and am comfortable depending on them and having them depend on me. I don't often worry about being abandoned or about someone getting too close to me.	
I am somewhat uncomfortable being close to others; I find it difficult to trust them completely, difficult to allow myself to depend on them. I am nervous when anyone gets too close, and often, love partners want me to be more intimate than I feel comfortable being.	

Answers: Box 1—anxious ambivalent/resistant; Box 2—secure; Box 3—anxious avoidant.

Hazen and Shaver found that the percentage of adults in their sample who fell into each of these categories was very similar to the percentages found in infant attachment research conducted in the United States (Campos, Barrett, Lamb, Goldsmith, & Stenberg, 1983). The secure classification described 56% of the adults and 62% of the infants, the anxious avoidant classification described 25% of the adults and 23% of the infants, and the anxious ambivalent/resistant category described 19% of the adults and 15% of the infants.

The respondents' perception of the quality of their relationship with their parents (and the parents' relationship with each other) was the best predictor of type of attachment, but Hazen and Shaver are careful to say that relationships are complex and personality variables such as attachment styles are not enough, on their own, to explain romantic attachment. Their results do, however, point to continuity in the quality of personal relationships.

Child Care and Attachment

Reading all of this information about mother-infant attachment may be making you wonder if mothers are the only ones who can or should take care of infants and young children. The issue of early child care has been a very controversial topic and is an excellent example of how the historical context influences opinions and practices. Many people believe that day care centers are a new invention. However, we have had day care centers in the United States since the 1800s. Initially child care was provided as an act of charity so that widows could work and support their families (Scarr & Weinberg, 1986). By the early 19th century the tide had turned and maternal employment was being denounced by social workers as neglectful (Rose, 1999), but the Great Depression of the 1930s again made maternal employment a necessity in many families. Later, during World War II, when many men were sent abroad to fight, women took over the jobs the men left behind to keep the country running. The ideal woman at that time was "Rosie the Riveter," a hardworking woman who was helping the war effort by working in the defense industry, and while she worked, child care facilities connected to schools and places of work took care of the children. An example is the Kaiser Shipyards in San Francisco, which employed 24,500 women while the federally funded Maritime Child Development Center provided care for 1,400 children between the ages of 18 months and 6 years (Hassan, 2005; National Park Service, n.d.).

Rosie the Riveter. During World War II, Rosie the Riveter was the ideal woman. While she worked in a factory to keep the country running and to support the troops, her children often were cared for in federally funded child care facilities.

When the war ended, the jobs that women had been doing were given back to the returning soldiers, and the women were encouraged, or forced, to go back into the home.

Today the United States is one of only a few Western countries that do not provide publicly funded child care for their citizens. One reason for this is a continuing belief that women should be at home taking care of their young children, but the reality is that over half of married mothers of children under the age of 6 are in the workforce (Cohany & Sok, 2007). Despite what some people think, most women work today out of necessity. Although many have jobs that they enjoy and that give them a sense of identity and feelings of accomplishment, their paychecks are necessary because their partners' salaries are too low to adequately support a family, their partners are unemployed, or the woman is the head of the household. For these women, child care may consist of care by relatives, a nanny or babysitter, a day care home, or a day care center. Figure 10.1 shows you both the historical rates of mothers who are working and the types of child care that they use. Each of these child care arrangements has its strengths and weaknesses.

Attachment to Nonparental Caregivers

One argument that has been made against the use of nonmaternal child care is that the quality of the child's attachment to the mother may suffer. As we have seen already in this chapter, secure attachment in the early years can have significant influence on the later nature of the child's development, so this is a very important issue to understand. In 1991, the National Institute of Child Health and Human Development (NICHD) began a large, longitudinal research project at 10 locations across the United States designed to examine the effects of early child care on child development. The findings turned out to be surprisingly complex in regard to security of attachment.

Insecure attachment to the mother was first and foremost linked to insensitive mothering rather than to the child being placed in nonmaternal care. However, three things magnified the negative effect of insensitive mothering: (a) The quality of the nonmaternal care was poor, (b) the infant spent more than 10 hours a week in care, or (c) the infant had experienced more than one child care arrangement within his or her first 15 months (Belsky, 2005; NICHD Early Child Care Research Network, 1997). In other words, poor-quality child care added to the negative effect of insensitive mothering on the development of secure attachment. Interestingly, in a different study, infants with difficult temperaments were *more* likely to have secure attachment with *more* out-of-home care (McKim, Cramer, Stuart, & O'Connor, 1999). Perhaps when mothers got a break from these difficult infants, they were able to provide care to their infants in their homes with more enthusiasm.

Quality of child care is also linked to the likelihood of a secure attachment relationship developing between a child and his caregiver (Elicker, Fortner-Wood, & Noppe, 1999). If an infant or a child is spending a good part of his day with a nonparental caregiver, we would hope that the child would find safety and security with that caregiver, just as he does with a parent. Although some parents are concerned that attachment to a child care provider will undermine the child's attachment to them, we have seen that children are capable of more than one secure

Figure 10.1

U.S. women in the workforce and child care arrangements. The number of women who have children and who are employed outside the home has steadily increased over the last three decades, until quite recently. Mothers of preschool children need to rely upon a variety of child care arrangements to care for their children while they are at work.

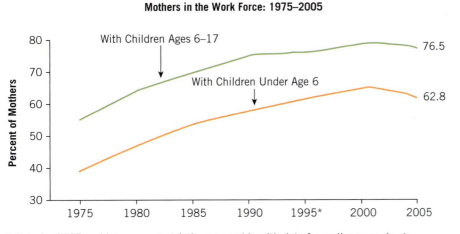

Mothers in the Work Force: 1975–2005

With Children Ages 6–17

With Children Under Age 6

76.5

62.8

* Data for 1995 and later are not strictly comparable with data for earlier years due to changes in the survey and estmation process.

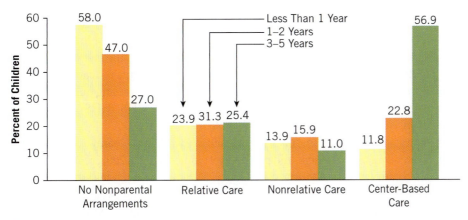

Weekly Child Care Arrangements* for Children Aged 5 Years and Younger,** by Age: 2005

Less Than 1 Year
1–2 Years
3–5 Years

58.0 47.0 27.0 23.9 31.3 25.4 13.9 15.9 11.0 11.8 22.8 56.9

No Nonparental Arrangements | Relative Care | Nonrelative Care | Center-Based Care

* Percents may equal more than 100 because children may have more than one type of nonparental care arrangement.

** Includes only children not yet enrolled in kindergarten.

attachment. Ahnert, Pinquart, and Lamb (2006) found that secure attachments between children and their caregiver were more likely in home-based than in center-based care. In child care centers, secure attachment was based more on the caregiver's involvement with the group of children as a whole and less on sensitivity to individual children.

Quality of Care

Clearly the quality of child care can have an impact on attachment and emotional development overall, but what is quality care? The National Child Care Information Center has identified these components as indicators of high-quality child care (Mitchell, 2005):

1. Staff qualifications that include formal education in early education, child development, or a related field, as well as opportunities for professional development of staff and administrators

2. A learning environment that uses a developmentally appropriate curriculum, has learning centers, and includes reading to children

3. Family involvement through parent-teacher conferences and regular communication with the family; also attitudes of friendliness toward families

4. A current valid license and a history of compliance with regulations governing care facilities

5. Group size and ratios in accordance with state requirements

6. Regular program evaluation leading to improvements

7. "Best practices" compensation for staff that rewards staff for qualifications and experience and includes benefits

8. Administrative policies and procedures that are clear and include regular staff meetings, annual staff evaluations, and written job descriptions and personnel policies

Although there are high-quality child care settings available that meet these standards, many child care settings have been found to be inadequate for providing for even the basic needs of the children, and this is more likely for children who come from low-income families (Shonkoff & Phillips, 2000). Although all of the criteria identified by the National Child Care Information Center are important, two are particularly important to consider when looking for high-quality care for infants and young children. They are the issue of *group size and the ratio of caregivers to children* and the issue of *best practices compensation for staff.*

Each state sets the standards for how many children may be cared for in a group and how many caregivers must be there. In 2006, child-to-caregiver ratios in the first year of life ranged from 3 infants per caregiver in Kansas and Massachusetts to 6 infants per caregiver in six other states. The majority of states mandated ratios of 4:1 or 5:1, with increasing numbers as the children get older (U.S. Department of Health and Human Services [USDHHS], 2008d). The goal for quality care is to keep this ratio as low as possible.

Regarding staff compensation, "on average, childcare workers . . . earn . . . less than amusement park attendants, car washers, and pest control workers" (Hall, 2008, p. 70). Consequently in many child care centers, the turnover of staff is a great problem. One study conducted in Maryland found that one third of all caregivers left their jobs during 1 year, which places child care among the highest rates of turnover of any profession (Maryland Committee for Children, 2006), and this is typical of the situation throughout the United States (Shonkoff & Phillips, 2000). When child care workers receive a living wage and health care benefits, staff members stay longer at their jobs (Shonkoff & Phillips, 2000). This is important because consistency of care allows a caregiver to get to know the infant and the infant to become attached to the caregiver.

Attachment Disorders

Most children develop secure attachments to their caregivers and some have insecure attachments, but a rare few have such difficulties in their attachment relationships that they require intervention.

The *Diagnostic and Statistical Manual of Mental Disorders* (American Psychiatric Association, 2000) recognizes a condition called **reactive attachment disorder (RAD)**. However, there has been a good deal of controversy over this particular diagnosis because "RAD is one of the least researched and most poorly understood disorders in the DSM" (Chaffin et al., 2006, p. 80).

There are two types of reactive attachment disorder. In the first, which is called the inhibited type, the child does not seem able to form any attachment. Symptoms include being withdrawn, being hyper-vigilant (that is, always looking for threats in the environment), or showing contradictory responses to possible attachment figures (similar to the behavior seen in children with a disorganized/disoriented attachment). Weir (2007) provides a description of an adopted boy who demonstrated this type of attachment disorder. "Aaron" was adopted at age 3 after having lived with an abusive mother. From the beginning he had difficulty forming a warm attachment, especially to his new mother. He would "scream, throw tantrums, hit, swear, and express hatred toward" her (Weir, 2007, p. 3). By age 8, the mother was ready to return him to the adoption agency.

In the second type, called the disinhibited type, the child is indiscriminate in whom he goes to. His reaction is the same, whether he is interacting with a stranger or someone he knows well. If he is frightened, he is just as likely to go to a stranger as to his caregiver. He does not seem to have any special relationship to his caregiver. Do you see how each type of behavior—either attaching to no one or indiscriminately attaching to everyone—indicates a disruption in the attachment process? These symptoms are very extreme, so we are not talking about children who are just shy or friendly.

Causes of Attachment Disorder

The diagnosis of reactive attachment disorder was developed in part in response to the observations made in the 1960s by Tizard and her colleagues of children raised in orphanages in England (Tizard & Rees, 1975; Zeanah, Smyke, Koga, Carlson, & Bucharest Early Intervention Project Core Group, 2005). These children were raised with multiple caretakers, rather than a few people who knew and understood each child well. When Tizard observed the children at age 4, only one third had formed secure attachments to a caregiver.

More recent research has focused on orphanages in Romania, a country in Eastern Europe that was under the control of a brutal dictator, Nicolae Ceausescu, from 1965 until his overthrow in 1989. In order to consolidate his hold on the country, Ceausescu wanted to increase the population and therefore abolished access to contraception and abortion and forced women to continue having children beyond the ability of their families to care for them. As a result, over 100,000 children were sent to Romanian orphanages that were not prepared to care for them. These children had inadequate food, clothing, heat, and personal caregiving (Kaler & Freeman, 1994). One study reported that an individual child would be cared for by as many as 17 different caregivers in a single week (Zeanah et al., 2005). Many children were fed by someone propping up a bottle for them, rather than someone holding them. They were not kept clean, and one adoptive mother said her child was covered with flies when she took her from the institution (O'Connor, Bredenkamp, Rutter, & The English and Romanian Adoptees (ERA) Study Team, 1999).

After reading earlier in this chapter about how an infant forms a secure attachment with a caregiver, you can see why children who were living in these orphanages could not form attachments. They never had the consistent, sensitive, or responsive caregiving that is necessary for this bond to form.

Video Link 10.4
Reactive attachment disorder.

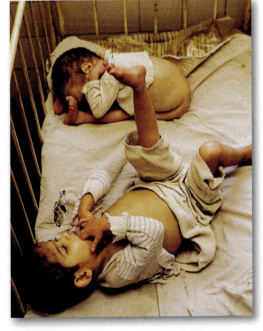

Romanian orphans. The terrible conditions in Romanian orphanages created lasting problems, even for children who were eventually adopted. The inability of these children to form emotional attachments was one of the most serious ones.

Families in England and the United States eventually adopted many of the Romanian children from these institutions. This gave researchers an opportunity to study the effects of severe early deprivation on later development (this is what we called a "natural experiment" in Chapter 3). The good news is that some of these children have been able to form secure attachment relationships with their adoptive parents. The bad news is that a large group of these children had great difficulty overcoming their earlier experience and forming secure adaptive attachments (Zeanah et al., 2005). As attachment theory would predict, those who were adopted before 6 months of age appeared to do much better than those who were adopted after 6 months (Kreppner et al., 2007). Do you know why? You learned earlier in this chapter that between 6 weeks and 6–8 months is the period of "attachment in the making." Beyond this stage in the attachment process, it becomes more difficult to reverse the effect of early experiences. Although early deprivation can form the basis for long-term problems in emotional development even when circumstances change for the better, a recent report from a task force of the American Professional Society on the Abuse of Children concluded that the outcome for these children is more hopeful than we had previously thought (Chaffin et al., 2006). Many of these adopted children do eventually form attachments to their adoptive parents (MacLean, 2003).

Prevention and Treatment of Attachment Disorders

The infant mental health movement begun by Selma Fraiberg and others in the 1970s focused on helping families in which infant attachment was not progressing (Fraiberg, Adelson, & Shapiro, 1975). Since that time, many programs have been developed to try to prevent and/ or treat attachment disorders in high-risk populations, such as children living in poverty or in abusive families. These programs help parents learn parenting skills that can be used with a child with attachment disorder or to prevent the development of the disorder. Bakermans-Kranenburg, van IJzendoorn, and Juffer (2003) found that the most effective therapies focused on developing the mother's sensitivity to her baby. As maternal sensitivity increased, so did infant-mother attachment. Although only a few programs to date have targeted the sensitivity of both mothers and fathers, those that did found an even greater effect than those that only intervened with the mother. For adopted children with attachment disorders, it is important for a family to know that much hard work will be needed to try to reverse the child's earlier experiences.

Development of Emotions

Self-conscious emotions Emotions that depend on awareness of oneself, such as pride, guilt, and shame.

Guilt Feelings children have when they think about the negative aspects of something they have done, particularly moral failures.

Shame A feeling that occurs as a result of personal failure or when children attribute their bad behavior to an aspect of themselves that they believe they cannot change.

From Basic to Complex Emotions

As we mentioned at the beginning of this chapter, infants within the first year of life demonstrate the basic emotions: happiness, sadness, fear, anger, surprise/interest, and disgust (Izard, 2007). Before age 3, most children recognize happiness when they see it in others, and by 4 or 5 they can identify the other basic emotions (Tracy, Robins, & Lagattuta, 2005).

It takes a bit longer for more complex emotions to develop. Some emotions depend on an awareness of self that very young children do not yet possess. Emotions such as pride, shame, and guilt all require children to think about how an emotional event affects their evaluation of themselves (Tracy et al., 2005). Children begin to experience **self-conscious emotions** such as pride by age 3, and by age 4 or 5 they can identify pride from others' nonverbal signals.

By one definition, **guilt** occurs when children think about the negative aspects of something they have done, whereas **shame** occurs when they attribute their bad behavior to an aspect of themselves that they believe they cannot change (Tracy & Robins, 2006). Shame has also been linked with personal failures, such as poor performance at school or in sports, whereas guilt is linked to moral issues, such as hurting others. Many researchers have claimed that children do not develop the complex abilities necessary to understand these emotions until well into middle childhood. Berti, Garattoni, and Venturini (2000) found that 5-year-old Italian children were just as likely as older children to understand that guilt is caused by something one has done wrong and can be dealt with by trying to repair the damage done. However, the 5-year-olds also tended to believe that they only had to feel guilty if someone else was there to see what happened. If no one was there, then they would feel happy! Older children's sense of guilt was not affected by whether someone else was there. In Chapter 11 we will talk more about the process of moral development and how children internalize the values of their culture and feel guilt or shame if they violate these internalized standards. You can see whether you are clear on this distinction by answering the question in **Active Learning: Shame and Guilt**.

Shame and Guilt

Read the following scenario and decide which answer would indicate guilt and which would indicate shame:

You are hurrying home one day to watch your favorite television program. You see your little brother outside. He is sitting on the sidewalk crying. He dropped a bag of marbles, and they are rolling all over the place. You don't stop to help him. You just keep on walking toward home.

Are you the kind of child who would think, "I am a mean kid for not helping?" Are you the kind of child who would feel you did something wrong?

Answer: Ferguson, Stegge, Miller, and Olsen (1999) suggest that thinking you are a "mean kid" is indicative of shame, and feeling "you did something wrong" is indicative of guilt.

Empathy

When Bill Clinton was president, he often reacted to the distress of others by saying, "I feel your pain." Sharing other people's feelings, whether pain or pleasure, is the essence of **empathy**. As we saw in Chapter 6, from their first days of life, infants imitate the actions of others. The same is true for emotions. If a baby hears another baby crying, he is quite likely to start crying himself (Sagi & Hoffman, 1976). Have you experienced something similar yourself? When you see someone crying on television or a movie, do you ever find your own eyes getting wet? Experiencing the feelings of others is a primitive form of empathy and is the basis for much human interaction. When we experience another's distress we are more likely to try to show **sympathy** to others by helping or comforting that person. We will discuss empathy further when we talk about moral development in Chapter 11, but for now you can see how empathy is expressed in children by completing **Active Learning: Empathy and Sympathy**.

Empathy   Sharing the feelings of other people.

Sympathy   Concern for others' welfare that often leads to helping or comforting them.

Empathy and Sympathy

You can carry out the following experiment designed by Carolyn Zahn-Waxler and her colleagues to look at empathy and sympathy in children (for more information, see Robinson, Zahn-Waxler, & Emde, 1994). When you are with a child you know, pretend to hurt yourself. You can pretend to pinch your finger in a drawer, stub your toe, or experience some other noticeable but minor "hurt." Practice beforehand so you can react in a realistic way.

(Continued)

(Continued)

How does the child respond? Young children may ignore you, laugh, look hurt or cry themselves, or show sympathy by asking if you need a Band-Aid or if you are OK. Think about what each type of behavior means in terms of the child's ability to take another's point of view as well as empathizing with another's pain. As children get older, they move from showing personal distress when they empathize with you (for example, crying themselves) to being more oriented to your feelings and helping you feel better.

After you note the child's reaction, be sure to reassure the child that you now are feeling much better and do not hurt anymore. Also thank the child if he or she tried to help you.

Empathy. Even young children can experience empathy and will attempt to soothe another person, like this sister is doing for her brother.

Social referencing
Using the reaction of others to determine how to react in ambiguous situations.

If you were to search the literature for research on empathy in older children and adolescents, what you would find is that there is much more research on adolescents who *lack* a sense of empathy than on those who have a well-developed sense of empathy. A lack of ability to empathize with others has been associated with adolescents who are sexually abusive, delinquent and antisocial, or bullies among their peers. One protection against this problem is a history of secure attachments. Adolescents who have had secure attachments have learned how to regulate their emotions in the context of interpersonal relationships, and their ability to empathize is linked to more prosocial and caring behaviors (Carlo, Raffaelli, Laible, & Meyer, 1999). Adolescents who report secure attachment with their parents and with their peers were found to be more emotionally aware, more sympathetic, more prosocial in their behavior, and more positive in their affect (Laible, 2007).

Social Referencing

One way that we develop emotion schemas is by looking at how others are reacting when we are uncertain about how we should react, a process called **social referencing**. Social referencing first develops between 9 and 12 months of age (Hennighausen & Lyons-Ruth, 2005). You may have seen a toddler fall and immediately look around for his parent. If his father gasps and runs over with fear on his face, the child is likely to begin crying. However, if his dad smiles and says, "You're OK" (if the child really isn't hurt), the toddler is likely to pick himself up and return to play. The child is learning to interpret his feeling of mild upset as either a very fearful emotion or a slight bump that he can manage and overcome. Of course any child who is truly hurt will cry and needs comfort!

Representation of Emotions

As children move into early childhood, they begin to represent events in their lives through language and images (for a description of symbolic thought, review the information on Piaget's preoperational stage in Chapter 7). Conversations with parents about events in their lives help shape the way in which children understand and cope with their emotions. Parents who use more words to label and describe emotions have children who are more comfortable talking about their feelings. In a study of children with asthma, Sales and Fivush (2005) found that children's emotional well-being was related to their mothers' use of emotion words and explanations in their conversations with their children about the child's disease.

Regulation of Emotions

We began this chapter by talking about one of the major developmental tasks for infants: learning to regulate their emotions so that they are not overwhelmed by them. When children (and adults) can control the expression of their emotions, they are more likely to be able to use them in a positive way. One example of an adult who is not in control of his emotions is a person who experiences road rage. This person may chase after someone who has cut him off in traffic, putting himself and others at risk. This level of anger also harms the person's health because high levels of anger and aggression are related to a higher likelihood of heart disease (Suarez, 2004). If you have ever experienced road rage yourself, you can now think with a clearer, calmer head about what would have been a better way to deal with your feelings. In children, we see a similar inability to control rage when the child has a temper tantrum. Remember this parallel and your own health the next time someone cuts you off in traffic.

Of course infants first learn to regulate their emotions only with the help of adults who soothe and care for them. However, even early in development infants begin to develop ways to soothe themselves through behaviors such as thumb sucking, holding a favorite "blankie," or avoidance of a feared or frustrating object by looking away (Eisenberg, Hofer, & Vaughan, 2007).

Some research has found that children in preschool who were more able to regulate their emotions were later found to have higher social competence in adolescence and adulthood (Mischel & Ayduk, 2004). Preschoolers' ability to regulate their emotions also was related to academic ability in third grade (Izard, 2007). These findings are consistent with the ideas expressed by Daniel Goleman (1995) in his book *Emotional Intelligence.* Goleman believes that the ability to deal with emotions is of equal importance to our success as our cognitive abilities, as reflected by an IQ score. Understanding and controlling one's own emotions, understanding those of others, and being able to use all of this understanding to navigate human interactions successfully are the basic tools of **emotional intelligence**.

Emotional intelligence
The ability to understand and control one's emotions, to understand the emotions of others, and to use this understanding in human interactions.

Normal Emotions and Emotional Problems

All children and adolescents must deal with their emotional responses to a wide variety of life experiences. Most often they can cope with these feelings and even use them to enhance their lives. However, sometimes children's emotional responses go beyond their ability to cope with and control them, resulting in psychological disorders (Feng et al., 2009). In these cases they need special help from others in their lives or from professionals, such as psychologists, social workers, psychiatrists, and counselors. We will describe how fear, sadness, and anger develop in childhood and adolescence. We also will describe some difficulties children may encounter when these feelings become overwhelming and undermine the child's development.

Fear and Anxiety

Fear of things like loud noises or novel items in the child's environment typically appears at around 7 months of age, and as the child moves through toddlerhood, fear of the dark or of the scary monsters in the closet is common. In a study by Muris, Merckelbach, Gadet, and Moulaert (2000) in the Netherlands, approximately three quarters of the 4-year-old children interviewed reported that they experienced fears, worries, and scary dreams. These fears were common in the youngest group, increased through age 8, and then decreased. Repeated exposure to frightening experiences that really do no harm, a growing understanding of the physical world, and increases in the ability to use coping strategies all contribute to this decline. Later in childhood fear of things in the environment is replaced by social anxieties and anxiety about school performance.

Fear and anxiety are not the same thing. **Anxiety** is a vague sense of fear or a feeling of dread. When we are feeling anxious, we often can't quite put our finger on what is bothering us or say exactly what it is that we are afraid of. Fear, on the other hand, tends to be specific. We feel anxious about what could happen in new situations, but we feel fear when we see spiders and snakes (or, at least, many of us do). Some level of anxiety, and even fear, from time to time during development is normal. As you learned earlier in this chapter, children experience stranger anxiety and separation anxiety during infancy, but most outgrow this type of anxiety. Some school-age children and even adolescents unexpectedly reexperience separation anxiety the first time they sleep over at a friend's house, go to overnight camp, or even head off to college (Kline, 2006).

Recent studies have found that a significant number of children go on to develop full-blown **anxiety disorders** from common childhood fears. Anxiety disorders are now among the most commonly diagnosed mental health problems among children and adolescents, affecting between 5% and 18% of them (Linares-Scott & Feeny, 2006). According to the Surgeon General of the United States (USDHHS, 1999), the most common forms of anxiety disorders are separation anxiety disorder (which is normal in young children but can become a disorder in older children or adolescents), generalized anxiety disorder, and social phobias. Longitudinal studies of children with anxiety disorders have found that these conditions in childhood predict the development of emotional disorders in adolescence, so they should not be ignored with the assumption that they will simply disappear with age (Bittner et al., 2007).

There also is evidence to suggest that in recent years anxiety disorders have increased greatly among children and adolescents. A meta-analysis of studies of children's anxiety that were conducted between 1952 and 1993 found that the increase in anxiety levels during that period was so great that samples of normal children in the 1980s had higher scores on the measures of anxiety than the scores of child psychiatric patients in the 1950s (Twenge, 2000). For today's children there are more than monsters under the bed. Although we do not know for sure what has caused this increase in anxiety, Twenge (2000) found correlations between measures of anxiety with both threats in the environment (such as high crime rates) and a lack of social connectedness (as indicated by factors such as divorce rates).

Girls are more likely than boys to have an anxiety disorder, as shown in Figure 10.2 (Yonkers & Gurguis, 1995), although the age of onset and the time to recovery for adolescents receiving treatment does not differ by gender (Lewinsohn, Gotlib, Lewinsohn, Seeley, & Allen, 1998). However, the cause for this gender difference—whether it is due to hormonal differences, differences in the way that girls and boys are socialized, or gender differences in the use of coping strategies—still is not known.

When there is no rational basis for a fear of something specific, and it is so severe that it interferes with day-to-day functioning, it is called a **phobia**. Some common phobias among adults include fear of spiders, snakes, heights, flying, water, and public speaking. Among children, however, school phobia needs to be added to that list. Because a phobia is an irrational fear, we are not talking here about children who are victims of bullies (and who, therefore, have

Anxiety A vague sense of fear or a feeling of dread.

Video Link 10.5
Separation anxiety.

Anxiety disorder A level of anxiety that interferes with normal functioning; includes separation anxiety disorder in older children or adolescents, generalized anxiety disorder, and social phobias.

TRUE/FALSE

7. The average child today reports more anxiety than a child in psychiatric treatment in the 1950s did.

True. Although we do not know the reason why children now experience more anxiety than they did in the past 50 years, some evidence points to an increase in threats from the environment combined with less social support from families.

Phobia An irrational fear of something specific that is so severe that it interferes with day-to-day functioning.

Figure 10.2

Cumulative hazard function for anxiety disorder for the age at onset by gender. The risk of being diagnosed with an anxiety disorder increases as children and adolescents get older. Note that at all ages beyond early childhood females are at a greater risk than males of being diagnosed with an anxiety disorder.

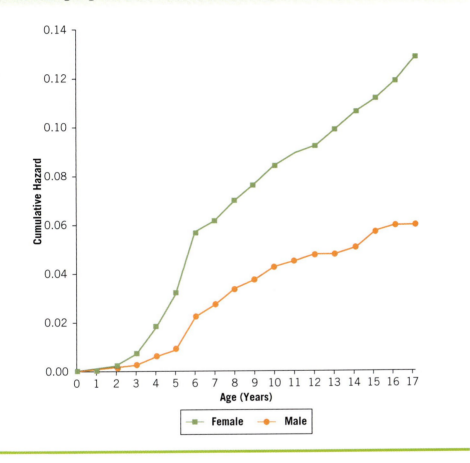

a good reason to fear going to school) or children who refuse to go to school following a violent incident such as a schoolyard fight or shooting. In such cases, there is a clearly identifiable and reasonable basis for their fear.

Estimates are that about 5% of the school-age population is affected by school phobia (Chitiyo & Wheeler, 2006; Tyrrell, 2005), and this phobia can arise from any of several different causes. It can be a form of separation anxiety based primarily on the child's fear of being away from the parents or a form of social phobia where the central concern for the child is worry about having to interact with other children or adults. Interestingly there are peaks in the rate of school phobias between the ages of 5 and 6 (when children first begin school) and again at about age 10 or 11 (when they transition from elementary school to middle school, a time when peer relationships are becoming increasingly important) (Tyrrell, 2005).

A study of 136 eleven-year-old Israeli children found a higher incidence of school phobias among children who had been classified as ambivalently attached at 12 months of age compared to children who had been classified as securely attached (Bar-Haim, Dan, Eshel, &

8. School phobias usually are the result of children worrying that they won't do well in school. **TRUE/FALSE**

False. Most children who suffer from school phobia are average to good students. Anxiety about separating from their parents or social anxiety is more likely to be the cause.

Sagi-Schwartz, 2007). Children who suffer from school phobias tend to be average to good students, so it doesn't seem that the children are avoiding school because they are afraid they will not do well (although they do tend to be perfectionists). A typical treatment often involves gradually returning the child to the classroom while equipping the child with strategies that help him manage his emotional distress (Chitiyo & Wheeler, 2006), and intervening as early as possible also contributes to the success of this approach (Tyrrell, 2005). The longer the child avoids school, the scarier it will seem to her. If a phobia is an irrational fear, it makes sense that getting the child back into the feared situation (in this case, a school classroom) where she can have some positive experiences and see for herself that there is no basis for her fear would be a sound approach to use. We will discuss other types of anxiety disorders in Chapter 15.

Sadness and Depression

Sadness is a normal reaction to experiences such as loss and disappointment. However, children who have difficulty regulating their sadness appear to be more likely than others to develop depression in early adolescence (Feng et al., 2009). Depression can run the gamut from something that is relatively mild and short-lived to something that is persistent and quite severe. When we talk about a **clinical depression**, we are referring to one that is long lasting and severe enough to affect the individual physically, emotionally, cognitively, and socially. Physically the person often has trouble sleeping (or may sleep all the time), feels tired, or loses her appetite. Emotionally she may feel worthless and sad. Cognitively, depression often interferes with a person's ability to concentrate, and, in severe cases, there can be reoccurring thoughts of death. The person loses interest in things that he or she previously enjoyed socially and wants to be alone, rather than with others (Hammen & Rudolph, 2003).

Depression in children prior to adolescence is relatively rare, affecting less than 1% to 3% of children (Hammen & Rudolph, 2003; Kazdin & Marciano, 1998), but this incidence increases to between 8% (Kazdin & Marciano, 1998) and 15% or higher for adolescents between the ages of 15 and 18 (Hammen & Rudolph, 2003). However, if we include in these estimates cases of subclinical levels of depression, the percentage of adolescents affected by depression grows considerably. A study conducted by Cooper and Goodyear (1993) found that 21% of 11- to 16-year-old females showed symptoms of depression that did not rise to the level necessary for a diagnosis of major depression but that still could interfere with the adolescent's adjustment and functioning.

It may surprise you to learn that before adolescence, boys are actually at a *greater* risk of suffering from depression than girls (Hankin et al., 1998). As you can see in Figure 10.3, the rate of clinical depression diagnosed in males is higher than the rate for females until early adolescence. During adolescence, however, girls become more likely to suffer from depression, and the gender difference that emerges in early adolescence continues to grow, with adolescent girls being 2 to 5 times more likely than boys to suffer from depression (Hankin et al., 1998).

A variety of explanations have been proposed to explain gender differences in depression, and these include biological, cognitive, and social explanations. Because of the sharp increase in depression in females at midpuberty, researchers have looked for biological causes, but there is not a great deal of support for this hypothesis (Hankin & Abramson, 1999), although there may be other genetic factors at work. Another relevant gender difference is how boys and girls deal with stress. When negative things happen to girls, they are more likely than boys to ruminate on the event, playing it over and over again in their minds, thereby increasing their distress. This is compounded by the fact that girls also are more likely than boys to experience negative life events (Hankin & Abramson, 1999). In adolescence girls become more dissatisfied with their physical appearance and with their peer relationships, which become increasingly intimate and take on greater importance. This leaves girls particularly vulnerable when these relationships go through rough times. Because girls tend to disclose intimate information

---

Clinical depression A condition marked by feelings of worthlessness and hopelessness, a lack of pleasure, sleep and appetite disturbances, and possibly suicidal thoughts.

TRUE/FALSE

9. Throughout childhood and adolescence, girls are more likely to suffer from depression than boys.

False. During childhood, boys are actually more likely to suffer from depression than girls. It isn't until adolescence that the risk of depression for girls becomes greater, for a variety of reasons.

TRUE/FALSE

10. Hormonal changes at puberty are a likely cause of adolescent depression.

False. There actually is *not* a great deal of support for underlying biological causes of adolescent depression. Cognitive, social, and developmental causes have much stronger support.

Figure 10.3

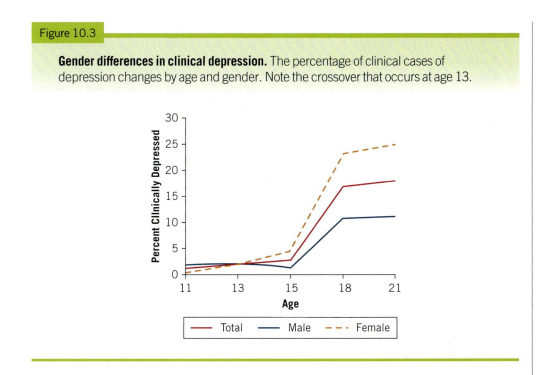

Gender differences in clinical depression. The percentage of clinical cases of depression changes by age and gender. Note the crossover that occurs at age 13.

within their peer relationships, a former friend could potentially betray them if the friendship ends. Finally, girls and boys are socialized differently, with boys being allowed to express their frustration and anger by acting out, while girls are socialized to keep these feelings inside in a way that may take a psychological toll on them in the form of depression. To date, there has not been a lot of research that looks at depression in children and adolescents from ethnic minorities. However, in a large epidemiological study of 5,423 students from sixth to eighth grade, Roberts, Roberts, and Chen (1997) found comparable rates of depression across nine ethnic groups, with the exception of higher rates among Mexican American children.

Depression that becomes chronic or severe is a serious emotional condition, but it also is one that is treatable. Unfortunately, it is estimated that between 70% and 80% of clinically depressed adolescents never receive treatment (Kazdin & Marciano, 1998). Psychotherapy can help depressed children and adolescents overcome their depression by helping them change how they think about and deal with their problems. Behavioral therapies can help them improve their coping and social skills or teach them relaxation techniques (Kazdin & Marciano, 1998). If the warning signs of a genuine problem are overlooked because they are mistaken for "normal" adolescent moodiness, the young person doesn't get help that he or she needs. Although antidepressant medications are frequently used in the treatment of depression in adults, they may not work as well for adolescents and may even carry additional risks (Wolfe & Mash, 2006). One particular difficulty in diagnosing and treating depression in adolescents is that adults may have trouble distinguishing between normal adolescent moodiness, a situational depression in response to some disappointment or loss, and true clinical depression.

Anger and Aggression

Angry feelings may be expressed as aggression. Most children learn to control their anger by channeling it in appropriate ways. However, some children are not able to control feelings that lead them into conflict with others. In a study of over 1,100 children who participated in the NICHD Study of Early Child Care and Youth Development (NICHD Early Child

Figure 10.4

Changes in levels of aggression with age. At the start of this study of aggression, 2-year-olds differed in their scores on a measure of aggression. While initial levels were moderate to low for most toddlers, they were high for one group. Over time, the level decreased for most groups, but for the group that started at the highest level, levels remained high throughout the study to age 9.

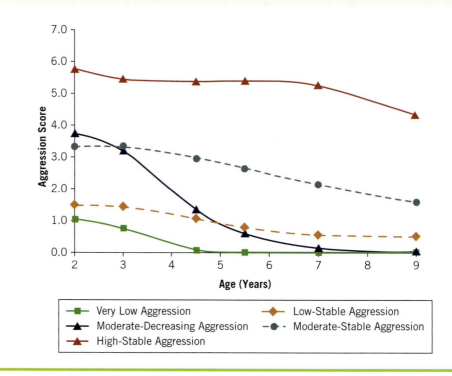

Care Research Network, 2004), the researchers identified trajectories of aggressive behavior between the time the children were 24 months old and when they were in third grade as shown in Figure 10.4. Most of the children displayed low levels of aggression as toddlers, and this level decreased across time, and children who began the study with moderate levels of aggression also tended to decline sharply over the course of the study as they learned to regulate these emotions. However, a small group of children showed high levels of aggression in toddlerhood that persisted through the ages studied. These children were more likely to come from families that faced a lot of adversity and to have parents who were less sensitive in their caregiving.

A similar pattern of persistent aggression was found for about one sixth of the children in another large, longitudinal study. Almost 11,000 Canadian children were followed from toddlerhood to preadolescence, and the majority of the children showed a pattern of physical aggression that was moderate in toddlerhood but declined to infrequent use by preadolescence (Cote, Vaillancourt, & LeBlanc, 2006). However, again there was a small group (about 16% of the entire sample) that showed a pattern that started at a high level of physical aggression in toddlerhood and remained stable at that level across time. Characteristics of this group included boys from low-income families where parents relied upon hostile or ineffective parenting strategies. Consistent, high levels of aggression can be linked with conduct disorders, a condition that will be described in Chapter 11.

Conclusion

From earliest infancy onward, we must all learn to understand, express, and control our emotions. In this chapter we have shown how our emotional experiences develop within the context of our close relationships with other people. Through our earliest attachment relationships we develop our basic understandings about emotions, which we take with us into our later relationships. At each stage of development we add new levels of understanding and experience that build upon each other to shape the nature of our feelings about others and about ourselves. In the next chapter, we will see how emotional, cognitive, and even language development all contribute as the infant begins to develop a first sense of self, which leads eventually to the adolescent's ongoing understanding of identity.

CHAPTER SUMMARY

1. **What are the characteristics of emotion?**
The experience of an emotion includes your body's physiological reaction to a situation, your interpretation of the situation, communication of the feeling to another person, and your own actions in response to the feeling.

2. **How do you define temperament, and what different types have been described?**
Temperament is the general way in which we respond to experiences in the world, such as being timid or fearless. Infant temperaments have been characterized as **easy**, **difficult**, or **slow to warm**. **Goodness of fit** characterizes the match between the temperament of an infant and the type of demands placed on the infant by the environment.

3. **What is attachment, and how is it adaptive for survival?**
Attachment is a strong, positive emotional bond with a particular person who provides a sense of security. It is adaptive because it provides children a safe place necessary for exploring the environment, learning, and emotional self-regulation. According to John Bowlby, attachment develops in four stages: **preattachment** (birth to 6 weeks), **attachment in the making** (6 weeks to 6–8 months), **clear-cut attachment** (6–8 months to 18 months–2 years), and **goal-corrected partnership** (or formation of reciprocal relationships; 18 months on).

4. **What are Ainsworth's four types of attachment?**
Based upon how an infant behaves when the mother is present and when the mother returns after a separation in the **Strange Situation**, the infant's attachment can be classified as **secure**, **anxious avoidant**, **anxious ambivalent/resistant**, or **disorganized/disoriented**.

5. **How do mother, father, and infant contribute to the development of attachment?**
Mothers' warm, responsive caretaking is related to secure attachment in the infant. Fathers develop their own attachment with their infants, which may or may not be of the same type as their partner's. Infant temperament, health issues, and other characteristics may all contribute to the quality of the infant's attachment. There are many factors that influence the family unit at different levels and at different times that contribute to the development of attachment.

6. **What roles do biology and culture play in attachment?**
Infants who are deprived of attachment have different neurochemical reactions to interaction with people around them than infants with normal attachment experiences. Although the percentage of infants with secure attachment does not differ much among cultures around the world, the ways that sensitive parenting and security in infancy are defined do differ.

7. **What effect does attachment have on children's development beyond infancy?**
For most infants, the type of attachment they experience does not change over time; however, infants can change from secure to insecure attachment or vice versa, depending on their circumstances. Securely attached infants become more resilient in the face of later stress, have a greater ability to form warm and trusting relationships, and show greater academic competence. Experiences they have later in life, such as positive relationships with peers, also can affect aspects of later development. Although older children do not need parents' physical presence as infants do, they still rely on an inner emotional connection, even as they develop strong attachments to peers. Insecure attachment to parents continues to be a risk factor even for adolescents.

8. **What effect does nonparental child care have on the development of attachment?**
Children are capable of forming a secure attachment to more than one person at a time. High-quality child care does not harm children's attachment to their parents, but

poor-quality child care can interact with poor mothering to create less secure attachment.

9. What is reactive attachment disorder?

Reactive attachment disorder occurs with children who have been deprived or abused early in their lives. They either withdraw from emotional connections to people or attach indiscriminately to anyone, not just to the people who take care of them.

10. How do emotions develop from basic to complex?

Within the first year of life, infants demonstrate the basic emotions: happiness, sadness, fear, anger, surprise/interest, and disgust. Other emotions that rely on self-awareness, including pride, shame, and guilt, do not develop until the preschool years or beyond.

11. How do emotions connect us to other people?

We share other people's feelings when we have **empathy** for them. Empathy leads to helping others and often keeps us from hurting others. **Social referencing** is the process by which children check with others to see how to react in an emotionally ambiguous situation.

12. How do children learn to control their emotions?

Both parental soothing and modeling of emotional control play important roles. Infants develop their own techniques of self-control including thumb sucking for self-soothing. Fear, anxiety, sadness, and anger are all normal emotions, and most children learn to deal with all of them as they develop appropriate coping strategies. Sometimes, however, children's emotions become unmanageable and develop into disorders such as **anxiety disorders**, **phobias**, **clinical depression**, and antisocial behavior, including high levels of aggression.

Go to **www.sagepub.com/levine** for additional exercises and video resources. Select **Chapter 10, Emotional Development and Attachment,** for chapter-specific activities.

chapter 11

Identity

The Self, Gender, and Moral Development

11

If you were asked to describe yourself, what would you say? Take a minute to write down your self-description so that you can use it as a point of comparison with the descriptions that we typically find for preschoolers, school-age children, and teenagers. Do children think about themselves in the same way as adults do? Clearly the answer is no. In this chapter we will look at many aspects of the "self" and how those different aspects change as the individual moves through childhood and adolescence.

We will start by looking at the self-concept, the totality of how you describe yourself and your relationships. Next, we will look at self-esteem, or how you evaluate and feel

Test Your Knowledge

Test your knowledge of child development by deciding whether each of the following statements is *true* or *false,* and then check your answers as you read the chapter.

1. **True/False:** When a toddler is struggling to do something like move a heavy object, an adult should help the toddler out so she doesn't experience a sense of failure.
2. **True/False:** Children's self-esteem is extraordinarily high in early childhood.
3. **True/False:** Programs that help build students' self-esteem not only improve their grades but also help reduce delinquency, drug use, and adolescent pregnancy.
4. **True/False:** The self-esteem of boys and girls is quite similar during adolescence.
5. **True/False:** If you put a 3-year-old boy in a dress and polished his nails, he would be afraid that it would make him a girl.
6. **True/False:** During adolescence, the most well-adjusted females are ones who score high

on measures of femininity, and the most well-adjusted males are ones who score high on measures of masculinity.

7. **True/False:** There is evidence that many gay teenagers today are more interested in the everyday concerns of adolescence (such as school and friends) than they are in their sexual orientation.
8. **True/False:** When children are asked to resist the temptation to peek at something they have been told *not* to look at, girls and boys give in to temptation at the same rates.
9. **True/False:** About one half of children who show problems with aggression or being impulsive during the preschool years will grow out of their problems by the time they enter school.
10. **True/False:** Programs that use a "tough-love" approach (for example, wilderness camps, boot camps) for adolescents with conduct problems have been highly successful at rehabilitating these young people.

Correct answers: (1) False, (2) True, (3) False, (4) True, (5) True, (6) False, (7) True, (8) True, (9) True, (10) False about those characteristics. We also will discuss several important aspects of a person's sense of who she is: her gender identity, ethnic identity, and moral identity. We will conclude the chapter by describing how children develop self-control and what happens when they have difficulty doing this.

Development of Self-Concept

The modern study of the self began back in the 1890s, when one of the major early figures in the study of psychology, William James (1892/1992), wrote about two aspects of the self: the "I" self and the "me" self. Just as the word *I* is used as the subject or actor in a sentence (for example, "I am reading this book"), James conceptualized *I* as the self that experiences or acts on the world. The word *me* is used as the object in a sentence (for example, "Look at me!"), and for James this second aspect was the self that we can think about and define with characteristics such as being a hard worker or an outgoing person. Both of these aspects of self change throughout childhood and adolescence.

Building on these ideas, another early psychologist, Charles Cooley (1902/1964), suggested that our sense of self is largely a reflection of how other people see us, what he termed a "looking-glass self." Cooley proposed that first we form a picture of ourselves and our characteristics, and then we see how others react to us and base our self-concept on our interpretation of the reactions of others. In other words, our sense of self is the product of our interaction with others in our social world.

Self-Concept and Culture

You should remember our discussion of individualistic and collectivist cultures from Chapter 4. As we saw, some cultures place a high value on the role of the individual and individual achievement. In the United States, we tend to see people as separate, autonomous individuals who choose their own paths in life. In contrast, collectivist cultures conceptualize the self as part of a group, and the goals of that group take priority. Read these two self-descriptions from 6-year-old children:

> I am a wonderful and very smart person. A funny and hilarious person. A kind and caring person. A good-grade person who is going to go to [a prestigious university]. A helpful and cooperative girl.

> I'm a human being. I'm a child. I like to play cards. I'm my mom and dad's child, my grandma and grandpa's grandson. I'm a hard working good child. (Wang, 2006, p. 182)

You could probably guess which description came from an American child and which came from a Chinese child. Euro American children typically include more traits and abilities ("I'm smart," "I am the fastest runner") in their descriptions, while Chinese children include more situational descriptions ("I play with my friend after school") and overt behaviors ("I like to tell stories"). Euro American children also are more likely to include positive evaluations like "beautiful" or "smart" while Chinese children use less evaluative descriptions like "work hard." Across the descriptions, Euro American children place more emphasis on the personal aspects of their lives, and Chinese children place more emphasis on the social aspects of theirs (Wang, 2006). In all societies, individuals define themselves both in terms of individual characteristics and in terms of their relationships to others, but the value of each aspect may differ (Raeff, 2004). Although both groups of children use both types of descriptions, the *ratio* of personal-to-social references is different between the groups, with Euro American children using more personal references relative to the number of social references Chinese children use. Figure 11.1 shows that these cultural differences appear early in development and persist into adulthood.

Figure 11.1

Ratio of personal-to-social statements in self-descriptions in two cultures. This figure shows the mean personal-to-social ratio of statements in the self-descriptions of young Euro American and Chinese children. Euro American children who live in an individualistic culture use more personal than social descriptions compared to Chinese children who live in a collectivist culture.

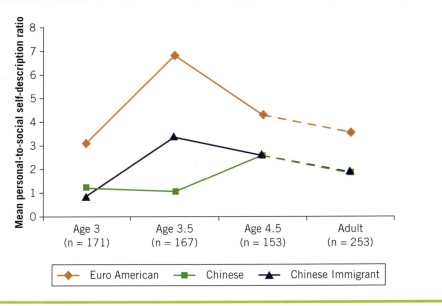

One important implication of these cultural differences is that how you embody and enact those characteristics that are valued by your society has a significant impact on how you feel about yourself (that is, on your self-esteem). We will return to this topic in the next section of the chapter.

Cultural values. Children are socialized into the values of their cultures, and these values become part of how they see themselves. Children in individualistic cultures (such as the United States) often take great pride in individual achievement and success, while children in collectivistic cultures (such as China) are more likely to see themselves as embedded in a rich network of social relationships that take precedence over individual needs or accomplishments.

The Self in Infants and Toddlers

What conception of "self" is present when we are born? Psychoanalyst Margaret Mahler argued that infants are not born with a sense that they have a "self" that is separate from those who take care of them (Mahler, Pine, & Bergman, 1975). Babies must develop this sense, and they appear to do it in two stages. The first understanding of self is based on the infant's growing ability to make things happen: "*I* make this mobile move" or "*I* make my mommy smile." The baby's *intention* to make things happen reflects her awareness that she is the agent of change. Rochat (2001) has argued that this first understanding then leads to a new concept of "me" when the child can begin to think *about* herself. Self-awareness means that the child is the object of her own perceptions and thoughts (Gallup, Anderson, & Shillito, 2002). This second type of awareness begins to develop in the second year of life. We will describe four ways in which this new sense of self is expressed: mirror self-recognition, use of the pronouns *I* and *you*, perceptual role-taking, and possessiveness with toys. All four develop at about the same time, somewhere near the child's second birthday (Rochat, 2001; Stipek, Gralinski, & Kopp, 1990).

That's me! Before their second birthday, toddlers begin to recognize their own image in the mirror. Before this, they may have been fascinated by the baby in the mirror, but now they know who that baby is—they are looking at themselves!

Mirror Self-Recognition

The classic experiment that has been carried out to determine whether a toddler has physical self-awareness is the "rouge on the nose" mirror self-recognition task. In this task, the toddler's parent pretends to wipe the toddler's nose, but she secretly puts rouge or lipstick on the Kleenex and marks the child's nose. The child is then placed in front of a mirror. If the child realizes that the image in the mirror is really herself and not another child, she will touch her own nose when she sees the funny red mark on it. Children at 1 year of age will not do this. Instead they react as if their mirror image were another child, with whom they can interact. Sometime between 18 and 24 months, most children understand that the mirror image is a reflection of themselves and they touch their own nose (Gallup et al., 2002).

Use of Pronouns

You may hear toddlers say something like "Daddy, pick you up, pick you up!" when what they mean is "Daddy, pick me up!" Using *I* and *you* appropriately is not something that can be learned by imitation. The child only *hears* Daddy say, "I'll pick you up," so he imitates what he hears. Only when he understands that *I* is different from *you* does he become able to use the pronouns correctly and say "Pick me up!" Toddlers develop this ability several months before or after their second birthday. Before this time, many resort to the strategy of referring to themselves by name—for example, "Ethan do it!" (Bates, 1990).

Perceptual Role-Taking

If you ask a toddler to show you her drawing, she may hold it up so that she can see it, but you cannot. You may have to ask her to turn it around so that you can see it too. The toddler assumes that because she can see it, you must be able to see it as well. The child must develop a clearer idea that you and she are separate people with different points of view in order to develop what is called **perceptual role-taking**. Ricard, Girouard, and Gouin Decairie (1999)

Perceptual role-taking
The ability to see things from someone else's perspective.

found that the development of this ability to see from another's perspective was linked with the ability to use *I* and *you* correctly as described in the previous paragraph.

Possessiveness

Two-year-olds are entering what Erik Erikson (1963) referred to as the stage of *autonomy versus shame and doubt.* Being "autonomous" means that you are independent and have some control over what happens to you. Toddlers assert their autonomy, or separation of self from others, through two of their favorite commands: "No!" and "Mine!" As they develop a clearer sense of themselves as separate from those around them, they are motivated to defend their own way of doing things and what they think belongs to them. In one study, Levine (1983) found that 2-year-old boys who recognized themselves in a mirror and were able to understand and use *I* and *you* accurately were more likely than those with a less clear self-concept to claim toys when interacting with an unfamiliar peer. According to Pierce, Kostova, and Dirks (2003), "The object is experienced as having a close connection with the self . . . becoming part of the 'extended self'" (p. 86). Caregivers who deal with toddlers should see this toy-claiming not as selfishness but as a first expression of the child's understanding that "I have a self that is different from yours." The adults can acknowledge this identification of self with toys by suggesting to the toddler that he pick one toy to put away and not share, while promoting the sharing of all the others. While mothers generally promote sharing in their toddlers, there are some differences for boys and girls. Ross, Tesla, Kenyon, and Lollis (1990) found that mothers of boys were more likely to support their toddlers' claims of ownership while mothers of girls were more likely to insist that the girls share.

It's mine! Possessiveness is another component of toddlers' growing sense of self. Once they know that they are a separate individual, they also understand that there are things that belong to them.

Toddlers who have a clearer sense of self are better able to play successfully with peers (Levine, 1983). They begin to imitate each other (Asendorpf & Baudonniere, 1993), and they can work together with a peer to solve a problem. For example, in one study two toddlers were shown a clear box containing toys. The only way to retrieve the toys was for one child to press a lever, while the other took the toys out of the box. One child could not physically do it alone. Toddlers who had shown a clearer sense of self-other differentiation were more able to coordinate with their partner to retrieve the toys successfully (Brownell & Carriger, 1990).

The Self in Preschoolers

For Erikson, the toddler is trying to become autonomous in relation to his parents; that is, he is becoming a separate self. For the preschooler, the self becomes tied to what the child can do. Erikson (1963) describes the central issue of this stage as *initiative versus guilt.* Preschoolers try to initiate activity; that is, they want to do things, to create, and to make things happen. However, they may fail at these attempts to do things by themselves, and that can lead to guilty

1. When a toddler is struggling to do something like move a heavy object, an adult should help the toddler out so she doesn't experience a sense of failure.

TRUE/FALSE

False. Toddlers are developing a sense of autonomy, and to do this, they need to take the initiative and find out what they can and can't do. Adults should be patient with these attempts so the child doesn't feel guilty about trying something that is difficult.

"I can do it myself!" During the preschool years, children struggle with becoming autonomous and being able to do things by themselves. Parents can support this growing autonomy by being patient with their children's attempts.

Autobiographical memory A coherent set of memories about one's life.

feelings that they have done something wrong, especially if parents are impatient with their failed attempts. The child's definition of self as "what I do" is reflected in Susan Harter's (1999) illustration of a preschooler's self-description:

> I'm 3 years old and I live in a big house with my mother and father. . . . I have blue eyes and a kitty that is orange. . . . I know all of my ABC's, listen: A, B, C, D, E, F, G, H, J, L, K, O, M, P, Q, X, Z. I can run real fast. . . . I can count up to 100. . . . I can climb to the top of the jungle gym, I'm not scared! I'm never scared! I'm always happy. . . . I'm really strong. I can lift this chair, watch me!" (p. 37)

Can you list the characteristics that make up this description? It includes physical description (blue eyes), possessions (a kitty), abilities (knowing ABCs, climbing, lifting a chair), feelings (never scared), and some basic information—the child's age and where he lives. Are these similar to the way you described yourself in the beginning of the chapter? In all likelihood there are some major differences.

At this age, children also begin to develop a more coherent set of memories about their lives, which is referred to as **autobiographical memory**. Research has shown that the way that parents talk with their children about what happens in their lives has an effect on how children remember their lives. Haden (2003) described two approaches that parents take in their conversations with children about their life experiences. The first is called *high elaborative* because these parents guide their children in complex discussions about events in their lives. The second approach is called *low elaborative* because these parents more often try to get the child to say exactly what happened, and when children do not, the parents just change the subject instead of discussing it with them further. The evidence is that children with high elaborative mothers are more able to remember details about their lives and may even understand their lives in more complex ways (Haden, 2003).

Autobiographical memories also reflect cultural differences. In conversations between American mothers and their child, the child is usually given the lead with the mother playing an auxiliary role in which she supports and elaborates on the child's description of what happened. In conversation between Chinese mothers and their child, however, the reverse is true. Those conversations tend to be directed by the mother. She introduces the topics, provides instructions, or teaches cultural rules and values (Wang, 2004). Another significant difference is that in Chinese dyads the parent may use the conversation to remind the child of an incident in which the child misbehaved or violated some rule or expectation (Miller, Fung, & Mintz, 1996), and this type of autobiographical story is often told in the presence of a third party. American mothers rarely do this, and almost never do it in front of a third party. On those rare occasions when an American mother talks about a child's misbehavior, it is likely done in a humorous way that implies that the incidence was funny or that the child's behavior was cute or clever, again emphasizing the uniqueness of the child rather than the violation of cultural expectations.

The Self in School-Age Children

As children enter middle childhood, they become able to think about themselves in more complex ways. Erikson (1963) describes this period as a conflict of *industry versus inferiority*. Erikson saw middle childhood as the time when children set aside childhood fantasies and begin the work that is needed to learn the "industry" of their society. In most modern societies, this means going to school to prepare for adult life. Erikson also saw that this is an age when children begin to compare themselves to others and don't always come out on top. In carrying out this social comparison, they can think, "I am better than Joe at arithmetic but not as good as Arina at reading." This reflects a new ability to coordinate two or more concepts at the same time. It is as if younger children can only think of one thing at a time, while older children can keep more than one thing in their mind: for example, one's performance and someone else's performance, as well as different types of performance, such as arithmetic and reading (Harter, 2006b). This is, of course, exactly what Piaget would say that children of this age can do cognitively. Parents and teachers also contribute to this type of social comparison when they emphasize how well some children are doing in relation to other children.

While young children tend to see themselves in an all-or-nothing way ("I'm never scared! I'm always happy"), children between 8 and 11 years of age are refining their self-concepts to include shades of gray; for example, "I get sad if there is no one to do things with" (Harter, 2006b, p. 527). They can also experience more than one feeling at a time; for example, "I was happy that I got a present but mad that it wasn't what I wanted" (Harter, 2006b, p. 527).

The Self in Adolescents

The cognitive changes that occur during the stage of formal operations are reflected in how the adolescent can think about the self. Self-descriptions become more abstract and focus more on enduring qualities or traits (Harter, 1999). Increasingly the adolescent develops a **differentiated self**. Adolescents now understand that they can show different characteristics in different situations but that these differences are all part of a unitary whole. For example, an adolescent might say, "I am usually a pretty friendly, outgoing person, but I really clam up when I am around adults." Adolescents have the cognitive ability to pull these divergent pieces of the self together into a coherent whole.

Differentiated self The understanding that one can show different characteristics in different situations but that these differences are all part of a unitary whole.

You will remember from Chapter 2 that the developmental crisis of adolescence is one of *identity versus role confusion*. According to Erikson (1963, 1968), in order for development to proceed in an optimal way, the young person must figure out who he is but also must think about the person he wants to become as he moves from adolescence into young adulthood. When adolescents are able to resolve this conflict by developing a strong sense of their own identity, they are in a good place to deal with a developmental issue that emerges in early adulthood: *intimacy versus isolation*. Individuals with a strong sense of self are able to enter into an intimate relationship and to connect their identity with another individual without losing their own sense of self in the process.

Teen identities. As part of the process of identity development, adolescents may "try on" different identities like "skater," "jock," or "brain."

An important part of this process of identity development involves the adolescent "trying on" different identities, and that helps explain some of the behaviors we associate with adolescence. Teenagers experiment with new activities or associate with new friends, and sometimes they even take on new identities as a part of this process. An adolescent who has held conventional views and attitudes may flirt briefly with the Goth culture or begin spending time with the skaters or the druggies at school. Sometimes, however, this experimentation becomes more than a flirtation as the young person finds that the new alternative identity feels right to him and it persists, supported by the new peer relationships that go along with it (Kerpelman & Smith, 1999). The result may be a **negative identity**, or an identity that is in direct opposition to an identity that parents or other adults would support (Erikson, 1963). When an adolescent has not been able to find an identity for himself, even a negative identity may seem preferable to remaining in a state of identity confusion. Being a gang member, a druggie, or a delinquent provides a ready-made identity in the sense that there is a clearly defined set of attitudes, values, and behaviors that comes with it.

Negative identity   An identity that is in direct opposition to an identity that parents or other adults would support.

Marcia's Identity Statuses

The Canadian developmental psychologist James Marcia extended Erikson's work on identity development by describing the process by which adolescents work toward achieving an identity. According to Marcia (1966), identity achievement requires adolescents to engage in a period of active exploration of the alternatives available to them, a process that he calls being in a crisis. Adolescents also have to make a personal investment in the choices that they make, a process Marcia calls commitment. By combining these two processes, Marcia named and described four identity statuses (see Figure 11.2).

Figure 11.2

Marcia's identity statuses. According to Marcia, identity development during adolescence reflects two processes: exploration of the alternatives available and commitment to an identity. Where an individual stands on these two processes determines the adolescent's identity status.

		Crisis (exploration)	
		Low	High
Commitment	Low	Identity Diffusion	Moratorium
	High	Foreclosure	Identity Achievement

Identity Diffusion. If you talk with some adolescents about their future, it becomes clear that they haven't spent much time thinking about it and, what is more, they don't seem overly concerned about it. For adolescents experiencing **identity diffusion** there is both a lack of crisis (or the perceived need to explore alternatives) and a lack of commitment to a future identity.

Identity diffusion   A lack of interest in developing an identity.

Moratorium. Other adolescents in the status of **moratorium** are actively exploring alternatives that can shape their future identity (so, in Marcia's terms, they are in a state of crisis), but they are not yet ready to commit to a specific choice.

Moratorium   A time of exploration in search of identity, with no commitment made yet.

Foreclosure. Some adolescents make a firm commitment to an identity, even before they have engaged in an active process of exploration. How can you feel that you already know who you will become in the future without having actively looked for an identity? Marcia says that this occurs when an adolescent accepts an identity that has been prescribed for him by someone else, such as his parents. For example, if you grew up in a family where from an early age it was clearly communicated to you that everyone expected you to become a doctor, a teacher, a police officer, or a pastry chef, and these expectations became an unquestioned part of how you saw yourself, you would have foreclosed (or cut off) other possibilities. In many parts of the world, **foreclosure** is the norm; you will become whatever your parents were. For instance, if your culture is based on farming, you are most likely to become a farmer just as your parents were. If your family worked in a trade, you too would learn that trade. You might not have the array of choices available in countries such as the United States.

Foreclosure
Commitment to an identity without any exploration of possibilities.

Identity Achievement. Finally, there are adolescents who have actively engaged in a process of exploring the alternatives available to them and are now ready to commit to one of the possible identities, so they are in the status of **identity achievement**.

Identity achievement
The choice of an identity following exploration of the possibilities.

There are a few important points to note about Marcia's theory. First, we often think of identity in terms of an occupational commitment, but it applies also to commitment to religious or political ideologies (Marcia, 1966), lifestyle, recreational choices, friendships, and gender roles (Bergh & Erling, 2005). Remember this point later in the chapter when we discuss the exploration of sexual preference. Second, it might sound like there is a steady progression through the statuses toward the final goal of identity achievement, but there actually can be movement between any of the statuses. In a follow-up study of the college students first interviewed by Marcia, 47% of them showed instability of their identity status over a 6-year period (Marcia, 1976). Not surprisingly, moratorium was the most unstable status, with 100% of the students moving into a different status during this period of time.

However, even adolescents who have an achieved identity status can have new experiences that shake up their commitment to an identity and push them back into a state of moratorium. Having a close relationship with someone who has different attitudes or values than you have, traveling to a part of the world you have never seen before and experiencing a new culture, or coming to college and being exposed to new ideas—any of these experiences could shake up a previously solid commitment to an identity. Adolescents also can move from actively exploring (moratorium) to a state of diffusion (where they give up their active exploration), only to relaunch their exploration at some point in the future. Finally, it is important to realize that people are likely to change at least some aspects of their identity throughout adult life. Beyond adolescence, significant life events such as the birth of a child, a divorce, or a change in health could result in a need to reevaluate identity.

Look back at Figure 11.2. Where would you place yourself in it? Where were you a year ago? Where do you think you'll be a year from now?

Self-Esteem

We began this chapter by talking about self-concept, or how you describe yourself. Now we turn our attention to self-esteem, or how you *feel* about those characteristics. Sometimes people confuse these terms, but they are distinct, and it is important that you understand that distinction. Remember that list of characteristics you wrote at the beginning of the chapter? Use it now in **Active Learning: The Difference Between Self-Concept and Self-Esteem** to examine the difference between self-concept and **self-esteem**.

Self-esteem How people feel about characteristics they associate with themselves.

The Difference Between Self-Concept and Self-Esteem

In the column below labeled "Self-Concept," make a list of 8 to 10 characteristics that describe you. They can include physical characteristics (such as your height, weight, or body build), your skills and abilities, or your personality characteristics. After you complete your list, go back and circle a number to indicate for each characteristic how much you like or dislike this characteristic in yourself.

Self-Concept	Self-Evaluation										
	Like	10	9	8	7	6	5	4	3	2	1	Dislike
	Like	10	9	8	7	6	5	4	3	2	1	Dislike
	Like	10	9	8	7	6	5	4	3	2	1	Dislike
	Like	10	9	8	7	6	5	4	3	2	1	Dislike
	Like	10	9	8	7	6	5	4	3	2	1	Dislike
	Like	10	9	8	7	6	5	4	3	2	1	Dislike
	Like	10	9	8	7	6	5	4	3	2	1	Dislike
	Like	10	9	8	7	6	5	4	3	2	1	Dislike
	Like	10	9	8	7	6	5	4	3	2	1	Dislike
	Like	10	9	8	7	6	5	4	3	2	1	Dislike

If you are like most people, you will find some variability in your self-evaluation. There are some things (probably a lot of things) that you like about yourself and some things that are important aspects of your self-concept that you don't like very much.

If you look carefully at the characteristics that you included in your self-concept, you also can understand how someone else with the same list of characteristics could end up with a different level of self-esteem. For instance, you may describe yourself as a very tall person, but you could love or hate that about yourself. Or you may see yourself as a very trusting person, but you could like the fact that you always think the best of everyone or hate the fact that you are so trusting that people take advantage of you all the time.

Remember that these self-evaluations occur in a cultural context. Is there anything on your list of characteristics that you like and your culture values that would *not* be seen as positively in another culture?

Self-Esteem During Childhood

If you look back at the self-description of the 3-year-old that appeared near the beginning of this chapter, you may be struck by how very positive and optimistic it was. This 3-year-old claimed that he knew *all* of his ABCs (although he clearly did not), could run *fast*, climb to the *top* of the jungle gym, and is *never* scared. Another example of this unrealistic self-appraisal comes from a little girl who was asked whether she knew how to swim. "Yes" was her reply, but when she was asked to swim over to the adult, she let go of the side of the pool and sank like a stone! Where does this unbounded optimism come from?

First, you need to consider the standard of comparison that young children use. Preschoolers are not yet able to compare themselves to others, a process called **social comparison**, which will emerge during the school years. Without a standard of comparison, almost everything they do can be the "best" in their eyes (Harter, 1999). Because young children do not take the perspective of other people, they focus on self-comparisons rather than social comparisons. When a 3-year-old compares what she can do now to what she could do just a year earlier, it is a very impressive improvement.

As children move from early childhood into middle childhood, their confidence in their own abilities often declines (Eccles, 1999; Harter, 2006a), and several factors contribute to this. First, children increasingly compare themselves to their peers, and consequently their self-evaluations become more realistic and drop from the inflated levels of early childhood. Second, remember that the psychosocial developmental task of middle childhood is *industry versus inferiority* and the "work" of these children is what they do in school. The constant feedback that children in elementary school receive from their teachers helps them develop a more accurate appraisal of their ability (Wigfield et al., 1997). Third, children during middle childhood often participate in a variety of organized activities in which they are evaluated. They may be taking music lessons or gymnastics, playing organized sports, or participating in competitive activities such as the chess club or the debate team at school. In all these situations, they are continually evaluated and told how they can improve their performance.

High self-esteem has been associated with a number of positive developmental outcomes, and low self-esteem has been associated with a number of negative ones. For instance, students who do well in school tend to have higher self-esteem than students who do more poorly (Baumeister, Campbell, Krueger, & Vohs, 2003). Based on this observed relationship, school systems have developed a number of programs designed to boost students' self-esteem, with the goal of eventually improving their academic performance. Collectively these efforts are referred to as the **self-esteem movement**. Learn about the history of this movement in **Journey of Research: The Self-Esteem Movement**.

2. Children's self-esteem is extraordinarily high in early childhood. ✔✗ **TRUE/FALSE**

True. Young children often have very high self-esteem because they do not yet compare their own performance to what others do, so they think they can do anything.

Social comparison The process of comparing oneself to others.

Self-esteem movement School-based programs designed to boost students' self-esteem, with the goal of eventually improving their academic performance.

The Self-Esteem Movement

JOURNEY *of* RESEARCH

TRUE/FALSE

3. Programs that help build students' self-esteem not only improve their grades but also help reduce delinquency, drug use, and adolescent pregnancy.

    False. Self-esteem programs have not been effective at improving school performance or reducing adolescent problems. Although good students usually have high self-esteem, improving a student's self-esteem does not necessarily result in improved grades.

The self-esteem movement had its roots in the efforts of California state assemblyman John Vasconcellos, who created the California Task Force to Promote Self-Esteem and Personal and Social Responsibility in 1986 (Mecca, Smelser, & Vasconcellos, 1989). The foreword to an edited volume titled *The Social Importance of Self-Esteem* produced by the members of the Task Force (Mecca et al., 1989) says that the data and testimony from public hearings they held led to "a consensus that a primary factor affecting how well or how poorly an individual functions in society is self-esteem" (p. vii). Other social problems as wide-ranging as alcohol and drug abuse, crime, and even child abuse also were linked to low self-esteem.

As a result of these findings, a number of school-based self-esteem programs were created. However, over the years critics charged that these were largely "feel good" programs that had little or no impact on actual school performance. While such programs emphasized the uniqueness and the value of the individual, their praise was not tied to specific achievements or accomplishments (and specifically was *not* tied to academic performance). Despite an expenditure of millions of dollars on these programs, research failed to find any significant positive outcomes that could be tied back to participating in esteem-building programs (Baumeister et al., 2003; Twenge, 2006).

In a review of the self-esteem literature in 2003, Roy F. Baumeister and his colleagues pointed out

that we may have gotten it backward. Self-esteem and positive outcomes may be correlated, but remember that we can't determine the direction of an effect from a correlation. Children who are good students often feel good about themselves (that is, they have high self-esteem), but the question is whether feeling good about yourself makes you a good student. Imagine for a moment what would happen if you felt *great* about yourself but were required to take a test on matrix algebra when you had never studied matrix algebra. Although the direction of the effect can theoretically move in either direction, most evidence supports the idea that high self-esteem is primarily an *outcome* that results from performing well, rather than being the *cause* of good performance (Baumeister, 1996; Baumeister et al., 2003; Dweck, 1999). High self-esteem also has not been found to "prevent children from smoking, drinking, taking drugs, or engaging in early sex" (Baumeister et al., 2003, p. 1), which were other goals of the self-esteem movement.

This does not mean that we shouldn't promote high self-esteem among children. We want children and adolescents to feel good about themselves. Rather it means that we need to help children base their esteem on actual achievement rather than on empty praise (Dweck, 1999). As adults, we need to help them find what they are good at or develop skills they need to succeed at things they care about.

Self-Esteem During Adolescence

Early adolescence is a time that is notoriously hard on a teen's self-esteem. Physical, social, and environmental factors come together in a way that is challenging for many adolescents (Eccles et al., 1997; Simmons & Blyth, 1987). Think of a time in your life when you were dealing with many changes all at the same time, and chances are that you will remember feeling overwhelmed, with little confidence in your ability to handle things in a competent way. Recalling this time in your life helps you understand why multiple changes during early adolescence can take a toll on an adolescent's self-esteem.

Young adolescents are dealing with the physical changes of puberty. As their body goes through rapid changes, they can feel clumsy and awkward and often are self-conscious about their physical appearance. This is so important that Susan Harter (1999) found that self-rated physical attractiveness accounted for 70% of the variance or difference in self-esteem in children and adolescents. At this same time, adolescents are moving from elementary school to middle school or junior high school. A number of researchers (Eccles et al., 1997; Fenzel, 2000; Simmons & Blyth, 1987) have noted a developmental mismatch between the demands of the middle/junior high school environment and the characteristics of young adolescents.

Middle school teachers have higher academic expectations for their students than teachers in elementary school have, so grades often decline after the transition, lowering the students' perception of their own academic competence. Consequently, young adolescents may need more help and support from their teachers, but in middle/junior high school they have different teachers for each of their subjects, so they have less opportunity to get to know their teachers well and for their teachers to know them. Some school districts have responded to this problem by dividing each grade level into smaller groups of students who have most of their classes together and who are taught by a core of teachers who consult with each other about the students and coordinate the curriculum. Middle/junior high schools also place a greater emphasis on discipline and control at a time when adolescents are striving for autonomy (Eccles, 1999). The school environment becomes more competitive and places more emphasis on assessment, increasing the social comparison between students at a time when students are already particularly sensitive about negative social comparisons.

The cognitive changes of adolescence also can affect self-esteem. Adolescents are better able to assess their abilities in multiple domains and can understand the complex patterns that emerge. They realize that they can be good students, fair volleyball players, and poor artists. Their global self-esteem is the product of these multiple assessments, but their ability to think hypothetically also allows them to think not only about their real selves (the characteristics they currently have) but also about their **ideal selves** (the characteristics they aspire to in the future). It is the discrepancy between the two and the importance of the domain to the individual that impact self-esteem (Harter, 2006b). For instance, if there is a fairly large discrepancy between how well you play basketball and how good you wish you could be at this game, but athletics is *not* an important domain for you, this large discrepancy may not have a negative effect on your self-esteem. However, there might be a relatively small discrepancy between your current weight and your ideal weight, but if the domain of physical appearance is very important to you, even a small discrepancy can have a large impact on your self-esteem.

After the decline in self-esteem that often accompanies the entrance into early adolescence, self-esteem typically improves throughout the remainder of adolescence (Impett, Sorsoli, Schooler, Henson, & Tolman, 2008). Figure 11.3 illustrates the pattern of change in self-esteem that has often been found (Robins, Trzesniewski, Tracy, Gosling, & Potter, 2002). Note that self-esteem is high in childhood (for the reasons we've already described) and there are no gender differences at this young age, but self-esteem declines for both boys and girls as children's self-evaluations become more realistic throughout childhood, reaching a low point in early adolescence. Also note that gender differences appear fairly early and persist until well into adulthood. However, as the figure shows, even the sharp drop from middle childhood through early adolescence is only about one-half point on the measure that was used in this research (from 3.8 to 3.4 for boys and to 3.2 for girls) and, even though girls' self-esteem is lower than that of boys, that is not the same thing as saying it is "low." A review of hundreds of studies on self-esteem that involved thousands of participants came to the conclusion that although boys score higher on measures of global self-esteem, the difference is actually quite small (Kling, Hyde, Showers, & Buswell, 1999). Figure 11.3 also shows that self-esteem for both boys and girls begins to rebound and increases over the rest of adolescence.

Ideal self The characteristics one aspires to in the future.

4. The self-esteem of boys and girls is quite similar during adolescence. **TRUE/FALSE**

    True. Although boys' self-esteem on average is higher than girls' self-esteem in adolescence, the magnitude of the difference between the genders is actually fairly small.

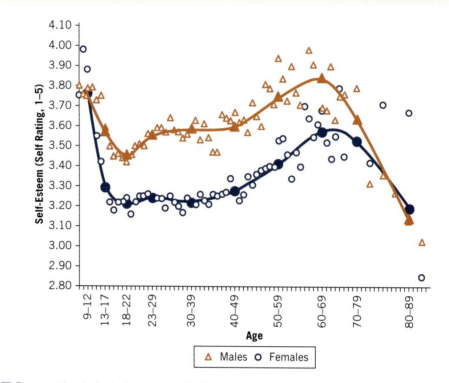

Figure 11.3

Changes in self-esteem. Self-esteem typically drops through childhood (as children engage in more social comparisons) and in early adolescence (when adolescents are dealing with multiple changes in their lives). However, it rebounds as they gain a stronger sense of identity and move toward adulthood.

NOTE: The open triangles (males) and open circles (females) are the results of individual studies that were pooled for this meta-analysis. The orange line and blue line show the average level of self-esteem at each age across these studies.

Gender Identity

"It's a boy!" "It's a girl!" One of the first and most central aspects of our identity is our gender. Our gender determines much about what our experiences in life will be. Every society prescribes certain roles and expectations for the behavior of men and women, girls and boys. Take a minute to think about what you connect with the concept of "boy" and the concept of "girl." Whether we are a boy or a girl biologically is determined by genes, hormones, and physical body parts. However, the concept of gender includes all the roles and stereotypes that our society connects with being a boy or a girl.

Theories of Gender Development

Numerous theories have contributed ideas about how children develop their concept of gender and their own gender identity. We will describe here the approach of four theories: psychoanalytic theory, behavioral and social learning theory, cognitive developmental theory, and gender schema theory.

Psychoanalytic Theory

According to psychoanalytic theory, children do not develop a clear gender identity until they are about 6 years old, when they are leaving the phallic stage of development. During this stage,

Freud said that boys go through the Oedipus crisis and girls go through the Electra crisis. In both cases, the child fantasizes about marrying the opposite-sex parent and doing away with the parent of the same sex. For boys, the Oedipus crisis is resolved when they realize that they cannot beat their more powerful father. Instead they identify with the father, deciding to be like him and hoping that someday they will find someone like their mother for themselves. For girls, the situation is more complicated. Essentially Freud believed that girls identify with their mothers, whom they believe to be damaged because they do not have a penis. There is little research evidence to support these ideas as the basis of gender identity in children (Golombok & Fivush, 1994).

Another approach to understanding gender identity that has emerged from psychoanalytic theory is that of Nancy Chodorow (1978). She theorized that infants develop a sense of self as they separate from their mother. Because mothers are most often the primary caretakers, little boys must develop their sense of self as a boy by moving away from their mother. Girls, however, can maintain a sense of self as a girl while remaining in close contact with their mother. Chodorow believed that boys may grow up to renounce closeness and intimacy as a threat to their masculinity, while girls' identity is centered more on their relationships and need for closeness.

Behavioral and Social Learning Theories

As we learned in Chapter 2, a central concept of the theory of behaviorism is reinforcement, those environmental responses that cause a behavior to continue or be repeated. For behaviorists, gender identity results from direct and indirect reinforcement of gender roles and activities. Adults may not intentionally reinforce gender-specific activities. They may claim that they do not discriminate between boys and girls and that all the differences that are seen between the sexes are due to biological reasons, but there is considerable research to show that parents do, in fact, reinforce sex-typed play activities and household chores (Lytton & Romney, 1991). While boys and girls receive positive reinforcement for gender-appropriate behavior, boys receive more active discouragement for behaviors and activities that are defined as feminine than girls do for their masculine activities, at least in part because "feminine" boys are expected to stay that way through adulthood, while "masculine" girls are expected to outgrow these characteristics (Martin, 1990; Sandnabba & Ahlberg, 1999). Fathers are more likely than mothers to respond negatively to cross-gender activities (Bussey & Bandura, 1999).

The central concept of social learning theory is the role of imitation, and children are exposed to numerous examples of gender roles and activities every day that they can imitate. Even when their parents do not demonstrate strongly differentiated gender roles, children still see these roles portrayed in the world around them and in the media. If you watch children's television shows and commercials you will see many models of masculine and feminine behavior. As just one example, in a study of superhero cartoons, male superheroes outnumbered females 2 to 1, and the male superheroes were rated as more likely to show anger while the female superheroes were more concerned about their appearance (Baker & Raney, 2007). The question remains as to why girls are more likely to imitate girls while boys imitate boys. This question is addressed in Kohlberg's cognitive developmental theory.

Cognitive Developmental Theory

Lawrence Kohlberg (1966) was the first theorist to examine the development of gender identity through the lens of cognitive theory. As a follower of Piaget, he believed that children's understanding of gender goes through stages as they mature. When they are younger, they do not understand that gender is a characteristic that is stable and permanent. He found that young children believed that gender could change over time ("I'm a boy, but I can be a mommy when I grow up") or because of changes in appearance, such as a hairstyle or clothing. The first stage,

5. If you put a 3-year-old boy in a dress and polished his nails, he would be afraid that it would make him a girl. **TRUE/FALSE**

True. Until children develop gender constancy at about age 5, they think that changing surface features to make them resemble the opposite sex (such as changing their hair, their clothes, or what they play with) might actually change their gender.

Gender identity Stage when children's concept of gender relies on external appearance.

Gender stability Stage when children understand that their gender is constant over time but don't understand that gender doesn't change even if they do activities usually performed by the other gender.

Gender constancy The understanding that one's gender remains constant even with external changes.

Video Link 11.1
Gender and toys.

called **gender identity**, begins at about age 2. In this stage children can identify gender—"I am a girl, and you are a boy"—but their concept of gender relies on external appearance. They may believe that if a girl were to wear a tie, she might become a boy. The second stage, called **gender stability**, begins at age 3 when children understand that their gender is constant over time—that is, that a girl cannot become a father and a boy cannot become a mother. However, they are still not clear that a girl playing with trucks does not become a boy. Finally, in the third stage, called **gender constancy**, 5-year-old children understand that gender remains constant even with external changes; for example, a boy with long hair is still a boy. Kohlberg believed that it is only when children have achieved full gender constancy that they begin to seek out specific information about what is appropriate for boys and girls to do and wear and to pay more attention to adults of the same gender.

In a recent study, Ruble et al. (2007) found support for these ideas. They also found that children who had achieved gender constancy were less likely to be rigid in their adherence to gendered characteristics. They asked the children questions such as "Is it wrong for boys to wear nail polish?" or "Would it be OK for a boy to wear nail polish if he didn't get into trouble and nobody laughed?" to determine how rigidly the children held gender role standards. It appears that before children have gender constancy, when there is still some question in their minds as to whether they can turn into the other sex, they are more likely to have rigid standards. Therefore, preschool children often have more rigid adherence to gender stereotypes than school-age children. Once the children are clear that they will forever be a boy or a girl, they are more flexible about external things like clothing, hairstyles, and nail polish. A boy may or may not want to wear nail polish, but he knows that he will still be a boy if he does. **Active Learning: Kohlberg's Cognitive Developmental Theory of Gender Development** is designed to show you how to test these concepts with a young child.

ACTIVE LEARNING

Kohlberg's Cognitive Developmental Theory of Gender Development

In order to determine what level of gender concept a child has according to Kohlberg's developmental theory, interview a child between the ages of 2 and 6 and ask the following questions:

1. Gender identity: Are you a girl or a boy? Whatever the child answers, ask the opposite; for example, if the child says she is a girl, ask if she is a boy.

2. Gender stability: When you were a little baby, were you a little girl or a little boy? Were you ever a little [opposite sex of child's first response]?

3. Gender stability: When you grow up, will you be a mommy or a daddy? Could you ever be a [parent of the opposite sex of child's first response]?

4. Gender constancy: If you wore [opposite sex of child—that is, "boys'" or "girls'"] clothes, would you be a girl or a boy?

5. Gender constancy: Do boys and girls play with different toys? If the child says yes, ask, "What toys do boys play with? What do girls play with?" After the child answers, say, "If you played with [a boy toy the child has mentioned], would you be a boy? If you played with [a girl toy the child has mentioned], would you be a girl?"

6. Gender constancy: Could you be a [opposite sex of child] if you wanted to be?

You can also ask the child the names of boys and girls with whom the child is friends. Substitute their names above instead of asking the child directly about him- or herself.

If the child can answer only Question 1 correctly, she is in the gender identity stage. If she can answer only the first three questions correctly, she is in the gender stability stage. If she can answer all five correctly, she has full gender constancy. Children who answer some but not all questions correctly within a stage are still working on the understanding in that stage. If possible, compare your results with those of classmates who interviewed children who were younger or older than the child you interviewed.

Video Link 11.2
Gender constancy.

Sandra Bem believed that much of what Kohlberg found about the stages of gender understanding was based on children's ignorance of the real physical differences between the sexes. In raising her own child, she made sure that he did know the difference. She tells the following story to illustrate the idea that when children understand the physical differences, they are not as affected by the superficial differences. Because Bem was trying to raise her son not to be gender stereotyped, she accepted his request to go to school with barrettes in his hair. One of his buddies told him, "You're a girl, because only girls wear barrettes." Her son decided to show him in no uncertain terms that he was a boy, not a girl, and pulled down his pants, but his friend replied, "Everybody has a penis; only girls wear barrettes!" (Bem, 1989, p. 662). Without the knowledge of physical differences between the sexes, his friend had to rely on superficial characteristics like barrettes to determine his friend's gender.

Gender Schema Theory

In Chapter 7 we described a schema as a way that we organize our understanding of the world. Gender is one important schema that guides the way that we see the world. The character "Pat" who appeared at one time on the television show *Saturday Night Live* plays on our need to divide people into males and females. Pat's sex is ambiguous, and people generally want to know "What sex is Pat really?" For some people, the ambiguity makes them very uncomfortable, and the humor comes from the way that the show plays on that discomfort. Look at this photo of Chris. What questions does this photo bring to your mind?

A gender schema contains more than simply whether someone is a male or a female. It also contains all the things that an individual connects with each gender, such as expected behaviors, abilities, and occupations. Sandra Bem believed that gender development does not follow stages based on cognitive development, as Kohlberg said. Instead, she believed that gender concepts are learned from one's particular society. Children's self-concepts are formed in part by what is assigned to their gender. Whereas in many Western cultures a boy is likely to have "strong" but not "nurturing" in his self-description, a girl is likely to have the opposite. Parents will exclaim how strong their little boy is or "what an arm" he has when he throws a ball. Little girls are unlikely to hear this. Rather, parents may talk with excitement about how their little girl is so loving to her dolls, a real "little mommy." As children learn what is expected for their gender, they try to do those

Meet Chris. Imagine you were just introduced to this child named Chris. What would your initial reaction be? What are the first questions you would ask this child? Does this child's appearance make you feel uncomfortable in any way, and, if so, what is the source of your discomfort? By the way, this is a picture of a 6-year-old boy.

Baby X. Would you think of this baby differently if you were told the baby was a boy or a girl? Would you dress the baby differently? How else might your behavior differ?

things. Eventually their self-esteem can become linked to their ability to fulfill gender-linked expectations (Bem, 1981). Although this is what happens in most cases, remember that if being a highly feminine girl or a highly masculine boy is not very important to you, not meeting these expectations may have relatively little impact on your self-esteem.

The question is whether children act in these gender-stereotyped ways and parents simply respond to what the children are doing, or whether children are reacting to parental cues and acting in ways that seem to please their parents. This is the "direction of effect" issue that we described in Chapter 3. To address this question, a series of experiments called the Baby X experiments were carried out. In one version, a 3-month-old child is dressed as a girl for one adult and as a boy for another adult. The adults are told to play with the "boy" or the "girl" and are provided with toys, some of which fit gender stereotypes. The result is that the adults choose different toys for the same children, a toy football if they think they are playing with a boy and a doll if they think they are playing with a girl (Sidorowicz & Lunney, 1980). In another study, adults were shown a movie of an infant being shown a jack-in-the-box and crying as a result. Especially for men, those who were told they were seeing a boy labeled the child's feeling as anger, while those who thought they were seeing a girl labeled the feeling as fear (Condry & Condry, 1976). Looking at a number of studies, Stern and Karraker (1989) found that the most consistent results were that parents and other adults would select stereotyped toys and activities for an infant based on whether the infant was labeled as a girl or a boy. However, there was more variability in other reactions, such as labeling of emotions, from study to study. It is apparent from this line of research that adults contribute to children's gender schemas through the way they interact and interpret the child's behavior based on the adults' own ideas about what to expect from boys and girls.

Gender Segregation

From an early age, boys and girls tend to prefer to spend time with peers who are the same gender as they are. This preference is pretty obvious from the preschool years until late

Gender segregation. On a typical elementary school playground, you would probably see boys playing with boys and girls playing with girls, just as they are in these photos.

childhood. You will read more about gender segregation in play in Chapter 13, but if you look at playgrounds in elementary school, you will see that the children spend the majority of their time in same-sex groups, and best friendships during childhood are almost exclusively between children of the same gender (Maccoby, 2002). In Chapter 13 we will describe the similarities and differences in more detail.

Puberty and Gender Intensification

We have seen that preschoolers may be more rigid about their gender role definitions than older children. A second period in which children may find it more important to cling to gender stereotypes is early adolescence. As children enter puberty and their bodies take on more of the characteristics of adult males or adult females, understanding and conforming to gender stereotypes becomes more important to them than when they were still children (Hill & Lynch, 1983). The changes in their physical appearance act as a signal to others that the young person is approaching adulthood, and so they receive increased social pressure to behave in ways that fit the stereotypes of male or female adults (Galambos, 2004). Some studies that have looked at short-term changes around the time of adolescence have found support for the idea that gender differences in behavior, attitudes, and psychological characteristics become greater than they were in childhood, through a process called **gender intensification** (Crouter, Manke, & McHale, 1995; Galambos, Almeida, & Petersen, 1990). However, a recent review of the literature on gender role development by Nancy Galambos (2004) raises the possibility that "when considered across the period of childhood and adolescence, gender intensification is not as strong or as wide-ranging a phenomenon as was first assumed" (p. 241). Galambos notes that there are many different aspects of gender role development that could be considered from the perspective of the gender intensification hypothesis but, since we don't yet have strong, longitudinal studies of all of them, we cannot yet reach a firm conclusion about the validity of the notion of gender intensification in early adolescence.

Young teens are often so uncertain about their gender identity that they look to very artificial means to resolve their anxieties. Before your high school years, you and your peers might have experienced some "tests" of gender such as the ones found in **Active Learning: A Masculinity/Femininity "Test" in Early Adolescence.**

Gender intensification
The idea that gender differences in behavior, attitudes, and psychological characteristics become greater in early adolescence than they were in childhood.

A Masculinity/Femininity "Test" in Early Adolescence

ACTIVE LEARNING

Look at your fingernails. Now stand up and look at the bottom of your shoes. This was a "test" made up and used by middle schoolers to assess their femininity or masculinity. The children's interpretation was that if you looked at your fingernails with your hands flat in front of you with palms down, you were feminine. If you looked at them with your hands curled, palms up, you were masculine. For the soles of your shoes, if you bent your knee up in front of you and twisted your foot over to look at the bottom of the shoe, you were masculine. If you looked over your shoulder as you bent your leg back, you were feminine.

Older children and young teens are at an age of great uncertainty about their sexual identity. When trying to figure out their own masculinity or femininity, meaningless "tests" such as these may loom large in their minds, and they may even tease each other about the results. Older teens will see them for the silliness that they are. Do you remember anything like these tests from your own early adolescence?

Gender Stereotyping and Androgyny

Consider this list of characteristics: *willing to take risks, competitive, sensitive to the needs of others, ambitious, sympathetic, understanding, warm, forceful, cheerful, has leadership abilities, self-reliant, willing to take a stand, soft-spoken, shy.*

If you were asked to divide these words into two groups, how would you do it? Do words like *willing to take risks, forceful,* and *has leadership abilities* end up in one group and words like *sensitive to the needs of others, warm,* and *soft-spoken* end up in the other? If you were asked to label these groups of words, it wouldn't be surprising if you used *male* and *female* or *masculine* and *feminine* as your labels. As we mentioned earlier in the chapter, gender stereotypes are very powerful influences on people's perceptions.

In 1974, Sandra L. Bem published an article that proposed a different way of thinking about masculinity and femininity that she called **androgyny**. In her own words, this is how Bem (1974) described this gender concept:

> Both in psychology and in society at large, masculinity and femininity have long been conceptualized as bipolar ends of a single continuum; accordingly, a person has had to be either masculine or feminine, but not both. This sex-role dichotomy has served to obscure two very plausible hypotheses: first, that many individuals might be "androgynous"; that is, they might be *both* masculine and feminine, *both* assertive and yielding, *both* instrumental and expressive—depending on the situational appropriateness of these various behaviors; and conversely, that strongly sex-typed individuals might be seriously limited in the range of behaviors available to them as they move from situation to situation. (p. 155)

Based on this perspective of gender roles, she developed the Bem Sex-Role Inventory (BSRI), which contains 20 adjectives on the Masculinity Scale, 20 adjectives on the Femininity Scale, and 20 Neutral Items. The items in the Masculinity Scale and Femininity Scale were selected based on the social desirability of each item for persons of each gender. Individuals who were classified as masculine by this measure not only selected a lot of items from the Masculinity Scale for their self-descriptions but also actively rejected items from the Femininity Scale. Likewise, individuals classified as feminine selected a lot of items from the Femininity Scale but actively rejected items from the Masculinity Scale. Individuals who equally selected items from the two scales were classified as androgynous.

Bem's hypotheses concerning the behavioral flexibility of androgynous individuals were later tested by research in which college students were placed in situations designed to elicit stereotypically feminine or masculine responses (Bem & Lewis, 1975). The first situation looked at the participant's ability to resist peer pressure (a stereotypically masculine behavior). Students were asked to rate whether a series of cartoons were funny or not funny. Although they thought other students also were rating the cartoons, they were actually listening to a tape recording in which, for some cartoons, the other voices expressed opinions that were not accurate (for example, everyone else seemed to agree that an unfunny cartoon *was* funny, or vice versa). The second situation gave participants an opportunity to be playful with a kitten (a stereotypical feminine behavior). As expected, both men and women who were androgynous showed resistance to pressure to conform and showed high levels of playfulness when interacting with the kitten. Bem concluded that there are androgynous individuals whose "sex role adaptability enables them to engage in situationally effective behavior without regard for its stereotype as masculine or feminine" (Bem & Lewis, 1975, p. 643).

However, not everyone agreed that an androgynous orientation was the most beneficial one for an individual (Rose & Montemayor, 1994; Whitley, 1983). As an alternative to the androgyny hypothesis, the **congruence model** says that it is having congruence (or a match) between your gender and your gender role orientation that would be most

Androgyny   The idea that both sexes can have the characteristics that are traditionally reserved for one sex.

Congruence model   The idea that having a match between your gender and your gender role orientation would be most beneficial to your psychological well-being.

Masculinity model   The idea that having masculine traits (regardless of your biological gender) would be associated with high self-esteem and well-being because it is masculine traits that are valued the most by Western society.

beneficial to your psychological well-being. And a third alternative, the **masculinity model**, suggests that having masculine traits (regardless of your biological gender) would be associated with high self-esteem and well-being because it is masculine traits that are valued the most by society.

When these alternative ideas were tested, one review of the literature came to the conclusion that there is not strong support for the congruence model (Whitley, 1983), but there is a fair amount of support for the masculinity model (Bassoff & Glass, 1982; Whitley, 1983). Allgood-Merten and Stockard (1991) found that androgyny was beneficial to the self-esteem of both boys and girls when they looked at fourth graders, but as children moved into adolescence, it was self-efficacy (a masculine trait), not relationality (a feminine one), that was most important for self-esteem, especially for girls. Markstrom-Adams (1989) also concluded that it was the masculine component of androgyny that was associated with psychological well-being for both male and female adolescents. Because it is more acceptable for girls to adopt some masculine characteristics than it is for boys to adopt feminine ones, androgyny seems to be advantageous for girls because they add these valued masculine traits to their feminine ones, but a more traditional masculine orientation remains beneficial for boys because boys don't benefit that much from adding the less-valued feminine traits (Markstrom-Adams, 1989).

Although you may already do some things that you consider to be outside of the stereotypes for your gender, it is instructive to consciously break down those stereotypes and watch the reactions of others and of yourself. To do so, try **Active Learning: Going Against Gender Stereotypes**.

6. During adolescence, the most well-adjusted females are ones who score high on measures of femininity, and the most well-adjusted males are ones who score high on measures of masculinity.

TRUE/FALSE

False. Although the balance of masculine to feminine traits is different for adolescent males and females, there seems to be some advantage to having at least some masculine traits for both, perhaps because masculine traits are more valued in Western cultures than feminine traits.

Going Against Gender Stereotypes

ACTIVE LEARNING

To experience for yourself how strongly gender stereotypes affect our behavior, choose an activity that goes against your own stereotype for your gender. First, you need to identify the behavior that you are going to "try on." It could be a leisure activity, a household task, or the use of media. We realize that students today may already have a good deal of gender flexibility, but for this activity choose something you associate with the opposite gender that you *don't* routinely do. Men might want to learn to braid hair or knit, or they might purchase and read fashion or bridal magazines. Women might want to learn how to change the oil in their car, mow the lawn, or use a snowblower (be sure you learn from someone who will make sure that you do this safely). Keep a diary record of how you feel taking on this new role, and make note of any resistance that you receive from others if they observe your behavior. How comfortable do you feel, and how likely are you to continue your new behavior beyond this brief experiment? If you have learned a new skill, how do you feel about your ability to do something that you never knew how to do before?

Development of Sexual Preference

Another important part of gender identity is **sexual orientation**, or preference for a same- or opposite-sex partner. As children enter adolescence, most of them find themselves attracted to members of the opposite sex, but some find themselves attracted to members of the same sex. It is difficult to estimate how many adolescents are in this situation because research done on sexual preference has used different methodologies or has measured different aspects of sexual orientation, so the results cannot be directly compared to each other to reach a single conclusion. The situation is further complicated by the fact that this research tries to measure

Sexual orientation
Preference for a sexual partner of the same or the opposite sex.

a behavior that often is kept secret, as well as the fact that individuals settle on a sexual orientation at different points in childhood, adolescence, or adulthood, so this estimate becomes a moving target. Given these difficulties, estimates of the prevalence of homosexuality are usually in the 3% to 5% range, but some researchers have made estimates that are 3 to 4 times higher than that (Kinsey Institute, 1999).

We begin by looking at the process that a young person goes through when exploring his or her sexual orientation and, in the case of gay, lesbian, or bisexual individuals, the process of "coming out." Gays and lesbians often recall that as early as childhood they began to feel that they were somehow different from their same-sex peers (Carver, Egan, & Perry, 2004; Savin-Williams & Diamond, 1999). They may have engaged in cross-sex-typed behaviors (for example, girls playing masculine competitive sports, boys playing with feminine dolls) or had cross-sex-typed interests. Some even begin to feel dissatisfied with their biological gender. At around age 10, when many children have their first romantic attraction, these children find themselves being drawn to someone of the same sex, and this experience triggers a period of sexual questioning, often before the child even enters puberty (Carver et al., 2004). As they work to come to terms with their sexual orientation, they may take the next step of exploring a same-sex relationship before finally adopting a gay, lesbian, or bisexual identity in late adolescence. In one study, half of the gay and bisexual men who were interviewed said they had fully accepted their sexual identities and had a homosexual romance or homosexual experiences during high school or college (Dube & Savin-Williams, 1999). This type of sexual exploration is not uncommon in adolescence and does not occur exclusively among young people who are homosexual.

Once young people have settled on a sexual orientation, the next test is to integrate their sexual orientation into their identity. An important part of that process involves disclosing this information to others (Savin-Williams & Ream, 2003). Young people today seem to be taking this step at younger ages than they did in the past. The first disclosure is still likely to be to a friend or a sibling, but it is much more likely that young people will disclose to their mother before disclosing to their father. Mothers are generally more accepting of this disclosure than fathers (Savin-Williams & Ream, 2003). Although there is relatively little information on how this disclosure affects the parent-child relationship in the long run, what information there is indicates that after an initial period of adjustment, most parent-child relationships rebound, and some even improve (Savin-Williams & Ream, 2003). Not surprisingly, acceptance and support from family members and friends is associated with better adjustment and mental health outcomes for the individual following disclosure of his or her sexual orientation (D'Augelli, 2003).

Before leaving this topic, it is important to point out that the topic of sexual orientation is a very complex one. Being gay, lesbian, or bisexual is a qualitatively different experience, but most of the research to date has looked at the experiences of gay men (Savin-Williams & Diamond, 1999). It is likely that we will need more complex and differentiated conceptualization of sexual identity development to adequately cover the range of experiences that includes lesbian and bisexual individuals (Diamond, 2006).

Although the process described here is typical for many individuals, it isn't the only way that finding a sexual orientation can happen. For instance, Diamond (2006) points out that we would make a mistake if we assumed that sexual questioning is something that happens at only one point in time and then is resolved. It is more likely that this is something the individual returns to from time to time to reexamine. When the process starts, when it ends, and how long it takes along the way are other dimensions that differ from one person to another.

Finally, remember that the process of exploring a sexual orientation takes place in a cultural context and at a particular point in historical time. Acceptance of homosexuality varies greatly from one culture to another, but, at least in some segments of society today, acceptance appears to be growing. An intriguing perspective on the long-term adjustment of gay youth is offered by Ritch Savin-Williams (2006) in his book *The New Gay Teenager*. Through interviews with a group of confident, upbeat teenagers who are gay, a picture emerges of teens who are

TRUE/FALSE

7. There is evidence that many gay teenagers today are more interested in the everyday concerns of adolescence (such as school and friends) than they are in their sexual orientation.

True. Recent research on gay teenagers has found that many of them appear to be confident, positive, and no more likely to suffer from problem behaviors than their heterosexual peers.

more concerned about the everyday issues of being an adolescent than about their sexual orientation. The possibility that many gay youth are happy and well adjusted is supported by longitudinal research that has found that the majority of them do not differ from their heterosexual peers on a number of problem behaviors. Rotheram-Borus and Langabeer (2001) conclude from their research that "substance use, problems at school, feelings of anxiety and depression, conduct problems, and the rate of delinquency appear normative among gay, lesbian, and bisexual youth" (p. 118). However, this generally positive picture is darkened by the significant fact that rates of suicide attempts continue to be higher among gay youth.

Gay and lesbian teens are often asked to explain their sexual orientation to others. To see what that might be like, try **Active Learning: The Heterosexual Questionnaire**.

The Heterosexual Questionnaire

ACTIVE LEARNING

Advocates for Youth (Rochlin, 1977/2008) developed the following activity to help create greater understanding of the experiences of gay, lesbian, and bisexual young people. When these youth are beginning to "come out," they are often asked questions that are nearly impossible to answer. The questions in the Heterosexual Questionnaire below are similar to the type of questions that these youths are expected to answer. Regardless of each student's sexual orientation, everyone should try to answer these questions from the point of view of a heterosexual. After you try to answer these questions, reflect on the questions that we have posed at the end of the questionnaire.

The Heterosexual Questionnaire

Please answer the following questions as honestly as possible.

1. What do you think caused your heterosexuality?
2. When and how did you first decide you were heterosexual?
3. Is it possible that your heterosexuality is just a phase you may grow out of?
4. Is it possible that your heterosexuality stems from a fear of others of the same sex?
5. If you have never slept with a member of your own sex, is it possible that you might be gay if you tried it?
6. If heterosexuality is normal, why are so many mental patients heterosexual?
7. Why do you heterosexual people try to seduce others into your lifestyle?
8. Why do you flaunt your heterosexuality? Can't you just be who you are and keep it quiet?
9. The great majority of child molesters are heterosexual. Do you consider it safe to expose your children to heterosexual teachers?
10. With all the societal support that marriage receives, the divorce rate is spiraling. Why are there so few stable relationships among heterosexual people?
11. Why are heterosexual people so promiscuous?
12. Would you want your children to be heterosexual, knowing the problems they would face, such as heartbreak, disease, and divorce?

Reflection Questions

1. Did you find the questions hard to answer? Were some harder than others? Which ones were especially difficult? What, specifically, was so difficult about these questions?
2. How did the questions make you feel?
3. What does it say about our society that gay, lesbian, and bisexual youth are asked similar questions?
4. What can you do in the future if you hear someone asking a homosexual youth such questions?

Our thoughts about the causes of homosexuality have changed substantially over the years. The evolution of our understanding is described in **Journey of Research: Explanations for Homosexuality**.

Explanations for Homosexuality

JOURNEY *of* **RESEARCH**

Homosexuality as a sexual orientation is as old as human history, but attempts to understand and explain it in a scientific manner are far more recent. In the late 1800s, Karl Heinrich Ulrichs proposed a scientific theory of homosexuality that claimed that there was a biological basis for it (Kennedy, 1997), but this view was quickly overshadowed by a psychoanalytic explanation that dominated the field for many years (Bieber et al., 1962).

The psychodynamic explanation is based upon a family dynamic that includes a dominant or seductive mother and a weak, hostile, or distant father, but the scientific validity of this proposition has been called into question. Research that tested this idea often was based upon the accounts of people who were already seeking help from a therapist, relied upon small samples or single-subject designs, or did not have a comparison group. The fact that these studies were conducted by clinicians who already subscribed to the notion that a neurotic family was a root cause of homosexuality further compromised the scientific value of this work. And, finally, it is hard to disentangle the fact that the distancing of a father from a child who is exhibiting some cross-gender traits could be a response to the child's gender orientation, rather than the cause of it (Isay, 1996).

The idea that homosexuality was pathological persisted until 1973, when the *Diagnostic and Statistical Manual of Mental Disorders* of the American Psychiatric Association (APA) officially excluded homosexuality as a disorder (Spitzer, 1981). Of course there continues to be debate within our society about whether homosexuality is "normal" or "natural" and about whether people make a conscious decision to adopt a heterosexual orientation.

Social learning theory provides a contemporary explanation for how children acquire their gender identity based on the processes of social reinforcement and observational learning (Bussey & Bandura, 1999). Although these ideas provide a helpful framework for understanding sexual orientation for children whose gender identity matches their biological sex, they are less satisfactory as an explanation for a homosexual or bisexual identity. Children in our culture are rarely positively reinforced for cross-gender behavior by parents or peers and are not likely to observe many homosexual role models that they would want to imitate. Even children who are raised by homosexual parents and, therefore, are exposed to homosexual role models daily are as likely to become heterosexual as children raised by heterosexual parents (Patterson, 2006).

Research has continued to explore a biological basis for sexual orientation. The possible role of genetics is supported by research on twins that has found that identical male twins are more likely to be similar in sexual preference than nonidentical male twins (Gladue, 1994; Griffin, Wirth, & Wirth, 1993). Other research has looked to neuroanatomy and neuroendocrinology as explanatory mechanisms (Byne, 1996). However, this research still has many unanswered questions. In all likelihood, the best possible explanation eventually will involve a complex set of interacting biological, social, and cognitive factors.

Finding an ethnic identity. Sharing family traditions—whether it is celebrating Kwanzaa, enjoying a birthday party with a piñata, or having a large Italian family dinner—helps children and adolescents form a sense of their ethnic identity. What family traditions did your family share while you were growing up?

Ethnic Identity

Developing a gender identity is a basic task that all children must deal with, but many children have an additional task to deal with. They also need to develop a sense of their **ethnic identity** or "the attitudes toward and feelings of belonging to an ethnic group" (Marks, Szalacha, Lamarre, Boyd, & Coll, 2007, p. 501). In early childhood ethnic identity is largely unexamined, but by the time children enter middle childhood, they have the cognitive capacity to begin to form ethnic identities (Ocampo, Knight, & Bernal, 1997). Phinney (1989) proposed a theory that describes the process beginning in adolescence. In her theory, the first stage is the stage of unexamined ethnic identity. The child or adolescent either has not thought about her ethnic identity and has no clear understanding of the issues (similar to Marcia's status of identity diffusion) or has accepted without question the values and attitudes that others hold about her ethnic group (similar to Marcia's status of foreclosure). In this stage, the adolescent often prefers the majority culture over her own ethnic culture (Marks et al., 2007).

The second stage is an ethnic identity search in which the adolescent actively tries to understand his culture and to explore the meaning of his ethnicity. The young person may read about his culture, talk to others who share his cultural heritage, visit ethnic museums, or take part

Ethnic identity The attitudes toward an ethnic group to which you feel you belong.

Table 11.1

Phinney's stages of ethnic identity development

Stage	Comment
Unexamined ethnic identity	"My past is just there; I have no reason to worry about it. I'm American now." (diffusion) "I don't go looking for my culture. I just go by what my parents say and do, and what they tell me to do, the way they are." (foreclosure)
Ethnic identity search	"There are a lot of non-Japanese around me and it gets pretty confusing to try and decide who I am." "I think people should know what Black people had to go through to get to where we are now."
Achieved ethnic identity	"People put me down because I'm Mexican, but I don't care anymore. I can accept myself more." "I used to want to be White, because I wanted long flowing hair. And I wanted to be real light. I used to think being light was prettier, but now I think there are pretty dark-skinned girls and pretty light-skinned girls. I don't want to be White now. I'm happy being Black."

in cultural events (Marks et al., 2007). He may even actively reject the majority culture during this process. The result of this exploration is the final stage, which is the achieved ethnic identity, in which the adolescent has "a clear, secure understanding and acceptance of one's own ethnicity" (Phinney, 1989, p. 38). This process is even more complex for the 5% or more of the school-age population that is multiracial (Brunsma, 2005). Table 11.1 illustrates the adolescent's thinking at each of these stages through some of the comments made by adolescents who were interviewed as a part of Phinney's research.

Progress through these stages has been associated with a number of positive outcomes for the adolescent, including higher scores on measures of self-esteem, mastery, psychological adjustment, social and peer interactions, and family relations (Crocetti, Rubini, & Meeus, 2008; Phinney, 1989; St. Louis & Liem, 2005). A strong sense of ethnic identity also can have a positive and protective role in the school context. Wong, Eccles, and Sameroff (2003) found that a strong positive connection to one's ethnic group reduced the impact of discrimination on academic self-concept and school achievement for African American adolescents and was associated with resistance to problem behaviors such as skipping classes, lying to parents about the adolescent's whereabouts, bringing alcohol or drugs to school, and cheating on exams. In an ethnically diverse population of high school students, Phinney, Cantu, and Kurtz (1997) found that ethnic identity status was associated with global self-esteem. For African American, Latino, and White adolescents, students who were committed to and who felt positively about their ethnic group had higher self-esteem than students who had negative attitudes or were uncommitted to their ethnic identity.

Moral Identity

In this section we examine development of a moral identity, based on one's understanding of and adherence to moral standards. Self-interest is a guiding force throughout our lives, but as we grow out of early childhood we learn to balance self-interest with concern for others. We learn to think about right and wrong not just in terms of what is good for us but in terms of what is good for everyone. This is the basis for the development of morality. Toddlers do what is right because they will be rewarded if they do or punished if they don't, but we want children to develop an internal sense of morality so that they will choose to do what is right because of their own thoughts and feelings, not because of the external consequences. Children develop a moral identity "to the extent that the self is organized around moral commitments" (Lapsley & Narvaez, 2004, p. vii). If moral concerns are central to their concept of themselves as a good person, their self-esteem will suffer if they violate their own moral standards. For some people, moral concerns are not central to their idea of themselves, so if they violate moral principles it may have little or no effect on their self-esteem.

In this section we will describe how children develop a sense of morality. We will describe how different theories have connected moral development with the influences of the environment, cognitive development, and emotional development. In addition, understanding morality is not the same as behaving in a moral fashion, so we will examine the development of moral thought but also the development of moral behavior.

The Role of the Environment

The theory of behaviorism offers an environmental explanation for how children first learn right from wrong. According to this theory, when a child does something good, like helping a friend, he may receive praise from an adult or a positive reaction from the friend. This reinforcement makes it more likely that he will behave this way again. However, when the child does something bad, like taking a toy away from a friend, he is likely to be scolded by an adult and receive a negative reaction from his friend. He will associate negative events with this behavior, and that should make it less

likely that the behavior will occur again in the future. Of course this can all go wrong when we unintentionally reinforce bad behavior. A young child who says a swearword, causing adults to laugh, is going to be more likely to repeat that word over and over again if it continues to get this reaction!

Developing a conscience. From the expression on this child's face, it looks like he knows he is doing something wrong. Do you think that internalized moral values are causing his concern, or does he simply fear that he will be punished if his misbehavior is discovered?

Social cognitive learning theory adds another learning mechanism for moral development. Children will imitate what they see others do, especially if the other person's behavior receives reinforcement. For example, children whose parents help out in the community are more likely to volunteer as well (Nolin, Chaney, & Chapman, 1997). Unfortunately children will also imitate immoral behavior they see. This has serious consequences when a parent is violent or otherwise abusive. Obviously parents need to watch their own behavior carefully so they only model behavior they would not mind seeing reflected in their children's behavior.

However, the biggest question in the development of morality is how children move from responding to external consequences, such as rewards and punishments, to internalizing a moral sense of right and wrong so that they do what is right even if no one is around. We want children to be able to behave morally because of their own feelings and thoughts about their actions, not just "because my mom said so." There are a number of theories that have attempted to explain how this happens, some of which emphasize the role of cognitive development while others emphasize the role of emotional development.

The Role of Cognitive Development

Cognitive theories link the development of moral thought to the development of thought in general. It has been argued that young children learn the basic rules of right and wrong by first grade. This **moral knowledge** is based on "intelligence, cultural background, and a desire to make a

Moral knowledge
Understanding of right and wrong.

Moral judgment The way people reason about moral issues.

good impression" (Kohlberg, 1987, p. 273). **Moral judgment** is not the same as moral knowledge. It is not the knowledge of what is right and wrong but how we think about moral issues and reach conclusions. For example, a child may know it is wrong to take a cookie without asking, because she knows that she will be punished if she does. A child at a higher level of judgment understands that taking the cookie is wrong because it breaks trust with a parent. Both children know what is wrong, but their moral judgment is based on their stage of cognitive development.

To test some of his ideas about moral development, Piaget (1965) posed moral dilemmas to children of different ages to see how they would respond. He believed that before the age of 4, young children were premoral; that is, they were unable to make their own moral judgments. For children from ages 4 through 7, he described moral thought as **heteronomous morality**. *Heteronomous* means "subject to external controls and impositions" (Merriam-Webster, 2010). In this stage, young children base their judgments on adult authority. They do not really understand why moral rules should be followed (Lapsley, 2006). Not surprisingly, rules are not applied in a consistent way. If you've ever played a board game like "Chutes and Ladders" with a preschooler, you know that the child may change the rules when it looks like he is going to lose the game. Piaget (1965) also believed that young children could not differentiate whether someone had done something on purpose or accidentally, and this limited their ability to judge the morality of certain behavior. For example, if a child broke many dishes by accident, preschoolers are likely to say that she should be punished more than a child who broke one dish on purpose.

Heteronomous morality Moral judgments based on the dictates of authority.

Immanent justice The belief that unrelated events are automatic punishment for misdeeds.

A second aspect of this level of moral thought is described as **immanent justice**. Piaget (1965) argued that young children believe in "the existence of automatic punishments which emanate from things themselves" (p. 251). For example, in one moral dilemma he says that a boy who stole apples ran away and then fell through a rotten bridge. He then asks the child whether the boy would have fallen if he had not stolen the apples. A child in this stage would say that the boy would not have fallen into the water if he had not stolen the apples. Falling into the water was a punishment for what he did. For young children, just as night comes "in order to put us to sleep," boards break in order to punish us (Piaget, 1965, p. 256). One difficulty with this kind of thinking is that children who have experienced a negative event, such as being hospitalized for an illness, may believe that this is a punishment for something bad that they did. In fact, many adults still show this kind of thinking when they ask "What did I do to deserve this?" when something terrible happens to them. It is as if they think they are being punished for something they did earlier that really has no connection with the bad event that happened.

Autonomous morality stage When children are aware of the rules and realize that they must adhere to them in order to maintain their interaction with others, rather than because an adult has told them what to do.

By age 7 or 8, children have generally moved on to the **autonomous morality stage** in which they are aware of the rules and realize that they must adhere to them in order to maintain their interaction with others. In Piaget's (1965) words, they come to understand that "everyone must play the same" (p. 44). The issue of fairness to all becomes central as children become less egocentric and more aware of others' points of view. Piaget believed that when children play with peers, everything must be negotiated, not handed down from adults, so children must figure out together how to play fair and treat each other decently if they want to continue playing.

Lawrence Kohlberg further developed Piaget's ideas on moral development. Kohlberg used a similar technique by presenting a series of moral dilemmas to children of different ages and came up with stages based on their responses to these dilemmas. His most famous story is titled "Heinz and the Drug":

> In Europe, a woman was near death from a rare form of cancer. There was one drug that the doctors thought might save her, a form of radium that a druggist in the same town had recently discovered. The druggist was charging $2,000, ten times what the drug cost him to make. The sick woman's husband, Heinz, went to everyone he knew to borrow the money, but he could only get together about half of what [the drug] cost. He told the druggist that his wife was dying, and asked him to sell it cheaper or let him pay later. But the druggist said, "No." So, Heinz got desperate and broke into the man's store to steal the drug for his wife. Should the husband have done that? Why? (Kohlberg, 2005, p. 214)

Video Link 11.3
Moral dilemma.

Some people read this dilemma and immediately say he should definitely break in to get the drug, while others believe it would be wrong to do so. In fact, Kohlberg was less interested in what people thought they would do than in understanding how they came to their decision. Someone who said that he would break in because his wife would be angry at him if he did not would be at quite a different level of moral thought than someone who said he would break in because human life is sacred. Likewise, someone who said he would not break in because he might get caught and sent to jail would be at a different level than someone who said he would not break in because it is important to respect each other's property.

Based upon these different types of reasoning, Kohlberg described three stages of moral judgment: preconventional, conventional, and postconventional. Two levels were found within each stage, and these are described in Table 11.2. We will describe here the broad outlines of the three major stages.

The first stage, **preconventional moral judgment**, is most characteristic of young children. It is marked by self-interest and motivation based on rewards and punishments. In some circumstances, we all continue to think in these terms. For example, if you are driving on the highway faster than the speed limit and you hit the brakes when you see a police car, you are not thinking about the underlying reasons for the speed limit (such as safety or conserving gasoline). You are trying to get somewhere as fast as you can without getting caught breaking the law, and you hit your brakes because you don't want to get an expensive speeding ticket.

In the second stage, **conventional moral judgment** moves beyond self-interest to take into account the good of those around you. In the first substage, a person bases moral decisions on the moral expectations of important people in his life. At this stage, "trust, loyalty, respect, and gratitude" are central values (Kohlberg, 1987, p. 284). In the second substage a person makes decisions based more on the expectations of society as a whole. Laws are to be followed because society would break down if everyone disobeyed them. In this stage, a person might respond to the Heinz dilemma by saying that he should not break in because if everyone did things like this, social order would break down.

Preconventional moral judgment Moral reasoning that is marked by self-interest and motivation based on rewards and punishments.

Conventional moral judgment Moral reasoning that moves beyond self-interest to take into account the good of others.

Table 11.2

Kohlberg's stages of moral development

Levels	Stages	Description (the basis for moral judgment)
I. Preconventional	1. Heteronomous morality	Obeying the word of authorities and fear of punishment
	2. Individualism, instrumental purpose, and exchange	Fairness—everyone's self-interest must be taken into account
II. Conventional	3. Mutual interpersonal expectations and conformity	Being "good" to those around you, in accordance with their expectations, including caring, loyalty, and gratitude
	4. Social system and conscience	Considering the good of society as a whole, maintaining order for the good of all
III. Postconventional	5. Social contract and individual rights	Understanding that the rules of society may differ for different groups and that some values, such as life and liberty, are universal
	6. Universal ethical principles	Following self-chosen principles involving equal rights even when they conflict with society's rules

Postconventional moral judgment
Independently formed moral judgments that are based on universal principles that apply to all people.

In the third stage, **postconventional moral judgment** moves beyond society as a defining factor of what is moral or right. Kohlberg believed that a person in this stage believes in the human rights of all people, so moral judgments are based on universal principles that apply to all. Often these principles will correspond with society's rules, but when they don't the person still chooses to follow the principles. For example, members of the organization called Greenpeace carry out actions that sometimes are against the laws of a particular country but that they believe are justified in the name of protecting the earth. In November 2009, Greenpeace members chained themselves to a crane that was used by a company they believe is destroying the forests of Indonesia. Their justification for their action was that deforestation produces the greenhouse gases that are contributing to global climate change that is endangering human life on the planet. However, their actions violate the laws of the country, and Indonesia is trying to deport them (Agence France-Presse, 2009). You will read about another situation where an individual chose to break the law on behalf of what he believed was a higher moral purpose when you read **Journey of Research: Kohlberg's Life History and His Theory**.

Although these stages are usually described in terms of children's development, Kohlberg believed that even adults may remain in the first stage of moral judgment, and many do not move beyond the stage of conventional moral judgment.

Kohlberg's Life History and His Theory

JOURNEY *of* **RESEARCH**

Many times individuals' life experiences influence the theories they develop and the research they carry out. Lawrence Kohlberg has a life history that is clearly connected to his research. Kohlberg served with the U.S. Merchant Marines after World War II. After his service, he volunteered to help sail ships that would move Jewish refugees out of Europe to the British-controlled territory of Palestine. In doing so, he was breaking British law, which made it illegal for these refugees to enter Palestine. He was captured and held in Cyprus until he was liberated by the Jewish fighting force known as the Haganah. Kohlberg's research in later years focused on how people make decisions about what is right and wrong. As was described above, the highest level in Kohlberg's theory is one in which a person develops universal moral principles that may or may not conform to what a particular country or group of people believes is right. Can you see how his life experiences shaped his theoretical ideas? (Adapted from Levine, 2002)

Gender Differences in Moral Thought

When Kohlberg did his original research, he studied only boys. When he did include girls, they tended to perform at a lower level of moral reasoning than the boys. Carol Gilligan believed that this was because Kohlberg's theory was gender-biased and reflected a masculine view of morality. Gilligan argued that women do not have a lower level of morality than men, but rather have a different type of morality than men. Her idea was that women base their moral judgments more on what she called the principle of care for the well-being of others and also oneself, while men base their judgments more on impersonal, abstract justice, which she believed was the basis for Kohlberg's stages. Although Gilligan did much of her research using real-life moral dilemmas, she also used hypothetical dilemmas, such as the following fable she used with children:

The Porcupine and the Moles

It was growing cold and a Porcupine was looking for a home. He found a most desirable cave, but saw it was occupied by a family of Moles. "Would you mind if I shared your home for the winter?" the Porcupine asked the Moles. The generous Moles consented, and the Porcupine moved in. But the cave was small, and every time the Moles moved around they were scratched by the Porcupine's sharp quills. The Moles endured this discomfort as long as they could. Then at last they gathered courage to approach their visitor. "Pray leave," they said, "and let us have our cave to ourselves once again." "Oh no!" said the Porcupine. "This place suits me very well."

After telling this fable, Gilligan would then ask, "What should the moles do? Why?" (Gilligan, 1987, p. 14).

Gilligan (1987) believed that girls and women would be more likely to respond in terms of everyone's needs: "Cover the porcupine with a blanket [so that the moles will not be stuck and the porcupine will have shelter]" or "Dig a bigger hole!" (p. 7). Boys would be more likely to respond in terms of absolute right and wrong: "The porcupine has to go definitely. It's the moles' house" (p. 7).

Although several studies have reported such gender differences, the majority have found that both boys and girls think about morality from both the justice and the care perspectives (Jaffee & Hyde, 2000), and Gilligan's idea that boys and girls differ in this respect was not borne out by research (Walker, 1984). In fact, Kohlberg's original findings that men were more moral than women also have not been borne out. In more recent research, the only gender differences found in Kohlberg's stages of moral reasoning have tended to favor girls, although these differences vary from country to country (Gibbs, Basinger, Grime, & Snarey, 2007). The major conclusion we can draw at the present time is that there is no clear gender difference in moral reasoning.

Cultural Differences in Moral Thought

Kohlberg believed that the same stages of moral development that he found in the United States would be found in cultures around the world. A review of studies carried out in 75 different countries found evidence for the universality of the move from preconventional to conventional morality (Gibbs et al., 2007). However, the universality of the move from conventional to postconventional moral reasoning has been much more controversial. Some have argued that the postconventional stage is reflective of Western and urban values. Other values may reach a higher level in a different way for other cultures. For example, in one study that compared Korean and British children, the researchers found that a concept that Koreans refer to as *chung* could not be scored according to Kohlberg's method. *Chung* is a central value in Korean society that translates as an emotional bond between people in which "the boundary between individuals was dimmed and a sense of one-ness, same-ness, affection, comfort, acceptance and so forth emerged" (Baek, 2002, p. 387). Although there are some cultural similarities, cross-cultural differences at the higher levels of moral thought may be caused by a Western bias in how moral reasoning is assessed rather than by any true differences in the level of moral reasoning found in different cultures.

Moral Thought and Moral Action

Would you describe yourself as an honest person? Do you help others whenever you can? People often believe that their behavior mirrors their values. In other words, they adopt a trait approach to understanding morality (Doris, 2002). They see themselves as a moral person and believe that they act based on that belief. However, there is a substantial amount of research that suggests that morality is more state-like than trait-like because any number of situational factors affect how likely it is that we behave in accordance with our moral values or beliefs. When you are posed with a hypothetical moral dilemma, you are largely free from the situational constraints that might determine your actual behavior, but real life is filled with constraints.

For example, divinity students were told they were going to give a practice sermon. Some were told to talk about the Good Samaritan who helped others in a time of need, while others were given unrelated topics. Then some students were told they were going to be late for their sermon, and some were not. On the way to deliver the sermon, each divinity student saw a man who appeared to be in pain and needed help. What do you think determined whether a student stopped to give help? According to Goleman (2007), it was not whether they had just been thinking about compassion and the Good Samaritan but rather whether they were going to be late for their sermon or not!

The Role of Emotional Development

Emotions enter into the development of morality in two ways. First, we don't want to do what is wrong because we will feel guilty about it, and that is a very uncomfortable emotion. Second, we want to do what is right because we will feel good about doing it. Freud's psychoanalytic theory described both the development of guilt and the development of what Freud called the ego ideal, which motivates us to do what is right. Freud's description of the origins of the superego, or conscience, through the resolution of the Oedipus and Electra complexes that was described in Chapter 2 has not received empirical support. However, modern research has continued to examine the role of the conscience in moral behavior.

Grazyna Kochanska and her colleagues have shown a link between conscience and moral behavior (Kochanska & Aksan, 2006). She defines conscience as guilty feelings following a bad action and the ability to control one's behavior to do the right thing even when no one else is around. She and her colleagues have examined the way that conscience develops. They found that responsiveness of the mother to her infant leads to the toddler's eager willingness to comply with the parent's guidance and rules. In preschoolers these rules become internalized to form the basis for the child's internal conscience. Children who develop an effective internal conscience are much less likely to engage in disruptive and negative behavior (Kochanska, Barry, Aksan, & Boldt, 2008). In this view, the importance of a warm, mutually responsive relationship with the parent (not the resolution of the Oedipus complex) is central in the child's ability to develop self-control and an internal conscience.

The central role of a different aspect of emotions in moral development is shown in the following simple example: A teacher sees a young child bump her head as she emerges from a play structure. The teacher says, "Oooh, ouch! That must hurt. Would you like me to rub it to make it feel better?" This example demonstrates the two basic aspects of emotional response that underlie prosocial behavior, described previously in Chapter 10: empathy and sympathy. The teacher is experiencing empathy when he says, "Oooh, ouch!" It is almost as if he too were experiencing the hurt. Even newborns seem to experience this type of emotional sharing. When they hear other babies crying, they are likely to start crying themselves (Sagi & Hoffman, 1976). However, unlike a newborn, the teacher is able to manage his own emotional response in order to react with concern for the child. This response is called sympathy (Eisenberg, Spinrad, & Sadovsky, 2006). If you feel empathy for other people, it is likely to lead to sympathy for their plight. You also are more likely to want to do something to help them (prosocial behavior) and less likely to want to hurt them (aggression).

Just as empathy and sympathy can lead to prosocial behaviors that we see as moral in nature, anger can lead to aggression in ways that violate moral standards. Aggression has been defined as any behavior that is intended to hurt someone, whether physically or emotionally. The use of aggression by children at different ages is related to the level of their moral understanding. We are less concerned by a preschooler who pushes a friend away to get to a toy than we are by a teenager who uses the Internet to destroy another teen's reputation in part because we don't expect the preschooler to understand how her behavior is hurtful to the other child.

Development of Self-Control

We began the preceding section on moral development by describing how children develop truly moral behavior by moving from the external controls of their parents and other adults to internal control of their own behavior. The ability to control oneself underlies moral behavior, but it is also important for many other aspects of life. In this section we will discuss the development of self-control and some difficulties when children do not develop effective self-control.

Self-Control in Infants and Toddlers

Infants have little or no self-control, and as adults we recognize and accept this. All that they know is what they are feeling and what they want at that very moment, but even young infants make some effort to exercise self-control. For instance, they signal in a subtle way when they are being overstimulated. If you are playing with an infant and the infant suddenly yawns, stretches, and turns away, that is a way of letting you know that he is feeling overwhelmed by what is going on and that you need to reduce the amount of stimulation he is trying to process. Being sensitive to the infant's signals—whether they are signals that the infant is hungry, tired, or uncomfortable—helps the infant learn to regulate his own emotions because he comes to know that he doesn't need to get frantic to get a response from his caregivers.

Modeling out-of-control behavior. Parents are powerful models for children. When parents lose control of their behavior, it indicates to their children that this type of behavior is acceptable. Remaining calm in the face of frustration models self-control.

Another way that parents help infants develop self-control is by providing an environment that has predictable routines. Parents don't need to be rigid about this, but regular times for meals, sleep, and play help keep an infant from becoming overly hungry, tired, or bored. You know from your own experience that it is more difficult to exercise self-control when you are feeling very tired or hungry, and the same is true for infants. Finally, parents have to help infants calm down when they can't do this for themselves. When you give an infant a pacifier, gently rub the infant's back, or cover her lightly with a blanket, you are helping her calm down before she can do this for herself.

As children become toddlers, the important adults in their lives continue to be powerful models for how to regulate and control emotions and behaviors. If parents react to their own frustrations with negative outbursts, toddlers learn that such behavior is acceptable. When parents are angry or become frustrated, they can stop for a minute to regain their composure and express their frustration in words before deciding what action to take. This type of response models exercising self-control rather than behaving impulsively for their children.

Toddlers also are increasingly able to do things to calm themselves down. If they are upset, they can find their own "blankie" or go to the place where they feel calm and safe. Parents can also help redirect their behavior. For instance, if a toddler bites in frustration, parents can give him an alternative behavior that works. People who work with young children know that biting at this age is not unusual, and you frequently hear them saying "Use your words" to remind children that they can express their frustration in other more acceptable ways than biting. As we've said, aggression between children is very common in the preschool years (Dodge, Coie, & Lynam, 2006), but as they grow they learn ways to effectively control these negative emotions. That is why we are so concerned about children and adolescents who fail to do this.

Executive Function, Effortful Control, and Delay of Gratification

Executive function entails a complex neurological process that plays a major role in the development of self-regulation. Just as the chief *executive* officer (CEO) of a business has to decide what tasks the business will undertake and then decide who will carry out each task, the *executive* function of the brain decides what goals to pursue and which parts of the brain will be used to pursue them. It is the coordinating function of the brain that allows us to choose our goals, initiate appropriate responses, inhibit inappropriate ones, monitor our success, and correct errors, if they occur (Zhou et al., 2007). We exercise executive function when we focus our attention on the classroom discussion rather than the noises in the hall or when we realize that we didn't really understand the paragraph we just read and decide to go back and read it again.

Executive control has been linked in children with **effortful control**, the ability to consciously control one's own behavior. In a well-known study, 4-year-old children were told that they could eat one marshmallow right away or they could wait and get two marshmallows (Eigsti et al., 2006). When tempted in this way, children actively tried to inhibit their immediate impulse to grab that marshmallow and eat it and to use other behaviors that could help them wait. They sat on their hands, looked away from the marshmallow, whistled a tune, or did whatever they thought would help them wait. **Active Learning: How Do Children Resist Temptation?** will show you how you can try this experiment yourself. Effortful control is used by children to help them delay immediate gratification in favor of waiting for a later, larger reward. A situation you may find familiar is when you are at a party with lots of wonderful food. Like many people, your impulse may be to eat as much as you can. However, you may decide to forgo this immediate gratification and eat more moderately in favor of a later reward of not feeling sick and an even more long-term reward of being healthier.

Effortful control The ability to consciously control one's behavior.

Video Link 11.4
Delay of gratification—long-term outcomes.

Video Link 11.5
How children resist temptation.

ACTIVE LEARNING

How Do Children Resist Temptation?

Walter Mischel and his colleagues found that children who exert active self-control at 4 years of age are more able to concentrate and tolerate frustration when they become teenagers (Eigsti et al., 2006). Infants have little ability to delay gratification, but by age 4 many children can use particular tactics to help themselves do so. Try the following task with a preschool child:

Equipment needed:

3 marshmallows (or other attractive reward)

A table and chair for the child

A bell (or other sound-maker)

1. In a room with no distractions (for example, no toys or books), ask whether the child would prefer to receive one marshmallow or two marshmallows. Then seat the child at a table with one marshmallow (or other treat) on a plate and a bell.

2. Tell the child you have to leave the room for a little while. Explain that if the child can wait until you come back the child will receive two marshmallows. However, if the child feels unable to wait, the child can eat the one marshmallow but will not receive the second marshmallow. Be sure the child understands the instructions.

3. Leave the room and secretly observe the child for up to 10 minutes or return if the child rings the bell and/or eats the marshmallow or if the child appears to be distressed. Ideally you would have a one-way mirror. Otherwise find a way to be sure the child cannot see you watching. Observe if and how the child tries to stop herself from taking the marshmallow. Does the child sit on her hands, look away from the marshmallow and around the room, sing to distract herself, and so on? These are all observable ways that the child may try to exercise active self-control.

4. If the child waited and did not eat the marshmallow, give the child both marshmallows. If the child rang the bell or ate one of the marshmallows, then he or she does not receive the second marshmallow.

5. Be sure to tell the child how helpful he or she was and thank the child regardless of whether the child got one marshmallow or two.

6. Compare your results with those of others in your class. Did children who had more tactics to try to control themselves have more success in waiting until the time was up to receive the marshmallows? Were there differences depending on the ages of the children; for example, were 4-year-olds able to wait longer than 3-year-olds? Reminder: Testing individual children does not "prove" or "disprove" a theory. That can only be done with a true experimental design (see Chapter 3). Activities such as these with individual children help illustrate the concepts we are discussing and add to your understanding of them.

Resisting temptation. Being able to control your emotions when faced with temptation is an important step in emotional development.

As they get older, children also become better able to delay gratification, and this is another indication of their maturing ability to control their behavior. McCabe and Brooks-Gunn (2007) recently looked at this topic by using **delay of gratification** tasks in a preschool classroom (rather than in a research laboratory). First they asked children to wait to eat an M&M candy until the researcher blew a whistle, and then they placed the children in groups of four and repeated the procedure. They also asked the children, first individually and then as part of a group, not to peek as the researcher wrapped a present for them. Not surprisingly, they found that older children were better able to regulate their behavior and delay gratification than younger children, whether they were tested individually or as part of a group. Although girls waited longer than boys before "peeking" on the gift wrap task, there was no gender difference in the likelihood that they would peek at some point during the test period. Finally the researchers note that there was *not* consistency across the different situations they tested. This highlights the fact that children's behavior is the result not only of the child's characteristics but rather of the child's characteristics in the context of a particular environmental situation. Ask yourself honestly what situation would be tempting enough that you too would "peek" even when you know you shouldn't.

Self-control at a young age has been associated with a number of positive outcomes (Zhou et al., 2007), but a lack of control and high negative emotionality in children as young as 3 to 5 years of age have been found to predict later delinquency and even adult criminal convictions (Henry, Caspi, Moffitt, Harrington, & Silva, 1999). Children who can regulate their emotions and behaviors are seen as more socially and academically competent, as more agreeable and more sympathetic, and as more resilient (McCabe & Brooks-Gunn, 2007). Emotional regulation is also linked to lower levels of problematic behaviors, such as impulsivity, delinquency, aggression, and several behavioral disorders that we will discuss later in the chapter, including conduct disorder and oppositional defiant disorder (McCabe & Brooks-Gunn, 2007). Because the ability to sustain attention and to persist when working on challenging tasks continues to develop through middle childhood and into early adolescence, there are opportunities for interventions that can change the course of the child's development before difficulties in these areas become a persistent pattern (Zhou et al., 2007). Such interventions can include helping the child develop coping skills, but they can also include helping parents learn behavioral management skills that support and assist their children's coping efforts.

Difficulties With Self-Regulation

There are several types of behavioral problems that we see in children and adolescents that are related to difficulties with regulating emotion and using executive control strategies. In

8. When children are asked to resist the temptation to peek at something they have been told *not* to look at, girls and boys give in to temptation at the same rates. **TRUE/FALSE**

True. Girls wait longer than boys before taking a peek, but there is no gender difference in the likelihood that they will peek at some point.

Delay of gratification
The ability to wait until later in order to get something desirable.

Externalizing behaviors
Behaviors in which the child or adolescent "acts out" on the environment such as aggressive or destructive behavior.

TRUE/FALSE

9. About one half of children who show problems with aggression or being impulsive during the preschool years will grow out of their problems by the time they enter school.

    True. Although aggression and impulsivity are the most common form of childhood maladjustment, half of aggressive or impulsive children will outgrow these problems by the time they are ready for school.

Oppositional defiant disorder   A persisting pattern of behavior marked by defiant, disobedient, and hostile behavior toward authority figures.

Conduct disorder   A persistent pattern of behavior marked by violation of the basic rights of others or of major age-appropriate social norms or rules.

Coercive family environment   A pattern of family interaction in which parents and children mutually train each other so that the child becomes increasingly aggressive and the parents become less effective in controlling the child's behavior.

this section we describe several forms that these problems can take, and we discuss the types of interventions that have been used to help children with these conditions. All of these conditions include **externalizing behaviors** or behaviors in which the child or adolescent "acts out" on the environment. This can include aggressive behavior, destructive behavior, attention problems, rule-breaking, and defiance of authority.

Problems with aggression and impulsivity have been described as "the most persistent and common forms of childhood maladjustment" (Olson, Bates, Sandy, & Lanthier, 2000, p. 119), but the good news is that about one half of preschool children who display symptoms of externalizing problems no longer show these symptoms by the time they have entered school (Campbell, Shaw, & Gilliom, 2000). However, when these symptoms do persist, they are associated with academic problems, relationship problems, peer rejection, and even later criminal behavior (Olson et al., 2000). As we discuss specific conditions, you will see that there is a fair amount of overlap in the symptoms associated with each, but there are also characteristics that differ between them (APA, 2000; Loeber, Keenan, Lahey, & Green, 1993).

Conduct Problems

The term *conduct problems* covers a wide range of acting-out behaviors (McMahon & Kotler, 2006). Figure 11.4 shows one way to conceptualize how several different conduct problems relate to each other (Frick et al., 1993). As you can see from the figure, behaviors as diverse as truancy, substance use, running away, being cruel to animals, stealing, setting fires, vandalism, lying, and being a bully can fit under this umbrella term. Two of the more frequently occurring behavior problems are **oppositional defiant disorder** and **conduct disorder**, and we will look at these two in more detail.

Oppositional Defiant Disorder. Young children can be oppositional and defiant, and adolescents can be argumentative. These behaviors may be annoying, but they are not usually a matter of clinical concern. We know that both toddlers and adolescents are dealing with psychosocial issues that reflect their growing sense of self and their need to become more independent and autonomous. Being oppositional or defiant from time to time is one way to assert that autonomy.

However, when confrontation, defiance, and argumentativeness become part of a persistent pattern of behavior, it may be an indication that a child has a behavioral disorder known as oppositional defiant disorder. The American Psychiatric Association (2000) defines oppositional defiant disorder as "a recurrent pattern of negativistic, defiant, disobedient, and hostile behavior toward authority figures that persists for at least 6 months" (p. 91). The behavior itself can take many different forms, including frequent temper tantrums, argumentativeness with adults, refusal to comply with adult requests, spiteful or vindictive behavior, aggressiveness toward peers, and difficulty maintaining friendships. Knowing when these behaviors have moved beyond the normal range into the problematic one and correctly identifying all underlying causes are two of the challenges with this condition.

It has been difficult to determine the cause of oppositional defiant disorder, but both the child's temperament and factors within the family environment play a role. Gerald Patterson and his colleagues at the Oregon Social Learning Center have described a pattern of interaction that frequently occurs in families with defiant children. They call this pattern a **coercive family environment**, and it involves parents and children mutually training each other to behave in ways that increase the likelihood of the child being aggressive and parents being less effective in controlling the aggressive behavior over time (Granic & Patterson, 2006). It starts when the child behaves in some way that irritates the parent, and the parent asks the child to stop what he is doing. For example, the child may be jumping on the furniture, and the parent tells the child to sit down and be quiet. Instead of complying with this request, the

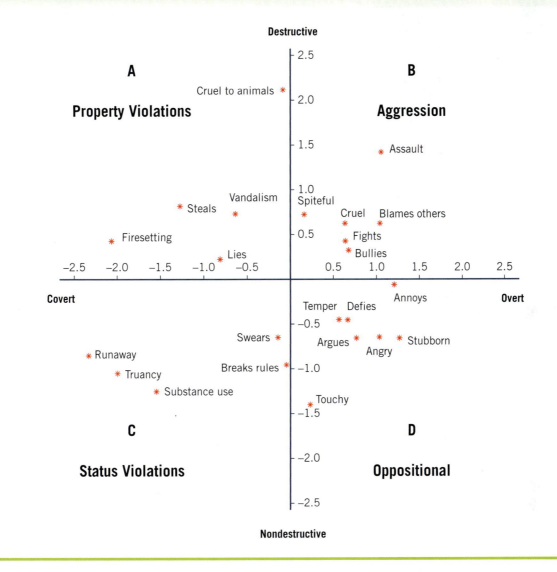

Figure 11.4

Classifying conduct problems. Frick et al. (1993) classified a number of conduct problems along two dimensions: whether the behavior was overt or covert and whether it was destructive or nondestructive. You can see where a number of conduct problems fall on these dimensions in this figure.

child engages in some other coercive behavior like whining or throwing a temper tantrum that annoys the parent even more. The child's behavior is so annoying that the parent finally gives up, perhaps with a statement like "You never listen to anything you are told to do." In the child's mind, he has won this battle because the parent stops trying to make him do something he doesn't want to do. When the parent gives up, it reinforces the child's coercive behavior. In addition, when giving in to the child stops the child's crying or whining, it reinforces the parent's ineffective parenting. This sets up a pattern of confrontation, followed by opposition, followed by defeat for the parent and success for the child, and this pattern repeats itself over and over again.

Oppositional defiant disorder typically is identified in preschool children (Shaw, Owens, & Giovannelli, 2001), but it can first appear in early adolescence (McMahon & Kotler, 2006; Patterson, Dishion, & Yoerger, 2000). Early onset is associated with

Video Link 11.6
Parenting.

Dealing with defiant behavior. It is normal for young children to assert themselves by being defiant from time to time, but it is how parents respond to this behavior that can lay the groundwork for later problems. Parents need to be firm and consistent in handling normal defiance.

ineffective parenting and a difficult temperament in the child. In this case, interventions that help parents provide structure in the home environment and establish daily routines can have some success in breaking the cycle, particularly if they are initiated before the child starts school (Egger, 2009; Shaw et al., 2001). In the case of late-onset oppositional defiant disorder, typically the adolescents have families who have done at least a marginally good job of setting limits and monitoring their child's behavior up to this point, but parental monitoring wanes in early adolescence and the influence of deviant peers becomes too strong, so the adolescent is drawn into deviant behaviors (Patterson & Yoerger, 2002).

Conduct Disorder. Some of the children with oppositional defiant disorder go on to develop a conduct disorder, which is more serious. The American Psychiatric Association (2000) describes a conduct disorder as a "repetitive and persistent pattern of behavior in which the basic rights of others or major age-appropriate social norms or rules are violated" (p. 98). A variety of specific behaviors are used to diagnose this condition, but they can be grouped into four broad categories: aggressiveness toward people and animals (this category includes behaviors such as cruelty to animals, bullying, fighting, and forced sexual activity), property destruction, deceptiveness or theft, and serious rule violations (including many instances of running away from home or being truant from school) (McMahon & Kotler, 2006). Although there are some behaviors that appear in the diagnostic criteria for both oppositional defiant disorder and conduct disorders, conduct disorders include the more serious violations of rights of others and societal norms (McMahon & Kotler, 2006).

Studies in different populations within the United States have found rates that vary from less than 1% to 10% of the population, and the rate is higher among males than females (APA, 2000). Similar to what we saw in the case of oppositional defiant disorder, there is a childhood-onset type and an adolescent-onset type of conduct disorder. The early-onset variety is associated with "inadequate parenting, neurocognitive problems, and temperament and behavior problems" (Moffitt & Caspi, 2001, p. 355), such as aggressiveness and irritability. The adolescent-onset variety is associated with ethnic minority status and time spent with deviant peers (McMahon & Kotler, 2006). Although the condition is 10 times more likely to affect boys than girls when we are talking about an onset during childhood, there is a 5-to-1 ratio of males to females for the adolescent-onset condition (Moffitt & Caspi, 2001).

Conduct disorders are one of the most difficult disorders to treat. One form of treatment known as multisystemic treatment (MST) has shown some promise. Based on Bronfenbrenner's ecological theory, this approach examines many levels of influence that may be contributing to the problem, including family, peers, school, and community. The design of the program is a partnership between the therapist and the family, building on strengths within

Conduct disorder. A conduct disorder involves aggression, a serious violation of another person's rights, or a major violation of societal rules. Drinking at this young age could be part of a pattern of behavior that indicates a potentially serious problem.

the family and the community to overcome problems **(**Henggeler, Melton, Brondino, Scherer, & Hanley, 1997). In a meta-analysis of 11 studies, MST made substantial improvements in family relations and decreased children's aggression toward peers, involvement with other conduct-disordered youth, and overall criminality (Curtis, Ronan, & Borduin, 2004).

Treatments such as MST that include the family seem to work better than those that remove the child from the family, often to programs based on confrontation or "tough love." Wilderness programs and boot camps are examples of such programs, but, as intuitive and appealing as these approaches may sound, they can actually be harmful (Lyman & Barry, 2006). While group treatments have sometimes been effective with younger children, this approach is more likely to produce some initial improvement but long-term worsening outcomes for older children and adolescents (Dishion, McCord, & Poulin, 1999).

The dilemma is similar to a problem associated with incarcerating adult criminals. These group interventions put adolescents who have been delinquent together in a setting where they have the opportunity to share information on their crimes and learn from each other, and these deviant peers actually reinforce each other's delinquent behavior (Dishion et al., 1999). Because the child or adolescent eventually needs to be able to function in his or her home, school, and community, treatment that keeps the family together as a unit makes achieving that goal more likely. Even if the adolescent were to acquire some positive skills as part of an out-of-home treatment program, if he or she returns to an environment that does not support those behavioral changes, they are not likely to persist.

10. Programs that use a "tough-love" approach (for example, wilderness camps, boot camps) for adolescents with conduct problems have been highly successful at rehabilitating these young people.

TRUE/FALSE

False. Unfortunately group interventions such as these put adolescents who have been delinquent together with other delinquent teens where they have the opportunity to learn bad behavior from each other and to reinforce each other's delinquent behavior.

Conclusion

In this chapter we have looked at an essential aspect of development: the development of the self. As part of that examination, we looked at how children and adolescents develop a sense of who they are as individuals (self-concept) as well as how they feel about themselves (self-esteem). We examined the development of both gender identity and ethnic identity. We explored many ideas about how children develop a moral identity. This growing sense of right and wrong develops along with the ability to control one's own impulses (self-control). By the end of adolescence, most young people have a complex concept of their own identity that combines all the elements we described above, as well as their hopes and aspirations for what they will become as adults.

CHAPTER SUMMARY

1 How is self-concept influenced by culture?

In cultures that have individualistic values, self-concept tends to be personal, with emphasis on individual achievement and success. In cultures based on collectivism, self-concept tends to be social, emphasizing how one is embedded in a rich network of social relationships.

2. How does the sense of self develop?

Infants have little self-awareness, but within the first 2 years of life they develop the ability to recognize themselves in a mirror, to use the pronouns *I* and *you* correctly, and to understand that other people see the world differently than they do (**perceptual**

role-taking). They also begin to claim toys. Preschoolers think about themselves in very concrete ways: possessions, size, abilities. School-age children begin to make **social comparison**, in which they compare themselves to others. Adolescents develop a **differentiated self** that takes into account their characteristics at various times and in different situations. They may also try out different identities before they settle on one.

3. Which of Erikson's stages of development contribute to the development of the self?

Erik Erikson's psychosocial stages of development are based in large part on the development of identity. Toddlers are dealing with *autonomy versus shame and doubt*, preschoolers deal with *initiative versus guilt*, school-age children have *industry versus inferiority*, and adolescents deal directly with *identity versus identity confusion*. Beginning with development of an autonomous self, children learn to initiate activity, work hard, and develop a deeper sense of who they are.

4. What are Marcia's four identity statuses?

According to Marcia, two processes are involved in forming an identity: exploring the possibilities and making a commitment. The four identity statuses he identified are **foreclosure** (no exploration, commitment made), **identity diffusion** (no exploration, no commitment), **moratorium** (exploration in process, no commitment), and **identity achievement** (exploration completed, commitment made).

5. How does self-esteem change from preschool through adolescence?

Preschoolers tend to have high self-esteem because they do not compare themselves to other people. When school-age children begin to use social comparisons, self-esteem often declines. In early adolescence self-esteem may drop with the physical changes of puberty and the new social and cognitive demands of middle school. Teens examine their real self in comparison to their **ideal self** and may find themselves lacking in what they want to be, but later in adolescence self-esteem often improves as their sense of identity develops.

6. How do different theories describe the development of gender identity?

The psychoanalytic theory connects gender development with resolution of the Oedipus or Electra complex. A newer approach in the psychoanalytic tradition links gender with boys' need to separate from the mother and girls' possibility of staying close to her to develop a sense of being a boy or a girl. Behavioral theories emphasize reinforcement and imitation of gender-appropriate behaviors. Cognitive developmental theory ties gender development to Piaget's stages of cognitive development. Gender schema theory emphasizes the development of ideas associated with each gender based on societal expectations and experiences.

7. What is androgyny?

Androgyny is the idea that both sexes can have the characteristics that are traditionally reserved for one sex. For example, both girls and boys can be strong *and* sensitive. However, in adolescence it is having more masculine than feminine traits (rather than being androgynous) that is associated with psychological well-being.

8. How do children and adolescents develop ethnic identity?

At first children may not think specifically about their ethnicity (unexamined ethnic identity). During adolescence ethnicity may become more meaningful, and teens may engage in an ethnic identity search, exploring the meaning of their ethnicity. Finally they reach a clear understanding and acceptance of their ethnic identity (achieved ethnic identity). Those adolescents with a strong sense of ethnic identity are more able to resist problem behaviors and more likely to have higher self-esteem.

9. What roles do environmental influences, cognitive development, and emotional development play in the development of morality?

Children learn from the reinforcements they receive from the environment what is right and what is wrong, while also learning what to do by imitation. Piaget and Kohlberg describe the process of development of moral judgment through a series of stages similar to Piaget's stages of cognitive development. For Piaget, these stages are premoral, **heteronomous morality**, and **autonomous morality.** Kohlberg's stages are **preconventional**, **conventional**, **and postconventional**. For both theories the progression is from judgments based on others' rules to internalized rules. The emotions of both empathy and guilt play a role in influencing children to behave in moral ways.

10. How do children develop self-control?

Parental modeling of controlled behavior is central to children learning to control themselves. Brain development also plays a role as executive function matures to allow the child to inhibit inappropriate responses in the service of a goal, known as **delay of gratification**. **Effortful control** comes into play when children develop the ability to consciously think about controlling their own behavior.

11. What problematic outcomes are associated with a lack of self-control?

Children who are generally defiant, negative, disobedient, and hostile to authority figures may have **oppositional defiant disorder**. Those who cross the line into breaking the rules of society and hurting others may have a **conduct disorder**. Both require intervention at many levels, including possible medication, psychotherapy, and intervention with the family, school, and community.

Go to **www.sagepub.com/levine** for additional exercises and video resources. Select **Chapter 11, Identity,** for chapter-specific activities.

Chapter Outline

chapter 12

Social Development
Parents, Peers, and Beyond

12

In this chapter we will explore the social world of children and adolescents. We begin by discussing how children understand their social world through the development of social cognition. We examine how social cognition changes with age and how this development influences the kinds of social interactions that children are able to have with others. We then look at two of the most important sources of socialization of the child: parents and peers. We will look at the nature of each type of relationship, how these relationships change over time, and why they are crucial for development. The chapter concludes with a description of nonparental adults in the social networks of children and adolescents. We discuss who these people are, the roles and functions they fill, and the impact they have on development.

Test Your Knowledge

Test your knowledge of child development by deciding whether each of the following statements is *true* or *false*, and then check your answers as you read the chapter.

1. **True/False:** An infant sees his mother smile when she eats broccoli and make a face when she eats an apple. Given a choice, the infant will still give his mother the apple because that is what *he* likes the best and that is all an infant understands.
2. **True/False:** In many parts of the world, spanking children has been outlawed.
3. **True/False:** Parental discipline that is based on reason and not force has been found to achieve the best outcomes for all children.
4. **True/False:** Mother-daughter relationships are the closest family relationship during adolescence, and father-daughter relationships have the greatest amount of conflict.
5. **True/False:** A good deal of parent-adolescent conflict is normal in families with adolescents.
6. **True/False:** Boys who are aggressive toward peers also can be some of the most popular boys in their school classroom.
7. **True/False:** Being rejected by peers doesn't bother some children.
8. **True/False:** In general, for adolescents, the more friends they have, the better.
9. **True/False:** Most adolescents say that they feel a good deal of peer pressure to do things that they know they shouldn't do.
10. **True/False:** School-wide programs that have attempted to reduce bullying in schools have been highly successful.

Correct answers: (1) False, (2) True, (3) False, (4) False, (5) False, (6) True, (7) True, (8) False, (9) False, (10) False

Social Cognition

Theory of Mind

Social cognition   How we think about and understand interactions between people.

As we learned in Chapter 7, cognition refers to how we think. When we study **social cognition**, we are looking at how we think about interactions between people. One important aspect of social cognition is how we understand what other people are thinking. For example, if you ask a child why she took her friend's toy away, she may answer, "Because I *wanted* it!" She explains her behavior in terms of her own mental state of *wanting* the toy. It takes children longer to understand that the other child is now crying because he, too, *wanted* it. **Theory of mind** refers to "young children's developing abilities to understand self and others as agents who act on the basis of their mental states (i.e., beliefs, desires, emotions, intentions)" (Astington & Filippova, 2005, p. 211). Children actively construct their ideas about what happens in their own and other people's minds (Wellman, 1990), and they become better at doing this as they get older. Over time, as we understand more and more about the motives, emotions, and thoughts of others, we all become pretty accomplished mind readers. See **Active Learning: Mind Reading and Mindblindness** to experience what it might be like if you did not have a theory of mind.

Theory of mind   The ability to understand self and others as agents who act on the basis of their mental states, such as beliefs, desires, emotions, and intentions.

Mind Reading and Mindblindness

Simon Baron-Cohen (1995) presents the following scenario in his book *Mindblindness:* "John walked into the bedroom, walked around, and walked out" (p. 1). Think about how you might try to explain this behavior. What could possibly be going on to make this happen?

Write down your ideas. Next, underline each word in your explanation that reflects something about John's possible mental state—for example, *wanted*, *heard*, *wanted to know*, *looked for*, *was confused*. After you do this, try to write an explanation for John's behavior that would *not* include anything about John's mental state. It is hard for us to do. Here is one attempt by Baron-Cohen: "Maybe John does this every day, at this time: he just walks into the bedroom, walks around, and walks out again" (p. 2). Not very satisfactory, is it? Most of us automatically put ideas about others' thoughts into our explanations for their behavior.

Mindblindness   The inability to understand and theorize about other people's thoughts; a basic characteristic of people who suffer from autism.

It is hard for us even to imagine what it would be like if we did not have theories about what goes on in other people's minds. Baron-Cohen describes **mindblindness**, the inability to understand and theorize about other people's thoughts, as a basic characteristic of people who suffer from autism, as we described in Chapter 6.

False belief paradigm   An experimental task used to assess a child's understanding of theory of mind in which the child predicts what someone else knows or believes.

A classic experiment designed to test whether children understand that what goes on in someone else's mind might be different from what is going on in their own is called the **false belief paradigm**. In these experiments, a child is shown a scene something like this: A doll named Louise is shown that a piece of candy is hidden in a certain drawer in a toy kitchen. Louise then leaves, and the experimenter takes the candy and moves it into the refrigerator. When Louise returns, she wants the candy. The child is asked where he thinks Louise will look for it. Children 3 years of age and younger are likely to say that Louise will look in the refrigerator. The child knows where the candy is and, if you don't yet have a theory of mind, it seems to you that Louise must know that too. At around age 4, children begin to understand that Louise has different thoughts in her mind than they do. They understand that Louise will look first in the drawer where she last saw the candy (Wellman, 1990). You can determine for yourself whether a young child has a developed a theory of mind or not by following the instructions in **Active Learning: False Beliefs**.

Video Link 12.1
Theory of mind.

False Beliefs

You can try the following simple experiment with a child between 3 and 4 years of age and another child who is older.

1. Before you see each child, take a box that a child would recognize as containing candy. Remove the candy and put something else inside: crayons, pennies, or marbles, for example.

2. Tell the child you want to ask her some questions and sit down with her. Ask her what she thinks is in the box. She should answer "candy" or something like that (for example, chocolates, gumdrops). Then show her what is really inside. Close the box again.

3. Ask her the following: "If [name of a friend] came into the room right now, what would she think is inside this box?"

If the child replies "candy" (or whatever she said the first time), then she has demonstrated a good understanding that a friend may think something different than she herself does. If she replies that her friend would know that it is not candy but is instead whatever you have put in the box, then she does not understand that her friend could have a false belief. Instead, she thinks her friend knows everything that she herself knows despite the fact that her friend never saw that you had replaced the candy with some other objects (adapted from Flavell, 1999).

"Mind reading" in childhood. This young child is beginning to understand that you must know what someone else is thinking in order to interact effectively with him (called theory of mind). He has picked up all the signals his father is sending that indicate that his father likes what the child is feeding him and he should continue.

Within the first 2 years of life, young children begin to use this understanding of some basic aspects of other people's minds in their interactions with them. For example, they seem to understand that they should give food to someone who has reacted with a smile to that food and not to someone who has reacted with disgust, even if they themselves prefer the rejected food (Repacholi & Gopnik, 1997). This growing understanding also helps the child's early language learning. Children have a primitive understanding of what an adult is thinking when the adult says "doll" while *looking* at an object. The child understands that the adult is labeling *that* object rather than something else (Baldwin & Moses, 2001). During the second year of life, infants also begin to develop language that is used to describe internal states, and they seem to progress from an understanding of wants and desires ("she wants that cookie") to an understanding of beliefs ("he thinks the cookie is over there") (Tardif & Wellman, 2000).

The ability to understand what others are thinking is a skill that families can promote. When parents discuss emotions with their children, the children are more likely to develop a theory of mind at a younger age (Lewis & Carpendale, 2002). In one study children were more likely to understand false beliefs if their parents' discipline techniques included asking the child to think about how another person felt (Ruffman, Perner, & Parkin, 1999).

Because differences in a child's experience have been shown to influence the development of theory of mind, it is not surprising that researchers also have looked at the impact of cultural

1. An infant sees his mother smile when she eats broccoli and make a face when she eats an apple. Given a choice, the infant will still give his mother the apple because that is what *he* likes the best and that is all an infant understands.

 TRUE/FALSE

False. Infants are beginning to develop a theory of mind, which means that they can understand the internal thoughts and feelings of another person. In this case, even though the infant would prefer the apple, he understands what his mother likes and would want to eat.

differences on this process (Vinden, 1999). Some have argued that understanding the mental state of another person (which is what is required to successfully complete a false-belief task) reflects the individualistic perspective found in Anglo European cultures (Lillard, 1998). In this perspective what individuals believe, think, and feel are important topics of conversation. In other societies, where harmony among people is valued highly, discussion of what goes on in individuals' minds may be less important, or even suppressed (Lillard, 1998). However, when researchers have studied children from a wide variety of different countries and cultures, few differences in the development of theory of mind were found. Wellman, Cross, and Watson (2001) concluded that "young children in Europe, North America, South America, East Asia and Africa, and from nonschooled 'traditional' as well as literate 'modern' cultures, all acquire these insights on roughly the same developmental trajectory" (p. 679).

Young children's theory of mind is still limited. For example, they do not understand that even when people appear to be doing nothing they are continuously thinking (Flavell, 1999). Also, it is not until middle childhood that children begin to understand that two people might interpret the same event differently (Carpendale & Chandler, 1996). This new understanding was demonstrated in one study in which children were presented with stories about sibling conflict such as the following:

> Peter and Helen are brother and sister. It is Halloween, and they are both taking costumes for the contest at school. The winner of the contest gets a really cool prize. Before they go to school, Peter realizes that he is missing one piece for his costume. He asks Helen: "Can you bring your bat to school for me? I have lots of other stuff that I need to carry." Helen says sure. Helen finds a baseball bat and a hairy rubber bat. She grabs the hairy rubber bat to take for Peter. Helen and Peter go to school. When the contest is starting, Helen gives Peter the hairy rubber bat. Peter is wearing a baseball player costume so he needs the baseball bat not a hairy rubber bat. "Oh no," Peter says, "You ruined my costume, you jerk!" (Ross, Recchia, & Carpendale, 2005, p. 591).

The children were asked who Peter thought was to blame and then who Helen thought was to blame and to explain each person's perspective. Finally they were asked whether it made sense that they had different points of view. By age 7 or 8 children were able to see that the two characters would have different ideas about who was at fault and that both views were valid.

Anyone who has played poker will know that understanding theory of mind gets even more complicated. A good poker player understands that not only does she have to intuit what the other players are thinking ("I have a good hand"), but she also has to keep in mind that the other players are trying to figure out what she is thinking. If she wants to bluff the others, she must make them think that she has different cards than she really does. In other words, she is thinking about their thinking about her thinking. This is called **recursive thinking** and is an ability that is still developing through adolescence (Grusec & Lytton, 1988).

So far we have seen that social cognition becomes more complex as children develop. A second important issue involves individual differences in how children interpret what other people think. Although the ability to understand what others are thinking is most often linked with greater ability to cooperate and interact in a positive fashion with others, there are children who have a tendency to understand others' intentions to be hostile rather than benign. This is called a **hostile attributional bias**. An attribution is the explanation or cause that we give to behavior. If you are nice to me, I can attribute it to my belief that you are a kind person or, if I have a hostile attributional bias, I might attribute it to my assumption that you want something from me. In one study children were presented with an ambiguous situation such as the following: A peer breaks a child's new radio while the child is out of the room, or a child overhears a friend talking about a birthday party to which she has not been invited. They were then presented with four possibilities, two attributing hostility (for example, "My friend wanted to get back at me for something") and two that did not (for example, "My friend did it by accident, or my friend will invite me later") (Crick, Grotpeter, & Bigbee, 2002, p. 1137). Children who had

Recursive thinking
The ability to think about other people thinking about your thinking.

Hostile attributional bias A tendency to interpret others' behaviors to be hostile and intentional rather than benign.

more hostile attributions tended to be more aggressive in the eyes of their peers (Crick et al., 2002). As we see from this example, social understanding is important for social relationships, yet there is more to social relationships than just social cognition. In the next sections we will explore the nature of children's relationships with parents and peers.

Interactions With Parents

In earlier chapters we spent a good deal of time talking about early relationships with parents, so in this section, we will just briefly remind you of some of those topics. Much less attention has been given to adolescents and their relationships with their parents, so we will devote more attention to topics relevant to adolescence in this chapter.

Early Social Interactions

It has become clear that infants are biologically "programmed" to be social from their earliest days of life. From Chapter 6, you'll remember that they can immediately imitate some facial expressions, they prefer to look at faces rather than inanimate objects, they respond to voices, and most babies love to be touched and held. Their cry is a signal that communicates their needs to those around them and draws others to care for them. Their first social smiles strengthen the bond that is already developing between parent and infant. Even at birth infants look at other people's eyes and begin to follow the direction in which someone is looking with their own gaze (Farroni, Massaccesi, Pividori, & Johnson, 2004). Within the first year, their attraction to eyes helps them engage in a process called **joint attention** (Flavell, 1999). In joint attention, the infant looks at the same object that someone else is looking at, but also looks at the person; that is, he monitors the other person's attention to make sure that they are both involved with the same thing (Akhtar, 2005). When infants engage in joint attention, they begin to explore the world together with their caregivers.

Joint attention
A process in which an individual looks at the same object that someone else is looking at, but also looks at the person to make sure that they are both involved with the same thing.

Joint attention. As this infant follows his mother's gaze and they share the experience of looking at this tree, the infant monitors his mother to be sure they are involved in the same thing.

Socialization in Childhood

In Chapter 10 we explored the importance of the attachment relationship between a child and his parents. We found that secure attachment is central to the formation of positive social relationships in the future. However, there is more to a child's relationship with his parents than the nature of their attachment. Parents are the first teachers and the first models of what social relationships are like. In a process called **socialization**, parents, peers, and other important figures in the child's world engage the growing child in learning how to interact in appropriate ways according to the rules and norms of their society (Damon, 2006). Of course, what is considered appropriate may vary from one culture to another. The main goal of socialization is to promote the child's acceptance and **internalization** of social norms. We will look at how parents promote their children's ability to understand society's expectations for their behavior, to act on this understanding, and to make those values a part of how to guide their own behavior.

Socialization The process by which parents, peers, and other important figures in the child's world teach a child how to interact in appropriate ways according to the rules and norms of their society.

Internalization The process by which individuals adopt the attitudes, beliefs, and values held by their society.

Parenting Strategies and Techniques

When we look at what parents do, there are many different techniques that they use to teach their children appropriate behavior. Which specific technique they choose will vary, of course,

Inductive discipline
A parenting technique that involves setting clear limits for children and explaining the consequences for negative behavior, why the behavior was wrong, and what the child might do to fix the situation.

Self-oriented induction A parenting technique in which the child is asked to think about the consequences that the child might experience as a result of his behavior.

Other-oriented induction A parenting technique in which the child thinks about consequences of the child's behavior for someone else.

Command strategy
A parenting technique in which the parent does not make any overt threats of punishment, but the child responds to the legitimate authority that the parent has to make a request of the child.

Relationship maintenance
A parenting technique in which the parents try to create a positive relationship with their child so that the parents will have a greater influence on the child's behavior.

Power assertion
A disciplinary technique that emphasizes control of the child's behavior through physical and nonphysical punishment.

Love withdrawal
A parenting technique in which parents threaten to withhold their love until a child conforms to the parents' expectations for his behavior.

based upon a number of factors including the parent's own personality characteristics, the characteristics of the child, the parent's understanding of the nature of child development, and the nature of the child's behavior.

Inductive discipline involves setting clear limits for children and giving consequences for negative behavior, but it is also based on explanations to the child about why the behavior was wrong and what he might do to fix the situation (Hoeve et al, 2009). Induction can be further divided into **self-oriented induction** in which the child is asked to think about the consequences that the child might experience as a result of his behavior—for example, "Put the cookie back [setting limits], or you will ruin your appetite for dinner [explaining why]," and **other-oriented induction** in which the child thinks about consequences of the child's behavior for someone else—for example, "Look how sad Joey looks when you said that mean thing to him. Can you help him feel better?" (Smith, 1988).

In many situations, parents can influence their children's behavior simply because children recognize and respect their parents' authority (Smith, 1988). When using the **command strategy**, the parent states what should be done. The parent does not make any overt threats of punishment, but the child responds to the legitimate authority that the parent has to make this request—for example, "It is time to turn off your computer and get ready for bed." Another positive parenting strategy is based upon social cognitive theory. You'll remember from Chapter 2 that according to social cognitive theory, behavior changes through the processes of modeling and imitation, and we are more likely to want to imitate models that we like or admire. In the technique of **relationship maintenance**, parents try to create a positive relationship with their child so that they will have a greater influence on the child's behavior or be a more attractive model for the child to imitate. When a parent displays affection toward a child, praises the child for things she has done well in the past, or shows that he understands how the child feels, it helps motivate the child to comply with what the parent wants the child to do (Smith, 1988).

In contrast to these types of positive discipline, **power assertion** is a technique that "relies on the adult-oriented, coercive, restrictive, and firm discipline techniques and emphasizes the negative aspects of control such as harsh punishment" (Hoeve et al., 2009, p. 750). Power assertion can rely upon physical or nonphysical threats of punishment. Another approach parents may use is **love withdrawal**, when they temporarily remove themselves emotionally from their child—for example, "I'm not speaking to you until you apologize." Martin Hoffman (1979) has argued that some power assertion or love withdrawal may be necessary to get the child's attention, but it is the explanations in inductive discipline that will help the child internalize the ideas about what is good and bad behavior.

What are the outcomes of each type of discipline? The use of inductive discipline has been related to the development of empathy. This increased level of empathy results in more prosocial behavior in children, meaning that they are more likely to share, and to show sympathy and other positive social behaviors (Krevans & Gibbs, 1996). However, the use of physical punishment has been linked with an increased level of bullying and fighting (Ohene, Ireland, McNeely, & Borowsky, 2006). In a large-scale meta-analysis of many studies on this topic conducted in North America, Europe, and Australia, power assertive techniques were related to an increased likelihood of delinquency in adolescents, while inductive discipline was related to less delinquency (Hoeve et al., 2009).

Although inductive discipline is beneficial to children in Western cultures, the same may not be true in all cultures. You can see how a discipline strategy that gives children the opportunity to make choices within certain limits and tells them how they can rectify a situation if they do something wrong fits well with cultural values that emphasize choice, independence, and self-motivation. The same would not be true for children in a culture that emphasizes interdependence, the importance of proper behavior in the eyes of others, and a hierarchical structure within the family. For instance, if a child misbehaves in the Japanese culture, rather than the child's mother reprimanding the child for the misbehavior, she is likely to apologize for the child's behavior to anyone who saw what happened (Miyake & Yamazaki, 1995). The mother's apology preserves the social harmony with the other individual while preserving the close emotional bond that the mother has with the child. The perception of parental behavior is affected by cultural expectations. Although Korean parents are seen by their adolescents as controlling (a situation that can trigger rebelliousness in American adolescents), Korean adolescents interpret strict discipline as a sign of warmth and love (Vinden, 2001). Vinden concludes her 2001 article by saying, "What we perceive, culturally, as good parenting is a cluster of attitudes and behaviors that result in children who are equipped to be productive exemplars of the culture in which they are raised" (p. 806). It will be important to remember this idea when we return to the broader topic of parenting styles in Chapter 14.

Although there is quite a bit of evidence that power assertion often has negative effects while inductive discipline has positive ones in Western cultures, many parents continue to believe in the old saying "spare the rod and spoil the child." In fact, 94% of parents in the United States say that they have spanked their children by the time they are 4 years old (Campbell, 2002). When we examine the issue of spanking from an international perspective, the results may surprise you. In 2006 the United Nations produced the *World Report on Violence Against Children*, which is directed at reducing violence in the home (Durrant, 2007; Pinheiro, 2006). The recommendations of the report include "changing cultural practices that contribute to violence against children, including the elimination of corporal punishment" (Durrant, 2007, p iii). There have been attempts in some states in the United States to make spanking, at least of very young children, illegal, but currently these attempts have not been successful. Table 12.1 shows that 24 countries have outlawed corporal punishment of children in all settings. A number of other countries permit corporal punishment in some situations (for example, in the child's home) but not in others (for example, in school or while the child is in a child care facility). A great number of countries, however, have no legal restrictions regarding the use of corporal punishment on children.

One of the reasons why many parents rely on spanking is that spanking can be effective at immediately stopping a behavior, but it is not an effective way to help children understand how to control themselves in the long run. Because parents may be out of control themselves when they spank their children, they model exactly the opposite of what they want their children to learn. One of the reasons why power assertion is ineffective in the long term is because when children become angry and resentful, their emotional distress gets in the way of hearing their parent's message about correct behavior. Under these circumstances, they are less likely to internalize the values that the parent is trying to instill in them and won't be able to use these values in the future.

With so many different strategies available, why do parents use one of these approaches rather than another? In part, this decision reflects personal characteristics of the parents themselves. Mothers are less likely to use power assertion if they have a high level of empathy for their babies. Mothers with less empathy are especially likely to use power assertion if their babies are irritable and therefore more difficult and stressful for the mother to handle (Clark, Kochanska, & Ready, 2000). In addition, mothers who have mutually responsive interaction patterns when their children are toddlers are less likely to use power assertion when the children are 5 years old (Kochanska, Aksan, Prisco, & Adams, 2008). You might wonder whether some parents are more strict and punitive with their children because their children are more difficult to control. In that case, the parents' punitive behavior would be a response to the child's behavior, rather than the cause of later problems. This is a very reasonable question to ask, but parents' use of power assertion has *not* been linked to their children's level of misbehavior at a younger age. Instead, it appears that the most important factor for parents who were more likely to use power assertion was whether they themselves were raised that way (Hoeve et al., 2009).

2. In many parts of the world, spanking children has been outlawed. **TRUE/FALSE**

True. In many countries, including Sweden, Denmark, Germany, New Zealand, and Costa Rica, spanking children is prohibited by law. The United States, Canada, and England are among the countries that still do not have anti-spanking legislation.

Table 12.1

Prohibition of corporal punishment at home, in school, and in alternative care settings. In August 2009, the Global Initiative to End All Corporal Punishment of Children compiled information to gauge world progress toward ending the use of corporal punishment against children in their homes, in their schools, and in child care settings. Data were collected on 207 countries. This table presents results from a selection of those countries.

Total	In homes	In schools	In alternative care settings
Prohibited	24	108	35
Not Prohibited	173	89	159
Prohibited	Yes	Yes	Yes
Selected List of Countries*	Austria, Bulgaria, Costa Rica, Croatia, Cyprus, Denmark, Finland, Germany, Greece, Hungary, Iceland, Israel, Latvia, Netherlands, New Zealand, Norway, Portugal, Republic of Moldova, Romania, Spain, Sweden, Ukraine, Uruguay, Venezuela		
	No	Yes	Yes
	Italy, Poland, Switzerland		
	No	Yes	Some**
	Belgium, Canada, Ecuador, Ethiopia, Ireland, Philippines, United Kingdom		
	No	Some**	Some**
	Australia, United States		
	No	No	Some**
	Barbados, Belize, Korea, Singapore		
	No	Yes	No
	Armenia, Cambodia, China, Republic of Congo, Dominican Republic, Egypt, El Salvador, India, Iran, Iraq, Japan, Jordan, Kenya, Mongolia, Nicaragua, Russian Federation, Senegal, South Africa, Taiwan, Thailand, Tonga, United Arab Emirates, Zambia		
	No	No	No
	Afghanistan, Argentina, Bangladesh, Bolivia, Botswana, Brazil, Chile, Colombia, Cuba, Czech Republic, France, Guatemala, Lebanon, Mexico, Nepal, Nigeria, Peru, Rwanda, Samoa, Saudi Arabia, Sri Lanka, Turkey, Uganda, Vietnam, Zimbabwe		

* This table shows the status of legislation outlawing corporal punishment for selected countries. Information on all 207 countries for which information is available can be found at http://www.endcorporalpunishment.org/pages/pdfs/charts/Chart-Global.pdf.

** "Some" indicates a mixed situation regarding prohibition. For instance, in the United States, some states prohibit corporal punishment in schools, but other states allow it. In some countries corporal punishment is prohibited in state-operated child care facilities but not in privately run facilities.

Parents are not always consistent in the way they discipline their children because their life circumstances also play a role in how they discipline. When parents are under stress, they are more likely to resort to using power assertion, especially when they are in a bad mood, when they believe the child's bad behavior was deliberate rather than accidental, or when the child has done something that is hurtful to others rather than some minor infraction of the rules (Critchley & Sanson, 2006).

There are differences among socioeconomic and ethnic groups in the use of power assertion and inductive discipline. African American parents are more likely than White parents to use power assertion. However, whereas White parents often combine power assertion with love withdrawal, for African American families this type of power assertion more often occurs in the context of a loving and warm relationship. Also, it appears that in this context power assertion does not have the same consequences for African American children. In fact, strong control is often linked with better outcomes for these children (Lansford, Deater-Deckard, Dodge, Bates, & Pettit, 2004). Some have argued that firm parental control is more important in dangerous neighborhoods, where it is necessary to keep children away from danger and negative influences; however, this difference has been found in middle-class as well as poor African American families. Instead, Lansford et al. (2004) argue that strong parental control is more often seen by African American parents and their children as a legitimate form of parental control that does not result in alienation between children and their parents. Of course, physical punishment or any other kind of power assertion can become abusive, and abuse is clearly linked with negative outcomes for children no matter what their ethnic, racial, or socioeconomic background, as we will discuss in Chapter 15 (Kazdin & Benjet, 2003; Lansford et al., 2004).

Changes in Relationships During Adolescence

Adolescence is a time of great change in biological, cognitive, and social aspects of development. It is not surprising that these changes are reflected in changes in adolescents' relationships with their parents. However, rather than there being a massive change in the relationship that has developed throughout childhood, what occurs is better described as a renegotiation of that relationship (Collins & Laursen, 2004).

Increasing Autonomy

For instance, adolescents are less willing than children to accept the unilateral authority of their parents, so decision making within the family moves toward becoming more of a shared process in most families (Hill, Bromell, Tyson, & Flint, 2007). While adolescents are typically allowed more independence, their parents in return expect more maturity, self-regulation, and good judgment from them. If parents tried to continue to exercise the same type of strict behavioral control that they used in childhood, this approach could backfire and result in adolescent misconduct and rebelliousness (Loeber & Stouthamer-Loeber, 1998). However, if parents relinquish some control and replace it with monitoring and tracking of the adolescent's activities, it is more likely to be accepted by the adolescent as legitimate (Dishion & McMahon, 1998), and adolescents are more likely to comply with their parents' expectations (Darling, Cumsille, & Martínez, 2008; Darling & Steinberg, 1993).

Other changes in the parent-adolescent relationship that have consistently been found include the fact that adolescents spend less time with their parents (Larson, Richards, Moneta, Holmbeck, & Duckett, 1996) and report less emotional closeness to their parents as they move through adolescence (Shearer, Crouter, & McHale, 2005; Steinberg & Silk, 2002). There also are some consistent differences between adolescents' relationships with their mother and with their father. Adolescents report spending less time with their father than with their mother, and report feeling closer to their mother than their father (Shearer et al., 2005; Steinberg & Silk, 2002). Father-daughter relationships are typically the most distant parent-adolescent relationship (Shearer et al., 2005). The time spent with fathers during adolescence is likely to be spent engaging in leisure activities or skill development, such as athletics (Collins & Russell, 1991).

You can see how these differences in how mothers and fathers interact with their adolescent reflect a continuation of the patterns that we described earlier in childhood. Interestingly,

3. Parental discipline that is based on reason and not force has been found to achieve the best outcomes for all children.

TRUE/FALSE

False. Although this type of discipline works best for many children, there is evidence that a more forceful approach has better outcomes for many African American children, perhaps because it occurs in the cultural context of a loving and warm relationship and is seen as a legitimate form of parental control.

4. Mother-daughter relationships are the closest family relationship during adolescence, and father-daughter relationships have the greatest amount of conflict.

TRUE/FALSE

False. Mother-daughter relationships *are* the closest, but they are also the ones that have the greatest amount of conflict.

although mother-daughter relationships are the closest parent-adolescent relationship, they also are marked by more conflict, particularly around the time of puberty (Steinberg & Silk, 2002). In fact, mothers of both sons and daughters are more likely to experience conflict with their adolescents than fathers do, perhaps because they spend more time in contact with their children (Shearer et al., 2005). However, one review of studies on parent-adolescent relationships found differences between parents' interactions with sons and daughters in only about 40% of studies (Russell & Saebel, 1997), so these gender differences may not be as great as is commonly believed.

It may *not* surprise you to learn that parents and adolescents often see their relationships quite differently (Gonzales, Cauce, & Mason, 1996; Larson & Richards, 1994; Steinberg, 2001). Who do you think is more accurate in their self-reports on the quality of this relationship? Would it surprise you to learn that it is the reports of adolescents (*not* their parents) that more closely match the observations made by impartial observers (Gonzales et al., 1996)? After we discuss the topic of parent-adolescent conflict later in this chapter, we'll talk some more about these differing perceptions and what can explain them.

Despite the emotional distancing that occurs in adolescence, parents remain important people in the lives of most adolescents (Gecas & Seff, 1990; Smetana, Metzger, & Campione-Barr, 2004; Steinberg, 2001; Steinberg & Silk, 2002). For instance, over half of adolescents in one study agreed with the statements "I can still learn a lot from my parents," "I count my parents among my best friends," and "I can communicate extremely well with my parents" (van Wel, 1994, p. 838).

TRUE/FALSE

5. A good deal of parent-adolescent conflict is normal in families with adolescents.

False. A good deal of parent-adolescent conflict occurs in *some* families, but conflict is neither overwhelming nor pervasive in most families. And, when conflict does occur, it is usually about everyday issues like homework or messy rooms rather than about explosive issues like sexual behavior or substance use.

Parent-Adolescent Conflict

Although there is a widely held belief that relationships between adolescents and their parents are marked with significant amounts of conflict, there is little research support for this idea (Arnett, 1999; Offer & Schonert-Reichl, 1992). Instead, we find that it is not unusual for there to be some level of conflict in most American families (Arnett, 1999), but that there is a good deal of variability from one family to another (Montemayor, 1983). The idea that adolescence is a time of conflict and alienation between adolescents and their families probably describes no more than 20% of families.

The *frequency* of conflict is highest in early adolescence and then declines as adolescents move into middle and late adolescence, but the *intensity* of conflict, when it does occur, tends to increase across adolescence (Arnett, 1999). In **Active Learning: Sources of Parent-Adolescent Conflict** you can explore the kinds of issues that cause conflict in families.

ACTIVE LEARNING   Sources of Parent-Adolescent Conflict

In 1994, Brian K. Barber conducted research in which he asked 1,828 White, Black, and Hispanic families of adolescents to rank order the frequency of conflict in their family about each of the topics below. Go through the list and rank from 1 (*most frequent*) to 10 (*least frequent*) how often you think *other families* with adolescents have conflict about each of these topics. Then go through the list again and think back to your own experiences when you were in middle adolescence (about 14 to 16 years of age) and rank how often you had conflict with your parents about each of these topics (again with *1* for the most frequent topic of conflict down to *10* for the least frequent topic of conflict). When you are done, you can check your rankings against Barber's results below.

Topics of Conflict	In Most Families	In My Family
	1 = most frequent 10 = least frequent	
How the adolescent dresses		
The adolescent's boyfriend/girlfriend		
The adolescent's friends		
How late the adolescent stays out at night		
Helping around the house		
The adolescent's sexual behavior		
The adolescent's drinking, smoking, or drug use		
Money		
School		
Getting along with other family members		

This is the rank ordering of actual conflict from Barber's (1994) sample: (1) helping around the house (*most frequent*), (2) family relations, (3) school, (4) how the adolescent dresses, (5) money, (6) how late the adolescent stays out, (7) the adolescent's friends, (8) the adolescent's boyfriend/girlfriend, (9) substance use, (10) sexual behavior (*least frequent*) (p. 379).

Many people believe that conflict between adolescents and their parents typically focuses on explosive issues like adolescent sexuality or substance use, but when conflict occurs between parents and teens, it is much more likely to occur around ordinary, everyday events like homework, curfews, loud music, and messy rooms (Barber, 1994; Eisenberg et al., 2008; Smetana, 1988). It would not be surprising if you identified more of these mundane issues as the most frequent sources of conflict in your family, even if you thought that *other families* were fighting about the big things. It seems that the things that create conflict between adolescents and their parents have not changed much over the last few decades. A 2008 study found that the four most frequent sources of conflict between adolescents and their parents were cleaning chores, getting along with family, respect/manners, and school issues and the least frequent sources of conflict were friends and dating and smoking or alcohol (Eisenberg et al., 2008). These findings are very similar to what Barber reported 14 years earlier.

Despite how it might feel to families when it is happening, conflict is *not* necessarily bad during adolescence. In individualistic societies, some level of conflict is an inevitable part of the individuation and identity development that normally occur during adolescence (Adams & Laursen, 2001). Adolescents also are at a time in their lives when they are moving toward greater autonomy, but the challenge for parents of adolescents is to find the right balance between granting them the autonomy they want and maintaining the connectedness or attachment that they need. Doing this is tricky because the "right" balance in early adolescence isn't the same as it will be in middle or late adolescence, so parents must be responsive to the developmental changes in their child. When conflict takes place in the context of a warm, supportive family environment, it can be a positive thing that fosters personal growth (Steinberg, 1993). Having a warm, supportive relationship with one's parents acts as a protective factor for the adolescent. Problem behaviors are reduced in this context, and mental well-being is enhanced, and this is true for both male and female adolescents (Hair, Moore, Garrett, Ling, & Cleveland, 2008).

How much conflict and what type of conflict will be tolerated differ from one cultural context to another. In countries that have more collectivist values, such as India, adolescents' conflict with their parents is handled in a different way. As we saw with Western samples, conflicts in Indian families also are most likely to be about minor things, like homework and household chores (Kapadia, 2008). However, there is more emphasis on maintaining harmony within the family and on honoring parents in the Indian culture. Consequently, adolescents are more likely to compromise to meet their parents' expectations and demands rather than believe that they should decide for themselves what is best for them. Similar patterns for resolving parent-adolescent differences have been found in other collectivist cultures, such as Mexico and Korea (Phinney, Kim-Jo, Osorio, & Vilhjalmsdottir, 2005).

Relationships with boyfriends or girlfriends are a possible source of conflict between American adolescents and their parents, so a statement made by a 19-year-old Vietnamese student living in the United States might surprise native-born Americans. He was asked what he would do if he fell in love with somebody but his choice did not fit with his family traditions. He answered, "This question is very difficult to answer. Since this situation hasn't happened to me yet, I really can't say anything about it. However, I would choose my family. You can have more than one lover in your life, but you only can have one blood-related [set of] parents" (T. Nguyen, personal communication, December 7, 2009). In this situation, there is little conflict to resolve because the young person willingly accepts what his parents want for him.

There is a good deal of evidence that supports the idea that parent-adolescent conflict is much harder on the parents than it is on the adolescent for a couple of reasons (Dekovic, 1999). First, parents and adolescents attach different meaning to conflict when it does occur. An issue that a parent may define in terms of right and wrong (either in moral terms or in terms of social conventions) may be one that the adolescent defines as a matter of personal choice (Steinberg, 2001). Because parents attach greater significance to this issue than the adolescent does, conflict around it is more distressing to them. Second, until adolescence the power differential within the family has definitely favored the parents (Adams & Laursen, 2001). The fact that adolescents now seem to want to question and debate everything can make parents feel like their authority is continually being challenged. Finally, parents have a deep investment in their parenting role (Dekovic, 1999), so being able to feel competent in that role is important to their sense of well-being. They want to do the right thing with regard to their adolescents. They know their adolescents are growing up, but worry about them growing up too fast. When they clash with their adolescents and hear from them that "everyone else is doing it," parents may begin to question their ability to pace their autonomy granting to their children. They also may worry that these clashes will permanently damage the quality of their relationship with their child, which is very important to them.

It's all a matter of how you see it. One thing that contributes to conflict between adolescents and their parents is the different ways that they define issues. To this teen, a messy room is a matter of personal choice and is nobody's business but her own, but to her parents, it may be seen as a violation of social conventions.

For these reasons, parents would be relieved to know that although conflict does cause some disruption in the parent-adolescent relationship, its effects are usually temporary. Most families successfully weather their children's transition through adolescence without conflict doing any serious harm to the quality of their relationship (Shearer et al., 2005). In fact, parents of adolescents report that their relationship with their adolescent children becomes closer during the process and that there are more positive changes than negative ones (Shearer et al., 2005). Families are able to handle moderate levels of conflict because patterns of positive interactions have been laid down throughout childhood (Holmbeck, 1996; McGue, Elkins, Walden, & Iacono, 2005). Thinking about it in this way, we see both continuity and change in parent-adolescent relationships. The relationship changes from one that is parent dominated to one that is more egalitarian, but the love, support, and responsiveness that were central to the earlier parent-child relationship remain strong as the child becomes an adolescent.

Interactions With Peers

The nature of children's early relationships with their parents becomes the foundation for their ability to engage successfully with other children. The ability to develop close relationships with peers is influenced by the nature of the children's attachment relationships with their parents. Toddlers and preschoolers who have secure attachments to their parents receive a more positive response from peers (Fagot, 1997; Jacobson & Wille, 1986). In a large study carried out by the National Institute of Child Health and Human Development (NICHD), children who had secure attachments to their mothers at age 3 were more likely to have high-quality friendships in third grade (McElwain, Booth-LaForce, Lansford, Wu, & Dyer, 2008), while insecurely attached children became increasingly withdrawn from their peers (Booth-LaForce & Oxford, 2008). It appears that children who have secure attachments to their parents have a higher sense of self-worth, and this translates into more confident interactions with peers (Booth-LaForce et al., 2006).

Infants and Toddlers

From infancy onward, there is something qualitatively different and special about children's interactions with other children their own age. When a child interacts with adults and even older children, it is the older people who are largely in charge of the interactions, both because they are more powerful and because they can keep the interaction going in spite of the young child's lesser social abilities. Peer interactions are different because children must work out how to maintain the relationship themselves, at their own level of social and cognitive functioning. The other reason that the relationship between peers is special is because peers are often more fun and exciting (Dunn, 2004). Mom and Dad will tire of "chase me" games long before two toddlers do. Preschoolers may share a deep interest in dinosaurs that the adults in their lives encourage but do not necessarily share. Teens can often share secrets with each other that they don't want to share with their parents.

What is the youngest age at which children are able to interact in a meaningful way with peers? While most people are very aware that preschoolers are able to play with other children, they often believe that infants and toddlers are not yet capable of real peer relationships. However, there is some evidence that even before age 2, infants are capable of forming relationships with other children. A classic study of peer relationships in very young children was carried out by Sigmund Freud's daughter Anna Freud and Sophie Dann. Children who had lost their parents during World War II were brought from Germany to England where they lived in group care in nurseries. Freud and Dann (1949) studied one particular group of children who had been separated from their parents early in infancy but had been kept together during their time in a concentration camp and then in the nursery in England. They were surprised to see that these young children showed clear signs of emotional attachment to each other. They were upset when they were separated and were soothed by each other's presence.

Video Link 12.2
Infant peer interaction.

Early social interactions. Toddlers' first interactions are often imitations of each other. Can you see how the imitative play of these two boys with the shape sorter might lead to turn taking and eventually cooperative interaction as they develop more social skills?

Babies are often very interested when they see other babies, smiling at them and trying to touch them (Hay, Nash, & Pedersen, 1983). As they become capable of moving around, one of the first ways in which infants begin to interact socially is that they imitate each other—for example, "I see you jump, it looks like fun, so I jump too." By 20–24 months of age, imitation becomes mutual (Asendorpf & Baudonniere, 1993; Eckerman & Peterman, 2001). For example, "You jump, then I jump, then you jump, then I jump, both of us laughing the whole time." At this age, children are quite aware of each other, and "imitation begets imitation" (Eckerman & Stein, 1990, p. 370).

Imitation helps create a sense that children are doing something fun together. As the children develop language, they add this new ability to their interactions. Language allows them to begin to coordinate their activities in a more cooperative way, planning what they will do together, or solving problems as they arise (Eckerman & Didow, 1996; Howes & Matheson, 1992). Language also indicates that children are developing the ability to use symbols, and this ability leads to pretend play. Now, instead of using just their bodies, as with the examples of imitative jumping given above, they can begin to arrange a tea party, with pretend tea and cookies or other make-believe games (Ungerer & Sigman, 1984).

All relationships have their conflicts, and we all know that our relationships with our peers are no exception. Adults who work with toddlers know that they have a large number of conflicts. "Mine!" and "No!" are two of a toddler's favorite things to say. Especially when these words are linked with hitting or biting, adults are not likely to see them in a positive light. However, being able to use these words reflects some positive aspects of toddlers' development. Claiming toys indicates a developing sense of self as an individual as we described in Chapter 11 (Levine, 1983). In addition, conflicts are not just about possessing objects. They also reflect a new social awareness. Research has shown that toddler conflicts are reciprocal in nature (Hay & Ross, 1982)—that is, "If you take my toy, the next time I see you, I will take yours." This becomes part of the way that children learn how to develop friends. If you want someone to play with you, you will not succeed if you take his toy.

Video Link 12.3
Toddler peer interaction.

Preschoolers

By the age of 3, children begin to show preferences for specific playmates, and friendships develop. **Friendship** has been defined as a mutual relationship, which means that both people must agree that they have a friendship. It is marked by companionship, closeness, and affection (Dunn, 2004). Although preschoolers are notoriously fickle, many form friendships that last months or even years (Dunn, 2004). Preschool children who are friends are more comfortable with each other, they have more fun when they play, and they can resolve conflicts and show sympathy and support for each other. Their interactions are more complex than those found among preschoolers who are not friends (Dunn, 2004). However, friendships at this age are not based on sophisticated qualities that will enter into relationships at an older age, such as how trustworthy the friend is. Preschoolers are more attracted to another child who enjoys the same kinds of play activities that they do.

As children develop special friendships it becomes more likely that some children will feel left out. It is common to hear statements such as that of little Emma to her playmate Marisol:

Friendship A mutual relationship marked by companionship, closeness, and affection.

"I can't be your friend now because I'm playing with Beth. I'll be your friend later."
Preschoolers have some difficulty relating to more than one person at a time.

Make-believe play is the hallmark of preschool peer interaction. Children take on different identities as they create a whole world of their own. As adults, we must appreciate the social skill this takes. One researcher has likened it to the level of coordination that must be achieved by a jazz quartet (Dunn, 2004). Children must learn to control their own impulses and understand others' intentions. At this stage, imitation is no longer enough to maintain an interaction. Instead the children develop complementary roles: "You be the mommy, and I'll be the baby." Judy Dunn (2004) believes that taking part in shared make-believe in which children can express and explore their feelings, including their fears, dreams, and disappointments, becomes the basis for the development of the trust and closeness that are essential to relationships among older children.

School-Age Children

As children enter school, two aspects of peer interaction become important: close friendships and general peer acceptance or rejection, which is referred to as **social status**. We begin by discussing the nature of childhood friendships. Children between the ages of 6 and 12 begin to value having a "best friend," and this friendship is more likely to be marked by a commitment to each other based on trust. Friends spend time together, like to do the same kinds of things, and increasingly offer each other emotional support. However, friendships will vary in the amount of loyalty and commitment, self-disclosure, and conflict they contain.

You'll remember from Chapter 11 that gender segregation (the tendency of children to play and become friends with other children of the same gender) begins in preschool, but as children get older, boys and girls become even less likely to have cross-gender friendships, and this is a choice made by children in many cultures around the world (Golombok & Hines, 2002). If the nature of all-girl friendships is different from the nature of all-boy friendships, that could mean that the friendships of boys and girls offer them different types of learning opportunities (Maccoby, 1998). However, as with most gender differences, those that have been found are often small compared to the amount of overlap, or similarity, between boys and girls. Some research has described boys' friendships as *extensive* while girls' are *intensive* because boys play in larger groups while girls play in pairs or smaller groups (Lewis & Phillipsen, 1998; Markovits, Benenson, & Dolenszky, 2001), but other studies have found no differences in the size of boys' and girls' friendship networks (Feiring & Lewis, 1991). One gender difference in friendships is that although both boys and girls are cooperative with friends, boys' friendships are more likely to also include competition and dominance, while girls' friendships are more likely to include self-disclosure and agreement (Zarbatany, McDougall, & Hymel, 2000).

The second dimension of peer interaction in school-age children is social status. Researchers have used a technique called **sociometry** to study peer acceptance. In this technique, researchers ask children to indicate their preferences for other children in one of two ways: (a) They choose a particular child in response to questions such as "Who do you play with?" or (b) they rate others in response to questions such as "How much do you like to play with _____?" (Hymel, Vaillancourt, McDougall, & Renshaw, 2002, pp. 266–267). Negative questions are also asked, such as "Who would you rather not play with?" (Hymel et al., 2002, p. 274). The choices of all the children are then combined to determine the overall level of social acceptance or rejection of each of the children in the peer group. Figure 12.1 shows how the dimensions of peer acceptance and peer rejection can be combined to describe different social statuses of individual children.

Video Link 12.4
Pretend play.

Social status   The level of peer acceptance or peer rejection of an individual in the peer group.

Sociometry   A research technique used to assess a child's social status within the peer group.

Figure 12.1

Determining sociometric status. After asking peers who they like the best (peer acceptance) and who they like the least (peer rejection), this information can be combined to produce the 5 sociometric status groups used in sociometric research (Coie et al., 1982).

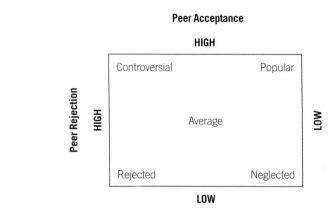

Popular children = High on peer acceptance, low on peer rejection
Rejected children = High on peer rejection, low on peer acceptance
Controversial children = High on peer acceptance, high on peer rejection
Neglected children = Low on peer acceptance, low on peer rejection
Average children = Average level of peer acceptance and peer rejection

Popular children
Children who receive a lot of nominations as "like most" and few as "like least" on a sociometric measure.

Rejected children
Children who receive a lot of nominations as "like least" and few as "like most" on a sociometric measure.

Average children
Children who receive a number of nominations for "like most" and "like least" that is close to the median in the peer group on a sociometric measure.

Neglected children
Children who receive relatively few nominations either as "like most" or as "like least" on a sociometric measure.

Controversial children
Children who receive both a large number of nominations for "like most" and a large number of nominations for "like least" from peers on a sociometric measure.

TRUE/FALSE

6. Boys who are aggressive toward peers also can be some of the most popular boys in their school classroom.

True. There is a small group of children who are aggressive but who also are admired by their peers because they often are physically competent and tend to dominate the peer group.

Children who receive a lot of nominations from the peer group for "like most" and few nominations for "like least" are classified as **popular** children. Those who receive a lot of nominations for "like least" and few for "like most" are classified as **rejected**. Children who receive a number of nominations close to the median for the group are classified as **average**, and those who receive relatively few nominations in either category are classified as **neglected**. The final group is a particularly interesting one. Some children receive both a large number of nominations for "like most" from some peers and a large number of nominations for "like least" from other peers. They are classified as **controversial** children (Coie, Dodge, & Coppotelli, 1982).

If these techniques make you uncomfortable, you are not alone. Although research has shown that asking these questions does not change children's interactions with each other, many continue to feel that it is unethical to ask children to name who they dislike. As a result, researchers who use sociometry have tried to minimize the possible negative effects in a variety of ways, including having discussions with the children afterward (Hymel et al., 2002).

We'll look at the characteristics of children who typically are placed in the different social statuses, as well as some of the developmental outcomes associated with each of the statuses. While popular children are seen as more helpful and cooperative, with greater problem-solving abilities, children who are rejected by their peers during middle childhood are likely to be either aggressive or withdrawn (La Greca & Prinstein, 1999). Children who are very shy, nervous, or depressed withdraw from contact with peers and are not very appealing playmates for other children, so friendships never develop. An alternative pathway to becoming a rejected child is to be aggressive, annoying, or socially unskilled (Sandstrom & Zakriski, 2004). For instance, the child may try to enter a game that other children are already playing by disrupting the game and annoying the potential playmates. Popular children are likely to be seen as having highly desirable characteristics, such as athletic ability or attractiveness. Which characteristics are seen as "desirable" may vary depending on the particular peer group. In some peer groups, aggressiveness is valued, so it does not result in rejection (Hymel et al., 2002). Recent research has identified two different types of popular boys (Rodkin, Farmer, Pearl, & Van Acker, 2000). **Prosocial-popular boys** are perceived by teachers and peers as having many of the positive characteristics associated with popular children, but there is another group of **antisocial popular boys** who are seen as aggressive but also as physically competent, disruptive, and "cool" and who are very well known within the peer group. These characteristics garner the boy a level of admiration and high social status within the group.

Some children who are not popular with the larger group of their peers may still have friendships that are able to buffer the negative effects of rejection or neglect by the peer group. Having one good friend can be enough to save a child from loneliness. On the other hand, there are children who are widely accepted by the group as a whole who do not have a close friend and who describe themselves as lonely (Dunn, 2004). Unpopular children tend to have friendships that are less stable and supportive than their more accepted peers, and they are less able to resolve conflicts in their peer relationships (Dunn, 2004; Lansford et al., 2006). Regarding the stability of peer status (that is, how likely that a child will remain in one category over time or from one setting to another), rejected children tend to maintain their status across various groups of peers and over time, but the status of neglected children may change when they move into a different peer group (Zettergren, 2005). That is because neglected children tend to be socially unskilled, so with a little more time to mature and develop these skills, a number of these children become more accepted within the peer group.

Both peer rejection and lack of friends are related to difficulties in adulthood while both peer acceptance and having a good friend are related to better outcomes. In one study, preadolescents who had friends were more likely to have a high sense of self-worth when they became

Prosocial-popular boys Boys who are perceived by teachers and peers as having many of the positive characteristics associated with popular children.

Antisocial popular boys Boys who are seen as aggressive but also as physically competent, disruptive, and "cool" and who are very well known within the peer group.

You gotta have friends! Popular children are liked by many of their peers, while rejected and neglected children are not. However, individual friendships are as important as social status for children's well-being.

TRUE/FALSE

7. Being rejected by peers doesn't bother some children.

True. Children differ in their sensitivity to rejection. For children for whom peer status or popularity isn't very important, neither is being rejected by peers.

adults. Preadolescents who were rejected by their peer group were more likely to have trouble with the law later in life, probably because rejected children tend to seek out and form friendships with deviant peers who are more likely to be involved with criminal behavior (Bagwell, Newcomb, & Bukowski, 1998).

Finally, the effects of peer rejection may be mediated by how sensitive the child is to rejection. All children experience rejection at some time in their lives, but some children respond more strongly than others. A child who doesn't notice rejection or doesn't care very much about it is less likely to be negatively affected than a child who has a high level of **rejection sensitivity**. **Active Learning: Rejection Sensitivity** gives you an opportunity to better understand how this affects a child's peer relationships.

ACTIVE LEARNING

Rejection Sensitivity

Begin by reading the following scenario:

"Do you want to go to the movies with me on Saturday?" Ruben asked Carla on the playground. "Sorry," she told him, "I'm busy on Saturday." Ruben angrily stormed off the playground, knocking over a trash can as he passed the gate. Then Tony approached her. "Do you want to go skating with me on Saturday?" he asked. "No, I can't. I'm busy on Saturday," Carla said. "How about on Sunday?" Tony asked. "OK," she said (Downey, Lebolt, Rincón, & Freitas, 1998, p. 1074).

1. Which boy demonstrates rejection sensitivity?
2. What is Ruben likely thinking about why Carla says she's busy? What is Tony thinking?
3. Think about what might explain the two boys' different reactions, including past experiences and current peer relationships.
4. How will the boys' reactions affect their future interactions with Carla?
5. Think about a time when you wanted to get together with someone and he or she said no. How did you interpret this response? What did you do? How did this affect your relationship with this person?

Rejection sensitivity
The extent to which a child is affected by peer rejection.

People who are particularly sensitive to rejection are more likely to interpret others' responses to them as hostile and a sign that the person doesn't like or respect them. They become either angry or anxious and may spend time ruminating about what has happened (London, Downey, Bonica, & Paltin, 2007). Other people may interpret the same incident quite differently. In the example in **Active Learning: Rejection Sensitivity**, Ruben sees Carla's response as an indication that she doesn't want to be with him, while Tony does not jump to that conclusion. If Ruben is generally rejected by his peers, his interpretation of Carla's response may be correct—maybe she really doesn't want to be with him. Children who experience more peer rejection over time come to expect rejection, and may see it even when it is not there (London et al., 2007). This may create a vicious cycle that perpetuates a child's rejection by potential friends. In one study children who became more accepted by their peers reduced their rejection sensitivity over time (London et al., 2007). Finally, rejection-sensitive children who were able to control the expression of their emotions had better long-term outcomes in adulthood (Ayduk et al., 2000). It appears that children who act aggressively or in a highly anxious and withdrawn manner may drive peers further away, but if the child can control these responses, they are less likely to do so.

Adolescents

Peer relationships become increasingly important contexts for development during adolescence. These relationships take a variety of forms, from individual friendships to association with large groups of adolescents who share reputations and interests. Although adolescents' relationships with their friends are different in some ways from children's relationships with their friends, adolescents enter the peer world of adolescence with the skills and level of social status that they had developed during childhood (Brown & Klute, 2003). Adolescents spend about twice as much time with their friends as they spend with their parents (Brown, 1993), and the amount of time spent with peers continues to increase across adolescence (Savin-Williams & Berndt, 1993).

Friendships

Almost all adolescents can report having at least one close friend. Although these adolescent friendships are not always stable, they tend to become more stable with age as teens become more skilled at maintaining relationships (Brown & Klute, 2003). Within the context of friendships, adolescents learn how to negotiate, to compromise, and to be more sensitive to the needs of others as they get older, so this helps preserve relationships over time. Adolescents who have high-quality peer relationships have been found to have better emotional adjustment.

Although friendships are important to adolescents, this is a case where more is not necessarily better (Savin-Williams & Berndt, 1993). Having a lot of friends is associated with popularity, but these relationships often are not intimate or close. The benefits that we normally associate with friendships may not be forthcoming from a large group that lacks closeness. Large networks also may be an indication that an adolescent is not able to establish and maintain close relationships. Adolescent girls generally have smaller, more exclusive friendship networks than boys, and they consider intimacy, loyalty, and commitment as important qualities in those relationships (Clark & Ayers, 1992; Savin-Williams & Berndt, 1993), whereas boys are more likely to base their friendships on qualities such as status or achievement (Clark & Ayers, 1992) and are more willing to admit new members to their friendship group (Savin-Williams & Berndt, 1993). Girls say that within their friendships they are truly understood and can be fully themselves. They feel liked and respected within these relationships, so simply spending time with their friends is very rewarding to them (Savin-Williams & Berndt, 1993). However, because girls do more intimate sharing and disclosing in their relationships, they understandably are more concerned about a possible betrayal by a friend, and this becomes one of the potential emotional costs of maintaining intimate relationships with friends.

In addition to the greater degree of intimacy in girls' friendships, some other general truths about adolescent friendships include the fact that both equality and reciprocity are expected in adolescent friendships, that adolescents are likely to select as friends people who they see as similar to themselves, and that close friendships are usually same-gender friendships (with a strong preference for friends from the same ethnic or racial background) (Brown & Klute, 2003). Of course, peer groups include more members of the opposite sex as the adolescent becomes older and begins dating (Brown, 1993). Beyond similarity in demographic characteristics such as age, gender, and ethnicity (Clark & Ayers, 1992), there also is evidence for similarity among friends in attitudes, values, and activity preferences (including engaging in anti-social behavior) (Solomon & Knafo, 2007).

Denise Kandel has written extensively on an explanation for why friends tend to be so similar to each other. She proposes two different mechanisms: selection and influence (Kandel, 1978). People tend to seek out friendships with people with whom they have things in common. Think of a time when you were in a new setting. It might have been after you moved to a new school, when you started a new job, or when you went to summer camp. If you didn't know anyone in that setting, you probably gravitated first toward people whom you saw as somewhat similar to yourself. Why? Because it is easier to initiate conversations when there is something in

8. In general, for adolescents, the more friends they have, the better. **TRUE/FALSE**

False. It takes a great deal of effort to maintain a large social network, but there may not be any more benefits from it than an adolescent could get from a few close friends. Also, there may be less closeness and intimacy among members of large networks, and these things are an important part of adolescent friendships.

Best friends. Friendships between teenage girls are marked with intimacy and disclosure. Friends also usually share a number of personal qualities.

common to talk about, whether it is your favorite band, which school you go to, or your favorite sports activity or team. However, once a relationship has formed, you now have some investment in continuing it, so friends begin to exert some pressure to keep everyone on the same page. If you begin to deviate from the group's expectations for your behavior, your attitude, or your style, you may feel pressure from the group to get back on track and in line with its behavior, attitudes, or style. Research has found that initially new friends are more similar to each other than just any two randomly matched set of peers (Urberg, Degirmencioglu, & Tolson, 1998), but those friends also become more similar over time. This means that friends can play a role in initiating friends into risky or problem behaviors, including sexual behavior (Billy & Udry, 1985), smoking (Kobus, 2003), substance use (Dishion & Owen, 2002), and delinquency (Dishion, Spracklen, Andrews, & Patterson, 1996). Peers do this by establishing the norms for the peer group (that is, what is expected or accepted within the group), but also through their direct modeling of these behaviors. We will talk about peer pressure a little later in this chapter.

Another possibility is that adolescents select friends who complement their own characteristics. An adolescent who is relatively shy or socially withdrawn could benefit from having a friend who is more outgoing and sociable. An adolescent who is not a strong student could benefit from having a friend who is a very strong student. Although this is possible, it is not as likely as birds of a feather flocking together. The shy adolescent and the socially outgoing adolescent are drawn toward different activities. The weak student and the strong student make different choices in how they want to spend their time. It can become very difficult to maintain a friendship under these circumstances. You can use **Active Learning: Friends—Similar or Different?** to explore these possibilities in your own adolescent friendships.

ACTIVE LEARNING

Friends—Similar or Different?

Think about your two best friends during your freshman or sophomore year of high school, and decide whether they were *similar to* or *different from* you on each of these characteristics.

	Friend #1		Friend #2	
Attitude toward school achievement	Similar	Different	Similar	Different
Level of participation in school activities	Similar	Different	Similar	Different
Hobbies or interests (for example, music, drama, video games, collections)	Similar	Different	Similar	Different
Religious values or beliefs	Similar	Different	Similar	Different
Attitude toward smoking	Similar	Different	Similar	Different
Attitude toward drinking	Similar	Different	Similar	Different
Crowd you were identified with (for example, populars, brains, jocks)	Similar	Different	Similar	Different
How shy or outgoing you were	Similar	Different	Similar	Different
Other characteristics that were important to you:				
1.	Similar	Different	Similar	Different
2.	Similar	Different	Similar	Different
3.	Similar	Different	Similar	Different

In what ways was the similarity between you and your friends beneficial to you? In what ways were any differences beneficial? Were there any differences that caused stress or tension in your relationship? Can you think of any way that either you or your friend changed over time as the result of your friendship?

Cliques and Crowds

When we move beyond the dyad, we begin to talk about peer groups. **Cliques** are small groups of friends who actually spend time together, and **crowds** are larger groups of adolescents in which membership is based on an individual's abilities or interests (Brown & Klute, 2003).

Cliques are typically groups of 3 to 10 age-mates (with an average of about 5 members) who "hang around together and develop close relationships" (Brown, 1993, p. 177). Cliques are most common during early adolescence, and membership in most cliques is fairly fluid, with members frequently moving in and out. In one study that followed adolescent cliques over 3 years, less than 10% of the groups were stable over that period of time (Engles, Knibbe, Drop, & deHaan, 1997). Within a clique, the members can hold different roles. A leader often emerges from the group, and this person may be able to control membership in the clique (Brown & Klute, 2003). Some are core members, and still others are "wannabes" who hang around the periphery of the clique (Brown, 1993). Some adolescents are members of more than one clique at a time and link the cliques together (Brown & Klute, 2003). And, of course, some adolescents are not a member of any clique. They may have only dyadic relationships or be socially isolated. Although cliques can be an important source of social support, they also can use techniques like ridicule or the threat of being ostracized to control their members.

Brown (1993) distinguishes between cliques and crowds by saying that a clique represents who the adolescent's friends are, but a crowd represents "who the adolescent *is*—at least in the eyes of peers" (p. 184). Crowds are large, reputation-based groups who share a stereotype but whose members do not necessarily spend time together. Think for a minute about the crowds that you would recognize at your high school. Some common adolescent crowds include the brains, jocks, skaters, populars, farmers, nerds, and druggies. In multiethnic communities there also may be crowds identified by ethnic labels, although this isn't always the case. The number of different crowds and how easily recognizable they are differs from one school setting to another.

One advantage of being part of a crowd is that it gives you a type of ready-made identity among your peers, although it might not be an identity that you like or one that you would necessarily choose for yourself (Brown, 1993). This is one reason why an adolescent might resist being identified as a member of a particular crowd. Other adolescents happily accept their crowd affiliation, struggle to align themselves with a different crowd, or drift from one crowd to another as they "try on" different identities. And, of course, there isn't always consensus about which crowd a particular adolescent is a member of (Brown & Klute, 2003). As Brown (1993) points out, adolescents choose their own cliques but are "thrust into" a crowd by their peers based upon their interests, their background, and their reputation (p. 183). Sometimes, however, the shared interests and attitudes that force an adolescent into a crowd become the foundation for friendships that lead to the formation of a new clique. As adolescents get older and develop a stronger sense of their own identity, crowds (just like cliques) become less important to them. **Active Learning: Recognizing a Crowd When You See One** gives you a chance to reflect on the crowd structure at your high school.

Cliques Small groups of friends who spend time together and develop close relationships.

Crowds Large, reputation-based groups that are based upon a shared stereotype but whose members do not necessarily spend time together.

Punks and populars and jocks, oh my! Teenage crowds are groups of teens who share a similar taste in fashion, music, and activities. Although the members of a particular crowd may not know each other or spend time together, their peers see them as a part of an identifiable crowd. It isn't difficult to guess which crowd this group represents.

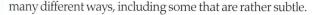

ACTIVE **LEARNING**

Recognizing a Crowd When You See One

Although most people report that they did not belong to just one clique or crowd in high school, most people are perceived this way. Name all the different crowds that existed in your high school. What determined who belonged in which group? How were these groups similar to and different from each other in how they dressed, what music they listened to, how they spent their time, their attitudes toward school, and other things you can think of? How did the crowds relate to each other? Did they do some things together or have some values in common?

If you have classmates who came from a different type of school than you attended, it might be interesting for you to compare notes. The number and types of crowds in a given school vary by the size of school, its ethnic/socioeconomic composition, rural/urban/suburban location, and a variety of other characteristics. Some of the crowds you were familiar with at your high school might not even exist in other high schools.

TRUE/FALSE

9. Most adolescents say that they feel a good deal of peer pressure to do things that they know they shouldn't do.

False. Most adolescents actually say that peer pressure tends to be subtle, rather than overt, and that there is more pressure to do positive things than there is to do negative ones. The exception is for adolescents who are members of deviant peer groups to begin with.

Peer pressure
Influence exerted by peers to get others to comply with their wishes or expectations.

Peer pressure. Peer pressure can be direct, or it can be subtle. The group norms that develop within a clique are one way that pressure is exerted on friends to adopt similar attitudes and behaviors.

Peer Pressure

Despite the concerns of parents or other adults that peers are a constant source of pressure for adolescents to behave in negative ways (for example, to be sexually active, to use drugs, to engage in delinquent behavior), there is *not* strong evidence to support this idea (Brown, 1993). **Peer pressure** can be direct (for instance, when peers use direct rewards or punishment for compliance) or more subtle (for instance, through modeling or by the establishment of group norms). Reports from adolescents themselves support the idea that peer pressure, when it does occur, is more likely to be subtle rather than direct. For instance, Brown (1993) describes how adolescents responded to a question about peer pressure to drink at a party where alcohol is available. They said, in effect, that it is there if you want it but "nobody gives you a hard time if you don't. Like, no one comes up and shoves a beer in your hand and says, 'Here, drink it!'" (Brown, 1993, p. 190). However, they also said that if everyone else is drinking, they felt a "little weird just sipping a soda" (Brown, 1993, p. 190). Brown concludes that peer pressure is "neither uniform nor overwhelming" (p. 193).

This level of influence was illustrated in a study on teen smoking in the United States. Ali and Dwyer (2009) studied a very large sample of teens and found that increases in the percentage of one's classmates and close friends who smoked were associated with small (3%–5%) but significant increases in the likelihood that a teen would smoke. In China, too, smoking by teens was related more to peer rather than parent smoking (Ma et al., 2008). Interestingly, in both urban and rural areas in China cigarettes are routinely offered as a gesture of goodwill, so Chinese youth risk being impolite by not accepting. This shows that peer pressure can be experienced in many different ways, including some that are rather subtle.

Adolescents are more resistant to pressure to behave in antisocial ways than in prosocial or neutral ways (Berndt, 1979; Brown, 1982; Clasen & Brown, 1985). However, the risk of antisocial behavior increases substantially when an adolescent is a part of an antisocial peer group. Within this group there is likely to be both direct peer pressure to engage in the behavior and more subtle forms of pressure like modeling of the behavior or peer endorsement of it. Again we see how selection and influence work together. In these cases, it is more likely that young adolescents who are aggressive or prone to deviance will gravitate toward other adolescents with similar inclinations (selection), and over time the norms that evolve within that group will reinforce antisocial behavior by group members (influence).

When adolescents have been asked how they would respond to peer pressure in hypothetical situations, young adolescents appear to be more susceptible than older adolescents (Berndt, 1979; Brown, 1993; Sumter, Bokhorst, Steinberg, & Westenberg, 2009). And, although this is not a consistent finding in all studies, girls report receiving more peer pressure than boys and being more susceptible to it (Brown, 1982, 1993). Adolescents who are not confident about their social skills also are more susceptible than more socially skilled adolescents (Brown, 1993).

It is important to keep in mind that peer pressure is not always negative. Although it is true that peers can initiate adolescents into drug or alcohol use, adolescents themselves report that peers often pressure them *away from* such behavior. And although peers can devalue academic achievement and draw adolescents away from their schoolwork, having high-achieving peers in fact exerts a positive influence on an adolescent's own academic achievement (Mounts & Steinberg, 1995). The type of influence that peers have on adolescents largely depends on whom the adolescent has selected as her peers. Our understanding of the relative influence that parents and peers have on adolescents has changed over time, and these changes are described in **Journey of Research: The Influence of Parents and Peers**.

The Influence of Parents and Peers

JOURNEY *of* RESEARCH

A dolescents have qualitatively different relationships with their parents and their peers. While relationships with parents are hierarchical and obligatory and have the balance of power on the side of the parents, relationships with peers are voluntary and egalitarian (Adams & Laursen, 2001). For a long time, the field has debated the relative influence of these two relationships on adolescents. Must adolescents break away from parents and follow peers before they can successfully become adults?

Initially the field assumed that parents were the primary influence on adolescent development and decision making. The goal of adolescents was to grow up and become adults, just like their parents, but as a separate teen culture evolved following World War II, developmentalists began to examine the effects of peer influences on adolescent development. The perception that came to dominate the thinking in our field was that adults and peers were two separate worlds, with little or no meeting ground in the middle. Adolescents were enticed away from their parents' world as they succumbed to the lure of peers. In 1970, Urie Bronfenbrenner reflected this sentiment

Teens in the 1950s. In the 1950s, the goal of many teenagers was to be as much like an adult as they possibly could be.

(Continued)

(Continued)

when he said that "where the peer group is to a large extent autonomous—as it often is in the United States—it can exert influence in opposition to values held by adult society" (p. 189). Kandel and Lesser (1972) popularized what became known as the hydraulic model, which was based on the assumption that there was a fixed amount of influence available so that increases in peer influence would necessarily mean that there would be compensating decreases in the influence of parents. The portrayal of adolescents as torn between two opposing forces continued to influence our thinking about adolescence for decades and is reflected in a large body of research that examines the relative influence of parents and peers.

In 1998, Judith Harris challenged many of these assumptions with the publication of her very controversial book *The Nurture Assumption: Why Children Turn Out the Way They Do.* Although she never claims that parents have no effect on their children, she does put forth very strong arguments for the idea that their influence has been significantly overestimated and that it is peers who are the primary force in the process of socialization. In a 1995 article in *Psychological Review,* she says, "What GS [group socialization] theory implies is that children would develop into the same sort of adults if we left them

in their homes, their schools, their neighborhoods, and their cultural or subcultural groups, but switched all the parents around" (p. 461). At the conclusion of this same article, she says, "GS theory can account for a growing body of data showing that the home environment has no lasting effects on psychological characteristics. The shared environment that leaves permanent marks on children's personalities is the environment they share with their peers" (pp. 482–483).

Harris's ideas represent a very extreme position on the relative influence of parents and peers, and there have been vigorous objections to them. However, Harris also has her supporters. Most contemporary research has walked the middle ground, finding that parents exert more influence than peers with regard to some areas of adolescent development, while peers exert more influence in other areas. For instance, peers have greater influence in areas related to the peer culture (for example, hairstyles, music preference, leisure activities), but parents continue to have the greater influence in more enduring aspects of adolescent development (for example, educational and career plans, religiosity, and personal values) (Brown, 1993, 2004). And parents and peers jointly influence adolescents in still other areas.

Bullying Being exposed repeatedly and over time to negative actions on the part of peers, including physical bullying, verbal bullying, and/or emotional bullying.

Bullying, Harassment, and Intimidation

Although peers usually are positive influences and an important source of support and companionship during childhood and adolescence, there is a darker side of peer relationships that includes bullying, harassment, and intimidation. Bullying has attracted increasing interest since the 1990s when several highly publicized cases of bullying led to tragic consequences that came to the attention of the public. In some cases the bullying resulted in the suicide of the victim, and in others the victims struck back violently through school shootings.

Bullying involves a victim "being exposed repeatedly and over time to negative actions on the part of one or more other students" (Olweus, 2003, p. 12). It is often unprovoked by victims, and there is a differential in power that makes it difficult for victims to defend themselves (Carney & Merrell, 2001; Harris, 2004; Olweus, 2003). There is quite a wide range of behaviors that are considered bullying including physical bullying such as hitting, pinching, or punching; verbal bullying such as name-calling or teasing; and emotional bullying such as threatening or intimidating someone.

Bullies. Bullying can take different forms including physical, verbal, and psychological abuse. Intimidating or threatening someone is a type of psychological bullying, even if the bully never carries out any threats to physically harm the person. What form of bullying do you think occurs most frequently?

A recent study that surveyed 7,182 adolescents in the United States found that 20.8% reported having been physically bullied at school at least once in the last 2 months, 53.6% reported having been verbally bullied, 51.4% reported social bullying, and 13.6% said they have been a victim of cyberbullying (Wang, Iannotti, & Nansel, 2009). Detailed information about the types of bullying reported by these students by

Table 12.2

Percentage of adolescents reporting different types of bullying by role and gender

Forms	Items	Total (N = 7,182)		Male (n = 3,395)		Female (n = 3,787)	
		Bully	Victim	Bully	Victim	Bully	Victim
Physical	Hit, kicked, pushed, shoved around, or locked indoors	13.3	12.8	18.1	17.2	8.8	8.7
Verbal	Called mean names, made fun of, or teased in a hurtful way	35.2	31.5	37.6	32.0	33.0	31.1
	Bullied with mean names and comments about race or color	9.1	13.1	12.0	15.2	6.5	11.3
	Bullied with mean names and comments about religion	5.8	8.5	8.4	9.7	3.3	7.5
Relational	Social isolation: excluded from a group of friends or ignored	24.0	25.6	24.3	23.6	23.8	27.4
	Spreading rumor: told lies or spread false rumors	11.2	31.9	12.0	27.1	10.5	36.3
Cyber	Bullied using computer or e-mail messages or pictures	6.1	8.1	7.6	7.9	4.7	8.3
	Bullied using cell phone	6.0	5.7	7.0	5.6	5.0	5.8

their role (victim or bully) and gender is presented in Table 12.2. However, one of the difficulties with trying to estimate the prevalence of bullying is that the estimate a researcher gets depends upon a number of factors in the research itself, including how bullying is defined, whether the definition includes the fact that the behavior is repeated or not, and the time period used for the research. For instance, you can easily understand that the estimate you would get would differ depending on whether you asked students to report on whether or not they had been bullied in the past 30 days or during the entire past school year. Despite these difficulties, the rates of bullying in the United States are fairly consistent from one study to another (Carney & Merrell, 2001).

Large-scale, systematic research on bullying in schools began in Scandinavia in the 1960s (Borntrager, Davis, Bernstein, & Gorman, 2009), but since then the topic has been studied in a number of different countries. Large differences in the self-reported rates of being a victim have been found, from 9% of students in Norway and Sweden, to 21.9% of students in Japan, to 42% of students in Italy. The number of children who self-identify as bullies also varies, from 7% in Scandinavia, to 28% of Italian primary school students, to 52% of Japanese elementary school students (Borntrager et al., 2009). Even taking into account these disparities, it appears that in many settings and across a number of cultures, the threat of being victimized by a bully is a significant concern for many school-age children.

Although both boys and girls can be bullies as well as victims, more bullies are male than female (Olweus, 2003), and boys bully others in different ways than girls do. Male bullies tend to use physical intimidation, and female bullies tend to use emotional and psychological intimidation (Wang et al., 2009). The incidence of bullying peaks in the middle school years (Grades 6–8) (Carney & Merrell, 2001; Nansel et al., 2001) and then decreases through adolescence. At all ages, there is far more emotional and psychological bullying than physical bullying (Harris, 2004; Olweus, 2003; Wang et al., 2009).

Bullying has always been a part of peer relations, but recently a new form of bullying has appeared. It is called **cyberbullying**. Cyberbullying involves the use of electronic technologies, including e-mails, text messages, digital images, webpages (including social network sites), blogs, and chat rooms, to harm others. Currently 97% of U.S. adolescents between the ages of 12 and 18 use the Internet (one half of them on a daily basis), almost one half of these teens have a cell phone, and one third of cell phone users send text messages (Kowalski & Limber,

Cyberbullying The use of electronic technologies, including e-mails, text messages, digital images, webpages (including social network sites), blogs, or chat rooms, to socially harm others.

2007). This creates a great potential for many adolescents to participate in—or to be the victim of—cyberbullying.

Research on this type of bullying is very new, but early studies indicate that between 11% and 25% of students report having been a victim of cyberbullying (Kowalski & Limber, 2007; Li, 2006; Wang et al., 2009). This can take the form of sending e-mails or text messages intended to embarrass or hurt someone's feelings; posting mean, false, or malicious information on websites or in blogs; or using someone else's user name to spread rumors or lies. A particularly hurtful form of cyberbullying is known as "sexting," which is the distribution of embarrassing photos. Teens sometimes exchange nude or seminude pictures with their boyfriend or girlfriend, but after the relationship ends, those photos can become ammunition in a vicious campaign of hurt and retribution as they are forwarded to others within the peer group or made available to the public.

Cyberbullying differs from other forms of bullying in ways that make it particularly damaging (Kowalski & Limber, 2007). First, electronic messages can be sent instantaneously to a large number of people, which means that the impact can be even greater than face-to-face bullying. Second, although a victim can try to avoid a bully at school or in the neighborhood, you can't hide from cyberbullying, which can "get you" at any time and in any place. Finally, the anonymity of being a cyberbully means that adolescents might say things electronically that they would not say to another person's face because they do not see the distress of their victim, which otherwise might make them stop their bullying. In fact, more than half of students who report that they have been a victim of cyberbullying say they do not know who the bully was (Kowalski & Limber, 2007).

Regardless of the form that bullying takes, bullies share some common characteristics. They are more likely to be depressed (Harris, 2004), to have relatively poor self-concepts (MacNeil & Newell, 2004), to lack self-control, and to have lower levels of social competence than their peers (Demaray & Malecki, 2003). Another very important characteristic is that bullies often have the negative perceptual bias we described earlier that causes them to see hostile intent in ordinary social interactions (Dodge, 1985). An accidental bump or an offhand comment is interpreted as an intentional affront. Based upon this misinterpretation, the bully then feels justified in attacking peers in retribution for the imagined offense. In terms of their behavior, bullies often engage in deviant behaviors, such as smoking, drinking, carrying a weapon, stealing, or damaging property (Nansel et al., 2001; Olweus, 1993). They also tend to have lower academic achievement, school adjustment, and bonding to the school environment (Demaray & Malecki, 2003; Harris, 2004; Sassu, Elinoff, Bray, & Kehle, 2004). Family characteristics include a lack of parental supervision, the use of punitive discipline, and family violence that models aggression as a way to resolve disputes (MacNeil & Newell, 2004). Parents of bullies may be uninvolved in their children's lives, and the child may feel unloved and uncared for (Demaray & Malecki, 2003).

Being a victim of bullying has serious emotional, psychological, and physical consequences for a child or an adolescent. Victims report feeling anxious and depressed and often have a poor self-concept (Sassu et al., 2004). Because victims often feel as though they have no friends, this sense of loneliness and powerlessness can contribute to thoughts of suicide or even a suicide attempt (Sassu et al., 2004). Being the victim of bullying also affects children's ability to be successful in school because victimization is associated with absenteeism, a lack of participation in extracurricular events (Harris, 2004), and a decline in academic performance (MacNeil & Newell, 2004). However, as some recent incidents of school violence have shown, a victim's response also can take the form of violence against others.

As adults, we could hope that a victim of bullying would tell an adult in school what is happening to him, but in one study, only 13% of high school students said they would tell a teacher or school administrator if they were the victim of bullying (Harris, 2004). Many of these students thought that administrators or teachers were not interested in stopping bullying.

Likewise, in a study of victims of cyberbullying, the majority of victims did not tell an adult about what happened (Li, 2006). Victimization can make people distrustful of other people, and this contributes to the child's unwillingness to tell others what is happening. And, finally, some victims claim that being bullied simply didn't bother them (Harris, 2004).

Bullying involves more than the interaction between a bully and a victim. To fully understand what happens—and why it happens—we need to look at the social context in which it occurs. Dan Olweus (2003) has provided such a description with the "bullying circle" (see Figure 12.2). As you can see, in addition to victim and bully, there are others who are passive or possible supporters of what is happening and others who are defenders or possible defenders of the victim, as well as curious onlookers. One goal of anti-bullying programs is to empower students so they can move in the direction of becoming someone who effectively acts as a defender in the face of bullying.

An important first step in developing a program to reduce bullying in school is awareness of the problem. However, many adults seem to be unaware of the problem or unconcerned about it (Banks, 1997; Sassu et al., 2004). It is difficult to know whether adults think that what is happening is unimportant (for instance, that bullying and being bullied are just a normal part of growing up) or whether they are truly unaware of what is happening.

In order to effectively reduce the incidence of bullying in a school, you need buy-in from all the parties: students, teachers, administrators, staff, and parents. Many individual states now have anti-bullying legislation (see Figure 12.3), but we still lack national legislation that treats bullying as a problem shared by all parts of the country.

Figure 12.2

The bullying circle. The bullying circle shows that bullying involves more than just a bully and a victim. A number of others are involved to a greater or lesser extent.

A. Students Who Bully
These students want to bully, start the bullying, and play a leader role.

B. Following or Henchmen
These students are positive toward the bullying and take an active part, but don't usually initiate it and do not play a lead role.

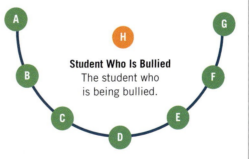

Student Who Is Bullied
The student who is being bullied.

C. Supporters or Passive Bullies
These students actively and openly support the bullying, for example, through laughter or calling attention to the situation, but they don't join in.

D. Passive Supporters or Possible Bullies
These students like the bullying but do not show outward signs of support.

E. Disengaged Onlookers
These students do not get involved and do not take a stand, nor do they participate actively in either direction. (They might think or say. "It's none of my business," or "Let's watch and see what happens.")

F. Possible Defenders
These students dislike the bullying and think they should help the student who is being bullied but do nothing.

G. Defenders
They dislike the bullying and help or try to help the student who is being bullied.

Figure 12.3

States with anti-bullying legislation. Does your state have laws that direct schools to develop policies to prevent and/or punish bullying? These are the states that had laws in place as of March 2009.

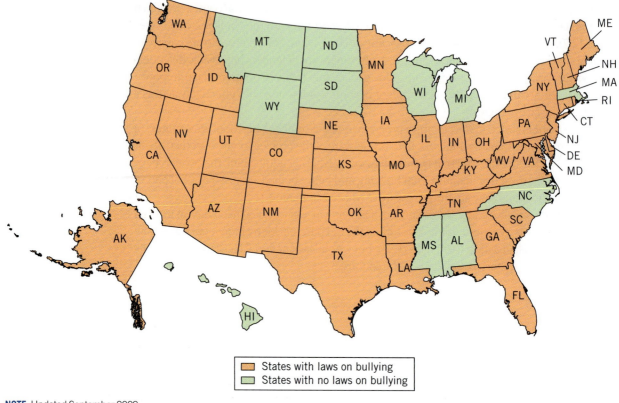

States with laws on bullying
States with no laws on bullying

NOTE: Updated September 2009.

Video Link 12.5
Peer mediation.

TRUE/FALSE

10. School-wide programs that have attempted to reduce bullying in schools have been highly successful.

False. Most programs that have been used to date have a relatively small impact on the incidence of bullying. There is a good deal of work that must be done to develop effective programs that will reduce this problem.

With public concern about bullying increasing, a number of different types of programs have been developed and implemented in U.S. schools, including (a) traditional programs such as the Olweus Bullying Prevention Program, which seeks to reduce the opportunities for bullying to occur while removing the rewards for it when it does happen (Olweus, 2003); (b) programs that increase social competence while reducing antisocial behavior such as aggression; (c) programs that teach students how to respond to conflict; and (d) restorative justice programs that try to restore a relationship between the victim and the bully through techniques such as reconciliation or peer mediation (Ferguson, San Miguel, Kilburn, & Sanchez, 2007).

In 2007 Ferguson and his colleagues conducted a meta-analysis of studies that evaluated the effectiveness of various anti-bullying programs. They found 42 published studies involving 34,713 participants that met their criteria for inclusion (the article was published between 1995 and 2006, had a control or comparison group, and evaluated a school-based program). The results of the meta-analysis showed that bullying programs have a small, but significant, effect ranging from less than 1% impact for low-risk children to 3.6% for high-risk children. The researchers concluded that although the programs produce a small amount of positive change, "it is likely that this change is too small to be practically significant or noticeable" (p. 408). (You can review the difference between statistical significance and practical significance in Chapter 3.) They acknowledge that their conclusion may be disappointing to policymakers and the general public who have embraced such programs, but this type of information serves a couple of useful purposes. First, it is not a good use of taxpayers' money to spend it on programs that do not produce the expected results. Second, such information should spur program developers and researchers to look for new programs that are more effective or to identify the elements of existing programs that do work and to strengthen their role in the program implementation.

Romantic Relationships in Adolescence

Adolescent romantic relationships are related to many of the developmental tasks of adolescence. They play an important role in the development of identity (including a sexual identity), influence the process of individuation from the family of origin, change the nature of peer relationships, and lay the groundwork for future intimate relationships.

Romantic relationships first emerge in adolescence, although the desire to have a boyfriend or girlfriend may begin before that. In one study of sixth, seventh, and eighth graders, there was no difference on a measure of how much the students wanted to have a boyfriend or girlfriend across the grades (Darling, Dowdy, VanHorn, & Caldwell, 1999), and the number of adolescents who report that they are in a romantic relationship increases across adolescence, from 36% of 13-year-olds to 70% of 17-year-olds (Carver, Joyner, & Udry, 2003).

Although romance seems to occupy a prominent place in the thoughts of many adolescents, there actually has been relatively little research done on the topic (Furman & Collins, 2009; Karney, Beckett, Collins, & Shaw, 2007). This is especially true when we compare the body of research on romantic relationships in adolescence to the body of research on adolescent sexual behavior described in Chapter 6. One of the reasons for this lack is the fact that we do not have a commonly accepted definition of what a romantic relationship is (Furman & Collins, 2009; Karney et al., 2007). Many studies simply allow the participants to decide for themselves whether they are in (or have had) a romantic relationship (Karney et al., 2007), but there clearly are problems with this methodology. For instance, in one national longitudinal study in which participants were asked to name up to three people with whom they had had a romantic relationship, the researchers found that a large percentage of the named relationships were not reciprocated (in other words, the person named as someone the adolescent had a romantic relationship with did *not* include that adolescent on *his* or *her* list of romantic partners) (Karney et al., 2007).

Another challenge in doing research on romantic relationships is that these relationships change a great deal over a relatively short amount of time. What a young adolescent wants from a romantic relationship and what makes that relationship satisfying or not is quite different from what an older adolescent wants. Younger adolescents place more importance on superficial characteristics such as physical appearance or having fun together, but older adolescents place a greater value on qualities such as commitment and intimacy as they search for someone who could become a life partner (Montgomery, 2005). Also, various aspects of dating have a different impact on adolescents depending upon their age. While intimacy and exclusivity in a dating relationship can be problematic when they are features of an early adolescent relationship, these same qualities are part of a strong romantic relationship in late adolescence (Karney et al., 2007).

Although adolescent romantic relationships differ in a number of ways, there is a general developmental pattern that describes how adolescents move into these relationships. First, teens begin the process by getting together in mixed-gender groups to do things such as going

I Love Lucy. It has been a long time since *I Love Lucy* was on television, but there was no problem that this glamorous couple couldn't solve in less than 30 minutes. Not much has changed in television's portrayal of romance—couples are beautiful and deeply in love, and every problem is handled quickly and simply.

to parties or hanging out. After they become comfortable with one another in these mixed-sex groups, individuals in the group pair off and begin dating. Finally, dyadic romantic relationships form (Connolly, Craig, Goldberg, & Pepler, 2004).

Where do adolescents get their ideas about what a romantic relationship is like? The endless discussion of the topic of romance with peers helps them form their ideas of what to expect in a romantic relationship. These discussions create the norms or expectations within the peer group for what will happen in a relationship. The other important source of information on romantic relationships for adolescents is the media. Research by Ward and Friedman (2006) showed that TV shows influence teens to see romance in a stereotypical way, with men as sexual predators and women as sex objects and both sexes as using manipulation and deceit to get the partner they desire. By contrast, the portrayal of marital relationships shows few serious conflicts and almost none that cannot be resolved easily through a bit of frank communication between the partners (Karney et al., 2007). Both types of portrayals distort the quality of relationships experienced by most couples and may leave adolescents unprepared for the reality they encounter when they find themselves in these situations. You can use **Active Learning: Romance as Seen on TV** to take a closer look at how romance is portrayed on a current television program.

ACTIVE LEARNING

Romance as Seen on TV

Watch a television program that focuses on the romantic relationship of a young couple. If you cannot find one specifically about adolescents, watching a program about young adults will do for this activity. An episode of a soap opera would be a perfect choice, but it is best to stay away from what purports to be "reality television."

As you watch it, make notes concerning the subtle, hidden messages about romantic relationships that are embedded in the program. Are they portrayed as blissful or as a constant source of conflict? Are they based on honesty or deceit and manipulation? How are any conflicts or disagreements resolved? How easy or difficult is it to resolve them? What are the rewards or benefits of being in this relationship? Does each partner benefit to the same extent? If there is sexual behavior in the program, does it occur in a committed relationship or a casual one?

Compare your observations with those of classmates who watch other programs. Do you see any patterns or themes in how romantic relationships are portrayed across different programs?

Researchers have been interested in understanding how romantic relationships are similar to or different from adolescents' other relationships. Friendships and romantic relationships have many qualities in common. Both relationships are voluntary, and adolescents enter or leave them as they will. In both, adolescents spend time together, confide in each other, provide social support, and share intimacy, but romantic relationships have an intensity and level of affection (as well as the potential for a sexual component of the relationship) that makes them different from other peer relationships (Furman & Collins, 2009). There also is a good deal of similarity in the quality of peer and romantic relationships. Adolescents with high-quality peer relationships are more likely to enjoy a high-quality relationship with their romantic partner, and likewise those with maladaptive peer relationships are more likely to have problematic romantic relationships (Karney et al., 2007; Kiesner, Kerr, & Stattin, 2004). Finally, just as we saw earlier in this chapter with regard to peer relationships, romantic partners are often similar to the adolescent on a number of characteristics, including age, race, ethnicity, attractiveness, academic interest, level of risk-taking behavior, and plans for attending college (Furman & Collins, 2009; Karney et al., 2007). With regard to age, however, boys are more likely to prefer partners who are within a year of their own age, but girls often prefer partners who are slightly older.

We also see a great deal of similarity between adolescents' relationships with their parents and their romantic relationships. From Chapter 10 you'll remember that attachment theory proposes that based upon the quality of our early relationships, we form an internal working model of close relationships that we carry forward with us into future relationships. If you also remember the characteristics of a secure attachment, you will easily understand this connection. One of the things that makes a romantic relationship different from other peer relationships is that the person uses his or her partner as a safe haven in times of stress and a secure base for exploring the environment and shows evidence of separation distress when away from his or her partner for a significant period of time (Furman & Collins, 2009), all characteristics of a secure attachment in early parent-child relationships. However, romantic relationships are different from parent-child relationships because in this attachment relationship, each partner becomes an attachment figure for his or her partner. Again, we find that the research evidence supports the idea of continuity in the quality of relationships. The quality of family relationships earlier in development is related to the quality of romantic relationships in adolescence (Karney et al., 2007; Laursen, Furman, & Mooney, 2006). Unfortunately we also see this continuity among adolescents who have been the victim of physical or sexual abuse while growing up (Karney et al., 2007). Being a victim of physical or sexual abuse during childhood places an adolescent at an increased risk of either experiencing or perpetrating violence within an intimate relationship as he or she moves through adolescence. This replication of violence in intimate relationships is not inevitable, but adolescents who are at risk in this way may benefit from intervention programs designed to help young people develop healthy and happy relationships.

We currently do not have research that examines how an adolescent's experiences in one romantic relationship affect subsequent romantic relationships. Without this, it is difficult to determine how early romantic experiences contribute to any possible modification in the expectations that the adolescent has for future relationships, but this would be an important topic for future research.

Beyond Parents and Peers

Research on social relations has largely focused on the relationships that children and adolescents have with parents and peers. These relationships are very important, but there is a piece of the picture that has been largely overlooked until fairly recently. If we simply ask children or adolescents to name the people who are important to them, they spontaneously include a wide range of relatives and nonrelated adults on their lists that go beyond parents and peers.

Relationships with nonparental adults. Many children and adolescents have adults other than their parents who are important to them. When asked to name these important nonparental adults, many include grandparents on their list.

Important Nonparental Adults

When we talk about nonparental adults, we are talking about both relatives and unrelated adults. A number of studies have examined whom children and adolescents name as the important nonparental adults in their lives. Relatives, such as grandparents, aunts and uncles, and older siblings or cousins frequently appear on those lists. Table 12.3 presents results that are typical of the findings from these studies. It shows whom the adolescents in a sample of 201 11th graders identified as "very important people" in their lives (Greenberger, Chen, & Beam, 1998, p. 321). Similar results have been reported by Rishel et al. (2007) for middle school and high school students and by Chen, Greenberger, Farruggia, Bush, and Dong (2003) for American and Chinese 11th graders. With regard to unrelated adults, it is not surprising that adolescents report that they have the most frequent contact with a favorite teacher (Rishel et al., 2007), but people like coaches, youth leaders, and clergy also appear on many lists.

Table 12.3

"Very important people." In research conducted in a large, ethnically diverse high school, these are the nonparental adults whom adolescents named as "very important people" in their lives. Relatives other than parents are important to many adolescents, but so are a number of other people who are not related to the adolescent.

Percentage of Respondents with VIPs in Various Role Relationships		
	Boys	**Girls**
Grandparent	5	18
Aunt/uncle	16	16
Cousin	10	3
Sibling	18	15
Parent's significant other	0	1
Friend's parent	8	8
Neighbor	5	2
Older friend	18	8
Relative of boyfriend/girlfriend	0	5
Teacher	10	10
Coach	5	5
Counselor	0	2
Church representative	5	7
Other/uncodable	2	0

Most of the research on nonparental adults has looked at adolescent samples, rather than samples of younger children, because younger children do not have the same opportunities to spend time with nonparental adults that adolescents have. In one study of over 200 adolescents from a large, ethnically diverse high school, the percentage of very important people who were relatives was similar for boys (48%) and girls (52%), but girls were more likely than boys to report that they had a very important person in their lives (Greenberger et al., 1998). Girls also report greater enjoyment in their relationships with the nonparental adults they name (Rishel et al., 2007) and greater psychological intimacy (Benson, 1993). Although it is most likely that the adult will be the same gender as the adolescent, boys had more cross-gender relationships than girls. Greenberger et al. (1998) did not find ethnic differences in whom the adolescents named or the functions they filled in their sample, although other research has found a preference for extended family members among African American adolescents (Benson, Mangen, & Williams, 1986).

Functions Filled by Nonparental Adults

Adolescents' relationships with nonparental adults fill a number of functional roles (Hamilton & Darling, 1989). They are important sources of social support when the adolescent is trying to cope with a stressful experience (Munsch & Blyth, 1993), as well as support for educational achievement, personal development, and trying new things (Chen et al., 2003). Nonparental adults are seen as role models, companions, teachers, guides and confidants by adolescents (Chen et al., 2003; Munsch & Blyth, 1993). Occasionally they are sources of more tangible support, such as financial assistance (Rhodes, Ebert, & Fischer, 1992). A very important question has been whether nonparental adults in an adolescent's life simply provide more of the same functions that parents provide or whether these relationships are qualitatively different from relationships with parents. Nancy Darling and her colleagues have maintained that unrelated adults provide a unique context for development because they represent an adult point of view (which distinguishes them from relationships with peers) but they are less judgmental than parents (Darling, Hamilton, & Shaver, 2003).

Most research has relied upon self-reports from adolescents about the characteristics of their social networks, but Rishel et al. (2007) asked both parents and adolescents to report on the strength of the adolescent's relationship with a number of people considered important in the adolescent's life. Interestingly, compared to the adolescents' perceptions, parents tended to underestimate the influence of extended family members but to overestimate the influence of unrelated adults who knew the adolescent in a formal or professional capacity, such as coaches, teachers, or clergy. Although people in these formal roles are devoted to working with young people, their time is often spread across many individuals, so their impact on any single adolescent may be diluted. Also, the role they play is more limited than the role that a relative might play. An adolescent may seek out the help of a teacher for a school-related problem but wouldn't be as likely to go to that person for help with a personal issue or general concerns (Benson et al., 1986).

Impact of Nonparental Adults

Adolescents' relationships with nonparental adults are important because these relationships can have a significant impact on development. In one study of young, single African American mothers, natural **mentors** are called an "overlooked resource" in the social networks of these women (Rhodes et al., 1992, p. 445). Women who had natural mentors in their lives reported less depression than those who did not and benefited more from the social support they received (Rhodes et al., 1992). When this relationship persisted for

Mentor A formal relationship in which a nonparental adult provides a range of functions to a younger person, or a naturally occurring relationship that provides the same functions.

2 years, the young women were more likely to stay in school or graduate from high school and saw more warmth in this relationship than even the relationship they had with their own mothers (Klaw, Rhodes, & Fitzgerald, 2003). These relationships also were characterized as being "remarkably unconflictual" (Rhodes et al., 1992, p. 456), although that may not be too surprising given that these are voluntary relationships that have persisted over time. Similar results were found for a group of inner-city Latina adolescent mothers (Rhodes, Contreras, & Mangelsdorf, 1994).

A wide range of studies have documented the protective effect that a relationship with a nonparental adult can have for an adolescent. A national longitudinal study of over 20,000 adolescents found that having a grandparent living in a family household was associated with lower levels of deviant behavior (Hamilton, 2005). Black children who had a grandparent living with the family also reported fewer depressive symptoms than other Black children. Having a natural mentor has been associated with lower levels of reported use of marijuana and nonviolent delinquency and higher levels of attachment to school (Zimmerman, Bingenheimer, & Notaro, 2002). This relationship may be so influential because a natural mentor has both a direct and an indirect effect on adolescent development. The natural mentor directly reduces the risk of problem behavior by monitoring and sanctioning the behavior of the adolescent but also has an indirect effect because the support that this relationship provides helps the adolescent resist pressure from peers to engage in negative behaviors. **Active Learning: Relationships With Nonparental Adults** gives you an opportunity to think about the people who have filled the role of natural mentor in your life and the impact they have had on your development.

ACTIVE LEARNING

Relationships With Nonparental Adults

Think about the relationships other than your relationship with your parents and your friends that were important to you while you were a teenager. Was there someone who was particularly influential, perhaps someone you would call a "natural mentor"? Were there different people who filled this role when you were in early, middle, and late adolescence, or did a single relationship continue throughout adolescence? What kinds of things did they do that made this relationship an important one to you? Were these the same types of things that you got from your parents and/or friends, or were there unique functions that they filled that you did not get from other relationships?

Conclusion

In this chapter we have seen how children's thinking about social concepts plays a role in how they manage their relationships with other people. Children develop their social worlds through the kinds of social interactions they experience but also by the sense they make out of those experiences. Young children first learn about social interaction from their relationships with their parents, but they must develop the social, emotional, and cognitive skills necessary to develop and maintain many kinds of relationships throughout their lives. Increasingly, peers become important, but parents continue to play a central role even in adolescence. The network of social relationships becomes more complex as nonparental adults and romantic partners enter the mix. When adolescents move on to adulthood, they are likely to be able to manage a very complex social world.

CHAPTER SUMMARY

1. What is social cognition?

Social cognition is how we understand and think about our social interactions with others. To do this, we need to develop a **theory of mind**. The development of theory of mind can be assessed using the **false belief paradigm.** Autistic children fail to develop a theory of mind, and their inability to read social interactions is called **mindblindness**.

2. What is socialization?

Socialization is the process by which children learn how to behave in accordance with the rules and norms of their society. Through the process of **internalization**, children make these rules and norms a part of who they are. Parents use a variety of parenting strategies and techniques to socialize their children. Positive strategies include **inductive discipline** (either **self-oriented induction** or **other-oriented induction**), **command strategies**, and **relationship maintenance**. In contrast, **power assertion** and **love withdrawal** are more negative strategies. Positive discipline has been associated with positive social outcomes and empathy, and negative strategies have been associated with increased aggression (although power assertion appears to be beneficial for children from some socioeconomic and ethnic backgrounds). Despite the negative consequences of power assertion, many parents still spank their children, which is not an effective way to help children learn how to control themselves.

3. How do parent-child relationships change as the child becomes an adolescent?

Adolescents and parents must renegotiate their relationship to maintain a balance between autonomy and connectedness with the family. Adolescents have qualitatively different relationships with their mothers and fathers, and adolescents and their parents see their relationship differently. Although conflict increases during adolescence, it is not a significant problem for the majority of families and, when it does occur, it is most likely to be about everyday issues. Some conflict is inevitable, but it often is more stressful for parents than for their adolescent children. In collectivist cultures that value harmony, adolescents are more likely to compromise to meet their parents' expectation so conflict is avoided.

4. What are peer relationships like during infancy and early childhood?

Infants who have secure attachments to their parents are likely to have more positive relationships with peers. Imitation and pretend play are important forms of play interaction in early childhood. The conflicts that occur between young playmates are part of the process of learning how to sustain a social relationship. By age 3 children can form **friendships**.

5. How do peer relationships change during middle childhood?

After children enter school, many find a best friend. There has been a question about whether girls' friendships and boys' friendships are qualitatively different, but gender differences in social relationships are usually small. **Sociometry** is a technique used to measure peer status. Based upon nominations by peers, children can be classified as **popular**, **rejected**, **average**, **neglected**, or **controversial**. Certain child characteristics are associated with different statuses, and there are different developmental outcomes for children in different statuses. Although the rejected status places a child at risk, some children have a low level of **rejection sensitivity**, so being rejected by peers may not distress them.

6. What types of positive peer relationships do adolescents have?

Adolescents spend an increasing amount of time with peers, and relationships become reciprocal and more intimate (especially for girls). There is a great deal of similarity between adolescent friends, and both selection and influence contribute to this similarity. Friends form **cliques**, and individual adolescents are placed within different **crowds** by their peers. Although peers exert **peer pressure**, the pressure is often subtle and is more likely to be for positive rather than negative behavior. Adolescents become more resistant to peer pressure as they get older. There is a debate over the relative influence of parents and peers, but it appears that peers have more influence in certain areas while parents have greater influence in others. Romantic relationships first emerge in adolescence. Adolescents' ideas about the nature of romantic relationships are influenced by friends and the media. The quality of romantic relationships usually is similar to the quality of the adolescents' relationships with others.

7. What is the darker side of adolescent peer relations?

Bullying is a threat to the well-being of a number of children and adolescents, and **cyberbullying** is a particularly vicious form of bullying. Bullies often have relatively poor self-concepts, lack self-control, and do poorly in school. Victims of bullies may feel anxious or depressed and may react by withdrawing from peers or striking out against them. Programs designed to reduce bullying have only had a small effect on reducing the incidence of bullying and could be improved.

8. What relationships beyond parents and peers are important for social development?

Many children and adolescents have nonparental adults (both relatives and unrelated adults) who they say are important in their lives. These adults can function as a **mentor** who provides some functions that are unique to this type of relationship. Having a mentor can benefit adolescent development or even act as a protective factor for adolescents who are at risk.

 Go to **www.sagepub.com/levine** for additional exercises and video resources. Select **Chapter 12, Social Development,** for chapter-specific activities.

part IV

Contexts for Development

chapter 13

Play, Extracurricular Activities, and Media Use

13

The Daily Lives of Children and Adolescents

The lives of children and adolescents contain much more than school, work, and family. Although in poverty-stricken areas around the world, even young children must work to help feed their families, in less desperate situations children and teens have some amount of time that is discretionary because they can decide for themselves how to spend it. For many children and adolescents, much of this time is used for leisure

Test Your Knowledge

Test your knowledge of child development by deciding whether each of the following statements is *true* or *false*, and then check your answers as you read the chapter.

1. **True/False:** If a child chooses to play alone, even when there are other children available to play with him, there is no reason for concern.
2. **True/False:** It is important for children to play because they have fun when they are playing, but the real learning happens in the classroom.
3. **True/False:** Educators in the United States agree that recess during the school day is important to allow students some "time out" to refresh themselves before returning to academic learning.
4. **True/False:** Middle-class adolescents are more likely to have paid employment than low-income adolescents.
5. **True/False:** Many children and teens these days are overscheduled, spending most of their time after school in multiple organized activities, like sports and music lessons.
6. **True/False:** Children who participate in organized sports develop skills that they use to keep them physically active throughout their lifetime.
7. **True/False:** Most families do not have any rules related to television viewing for their children.
8. **True/False:** Babies 8 to 16 months of age who watch videotapes designed to improve cognitive development (like Baby Einstein videos) have larger vocabularies than babies who don't watch these videos.
9. **True/False:** The fast pace used on the television program *Sesame Street* shortens the attention span of children who watch it.
10. **True/False:** European and Asian teens are just now starting to catch up with American teens in terms of how much they text message.

Correct answers: (1) True, (2) False, (3) False, (4) True, (5) False, (6) False, (7) True, (8) False, (9) False, (10) False activities. The way in which young people spend their leisure time varies between cultures and reflects their culture's values. In Taiwan, academics outside of school make up a relatively large portion of the day, and many activities for Taiwanese children are chosen and/or directed by adults (Newman et al., 2007). By comparison, American children are more likely to choose their own activities, and the one area they choose more than children in most other cultures is sports. Larson (2004) has studied how teens in the United States and other countries use their time outside of school. In general, American youth do far less homework and have much more free time. He describes three ways in which they use this free time: (a) playing or "hanging out" with others in unstructured activities; (b) engaging in structured activities, such as sports, drama or musical productions, or interest-based clubs; and (c) using media, such as television, video games, and computers. Table 13.1 shows the daily activities of children and adolescents in many different cultures. Try **Active Learning: The Daily Life of a Teen** to see how an adolescent you know uses his or her time and how much of that is leisure time.

Table 13.1

Average daily time use of adolescents in 45 studies

Activity	Nonindustrial, unschooled populations	Postindustrial, schooled populations		
		United States	**Europe**	**East Asia**
Household labor	5–9 hours	20–40 minutes	20–40 minutes	10–20 minutes
Paid labor	0.5–8 hours	40–60 minutes	10–20 minutes	0–10 minutes
Schoolwork	–	3.0–4.5 hours	4.0–5.5 hours	5.5–7.5 hours
Total work time	6–9 hours	4–6 hours	4.5–6.5 hours	6–8 hours
TV viewing	Insufficient data	1.5–2.5 hours	1.5–2.5 hours	1.5–2.5 hours
Talking	Insufficient data	2–3 hours	Insufficient data	45–60 minutes
Sports	Insufficient data	30–60 minutes	20–80 minutes	0–20 minutes
Structured voluntary activities	Insufficient data	10–20 minutes	10–20 minutes	0–10 minutes
Total free time	4–7 hours	6.5–8 hours	5.5–7.5 hours	4.0–5.5 hours

NOTE: The estimates in the table are averaged across a 7-day week, including weekdays and weekends. Time spent in maintenance activities like eating, personal care, and sleeping is not included. The data for nonindustrial, unschooled populations come primarily from rural peasant populations in developing countries (Larson, 2004, p. 136).

ACTIVE **LEARNING**

The Daily Life of a Teen

Ask a teenager to keep a journal reporting what she is doing every hour for 2 days (one school day and one weekend day). You might want to give her two sheets of paper divided into the hours of the day so she can note when she wakes up and goes to sleep (so you'll know how much time she was awake) and with one block of space for each hour. If this is not possible, think back to a typical day when you were in high school and describe for each hour what you were likely to be doing.

In either case, for each hour, decide whether you would classify the activity as school, paid work, or leisure time. Total the number of waking hours and divide the number of "leisure" hours by the total number of waking hours to find out the percentage of the time that was "leisure time."

For example, the teen below has a total of 18 hours in her day. She has 7 hours of leisure time, including sports, hanging out, dinner, and TV time. Therefore, seven eighteenths or .39 (almost 40%) of her day was spent in leisure activity.

8 a.m.	9 a.m.	10 a.m.	11 a.m.	12 p.m.	1 p.m.	2 p.m.	3 p.m.	4 p.m.
school	school	school	school	school	school	hanging out with friends	sports	sports
5 p.m.	6 p.m.	7 p.m.	8 p.m.	9 p.m.	10 p.m.	11 p.m.	12 a.m.	1 a.m.
homework	dinner with family	homework	TV with family	TV	homework	TV/ Facebook/ phone	homework	sleep

Next try to categorize each leisure hour as one of the following: media use, structured activities like sports or school clubs, "hanging out" with friends, or interacting with family. Calculate the percentage of time spent on each type of activity by totaling the number of hours you decided are spent in leisure activities and dividing the number of hours in each type of leisure activity by the total number of hours. For example, if you decide that the teen spent 6 hours in leisure activities and 2 of those hours were spent "hanging out," divide 2 hours (time spent hanging out) by 6 hours (the total leisure time) to get 33% or one third of the teen's leisure time. The teen shown in the chart above spends 3 hours watching TV; therefore three sevenths or .43 of her leisure time is spent watching TV.

American teens have been found to spend 40%–50% of their day in leisure activities, compared with 25%–35% for East Asians and 35%–45% for Europeans (Larson, 2004). The particular type of activity that occurs during these leisure hours has an effect on teens' development, as we will see later in this chapter.

In this chapter we will first describe children's play and its effects on their development. We will then discuss the nature of structured activities and unstructured time for children and adolescents and examine the controversy about how much is too much structured activity. Finally, we will describe media use and the impact that both old and new media are having on children and teens.

The Role of Play

Children and adolescents spend their time on a number of different activities, but play is an important childhood activity in most cultures. Some have argued that it is a universal human behavior, though play is not unique to humans, as anyone with a puppy knows. Even children who must work at an early age find ways to play while they are working (Drewes, 2005). For example, fantasy play was found among both poor and middle-class Brazilian children regardless of their ethnic group and location within the country (Gosso, Morais, & Otta, 2007). The United Nations Committee on the Rights of the Child (1999) included the following statement to promote the importance of play for children's development around the world:

Parties recognize the right of the child to rest and leisure, to engage in play and recreational activities appropriate to the age of the child and to participate freely in cultural life and the arts. (p. 19)

How does play differ from the other activities in which children take part? See **Active Learning: What Is Play?** to try to define the characteristics of play for yourself.

What Is Play?

Read the following descriptions of two play situations with 4-year-olds in two different cultures.

Scenario #1.   In the following translated dialogue, a 4-year-old boy (Dagiwa) and girl (Hoyali) in Papua New Guinea are pretending to be doctors taking care of patients, which are represented by the visiting anthropologist's feet and then by a tree stump:

Dagiwa: (addresses foot-patient) Are you also sick?

Hoyali: Hold this one (takes foot in hands and places it down on ground). I am letting it stay here.

Dagiwa: Has this one also been sick, eh?

Hoyali: Yes, this one has been sick.

Dagiwa: (pretends to give the foot-patient an injection) The injection is finished.

(Dagiwa leaves Hoyali and focuses his attention on a small banana stump . . . which is treated as if it is a new patient. Hoyali moves to join him.)

Dagiwa: Is this one ill?

Hoyali: I am giving it an injection (adapted from Goldman & Smith, 1998).

Scenario #2.   In this second example, a group of 4-year-olds is interacting in a day care center in the United States.

Elisha and Max are in their make-believe library in their day care center pretending to read a book about building castles. Elisha counts the blocks as she hands them to Max, who repeats the numbers as he places each block in the structure. Max is growing impatient, however, and says that he will be the castle's "big green dragon." Elisha responds, "OK, I will be the princess with a purple dress, but let's finish making the castle." Juan joins them and wants to play. Max agrees and offers Juan a role as the prince. But Juan wants to be the green dragon. Much negotiating takes place. Finally, Juan agrees to assume this role, but he insists on wearing a gold crown (Bellin & Singer, 2006, p. 101).

Based upon these scenarios, answer these questions:

1. How would you define play based on these two examples? What are the characteristics that make this play rather than some other kind of activity?

2. What cognitive, language, social, and emotional abilities must children have to be able to play in these ways?

3. Finally, how does this play help children develop physically, cognitively, linguistically, socially, and emotionally? What are they learning in each of these domains?

You will find answers to these questions as you continue reading this section of the chapter.

What definition of "play" did you come up with? Perhaps the chief characteristic of play is that it is fun. Children are actively and fully involved in the "private reality" that makes up their play (Segal, 2004, p. 38). Other characteristics that have been proposed include the following:

1. Play is done for its own sake, not for any outside goal or purpose.

2. Even when it is an imitation of adult work, play is marked as being different through signals such as exaggeration of activities, role reversals, or laughing.

3. Play is voluntary and spontaneous (Burghardt, 2004, p. 294).

There are two ways in which play has been examined developmentally: as a reflection of a child's level of development and as a necessary activity for the promotion of children's development (Scarlett, Naudeau, Salonius-Pasternak, & Ponte, 2005). As we will see, it is difficult to determine which of these is the *cause* of what we observe and which is the *effect.* In the following sections we will first discuss the ways in which types of play reflect the level of the child's development and then discuss the effects that play has on promoting children's development.

Types of Play and Levels of Development

Two-year-old children obviously play differently than 8-year-olds. The 2-year-old's cognitive, social, emotional, and language skills are not as sophisticated as those of the older child. Several theorists have attempted to relate the level of children's social and cognitive ability to the way that children play at different ages.

Parten's Stages of Social Play

In the 1930s, Mildred Parten (1932) described the following levels of play that researchers still use today.

1. **Unoccupied behavior:** looking around at whatever occurs, but engaging in no activity

2. **Onlooker behavior:** watching others play

3. **Solitary independent play:** engaging actively with toys that are different from those being used by other children

4. **Parallel play:** playing next to, but not in interaction with each other, often using the same type of materials—for example, blocks or dolls

5. **Associative play:** playing with other children, sharing toys, and interacting, but with no overall organization of the group to achieve a common goal

6. **Cooperative play:** playing as part of a group that has a common goal, such as building a building, creating a make-believe scene such as "house" with assigned roles, or playing sports

For examples of current studies that use Parten's stages, see Dyer and Moneta (2006), Freeman and Somerindyke (2001), and Krafft and Berk (1998). Many studies have provided support for Parten's idea that children become more interactive and more cooperative with age and that the tendency to take part in more socially interactive play reflects better social adjustment (Provost & LaFreniere, 1991). However, the exact stages Parten proposed have been called into question. Specifically, solitary and parallel play have not been found to reflect distinct levels of social maturity.

Whereas unoccupied and onlooker activities have been linked to immaturity and lack of social skills, solitary independent play, such as when a child plays imaginatively with dolls or creates block buildings, has been linked with positive development, autonomy, and maturity (Luckey & Fabes, 2005; Provost & LaFreniere, 1991). Also, the meaning of solitary play is in part determined by the reason behind it. Children may prefer to play alone because they can be in control of what happens, they need time to think about their feelings and reactions, or they just prefer a break from the social world. However, children may be found playing alone because they have been rejected by others, are too shy to approach other children, or lack the

Unoccupied behavior
Looking around at whatever occurs, but engaging in no activity.

Onlooker behavior
Watching others play.

Solitary independent play Engaging actively with toys that are different from those being used by other children.

Parallel play Playing next to a peer with the same type of materials, but not interacting with the other child.

Associative play
Sharing toys and interacting with peers, but without a common goal.

Cooperative play Play with peers that has a common goal.

1. If a child chooses to play alone, even when there are other children available to play with him, there is no reason for concern.  **TRUE/FALSE**

    True. Children may choose to play alone for several positive reasons, including the fact that they just need some time alone to think about their feelings. Solitary play is *not* necessarily a sign of a problem.

social skills to initiate contact with others. The context of a child's solitary play has to be taken into account when evaluating whether it reflects difficulties with social development.

For the stage of parallel play, contrary to what Parten proposed, research has not consistently shown that it is a higher level of social interaction than solitary play. Parallel play is prevalent throughout the preschool years and may be more related to the nature of the school curriculum than to the children's social skills. In one study, children were more likely to be involved in parallel play if the school provided many activities that promoted an individual task orientation rather than less structured or more cooperative activities (Provost & LaFreniere, 1991). To test yourself on your understanding of Parten's stages of play, see **Active Learning: Parten's Stages of Play.**

ACTIVE LEARNING

Parten's Stages of Play

Connect each level of Parten's play scale with the statement or description that best matches it:

Unoccupied behavior	1. Francisco and Martha decide to play house and agree that Ted will be the baby.
Onlooker behavior	2. Sepanta sucks her thumb while following the teacher around the room.
Solitary independent play	3. Jon and Claudia sit at the table playing with puzzles, occasionally looking at and commenting on each other's work.
Parallel play	4. Jacob paints at the easel with great intensity.
Associative play	5. Carol is new in class. She watches the children play with great interest.
Cooperative play	6. Sadie and Azucena play in the sandbox, talking with each other, exchanging the tools and cups they need for their projects.

Answers: Unoccupied behavior—2; Onlooker behavior—5; Solitary independent play—4; Parallel play—3; Associative play—6; Cooperative play—1

Piaget's Cognitive Levels of Play

Jean Piaget (1962) described a different developmental sequence of play, based on cognitive rather than social maturity. Piaget hypothesized that the nature of children's play would change as the level of their thinking changed. You can review Piaget's stages of cognitive development in Chapter 7. Based upon this sequence, he proposed three levels of play:

Practice play
Performing a certain behavior repetitively for the mere pleasure of it.

Symbolic/sociodramatic play Using symbolic representations and imagination for play.

1. **Practice play:** performing a certain behavior repetitively for the mere pleasure of it—for example, jumping back and forth over a puddle for no purpose other than the enjoyment of doing so. An infant in the sensorimotor stage of development is capable of practice play such as dropping a ball over and over again just to see it happen.

2. **Symbolic/sociodramatic play:** using symbolic representations and imagination for play—for example, pretending to talk on the telephone. Toddlers begin to use symbols in play at the end of the sensorimotor period, and preschoolers in the preoperational stage of cognition develop fantasy play to a much greater extent.

3. **Games with rules:** making up rules for a game or playing games with preestablished rules, such as baseball or soccer. This type of play is developed most clearly in the stage of concrete operations. Piaget argued that younger children try to fit reality to their own purposes through fantasy, while older children begin to fit themselves into the larger reality of the social world around them by following rules. We mentioned in Chapter 11 that preschoolers are likely to bend the rules if they are about to lose a game or suffer a serious setback.

In the time since Piaget proposed these three broad stages, researchers have further developed his ideas about the cognitive levels necessary for different types of play. Sara Smilansky (1968) added a stage after practice play, which she labeled **constructive play**, consisting of building or making something for the purposes of play. Others have looked separately at the development of each of the types of play.

The second stage of symbolic/sociodramatic play has received a good deal of attention. Fantasy or imaginative play appears in infants during the second year of life in very diverse cultures around the world, but the content of fantasy play reflects the larger culture. For example, in one study American children based their play on toys and the ideas they represented. For example, a toy rocket might trigger fantasy about a trip into outer space. By contrast, Chinese children tended not to use objects, but rather based their play on the complex social routines they experience in their society (Haight & Black, 2001).

While the content of fantasy play differs, the development of the ability to use symbols and understand social roles, both of which are used in fantasy play, may have a more universal pattern. Watson and Fischer (1977, 1980) proposed that fantasy play involving the use of symbols goes through several stages in accordance with the child's level of cognitive development. They proposed a sequence of steps based on the toddler's development from a focus only on himself to greater ability to take the role of another as follows:

1. The child performs the action—for example, pretending to sleep (18 months).

2. The child acts upon the other—for example, combing the doll's hair (18 months–2 years).

3. The child has the other perform an action—for example, the doll washes its face (2 years).

Preschoolers then build upon these skills as they learn to perform social roles:

1. The child performs or has a doll perform several different actions linked to a social role, such as doctor (3 years).

2. The child performs a social role with another person performing a complementary role—for example, doctor and patient (4 years).

3. The child performs more than one role—for example, she is the doctor and then the mother of the patient (6 years).

Stages of play. Which stages of fantasy play do these photographs represent?

It is apparent that both social and cognitive abilities contribute to a child's ability to play. Play becomes more sophisticated and complicated as children can coordinate activities with others socially while at the same time developing the ability to use symbols and understand rules.

The inability to play can be an indication of a variety of behavioral problems in childhood. In the *Diagnostic and Statistical Manual of Mental Disorders* (DSM-IV-TR) of the American Psychiatric Association (2000), one characteristic of autistic disorder is a "lack of varied, spontaneous make-believe play or social imitative play appropriate to developmental level" (p. 75). Children with autism have difficulty understanding and engaging in fantasy play (Bigham, 2008; Kroeger, Schultz, & Newsom, 2007). Other children who are highly stressed and anxious may have the cognitive and social abilities to play, but may experience **play disruption**, an inability to play because their emotions are preventing the kind of free expression linked with the fun of play (Scarlett et al., 2005). Play is such a central aspect of children's lives that difficulties with play often indicate larger problems in the child's life. We will discuss how play is used to help children's healthy development in the next section of this chapter.

The Effects of Play on Children's Development

In recent years there has been an increasing tendency to devalue play, as schools eliminate recess in order to make room for increased hours of academic instruction. This is unfortunate because play has been found to have many benefits for all aspects of development: physical, emotional, social, and cognitive. Although we would not be able to describe all of the benefits associated with play, we will give an example in each of four areas of development.

Physical Development

Play contributes directly to physical development in several ways. One way in which this happens is through **physical activity play**, the type of play that involves large muscle activity. Physical activity play goes through three stages (Smith, 2010). In infants we see patterns of activity called **rhythmic stereotypies**. These consist of repeated large muscle movements that have no purpose, such as kicking the legs or waving the hands. The development of these behaviors seems to be guided by neuromuscular maturation. Infants engage in these types of movements shortly before they gain voluntary control of the specific body parts they are exercising (Smith, 2010).

During toddlerhood, we see what is called **exercise play**. This type of play involves large muscle movement, such as running or jumping in the context of play, and not surprisingly peaks at age 4 or 5 and declines as children enter school. The function of exercise play may be to train the muscles and to build strength and endurance (Smith, 2010). The age range when exercise play is most prevalent is also the period of time in development when the muscles and bones in arms and legs are growing very rapidly (Smith, 2010).

The third type of physical activity play is **rough-and-tumble play**. Common games throughout the world, especially for boys, are based on this type of play. In Chapter 2 we described rough-and-tumble play in groups of boys but told you that we also see this type of play in groups of animals. This type of play increases during the early school years and continues although at a greatly reduced level into early adolescence. Clearly these activities promote physical strength and endurance, but they also may affect brain development. In rats, the greatest amount of neuronal growth was found during times in their lives when the rats were most involved with rough-and-tumble play and exploration (Haight & Black, 2001). The function of rough-and-tumble play changes from childhood to adolescence. For younger children (especially boys), it is a fun activity for friends, it helps build fighting skills, and it helps children develop emotional control, but in adolescents it becomes a safe way to establish social dominance within the peer group (Pelligrini, 2002).

Physical play in the schools has been reduced as recess has been cut back in recent years to accommodate increased academic time (Story,

Play disruption An inability to play because the child's emotions are preventing the kind of free expression linked with the fun of play.

Physical activity play The type of play that involves large muscle activity.

Rhythmic stereotypies Repeated large muscle movements that have no purpose, such as kicking the legs or waving the hands, usually seen in infants.

Exercise play Play in young children that involves large muscle movement, such as running or jumping.

Rough-and-tumble play Play that looks like fighting or wrestling, where the goal is not to hurt or win, but to have fun.

Physical play. Play can promote physical development in children. This type of rough-and-tumble play builds strength and coordination, and also helps establish a hierarchy within the peer group without the need to resort to real fights or struggles.

Kaphingst, & French, 2006). This may be a factor contributing to the obesity problem among American children. Rates of obesity in children have tripled since 1960. In 2000 only 29% of elementary schools scheduled regular recess, and only 49% of schools provided after-school sports. To make matters worse, only 22% of schools provided transportation home after sports, which disproportionately affects low-income children's ability to take part in these activities (Story et al., 2006). We discuss other effects of the reductions in school recess further in the section on cognitive development.

Emotional Development

In the psychoanalytic tradition of Sigmund Freud, play is seen as the expression of the child's inner emotional conflicts (Scarlett et al., 2005). Children play out in fantasy what is bothering them in real life. For example, a child may become the "mean mother" with her dolls to express her frustration with parental discipline she has experienced. This fantasy gives the child some sense of control that helps her deal with real situations in which she feels helpless, as all children do at some times when dealing with the powerful adults in their lives. It also allows her to express in play certain emotions that might be unacceptable in real life, such as anger at a baby sibling (Haight, Black, Ostler, & Sheridan, 2006).

Play has been associated with emotional expression, emotional regulation, and emotional understanding. Research has shown that children who spend more time in fantasy play have more understanding of the emotions of self and others (Lindsey & Colwell, 2003). Normally, play helps children express their feelings and deal with them; however, when children have more severe emotional difficulties, they may not be able to play, or they may use play to reenact traumatic scenes over and over again with little emotional relief (Haight et al., 2006). **Play therapy** developed as a way to help children work through difficult feelings with the help of an adult who is trained to understand play as a type of communication.

Many children, especially young children, are unlikely to be able to sit and talk with a therapist about their feelings as adults do. Instead they present their thoughts and emotions in symbolic form through their play. As their thoughts and feelings become clear in their play, the therapist helps the children manage them in more adaptive ways. One example was provided by Jones and Landreth (2002) in a study on play therapy for children with chronic, insulin-dependent diabetes. These children often suffer from anxiety as they experience frightening symptoms, such as diabetic coma, along with many mystifying and painful interventions from doctors and nurses. In one case, a child was experiencing stomachaches every day. Over five sessions of play therapy, he acted out battle scenes, which initially used play soldiers but eventually came to involve doctors and nurses as the "bad guys" who would never go away, because "they just keep coming back!" (Jones & Landreth, 2002, p. 127). After expressing his feelings in this symbolic way, he was able to talk about the "anxiousness" in his stomach. When the therapist clarified that "feeling worried or nervous" could be experienced as a stomachache, the boy was able to move on to a less conflicted and less compulsive type of play, and his stomachaches did not return.

In a meta-analysis of studies on the efficacy of play therapy, Bratton, Ray, and Rhine (2005) found that this type of treatment was generally very helpful to children and resulted in changes in their maladaptive behavior. Treatment was especially effective when parents were involved in the treatment so that they too could begin to understand what their child was communicating to them through play. When parents can see more clearly how things appear from their child's point of view, they are better able to help the child resolve conflicts rather than acting them out in negative ways, such as fighting with other children or experiencing stomachaches.

Social Development

Although children play when they are alone, most play is social. Infants and toddlers play most often with adults, and this play appears to be connected to their later ability to play with peers.

Video Link 13.1
Rough and tumble.

Play therapy A way to help children work through difficult feelings with the help of an adult who is trained to understand play as a type of communication.

Video Link 13.2
Play therapy.

Parents from many different cultures engage in fantasy play with their young children (Haight et al., 2006), and this play is associated with the development of social skills in children's interactions with peers. Research has shown a link between the amount and nature of parent-child play and children's competence in social interactions with other children. One example is the research by Lindsey and Mize (2000), who studied play between parents and their 3- to 6-year-old children. They found that children who engaged in more pretend play with their parents that was mutually responsive (that is, parent and child each responded effectively to each other's cues) had higher social competence with their peers in their preschools.

By age 3, children turn their attention from play with parents to play with peers (Haight & Miller, 1992). Play with other children is intrinsically social, so it is no surprise that it has been linked with the development of social skills and the formation of friendships. Friendships develop through play because young children define a friend as someone who likes to play the same way that they do. Rubin, Lynch, Coplan, Rose-Krasnor, and Booth (1994) studied the role of play in the very beginnings of friendship. They brought together groups of four previously unacquainted 7-year-old children to play. Children were then asked which child they liked to play with the most. The researchers found that children were drawn to other children who shared their same play style. If one child took part in fantasy play, they preferred to play with another child who also played this way, while a child who liked to build things (constructive play) preferred playing with another who also liked this activity.

Play and social development are inextricably linked, but research in this area has difficulty in determining what comes first, play or social competence. While play undoubtedly contributes to social development in children, children who are more advanced in their social development also probably make better playmates. For example, Taylor and Carlson (1997) found that preschool children who were more likely to engage in fantasy play were also more likely to demonstrate the social skill called theory of mind (as described in Chapter 12). However, the question remains whether understanding of theory of mind underlies the ability to take part in fantasy play, or whether fantasy play promotes children's understanding of theory of mind. It seems likely that a complex interaction occurs, but we need more research to tease out these effects.

Cognitive Development

Once a topic that provoked much research, play with peers has received less attention in recent years. Hay, Payne, and Chadwick (2004) have suggested that "it is time for psychologists and psychiatrists to turn their attention once again to the serious study of fun. . . . Play with peers was once a major topic in developmental psychology, and deserves to be studied anew" (p. 100).

One explanation for the waning interest in play is that increasingly play is seen as something that simply takes time from the "important work" of childhood: academic learning (Pellegrini, 2005). For example, several years ago the U.S. government wanted to narrow the focus of the Head Start preschool program for disadvantaged children to one outcome: literacy. While literacy is definitely a core skill all children should have, this narrow focus ignores the developmental need that preschoolers have to learn through exploration and play (Zigler & Bishop-Josef, 2006).

Another indication of this shift in emphasis is the fact that schools are cutting back on recess or eliminating it altogether in favor of fitting more academic work into the day. However, there has also been a reaction to this pressure to remove play from the school curriculum because some educators are convinced that play and recess are essential to children's positive development, including their academic achievement. As Joan Almon (2003) of the Alliance for Childhood said, "The child's love of learning is intimately linked with a zest for play" (p. 18). The national Parent Teacher Association (PTA) was so concerned about the trend toward eliminating playtime that it began a program called Rescuing Recess to convince the 40% of public

TRUE/FALSE

2. It is important for children to play because they have fun when they are playing, but the real learning happens in the classroom.

    False. Children *do* have fun while they play, but it also is one important way that they learn about the world.

TRUE/FALSE

3. Educators in the United States agree that recess during the school day is important to allow students some "time out" to refresh themselves before returning to academic learning.

    False. About 40% of public schools have eliminated, or are planning to eliminate, recess. Educators and those who make educational policy increasingly see recess as simply time lost from academic programming.

schools that have eliminated or are planning to eliminate recess to rethink their priorities (PTA, 2006). Together with the Cartoon Network, the national organization has awarded thousands of dollars in grant money to PTAs around the country that participated in programs promoting recess.

Video Link 13.3
Recess.

In Chapter 7 we discussed Vygotsky's concept of private speech, which is when young children talk out loud to direct themselves. Fantasy play seems to promote this self-talk more than other activities do. In one study researchers observed children's play with their mothers. They found that children often incorporated what their mothers had said during play when they talked to themselves during their own private fantasy play (Haight & Miller, 1992). If you have been with preschoolers, you have most likely seen the way that they talk to themselves as they make-believe, giving voice to different characters and having whole conversations all by themselves. Krafft and Berk (1998) found that children used private speech twice as often in make-believe play as in other tasks and that children who took part in more make-believe play were more likely to use private speech to guide themselves during realistic tasks.

Fantasy play has been used as an intervention strategy to help young children learn preacademic skills. Together with colleagues, Dorothy Singer, professor of psychology at Yale University and a longtime proponent of the importance of make-believe play, developed a program called *My Magic Story Car* in which parents and caregivers of low-income children are taught to use fantasy play to help their children develop the skills necessary for school (Bellin & Singer, 2006). For example, in the Trip to Mars game, the parent or caregiver helps children teach Martian children about life on earth by creating a book explaining it in their own words. The children then fly to Mars and pretend to teach the Martian children how to use the book. Clearly, children should and do respond with more enthusiasm to this way of learning literacy than by using worksheets to learn letters. Research has shown this program to be successful in improving young children's school readiness.

Playtime continues to be important for school-age children. In Taiwan and Japan, whose educational systems are often praised for their high level of academic focus and achievement, children are given 10- to 15-minute breaks from their academic tasks each hour (Stevenson, Lee, & Chen, 1990). Research by Pellegrini (2005) has demonstrated that children become less attentive to their schoolwork the longer they go without a break. When they are allowed some free time for play during the school day, they return to their academic tasks with increased attention. One theory is that children have limited attention spans and go into cognitive overload after working continually on their academic tasks (Smith, 2010). Play helps children maintain their attention as a result of letting off steam during recess, and research has shown that children who have at least one recess during the day have better behavior while they are in class (Barros, Silver, & Stein, 2009). A final factor in regard to play and cognitive development is that children are intrinsically motivated to play. It is fun and they want to do it, rather than being forced to do it. Children who learn through play maintain their motivation for learning, rather than getting burned out as a result of the pressure put upon them by others to learn skills that would be learned just as well through this natural behavior of childhood.

We have made the argument that play supports children's development in physical skills and brain development, emotional expression,

Recess. In Japan and Taiwan, recess is seen as a very important part of the school day. When these children return to the classroom, will they be more or less ready to learn than children who have been working straight through?

A universal playground. This playground has been specifically designed to be accessible to all children and adults—both those with disabilities and those without. Look at the bottom photo carefully. What accommodations can you see? The young girl in the second photo has a chance to play that she would not have had on a normal playground with all its steps and uneven surfaces.

social skills, cognitive abilities, and motivation for learning. Clearly, play should be available for the benefit of all children. However, there are children for whom play may be limited because of disabilities. In the next section we will discuss one program designed to help all children play.

Playgrounds That Accommodate Children (and Adults) With Disabilities

Amy Jaffe Barzach's life changed after she saw a little girl in a wheelchair watching other children play on a playscape, unable to join in. If you imagine the usual playground available to children, you will quickly realize that children who cannot walk or who have other physical limitations would never be able to get to the slide or play on a swing. Barzach believed that play should be every child's right, and she set out to make it so. She developed a program called Boundless Playgrounds© that creates playgrounds accessible to all children, regardless of their physical and mental conditions. One such playground was established at an army base. Barzach quickly realized that typical playscapes also limit the interaction that parents with disabilities can have playing with their children in these places. In the Boundless Playground on the army base, soldiers who were missing limbs or who were in wheelchairs were able to join in the fun with their children, creating a priceless opportunity to cement the bonds that may have been threatened when a parent who has been gone for a long time returns to his or her family but is very changed.

Gender and Play

The social world of girls and the social world of boys have been described as "the two cultures of childhood" (Maccoby, 1998, p. 32). How you play and with whom you play are affected to some degree by whether you are a boy or a girl. Across many cultures, boys play with boys and girls play with girls; boys are more physically active and exploratory than girls, while girls may take part in more make-believe play; and toy choices differ between the two sexes.

By age 3, boys begin to prefer to play with children of their own gender (Fabes, Gaertner, & Popp, 2006). Although there is plenty of play that goes on that involves both boys and girls, the preference for same-sex play interaction has been found in many cultures and even among nonhuman primates (Maccoby, 2002). It becomes even stronger in middle childhood, especially for boys (Maccoby, 1990; Munroe & Romney, 2006). Gender segregation during play is most likely to happen when there are many children to choose from, for instance in school. At home and in neighborhoods, choices may be more limited, so more mixed gender play occurs (Thorne, 1994). Often a boy and girl who play happily together at home actually hide this fact from their peers to avoid being teased at school.

One of the reasons why boys and girls play separately is because they have different styles of play. Many girls do not like the rough kind of play preferred by many boys. Another possible reason is that boys do not respond to girls' style of communication during play, which is more likely to be in the form of suggestions rather than commands. When girls realize they can't influence boys as play partners, they turn to partners who *will* respond: other girls (Maccoby, 1990). Beginning at about age 5, many girls prefer to interact in pairs or small groups, while boys are more likely to interact in large groups and involve themselves in organized games or projects. As we pointed out in Chapter 12, this difference in group size means that boys and girls are also engaging in different types of interactions. Large groups involve cooperation and competition, and conflict and coordination, while small groups allow for intimate connection, with attention to the individual needs and feelings of the participants (Maccoby, 2002). Barrie Thorne's (1994) observations conducted on playgrounds showed that girl and boy groups played different games and the separation was policed by taunts directed at those who crossed the boundaries: "Johnny is a *girl!*" "Sarah and Carlos are in love!" Sexual attraction and its rejection are shown in chasing and kissing games between girls and boys.

Although we know that girls and boys tend to choose to play with other children of their own sex, there is a question whether this is due to a simple choice of someone who is physically like themselves or whether it results from common interests held by each gender. To examine this question, try **Active Learning: Gender Play Preferences**.

Video Link 13.4
Universal playground.

Gender Play Preferences

ACTIVE LEARNING

Interview a child between ages 4 and 8 using the following procedure, based on the *Playmate and Play Style Preferences Structured Interview* developed by Alexander and Hines (1994):

1. Prepare materials: Take four blank cards or pieces of paper. On two cards draw a plain stick figure. On the third card draw a "female" stick figure (for example, with a skirt and long hair) and on the fourth card draw a "male" stick figure (for example, with a cap and bow tie). Then take a few more cards, and on separate cards draw a few gender-stereotyped toys, such as a baby doll and a toy truck, and a few gender-neutral toys, such as a slide and a puzzle. (You could also glue pictures of toys from magazines or catalogs, if you prefer.)

2. After reassuring the child that there are no right or wrong answers to these questions, show the child the two plain stick figures, one paired with a male gender-typed toy and the other with a female gender-typed toy. Explain that each figure is a child and the toy shows what that child likes to play with. Then ask the child to pick which figure he or she would want to play with. Do this with several toy pairs. Then use the gender-identified stick figures with gender-neutral toys and ask which figure he or she would choose to play with. Finally, pair the gendered figures with opposite sex-typed toys and ask the child to choose the playmate they'd prefer.

Did the child prefer to play with a figure who was using toys stereotyped for his or her own gender? Did the child prefer to play with a child of his or her own gender? When forced to choose, did he or she select a child of the same gender or the child who played with the gender-stereotyped toy? Alexander and Hines (1994) found that boys consistently chose the activity regardless of whether a boy or a girl was playing with it, perhaps rejecting boys who play outside of the accepted range of activities. Younger girls (4–5 years old) chose to play with girls, regardless of the supposed toy preference of the figure. Older girls (6–8 years old) chose the activity over the gender of the figure.

Similar differences in play styles between boys and girls have been found for non-Western cultures. A study conducted in four non-Western cultures found that boys played farther from home than girls and engaged in more physical play (Munroe & Romney, 2006). In many cultures it has been found that boys' play is more likely to be exploratory than girls' play, perhaps because adults put more limitations on where girls can go on their own. For fourth-grade children in Bulgaria, Taiwan, and the United States, boys spent more time in free play and with computer games, while girls did more adult-chosen activities, chores, extracurricular activities, and reading (Newman et al., 2007). Girls also tend to engage in more make-believe play (Drewes, 2005). In one study, 3- to 5-year-old girls carried out twice as much pretend play as boys of the same age (Werebe & Baudonniere, 1991).

Extracurricular Activities

So far, we have focused on play, but as children grow older play gives way to other activities. Some of these activities are structured, such as sports, music lessons, and dramatic performances. Other activities are unstructured and include "hanging out" with friends and watching TV. Some concern has been raised that children are spending too much time in structured activities and too little time in unstructured play (Elkind, 2007b). Being overscheduled with structured activities does not allow enough time for child-structured play that promotes later creativity and imagination (Elkind, 2007b). However, there is some risk with too much unstructured time because some research has found that teens who spend more unstructured time with friends show more problem behaviors, such as theft, assault, and vandalism (Osgood, Wilson, O'Malley, Bachman, & Johnston, 1996). In this section, we will examine the pros and cons of each type of activity.

Video Link 13.5
Unstructured play.

Unstructured Time

In the past 50 years, the likelihood that children will just go outside to play with friends in the neighborhood has decreased. The author Bill Bryson (2006), in his memoir of growing up in the 1950s in Des Moines, Iowa, describes his experience when he went back to see his childhood home. See whether this description corresponds to your own experience in your neighborhood:

> My peerless Little League park, with its grandstand and press box, was torn down so that somebody could build an enormous apartment building in its place. A new, cheaper park was built . . . but the last time I went down there it was overgrown and appeared to be abandoned. There was no one to ask what happened because there are no people outdoors anymore—no kids on bikes, no neighbors talking over fences, no old men sitting on porches. Everyone is indoors. (p. 263)

Hanging out at the mall. Children and teens need some unstructured time to spend in activities that they choose. Although too much unsupervised time is associated with problem behaviors, some time to "hang out" and enjoy being with friends is a positive thing for young people.

Kleiber and Powell (2005) have described three reasons for this decline in unstructured, child-directed, outdoor play: safety concerns, media use, and paid work for teens. The first factor reflects a parental concern for safety. Children are less likely to be able to roam their neighborhood safely as more and more open space is developed, with more traffic as a result. Parents are also less likely to be home monitoring their children's behavior because both parents are working or there is only a single parent to manage the home.

Parents of teens are especially concerned about risky or negative behaviors that can result from unsupervised time spent with peers. When teens spend unstructured time socializing with peers away from adult supervision, the likelihood of criminal behavior, teen sexuality and pregnancy, and drug and alcohol use increases (Mahoney, Stattin, & Lord, 2004), but even those who argue for the value of structured activities acknowledge that children and teens need some unstructured time. Just as younger children need free time to play, adolescents need time to just "hang out." Unstructured time with peers allows adolescents to develop an identity separate from their parents and to learn how to manage themselves with their peers, and that includes some experimentation with somewhat risky behaviors. The trick is to provide teens with an appropriate balance of freedom along with structured time so that they develop a sense of self-direction while minimizing risk (Osgood, Anderson, & Shaffer, 2005). As teens get older, parents increasingly allow them to spend time away from home in unstructured time with peers, but this is truer for boys than for girls and for Whites than for African American teens (Osgood et al., 2005).

Another reason there is less child-structured, outdoor play is because a great deal of leisure time is taken up by television and, increasingly, by other media such as computers and video games. This issue was a topic of an episode of the television show *The Simpsons*. In this episode, the producers of the violent *Itchy & Scratchy Show* are persuaded to eliminate the violence from their cartoon. Children are so bored with the new "nice" show that they turn off their TVs and emerge from their homes to run around outside and play with friends (with a lyrical Beethoven symphony playing in the background). Of course, once Itchy and Scratchy return to their violent ways, the children return to the TV, and the neighborhoods are again empty (Swartzwelder, 1994).

Finally, as children reach adolescence, paid work takes over some of what was leisure time in childhood. Most teens who work report that they do not need to work, but are doing so in order to have extra money. In fact, middle-class adolescents are more likely to have paid employment than low-income adolescents (Casey, Ripke, & Huston, 2005). Unless the work the teen is doing is tied to the development of school-related skills, the evidence that employment promotes positive development for teenagers is mixed. Some research shows that teens who work have higher earnings 4 years after high school, but are less likely to succeed in higher education. However, for teens from low-income families, work was related to higher academic achievement, but had no effect on adult income level (Casey et al., 2005).

Adolescent employment. Most teens work to have extra money. What do you think are the benefits and the drawbacks of teen employment?

Structured Time

Some people have blamed the loss of unstructured playtime on the development of organized activities for children and teens, such as team sports, which were once just informal pick-up games but now are highly structured by adults. We'll look at the amount of time that children and adolescents spend in organized activities and the impact that different types of organized activities have on development.

4. Middle-class adolescents are more likely to have paid employment than low-income adolescents.

TRUE/FALSE

True. Middle-class adolescents have less leisure time because they are more likely to have paid employment than low-income adolescents. They generally work for extra spending money rather than out of necessity.

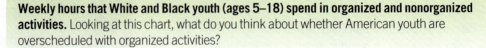

Figure 13.1

Weekly hours that White and Black youth (ages 5–18) spend in organized and nonorganized activities. Looking at this chart, what do you think about whether American youth are overscheduled with organized activities?

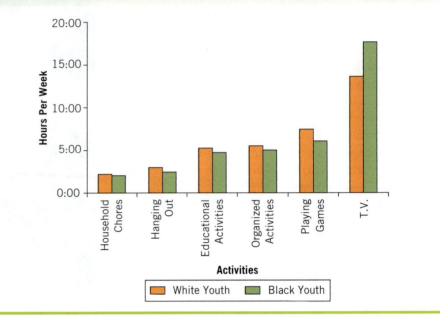

5. Many children and teens these days are overscheduled, spending most of their time after school in multiple organized activities, like sports and music lessons.

False. A minority of children and teens could be described as overscheduled, but 40% are not involved in any after-school activities.

The Amount of Scheduled Time

Although some people claim that children are "doing too much," research has shown that relatively few children appear to be overscheduled with organized activities. Figure 13.1 gives an overview of teen activities. According to Mahoney, Harris, and Eccles (2006), about 40% of children ages 5–18 do not participate in *any* organized, out-of-school activity, and most of the ones who do participate in such activities spend 10 hours a week or less on them. Not surprisingly, adolescents tend to be involved in more activities than younger children. In one national survey, 92.4% of American teens took part in at least one activity, 27.1% took part in one to three activities, 31.4% took part in four to six activities, and 33.9% participated in seven or more activities in the previous year (Substance Abuse and Mental Health Services Administration, Office of Applied Studies, 2007). However, Mahoney et al. (2006) found that only a small percentage (between 3% and 6%) of youth, ages 5–18, report spending more than 20 hours a week in organized activities. These authors conclude that only 1 in 10 children could be described as "overscheduled." It is true that 1 in 10 still might be too many, but overscheduling doesn't seem to be a typical pattern for children. Perhaps more important, when children and adolescents ages 9 through 19 were asked to describe *why* they participated in activities such as sports, after-school programs, clubs, and religious youth groups, the reasons they gave included enjoyment and excitement, encouragement and support from parents and friends, opportunities to challenge themselves and build skills, and anticipated social interactions with others. Mahoney et al. (2006) point out that in most cases it appears that children and adolescents have their own internal motivations for seeking out and participating in these experiences. Involvement in these activities is related to a number of positive outcomes for teens, including higher levels of achievement in school (high school graduation rates and entrance to college), lower levels of substance abuse, and better overall psychological adjustment (Mahoney et al., 2006).

For the small number of children and adolescents who are overscheduled, often by well-intentioned parents, there is a price to pay. According to David Elkind, the author of *The Power*

Organized activities. Children and adolescents get many benefits from participating in organized sports and activities, but the activities they participate in should be ones that the children enjoy, and adults need to be careful not to put too much pressure on them to perform. What organized activities influenced you when you were growing up, and in what ways did they impact your development?

of Play and *The Hurried Child*, "It may be intuitively clear to parents that they have to push kids because it's a very competitive world, but they may be doing more harm than good because they may not be nourishing the kinds of abilities and skills that are most necessary in today's world" (Joiner, 2007, para. 9). Elkind reminds us that children acquire other important skills such as creativity and innovation during free, unstructured playtime.

Mixed outcomes for teens' healthy development have been found for structured activities, so it is clear that these activities must be carefully planned if they are going to be beneficial rather than potentially harmful. Although such involvement is correlated with positive social and academic development, it also has been linked with higher rates of alcohol use in high school (Mahoney et al., 2006). Programs should be designed to occur during times when the teens would otherwise be hanging out with friends outside of adult supervision, usually the hours directly after the school day is over. Most problematic behavior for teens, including crime and sexuality, occurs between the hours of 3 and 6 in the afternoon (Osgood et al., 2005). One criticism of the midnight basketball program that became popular during the 1990s is that it took place when most of the teens would otherwise have been at home sleeping or watching television. Being on the streets together with peers after the program was over could actually become an opportunity for problem behavior (Osgood et al., 2005).

How do parents use this information? Moderation and balance are probably the keys. Beyond that, listening to your children to find out what they like and are interested in, encouraging them to try new things to expand their horizons and experiences but not pushing them to do what *you* want, and trying to find a balance between safe, constructive free playtime and organized activities is a very good start. In the next sections we will examine the nature and outcomes of two particular types of extracurricular activity: sports and the arts.

Organized Sports

Youth participation in sports encompasses a wide range of experiences. It can involve highly structured, adult-supervised, competitive activities, or it can involve informal activities organized by the children themselves that only loosely follow a set of rules. There are team sports like football, basketball, or hockey and individual sports like track, swimming, or gymnastics. Not all children want to participate in a team sport, but an individual sport can help them achieve many of the same benefits.

When sports are organized and supervised by adults, there is an opportunity for coaching and mentoring by positive adult role models. It also is likely that there will be rules to protect the safety of the participants, such as rules that determine eligibility or that match competitors by size or weight (American Academy of Pediatrics [AAP], 2001). The issue of safety in children's sports is not inconsequential. Sports-related injuries send 4 million children to the emergency room each year, and an additional 8 million are treated by family physicians (Engle, 2004). In a study of visits to emergency rooms in 25 states in 2006, the Health Care and Utilization Report determined that 1 in 5 visits for children between the ages of 5 and 17 were for sports-related injuries (Wier, Miller, & Steiner, 2009). As Figure 13.2 shows, the risk of sports-related injuries increases as children get older, and at all ages the risk is greater for boys than girls.

Connecting children and adolescents to positive role models is often listed as one of the benefits of participating in organized sports, but how adults see what they are doing in this role and how the children see it can be quite different. It is possible that coaches will have demands and expectations for performance that exceed the children's capabilities (AAP, 2001), which can result in frustration, stress, and a lowered sense of self-esteem for the participants. In one

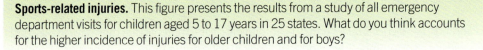

Figure 13.2

Sports-related injuries. This figure presents the results from a study of all emergency department visits for children aged 5 to 17 years in 25 states. What do you think accounts for the higher incidence of injuries for older children and for boys?

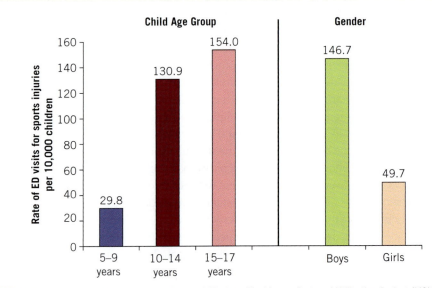

SOURCE: AHRQ, Center for Delivery, Organization, and Markets, Healthcare Cost and Utilization Project (HCUP), State Emergency Department Databases (SEDD) and State Inpatient Databases (SID) for the following 25 states: Arizona, California, Connecticut, Florida, Georgia, Hawaii, Indiana, Iowa, Kansas, Maine, Maryland, Minnesota, Missouri, Nebraska, New Hampshire, New Jersey, New York, Ohio, Rhode Island, South Carolina, South Dakota, Tennessee, Utah, Vermont, and Wisconsin; denominator data for rates were based on 2006 Claritas data for the 25 study states.

study of families involved in competitive hockey, mothers, fathers, and sons were asked to describe how much pressure parents exerted on their children and how much support the parents provided (Kanters, Bocarro, & Casper, 2008). Across all of the questions, the boys consistently reported feeling more pressure and perceiving less support than their parents reported. When there is this kind of lack of agreement between the experience of the children and the perception of the parents, it can become another source of stress that contributes to eventual burnout in the sport.

Most adults who volunteer their time to coach organized activities for children have the best interests of the children at heart, but many of them do not have experience working with children and adolescents and may not have a good understanding of child development. For example, as we saw when we discussed Piaget's stages of play in this chapter, very young children do not yet understand games with rules. Involving them in games like baseball can be an exercise in frustration because coaches and parents cannot understand why the child is playing with the dirt in the outfield rather than catching the ball! Even with older children, this misunderstanding of the child's developmental level sets up the possibility that what the adult is trying to accomplish and how the children interpret the coach's behavior are very different. You can see how, with the best intentions, an adult coach might push a young player, thinking that this push will help the child develop skills or will give him or her a sense of accomplishment, but the pushing is not seen in that same way by the child, who is just looking for a way to have fun and spend some time with friends.

While children find a lot to like and respect about their coaches, they also see a dark side. When children who were participating in sports programs were asked what they *liked* about their coaches, they said their coach was nice, was fair, and "teaches us good things" (for boys) or "helps us play better" (for girls). However, when they were asked what they *liked least* about their coaches, they said the coach "gets mad and yells at us," "works us too hard," "does not let me play enough" (for boys), or "doesn't teach us much" (for girls) (Humphrey, 2003, p. 58). Coaches may not be aware of how their well-intended efforts to "motivate" their players are seen by their young players.

If we think of organized sports as a way to keep children physically active and to set a pattern of lifelong physical activity, it is sad to note that 70% of children drop out of organized sports by the age of 13 (Engle, 2004). Maybe we could improve the retention rate if we listened more to what children are telling us about their experiences. As we've seen, it sounds like emphasizing skills, teamwork, and fun (rather than winning) is a good way to start to put some of the spontaneity and joy back into organized sports for children and teens.

6. Children who participate in organized sports develop skills that they use to keep them physically active throughout their lifetime.

TRUE/FALSE

False. Of children who participate in organized sports, 70% drop out by age 13. Children may be more likely to continue sports and types of physical activity that are not team-based into adulthood because they can do these things on their own.

Positive youth development An approach to finding ways to help all young people reach their full potential.

Positive Youth Development

In recent years a new way of thinking about development has emerged, and it has added a great deal to our understanding of the role that activities play in the lives of young people. This approach is often called the **positive youth development** approach because its primary focus is on finding ways to help young people reach their full potential (Catalano, Berglund, Ryan, Lonczak, & Hawkins, 1998; U.S. Department of Health and Human Services [USDHHS], 2007). Participation in well-planned and supervised activities can do far more than help children avoid the pitfalls associated with too much unsupervised time; it can promote positive youth development (Eccles & Templeton, 2002; National Research Council and Institute of Medicine, 2004;

Developmental assets. A relationship with a supportive and caring adult is one of the developmental assets identified by the Search Institute as a way to promote positive youth development.

Roeser & Peck, 2003). For instance, Roeser and Peck (2003) looked at patterns of involvement in positive activities in a group of adolescents who were at risk of academic failure. They found that vulnerable youth who were involved in high levels of both school and community sports activities were twice as likely to graduate high school and go on to college as students who did not have this level of involvement.

For a long time in the field of child development, we were primarily concerned about problems that affected our young people. Dropping out of school, juvenile delinquency, teenage pregnancy, and substance abuse were the kinds of issues that captured people's attention. Once we became aware of the magnitude of these problems, the next step was to think about ways that they could be fixed. There have been many efforts over the years to develop intervention programs that would remediate or rehabilitate children and adolescents who had these problems. As these attempts continued, our emphasis slowly shifted from *fixing* problems to trying to find ways to *prevent* them. Effort and energy then went into designing and implementing programs that were intended to support youth in ways that could prevent problems from developing in the first place (Catalano et al., 1998). Increasingly we have tried to understand the origins of problems and to target the risk factors for those problems so we can steer the developmental pathway in a new and better direction.

Deficit model of youth development The assumption that problems are caused by something lacking in the child or teen that needs to be fixed.

Both intervention programs and prevention programs use a **deficit model of youth development** (Lerner, Brentano, Dowling, & Anderson, 2002). The assumption is that there is something in the person that is lacking or missing. A positive youth development approach is based on a different way of thinking about how young people grow into adulthood. Similar to the way that people recognize that health is more than the absence of illness, we now recognize that positive youth development is more than the absence of problems (Catalano et al., 1998). This approach strives to identify the people, contexts, circumstances, and activities that help youth develop to their maximum potential. When organizations and communities give children and adolescents the chance to exercise leadership, to build their skills, and to get involved in positive and productive activities, youth have the building blocks that they need to grow into "healthy, happy, self-sufficient adults" (USDHHS, 2007, para. 1).

Developmental assets Common sense positive experiences and qualities that help young people become caring, responsible adults.

The Search Institute in Minneapolis has been a leader in identifying what these building blocks are. It has identified a set of 40 **developmental assets**. It defines a developmental asset as "common sense, positive experiences and qualities that help influence choices young people make and help them become caring, responsible adults" (Search Institute, n.d., para. 1). Constructive use of time is one of the sets of assets the Search Institute has identified, and this is how it describes those activities:

- Creative activities—Young person spends 3 or more hours per week in lessons or practice in music, theater, or other arts.
- Youth programs—Young person spends 3 or more hours per week in sports, clubs, or organizations at school and/or in the community.
- Religious community—Young person spends 1 or more hours per week in activities in a religious institution.
- Time at home—Young person is out with friends "with nothing special to do" two or fewer nights per week.

To determine how many adolescents have these assets in their lives, the Search Institute has administered its Attitudes and Behaviors survey to almost 150,000 youth in Grades 6–12 living in 202 communities across the United States. Based upon those survey data, the Search Institute has found that 21% of the youth surveyed said they participated in creative activities at least at the level that the Search Institute considers adequate to support youth development, 57% participate in youth programs, 58% participate in a religious community, and 51% do not spend more than 2 days a week outside of their home just "hanging out" with friends. These numbers indicate that for many young people, there still is room in their lives for higher levels of participation in various activities in their community that can support their positive development, and there is particularly room for more adolescents to find creative outlets through the arts.

In the previous section we noted that 70% of youth drop out of organized sports by the age of 13. If you have ever participated in organized sports, you probably know some of the reasons why. As you move from one level of competition to another—from elementary to middle school, then to high school, and possibly even to college—the skill level required to effectively compete gets greater and greater, and so does the commitment of time and energy required to be successful. In contrast, if you look at the kind of activities included on the list of developmental assets, you will see that many of them are lifelong activities. Young people who develop their creativity or become active in their communities or at their place of worship can continue to be engaged in these activities as they move through adolescence and into adulthood.

Creative Activities

Creative activities, such as painting, music, dance, and drama, are avenues for the expression of thoughts and emotions for people of all ages. Creative activities are also used as a very important part of positive youth development, helping children and adolescents express themselves and become involved with

Teens in the arts. What benefits do you think these teens may get from involvement in this play?

their peers both within and outside of their schools, with the supervision of a caring and often skilled adult.

Compared to the amount of research done on unstructured time and structured activities such as sports, there is relatively little research on participation in creative activities such as art, music, or drama. Much of the work that has been published has been theoretical rather than empirical (Gullatt, 2008). The most relevant theory for understanding the impact of creative activities on development is Howard Gardner's theory of multiple intelligences. You'll remember from Chapter 8 that Gardner proposed that there are different types of intelligence and that any individual can be strong or weak on any of them. While academic subjects in school typically emphasize logical-mathematical and linguistic intelligences, creative arts rely on and enhance others, such as musical intelligence, spatial intelligence, and bodily-kinesthetic intelligence (Gullatt, 2008).

Participating in the arts, whether it is through lessons or group performances, may be associated with many different outcomes for children and adolescents, but the information on the relationship between participation in the arts and academic achievement is mixed (Gullatt, 2008). Recent research on music training in children has shown that children who take music lessons show changes in their brain structure in regard to musical perception, and they also show more general improvements in auditory and language skills (Ho, Cheung, & Chan, 2003; Hyde et al., 2009; Lappe, Herholz, Trainor, & Pantev, 2008; Moreno et al., 2009). How these effects translate into actual school performance is not yet clear.

Art enrichment programs, which add creative art to the existing curriculum, have helped low-income preschoolers develop their school readiness skills (Brown, Benedett, & Armistead, 2010) and English-language learners develop their literacy skills (Rieg & Paquette, 2009). The advantage may come from the fact that these enhancement activities engage different modes of learning. A child with high musical intelligence, in Gardner's terms, but lower logical-mathematical skills may learn about math more easily through the use of music. However, Elliott Eisner (1998) claims that much of the research that purports to find positive effects for school-based programs is poorly conducted and does not provide strong support for them. What he suggests instead is that the goals of art educators should be to help children and adolescents develop their sense of aesthetics. In his view, the goal should be to create dispositional changes, meaning that we help children develop "a willingness to imagine possibilities . . . a desire to explore ambiguity . . . [and] . . . to recognize and accept the multiple perspectives and resolutions that work in the arts celebrate[s]" (pp. 14–15). In other words, we teach and do art for art's sake because it is a central aspect of the human experience.

Larson and Brown (2007) looked in detail at a group of teens who were involved in a theater program. They found three characteristics that described this program: (a) a high level of commitment by all involved, (b) clear expectations that the creative process would raise strong emotions, and (c) provision of emotional support. They found that the teens learned valuable lessons about understanding and managing emotions. They found new ways to deal with frustration as well as celebrate successes together.

Strong bonds and a positive group identity can be created among teens involved in group performances, whether they are dramatic, musical, or dance performances. Creating a play or a musical program has been found to be an effective way to bring students from many different backgrounds together with a common goal, while drawing upon a variety of their talents. Often they gain a new respect for the people they work with, regardless of their background. The public recognition that comes from a performance serves as a source of pride for those who take part in it. Dutton (2001) has found that goals of positive youth development, including exploration in a safe environment, a sense of connection to others and of contribution to something worthwhile, and a feeling of competence, are all enhanced by involvement in the arts.

Media Use

7. Most families do not have any rules related to television viewing for their children.

True. More than half of the families in one survey on television viewing said they have no rules for their children regarding what they watch or how much they watch.

In addition to play and structured activities, the third use of leisure time we will discuss is the growing role of media. When we discuss media, we include electronic sources like television, computers, and iPods as well as nonelectronic sources such as books and magazines. Although there is now a 50-year history of research on children and electronic media, mainly television, this is an area that is changing rapidly. The new electronic media have been hailed as great innovations, but also are viewed with suspicion regarding what their effects on children and adolescents will be. In this section we will look at the effects of media use that have been examined through research so far in this quickly changing field. We will begin by taking a look at what surveys have shown about how much and what type of media American children are using.

In spite of the explosion of new forms of media, TV still takes more time in children's lives than any other form. Based on a national sample of 8- to 18-year-olds in 2009, the Kaiser Family Foundation (KFF) found that children are watching an average of almost 4 and a half hours of TV and videos or DVDs per day, some of it on handheld devices such as a cell phone (Rideout, Foehr, & Roberts, 2010). This compares to 1 hour and 45 minutes of physical activity per day and 40 minutes of reading books, magazines, and newspapers. In almost half of homes the television is always on and rules set by parents for media use tend to monitor content, not amount of time (Rideout et al., 2010). In those families that do have rules about media use, children use media an average of almost 3 hours less per day. A reduction of just 1 hour a day is the equivalent of 365 hours in just 1 year, or more than 2 full weeks, so it is not an inconsequential amount of time to shift to other activities. Seventy-one percent of American children have a TV in their bedroom. These children spend significantly more time watching TV and less time reading than those who do not have their own TVs, although the average amount of time spent reading for both groups is less than 1 hour per day.

Table 13.2

Forms of electronic communication. This table summarizes common forms of electronic communication used by large numbers of children and adolescents. Newer technologies can continue to be added to this list.

Communication Form	Electronic Hardware That Supports It	Functions Enabled
E-mail	Computers, cell phones, personal digital assistants (PDAs)	Write, store, send, and receive asynchronous messages electronically; can include attachments of Word documents, pictures, audio, and other multimedia files
Instant messaging	Computers, cell phones, PDAs	Allows for the synchronous exchange of private messages with another user; messages primarily are in text but can include attachments of Word documents, pictures, audio, and other multimedia files
Text messaging	Cell phones, PDAs	Short text messages sent using cell phones and wireless handheld devices
Chat rooms	Computers	Synchronous conversations with more than one user that primarily involve text; can be either public or private
Bulletin boards	Computers	Online public spaces, typically centered on a topic (such as health, illnesses, religion), where people can post and read messages; many require registration, but only screen names are visible (such as www.collegeconfidential.com)
Blogs	Computers	Websites where entries are typically displayed in reverse chronological order (such as www.livejournal.com); entries can be either public or private only for users authorized by the blog owner/author
Social networking utilities	Computers	Online utilities that allow users to create profiles (public or private) and form a network of friends; allow users to interact with their friends via public and private means (such as messages, instant messaging); also allow for the posting of user-generated content such as photos and videos (such as www.facebook.com)
Video sharing	Computers, cell phones, cameras with wireless	Allows users to upload, view, and share video clips (such as www.youtube.com)
Photo sharing	Computers, cell phones, cameras with wireless	Allows users to upload, view, and share photos (such as www.flickr .com); users can allow either public or private access
Massively multiplayer online games (MMOGs)	Computers	Online games that can be played by large numbers of players simultaneously; the most popular type are the massively multiplayer online role-playing games (MMORPGs) such as *World of Warcraft*
Virtual worlds	Computers	Online simulated 3-D environments inhabited by players who interact with each other via avatars (such as Teen Second Life)

You can add other types of electronic technologies not included in the table here:

Multitasking. When we split our attention between different tasks (for example, reading a book while watching TV), we lower our capacity to process information, and we retain less information. However, many of us still do it anyway, don't we?

Multitasking Doing several different activities at the same time, often involving several forms of media.

Video Link 13.6
Multitasking.

Although TV is still the most frequently used medium, media use is constantly changing as new technologies develop at a faster and faster rate. Subrahmanyam and Greenfield's most current (2008) description of electronic media used by youth is found in Table 13.2, but you can add at the bottom of the list any newer technologies you are using that were developed after this list was made.

Not only are children and teens using more different forms of media than in the past, but they are also more likely to use several of these forms at the same time, a process known as **multitasking**. The Pew Internet & American Life Project carried out phone surveys in 2000 with 754 youth aged 12 to 17 years old concerning their use of the Internet and found that teens were often multitasking: instant messaging three or more people and also e-mailing, surfing the web, and talking on the phone. One 17-year-old girl in an online group discussion stated: "I get bored if it's not all going at once, because everything has gaps—waiting for someone to respond to an IM [instant message], waiting for a website to come up, commercials on TV, etc." (Lenhart, Rainie, & Lewis, 2001, p. 13). In 2010, the Kaiser Family Foundation (KFF) found that children and teens were using media for almost 7 and a half hours per day. Because they used more than one media source at a time, this accounted for 10 hours and 45 minutes of media content daily (Rideout et al., 2010). As we will see later in this chapter, all of this multitasking of electronic media may have implications for children's developing ability to focus intensely and for long periods of time on just one thing, such as reading a book or doing a homework assignment. Even more frightening, teens believe that they can use electronic media successfully while they are driving. Recent studies have shown that teens who talk on cell phones while driving have delayed reaction times to events on the road, waver between lanes, and are much more likely to have an accident. Teens who text message while driving increase their chances of being in an accident even more (Drews, Yazdani, Godfrey, Cooper & Strayer, 2009).

While the KFF study found that 8- to 18-year-olds read voluntarily for an average of 40 minutes a day, the situation seems to worsen in late adolescence, declining from 46 to 33 minutes of reading per day (note that this does not include time spent reading for school). A survey by the National Endowment for the Arts (2007) showed that in all age groups and at all levels of education, the ability to read well fell significantly between 1992 and 2003, which is hardly surprising given that reading itself promotes proficiency. The more we read, the better we become at reading.

Clearly children's and teens' use of electronic media fills many hours of their day. With the increasing mobility of these media, through laptop computers, electronic notebooks, iPods, iPhones, and whatever the next innovation is, it is likely that media will continue to play a bigger and bigger role in their lives. However, although the statistics give a clear impression of extensive media use by children and teens, averages hide the fact that there are significant numbers of children who use media only infrequently. For example, 21% of those surveyed by KFF reported watching no TV on an average day (Rideout et al., 2010), so we should not assume that all children are "plugged in." When we look at the effects of media use, we will see that the amount, as well as the type and content, of media used has consequences in many areas of development.

We will start by reviewing the evidence concerning the impact that media use has on children's physical, cognitive, and social development and on their self-concept. We conclude this section with a discussion about media literacy, or how children can be taught to understand the effects of media in order to use it most effectively and with the least harm to their ongoing development.

Media and Physical Development

There has been a good deal of research that has linked television viewing with obesity, a problem that affects about 20% of children and teens in the United States, as we saw in Chapter 6. Using a national sample, Crespo et al. (2001) found a significant relation between amount of television viewed by children 8 to 16 years of age and the prevalence of obesity. The assumption has been that children eat more and are less active when they sit in front of the TV, but the evidence is mixed about which factor is most important (Epstein et al., 2008; Jago, Baranowski, Baranowski, Thompson, & Greaves, 2005; Taveras et al., 2007). However, whether it is from reduced exercise or increased eating, there is a growing body of evidence that watching more television appears to cause greater problems with weight as children grow and develop, so limiting their television viewing should be helpful and healthful under any circumstances.

TV viewing and obesity. There is an association between the amount of TV children watch and their weight. Whether it is because children eat while they are watching TV or because watching TV keeps them from being more physically active is still an open question, but both factors are probably at work.

It is ironic that watching television contributes to obesity in children, while at the same time promoting the concept of thinness as the ideal for everyone, especially girls and women. Messages from the media are implicated in the increase in body dissatisfaction and eating disorders that we see among girls and increasingly among boys (Grabe, Ward, & Hyde, 2008). In Chapter 6 we described some factors, such as early puberty, that may underlie the development of anorexia nervosa or bulimia, but that list needs to include the influence of images in movies, in magazines, and on TV that promote the **thin ideal**. The relationship between thin ideal messages and eating disorders in teenage girls has been well documented (Harrison, 2000; Thompson & Heinberg, 1999). The impact of television on bulimic symptoms was demonstrated on the island of Fiji. Before television was introduced, 3% of girls had such symptoms. Three years after TV was introduced, 15% of girls used vomiting to control weight. Although there could be other variables that changed along with the introduction of TV on the island, it does appear that the introduction of the Western thin ideal affected Fiji women's traditional idea of the beauty of a more rounded body (Walcott, Pratt, & Patel, 2003).

Media, Cognitive Development, and Academic Achievement

Not all television viewing has the same effect on children's development. There is evidence that educational TV improves cognitive functioning and academic performance for some children, while entertainment TV makes academic performance worse. However, with infants there is *no evidence* that TV of any kind is helpful (Kirkorian, Wartella, & Anderson, 2008). The American Academy of Pediatrics Committee on Public Education (2001) recommends that pediatricians "discourage television-viewing for children younger than 2 years and encourage more interactive activities that will promote proper brain development, such as talking, playing, singing, and reading together" (p. 424). While 32% of children under 2 do not watch any screen-based programming, 68% do watch TV (Vandewater et al., 2007), and 43% watch TV, including recorded programming, every day (Rideout & Hamel, 2006). The research evidence shows that infants and toddlers learn much more effectively from real-life interaction than from on-screen programs (Anderson & Pempek, 2005; Krcmar, Grela, & Lin, 2007). Babies age 8–16 months who watched videotapes designed specifically to improve cognitive development, such as the Baby Einstein videos, actually had smaller vocabularies than those who did not (Zimmerman, Christakis, &

Thin ideal The idea that it is best for girls and women to be thin.

8. Babies 8 to 16 months of age who watch videotapes designed to improve cognitive development (like Baby Einstein videos) have larger vocabularies than babies who don't watch these videos.

 TRUE/FALSE

False. In fact, babies who watch these videotapes have *smaller* vocabularies than babies who don't watch them. Babies learn best when they are interacting with other people, not watching videotapes. The American Academy of Pediatrics recommends that children under 2 not watch *any* screen media.

Meltzoff, 2007). Although the reasons behind this relationship are not clear, it is possible that parents are talking less to children when they are watching these videos.

Even when young children are not watching TV, but the TV is on in the background, their play is disrupted. When 1- to 3-year-old children played with background TV on, their play episodes lasted for shorter periods of time and they were less able to focus their attention on their play than when there was no TV on (Schmidt, Pempek, Kirkorian, Lund, & Anderson, 2008). Think about being in a room or a restaurant where a TV is on that you are not even watching. Do you find your eyes drawn to the TV over and over again, distracting you from your conversation or other work? The same appears to be true for young children, to the detriment of their ability to develop their play.

From age 2 on, educational (but not entertainment) TV does seem to affect learning in a positive way. For example, research on *Sesame Street* has found even greater positive effects on preacademic skills when children watched beginning at ages 2 and 3 rather than at age 4 (Wright, Huston, Scantlin, & Kotler, 2001). Although there are many educational programs on television, *Sesame Street* has included a research component since the very beginning of its programming and, as a result, has more research on its effectiveness than any other program. See **Journey of Research: Educational TV and *Sesame Street*** for additional information about the history and effectiveness of *Sesame Street*.

Sesame Street around the world. In November 2009, *Sesame Street* celebrated its 40th anniversary. It now appears in 120 countries around the world. In each country, the cast of Muppets is adapted to the local culture. In 2002, *Sesame Street* in South Africa introduced Kami, a Muppet who is living with HIV.

JOURNEY of RESEARCH

Educational TV and *Sesame Street*

Our romance with the television set began in the mid-1900s. Although the television had been invented in the 1930s, production of TV sets was halted during World War II. After the war, production resumed and sales of 44,000 TV sets in 1947 quickly became over 8,000,000 TV sets in the homes of American families by the late 1950s (Levine & Waite, 2002). Even when television was first introduced, attempts were made to produce educational programs for children. In those days, the format often involved a teacher leading activities such as one might find in a preschool or kindergarten. The teachers in these programs were not trained actors, and surveys at that time showed that children greatly preferred commercial TV to these early educational TV shows (Lemish, 2007).

In 1964, President Lyndon Johnson made a speech at the graduation ceremony at the University of Michigan declaring the War on Poverty and the creation of the Great Society, dedicated to the well-being of all its citizens. At this point it had become apparent that children who lived in poverty entered kindergarten at a great disadvantage compared with other children. One government program that resulted from the War on Poverty was the preschool program Head Start, which we described in Chapter 8. However, Head Start could not serve all the children who could benefit from it. Research by Joan Ganz Cooney for the Carnegie Corporation found that preschoolers were watching a great deal of television every day (Friedman, 2006) and the vast majority of American homes had a television, regardless of their income level.

Cooney and her colleagues developed the idea that a different kind of TV show could be used to engage and teach young children, especially those being raised in poverty, to help get them ready for school. She developed the Children's Television Workshop (now called the Sesame Workshop), which used research to determine the most effective ways to teach young children. Bringing together top educators, psychologists, and television producers, the group used the latest research to determine how children would best learn from this relatively new medium (Lemish, 2007). From the observation that children are greatly attracted to watching commercials, the Sesame Workshop developed a show that would use the same techniques found in commercials, such as short segments, bright colors, and music, but with educational, rather than commercial, goals in mind. With the addition of Jim Henson's Muppets, this show became *Sesame Street*, which first aired in 1969 (Friedman, 2006; Williams-Rautiolla, 2008).

Today the U.S. version of *Sesame Street* is watched by about 8 million people each week, but *Sesame Street* has gone far beyond the borders of the United States. Twenty versions of the show appear in 120 countries around the world (Friedman, 2006). In each version, *Sesame Street* staff members from the United States work together with local producers, artists, and actors to create a program appropriate for that culture.

Sesame Street sets very specific goals based on research-supported knowledge about children's development. For example, it has been shown that children learn more from TV when they interact with an adult about what they've seen, so *Sesame Street* has designed segments that will engage parents as well as their preschoolers (Wright et al., 2001). One way that *Sesame Street* does this is through its use of adult-level humor and content. For example, one segment introduces the letter *B* with a voice singing "Letter B" to the tune of The Beatles' song "Let It Be" and another segment plays on the popular TV series *Desperate Housewives* with the title *Desperate Houseplants*. Three- and 4-year-old children are not going to understand these jokes, but their parents will. The idea has been to encourage parents to watch with their children so they can discuss and reinforce what the show teaches.

Sesame Street is designed to teach preacademic skills that prepare children for reading, writing, and arithmetic, so each show is "sponsored" by a particular letter and number, but the show teaches much more than preacademic skills. For example, diversity has always been a central value, with characters from all backgrounds represented in the cast. *Sesame Street* also has not shied away from the big issues that impact children's lives. For example, in South Africa, on *Takalani Sesame,* the show introduced a Muppet character, Kami, who was HIV positive and showed both the prejudice Kami experienced and the love and fun the character could have with others (Hawthorne, 2002). "Social, moral and affective" teaching goals have guided the programming throughout *Sesame Street*'s history (Mielke, 2001, p. 84).

There is much research evidence that watching *Sesame Street* does make a difference for young children who would otherwise be unprepared for entering school. These children were more prepared to learn to read and to do arithmetic, and this seemed to be truly a result of watching the show and not a result of other variables, such as how educated parents were or how much they read to their children. This advantage continued even through high school. Children who watched the program at age 5 had higher grades in English, math, and science in high school (Huston, Anderson, Wright, Linebarger, & Schmitt, 2001; Schmidt & Anderson, 2007). You might wonder how watching one TV series could have such a long-term effect. Longitudinal research has shown that watching *Sesame Street* is related not just to preacademic skills but also to a greater sense of competence, less aggression, and more motivation for academic achievement (Huston et al., 2001). Teens who are less aggressive can take part in school more effectively, feel good about what they are accomplishing there, and maintain their motivation to achieve.

Criticisms of *Sesame Street* have focused on the fast pacing of the program, which some have claimed may contribute to shortening the attention span of the children who watch it. However, research by Anderson, Levin, and Lorch (1977) found no immediate effects of pacing in *Sesame Street* on impulsivity or task persistence, and these researchers argue that the increase in academic competence for those who watch the show is evidence that attention is not harmed.

Sesame Street remains a major force in children's educational television. To keep pace with rapidly changing media, today *Sesame Street* has added a website (http://www.sesameworkshop.org) with podcasts, computer games, and other activities and ideas for parents and caregivers to help children develop all types of abilities that will help when they enter school.

9. The fast pace used on the television program *Sesame Street* shortens the attention span of children who watch it. **TRUE/FALSE**

False. The fast pace of *Sesame Street* does not seem to shorten children's attention span. To the contrary, children who watch this program have increased academic competence, so the pace must be working for them.

Orienting response   The tendency to pay attention automatically to novel, moving, meaningful, or surprising stimuli.

Television programs are designed to grab and hold your attention. To do so, they take advantage of a natural tendency we have to respond automatically to "novel, moving, meaningful, or surprising" stimuli, which is called the **orienting response** (Diao & Sundar, 2004, p. 539). Our minds are designed to react, or orient, to anything new in the environment so we can evaluate what our response to it should be. Television uses editing to make us attend to the images on the screen. "Jump cuts" (shifting from one scene to another) are used to provide motion, novelty, and surprise that keep attracting our attention. In the early days of TV, there was just one camera that stayed in place and focused on one scene for a long time. As technology developed, directors began to move the camera and "jump" from one scene to another. These jumps elicit the orienting response and draw the viewer's attention. However, over time, as people got used to these scene shifts, they became less novel and surprising. TV programs, and in particular commercials, which are designed to make the viewer pay attention to their product, began to pick up the pace in order to grab the viewer's attention. TV producer Quinn Martin has said, "As commercials got people used to absorbing information quickly, I had to change my style to give them more jump cuts or they'd be bored. . . . The whole art form has speeded up" (Kubey & Csikszentmihalyi, 1990, p. 140). You can examine the pacing of children's programming for yourself in **Active Learning: The Pace of TV**.

ACTIVE LEARNING

The Pace of TV

While you are watching your favorite television show, place a check mark on a sheet of paper each time there is a shift from one scene or point of view to another. Note the name and type of show, and the time you start and finish. In a different place on your paper, record the same information on pacing during the commercials, making note of when the commercial started and finished. See if there is a difference when you average the number of jump cuts per minute for the show and the commercial.

Finally, watch a children's television show to compare the number of jump cuts or scene shifts shown to children. You may be surprised at how many jump cuts are found. Each one is designed to capture your attention by activating your orienting response so that you do not turn away from the TV. Compare your findings with those of others in your class. Were there differences in pacing between different types of shows or between the adult- and child-oriented shows? Did violent shows have more or fewer jump cuts than nonviolent shows? Becoming aware of the techniques used in media to affect you in this and a variety of ways is the beginning of what is known as media literacy.

Although educational TV has been shown to have a positive effect on children's cognitive development and school achievement, entertainment TV, which is the majority of viewing for school-age children, appears to have a negative effect. Other recreational media, such as video games, also are linked with poorer school performance. There are several explanations that have been proposed to explain this link. The simplest is that children and teens may be spending their time using media in place of doing homework (Van Evra, 2004). This idea found support from a national sample surveyed by the Kaiser Family Foundation, in which light TV viewers spent more time each day doing homework, while children who used media more spent less time doing work for school (Rideout, Roberts, & Foehr, 2005).

Particularly in the early years, when children are learning to read, school achievement declines as the amount of entertainment TV viewing increases (Schmidt & Anderson, 2007). Shin (2004) found that the more TV 6- to 13-year-olds watched, the less leisure reading, homework, and studying they did, but Huston, Wright, Marquis, and Green (1999) found this relationship only for entertainment TV, not educational TV. MacBeth

(1996) found that the more television Canadian children watched, the fewer books they read, and the poorer their reading skills were. Other media besides TV may also displace time spent doing homework. In a somewhat older sample consisting of 8- to 18-year-olds, the Kaiser Family Foundation also found that heavier media users had lower grades, and they were also less happy, more likely to be bored, and more likely to get into trouble than medium or light media users (Rideout et al., 2010). There is growing support for the idea that time spent on recreational media is cutting into time that could be spent—perhaps could be *better* spent—doing homework.

A second possible reason for a link between media use and lower academic performance is that many children and teens are using a variety of types of media *while* they are doing their homework. The KFF study found that almost one third of 8- to 18-year-olds said they multitask most of the time while doing homework (Rideout et al., 2010). But, similar to the distracting effect that a TV in the background had on preschoolers, TV that is on in the background can affect academic performance in older children. A study by Pool, Koolstra, and van der Voort (2003) in the Netherlands found that high school students who did an academic task while soap operas were shown on television took longer to carry out the task than those with no distractions and had less understanding of the material they had studied. One possible explanation is that distraction, such as a TV show, engages working memory and reduces its capacity to process other information so that less information can be put into the memory system (Foerde, Knowlton, & Poldrack, 2006). Try **Active Learning: Studying and Distractions** to see whether your studying style is interfering with how efficiently you study.

Studying and Distractions

ACTIVE LEARNING

1. Set a goal of reading 10 pages of this textbook when you are likely to have distractions. Note the time when you start reading. Every time you are interrupted, note how long the interruption lasts and write down what the interruption was. Be sure to include when you interrupt yourself by text messaging someone, getting a snack, making a phone call, looking up at the TV, and so forth. Write down the time when you finish reading the 10 pages. Subtract your starting time from your ending time and then subtract the total time it took for all of the interruptions.

2. Now find a time and place to read 10 more pages of this textbook where you are reasonably certain not to be interrupted and not to be tempted to interrupt yourself. Write down the time that you start reading and the time that you finish the 10 pages. Subtract to find out how long it took you.

3. Compare the results of studying both ways. Was one way more efficient than the other?

Bowman, Levine, Waite, and Gendron (2010) found that students who were interrupted with instant messages while reading a textbook online took much longer than students who were not interrupted to do the same amount of reading. If you are used to studying with the television, computer, and cell phone on, look at your results and decide for yourself whether the interruptions made you slower. You may want to consider putting off your other activities until you have finished studying. The end result is likely to be more efficient studying and more free time for you!

A third possible reason for a link between media use and poor academic performance is that children are having more difficulty focusing attention on just one thing in depth because they are used to the attention-grabbing techniques used on television. Geist and Gibson (2000) found that preschoolers were more likely to jump from one play object to the next after they watched entertainment television rather than educational TV or no TV. Longitudinal studies have found that the amount of TV that preschoolers, school-age children, and teens watch is associated with attention problems later in their lives (Johnson, Cohen, Kasen, & Brook, 2007; Landhuis, Poulton, Welch, & Hancox, 2007; Zimmerman & Christakis, 2007). Shin (2004) found that children who watched more TV were more impulsive and this impulsiveness contributed to poorer school performance. Although it is clear that TV viewing and attention problems are correlated, the question of causality remains unanswered. The studies above suggest that TV viewing comes before the development of attention problems. However, Acevedo-Polakovich, Lorch, and Milich (2007) argue that children with severe attention problems that result in a diagnosis of attention deficit hyperactivity disorder choose to watch more TV than other children because TV is one of the few things that will hold these children's attention. However, these researchers still recommend removing the TV from children's bedrooms in order to limit the amount they watch.

Media and Social Development

Aggression and Prosocial Behavior

The study of media's impact began with Albert Bandura's study on aggression described in Chapter 2, in which children watched an adult attack a Bobo doll. Since that time "a clear and consistent pattern of empirical results has emerged from over four decades of research on the effects of media violence," namely that watching violence or taking part in media violence promotes aggression in young viewers (Gentile, 2003, p. ix). Meta-analyses, in which the results of many studies can be combined, demonstrate clearly that media violence promotes aggression and antisocial behavior (Comstock & Scharrer, 2003). Two of these studies demonstrate such findings specifically with regard to television. In one study, Christakis and Zimmerman (2007) followed children longitudinally and concluded that viewing violent television at ages 2–5 was linked with greater aggression at ages 7–10. In another study children were assigned to watch either Batman and Superman cartoons or *Mr. Rogers' Neighborhood* over a period of 4 weeks. The researchers found that watching Batman and Superman increased aggressive behavior for children who were already more aggressive, while *Mr. Rogers' Neighborhood* increased prosocial behavior (Friedrich & Stein, 1973). This relationship has been found for teens as well. Fourteen-year-olds who watched more television were more likely later in adolescence to be involved in violence and aggressive acts that hurt other people. This relationship was found even when other factors like the child's previous level of aggression and living situations were taken into account (Johnson, Cohen, Smailes, Kasen, & Brook, 2002).

In recent years, there have been several high-profile cases of school violence in which the role of violent video games in promoting extremely violent actions has been questioned. Violent video games increase aggressive tendencies even more than TV because players are acting out the violence rather than just viewing it (Polman, de Castro, & van Aken, 2008). In a review of studies on violent video games, Anderson and Bushman (2001) concluded that they increase the player's actual aggression, raise arousal levels, increase aggressive thoughts and feelings, and decrease

Violent video games. Research has found that playing violent video games brings out aggressive tendencies in children who are already aggressive but also in those who are not.

prosocial behavior. The more blood there is in the game, the more intense these effects appear to be (Barlett, Harris, & Bruey, 2008). When the player identifies with and acts out the role of the "shooter," these effects are even stronger (Konijn, Bijvank, & Bushman, 2007). Although there is some evidence that children who are already more hostile and aggressive are more likely than others to be further affected by playing violent video games, it appears that even children who do not fit this profile become more violent. In one study, the least hostile children who played video games got into more fights than the most hostile children who did not. In all cases, when parents limited the amount of time and controlled the content of the video games their children played, children had lower levels of aggression (Gentile & Anderson, 2003).

Clearly not all media are violent, and research has shown that viewing other types of programming can be related to children's prosocial behavior such as sharing and cooperation. In one study, 4-year-old children who watched more educational programming were more prosocial in their interactions 2 years later (Ostrov, Gentile, & Crick, 2006). However, even educational programs had their risks. Girls who watched more educational shows were also more likely than other girls to take part in relational aggression (for example, "*We* don't want to play with *you!*"). The authors speculate that even educational shows model this type of behavior, although they usually show the characters making up by the end of the show. They speculate that preschool children do not understand the story line in the same way that adults do. They don't connect the positive resolution with the earlier aggression, so they only see the relational aggression as a model to imitate.

Communication

Electronic media have become an important form of communication among friends for teenagers. Teens stay in touch with friends by contacting them online, using instant messaging, e-mailing, text messaging, blogging, playing interactive games together, and viewing online social networking sites such as Facebook and MySpace. American teens are just now catching up with European and Asian teens in their use of text messaging (Subrahmanyam & Greenfield, 2008). Girls are more likely than boys to use the media to maintain existing friendships, while boys are more likely to use the media for flirting and for making new friends (Lenhart & Madden, 2007). Overall, teens report an enhanced sense of well-being as a result of maintaining friendships in this way (Valkenburg & Peter, 2007). Use of social networking sites is changing the nature of social communication because of the public announcements found there of whom each person is "friends" with and even the exact conversations between friends (Subrahmanyam & Greenfield, 2008). These online connections may lead to new relationships, as "friends of a friend" make contact with each other. Social networking sites are also used to develop groups of people with common interests who may help each other. One study found that teens with cancer often used their websites to make contact with others who have cancer and to share information about their disease (Suzuki & Beale, 2006). Teens have also been found to use an online peer advice bulletin board to share information about general and sexual health and development. In this anonymous setting, they often feel freer to ask questions they may be too embarrassed to ask their parents or even their friends; for example, what is it like to have a Pap smear? (Suzuki & Calzo, 2004).

However, the underside of these positive aspects of online communication includes predators and cyberbullying. We discussed cyberbullying in some detail in the previous chapter, so you understand that it can be a particularly vicious way to attack young people and their reputation. Online predators present a different type of risk. A study of online predators determined that most cases involve adults who create relationships with teenagers by developing trust over a long period of time (Wolak, Finkelhor, Mitchell, & Ybarra, 2008). In most cases teens who eventually meet with the adult in person believe that they are having a romantic, sexual relationship with someone who cares for them. Most crimes that result are statutory rapes rather than forced rapes, meaning that an adult has sex with someone who is legally too young to be able to give consent

Video Link 13.7
Violent video games.

10. European and Asian teens are just now starting to catch up with American teens in terms of how much they text message.

TRUE/FALSE

False. In fact it is American teens who are still catching up with European and Asian teens in this regard.

to have sex. Clearly teens need to be better educated about the potential dangers of relationships with adults that are created through electronic communications, but it is difficult for parents to know how to monitor the safety of their children's interactions online, especially when the children often know more about how it all works than they do. ProtecTeens is a project designed to help parents become more knowledgeable. A family contract that can be used as a mechanism to discuss and agree on guidelines for the use of social networking sites appears in Figure 13.3.

Figure 13.3

Family Contract for Internet Safety. This is a contract prepared by the Office of the Attorney General of the State of Idaho that can be used by parents and children to lay out some guidelines for the use of the Internet.

ProtecTeens™

OFFICE OF ATTORNEY GENERAL LAWRENCE WASDEN

Family Contract for Internet Safety

Child's Agreement

I know that there are strangers and dangers on the Internet. To help keep me safe, I promise to follow these steps whenever I am online.

- I will create safe and polite screen and profile names that do not tell people anything about me or my family, and are not rude or sexually suggestive.
- I will not give out or put any personal information about me or my family anytime I am online, including my address, telephone number, what school I go to, or how old I am.
- I will not add people as "friends" to my profile that I do not know personally and in real life.
- I will not be a cyberbully. I will treat others with respect, use good language, and not post or send anyone mean or threatening words that might hurt or embarrass them.
- I will not send pictures or videos of myself to anyone without asking my parents first.
- I will tell my parents about people I meet online. I know there are adults that will pretend to be kids to get me to talk to them.
- I will not call or agree to meet anyone I met online without asking my parents first.
- I will tell my parents immediately if someone sends or posts any pictures, videos, or words that make me uncomfortable, sad or upset.
- I will keep my screen names, profiles names and passwords secret from everyone except my parents
- I will tell my parents if someone online asks me to do something I am not supposed to do or that makes me uncomfortable or embarrassed.
- I will not download anything from the Internet unless first asking my parents.
- I know that it is illegal to send or post sexually suggestive photos or videos of myself or friends.
- I will not buy or order anything online without asking my parents' permission first.
- I will follow my parents' guidelines for my Internet use anytime I am connected, whether I am at home, at school, or at a friend's house.

Parent Agreement

I know that the Internet can be a dangerous place, but that it can be very useful and entertaining. I will help my child stay safe online by following these guidelines.

- I will be involved in my child's Internet activity, and get to know the websites they visit.
- I will set reasonable rules for my child's Internet use.
- I will listen to my child. If they have made an error in judgement using the Internet, I will react reasonably.
- I will keep a list of my child's profile names, e-mail addresses, and passwords.
- I will take steps to keep my family safe from strangers and inappropriate material on our computers.
- I will report any suspicious, inappropriate, or illegal activity to the proper authorities.
- I will frequently check to see what sites my child is visiting on the Internet.
- I will continue to learn about new ways to protect my family when they are online.

| _____ | | _____ | |
| Child's Signature | Date | Parent's Signature | Date |

Media and Self-Concept

As we discussed in Chapter 11, children and teens are vulnerable to many influences as they develop their self-concept and build their self-esteem. The way they see themselves and the way they value themselves is certain to be affected by the media they use for so many hours each day. For many years Fred Rogers (better known by his television name of Mr. Rogers) made it his goal to make children feel "special" and to enhance their self-esteem through his television program *Mr. Rogers' Neighborhood.* This is a tribute that was written about Mr. Rogers after his death in 2003.

Mr. Rogers: A Personal Tribute

Fred Rogers was a remarkable man whose show *Mister Rogers' Neighborhood* impacted millions of children over 33 years. Although his program did not have the high "production values" found in *Sesame Street,* his personal touch reached children in a very comforting way. When he was awarded the Presidential Medal of Freedom in 2002, he said, "The whole idea . . . is to look at the television camera and present as much love as you possibly could to a person who needs it" (McFeatters, 2002, para. 2).

When my son was 3 years old, we sat together comfortably watching Mr. Rogers on TV. At the end of the show, my son turned to me and said, "Mom, I think he knows my name." I was so moved by his sense that his "friend" on TV knew him personally that I told my sister about what he'd said. My sister is a freelance writer and subsequently interviewed Fred Rogers about a book he had written. He agreed to the interview, but only on the condition that she allow him to find out about her as well. So they talked and they wrote several letters to each other. She eventually wrote to Mr. Rogers about what my son had said about him. He replied, "How perceptive your 3-year-old nephew is! When he said, 'I think he knows my name,' little did he know that *name* and *nature* are the exact same word in Old Testament Hebrew. I've spent much of my professional life trying to know the nature of children like your nephew. Please give him a hug for me when you see him" (F. M. Rogers, personal communication, June 12, 1989).

Several years later, as a clinical psychologist, I was involved in therapy with a woman suffering from depression. During the time that we worked together, she gave birth to a child. When he was about 18 months old she came to her therapy session and told me about her experience watching Mr. Rogers with her son. Struggling with her own self-esteem, she told me that she felt so much better after watching Mr. Rogers on TV. With a laugh she said that he really did make her feel special.

Research has confirmed the wisdom of Mr. Rogers's approach. Several studies have shown that watching *Mr. Rogers' Neighborhood* increases positive peer interactions, the ability to deal with fear and anger, and the ability to delay gratification among young children (Cantor, Sparks, & Hoffner, 1988; Coates, Pusser, & Goodman, 1976; Friedrich & Stein, 1973). (Adapted from Levine, 2003)

Although self-esteem can be raised by shows such as *Mr. Rogers' Neighborhood,* we know that there are many ways in which TV can be harmful to the self-esteem of children and teens. We have already discussed the research showing that even young girls begin to have lower self-esteem when they are constantly exposed to the thin ideal shown on television and in magazines. Media can affect children's self-concept in another way by limiting the options that they see for their life. Harrison (2006) has argued that television shows and movies are less diverse than real life in many ways. People from minority groups are underrepresented and are often portrayed in negatively stereotyped ways. However, diversity is also absent in other ways. The types of stories told tend to show the same types of characters with the same types of goals over and over again. If you think of cartoons, Wile E. Coyote, who is mainly unintelligent and aggressive, has only one goal in life: to catch the Road Runner. Shows for teens can be just as limited, showing little complexity in either character or plot. As children watch hours of these programs, do they become so focused on these few characteristics that they define themselves according to these few possibilities as well?

Self-complexity The number of different ways in which an individual defines herself.

Harrison argued that a positive self-concept relies to some extent on **self-complexity**—that is, the number of different ways in which an individual defines herself. For example, an individual with high self-complexity sees herself as someone who is an attractive person, a fairly good athlete, an excellent student, and a good friend (most of the time). Someone with low self-complexity might tie her identity to her appearance and little else. In research with a largely nonminority sample of teens, Harrison found that the more television teens watched, the less complex their self-image was (see Figure 13.4). These limitations can cause trouble for teens when they experience stressful situations. For example, a boy whose identity is limited to being "a loving boyfriend" may become distraught when his girlfriend breaks up with him. Another boy with a more complex identity who is also very proud of his achievements in academics may be able to turn to this aspect of himself when faced with a breakup with his girlfriend.

One area that has received less attention is the impact of the media on the self-concept of minority youngsters. Television and movies, whose goal is to attract the most viewers, have tended to portray White, non-Latino characters more often than minorities. When minorities are presented in the media, they are often shown in a negative light. For example, African American characters are often characterized by criminality, lack of intelligence, laziness, or inappropriate behavior (Ward, 2004). Latino characters are 4 times as likely as others to be represented as domestic workers. They, too, are associated with crime and stereotypes, such

---

Figure 13.4

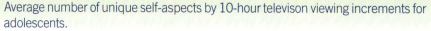

TV viewing and self-complexity. Research conducted by Harrison (2006) found that the more hours per week that teens watched television, the less complex their self-images. This may reflect the stereotypical portrayal of characters and plots in many television shows.

Average number of unique self-aspects by 10-hour televison viewing increments for adolescents.

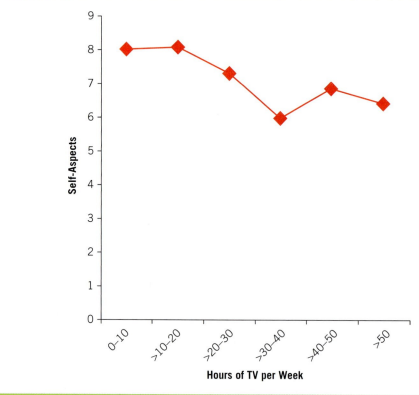

as having a "hot temper" (Rivadeneyra, Ward, & Gordon, 2007). In magazine ads, minority women are more likely to be represented as wild animals (Plous & Neptune, 1997). These portrayals are likely to affect minority youth, who are greater consumers of media than non-minorities (Rivadeneyra et al., 2007; Ward, 2004). Research by Ward and her colleagues has confirmed this relationship, but also has shown its complexity. For Latino teens, the more media they viewed, the lower their social and body self-esteem was, but this relationship was strongest for women and for those who were more highly identified with Latino culture (Rivadeneyra et al., 2007). For African American teens, only two types of television viewing, sports and music videos, were related to lower self-esteem. In addition, those who identified with Black characters on TV tended to have higher self-esteem, while those who identified with White characters had lower self-esteem. Finally, these relationships held only for those who reported themselves to be less religious. It appears that the individual's background, the kind of TV programs the person watches, and the reactions the person has to TV all play a role in how TV viewing is related to self-concept for African American adolescents (Ward, 2004).

Helping Children and Adolescents Use Media Wisely

Parental Guidance

Fred Rogers's advice to parents in regard to TV viewing was very simple: Do you want your child to act like the characters he or she sees on TV? (Franklin, Rifkin, & Pascual, 2001). There are three ways in which parents can interact with children around TV: (a) active mediation and guidance, which involves talking with the child about what he or she is watching; (b) setting limitations on what the child watches; and (c) actually coviewing programs with the child (Nathanson, 1999). Nathanson found that children were less likely to absorb messages of violence and aggression and perform them when parents discussed these messages with their children. Although there was a positive effect of limiting viewing, there also was some evidence that too much limitation might make the programs "forbidden fruit" and therefore even more appealing to children. Children between 8 and 22 years reported being *more* attracted to programs that were given restrictive ratings (Bushman & Cantor, 2003). Remember, however, that many families report that they have no rules for their children in regard to TV viewing, and over 70% of children have TV and/or other media in their bedrooms, where no direct parental supervision occurs (Rideout et al., 2010).

Parents need to find a comfortable medium between being overly restrictive and having no restrictions at all. Finally, when parents watched shows containing violence with children without commenting on the show's content, children's aggression increased, possibly because it appeared to them that the parents tacitly approved of the messages they were seeing. We might speculate that giving children unfettered access to TV in the bedroom may also give the clear message of parental acceptance of all TV content (Barkin et al., 2006).

Teaching Media Literacy

Media literacy or media education is designed to provide children with the skills to understand the underlying purposes and messages of media they use. For example, it has been found that the more young teens watch movies in which there is a lot of smoking, the more likely they are to begin smoking themselves (Jackson, Brown, & L'Engle, 2007). Even controlling for parent and peer smoking, those who watched the most smoking were 2.6 times more likely to start smoking than those who watched at the lowest level (Wills, Sargent, Stoolmiller, Gibbons, & Gerrard, 2008). One solution would be for the movie industry to reduce the amount of smoking portrayed or to provide warning labels to indicate that smoking is shown in the movie (similar to the warnings that movies contain sex, violence, or adult language). However, another approach is to use media education to teach children and teens about why movies contain so much smoking. *Blowing Smoke* is the name of one project designed to teach sixth and eighth

Media literacy
Providing children with the skills to understand the underlying purposes and messages of media.

graders about smoking in movies (Bergsma & Ingram, 2001). The researchers found that most children initially believed that smoking in movies was a random event with no particular purpose. *Blowing Smoke* taught the children that when they see smoking in films it reflects a form of advertising, sometimes even including brand names. In the past, tobacco companies paid for such placement of their product in films or gave free tobacco products to actors and others involved with the film. It is unclear whether this practice persists, but the level of smoking has not changed since a voluntary ban was introduced in 1990 (Sargent et al., 2001). By helping children understand the motivation behind showing people smoking in movies and helping them think critically about it, children's tendency to want to emulate admired movie stars when they smoke can be changed (Bergsma & Ingram, 2001). Try **Active Learning: Cigarettes in the Movies** to see how much smoking there is in the movies and TV programs that you watch and how you might talk with children about what you see.

ACTIVE LEARNING

Cigarettes in the Movies

In the next 2 weeks, notice how many characters in movies and TV shows that you watch smoke cigarettes. Do you see the same amount of smoking occurring in real life as you see in these programs? Can you explain why the directors of the show would choose to have each character smoke? What, if anything, does it convey about the person? Can you think of any reasons, besides artistic ones, for the decision to have a character smoke?

At the following website you can find information and research on how teens are affected by seeing smoking in the media and how the tobacco companies have influenced the placement of tobacco products in films and TV shows: http://www.scenesmoking.org/frame.htm. You will also find ratings of current movies based on their presentation of tobacco use at this site.

Media education can help make children more savvy consumers of media so they can sort out what the producers are trying to do and decide for themselves whether they want to go along with it. Some resources for parents and others who would like to teach media literacy to children include the following:

- The American Academy of Pediatrics lists a wide selection of sites (http://www.aap.org/health topics/mediause.cfm) designed to help parents make sure that their children are using media in a healthy way.
- The American Psychological Association maintains a website (http://www.apa.org/topics/kids media/index.aspx) on kids and the media.
- The Kaiser Family Foundation funds a great deal of research with national samples on children and media. The KFF website (http://www.kff.org/entmedia/index.cfm) is an excellent source of information on how children and teens are using media.

Conclusion

We have seen that children and teens spend their leisure time in a variety of ways. Young children play, while older children become involved in more structured extracurricular activities, as well as "hanging out" with friends. Children of all ages are using media, including television, computers, and many other new technologies. Each of these types of activities has certain outcomes for child development. It is important that we continue to examine the entire context of children's lives in order to understand and help children use all the resources available to them and their families in the most positive way.

CHAPTER SUMMARY

1. **What do children and adolescents do when they are not in school?**

   In cultures in which children are not required to work to help feed their families, leisure time is spent in different ways. In Asia children are required by parents to do more academic work. In the United States, children take part in unstructured play, participate in structured activities such as sports or the arts, and use media.

2. **What is play, and how does it develop?**

   Play is self-chosen activity that is done for its own sake because it is fun. Parten described the social stages of play based on children's developing ability to coordinate their activity with a peer: **unoccupied behavior**, **onlooker behavior**, **solitary independent play**, **parallel play**, **associative play**, and **cooperative play**. Piaget described stages of play as based on cognitive levels of understanding: **practice play**, **symbolic/sociodramatic play**, and **games with rules**.

3. **How does play affect children's development?**

   Through physical activity, it promotes health and brain development. Play allows for emotional expression, emotional regulation, and emotional understanding. Play also develops social skills and friendships. Play is one of the best ways to learn because children remain enthusiastic about what they are learning. Recess is also important as a time during the school day to recharge energy for learning.

4. **How do boys and girls differ in play?**

   Gender segregation is associated with some differences in play between boys and girls. Boys tend to play farther away from home base and are more competitive in their play with larger groups involved. Girls tend to play with a small group of friends and are involved with more make-believe play. However, there is much overlap in what boys and girls do with their unstructured time.

5. **What are the benefits and risks of unstructured and structured time for children and teens?**

   Unstructured and unsupervised time has been declining because of safety concerns, media use, and paid work for teens, which is a concern because free playing time for children promotes creativity and imagination. For teens, unsupervised time may lead to problem behaviors, but some amount of autonomy is necessary for development of identity.

   Relatively few children have too many structured activities in their lives, despite fears that this is a problem. Well-supervised activities provide opportunities for achievement, socialization with peers and adults, and excitement shared with a group. However, organized sports may cause injuries, and children may be pressured to win. Many drop out by age 13. Creative activities have been linked with brain development, but the links with academic achievement are not as clear. **Positive youth development** focuses on using positive activities to help children and teens reach their maximum potential.

6. **What positive and negative effects does media use have on children and teens?**

   American children and teens use media for almost 7 and a half hours per day. TV viewing promotes obesity due to lack of physical activity or overeating in front of the TV. Paradoxically it also promotes eating disorders because of images of ultrathin models. For cognitive development, no positive effects of TV viewing are found for children under age 2. After that, educational TV and other media can promote positive cognitive and social development, but entertainment TV has a negative effect on academic achievement. Violent media promote aggressive thoughts and behavior, but prosocial messages in the media can have a positive effect. Social networking can enhance friendships, but there is a danger of adult predators when children and teens talk with people they don't know. Media can constrict **self-complexity** for teens, and minority children may be hurt by stereotypes shown in the media. It is important to teach **media literacy** to help children understand how the media are trying to manipulate their thinking in subtle ways.

Go to **www.sagepub.com/levine** for additional exercises and video resources. Select **Chapter 13, Play, Extracurricular Activities, and Media Use,** for chapter-specific activities.

chapter 14

Families

14

In this chapter we will examine the influence that families have on children's development. We will begin by exploring the diversity of types of families that exist in American society, with a focus on the children who live within them. We will examine issues of divorce, single parenting, noncustodial parents, stepfamilies, and the role of grandparents, gay and lesbian parents, adoptive parents, and foster families. We will then look at the functioning of families—both what they do and how they do it. Finally we will discuss things that can help the family be the best possible context for the development of children.

Test Your Knowledge

Test your knowledge of child development by deciding whether each of the following statements is *true* or *false,* and then check your answers as you read the chapter.

1. **True/False:** The incidence of stepfamilies in the United States has not changed much from 1900 to today.
2. **True/False:** The majority of women who are single but living with the father of their baby when their baby is born will marry the baby's father shortly after the baby's birth.
3. **True/False:** Adolescents from single-parent families spend just as much time with their families as children from two-parent families.
4. **True/False:** Having their parents divorce has been found to cause behavioral problems and emotional problems like depression in children following the divorce.
5. **True/False:** Open adoption, in which the adopted child has contact with his or her birth mother, does not weaken the attachment of the child to his or her adoptive mother.
6. **True/False:** American families on average eat a meal together as a family only once a week.
7. **True/False:** Children who are raised by permissive parents are most likely to grow up to be self-reliant, confident, and explorative.
8. **True/False:** Based upon the research done on parenting styles, it is clear that children are the way they are because their parents make them that way.
9. **True/False:** Good parenting is good parenting, so the same parenting strategies should work equally well for all children.
10. **True/False:** Children who grow up without siblings tend to be more self-centered, maladjusted, lonely, and neurotic than children who have siblings.

Correct answers: (1) True, (2) False, (3) True, (4) False, (5) True, (6) False, (7) False, (8) False, (9) False, (10) False

What Constitutes a Family?

Differing Cultural Definitions

Family Any two or more individuals living together who are related by birth, marriage, or adoption.

"Few would dispute that the family is the basic social unit in the organization of human society and a primary context for the development and socialization of society's children" (McLoyd, Hill, & Dodge, 2005, p. 3), yet the definition of **family** may differ widely. Before reading on, write down your thoughts about what makes a family. Think about how a family is created and who its members might be. The following examples illustrate some of the diversity in the forms that families can take in different cultures. Some of these examples may be family forms that you have not encountered before. Which of the following would you include in a definition of family?

- A Toda woman of south India marries all of her husband's brothers, and her children are each assigned to one of the brothers, not necessarily the biological father (Coontz, 2000).
- A Gusii woman of Kenya raises her children on a small farm where she cultivates her food. She is one of several wives of one man (LeVine et al., 1994).
- An Ifaluk family of Micronesia consists of two sets of parents: biological and adoptive. Anyone can ask a pregnant woman for permission to adopt her baby. The baby will live with its mother until age 3 when it will move in with the adoptive family. Both families are involved with the child's upbringing (DeLoache & Gottlieb, 2000).

These examples show that ideas about what constitutes a family include many possibilities in countries around the world. Families differ in many ways within the United States as well, and we will look at a wide variety of families in this chapter. The U.S. Census Bureau (2008a) defines a family as any two individuals living together who are related by birth, marriage, or adoption. Many people will think of a husband and wife living with their biological and/or adopted children, or what is called a **nuclear family**. Anything else is often seen as deviant, yet it is likely that in your own class there are many students from families that do not look like the 1950s stereotype shown in TV shows such as *Leave It to Beaver* and *The Adventures of Ozzie & Harriet*, and even in current shows such as *The Simpsons*. Can you think of families that you know who do not fit the Census Bureau's definition? Would an unmarried couple who has taken in a neighbor's child be a family by your definition? Although families differ in how many people they contain or in members' relationship to each other, families all share some of the same important functions. We'll return to this topic in the second section of this chapter, but first we will look at some of the family forms that are common in the United States.

Nuclear family A family consisting of a husband, a wife, and their biological and/or adopted children.

Changes in the American Family and Their Impact on Children

We are often tempted to think of "the good old days" as a time when families stayed together and life was much better for children. It is important that we begin this chapter with some perspective on what families are like now and what they were like in the last 150 years.

The divorce rate has risen dramatically in the past century, but we must remember that divorce is only one way in which a marriage is dissolved. In earlier times marital desertion, in which one parent simply ran away, was more common than it is today (Duncan, 1994). Beverly Schwartzberg (2004) describes many marriages in the 1850s as "'fluid marriage,' for they demonstrate that the seemingly rigid marriage contract contained many escape clauses" (pp. 573–574). Husbands and wives would simply disappear and might remarry even without a prior divorce, which was very difficult to obtain. "Fluid marriages bespoke a world where acceptance of marriage as a fundamental legal, social, and cultural institution was accompanied by a pragmatic flexibility that demonstrated both respect for marriage and a willingness to adapt households to meet need and fortune" (Schwartzberg, 2004, p. 574).

It may also surprise you to learn that the incidence of stepfamilies in this country has probably not risen very much from the early 1900s. While stepfamilies now are the result of divorce, in earlier times they could be the result of abandonment and remarriage as described above, or they could result from parental death. In the years between 1901 and 1910, 22.6% of children under age 18 experienced the death of either their mother or their father (Chadwick & Heaton, 1987). In the early 20th century, the death rate of parents with young children was much higher than it is today. In 1915, over 600 pregnant women died for every 100,000 births, but by 2003, this rate had dropped to 12 maternal deaths per 100,000 births (Hoyert, 2007). "In 2000 it was more likely that 20-year-olds would have a *living grandmother* than it was that 20-year-olds in 1900 would have a *living mother*" (Coleman, Ganong, & Warzinik, 2007, p. 34). A 20-year-old who married in 1900 could expect to live with that spouse for an average of 25 years before that partner died. In 2000, newlyweds could expect to share over 50 years of life with their partner if they did not divorce (Coleman et al., 2007). In a mostly agricultural society it was considered essential to have two parents present to raise children, so remarriage was very common. It was not until 1970 that the number of marriages that were ended by divorce outnumbered the number ended by death (Fischer, Hout, & Stiles, 2006).

Stephanie Coontz (2000) has concluded that the major difference between current and earlier levels of diversity in family types is "not occasioned by the *existence* of diversity but by its increasing *legitimation*" (Coontz, 2000, p. 28). Diverse forms of family life are no longer hidden in the shadows, but are increasingly recognized as acceptable ways to raise children.

Single Parenting

There are many reasons why parents may raise their children without a partner. They may have been divorced, lost a partner to death, or never been married. Each of these has different consequences for children. As shown in Figure 14.1, the percentage of families headed by a single parent in the United States has more than doubled since 1970 when 10% of families were headed by a single parent. For African American women, the change over time is even more dramatic. While 85% of African American women were married when they gave birth to their first child in 1950, in 2000 approximately 70% were not married (Coleman et al., 2007). African American women are more likely to be single parents because they never married, while White women are more likely to become single parents following a divorce (Coleman et al., 2007). Most single custodial parents are women, but the number of fathers raising children on their own has also risen. In 2006, 19% of single-parent households (2.5 million) were headed by fathers (U.S. Census Bureau, 2008b).

Children used to jump rope and sing "First comes love, then comes marriage, then comes Susie with a baby carriage." Not necessarily anymore. Increasingly women are having children first and getting married later. In 2007, 40% of births in the United States were to unmarried women (Federal Interagency Forum on Child and Family Statistics, 2009). Of course, being unmarried does not necessarily mean that the mother is not living with the child's father. In fact, much of the increase in single-parent births is due to cohabitation with the child's father rather than marriage to him, with 50% of single mothers reporting that they lived with their new baby's father (Coltrane, 2004). Although many women in this situation plan eventually to marry the father of their child, in one large-scale study it was found that 1 year later only 10% of the fathers in this situation had actually married the mother and only 20% maintained regular contact with the child (McLanahan & Carlson, 2004). Partner instability was found to be greater for single mothers during the first 3 years of their child's life than for married mothers (Osborne & McLanahan, 2007).

1. The incidence of stepfamilies in the United States has not changed much from 1900 to today. **TRUE/FALSE**

   True. The incidence (or likelihood of occurrence) is probably similar, but the reason for the creation of stepfamilies has changed. Today they are primarily due to divorce, but in the past they were due to death of one of the parents or marital desertion.

2. The majority of women who are single but living with the father of their baby when their baby is born will marry the baby's father shortly after the baby's birth. **TRUE/FALSE**

   False. Survey research shows that only 10% of women in this situation marry the father of their baby within a year of the birth of their child.

Video Link 14.1
Single parents and poverty.

TRUE/FALSE

3. Adolescents from single-parent families spend just as much time with their families as children from two-parent families.

True. In single-parent families time is spent with the noncustodial fathers and with custodial mothers and their extended family members while in two-parent families the time is spent with the two parents together, but amount of time spent with families is similar in these two family structures.

Emotional parentification
A situation in which children become more concerned about their parent's emotional needs than their own.

Extended family
A family that includes both nuclear family members and other relatives.

| Figure 14.1 |

Statistics on the rise in number of single mothers. This figure shows the dramatic rise in the number of births to single mothers in the United States since 1940. In 2007, nearly 4 in 10 births were to unmarried women. The rate for 2007 was 80% higher than the rate for 1980.

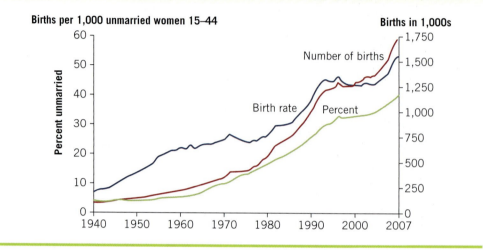

Whether there are one or two parents in a household is important because of the living situation it creates. Single-parent families are much more likely than two-parent families to fall below the poverty line. In 2007, while 8.5% of children in two-parent families had poverty-level incomes, 42.9% of single-parent families headed by women and 21.3% headed by men were at the poverty level (U.S. Census Bureau, 2007). As we will discuss in Chapter 15, poverty has both direct and indirect effects on children. It increases parental stress and reduces parenting skill, which then affects child well-being. According to Martin, Emery, and Peris (2004), negative effects attributed to single parenting, such as lower academic achievement and more psychological problems, are due at least in part to the effects of poverty (Martin et al., 2004).

Single parents must be both mother and father to their children. All of the tasks that would otherwise be shared by two parents must be accomplished by one. This stress often affects the parent's ability to parent effectively. Both closeness and discipline may suffer. One particular concern raised in these situations is called **emotional parentification**, in which children become more concerned about their parent's emotional needs than their own by becoming a confidant, or by needing to mediate between their parents (Jurkovic, Thirkield, & Morrell, 2001; Martin et al., 2004). Parentification can also take an instrumental form in which children take on the responsibility for managing the household (for example, taking care of siblings, shopping or cleaning for the family) (Jurkovic et al., 2001). These children may appear to others to be doing well, but are actually forced to take on a role for which they are not ready. This added responsibility can contribute to the development of competence and maturity in older children, but can be an overwhelming burden to younger children (Jurkovic et al., 2001).

How does life in a one-parent family differ from life with two parents? Asmussen and Larson (1991) carried out a study to compare the daily experiences of young teens in single-mother and two-parent families. These White, middle- and working-class teens reported their daily activities when they were paged throughout the day for 1 week. The researchers found that there were no differences in the amount of time that teens from the two groups spent with their parents. In fact, both groups spent the same amount of time with family. The major difference was that those in single-parent families spent time with their mother and **extended family**, such as grandparents and aunts and uncles, while the other children spent that time with both parents together. In single-parent families, young adolescents were found to spend more time with their mothers carrying out tasks and more time with their fathers in pleasurable activities. In this same study, teens in single-parent families experienced their parents as being friendlier than teens in two-parent families.

Time together. Children who live only with their mother spend more time doing chores with her. As you can see in this picture, this time together can be positive and help build a closer relationship.

We mentioned at the beginning of this section that whether a single-parent family is created by divorce, unmarried status, or death of a spouse has different consequences for the children in that single-parent family. Generally children whose parent has died tend to do better in terms of education and emotional adjustment in the long run. Once again we find that financial well-being may play an important role in this difference. In one large-scale study, there were no differences between widowed and divorced women in their values and parenting of their children, but widows tended to have a higher family income, whether they were working or stayed at home (Biblarz & Gottainer, 2000). Society has established ways to support those who have lost a loved one, but it does not have comparable ways of supporting those who have undergone a divorce. For example, widows receive Social Security survivor's benefits (Tillman, 2007). On an emotional level, children are more likely to be able to hold onto positive thoughts about the lost parent, while children of divorce are more likely to struggle with their feelings about both their parents. Let's look more closely at the impact that divorce has on children.

Divorce

Every year, over 1 million children in the United States experience the divorce of their parents (Kunz, 2001). Between 40% and 50% of all marriages end in divorce (Cherlin, 2010). The earliest research on divorce tended to treat it as a single event. Children from divorced families and children from intact families were compared, and many negatives were found about how children from divorced families fared. However, current thinking defines divorce as a process, rather than as one event (Greene, Sullivan, & Anderson, 2008). The divorce itself may be just one of a chain of upheavals in a child's life. It is usually preceded by family events that may include a great deal of conflict or distance among family members. Parents may handle the divorce itself very differently, taking their children's needs into consideration or not. After the divorce there will likely be additional changes, including residential moves, new caretakers, custody changes, parental dating relationships, cohabitation, stepparents, new siblings, and more. All of these factors play a role in how children fare following a divorce.

We must also remember that research on children and divorce has, by necessity, been correlational (because we cannot randomly assign children to divorced or intact families to create an experimental research design); therefore we cannot assume that differences between children from divorced and intact families are *caused* by the divorce. As we learned in Chapter 3 when we studied the nature of correlational and experimental research, there might be a third factor causing both the likelihood of divorce and poorer child outcomes. For example, depression might have a genetic underpinning within a particular family. This tendency toward depression might contribute to the likelihood of a divorce in the family and might also result in depression in the children of divorced parents as adults. We might conclude that divorce caused the subsequent depression, when it was genetic influences that may have played the stronger role, contributing both to depression and to the incidence of divorce (Cherlin,

4. Having their parents divorce has been found to cause behavioral problems and emotional problems like depression in children following the divorce.

TRUE/FALSE

False. Although experiencing a parental divorce is *associated* with certain problems in children following a divorce, with our research techniques we cannot say that the divorce is the *cause* of the child's problems. Some of these problems may have existed prior to the divorce and simply continue after it.

Video Link 14.2
Talking about divorce.

Video Link 14.3
Children and divorce.

Chase-Lansdale, & McRae, 1998). Another way that the results of correlational studies of the effects of divorce on children can be misinterpreted is that we get it backward. That is, when children from divorced families have higher levels of misbehavior, we might conclude that the divorce caused the behavioral problems. However, being parents of a child who does a lot of acting out can be very stressful on a marriage. It is possible that these children contributed to their parents' decision to divorce and that the child's misbehavior predated the divorce itself rather than resulting from it. While children should never be blamed for their parents' divorce, any stress within the family system can contribute to the breakup of a marriage.

On average, children whose parents divorce experience more adjustment problems as they grow and develop. It is estimated that 20%–25% of children from divorced parents experience high levels of behavior problems compared to 10% of children from intact families (Greene, Anderson, Hetherington, Forgatch, & DeGarmo, 2003). However, the average differences between children of divorce and children from intact families are quite small, and most children from divorced families score within the normal range of functioning on many measures (APA, 2004a). High levels of conflict between parents, whether before, during, or after divorce, are consistently related to poorer outcomes for the children. However, when high levels of conflict are resolved by divorce, children often do better following the divorce (Booth & Amato, 2001; Hetherington & Stanley-Hagan, 1999).

Certain factors that often accompany divorce are related to worse outcomes for children of divorced families. They include:

1. Financial difficulties and poverty

2. Ongoing conflict between divorced parents

3. High levels of parental distress

4. A greater number of life changes and disruptions (APA, 2004a; Greene et al., 2008; Martinez & Forgatch, 2002)

Family conflict. What would it feel like to be this boy, listening to his parents fight?

Consider how these factors are related. As parents deal with the stress of decreased income, the emotional distress from the breakup of their relationship (including depression and anger), changes in work situations, and more, their parenting skills often suffer, and children's well-being also declines. Parents who are highly stressed often exhibit less positive support for the child, use less effective communication, and provide less monitoring and control over the child's behavior (Greene et al., 2008; Martinez & Forgatch, 2002; Pett, Wampold, Turner, & Vaughan-Cole, 1999). However, for some parents the divorce brings relief, new opportunities, or more healthy relationships (Greene et al., 2008).

Because children are negatively affected by high levels of marital conflict, parents' inability to resolve conflict using compromise and negotiation is related to children's fears and insecurities. Parents who attack each other, whether verbally or physically, have children who have more difficulty in many areas of life. Children respond not only to the high level of conflict, but also to parents who are more likely to be depressed and withdrawn, rejecting, and harsh in their interactions with their children (APA, 2004a). However, not all family conflict has the same impact on children. Recently attention has been given to what is called **constructive conflict**. There is evidence that when parents disagree, but handle it in a positive way (for example, they are affectionate despite their disagreement, they resolve conflict through problem solving, and they remain emotionally supportive of each other), it is associated with positive emotional development in the children in the family

Constructive conflict
Family conflict that is resolved in a positive way using affection, problem solving, and emotional support.

(McCoy, Cummings, & Davies, 2009). Conflict in the context of a generally satisfying marriage does not threaten children's sense of security and well-being, so it does not have the same negative impact that conflict that involves yelling, threatening, and insulting does (Cummings, Goeke-Morey, & Papp, 2003).

Research has examined numerous aspects of the well-being of children whose parents are divorced: academic functioning, social interactions, problem behaviors, and emotional difficulties. In many studies it has been found that academic achievement suffers and this leads to other consequences later in life. The biggest impact is on school completion. Children from single-parent families formed by divorce are twice as likely as those with two parents to leave school before high school graduation (Martin et al., 2004), they are less than half as likely to attend college (Elliott, 2009), and they are less likely to complete college if they do begin (Biblarz & Gottainer, 2000).

Two types of behavior problems have been examined: externalizing and internalizing. **Externalizing behavior problems**, such as aggression, are directed at other people, while **internalizing behavior problems**, such as anxiety, are directed at oneself. Children, especially boys, from divorced and single-parent families have generally been found to be more "disobedient, aggressive, demanding and lacking in self-control" (Martin et al., 2004, p. 284) both in early childhood and later in life, which is evidence of externalizing behavior problems. The evidence concerning internalizing behavior problems and divorce is more mixed. In one longitudinal study people were studied at age 7, before any of them had experienced a divorce; then again at age 11, when some had experienced divorce; and finally again at age 33 (Cherlin et al., 1998). When these children were 11, there were few differences directly attributable to the divorce, rather than to preexisting problems in the child and the family. However, by age 33, the earlier problems seemed to have been compounded by the long-term effects of the divorce. Those who had experienced divorce in childhood were more likely to be depressed at age 33.

Another effect of divorce that cannot be assessed until the children have reached adulthood is the ability to be involved in and committed to a long-term intimate relationship. A characteristic that many children whose parents divorced have in common is that they did not have a model of their own parents as a well-functioning, caring intimate partnership. When they reach adulthood they are more likely to have difficulty creating their own long-term, intimate relationships. In a number of studies, young adults whose parents had divorced were more wary of intimate relationships (Burns & Dunlop, 2002) and more likely to have many short-term relationships (Jónsson, Njardvik, Ólafsdóttir, & Grétarsson, 2000). Once they were married, they were less satisfied (Jacquet & Surra, 2004) and more likely to experience divorce themselves (Wauterickx, Gouwy, & Bracke, 2006). However, it is important to keep in mind that, although more children of divorced parents experience these problems, the majority of them do succeed in creating committed relationships.

One important factor in children's adjustment is the age of the child when the parents divorce. Children's understanding and ability to process the changes that are occurring will differ depending on their level of development. The following paragraphs describe some typical responses of children at different ages.

Infants and toddlers do not understand what is happening when parents separate. Instead they resonate to their parents' feelings and to disruptions in their normal routines, resulting in behaviors such as anger and aggression, separation anxiety, eating or sleep problems, or loss of recent developmental achievements such as toilet training or language development (Cohen & the American Academy of Pediatrics Committee on Psychosocial Aspects of Child and Family Health, 2002; Kalter, 1990).

As we have learned, preschoolers are egocentric, seeing the world only from their own point of view. Therefore, many preschoolers, as well as some older children, believe that they had something to do with causing the divorce. Because their logical thinking is limited, they may also develop illogical reasoning to explain the events. Like younger children, preschoolers may also

Externalizing behavior problems Behaviors in which the child or adolescent "acts out" on the environment such as aggressive or destructive behavior.

Internalizing behavior problems Negative or aggressive behaviors that are directed inward at oneself, such as anxiety or depression.

A child's view of divorce. When parents of school-age children divorce, it is important that parents help them understand that they are still loved by both parents and they will be cared for by them.

experience separation anxiety as they reason that one parent has left, so the other could also abandon them. Nightmares may become more common. Finally, children may become aggressive toward peers as a result of anger at what has happened at home or in imitation of parental aggression toward each other (Cohen et al., 2002; Kalter, 1990).

School-age children may react to divorce with sadness and depression. Their efforts to keep the fantasy that their parents will reunite are often an attempt to fight off this sadness (Kalter, 1990). For school-age children, academic performance may decline. Children at this age may be more affected by the divided loyalties they feel toward mother and father. Anger may be expressed toward parents directly or indirectly, through negative behaviors such as "whining, complaining, [or] 'accidentally' spilling drinks repetitively," or the anger and aggression may be displaced onto peers (Kalter, 1990, p. 201).

Adolescence is a time for becoming more independent of parents, a task that is easier when the parents are in a position to give both support and control as needed to help their teens become independent young adults. When parents are themselves embroiled in the emotional conflicts of a divorce, parenting becomes much more difficult. Adolescents may respond with problem behaviors, as their disappointment with their parents is acted out. Teen pregnancy is twice as high in divorced families as in married families (Martin et al., 2004). Depression, delinquent behavior, and substance abuse are also more likely to occur for these teens than for teens in families that are not in crisis (Cohen et al., 2002).

Helping Children Cope With Divorce. Just as there is successful and unsuccessful marriage, there also is successful and unsuccessful divorce. In a successful divorce, parents are able to disengage from each other while maintaining warm and consistent parenting with their children. In unsuccessful divorce, the marital conflict continues for years, the children are brought into it in many ways, and nothing seems resolved. Parents "bad-mouth" each other to the children or use the children to spy on the other parent's activities. These high-conflict divorces create anxiety in children. The good news is that when parents are able to resolve their conflicts and recover emotionally from the divorce and their experiences in the marriage, then it is more likely that the children will be able to have a positive relationship with both parents. In this situation, children's cognitive and social development is less likely to be negatively affected by the divorce in the long term (APA, 2004a; Whiteside & Becker, 2000).

Active Learning: Parenting and Divorce gives you several scenarios to examine in order to apply the principles you are learning about to understand what is harmful and what is helpful to children whose parents are divorcing.

ACTIVE LEARNING

Parenting and Divorce

Perfectly reasonable people, who believe that they are handling their divorce well, may say things such as the following in front of their children:

Spouse A: [when the child is being dropped off for a visit] I told you I was taking Greg to a movie tonight at 7:00. You're late.

Spouse B: You didn't tell me that. You must have forgotten to mention it. Sometimes your memory goes as you get older.

Spouse A: Maybe it's your hearing that's going! Next time I'll write it down for you.

Spouse B: Maybe it's your thinking that's going! Besides, he's seen that movie already. Don't you know what your son has seen? Don't you listen to him?

(Kalter, 1990, p. 7)

Or they might say the following to their children:

Mother: I'm sorry you can't go to camp this summer. Your dad's still drinking away his money instead of thinking about you. That's why we got divorced in the first place. I hope you don't wind up like the bum he is.

Father: Is your mom going out with that same guy? Does he stay overnight sometimes? Someone ought to tell her that she's acting like a real jerk.

(Kalter, 1990, p. 13)

A very different way of talking with children about some of the consequences of divorce is the following:

Father: I've heard that when a guy's parents get divorced and then one of them starts dating, it's hard. And one reason it is especially hard . . . is that they start to see that their parents really aren't going to make up and get back together. Most teenagers want their parents to quit being divorced and get back together. But when one parent starts dating, it gets pretty clear that they're going to stay divorced.

(Kalter, 1990, p. 373)

Look at the examples above and make a list of what each parent is doing to either foster or hurt his or her child's adjustment to the divorce and the child's overall development. With each item on your list, put ideas about how children at various ages might react to hearing what the parents said.

Answers: The following parent behaviors that have been found to harm children whose parents are divorcing all appear in the examples above: asking children about the other parent (using them as spies), involving children in financial disputes, talking negatively about the other parent, and engaging in conflict in front of the children (Brandon, 2006). Behaviors that help children include encouraging the child to talk about what he is feeling and accepting those feelings.

There are some basic things that parents can do to help their children cope with a divorce:

1. Encourage them to talk about how they are feeling about the events that make up a divorce.
2. Don't bad-mouth the other parent to the children.
3. Don't use the children as messengers between parents.
4. Make sure the children know that both parents still love them and that the divorce is not their fault.
5. Help the children keep contact with both parents.
6. Get emotional support and help for themselves. Don't let the children become the parent's caretaker or confidant.
7. Keep up with child support payments, but don't discuss the status of these payments with the children (American Academy of Matrimonial Lawyers, 2009; Nemours Foundation, 1995–2009).

Noncustodial Parents. When children grow up in mother-only households as a result of divorce or because the mother never married, we should not presume that because a father does not reside in the same household as his children he is not part of their lives. In many cases this may be true, but there are a variety of ways in which a father who does not reside with his children can sustain a relationship with them. A great deal of the research that has been done on nonresident fathers has looked at the amount of face-to-face contact the father has with his children (for example, the frequency of contact or length of time they spend together) or the father's provision of financial support to the family. Much less of it has looked at the quality of the relationship maintained despite the physical separation (Dunn, Cheng, O'Connor, & Bridges, 2004). One explanation for why there is so much variability in the outcomes for children of divorce is that simple measures of paternal contact may not be adequate to assess the impact of nonresident fathers on their children's development. Instead we need to look at the *quality* of the relationship that is maintained over time (Amato & Gilbreth, 1999).

The amount of contact that children have with nonresident fathers varies greatly, with many children losing virtually all contact with their fathers after a few years (Dunn et al., 2004), although there is some evidence that this may be changing in younger cohorts of fathers (Amato & Gilbreth, 1999). Younger fathers may be taking to heart the recommendation just made not to give up on the relationship, even if they are separated by distance from their children.

In a study of young adolescents in which about half of the sample resided with their father and the other half lived apart from their father, the adolescents were asked to describe the perceived quality of their relationship with their father on a number of dimensions (Munsch, Woodward, & Darling, 1995). Among the 177 adolescents who lived apart from their father, half of them indicated that they did not have any contact with their father. When the other half of this group was asked to describe the quality of their relationship with their nonresidential father, there were surprisingly few differences between their perceptions and the perceptions of the children who lived in the same household as their father. The adolescents in both groups were equally likely to say that they had used their father as a source of social support when dealing with a recent stressful event, and both groups saw their father as equally helpful in this situation. The adolescents also reported on the extent to which they felt their father filled certain functional roles in their lives (for example, being a teacher, role model, or companion) and the extent to which their father provided specific types of social support to their children in a time of stress (for example, providing problem-solving help, instrumental support, or esteem enhancement). Finally, they were asked to evaluate some general qualities of the relationship they had with their father (for example, how helpful, accepting, and understanding their father was). In all, 21 comparisons were made, and only three significant differences were found between the two groups of children—and in all three of those cases the children who lived apart from their father saw them as being *more* supportive or functional than the children who lived with their father. The authors conclude that it takes effort for a father who does not reside with his children to maintain a relationship with them, and therefore negative talk about "deadbeat dads" or the suggestion that nonresidential fathers are unimportant in the lives of their children only makes it easier for fathers to give up and walk away from their children. Instead nonresidential fathers need to hear the message that they can be—and often are—important people in the lives of their children. How positive these relationships with noncustodial fathers are continues to be supported by research (Dunn et al., 2004; Furstenberg & Cherlin, 1991; Mandel & Sharlin, 2006).

Noncustodial fathers. Many fathers remain important people in their children's lives, even if they don't live with them. If noncustodial fathers understood this, they might be more motivated to work at maintaining a relationship with their children following a divorce.

About 19% of single-parent families are headed by fathers, so the mother is not the custodial parent in these families (U.S. Census Bureau, 2008b), but considerably less research has been done on noncustodial mothers. A particular challenge for a noncustodial mother is dealing with the negative assumptions that people often make about why she does not have custody of her children (Greif, 1997). People tend to be more judgmental and harder on noncustodial mothers than they are on noncustodial fathers, but in most cases the mother is emotionally or financially unable to care for her children and often has voluntarily relinquished custody to the children's father.

There are a number of ways in which the relationship with a noncustodial mother differs from that with a noncustodial father. Compared to noncustodial fathers, noncustodial mothers are seen as maintaining greater emotional involvement in the lives of their children, even when they live apart, and as being more sensitive to their child's needs, more effective at providing support and comfort, and more knowledgeable about the child's day-to-day activities (Gunnoe & Hetherington, 2004). There also is some evidence that the relationship with a noncustodial mother plays a bigger role in the child's postdivorce adjustment (Clarke-Stewart & Hayward, 1996; Gunnoe & Hetherington, 2004).

Stepfamilies and Blended Families

As we have seen, divorce is very prevalent in Western society, but 3 out of 4 people who divorce also remarry (Coleman et al., 2007), and when children are involved, **stepfamilies** form. At the end of the 20th century, in 50% of all marriages in the United States, one of the partners was previously divorced, and in 10% of marriages one of the partners had previously been married two or more times before (Coleman et al., 2007). These numbers do not include the large number of families in which a parent lives with a new partner without marriage (Tillman, 2007), nor do they include stepfamilies formed when the mother was never previously married.

Stepfamilies Families in which there are two adults and at least one child from a previous relationship of one of the adults; there also may be biological children of the couple.

One definition of a stepfamily is "a family of two adults in a formal or informal marriage where at least one of the adults has children from a previous relationship. There may be children from the current union. Children may live-in full-time or part-time or may not currently have contact" (Howden, 2007, p. 2). New families that form may be very complex as the following example shows:

> A "his," "hers" and "ours" family. The father has one biological son (11), and the mother has two biological children, a boy, 16, and girl, 13, who all live in the same household. They have an "ours" three-year-old daughter. Shared parenting arrangements see children moving in and out for five and four days each week. The whole stepfamily is together on two separate nights each week. One ex-partner has re-partnered and has two young adult stepchildren. (Howden, 2007, para. 15)

It is understandable that these relationships can sometimes be quite confusing to children. For example, one 4-year-old boy lived in a family with his mother and with his father who had been married before and had two daughters, his half-sisters, who visited on a regular basis. One day, when the girls' mother dropped them off at the house, the little boy became very angry that the girls' mother was not taking him with her. Apparently, the boy had reasoned that since his two sisters had *his* mother as a stepmother, then *their* mother must be also *his* stepmother. His sisters visited with his father and mother, so he figured he should go visit with their mother. When told this wouldn't happen he became angry and accused his parents of depriving him of a stepmother! Children may also become confused about whom they refer to as Mom and Dad. The cartoon in Figure 14.2 shows that confusion may arise in other situations as well.

Figure 14.2

Stepfamilies are complicated. Children may become confused when they deal with all the complexity they find in their family structures.

"When you say you want to speak to my parents, do you mean my mommy and her new husband or my daddy and his new wife or my mommy and my daddy?"

SOURCE: www.CartoonStock.com.

In one study, 16- to 18-year-olds from divorced and remarried families were asked who made up their family. For these teens, four patterns were described:

1. Both biological parents

2. Both biological parents and at least one stepparent

3. One biological parent and the new spouse

4. One biological parent

Try **Active Learning: Diagram Your Family** to see how complex your own family is by using a genogram to diagram these relationships.

ACTIVE LEARNING

Diagram Your Family

A genogram is a mapping of your biological family; however, many families are much more complex than a simple genogram would indicate. Try the following activity to map your family.

Using circles for females and squares for males, put yourself in the middle of a page. Draw your family relationships around you. Put horizontal solid lines to indicate marriages, and use dashed lines to indicate cohabiting, committed relationships. A horizontal line with a ———//——— indicates a divorce or separation. Put an X over anyone who has died. Put vertical or slanted solid lines to show biological children, and use dashed lines to show adoption, steprelations, or other nonbiological parent-child relationships (adapted from Gerlach, 2010). Does your family look like the traditional nuclear family or more like the multigenerational stepfamily shown in Figure 14.3?

Figure 14.3

Genogram for a nuclear family and partial genotype of a multigenerational stepfamily.

Does your family look like this traditional three-generation nuclear family?

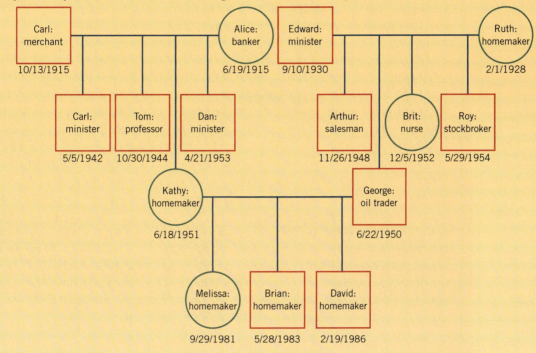

Or does it look more like this multigenerational three-home stepfamily?

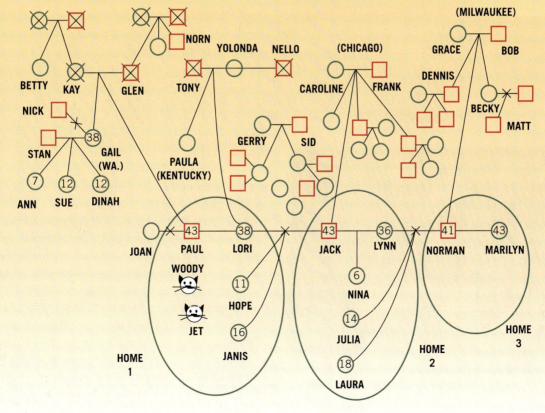

Relationships within stepfamilies are as variable as the stepparents and children themselves. As you might expect, it is more difficult for a stepparent to feel close to a stepchild than for a parent to feel close to a biological child (Pasley & Moorefield, 2004). It is not uncommon for children to show dislike or challenging behavior to a new stepparent in order to avoid loyalty conflicts with their biological parent (Kalter, 1990). Children may continue to harbor the fantasy that their parents will get back together, or they may simply resent the attention that their parent now pays to the new partner. In either case, children may do their best to annoy or irritate the stepparent so much that the stepparent leaves. In fact, 60% of remarried couples experience a second divorce, and the rate is 50% higher for families with children (Hetherington & Stanley-Hagan, 1999). If the stepparent can ride out this period of adjustment, which lasts for 5 to 7 years on average, a better relationship may ultimately develop. On the positive side, a parent's second marriage may be better than the first, providing the child with a new model of what a loving relationship can be (Kalter, 1990).

Research comparing children in stepfamilies to other groups of children has not shown any conclusive differences (Pasley & Moorefield, 2004). Academic performance is somewhat lower than for children in intact families, and remarriage of a parent does not increase academic performance of the children over the level they achieved in a single-parent family (Tillman, 2007). Overall adjustment and well-being of children in stepfamilies is slightly lower on average than that of children in well-functioning biological families, but individual differences are very large, which means that many children in stepfamilies are thriving (Dunn, 2002). As we discussed in regard to the effects of divorce, the most important factors that relate to children's well-being are the number of transitions and stresses a child has been exposed to and the nature of the parent-child relationship (Dunn, 2002). Parents and others need to be open to listening to children's thoughts and feelings about their complicated family lives.

Grandparents Raising Grandchildren

Almost 2.5 million grandparents in the United States are acting as parents to their grandchildren (U.S. Census Bureau, 2006). In addition, about 30% of children under 5 whose mothers work are cared for by grandparents (U.S. Census Bureau, 2008d).

Grandparents become their grandchildren's main caretakers for many reasons: death of the parents, illness, incarceration, drug addiction, or other difficulties that prevent parents from filling their parental role (Barger, 2008). Nationally, 460,000 of these grandparents are living below the poverty line, and 700,000 have some disability (U.S. Census Bureau, 2006). Sometimes the grandparents are assigned to be the major caretakers by child welfare agencies, but more often these are informal arrangements. In these cases, the agencies that are intended to support families may not know about the arrangements; therefore few services are provided to help the grandparents raise these children (Raphel, 2008). Without formal legal rights, grandparents can be hindered in taking care of their grandchildren's needs. For instance, they cannot give permission for medical care and may have difficulty enrolling the child in school (American Association of Retired Persons, 2004).

Often these families are marginalized, with few services available to them, but there are some programs designed to help them. An organization called Generations United (2009) has a National Center on Grandparents and Other Relatives Raising Children that provides information, support, and advocacy on a national level. At the local level, in Hartford, Connecticut, a program called Generations provides help to

Grandparents raising their grandchildren. Grandparents are often involved in the care of their grandchildren, and sometimes are the ones who raise them. What issues arise when a grandparent becomes the child's major caregiver?

24 families in which grandparents are raising their grandchildren (Barger, 2008). Housing is provided with rent on a sliding scale, along with free child care on a campus that is separated from the dangerous neighborhood that surrounds it. Classes on everything from parenting skills to sewing skills are provided, and social workers help the grandparents find the resources they need to provide a better future for their grandchildren and for themselves. For example, one grandmother enrolled in college and planned to use her degree to help others in her situation.

Even when grandparents are not the main caregivers for their grandchildren, their role has been expanding to fill gaps in single-parent and divorced families or when both parents work outside the home (Bengtson, 2001; Dunn, Fergusson, & Maughan, 2006). In addition, parents often stay close, both emotionally and physically, to their own parents, who are living longer than in the past. Women tend to maintain more close-knit relationships with their parents than men do (Bengtson, 2001). In one large study in the United Kingdom, almost 25% of mothers of infants saw their own mothers every day (Dunn et al., 2006). When parents are close to their own parents, then grandparent-grandchildren relationships are likely to be close as well, with help going both ways: The children help the grandparents, and the grandparents also care for their grandchildren (Dunn et al., 2006). There are cultural differences in these relationships. In the United States, African American parents are more likely than European Americans to have a close relationship with their own mothers (Bengtson, 2001). In the United Kingdom, White mothers of infants were likely to see their own mothers once a week, Black mothers saw them only once a month, but Pakistani mothers were likely to see their own mothers every day (Dunn et al., 2006).

Gay and Lesbian Parents

Unlike the other types of families we have discussed, we do not have reliable figures to tell us how many children are growing up with gay or lesbian parents (Kurdek, 2004). The vast majority of children who are living in households with gay or lesbian parents were born when one of the parents was in a heterosexual marriage and only later "came out." However, increasingly gay and lesbian couples are having children through pregnancy or adoption (Elliott & Umberson, 2004).

Research on children who are raised by gay or lesbian parents has shown few differences between these children and those raised by heterosexual couples (Patterson, 2009). Emotional well-being and cognitive skills show no differences (Stacey & Biblarz, 2001). Children's adjustment in these families is linked to the quality of the relationship between parents and child, just as it is in heterosexual families, rather than to the sexual preference of the parents. Sexual identity and sexual preferences of these children seem to be less restricted than children of heterosexual couples, and parents are less likely to promote only gender-stereotyped behaviors (Stacey & Biblarz, 2001). In early adulthood, they were more open to homosexual as well as heterosexual experiences, but were no more likely than other teens to identify themselves as gay or lesbian (Golombok & Tasker, 1996). One concern has been that these children will be teased and even bullied more than other children. While children and teens do report hearing negative remarks about their families, no overall differences are found in their friendships, their popularity, or any other aspect of their peer relationships (Patterson, 2009).

Growing up with two dads. Children who grow up with gay parents are likely to be as happy and well adjusted as children of heterosexual parents. It is the quality of the parent-child relationship (rather than the parents' sexual preference) that is important to the child.

Video Link 14.4
Gay and lesbian parents.

Adoptive Families

As we said in Chapter 12, young teens often have conflicts with their parents. When these families were formed by adoption, they deal with additional issues, as illustrated by the conversation below between a mother and a tall, red-haired boy who was adopted at birth by his much shorter, dark-haired parents:

Mother: Jack, you need to do your homework *now*.

Jack: *You* can't make me do my homework. I'm going to go find my *real* mother!

Mother: Your *real* mother is yelling at you right now!

Although we certainly don't recommend yelling at children, this interchange illustrates some of the issues in families formed by adoption. Jack is dealing with the normal issues of independence and identity found in early adolescence. This mother's response could have been defensive, based on her fear of abandonment (Rampage, Eovaldi, Ma, & Weigel-Foy, 2003): "Go ahead, find your real mother." The implication of this response would be "You were never really mine." Instead, she is comfortable with being his real mother and knows that he needs her to acknowledge their firm connection. He can express his independence with the security of knowing that he cannot really push her away; their bond is real and strong.

Jack is probably also wondering about his identity and where he came from. He clearly does not resemble his parents, as will be true whenever the child is of a different race than the parents, and he is reminded of this fact every time he sees his own reflection. In 2007 40% of adopted children were of a different race than their parents (Vandivere, Malm, & Radel, 2009). Especially during adolescence, adoptees need to know as much as the adoptive parents know about their birth parents (Rampage et al., 2003). Professionals who study and work with adoptive families point to the importance of developing the "family story." Every family has its stories about its history, but this aspect of family life is especially important when adoption plays a role. Parents can begin to tell children, in simple terms and in a loving context, the story of their adoption, even before they can really understand it. This sets the stage to fill in details as the child grows and is able to understand more. When the details are difficult, the parents walk a fine line between "honoring the birthparent and acknowledging hardships and limitations" (Rampage et al., 2003, p. 217).

Respecting the child's cultural origins becomes an issue especially in international adoptions. In 2007, there were 1.8 million adopted children under the age of 18 in the United States; 25% of these were foreign born and 60% of those children were from Asia, mostly from China (Vandivere et al., 2009). In the family pictured on this page, Chinese studies are part of the family's tribute to their daughter's background. During a visit to China, they visited an orphanage similar to the one in which their daughter had lived as an infant.

Open adoptions, in which the child and the birth and adoptive families have access to each other, are much more common than they were in the past (Berge, Mendenhall, Wrobel, Grotevant, & McRoy, 2006). In one study, adolescents who had been adopted as infants were interviewed about their feelings about the openness of their adoptions. The authors of the study concluded that contact with the birth mother was appreciated by the majority of teens and did not interfere with their attachment to their adoptive mothers. In the words of one boy in describing his relationship with his birth mother: "Mainly a friend, I guess, I mean she doesn't have like a parental role, because I already have that. She's mainly just another person who loves me" (Berge et al., 2006, p. 1033). It is not unusual for adoptive children to have fantasies about their birth families, and these fantasies can affect their relationships with their adoptive families (Rampage et al., 2003), but when children have contact with their birth parents, many of these fantasies are replaced by the realities. As we saw above, these realities can be positive and the child finds "another person who loves me," or they may be negative, as when the child finds that there was good reason why his birth parents were unable to care for a child.

TRUE/FALSE

5. Open adoption, in which the adopted child has contact with his or her birth mother, does not weaken the attachment of the child to his or her adoptive mother.

    True. This is what the results from at least one study of open adoptions have shown. This contact helps the child have a stronger sense of his or her identity.

Open adoptions
Adoptions in which the children and their biological and adoptive families have access to each other.

Video Link 14.5
Open adoption.

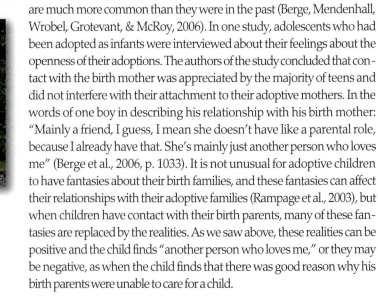

Multicultural adoptive family. This picture shows a family with two adopted children, one from Colombia and one from China. For international adoptions, acknowledging the children's background is important in their developing ethnic identity. This family took a trip to China and visited an orphanage similar to the one in which the daughter had lived before she was adopted.

Contact with their birth parents also helped adolescents develop their sense of identity. For Jack, the boy at the beginning of this section, knowing where his height and red hair came from might give him more of a sense of who he is. As one adopted girl stated,

> My mom's family looks a lot alike, and I don't look anything like them. . . . When I see the pictures of my birthmother or visit, I see the similarities and can say I look more like her. Or my birthmother would write me in a letter something that would sound like me and I'd say, "Well, oh that is where I get this from." That's, I think, the part that interests me the most about it. It's discovering why I am the way that I am. (Berge et al., 2006, pp. 1023–1024)

Foster Care

There are circumstances in which children must be removed from their homes for their own well-being. They may be in situations of abuse or neglect, or their parent may be unable to care for them because of mental or physical illness, incarceration, substance abuse, or even death (American Academy of Child and Adolescent Psychiatry [AACAP], 2005). When there are no alternative caregivers within the family, these children are likely to enter the **foster care** system and will be placed with a foster family, which receives financial support from the state. Everyone involved, including the child, knows that this is a temporary situation. The child may return home, move to another foster home or institution, or eventually be legally released for adoption.

Everyone agrees that children do best when they have consistent, reliable care. In 1980, Congress passed the Adoption Assistance and Child Welfare Act to promote efforts to provide consistent care, either by returning children to their families when possible or through permanent adoption. The Adoption and Safe Families Act of 1997 followed with financial support for reunification programs provided to children's birth families to enhance the possibility that they might be able to return. It also sets time limits on this support. If the child has been in foster care for 15 of the previous 22 months, the act stipulates that efforts to establish a permanent adoptive family must proceed (Child Welfare League of America, n.d.). At this point, if the parents are still unable to provide care in a positive and consistent manner, parental rights may be terminated. In most cases, an attempt will be made to place the child with relatives, with the hope that they will eventually adopt the child (AACAP, 2005). About one third of all foster children are officially placed with family members, and there are many more who are informally in these living situations (Raphel, 2008).

Children in foster care have undergone the trauma that preceded their removal from their home, as well as the removal itself (Bruskas, 2008). Many suffer serious emotional problems, including posttraumatic stress disorder, anxiety, and depression. The American Academy of Child and Adolescent Psychiatry (2005) lists the following emotional issues that these children may deal with:

- Blaming themselves and feeling guilty about their removal from their birth parents
- Wishing to return to their birth parents, even if they were abused by them
- Feeling unwanted if they need to wait a long time for an adoption
- Feeling helpless about multiple changes in foster parents over time
- Having mixed emotions about attaching to foster parents
- Feeling insecure and uncertain about their future
- Reluctantly acknowledging positive feelings for foster parents

The foster parents with whom the children are placed also have to deal with important challenges:

- Recognizing the limits of their emotional attachment to the child
- Understanding mixed feelings toward the child's birth parents
- Recognizing their difficulties in letting the child return to his or her birth parents
- Dealing with the complex needs (emotional, physical, etc.) of children in their care
- Working with sponsoring social agencies
- Finding needed support services in the community
- Dealing with the child's emotions and behavior following visits with his or her birth parents

Foster care The temporary placement of children in a family that is not their own because of unhealthy situations within their birth family.

Children's education is also affected by their entry into the foster care system. With changes of schools, records can be lost, days are missed, and new situations may be uncomfortable for the children. These disruptions in the educational process are reflected in the fact that only 50% of children who have been in foster care either graduate high school or pass the General Educational Development (GED) test. Less than 2% of these children go on to college (Bruskas, 2008).

The best hope for foster children is to find a stable family with which to live. However, actual adoption is difficult in cases such as these because these children have had many disruptions in their lives or have been the victims of physical, emotional, and/or sexual abuse. The effects of these experiences cannot necessarily be overcome by entering a well-meaning, loving family. Children who have had such experiences are very cautious about getting attached to anyone, are constantly on the lookout for problems, and have difficulty regulating their emotions. As we described in Chapter 10, in extreme cases they may suffer from reactive attachment disorder as a result of their experiences. Families who adopt these children must be adequately prepared for the challenge they are taking on and supported throughout the process in order to raise them (Rampage et al., 2003).

At age 18, many of these children leave the foster care system with few supports or skills. Many eventually return to their families of origin (Courtney, 2009), but a disproportionate number will be homeless and may turn to criminal behavior (Bruskas, 2008). In 2008 Congress passed the Fostering Connections to Success and Increasing Adoptions Act that allows states to provide support for foster children beyond age 18. Acknowledging that families in the United States now help their children move into adulthood with both financial and emotional support, this new act continues the role of government in providing care until these adolescents reach age 21 if they are in school, in employment training, or employed at least 80 hours per month (Courtney, 2009). Research on the effectiveness of the programs that result from this new act will eventually give us an idea of what works to help children move from the foster care system into a successful adulthood.

TRUE/FALSE

6. American families on average eat a meal together as a family only once a week.

   False. There is room for improvement in this regard, but about half of American families with children eat dinner together at least 3–5 times per week.

How Do Families Function?

Family Time

The major question in regard to all the types of families that we have described so far is "What is the function of a family in regard to children's well-being?" Families provide children with many things: the basic necessities of life, love, education, supervision, and control. In the United States, many of these functions come together at family mealtimes. About half of families with children eat dinner together at least 3 to 5 times per week. Although these meals tend to last only about 20 minutes, evidence has shown that families who share meals have children who are less likely to be obese or have other eating disorders, less likely to use drugs and alcohol, and more likely to succeed in school (Fiese & Schwartz, 2008). In one longitudinal study of adolescents, female adolescents who had meals with their families 5 or more times a week were less likely to develop eating disorders or to use extreme weight control behavior such as self-induced vomiting or the use of laxatives 5 years later (Neumark-Sztainer, Eisenberg, Fulkerson, Story, & Larson, 2008).

Food itself acts as a positive reinforcement, but the impact of family dinners is strongest when the atmosphere is one of responsiveness and organization. Dinner is often a good time for everyone to check in at the end of the day, share experiences, and reconnect. The storytelling that may occur (for example, "You'll never guess what happened when . . .") is a likely contributor to children's increased literacy, as they learn more about language from the conversations (Larson, 2008). It may surprise

Family dinnertime. Families exchange more than food when they sit down to meals together. This girl may be learning many things, such as how to take part in a conversation and what her parents do during their day.

you to hear that most teens report enjoying meals with their families and eat more healthfully when they share family meals (Neumark-Sztainer, 2008). The positive sharing that may go on contributes to the lower level of risk taking and emotional problems that teens in these families have (Larson, 2008). Many families have a television in their eating area and use it for information like the news or to distract younger children, but it appears that having the TV on has negative consequences because it disrupts the family's interactions. It also promotes obesity because people pay less attention to whether they are full and have eaten enough when they are watching television (Fiese & Schwartz, 2008). **Active Learning: Family Mealtime** will guide you in thinking about your own family's experiences with mealtimes.

Family Mealtime

ACTIVE LEARNING

Think about your own family when you were a child and a teenager. How often did your family eat together? Did the frequency of eating together change from childhood to adolescence for you and, if it did, how did it change? When you ate together, remember what types of things were discussed and what the atmosphere was. What kinds of things interfered with your family eating together: job responsibilities, sports, or other extracurricular activities? Was the TV on in the room on a regular basis? If so, what impact did this have on family interaction? What kind of food was served—homemade, frozen, or fast food? Now consider your own experience in light of the general findings that connect family dinners with positive outcomes. How does your experience fit or not fit with this research? What does this exercise tell you about your own experience, but also what does it tell you about how the research might be refined so that it could capture other pertinent issues?

Family mealtime is just one type of ritual that helps connect the members of a family together. Think for a minute about other routines and rituals that were part of your family experiences while you were growing up. With younger children we often have bedtime rituals that might include a bath and some time to read a story, there may be special ways that birthdays are marked that the children look forward to from year to year, and for adolescents we celebrate the milestones in their lives. Rituals and routines are important because they help establish a rhythm in family life and make life organized and predictable (Spagnola & Fiese, 2007). They also help strengthen families by providing a sense of belonging and connection between generations (Nelms, 2005). They often reflect a family's cultural and religious values and provide opportunities for members of the family to emotionally bond with one another through shared memories.

Families add or lose traditions as family structure changes, and this requires adaptation on the part of everyone (Moriarty & Wagner, 2004). For example, if everyone had gathered at a grandparent's home to celebrate Thanksgiving each year, the death of that grandparent would make the family decide whether someone else will assume that role or whether the tradition will be abandoned or transformed in some way. Stepfamilies also need to renegotiate family traditions. In blended families, do they adopt the traditions of one of the families or the other? Do they try to combine elements from both traditions and create a hybrid? Or do they develop new traditions that are unique to the new blended families? This type of adjustment is part of the restabilization process that stepfamilies go through.

In the next section of this chapter we will look at two of the basic relationships that children have within families, those with parents and those with siblings.

The Changing Roles of Mothers and Fathers

One of the biggest changes in the American family in recent history has been the movement of mothers into the world of work outside the family home, as illustrated in Figure 14.4. In 1950,

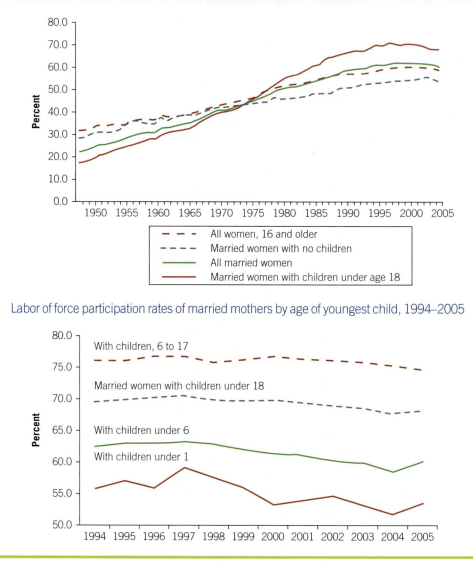

Figure 14.4

Labor force participation by mothers. Chart 1 shows how labor force participation has changed from the 1950s into the 2000s. Note that married women with children under the age of 18 have outpaced other groups of women in entering the world of work. Chart 2 shows how the age of a woman's children affects her likelihood of being employed. Women with children who are school-aged or older are more likely than mothers with younger children to work.

Labor force participation rates of women by marital status and presence of children, March 1948–2005

Labor of force participation rates of married mothers by age of youngest child, 1994–2005

16% of children had mothers who worked for pay. By 1991, 59% of children, including a majority of preschoolers, had mothers who worked outside the home (Coontz, 2000), and by 2005, between 55% and 75% of married mothers were working (Cohany & Sok, 2007). Between two thirds and three fourths of married couples with children are now dual earners (Fraenkel, 2003). One issue that arises is how families manage the balance between work and family life. As we all know, work and family each create both stresses and joys. These two aspects of our lives will interact. Few people can simply turn off their work when they enter their homes. If parents experience stress at work, they are less likely to have the same energy for their children, resulting in more conflict and more child behavioral and emotional problems (Fraenkel, 2003).

The effects of mothers working outside the home on children's well-being differ according to the age of the child. In one study, children whose mothers worked full-time during their first or second years of life were found to be less compliant with adult expectations in their preschool years (Belsky & Eggebeen, 1991). However, another study found that mothers working long hours were associated with slightly lower levels of cognitive development and academic achievement, but they did not have a significant effect on compliance, problem behaviors, or self-esteem (Harvey, 1999). In more recent research, no differences in cognitive development were found between those children with working mothers and those whose mothers stayed home except for a small but consistently lower level for children whose mothers had worked full-time during their first year of life (Hill, Waldfogel, Brooks-Gunn, & Han, 2005).

A study conducted by Hoffman and Youngblade (1999) with European American and African American third and fourth graders from diverse socioeconomic backgrounds found no differences between children of employed and stay-at-home mothers on several measures of cognitive achievement. This lack of significant difference held across gender, socioeconomic status, and marital status. With regard to socioemotional development, the girls of employed mothers in their study were less shy and more independent, had a stronger sense of self-efficacy, and were more assertive than girls with stay-at-home mothers. Both boys and girls of employed mothers held less traditional views of gender roles and were more likely to agree that men could do things that are traditionally feminine and that women could do things that are traditionally masculine.

Research on the effect of maternal employment on adolescents has largely focused on the fact that adolescents with employed mothers often spend time at home without adult supervision. Children are more likely to take care of themselves if their mothers are employed, and the older the children, the greater the likelihood of them spending time alone when their parents are at work. The good news for working mothers is that there is accumulating evidence that maternal employment has "only a small and indirect effect on delinquency" (Vander Ven, Cullen, Carrozza, & Wright, 2001, p. 252). Aughinbaugh and Gittleman (2003) also found little association between maternal employment and adolescents' decision to drink alcohol, smoke, use drugs, become sexually active, or commit delinquent acts (see also Armistead, Wierson, & Forehand, 1990). Perhaps not surprisingly, when adolescents are supervised at a distance (for example, by phone), do not associate with delinquent peers, and feel an attachment to school, they are less likely to become involved in delinquency (Vander Ven et al., 2001).

When we look at trends for fathers in the United States, there appear to be some contradictions. On the one hand, married fathers are more involved with their children than in the past (Coltrane, 2004). There also are increasing numbers of men who are the primary caretakers of their children while their wives work outside the home, although these numbers are still small. In 2006, more than a quarter-million children in the United States were cared for by stay-at-home fathers. In addition, even if the fathers also worked outside the home, they were the primary caregivers for almost 3 million preschoolers during the hours that their mothers worked (U.S. Census Bureau, 2008b). However, as we've seen, there are more single-parent families headed by mothers, with little or no involvement of fathers. What impact do fathers have on children's development? Research has shown that fathers with positive parenting skills and greater involvement with their children foster greater cognitive skills, self-control, and empathy and less gender stereotyping in both preschoolers and adolescents (Coltrane, 2004).

Some differences in the parenting by mothers and fathers persist, however. On average, mothers spend more time with their infants and

The changing role of American fathers. Young fathers are now playing a larger role in the physical care of their children than was true a generation or two ago.

Video Link 14.6
Changing roles.

young children than fathers do, and they are more involved in caregiving activities. Mothers are often found to be more sensitive to their young children, especially their daughters, than fathers are (Lovas, 2005; Schoppe-Sullivan et al., 2006). By contrast, fathers' role with children has been described as moving the child away from the protection of the mother into the wider world of social relationships. Fathers engage in more physical play with their children than mothers, but this role for fathers is not universal. Fathers have been found to be more playful than mothers in France, Switzerland, Italy, and India, but not in Germany, Sweden, or Taiwan (Lewis & Lamb, 2003). Even in the United States, some fathers tend to be more playful, while others see their role more as a caretaker or disciplinarian, or are simply disengaged from child rearing (Jain, Belsky, & Crnic, 1996).

The way we have thought about parents and parenting has changed over time, reflecting changes in both our philosophical beliefs about the nature of children and families and our growing understanding of the factors that influence child development. **Journey of Research: Changing Views of Parenting** describes how ideas about parenting have changed over time.

Changing Views of Parenting

JOURNEY *of* RESEARCH

Parent effects model
A model of parenting effects that assumes that parents cause the characteristics that we see in their children.

We can trace some of the earliest advice for parents back to philosophers like Thomas Hobbes and John Calvin, who portrayed children as sinful by nature and in need of firm discipline in order to build good character, or to Jean-Jacques Rousseau, who portrayed children as basically good and innocent by nature and in need of nurturance and guidance (Heath, 2005). As you already know, Freud's theory portrayed childhood as a critical time for meeting the needs of children. Compared to earlier ideas, Freudian ideas of parenting were indulgent and lenient, but these ideas were never widely embraced in the United States (Heath, 2005). Instead American parents in the early 20th century looked to science for information on how to best raise their children, and they found it in the work of John Watson.

In Chapter 2 we quoted from Watson's (1928) book on child rearing in which he claimed that he could take any healthy infant and make the infant anything he wanted the infant to be. In a chapter from that book titled "The Dangers of Too Much Mother Love," he warned parents against showing too much affection toward their children because it would make them overly dependent on their parents. Instead he advocated for maintaining a strict schedule and for treating even very young children like young adults. Throughout the 1930s, 1940s, and 1950s, Watson

promoted the ideas in his book through articles he published in popular magazines and speeches he gave at professional conferences and meetings (Heath, 2005), and the public readily embraced this "scientific approach" to child rearing.

Several ideas converged in the 1940s and 1950s which turned parents' attention toward the importance of responsiveness and warmth in their relationships with their children. You have read about the research in the 1940s and 1950s by Bowlby and Ainsworth on attachment, which advocated for parents being sensitive and responsive to the needs of their children, rather than making them adhere to a strict schedule. Dr. Benjamin Spock popularized an approach to parenting that struck a middle ground between Freud's leniency and Watson's unresponsiveness (Heath, 2005), and his ideas remained popular through the 1970s. Beginning in the 1960s, the most comprehensive and influential research on parenting was conducted by Diana Baumrind, and her research continues to shape the way we think about parenting.

Note that all of these different approaches to parenting share one thing in common: They all assume that what parents do makes their children the type of people they become. This is called a **parent effects model** because it assumes that parents cause the characteristics that we see in their children. However, as our understanding of parenting grew, it became clear that in some cases it was characteristics of the child that seemed to be driving the process and determining the parenting style that the parents used. This is called a **child effects model**. For instance, a very defiant and oppositional child may evoke a harsher style of parenting than a child who is more compliant and obedient would evoke. Today, most developmentalists think of parenting as a transactional process (or use a **transactional model**), in which the influence moves in both directions as part of an ongoing process. Parents certainly do influence their children's behavior, but children also influence their parents' behavior.

Finally, the research has increasingly recognized the role that context plays in influencing parental behavior. Parenting styles research has begun looking at the powerful role of cultural values, expectations, and customs in parenting styles, as well as how parents adapt their parenting style not only to the characteristics of their children but also to the characteristics of the communities and neighborhoods in which they live. This is another situation where, as we described in Chapter 10, the best situation is one in which there is a goodness of fit between the characteristics of the environment and the characteristics of the child.

Child effects model
A model of parenting effects that assumes that it is the characteristics of the child that determine the parenting style that the parents use.

Transactional model
A model of parenting effects that assumes that influence moves from parent to child but also from child to parent in a reciprocal process.

Parenting Styles

So far we have discussed two basic aspects of parenting that influence how children develop. In Chapter 10 we discussed the importance of the development of secure attachment between parents and their children, and in Chapter 12 we looked at the important role of parental control techniques and strategies in helping children learn appropriate behavior for their society. Diana Baumrind took dimensions that had appeared repeatedly in previous research on parenting and combined them to describe four different parenting styles. The first dimension is parental acceptance/responsiveness, and the second is parental demandingness/control (Maccoby & Martin, 1983). Parents can be high or low on each of these dimensions. Parents who are high on **acceptance/responsiveness** show a good deal of warmth and affection in their relationship with their child and provide a lot of praise and encouragement. In contrast, parents who are low on this dimension can be cool and even rejecting (sometimes ignoring the child completely), and they are more likely to criticize or punish the child than to praise him. Parents who are high on the **demandingness/control** dimension impose a lot of demands and restrictions on their children and often have a great number of rules that control their children's behavior. In contrast, parents who are low on this dimension impose much less structure and fewer limits on their children. If we combine these two dimensions, we get the four distinct parenting styles shown in Figure 14.5.

   Authoritative parents combine high levels of control with a good deal of warmth and encouragement (Baumrind, 1971). Although they do make demands upon their children,

Acceptance/ responsiveness
A dimension of parenting that measures the amount of warmth and affection in the parent-child relationship.

Demandingness/ control A dimension of parenting that measures the amount of restrictiveness and structure that parents place on their children.

Authoritative parents
A parenting style that combines high levels of control with a good deal of warmth and encouragement, marked with reasonable expectations and explanation of the parents' rules.

Figure 14.5

Baumrind's parenting styles. By combining two important dimensions of parenting (acceptance/responsiveness and demandingness/control), it is possible to describe four different parenting styles.

		Acceptance/Responsiveness	
		High	**Low**
Demandingness/Control	**High**	Authoritative	Authoritarian
	Low	Permissive	Uninvolved

Authoritarian parents
A parenting style that combines high levels of control and low levels of warmth, marked by an expectation of compliance from the child.

Permissive parents
A parenting style that provides a great deal of warmth and acceptance but few, if any, rules or restrictions.

Uninvolved or neglectful parents A parenting style that is low both on the dimension of warmth and on the dimension of control; parents may be disinterested in parenting or actively reject their children.

Parenting styles Fairly regular and consistent patterns of interacting with children.

TRUE/FALSE

7. Children who are raised by permissive parents are most likely to grow up to be self-reliant, confident, and explorative.

False. Contrary to what you might think (or what permissive parents might expect), children raised with a permissive parenting style have been described as less self-reliant, explorative, and self-controlled than children reared by other parenting styles.

their expectations are reasonable and appropriate for the child's age. A hallmark of this style is that authoritative parents are willing to provide rationales for their rules and expectations and are open to listening to their children's point of view (Heath, 2005). Sometimes they are even persuaded by their children to be flexible about the rules because the situation warrants it. Overall these parents treat their children with respect and respond to their child's unique characteristics.

Authoritarian parents are high on control and often have a large number of rules that they expect their children to obey. In fact, these parents highly value unquestioning compliance from their children. They feel no obligation to explain the reasons for their rules and are generally unyielding about the rules themselves. These parents are not sensitive to the feelings of their children and are, therefore, considered low on the dimension of acceptance/responsiveness.

Permissive parents provide a great deal of warmth and acceptance to their children, but this acceptance is coupled with few, if any, rules or restrictions. Children are free to express their ideas and opinions (often having an equal say with parents in decision making in the family), and parents usually do little monitoring or restricting of the child's activities.

Baumrind did not identify **uninvolved or neglectful parents** in her original research, but these parents provide neither control nor warmth to their children (Maccoby & Martin, 1983). They do not make demands on their children for good behavior and do not sets rules or limits for them. They also are not emotionally connected to their children. They may be disengaged or disinterested, or they may actively reject their children. They do not monitor or supervise their children's behavior and do not support or encourage self-regulation (Maccoby & Martin, 1983). Some parents in this category are so consumed with problems in their own lives that they appear to have nothing left to give to their relationship with their children.

These brief descriptions provide a good sense of these different parenting styles, but parents do not always fit neat, clear-cut textbook descriptions. Even the most authoritarian parent might relent and show some flexibility occasionally, and even the most permissive parent might have to draw the line at some point and stop a child's behavior. However, **parenting styles** are fairly regular and consistent patterns that play themselves out in a variety of situations. It would not be surprising if, as you read these descriptions, some parents you know came to mind for at least a couple of them.

A great deal of research has been done on the consequences of each of these different parenting styles. We will describe what the research has shown, but bear in mind that most of this research has been done on White, middle-class children from Western cultures. The characteristics of individualistic cultures that differ from collectivist cultures might influence parenting styles and their outcomes. We will discuss some of these differences after we outline the original research.

Beginning with some of Baumrind's (1971) original research, children who were raised by authoritative parents were described as having a number of positive characteristics. They were found to be "the most self-reliant, explorative, and content" (p. 1). In comparison, children raised by authoritarian parents were described as "discontent, withdrawn, and distrustful" (p. 2), and children raised by permissive parents were described as "the least self-reliant, explorative, and self controlled" (p. 2). Subsequent research conducted by many other researchers has supported the conclusion that children raised with an authoritative style develop very well on a number of dimensions, and children raised by other styles fare more poorly in comparison.

The achievement orientation that Baumrind (1967) found in preschool children raised by authoritative parents continues to be reflected in older children and adolescents in their academic achievement (Aunola, Stattin, & Nurmi, 2000; Dornbusch, Ritter, Leiderman, & Roberts, 1987; Gray & Steinberg, 1999). These children also are more socially skilled, show greater psychosocial maturity, and exhibit fewer internalizing and externalizing problems. For example, they are more likely to be seen as outgoing, as leaders (Baumrind, 1991a), as more cooperative with peers, siblings, and adults (Denham, Renwick, & Holt, 1991), and as more empathetic and altruistic (Aunola et al., 2000). They also have been found to have higher self-esteem (Abraham & Christopherson, 1984; McClun & Merrell, 1998), to be more self-reliant (Steinberg, Mounts, Lamborn, & Dornbusch, 1991), and to have a stronger internal locus of control (McClun & Merrell, 1998). Children reared by authoritative parents also have fewer behavior problems and less psychological distress (Gray & Steinberg, 1999; Steinberg et al., 1991) and are less likely to use substances (Adamczyk-Robinette, Fletcher, & Wright, 2002; Baumrind, 1991b; Fletcher & Jefferies, 1999; Gray & Steinberg, 1999).

Children who are reared with an authoritarian style are not encouraged to think for themselves and are not allowed to make their own decisions. Baumrind described their situation as being one in which they feel trapped and angry, but also one in which they are afraid to protest because of the possible negative consequences. This may help explain why authoritarian parenting has been associated with a child becoming a bully (Baldry & Farrington, 2000). Authoritarian parents often rely on physical punishment, so they model aggressive behaviors for their children. A child who has, in effect, been bullied by authoritarian parents may vent the resulting anger and frustration he or she feels on other weaker victims. Authoritarian parenting also predicts convictions for criminal offenses in young adolescents (Farrington & Hawkins, 1991), which can be thought of as another way of striking out at people and property. Children of authoritarian parents have lower self-esteem (Martinez & Garcia, 2008; Rudy & Grusec, 2006), lower psychosocial maturity (Mantzicopoulos & Oh-Hwang, 1998), a lower level of moral reasoning (Boyes & Allen, 1993), and poorer academic grades (Dornbusch et al., 1987). The picture that emerges suggests that across a range of developmental outcomes, authoritarian parenting has negative repercussions for child development.

Permissive parents are the other extreme on the dimension of control, although the low level of control that they exercise is combined with a good deal of warmth and affection. Parents may choose this style with the best of intentions, but the child outcomes are not particularly positive. According to Lamborn, Dornbusch, and Steinberg (1996), large amounts of autonomy during adolescence have been associated with "higher rates of deviant behavior, lower academic competence, and poorer psychosocial functioning" (p. 295) (see also Dornbusch et al., 1987). Nijhof and Engels (2007) describe these children as "self-centered, impulsive and aggressive" (p. 711), as having poor social skills, and as feeling unworthy of the love of another person. On a test of moral reasoning, they fell below the scores of children raised by authoritative parents (although they scored higher than children raised by authoritarian parents) (Boyes & Allen, 1993). Remember that permissive parents do not exercise control over their children's behavior but also may not offer guidance or direction. It is understandable how this underinvolvement could contribute to a child's low expectations for interpersonal relationships. Aunola et al. (2000) found that children with underinvolved parents are more prone to depression.

A growing body of research has found that children with uninvolved (sometimes also referred to as *neglectful*) parents do the worst in terms of their outcomes. Both young children and young adolescents who are raised by parents who are less warm and less involved have been found to be more angry and defiant (Miller, Cowan, Cowan, Hetherington, & Clingempeel, 1993). Lamborn, Mounts, Steinberg, and Dornbusch (1991) found that adolescents from uninvolved households scored more poorly than other adolescents on measures of psychosocial development (self-reliance, work orientation, social competence), school achievement (grade point average, school orientation), internalized distress (psychological and somatic symptoms), and problem behavior (drug use, delinquency).

You are likely to have some reaction when you see the photo on the next page. Use **Active Learning: How Parents React** to better understand how parents with different parenting styles would deal with this situation. How would you react?

ACTIVE LEARNING

How Parents React

Imagine that a parent comes into the living room to find this scene. Now think about each parenting style that Diana Baumrind has identified. Describe what you think an authoritative parent would say and do. Now do the same for an authoritarian parent, a permissive parent, and an uninvolved parent. Now imagine that you are that 3-year-old and think about what you would learn from the response of each type of parent. In the long run, which type of response is likely to be most effective in making you want to behave differently in the future? Why?

TRUE/FALSE

8. Based upon the research done on parenting styles, it is clear that children are the way they are because their parents make them that way.

False. Parenting is a very complex process. Although parents affect their children, they also respond to their children's characteristics. Children also influence how their parents treat them. The parenting process works in both directions, with parents shaping children and children shaping their parents.

Parenting Models

In **Journey of Research: Changing Views of Parenting**, we introduced the idea that there has been an evolution from an initial view that parents cause children's behavior to a more interactional view that parents and children influence each other. So far, the way we have described parenting styles and child outcomes could be seen as an example of the parent-effects model. We were careful in our descriptions to say that certain parental behaviors are "associated with" or "related to" certain child outcomes, and you'll remember that when two things are correlated, we do not know the direction of the effect. We cannot say what has caused what. However, when people read the research on parenting, it is easy to slip into thinking about it in those terms: that what parents do *causes* their children to turn out in certain ways. But as research on parenting styles has continued, we have increasingly recognized the essential role that children's characteristics play in this process.

We can find examples of a child-effects model in the literature, but before we describe them, stop for a minute and think about what characteristics of a child would be so powerful that they could determine a parent's parenting style. Did you think about the child's age and gender? Both of these child characteristics influence how parents treat different children, even within the same family (Furman, 1995). For instance, as infants become toddlers and begin to do more things on their own, their growing independence affects their parents, who react by exerting greater control over their child's behavior (Kuczynski & Kochanska, 1995). Parents also begin to expect more conventional behavior from their children and greater compliance to the parents' requests. When children become adolescents, parents typically respond to their growing maturation with more autonomy granting. The balance of power within the parent-child relationship, which clearly favored the parent during childhood, now shifts in the direction of a more egalitarian relationship (Holmbeck, Paikoff, & Brooks-Gunn, 1995).

The child's gender is another important characteristic that elicits different types of parenting behavior. Parents often exercise more control over their daughters and show more warmth and affection to them, while granting greater autonomy to (or exercising less control over) their sons.

Another situation in which the child can drive the parenting process is one in which the child has some extreme characteristics that parents react to. Parents' style may be affected if their child has a physical, a mental, or an emotional disability. Children who have temperaments that are extremely defiant or oppositional evoke harsher and more controlling behavior from their parents than children who are more obedient or compliant. One example of how children can shape their parents comes from a study of mothers of young children who were oppositional or defiant. These mothers had an **external locus of control** (that is, they had come to believe that they, as parents, had no control over what was happening with their children) (Roberts, Joe, & Rowe-Hallbert, 1992). Under these circumstances, parents might give up on any efforts to change their child's behavior (Crockenberg & Litman, 1991), in which case parenting becomes a child-driven process.

The model of parenting that is used most often today is the transactional model, in which the influence of the child and the influence of the parents are reciprocal and mutual. Parents certainly respond to characteristics of their children (for example, age, gender, temperament) and exert effort to shape their behavior, but children are not passive recipients of these efforts. Their responses to these efforts feed back and influence future parenting behaviors, as parents try to adapt to changing characteristics of their child. In Chapter 11, we provided an example of a negative transactional process in which a child's oppositional behavior resulted in parents escalating their efforts to forcefully control the child's misbehavior, which, in turn, only provoked greater misbehavior on the part of the child. Fortunately this process can (and usually does) work in a positive direction. When a child or an adolescent behaves in a responsible or competent way, parents are likely to respond by granting more autonomy or relinquishing some parental control, which, in turn, gives the child or adolescent the new opportunity to continue developing autonomy as he or she moves toward greater maturity.

Congruence of Parenting Styles

Much of the research on parenting has looked at mothers' parenting styles (Winsler, Madigan, & Aquilino, 2005), but once researchers began to look at fathers' parenting styles as well, the issue of how much agreement there was between mothers and fathers arose. Several consistent differences between mothers and fathers have been found. Mothers are more likely than fathers to use an authoritative style, and fathers are more likely than mothers to use an authoritarian style (Holmbeck et al., 1995; Russell, Hart, Robinson, & Olsen, 2003; Winsler et al., 2005).

Within the same family, the congruence between parents' styles is only modest. In one study, there was fairly high agreement between parents who were permissive, moderate agreement between parents in families where one parent was authoritarian, and no agreement in families where one parent was authoritative (Winsler et al., 2005). What can explain these differences? Being a permissive parent is often an intentional choice by parents who want to create a specific type of child rearing environment, so individuals who share this goal may be more likely to find each other, or one permissive parent may convince the other parent of the wisdom in adopting this style. In other families, one parent may adopt a style that balances the style of the other parent. If one parent is authoritarian, it may be more important that the second parent balance that style by being authoritative or even permissive. However, if one parent is authoritative, it may matter less which style the second parent adopts.

Fortunately children can adapt to the fact that their parents have different styles of interacting with them, and, of course, children sometimes try to use these differences to their own advantage. When children want something from their parents, they often have a pretty good idea of which parent to approach with their request and just how to frame that request to increase the chance that they will get what they want. The one potential problem with this is if the lack of agreement between parents becomes a source of conflict within the family.

Parenting in Context

Parenting is not something that happens in a vacuum. It happens in a context—whether a cultural, socioeconomic, or familial context—and it reflects the values and beliefs of that context. Although we have said broadly that authoritative parenting is associated with the most

Video Link 14.7
Parenting style.

9. Good parenting is good parenting, so the same parenting strategies should work equally well for all children. **TRUE/FALSE**

False. What is "good parenting" can differ from one culture to another. Parents reflect the values and beliefs of their culture, so in a culture that values obedience from children, parenting that requires more compliance from children is probably the best.

positive outcomes, we still need to take context into account. Is this the most effective style for children in all situations? There is some research that supports the idea that it is. In one study of over 10,000 American adolescents from a variety of ethnic and socioeconomic backgrounds who were living in a variety of family structures, the authors concluded that "analyses indicate that the positive correlates of authoritative parenting transcend ethnicity, socioeconomic status, and family structure. Virtually regardless of their ethnicity, class, or parents' marital status, adolescents whose parents are firm, accepting and democratic earn higher grades in school, are more self-reliant, report less anxiety and depression, and are less likely to engage in delinquent behavior" (Steinberg et al., 1991, p. 19; see also Radziszewska, Richardson, Dent, & Flay, 1996). Other research supports the idea that authoritative parenting benefits adolescents in other cultures as well (for example, for Korean adolescents see Mantzicopoulos & Oh-Hwang, 1998, and for Brazilian adolescents see Martinez & Garcia, 2008). But two important exceptions to this conclusion have been found. The first is in the case of ethnic minorities living in disadvantaged neighborhoods, and the second is in the case of some collectivist cultures.

Similar to what we said in Chapter 12 when we discussed parental discipline and the use of control, in dangerous neighborhoods children are much more likely to have a negative outcome when their parents are more disengaged or permissive, but they are *not* negatively affected by relatively punitive parenting (Roche, Ensminger, & Cherlin, 2007). In a high-risk community, greater parental restriction, stronger behavioral control, and stricter punishment may be understood by both parent and child as necessary for survival. However, there is a good deal of variation in terms of how heavily minority parents rely on restriction and punishment. Among middle-class working African American parents, where the environment presents less of a threat, physical punishment was used sparingly, in conjunction with more child-centered strategies like reasoning, and in the context of a warm parent-child relationship (Bluestone & Tamis-LeMonda, 1999).

Compared to Western parents, Asian parents are relatively more controlling, a primary aspect of authoritarian parenting. Although an authoritarian parenting style has been associated with poorer school performance among Euro American children and adolescents, this is not the case for Chinese children. Although Chinese parents are more controlling, their children typically do well in school. Ruth Chao (1994) explains this paradox by describing the Chinese concept of *chiao shun* or the expectation that parents will train their children "to adhere to socially desirable and culturally approved behavior" (p. 1112). When children reach school age, mothers provide the drive for their efforts to succeed in school, but this is done in a context of a warm, supportive, and physically close relationship that was established when the child was much younger. Another important concept in this culture is *guan*, which literally means "to govern" but can also mean "to care for" or even "to love" (p. 1112). From this perspective, even close monitoring and correcting of a child's behavior by adults is seen by both parent and child as a fulfillment of their responsibilities to the child and in the child's best interest.

Latino families are not a singular group, but whether they have immigrated from Mexico, Cuba, Puerto Rico, or Central or South America, there are several shared cultural values in Latino families that influence how parents raise their children (Halgunseth, Ispa, & Rudy, 2006). The first is *familismo*, which includes a strong desire to maintain family ties, to be loyal to the family, and to give the needs of the family priority over one's own needs, together with a belief that one's family will be available to provide instrumental and emotional support when one needs it. The second is *respeto*, which requires that individuals fulfill the expectations for their social roles and maintain harmonious interpersonal relationships through respect of themselves and others. The third is *educación*, which is a broader concept than academics. It involves "training in responsibility, morality and interpersonal relationships" (Halgunseth et al., 2006, p. 1286).

We see these cultural values reflected in several specific parenting behaviors. Latino parents engage in more physical guidance of young children, more parental direction and modeling for school-age children, and more rule setting and monitoring for adolescents, and all of these behaviors have been associated with good outcomes for their children (Halgunseth et al., 2006). Because of the position of respect that Latino fathers occupy within the family, it is the father's responsibility to set the family rules. Although there are more rules in Latino families, adolescents are less willing to confront their fathers about the rules and suffer greater distress when there is conflict within the family (Crean, 2008). Because cultural values can change as families become more acculturated to their new countries, the role of fathers in Latino families may be undergoing some change. There is some evidence that Latino fathers are becoming more nurturant and less authoritarian than they were in the past (Jambunathan, Burts, & Pierce, 2000).

In conclusion, the relationship between parenting behaviors and children's outcomes is complex and multidimensional. In addition to considering the direction of the effect, we need to consider characteristics of both the children and the situation. Cultural values, neighborhood characteristics, and socioeconomic status will have an impact on these outcomes, but it is clear that one reason that we see the variations that we do is because parents try to adjust and adapt their parenting to find what works best for their children. **Active Learning: Exploring Your Parents' Style** guides you in connecting your own experiences with your parents to the ideas presented here.

Exploring Your Parents' Style

ACTIVE LEARNING

Based upon what you have learned about parenting styles, reflect on how you were parented while you were growing up by thinking about these questions:

- What style of parenting did each of your parents use? Did they use the same or different styles?
- If you have siblings, were there any differences in the styles your parents used with your siblings? Can you think of reasons why they may have treated siblings differently?
- How did your parents' parenting style affect you?
- Did their parenting style change as you grew older? If so, *how* did it change?
- What would you do differently with your own children? What would you do the same? Why?

Relationships With Siblings

Siblings are the longest-lasting relationship that you will have in your life. On average sibling relationships last longer than parent-child relationships or marital relationships. About 80% of children in the United States have at least one sibling and, as you would guess from the description earlier in this chapter about family configurations, sibling relationships have become quite complicated. It is not simply a question of how many siblings you have because who those siblings are makes a difference. Sister-sister relationships are different from brother-brother relationships or sister-brother relationships, siblings who are quite a few years different in age have a different type of relationship than siblings who are born close together, and finally, in addition to birth siblings, there are qualitatively different relationships with stepsiblings, half-siblings, and adoptive siblings.

He's my brother! There is much more to sibling relationships than sibling rivalry. Most relationships are warm and supportive, and siblings learn a great deal from each other.

Siblings occupy a special place in a child's social world. Some of the functions they fill overlap with those of parents and others overlap with those of peers, but the combination of roles they fill is unique. According to Cicirelli (1980), "Siblings have been viewed as parent substitutes, rivals, teachers, stimulators, challengers, role models, confidantes, companions, and so on" (p. 111). To varying degrees, older siblings may act as caregivers to their younger siblings. It is within the sibling relationship that we learn much of what we know about social relationships. In fact, one of the concerns expressed about only children is that they do not have the opportunity to learn social skills such as negotiation, compromise, and how to get along with others because they do not have this day-to-day interaction with siblings. The function of being a teacher is so pervasive within the sibling relationship that Cicirelli (1994) says "younger siblings learn values, knowledge and skills that help them to develop cognitively, socially and emotionally, as well as values and knowledge about the larger society (such as respect for elders) that prepare them for future living" (p. 11).

Siblings' relationships vary along the dimensions of closeness/distance and cooperation/conflict. Children's relationships with their brothers and sisters may be marked *both* by closeness and by conflict; one does not rule out the other. Because of the intimacy and frequency of contact, the sibling relationship can be marked by levels of jealousy and rivalry that are not usually seen in more discretionary relationships, like those between peers. Finally, to varying degrees a sense of obligation is a part of the sibling relationship. There is an expectation that siblings will be there to provide support and resources to each other in times of need (Cicirelli, 1994), although siblings with more detached, distant relationships are much less likely to support each other (McHale, Whiteman, Kim, & Crouter, 2007).

Sibling relationships often reflect the nature of the relationship between parents and their children. For example, McHale et al. (2007) found that a warmer relationship with parents was related to more positive sibling relationships. However, siblings can sometimes compensate for difficulties in relationships with the parents. Warm sibling relationships can help children deal with stress in their lives, even when their relationship with their mother is not warm (Gass, Jenkins, & Dunn, 2007).

Siblings can have both positive and negative effects on each other. Boys in particular have higher levels of antisocial behavior when they experience higher levels of conflict with siblings (Dunn, 2005a). Siblings may also become "partners in crime," influencing each other to become more involved with negative behavior (Richmond, Stocker, & Rienks, 2005, p. 556). Younger siblings may learn negative behaviors from their older brothers and sisters, but older siblings can also be affected by their experience of successfully bullying their younger sibling. In either case the children in these relationships are not learning self-control and empathy through their interactions with their siblings (Criss & Shaw, 2005). On the positive side, children and teens are less depressed when they have warm, supportive sibling relationships (Richmond et al., 2005).

Birth Order and Sibling Roles

There have been several broad descriptions of differences between siblings by birth order, based on the idea that children have different experiences and play different roles in the family depending on whether they were born first, in the middle, or last. Alfred Adler (1956) originally suggested that the firstborn child is dethroned from his privileged position by the birth of a sibling, and this motivates the child to continue to strive for excellence throughout his life, while the youngest child in a family is pampered and spoiled. These ideas led to a considerable amount of research that explored the effect of birth order on development. Later personality research went on to describe firstborn children as high achievers who behaved responsibly, middle children as the ones who are more socially skilled and popular, and youngest children as the ones who are more spoiled (Pulakos, 1987). Sulloway (1997) reopened the debate on birth order with his book *Born to Rebel*, in which he contends that firstborns are also seen as more conservative and conforming and later-borns as more unconventional and rebellious. However, the evidence for these differences is mixed, at best. Harris (2000) presents evidence that the kinds of behaviors learned in a family from siblings are not transferred to other situations. In other words, a child may be a leader in the family, but not in situations outside of the family, and large-scale studies have not consistently confirmed overall personality differences based on birth order.

Another way of classifying sibling roles comes from research done with families in which alcoholism is a problem. The dysfunction within the family may force children into more extreme and clearly delineated roles than happens in more functional families (Fischer, Pidcock, Munsch, & Forthun, 2005). The *Children's Roles Inventory* (Potter & Williams, 1991) identifies siblings within a family who fill a variety of roles, including the role of *hero* (the sibling who is the responsible one who takes care of other people and is successful at what he or she does); the *scapegoat* (the problem child who acts out to get attention from the family through bad behavior); the *lost child* (the sibling who is isolated and tries not to cause the family any additional problems or concerns); and the *mascot* (the sibling who seeks attention and approval from others and distracts the family from its problems by being the family clown). The *hero* is often the oldest child in the family, while younger siblings assume the roles of *scapegoat*, *lost child*, or *mascot*. The roles of both hero and mascot are considered positive because people like and approve of the behaviors associated with them, but the other roles are negative ones.

Differential Parental Treatment

Despite evidence that children within a family differentiate themselves from each other, parents are often quick to say that they treat all the children in their family the same. The children themselves, however, often disagree. Although parents may *love* their children the same, the way they actually treat their children can be quite variable. We have already said that parents may adopt different parenting styles with different children within the same family. This really shouldn't be surprising given that children within the same family differ by age and gender, and may also differ by a number of personality and temperament characteristics (Baskett, 1984; McHale & Pawletko, 1992; Plomin, Asbury, & Dunn, 2001). However, siblings who are treated in a less favorable way—or *perceive* that they are treated less favorably—show lower levels of adjustment and more conflicted sibling relationships (McHale, Crouter, McGuire, & Updegraff, 1995; Neiderhiser, Reiss, Hetherington, & Plomin, 1999; Reiss et al., 1995), or can even be at an increased risk of engaging in delinquent activities (Scholte, Engles, de Kemp, Harakeh, & Overbeek, 2007). Of course there is one situation in which differential treatment between siblings is almost inevitable, and that is in the case of stepsiblings (Beer, 1989). Each parent in the family likely has a qualitatively different relationship with his or her biological children and his or her stepchildren; plus, each stepsibling has a different biological parent he or she doesn't live with who comes into the mix. Under these complex circumstances, it is not surprising if rivalries or conflicts develop.

The impact of differential parental treatment of siblings is lessened if a child who receives less attention or is treated more harshly sees the differential treatment as legitimate or justified. For instance, when one of the siblings in a family has a developmental disability or other conditions that necessitate the special treatment by the parents, the healthy sibling usually recognizes and accepts that difference in treatment (McHale & Pawletko, 1992; Schuntermann, 2007).

Shared and Nonshared Environments

The assumption underlying much of the research done on siblings has been that siblings share the same environment and that what is different between them is their degree of genetic similarity (Plomin, Chipuer, & Neiderhiser, 1994). Identical twins share 100% of their genes in common, but fraternal twins and siblings share only 50% of their genes in common. When we compare identical twins to fraternal twins and we find more differences between fraternal twins, we have tended to attribute those differences to their genetic differences. After all, twins grow up in the same family, don't they?

Increasingly we have realized that each child in the family has many different experiences within the same family environment, so we have become interested in understanding the impact of what is called the **nonshared environment**. How important is the effect of these nonshared influences? They are so great that one group of researchers in this area has concluded that "one of the most notable findings in contemporary behavior genetics is that children growing up in the same family are not very similar" (Hetherington, Reiss, & Plomin, 1994, p. vii). In fact, once the effects of genetics are taken into account, siblings are no more similar to each other than almost any two other children chosen at random (Turkheimer & Waldron, 2000). It is almost as though they were reared in completely different environments.

Previously we had assumed that things like the quality of the parents' marital relationship, the neighborhood the children grew up in, and the family's socioeconomic status were important influences on development that equally affected all children in a family, but are these really the same thing for all children in the family? You were born into a family at a certain point in your family's life history, but each of your siblings was born at a different point in that timeline. Let's assume that you are the oldest child in the family (although this works the same if you are a middle child or youngest child in a family). If you were a firstborn child, your family might still have been struggling to establish itself financially at the time of your birth, and money may have been tight during your early childhood. By the time your siblings were born, your family might have been better off financially, so their childhood was spent in more affluent circumstances than yours. Likewise your parents' relationship could have gotten stronger or become more troubled in the interval between the time of your birth and the birth of your siblings. Your family may have moved to a better—or poorer—neighborhood during this interval. Any of these changes mean that the family environment that you experienced in your early childhood would not necessarily be the same environment that your siblings experienced during theirs. As children get older, they have increasing opportunities to select their own experiences outside of the family, and this also contributes to children in the same family growing up in different environments. If you chose to play soccer, join the band, and hang out with the cool kids, did all of your siblings make the same choices? Or did they pick different activities, have different interests, and choose different friends than you did? **Active Learning: Examining Nonshared Environments** allows you to continue thinking about ways in which you and your siblings grew up in separate worlds even though you grew up in the same family.

Nonshared environment
The environmental experiences that are different for each child in a family, including the differential impact of family events that occur at different ages for siblings.

Examining Nonshared Environments

For this activity, choose one of your siblings as your focus. You might want to choose the sibling that you feel is most different from you, but you don't need to do this. We apologize to only children for not being able to include them in this activity. We suggest that you do not write any personal identifying information in your textbook if you might sell it at some time in the future.

For each item, write a brief description (just words or phrases) of your experiences and the experiences of your sibling as you see them. Then think about how these differences may have affected the two of you.

Event/Experience	You	Your Focus Sibling
Family interactions—The amount of each given by your parents: • Affection • Control/strictness • Responsibility		
Academic success		
Social relationships • Number of close friends • Quality of friendships (supportive, conflictual, etc.) • Peer group you spent time with (jocks, brains, populars, druggies, nerds, etc.)		
Participation in activities (list which ones) • At school • In the community • Lessons • Work (If "yes," at what age?)		
Major family life events (residential moves, major changes in finances, serious illness/injury of family members, parental separation or divorce, etc.). For each event, indicate the age at which this occurred for you and your sibling.		

Based on this comparison, what did you conclude about the nature of the shared environment between you and your sibling? In what ways did you have environments that were *not* shared that may have contributed to differences between you and your sibling?

Only Children

American families have gotten smaller in recent years for a number of reasons. Women may choose to remain childless, couples marry and begin their childbearing at later ages, and the cost of raising children continues to climb. Currently there are over 20 million one-child households in the United States (Nichols, 2008). There are a number of negative ideas about what only children are like, and those biases arise from three different perspectives (Falbo & Polit, 1986). First, if siblings teach each other so much, perhaps the only child has a social disadvantage. Second, only children are unique (for instance, they are both the firstborn and the last-born child in their families), and perhaps this uniqueness places them at a disadvantage. Third, the quality of the parent-child relationship is unique because only children are exposed to all the anxiety of first-time parents but also have the advantage of exclusive access to their parents' time and attention. You can see how these theories connect to some of the negative characteristics associated with only children. If only children have their parents' exclusive attention, won't they be selfish or totally dependent on others when they grow up? If they don't have social interactions with siblings, won't they lack communication skills or social skills? Could this lack of interaction with siblings lower their intellectual achievement?

10. Children who grow up without siblings tend to be more self-centered, maladjusted, lonely, and neurotic than children who have siblings.

TRUE/FALSE

False. Contrary to the popular stereotype, children who have no siblings usually have very good outcomes. They have been found to have high achievement, good adjustment, strong character, and positive social relationships.

Video Link 14.8
Children with no siblings.

In general, research has failed to support these negative predictions. Rather it has found that only children show high achievement, good adjustment, strong character, and positive social relationships (Falbo & Polit, 1986). In many comparisons between only children and children with siblings, only children share the positive advantages that firstborn children enjoy or are indistinguishable from children in small families. That also suggests that they are *not* unique. Rather they look like other children who have had the same advantage of having parent-child relationships that support positive development and high achievement.

Interventions for a Better Family Life

As we have learned, children thrive when they grow up in families in which they have positive relationships with their caregivers in an organized living situation with clear expectations and opportunities to learn (Shonkoff & Phillips, 2000). When we studied the ecological theory of Urie Bronfenbrenner in Chapter 2, we saw that children and their families are affected by influences at many different levels, from broad cultural expectations, to government policies, to the neighborhoods in which they live, to their own individual, even internal experiences in life. When a family is struggling, intervention may occur at any of these levels. Also, support can be provided to families at different points in the development of the family; some start before the first baby is born, and some focus on dealing with teenagers. Some programs pick high-risk populations and try to intervene in order to prevent the development of problems, while other programs are responses to problems that already exist. Many types of programs have been instituted to help promote better family life with the ultimate goal of improving children's well-being. We obviously cannot describe all of these programs, but we will give you a few examples to illustrate these alternative approaches.

Video Link 14.9
Intervention for families.

At the level of government, some of the central policies that influence families include those that are concerned with economic security, provision of child care and education, health care policies, and policies concerning reproductive rights (Hartman, 2003). For example, the Family and Medical Leave Act of 1993 was passed to allow workers up to 12 weeks of unpaid leave, with the guarantee of return to the same or a comparable job, when they give birth, adopt, or take a child into foster care, or to care for a family member with a serious health problem (U.S. Department of Labor, 2010). This act was designed to provide parents with the possibility of staying home with their new babies to begin forming the secure attachment relationships that are so important to later child development, while protecting employment that may be essential for their family's financial security. It was clearly an improvement from the prior situation, in which there was no job protection for women who had children, and yet it provides much less protection than that provided by governments in other countries. In France, parents can take off 16–26 weeks at 100% of their current salary (Stebbins, 2001), and they may take up to 2 years of unpaid leave. In Sweden, either parent can take up to 12 months of paid leave to care for a new baby (Wetzels, 2001).

Intervention for families can also come at the level of the community. One example is the Safe Start demonstration program sponsored by the U.S. Department of Justice. This program was set up in 11 communities to help children 6 and younger and their families who had been exposed to violence. Described as a **wraparound program**, it included services from the justice system, health and mental health care providers, and other human services (Arteaga & Lamb, 2008). In communities that implemented this program successfully, new screening protocols used by police, schools, and others involved with children were able to identify more children who had been exposed to violence. Researchers found that the program resulted in less exposure to violence and fewer psychological symptoms for the children. Parents experienced less stress and showed a better understanding of the effects of violence on their children (Hyde, Lamb, Arteaga, & Chavis, 2008).

Wraparound program
A comprehensive set of services offered to families to strengthen them or reunite them.

Interventions with families at the level of the individual family may consist of family therapy for those with identified difficulties. With family therapy, there is often a child who presents with a problem, but the therapist, who might be a psychiatrist, psychologist, social worker, or marriage and family therapy counselor, meets with the whole family or with various combinations, such as father and daughter or parents and one son (Fox, 2006). Family therapy, as with any psychotherapy, begins with evaluation, examining "medical, academic, social, and family history"; the nature of the problem and the nature of the "strengths within the child, family, school and larger community; and potential barriers to treatment" (Eyberg, Nelson, & Boggs, 2008, p. 233). Depending on the initial evaluation, interventions can include teaching parenting skills, helping parents understand their children's behavior, or helping parents with their own emotional disorders. Therapists may help families reflect on their interactions or may coach the families while they interact. Eyberg et al. (2008) found evidence for the effectiveness of family therapy with young children with oppositional defiant disorder and conduct disorder and

Family therapy. Family therapy often helps an adolescent by helping the family understand and change interactions within the whole family unit.

Eisler, Simic, Russell, and Dare (2007) reported successful treatment of teens with eating disorders at a 5-year follow-up using family therapy.

Another type of family-based program targets those families whose children are at high risk for developing psychological and behavioral problems and attempts to intervene before those problems emerge. These early intervention programs will target families for a variety of reasons, including poverty, maternal depression, and premature birth (Landry, Smith, Swank, & Guttentag, 2008). For example, Landry et al. (2008) have used the Play and Learning Strategies (PALS I) infant intervention program to improve parents' responsiveness to their infants and toddlers who were born with very low birth weight, a high risk factor for later developmental problems. This program includes "educational videotapes featuring mothers with similar backgrounds, facilitator coaching of parents' use of key behaviors during videotaped interactions with their infants, supporting mothers to critique their videotaped practiced behaviors, and planning for how to use the target behaviors across the week" (Landry et al., 2008, p. 1336). This program promotes more warmth and enjoyment between these mothers and their infants, which, in turn, promotes social and language development in their infants.

The authors of the book *From Neurons to Neighborhoods* conclude that intervention with families works best when it consists of "empowering parents as the true experts with respect to their own child's and family's needs and . . . building a strong, mutually respectful, working partnership in which parents and professionals relate comfortably in a collaborative effort to achieve family-driven objectives" (Shonkoff & Phillips, 2000, p. 366).

To find and evaluate intervention programs available to families in your community, try **Active Learning: Finding Community Interventions**.

Finding Community Interventions

ACTIVE LEARNING

Most communities have a number of programs available that can assist families and children, but locating these services when you need them is not always easy. Find an intervention program in your own community that provides therapeutic services to children and families. You might look for information on programs that is posted on public bulletin boards or included in flyers handed out at a physician's office, or by searching the Internet. If you do a web search, remember to include the name of your community in your search terms so that you find a local program. Particularly in larger communities, there may be a local guide to community resources published by a social services agency.

Answer as many of these questions as you can:

- Who provides the services? (This could be a community hospital, an agency or organization, a school, or a private service provider, such as a counselor or psychologist.)
- What types of family problems or concerns are addressed through this program?
- What types of services are provided? (This could include group counseling, workshops, individual sessions, online delivery, or some other type of delivery.)
- Is there a charge for receiving services? If so, what is it? Is there a sliding scale (that is, does the amount that is charged depend upon the income level of the family)?

Conclusion

In this chapter we have examined some of the types of families found in modern American society. Although each type provides its own rewards and challenges, the overall conclusion in regard to children's well-being is that positive parenting and low levels of family conflict are more important than the structure of the family in which a child is raised (Hetherington & Stanley-Hagan, 1999). It appears that when parents and other caregivers are able to maintain loving relationships and provide appropriate supervision, the type of family structure seems to matter less for children's well-being. It is these characteristics that must be developed and supported in programs designed to help families. Repeated familial disruptions affect children negatively both directly and indirectly through their effects on the parents' ability to care for their children effectively.

CHAPTER SUMMARY

1. **What constitutes a family?**
A **family** is the basic social unit in human society, but it can take different forms from one culture to another. In the United States, a family is any two individuals living together who are related by birth, marriage, or adoption. There are **nuclear families** and **extended families.**

2. **How are single-parent families different from two-parent families?**
The number of single-parent families in the United States has increased substantially in recent years. Many single-parent families live below the poverty level, and this affects children directly and indirectly. Single parents must fill all of the parenting roles by themselves, and this can result in **emotional parentification** of the children. Children in single-parent families spend more time with extended family than children in two-parent families do.

3. **How does divorce affect families?**
Divorce affects over 1 million children in the United States each year. Because divorce is a process, it takes time for everyone to adjust to the changes it brings. It also necessitates many changes in the lives of children. Parenting skills

often suffer following a divorce. Although divorce has been associated with a number of adjustment problems for the children, including both **externalizing behavior problems** and **internalizing behavior problems**, most children from divorced families function in the normal range. Conflict between parents is related to poorer outcomes for the children, but **constructive conflict** can reduce or eliminate them.

4. **How can we help children cope with a divorce?**
The age at which children experience parental divorce affects their response to it. Some of the ways that parents can help their children cope with a divorce include encouraging them to talk about their feelings, not making them choose between their parents, and making sure they know that their parents still love them.

5. **What is the role of a noncustodial parent following a divorce?**
Noncustodial parents continue to be important people in the lives of their children, although many children eventually lose contact with their fathers following a divorce. How the noncustodial parent functions is more important than

simply how much time the parent spends with the child. A child's relationship with a noncustodial mother plays a big role in a child's postdivorce adjustment, but there is little research on this topic.

6. **How does living in a stepfamily affect its members?**
A stepfamily is a complex family arrangement. Stepchildren may dislike or resent their stepparents, but the relationship usually improves with time. Research comparing children in stepfamilies to other groups of children has not shown strong conclusive differences, although academic performance may be somewhat lower.

7. **What other forms do families take?**
Other family forms include families headed by grandparents, headed by gay or lesbian partners, formed through adoption, or formed through foster care. Each family form has its own challenges. Children raised by gay or lesbian parents are as happy and well adjusted as children in other types of families and are no more likely than others to identify themselves as gay or lesbian. Adopted children need to know that their bond with their adoptive parents is real and strong. If the adopted child comes from a different cultural background, the adoptive parents need to help the child understand and respect the child's cultural identity. Children in **open adoptions** appreciate knowing their birth parents because it helps them develop a sense of identity. Children in **foster care** are only temporarily placed with a family, so it is often difficult for these children and the foster parents to bond.

8. **How do family time, rituals, and routines benefit children?**
Family time at meals gives families a chance to connect and share the stories of their day. Rituals and routines establish a family rhythm and help make life organized and predictable for children. They strengthen families by providing a sense of belonging and connection between generations. When a family gains or loses a member, traditions often need to be transformed or renegotiated.

9. **How have the roles of mothers and fathers changed?**
Today more mothers are employed in the workforce, and many fathers are more involved with caretaking of their children than in past generations. Some fathers are the primary caregivers in their families. Positive parenting by fathers is associated with a number of positive outcomes. Parents' roles in the United States continue to differ in that mothers are often more responsive to the emotional needs of their children while fathers engage in play and encourage exploration.

10. **What are the different parenting styles that parents use?**
Based upon the amount of parental **acceptance/responsiveness** and the amount of parental **demandingness/control**, we can describe four styles of parenting: **authoritative parents**, **authoritarian parents**, **permissive parents**, and **uninvolved or neglectful parents**. Although **parenting style** is a consistent pattern of behaviors, parents sometimes deviate from these patterns. Authoritative parenting is associated with a number of positive characteristics, and children raised by parents with other styles do more poorly in comparison, with children raised by uninvolved or neglectful parents doing the worst. Our models of parenting have included the **parent effects model** and the **child effects model**, but today most developmentalists support a **transactional model**. Which parenting style works best for a child is influenced by the goodness of fit between the demands of the environment and the child's characteristics.

11. **How are sibling relationships similar to and different from other family relationships?**
Siblings are our longest-lasting relationship. The nature of these relationships is affected by the gender configuration and age spacing of the siblings and can be both close and conflictual. When parents treat siblings differently, it can be problematic for the sibling who is treated more poorly, unless the differential treatment is justified by some special need of the preferred sibling. Siblings are not as similar as we might think because there is a significant impact of their **nonshared environment**. Although only children do not have siblings, they are just as likely to be well adjusted and happy as children who do have siblings.

12. **How can we strengthen and support families?**
Programs to promote better family life can be implemented at the community, national, or family level, and they aim to prevent problems or to help families recover from problems. At the family level, intervention may include family therapy. Effective programs empower parents to advocate for their children and to build a working relationship with professionals.

Go to **www.sagepub.com/levine** for additional exercises and video resources. Select **Chapter 14, Families,** for chapter-specific activities.

chapter 15

Health, Well-Being, and Resilience

15

Health is more than the absence of illness. It is a general state of well-being that includes not only physical well-being but also mental and social well-being. In this chapter we describe some of the common threats to children's health and well-being and review some recommendations that can help parents ensure that their children are healthy. We also look at how children and adolescents learn to cope with the stress that they experience. For most children, their stress is the normal stress that everyone experiences (for example, taking an important test, starting a new school, struggling to master a difficult task), but for others the stress they experience is extraordinary. We look at how growing up in poverty, being a victim of child abuse or neglect, experiencing racism, or suffering from a mental disorder can affect a child's well-being. The chapter concludes, however, with a look at how resilient children and adolescents can be and at some of the factors that help build that resiliency.

1. The best way to define being "healthy" is to say that you don't have any illnesses.

TRUE/FALSE

False. Being healthy is much more than not being sick. It is a general state of well-being that includes your physical, social, and mental well-being.

Test Your Knowledge

Test your knowledge of child development by deciding whether each of the following statements is *true* or *false*, and then check your answers as you read the chapter.

1. **True/False:** The best way to define being "healthy" is to say that you don't have any illnesses.
2. **True/False:** When you are trying to deal with a stressful situation, you should try to ignore your emotional response and focus on solving the problem.
3. **True/False:** Because children are still growing, they are more resistant to the effects of environmental toxins than adults are.
4. **True/False:** The incidence of childhood cancer has increased in recent years.
5. **True/False:** If you are one of the 4,400 adolescents who smoked their first cigarette today, there is a 1-in-10 chance that you will eventually die from a smoking-related illness.
6. **True/False:** More White children than minority children live in poverty in the United States.
7. **True/False:** In the United States, one child dies from child abuse or neglect every 4 days.
8. **True/False:** When asked, children who have been sexually abused are likely to deny their abuse.
9. **True/False:** Adults who were abused as children are likely to become abusive parents themselves.
10. **True/False:** Children who are able to rise above great adversity like poverty or child abuse have a number of unique abilities.

Correct answers: (1) False, (2) False, (3) False, (4) True, (5) False, (6) True, (7) False, (8) False, (9) False, (10) False

Stress and Coping

What Is Stress?

Stress Anything that places excessive demands on our ability to cope.

Stress is a normal—and inevitable—part of life. In the broadest sense, stress is anything that places excessive demands on our ability to cope (Lazarus, 1999). That could include fairly minor things like writing a paper for class, running to catch a bus, or having to speak in front of a group, but it also can include serious things like living in poverty, going through a divorce, or having a chronic health problem. When you experience stress, your body responds to help you deal with it by releasing hormones that affect you physiologically. Think for a moment about what it feels like when you are under stress. Your heart rate speeds up and pumps more blood through your body. Your blood vessels open wider to allow this increased volume of blood to reach your muscles, and your pupils dilate to let more light into your eyes. Your breathing rate also speeds up so that you take in more oxygen. Your liver releases stored glucose to provide energy to your body. And why do you

Fight-or-flight response The physiological response to threat.

sweat when you are under stress? Because it helps cool the body (Nemours Foundation, 2007). All of these responses evolved as a part of the **fight-or-flight response** that was meant to protect us from real, physical threats in the environment. When we are dealing with short-term sources of stress, this response works the way it should—it energizes us just when we need it. The trouble occurs when our stress isn't brief or acute but instead becomes long-term or chronic. When stress continues over time and the body tries to maintain this elevated level of readiness, it can begin to take a toll on us physically. You know that stress can be exhausting.

There are some things that we all recognize and agree are stressful, but other things that create stress for us are pretty subjective (Johnson, 1986). Some people find speaking before a crowd to be energizing and even fun, but others are nearly paralyzed with fright at the prospect of having to take the stage. Millions of people drive on to freeways every day without giving it a thought, but others grip the steering wheel tightly and hold their breath as their palms begin to sweat when they see the entrance ramp. The types of things that are experienced as stressful by children and adolescents change as a function of their age (Humphrey, 2004).

Coping with school stress. Children may respond differently to similar situations. Which boy in these pictures looks like school is a stressful place for him to be?

Many people look back at their childhood and romanticize it as an idyllic time when they had no cares or worries. The truth is that children and teens have plenty of worries, but they are often quite different from the ones we experience as adults. For young children, being separated from their parents is a stressful experience, and dealing with new things in their environment can also be difficult. When children get older and enter school, situations that test their competence can be stressful, and so can the need to make new friends. For adolescents, social experiences are important, so situations that involve peer rejection can be stressful, and all adolescents need to cope with the changes that their bodies go through as they enter puberty.

Normative Stress Versus Non-normative Stress

Most of the stress that we experience is **normative stress**. This type of stress is caused by things that happen to everyone (or almost everyone), is often something we can anticipate and prepare for, and does not overwhelm our ability to cope. Starting kindergarten or middle school or college is a normative event, even though it usually creates some amount of stress. Going through puberty, learning to drive, and going out on your first date are other examples. By contrast, **non-normative stress** is the result of a relatively rare occurrence that creates a great deal of stress, often overwhelming the individual, at least for a period of time. You do not anticipate these events and may not have had the chance to see how other people cope with similar events. The death of a parent, a serious illness or hospitalization, and living through a natural disaster are all examples of non-normative stress.

Coping with either type of stress can occur in the short term or over the long term. Recovering from a serious injury could be very intensive, but you also could have a full and complete recovery within a relatively short amount of time so that the stress comes to an end. Coping effectively with short-term stress builds coping skills and develops competence. By contrast, coping with a chronic life-threatening condition creates a great deal of stress, but that stress continues without relief. Situations that are highly stressful and that continue over an extended period are the most damaging to the course of normal development. Living in a war zone, being a victim of child abuse, or experiencing the death of a close family member tests the limits of endurance for all children.

As the number of stressful life events increases in a child's life, so does the likelihood that the child will experience a mental health problem like anxiety or depression, a behavioral problem such as poor school performance or delinquency, lower self-esteem, or problems with physical health (Johnson, 1986). A number of characteristics or circumstances can help moderate the effect of life stress so that the impact on the child is not as negative as it would be otherwise. The topic of resiliency is discussed later in this chapter, but for now we can tell you that characteristics of the child (such as having an easygoing temperament or good problem-solving skills) or characteristics of the child's environment (such as having a secure attachment figure or a strong network available that can provide social support) help in this process.

Coping

Coping is defined as "the cognitive and behavioral efforts made to master, tolerate or reduce external and internal demands" (Folkman & Lazarus, 1980, p. 223), and the strategies that are used to try to do this can be described as problem-focused or emotion-focused. **Problem-focused strategies** are designed to alter the situation to reduce your stress, while **emotion-focused strategies** are designed to reduce or manage the emotional distress that you are feeling. Most stressful situations elicit both types of coping (Carver, Scheier, & Weintraub, 1989). Table 15.1 provides examples of some types of strategies that children and adolescents use to deal with their stress. For instance, you could try to improve a stressful situation by finding information that you can use, learning some new skills, using problem-solving strategies, or mobilizing social support for assistance. Problem-focused strategies like these are more effective when the situation is one that you can realistically change or control. However, sometimes situations are beyond our control, and there aren't effective ways to change the situation in order to reduce stress. In those situations, you can reduce some of the stress by using emotion-focused strategies like sharing your feelings with trusted friends or by changing your perception of the situation. Coping is a process, so you may need to manage your emotional distress before you are able to take action to solve a problem.

Normative stress
Stresses that are predictable and that most children go through.

Non-normative stress
The experience of unusual and unexpected distressing events.

Video Link 15.1
Children's stress.

2. When you are trying to deal with a stressful situation, you should try to ignore your emotional response and focus on solving the problem. **TRUE/FALSE**

False. People generally deal with their emotional response as part of solving the problem that is causing stress. Some stresses cannot be resolved, but you can manage the way you think about them to reduce your distress.

Coping Efforts made to master, tolerate, or reduce stress.

Problem-focused strategies Coping that focuses on solving a stressful problem.

Emotion-focused strategies Coping that is designed to reduce or manage emotional distress.

Table 15.1

Coping strategies. This table contains examples of strategies that adolescents might use to cope with their problems.

Problem-Focused Coping Strategies (efforts to change the source of the stress or your relationship to it)	
Strategy	**Example**
Active coping—taking action to remove the source of the stress or soften its effect	I put more time and effort into overcoming this problem.
Planning—thinking about the best way to handle the situation	I think about what I can do, step by step, to make the situation better.
Seeking instrumental social support—seeking advice, assistance, or information from others	I talk to others who have the same problem to get some advice from them.
Restraint coping—waiting for the right opportunity to take action	I make myself be patient until it is the right time to act.
Emotion-Focused Coping Strategies (attempts to manage or regulate the emotions caused by the situation)	
Strategy	**Example**
Expressing or venting your feelings—To release your feelings.	When I get upset, I just let it all out because it makes me feel better.
Seeking emotional support—Seeking moral support, sympathy or understanding	I talk to my best friend because she is always there for me when I need her.
Acceptance of the situation	I just learn how to live with those things I can't change.
Positive reframing or reappraisal	I realize that what has happened to me is really all for the best in the long run.

In most situations, people use a combination of strategies as part of their coping efforts, and mix together problem-focused and emotion-focused strategies (Folkman & Lazarus, 1980). And, while we would expect to see some individual differences in how people cope (that is, that some people would be more action-oriented and rely more on problem-focused coping and other people would be more contemplative and rely more on emotion-focused or reappraisal coping), it appears that the characteristics of the situation are also a powerful influence on the choice of coping strategies (Folkman & Lazarus, 1980). Situations that are seen as more controllable are more often met with problem-focused coping strategies, while those seen as uncontrollable are met with emotion-focused coping strategies (Compas, Malcarne, & Fondacaro, 1988).

Just as the types of things that are stressful change with the age of the child, so do the ways children try to cope with their stress. Young children are more likely to rely upon problem-focused approaches when they are in distress. They don't have the cognitive ability yet to fully understand the sources of their stress. If they don't want to be separated from their parents, they run after them or wave to them to come back. When they use emotion-focused strategies, those strategies are pretty simple and direct. They might grab a favorite blanket or toy to soothe themselves or say "Mommy come home" to reassure themselves that their mother will come back. Emotion-focused strategies develop more rapidly in later childhood and early adolescence (Compas, Banez, Malcarne, & Worsham, 1991). Developing cognitive capabilities enables older children to better understand what is happening to them, and their metacognitive ability helps them identify what is most likely to work for them.

Ways to Help Children Cope With Stress

Parents and people who work with children and adolescents want to help them deal with stress in their lives, and there are a number of things they can do. First they need to simply watch the child for signs of stress. They will differ with the age of the child. A young child might regress to more immature behavior (for example, thumb sucking or beginning to wet himself again after he has been toilet trained). Routine patterns of eating, sleeping, and leisure activities can be disrupted for children or adolescents at any age. Older children and adolescents might begin having trouble at school because they can't concentrate or pay attention. There may be changes in their emotions. Children may become more aggressive than they usually are, or more clingy or withdrawn. They may have vague physical complaints about headaches or upset stomachs. Any of these changes should signal to a concerned adult to ask the child how she is feeling and if something is bothering her. Disclosure is the first essential step for getting social support in a time of stress, and we can encourage children to take this step.

Emotion-focused coping. This child might find flying stressful. Her stuffed animals help her feel comforted and cope with the stress.

Then parents or professionals can help children think about problem-solving strategies that might work for them, or they can help them reappraise the stressful situation if it has been blown out of proportion. If stress is chronic, there are other behavior management strategies that can be helpful. Depending upon the age of the child, learning relaxation techniques, using meditation, or learning biofeedback can be helpful (Humphrey, 2004). Even young children can learn that they can stop and take some slow, deep breaths when they are feeling stressed or can think for a few minutes about something that is very pleasant for them. Some of the same things help all of us—children, adolescents, and adults—cope with stress. They include getting enough rest, eating a healthy diet, and getting some exercise. **Active Learning: Finding Resources to Cope With Stress** gives you the opportunity to explore some of the resources available to you on your campus if you are dealing with a good deal of stress.

Finding Resources to Cope With Stress

You may be well aware of the fact that being a college student can be stressful! Other people also recognize this, so that is why most colleges and universities offer a wide range of services to their students to help them cope (and these services are usually free of charge).

Go to your college's home page and search for terms like *student workshops* or *counseling services* to see what your campus offers. On one campus, searching for the term *counseling services* found this information on the webpage for University Counseling Services:

- Counseling services—individual counseling, couples counseling, group counseling, psychiatric consultation, and urgent care
- Group therapy—Relationship Support, Gay/Lesbian/Bisexual Support, Men's Support, Making Peace with Your Body (body image, eating disorders), Saying Goodbye to Shy, First-Year College Experience
- Personal improvement workshops—Choice or Chance: Career Development, Improving Your Sleep, Relaxation Enhancement, Building Self-Esteem, Overcoming Procrastination

If you are aware that you are experiencing a high level of stress, you may want to look into the services that your college offers to prevent future health problems.

These general issues of stress and coping give you some preparation for understanding specific causes of stress in childhood. We will next discuss the impact of some major causes of stress: physical health problems, poverty, child abuse, racial discrimination, and mental health problems.

Illnesses and Other Health Threats

We have already discussed some important topics related to health in earlier chapters. In Chapter 5 you learned about the importance of a good maternal diet during pregnancy, especially for optimal brain development, and about threats to prenatal development, such as maternal use of alcohol, tobacco, and drugs. In Chapter 6, you learned how both malnourishment and obesity threaten children's health in different ways. We begin this section of the chapter by looking at some of the most common illnesses experienced by children and adolescents.

Common Illnesses

If you are not a parent yourself, you may have wondered why parents of young children seem so preoccupied with their children's bladders and bowels. That's because this is one good day-to-day indicator of their children's health. When children have diarrhea, they can run the risk of becoming dehydrated. Diarrhea can be caused by a gastrointestinal infection or by a reaction to something the child ate. As adults, diarrhea is often experienced as an annoying symptom of an illness, but it is a much more serious problem for children worldwide. In fact, it is the second leading cause of death in children, linked with 25% of childhood deaths around the world. It is especially prevalent in poor countries that have inadequate sanitation and few medical resources (Werner, Sanders, & Brelsford, 1997). Sometimes doctors recommend an oral rehydrating solution to keep the child adequately hydrated, and severe diarrhea (especially if the child has a fever) requires a visit to the doctor.

Even a low-grade fever can be a medical concern for infants and young children because it could be a sign of a serious infection, so parents should consult their doctor. Any temperature of 105° or higher taken with an oral thermometer requires immediate medical attention. If the child has a runny nose and a low-grade fever, it might indicate something as simple as a cold, but a fever can be associated with a whole range of other symptoms, and some of them represent very serious health threats. For instance, if the fever is accompanied by pain in the lower right side of the abdomen and vomiting occurs, it can indicate appendicitis. A low-grade fever together with a sore throat could be symptomatic of strep throat, which usually requires treatment with an antibiotic. A high fever with chills, chest pains, and coughing can indicate pneumonia. You can see from this description that a fever can indicate a number of relatively minor concerns but also some very serious ones, so parents should consult a doctor with a specific description of what other symptoms they have observed in their child.

Few signs of illness get a parent's attention as quickly as a child who has nausea or who is vomiting. When infants drink milk too quickly or swallow too much air as they drink, they may spit up small amounts of milk, but this is not a reason for concern. However, an infant who forcefully vomits large volumes of milk could have a blockage at the end of the stomach, a condition that requires surgery. When a child is vomiting and it is accompanied by diarrhea, dehydration becomes a concern, and parents need to be sure that the child is getting enough fluids. When vomiting occurs repeatedly over a period of several hours, it is time to contact a doctor for professional advice.

The common illnesses described thus far primarily involve health concerns with infants and young children, but these symptoms are concerns for children and adolescents of any age. It is just that infants are not able to tell us what they are feeling, so adults have an extra obligation to watch for and correctly interpret these symptoms of illness when they occur in young children. All infants should receive frequent well-baby checkups for the first year of their lives because this is a chance for a doctor to monitor the infant's physical growth and weight gain, and an excellent opportunity for parents to ask any health-related questions that they have. The American Academy of Pediatrics (2009b) recommends checkups every 3–6 months between ages 1 and 3, and on a yearly basis thereafter.[1]

As children get older and especially once they enter school, different types of common illnesses occur because children have contact with many other people over the course of a day. According to the Mayo Clinic (2008), the top five reasons why children miss school include the common cold, the stomach flu, ear infections, pink eye (or conjunctivitis), and sore throats. Whenever children are together in groups, whether it is in a classroom or in a day care facility, there are plenty of opportunities for infections to spread, so children need to be taught some ways that they can protect themselves. Thorough hand washing is one of those simple—but important—precautions.

There isn't much that can be done to treat or speed up the progress of colds or the flu, but parents can be sure that their children stay well hydrated, get plenty of rest, and perhaps use a humidifier or saline nose drops to make them more comfortable. However, contrary to what many parents may believe, over-the-counter cough and cold medicines should *not* be given to young children. In 2008, the U.S. Food and Drug Administration issued a Public Health Advisory recommending that "over-the-counter (OTC) cough and cold products should not be used to treat infants and children less than 2 years of age because serious and potentially life-threatening side effects can occur from such use" (USFDA, 2008b, para. 1). It also concluded that there is no evidence that these products benefit infants. In October 2008, the Consumer Healthcare Products Association voluntarily agreed to relabel these over-the-counter products to indicate they shouldn't be used in children younger than age 4. Further, children under the age of 18 should not be given aspirin to treat viral infections because of a possible link between aspirin and Reye's syndrome, a rare but dangerous condition that involves swelling of the liver and the brain (Mayo Clinic, 2009a).

How to help prevent spreading colds and the flu. These photos show two precautions children are taught to help prevent the spread of illness: coughing or sneezing into the crook of their arm instead of into their hand or the air and frequently washing their hands.

Ear infections occur when fluid builds up behind the eardrum and becomes a breeding ground for viruses or bacteria (Mayo Clinic, 2008). Bacterial infections will respond to antibiotics, but in most cases this is not necessary. Warm compresses may give the child some relief from the pain without overusing antibiotics. Repeated ear infections are a concern because they can affect a child's hearing. Accurate hearing is essential for the development of language in the early years, so repeated ear infections may be a cause for concern. In one study, children who had repeated ear infections that started before age 2, and especially those who continued

1. General information on elimination problems, diarrhea, vomiting, and nausea was taken from Shelov and Altmann (2009).

to have them through age 6, were more likely than other children to have difficulty discriminating sounds and learning to read (Shapiro, Hurry, Masterson, Wydell, & Doctor, 2009). Shapiro and her colleagues compare the experience of children with chronic ear infections to being in a foreign language class that is too difficult for us; we eventually just give up trying. Doctors may perform surgery in which tubes are placed in the ears to keep the fluids from building up. This surgery can restore hearing and enable children to develop language normally (Kogan, Overpeck, Hoffman, & Casselbrant, 2000).

Sore throats usually run their course in a few days, but if they last longer than a week, if they are accompanied by a fever, or if the child's tonsils are red and swollen, the child may have strep throat. Strep throat is a bacterial infection that can be treated by antibiotics (Mayo Clinic, 2008) and needs to be seen by a medical professional.

Immunizations help protect children from contagious diseases. Vaccines have virtually eliminated diseases like diphtheria, measles, polio, and whooping cough in the United States. These diseases had taken many young lives in the past. No vaccine can be 100% effective, and immunizations have both costs and benefits, but side effects are usually mild and short-lived (although serious reactions do rarely occur) (USFDA, 2008a). For that reason, doctors may advise that children not be vaccinated if they are ill or have certain types of allergies. Infants receive a series of immunizations during their first 2 years, and school districts require that children are current on their immunizations before they enter school. As we discussed in Chapter 6, there is no scientific evidence that connects immunization to an increased risk of autism in children.

Recently a vaccine that helps prevent infections by the human papillomavirus (HPV) has been developed. The recommendation is that a series of three shots be administered to girls between the ages of 11 and 13 before they become sexually active to offer them protection that helps prevent "cervical cancer, abnormal and precancerous cervical lesions, abnormal and precancerous vaginal and vulvar lesions and genital warts" (USFDA, 2008a). The vaccination can also be given between ages 13 and 26 if the girl did not receive it earlier. This vaccine has been thoroughly tested, and the FDA has found it to be both safe and effective. However, there still has been controversy about this recommendation because parents have difficulty accepting the fact that their 11- or 12-year-old daughter might need protection from a sexually transmitted disease. However, national statistics from 2007 found that 33% of ninth graders reported ever having had sexual intercourse (Federal Interagency Forum on Child and Family Statistics, 2009), so early inoculation is important if this is to be a preventative measure.

Video Link 15.2
HPV vaccination.

Chronic Illnesses

The types of common illnesses we just described are called self-limiting or acute illnesses because they usually run their course in a fairly short amount of time, often without any medical intervention. By contrast, chronic illnesses are ones that are long-lasting, do not resolve themselves, and cannot be cured completely in most cases (National Center for Chronic Disease Prevention and Health Promotion, 2009). Chronic illnesses in children and adolescents include conditions such as asthma (the most common chronic illness), diabetes, sickle cell anemia, cancer, HIV/AIDS, cystic fibrosis, epilepsy, congenital heart problems, cerebral palsy, and seizure disorders. Estimates of the number of children living with chronic conditions will vary depending on the definition used, but by one estimate 15% to 18% of children in the United States live with at least one of these conditions (Perrin, Bloom, & Gortmaker, 2007).

Because a chronic illness negatively affects a child's normal activities, children and their families need help in coping with the ongoing challenges such illnesses present (Kratz, Uding, Trahms, Villareale, & Kierkhefer, 2009). Everyone in the family is affected by a child's chronic illness, including the child's healthy siblings. Parents experience stress because they need to be constantly vigilant of their child's condition and because they may worry about the additional medical expenses incurred by the family. The child obviously suffers from whatever pain, discomfort, or limitations the condition brings with it, as well as the need to visit the doctor or be hospitalized frequently. When hospitalization is required, being in a strange environment, often separated from their parents, is stressful to children, especially younger children who cannot fully understand all that is happening to them. Medical procedures can be both painful and frightening. Fortunately more hospitals and medical offices now offer families the services of professionals such as pediatric psychologists and child life specialists.

Pediatric psychologists provide therapeutic intervention to help with the emotional and behavioral difficulties that children experience in connection with medical disorders. They also work to develop effective ways to help children deal with painful and frightening medical procedures (American Psychological Association, 2010). **Child life specialists** are experts in child development who promote optimal development in children by providing information, support, and guidance to children and family members who are dealing with serious health threats (American Academy of Pediatrics, 2006a). To do this, they use a variety of techniques, including play, preparing children for medical procedures by providing developmentally appropriate information, and creating opportunities for self-expression. They also help families understand the medical procedures that are being used to treat their children.

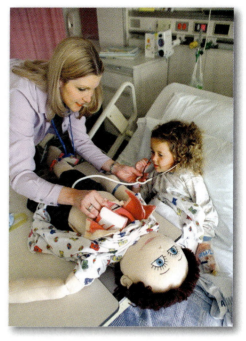

The work of a child life specialist. How do you think the child life specialist in this picture is helping this boy cope with his stay in the hospital?

Pediatric psychologists
Child psychologists who provide therapeutic interventions for children with medical disorders.

Child life specialists
Experts in child development who promote optimal development in children in medical settings.

How a child copes with a chronic illness depends on several factors, including the age of the child, the child's personality, and the nature of the illness itself. Another factor that is important in the coping process is the fact that children with chronic illnesses feel different from other children their same age. Other children may avoid the sick children because they mistakenly fear that the child is contagious. It is difficult for school-age children to establish and maintain friendships if they are frequently absent from school or cannot participate in the same activities that other children do. And, frankly, sometimes peers can just be mean. Medical procedures may disfigure a child or cause changes in a child's appearance (such as the loss of hair or facial puffiness) or can stunt children's normal growth process so that they are smaller or lighter than other children of the same age.

At a time when adolescents would ordinarily be developing autonomy and independence from parents, an adolescent with a chronic illness may still need a great deal of parental monitoring and supervision, and teenage rebelliousness in a chronically ill child could take the form of a rebellion about the medical regime that is essential to his or her health. For instance, a diabetic teenager who doesn't watch her diet and eats what everyone else does or refuses to regularly test her blood glucose level may temporarily feel more normal, but this rebellion can take a serious toll on her health.

Families are systems, so a chronic illness or disability in one family member affects everyone else in the family because system members are interconnected and what affects one of them also reverberates with the others. Family routines and priorities may need to be adjusted to accommodate the needs of the ill child. Parents understandably may feel disappointment or experience a sense of grief at the loss of the life they had imagined for their child. The need for constant vigilance of a child's medical condition can place a tremendous strain on a marriage, and caregiver burnout is a real possibility if parents don't make time to meet some of their own needs. Healthy siblings may resent that they don't get the same amount of time or attention from their parents that their ill sibling does (Boyse, Boujaoude, & Laundy, 2010). A recent, promising intervention has targeted developing coping skills in healthy siblings while also developing problem-solving communication in the parents and a strengthening of family time and routines for the entire family (Giallo & Gavidia-Payne, 2008). The focus is not just

Video Link 15.3
Child life specialists.

on the sick child, but on the whole family and the supports it needs. Some programs that may be helpful to families include support groups specific to the disorder the child has, such as the American Cancer Society, as well as respite care, which allows other family members some time to relax knowing that their child is being cared for by a trained health care professional (Sayger, Bowersox, & Steinberg, 1996).

Many chronic illnesses run in families. How much do you know about your own health history? You are routinely asked for this information when you see a new physician. **Active Learning: Creating a Personal Health History** will help you compile this information.

ACTIVE LEARNING

Creating a Personal Health History

You might want to use this activity as an opportunity to track down information from your childhood that you may not have or to ask questions about your family's health history that you have never discussed with your parents before. The Surgeon General of the United States maintains a webpage where you can compile a detailed family health history at https://familyhistory.hhs.gov/fhh-web/home.action, but you also can do this more informally by finding answers to these general questions:

- What childhood illnesses did you have (for example, mumps, rubella or German measles, chicken pox, rheumatic fever, or strep throat)? At which age did you have each illness, and how severe was it?
- Are you current with your immunizations (for example, tetanus, polio, rubella, and diphtheria)? Find out the date that you received each immunization (and remember that immunizations need to be updated from time to time).
- What are the names and dates of any surgical procedures you have had?
- What are the dates and reasons for any hospitalizations?
- What allergies (if any) do you have?
- What medications do you take (both by prescription and over the counter), and what is the amount and frequency of using them?
- It also is important that you know about your family's medical history and the major illnesses such as arthritis, diabetes, hypertension (high blood pressure), heart disease, kidney problems, seizure disorders, major depression, alcoholism, or other substance abuse problems that have affected your parents, grandparents, and siblings.

TRUE/FALSE

3. Because children are still growing, they are more resistant to the effects of environmental toxins than adults are.

False. Because they are still growing, children are more vulnerable to the effect of toxins. Also, toxins have a greater impact on children than adults because of children's smaller size.

Video Link 15.4
Toxins.

Environmental Toxins and Threats

Because children are still growing and because they eat and drink more in proportion to their body size than adults, they are even more vulnerable than adults to environmental toxins (U.S. Environmental Protection Agency, 2009a). A large number of environmental hazards have been identified, including asbestos, dioxin, household chemicals, lead, mercury, molds, pesticides, radon, and secondhand smoke. As an estimate of the impact of the environment on health, in her 2000 presidential address to the Ambulatory Pediatric Association, Dr. Ellen Crain made the claim that "the environment may account for 25% to 40% of the global burden of disease" (p. 871).

As an example of the nature of that exposure, a report from the U.S. Environmental Protection Agency (Egeghy et al., 2007) said that pesticide products were found in 90% of the homes studied. This report also concluded that pesticides that were present in food and in household dust (which is unintentionally ingested by children) were the primary means of exposure to this toxin.

As another example, children may also be exposed to lead in their environment. In recent years the amount of lead that children are exposed to has been greatly reduced by the elimination of lead as an ingredient in household paint and in motor fuel (Federal Interagency Forum on Child and Family Statistics, 2009). However, the risk of exposure to lead is not evenly distributed among the population. Because lead was an additive in paint until the 1980s, many older houses still have surfaces covered in lead-based paint. Lead was outlawed as an additive to motor fuels in 1995 (with some exceptions, such as its continued use in aviation fuel), but prior to that time, millions of metric tons of lead were poured into the environment, and lead continues to be found in the soil near roadways. This places children who live today in older housing and in traffic-congested areas at the greatest risk of exposure to lead in the environment.

The differential exposure to risk from this toxin is illustrated by the fact that in 2003–2006, blood lead levels at or above 5 micrograms per deciliter of blood were found in 12% of Black children versus 2% of White and Mexican American children (Federal Interagency Forum on Child and Family Statistics, 2009). In 1997, the Centers for Disease Control and Prevention (CDC) estimated that 1 in 20 American children suffer from subclinical levels of lead poisoning (Crain, 2000), and even subclinical levels can have a negative effect on several aspects of cognitive functioning (Jusko et al., 2008; Surkan et al., 2007).

We also see the impact of environmental factors on several of the chronic illnesses that affect a significant number of children each year. You probably know that the incidence of children with **asthma** has increased substantially in recent years. The increase in the incidence of asthma and related respiratory problems has paralleled the increase in the use of fossil fuels, and today the incidence is highest among poor children who live in urban environments filled with coal-burning furnaces and diesel-fueled vehicles (Crain, 2000). By current estimates, about 9% of children under the age of 17 have asthma (Federal Interagency Forum on Child and Family Statistics, 2009), an incidence that has doubled since the 1980s (Perrin et al., 2007). As we have already noted, this makes it the most common chronic illness among children in the United States. Asthma places more limits on children's activity than any other disease (Mayo Clinic, 2010). Over 6 million children in the United States have asthma, and asthma was responsible for almost 13 million missed days of school in 2003, and 7 million outpatient visits to physicians or hospitals and almost 200,000 hospitalizations in 2004 (Akinbami, 2010).

Asthma is caused by an inflammation of the bronchial airways that produces chest tightness, coughing and wheezing, and shortness of breath. Although more than half of all cases are caused by allergies, exposure to secondhand smoke in the environment also poses a risk. Even a mother smoking during her pregnancy has been associated with an increased risk of a child developing asthma, possibly as a result of stunted growth of the lungs prenatally (Jaakola & Gissler, 2007). Because the number of adult smokers has decreased in recent years, the percentage of children who are regularly exposed to cigarette smoke within their own homes has decreased by more than half (from 27% in 1994 to 11% in 2003) (U.S. Environmental Protection Agency, 2009b), but exposure to air pollutants such as ozone, particulates, nitrogen dioxide, and sulfur dioxide remains an ongoing risk for children with asthma because these pollutants can trigger an attack.

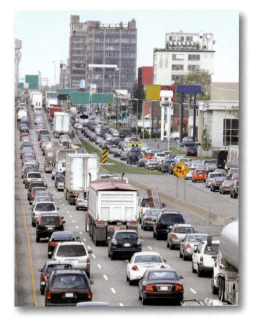

Environmental toxins. Environmental toxins come in many different forms. What toxins would a child who lived near this highway be exposed to? What outcomes might result from this exposure?

Asthma The most common chronic illness in childhood, in which a child's airways constrict, making it difficult to breathe.

Video Link 15.5
Asthma.

Childhood asthma. This boy has asthma and must use an inhaler when he has difficulty breathing. Asthma is the most common chronic illness among children in the United States.

4. The incidence of childhood cancer has increased in recent years.

True. Unfortunately the incidence of childhood cancer has continued to increase in recent years, but fortunately the mortality rate for childhood cancer decreased during the same time. More children are surviving many types of cancer than survived in the past.

The causes of childhood cancer are still poorly understood, but there is evidence that exposure to toxins, such as radiation and pesticides, may be one factor that contributes to some types of childhood cancer (U.S. Environmental Protection Agency, 2008). Recent statistics on childhood cancers contain both good news and bad news. As you can see from Figure 15.1, the good news is that the number of fatalities due to childhood cancer has decreased over the last 30 years, but the bad news is that the incidence of childhood cancers has continued to climb during that same period (U.S. Environmental Protection Agency, 2008). Research will need to continue to identify the environmental conditions associated with this increase.

Figure 15.1

Incidence and mortality rates of childhood cancer. The number of cases of diagnosed cancer in children has gone up over time, but fortunately with better treatment, the death rate has gone down.

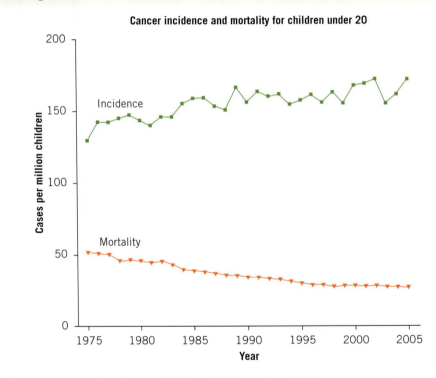

Accidents

Recent years have seen a dramatic decrease in the rate of childhood injury, as shown in Figure 15.2. According to Wallis, Cody, and Mickalide (2003), deaths from injury declined from 15.4 per 100,000 children in 1987 to 8.5 per 100,000 children in 2005, a decline of 45%. Table 15.2 shows some specific causes of childhood deaths and their rate of decrease since 1987. We can easily think of societal changes that have contributed to this overall decline. Laws now require that children be restrained while riding in motor vehicles, school and community programs promote bicycle safety (including wearing helmets and safety gear), organized sports for children pay more attention to the safety of participants, and toys are screened for health and safety hazards. This is all progress, but there is still room for improvement. Unintentional injury is still the leading cause of death in the United States among children between the ages of 1 and 14 (Wallis et al., 2003). According to the National Center for Injury Prevention and Control, over 12,000 children die each year in this country from unintentional injuries (Borse et al., 2008).

Boys are twice as likely to die from an injury as girls (Borse et al., 2008). The cause of death from injury varies by age group. For children younger than 1 year of age, suffocation is the most common cause of death; for children ages 1 to 4 years, drowning is the most common cause; and for children ages 5 to 19 years, injuries from traffic accidents are the leading cause (Borse et al., 2008).

Of course the number of nonfatal injuries greatly exceeds the number of fatal ones. There are 33 hospitalizations and 1,350 emergency room visits for nonfatal injuries for every fatality

Figure 15.2

Number of deaths due to accidents. This figure shows that there has been a 43% decrease in the deaths of children occurring because of accidents between 1987 and 2004. Think about what might account for this welcome change and then look at Table 15.2 to see what causes of death from injury have decreased over this time period.

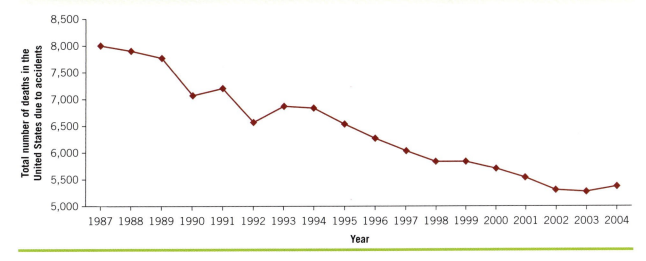

Table 15.2

Causes of childhood accidental deaths. All of the following types of accidental deaths have decreased since 1987, with the exception of suffocation. How would you explain these changes?

Type of Incident	Number of Deaths in Year 1987	Number of Deaths in Year 2004	Percent Decrease/ Increase
Motor vehicle crash	3,587	2,431	↓32%
Drowning	1,363	761	↓44%
Pedestrian injury	1,283	583	↓55%
Fire and/or burn injury	1,233	512	↓58%
Suffocation	690	963	↑28%
Falls	149	107	↓28%
Poisoning	100	86	↓14%
Firearm	247	63	↓74%

among children between the ages of 1 and 14 years (Federal Interagency Forum on Child and Family Statistics, 2009). Falls are the leading cause of nonfatal injuries for children under the age of 15 and account for over 50% of the injuries to children under the age of 1 year (see Figure 15.3a). The other top causes of nonfatal injuries in children younger than age 9 include being struck by or against an object (for example, being hit by a baseball or running into a wall), animal bites, and insect stings. Being struck by or against an object and overexertion are the leading causes of injuries for older children between the ages of 10 and 14, and being struck by

Figure 15.3a

Emergency department visit rates for children ages 1–4 and 5–14 by leading causes of injury visits, 2005–2006

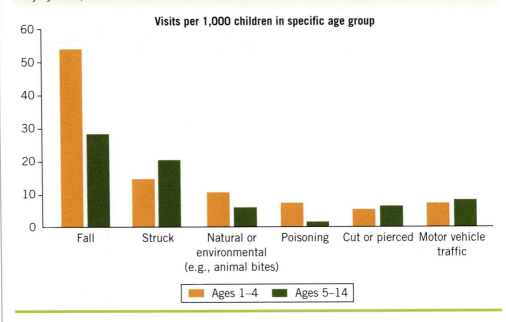

Figure 15.3b

Emergency department visit rates for adolescents ages 15–19 by leading causes of injury visits, 2005–2006

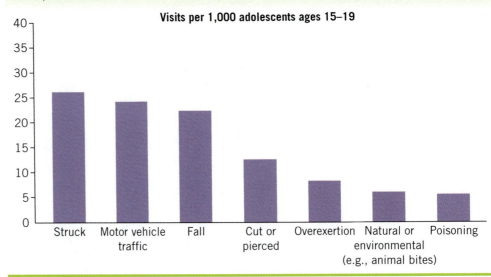

or against an object, falls, and injuries related to being an occupant of a motor vehicle are the leading causes of nonfatal injuries among adolescents between the ages of 15 and 19 (see Figure 15.3b) (Borse et al., 2008). Violence and sports-related injuries are also more frequent at older ages (Federal Interagency Forum on Child and Family Statistics, 2009). At all ages beyond age 1, boys have a higher rate of nonfatal injuries than girls.

Smoking, Alcohol, and Drugs

As children move into adolescence, they begin to make lifestyle choices that directly affect their health and well-being. Some of the choices that have serious implications for adolescent health are their decisions about the use of substances. According to *America's Children: Key National Indicators of Well-Being*, prepared by the Federal Interagency Forum on Child and Family Statistics (2009),

- 3.1% of eighth graders, 5.9% of tenth graders, and 11.4% of twelfth graders reported smoking daily in the previous 30 days (with more than twice as many White adolescents as Black or Hispanic adolescents reporting smoking on a daily basis);
- 8.1% of eighth graders, 16% of tenth graders, and 24.6% of twelfth graders reported having five or more alcoholic beverages in a row during the last 2 weeks; and
- 7.6% of eighth graders, 15.8% of tenth graders, and 22.3% of twelfth graders reported using illicit drugs in the previous 30 days.

Fortunately, the same report documents a decline in these percentages from previous reports. For instance, the percentage of adolescents who reported smoking on a daily basis is about one-half the percentage reported in 1995. Unfortunately, although the percentage of adolescents reporting heavy drinking has declined slightly since 1995, these percentages still remain fairly high.

For many adolescents, drinking becomes a way to challenge the limitations put on young people. Many adolescents have their first drink between the ages of 13 and 15, and about 15% of eighth graders report having had at least one drink in the past month (Johnston, O'Malley, Bachman, & Schulenberg, 2009). Surveys consistently show that males report higher levels of both heavy drinking and daily drinking than females, and that White students report the highest levels and Blacks the lowest. By the time adolescents become college students, almost half of them engage in binge drinking (55.5% of males and 48% of females) (Wechsler et al., 2002), and the gender gap appears to be decreasing (Johnston, O'Malley, Bachman, & Schulenberg, 2007). For some of these young people, alcohol becomes a lifelong problem.

Heavy alcohol consumption is a risk factor for other health threats, such as motor vehicle accidents, injuries, and fighting. Early onset of this behavior (remember, more than 8% of eighth graders reported having five or more alcoholic beverages in a row in the previous 30 days) is particularly problematic because young adolescents are still immature in their decision-making skills and may not fully appreciate the consequences of their decision to drink. Also, adolescents who start drinking at a young age have a longer period of exposure to alcohol compared to adolescents who wait to start drinking, so there is a greater cumulative toll taken by their alcohol consumption.

The decision to drink alcohol may have the most immediate and serious consequences for adolescents. A single episode of binge drinking or of driving while drunk can be lethal, but the decision to smoke may be the one that has the most serious long-term consequences. In the *Morbidity and Mortality Weekly Report*, the Centers for Disease Control and Prevention (2003) report that about 4,400 adolescents try their first cigarette each day, and estimate that one third of these young people will eventually die from a smoking-related disease. In 2008, 6% of 10th graders and 11% of 12th graders reported smoking cigarettes on a daily basis

5. If you are one of the 4,400 adolescents who smoked their first cigarette today, there is a 1-in-10 chance that you will eventually die from a smoking-related illness. **TRUE/FALSE**

False. The chance is 1 in 3 that you will eventually die from an illness that is related to your smoking, like emphysema, heart disease, cancer, or stroke.

in the previous 30 days (Federal Interagency Forum on Child and Family Statistics, 2009). Although rates of smoking are similar for males and females, the rate differs substantially by ethnic and racial group, with White students reporting the highest rate of daily smoking (14.3%) and a considerably smaller proportion of Hispanics (6.7%) and Black students (5.8%) reporting the same thing (Federal Interagency Forum on Child and Family Statistics, 2009). Because it is so difficult to stop smoking once the habit has been established, efforts designed to prevent young people from starting to smoke seem the wisest course. Some prevention efforts, such as the "truth®" campaign created by the American Legacy Foundation, have been quite successful. This campaign accounted for 22% of the decline in youth smoking over a 3-year period (Farrelly, Davis, Haviland, Messeri, & Healton, 2005). However, as we discussed in Chapter 13, any prevention effort must compete with advertising that continues to portray smoking as pleasurable, product placement in movies that pairs cigarettes with attractive young actors and actresses, and the continuing perception by teens that smoking is "cool" and a sign of adulthood.

Video Link 15.6
Anti-smoking campaign.

Illicit drug usage is associated with a wide range of negative health outcomes, with the specific effects depending upon the particular substance used, its frequency, and dosage. Cocaine has been linked to serious health problems that include heart attack and stroke, marijuana use is associated with both physical (for example, lung damage) and cognitive impairment (for example, memory loss), and hallucinogens are associated with problems in learning and retaining information (Federal Interagency Forum on Child and Family Statistics, 2009). Of course the use of any substance that affects physical or cognitive functioning can have collateral damage for your health. If your reaction time is slowed, you put yourself (and others) at risk when you get behind the wheel and drive. If your decision making is impaired, you put yourself (and others) at risk when you engage in behaviors that can impair your health (for example, engaging in unprotected sex, taking foolish dares). The self-reported use of illicit drugs has declined slightly since a peak in the mid-1990s (Federal Interagency Forum on Child and Family Statistics, 2009), so that is an encouraging sign.

Violence

We discuss child abuse later in this chapter, but children and adolescents also can be victims of violence perpetrated by people outside of the family. It can even occur in the context of a romantic relationship. According to the National Youth Violence Prevention Resource Center (2007), about one quarter of high school students (males and females) and almost one-third of college students report having been a victim of nonsexual dating violence (that is, physical assault and battery or verbal and emotional abuse). Also, nearly one half of the 500,000 sexual assaults reported to police each year are committed by friends or acquaintances. Adolescent girls are 4 times more likely to be the victim of a sexual assault than any other age groups (National Youth Violence Prevention Resource Center, 2007). Beginning to date at a younger age, becoming sexually active at a younger age, and having been a victim of sexual abuse are factors that place a girl at an increased risk of dating violence. The use of alcohol or other drugs is another contributing factor to that risk.

School violence is another threat to the well-being of children and adolescents that has captured headlines in recent years, but schools are safe for most children and adolescents and have become safer in recent years as the overall rates of school violence have fallen (National Youth Violence Prevention Resource Center, 2008). That being said, we can't ignore the fact that some schools do have serious problems with violence in its many different forms. Although school-related deaths remain rare, school violence also includes assaults (with or without weapons), physical fights, threats, bullying, and gang violence. In 2006, there were 767,000 victims of violent crimes at school (Dinkes, Kemp, & Baum, 2009), and the Centers for Disease Control and Prevention (2008e) report that in a nationwide survey of high school students,

7.9% of the students said that during the previous 12 months they had been threatened or injured with a weapon on school property, and 13.6% said they had been involved in a physical fight.

Efforts to reduce school violence have included services that are designed to help individual children who are at risk of perpetrating violence and school-wide interventions designed to change the school climate in a more positive direction, as well as broad-based community interventions designed to reduce violence in the community in which an individual school is located. A number of schools have used peer-mediation programs to facilitate nonviolent solutions to conflicts between students. In these programs, students are trained to use communication skills, problem solving, and conflict resolution skills to help other students negotiate agreements that satisfy both parties in a dispute. A meta-analysis of 43 studies on peer-mediation programs in elementary and secondary schools found a positive impact of such programs on school climate and on the perception of the level of conflict at the schools, and an actual reduction in the number of conflicts in the schools that required disciplinary action (Burrell, Zirbel, & Allen, 2003). In **Active Learning: School Violence From a Student's Perspective** you can compare your own experience of school violence with those of classmates.

School Violence From a Student's Perspective

Think about your own experience with violence in your elementary, middle, and high school. Talk with several friends and/or classmates who came from different high schools and compare your experiences. This activity will be most effective if the members of each group have had experiences in different types of schools. Violence on average is greater in middle school and high school than in elementary school, and in urban schools than in suburban or rural schools. Males are more likely than females to be both perpetrators and victims. Fewer than half of public schools report a violent crime each year, and only 10% report a serious violent crime (National Youth Violence Prevention Resource Center, 2008), but in your discussion, remember to think about a full range of violent behavior, including threats of violence, assaults, and bullying in addition to other more clearly criminal acts. Also discuss what, if any, efforts were made by your schools to reduce school violence or to improve the school climate.

The Impact of Poverty

UNICEF (2005) has described poverty as the single most important indicator of child well-being. In the United States, 18% of children live in poverty, a rate much higher than in any other industrialized nation (Sherrod, 2009; U.S. Census Bureau, 2008c). There is a very large racial divide within these numbers. Although most low-income children are White, the percentages within each racial group are very different (McLoyd, 1998). About 10% of White children, 11% of Asian children, 28% of Hispanic children, and 34% of Black children live in poverty (U.S. Census Bureau, 2008c). Children are much more likely to live in poverty if they are raised in a single-mother household; almost 60% of these children live below the poverty line. Unfortunately, children under the age of 6 are more likely to live in poverty than older children, setting the stage for developmental problems in the years that follow if the family remains in poverty (U.S. Census Bureau, 2008c).

Poverty is related to higher levels of mental retardation and developmental delay, learning disabilities and failure in school, health problems, and behavior problems (Shonkoff & Phillips, 2000). Figure 15.4 illustrates some of the health disparities in children from different

6. More White children than minority children live in poverty in the United States. **TRUE/FALSE**

True. This is true because there are more White children than minority children in the United States. However, the percentage of minority children who live in poverty is greater than the percentage of White children in poverty.

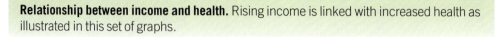

Figure 15.4

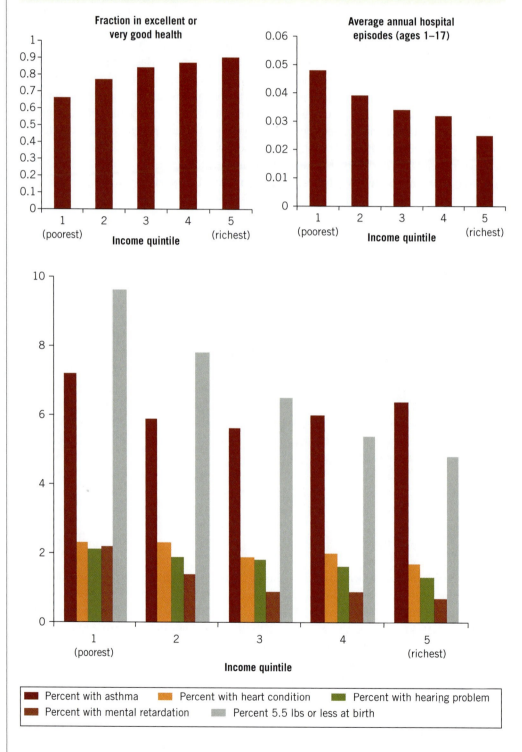

Relationship between income and health. Rising income is linked with increased health as illustrated in this set of graphs.

socioeconomic backgrounds. Poverty is not a static condition. Families move in and out of poverty as their circumstances change but, in general, the more extreme the poverty is and the longer the child spends in poverty, the worse the outcome (Brooks-Gunn & Duncan, 1997; Duncan, Brooks-Gunn, & Klebanov, 1994; Korenman, Miller, & Sjaastad, 1995). Children also seem to do worse if they live in poverty early in their childhood. If poverty develops later, the negative consequences for children are somewhat reduced, especially in terms of academic achievement (Brooks-Gunn & Duncan, 1997). Poverty delivers a double disadvantage: It creates more problems, and people then have fewer resources to help them cope with these problems.

Poverty's impact begins for children before birth. Lack of adequate health services and poor nutrition contribute to prenatal problems and premature birth (McLoyd, 1998). Prematurity is a high risk factor for later health problems and cognitive limitations. These problems are often overcome when the family has access to adequate resources, but the outcome is less likely to be positive when the family does not. In addition, poor infants are more likely to be exposed to drugs and/or alcohol prenatally. As we learned in Chapter 5, fetal alcohol syndrome is a major cause of intellectual disability in the United States.

Poverty creates enormous stress in parents, which results in high rates of depression. Depressed parents are much less able to adequately care for their children to support their optimal growth (Shonkoff & Phillips, 2000), and poverty decreases the resources available to help mothers with depression, resulting in worse outcomes for the children (Petterson & Albers, 2001). Low-income parents are also less likely to provide a cognitively stimulating environment, with the toys and books that promote academic achievement (McLoyd, 1998). As we learned in Chapter 9, low-income mothers are less likely to talk with their children than mothers who are more well-off (McLoyd, 1998). The result is a lower level of verbal proficiency in the children, which has an important impact on later academic achievement.

The many risk factors associated with poverty, such as dangerous neighborhoods, parental mental health issues, and exposure to family violence (Evans & English, 2002), are also linked to behavioral problems in poor children. Also parents who are dealing with the issues associated with poverty are more likely to be highly punitive and less warm toward their children, and this pattern of parenting is linked with behavioral problems (Bradley, Corwyn, McAdoo, & Garcia Coll, 2001). There is more evidence for a link with children's externalizing problems, such as aggression, than with their internalizing problems, such as depression, but both are elevated in poor children and increase the longer the child lives in poverty (Allhusen et al., 2005; McLoyd, 1998).

Biological response appears to play a mediating role in the unhealthy outcomes of poverty. Cortisol is a hormone that is linked to the experience of stress, but it also is linked with problems such as depression, posttraumatic stress disorder, obesity, and diabetes. Research has shown that children in low-socioeconomic-status families develop much higher levels of cortisol in response to ambiguous situations that the children interpret as threatening, and in response to a chaotic home life. This, in turn, puts them at higher risk for both psychological and physical problems (Chen, Cohen, & Miller, 2010).

Research has shown that when income relative to family needs increases in low-income families, child outcomes improve. In a large study carried out by the National Institute of Child Health and Human Development, children were followed from birth to age 3 (Dearing, McCartney, & Taylor, 2001). Although increases in income

Homelessness. One outcome of poverty can be homelessness. The mother cuddling her daughter in this photo searched for work for 6 months and then was unable to pay her rent, so the family lost their house.

for middle- and upper-income families did not affect children's abilities at age 3, increases in income for low-income families had a large effect. Children's language abilities, readiness for school, and social behaviors all improved, even to the same level as that for children in families who were not deprived. It was also true that poor families who became poorer had children with even worse outcomes. These same results were found when these children were retested at age 9. Chronically poor children had worse outcomes than those who had brief periods of economic disadvantage, while those with even brief experiences of poverty did worse than those who had never experienced poverty (Allhusen et al., 2005). In a separate study, antisocial behavior was found to decrease in 4- to 7-year-olds when their families moved out of poverty and to increase the longer the families remained in poverty (MacMillan, McMorris, & Kruttschnitt, 2004).

There are some factors that are linked with better outcomes for children in low-income families. When parents are very loving, but also very strict, this seems to help children succeed in difficult circumstances (McLoyd, 1998). Attendance at an early education program, such as Head Start, also helps. However, McLoyd (1998) argues that direct financial aid to low-income families, as is found in many European countries, is likely to be the most direct and effective way to improve the lot of children in those families. Evidence for this approach is found in one study of families who had experienced a rise in their income. The older siblings in these families, who had spent more of their time in poverty, were less likely to graduate high school than their younger siblings who had spent less of their life in poverty (Duncan, Yeung, Brooks-Gunn, & Smith, 1998). One intervention program called New Hope was designed to help low-income families get jobs, and to provide them with income support, health care, and child care (Huston et al., 2005). There were many positive results of this program. Children, particularly boys, aged 6 to 10 improved over time in school achievement and social skills. The parents in these families described having more support, less stress, and more optimism about their future (Huston et al., 2001). The children spent more time in structured child care and other activities, while children from comparable families who were not in the program spent more time on their own or with young babysitters. All of these factors combined to produce positive outcomes for children that were maintained at a follow-up 5 years later (Huston et al., 2005).

Child Abuse and Neglect

What Is Abuse?

Many people think that abusing a child is about the most horrible crime an adult can commit, but in 2006 more than 3.3 million reports of suspected abuse or neglect were made to agencies in the United States that are responsible for protecting children (U.S. Department of Health and Human Services [USDHHS], 2008a). Stop for a moment and count slowly to 10. In the time it took you to count to 10, it is likely that another report of suspected maltreatment was made because a new report comes into the system on an average of once every 10 seconds. The reports of suspected maltreatment include a variety of allegations. **Maltreatment** is a broad term that includes several types of abuse (physical, sexual, and emotional), as well as several types of neglect (physical, emotional, and educational). The Centers for Disease Control and Prevention (2008d) provide these definitions of the four largest categories of maltreatment:

Maltreatment Physical abuse, sexual abuse, emotional abuse, or neglect.

- *Physical abuse* occurs when a child's body is injured as a result of hitting, kicking, shaking, burning, or other use of force.
- *Sexual abuse* involves engaging a child in sexual acts. It includes fondling, rape, and exposing a child to other sexual activities.

- *Emotional abuse* refers to behaviors that harm a child's self-worth or emotional well-being. Examples include name-calling, shaming, rejection, withholding love, and threatening.
- *Neglect* is the failure to meet a child's basic needs. These needs include housing, food, clothing, education, and access to medical care (para. 2–5).

Physical child abuse. Child abuse may have immediate consequences such as those seen in the girl above, but it also has many long-term, psychological consequences for many of its victims.

When a report of suspected abuse or neglect is received by a child protective agency, the first step is determining whether the report involves an allegation that is covered by child protective legislation. About 63% of all allegations received are forwarded to a local child protective agency for further investigation (USDHHS, 2008a). Investigations usually involve interviews with the child or children involved in the report, their parents or caregivers, and other people who know the family. Following the investigation, a determination is made as to whether the allegations are substantiated (that is, there is evidence that supports the allegations) or are unsubstantiated. In about 24% of the investigations, at least one child is found to be a victim of abuse or neglect (USDHHS, 2008a). Depending on the findings from the investigation, children can be removed from the family if they are considered to be in imminent danger, or services can be provided to the family to prevent further maltreatment. The balance between child protection and family preservation is a central concern of child welfare agencies (Roberts, 2002), so agencies are reluctant to remove children unless they are clearly in danger.

As you will read in **Journey of Research: Child Protective Legislation**, when the public's attention was first drawn to the magnitude of the problem of child abuse and neglect, there was a great deal of outrage over the ways in which children had been let down by the system, so the original legislation was intended to uncover every possible case in which abuse was occurring. To this end, each state maintains a toll-free hotline to receive reports of suspected maltreatment. Any concerned citizen can report his or her suspicions to authorities, who then are responsible for conducting an investigation, so neighbors, relatives, and family friends can all make reports, and most states also accept anonymous reports. Although there was initially some concern that making a false report would become a way for disgruntled neighbors or vindictive ex-spouses to harass a parent, you will be relieved to know that only one tenth of one percent of all reports are typically determined to be intentionally false (USDHHS, 2008a), and people who knowingly file false reports can be prosecuted.

The legislation also classifies a number of professionals who work with children and families as **mandatory reporters** who are required by law to report their suspicions to authorities (USDHHS, 2008a). These mandatory reporters include health care providers, teachers, child care providers, social workers, and police officers. Slightly more than half of all reports come from professionals. Failure by a professional to report a suspicion of maltreatment carries a legal penalty (either a fine or imprisonment), but all states provide immunity from civil liability and criminal penalties for mandatory reporters who contact protective services because their reports are considered to have been made in good faith (Crosson-Tower, 2003). The identity of the source of a report is not disclosed to the family.

A consequence of the original decision to cast a wide net to uncover any abuse that was occurring is that the system has often been close to overwhelmed by the number of reports it receives. It takes a great deal of resources to screen and investigate over 3 million reports annually, and remember that only one quarter of the reports that are investigated will eventually find evidence of maltreatment. We could change the legislation to make reporting abuse

Mandatory reporters
Individuals who work with children who are required by law to report suspicions of child maltreatment to authorities.

more difficult, but that would mean that more cases of abuse or neglect would go undetected. So far we have not been willing to make this trade-off, so we continue to have a broad-based approach designed to discover as many families in which abuse is occurring as possible.

Incidence of Maltreatment

TRUE/FALSE

7. In the United States, one child dies from child abuse or neglect every 4 days.

   False. In fact, 4 children die every single day from child abuse or neglect in the United States. That is over 1,500 child deaths each year.

The incidence of neglect is much higher than the incidence of abuse. In 2008, more than 70% of the substantiated cases of maltreatment involved neglect (USDHHS, 2008a). Physical abuse accounted for another 15%, sexual abuse accounted for 9.1%, and psychological maltreatment accounted for 7.3%. An additional 2.2% of the cases were medical neglect, and 9% of victims experienced other types of maltreatment (cases can be substantiated on more than one allegation, which is why the total is greater than 100%) (USDHHS, 2008a). In this same year, 1,740 children in the United States died from abuse and neglect (USDHHS, 2008a). That means that over 4 children each day died as the result of abuse or neglect, and 13.1% of the fatalities involved children in families that had already received family preservation services from Child Protective Services in the past 5 years (USDHHS, 2008a). Children under the age of 4 were at the greatest risk of dying at the hands of their own parents and account for 79% of the childhood fatalities (Centers for Disease Control and Prevention, 2008a).

In 2008, over 758,000 children were victims of abuse or neglect (USDHHS, 2008a). However, when we try to estimate the magnitude of the problem, we need to remember that statistics reflect only those cases that are actually reported to protective services in any given year. For this reason they represent only a portion of the actual cases of maltreatment that occur. By some estimates, the actual number of cases is 3 times greater than the number of reports made to protective services (American Psychological Association, 2004b). To estimate the actual incidence, one survey interviewed a nationally representative sample of children or parents of children between the ages of 2 and 17 years of age. Based on that survey, the researchers estimated that 1 in 7 children was a victim of maltreatment in the previous year (Finkelhor, Ormrod, Turner, & Hamby, 2005). Emotional abuse in the form of name-calling or denigrating the child was by far the most frequently identified type of maltreatment in this study.

Victims and Perpetrators

Figure 15.5 shows that younger children are at a greater risk of being a victim of abuse than older children, and Figure 15.6 shows that African American children are at the highest risk and Asian American children are at a substantially lower risk than children from other ethnic groups. Neglect, however, occurs at similar rates among children and adolescents (Finkelhor et al., 2005). Although the risk does not differ substantially between boys and girls for most types of maltreatment (Finkelhor et al., 2005; USDHHS, 2008a), the risk of being a victim of sexual abuse is 4 times higher for girls than for boys. Because cases of sexual abuse are different in several ways from other types of child maltreatment, we will discuss this topic separately a little later in the chapter.

As you can see from Figure 15.7, mothers alone are the most frequent perpetrators of child maltreatment, followed by mothers and fathers together, and fathers alone. Taken together, this means that over 80% of perpetrators of abuse or neglect are the parents of the child. Other relatives (for example, grandparents, aunts, or uncles) were listed as the perpetrator of the abuse in 4.7% of the indicated cases in 2008, and unmarried partners of a parent were listed in another 2.5% of the cases (USDHHS, 2008a). Also note that nonparental caregivers are listed as the perpetrator for about 10% of the reports. This category of perpetrator could include a child's care provider (for example, a babysitter or child care worker) or some other adult who has authority over the child (for example, a teacher or an adult in a community organization). It is not surprising that mothers top this list because they spend more time with children

Figure 15.5

Maltreatment by age of victim. Are you surprised to see that the highest rate of child abuse is among infants and toddlers younger than age 3?

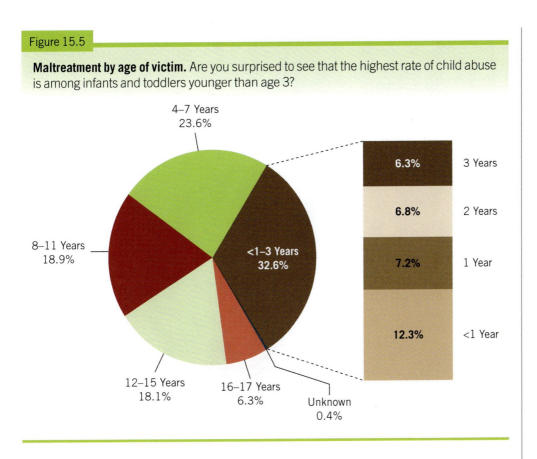

Figure 15.6

Maltreatment by race/ethnicity of victim. As you can see, there are large disparities in rates of child abuse among different racial and ethnic groups.

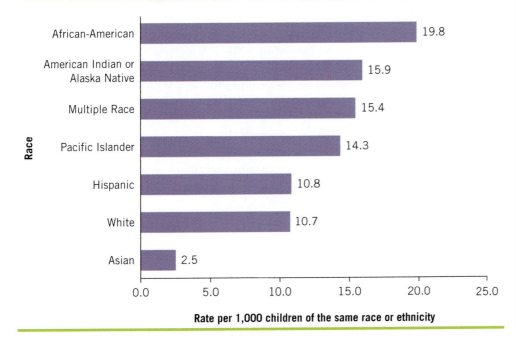

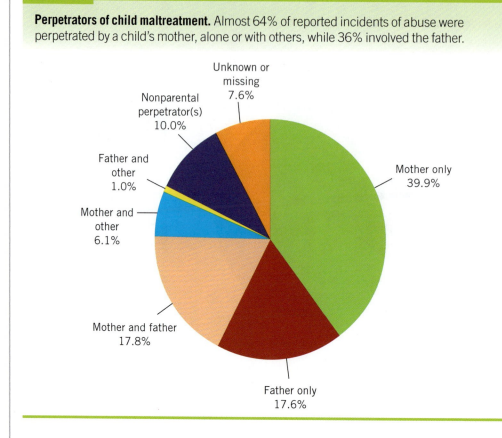

Figure 15.7

Perpetrators of child maltreatment. Almost 64% of reported incidents of abuse were perpetrated by a child's mother, alone or with others, while 36% involved the father.

Unknown or missing
7.6%

Nonparental perpetrator(s)
10.0%

Father and other
1.0%

Mother and other
6.1%

Mother only
39.9%

Mother and father
17.8%

Father only
17.6%

(especially younger children) than any other caregiver, and in addition to directly committing the abuse, mothers can be charged with maltreatment if they fail to protect their children from harm by others.

Child abuse and neglect certainly can occur at any socioeconomic level in society, but low-income families are at greater risk of being reported. It is also likely that maltreatment actually occurs more frequently in poorer families. As we have seen, there are a number of circumstances associated with being poor that contribute to this increased risk. Poorer families, in general, are exposed to more life stressors, and increased stress makes it more likely that parents could lose control and strike out at their children. And, of course, fewer financial resources can result in living conditions that represent neglect. When the economy takes a downturn, reports of both abuse and neglect typically increase (Freisthler, Merritt, & LaScala, 2006; Steinberg, Catalano, & Dooley, 1981). Parents who have substance abuse problems are both more likely to be living in marginal conditions and more likely to be abusing or neglecting the children in their households. Finally, it is much more likely that low-income families will be in contact with agencies such as welfare agencies, probation services, or public health clinics that are mandatory reporters of suspected abuse or neglect.

Sexual Abuse

Although we know that many cases of child maltreatment are never detected or reported to authorities, the problem of underreporting is even greater for cases of sexual abuse (Flinn, 1995). Sexual abuse that is committed by someone who is not a member of the child's family or responsible for caring for the child is typically handled by the criminal justice system, rather than Child Protective Services, so these cases do not become part of the national child abuse reporting statistics. However, most children who are sexually abused are victimized by someone they know (Finkelhor et al., 2005), and they often have been threatened with harm to themselves or their family if they disclose what has happened. This lowers the chance of the child telling someone about the abuse. Boys who are sexually abused are even less likely to disclose what has happened to them than girls are (Finkelhor, Hotaling, Lewis, & Smith, 1990; Ullman & Filipas, 2005).

Although both boys and girls might fear that they won't be believed or that they won't receive help in response to their disclosure, males have some additional issues tied to our cultural expectations for males. In a recent article that reports the results of interviews with male survivors of childhood sexual abuse, the authors describe the societal demands for acceptable masculine behavior as "strength, silence, and stoicism" (Sorsoli, Kia-Keating, & Grossman, 2008, p. 342). Males are raised to believe that they shouldn't be weak and shouldn't allow themselves to be victims and, if they have been victimized, that they should keep it to themselves. Such attitudes work against the chance that a boy will disclose to a trusted adult that sexual abuse has happened, but disclosure is the necessary first step in protecting the child from further abuse and to get the child access to therapeutic services. Sexual abuse continues on average for 4 years (Flinn, 1995), so early disclosure is a critical step in stopping the abuse as soon as possible.

Although most children do not voluntarily report their abuse, they are likely to admit it if a caring adult introduces the topic and asks them about it (Bruck & Ceci, 2004; London, Bruck, Wright, & Ceci, 2008). Because so many adults have gone years and years without admitting the abuse that happened to them, we came to believe that it would be difficult to get children to admit the abuse, but it turns out that children are not in denial about the reality of their abuse, nor do they need specific suggestions about what happened to get them to talk about it. Lamb et al. (2003) found that 83% of 4- to 8-year-old children willingly answered open-ended questions about their abuse, and 66% were willing to name the perpetrator when questioned by specially trained police.

An analysis of reports of suspected sexual abuse found that reports involving female victims were more likely to be substantiated than reports involving male victims (Dersch & Munsch, 1999). It is possible that male victims are not as cooperative or forthcoming during the investigation as female victims, but in this research the difference was attributed to the fact that more reports involving female victims came from mandatory reporters. Because mandatory reporters have a better understanding of what is necessary for Child Protective Services to substantiate a report, their reports tend to be substantiated at a higher rate than reports from members of the general public. The recommendation from this research was to better educate mandatory reporters about the incidence and indications of sexual abuse in boys so that they could recognize and make reports of cases involving male victims that require investigation, just as they do in the case of suspected sexual abuse involving female victims.

Children are at greatest risk of being a victim of sexual abuse between the ages of 8 and 12 years, although in over 20% of the cases, the abuse begins before the age of 8 (Flinn, 1995). Some of the other factors that place a child at risk of being sexually abused (especially for older children and adolescents) include having few friends, having parents who are absent or unavailable, drug or alcohol abuse in the family, having a household with transient adults living in it, or having a parent who was physically or sexually abused as a child (Flinn, 1995). Sexual abuse occurs in families from all ethnic and racial backgrounds and at all socioeconomic levels. It occurs in countries around the world, in many different cultures, with rates that average below 10% for boys and between 10% and 20% for girls. However, rates as high as 50% to 60% have been found in studies in the United States and South Africa (Pereda, Guilera, Forns, & Gómez-Benito, 2009).

Of great concern worldwide is the sexual exploitation of young people for prostitution and pornography. Sex trafficking involves the forcible removal of children from their families for the purposes of prostitution. Estimates are that 200,000 girls from Nepal are currently working in

8. When asked, children who have been sexually abused are likely to deny their abuse. **TRUE/FALSE**

False. Although many adults have never revealed the abuse that occurred when they were children, it is likely that no one ever asked them about it. The evidence shows that most children will reveal abuse when asked about it directly.

brothels in India (Crawford & Kaufman, 2008). These are instances of severe and long-lasting abuse that have devastating consequences for the girls involved.

The Impact of Child Abuse and Neglect

Experiencing abuse during childhood has been associated with a number of behavioral and mental health problems. Sexual abuse has been associated with higher rates of depression, anxiety disorders, antisocial behavior, substance abuse, and attempted suicides (Fergusson & Mullen, 1999; Finkelhor & Hashima, 2001; Putnam, 2003), and outcomes are poorer for sexual abuse survivors who suffered more severe abuse (for example, the abuse began at a younger age, it continued for longer, it involved penetration, or there was little or no support following the child's disclosure of the abuse) (Browne & Finkelhor, 1986). The consequences of physical abuse are not as clear (Fergusson, Boden, & Horwood, 2008). Although some research has found reports of suicidal thoughts, depression, antisocial behavior, and substance abuse, other studies have not found differences in these outcomes between physically abused children and matched control samples of children who were not abused. There are few studies that have examined the long-term impact of neglect on children's development.

Although it isn't surprising to learn that being a victim of sexual abuse has later negative repercussions for children, it is important that you understand the nature and the magnitude of those repercussions. Although these experiences increase a child's risk of suffering from mental and psychosocial problems, one recent estimate of the magnitude of the effect was that childhood sexual abuse accounted for 13% of the mental health problems experienced by the participants in the study (Fergusson et al., 2008). A similar estimate for the effect of childhood physical abuse was that 5% of the mental health problems experienced by participants were attributable to their abuse. So, although abuse contributes to an increased risk, the abuse is not the sole cause of these negative outcomes.

The research conducted by Fergusson and his colleagues (2008) was particularly important because it controlled for a number of other life experiences that are known to be associated with the same negative mental health and psychosocial outcomes that we associate with physical and sexual abuse. For instance, we know that children who grow up in families that are unstable, who are not securely attached to their caregivers, who live in poverty, or who live in difficult and dangerous environments are more prone to these types of mental health problems. When Fergusson et al. (2008) controlled for these factors within their sample, the relationship between childhood physical abuse and later mental health problems became non-significant. By contrast, the relationship between childhood sexual abuse and mental health outcomes was reduced in strength but still remained statistically significant. This type of analysis helps us understand how the factors that often co-occur with abuse contribute to the negative outcomes that we see in these children. The fact that sexual abuse often occurs over a period of years and escalates in its severity over time is another possible explanation for why its effect on developmental outcomes is larger than the effect for physical abuse.

What can we take from this research on child outcomes? First, as traumatic as childhood experiences of abuse are, this research highlights the fact that many children find some way to recover from them. While it is extremely important that we continue to do whatever we can to prevent abuse from occurring and to stop it when it does, children have a great deal of resiliency, and with appropriate help they can recover. Second, this research also reminds us of the fact that children growing up in difficult circumstances are often faced with multiple threats to their healthy development. The fact that inadequate parenting, domestic violence, poverty, and abuse occur together is not surprising, but these life circumstances multiply the amount of stress that a child has to deal with, so most children who are the victims of abuse are not dealing with a singular problem. Children who face fewer developmental challenges are more likely to overcome them and have a more positive prognosis for their future, so children growing up in less stressful situations definitely have an advantage.

One of the consequences of abuse that you have probably heard about is the idea that abused children grow up to become abusive parents. It is not as simple as that. When we look at the histories of parents who have abused their children, it is true that many of them were victims of abuse themselves, but most estimates are that about 30% of children with a history of abuse perpetuate the cycle with their own children. This would mean that 70% (or over two thirds) manage to find some way to break the cycle and do not repeat the pattern with their own children (Kaufman & Zigler, 1993; Leifer & Smith, 1990). It is encouraging to know that many adults who have experienced the pain of abuse manage to overcome these experiences to become positive, effective parents.

Preventing child maltreatment can be expensive, but a 2007 estimate of the annual direct and indirect costs of child abuse was $103.8 billion (Wang & Holton, 2007). This is considered a conservative estimate because it is based only on the number of cases included in national reporting statistics and not the total number of actual cases. Additionally, beyond the monetary cost, there are incalculable "intangible losses" in terms of "pain, suffering and reduced quality of life" (Wang & Holton, 2007, p. 2) associated with it.

You can read about the history of efforts to protect children from abuse or neglect at the hands of their own parents or caregivers in **Journey of Research: Child Protective Legislation**.

9. Adults who were abused as children are likely to become abusive parents themselves.

TRUE/FALSE

False. This is one of the most serious misunderstandings about child abuse. About 30% of abused children perpetuate the cycle by repeating abuse in the next generation, but the majority of abused children do not. They successfully break that vicious cycle when they reach adulthood.

Child Protective Legislation

JOURNEY *of* RESEARCH

The unfortunate truth is that child abuse has occurred throughout human history, and continues today in a variety of forms. For much of that time, children were considered the property of their parents (more specifically, property of their fathers) and, as such, their parents were free to do whatever they wanted to do to them. Children who were sickly, disabled, deformed, or simply unwanted could be killed, abandoned, or sold into servitude or slavery (Krug, Dahlberg, Mercy, Zwi, & Lozano, 2002). As long as children were seen as property, society chose not to interfere with decisions made by individual families about how they treated their children.

When families lived on farms, everyone in the family—including the children—was expected to work productively at the day-to-day tasks that needed to be done. However, with the advent of the Industrial Revolution, the nature of work changed, and so did the role of children in an increasingly industrialized society. Many families moved off of farms and into cities, and children took their place alongside adult workers in factories, mines, and mills. Often it was the most dangerous, dirty, and

menial jobs that were left to the children. In England, a 5-year-old child might be expected to work a 16-hour day, and to receive a beating in the process if he wasn't working hard enough (Barriere, n.d.). In a way, this harsh treatment was a reflection of the attitudes toward children at the time. Today we think of children as individuals who need to be nurtured and protected, but in many areas of the world the view of children in the 1800s was that they needed hard work and strict discipline if they were to be kept on the straight and narrow path and to grow up to be honest, moral people (Bagnell, 2001).

In the United States, a pivotal event in the history of child protection occurred in 1873, when a church worker became aware of a 9-year-old girl named Mary Ellen who was being horribly mistreated by her family. The worker saw that Mary Ellen was malnourished, had been beaten, and was routinely shackled to her bed (Miller-Perrin & Perrin, 1999). However, when the church worker tried to have Mary Ellen removed from her home, she found that there was no legal precedence for such an action, and the authorities refused to act. Being persistent, the church worker next turned to

(Continued)

(Continued)

the American Society for the Prevention of Cruelty to Animals (ASPCA) for help, arguing that Mary Ellen, as a member of the animal kingdom, deserved at least the same protection that would be offered to a mule that was being mistreated. With the help of the ASPCA, Mary Ellen was removed from her abusive home and placed in foster care (Miller-Perrin & Perrin, 1999). The following year, in 1874, the Society for Prevention of Cruelty to Children was formed with the mission of protecting children from abuse and maltreatment (Miller-Perrin & Perrin, 1999). The case of Mary Ellen is considered the first child abuse case in North America, but it did not lead directly to broadly based efforts to protect children.

That had to wait for almost another 100 years. In the 1960s, Dr. Henry Kempe, a pediatrician in Denver, Colorado, found evidence in the X-rays of some children he treated of broken bones and fractures in different stages of healing, indicating that whatever had caused them had happened repeatedly over a period of time. It was Dr. Kempe and some of his colleagues who published the groundbreaking article "The Battered Child Syndrome" in 1962 and began a campaign to raise awareness not only among doctors but also among the general public of a situation that had remained hidden behind the closed doors of private homes before this (Leventhal, 2003).

Even with the growing acknowledgement that child abuse existed and might be widespread, it took more than another decade before the United States passed comprehensive legislation intended to protect children from abuse. In 1974, Public Law 93–247 (the Child Abuse Prevention and Treatment Act—CAPTA) was enacted by Congress. This legislation established a mechanism for reporting cases of suspected abuse or neglect to child protection agencies and for tracking the disposition of those cases. The act has been amended several times, most recently in 2003, but it remains the foundation for our efforts to identify and protect children who are being mistreated, and to provide support to families so that children can safely remain in their homes with their parents.

Racial Stereotyping, Prejudice, and Discrimination

Racism A pervasive system of advantage and disadvantage based on race.

Stereotypes
Conclusions made about someone based solely on the group with which he or she is identified.

Prejudices Negative attitudes toward individuals based on their race, ethnicity, religion, or other factors.

Discrimination
Negative behavior directed at people on the basis of their race, ethnicity, religion, or other factors.

A group of teenagers presented a skit in which an African American teen enters a store and is harassed by the store owner, who clearly assumes that the teen is going to steal something. When the students watching this skit were asked to write their responses to it, the White students indicated that they thought this was ridiculous and inaccurate, but the African American students in the class wrote that "this happens all the time." Although there are many who believe that racism is no longer an issue in the United States, those who experience it have a very different perception. In a variety of studies, between 49% and 90% of African American adolescents report having had experiences of racial discrimination involving harassment, poor treatment in public settings, or assumptions of lower ability or more violent behavior (Cooper, McLoyd, Wood, & Hardaway, 2008).

Racism has been defined as "a pervasive system of advantage based on race" (Tatum, 1997, p. 92). There are three aspects: **stereotypes**, which are fixed beliefs about a particular racial group; **prejudices**, which are negative attitudes about that group; and **discrimination**, which is negative behavior directed at that group (Cooper et al., 2008). Racism can be overt, meaning it is openly accepted and acted upon, or it can be covert. When it is covert, it is not acknowledged, and the individual who carries the racist attitudes may not even be aware of them but continues to be affected by them. Racism is found in individuals, but it can also be found in the way that institutions are created and operate. For example, in a large study carried out in Baltimore, it was found that African American youth applied more often for jobs but had lower rates of employment, even when they had the same socioeconomic status and academic achievement as their White peers (Entwisle, Alexander, & Olson, 2000). This may result when employers do not recruit in inner-city high schools, but do so in suburban schools (Cooper et al., 2008). The result of this institutional racism is to provide fewer opportunities for African American youth, which then has an impact on later achievement and economic well-being.

For adolescents, the perception that they are being treated unfairly because of their race is linked with a number of negative outcomes: lower levels of self-esteem and higher levels of depression, anxiety, and conduct disorders. In one study, 10- to 12-year-olds reported on whether they had had experiences such as the following:

- "Someone said something insulting to you because you are African American."
- "A store owner or sales person working at a business treated you in a disrespectful way because you are African American."
- "Someone yelled a racial insult at you because you are African American."
- "You encountered Whites who didn't expect you to do well because you are African American." (Brody et al., 2006, p. 1176)

When these children were studied 5 years later, those who reported experiencing more racial discrimination were more likely to have conduct disorders and depression. Discrimination experienced in school can interfere with students' willingness to engage in academic pursuits, and substance abuse or violence may become a way to avoid or fight against feelings of a lack of control over their lives (Cooper et al., 2008).

There are two issues with racism. One is how those who suffer racism can overcome its effects. The other is how society can prevent racism. We will address these two questions separately.

Some teens who experience discrimination develop an attitude of "no one is going to stand in the way of my success" and take enormous pride in their ability to overcome adversity. Several factors contribute to the ability to take this approach. First, parental warmth and support as well as positive social support from others in their lives plays a role in helping minority teens maintain their self-esteem in the face of negative events. Second, through a process called **racial socialization**, minority parents teach their children about discrimination that they may experience and prepare them with ideas and tactics that can help them deal with these experiences. In addition, they emphasize the pride that their children should have in their ethnic and racial heritage to promote positive racial identification. Both parental support and racial socialization have been found to improve the outcomes for children who have experienced racial discrimination (Brody et al., 2006; Cooper et al., 2008; Sellers, Copeland-Linder, Martin, & Lewis, 2006).

The central issue in regard to racial discrimination is how we can reduce or eliminate it so that minority youth do not have to undergo these experiences that can affect them so negatively. Researchers have focused on children in an attempt to influence racial attitudes before they harden into prejudice and discrimination. It was long assumed that racial discrimination was learned from the attitudes of adults and that children do not naturally develop these attitudes. However, recent research has shown that a variety of factors, including the cognitive limitations of young children, contribute to a natural tendency to differentiate among people on the basis of observable characteristics such as skin color. Children's ideas about groups of people become increasingly stereotypical and prejudiced up to age 4 or 5, after which time this bias decreases. This corresponds to the idea found in Piaget's cognitive theory that young children have difficulty sorting objects in more than one way. They might categorize blocks by color, but they are not able to simultaneously categorize them by shape. In the same way, they may categorize people by color, ignoring other factors that make people similar or dissimilar to each other. As children develop the ability to classify objects in multiple ways, they become more able to classify people in multiple ways; that is, they can see that people may belong to a

Racial socialization
Efforts by minority parents to teach their children about discrimination, prepare them to deal with these experiences, and teach them to take pride in their heritage.

certain ethnic or racial group and yet have characteristics that are not stereotypically associated with that group. Racial stereotyping declines when the multiple classification ability increases (Bigler & Liben, 1993). Role-taking ability and empathy develop as children move beyond the preschool years, and these abilities also contribute to less stereotyping and prejudice.

Several types of intervention that have been evaluated in schools include multicultural education, cooperative learning experiences, and antibias social cognitive skills training (Pfeifer, Brown, & Juvonen, 2007). In multicultural education, children are introduced to positive ideas about children from racial or ethnic groups other than their own. These programs are often carried out in schools in which there is little diversity in the student body. The results have been disappointing because there is little change found in students' racial attitudes (Pfeifer et al., 2007). A different approach encourages interaction among children of different races and backgrounds through cooperative learning experiences. In these programs, multiracial groups of students must work together on a learning project in school to ensure that everyone in the group masters the material. Groups compete with one another, and rewards are given for group, not individual, performance. These programs have been more successful than multicultural education in promoting cross-race friendships that seem to last beyond the particular group project in which the students are involved. These programs, as well as extracurricular activities such as sports and theater, may correspond to Gordon Allport's (1954) classical writing describing four requirements for positive intergroup contact: equal status of all members, common goals for the group, no competition within the group, and the support of authorities.

Breaking down discrimination. Racial discrimination is reduced when multiracial groups work together toward a common goal. That is exactly what happens on a sports team. Have you been involved in activities that helped break down barriers between children from different backgrounds?

A third approach to reducing racism and discrimination teaches children specifically about prejudice and discrimination and their effects. These antibias programs are often combined with education designed to promote role-taking skills and empathy. Many of these programs have been found to be successful in changing children's prejudiced attitudes, especially when the children were in integrated schools where they had the opportunity to interact with children from different backgrounds (Pfeifer et al., 2007).

Mental Health and Mental Disorders

In any one year, 20% of children and adolescents experience mental health problems (Mash & Hunsley, 2007). In this book we have already discussed several types of psychopathology found in childhood and adolescence as they were relevant to the topics of each chapter. You can use the following list to review those topics:

- Motor coordination disorders such as cerebral palsy: Chapter 6
- Eating disorders: Chapter 6
- Autism: Chapters 6 and 9
- Mental retardation/intellectual disability: Chapter 8
- Attention deficit hyperactivity disorder: Chapter 8
- Learning disabilities: Chapters 8 and 9
- Communication disorders: Chapter 9
- Reactive attachment disorder: Chapter 10
- Depression: Chapter 10
- Anxiety disorders: Chapter 10
- Conduct disorder and oppositional defiant disorder: Chapter 11

In this chapter we will examine several other types of disorders that can occur in adolescence and childhood: the mood disorder known as bipolar disorder, several types of anxiety disorders, the tic disorders including Tourette's disorder, and the psychotic disorder of schizophrenia.

There are some common factors to all of these disorders. Most often the symptoms are not unlike behavior that many people exhibit from time to time. The difference in diagnosing these disorders is that the behaviors, thoughts, and feelings are more extreme and of longer duration than most people experience. Also, they cause significant distress and/or disruption to the lives of the children and adolescents who experience them. For many of these disorders, early onset in childhood has a worse prognosis for later well-being. However, children can be flexible and resilient, and the drive to develop may help them have a better chance for recovery. Treatment for these disorders often includes both psychiatric medicines and psychosocial interventions with the child and the family.

Mood Disorders

We all have times when we are sad and times when we are elated; our moods reflect our circumstances, thoughts, and experiences. Generally we are able to regulate our moods so that they don't interfere with our daily existence. However, for some people, their ability to regulate their moods decreases, and depression or bipolar disorder may result. We described depression in Chapter 10 when we discussed emotional development, so we will just briefly summarize that information here.

Depression is characterized by sadness and/or irritability, a loss of interest and pleasure in activities that were formerly enjoyed, changes in appetite and sleep, feelings of guilt or worthlessness, difficulty concentrating, and suicidal ideas (American Psychiatric Association [APA], 2000). Bipolar disorder is characterized by both depression and the other extreme of excitation and elation called mania. Rather than simply feeling happy, people who are experiencing a manic episode feel grandiose and like they can do anything, with no limits. They sleep little, talk fast, and jump from one idea to another (APA, 2000). They may do what is pleasurable regardless of the consequences, like charging thousands of dollars to their credit cards when they know they can't pay for these purchases. When someone stands in the way of their often unrealistic plans, they become irritable. These symptoms may reach the level of delusions, meaning that the person has lost contact with reality and believes ideas that could not be true, such as having a close, personal friendship with the pope.

Until the mid-1990s, **bipolar disorder** was not a diagnosis given to children and adolescents, but in recent years there has been an explosion in its prevalence. Although older adolescents are now seen as having symptoms that look much like those of adults, diagnosis in children is still somewhat controversial (Quinn, 2007). In a review of seven studies, children and adolescents were found to have the same symptoms as adults. During manic phases, they sleep little, talk fast and in a pressured way, and do risky things because they believe they are capable of much more than they really are (Kowatch, Youngstrom, Danielyan, & Findling, 2005). During depressive phases, they may sleep either too much or too little, eat too much or too little, withdraw from activities and social contacts, and think about suicide (National Institute of Mental Health, 2009a). However, children are also diagnosed with bipolar disorder when they do not show discrete episodes of depression and mania. Instead, they show general dysregulation of mood, including irritability, extreme temper storms or rages, and hyperactivity as a general characteristic (Smith, 2007). In addition, there is more likely to be a mixing of symptoms of depression and mania at the same time, such as hopelessness combined with racing thoughts, which may contribute to the risk of suicide (Youngstrom, 2007). Much more research is needed to see whether children with these behaviors become adults with the characteristics of adult bipolar disorder, or whether this pattern of behaviors will be linked to

Bipolar disorder A psychiatric disorder characterized by both depression and mania.

different outcomes (Smith, 2007). There already is some indication that bipolar disorder is continuous from childhood to adolescence (Chang, 2007).

Bipolar disorder appears to have a strong genetic component, but genetics alone do not account for the development of the disorder. Children who have a parent who is bipolar are 4 times as likely as children whose parents do not have any mental disorder to develop a mood disorder themselves (Lapalme, Hodgins, & LaRoche, 1997), but the experience of child abuse also appears to be related to early development of bipolar disorder. In one study, about 50% of 100 people diagnosed with bipolar disorder reported having experienced severe abuse when they were children (Garno, Goldberg, Ramirez, & Ritzler, 2005).

Bipolar disorder is chronic, and therefore treatment is focused on improvement rather than cure. Periods of both recovery and relapse are likely to continue (Youngstrom, 2007). Medications used to treat this disorder include mood stabilizers and antipsychotic medication, plus psychoeducational treatment for the child and family. This treatment is designed to help both the child and the family understand the disorder, to promote social skills and self-control in the child, and to promote improved communication within the family (Roberts, Bishop, & Rooney, 2008).

Separation anxiety. Young children normally are distressed when they are separated from their caregivers. However, when a child reaches school age and the fear of separation is still overwhelming, it becomes a concern that may require professional help.

Anxiety Disorders

Some children are more prone to anxiety than others, and there are circumstances that promote greater anxiety. However, when individuals experience an abnormal level of fear or worry, they are likely suffering from an anxiety disorder. These disorders include separation anxiety disorder, panic anxiety, phobias, obsessive-compulsive disorder (OCD), posttraumatic stress disorder (PTSD), and generalized anxiety disorder (APA, 2000). Each type of anxiety disorder is likely to begin at a different age. At age 7, children may suffer from separation anxiety and specific phobias for things like animals and monsters. At age 9 or 10, generalized anxiety and OCD may begin, and at about age 15, panic disorder may begin. Obviously PTSD can occur whenever trauma is experienced.

In Chapter 10, you learned that separation anxiety is seen as normal behavior through age 6, but it is treated as a disorder when it continues at high levels beyond that age. It consists of heightened or extreme fear of being away from parents or other caregivers. Often children refuse to go to school because of their fears of being without those to whom they are emotionally attached.

Phobias are unreasonable fears, such as a fear of going outside, known as agoraphobia. One of the most common fears is of public speaking, and when this fear becomes incapacitating it is known as social phobia. Social phobia may also include fear of other social situations. Other common phobias include spiders, snakes, air travel, elevators, and bridges. See Chapter 10 for a discussion of school phobias.

Generalized anxiety disorder is marked by general, ongoing worried feelings. It is less common in younger children, who may worry about their physical well-being, and more common in older children, who worry disproportionately about living up to standards academically, socially, or in other ways (Southam-Gerow & Chorpita, 2007). Children may express their fears through their body, experiencing stomachaches or headaches.

Many people who suffer **panic anxiety** or panic attacks believe that they are having a heart attack, because the symptoms include sudden fear, rapid heartbeat, sweating, difficulty

Generalized anxiety disorder General, ongoing worried feelings that limit a person's ability to function well.

Panic anxiety Sudden fear, rapid heartbeat, sweating, difficulty breathing, chest pain, and other physical symptoms that are not linked to a physical cause such as a heart attack.

breathing, chest pain, and other physical symptoms (APA, 2000). This condition is not likely to appear until late adolescence. Because sufferers feel that they cannot control when this feeling will come upon them, the fear that it will occur again may begin to limit their activity (Southam-Gerow & Chorpita, 2007). For example, teens may want to avoid going to school for fear that it will happen to them there and embarrass them in front of their peers.

Obsessive-compulsive disorder (OCD) consists of two symptoms. Obsessions are intrusive thoughts that continue to pop up in a person's mind time and time again. Often these thoughts are about germ contamination, aggressive impulses, or a need for extreme order. Compulsions are repeated behaviors that people feel they must do; if they do not do them, enormous anxiety results. For example, a person may wash his hands over and over to the point of scrubbing the skin until it is raw. People with this disorder know that what they are doing is unreasonable, but they cannot stop themselves (APA, 2000) because engaging in these behaviors provides some temporary relief from their obsessive thoughts.

Young children often enjoy rituals with their parents. For example, when leaving a child at child care, the parent may need to give the child a kiss and then go out the door but "touch" hands through the glass window in the door before leaving. Rituals are reassuring to the child and help with the transition to the new setting. However, when a child has OCD, these rituals become hardened into absolute requirements, resulting in great fear if they are not carried out. The rituals eventually take up a significant amount of time and interfere with other activities (APA, 2000).

The most well-known tic disorder is **Tourette's disorder**. A tic is a "sudden, rapid, recurrent, nonrhythmic, stereotyped motor movement or vocalization" (APA, 2000, p. 108). It is not uncommon for children to experience tic-like behaviors, such as repetitively shrugging their shoulders or lowering their head, but the diagnosis of tic disorder is not made until the behavior has continued for at least a year. Tic disorder is most commonly diagnosed in childhood and reaches its peak in early adolescence, but only 25% of cases continue into adulthood (Chang & Piacentini, 2002). Tourette's disorder is diagnosed when an individual has many motor tics and at least one vocal tic and the disorder begins before the age of 18. Although Tourette's disorder is most well known for the vocal tic in which an individual says or shouts obscenities, only 10% of people with the disorder have this particular symptom. Vocal tics may be simple grunts, clicks, or snorts (APA, 2000).

Posttraumatic stress disorder (PTSD) is an anxiety disorder that follows the experience of or exposure to an event marked by physical harm or the threat of physical harm to oneself or others. These events range from abuse to war to natural disasters. People with PTSD experience enormous fear and a sense of helplessness when the event occurs. Later they begin to have nightmares, and may relive the experience both while sleeping and while awake. Unwanted memories may intrude unexpectedly. **Active Learning: Intrusive Thoughts** gives you a bit of the experience of what having an intrusive thought might feel like. Although children are less likely than adults to have complete amnesia for the triggering events, they may have "time skew" so that they do not remember events in their correct sequence (Hamblen & Barnett, 2009). Children are more likely to have "disorganized or agitated behavior" (APA, 2000, p. 463). They often have sleep problems and angry outbursts. In their play, they may reenact these traumatic experiences over and over, in direct or disguised form. Although play often helps children work out emotional problems, this type of play is a rigid reenactment of events that does not seem to give relief to the child (Hamblen & Barnett, 2009). Children, like adults, can become hypervigilant; that is, they are constantly on the lookout for threatening events and may interpret occurrences as threatening even when they are not (Fletcher, 2007). They may develop a sense that there were signs or omens that predicted the event and believe that they can avoid a recurrence if they can just see those signs ahead of time (Hamblen & Barnett, 2009).

Children will be less likely to develop PTSD when they experience a one-time trauma rather than ongoing traumatic experiences. The exception to this is when the one-time trauma is an

Obsessive-compulsive disorder (OCD) A disorder marked by obsessions or intrusive thoughts and repeated behaviors that people feel compelled to do to control the obsessive thoughts.

Tourette's disorder A disorder that begins before the age of 18 in which an individual has many motor tics and at least one vocal tic.

Posttraumatic stress disorder (PTSD) An anxiety disorder that follows exposure to an event marked by great harm or the threat of harm to oneself or others.

important loss, such as the death of a parent (Fletcher, 2007). Children are also helped when their parents maintain a warm relationship with them throughout the trauma and when the parents themselves are coping effectively (Hamblen & Barnett, 2009). Cognitive reappraisal, in which children reinterpret the circumstances and their role in them in a different way, also is helpful (Fletcher, 2007). For example, Mary (not her real name) was a child who had been a victim of ongoing tribal violence in Africa. She had experienced her mother's murder in addition to many other traumas. It was clear that Mary felt that she was evil because she should have done something to prevent her mother's death. With cognitive reappraisal she was able to reinterpret the event as a tragedy that she had survived and "that was not my fault" (Vickers, 2005, p. 227). This new insight was one factor that helped her symptoms of PTSD subside.

ACTIVE LEARNING Intrusive Thoughts

Sit quietly for several minutes with your eyes closed and think about anything you want, except do *not* think about the green rabbit on this page.

Were you able to keep this rabbit out of your mind? People with PTSD often try very hard not to think about the traumatic events they have experienced. In fact, some actually develop amnesia for those events. However, for many, the more they try to keep the memories and thoughts out of their minds, the more these thoughts and emotions intrude in a way that is out of their control. This has been likened to a messy closet, with toys and clothes falling out. When items are examined and put back in a more orderly way, the closet can be kept closed and only opened when you choose to take something out. In a similar way, examining and understanding your thoughts, emotions, and memories allows you to put them in the past so you can fully engage in your current life (adapted from Vickers, 2005).

Psychotic Disorders: Childhood Schizophrenia

Schizophrenia A psychotic disorder marked by disorganized thinking, hallucinations, and delusions.

Schizophrenia is a very serious psychological disorder that most often begins in late adolescence or early adulthood in which individuals become less able to discriminate external reality from their own internal states. When children and younger teens develop this disorder, it is referred to as early-onset schizophrenia (McDonell & McClellan, 2007). Diagnosis of schizophrenia in children is very uncommon, although it has been found in children as young as age 5 (APA, 2000). Children with early-onset schizophrenia are likely to experience hallucinations, particularly hearing voices that aren't there. They have trouble maintaining their focus on a task, and their speech may not follow a logical pattern. Their speech may contain loose associations, which are "frequent, sudden, and apparently unrelated changes in the subject of a conversation" (McDonell & McClellan, 2007, p. 527). Both illogical thoughts and loose associations are common for all children under the age of 7, so they are considered a thought disorder only after that age (Caplan, 1994). As the symptoms of schizophrenia develop, children's general level of cognitive, social, and emotional functioning decreases. They begin to show a lack of emotion and lowered motivation (McDonell & McClellan, 2007).

Later adolescence is a more common time for the first diagnosis of schizophrenia, but schizophrenia still is not a very common disorder. Worldwide, it is estimated that between 0.5% and 1.5% of the population suffers from schizophrenia (APA, 2000). Most people who develop schizophrenia will first develop behaviors such as social withdrawal, unusual behavior, and sudden rages before developing the symptoms of the disorder (APA, 2000). Symptoms include those listed above for early-onset schizophrenia, but adolescents may also experience delusions, which are strong beliefs in something that does not fit reality. For example, a paranoid delusion might be that the FBI is plotting against you. The mental disorganization of schizophrenia results in difficulty with social, academic, and occupational functioning (APA, 2000).

Schizophrenia, like bipolar disorder, has a very large genetic component. If one identical twin is schizophrenic, there is a 40% to 60% chance that the other will be as well, while nonidentical twins are only 5% to 15% as likely to share this condition with their twin (McDonell & McClellan, 2007). Prenatal environment may also play a role. Brain development may be disrupted prenatally by factors such as the mother's experience of starvation and influenza, and these factors have been related to a greater possibility of developing schizophrenia in these mothers' children (Brown & Susser, 2008; Limosin, Rouillon, Payan, Cohen, & Strub, 2003).

Also like bipolar disorder, schizophrenia is a chronic disorder, with acute and less acute phases, but with little likelihood of a cure. Treatment must include work with the child's family to promote understanding of the disorder, as well as psychiatric medications for the child to help control the symptoms, and a comprehensive educational program for the child to promote the most positive outcome possible (Volkmar & Tsatsanis, 2002).

Resilience

Throughout this chapter we have described a number of experiences that challenge the growth and development of children and adolescents, from physical threats to emotional disorders to poverty. At this point you may be thinking that it is amazing that children who experience such great adversity can thrive and grow up to be what Emmy Werner (2005) has described as "competent, confident, and caring adults" (p. 98). Throughout this discussion of threats to children's well-being, we have tried to point out the essential **resilience** or self-righting tendency that children have. It is always our hope that children are spared these types of challenges, but children do have the ability to face challenges, cope with them and learn from the experiences, and then use what they have learned in the future. **Journey of Research: Invincible, Invulnerable, and Resilient** describes how our understanding of children's ability to cope with developmental challenges has changed over the years.

Resilience The ability to bounce back from adversity or to thrive despite negative life circumstances.

Invincible, Invulnerable, and Resilient

JOURNEY *of* **RESEARCH**

An important and interesting shift occurred in the field of child development in the 1970s. Prior to that time, psychologists and psychiatrists had primarily been focused on understanding circumstances that threatened or disrupted the developmental process, using what is known as a deficit model or risk perspective. We wanted to understand the factors (for example, environmental circumstances or individual characteristics) that placed a child at risk for less-than-optimal development. With that understanding, we hoped to be able to intervene in ways that would prevent problems or correct ones that already existed.

A change in perspective emerged in the 1970s and 1980s when several researchers caught people's attention with stories of children who had overcome

(Continued)

(Continued)

great adversity and went on to become extraordinary individuals in the process. In one of the most widely known studies, Emmy Werner (1992) followed a cohort of almost 700 children on the island of Kauai from birth until they were in their 30s. Almost one third of the children were initially considered to be at high risk because of their life circumstances. These children had difficult births, lived in poverty, had parents who were impaired by alcoholism or mental illness, or experienced parental divorce or discord, and many of them had multiple risk factors. But as Werner and Smith (1985) tracked these high-risk children over time, they found that one third of them had very good outcomes by the time they entered adulthood. With the advent of this type of resiliency research, the focus in the field began to shift from what could go wrong in development to what could go right. What helps a child recover or bounce back from adversity?

Protective factors that have been identified in resiliency research include having an active, outgoing personality that engages other people (both adults and peers); having good communication and problem-solving skills; having a talent or an ability that attracts other people; and having faith in one's own ability to make good things happen (Werner, 2005). These children also are emotionally stable and not easily upset. Often they make good use of whatever resources are available to them, and they form affectional bonds with alternative caregivers when their own parents are unavailable to provide support.

Another important protective factor that has emerged from longitudinal research has been the ability to take advantage of major life transitions as opportunities to redirect one's life (Werner, 2005). Entering into a supportive marriage, returning to school, and deciding to enter military service are all opportunities for a second chance, and resilient individuals seize those opportunities. Emmy Werner (2005) summarized the process by saying that the resilient children in her study "had relied on sources of support within the family and community that *increased* their competence and efficacy, *decreased* the number of stressful life events they subsequently encountered, and *opened up* new opportunity for them" (author's emphasis, p. 99).

The next shift in perspective came with the advent of the *positive youth development* perspective. This approach was discussed in Chapter 13, when we looked at the impact of participation in positive community-based activities as a way to build strengths in children and adolescents. It seeks to understand circumstances that promote optimal development, rather than just to identify circumstances that place a child at risk or protect a child from harm. We could think of protective factors as those factors that are at work when a child is already at risk for some negative developmental outcome, but the developmental assets framework adopted by the positive youth development perspective presumes that assets work in *any* circumstance for *any* child, whether there is risk or not, to maximize the child's positive potential for growth. From this perspective, the goal is not surviving in the face of adversity or protecting children from risk, but rather finding ways to help all children thrive regardless of their life situation. Sesma, Mannes, and Scales (2005) sum up this approach by saying, "The concept of thriving encompasses not only the relative absence of pathology, but also more explicit indicators of healthy and even optimal development" (p. 288).

TRUE/FALSE

10. Children who are able to rise above great adversity like poverty or child abuse have a number of unique abilities.

False. The strengths that resilient children draw upon to overcome adversity are the same abilities that are beneficial to any child. Although the abilities themselves are not unique (because they are ones that many successful people share), what is extraordinary is the ability of these children to draw upon those strengths even when they are living in such challenging situations.

Characteristics of Resilient Children

When research on resiliency first entered the literature (and later entered the mind of the public), the portrayal of resilient children suggested that they were remarkable—even heroic—in some way. Words like *invulnerable* and *invincible* were used to describe them, as though nothing could harm them (Masten, 2001). But as research on these children has matured, the picture that emerges is quite different from that of a superhero overcoming impossible odds. Anne Masten (2001), a researcher who has worked for many years with colleagues studying resiliency, has concluded that resiliency is the product of what she calls "ordinary magic" (p. 227). She says, "The greatest surprise of resilience research is the ordinariness of the phenomena. Resilience appears to be a common phenomenon that results in most cases from the operation of basic human adaptational systems" (Masten, 2001, p. 227). Those systems include "connection to competent and caring adults in the family and community, cognitive and self-regulation skills, positive views of self, and motivation to be effective in the environment" (Masten, 2001, p. 234).

We have discussed each of these characteristics at some point in this book. Recall what you have learned about the role of attachment, effective parenting, self-esteem, self-regulation, intrinsic motivation, and a drive to master the environment on the course of development. These are aspects of development that we get right most of the time, and aspects that try to reassert themselves when things go wrong. Thinking about the "power of the ordinary" leads us to the conclusion that "resilience does not come from rare and special qualities, but from the everyday magic of ordinary, normative human resources in the minds, brains, and bodies of children, in their families and relationships, and in their communities" (Masten, 2001, p. 235), but these adaptational systems need to be nurtured so they are available to children when they are needed. **Active Learning: Resilience** gives you a chance to think about where and when you have seen this "ordinary magic" happen in your own experiences.

Resilience

ACTIVE LEARNING

Children and adolescents may experience many types of traumatic events or life circumstances, such as poverty, a natural disaster, child abuse, or a difficult parental divorce. Think about someone you know who appears to be doing well despite difficult life experiences that could have put that person at risk for emotional disturbance, criminal behavior, or other negative outcomes. If there have been potentially traumatic events or circumstances in your life, you can reflect upon your own experiences.

Then think about what factors in that person's life may have contributed to his or her apparent resilience. For example, one young teenager was part of a tough, inner-city gang and was headed for trouble. Instead he ended up going to college. He attributes his change in direction and resilience to the guidance of his stepfather, who got him into football, where he found a different way to succeed, a positive group of peers, and a reason to do well in school. His resilience came from the interest of a caring adult, plus his own talents. The factors you see for the individual you describe may come from the outside, such as loving support from one individual; they may come from the child, such as a lively intelligence or social skills; or, most likely, they may come from a combination of the two.

One of the greatest challenges to our understanding of the concept of resiliency is the great variability that we see in child outcomes. For example, many Romanian orphans who are adopted by well-functioning families show an incredible amount of recovery when their life circumstances change (Masten, 2001), but some continue to show serious pathologies despite their improved living conditions. Most children who experience abuse while growing up do not perpetuate that pattern with their own children (Kaufman & Zigler, 1993; Leifer & Smith, 1990), but some do. Children of mothers who are clinically depressed have a high incidence of psychiatric disorders themselves, but a sizeable proportion are able to function adequately in their own lives (Goldstein & Brooks, 2005). Although children growing up in poverty are likely to have psychological and academic difficulties that could limit their achievements, the list of children who have been able to overcome their early experiences of poverty includes people who have been successful in all fields of endeavor, and includes several presidents of the United States.

What resiliency research shows us is that recovery is possible, even if it is not inevitable. However, the range of circumstances that can challenge or threaten healthy development is vast, and the mechanisms that can protect children are numerous. As of now, we have not identified all the critical factors, and the course of development is so complex that it is unlikely that we will ever be able to devise a formula for resiliency that can correct every possible negative trajectory. What is important, however, is that work continues within the field to identify and understand the complex interactions between the individual and his or her environment that help children reach their full and unique potential whatever their life circumstances happen to be.

Conclusion

As children grow, they face a multitude of risk factors, but also encounter many factors that help protect them from risk. In this chapter we have discussed some of the experiences that may challenge children, including physical and mental illness, poverty, racial discrimination, and child abuse. Any child who experiences these problems will be affected by them, and usually the greater the number of risk factors children experience, the less likely it is that they will emerge with the physical, cognitive, social, and emotional skills they need for a successful life. However, some children are able to cope well and show remarkable resilience. As a society and as individuals, we owe it to all our children to do whatever we can to improve their chances.

As you finish this course in child development, you are now armed with some tools that will help you make a difference, whether you work with an individual child, have your own children, teach in a classroom, develop programs for families or neighborhoods, advocate for children in the courts or the government, or carry out research to continue to add to our body of knowledge about children and their development. We hope that what you have learned will become the basis for your work (and play) with children in the future and that we have given you a solid foundation of knowledge that you can build upon in the future.

CHAPTER SUMMARY

1. **What is stress, and how do we cope with it?**
   Stress is anything that places excessive demands on our ability to cope. Children may experience **normative stress** that most children go through, or they may experience **non-normative stress** when they experience unusual distressing events. The more stress children experience, the more likely they are to develop mental health disorders or other behavioral and emotional problems. Children can use **problem-focused strategies** or **emotion-focused strategies** to cope with the stress.

2. **What types of health threats can children and their families face?**
   Children may experience common, short-term illnesses or long-term, chronic illnesses. Environmental toxins may contribute to the development of some illnesses. Rates of injury and death from accidents in childhood have been rising. In adolescence, smoking, alcohol, and drugs have negative effects on health. Violence is another threat that can result in disabling conditions, both physically and emotionally.

3. **What impact does poverty have on children's development?**
   Poverty is related to higher levels of mental retardation and developmental delay, learning disabilities and failure in school, health problems, and behavior problems. The longer and the earlier that a child lives in poverty, the worse the outcomes tend to be. However, when income increases for low-income families, child outcomes often improve.

4. **What are child abuse and neglect, and what effects do they have?**
   Child abuse includes physical, sexual, and emotional abuse, while child neglect includes the failure to provide for the physical, emotional, and educational needs of children. **Mandatory reporters** are required to report suspected abuse and neglect to child welfare agencies. Children whose abuse is reported may receive services to help their family, or they may be removed from the family. Parents and other relatives are responsible for almost all abuse of children. Although child abuse is more common in low-income families, child sexual abuse is equally common among all income levels. Sexual exploitation of children, including sex trafficking, is a major concern around the world. Sexual abuse is more clearly linked to negative outcomes, such as depression, anxiety disorders, antisocial behavior, substance abuse, and attempted suicides, than are physical abuse and neglect. Mental health professionals work to prevent child maltreatment and treat the outcomes of it.

5. **What effects does racism have on children?**
   Racism includes **stereotypes**, **prejudices**, and **discrimination** against people of a certain race. For African Americans, the experience of racism is linked with lower self-esteem, more depression, and more anxiety and conduct disorders. Schools have instituted multicultural education, cooperative learning experiences, and antibias social cognitive skills training to reduce racism and other forms of discrimination.

6. What types of mental health disorders can children experience?

Mood disorders include depression and **bipolar disorder**. Anxiety disorders include separation anxiety disorder, **panic anxiety**, phobias, **obsessive-compulsive disorder (OCD)**, **posttraumatic stress disorder (PTSD)**, and **generalized anxiety disorder**. **Schizophrenia** is a psychotic disorder that is very rare in children, but more likely to be diagnosed in late adolescence.

7. What makes some children resilient in the face of adversity?

Resilient children, who thrive despite adversity, often have an engaging, emotionally stable personality, good communication and problem-solving skills, and a talent or an ability that attracts other people, and they have faith in their ability to make good things happen. These children are able to take advantage of major life transitions as opportunities to change the direction of their life.

Go to **www.sagepub.com/levine** for additional exercises and video resources. Select **Chapter 15, Health, Well-Being, and Resilience,** for chapter-specific activities.

Glossary

A-not-B task   A test for object permanence in which an object is hidden under cloth A and then moved under cloth B.

Ability tests   Standardized measures of intellectual ability.

Accelerated program   A type of program that allows gifted students to move through the standard curriculum but more quickly than is typical.

Acceptance/responsiveness   A dimension of parenting that measures the amount of warmth and affection in the parent-child relationship.

Accommodation   Changing your mental schemas so they fit new experiences.

Achievement tests   Standardized measures of learning connected with academic subjects.

Active gene-environment interaction   When one's genetic endowment becomes a driving force for children to seek out experiences that fit their genetic endowments.

Active labor   The second phase in the first stage of labor in which contractions become longer, stronger, and more frequent and a woman may require pain medication; begins when the cervix has dilated to 4 centimeters and lasts on average 3 to 8 hours.

Active niche picking   A process in which people express their genetic tendencies by finding environments that match and enhance those tendencies.

Adaptive functioning   A person's ability to function independently.

Adolescent growth spurt   The period of rapid increase in height and weight that occurs in early adolescence.

Amniocentesis   A test to look for genetic abnormalities prenatally, in which a physician uses a long, thin needle to extract amniotic fluid, which is then tested.

Amnion   The inner fetal membrane that surrounds the fetus and is filled with amniotic fluid.

Anal stage   Freud's second stage of development during which toddlers' sexual energy is focused on the anus. Toilet training and control are major issues.

Analytical intelligence   The type of intelligence that is the one closest to "g" or general intelligence and the one prized highly in most schools.

Androgyny   The idea that both sexes can have the characteristics that are traditionally reserved for one sex.

Animism   Giving human characteristics, such as thought and intention, to inanimate or natural things.

Anorexia nervosa   A condition in which individuals become obsessed with their weight and intentionally restrict food intake to a point that it may become life threatening.

Antisocial popular boys   Boys who are seen as aggressive but also as physically competent, disruptive, and "cool" and who are very well known within the peer group.

Anxiety   A vague sense of fear or a feeling of dread.

Anxiety disorder   A level of anxiety that interferes with normal functioning; includes separation anxiety disorder in older children or adolescents, generalized anxiety disorder, and social phobias.

Anxious ambivalent/resistant attachment   An attachment classification in which the infant is reluctant to move away from his mother to explore and is very distressed when his mother leaves, but when his mother returns, he wants to approach her but also angrily resists her attempt to pick him up.

Anxious avoidant attachment An attachment classification in which the infant is not distressed when his mother leaves, is just as comfortable with the stranger as with his mother, and, when his mother returns, does not rush to greet her.

Apgar Scale An assessment of a newborn's overall condition at 1 minute and 5 minutes after birth that is based upon the newborn's activity level, pulse, grimace, appearance, and respiration.

Applied research Research that has the primary goal of solving problems or improving the human condition.

Archival records Data collected at an earlier date that are used for research purposes.

Asperger's disorder A pervasive developmental disorder at the mild end of the autism spectrum, marked by a relatively high level of functioning but repetitive routines, inappropriate social and emotional behavior, and uncoordinated motor movements.

Assimilation Fitting new experiences into existing mental schemas.

Associative play Sharing toys and interacting with peers, but without a common goal.

Asthma The most common chronic illness in childhood, in which a child's airways constrict, making it difficult to breathe.

Attachment An emotional bond to a particular person.

Attachment in the making The stage from 6 weeks to 6–8 months in which infants develop stranger anxiety, differentiating those they know from those they don't.

Attention deficit hyperactivity disorder (ADHD) A disorder marked by extreme difficulty with inattention, impulsivity, or a combination of both.

Attrition The loss of participants over the course of a longitudinal study.

Authoritarian parents A parenting style that combines high levels of control and low levels of warmth, marked by an expectation of compliance from the child.

Authoritative parents A parenting style that combines high levels of control with a good deal of warmth and encouragement, marked with reasonable expectations and explanation of the parents' rules.

Autism A pervasive developmental disorder that is characterized by difficulties with social interaction, problems with verbal and nonverbal communication, and deficits in symbolic and imaginative play.

Autism spectrum disorders A group of conditions ranging from severe (autistic disorder) to mild (Asperger's disorder) and characterized by pervasive impairment in thinking, feeling, language, and the ability to relate to others.

Autobiographical memory A coherent set of memories about one's life.

Automaticity The process by which skills become so well practiced that you can do them without much conscious thought.

Autonomous morality stage When children are aware of the rules and realize that they must adhere to them in order to maintain their interaction with others, rather than because an adult has told them what to do.

Average children Children who receive a number of nominations for "like most" and "like least" that is close to the median in the peer group on a sociometric measure.

Axons The parts of a nerve cell that conduct impulses away from the cell body.

Baby diary A careful recording of the development of one's own children.

Balanced reading approach An approach to teaching reading that combines elements of the whole language approach (which emphasizes comprehension and meaning) with elements of the phonics approach (which emphasizes decoding of words).

Basic research Research that has the primary goal of adding to our body of knowledge rather than having immediate direct application.

Behavioral genetics Research to determine the degree of genetic basis for a behavior, a trait, or an ability through means including twin studies and adoption studies.

Behavioral genomics Research that links behaviors with specific genes.

Behaviorism The theory developed by John B. Watson that focuses on environmental control of observable behavior.

Bidirectional effect   Mutual influence between two individuals.

Bipolar disorder   A psychiatric disorder characterized by both depression and mania.

Blastocyst   A hollow ball of cells that consists of the inner cell mass (which becomes the embryo) and an outer ring of cells (which becomes the placenta and chorion).

Broca's area   The part of the brain that is involved in the physical production of speech.

Bulimia   An eating disorder characterized by eating binges, followed by purging (for example, self-induced vomiting or the excessive use of laxatives) to get rid of the food.

Bullying   Being exposed repeatedly and over time to negative actions on the part of peers, including physical bullying, verbal bullying, and/or emotional bullying.

Canalization   The degree to which the expression of a gene is influenced by the environment.

Cathexis   In psychoanalytic theory, the direction of someone's emotional energy to a particular person or object.

Centration   Focusing on only one aspect of a situation.

Cephalocaudal development   A principle whereby development proceeds from the head region down through the body.

Cerebral palsy   A chronic condition that appears early in development and primarily involves problems with body movement and muscle coordination.

Child effects model   A model of parenting effects that assumes that it is the characteristics of the child that determine the parenting style that the parents use.

Child life specialists   Experts in child development who promote optimal development in children in medical settings.

Child-directed speech   Speech that is tailored to fit the sensory and cognitive capabilities of infants and children so that it holds their attention; includes speaking in a higher pitch with exaggerated intonation and a singsong rhythm and using a simplified vocabulary.

Chorion   The outer fetal membrane that surrounds the fetus and gives rise to the placenta.

Chorionic villus sampling (CVS)   A test to look for genetic abnormalities prenatally, in which a small tube is inserted either through the vagina and cervix or through a needle inserted in the abdomen, and a sample of cells from the chorion is retrieved for testing.

Chromosome disorders   Disorders that result when too many or too few chromosomes are formed or when there is a change in the structure of the chromosome caused by breakage.

Chromosomes   The strands of genes that constitute the human genetic endowment.

Chronosystem   The dimension of time, including one's age and the time in history in which one lives.

Circular reaction   An infant's repetition of a reflexive action that results in a pleasurable experience.

Classical conditioning   The process by which a stimulus (the unconditioned stimulus) that naturally evokes a certain response (the unconditioned response) is paired repeatedly with a neutral stimulus. Eventually the neutral stimulus becomes the conditioned stimulus and evokes the same response, now called the conditioned response.

Classification   The ability to organize objects into hierarchical conceptual categories.

Clear-cut attachment   The stage from 6–8 months to 18 months–2 years, when an infant develops separation anxiety when a person he is attached to leaves him.

Clinical depression   A condition marked by feelings of worthlessness and hopelessness, a lack of pleasure, sleep and appetite disturbances, and possibly suicidal thoughts.

Clinical interview   An interview strategy in which the interviewer can deviate from a standard set of questions to gather additional information.

Cliques   Small groups of friends who spend time together and develop close relationships.

Coercive family environment   A pattern of family interaction in which parents and children mutually train each other so that the child becomes increasingly aggressive and the parents become less effective in controlling the child's behavior.

Cognitive development   The study of the changes that occur in how we think and learn as we grow.

Cognitive flexibility   The ability to switch focus as needed in order to complete a task.

Cognitive processing theory   The theory that learning language is a process of "data crunching," in which the actual process of learning words and their meanings relies on the computational ability of the human brain.

Cohort effect   Differences between groups in a cross section or cross-sequential study that are attributable to the fact that the participants have had different life experiences.

Collectivism   The cultural value that emphasizes obligations to others within your group.

Command strategy   A parenting technique in which the parent does not make any overt threats of punishment, but the child responds to the legitimate authority that the parent has to make a request of the child.

Concordance rate   The degree to which a trait or an ability of one individual is similar to that of another; used to examine similarities between twins and among adopted children and their biological and adoptive parents.

Concrete operations   The third stage in Piaget's theory in which children between 6 and 12 years of age develop logical thinking that is still not abstract.

Conduct disorder   A persistent pattern of behavior marked by violation of the basic rights of others or of major age-appropriate social norms or rules.

Congruence model   The idea that having a match between your gender and your gender role orientation would be most beneficial to your psychological well-being.

Connectionist/network model   In this model of memory, the process is envisioned as a neural network that consists of concept nodes that are interconnected by links.

Conservation   The understanding that a basic quantity of something (amount, volume, mass) remains the same regardless of changes in appearance.

Constraints   Assumptions that language learners make that limit the alternative meanings that they attribute to new words.

Constructive conflict   Family conflict that is resolved in a positive way using affection, problem solving, and emotional support.

Constructive play   Building or making something for the purposes of play.

Constructivism   The idea that humans actively construct their understanding of the world, rather than passively receiving knowledge.

Control group   The group in an experiment that does not get the special treatment and provides a baseline against which the experimental group can be compared.

Controversial children   Children who receive both a large number of nominations for "like most" and a large number of nominations for "like least" from peers on a sociometric measure.

Conventional moral judgment   Moral reasoning that moves beyond self-interest to take into account the good of others.

Convergent thinking   Finding one correct solution for a problem.

Cooperative learning   An educational strategy that allows groups of students who are at different ability levels to work together on a common goal, such as a project or an assignment.

Cooperative play   Play with peers that has a common goal.

Coping   Efforts made to master, tolerate, or reduce stress.

Corpus callosum   The band of fibers that connects the two hemispheres of the brain.

Correlations   A measure of the strength and direction of the relationship between two variables.

Couvade   A sympathetic pregnancy in which a man experiences a variety of symptoms associated with pregnancy or childbirth while his partner is pregnant.

Creative intelligence   The ability to generate ideas and to deal successfully with novelty (sometimes referred to as divergent thinking).

Creativity   Thinking that is novel and that produces ideas that are of value.

Critical period   A period of time during which development is occurring rapidly and the organism is especially sensitive to damage, which often is severe and irreversible.

Cross-sectional design   A research design that uses multiple groups of participants who represent the age span of interest to the researcher.

Cross-sequential design   A research design that uses multiple groups of participants and follows them over a period of time, with the beginning age of each group being the ending age of another group.

Crowds   Large, reputation-based groups that are based upon a shared stereotype but whose members do not necessarily spend time together.

Crystallized intelligence   What we already know and can draw upon to solve problems.

Culture   Culture is the system of behaviors, norms, beliefs, and traditions that form in order to promote the survival of a group that lives in a particular environmental niche. It is a way of describing similarities within one group of people and differences between groups of people.

Cyberbullying   The use of electronic technologies, including e-mails, text messages, digital images, webpages (including social network sites), blogs, or chat rooms, to socially harm others.

Decentration   The ability to think about more than one aspect of a situation at a time.

Deficit model of youth development   The assumption that problems are caused by something lacking in the child or teen that needs to be fixed.

Delay of gratification   The ability to wait until later in order to get something desirable.

Demandingness/control   A dimension of parenting that measures the amount of restrictiveness and structure that parents place on their children.

Dendrites   The portions of a neuron that receive impulses from other neurons.

Dependent variable   The outcome of interest to the researcher that is measured at the end of an experiment.

Developmental assets   Common sense positive experiences and qualities that help young people become caring, responsible adults.

Developmental bilingual program   A program for English language learners in which students initially receive instruction in core subjects in their native language and receive instruction in art, physical education, and music in English until they have the language skills to be instructed in the core subjects in English.

Developmental psychopathology   An approach to understanding mental and behavioral problems based on the idea that biological, psychological, and social influences affect development to produce adaptive or maladaptive outcomes.

Deviation IQ   A measure of intelligence that is based upon the individual's deviation from the norms for a given test.

Dialogic reading   A technique used to facilitate early literacy, which involves an adult and a child looking at a book together while the adult asks questions and encourages a dialogue, followed by switching roles so the child asks questions of the adult.

Differentiated self   The understanding that one can show different characteristics in different situations but that these differences are all part of a unitary whole.

Difficult temperament   A child's general responsiveness marked by more negative mood, frustration and intense responses, slow adaptation to change, and irregular patterns of eating, sleeping, and elimination.

Discrimination   Negative behavior directed at people on the basis of their race, ethnicity, religion, or other factors.

Disequilibrium   A state of confusion in which your schemas do not fit your experiences.

Disorganized/disoriented attachment   An attachment classification in which behavior is unpredictable and odd and shows no coherent way of dealing with attachment issues, often linked with parental abuse or neglect.

Divergent thinking   The ability to find as many possible solutions to a problem as possible, rather than the one "correct" solution.

Dizygotic (DZ) twins   Formed when a woman produces two ova or eggs, which are fertilized by two sperm; genetically DZ twins are as similar as any siblings.

Doula   A trained, knowledgeable companion who is present at a birth to support the woman through her labor and delivery.

Drive reduction   The idea that human behavior is determined by the motivation to satisfy or reduce the discomfort caused by biological needs or drives.

Dual language program   Programs in which children who are native speakers of English and children who are not work together in a classroom where both English and the children's other native languages are used.

Dynamic systems theory   Esther Thelen's theory that biological maturation is not independent of the environmental influences that surround the developing child.

Dysgraphia   A learning disability characterized by difficulties with writing, including trouble with spelling, handwriting, or expressing thoughts on paper.

Dyslexia   A learning disability in which individuals have difficulty distinguishing or separating the sounds in spoken words, creating problems with spelling and reading.

Early labor   The first phase in the first stage of labor in which contractions are usually not painful but the cervix begins to thin out and dilate.

Easy temperament   A child's general responsiveness marked by positive mood, easy adaptation to change, and regularity and predictability in patterns of eating, sleeping, and elimination.

Echolalia   A condition often seen in autistic children in which they repeat what has been said to them instead of responding appropriately.

Ectoderm   The outermost layer of the inner cell mass that later becomes the skin, sense organs, brain, and spinal cord.

Effortful control   The ability to consciously control one's behavior.

Ego   The part of the personality that contends with the reality of the world and controls the basic drives.

Egocentric speech   A limitation of young children's communication due to their inability to take the perspective of other people into account.

Egocentrism   The inability to see or understand things from someone else's perspective.

Elaboration   A memory strategy that involves creating extra connections, like images or sentences, that can tie information together.

Electra complex   According to Freud, the desire of the young girl to marry her father and kill her mother.

Embryo   The developing organism from conception to the beginning of the third month of a pregnancy.

Embryonic stage   The prenatal stage that lasts from 2 weeks to 2 months postconception.

Emergent literacy   The set of skills that develop before children begin formal reading instruction, which provide the foundation for later academic skills.

Emotion   The body's physiological reaction to a situation, the cognitive interpretation of the situation, communication to another person, and actions.

Emotion schemas   All the associations and interpretations that an individual connects to a certain emotion.

Emotion-focused strategies   Coping that is designed to reduce or manage emotional distress.

Emotional intelligence   The ability to understand and control one's emotions, to understand the emotions of others, and to use this understanding in human interactions.

Emotional parentification   A situation in which children become more concerned about their parent's emotional needs than their own.

Empathy   Sharing the feelings of other people.

Encoding processes   The transformation processes through which new information is stored in long-term memory.

Endoderm   The innermost layer of the inner cell mass that later becomes the respiratory system, digestive system, liver, and pancreas.

Enrichment approach   An educational approach for gifted children in which the curriculum is covered but in greater depth, breadth, or complexity than is done in a typical classroom.

Epigenetics   A system by which genes are activated or silenced in response to events or circumstances in the individual's environment.

Equifinality   Different developmental pathways may result in the same outcome.

Equilibration   An attempt to resolve uncertainty to return to a comfortable cognitive state.

Ethnic identity   The attitudes toward an ethnic group to which you feel you belong.

Ethology   The study of animal and human behavior in the natural environment.

Eugenics   The concept that desirable traits can be bred into human beings, while undesirable ones can be bred out.

Event sample   A data collection technique in which a researcher records information about all occurrences of a coherent set of behaviors being investigated.

Evocative gene-environment interaction   When children's genetic endowment causes them to act in a way that draws out or "evokes" certain responses from those around them.

Executive function   The aspect of brain organization that coordinates attention and memory and controls behavioral responses for the purpose of attaining a certain goal.

Exercise play   Play in young children that involves large muscle movement, such as running or jumping.

Exosystem   Settings that the child never enters (*external* to the child) but that affect the child's development nevertheless, such as the parents' place of work.

Expectancy effects   The effect that the expectations of others can have on one's self-perception and behavior.

Experience-dependent brain development   Development that occurs in response to specific learning experiences.

Experience-expectant brain development   Development that occurs when we encounter experiences that our brain *expects* as a normal event.

Experimental group   The group in an experiment that gets the special treatment that is of interest to the researcher.

Expressive language   The written or spoken language that we use to convey our thoughts, emotions, or needs.

Expressive language disorder   A disorder involving a limited vocabulary and difficulty using tense correctly, recalling words, or producing sentences of the length and complexity that would be expected of a child of that age.

Extended family   A family that includes both nuclear family members and other relatives.

External locus of control   The belief that events are outside of one's own control.

Externalizing behavior problems   Behaviors in which the child or adolescent "acts out" on the environment such as aggressive or destructive behavior.

Extinction   In operant conditioning, the process by which a behavior stops when it receives no response from the environment.

False belief paradigm   An experimental task used to assess a child's understanding of theory of mind in which the child predicts what someone else knows or believes.

Family   Any two or more individuals living together who are related by birth, marriage, or adoption.

Fast mapping   A process by which children apply constraints and their knowledge of grammar to learn new words very quickly, often after a single exposure.

Fertilization   The process by which a sperm penetrates an egg.

Fetal alcohol spectrum disorders (FASDs)   A range of impairments in a child resulting from consumption of alcohol during a pregnancy; associated with any subset of characteristics of fetal alcohol syndrome at varying levels of severity and other more subtle or functional deficits.

Fetal alcohol syndrome (FAS)   A condition in the child resulting from heavy or binge consumption of alcohol during a pregnancy; associated with characteristic facial features, small stature, and a small head, as well as cognitive deficits and trouble controlling behavior and regulating emotions.

Fetal stage   The prenatal stage that lasts from 2 months postconception until birth.

Fetus   The developing organism from the end of the eighth week after conception until birth.

Fight-or-flight response   The physiological response to threat.

Fine motor skills   Skills that involve small movements, mostly of the hands and fingers, but also of the lips and tongue.

Fluid intelligence   Intelligence that allows us to solve novel problems for which we have little training quickly and effectively.

Flynn effect   The increase in intelligence test scores that has occurred over time, necessitating the renorming of the tests.

Folk wisdom   Knowledge that is widely accepted but has not been scientifically tested.

Food insecurity   A situation in which food is often scarce or unavailable, causing people to overeat when they do have access to food.

Foreclosure   Commitment to an identity without any exploration of possibilities.

Forgotten half   High school students who graduate from high school and do not continue their education by going to college but are not well prepared for the transition to work.

Formal operations   Piaget's fourth stage in which people 12 and older think both logically and abstractly.

Foster care   The temporary placement of children in a family that is not their own because of unhealthy situations within their birth family.

Free association   The process used by psychoanalysis in which one thinks of anything that comes to mind in relation to a dream or another thought in order to discover the contents of the unconscious mind.

Friendship   A mutual relationship marked by companionship, closeness, and affection.

Games with rules   Making up rules for a game or playing games with preestablished rules.

Gender constancy   The understanding that one's gender remains constant even with external changes.

Gender identity   Stage when children's concept of gender relies on external appearance.

Gender intensification   The idea that gender differences in behavior, attitudes, and psychological characteristics become greater in early adolescence than they were in childhood.

Gender stability   Stage when children understand that their gender is constant over time but don't understand that gender doesn't change even if they do activities usually performed by the other gender.

Gene   The basic unit of inheritance, genes are made of DNA and they give the messages to the body to create proteins that are the basis for the body's development and functioning.

Gene therapy   Treatment of genetic disorders through implanting or disabling specific genes.

Generalize   To draw inferences from the findings of research on a specific sample about a larger group or population.

Generalized anxiety disorder   General, ongoing worried feelings that limit a person's ability to function well.

Genetic-epistemology   Piaget's theory that development of knowledge is based on both genetics (from biology) and epistemology (a philosophical understanding of the nature of knowledge).

Genital stage   Freud's fifth and final stage in which people 12 and older develop adult sexuality.

Genotype or genome   All of a person's genes, including those that are active and those that are silent.

Germinal stage   The prenatal stage that lasts from conception to 2 weeks postconception.

Gestational age   The length of time since the conception of a developing organism.

Gifted (or talented) children   Children and youth who exhibit high performance capability in intellectual, creative, and/or artistic areas; possess an unusual leadership capacity; or excel in specific academic fields.

Goal-corrected partnership   The stage of development of attachment from 18 months on, when toddlers create reciprocal relationships with their mothers.

Goodness of fit   How well a child's temperamental characteristics match with the demands of the environment.

Gross motor skills   Skills that involve the large muscle groups of the body—for example, the legs and arms.

Guilt   Feelings children have when they think about the negative aspects of something they have done, particularly moral failures.

Habituation   The reduction in the response to a stimulus that is repeated.

Hemispheres   The two halves of the cerebellum.

Heteronomous morality   Moral judgments based on the dictates of authority.

Hostile attributional bias   A tendency to interpret others' behaviors to be hostile and intentional rather than benign.

Hypothesis   A prediction, often based upon theoretical ideas or observations, that is tested by the scientific method.

Hypothetico-deductive reasoning   The ability to form hypotheses about how the world works and to reason logically about these hypotheses.

Id   According to psychoanalytic theory, the basic drives, such as sex and hunger.

Ideal self   The characteristics one aspires to in the future.

Identity achievement   The choice of an identity following exploration of the possibilities.

Identity diffusion   A lack of interest in developing an identity.

Imaginary audience   The belief that one is the center of other people's attention much of the time.

Immanent justice   The belief that unrelated events are automatic punishment for misdeeds.

Immersion programs   A program for English language learners in which the students are taught academic subjects in English, with teachers tailoring the language they use to the current language level of their students.

Imprinting   In ethology, the automatic process by which animals attach to their mothers.

Independent variable   The variable in an experiment that the researcher manipulates.

Individualism   The cultural value that emphasizes the importance of the individual with emphasis on independence and reliance on one's own abilities.

Inductive discipline   A parenting technique that involves setting clear limits for children and explaining the consequences for negative behavior, why the behavior was wrong, and what the child might do to fix the situation.

Infant mortality   The rate of infant death within the first year of life.

Infant states   Different levels of consciousness used to regulate the amount of stimulation an infant receives; states range from crying to deep sleep.

Infantile amnesia   The inability to remember experiences that happened to us before we were about 3 years of age.

Infertility   The inability to conceive within 1 year of frequent, unprotected sex.

Informed consent   Informing research participants of the risks and benefits of participating in the research and guaranteeing them the right to withdraw from participation if they wish.

Inhibition   The ability to stay on task and ignore distractions.

Inner cell mass   A solid clump of cells in the blastocyst, which later develops into the embryo.

Intelligence   Those qualities that help us adapt successfully so that we achieve our goals in life.

Intelligence quotient   Originally a measure of intelligence calculated based on the ratio of a child's mental age to chronological age, largely replaced now by the deviation IQ.

Interactionism   A theory of language development that proposes that the child's biological readiness to learn language interacts with the child's experiences with language in the environment to bring about the child's language development.

Internal working model   Mental representations of the particular attachment relationships that a child has

experienced that become the model for expectations of future relationships.

Internalization   The process by which individuals adopt the attitudes, beliefs, and values held by their society.

Internalizing behavior problems   Negative or aggressive behaviors that are directed inward at oneself, such as anxiety or depression.

Interrater reliability   A measure of consistency in the data gathered by multiple observers.

Intervention   Treatment of a problem after it has been identified.

Job shadowing   A way to learn about a career by spending time watching a person who is working in that career.

Joint attention   A process in which an individual looks at the same object that someone else is looking at, but also looks at the person to make sure that they are both involved with the same thing.

Kangaroo care   A practice where the baby is placed in skin-to-skin contact with the parent's bare chest or breasts and draped with a blanket.

Knowledge telling   A style of writing (typical of younger children) in which the writer proceeds with little or no evidence of planning or organization of ideas, with the goal of telling as much as he knows about a topic.

Knowledge transforming   A style of writing (typical of older children and adolescents) in which the goal is to convey a deeper understanding of a subject by taking information and transforming it into ideas that can be shared with a reader so that the reader understands and learns from those ideas.

Language   A system of symbols that is used to communicate with others or in our thinking.

Latency stage   Freud's fourth stage, involving children ages 6–12, when the sex drive goes underground.

Learning disability   A disorder in one or more of the basic psychological processes involved in understanding or using language, spoken or written, that may manifest itself in an imperfect ability to listen, think, speak, read, write, spell, or do mathematical calculations.

Long-term memory   The capacity for nearly permanent retention of memories.

Longitudinal design   A research design that follows one group of individuals over time and looks at the same or similar measures at each point of testing.

Love withdrawal   A parenting technique in which parents threaten to withhold their love until a child conforms to the parents' expectations for his behavior.

Low birth weight   A full-term infant who weighs less than 5 pounds, 4 ounces.

Macrosystem   Cultural norms that guide the nature of the organizations and places that make up one's everyday life.

Maltreatment   Physical abuse, sexual abuse, emotional abuse, or neglect.

Mandatory reporters   Individuals who work with children who are required by law to report suspicions of child maltreatment to authorities.

Masculinity model   The idea that having masculine traits (regardless of your biological gender) would be associated with high self-esteem and well-being because it is masculine traits that are valued the most by Western society.

Media literacy   Providing children with the skills to understand the underlying purposes and messages of media.

Memes   Units of culture that are handed down from one generation to the next.

Menarche   A girl's first menstrual period.

Mental age   In early intelligence tests, the ability of a child to successfully pass measures designed to assess intelligence at particular ages.

Mentally retarded (or intellectually disabled)   A degree of intellectual impairment that includes a low score on a standardized test of intelligence (usually 70 to 75 or lower) and impaired adaptive functioning.

Mentor   A formal relationship in which a nonparental adult provides a range of functions to a younger person, or a naturally occurring relationship that provides the same functions.

Mesoderm   The middle layer of the inner cell mass that later becomes the muscles, bones, blood, heart, kidney, and gonads.

Mesosystem   The interaction among the various settings in the microsystem, such as a child's school and home.

Meta-analysis   A statistical procedure that combines data from different studies to determine whether there is a consistent pattern of findings across studies.

Metacognition   The ability to think about and monitor one's own thoughts and cognitive activities.

Metalinguistic abilities   The ability to think about and talk about language.

Metamemory   The understanding of memory, how it works, and how to use it effectively.

Microsystem   In ecological theory, the interaction of the person in her immediate settings, such as home, school, or friendship groups.

Mindblindness   The inability to understand and theorize about other people's thoughts; a basic characteristic of people who suffer from autism.

Mirror neurons   Neurons that fire both when an individual acts and when the individual observes the same action performed by another.

Miscarriage   The natural loss of a pregnancy before the fetus reaches a gestational age of 20 weeks.

Molecular genetics   Research focused on the identification of particular genes to identify how these genes work within the cell.

Monozygotic (MZ) twins   Formed when a woman produces one egg that is fertilized by one sperm and then splits to form two individuals with the same genes.

Moral judgment   The way people reason about moral issues.

Moral knowledge   Understanding of right and wrong.

Moratorium   A time of exploration in search of identity, with no commitment made yet.

Morpheme   The smallest unit in a language that has meaning.

Motor schema   Infants' understanding of the world through their action on it.

Multifactorial inheritance disorders   Disorders result from the interaction of many genes and also environmental influences.

Multifinality   The same pathways may lead to different developmental outcomes.

Multitasking   Doing several different activities at the same time, often involving several forms of media.

Mutations   Changes in the formation of genes that occur as cells divide.

Mutual exclusivity constraint   An assumption made by language learners that there is one (and only one) name for an object.

Myelination   The process of laying down a fatty sheath of myelin on the neurons.

Nativism   A theory of language development that hypothesizes that human brains are innately wired to learn language and that hearing spoken language triggers the activation of a universal grammar.

Natural or "quasi" experiment   Research in which the members of the groups are selected because they represent different "treatment" conditions.

Nature   The influence of genetic inheritance on children's development.

Negative correlation   A correlation in which increases in one variable are associated with decreases in another variable.

Negative identity   An identity that is in direct opposition to an identity that parents or other adults would support.

Negative reinforcement   In operant conditioning, the removal of an unpleasant stimulus makes a behavior more likely to happen again.

Neglected children   Children who receive relatively few nominations either as "like most" or as "like least" on a sociometric measure.

Neurons   The cells that make up the nervous system of the body.

Neuropsychological tests   Tests used to assess brain function.

Neuropsychology   The study of the interaction of the brain and behavior.

Neurotransmitters   Chemicals that transmit nerve impulses across a synapse from one nerve cell to another.

Niche-picking   Individuals choose the part of their environment (the "niche") in which they feel comfortable, based on their genetic predispositions.

Non-normative stress   The experience of unusual and unexpected distressing events.

Nonshared environment   The environmental experiences that are different for each child in a family, including the differential impact of family events that occur at different ages for siblings.

Normative stress   Stresses that are predictable and that most children go through.

Norms   The average or typical performance of an individual of a given age on a test.

Nuclear family   A family consisting of a husband, a wife, and their biological and/or adopted children.

Null hypothesis   The hypothesis tested by an experiment that there will be no difference in the outcome for the groups in an experiment.

Nurture   The influence of learning and the environment on children's development.

Obesity   Being 20% or more over an individual's ideal body weight.

Object permanence   The understanding that objects still exist when an infant does not see them.

Observer bias   The tendency for an observer to notice and report events that he is expecting to see.

Obsessive-compulsive disorder (OCD)   A disorder marked by obsessions or intrusive thoughts and repeated behaviors that people feel compelled to do to control the obsessive thoughts.

Oedipus complex   In Freudian theory, young boys want to marry their mothers and kill their fathers. They fear castration at the hands of their fathers in retaliation for their wish to possess their mother.

Onlooker behavior   Watching others play.

Open adoptions   Adoptions in which the children and their biological and adoptive families have access to each other.

Operant conditioning   The process that happens when the response that follows a behavior causes that behavior to happen more.

Operationalize   To define a concept in a way that allows it to be measured.

Operations   Mental actions that follow systematic, logical rules.

Oppositional defiant disorder   A persisting pattern of behavior marked by defiant, disobedient, and hostile behavior toward authority figures.

Oral stage   Freud's first stage in which the sexual drive is located in the mouth for infants.

Organogenesis   The process in prenatal development by which all of the major organ systems of the body are laid down.

Orienting response   The tendency to pay attention automatically to novel, moving, meaningful, or surprising stimuli.

Other-oriented induction   A parenting technique in which the child thinks about consequences of the child's behavior for someone else.

Overregularization   A type of grammatical error in which children apply a language rule to words that don't follow that rule or pattern (for example, adding an *s* to make the plural of a word like *foot*).

Ovulation   The release of a mature egg from an ovary.

Ovum   An unfertilized egg.

Panic anxiety   Sudden fear, rapid heartbeat, sweating, difficulty breathing, chest pain, and other physical symptoms that are not linked to a physical cause such as a heart attack.

Parallel play   Playing next to a peer with the same type of materials, but not interacting with the other child.

Parent effects model   A model of parenting effects that assumes that parents cause the characteristics that we see in their children.

Parenting styles   Fairly regular and consistent patterns of interacting with children.

Passive gene-environment interaction   When a child's family shares his own genetically determined abilities and interests.

Pediatric psychologists   Child psychologists who provide therapeutic interventions for children with medical disorders.

Peer pressure   Influence exerted by peers to get others to comply with their wishes or expectations.

Peer review   A process by which professional peers review research results prior to their publication or dissemination.

Perception   The process of interpreting and attaching meaning to sensory information.

Perceptual bias   The tendency to see and understand something in the way you expected.

Perceptual role-taking   The ability to see things from someone else's perspective.

Perinatal   At the time of birth.

Permissive parents   A parenting style that provides a great deal of warmth and acceptance but few, if any, rules or restrictions.

Personal fable   The belief (often held by teenagers) that you are in some way unique and different from all other people.

Personality tests   Tests that evaluate the thoughts, emotions, attitudes, and behavioral traits that comprise personality.

Phallic stage   Freud's third stage, involving children 3–6 years of age, in which boys experience the Oedipus complex and girls experience the Electra complex.

Phenotype   The genetically based characteristics that are actually shown in one's body.

Phobia   An irrational fear of something specific that is so severe that it interferes with day-to-day functioning.

Phoneme   The smallest distinct sound in a particular language that signals differences between words.

Phonics (or basic skills) approach   An approach to teaching reading that starts with basic elements like letters and phonemes and teaches children that phonemes can be combined into words before moving on to reading as a whole.

Phonological awareness   Learning to recognize the letters of the alphabet and the sounds associated with them.

Phonological disorder   A language disorder in which the child has difficulty with producing sounds or using sounds correctly.

Phonology   The study of the sounds of a language.

Physical activity play   The type of play that involves large muscle activity.

Physical development   Biological changes that occur in the body and brain, including changes in size and strength, integration of sensory and motor activities, and development of fine and gross motor skills.

Placenta   The organ that supports a pregnancy by bringing oxygen and nutrients to the embryo from the mother through the umbilical cord and carrying away fetal waste products.

Plasticity   The ability of an immature brain to change in form and function.

Play disruption   An inability to play because the child's emotions are preventing the kind of free expression linked with the fun of play.

Play therapy   A way to help children work through difficult feelings with the help of an adult who is trained to understand play as a type of communication.

Pleasure principle   The idea that the id seeks immediate gratification for all of its urges to feel pleasure.

Pleiotropic effects   Any single gene may have many different influences.

Polygenic inheritance   Numerous genes may interact together to promote any particular trait or behavior.

Popular children   Children who receive a lot of nominations as "like most" and few as "like least" on a sociometric measure.

Population   A set that includes everyone in a category of individuals that we are interested in studying (for example, all toddlers, all teenagers with learning disabilities).

Positive correlation   A correlation in which increases in one variable are associated with increases in another variable.

Positive youth development   An approach to finding ways to help all young people reach their full potential.

Postconventional moral judgment   Independently formed moral judgments that are based on universal principles that apply to all people.

Postformal or dialectical thinking   The ability to analyze and bring together contradictory thoughts and emotions.

Postpartum depression   A severe depression anytime in the first year after childbirth that lasts for more than 2 weeks; symptoms are severe enough that they interfere with the woman's ability to function.

Posttraumatic stress disorder (PTSD)   An anxiety disorder that follows exposure to an event marked by great harm or the threat of harm to oneself or others.

Power assertion   A disciplinary technique that emphasizes control of the child's behavior through physical and nonphysical punishment.

Practical intelligence   The ability to solve everyday problems by changing yourself or your behavior to fit the environment better, changing the environment, or moving to a different environment in which you can be more successful.

Practice play   Performing a certain behavior repetitively for the mere pleasure of it.

Pragmatics   The rules that guide how we use language in social situations.

Preattachment   The stage of development of attachment from birth to 6 weeks, in which infant sensory preferences bring infants into close connection with parents.

Precocious puberty   A condition in which pubertal changes begin at an extraordinarily early age (as young as 6 or 7 years of age).

Preconventional moral judgment   Moral reasoning that is marked by self-interest and motivation based on rewards and punishments.

Prejudices   Negative attitudes toward individuals based on their race, ethnicity, religion, or other factors.

Prematurity   A birth that occurs before a gestational age of 37 weeks.

Preoperational stage   Piaget's second stage of development, in which children ages 2–7 do not yet have logical thought, instead thinking magically and egocentrically.

Primary sex characteristics   Changes that occur in the organs necessary for reproduction.

Private speech   Talking to oneself, often out loud, in order to guide one's own actions.

Problem-focused strategies   Coping that focuses on solving a stressful problem.

Processing capacity   The amount of information that you can think about at one time.

Processing efficiency   The speed and accuracy with which one can process information.

Projective tests   Assessments based on an individual's projections of aspects of his or her personality onto ambiguous external stimuli, such as an inkblot.

Prosocial-popular boys   Boys who are perceived by teachers and peers as having many of the positive characteristics associated with popular children.

Protective factors   Aspects of life that increase the health and well-being of children and families.

Proximodistal   Development that proceeds from the central axis of the body toward the extremities.

Pruning The deterioration and disappearance of synapses that are not used.

Psychosexual stages Freud's stages that are based on the idea that at each stage sexual energy is invested in a different part of the body.

Psychosocial stages Erikson's stages that are based on a central conflict to be resolved involving the social world and the development of identity.

Puberty The physical changes that occur in adolescence that make an individual capable of sexual reproduction.

Punishment Administering a negative consequence or taking away a positive reinforcement to reduce the likelihood of an undesirable behavior occurring.

Qualitative changes Changes in the overall nature of what you are examining.

Quantitative changes Changes in the amount or quantity of what you are measuring.

Questionnaires A written form of a survey.

Racial socialization Efforts by minority parents to teach their children about discrimination, prepare them to deal with these experiences, and teach them to take pride in their heritage.

Racism A pervasive system of advantage and disadvantage based on race.

Random assignment Assigning participants to the experimental and control groups by chance so that the groups will not systematically differ from each other.

Range of reaction The range of potential outcomes for any given genotype.

Reactive attachment disorder (RAD) A disorder marked by inability to form attachments to caregivers.

Reality principle The psychoanalytic concept that the ego has the ability to deal with the real world and not just drives and fantasy.

Recast To facilitate language learning, adults often repeat what children say but put it into more advanced grammar.

Receptive language The ability to understand words or sentences.

Receptive-expressive language disorder A disorder in which a child has difficulty with both expressive language (using words and language) and receptive language (understanding words and sentences).

Recursive thinking The ability to think about other people thinking about your thinking.

Reflexes Patterned, involuntary motor responses that are controlled by the lower brain centers.

Rehearsal Repeating information in order to remember it.

Reinforcement A response to a behavior that causes that behavior to happen more.

Rejected children Children who receive a lot of nominations as "like least" and few as "like most" on a sociometric measure.

Rejection sensitivity The extent to which a child is affected by peer rejection.

Relationship maintenance A parenting technique in which the parents try to create a positive relationship with their child so that the parents will have a greater influence on the child's behavior.

Reliability The ability of a measure to produce consistent results.

Replicate To find the same results as in a previous research study.

Representative sample A group of participants in a research study who have individual characteristics in the same distribution that exists in the population.

Resilience The ability to bounce back from adversity or to thrive despite negative life circumstances.

Reversibility The ability to reverse mental operations.

Rhythmic stereotypies Repeated large muscle movements that have no purpose, such as kicking the legs or waving the hands, usually seen in infants.

Rites of passage Rituals that publicly mark a change in status from child to adult.

Rough-and-tumble play Play that looks like fighting or wrestling, where the goal is not to hurt or win, but to have fun.

Sample bias Changes in the makeup of the sample in a longitudinal or cross-sequential study that make the sample less representative over time.

Scaffolding The idea that more knowledgeable adults and children support a child's learning by providing help to move the child just beyond his current level of capability.

Schedules of reinforcement Schedules (ratio or interval) on which reinforcement can be delivered based upon a fixed or variable number of responses or fixed or variable lengths of time.

Schema A cognitive framework that places concepts, objects, or experiences into categories or groups of associations.

Schizophrenia A psychotic disorder marked by disorganized thinking, hallucinations, and delusions.

Scientific method The process of formulating and testing hypotheses in a rigorous and objective manner.

Scripts Memory for the way a common occurrence in one's life, such as grocery shopping, takes place.

Secondary sex characteristics Characteristics that are associated with gender but do not directly involve the sex organs.

Secular trend The downward movement of the age at which girls experience menarche in industrialized countries since the mid-1800s.

Secure attachment A strong, positive emotional bond with a person who provides comfort and a sense of security.

Secure base for exploration The use of a parent to provide the security that an infant can rely on as she explores the environment.

Secure base script The expectation that a child develops that distress will or will not be met with care, concern, and support.

Selective attention Tuning in to certain things while tuning out others.

Self-complexity The number of different ways in which an individual defines herself.

Self-conscious emotions Emotions that depend on awareness of oneself, such as pride, guilt, and shame.

Self-efficacy Bandura's concept of a belief in our power to influence our own functioning and life circumstances.

Self-esteem How people feel about characteristics they associate with themselves.

Self-esteem movement School based programs designed to boost students' self-esteem, with the goal of eventually improving their academic performance.

Self-fulfilling prophecy The process by which expectations or beliefs lead to behaviors that help ensure that you fulfill the initial prophecy or expectation.

Self-oriented induction A parenting technique in which the child is asked to think about the consequences that the child might experience as a result of his behavior.

Semantic bootstrapping The use of conceptual categories to create grammatical categories.

Semantics The study of the meanings of words.

Sensations The information from the environment that is picked up by our sense organs.

Sensorimotor stage Piaget's first stage in which infants learn through their senses and their actions upon the world.

Sensory memory The capacity for information that comes in through our senses to be retained for a very brief period of time in its raw form.

Separation anxiety Distress felt when separated from parent.

Sexual orientation Preference for a sexual partner of the same or the opposite sex.

Sexually transmitted infection (STI) A disease or infection that is transmitted by direct sexual contact.

Shame A feeling that occurs as a result of personal failure or when children attribute their bad behavior to an aspect of themselves that they believe they cannot change.

Single gene disorders Genetic disorders caused by recessive genes or mutations.

Slow-to-warm temperament A general responsiveness marked by a slow adaptation to new experiences and moderate irregularity in eating, sleeping, and elimination.

Social cognition How we think about and understand interactions between people.

Social cognitive theory The theory that individuals learn by observing others and imitating their behavior.

Social comparison The process of comparing oneself to others.

Social policy Government or private policies for dealing with social issues.

Social promotion Promoting a child who has not mastered grade-level material to keep the child in a class with same-age peers.

Social referencing Using the reaction of others to determine how to react in ambiguous situations.

Social status The level of peer acceptance or peer rejection of an individual in the peer group.

Social-emotional development The ways we connect to other individuals and understand emotions.

Socialization The process by which parents, peers, and other important figures in the child's world teach a child how to interact in appropriate ways according to the rules and norms of their society.

Sociobiology A theory that proposes that social behavior is determined by genes that evolved to promote adaptation.

Sociometry A research technique used to assess a child's social status within the peer group.

Solitary independent play Engaging actively with toys that are different from those being used by other children.

Spermarche The beginning of production of viable sperm.

Stage theories Theories of development in which each stage in life is seen as qualitatively different from the ones that come before and after.

Stepfamilies Families in which there are two adults and at least one child from a previous relationship of one of the adults; there also may be biological children of the couple.

Stereotype threat The anxiety that results when individuals feel they are behaving in ways that confirm stereotyped expectations of a group with which they identify.

Stereotyping Conclusions made about someone based solely on the group with which he or she is identified.

Stores model The idea that information is processed through a series of mental locations (sensory to short-term to long-term memory "stores").

Strange Situation Mary Ainsworth's experimental procedure designed to assess security of attachment in infants.

Stranger anxiety Fearfulness that infants develop toward people they do not know.

Stress Anything that places excessive demands on our ability to cope.

Sudden infant death syndrome (SIDS) The unexpected death of an apparently healthy infant; the rate of SIDS peaks between the ages of 2 months and 4 months.

Superego Freud's concept of the conscience or sense of right and wrong.

Surveys A data collection technique that asks respondents to answer questions.

Sustained attention Maintaining focus over time.

Symbolic/sociodramatic play Using symbolic representations and imagination for play.

Sympathy Concern for others' welfare that often leads to helping or comforting them.

Synapse The place where the axon from one neuron meets the dendrite of another neuron.

Synaptogenesis The development of new synapses.

Syntactic bootstrapping The use of syntax to learn the meaning of new words (semantics).

Syntax The grammar of a language.

Taxonomic constraint An assumption language learners make that two objects that have features in common can have a name in common, but that each object also can have its own individual name.

Telegraphic speech A stage in language development in which children only use the words necessary to get their point across and omit small words that are not necessary (for example, *Go up*).

Temperament The general emotional style an individual displays in responding to events.

Teratogens Agents that can disrupt prenatal development and cause malformations or termination of the pregnancy.

Theory of core knowledge The theory that basic areas of knowledge are innate and built into the human brain.

Theory of mind The ability to understand self and others as agents who act on the basis of their mental states, such as beliefs, desires, emotions, and intentions.

Theory of multiple intelligences The idea that there are a number of different types of intelligence that are all relatively independent of each other.

Thin ideal The idea that it is best for girls and women to be thin.

Threshold theory The theory that intelligence and creativity are related up to approximately an IQ score of 120 but not beyond that.

Time sample A data collection technique in which a researcher observes an individual for a predetermined period of time and records the occurrence of specific behaviors of interest to the research during that period.

Tourette's disorder A disorder that begins before the age of 18 in which an individual has many motor tics and at least one vocal tic.

Transactional effect   A bidirectional effect in which there are changes over time as a result of the ongoing interaction between the individuals.

Transactional model   A model of parenting effects that assumes that influence moves from parent to child but also from child to parent in a reciprocal process.

Transductive reasoning   Thought that connects one particular observation to another by creating causal links where none exist.

Transition   The third phase in the first stage of labor in which contractions come in rapid succession and last up to 90 seconds each, with little or no pause between them; lasts on average between 15 minutes and 3 hours and ends when cervix has dilated 10 centimeters.

Transitional bilingual education programs   Programs for English language learners in which students receive some instruction in their native language while they also receive concentrated instruction in learning English.

Triarchic theory   Sternberg's idea that intelligence represents a balance of analytical, creative, and practical abilities.

Trophoblast   The outer ring of cells in the blastocyst that later develops into the support system for the pregnancy.

Unconscious mind   The thoughts and feelings about which we are unaware.

Undernutrition   A deficiency of calories or of one or more essential nutrients.

Unidirectional effect   Influence that runs in only one direction (for example, from a parent to his or her child).

Uninvolved or neglectful parents   A parenting style that is low both on the dimension of warmth and on the dimension of control; parents may be disinterested in parenting or actively reject their children.

Universal grammar   A hypothesized set of grammatical rules and constraints proposed by Chomsky that is thought to underlie all languages and that is hardwired in the human brain.

Unoccupied behavior   Looking around at whatever occurs, but engaging in no activity.

Validity   A measure that accurately measures what it purports to measure.

Variable   A characteristic that can be measured and that can have different values.

Violation of expectation   Research based on the finding that babies look longer at unexpected or surprising events.

Virginity pledge   A promise made by children or adolescents to abstain from becoming sexually active before marriage.

Visual acuity   The ability to see things in sharp detail.

Vocabulary burst   The rapid growth of a child's vocabulary that often occurs in the second year.

Wernicke's area   The part of the brain that has to do with understanding the meaning in speech.

Whole language instruction   A way to teach reading that emphasizes understanding the meaning of words from the context in which they appear.

Whole word bias   An assumption made by language learners that a word describes an entire object, rather than just some portion of it.

Working (or short-term) memory   Memory capacity that is limited to only a brief time but that also allows the mind to process information in order to move it into long-term memory.

Wraparound program   A comprehensive set of services offered to families to strengthen them or reunite them.

Zone of proximal development   According to Vygotsky, this is what a child cannot do on her own but can do with a little help from someone more skilled or knowledgeable.

Zygote   The fertilized egg that begins to divide into the cells that will develop into the embryo.

Credits

Features, Figures, and Tables

Chapter 1

Figure 1.1, page 11. Copyright © 1999 Society for Research in Child Development.
Figure 1.2, page 16. Dubow, Boxer, & Huesmann (2008, p. 44). Copyright © 2008 Society for the Study of Addiction.

Chapter 2

Figure 2.1, page 37. ©iStockphoto.com/ HelgaMariah.
Figure 2.2, page 43. ©Jupiterimages/ Comstock/Thinkstock; ©Comstock/ Thinkstock; ©Stockbyte/Thinkstock.
Figure 2.4, page 57. Copyright © 1982. Printed and electronically reproduced by permission of Pearson Education, Inc., Upper Saddle River, New Jersey.
Figure 2.5, page 63. ©Photos.com/Thinkstock; ©Ted Streshinsky/Corbis; ©Farrell Grehan/ Corbis; ©Cornell University.
Figure 2.6, page 64. ©iStockphoto.com/ PictureLake; ©iStockphoto.com/Tomacco.
Table 2.1, page 35. Compiled from Erikson (1963) and Kahn (2002).

Chapter 3

Figure 3.1, page 79. Barkley (1991). Copyright © 1991 by Guilford Publications, Inc. Reproduced with permission via Copyright Clearance Center.
Figure 3.2, page 91. Based on research conducted by Whitehurst et al. (1988).
Figure 3.3, page 94. Barcelona Field Studies Centre (2010). Copyright 2009 Barcelona Field Studies Centre S.L. Reprinted with permission. All rights reserved. http://geographyfieldwork.com.

Figure 3.4, page 98. Tram & Cole (2006, p. 683). Copyright © 2006 American Psychological Association.
Table 3.2, page 85. Calculated by FairTest.org (2008). Reprinted with permission of FairTest.
Table 3.3, page 105. Kapoun (1998). Reprinted by permission of Jim Kapoun.

Chapter 4

Figure 4.1, page 116. Human Genome Project Information (n.d.); U.S. Department of Energy Genome Programs (2003), http://genomics .energy.gov.
Figure 4.2, page 117. ©Biophoto Associates/ Photo Researchers, Inc.
Figure 4.3, page 120. U.S. National Library of Medicine (n.d.).
Figure 4.5, page 124. National Heart, Lung and Blood Institute (2007).
Figure 4.6, page 128. ©Biophoto Associates/ Photo Researchers, Inc.
Figure 4.7, page 130. ©VEM/Photo Researchers, Inc.
Table 4.1, page 123. BabyMed (2001).
Table 4.2, page 128. Source: DeLalla (1998); National Human Genome Research Institute (2007c); Saul & Tarleton (1998).
Table 4.3, page 129. March of Dimes (2008). Copyright © 2010 March of Dimes. Used by permission.

Chapter 5

Figure 5.1, page 149. ©BSIP/Photo Researchers, Inc.
Figure 5.2, page 149. ©Jim Dowdalls/Photo Researchers, Inc.

Figure 5.3, page 151. ©Visuals Unlimited/Corbis.
Figure 5.4, page 152. DevelopmentalBiology .net (n.d.).
Figure 5.5, page 158. March of Dimes Perinatal Data Center (2002). Copyright © 2010 March of Dimes. Used by permission.
Figure 5.6, page 162. Bobo, Klepinger, & Dong (2006, p. 1066). Copyright © 2006, Mary Ann Liebert, Inc. Publishers. Reprinted with permission.
Figure 5.7, page 166. Centers for Disease Control and Prevention (2009a).
Figure 5.8, page 177. U.S. Department of Health and Human Services, Health Resources and Services Administration, Maternal and Child Health Bureau (2004).
Table 5.1, page 150. Kalb (2004); Turkington (2002).

Chapter 6

Figure 6.1, page 192. ©Purestock/Getty Images.
Figure 6.3, page 195. ©3DClinic/Collection Mix: Subjects/Getty Images.
Figure 6.4, page 202. Merck Manual (2008). Reprinted with permission from *The Merck Manual of Diagnosis and Therapy*, Edition 18, edited by Robert Porter. Copyright 2008 by Merck & Co., Inc., Whitehouse Station, NJ. Available at: http://www.merck.com/mmpe.
Figure 6.5, page 213. ©BSIP/Photo Researchers, Inc.
Figure 6.6, page 218. Alan Guttmacher Institute (2010).
Figure 6.7, page 220. Centers for Disease Control and Prevention (2009c).
Figure 6.8, page 221. Alford & Hauser (2009). Used with permission of Advocates for Youth, Washington, DC. www.advocatesforyouth.org.

Figure 15.3b, page 550. Federal Interagency Forum on Child and Family Statistics (2009, p. 36).

Figure 15.4, page 554. National Children's Study (2003, p. 4).

Figure 15.5, page 559. U.S. Department of Health and Human Services (2008a).

Figure 15.6, page 559. U.S. Department of Health and Human Services (2006).

Figure 15.7, page 560. U.S. Department of Health and Human Services (2008a). U.S. Department of Health and Human Services, Administration on Children, Youth and Families. *Child Maltreatment 2006* (Washington, DC: U.S. Government Printing Office, 2008).

Table 15.1, page 540. Adapted for use with adolescents from Carver, Scheier, & Weintraub (1989).

Table 15.2, page 549. Safe Kids Worldwide (2007). Reprinted by permission of Safe Kids Worldwide, www.safekids.org.

Active Learning: Finding Resources to Cope With Stress, page 541. California State University at Northridge (2009a, 2009b).

Photos

Part I

Photos, pages xxx–1. Kane Skennar/Digital Vision/Thinkstock; Jupiterimages/Comstock/Thinkstock; Jupiterimages/Comstock/Thinkstock.

Chapter 1

Photos, page 2. Jupitees/Brand X Pictures/Thinkstock; ©Istockphoto.com/Damir Cudic.

Photo, page 5. ©David Young-Wolff/Photographer's Choice/Getty Images.

Photo, page 5. ©Jupiterimages/Brand X Pictures/Thinkstock.

Photos, page 8. ©Flying Colours Ltd/Photodisc/Thinkstock; ©Jupiterimages/Comstock/Thinkstock; ©Michael Blann/Valueline/Thinkstock.

Photo, page 9. ©Jupiterimages/Creatas/Thinkstock.

Photo, page 12. ©Comstock Images/Thinkstock.

Photos, page 14. ©Digital Vision/Thinkstock; ©Creatas/Thinkstock.

Photo, page 15. ©Comstock/Thinkstock.

Photo, page 21. ©Steve Liss/TIME & LIFE Images/Getty Images.

Photos, page 22. ©Jupiterimages/Comstock/Thinkstock; ©Katy McDonnell/Digital Vision/Thinkstock.

Photo, page 24. ©Digital Vision/Thinkstock.

Chapter 2

Photos, page 28. Jupiterimages/Pixland/Thinkstock; © Ron Nickel/Design Pics/Corbis.

Photo, page 34. ©Jupiterimages/Pixland/Thinkstock.

Photos, page 40. ©B. Pepone/Corbis; ©Center for High Performance Computing and Visualization, University of Groningen.

Photo, page 41. ©Steve Mason/Digital Vision/Thinkstock.

Photo, page 44. ©Keith Dannemiller/CORBIS.

Photos, page 45. ©Albert Bandura.

Photo, page 52. ©Photos.com/Thinkstock.

Photos, page 53. ©Jupiterimages/Photos.com/Thinkstock; ©Nina Leen/Time & Life Pictures/Getty Images.

Photos, page 54. ©iStockphoto.com/Stefan1234; ©Robert van der Hilst/CORBIS; ©iStockphoto.com/ArtisticCaptures.

Photo, page 61. ©Herbert Gehr/Time & Life Pictures/Getty Images.

Photo, page 62. ©Jennie Woodcock; Reflections Photolibrary/CORBIS.

Photo, page 64. ©iStockphoto.com/lisafx.

Chapter 3

Photos, page 68. Richard T. Nowitz/Photo Researchers, Inc.; ©Laura Dwight/Corbis.

Photo, page 71. ©Jupiterimages/Creatas/Thinkstock.

Photos, page 72. ©istockphoto/MichaelBlackburn; ©Martin Ruetschi/Keystone/Corbis; ©iStockphoto.com/aabejon.

Photo, page 72. ©Jupiterimages/Brand X Pictures/Thinkstock.

Photo, page 75. ©Louie Psihoyos/Science Faction/Corbis.

Photo, page 82. ©Chip Simons/Workbook Stock/Getty Images.

Photo, page 86. ©Jon Wilson/Photo Researchers, Inc..

Photos, page 87. ©iStockphoto.com/bravajulia; ©Visuals Unlimited/Corbis.

Photo, page 92. ©Jupiterimages/Pixland/Thinkstock.

Photos, page 93. ©Amanda Koster/Corbis; ©Karen Kasmuski/CORBIS.

Photos, page 96. ©BananaStock/Thinkstock; ©Photodisc/Thinkstock; ©Jupiterimages/Comstock/Thinkstock.

Photo, page 99. ©Tim Cowie/Icon SMI/Corbis.

Photo, page 100. ©BananaStock/Thinkstock.

Part II

Photos, page 112–113. Marc Debnam/Digitial Vision/Thinkstock; Siri Stafford/Photodisc/Thinkstock; Marili Forastieri/Photodisc/Thinkstock; Jupiterimages/Comstock/Thinkstock.

Chapter 4

Photos, page 114. Barbara Penoyar/Photodisc/Thinkstock; © Istockphoto.com/JohnPrescott.

Photos, page 119. ©Barbara Penoyar/Photodisc/Thinkstock; ©Barbara Penoyar/Photodisc/Thinkstock; ©iStockphoto.com/digitalskillet.

Photo, page 121. ©Jupiterimages/Brand X Pictures/Thinkstock.

Photo, page 126. ©Gary Meszaros/Visuals Unlimited/Getty Images.

Photo, page 127. © Biophoto Associates/Photo Researchers, Inc.

Photo, page 129. ©George Doyle/Stockbyte/Thinkstock.

Photo, page 134. ©Bettmann/CORBIS; ©Bettmann/CORBIS.

Photos, page 140. ©Per-Anders Pettersson/Getty Images News/Getty Images; ©Jupiterimages/Creatas/Thinkstock.

Photo, page 143. ©Diane Cook & Len Jenshel/Corbis.

Photos, page 144. ©M. Langer/plainpicture/Corbis; ©REB Images/Blend Images/Corbis.

Chapter 5

Photos, page 146. Marili Forastieri/Digital Vision/Thinkstock; Jupiterimages/Brand X Pictures/Thinkstock.

Photo, page 153. ©Claude Edelmann/Photo Researchers, Inc.

References

Abbeduto, L., & Symons, F. (Eds.). (2008). *Taking sides: Clashing views in educational psychology* (5th ed.). Boston, MA: McGraw-Hill.

Abma, J. C., Martinez, G. M., Mosher, W. D., & Dawson, B. S. (2004). Teenagers in the United States: Sexual activity, contraceptive use, and childbearing. *Vital and Health Statistics, 23*(24), 1–48. Washington, DC: Centers for Disease Control and Prevention.

Abraham, K. G., & Christopherson, V. A. (1984). Perceived competence among rural middle school children: Parental antecedents and relation to locus of control. *Journal of Early Adolescence, 4*(4), 343–351.

Abreu-Villac, Y., Seidler, F. J., Tate, C. A., Cousins, M. M., & Slotkin, T. A. (2004). Prenatal nicotine exposure alters the response to nicotine administration in adolescence: Effects on cholinergic systems during exposure and withdrawal. *Neuropsychopharmacology, 29*, 879–890.

Acevedo-Polakovich, I. D., Lorch, E. P., & Milich, R. (2007). Comparing television use and reading in children with ADHD and non-referred children across two age groups. *Media Psychology, 9*, 447–472.

Achiron, R., Lipitz, S., & Achiron, A. (2001). Sex-related differences in the development of the human fetal corpus callosum: In utero ultrasonographic study. *Prenatal Diagnosis, 21*, 116–120.

Ackerman, B. P. (1997). The role of setting information in children's memory retrieval. *Journal of Experimental Child Psychology, 65*(2), 238–260.

Adamczyk-Robinette, S. L., Fletcher, A. C., & Wright, K. (2002). Understanding the authoritative parenting-early adolescent tobacco use link: The mediating role of peer tobacco use. *Journal of Youth and Adolescence, 31*(4), 311–318.

Adams, R., & Laursen, B. (2001). The organization and dynamics of adolescent conflict with parents and friends. *Journal of Marriage and Family, 63*(1), 97–110.

Adler, A. (1956). *The individual psychology of Alfred Adler* (H. L. Ansbacher & R. R. Ansbacher, Eds.). New York, NY: Basic Books.

Agence France-Presse. (2009). *Indonesia to deport Greenpeace activists including Pinoy: leader*. ABS-CBN News. Retrieved from http://www.abs-cbnnews.com/pinoy-migration/11/26/09/indonesia-deport-greenpeace-activists-including-pinoy-leader

Agras, W. S., Bryson, S., Hammer, L. D., & Kraemer, H. C. (2007). Childhood risk factors for thin body preoccupation and social pressure to be thin. *Journal of the American Academy of Child and Adolescent Psychiatry, 46*(2), 171–178.

Ahmed, R. A. (2010). North Africa and the Middle East. In M. H. Bornstein (Ed.), *Handbook of cultural developmental science* (pp. 359–381). New York, NY: Psychology Press.

Ahnert, L., Pinquart, M., & Lamb, M. E. (2006). Security of children's relationships with nonparental care providers: A meta-analysis. *Child Development, 77*(3), 664–679.

Ainsworth, M. D. S. (1979). Infant-mother attachment. *American Psychologist, 34*(10), 932–937.

Ainsworth, M. D. S., & Bell, S. M. (1970). Attachment, exploration and separation: Illustrated by the behavior of one-year-olds in a strange situation. *Child Development, 41*(1), 49–67.

Ainsworth, M. D. S., Blehar, M. C., Waters, E., & Wall, S. (1978). *Patterns of attachment*. Hillsdale, NJ: Erlbaum.

Ainsworth, M. D. S., & Bowlby, J. (1989). An ethological approach to personality development. *American Psychologist, 46*(4), 333–341.

Akhtar, N. (2005). Is joint attention necessary for early language learning? In B. D. Homer & C. S. Tamis-LeMonda (Eds.), *The development of social cognition and communication* (pp. 165–179). Mahwah, NJ: Erlbaum.

Akinbami, L. (2010). *Asthma prevalence, health care use and mortality: United States, 2003-05.* Retrieved from http://www.cdc.gov/nchs/data/hestat/asthma03-05/asthma03-05.htm

Alan Guttmacher Institute. (2009). *Facts on sexually transmitted infections in the United States*. Retrieved from http://www.guttmacher.org/pubs/2009/06/09/FIB_STI_US.pdf

Alan Guttmacher Institute. (2010). *Facts on American teens' sexual and reproductive health*. Retrieved from http://www.guttmacher.org/pubs/fb_ATSRH.html

Alberts, A., Elkind, D., & Ginsberg, S. (2007). The personal fable and risk-taking in early adolescence. *Journal of Youth and Adolescence, 36*, 71–76.

Alberts, B., Johnson, A., Lewis, J., Raff, M., Roberts, K., & Walter, P. (2002). *Molecular biology of the cell* (4th ed.). New York, NY: Garland Science.

Alexander, G. M., & Hines, M. (1994). Gender labels and play styles: Their relative contribution to children's selection of playmates. *Child Development, 65*, 869–879.

Alexander-Passe, N. (2006). How dyslexic teenagers cope: An investigation of self-esteem, coping and depression. *Dyslexia: An International Journal of Research and Practice, 12*(4), 256–275.

Alford, S., & Hauser, D. (2009). *Adolescent sexual health in Europe and the U.S.—Why the difference?* (3rd ed.). Washington, DC: Advocates for Youth. (Updated from *Adolescent sexual health in Europe and the U.S.—Why the difference?* by A. Feijoo, 2000 [1st ed.] and 2001 [2nd ed.], Washington DC: Advocates for Youth)

Ali, M. M., & Dwyer, D. S. (2009). Estimating peer effects in adolescent smoking behavior: A longitudinal analysis. *Journal of Adolescent Health, 45*(4), 402–408.

Allen, J. P., Seitz, V., & Apfel, N. H. (2007). The sexually mature teen as a whole person: New directions in prevention and intervention for teen pregnancy and parenthood. In J. L. Aber, S. J. Bishop-Josef, S. M. Jones, K. T. McLearn, & D. A. Phillips (Eds.), *Child development and social policy: Knowledge for action* (pp. 185–200). Washington, DC: American Psychological Association.

Allen, R. E., & Hanson, R. W., Jr. (2005). Episiotomy in low-risk vaginal deliveries. *Journal of the American Board of Family Physicians, 18*(1), 8–12.

Allgood-Merten, B., & Stockard, J. (1991). Sex role identity and self-esteem: A comparison of children and adolescents. *Sex Roles, 25*(3–4), 129–139.

Allhusen, V., Belsky, J., Booth-LaForce, C., Bradley, R., Brownell, C. A., Burchinal, M., . . . Weinraub, M. (2005). Duration and developmental timing of poverty and children's cognitive and social development from birth through third grade. *Child Development, 76*(4), 795–810.

Allix, N. M. (2000). The theory of multiple intelligences: A case of missing cognitive matter. *Australian Journal of Education, 44,* 272–288.

Allport, G. (1954). *The nature of prejudice.* Reading, MA: Addison Wesley.

Almli, C. R., Rivkin, M. J., McKinstry, R. C., & Brain Development Cooperative Group. (2007). The NIH MRI study of normal brain development (Objective-2): Newborns, infants, toddlers, and preschoolers. *NeuroImage, 35*(1), 308–325.

Almon, J. (2003). The vital role of play in early childhood education. In S. Olfman (Ed.), *All work and no play: How educational reforms are harming our preschoolers* (pp. 17–42). Westport, CT: Praeger.

Alomar, L., & Zwolinski, M. (2002). Quinceañera! A celebration of Latina womanhood. *Voices: The Journal of New York Folklore, 28.* Retrieved from http://www.nyfolklore.org/pubs/voic28-3-4/onair.html

Alvino, J. (1995). *Considerations and strategies for parenting the gifted child* (Publication RM95218). Storrs, CT: The National Research Center on the Gifted and Talented, University of Connecticut.

Amato, P., & Gilbreth, J. G. (1999). Nonresident fathers and children's well-being: A meta-analysis. *Journal of Marriage and Family, 61,* 557–573.

Ambert, A. (1997). *Parents, children and adolescents.* New York, NY: Haworth Press.

America's Promise Alliance. (2009). *Cities in crisis 2009: Closing the graduation gap.* Retrieved from http://www.americaspromise.org/Our-Work/Dropout-Prevention/Cities-in-Crisis.aspx

American Academy of Child and Adolescent Psychiatry. (2005). *Foster care.* Retrieved from http://www.aacap.org/cs/root/facts_for_families/foster_care

American Academy of Family Physicians. (2009). *Familydoctor.org.* Retrieved from http://familydoctor.org/online/famdocen/home/tools/symptom.html

American Academy of Matrimonial Lawyers. (2009). *Ten tips for divorcing parents.* Retrieved from http://www.aaml.org/go/library/publications/stepping-back-from-anger/ten-tips-for-divorcing-parents/

American Academy of Pediatrics. (2001). Organized sports for children and preadolescents. *Pediatrics, 107*(6), 1459–1462.

American Academy of Pediatrics. (2006a). Child life services. *Pediatrics, 118*(4), 1757–1763.

American Academy of Pediatrics. (2006b). *Choking prevention and first aid for infants and children.* Elk Grove Village, IL: Author.

American Academy of Pediatrics. (2009a). Policy statement. *Pediatrics, 123*(1), 188.

American Academy of Pediatrics. (2009b). Recommendations for preventive pediatric health care. *Pediatrics, 96,* 373–374.

American Academy of Pediatrics Committee on Adolescence. (2001). Condom use by adolescents. *Pediatrics 107*(6), 1463–1469.

American Academy of Pediatrics Committee on Drugs. (2001). The transfer of drugs and other chemicals into human milks. *Pediatrics, 108*(3), 776–789.

American Academy of Pediatrics Committee on Public Education. (2001). American Academy of Pediatrics: Children, adolescents and television. *Pediatrics, 107*(2), 423–426.

American Academy of Pediatrics: Task Force on Sudden Infant Death Syndrome. (2005). The changing concept of sudden infant death syndrome: Diagnostic coding shifts, controversies regarding the sleeping environment, and new variables to consider in reducing risk. Policy statement. *Pediatrics, 116,* 1245–1255.

American Association of Intellectual and Developmental Disabilities. (2008). *Frequently asked questions on intellectual disability and the AAIDD definition.* Retrieved from http://www.aamr.org/Policies/faq_mental_retardation.shtml

American Association of Retired Persons. (2004). *Legal issues for grandparents raising grandchildren.* Retrieved from http://www.aarp.org/family/grandparenting/articles/grandparents-legal.html

American Association of University Women. (2009). *Position on single sex education.* Retrieved from http://www.aauw.org/act/issue_advocacy/actionpages/singlesex.cfm

American Association of University Women Educational Foundation. (2004). *Under the microscope—A decade of gender equity projects in the sciences.* Washington, DC: Author.

American Congress of Obstetricians and Gynecologists. (2005). *Smoking cessation during pregnancy. ACOG Committee Opinion (No. 316).*

American Congress of Obstetricians and Gynecologists. (2007). *You and your baby: Prenatal care, labor and delivery, and postpartum care.* Retrieved from http://www.acog.org/publications/patient_education/ab005.cfm

American Congress of Obstetricians and Gynecologists. (2009). *Labor induction.* Retrieved from http://www.acog.org/publications/patient_education/bp154.cfm

American Medical Association. (2008). *Prenatal screening questionnaire.* Retrieved from http://www.ama-assn.org/ama1/pub/upload/mm/464/ped_screening.pdf

American Pregnancy Association. (2007). *Epidural anesthesia.* Retrieved from http://www.americanpregnancy.org/labornbirth/epidural.html

American Psychiatric Association. (1980). *Diagnostic and statistical manual of mental disorders* (3rd ed.). Washington, DC: Author.

American Psychiatric Association. (1994). *Diagnostic and statistical manual of mental disorders* (4th ed.). Washington, DC: Author.

American Psychiatric Association. (2000). *Diagnostic and statistical manual of mental disorders* (4th ed., text rev.). Washington, DC: Author.

American Psychological Association. (2004a). *Briefing sheet: An overview of the psychological literature on the effects of divorce on children.* Retrieved from http://www.apa.org/about/gr/issues/cyf/divorce.aspx

American Psychological Association. (2004b). *Child abuse prevention and treatment act (CAPTA).* Retrieved from http://www.apa.org/divisions/div37/CAPTA%20and%20ESSSSCP.pdf

American Psychological Association. (2009). *PsycINFO: July 2009 update.* Retrieved from http://www.apa.org/pubs/databases/psycinfo/index.aspx

American Psychological Association. (2010). *Society of Pediatric Psychology.* Retrieved from http://www.apa.org/about/division/div54.aspx

American Social Health Association. (1996). *Herpes resource center.* Retrieved from http://www.ashastd.org/herpes/herpes_learn_pregnancy.cfm

American Speech-Language-Hearing Association. (1997–2009). *Speech and language disorders and diseases.* Retrieved from http://www.asha.org/public/speech/disorders/

Anderson, C. A., & Bushman, B. J. (2001). Effects of violent video games on aggressive behavior, aggressive cognition, aggressive affect, physiological arousal, and prosocial behavior: A meta-analytic review of the scientific literature. *Psychological Science, 12*(5), 353–359.

Anderson, D. R., Levin, S. R., & Lorch, E. P. (1977). The effects of TV program pacing on the behavior of preschool children. *Educational Communication & Technology, 25*(2), 159–166.

Anderson, D. R., & Pempek, T. A. (2005). Television and very young children. *American Behavioral Scientist, 48*(5), 505–522.

Anderson, D. I., Roth, M. B., & Campos, J. J. (2005). Reflexes. In *Encyclopedia of human development.* Thousand Oaks, CA: Sage. Retrieved from http://www.sage-eference.com/humandevelopment/Article_n517.html

Anderson, K. (2005). *US "whittling away at death penalty."* Washington, DC: BBC News website. Retrieved from http://news.bbc.co.uk/2/hi/americas/4314207.stm

Andreou, G., & Karapetsas, A. (2004). Verbal abilities in low and highly proficient bilinguals. *Journal of Psycholinguistic Research, 33*(5), 357–364.

The Annie E. Casey Foundation. (2009). *About us: Mission and history*. Retrieved from http://www.aecf.org/Home/AboutUs/MissionAndHistory.aspx

Anthony, L. G., Anthony, B. J., Glanville, D. N., Naiman, D. Q., Waanders, C., & Shaffer, S. (2005). The relationships between parenting stress, parenting behaviour and preschoolers' social competence and behaviour problems in the classroom. *Infant and Child Development, 14*(2), 133–154.

Arifeen, S., Black, R. E., Antelman, G., Baqui, A., Caulfield, L., & Becker, S. (2001). Exclusive breastfeeding reduces acute respiratory infection and diarrhea deaths among infants in Dhaka slums. *Pediatrics, 108*(4), e67.

Armbruster, B. B., Lehr, F., & Osborn, J. M. (2001). *Putting reading first: The research building blocks for teaching children to read*. Washington, DC: National Institute for Literacy.

Armistead, L., Wierson, M., & Forehand, R. (1990). Adolescents and maternal employment. *Journal of Early Adolescence, 10*(3), 260–278.

Armsden, G. C., & Greenberg, M. T. (1987). The Inventory of Parent and Peer Attachment: Individual differences and their relationship to psychological well-being in adolescence. *Journal of Youth and Adolescence, 16*(5), 427–454.

Arnett, J. J. (1999). Adolescent storm and stress, reconsidered. *American Psychologist, 54*(5), 317–326.

Arnold, D. H., Fisher, P. H., & Doctoroff, G. L. (2002). Accelerating math development in Head Start classrooms. *Journal of Educational Psychology, 94*(4), 762–770.

Arteaga, S. S., & Lamb, Y. (2008). Expert review of key findings on children exposed to violence and their families from the Safe Start Demonstration Project. *Best Practices in Mental Health: An International Journal, 4*(1), 99–107.

Asendorpf, J. B., & Baudonniere, P. (1993). Self-awareness and other-awareness: Mirror self-recognition and synchronic imitation among unfamiliar peers. *Developmental Psychology, 29*(1), 88–95.

Asher, J. J., & Garcia, R. (1969). The optimal age to learn a foreign language. *Modern Language Journal, 53*(5), 334–341.

Aslin, R. N., Saffran, J. R., & Newport, E. L. (1998). Computation of conditional probability statistics by 8-month-old infants. *Psychological Science, 9*(4), 321–324.

Asmussen, L., & Larson, R. (1991). The quality of family time among young adolescents in single-parent and married-parent families. *Journal of Marriage and Family, 53*, 1021–1030.

Associated Press. (2006). *Woman kicked off plane for breast-feeding baby*. Retrieved from http://www.msnbc.msn.com/id/15720339/

Astington, J. W., & Filippova, E. (2005). Language as the route into other minds. In B. F. Malle & S. D. Hodges (Eds.), *Other minds* (pp. 209–222). New York, NY: Guilford.

Aughinbaugh, A., & Gittleman, M. (2003). *Maternal employment and adolescent risky behavior*. U.S. Bureau of Labor Statistics Working Paper #366.

Aunola, K., Stattin, H., & Nurmi, J. (2000). Parenting styles and adolescents' achievement strategies. *Journal of Adolescence, 23*(2), 205–222.

Avis, J., & Harris, P. L. (1991). Belief-desire reasoning among Baka children: Evidence for a universal conception of mind. *Child Development, 62*(3), 460–467.

Ayduk, O., Mendoza-Denton, R., Mischel, W., Downey, G., Peake, P. K., & Rodriguez, M. (2000). Regulating the interpersonal self: Strategic self-regulation for coping with rejection sensitivity. *Journal of Personality and Social Psychology, 79*(5), 776–792.

BabyMed. (2001). *Baby eye color calculator and predictor*. Retrieved from http://babymed.com/Tools/Other/Eye_Color/Default.aspx

Baek, H. (2002). A comparative study of moral development of Korean and British children. *Journal of Moral Education, 31*(4), 373–391.

Bagnell, K. (2001). *The little immigrants: The orphans who came to Canada*. Toronto, ON, Canada: Dundurn Press.

Bagwell, C. L., Newcomb, A. F., & Bukowski, W. M. (1998). Preadolescent friendship and peer rejection as predictors of adult adjustment. *Child Development, 69*(1), 140–153.

Bahl, R., Frost, C., Kirkwood, B. R., Edmond, K., Martines, J., Bhandari, N., & Arthur, P. (2005). Infant feeding patterns and risks of death and hospitalization in the first half of infancy: Multicentre cohort study. *Bulletin of the World Health Organization, 83*(6), 418–426.

Bailey, A., LeCouteur, A., Gottesman, I., & Bolton, P. (1995). Autism as a strongly genetic disorder: Evidence from a British twin study. *Psychological Medicine, 25*(1), 63–77.

Bailey, J. A., Hill, K. G., Hawkins, J. D., Catalano, R. F., & Abbott, R. D. (2008). Men's and women's patterns of substance use around pregnancy. *Birth: Issues in Perinatal Care, 35*(1), 50–59.

Baillargeon, R. (2008). Innate ideas revisited: For a principle of persistence in infants' physical reasoning. *Perspectives on Psychological Science, Special Issue: From Philosophical Thinking to Psychological Empiricism, 3*(1), 2–13

Baillargeon, R., Needham, A., & DeVos, J. (1992). The development of young infants' intuitions about support. *Early Development & Parenting, 1*(2), 69–78.

Baillargeon, R., Spelke, E. S., & Wasserman, S. (1985). Object permanence in five-month-old infants. *Cognition, 20*(3), 191–208.

Baker, K., & Raney, A. A. (2007). Equally super? Gender-role stereotyping of superheroes in children's animated programs. *Mass Communication and Society, 10*(1), 25–41.

Bakermans-Kranenburg, M. J., van IJzendoorn, M. H., & Juffer, F. (2003). Less is more: Meta-analyses of sensitivity and attachment interventions in early childhood. *Psychological Bulletin, 129*(2), 195–215.

Balaban, M. T., & Reisenauer, C. D. (2005). Sensory development. In *Encyclopedia of human development*. Thousand Oaks, CA: Sage. Retrieved from http://www.sage-ereference.com/humandevelopment/Article_n555.html

Baldry, A. C., & Farrington, D. P. (2000). Bullies and delinquents: Personal characteristics and parental styles. *Journal of Community & Applied Social Psychology, 10*(1), 17–31.

Baldwin, D. A., & Moses, L. J. (2001). Links between social understanding and early word learning: Challenges to current accounts. *Social Development, 10*(3), 309–329.

Bali Travel Guidebook. (2002). *Royal Odalan and tooth filing ceremony (Mepandes)*. Retrieved from http://www.klubkokos.com/guidebook/royal_odalan.htm

Banaschewski, T., & Brandeis, D. (2007). What electrical brain activity tells us about brain function that other techniques cannot tell us—A child psychiatric perspective. *Journal of Child Psychology and Psychiatry, 4*(5), 415–435.

Bandura, A. (1986). *Social foundations of thought and action*. Englewood Cliffs, NJ: Prentice Hall.

Bandura, A., Caprara, G. V., Barbaranelli, C., Pastorelli, C., & Regalia, C. (2001). Sociocognitive self-regulatory mechanisms governing transgressive behavior. *Journal of Personality and Social Psychology, 80*(1), 125–135.

Bandura, A., Ross, D., & Ross, S. A. (1963). Imitation of film-mediated aggressive models. *Journal of Abnormal and Social Psychology, 66*(1), 3–11.

Banks, R. (1997). *Bullying in schools*. Eric Document ED 407154.

Bar-Haim, Y., Dan, O., Eshel, Y., & Sagi-Schwartz, A. (2007). Predicting children's anxiety from early attachment relationships. *Journal of Anxiety Disorders, 21*(8), 1061–1068.

Barber, B. K. (1994). Cultural, family, and personal contexts of parent-adolescent conflict. *Journal of Marriage and Family, 56*(2), 375–386.

Barcelona Field Studies Centre. (2010). *Data presentation: Scatter graphs*. Retrieved from http://geographyfieldwork.com/DataPresentationScatterGraphs.htm

Barger, T. S. (2008). Raising their profile. *Hartford Courant*, p. A1.

Barker, L. (2006). Teaching evolutionary psychology: An interview with David M. Buss. *Teaching of Psychology, 33*(1), 69–76.

Barker, R. D., & Wright, H. F. (1951). *One boy's day: A specimen record of behavior*. New York, NY: Harper.

Barker, R. G., & Associates. (1978). *Habitats, environments, and human behavior.* San Francisco, CA: Jossey-Bass.

Barkin, S., Ip, E., Richardson, I., Klinepeter, S., Finch, S., & Krcmar, M. (2006). Parental media mediation styles for children aged 2 to 11 years. *Archives of Pediatrics & Adolescent Medicine, 160*(4), 395–401.

Barkley, R. A. (1991). *Attention deficit and hyperactivity disorder—A clinical workbook.* New York, NY: Guilford.

Barkley, R. A. (2006). Attention-deficit/hyperactivity disorder. In D. A. Wolfe & E. J. Mash (Eds.), *Behavioral and emotional disorders in adolescents* (pp. 91–152). New York, NY: Guilford.

Barkley, R. A. (2008). *ADHD in adults: What the science says.* New York, NY: Guilford.

Barlett, C. P., Harris, R. J., & Bruey, C. (2008). The effect of the amount of blood in a violent video game on aggression, hostility, and arousal. *Journal of Experimental Social Psychology, 44*(3), 539–546.

Baron-Cohen, S. (1995). *Mindblindness.* Cambridge, MA: MIT Press.

Baron-Cohen, S. (2001). Theory of mind and autism: A review. In L. M. Glidden (Ed.), *International Review of Research in Mental Retardation: Autism* (Vol. 23, pp. 169–184). San Diego, CA: Academic Press.

Barr, R. G. (1995). Infant crying and colic: It's a family affair: Invited commentary. *Infant Mental Health Journal, 16*(3), 218–220.

Barriere, D. (n.d.). *History of child abuse.* Retrieved from http://www.child-abuse-effects.com/history.html

Barros, R. M., Silver, E. J., & Stein, R. E. K. (2009). School recess and group classroom behavior. *Pediatrics, 123*(2), 431–436.

Bartlett, E. E. (2004). The effect of fatherhood on the health of men: A review of the literature. *Journal of Men's Health and Gender, 1*(2–3), 159–169.

Bartsch, R. A., Judd, C. M., Louw, D. A., Park, B., & Ryan, C. S. (1997). Cross-national outgroup homogeneity: United States and South African stereotypes. *South African Journal of Psychology, 27*(3), 166–170.

Baskett, L. M. (1984). Ordinal position differences in children's family interactions. *Developmental Psychology, 20,*1026–1031.

Bassoff, E. S., & Glass, G. V. (1982). The relationship between sex roles and mental health: A meta-analysis of twenty-six studies. *Counseling Psychologist, 10*(4), 105–112.

Bates, E. (1990). Language about me and you: Pronominal reference and the emerging concept of self. In D. Cicchetti & M. Beeghly (Eds.), *The self in transition* (pp. 165–182). Chicago, IL: University of Chicago Press.

Bauer, P. J. (2007). Recall in infancy: A neurodevelopmental account. *Current Directions in Psychological Science, 16*(3), 142–146.

Baumeister, R. F. (1996). Should schools try to boost self-esteem? Beware the dark side. *American Educator, 20*(2), 14–19, 43.

Baumeister, R. F., Campbell, J. D., Krueger, J. I., & Vohs, K. D. (2003). Does high self-esteem cause better performance, interpersonal success, happiness, or healthier lifestyles? *Psychological Science in the Public Interest, 4*(1), 1–44.

Baumrind, D. (1967). Child care practices anteceding three patterns of preschool behavior. *Genetic Psychology Monographs, 75*(1), 43–88.

Baumrind, D. (1971). Current patterns of parental authority. *Developmental Psychology Monograph, 4*(1), Part 2, 1–103.

Baumrind, D. (1991a). Effective parenting during the early adolescent transition. In P. A. Cowan & E. M. Hetherington (Eds.), *Family transitions* (pp. 111–163). Hillsdale, NJ: Erlbaum.

Baumrind, D. (1991b). The influence of parenting style on adolescent competence and substance use. *Journal of Early Adolescence, 11*(1), 56–95.

BBC News. (1998). *Evel Knievel's son smashes stunt record.* Retrieved from http://news.bbc.co.uk/2/hi/in_depth/60039.stm

BBC News. (2005). *Why do Kenyans dominate marathons?* Retrieved from http://news.bbc.co.uk/2/hi/africa/4405082.stm

Bear, M. F., Connors, B. W., & Paradiso, M. A. (2007). *Neuroscience exploring the brain* (3rd ed.). Baltimore, MD: Lippincott, Williams & Wilkins.

Bearman, P. S., & Brucker, H. (2001). Promising the future: Virginity pledges and first intercourse. *American Journal of Sociology, 106*, 859–912.

Beasley, N. M. R., Hall, A., Tomkins, A. M., Donnelly, C., Ntimbwa, P., Kivuga, J., . . . Bundy, D. A. P. (2000). The health of enrolled and non enrolled children of school age in Tanga, Tanzania. *Acta Tropica, 76*(3), 223.

Becher, J. C. (2006). *Insights into early fetal development.* Royal College of Physicians of Edinburgh and Royal College of Physicians and Surgeons of Glasgow. Retrieved from http://behindthemedicalheadlines.com/articles/insights-into-early-fetal-development

Beck, H. P., Levinson, S., & Irons, G. (2009). Finding Little Albert: A journey to John B. Watson's infant laboratory. *American Psychologist, 64*(7), 605–614.

Beeler, S. B., & Karas, G. B. (2001). *Throw your tooth on the roof: Tooth traditions from around the world.* Boston, MA: Houghton Mifflin.

Beemsterboer, S. N., Homburg, R., Gorter, N. A., Schats, R., Hompes, P. G. A., & Lambalk, C. B. (2006). The paradox of declining fertility but increasing twinning. *Human Reproduction, 21*(6), 1531–1532.

Beer, W. R. (1989). *Strangers in the house: The world of stepsiblings and half-siblings.* New Brunswick, NJ: Transaction.

Bell, J. (2008). *Yale professor recognized for commitment to children and youth.* Retrieved from http://ziglercenter.yale.edu/documents/CTVoicesaward-Gilliam.pdf

Bell, S. M., & Ainsworth, M. D. (1972). Infant crying and maternal responsiveness. *Child Development, 43*(4), 1171–1190.

Bellin, H. F., & Singer, D. G. (2006). My magic story car: Video based play intervention to strengthen emergent literacy of at-risk preschoolers. In D. G. Singer, R. M. Golinkoff, & K. Hirsh-Pasek (Eds.), *Play=learning* (pp. 101–123). New York, NY: Oxford University Press.

Belsky, J. (2005). Attachment theory and research in ecological perspective. In K. E. Grossmann, K. Grossmann, & E. Waters (Eds.), *Attachment from infancy to adulthood: The major longitudinal studies* (pp. 71–97). New York, NY: Guilford.

Belsky, J., Burchinal, M., McCartney, K., Vandell, D. L., Clarke-Stewart, K. A., Owen, M. T., & the NICHD Early Child Care Research Network. (2007). Are there long-term effects of early child care? *Child Development, 78*(2), 681–701.

Belsky, J., & Eggebeen, D. (1991). Early and extensive maternal employment and young children's socioemotional development: Children of the National Longitudinal Survey of Youth. *Journal of Marriage and Family, 53*, 1083–1098.

Belsky, J., & Kelly, J. (1994). *The transition to parenthood: How a first child changes a marriage.* New York, NY: Delacorte Press.

Belsky, J., Steinberg, L. D., Houts, R. M., Friedman, S. L., DeHart, G., Cauffman, E., . . . NICHD Early Child Care Research Network. (2007). Family rearing antecedents of pubertal timing. *Child Development, 78*(4), 1302–1321.

Bem, S. L. (1974). The measurement of psychological androgyny. *Journal of Consulting and Clinical Psychology, 42*(2), 155–162.

Bem, S. L. (1981). Gender schema theory: A cognitive account of sex typing. *Psychological Review, 88*(4), 354–364.

Bem, S. L. (1989). Genital knowledge and gender constancy in preschool children. *Child Development, 60*(3), 649–662.

Bem, S. L., & Lewis, S. A. (1975). Sex role adaptability: One consequence of psychological androgyny. *Journal of Personality and Social Psychology, 31*(4), 634–643.

Bengtson, V. L. (2001). Beyond the nuclear family: The increasing importance of multigenerational bonds [The Burgess Award Lecture]. *Journal of Marriage and Family, 63*, 1–16.

Bengtsson, S. L., Nagy, Z., Skare, S., Forsman, L., Forssberg, H., & Ullén, F. (2005). Extensive piano practicing has regionally specific effects on white matter development. *Nature Neuroscience, 8*(9), 1148–1150.

Benight, C. C., & Bandura, A. (2004). Social cognitive theory of posttraumatic recovery: The role of perceived self-efficacy. *Behaviour Research and Therapy, 42*, 1129–1148.

Benson, A. (n.d.). *Statistical significance versus practical significance.* Retrieved from http://

www.umich.edu/~numbers/statistics/statistics2.html

Benson, E. (2003). Intelligent intelligence testing. *Monitor on Psychology, 34*(2), 48.

Benson, P. L. (1993). *The troubled journey: A portrait of 6th-12th grade youth.* Minneapolis, MN: Search Institute.

Benson, P. L., Mangen, D. J., & Williams, D. L. (1986). *Adults who influence youth: Perspective from 5th-12th grade students.* Minneapolis, MN: Search Institute.

Berg, S. J., & Wynne-Edwards, K. E. (2001). Changes in testosterone, cortisol, and estradiol levels in men becoming fathers. *Mayo Clinic Proceedings, 76,* 582–592.

Berge, J. M., Mendenhall, T. J., Wrobel, G. M., Grotevant, H. D., & McRoy, R. G. (2006). Adolescents' feelings about openness in adoption: Implications for adoption agencies. *Child Welfare Journal, 85*(6), 1011–1039.

Berger, L., Brooks-Gunn, J., Paxson, C., & Waldfogel, J. (2008). First-year maternal employment and child outcomes: Differences across racial and ethnic groups. *Children and Youth Services Review, 30*(4), 365–387.

Bergh, S., & Erling, A. (2005). Adolescent identity formation: A Swedish study of identity status using the EOM-EIS-II. *Adolescence, 40*(158), 377–396.

Bergsma, L., & Ingram, M. (2001). *Blowing smoke—Project evaluation final report.* Retrieved from http://www.scenesmoking.org/research/BlowingSmoke.pdf

Berk, L. E., Mann, T. D., & Ogan, A. T. (2006). Make-believe play: Wellspring for development of self-regulation. In D. G. Singer, R. M. Golinkoff, & K. Hirsh-Pasek (Eds.), *Play=learning* (pp. 74–100). New York, NY: Oxford University Press.

Berk, L. E., & Winsler, A. (1995). *Scaffolding children's learning: Vygotsky and early childhood education.* Washington, DC: National Association for the Education of Young Children.

Bernard, J. (1972). *The future of marriage.* New Haven, CT: Yale University Press.

Berndt, T. (1979). Developmental changes in conformity to peers and parents. *Developmental Psychology, 15*(6), 608–616.

Berti, A. E., Garattoni, C., & Venturini, B. (2000). The understanding of sadness, guilt, and shame in 5-, 7-, and 9-year-old children. *Genetic, Social, and General Psychology Monographs, 126*(3), 293–318.

Bhanot, R., & Jovanovic, J. (2005). Do parents' academic gender stereotypes influence whether they intrude on their children's homework? *Sex Roles, 52*(9–10), 597–607.

Bialystok, E. (2001). *Bilingualism in development: Language, literacy, and cognition.* New York, NY: Cambridge University Press.

Bialystok, E. (2007). Acquisition of literacy in bilingual children: A framework for research. *Language Learning, 57,* 45–77.

Bialystok, E., & Viswanathan, M. (2009). Components of executive control with advantages for bilingual children in two cultures. *Cognition, 112*(3), 494–500.

Bianchi, S. M., Robinson, J. P., & Milkie, M. A. (2006). *Changing rhythms of American family Life.* New York, NY: Russell Sage Foundation.

Biasini, F. J., Grupe, L., Huffman, L., & Bray, N. W. (1999). Mental retardation: A symptom and a syndrome. In S. Netherton, D. Holmes, & C. E. Walker (Eds.), *Comprehensive textbook of child and adolescent disorders* (pp. 6–23). New York, NY: Oxford University Press.

Biblarz, T. J., & Gottainer, G. (2000). Family structure and children's success: A comparison of widowed and divorced single-mother families. *Journal of Marriage and Family, 62,* 533–548.

Biddle, B. J., & Berliner, D. C. (2002). Small class size and its effects. *Educational Leadership, 59*(5), 12–23.

Bieber, L., Dince, P., Drellich, M., Grand, H., Gundlach, R., Kremer, M., . . . Bieber, T. (1962). *Homosexuality: A psychoanalytic study of male homosexuals.* New York, NY: Basic Books.

Bigham, S. (2008). Comprehension of pretence in children with autism. *British Journal of Developmental Psychology, 26*(2), 265–280.

Bigler, R. S., & Liben, L. S. (1993). A cognitive-developmental approach to racial stereotyping and reconstructive memory in Euro-American children. *Child Development, 64*(5), 1507–1518.

Billy, J. O., & Udry, J. R. (1985). Patterns of adolescent friendship and effects on sexual behavior. *Social Psychology Quarterly, 48*(1), 27–41.

Binder, E. B., Bradley, R. G., Liu, W., Epstein, M. P., Deveau, T. C., Mercer, K. B., . . . Ressler, K. J. (2008). Association of *FKBP5* polymorphisms and childhood abuse with risk of posttraumatic stress disorder symptoms in adults. *JAMA, 299*(11), 1291–1305.

Bingham, A., & Pennington, J. L. (2007). As easy as ABC: Facilitating early literacy enrichment experiences. *Young Exceptional Children, 10*(2), 17–29.

Birdsong, D., & Molis, M. (2001). On the evidence for maturational constraints in second-language acquisition. *Journal of Memory and Language, 44*(2), 235–249.

Bishop, S. L., Luyster, R., Richler, J., & Lord, C. (2008). Diagnostic assessment. In K. Chawarska, A. Klin, & F. R. Volkmar (Eds.), *Autism spectrum disorders in infants and toddlers: Diagnosis, assessment, and treatment* (pp. 23–49). New York, NY: Guilford.

Bittner, A., Egger, H. L., Erkanli, A., Costello, E. J., Foley, D. L., & Angold, A. (2007). What do childhood anxiety disorders predict? *Journal of Child Psychology and Psychiatry, 48*(12), 1174–1183.

Black, M. M., Hess, C. R., & Berenson-Howard, J. (2000). Toddlers from low-income families have below normal mental, motor, and behavior scores on the Revised Bayley Scales. *Journal of Applied Developmental Psychology, 26*(6), 655–666.

Blackwell, G. L. (2010). A little help along the way. *Outlook, 104*(1), 16–19.

Blair, C., Zelazo, P. D., & Greenberg, M. T. (2005). The measurement of executive function in early childhood. *Developmental Neuropsychology, 28*(2), 561–571.

Blakeslee, S. (1997). When an adult adds a language, it's one brain, two systems. *The New York Times,* p. C4.

Blasi, C. H., & Bjorklund, D. F. (2003). Evolutionary developmental psychology: A new tool for better understanding human ontogeny. *Human Development, 46,* 259–281.

Blass, E. M., & Hoffmeyer, L. B. (1991). Sucrose as an analgesic in newborn humans. *Pediatrics, 87,* 215–218.

Blatt-Eisengart, I., Drabick, D. A. G., Monahan, K. C., & Steinberg, L. (2009). Sex differences in the longitudinal relations among family risk factors and childhood externalizing symptoms. *Developmental Psychology, 45*(2), 491–502.

Blood, D. C., Studdert, V. P., & Gay, C. C. (Eds.). (2007). *Saunders comprehensive veterinary dictionary* (3rd ed.). London, England: Elsevier.

Bloom, C. M., & Lamkin, D. M. (2006). The Olympian struggle to remember the cranial nerves: Mnemonics and student success. *Teaching of Psychology, 33*(2), 128–129.

Bluestone, C., & Tamis-LeMonda, C. S. (1999). Correlates of parenting styles in predominantly working- and middle-class African American mothers. *Journal of Marriage and Family, 61*(4), 881–893.

Bobo, J. K., Klepinger, D. H., & Dong, F. B. (2006). Changes in the prevalence of alcohol use during pregnancy among recent and at-risk drinkers in the NLSY cohort. *Journal of Women's Health, 15*(9), 1061–1070.

Bohannon, J. N., & Bonvillian, J. D. (2005). Theoretical approaches to language acquisition. In J. B. Gleason (Ed.), *The development of language* (6th ed., pp. 230–291). Boston, MA: Pearson.

Boksa, P. (2008). Maternal infection during pregnancy and schizophrenia. *Journal of Psychiatry & Neuroscience, 33*(3), 183–185.

Booth, A., & Amato, P. R. (2001). Parental predivorce relations and offspring postdivorce well-being. *Journal of Marriage and Family, 63*(1), 197–212.

Booth-LaForce, C., Oh, W., Kim, A. H., Rubin, K. H., Rose-Krasnor, L., & Burgess, K. (2006). Attachment, self-worth, and peer-group functioning in middle childhood. *Attachment & Human Development, 8*(4), 309–325.

Booth-LaForce, C., & Oxford, M. L. (2008). Trajectories of social withdrawal from grades 1 to 6: Prediction from early parenting, attachment, and temperament. *Developmental Psychology, 44*(5), 1298–1313.

Bornstein, M. H., Hahn, C., Bell, C., Haynes, O. M., Slater, A., Golding, J., . . . ALSPAC Study Team. (2006). Stability in cognition across early childhood: A developmental cascade. *Psychological Science, 17*(2), 151–158.

Bornstein, M. H., & Sigman, M. D. (1986). Continuity in mental developmental from infancy. *Child Development, 57,* 251–274.

Borntrager, C., Davis, J. L., Bernstein, A., & Gorman, H. (2009). A cross-national perspective on bullying. *Child & Youth Care Forum, 38*(3), 121–134.

Borse, N. N., Gilchrist, J., Dellinger, A. M., Rudd, R. A., Ballesteros, M. F., & Sleet, D. A. (2008). *CDC childhood injury report: Patterns of unintentional injuries among 0–19 year olds in the United States, 2000–2006.* Atlanta, GA: Centers for Disease Control and Prevention, National Center for Injury Prevention and Control.

Bortolus, R., Parazzini, F., Chatenoud, L., Benzi, G., Bianchi, M. M., & Marini, A. (1999). The epidemiology of multiple births. *Human Reproduction Update, 5*(2), 179–187.

Bosma, H., & Gerlsma, C. (2003). From early attachment relations to the adolescent and adult organization of self. In J. Walsiner & K. J. Connolly (Eds.), *Handbook of developmental psychology* (pp. 450–488). Thousand Oaks, CA: Sage.

Bosman, J. (2007). A plan to pay for top scores on some tests gains ground. *The New York Times.* Retrieved from http://www.nytimes.com/2007/06/09/nyregion/09schools.html

Bouchard, T., Lykken, D. T., McGue, M., & Segal, N. (1990). Sources of human psychological differences: The Minnesota Study of Twins Reared Apart. *Science, 250*(4978), 223–228.

Bouchard, T. J., Jr., & McGue, M. (1981). Familial studies of intelligence: A review. *Science, 212*(29), 1055–1059.

Bower, B. (2004). The brain's word act: Reading verbs revs up motor cortex areas. *Science News, 165*(6), 83.

Bower, B. (2005). Investing on a whiff. *Science News, 167*(23), 356–357.

Bower, B. (2006). In sickness and in death: Spouses' ills imperil partners' survival. *Science News, 169*(7), 99. Retrieved from http://www.sciencenews.org/articles/20060218/fob1.asp

Bowlby, J. (1958). The nature of the child's tie to his mother. *International Journal of Psycho-Analysis, 39,* 350–373.

Bowlby, J. (1969). *Attachment and loss: Vol. 1. Attachment.* New York, NY: Basic Books.

Bowman, L. L., Levine, L. E., Waite, B. M., & Gendron, M. (2010). Can students really multitask? An experimental study of instant messaging while reading. *Computers & Education, 54*(4), 927–931.

Boyd, R. (2008). Do people only use 10 percent of their brains? *Scientific American.* Retrieved from http://www.scientificamerican.com/article.cfm?id=people-only-use-10-percent-of-brain

Boyes, M. C., & Allen, S. G. (1993). Styles of parent-child interaction and moral reasoning in adolescence. *Merrill-Palmer Quarterly, 39*(4), 551–570.

Boyse, K., Boujaoude, L., & Laundy, J. (2010). *Children with chronic conditions.* University of Michigan Health System. Retrieved from http://www.med.umich.edu/yourchild/topics/chronic.htm

Bradley, R. H., Corwyn, R. F., McAdoo, H. P., & Garcia Coll, C. (2001). The home environments of children in the United States: Part I. Variations by age, ethnicity, and poverty status. *Child Development, 72*(6), 1844–1867.

Branch, D. W., & Scott, J. R. (2003). Early pregnancy loss. In J. S. Scott, R. S. Gibbs, B. Y. Karlan, & A. F. Haney (Eds.), *Danforth's obstetrics and gynecology* (9th ed., pp. 75–87). Philadelphia, PA: Lippincott.

Brandon, D. J. (2006). Can four hours make a difference? Evaluation of a parent education program for divorcing parents. *Journal of Divorce & Remarriage, 45*(1–2), 171–185.

Bratton, S. C., Ray, D., & Rhine, T. (2005). The efficacy of play therapy with children: A meta-analytic review of treatment outcomes. *Professional Psychology: Research and Practice, 36*(4), 376–390.

Braungart-Rieker, J., Courtney, S., & Garwood, M. M. (1999). Mother- and father-infant attachment: Families in context. *Journal of Family Psychology, 13*(4), 535–553.

Bregman, J. (2005). Apgar Score. *Encyclopedia of Human Development.* Thousand Oaks, CA: Sage. Retrieved from http://www.sage-eref erence.com/humandevel opment/Article_n

Bremner, J. G., Johnson, S. P., Slater, A., Mason, U., Foster, K., Cheshire, A., & Spring, J. (2005). Conditions for young infants' perception of object trajectories. *Child Development, 76*(5), 1029–1043.

Brennan, A., Marshall-Lucette, S., Ayers, S., & Ahmed, H. (2007). A qualitative exploration of the Couvade syndrome in expectant fathers. *Journal of Reproductive & Infant Psychology, 25*(1), 18–39.

Brisch, K. H., Bechinger, D., Betzler, S., Heinemann, H., Kächele, H., Pohlandt, F., . . . Buchheim, A. (2005). Attachment quality in very low-birthweight premature infants in relation to maternal attachment representations and neurological development. *Parenting: Science and Practice, 5*(4), 311–331.

Britsch, B., Callahan, N., & Peterson, K. (2010). The power of partnerships. *Outlook, 104*(1), 13–15.

Broadbent, D. E. (1987). *Perception and communication.* New York, NY: Oxford University Press. (Original work published in 1958; Elmsford, NY: Pergamon Press)

Brody, G. H., Chen, Y., Murry, V. M., Ge, X., Simons, R. L., Gibbons, F. X., . . . Cutrona, C. E. (2006). Perceived discrimination and the adjustment of African-American youths: A five year longitudinal analysis with contextual moderation effects. *Child Development, 77*(5), 1170–1189.

Brody, L. E. (2005). The study of exceptional talent. *High Ability Studies, 16*(1), 87–96.

Bronfenbrenner, U. (1970). *Two worlds of childhood: U.S. and U.S.S.R.* New York, NY: Russell Sage Foundation.

Bronfenbrenner, U. (1975). Reality and research in the ecology of human development. *Proceedings of the American Philosophical Society, 119*(6), 439–469.

Bronfenbrenner, U. (1977). Toward an experimental ecology of human development. *American Psychologist, 32*(7), 513–531.

Bronfenbrenner, U. (1986). Ecology of the family as a context for human development: Research perspectives. *Developmental Psychology, 22*(6), 723–742.

Brooks-Gunn, J., & Duncan, G. J. (1997). The effects of poverty on children. *The Future of Children, 7*(2), 55–71.

Brophy, J. E. (1983). Research on the self-fulfilling prophecy and teacher expectations. *Journal of Educational Psychology, 75*(5), 631–661.

Brophy-Herb, H. E., Lee, R. E., Nievar, M. A., & Stollak, G. (2007). Preschoolers' social competence: Relations to family characteristics, teacher behaviors and classroom climate. *Journal of Applied Developmental Psychology, 28*(2), 134–148.

Brotherson, S. E. (2004). *The transition from partners to parents.* North Dakota State University Extension Publication, FS-604.

Brotherson, S. E. (2007). From partners to parents: Couples and the transition to parenthood. *International Journal of Childbirth Education, 22*(2), 7–12.

Brouwers, S. A., Mishra, R. C., & Van de Vijver, F. J. R. (2006). Schooling and everyday cognitive development among Kharwar children in India: A natural experiment. *International Journal of Behavioral Development, 30*(6), 559–567.

Brown, A. S., & Susser, E. (2008). Prenatal nutritional deficiency and risk of adult schizophrenia. *Schizophrenia Bulletin, 34*(6), 1054–1063.

Brown, B. B. (1982). The extent and effect of peer pressure among high school students: A retrospective study. *Journal of Youth and Adolescence, 11,* 121–133.

Brown, B. B. (1993). Peer groups and peer cultures. In S. S. Feldman & G. R. Elliott (Eds.), *At the threshold: The developing adolescent* (pp. 171–196). Cambridge, MA: Harvard University Press.

Brown, B. B. (2004). Adolescents' relationships with peers. In R. M. Lerner & L. Steinberg (Eds.), *Handbook of adolescent psychology* (2nd ed., pp. 363–394). Hoboken, NJ: Wiley.

Brown, B. B., & Klute, C. (2003). Friendships, cliques, and crowds. In G. R. Adams & M. D. Berzonsky (Eds.), *Blackwell handbook of adolescence* (pp. 330–348). Malden, MA: Blackwell.

Brown, E. D., Benedett, B., & Armistead, M. E. (2010). Arts enrichment and school readiness for children at risk. *Early Childhood Research Quarterly, 25,* 112–124.

Brown University Department of Cognitive & Linguistic Sciences. (n.d.). Image of Piaget's three mountains task. Retrieved from http://www.cog.brown.edu/courses/cg63/images/3_mountains.gif

Browne, A., & Finkelhor, D. (1986). Initial and long-term effect: A review of the research. In D. Finkelhor & Associates (Eds.), *A sourcebook on child sexual abuse* (pp. 143–179). Beverly Hills, CA: Sage.

Browne, J. V. (2005). Preterm infants. *Encyclopedia of human development.* Thousand Oaks, CA: Sage. Retrieved from http://www.sage-ereference.com/humandevelopment/Article_n496.html

Brownell, C., & Carriger, M. S. (1990). Changes in cooperation and self-other differentiation during the second year. *Child Development, 61,* 1164–1174.

Bruck, M., & Ceci, S. (2004). Forensic developmental psychology: Unveiling four common misconceptions. *Current Directions in Psychological Science, 13*(6), 229–232.

Bruder, C. E. G., Piotrowski, A., Gijsbers, A. A. C. J., Andersson, R., Erickson, S., Diaz de Stahl, T., . . . Dumanski, J. P. (2008). Phenotypically concordant and discordant monozygotic twins display different DNA copy-number-variation profiles. *The American Journal of Human Genetics, 82*(3), 763–771.

Brunsma, D. L. (2005). Interracial families and the racial identification of mixed-race children: Evidence from the Early Childhood Longitudinal Study. *Social Forces, 84*(2), 1131–1157.

Brunton, P. J., & Russell, J. A. (2008). The expectant brain: Adapting for motherhood. *Nature Reviews Neuroscience, 9*(1), 11–25.

Bruskas, D. (2008). Children in foster care: A vulnerable population at risk. *Journal of Child and Adolescent Psychiatric Nursing, 21,* 70–77.

Bryson, B. (2006). *The life and times of the Thunderbolt Kid: A memoir.* New York, NY: Broadway Books.

Bryson, M., & Scardamalia, M. (1991). *Teaching writing to students at risk of academic failure.* ERIC Document No. ED338725.

Buckley, K. W. (1989). *Mechanical man: John Broadus Watson and the beginnings of behaviorism.* New York, NY: Guilford.

Bureau of Labor Statistics. (2010). *Occupational outlook handbook.* Retrieved from http://www.bls.gov/OCO/

Burghardt, G. M. (2004). Play and the brain in comparative perspective. In R. L. Clements & L. Fiorentino (Eds.), *The child's right to play—A global approach* (pp. 293–308). Westport, CT: Praeger.

Burns, A., & Dunlop, R. (2002). Parental marital quality and family conflict: Longitudinal effects on adolescents from divorcing and non-divorcing families. *Journal of Divorce & Remarriage, 37*(1–2), 57–74.

Burrell, N. A., Zirbel, C. S., & Allen, M. (2003). Evaluating peer mediation outcomes in educational settings: A meta-analytic review. *Conflict Resolution Quarterly, 21*(1), 7–26.

Bushman, B. J., & Cantor, J. (2003). Media ratings for violence and sex. *American Psychologist, 58*(2), 130–141.

Buss, A. H., & Plomin, R., & Willerman, L. (1973). The inheritance of temperaments. *Journal of Personality, 41*(4), 513–524.

Bussey, K., & Bandura, A. (1999). Social cognitive theory of gender development and differentiation. *Psychological Review, 106*(4), 676–713.

Butterworth, G. (2003). Pointing is the royal road to *language* for babies. In S. Kita (Ed.), *Pointing: Where language, culture, and cognition meet* (pp. 9–33). Mahwah, NJ: Erlbaum.

Byne, W. (1996). Biology and homosexuality: Implications of neuroendocrinological and neuroanatomical studies. In R. P. Cabaj & T. S. Stein (Eds.), *Textbook of homosexuality and mental health* (pp. 129–146). Washington, DC: American Psychiatric Association.

Cacciatore, J. (2009). Appropriate bereavement practice after the death of a Native American child. *Families in Society, 90*(1), 46–50.

Cadoret, R. J., Troughton, E., & O'Gorman, T. W. (1987). Genetic and environmental factors in alcohol abuse and antisocial personality. *Journal of Studies on Alcohol, 48,* 1–8.

Cadoret, R. J., Yates, W. R., Troughton, E., Woodworth, G., & Steward, M. A. (1995). Genetic-environmental interaction in the genesis of aggressivity and conduct disorders. *Archives of General Psychiatry, 52*(11), 916–924.

Calhoun, F., & Warren, K. (2006). Fetal alcohol syndrome: Historical perspectives. *Neuroscience and Biobehavioral Reviews, 31,* 168–171.

California Department of Developmental Services. (1999). *Changes in the population of persons with autism and pervasive developmental disorders in California's developmental services system: 1987 through 1998.* Sacramento, CA: Author.

California State University at Northridge. (2009a). *Services offered.* Retrieved from http://www.csun.edu/counseling/services/offered.htm

California State University at Northridge. (2009b). *Groups & workshops.* Retrieved from http://www.csun.edu/counseling/group/

Camilli, G., Vargas, S., & Yurecko, M. (2003, May 8). Teaching children to read: The fragile link between science and federal education policy. *Education Policy Analysis Archives, 11*(15). Retrieved from http://epaa.asu.edu/epaa/v11n15/

Campbell, S. (2002). Spare the rod? *Psychology Today.* Retrieved from http://www.psychologytoday.com/articles/200210/spare-the-rod

Campbell, S. B., Shaw, D. S., & Gilliom, M. (2000). Early externalizing behavior problems: Toddlers and preschoolers at risk for later maladjustment. *Development and Psychopathology, 12,* 467–488.

Campbell, S. B., Spieker, S., Burchinal, M., Poe, M. D., & NICHD Early Child Care Research Network. (2006). *Journal of Child Psychology and Psychiatry, 47*(8), 791–800.

Campos, J. J., Barrett, K. C., Lamb, M. E., Goldsmith, H. H., & Stenberg, C. (1983). Socioemotional development. In M. M. Haith & J. J. Campos (Eds.), *Handbook of child psychology: Vol. 2. Infancy and psychobiology* (pp. 783–915). New York, NY: Wiley.

Cano, F., & Cardelle-Elawar, M. (2004). An integrated analysis of secondary school students' conceptions and beliefs about learning. *European Journal of Psychology of Education, 19*(2), 167–187.

Cantor, J., Sparks, G. G., & Hoffner, C. (1988). Calming children's television fears: Mr. Rogers vs. The Incredible Hulk. *Journal of Broadcasting and Electronic Media, 32*(3), 271–288.

Caplan, R. (1994). Communication deficits in childhood schizophrenia spectrum disorders. *Schizophrenia Bulletin, 20*(4), 671–683.

Carbo, M. (1996). Whole language vs. phonics: The great debate. *Principal, 75,* 36–38.

Carlo, G., Raffaelli, M., Laible, D. J., & Meyer, K. A. (1999). Why are girls less physically aggressive than boys? Personality and parenting mediators of physical aggression. *Sex Roles, 40*(9–10), 711–729.

Carlson, K. J., Eisenstat, S. A., & Ziporyn, T. (2004). *The new Harvard guide to women's health.* Cambridge, MA: Harvard University Press.

Carlson, V. J., & Harwood, R. L. (2003). Attachment, culture, and the caregiving system: The cultural patterning of everyday experiences among Anglo and Puerto Rican mother-infant pairs. *Infant Mental Health Journal, 24*(1), 53–73.

Carney, A. B., & Merrell, K. W. (2001). Bullying in schools: Perspectives on understanding and preventing an international problem. *School Psychology International, 22*(3), 364–382.

Carpendale, J. I., & Chandler, M. J. (1996). On the distinction between false belief understanding and subscribing to an interpretive theory of mind. *Child Development, 67*(4), 1686–1706.

Carper, R. A., & Courchesne, E. (2005). Localized enlargement of the frontal cortex in early autism. *Biological Psychiatry, 57*(2), 126–133.

Carter, C. S. (2005). The chemistry of child neglect: Do oxytocin and vasopressin mediate the effects of early experience? *Proceedings of the National Academy of Sciences, 102*(51), 18247–18248.

Carter, D. B., & Levy, G. D. (1988). Cognitive aspects of early sex role development: The influence of gender schemas on preschoolers' memories and preferences for sex-typed toys and activities. *Child Development, 59*, 782–792.

Carver, C. S., Scheier, M. F., & Weintraub, J. K. (1989). Assessing coping strategies: A theoretically based approach. *Journal of Personality and Social Psychology, 56*(2), 267–283.

Carver, K., Joyner, K., & Udry, J. R. (2003). National estimates of adolescent romantic relationships. In P. Florsheim (Ed.), *Adolescent romantic relations and sexual behavior: Theory, research, and practical implications* (pp. 23–56). Mahwah, NJ: Erlbaum.

Carver, P. R., Egan, S. K., & Perry, D. G. (2004). Children who question their heterosexuality. *Development Psychology, 40*(1), 43–53.

Case, R. (1985). *Intellectual development: Birth to adulthood*. Orlando, FL: Academic Press.

Case, R. (1998). The development of central conceptual structures. In D. Kuhn & R. Siegler (Eds.), *Handbook of child psychology: Vol. 2—Cognition, perception and language* (5th ed., pp. 745–800). New York, NY: Wiley.

Casey, D. M., Ripke, M. N., & Huston, A. C. (2005). Activity participation and the well-being of children and adolescents in the context of welfare reform. In J. L. Mahoney, R. W. Larson, & J. S. Eccles (Eds.), *Organized activities as contexts of development* (pp. 65–84). Mahwah, NJ: Erlbaum.

Caspi, A., Lynam, D., Moffitt, T. E., & Silva, P. A. (1993). Unraveling girls' delinquency: Biological, dispositional, and contextual contributions to adolescent misbehavior. *Developmental Psychology, 29*, 19–30.

Caspi, A., McClay, J., Moffitt, T. E., Mill, J., Martin, J., Craig, I. W., . . . Poulton, R. (2002). Role of genotype in the cycle of violence in maltreated children. *Science, 297*(5582), 851–854.

Caspi, A., Sugden, K., Moffit, T., Taylor, A., Craig, I. W., Harrington, H., . . . Poulton, R. (2003). Influence of life stress on depression: Moderation by a polymorphism in the 5-HTT gene. *Science, 301*, 386–389.

Catalano, R. F., Berglund, M. L., Ryan, J. A. M., Lonczak, H. S., & Hawkins, J. D. (1998). *Research findings on evaluations of positive youth development programs*. Retrieved from http://aspe.hhs.gov/hsp/PositiveYouthDev99/index.htm

Catsambis, S. (1994). The path to math: Gender and racial-ethnic differences in mathematics participation from middle school to high school. *Sociology of Education, 67*(3), 199–215.

Cattell, R. B. (1963). Theory of fluid and crystallized intelligence: A critical experiment. *Journal of Educational Psychology, 54*, 1–22.

Causey, K., Gardiner, A., & Bjorklund, D. F. (2008). Evolutionary developmental psychology and the role of plasticity in ontogeny and phylogeny. *Psychological Inquiry, 19*(1), 27–30.

Ceci, S. J., & Bruck, M. (1995). *Jeopardy in the courtroom: A scientific analysis of children's testimony*. Washington, DC: American Psychological Association.

Ceci, S. J., Bruck, M., & Loftus, E. F. (1998). On the ethics of memory implantation research. *Applied Cognitive Psychology, 12*(3), 230–240.

Celce-Murcia, M., & Olshtain, E. (2001). *Discourse and context in language teaching: A guide for language teachers*. New York, NY: Cambridge University Press.

Centers for Disease Control and Prevention. (1994). Zidovudine for the prevention of HIV transmission from mother to infants. *Morbidity and Mortality Weekly Report, 43*(16), 285–287.

Centers for Disease Control and Prevention. (2000). *Highlights: Tobacco use and reproductive outcomes*. Retrieved from http://www.cdc.gov/tobacco/data_statistics/sgr/2001/highlights/outcomes/

Centers for Disease Control and Prevention. (2003). Tobacco use among middle and high school students—United States, 2002. *Morbidity and Mortality Weekly Report, 52*(45), 1096–1109.

Centers for Disease Control and Prevention. (2005c). *Alcohol use and pregnancy*. Retrieved from http://www.cdc.gov/ncbddd/factsheets/FAS_alcoholuse.pdf

Centers for Disease Control and Prevention. (2005b). *Intellectual disability*. Retrieved from http://www.cdc.gov/ncbddd/dd/mr2.htm

Centers for Disease Control and Prevention. (2005c). *Trends in reportable sexually transmitted diseases in the United States, 2005: National surveillance data for chlamydia, gonorrhea, and syphilis*. Washington, DC: Author.

Centers for Disease Control and Prevention. (2006). *Fetal alcohol spectrum disorders*. Retrieved from http://www.cdc.gov/ncbddd/fas/fasask.htm#character

Centers for Disease Control and Prevention. (2007a). Distribution of births, by gestational age—United States. *Morbidity and Mortality Weekly Report, 56*(14), 344.

Centers for Disease Control and Prevention. (2007b). *HIV/AIDS*. Retrieved from http://www.cdc.gov/hiv/topics/perinatal/index.htm

Centers for Disease Control and Prevention. (2007c). *What do we know about tobacco use and pregnancy?* Retrieved from http://www.cdc.gov/reproductivehealth/TobaccoUsePregnancy/index.htm

Centers for Disease Control and Prevention. (2008a). *Child maltreatment: Facts at a glance*. Retrieved from http://www.cdc.gov/ncipc/dvp/CM_Data_Sheet.pdf

Centers for Disease Control and Prevention. (2008b). *Physical activity for everyone*. Retrieved from http://www.cdc.gov/physical activity/everyone/guidelines/what_counts.html

Centers for Disease Control and Prevention. (2008c). *STDs and pregnancy—CDC fact sheet*. Retrieved from http://www.cdc.gov/std/STDFact-STDs&Pregnancy.htm

Centers for Disease Control and Prevention. (2008d). *Understanding child maltreatment: Fact sheet 2008*. Retrieved from http://www.cdc.gov/ncipc/pub-res/CMFactsheet.pdf

Centers for Disease Control and Prevention. (2008e). *Understanding school violence: Fact sheet*. Retrieved from http://www.cdc.gov/ncipc/dvp/YVP/SV_FactSheet.pdf

Centers for Disease Control and Prevention. (2009a). *Pediatric HIV/AIDS surveillance (through 2007)*. Retrieved from Centers for Disease Control and Prevention. (2007). *Does breastfeeding reduce the risk of pediatric overweight?* Research to Practice Series No. 4. Atlanta, GA: Author.

Centers for Disease Control and Prevention. (2009b). Prevalence of autism spectrum disorder—Autism and developmental disabilities monitoring network, United States, 2006. *Morbidity and Mortality Weekly Report, 58*(SS-10), 1–20.

Centers for Disease Control and Prevention. (2009c). Quick stats: Birth rates for teens aged 15–19 years, by age group: United States, 1985–2007. *Morbidity and Mortality Weekly Report, 58*(12), 313.

Centers for Disease Control and Prevention. (2010a). Attention-deficit/hyperactivity disorder (ADHD). Retrieved from http://www.cdc.gov/ncbddd/adhd/

Centers for Disease Control and Prevention. (2010b). Youth Risk Behavior Surveillance—United States, 2009. *Morbidity and Mortality Weekly Report, 59*(No. SS-5). Retrieved from http://www.cdc.gov/hiv/topics/surveillance/resources/slides/pediatric/index.htm

Cernoch, J. M., & Porter, R. H. (1985). Recognition of maternal axillary odors by infants. *Child Development, 56*(6), 1593–1598.

Chadwick, B. A., & Heaton, T. B. (1987). *Statistical handbook on the American family*. Phoenix, AZ: Oryx Press.

Chaffin, M., Hanson, R., Saunders, B. E., Nicholls, R., Barnett, D., Zeanah, C., . . . Miller-Perrin, C. (2006). Report of the APSAC task force on attachment therapy, reactive attachment disorder, and attachment problems. *Child Maltreatment, 11*(1), 76–89.

Chang, K. (2007). Adult bipolar disorder is continuous with pediatric bipolar disorder. *The Canadian Journal of Psychiatry /La Revue canadienne de psychiatrie, 52*(7), 418–425.

Chang, S., & Piacentini, J. (2002). Childhood obsessive-compulsive disorder and tic disorders. In D. T. Marsh & M. A. Fristad (Eds.), *Handbook of serious emotional disturbance* (pp. 266–283). New York, NY: Wiley.

Chao, R. K. (1994). Beyond parental control and authoritarian parenting style: Understanding Chinese parenting through the cultural notion of training. *Child Development, 65*(4), 1111–1119.

Cheatham, S. K., Rucker, H. N., & Polloway, E. A. (1995). Savant syndrome: Case studies, hypotheses, and implications for special education. *Education & Training in Mental Retardation & Developmental Disabilities, 30*(3), 243–353.

Chen, C., Greenberger, E., Farruggia, S., Bush, K., & Dong, Q. (2003). Beyond parents and peers: The role of important non-parental adults (VIPs) in adolescent development in China and the United States. *Psychology in the Schools, 40*(1), 35–50.

Chen, E., Cohen, S., & Miller, G. E. (2010). How low socio-economic status affects 2-year hormonal trajectories in children. *Psychological Science, 21*(1), 31–37.

Cherlin, A. J. (2010). Demographic trends in the United States: A review of research in the 2000s. *Journal of Marriage and Family, 72*(3), 403–419.

Cherlin, A. J., Chase-Lansdale, P. L., & McRae, C. (1998). Effects of parental divorce on mental health throughout the life course. *American Sociological Review, 63,* 239–249.

Chernella, J. M. (1991). Symbolic inaction in rituals of gender and procreation among the Garifuna (Black Caribs) of Honduras. *Ethos, 19*(1) 52–67.

Chess, S., & Thomas, A. (1999). *Goodness of fit: Clinical applications from infancy through adult life.* Philadelphia, PA: Brunner/Mazel.

Chess, S., Thomas, A., & Birch, H. G. (1965). *Your child is a person: A psychological approach to childhood without guilt.* New York, NY: Viking Press.

Chew, S. L. (2006). Seldom in doubt but often wrong: Addressing tenacious student misconceptions. In D. S. Dunn & S. L. Chew (Eds.), *Best practices for teaching introduction to* (pp. 211–223). Mahwah, NJ: Erlbaum.

Chi, M. T. H. (1978). Knowledge structures and memory development. In R. S. Siegler (Ed.), *Children's thinking: What develops?* (pp. 73–96). Hillsdale, NJ: Erlbaum.

Child Trends. (2010). *High school dropout rates.* Retrieved from www.childtrendsdatabank .org/alphalist?q=node/162

Child Welfare League of America. (n.d.) *Summary of the Adoption and Safe Families Act of 1997.* Retrieved from http://library .adoption.com/Resources-and-Information/ Summary-of-The-Adoption-And-Safe-Families-Act-of-1997/article/3522/1.html

Chitiyo, M., & Wheeler, J. J. (2006). School phobia: Understanding a complex behavioural response. *Journal of Research in Special Educational Needs, 6*(2), 87–91.

Chodorow, N. J. (1978). *The reproduction of mothering: Psychoanalysis and the socialization of gender.* Berkeley: University of California Press.

Chomsky, N. (1968). *Language and mind.* New York, NY: Harcourt, Brace & World.

Choy, Y., Fyer, A. J., & Lipsitz, J. D. (2007). Treatment of specific phobia in adults. *Clinical Psychology Review, 27*(3), 266–286.

Christakis, D. A., & Zimmerman, F. J. (2007). Violent television viewing during preschool is associated with antisocial behavior during school age. *Pediatrics, 120*(5), 993–999.

Churchill, J. (2006). Why are teeth the only bones we lose? *HHMI Bulletin, 19*(3), 51.

Chye, T. T., Teng, T. K., Hao, T. H., & Seng, J. T. C. (2008). *The new art and science of pregnancy and childbirth: What you want to know from your obstetrician.* Hackensack, NJ: World Scientific.

Cianciolo, A. J., & Sternberg, R. J. (2004). *Intelligence: A brief history.* Malden, MA: Blackwell.

Cicchetti, D., & Toth, S. L. (2009). The past achievements and future promises of developmental psychopathology: The coming of age of a discipline. *Journal of Child Psychology and Psychiatry, 50*(1–2), 16–25.

Cicirelli, V. G. (1980). A comparison of college women's feelings toward their siblings and parents. *Journal of Marriage and Family, 42*(1), 111–118.

Cicirelli, V. G. (1994). Sibling relationships in cross-cultural perspective. *Journal of Marriage and Family, 56*(1), 7–20.

Clark, L. A., Kochanska, G., & Ready, R. (2000). Mothers' personality and its interaction with child temperament as predictors of parenting behavior. *Journal of Personality and Social Psychology, 79*(2), 274–285.

Clark, M. L., & Ayers, M. (1992). Friendship similarity during early adolescence: Gender and racial patterns. *Journal of Psychology: Interdisciplinary and Applied, 126*(4), 393–405.

Clarke-Stewart, K. A., & Hayward, C. (1996). Advantages of father custody and contact for the psychological well-being of school-age children. *Journal of Applied Developmental Psychology, 17,* 239–270.

Clasen, D. R., & Brown, B. B. (1985). The multidimensionality of peer pressure in adolescence. *Journal of Youth and Adolescence, 14*(6), 451–468.

Clemens, J., Elyazeed, R. A., Rao, M., Savarino, S., Morsy, B. Z., Kim, Y., . . . Lee, Y. J. (1999). Early initiation of breastfeeding and the risk of infant diarrhea in rural Egypt. *Pediatrics, 104*(1), e3.

Coates, B., Pusser, H. E., & Goodman, I. (1976). The influence of "Sesame Street" and "Mister Rogers' Neighborhood" on children's social behavior in the preschool. *Child Development, 47*(1), 138–144.

Coe, C. L., & Lubach, G. R. (2008). Fetal programming: Prenatal origins of health and illness. *Current Directions in Psychological Science, 17*(1), 36–41.

Cohany, S. R., & Sok, E. (2007). Trends in labor force participation of married mothers of infants. *Monthly Labor Review, 130,* 9–16.

Cohen, G. J., & the American Academy of Pediatrics Committee on Psychosocial Aspects of Child and Family Health. (2002). Helping children and families deal with divorce and separation. *Pediatrics, 110,* 1019–1023.

Cohen, L. B., Chaput, H. H., & Cashon, C. H. (2002). A constructivist model of infant cognition. *Cognitive Development, 17*(3–4), 1323–1343.

Coie, J. D., Dodge, K. A., & Coppotelli, H. (1982). Dimensions and types of social status: A cross-age perspective. *Developmental Psychology, 18*(4), 557–570.

Cole, M., & Cagigas, X. E. (2010). Cognition. In M. H. Bornstein (Ed.), *Handbook of cultural developmental science* (pp. 127–142). New York, NY: Psychology Press.

Coleman, M., Ganong, L. H., & Warzinik, K. (2007). *Family life in twentieth century America.* Westport, CT: Greenwood Press.

College Board. (2008). *2008 College bound seniors—Total group profile report.* Retrieved from http://professionals.collegeboard.com/ profdownload/Total_Group_Report.pdf

Collins, W. A., & Laursen, B. (2004). Parent-adolescent relationships and influences. In R. M. Lerner & L. Steinberg (Eds.), *Handbook of adolescent psychology* (2nd ed., pp. 331–361). Hoboken, NJ: Wiley.

Collins, W. A., & Russell, G. (1991). Mother-child and father-child relationships in middle childhood and adolescence: A developmental analysis. *Developmental Review, 11*(2), 99–136.

Colombo, J., & Mitchell, D. W. (2009). Infant visual habituation. *Neurobiology of Learning and Memory, 92*(2), 225–234.

Coltrane, S. (2004). Fathering. In M. Coleman & L. H. Ganong (Eds.), *Handbook of contemporary families* (pp. 224–243). Thousand Oaks, CA: Sage.

Compas, B. E., Banez, G. A., Malcarne, V., & Worsham, N. (1991). Perceived control and coping with stress: A developmental perspective. *Journal of Social Issues, 47*(4), 23–34.

Compas, B. E., Malcarne, V. L., & Fondacaro, K. M. (1988). Coping with stressful events in older children and young adolescents. *Journal of Consulting and Clinical Psychology, 56*(3), 405–411.

Comstock, G., & Scharrer, E. (2003). Meta-analyzing the controversy over television violence and aggression. In D. A. Gentile (Ed.), *Media violence and children* (pp. 205–226). Westport, CT: Praeger.

Condry, J., & Condry, S. (1976). Sex differences: A study of the eye of the beholder. *Child Development, 47*(3), 812–819.

Conkle, A. (2009). Keynote address—Nancy Kanwisher: Sharpening the focus on brain function. *APS Monitor,* 7–9.

Connolly, C. J., Craig, W., Goldberg, A., & Pepler, D. (2004). Mixed-gender groups, dating, and romantic relationships in early adolescence. *Journal of Research on Adolescence, 14*(2), 185–207.

Cooley, C. H. (1964). *Human nature and the social order.* New York, NY: Schocken

Books. (Original work published in 1902 by Scribner)

Coontz, S. (2000). Historical perspectives on family diversity. In D. H. Demo, K. R. Allen, & M. A. Fine (Eds.), *Handbook of family diversity* (pp. 15–31). New York, NY: Oxford University Press.

Cooper, P. J., & Goodyear, I. (1993). A community study of depression in adolescent girls. I. Estimates of symptom and syndrome prevalence. *British Journal of Psychiatry, 163,* 369–374.

Cooper, S. M., McLoyd, V. C., Wood, D., & Hardaway, C. R. (2008). Racial discrimination and mental health. In S. M. Quintana & C. McKown (Eds.), *Handbook of race, racism, and the developing child* (pp. 278–312). Hoboken, NJ: Wiley.

Coplan, J. (2000). Counseling parents regarding prognosis in autism spectrum disorder. *Pediatrics, 105*(5), e65.

Corenblum, B. (2003). What children remember about ingroup and outgroup peers: Effects of stereotypes on children's processing of information about group members. *Journal of Experimental Child Psychology, 86*(1), 32–66.

Correll, S. J. (2004). Constraints into preferences: Gender, status, and emerging career aspirations. *American Sociological Review, 69*(1), 93–113.

Cosden, M., Zimmer, J., & Tuss, P. (1993). The impact of age, sex and ethnicity on kindergarten entry and retention decisions. *Educational Evaluation and Policy Analysis, 15*(2), 209–222.

Costin, C. (1999). *The eating disorder sourcebook: A comprehensive guide to the causes, treatments, and prevention of eating disorders.* Los Angeles, CA: Lowell House.

Cote, S. M., Vaillancourt, T., & LeBlanc, J. C. (2006). The development of physical aggression from toddlerhood to pre-adolescence: A nation wide longitudinal study of Canadian children. *Journal of Abnormal Child Psychology, 34*(1), 71–85.

Cotton, K. (1989). *Expectations and student outcomes.* Northwest Regional Educational Laboratory, School Improvement Research Series Close-Up #7. Portland, OR: Northwest Regional Education Laboratory.

Council for Exceptional Children. (2009). *Learning disabilities.* Retrieved from http://www.cec.sped.org/AM/Template.cfm?Section=Learning_Disabilities&Template=/TaggedPage/TaggedPageDisplay.cfm&TPLID=37&ContentID=5629

Courage, M. L., Reynolds, G. D., & Richards, J. E. (2006). Infants' attention to patterned stimuli: Developmental change from 3 to 12 months of age. *Child Development, 77*(3), 680–695.

Courtney, M. E. (2009). The difficult transition to adulthood for foster youth in the US: Implications for the state as corporate parent. *Society for Research in Child Development Social Policy Report, 23*(1), 3–11, 14–18.

Cowan, C. P., & Cowan, P. A. (1992). *When partners become parents.* New York, NY: Basic Books.

Cowan, C. P., & Cowan, P. A. (1995). Interventions to ease the transition to parenthood: Why they are needed and what they can do. *Family Relations, 44*(4), 412–423.

Cox, M., Paley, B., Payne, C. C., & Burchinal, M. (1999). The transition to parenthood: Marital conflict and withdrawal and parent-infant interactions. In M. J. Cox & J. Brooks-Gunn (Eds.), *Conflict and cohesion in families: Causes and consequences* (pp. 87–104). Mahwah, NJ: Erlbaum.

Crain, E. F. (2000). Environmental threats to children's health: A challenge for pediatrics: 2000 Ambulatory Pediatric Association (APA) presidential address. *Pediatrics, 106*(4, Part 2), 871–875.

Crain, W. (2005). *Theories of development: Concepts and applications* (5th ed.). Upper Saddle River, NJ: Pearson Prentice Hall.

Crawford, J. (1995). *Bilingual education: History, politics, theory and practice.* Los Angeles, CA: Bilingual Educational Services.

Crawford, M., & Kaufman, M. R. (2008). Sex trafficking in Nepal: Survivor characteristics and long-term outcomes. *Violence Against Women, 14*(8), 905–916.

Crean, H. F. (2008). Conflict in the Latino parent-youth dyad: The role of emotional support from the opposite parent. *Journal of Family Psychology, 22*(3), 484–493.

Crespo, C. J., Smit, E., Troiano, R. P., Bartlett, S. J., Macera, C. A., & Andersen, R. E. (2001). Television watching, energy intake, and obesity in US children: Results from the third National Health and Nutrition Examination Survey, 1988–1994. *Archives of Pediatrics and Adolescent Medicine, 155*(3), 360–365.

Crick, N. R., Grotpeter, J. K., & Bigbee, M. A. (2002). Relationally and physically aggressive children's intent attributions and feelings of distress for relational and instrumental peer provocations. *Child Development, 73*(4), 1134–1142.

Criss, M. M., & Shaw, D. S. (2005). Sibling relationships as contexts for delinquency training in low-income families. *Journal of Family Psychology, 19*(4), 592–600.

Critchley, C. R., & Sanson, A. V. (2006). Is parent disciplinary behavior enduring or situational? A multilevel modeling investigation of individual and contextual influences on power assertive and inductive reasoning behaviors. *Journal of Applied Developmental Psychology, 27*(4), 370–388.

Crocetti, E., Rubini, M., & Meeus, W. (2008). Capturing the dynamics of identity formation in various ethnic groups: Development and validation of a three-dimensional model. *Journal of Adolescence, 31*(2), 207–222.

Crockenberg, S., & Leerkes, E. (2003). Infant negative emotionality, caregiving, and family relationships. In A. C. Crouter & A. Booth (Eds.), *Children's influence on family dynamics* (pp. 57–78). Mahwah, NJ: Erlbaum.

Crockenberg, S., & Litman, C. (1991). Effects of maternal employment on maternal and two-year-old child behavior. *Child Development, 62*(5), 930–953.

Crockenberg, S. B. (1981). Infant irritability, mother responsiveness, and social support influences on the security of infant–mother attachment. *Child Development, 52*(3), 857–865.

Cromwell, S. (1998a). *The bilingual education debate: Part I.* Retrieved from http://www.education-world.com/a_curr/curr047.shtml

Cromwell, S. (1998b). *The bilingual education debate: Part II.* Retrieved from http://www.education-world.com/a_curr/curr049.shtml

Crosnoe, R., Riegle-Crumb, C., Field, S., Frank, K., & Muller, C. (2008). Peer group contexts of girls' and boys' academic experiences. *Child Development, 79*(1), 139–155.

Crosson-Tower, C. (2003). *The role of educators in preventing and responding to child abuse and neglect.* Washington, DC: U.S. Department of Health and Human Services, Office on Child Abuse and Neglect.

Crouter, A. C., Manke, B. A., & McHale, S. M. (1995). The family context of gender intensification in early adolescence. *Child Development, 66,* 317–329.

Culp, A. M., Culp, R. E., Blankemeyer, M., & Passmark, L. (1998). Parent Education Home Visitation Program: Adolescent and nonadolescent mother comparison after six months of intervention. *Infant Mental Health Journal, 19*(2), 111–123.

Cummings, E. M., Goeke-Morey, M., & Papp, L. (2003). Children's responses to everyday marital conflict tactics in the home. *Child Development, 74,* 1918–1929.

Cunningham, F. G., Leveno, K. J., Bloom, S. L., Hauth, J. C., Gilstrap, L., III., & Wenstrom, K. D. (2005). *Williams obstetrics* (22nd ed.). New York, NY: McGraw-Hill.

Curtis, N. M., Ronan, K. R., & Borduin, C. M. (2004). Multisystemic treatment: A meta-analysis of outcome studies. *Journal of Family Psychology, 18*(3), 411–419.

D'Augelli, A. R. (2003). Lesbian and bisexual female youth aged 14 to 21: Developmental challenges and victimization experiences. *Journal of Lesbian Studies, 7*(4), 9–29.

Dai, D. Y. (2006). There is more to aptitude than cognitive capacities: Comment. *American Psychologist, 61*(7), 723–724.

Dailard, C. (2006). The public health promise and potential pitfalls of the world's first cervical cancer vaccine. *Guttmacher Policy Review, 9*(1), 6–9.

Dales, L., Hammer, S. J., & Smith, N. J. (2001). Time trends in autism and in MMR immunization coverage in California. *Journal of the American Medical Association, 285*(9), 1183–1185.

Damon, W. (2006). Socialization and individuation. In G. Handel (Ed.), *Childhood socialization* (pp. 3–9). New Brunswick, NJ: Aldine Transaction.

Darke, K., Clewell, B., & Sevo, R. (2002). Meeting the challenge: The impact of the National Science Foundation's program for women and girls. *Journal of Women and Minorities in Science and Engineering, 8*(3–4), 285–303.

Darling, N., Cumsille, P., & Martínez, M. L. (2008). Individual differences in adolescents' beliefs about the legitimacy of parental authority and their own obligation to obey: A longitudinal investigation. *Child Development, 79*(4), 1103–1118.

Darling, N., Dowdy, B. B., VanHorn, M. L., & Caldwell, L. L. (1999). Mixed-sex settings and the perception of competence. *Journal of Youth and Adolescence, 28*(4), 461–480.

Darling, N., Hamilton, S. F., & Shaver, K. H. (2003). Relationship outside the family: Unrelated adults. In G. R. Adams & M. D. Berzonsky (Eds.), *Blackwell handbook of adolescence* (pp. 349–370). Malden, MA: Blackwell.

Darling, N., & Steinberg, L. (1993). Parenting style as context: An integrative model. *Psychological Bulletin, 113*(3), 487–496.

Darroch, J. E., & Singh, S. (1999). *Why is teenage pregnancy declining? The roles of abstinence, sexual activity, and contraceptive use* [Occasional Report, No. 1]. New York, NY: Alan Guttmacher Institute.

Darwin, C. (1859). *On the origin of species.* London: John Murray.

Darwin, C. R. (1877). A biographical sketch of an infant. *Mind: A Quarterly Review of Psychology and Philosophy, 2*(7), 285–294.

Dasen, P. R. (1972). Cross-cultural Piagetian research: A summary. *Journal of Cross-Cultural Psychology, 3*(1), 23–40.

Dasen, P. R. (1977). *Piagetian psychology: Cross-cultural contributions.* Oxford, England: Gardner.

Davies, P. G., Spencer, S. J., Quinn, D. M., & Gerhardstein, R. (2002). Consuming images: How television commercials that elicit stereotype threat can restrain women academically and professionally. *Personality and Social Psychology Bulletin, 28*(12), 1615–1628.

Davis, B. E., Moon, R. Y., Sachs, H. C., & Ottolini, M. C. (1998). Effects of sleep position on infant motor development. *Pediatrics, 102*(5), 1135–1140.

Davis, B. G. (1993). *Tools for teaching.* San Francisco, CA: Jossey-Bass.

de Baulny, H. O., Abadie, V., Feillet, F., & de Parscau, L. (2007). Management of phenylketonuria and hyperphenylalaninemia. *Journal of Nutrition, 137,* 1561S–1563S.

de Groot, M. J., Hoeksma, M., Blau, N., Reijngoud, D. J., & van Spronsen, F. J. (2010). Pathogenesis of cognitive dysfunction in phenylketonuria: Review of hypotheses. *Molecular Genetics and Metabolism, 99,* S86–S89.

de Haan, M. (2007). *Infant EEG and event-related potentials.* New York, NY: Psychology Press.

de Medina, P. G. R., Visser, G. H. A., Huizink, A. C., Buitelaar, J. K., & Mulder, E. J. H. (2003). Fetal behaviour does not differ between boys and girls. *Early Human Development, 73*(1–2), 17–26.

de Paula Careta, F., & Louro, I. D. (2005). Cerebral palsy. In S. L. Chamberlin & B. Narins (Eds.), *Gale encyclopedia of neurological disorders* (Vol. 1, pp. 218–223). Detroit, MI: Gale.

Dearing, E., McCartney, K., & Taylor, B. A. (2001). Change in family income-to-needs matters more for children with less. *Child Development, 72*(6), 1779–1793.

DeCasper, A., & Fifer, W. P. (1987). Of human bonding: Newborns prefer their mothers' voices. In J. Oates & S. Sheldon (Eds.), *Cognitive development in infancy* (pp. 111–118). Hillsdale, NJ: Erlbaum.

DeCasper, A. J., & Spence, M. J. (1986). Prenatal maternal speech influences newborns' perception of speech sounds. *Infant Behavior & Development, 19*(2), 133–150.

Dekovic, M. (1999). Parent-adolescent conflict: Possible determinants and consequences. *International Journal of Behavioral Development, 23*(4), 977–1000.

DeLalla, L. F. (1998). *Behavioral genetics.* Mahwah, NJ: Erlbaum.

DeLoache, J., & Gottlieb, A. (2000). *A world of babies.* New York, NY: Cambridge University Press.

Del Rio, P., & Alvarez, A. (2007). Inside and outside the zone of proximal development. In H. Daniels, M. Cole, & J. V. Wertsch (Eds.), *The Cambridge companion to Vygotsky* (pp. 276–303). New York, NY: Cambridge University Press.

Demaray, M. K., & Malecki, C. K. (2003). Perceptions of the frequency and importance of social support by students classified as victims, bullies, and bully/victims in an urban middle school. *School Psychology Review, 32*(3), 471–489.

Demetriou, A., Christou, C., Spanoudis, G., & Platsidou, M. (2002). The development of mental processing: Efficiency, working memory, and thinking. *Monographs of the Society for Research in Child Development, 67*(1, Serial No. 268).

Dempster, F. N. (1981). Memory span: Sources of individual and developmental differences. *Psychological Bulletin, 89*(1), 63–100.

Demuth, K. (1990). Subject, topic, and Sesotho passive. *Journal of Child Language, 17*(1), 67–84.

DeNavas-Walt, C., Proctor, B. D., & Smith, J. C. (2008). *Income, poverty, and health insurance coverage in the United States: 2007* (p. 12). U.S. Census Bureau. Retrieved from http://www.census.gov/prod/2008pubs/p60-235.pdf

Denham, S. A., Renwick, S. M., & Holt, R. W. (1991). Working and playing together: Predictions of preschool social-emotional competence from mother-child interaction. *Child Development, 62*(2), 242–249.

Dennissen, J. J. A., Asendorpf, J. B., & van Aken, M. A. G. (2008). Childhood personality predicts long-term trajectories of shyness and aggressiveness in the context of demographic transitions in emerging adulthood. *Journal of Personality, 76*(1), 67–99.

DeRamirez, R. D., & Shapiro, E. S. (2007). Cross-language relationship between Spanish and English oral reading fluency among Spanish-speaking English language learners in bilingual education classrooms. *Psychology in the Schools, 44*(8), 795–806.

Dersch, C. A., & Munsch, J. (1999). Male victims of sexual abuse: An analysis of substantiation of Child Protective Services reports. *Journal of Child Sexual Abuse, 8*(1), 27–48.

Desmarais, C., Sylvestre, A., Meyer, F., Bairati, I., & Rouleau, N. (2008). Systematic review of the literature on characteristics of late-talking toddlers. *International Journal of Language & Communication Disorders, 43*(4), 361–389.

Desrochers, S. (2008). From Piaget to specific Genevan developmental models. *Child Development Perspectives, 2*(1), 7–12.

Detterman, D. K., & Thompson, L. A. (1997). What is so special about special education? *American Psychologist, 52*(10), 1082–1090.

DevelopmentalBiology.net. (n.d.). *Ectoderm, mesoderm, endoderm.* Retrieved from http://www.developmentalbiology.net/images/neurulasm.jpg

DeVito, D. (Producer), & Niccol, A. (Director). (1997) *Gattaca* [Motion picture]. USA: Columbia Pictures.

Dewey, K. G. (2003). Is breastfeeding protective against child obesity? *Journal of Human Lactation, 19*(1), 9–18.

Diamond, A. (2006). The early development of executive functions. In E. Bialystok & F. I. M. Craik (Eds.), *Lifespan cognition: Mechanisms of change* (pp. 70–95). Oxford, England: Oxford University Press.

Diamond, A. (2009). The interplay of biology and the environment broadly defined. *Developmental Psychology, 45*(1), 1–8.

Diamond, L. M. (2006). What we got wrong about sexual identity development: Unexpected findings from a longitudinal study of young women. In A. M. Omoto & H. S. Kurtzman (Eds.), *Sexual orientation and mental health: Examining identity and development in lesbian, gay, and bisexual people* (pp. 73–94). Washington, DC: American Psychological Association.

Diao, F., & Sundar, S. S. (2004). Orienting response and memory for web advertisements: Exploring effects of pop-up window and animation. *Communication Research, 31,* 537–567.

Dick, D. M., & Rose, R. J. (2004). Behavior genetics: What's new? What's next? In J. Lerner & A. E. Alberts (Eds.), *Current directions in developmental psychology* (pp. 3–10). Upper Saddle River, NJ: Pearson Prentice Hall.

Diego, M. A., Hernandez-Reif, M., Field, T., Friedman, L., & Shaw, K. (2001). HIV adolescents show improved immune function following massage therapy. *International Journal of Neuroscience, 106*, 35–45.

Dieter, J. N. I., Field, T., Hernandez-Reif, M., Emory, E. K., & Redzepi, M. (2003). Stable preterm infants gain more weight and sleep less after five days of massage therapy. *Journal of Pediatric Psychology, 28*(6), 403–411.

DiLalla, L. F., Thompson, L. A., Plomin, R., Phillips, K., Fagan, J. F., III, Haith, M. M., . . . D. W. (1990). Infant predictors of preschool and adult IQ: A study of infant twins and their parents. *Developmental Psychology, 26*(5), 759–769.

Dilworth-Bart, J. E., Khurshid, A., & Vandell, D. L. (2007). Do maternal stress and home environment mediate the relation between early income-to-need and 54-months attentional abilities? *Infant and Child Development, 16*(5), 525–552.

Dinkes, R., Kemp, J., & Baum, K. (2009). *Indicators of school crime and safety: 2008 (NCES 2009-002/NCJ 226343).* National Center for Educational Statistics, Institute for Educational Sciences, U.S. Department of Education, and Bureau of Justice Statistics, Office of Justice Programs, U.S. Department of Justice. Washington, DC.

Diorio, J., & Meaney, M. J. (2007). Maternal programming of defensive responses through sustained effects on gene expression. *Journal of Psychiatry and Neuroscience, 32*(4), 275–284.

DiPietro, J. A., Bornstein, M. H., Costigan, K. A., Pressman, E. K., Hahn, C., Painter, K., . . . Yi, L. J. (2002). What does *fetal* movement predict about behavior during the first two years of life? *Developmental Psychobiology, 40*(4), 358–371.

DiPietro, J. A., Caulfield, L., Costigan, K. A., Merialdi, M., Nguyen, R. H. N., Zavaleta, N., & Gurewitsch, E. D. (2004). Fetal neurobehavioral development: A tale of two cities. *Developmental Psychology, 40*(3), 445–456.

Dishion, T. J., McCord, J., & Poulin, F. (1999). When interventions harm: Peer groups and problem behavior. *American Psychologist, 54*(9), 755–764.

Dishion, T. J., & McMahon, R. J. (1998). Parental monitoring and the prevention of child and adolescent problem behavior: A conceptual and empirical formulation. *Clinical Child and Family Psychology Review, 1*(1), 61–75.

Dishion, T. J., & Owen, L. D. (2002). A longitudinal analysis of friendships and substance use: Bidirectional influence from adolescence to adulthood. *Developmental Psychology, 38*(4), 480–491.

Dishion, T. J., Spracklen, K. M., Andrews, D. W., & Patterson, G. R. (1996). Deviancy training in male adolescents friendships. *Behavior Therapy, 27*(3), 373–390.

Dodge, K. A. (1985). Attributional bias in aggressive children. In P. C. Kendall (Ed.), *Advances in cognitive-behavioral research and therapy* (Vol. 4, pp. 73–110). San Diego, CA: Academic Press.

Dodge, K. A., Coie, J. D., & Lynam, D. (2006). Aggression and antisocial behavior in youth. In N. Eisenberg, W. Damon, & R. M. Lerner (Eds.), *Handbook of childhood psychology: Vol. 3. Social, emotional and personality development* (6th ed., pp. 719–788). Hoboken, NJ: John Wiley & Sons.

Dombrowski, S. C., Noonan, K., & Martin, R. P. (2007). Low birth weight and cognitive *outcomes*: Evidence for a gradient relationship in an urban, poor, African American birth cohort. *School Psychology Quarterly, 22*(1), 26–43.

Doris, J. M. (2002). *Lack of character: Personality and moral behavior.* New York, NY: Cambridge University Press.

Dornbusch, S. M., Ritter, P. L., Leiderman, P. H., & Roberts, D. F. (1987). The relation of parenting style to adolescent school performance. *Child Development, 58*(5), 1244–1257.

Doss, B. D., Rhoades, G. K., Stanley, S. M., & Markman, H. J. (2009). The effect of the transition to parenthood on relationship quality: An 8-year prospective study. *Journal of Personality and Social Psychology, 96*(3), 601–619.

Dowling, W. C. (1999). Enemies of promise: Why America needs the SAT. *Academic Questions, 13*(1), 6–24.

Downey, G., Lebolt, A., Rincón, C., & Freitas, A. L. (1998). Rejection sensitivity and children's interpersonal difficulties. *Child Development, 69*(4), 1074–1091.

Dr. Seuss Enterprises. (2002–2004). *All about Dr. Seuss.* Retrieved from http://www.catinthehat.org/history.htm

Drewes, A. A. (2005). Play in selected cultures: Diversity and universality. In E. Gil & A. A. Drewes (Eds.), *Cultural issues in play therapy* (pp. 26–71). New York, NY: Guilford.

Drews, F. A., Yazdani, H., Godfrey, C. N., Cooper, J. M., & Strayer, D. L. (2009). Text messaging during simulated driving. *Human Factors, 51*(5), 762–770.

Drouin, M., & Davis, C. (2009). R u txting? Is the use of text speak hurting your literacy? *Journal of Literacy Research, 41*(1), 46–67.

Dube, E. M., & Savin-Williams, R. D. (1999). Sexual identity development among ethnic sexual-minority male youth. *Developmental Psychology, 35*(6), 1389–1398.

Dublin, S., Lydon-Rochelle, M., Kaplan, R. C., Watts, D. H., & Critchlow, C. W. (2000). Maternal and neonatal outcomes after induction of labor without an identified indication. *American Journal of Obstetrics & Gynecology, 183*(4), 986–994.

Dubow, E. F., Boxer, P., & Huesmann, L. R. (2008). Childhood and adolescent predictors of early and middle adulthood alcohol use and problem drinking: The Columbia County Longitudinal Study. *Addiction, 103*(Supp. 11), 36–47.

Duckworth, A. L., & Seligman, M. E. P. (2005). Self-discipline outdoes IQ in predicting academic performance of adolescents. *Psychological Science, 16*(12), 939–944.

Duncan, G. J., Brooks-Gunn, J., & Klebanov, P. K. (1994). Economic deprivation and early childhood development. *Child Development, 65*(2), 296–318.

Duncan, G. J., Yeung, W., Brooks-Gunn, K., & Smith, J. R. (1998). How much does childhood poverty affect the life chances of children? *American Sociological Review, 63*(3), 406–423.

Duncan, R. M., & Cheyne, J. A. (2002). Private speech in young adults: Task difficulty, self-regulation, and psychological predication. *Cognitive Development, 16*, 889–906.

Duncan, S. W. (1994). Economic impact of divorce on children's development: Current findings and policy implications. *Journal of Clinical Child Psychology, 23*, 444–457.

Dunn, J. (2002). The adjustment of children in stepfamilies: Lessons from community studies. *Child and Adolescent Mental Health, 7*(4), 154–161.

Dunn, J. (2004). *Children's friendships.* Malden, MA: Blackwell.

Dunn, J. (2005a). Commentary: Siblings in their families. *Journal of Family Psychology, 19*(4), 654–657.

Dunn, J. (2005b). Naturalistic observation of children and their families. In S. Greene & D. Hogan (Eds.), *Researching children's experience: Methods and approaches* (pp. 87–101). Thousand Oaks, CA: Sage.

Dunn, J., Cheng, H., O'Connor, T. G., & Bridges, L. (2004). Children's perspectives on their relationships with their non-resident fathers: Influences, outcomes and implications. *Journal of Child Psychology and Psychiatry, 45*(3), 553–566.

Dunn, J., Fergusson, E., & Maughan, B. (2006). Grandparents, grandchildren, and family change. In A. Clarke-Stewart & J. Dunn (Eds.), *Families count* (pp. 299–318). New York, NY: Cambridge University Press.

Durgunoglu, A. Y. (2002). Cross-linguistic transfer in literacy development and implications for language learners. *Annals of Dyslexia, 52*, 189–204.

Durrant, J. E. (2007). *Positive discipline: What it is and how to do it.* Bangkok, Thailand: Save the Children Sweden.

Dutton, S. E. (2001). Urban youth development—Broadway style: Using theatre and group work as vehicles for positive youth development. *Social Work with Groups, 23*(4), 39–58.

Dweck, C. S. (1999). Caution—Praise can be dangerous. *American Educator, 23*(1), 1–5.

Dwyer, C. A., & Johnson, L. M. (1997). Grades, accomplishments, and correlates. In W. W. Willingham & N. S. Cole (Eds.), *Gender and fair assessment* (pp. 127–156). Mahwah, NJ: Erlbaum.

Dyer, S., & Moneta, G. B. (2006). Frequency of parallel, associate, and cooperative play in British children of different socioeconomic status social behavior and personality. *Social Behavior and Personality, 34*(5), 587–592.

Eccles, J. S. (1999). The development of children ages 6 to 14. *The Future of Children, 9*(2), 30–44.

Eccles, J. S., Midgley, C., Wigfield, A., Buchanan, C. M., Reuman, D., Flanagan, C., & Iver, D. M. (1997). Development during adolescence: The impact of stage-environment fit on young adolescents' experiences in schools and in families. In J. Nottermann (Ed.), *The evolution of psychology: Fifty years of the American Psychologist* (pp. 475–501). Washington, DC: American Psychological Association.

Eccles, J. S., & Templeton, J. (2002). Extracurricular and other after-school activities for youth. *Review of Educational Research, 26,* 113–180.

Eckerman, C. O., & Didow, S. M. (1996). Nonverbal imitation and toddlers' mastery of verbal means of achieving coordinated action. *Developmental Psychology, 32*(1), 141–152.

Eckerman, C. O., & Peterman, K. (2001). Peers and infant social/communicative development. In G. Bremner & A. Fogel (Eds.), *Blackwell handbook of infant development* (pp. 326–350). Malden, MA: Blackwell.

Eckerman, C. O., & Stein, M. R. (1990). How imitation begets imitation and toddlers' generation of games. *Developmental Psychology, 26*(3), 370–378.

Edgren, A. R. (2002). Prematurity. In D. S. Blanchfield & J. L. Longe (Eds.), *Gale encyclopedia of medicine* (Vol. 4, 2nd ed., pp. 2706–2708). Detroit, MI: Gale.

Education Resources Information Center. (n.d.). *About the ERIC collection.* Retrieved from http://www.eric.ed.gov/ERICWebPortal/resources/html/collection/about_collection.html

Education Week. (2004). *Reading.* Retrieved from http://www.edweek.org/rc/issues/reading/

Egeghy, P. P., Sheldon, D. M., Stout, E. A., Cohen-Hubal, N. S., Tulve, L. J., Melnyk, M. K., . . . Coan, A. (2007). *Important exposure factors for children: An analysis of laboratory and observational field data characterizing cumulative exposure to pesticides* (EPA Report 600/R-07/013). Washington, DC: Environmental Protection Agency.

Egger, H. (2009). Toddler with temper tantrums: A careful assessment of a dysregulated preschool child. In C. A. Galanter & P. S. Jensen (Eds.), *DSM-IV-TR casebook and treatment guide for child mental health* (pp. 365–384). Arlington, VA: American Psychiatric Publishing.

Eigsti, I., Zayas, V., Mischel, W., Shoda, Y., Ayduk, O., Dadlani, M. B., . . . Casey, B. J. (2006) Predicting cognitive control from preschool to late adolescence and young adulthood. *Psychological Science, 17*(6), 478–484.

Eisenberg, N., Hofer, C., Spinrad, T. L., Gershoff, E. T., Valiente, C., Losoya, S. H., . . . Maxon, E. (2008). Understanding mother-adolescent conflict discussions: Concurrent and across-time prediction from youths' dispositions and parenting: III. Descriptive analyses and correlations. *Monographs of the Society for Research in Child Development, 73*(2), 54–80.

Eisenberg, N., Hofer, C., & Vaughan, J. (2007). Effortful control and its socioemotional consequences. In J. J. Gross (Ed.), *Handbook of emotion regulation* (pp. 287–306). New York, NY: Guilford.

Eisenberg, N., Spinrad, T. L., & Sadovsky, A. (2006). Empathy-related responding in children. In M. Killen & J. Smetana (Eds.), *Handbook of moral development* (pp. 517–549). Mahwah, NJ: Erlbaum.

Eisler, I., Simic, M., Russell, G. F. M., & Dare, C. (2007). A randomised controlled treatment trial of two forms of family therapy in adolescent anorexia nervosa: A five-year follow-up. *Journal of Child Psychology and Psychiatry, 48,* 552–560.

Eisner, E. W. (1998). Does experience in the arts boost academic achievement? *Art Education, 51*(1), 7–15.

Elbert, T., Pantev, C., Wienbruch, C., Rockstroh, B., & Taub, E. (1995). Increased cortical representation of the fingers of the left hand in string players. *Science, 270*(5234), 305–307.

Elicker, J., Fortner-Wood, C., & Noppe, I. C. (1999). The context of infant attachment in family childcare. *Journal of Applied Developmental Psychology, 20*(2), 319–336.

Eliot, L. (1999). *What's going on in there? How the brain and mind develop in the first five years of life.* New York, NY: Bantam Books.

Elkind, D. (2007a). *The hurried child.* Cambridge, MA: DaCapo.

Elkind, D. (2007b). *The power of play.* Cambridge, MA: DaCapo.

Elkind, D., & Bowen, R. (1979). Imaginary audience behavior in children and adolescents. *Developmental Psychology, 15*(1), 38–44.

Elliott, W. (2009). Children's college aspirations and expectations: The potential role of children's development accounts (CDAs). *Children and Youth Services Review, 31,* 274–283.

Elliott, S., & Umberson, D. (2004). Recent demographic trends in the US and implications for well-being. In J. Scott, J. Treas, & M. Richards (Eds.), *The Blackwell companion to the sociology of families* (pp. 34–53). Malden, MA: Blackwell.

Ellis, B. J., & Essex, M. J. (2007). Family environments, adrenarche, and sexual maturation: A longitudinal test of a life history model. *Child Development, 78*(6), 1799–1817.

Ellsworth, C. P., Muir, D. W., & Hains, S. M. J. (1993). Social competence and person-object differentiation: An analysis of the still-face effect. *Developmental Psychology, 29*(1), 63–73.

Else-Quest, N. M., Hyde, J. S., & Linn, M. C. (2010). Cross-national patterns of gender differences in mathematics: A meta-analysis. *Psychological Bulletin, 136*(1), 103–127.

Ely, R. (2005). Language and literacy in the school years. In J. B. Gleason (Ed.), *The development of language* (6th ed., pp. 396–443). Boston, MA: Pearson.

Engle, M. (2004). Kids and sports. *New York University Child Study Center Letter, 9*(1), 1–7.

Engles, R. C. M. E., Knibbe, R. A., Drop, M. J., & deHaan, Y. T. (1997). Homogeneity of cigarette smoking within peer groups: Influence or selection? *Health Education and Behavior, 24*(6), 801–811.

Entwisle, D. R., Alexander, K. L., & Olson, L. S. (2000). Early work histories of urban youth. *American Sociological Review, 65*(2), 279–297.

Epstein, L. H., Roemmich, J. N., Robinson, J. L., Paluch, R. A., Winiewicz, D. D., Fuerch, J. H., & Robinson, T. H. (2008). A randomized trial of the effects of reducing television viewing and computer use on body mass index in young children. *Archives of Pediatric and Adolescent Medicine, 162*(3), 239–245.

Erikson, E. H. (1963). *Childhood and society* (2nd ed.). New York, NY: Norton.

Erikson, E. H. (1968). *Identity, youth and crisis.* New York, NY: Norton.

Ersoy, B., Balkan, C., Gunay, T., & Egemen, A. (2005). The factors affecting the relation between the menarcheal age of mother and daughter. *Child: Care, Health and Development, 31*(3), 303–308.

Evans, G. W., & English, K. (2002). The environment of poverty: Multiple stressor exposure, psychophysiological stress, and socioemotional adjustment. *Child Development, 73*(4), 1238–1248.

Ewing, A. T. (1995). *A cooperative learning approach to demonstrate operant conditioning and experimental methodology.* Paper presented at annual convention of the American Psychological Association, New York, August 11.

Eyberg, S. M., Nelson, M. M., & Boggs, S. R. (2008). Evidence-based psychosocial treatments for children and adolescents with disruptive behavior. *Journal of Clinical Child and Adolescent Psychology, 37,* 215–237.

Eyer, D. (1992). *Mother-infant bonding: A scientific fiction.* New Haven, CT: Yale University Press.

Fabes, R. L., Gaertner, B. M., & Popp, T. K. (2006). Getting along with others: Social competence in early childhood. In K. McCartney & D. Phillips (Eds.), *Blackwell handbook of early childhood development* (pp. 297–316). Malden, MA: Blackwell.

Fagan, J. F., Holland, C. R., & Wheeler, K. (2007). The prediction, from infancy, of adult IQ and achievement. *Intelligence, 35*(3), 225–231.

Fagot, B. I. (1997). Attachment, parenting, and peer interactions of toddler children. *Developmental Psychology, 33*(3), 489–499.

Fahlman, S. E. (n.d.). *Smiley lore :-).* Retrieved from http://www.cs.cmu.edu/~sef/sefSmiley.htm

FairTest.org. (2008). *2008 College bound seniors average SAT scores*. Retrieved from http://www.fairtest.org/files/2008%20COLLEGE%20BOUND%20SENIORS%20AVERAGE%20SAT%20SCORES.pdf

Falbo, T., & Polit, D. F. (1986). Quantitative review of the only child literature: Research evidence and theory development. *Psychological Bulletin, 100*(2), 176–189.

Fan, J., Gu, X., Guise, K. G., Liu, X., Fossella, J., Wang, H., & Posner, M. I. (2009). Testing the behavioral interaction and integration of attentional networks. *Brain and Cognition, 70*(2), 209–220.

Farrelly, M. C., Davis, K. C., Haviland, M. L., Messeri, P., & Healton, C. G. (2005). Evidence of a dose-response relationship between "*truth*" antismoking ads and youth smoking prevalence. *American Journal of Public Health, 95*(3), 425–431.

Farrington, D. P., & Hawkins, J. D. (1991). Predicting participation, early onset and later persistence in officially recorded offending. *Criminal Behaviour and Mental Health, 1*(1), 1–33.

Farroni, T., Massaccesi, S., Pividori, D., & Johnson, M. (2004). Gaze following in newborns. *Infancy, 5*(1), 39–60.

Farroni, T., Menon, E., & Johnson, M. H. (2006). Factors influencing newborns' preference for faces with eye contact. *Journal of Experimental Child Psychology, 95*(4), 298–308.

Fast, I. (1985). Infantile narcissism and the active infant. *Psychoanalytic Psychology, 2*(2), 153–170.

Federal Interagency Forum on Child and Family Statistics. (2008). *America's children in brief: Key national indicators of well-being, 2008. Economic circumstances figures (Figure Econ3.B)*. Retrieved from http://www.childstats.gov/americaschildren08/econ_fig.asp

Federal Interagency Forum on Child and Family Statistics. (2009). *America's children: Key national indicators of well-being*. Washington, DC: U.S. Government Printing Office.

Feeney, B. C., Cassidy, J., & Ramos-Marcuse, F. (2008). The generalization of attachment representations to new social situations: Predicting behavior during initial interactions with strangers. *Journal of Personality and Social Psychology, 95*(6), 1481–1498.

Feinberg, M. E., Reiss, D., Neiderhiser, J. M., & Hetherington, E. M. (2005). Differential association of family subsystem negativity on siblings' maladjustment: Using behavior genetic methods to test process theory. *Journal of Family Psychology, 19*(4), 601–610.

Feiring, C., & Lewis, M. (1991). The development of social networks from early to middle childhood: Gender differences and the relation to school competence. *Sex Roles, 25*(3–4), 237–253.

Feist, G. J., & Barron, F. X. (2003). Predicting creativity from early to late adulthood:

Intellect, potential, and personality. *Journal of Research in Personality, 37*(2), 62–88.

Feld, S., & Schieffelin, B. B. (1998). Hard words: A functional basis for Kaluli discourse. In D. Brenneis & R. K. S. Macauley (Eds.), *The matrix of language* (pp. 56–74). Boulder, CO: Westview Press.

Feldhusen, J. F., & Dai, D. Y. (1997). Gifted students' attitudes and perceptions of the gifted label, special programs, and peer relations. *Journal of Secondary Gifted Education, 9*(1), 15–20.

Fendrich-Salowey, G., Buchanan, M., & Drew, C. J. (1982). Mathematics, quantitative and attitudinal measures for elementary school boys and girls. *Psychological Reports, 51*(1), 155–162.

Feng, X., Keenan, K., Hipwell, A. E., Henneberger, A. K., Rischall, M. S., Butch, J., . . . Babinski, D. E. (2009). Longitudinal associations between emotion regulation and depression in preadolescent girls: Moderation by the caregiving environment. *Developmental Psychology, 45*(3), 798–808.

Fenzel, L. M. (2000). Prospective study of changes in global self-worth and strain during the transition to middle school. *Journal of Early Adolescence, 20*(2), 93–116.

Ferguson, C. J., San Miguel, C., Kilburn, J. C., Jr., & Sanchez, P. (2007). The effectiveness of school-based anti-bullying programs: A meta-analytic review. *Criminal Justice Review, 32*(4), 401–414.

Ferguson, T. J., Stegge, H., Miller, E. R, & Olsen, M. E. (1999). Guilt, shame, and symptoms in children. *Developmental Psychology, 35*(2), 347–357.

Fergusson, D. M., Boden, J. M., & Horwood, L. J. (2008). Exposure to childhood sexual and physical abuse and adjustment in early adulthood. *Child Abuse & Neglect, 32*(6), 607–619.

Fergusson, D. M., & Mullen, P. E. (1999). *Childhood sexual abuse: An evidence-based perspective*. Thousand Oaks, CA: Sage.

Fernald, A. (1985). Four-month-olds prefer to listen to motherese. *Infant Behavior and Development, 8*, 181–195.

Fernald, A., & Morikawa, H. (1993). Common themes and cultural variation in Japanese and American mothers' speech to infants. *Child Development, 64*, 637–656.

Fernald, A., Pinto, J. P., Swingley, D., Weinberg, A., & McRoberts, G. W. (2001). Rapid gains in speed of verbal processing by infants in the 2nd year. In M. Tomasello & E. Bates (Eds.), *Language development: The essential readings* (pp. 49–56). Malden, MA: Blackwell.

Fernyhough, C., & Fradley, E. (2005). Private speech on an executive task: Relations with task difficulty and task performance. *Cognitive Development, 20*(1), 103–120.

Field, T. (2007). *The amazing infant*. Malden, MA: Blackwell.

Field, T., Diego, M., & Hernandez-Reif, M. (2007). Massage therapy research. *Developmental Review, 27*(1), 75–89.

Field, T., Hernandez-Reif, M., Diego, M., Feijo, L., Vera, Y., & Gil, K. (2004). Massage therapy by parents improves early growth and development. *Infant Behavior & Development, 27*(4), 435–442.

Field, T., Morrow, C., Valdeon, C., Larson, S., Kuhn, C., & Schanberg, S. (1992). Massage reduces anxiety in child and adolescent psychiatric patients. *Journal of the American Academy of Child and Adolescent Psychiatry, 31*, 125–131.

Fiese, B. H., & Schwartz, M. (2008). Reclaiming the family table: Mealtime and child health and well-being. *Society for Research in Child Development Social Policy Report, 22*(4), 3–9, 13–18.

Fifer, W. P., Monk, C. E., & Grose-Fifer, J. (2004). Prenatal development and risk. In G. Bremner & A. Fogel (Eds.), *Blackwell handbook of infant development* (pp. 505–542). Malden, MA: Blackwell.

Filipek, P. A., Accardo, P. J., Baranek, G. T., Cook, E. H., Jr., Dawson, G., Gordon, B., . . . Volkmar, F. R. (1999). The screening and diagnosis of autism spectrum disorders. *Journal of Autism and Developmental Disorders, 29*(2), 439–484.

Finkelhor, D., & Hashima, P. Y. (2001). The victimization of children and youth: A comprehensive overview. In S. O. White (Ed.), *Handbook of youth and justice* (pp. 48–78). New York, NY: Kluwer Academic.

Finkelhor, D., Hotaling, G., Lewis, I. A., & Smith, C. (1990). Sexual abuse in a national survey of adult men and women: Prevalence, characteristics, and risk factors. *Child Abuse and Neglect, 14*, 19–28.

Finkelhor, D., Ormrod, R., Turner, H., & Hamby, S. L. (2005). The victimization of children and youth: A comprehensive, national survey. *Child Maltreatment, 10*(1), 5–25.

First Candle. (n.d.). *When a baby has died: Friends and relatives*. Retrieved from http://www.firstcandle.org/grieving-families/friends-relatives/

Fischer, C. S., Hout, M., & Stiles, J. (2006). How Americans lived: Families and life courses in flux. In C. S. Fischer & M. Hout (Eds.), *Century of difference* (pp. 57–95). New York, NY: Russell Sage.

Fischer, J. L., Pidcock, B. W., Munsch, J., & Forthun, L. (2005). Parental abusive drinking and sibling role differences. *Alcoholism Treatment Quarterly, 23*(1), 79–97.

Flavell, J. H. (1999). Cognitive *development:* Children's knowledge about the mind. *Annual Review of Psychology, 50*, 21–45.

Flavell, J. H., Miller, P. H., & Miller, S. A. (2002). *Cognitive development* (4th ed.). Upper Saddle River, NJ: Prentice Hall.

Fleming, A. S., Corter, C., Stallings, J., & Sneider, M. (2002). Testosterone and prolactin are associated with emotional responses to infant cries in new fathers. *Hormones and Behavior, 42*, 399–413.

Fletcher, A. C., & Jefferies, B. C. (1999). Parental mediators of associations between perceived authoritative parenting and early adolescent substance use. *Journal of Early Adolescence, 19*(4), 465–487.

Fletcher, G. E., Zach, T., Pramanik, A. K., & Ford, S. P. (2009). Multiple births. *E-Medicine.* Retrieved from http://www.emedicine.com/ped/TOPIC2599.HTM

Fletcher, K. E. (2007). Posttraumatic stress disorder. In E. J. Mash & R. A. Barkley (Eds.), *Assessment of childhood disorders* (pp. 398–486). New York, NY: Guilford.

Flinn, S. K. (1995). *Child sexual abuse I: An overview.* Retrieved from http://www.advocatesforyouth.org/publications/factsheet/fsabuse1.htm

Flynn, J. R. (1984). The mean IQ of Americans: Massive gains 1932 to 1978. *Psychological Bulletin, 95,* 29–51.

Flynn, J. R. (2007). What is intelligence? *Beyond the Flynn effect.* New York, NY: Cambridge University Press.

Foa, E. B., & Kozak, M. J. (1986). Emotional processing of fear: Exposure to corrective information. *Psychological Bulletin, 99*(1), 20–35.

Foerde, K., Knowlton, B. J., & Poldrack, R. A. (2006). Modulation of competing memory systems by distraction. *Proceedings of the National Academy of Sciences, 103*(31), 11778–11783.

Fogel, A. (2002). *Infancy* (4th ed.). Belmont, CA: Wadsworth.

Folkman, S., & Lazarus, R. S. (1980). An analysis of coping in a middle-aged community sample. *Journal of Health and Social Behavior, 21,* 219–239.

Fombonne, E. (2005). The changing epidemiology of autism. *Journal of Applied Research in Intellectual Disabilities, 18*(4), 281–294.

Fombonne, E., Zakarian, R., Bennett, A., Meng, L., & McLean-Heywood, D. (2005). Pervasive developmental disorders in Montreal, Quebec, Canada: Prevalence and links with immunizations. *Pediatrics, 118*(1), 139–150.

Fonagy, P., Target, M., & Gergely, G. (2006). Psychoanalytic perspectives on developmental psychology. In D. J. Cohen & D. Cicchetti (Eds.), *Developmental psychopathology: Theory and method* (Vol. 1, pp. 701–749). Hoboken, NJ: Wiley.

Forbes, G. B. (1989). Assessment and significance of body composition in infants and children. In B. Schürch & N. S. Scrimshaw (Eds.), *Activity, energy expenditure and energy requirements of infants and children.* Proceedings of an I/D/E/C/G Workshop held in Cambridge, MA, November 14–17.

Ford-Martin, P. (2006). Psychological tests. In K. Krapp & J. Wilson (Eds.), *Gale encyclopedia of children's health* (Vol. 3, pp. 1530–1532). Detroit, MI: Thomson/Gale.

Fox, B. (2001). The formative years: How parenthood creates gender. *Canadian Review of Sociology and Anthropology, 28*(4), 373–390.

Fox, G. (2006). Development in family contexts. In L. Combrinck-Graham (Ed.), *Children in family contexts* (pp. 26–50). New York, NY: Guilford.

Fraenkel, P. (2003). Contemporary two-parent families. In F. Walsh (Ed.), *Normal family processes* (3rd ed., pp. 61–95). New York, NY: Guilford.

Fraiberg, S., Adelson, E., & Shapiro, V. (1975). Ghosts in the nursery: A psychoanalytic approach to the problem of impaired infant-mother relationships. *Journal of the American Academy of Child Psychiatry, 14,* 387–422.

Franklin, J., Rifkin, L., & Pascual, P. (2001). Serving the very young and the restless. In D. G. Singer & J. L. Singer (Eds.), *Handbook of children and the media* (pp. 507–520). Thousand Oaks, CA: Sage.

Freeman, N. K., & Somerindyke, J. (2001). Social play at the computer: Preschoolers scaffold and support peers' computer competence. *Information Technology in Childhood Education Annual, 12,* 203–213.

Freisthler, B., Merritt, D. H., & LaScala, E. A. (2006). Understanding the ecology of child maltreatment: A review of the literature and directions for future research. *Child Maltreatment, 11*(3), 263–280.

Freud, A. (1965). *Normality and pathology in childhood.* New York, NY: International Universities Press.

Freud, A., & Dann, S. (1949). An experiment in group upbringing. *Psychoanalytic Study of the Child, 3/4,* 127–168.

Freud, S. (1950). A note on the unconscious in psycho-analysis (1912). In *Collected papers* (Vol. IV, pp. 22–29). London, England: Hogarth Press.

Freud, S. (1953a). Female sexuality (1931). In *Collected papers* (Vol. V, pp. 252–272). London, England: Hogarth Press.

Freud, S. (1953b). Some psychological consequences of the anatomical distinction between the sexes (1925). In *Collected papers* (Vol. V, pp. 186–197). London, England: Hogarth Press.

Freud, S. (1953c). Two encyclopedia articles (1922): (a) Psycho-analysis. In *Collected papers* (Vol. V, pp. 107–130). London, England: Hogarth Press.

Freud, S. (1959). Character and anal erotism (1908). In *Collected papers* (Vol. II, pp. 45–50). London, England: Hogarth Press.

Frey, N. (2005). Retention, social promotion, and academic redshirting: What do we know and need to know? *Remedial and Special Education, 26*(6), 332–346.

Frick, P. J., Lahey, B. B., Loeber, R., Tannenbaum, I. E., VanHorn, Y., Christ, M. A. G., . . . Hanson, K. (1993). Oppositional defiant disorder and conduct disorder: A meta-analytic review of factor analyses and cross-validation in a clinic sample. *Clinical Psychology Review, 13*(4), 319–340.

Fried, P. A., & Makin, J. E. (1987). Neonatal behavioural correlates of prenatal exposure to marihuana, cigarettes and alcohol in a low risk population. *Neurotoxicology and Teratology, 9*(1), 1–7.

Friedman, H. S., Tucker, J. S., Schwartz, J. E., Martin, L. R., Tomlinson-Keasey, C., Wingard, D. L., & Criqui, M. H. (1995). Childhood conscientiousness and longevity. *Journal of Personality & Social Psychology, 68,* 696–703.

Friedman, M. J. (2006). *Sesame Street educates and entertains internationally.* Retrieved from http://www.america.gov/st/washfile-english/2006/April/20060405165756jmnamdeirf0.4207117.html

Friedrich, L. K., & Stein, A. H. (1973). Aggressive and prosocial television programs and the natural behavior of preschool children [Special issue]. *Monographs of the Society for Research in Child Development, 38*(4, Serial No. 151).

Fries, A. B. W., Ziegler, T. E., Kurian, J. R., Jacoris, S., & Pollak, S. D. (2005). Early experience in humans is associated with changes in neuropeptides critical for regulating social behavior. *Proceedings of the National Academy of Sciences, 102*(47), 17237–17240.

Frith, U. (2003). *Autism: Explaining the enigma.* Malden, MA: Blackwell.

Frodi, A. M., & Lamb, M. E. (1980). Child abusers' responses to infant smiles and cries. *Child Development, 51*(1), 238–241.

Froschl, M., & Sprung, B. (2008). A positive and pro-active response to young boys in the classroom. *Exchange: The Early Childhood Leaders' Magazine, 182,* 34–36.

Fry, D. P. (2005). Rough-and-tumble social play in humans. In A. D. Pellegrini & P. K. Smith (Eds.), *The nature of play* (pp. 54–85). New York, NY: Guilford.

Fuchs, L. S., Fuchs, D., Hamlett, C. L., & Karns, K. (1998). High-achieving students' interactions and performance on complex mathematical tasks as a function of homogeneous and heterogeneous pairings. *American Educational Research Journal, 35*(2), 227–267.

Furman, W. (1995). Parenting siblings. In M. H. Bornstein (Ed.), *Handbook of parenting: Vol. 1. Children and parenting* (pp. 143–162). Mahwah, NJ: Erlbaum.

Furman, W., & Collins, W. A. (2009). Adolescent romantic relationships and experiences. In K. H. Rubin, W. M. Bukowski, & B. Laursen (Eds.), *Handbook of peer interactions, relationships, and groups* (pp. 341–360). New York, NY: Guilford.

Furstenberg, F. F., Jr., & Cherlin, A. J. (1991). *Divided families: What happens to children when parents part.* Cambridge, MA: Harvard University Press.

The Future of Children. (2010). *About the Future of Children.* Retrieved from http://futureofchildren.org/futureofchildren/about/

Gadgil, A. (n.d.). *The gray zone.* Retrieved from http://www.lbl.gov/Education/ELSI/research-main.html

Galambos, N. L. (2004). Gender and gender role development in adolescence. In R. M. Lerner & L. Steinberg (Eds.), *Handbook of adolescent development* (2nd ed., pp. 233–262). Hoboken, NJ: Wiley.

Galambos, N. L., Almeida, D. M., & Petersen, A. C. (1990). Masculinity, femininity, and sex role attitudes in early adolescence: Exploring gender intensification. *Child Development, 61*, 1905–1914.

Galan, H. L., & Hobbins. J. C. (2003). Intrauterine growth restriction. In J. S. Scott, R. S. Gibbs, B. Y. Karlan, & A. F. Haney (Eds.), *Danforth's obstetrics and gynecology* (9th ed., pp. 203–217). Philadelphia, PA: Lippincott.

Gallagher, S. K., & Gerstel, N. (2001). Connections and constraints: The effects of children on caregiving. *Journal of Marriage and Family, 63*(1), 265–275.

Gallup, G. G., Anderson, J. R., & Shillito, D. J. (2002). The mirror test. In M. Bekoff, C. Allen, & G. M. Burghardt (Eds.), *The cognitive animal: Empirical and theoretical perspectives on animal cognition* (pp. 325–334). Cambridge, MA: MIT Press.

Ganger, J., & Brent, M. R. (2004). Reexamining the vocabulary spurt. *Developmental Psychology, 40*(4), 621–632.

Garan, E. M. (2001). Beyond the smoke and mirrors. *Phi Delta Kappan, 82*(7), 500–506.

Gardephe, C. D., & Ettlinger, S. (1993). *Don't pick up the baby or you'll spoil the child and other old wives' tales about pregnancy and parenting.* San Francisco, CA: Chronicle Books.

Gardner, H. (1976). *The shattered mind.* New York, NY: Vintage Books.

Gardner, H. (1993). *Frames of mind: The theory of multiple intelligences.* New York, NY: Basic Books.

Gardner, H. (1999). *Intelligence reframed.* New York, NY: Basic Books.

Gardner, H., & Connell, M. (2000). Response to Nicholas Allix. *Australian Journal of Education, 44,* 288–293.

Gardner, H., & Moran, S. (2006). The science of multiple intelligences theory: A response to Lynn Waterhouse. *Educational Psychologist, 41*(4), 227–232.

Gardner, R. M., Stark, K., Friedman, B. N., & Jackson, N. A. (2000). Predictors of eating disorder scores in children ages 6 through 14: A longitudinal study. *Journal of Psychosomatic Research, 49*(3), 199–205.

Garno, J. L., Goldberg, J. F., Ramirez, P. M., & Ritzler, B. A. (2005). Impact of childhood abuse on the clinical course of bipolar disorder. *British Journal of Psychiatry, 186*(2), 121–125.

Garven, S., Wood, J. M., Malpass, R. S., & Shaw, J. S. (1998). More than suggestion: The effect of interviewing techniques from the McMartin Preschool case. *Journal of Applied Psychology, 83*(3), 347–359.

Gaskins, I. W., & Pressley, M. (2007). Teaching metacognitive strategies that address executive function processes within a schoolwide curriculum. In L. Meltzer (Ed.), *Executive function in education: From theory to practice* (pp. 261–286). New York, NY: Guilford.

Gass, K., Jenkins, J., & Dunn, J. (2007). Are sibling relationships protective? A longitudinal study. *Journal of Child Psychology and Psychiatry, 48*(2), 167–175.

Gauvain, M., & Parke, R. D. (2010). Socialization. In M. H. Bornstein (Ed.), *Handbook of cultural developmental science* (pp. 239–258). New York, NY: Psychology Press.

Gay, P. (1988). *Freud: A life for our time.* New York, NY: Norton.

Gay, P. (1999). Sigmund Freud. *Time.* Retrieved from http://205.188.238.181/time/time100/scientist/

Ge, X., Brody, G. H., Conger, R. D., Simons, R. L., & Murry, V. M. (2002). Contextual amplification of pubertal transition effects on deviant peer affiliation and externalizing behavior among African-American children. *Developmental Psychology, 38*(1), 42–54.

Gecas, V., & Seff, M. A. (1990). Families and adolescents: A review of the 1980s. *Journal of Marriage and Family, 52*(4), 941–958.

Geist, E. A., & Gibson, M. (2000). The effect of network and public television programs on four and five year olds' ability to attend to educational tasks. *Journal of Instructional Psychology, 27,* 250–262.

Generations United. (2009). *GU action center.* Retrieved from http://www.gu.org//action-center.asp

Genesee, F., & Cloud, N. (1998). Multilingualism is basic. *Educational Leadership, 55*(6), 62–65.

Gentile, D. A. (2003). Introduction. In D. A. Gentile (Ed.), *Media violence and children* (pp. ix–xi). Westport, CT: Praeger.

Gentile, D. A., & Anderson, C. A. (2003). Violent video games: The newest media violence hazard. In D. A. Gentile (Ed.), *Media violence and children* (pp. 131–152). Westport, CT: Praeger.

Gerard, M. (2004). What's a parent to do? Phonics and other stuff. *Childhood Education, 83*(3), 159–160.

Gerber, P. J., Schneiders, C. A., Paradise, L. V., Reiff, H. B., Ginsberg, R. J., & Popp, P. A. (1990). Persisting problems of adults with learning disabilities: Self-reported comparisons from their school-age and adult years. *Journal of Learning Disabilities, 23*(9), 570–573.

Gerlach, P. K. (2010). *Make a family map (genogram) to see who you all are.* Retrieved from http://sfhelp.org/sf/basics/geno.htm

Gernsbacher, M. A., Dawson, M., & Goldsmith, H. H. (2005). Three reasons not to believe in an autism epidemic. *Current Directions in Psychological Science, 14*(2), 55–58.

Gesell, A., & Ilg, F. L. (1943). *Infant and child in the culture of today.* London, England: Harper and Brothers.

Gesell, A., & Ilg, F. L. (1946). *The child from five to ten.* New York, NY: Harper and Brothers.

Ghoting, S. N., & Martin-Díaz, P. (2006). *Early literacy storytimes @ your library: Partnering with caregivers for success.* Chicago, IL: American Library Association.

Giallo, R., & Gavidia-Payne, S. (2008). Evaluation of a family-based intervention for siblings of children with a disability or chronic illness. *Australian e-Journal for the Advancement of Mental Health, 7*(2), 1–13.

Gibbs, J. C., Basinger, K. S., Grime, R. L., & Snarey, J. R. (2007). Moral judgment development across cultures: Revisiting Kohlberg's universality claims. *Developmental Review, 27*(4), 443–500.

Giedd, J. N. (2004). Structural magnetic resonance imaging of the adolescent brain. *Annals of the New York Academy of Sciences, 1021,* 77–85.

Gilbert, S. F. (2000). *Developmental biology.* Sunderland, MA: Sinauer.

Gilbert, S. F. (2006). *Developmental biology* (8th ed.). Sunderland, MA: Sinauer.

Gilliam, W. S. (2005). Prekindergarteners left behind: Expulsion rates in state prekindergarten systems. Retrieved from http://childstudycenter.yale.edu/faculty/pdf/Gilliam05.pdf

Gilligan, C. (1987). *Adolescent development reconsidered.* 10th Annual Konopka Lecture. Retrieved from http://www.konopka.umn.edu/peds/ahm/prod/groups/med/@pub/@med/documents/asset/med_21792.pdf

Ginn, J. D. (2008). *At issue: Bilingual education.* Detroit, MI: Thomson-Gale.

Gjerdingen, D. K., & Center, B. A. (2005). First-time parents' postpartum changes in employment, childcare, and housework responsibilities. *Social Science Research, 34,* 103–116.

Gladue, B. A. (1994). The biopsychology of sexual orientation. *Current Directions in Psychological Science, 3,* 150–154.

Glaser, S. (1993). Intelligence testing. *Congressional Quarterly Researcher, 3,* 649–672.

Gleason, J. B. (2005). The development of language: An overview and a preview. In J. B. Gleason (Ed.), *The development of language* (6th ed., pp. 1–38). Boston, MA: Pearson.

Gleason, P., & Suitor, C. (2001). *Food for thought: Children's diets in the 1990s* [Policy brief]. Princeton, NJ: Mathematica Policy Research.

Gleitman, L. (1990). The structural sources of verb meaning. *Language Acquisition, 1,* 3–50.

Global Initiative to End All Corporal Punishment of Children. (2009). *Global progress toward prohibiting all corporal punishment.* Retrieved from http://www.endcorporalpunishment.org/pages/pdfs/charts/Chart-Global.pdf

Gogtay, N., Giedd, J. N., Lusk, L., Hayashi, K. M., Greenstein, D., Vaituzis, A. C., . . .

Thompson, P. M. (2004). Dynamic mapping of human cortical development during childhood through early adulthood. *Proceedings of the National Academy of Sciences, 101*(21), 8174–8179.

Gokhale, A. A. (1995). Collaborative learning enhances critical thinking. *Journal of Technology Education, 7*(1), 22–30.

Goldberg, R. J., Higgins, E. L., Raskind, M. H., & Herman, K. L. (2003). Predictors of success in individuals with learning disabilities: A qualitative analysis. *Learning Disabilities Research and Practice, 18*(4), 222–236.

Goldfield, B. A., & Snow, C. E. (2005). Individual differences—Implications for the study of language acquisition. In J. B. Gleason (Ed.), *The development of language* (6th ed., pp. 292–323). Boston, MA: Pearson.

Goldman, L., & Smith, C. (1998). Imagining identities: Mimetic constructions in Huli child fantasy play. *Journal of the Royal Anthropological Institute, 4*(2), 207–234.

Goldsmith, H. H., Lemery, K. S., Aksan, N., & Buss, K. A. (2000). Temperamental substrates of personality. In V. J. Molfese & D. L. Molfese (Eds.), *Temperament and personality development across the life span* (pp. 1–32). Mahwah, NJ: Erlbaum.

Goldstein, S., & Brooks, R. B. (2005). The future of children today. In S. Goldstein & R. B. Brooks (Eds.), *Handbook of resilience in children* (pp. 397–400). New York, NY: Springer.

Goleman, D. (1995). *Emotional intelligence.* New York, NY: Bantam Books.

Goleman, D. (2007). *Daniel Goleman on compassion—A lecture at the TED conferences.* Retrieved from http://www.ted.com/talks/daniel_goleman_on_compassion.html

Golombok, S., & Fivush, R. (1994). *Gender development.* New York, NY: Cambridge University Press.

Golombok, S., & Hines, M. (2002). Sex differences in social behavior. In P. K. Smith & C. H. Hart (Eds.), *Blackwell handbook of childhood social development* (pp. 117–136). Malden, MA: Blackwell.

Golombok, S., & Tasker, F. (1996). Do parents influence the sexual orientation of their children? Findings from a longitudinal study of lesbian families. *Developmental Psychology, 32,* 3–11.

Gonzales, N. A., Cauce, A. M., & Mason, C. A. (1996). Inter-observer agreement in the assessment of parental behavior and parent-adolescent conflict: African American mothers, daughters, and independent observers. *Child Development, 67*(4), 1483–1498.

Good, C., Aronson, J., & Inzlicht, M. (2003). Improving adolescents' standardized test performance: An intervention to reduce the effects of stereotype threat. *Journal of Applied Developmental Psychology, 24*(6), 645–662.

Good, T. L. (1987). Two decades of research on teacher expectations: Findings and future directions. *Journal of Teacher Education, 38,* 32–47.

Goodlett, C. R., & Horn, K. H. (2001). Mechanisms of alcohol-induced damage to the developing nervous system. *Alcohol Research & Health, 25*(3), 175–184.

Goodman, G. S., & Schaaf, J. M. (1997). Over a decade of research on children's eyewitness testimony: What have we learned? Where do we go from here? *Applied Cognitive Psychology, 11,* S5–S20.

Goodman, R., & Stevenson, J. (1989). A twin study of hyperactivity: II. The aetiological role of genes, family relationships and perinatal adversity. *Journal of Child Psychology and Psychiatry, 30*(5), 691–709.

Goodwin, C. J. (2005). *A history of modern psychology* (2nd ed.). Hoboken, NJ: Wiley.

Goodwyn, S. W., Acredolo, L. P., & Brown, C. A. (2000). Impact of symbolic gesturing on early language development. *Journal of Nonverbal Behavior, 24*(2), 81–103.

Gopnik, A., Meltzoff, A. N., & Kuhl, P. K. (1999). *The scientist in the crib.* New York, NY: William Morrow.

Gordon, J. D., Rydfors, J. T., Druzin, M., & Tadir, Y. (2001). *Obstetrics, gynecology and infertility: Handbook for clinicians-resident survival guide* (5th ed.). Arlington, VA: Scrub Hill Press.

Gosso, Y., Morais, M. L. S., & Otta, E. (2007). Pretend play of Brazilian children: A window into different cultural worlds. *Journal of Cross-Cultural Psychology, 38*(5), 539–558.

Gottfredson, L. (1998). The general intelligence factor. *Scientific American Presents,* 24–29.

Gottlieb, G. (1991). Experiential canalization of behavioral development: Theory. *Developmental Psychology, 27*(1), 4–13.

Gould, S. J. (1996). *The mismeasure of man.* New York, NY: Norton.

Gove, M. K. (1983). Clarifying teachers' beliefs about reading. *Reading Teacher, 37*(3), 261–268.

Gowers, S., & Doherty, F. (2007). Outcome and prognosis. In B. Lask & R. Bryant-Waugh (Eds.), *Eating disorders in childhood and adolescence* (3rd ed., pp. 75–96).

Grabe, S., Ward, L. M., & Hyde, J. S. (2008). The role of the media in body image concerns among women: A meta-analysis of experimental and correlational studies. *Psychological Bulletin, 134*(3), 460–476.

Grady, D. (2007). Promising dystrophy drug clears early test. *The New York Times.* Retrieved from http://www.nytimes.com/2007/12/27/health/27drug.html

Granic, I., & Patterson, G. R. (2006). Toward a comprehensive model of antisocial development: A dynamic systems approach. *Psychological Review, 113*(1), 101–131.

Gray, L., Watt, L., & Blass, E. M. (2000). Skin-to-skin contact is analgesic in healthy newborns. *Pediatrics, 105*(1), e14.

Gray, M. R., & Steinberg, L. (1999). Unpacking authoritative parenting: Reassessing a multidimensional construct. *Journal of Marriage and Family, 61,* 574–587.

Gredler, M. E., & Shields, C. C. (2008). *Vygotsky's legacy.* New York, NY: Guilford.

Greenberger, E., Chen, C., & Beam, M. R. (1998). The role of "very important" non-parental adults in adolescent development. *Journal of Youth and Adolescence, 27*(3), 321–343.

Greene, A. (2004). *From first kicks to first steps: Nurturing your baby's development from pregnancy through the first year of life.* New York, NY: McGraw-Hill.

Greene, S. M., Anderson, E. R., Hetherington, E. M., Forgatch, M. S., & DeGarmo, D. S. (2003). Risk and resilience after divorce. In F. Walsh (Ed.), *Normal family processes* (3rd ed., pp. 96–120). New York, NY: Guilford.

Greene, S. M., Sullivan, K., & Anderson, E. R. (2008). Divorce and custody. In M. Hersen & A. M. Gross (Eds.), *Handbook of clinical psychology: Vol. 2. Children and adolescents* (pp. 833–855). Hoboken, NJ: Wiley.

Greenfield, T. A. (1997). Gender- and grade-level differences in science interest and participation. *Science Education, 81*(3), 259–275.

Greenglass, E. R. (2002). Work stress, coping and social support: Implications for women's occupational well being. In D. L. Nelson & R. J. Burke (Eds.), *Gender work stress and health* (pp. 85–96). Washington, DC: American Psychological Association.

Greenough, W. T., Black, J. E., & Wallace, C. S. (1987). Experience and brain development. *Child Development, 58*(3), 539–559.

Greif, G. L. (1997). Working with noncustodial mothers. *Families in Society, 78*(1), 46–51.

Griffin, C. W., Wirth, J. J., & Wirth, A. G. (1993). Parent-child relationships do not affect homosexuality. In W. Dudley (Ed.), *Homosexuality: Opposing viewpoints* (pp. 36–44). San Diego, CA: Greenhaven Press.

Grimm, L. G. (1993). *Statistical applications for the behavioral sciences.* New York, NY: Wiley.

Groome, L. J., Swiber, M. J., Holland, S. B., Bentz, L. S., Atterbury, J. L., & Trimm, R. F. (1999). Spontaneous motor activity in the perinatal infant before and after birth: Stability in individual differences. *Developmental Psychobiology, 35*(1), 15–24.

Grossmann, K., Grossmann, K. E., Spangler, G., Suess, G., & Unzner, L. (1985). Maternal sensitivity and newborns' orientation responses as related to quality of attachment in northern Germany. *Monographs of the Society for Research on Child Development, 50,* 233–256.

Grusec, J., & Lytton, H. (1988). *Social development.* New York, NY: Springer.

Grusec, J. E. (1992). Social learning theory and developmental psychology: The legacies of Robert Sears and Albert Bandura. *Developmental Psychology, 28*(5), 776–786.

Guglielmi, R. S. (2008). Native language proficiency, English literacy, academic achievement, and occupational attainment in limited-English-proficient students: A latent growth modeling perspective. *Journal of Educational Psychology, 100*(2), 322–342.

Guilford, J. P. (1950). Creativity. *American Psychologist, 5,* 444–454.

Gullatt, D. E. (2008). Enhancing student learning through arts integration: Implications for the profession. *The High School Journal, 91*(4), 12–25.

Gunn, B., Simmons, D., & Kameenui, E. (1995). *Emergent literacy: Synthesis of the research (Technical Report No. 19).* University of Oregon: National Center to Improve the Tools of Educators.

Gunnar, M. R. (2007). Stress effects on the developing brain. In D. Romer & E. F. Walker (Eds.), *Adolescent psychopathology and the developing brain: Integrating brain and prevention science* (pp. 127–147). New York, NY: Oxford University Press.

Gunnar, M. R., & Cheatham, C. L. (2003). Brain and behavior interface: Stress and the developing brain. *Infant Mental Health Journal, 24*(3), 195–211.

Gunnar, M. R., & Quevedo, K. (2007). The neurobiology of stress and development. *Annual Review of Psychology, 58,* 145–173.

Gunnoe, M. L., & Hetherington, E. M. (2004). Stepchildren's perceptions of noncustodial mothers and noncustodial fathers: Differences in socioemotional involvement and associations with adolescent adjustment problems. *Journal of Family Psychology, 18*(4), 555–563.

Gurung, R. A. R. (2005). How do students really study (and does it matter)? *Teaching of Psychology, 32*(4), 239–241.

Gustafson, G. E., Wood, R. M., & Green, J. A. (2000). Can we hear the causes of infants' crying? In R. G. Barr, B. Hopkins, & J. A. Green (Eds.), *Crying as a sign, a symptom, & a signal: Clinical emotional and developmental aspects of infant and toddler crying* (pp. 8–22). New York, NY: Cambridge University Press.

Haden, C. A. (2003). Joint encoding and joint reminiscing: Implications for young children's understanding and remembering of personal experiences. In R. Fivush & C. A. Haden (Eds.), *Autobiographical memory and the construction of a narrative self* (pp. 49–69). Mahwah, NJ: ErlbHaight, W., Black, J., Ostler, T., & Sheridan, K. (2006). Pretend play and emotion learning. In D. G. Singer, R. M. Golinkoff, & K. Hirsh-Pasek (Eds.), *Play=learning* (pp. 209–230). New York, NY: Oxford University Press.

Haight, W., & Miller, P. J. (1992). The development of everyday pretend play: A longitudinal study of mothers' participation. *Merrill-Palmer Quarterly, 38*(3), 331–349.

Haight, W. L., & Black, J. E. (2001). A comparative approach to play: Cross-species and cross-cultural perspectives of play in development. *Human Development, 44,* 228–234.

Hair, E. C., Moore, K. A., Garrett, S. B., Ling, T., & Cleveland, K. (2008). The continued importance of quality parent-adolescent relationships during late adolescence. *Journal of Research on Adolescence, 18*(1), 187–200.

Haith, M. M., Bergman, T., & Moore, M. (1977). Eye contact and face scanning in early infancy. *Science, 198,* 853–855.

Hakuta, K. (1987). Degree of bilingualism and cognitive ability in mainland Puerto Rican children. *Child Development, 58*(5), 1372–1388.

Hakuta, K., & Garcia, E. E. (1989). Bilingualism and education. *American Psychologist, 44*(2), 374–379.

Halgunseth, L. C., Ispa, J. M., & Rudy, D. (2006). Parental control in Latino families: An integrated review of the literature. *Child Development, 77*(5), 1282–1297.

Hall, D. M. (2008). Feminist perspectives on the personal and political aspects of mothering. In J. C. Chrisler, C. Golden, & P. D. Rozee (Eds.), *Lectures on the psychology of women* (4th ed., pp. 58–79). Boston, MA: McGraw-Hill.

Halle, C., Dowd, T., Fowler, C., Rissel, K., Hennessy, K., MacNevin, R., & Nelson, M. A. (2008). Supporting fathers in the transition to parenthood. *Contemporary Nurse, 31*(1), 57–70.

Hamblen, J., & Barnett, E. (2009). *PTSD in children and adolescents.* U.S. Department of Veterans' Affairs. Retrieved from http://www.ptsd.va.gov/professional/pages/ptsd_in_children_and_adolescents_overview_for_professionals.asp

Hamilton, B. E., Martin, J. A., & Ventura, S. J. (2009). Births: Preliminary data for 2007. *Morbidity and Mortality Weekly Report, 58*(12), 313.

Hamilton, H. A. (2005). Extended families and adolescent well-being. *Journal of Adolescent Health, 36,* 260–266.

Hamilton, M. A., & Hamilton, S. F. (1997). *Learning well at work: Choices for quality.* Washington, DC: U.S. Department of Education/U.S. Department of Labor.

Hamilton, S. F., & Darling, N. (1989). Mentors in adolescents' lives. In K. Hurrelmann & U. Engel (Eds.), *The social world of adolescents: International perspectives* (pp. 121–139). Oxford, England: Walter De Gruyte.

Hamilton, S. F., & Hamilton, M. A. (1999). *Building strong school-to-work systems: Illustrations of key components.* Washington, DC: U.S. Department of Education/U.S. Department of Labor.

Hammen, C., & Rudolph, K. D. (2003). Childhood mood disorders. In E. J. Mash & R. A. Barkley (Eds.), *Child psychopathology* (2nd ed., pp. 233–278). New York, NY: Guilford.

Hankin, B. L., & Abramson, L. Y. (1999). Development of gender differences in depression: Description and possible explanations. *Annals of Medicine, 31*(6), 372–379.

Hankin, B. L., Abramson, L. Y., Moffitt, T. E., Silva, P. A., McGee, R., & Angell, K. E. (1998). Development of depression from preadolescence to young adulthood: Emerging gender differences in a 10-year longitudinal study. *Journal of Abnormal Psychology, 107*(1), 128–140.

Hanrahan, C. (2006). Sleep. In K. Krapp & J. Wilson (Eds.), *Gale encyclopedia of children's health: Infancy through adolescence* (Vol. 4, pp. 1676–1680). Detroit, MI: Gale.

Hansen, M. B., & Markman, E. M. (2009). Children's use of mutual exclusivity to learn labels for parts of objects. *Developmental Psychology, 45*(2), 592–596.

Harlow, H. F. (1958). The nature of love. *American Psychologist, 13*(12), 673–685.

Harris, B. (1979). Whatever happened to Little Albert? *American Psychologist, 34*(2), 151–160.

Harris, J. R. (1995). Where is the child's environment? A group socialization theory of development. *Psychological Review, 102*(3), 458–489.

Harris, J. R. (1998). *The nurture assumption: Why children turn out the way they do.* New York, NY: Free Press.

Harris, J. R. (2000). Context-specific learning, personality, and birth order. *Current Directions in Psychological Science, 9*(5), 174–177.

Harris, S. (2004). Bullying at school among older adolescents. *Prevention Researcher, 11*(3), 12–14.

Harrison, J. (2008, September). UA study sheds light on relationship between absent fathers and early puberty. *UANews.* Retrieved from http://uanews.org/node/21474

Harrison, K. (2000). The body electric: Thin ideal media and eating disorders in adolescents. *Journal of Communication, 50*(3), 119–143.

Harrison, K. (2006). Scope of self: Toward a model of television's effects on self-complexity in adolescence. *Communication Theory, 16*(2), 251–279.

Hart, B., & Risley, T. R. (1995). *Meaningful differences in the everyday experience of young American children.* Baltimore, MD: Paul H. Brookes.

Harter, S. (1999). *The construction of the self.* New York, NY: Guilford.

Harter, S. (2006a). The development of self-esteem. In M. H. Kernis (Ed.), *Self-esteem issues and answers: A sourcebook of current perspectives* (pp. 144–150). New York, NY: Psychology Press.

Harter, S. (2006b). The self. In N. Eisenberg, W. Damon, & R. M. Lerner (Eds.), *Handbook of child psychology: Vol. 3. Social, emotional, and personality development* (6th ed., pp. 505–570). Hoboken, NJ: Wiley.

Hartman, A. (2003). Family policy: Dilemmas controversies, and opportunities. In F. Walsh (Ed.), *Normal family processes* (3rd ed., pp. 635–662). New York, NY: Guilford.

Harvey, E. (1999). Short-term and long-term effects of early parental employment on children of the National Longitudinal Survey of Youth. *Developmental Psychology, 35*(2), 445–459.

Hassan, A. (2005). *Rosie re-riveted in public memory: A rhetorical study of the shipyard childcare in Richmond California and the 1946–1957 campaign to preserve public supported childcare.* Doctoral dissertation, College of Communication of Ohio University. Ann Arbor, MI: UMI Dissertation Services.

Hawthorne, P. (2002). Positively *Sesame Street. Time.* Retrieved from http://www.time.com/time/magazine/article/ 0,9171,901020930-353521,00.html

Hay, D. F., Nash, A., & Pedersen, J. (1983). Interaction between six-month-old peers. *Child Development, 54,* 557–562.

Hay, D. F., Payne, A., & Chadwick, A. (2004). Peer relations in childhood. *Journal of Child Psychology and Psychiatry, 45*(1), 84–108.

Hay, D. F., & Ross, H. S. (1982). The social nature of early conflict. *Child Development, 53*(1), 105–113.

Hazen, C., & Shaver, P. (1987). Romantic love conceptualized as an attachment process. *Journal of Personality and Social Psychology, 52*(3), 511–524.

Head Start Family and Child Experiences Survey (FACES). (2007). Retrieved from http://www.acf.hhs.gov/programs/opre/hs/faces/reports/faces_findings_06/faces06_children.html

Heath, P. (2005). *Parent-child relations: History, theory, research, and context.* Upper Saddle River, NJ: Pearson.

Hechtman, P., Kaplan, F., Ayleran, J., Boulay, B., Andermann, E., de Braekeleer, M., . . . Scriber, C. (1990). More than one mutant allele causes infantile Tay-Sachs disease in French-Canadians. *American Journal of Human Genetics, 47*(5), 815–822.

Hedden, T., Ketay, S., Aron, S., Markus, H. R., & Gabrieli, J. D. E. (2008). Cultural influences on neural substrates of attentional control. *Psychological Science, 19*(1), 12–17.

Henggeler, S. W., Melton, G. B., Brondino, M. J., Scherer, D. G., & Hanley, J. H. (1997). Multisystemic therapy with violent and chronic juvenile offenders and their families: The role of treatment fidelity in successful dissemination. *Journal of Consulting and Clinical Psychology, 65*(5), 821–833.

Hennessey, B. A. (2007). Promoting social competence in school-aged children: The effects of the Open Circle Program. *Journal of School Psychology, 45*(3), 349–360.

Hennighausen, K. H., & Lyons-Ruth, K. (2005). Disorganization of behavioral and attentional strategies toward primary attachment figures: From biologic to dialogic processes. In C. S. Carter, L. Ahnert, K. E. Grossmann, S. B. Hrdy, M. E. Lamb, S. W. Porges, & N. Sachser (Eds.), *Attachment and bonding: A new synthesis* (pp. 269–300). Cambridge, MA: MIT Press.

Hennighausen, K. H., & Lyons-Ruth, K. (2010). Disorganization of attachment strategies in infancy and childhood. In *Encyclopedia on early childhood development.* Centre of Excellence for Early Childhood Development. Retrieved from http://www.enfant-encyclopedie.com/pages/PDF/Hennighausen-LyonsRuthANGxp_rev.pdf

Henry, B., Caspi, A., Moffitt, T. E., Harrington, H. L., & Silva, P. A. (1999). Staying in school protects boys with poor self-regulation in childhood from later crime: A longitudinal study. *International Journal of Behavioral Development, 23*(4), 1049–1073.

Hepper, P. G., Wells, D. L., & Lynch, C. (2005). Prenatal thumb sucking is related to postnatal handedness. *Neuropsychologia, 43*(3), 313–315.

Herrnstein, R. J., & Murray, C. (1994). The bell curve: Intelligence and class structure in American life. New York, NY: Free Press.

Hetherington, E. M. (1991). Presidential address: Families, lies and videotapes. *Journal of Research on Adolescence, 1*(4), 323–348.

Hetherington, E. M., Reiss, D., & Plomin, R. (Eds.). (1994). *Separate social words of siblings: The impact of nonshared environment on development.* Hillsdale, NJ: Erlbaum.

Hetherington, E. M., & Stanley-Hagan, M. (1999). The adjustment of children with divorced parents: A risk and resiliency perspective. *Journal of Child Psychology and Psychiatry, 40,* 129–140.

Hickman, G. R., Bartholomew, M., Mathwig, J., & Heinrich, R. S. (2008). Differential developmental pathways of high school dropouts and graduates. *Journal of Educational Research, 102*(1), 3–14.

Hill, C., Corbett, C., & St. Rose, A. (2010). *Why so few? Women in science, technology, engineering and mathematics.* Washington, DC: AAUW. Retrieved from http://www.aauw.org/learn/research/upload/whysofew.pdf

Hill, J. L., Brooks-Gunn, J., & Waldfogel, J. (2003). Sustained effects of high participation in early intervention for low-birth-weight premature infants. *Developmental Psychology, 39*(4), 730–744.

Hill, J. L., Waldfogel, J., Brooks-Gunn, J., & Han, W. J. (2005). Maternal employment and child development: A fresh look using newer methods. *Developmental Psychology, 41,* 833–850.

Hill, J. P., & Lynch, M. E. (1983). The intensification of gender-related role expectations during early adolescence. In J. Brooks-Gunn & A. C. Petersen (Eds.), *Girls at puberty: Biological and psychosocial perspectives* (pp. 201–228). New York, NY: Plenum.

Hill, M. S. (1992). *The panel study of income dynamics: A user's guide.* Newbury Park, CA: Sage.

Hill, N. E., Bromell, L., Tyson, D. F., & Flint, R. (2007). Developmental commentary: Ecological perspectives on parental influences during adolescence. *Journal of Clinical Child and Adolescent Psychiatry, 36*(3), 367–377.

Hillman, C. H., Buck, S. M., Themanson, J. R., Pontifex, M. B., & Castelli, D. M. (2009). Aerobic fitness and cognitive development: Event-related brain potential and task performance indices of executive control in preadolescent children. *Developmental Psychology, 45*(1), 114–129.

Hinde, E. R., & Perry, N. (2007). Elementary teachers' application of Jean Piaget's theories of cognitive development during social studies curriculum debates in Arizona. *The Elementary School Journal, 108*(1), 63–79.

Ho, Y. C., Cheung, M. C., & Chan, A. S. (2003). Music training improves verbal but not visual memory: Cross-sectional and longitudinal explorations in children. *Neuropsychology, 17,* 439–450.

Hodapp, R. M., Maxwell, M. A., Sellinger, M. H., & Dykens, E. M. (2006). Persons with mental retardation: Scientific, clinical and policy advances. In T. G. Plante (Ed.), *Mental disorders of the new millennium: Volume 3. Biology and function* (pp. 25–54). Westport, CT: Praeger.

Hoeve, M., Dubas, J. S., Eichelsheim, V. I., van der Laan, P. H., Smeenk, W., & Gerris, J. R. M. (2009). The relationship between parenting and delinquency: A meta-analysis. *Journal of Abnormal Child Psychology, 37*(6), 749–775.

Hoff, E., & Naigles, L. (2002). How children use input to acquire a lexicon. *Child Development, 73*(2), 418–433.

Hoffman, K., Marvin, R. S., Cooper, G., & Powell, B. (2006). Changing toddlers' and preschoolers' attachment classifications: The circle of security intervention. *Journal of Consulting and Clinical Psychology, 74*(6), 1017–1026.

Hoffman, L. W., & Youngblade, L. M. (1999). *Mothers at work: Effects on children's well-being.* Cambridge, UK: Cambridge University Press.

Hoffman, M. L. (1979). Development of moral thought, feeling, and behavior. *American Psychologist, 34*(10), 958–966.

Hoge, R. D., & Renzulli, J. S. (1991). *Self-concept and the gifted child* (RBDM 9104). Storrs, CT: The National Research Center on the Gifted and Talented, University of Connecticut.

Holcombe, E., Peterson, K., & Manlove, J. (2009). Ten reasons to still keep the focus on teen childbearing. *Child Trends Research Brief.* Retrieved from http://www.childtrends.org/Files//Child_Trends-2009_04_01_RB_KeepingFocus.pdf

Hollich, G., Golinkoff, R. M., & Hirsh-Pasek, K. (2007). Young children associate novel words with complex objects rather than salient parts. *Developmental Psychology, 43*(5), 1051–1061.

Holmbeck, G. N. (1996). A model of family relational transformation during the transition to adolescence: Parent-adolescent conflict and adaptation. In J. A. Graber, J. Brooks-Gunn, & A. C. Petersen (Eds.), *Transitions through adolescence: Interpersonal domains and context* (pp. 167–199). Mahwah, NJ: Erlbaum.

Holmbeck, G. N., Paikoff, R. L., & Brooks-Gunn, J. (1995). Parenting adolescents. In M. H. Bornstein (Ed.), *Handbook of parenting: Vol. 1. Children and parenting* (pp. 91–118). Mahwah, NJ: Erlbaum.

Honein, M. A., Paulozzi, L. J., & Erickson J. D. (2001). Continued occurrence of Accutane-exposed pregnancies. *Teratology, 64*(3), 142–147.

Hoover Institution. (2007). *Facts on policy: Infant mortality rate II: International comparison.* Retrieved from http://www.hoover.org/research/factsonpolicy/facts/7088621.html

Hopkins, B., & Johnson, S. P. (2005). *Prenatal development of postnatal functions.* Westport, CT: Praeger.

Hopson, J. L. (1998, September/October). Fetal psychology: Your baby can feel, dream and even listen to Mozart in the womb. *Psychology Today, 31,* 44–48.

Howden, M. (2007). *Stepfamilies: Understanding and responding effectively.* Australian Family Relationships Clearinghouse Briefing No. 6.

Howe, M. L., & Courage, M. L. (1993). On resolving the enigma of infantile amnesia. *Psychological Bulletin, 113*(2), 305–326.

Howell, E. A., Mora, P., & Leventhal, H. (2006). Correlates of early postpartum depressive symptoms. *Maternal & Child Health Journal, 10*(2), 149–157.

Howes, C., & Matheson, C. C. (1992). Sequences in the development of competent play with peers: Social and social pretend play. *Developmental Psychology, 28*(5), 961–974.

Hoyert, D. L. (2007). *Maternal mortality and related concepts.* National Center for Health Statistics. *Vital Health Stat 3*(33).

Hubel, D. H., & Wiesel, T. N. (1965). Comparison of the effects of unilateral and bilateral eye closure on cortical unit responses in kittens. *Journal of Neurophysiology, 28,* 1029–1040.

Huizink, A. C., & Mulder, E. J. H. (2006). Maternal smoking, drinking or cannabis use during pregnancy and neurobehavioral and cognitive functioning in human offspring. *Neuroscience & Biobehavioral Reviews, 30*(1), 24–41.

Human Genome Project Information. (2003). *CFTR: The gene associated with cystic fibrosis.* Retrieved from http://www.ornl.gov/sci/techresources/Human_Genome/posters/chromosome/cftr.shtml

Human Genome Project Information. (2008a). *Gene therapy.* Retrieved from http://www.ornl.gov/sci/techresources/Human_Genome/medicine/genetherapy.shtml

Human Genome Project Information. (2008b). *Insights learned from the human DNA sequence.* Retrieved from http://www.ornl.gov/sci/techresources/Human_Genome/project/journals/insights.html

Human Genome Project Information. (2008c). *U.S. Human Genome Project research goals.* Retrieved from http://www.ornl.gov/sci/techresources/Human_Genome/hg5yp/index.shtml

Human Genome Project Information. (2009). *Site index.* Retrieved from http://www.ornl.gov/sci/ techresources/Human_Genome/home.shtml

Human Genome Project Information. (n.d.). *Human genome landmarks poster: Chromosome viewer.* Retrieved from http://www.ornl.gov/sci/techresources/Human_Genome/posters/chromosome/chooser.shtml

Humphrey, J. H. (2003). *Child development through sport.* New York, NY: Haworth Press.

Humphrey, J. H. (2004). *Childhood stress in contemporary society.* New York, NY: Haworth Press.

Hunt, J. M. (1988). Relevance to educability: Heritability or range of reaction. In S. G. Cole & R. G. Demaree (Eds.), *Applications of interactionist psychology: Essays in honor of Saul B. Sells* (pp. 59–108). Hillsdale, NJ: Erlbaum.

Huston, A. C., Anderson, D. R., Wright, J. C., Linebarger, D. L., & Schmitt, K. L. (2001). *Sesame Street* viewers as adolescents: The recontact study. In S. M. Fisch & R. T. Truglio (Eds.), *"G" is for growing—Thirty years of research on children and* Sesame Street (pp. 131–146). Mahwah, NJ: Erlbaum.

Huston, A. C., Duncan, G. J., Granger, R., Bos, J., McLoyd, V., Mistry, R., . . . Ventura, A. (2001). Work-based antipoverty programs for parents can enhance the school performance and social behavior of children. *Child Development, 72*(1), 318–336.

Huston, A. C., Duncan, G. J., McLoyd, V. C., Crosby, D. A., Ripke, M. N., Weisner, T. S., & Eldred, C. A. (2005). Impacts on children of a policy to promote employment and reduce poverty for low-income parents: New hope after 5 years. *Developmental Psychology, 41*(6), 902–918.

Huston, A. C., Wright, J. C., Marquis, J., & Green, S. B. (1999). How young children spend their time: Television and other activities. *Developmental Psychology, 35*(4), 912–925.

Huttenlocher, P. E. (1999). Synaptogenesis in human cerebral cortex and the concept of critical periods. In N. A. Fox, L. A. Leavitt, & J. G. Warhol (Eds.), *The role of early experience in infant development* (pp. 15–28). New York, NY: Johnson & Johnson.

Huttenlocher, P. E., & Dabholkar, A. S. (1997). Regional differences in synaptogenesis in human cerebral cortex. *Journal of Comparative Neurology, 387*(2), 167–178.

Hyde, K. L., Lerch, J., Norton, A., Forgeard, M., Winner, E., Evans, A. C., & Schlaug, G. (2009). Musical training shapes structural brain development. *Journal of Neuroscience, 29*(10), 3019–3025.

Hyde, M. M., Lamb, Y., Arteaga, S. S., & Chavis, D. (2008). National evaluation of the Safe Start Demonstration Project: Implications for mental health practice. *Best Practices in Mental Health, 4*(1), 108–122.

Hymel, S., Vaillancourt, T., McDougall, P., & Renshaw, P. D. (2002). Peer acceptance and rejection in childhood. In P. K. Smith & C. H. Hart (Eds.), *Blackwell handbook of childhood social development* (pp. 265–284). Malden, MA: Blackwell.

Impett, E. A., Sorsoli, L., Schooler, D., Henson, J. M., & Tolman, D. L. (2008). Girls' relationship authenticity and self-esteem across adolescence. *Developmental Psychology, 44*(3), 722–733.

Institute of Education Sciences. (2007). *Intervention: Dialogic reading.* Retrieved from http://ies.ed.gov/ncee/wwc/reports/early_ed/dial_read/

Ip, S., Chung, M., Raman, G., Chew, P., Magula, N., DeVine, D., Trikalinos, T., & Lau, J. (2007). *Breastfeeding and maternal and infant health outcomes in developed countries.* Evidence Report-Technology Assessment No. 153. AHRQ Publication No. 07-E007. Rockville, MD: Agency for Health Care Research and Quality.

Ireson, J., Hallam, S., & Plewis, I. (2001). Ability grouping in secondary schools: Effects on pupils' self-concepts. *British Journal of Educational Psychology, 71*(2), 315–326.

Isay, R. A. (1996). Psychoanalytic therapy with gay men: Developmental considerations. In R. P. Cabaj & T. S. Stein (Eds.), *Textbook of homosexuality and mental health* (pp. 451–469). Washington, DC: American Psychiatric Association.

Ito, T., Ando, H., Suzuki, T., Ogura, T., Hotta, K., Imamura, Y., . . . Handa, H., (2010). Identification of a primary target of thalidomide teratogenicity. *Science, 327*(5971), 1345–1350.

Iverson, J. M., Capirci, O., Volterra, V., & Goldin-Meadow, S. (2008). Learning to talk in a gesture-rich world: Early communication in Italian vs. American children. *First Language, 28*(2), 164–181.

Iverson, J. M., & Goldin-Meadow, S. (2005). Gesture paves the way for language development. *Psychological Science, 16,* 368–371.

Izard, C. E. (2007). Basic emotions, natural kinds, emotion schemas and a new paradigm. *Perspectives on Psychological Science, 2*(3), 260–280.

Jaakola, J. K., & Gissler, M. (2007). Are girls more susceptible to the effects of prenatal exposure to tobacco smoke on asthma? *Epidemiology, 18,* 573–576.

Jack, F., MacDonald, S., Reese, E., & Hayne, H. (2009). Maternal reminiscing style during early childhood predicts the age of adolescents' earliest memories. *Child Development, 80*(2), 496–505.

Jack, R. E., Blais, C., Scheepers, C., Schyns, P. G., & Caldara, R. (2009). Cultural confusions show that facial expressions are not universal. *Current Biology, 19*(18), 1543–1548.

Jackson, C., Brown, J. D., & L'Engle, K. L. (2007). R-rated movies, bedroom televisions, and initiation of smoking by white and black adolescents. *Archives of Pediatrics & Adolescent Medicine, 161*(3), 260–268.

Jackson, K. M., & Nazar, A. M. (2006). Breastfeeding, the immune response, and long-term health. *Journal of the American Osteopathic Association, 106*(4), 203–207.

Jacobs, B. A., & Lefgren, L. (2004). Remedial education and student achievement: A regression continuity analysis. *The Review of Economics and Statistics, 86*(1), 226–244.

Jacobs, J. E., Davis-Kean, P., Bleeker, M., Eccles, J. S., & Malanchuk, O. (2005). I can, but I don't want to: The impact of parents, interests, and activities on gender differences in math. In A. Gallagher & J. Kaufman (Ed.), *Gender differences in mathematics* (pp. 246–263). New York, NY: Cambridge University Press.

Jacobson, J. L., & Wille, D. E. (1986). The influence of attachment pattern on developmental changes in peer interaction from the toddler to the preschool period. *Child Development, 57*(2), 338–347.

Jacquet, S. E., & Surra, C. A. (2004). Parental divorce and premarital couples: Commitment and other relationship characteristics. *Journal of Marriage and Family, 63*(3), 627–638.

Jaffee, S., & Hyde, J. S. (2000). Gender differences in moral orientation: A meta-analysis. *Psychological Bulletin, 126*(5), 703–726.

Jago, R., Baranowski, T., Baranowski, J. C., Thompson, D., & Greaves, K. A. (2005). BMI from 3–6 years of age is predicted by TV viewing and physical activity, not diet. *International Journal of Obesity, 29,* 557–564.

Jain, A., Belsky, J., & Crnic, K. (1996). Beyond fathering behaviors: Types of dads. *Journal of Family Psychology, 10*(4), 431–442.

Jambunathan, S., Burts, D. C., & Pierce, S. (2000). Comparisons of parenting attitudes among five ethnic groups in the United Sates. *Journal of Comparative Family Studies, 31*(4), 395–406.

James, W. (1990). *The principles of psychology.* Cambridge, MA: Harvard University Press. (Original work published in 1890)

James, W. (1992). The self. In W. James (Ed.), *Psychology: Briefer course* (pp. 174–209). New York, NY: Library Classics of the United States. (Original work published in 1892)

Jauniaux, E., & Greenough, A. (2007). Short and long term outcomes of smoking during pregnancy. *Early Human Development, 83*(11), 697–698.

Jennings, J., & Rentner, D. S. (1998). Youth and school reform: From the forgotten half to the forgotten third. In S. Halperin (Ed.), *The forgotten half revisited: American youth and young families, 1988–2008* (pp. 83–100). Washington, DC: American Youth Policy Forum.

Jensen, A. R. (1972). *Genetics and education.* New York, NY: Harper & Row.

Jepsen, J., & Martin, H. (2006). *Born too early: Hidden handicaps of premature children.* London, England: Karnac Books.

Johnson, C. P., & Walker, W. O. (2006). Mental retardation: Management and prognosis. *Pediatrics in Review, 27,* 249–256.

Johnson, D., & Sulzby, E. (1999). Addressing the literacy needs of emergent and early readers. *Pathways to School Improvement.* Retrieved from http://www.ncrel.org/sdrs/areas/issues/content/cntareas/reading/li100.htm

Johnson, J. G., Cohen, P., Kasen, S., & Brook, J. S. (2007). Extensive television viewing and the development of attention and learning difficulties during adolescence. *Archives of Pediatrics & Adolescent Medicine, 16*(5), 480–486.

Johnson, J. G., Cohen, P., Smailes, E. M., Kasen, S., & Brook, J. S. (2002). Television viewing and aggressive behavior during adolescence and adulthood. *Science, 295*(5564), 2468–2471.

Johnson, J. H. (1986). *Life events as stressors in childhood and adolescence.* Newbury Park, CA: Sage.

Johnson, J. S., & Newport, E. L. (1989). Critical period effects in second language learning: The influence of maturational state on the acquisition of English as a second language. *Cognitive Psychology, 21*(1), 60–99.

Johnson, K. (2000). *Do small classes influence academic achievement? What the National Assessment of Education Progress shows* [Center for Data Analysis Report #00–07]. Washington, DC: Heritage Foundation.

Johnson, V. E., & de Villiers, J. G. (2009). Syntactic frames in fast mapping verbs: Effects of age, dialect, and clinical status. *Journal of Speech, Language, and Hearing Research, 52*(3), 610–622.

Johnston, L. D., O'Malley, P. M., Bachman, J. G., & Schulenberg, J. E. (2007). *Monitoring the Future national survey results on drug use, 1975–2006: Volume I, Secondary school students* (NIH Publication No. 07-6205). Bethesda, MD: National Institute on Drug Abuse.

Johnston, L. D., O'Malley, P. M., Bachman, J. G., & Schulenberg, J. E. (2009). *Teen marijuana use tilts up, while some drugs decline in use.* University of Michigan News Service: Ann Arbor, MI. Retrieved from http://www.monitoringthefuture.org

Joiner, L. L. (2007). The road to stress is paved with good parental intentions. *Gannett News Service, USA Today.* Retrieved from http://www.usatoday.com/news/education/2007-08-15-kids-scheduling_N.htm

Jones, E. G., Renger, R., & Kang, Y. (2007). Self-efficacy for health-related behaviors among deaf adults. *Research in Nursing & Health, 30*(2), 185–192.

Jones, E. M., & Landreth, G. (2002). The efficacy of intensive individual play therapy for chronically ill children. *International Journal of Play Therapy, 11*(1), 117–140.

Jones, M. C. (1924). A laboratory study of fear: The case of Peter. *Pedagogical Seminary, 31,* 308–315.

Jones, M. G., & Wheatley, J. (1990). Gender differences in teacher-student interactions in science classrooms. *Journal of Research in Science Teaching, 27*(9), 861–874.

Jónsson, F. H., Njardvik, U., Ólafsdóttir, G., & Grétarsson, S. J. (2000). Parental divorce: Long-term effects on mental health, family relations and adult sexual behavior. *Scandinavian Journal of Psychology, 41*(2), 101–105.

Jorde, L. B., Carey, J. C., Bamshad, M. J., & White, R. L. (2006). *Medical genetics* (3rd ed.). St. Louis, MO: Mosby.

Jose-Miller, A. B., Boyden, J. W., & Frey, K. A. (2007). Infertility. *American Family Physician, 75*(6), 849–856.

Joseph, J. (2001). Separated twins and the genetics of personality differences: A critique. *American Journal of Psychology, 114*(1), 1–30.

Jurkovic, G. J., Thirkield, A., & Morrell, R. (2001). Parentification of adult child of divorce: A multidimensional analysis. *Journal of Youth and Adolescence, 30*(2), 245–257.

Jusko, T. A., Henderson, C. R., Lanphear, B. P., Dory-Slechta, D. A., Parsons, P. J., & Canfield, R. L. (2008). Blood lead concentrations < 10 μg/dL and child intelligence at 6 years of age. *Environmental Health Perspectives, 116*(2), 243–248.

Kagan, J. (2008). In defense of qualitative changes in development. *Child Development, 79*(6), 1606–1624.

Kahle, J. B., & Lakes, M. K. (1983). The myth of equality in science classrooms. *Journal of Research in Science Teaching, 20*(2), 131–140.

Kahn, M. (2002). *Basic Freud.* New York, NY: Basic Books.

Kail, R. V., & Ferrer, E. (2007). Processing speed in childhood and adolescence: Longitudinal models for examining developmental change. *Child Development, 78*(6), 1760–1770.

Kaiser, L. L., Melgar-Quiñonez, H., Townsend, M. S., Hicholson, Y., Fujii, M. L., Martin, A. C., & Lamp, C. L. (2003). Food insecurity and food supplies in Latino households with young children. *Journal of Nutrition Education & Behavior, 35*(3), 148–153.

Kaiser Family Foundation. (2007). *Health care spending in the United States and OECD countries.* Retrieved from http://www.kff.org/insurance/snapshot/chcm010307oth.cfm

Kalb, C. (2004, January 26). Brave new babies. *Newsweek,* pp. 45–53.

Kalb, C. (2005, February 28). When does autism start? *Newsweek,* pp. 45–47, 50–53.

Kalben, B. B. (2002). *Why men die younger: Causes of mortality differences by sex.* SOA Monograph M-LI01-1. Schaumberg, IL: Society of Actuaries.

Kaler, S. R., & Freeman, B. J. (1994). Analysis of environmental deprivation: Cognitive and social development in Romanian orphans. *Journal of Child Psychology and Psychiatry, 35*(4), 769–781.

Kalter, N. (1990). *Growing up with divorce.* London, England: Collier Macmillan.

Kaltiala-Heino, R., Kosunen, E., & Rimpela, M. (2003). Pubertal timing, sexual behaviour and self-reported depression in middle adolescence. *Journal of Adolescence, 26,* 531–545.

Kamii, C., Rummelsburg, J., & Kari, A. (2005). Teaching arithmetic to low-performing, low-SES first graders. *Journal of Mathematical Behavior, 24*(1), 39–50.

Kanaya, T., Ceci, S. J., & Scullin, M. H. (2003). The rise and fall of IQ in special ed: Historical trends and their implications. *Journal of School Psychology, 41*(6), 453–465.

Kandel, D. B. (1978). Homophily, selection, and socialization in adolescent friendships. *American Journal of Sociology, 84*(2), 427–436.

Kandel, D. B., & Lesser, G. S. (1972). *Youth in two worlds.* San Francisco, CA: Jossey-Bass.

Kanner, L. (1949). Problems of nosology and psychodynamics of early infantile autism. *American Journal of Orthopsychiatry, 19,* 416–426.

Kanters, M. A., Bocarro, J., & Casper, J. (2008). Supported or pressured? An examination of agreement among parents and children on parent's role in youth sports. *Journal of Sport Behavior, 31*(1), 64–80.

Kapadia, S. (2008). Adolescent-parent relationships in Indian and Indian immigrant families in the US: Intersections and disparities. *Psychology and Developing Societies, 20,* 257–275.

Kapoun, J. (1998, July/August). Teaching undergrads WEB evaluation: A guide for library instruction. *C&RL News,* 522–523. Available from http://www.ala.org/ala/mgrps/divs/acrl/publications/crlnews/1998/jul/teachingundergrads.cfm

Karmiloff, K., & Karmiloff-Smith, A. (2001). *Pathways to language.* Cambridge, MA: Harvard University Press.

Karney, B. R., Beckett, M. K., Collins, R. L., & Shaw, R. (2007). *Adolescent romantic relationships as precursors of healthy adult marriages: A review of theory, research, and programs.* Santa Monica, CA: RAND Corporation TR-488-ACF. (Technical report prepared by the RAND Labor and Population Program for the U.S. Department of Health and Human Services).

Karwelt, N. L. (1999). *Grade retention: Prevalence, timing, and effects* [CRESPAR Report No. 33]. Baltimore, MD: Johns Hopkins University.

Katz, V. L. (2003). Prenatal care. In J. S. Scott, R. S. Gibbs, B. Y. Karlan, & A. F. Haney (Eds.), *Danforth's obstetrics and gynecology* (9th ed., pp. 1–33). Philadelphia, PA: Lippincott.

Kaufman, J., & Zigler, E. (1993). The intergenerational transmission of abuse is overstated. In R. J. Gelles & D. R. Loseke (Eds.), *Current controversies on family violence* (pp. 209–221). Newbury Park, CA: Sage.

Kavšek, M. (2004). Predicting later IQ from infant visual habitation and dishabituation: A meta-analysis. *Journal of Applied Developmental Psychology, 25*(3), 369–393.

Kazdin, A. E., & Benjet, C. (2003). Spanking children: Evidence and issues. *Current Directions in Psychological Science, 12*(3), 99–103.

Kazdin, A. E., & Marciano, P. L. (1998). Childhood and adolescent depression. In E. J. Mash & R. A. Barkley (Eds.), *Treatment of childhood disorders* (2nd ed., pp. 211–248). New York, NY: Guilford.

Kemp, N., & Bryant, P. (2003). Do beez buzz? Rule-based and frequency-based knowledge in learning to spell plurals. *Child Development, 74*(1), 63–74.

Kennedy, H. (1997). Karl Heinrich Ulrichs: First theorist of homosexuality. In V. A. Rosario (Ed.), *Science and homosexualities* (pp. 26–45). New York, NY: Routledge.

Kennell, J., Klaus, M., McGrath, S., Robertson, S., & Hinkley, C. (1991). Continuous emotional support during labor in a US hospital. A randomized controlled trial. *Journal of the American Medical Association, 265*(17), 2197–2201.

Kennell, J. H., & Klaus, M. H. (1979). Early mother–infant contact: Effects on the mother and the infant. *Bulletin of the Menninger Clinic, 43*(1), 69–78.

Kenney-Benson, G. A., Pomerantz, E. M., Ryan, A. M., & Patrick, H. (2006). Sex differences in math performance: The role of children's approach to schoolwork. *Developmental Psychology, 42*(1), 11–26.

Kent, J. S., & Clopton, J. S. (1992). Bulimic women's perceptions of their family relationships. *Journal of Clinical Psychology, 48*(3), 281–292.

Keogh, B. K., & MacMillan, D. I. (1996). Exceptionality. In D. C. Berliner & R. C. Calfee (Eds.), *Handbook of educational psychology* (pp. 311–330). New York, NY: Macmillan.

Kerpelman, J. L., & Smith, S. L. (1999). Adjudicated adolescent girls and their mothers: Examining identity perceptions and processes. *Youth & Society, 30*(3), 313–347.

KidsHealth. (2008). *10 things that might surprise you about being pregnant.* Retrieved from http://kidshealth.org/parent/pregnancy_newborn/pregnancy/pregnancy.html

Kiesner, J., Kerr, M., & Stattin, H. (2004). "Very important persons" in adolescence: Going beyond in-school, single friendships in the study of peer homophily. *Journal of Adolescence, 27,* 545–560.

Kim, K. H. (2005). Can only intelligent people be creative? A meta-analysis. *Journal of Secondary Gifted Education, 16*(2–3), 57–66.

Kim, K. H. (2008). Meta-analyses of the relationship of creative achievement to both IQ and divergent thinking test scores. *Journal of Creative Behavior, 42*(2), 106–130.

Kim-Cohen, J., Caspi, A., Taylor, A., Williams, B., Newcombe, R., Craig, I. W., & Moffitt, T. E. (2006). MAOA, maltreatment, and gene-environment interaction predicting children's mental health: New evidence and a meta-analysis. *Molecular Psychiatry, 11*(10), 903–913.

Kinsbourne, M. (2009). Development of cerebral lateralization in children. In C. R. Reynolds & E. Fletcher-Janzen (Eds.), *Handbook of clinical child neuropsychology* (3rd ed., pp. 47–66). New York, NY: Springer.

Kinsey Institute. (1999). *Prevalence of homosexuality.* Retrieved from http://www.kinseyinstitute.org/resources/bib-homoprev.html#reviews

Kirkorian, H. L., Wartella, E. A., & Anderson, D. R. (2008). Children and electronic media. *The Future of Children, 18*(1), 39–62.

Kirschner, F., Paas, F., & Kirschner, P. A. (2009). A cognitive load approach to collaborative learning: United brains for complex tasks. *Educational Psychology Review, 21*(1), 31–42.

Kisilevsky, B. S., & Low, J. A. (1998). Human fetal behavior: 100 years of study. *Developmental Review, 18,* 1–29.

Klaw, E. L., Rhodes, J. E., & Fitzgerald, L. F. (2003). Natural mentors in the lives of African American adolescent mothers: Tracking relationships over time. *Journal of Youth and Adolescence, 32*(3), 223–232.

Kleiber, D. A., & Powell, G. M. (2005). Historical change in leisure activities during after-school hours. In J. L. Mahoney, R. W. Larson, & J. S. Eccles (Eds.), *Organized activities as contexts of development* (pp. 23–44). Mahwah, NJ: Erlbaum.

Klein, P. D. (1997). Multiplying the problems of intelligence by eight: A critique of Gardner's theory. *Canadian Journal of Education, 22*(4), 377–394.

Kline, W. H. (2006). The re-emergence of separation fears in the college bound adolescent: From disruption to resolution. *Journal of Infant, Child & Adolescent Psychotherapy, 5*(4), 420–436.

Kling, K. C., Hyde, J. S., Showers, C. J., & Buswell, B. N. (1999). Gender differences in self-esteem: A meta-analysis. *Psychological Bulletin, 125,* 470–500.

Klump, K. L., Kaye, W. H., & Strober, M. (2001). The evolving genetic foundations of eating disorders. *Psychiatric Clinics of North America, 24*(2), 215–225.

Kobus, K. (2003). Peers and adolescent smoking. *Addiction, 98,* 37–55.

Kochanska, G., & Aksan, N. (2006). Children's conscience and self-regulation. *Journal of Personality, 74*(6), 1587–1617.

Kochanska, G., Aksan, N., Prisco, T. R., & Adams, E. E. (2008). Mother-child and father-child mutually responsive orientation in the first 2 years and children's outcomes at preschool age: Mechanisms of influence. *Child Development, 79*(1), 30–44.

Kochanska, G., Barry, R. A., Aksan, N., & Boldt, L. J. (2008). A developmental model of maternal and child contributions to disruptive conduct: The first six years. *Journal of Child Psychology and Psychiatry, 49*(11), 1220–1227.

Kogan, M. D., Overpeck, M. D., Hoffman, H. J., & Casselbrant, M. L. (2000). Factors associated with tympanostomy tube insertion among preschool-age children in the United States. *American Journal of Public Health, 90*(2), 245–250.

Kohlberg, L. (1966). A cognitive-developmental analysis of children's sex-role concepts and attitudes. In E. E. Maccoby (Ed.), *The development of sex differences* (pp. 82–173). Palo Alto, CA: Stanford University Press.

Kohlberg, L. (1987). The development of moral judgment and moral action. In L. Kohlberg (Ed.), *Child psychology and childhood education* (pp. 259–328). White Plains, NY: Longman.

Kohlberg, L. (2005). Moral stages and moralization: The cognitive-developmental approach. In C. Lewis & J. G. Bremner (Eds.), *Developmental psychology II: Social and language development* (Vol. 5, pp. 201–231). Thousand Oaks, CA: Sage.

Kohlberg, L., Yaeger, J., & Hjertholm, E. (1968). Private speech: Four studies and a review of theories. *Child Development, 39,* 691–736.

Kokko, K., & Pulkkinen, L. (2005). Stability of aggressive behavior from childhood to middle age in women and men. *Aggressive Behavior, 31*(5), 485–497.

Konijn, E. A., Bijvank, M. N., & Bushman, B. J. (2007). I wish I were a warrior: The role of wishful identification in the effects of violent video games on aggression in adolescent boys. *Developmental Psychology, 43*(4), 1038–1044.

Koplan, J. P., Liverman, C. T., & Kraak, V. I. (Eds.). (2005). *Preventing childhood obesity: Health in the balance.* Washington, DC: National Academies Press.

Korenman, S., Miller, J. E., & Sjaastad, J. E. (1995). Long-term poverty and child development in the United States: Results from the NLSY. *Children and Youth Services Review, 17*(1–2), 127–155.

Kovács, Á. M., & Mehler, J. (2009). *Cognitive gains in 7-month-old bilingual infants. Proceedings of the National Academy of Sciences of the United States of America, 106*(16), 6556–6560.

Kowalski, R. M., & Limber, S. P. (2007). Electronic bullying among middle school students. *Journal of Adolescent Health, 41*(6 Supplement), S22–S30.

Kowatch, R. A., Youngstrom, E. A., Danielyan, A., & Findling, R. L. (2005). Review and meta-analysis of the phenomenology and clinical characteristics of mania in children and adolescents. *Bipolar Disorders, 7*(6), 483–496.

Krabbe, S., Christiansen, C., Rødbro, P., & Transbol, I. (1979). Effect of puberty on rates of bone growth and mineralisation: With observations in male delayed puberty. *Archives of Disease in Childhood, 54*(12), 950–953.

Krafft, K. C., & Berk, L. E. (1998). Private speech in two preschools: Significance of open-ended activities and make-believe play for verbal self-regulation. *Early Childhood Research Quarterly, 13*(4), 637–658.

Kratz, L., Uding, N., Trahms, C. M., Villareale, N., & Kierkhefer, G. M. (2009). Managing childhood chronic illness: Parent perspectives and implications for parent-provider relationships. *Families, Systems, & Health, 27*(4), 303–313.

Krcmar, M., Grela, B., & Lin, K. (2007). Can toddlers learn vocabulary from television? An experimental approach. *Media Psychology, 10*(1), 41–63.

Kreppner, J. M., Rutter, M., Beckett, C., Castle, J., Colvert, E., Groothues, C., . . . Sonuga-Barke, E. J. S. (2007). Normality and impairment following profound early institutional deprivation: A longitudinal follow-up into early adolescence. *Developmental Psychology, 43*(4), 931–946.

Krevans, J., & Gibbs, J. C. (1996). Parents' use of inductive discipline: Relations to children's empathy and prosocial behavior. *Child Development, 67*(6), 3263–3277.

Kroeger, K. A., Schultz, J. R., & Newsom, C. (2007). A comparison of two group-delivered social skills programs for young children with autism. *Journal of Autism and Developmental Disorders, 37*(5), 808–817.

Kronk, C. M. (1994). Private speech in adolescents. *Adolescence, 29*(116), 781–804.

Krug, E. G., Dahlberg, L., Mercy, J., Zwi, A., & Lozano, R. (2002). *World report on violence and health.* Geneva, Switzerland: World Health Organization.

Kubey, R., & Csikszentmihalyi, M. (1990). *Television and the quality of life.* Hillsdale, NJ: Erlbaum.

Kuczynski, L., & Kochanska, G. (1995). Function and content of maternal demands: Developmental significance of early demands for competent action. *Child Development, 66*(3), 616–628.

Kulik, J. A., & Kulik, C. C. (1984). Effects of accelerated instruction on students. *Review of Educational Research, 54,* 409–425.

Kunz, J. (2001). Parental divorce and children's interpersonal relationships: A meta-analysis. *Journal of Divorce & Remarriage, 34*(3/4), 19–47.

Kunzinger, E. L. (1985). A short-term longitudinal study of memorial development during early grade school. *Developmental Psychology, 21*(4), 642–646.

Kurdek, L. A. (2004). Gay men and lesbians. In M. Coleman & L. H. Ganong (Eds.), *Handbook of contemporary families* (pp. 96–115). Thousand Oaks, CA: Sage.

Kutscher, M. (2008). *ADHD—Living without brakes.* Philadelphia, PA: Jessica Kingsley.

La Greca, A. M., & Prinstein, M. J. (1999). Peer group. In W. K. Silverman & T. H. Ollendick (Eds.), *Developmental issues in the treatment of children* (pp. 171–198). Boston, MA: Allyn & Bacon.

Labouvie-Vief, G. (2006). Emerging structures of adult thought. In J. A. Arnett & J. L. Tanner (Eds.), *Emerging adults in America: Coming of age in the 21st century* (pp. 59–84). Washington, DC: American Psychological Association.

Lachance, J. A., & Mazzocco, M. M. M. (2006). A longitudinal analysis of sex differences in math and spatial skills in primary school age children. *Learning and Individual Differences, 16*(3), 195–216.

LaGravenese, R. (Director). (2007). *Freedom writers* [Motion picture]. United States: Paramount.

Laible, D. (2007). Attachment with parents and peers in late adolescence: Links with emotional competence and social behavior. *Personality and Individual Differences, 43*(5), 1185–1197.

Laird, J. A., & Feldman, S. S. (2004). Evaluation of the Summerbridge Intervention Program: Design and preliminary findings. In G. D. Borman & M. Boulay (Eds.), *Summer learning: Research, policies, and programs* (pp. 199–229). Mahwah, NJ: Erlbaum.

Lamaze International. (2010). *Lamaze's approach to birth.* Retrieved from http://www.lamaze .org/AboutLamaze/MissionandVision/ LamazePhilosophyofBirth/tabid/378/ Default.aspx

Lamaze International. (n.d.). *What is Lamaze?* Retrieved from http://www.lamazevideo .com/asprog.html

Lamb, M. E., Sternberg, K., Orbach, Y., Esplin, P., Stewart, H., & Mitchell, S. (2003). Age differences in children's responses to open ended invitations in the course of forensic interviews. *Journal of Consulting and Clinical Psychology, 71,* 926–934.

Lamborn, S. D., Dornbusch, S. M., & Steinberg, L. (1996). Ethnicity and community context as moderators of the relations between family decision making and adolescent adjustment. *Child Development, 67*(2), 283–301.

Lamborn, S. D., Mounts, N. S., Steinberg, L., & Dornbusch, S. M. (1991). Patterns of competence and adjustment among adolescents from authoritative, authoritarian, indulgent, and neglectful families. *Child Development, 62*(5), 1049–1065.

Landhuis, C. E., Poulton, R., Welch, D., & Hancox, R. J. (2007). Does childhood television viewing lead to attention problems in adolescence? Results from a prospective longitudinal study. *Pediatrics, 120*(3), 532–537.

Landry, S. H., Smith, K. E., Swank, P. R., & Guttentag, C. (2008). A responsive parenting intervention: The optimal timing across early childhood for impacting maternal behaviors and child outcomes. *Developmental Psychology, 44,* 1335–1353.

Lane, J. (1994). *History of genetics timeline.* Retrieved from http://www.accessexcellence.org/AE/AEPC/WWC/1994/genetic stln.php

Langercrantz, H., & Slotkin, T. A. (1986). The "stress" of being born. *Scientific American, 254,* 100–107.

Lansford, J. E., Deater-Deckard, K., Dodge, K. A., Bates, J. E., & Pettit, G. S. (2004). Ethnic differences in the link between physical discipline and later adolescent externalizing behaviors. *Journal of Child Psychology and Psychiatry, 45*(4), 801–812.

Lansford, J. E., Putallaz, M., Grimes, C. L., Schiro-Osman, K. A., Kupersmidt, J. B., & Coie, J. D. (2006). Perceptions of friendship quality and observed behaviors with friends: How do sociometrically rejected, average, and popular girls differ? *Merrill-Palmer Quarterly, 52*(4), 694–720.

Lapalme, M., Hodgins, S., & LaRoche, C. (1997). Children of parents with bipolar disorder: A metaanalysis of risk for mental disorders. *Canadian Journal of Psychiatry/ La Revue canadienne de psychiatrie, 42*(6), 623–631.

Lappe, C., Herholz, S. C., Trainor, L. J., & Pantev, C. (2008). Cortical plasticity induced by short-term unimodal and multimodal musical training. *Journal of Neuroscience, 28*(39), 9632–9639.

Lapsley, D. K. (2006). Moral stage theory. In M. Killen & J. Smetana (Eds.), *Handbook of moral development* (pp. 37–66). Mahwah, NJ: Erlbaum.

Lapsley, D. K., & Narvaez, D. (2004). Preface. In D. K. Lapsley & D. Narvaez (Eds.), *Moral development, self and identity* (pp. vii–xiii). Mahwah, NJ: Erlbaum.

Lara-Torre, E. (2009). Update in adolescent contraception. *Obstetrics & Gynecology Clinics of North America, 36*(1), 119–128.

Larsen, M. D., Griffin, N. S., & Larsen, L. M. (1994). Public opinion regarding support for special programs for gifted children. *Journal for the Education of the Gifted, 17*(2), 131–142.

Larson, J. P. (2002). Genetic counseling. In D. S. Blachfield & J. L. Longe (Eds.), *Gale encyclopedia of medicine* (Vol. 3, 2nd ed., pp. 1429–1431). Detroit, MI: Gale.

Larson, R. (2004). How U.S. children and adolescents spend time: What it does (and doesn't) tell us about their development. In J. Lerner & A. E. Alberts (Eds.), *Current directions in developmental psychology* (pp. 134–144). Upper Saddle River, NJ: Pearson Prentice Hall.

Larson, R. (2008). Family mealtimes as a developmental context. *Society for Research in Child Development Social Policy Report, 22*(4), 12.

Larson, R., & Richards, M. H. (1994). *Divergent realities: The emotional lives of mothers, fathers, and adolescents.* New York, NY: Basic Books.

Larson, R. W., & Brown, J. R. (2007). Emotional development in adolescence: What can be learned from a high school theater program? *Child Development, 78*(4), 1083–1099.

Larson, R. W., Richards, M. H., Moneta, G., Holmbeck, G., & Duckett, E. (1996). Changes in adolescents' daily interactions with their families from ages 10 to 18: Disengagement and transformation. *Developmental Psychology, 32,* 744–754.

Laursen, B., Furman, W., & Mooney, K. A. (2006). Predicting interpersonal competence and self-worth from adolescent relationships and relationship networks: Variable-centered and person-centered perspectives. *Merrill-Palmer Quarterly, 52*(3), 572–600.

Lavallee, M., & Dasen, P. (1980). Apprenticeship of the concept of class inclusion among Baoulé children (Ivory Coast). *International Journal of Psychology, 15*(1), 27–41.

Law, K. L., Stroud, L. R., LaGasse, L. L., Niaura, R., Liu, J., & Lester, B. (2003). Smoking during pregnancy and newborn neurobehavior. *Pediatrics, 111*(6), 1318–1323.

Lawrence, E., Rothman, A. D., Cobb, R. J., Rothman, M. T., & Bradbury, T. N. (2008). Marital satisfaction across the transition to parenthood. *Journal of Family Psychology, 22*(1), 41–50.

Lazarus, R. S. (1999). *Stress and emotion: A new synthesis.* New York, NY: Springer.

LD OnLine. (2008a). *Celebrity quiz.* Retrieved from http://www.ldonline.org/article/5938

LD OnLine. (2008b). *LD basics: What is a learning disability?* Retrieved from http://www.ldonline.org/ldbasics/whatisld

Le, H. (2000). Never leave your little one alone—Raising an Ifaluk child. In J. DeLoache & A. Gottlieb (Eds.), *A world of babies* (pp. 199-222). New York, NY: Cambridge University Press.

Learning Disabilities Association of America. (2006). *Defining learning disabilities.* Retrieved from http://www.ldanatl.org/new_to_ld/defining.asp

Lecanuet, J., Graniere-Deferre, C., & DeCasper, A. (2005). Are we expecting too much from prenatal sensory experiences? In B. Hopkins & S. P. Johnson (Eds.), *Prenatal development of postnatal functions* (pp. 31–49). Westport, CT: Praeger.

Lee, J., Grigg, W., & Donahue, P. (2007). *The nation's report card: Reading 2007* (NCES 2007–496). Washington, DC: National Center for Education Statistics, Institute of Education Sciences, U.S. Department of Education.

Lee, M. D., MacDermid, S. M., Dohring, P. L., & Kossek, E. E. (2005). Professionals becoming parents: Socialization, adaptation and identity transformation. In E. E. Kossek & S. J. Lambert (Eds.), *Work and life integration: Organization, cultural and individual perspectives* (pp. 287–317). Mahwah, NJ: Erlbaum.

Lehman, E. B., & Erdwins, C. J. (2004). The social and emotional adjustment of young, intellectually gifted children. In S. M. Moon (Ed.), *Social/emotional issues, underachievement, and counseling of gifted and talented students* (pp. 1–8). Thousand Oaks, CA: Corwin Press.

Lehmann, C. (2004). Brain studies could affect death penalty case outcome. *Psychiatric News, 39*(24), 10–34.

Leifer, M., & Smith, S. (1990). Towards breaking the cycle of intergenerational abuse. *American Journal of Psychotherapy, 44*(1), 116–128.

Lemish, D. (2007). *Children and television: A global perspective.* Oxford, England: Blackwell.

Lenhart, A., & Madden, M. (2007). *Social networking websites and teens: An overview.* Retrieved from http://www.pewinternet.org/PPF/r/198/report_display.asp

Lenhart, A., Rainie, L., & Lewis, O. (2001). *Teenage life online: The rise of the instant-message generation and the Internet's impact on friendships and family relationships.* Retrieved from http://www.pewinternet.org/Reports/2001/Teenage-Life-Online/Introduction/A-general-portrait-of-wired-teens.aspx?r=1

Lenroot, R. K., Greenstein, D. K., Gogtay, N., Wallace, G. L., Clasen, L. S., Blumenthal, J. D., . . . Giedd, J. N. (2007). Sexual dimorphism of brain developmental trajectories during childhood and adolescence. *NeuroImage, 36,* 1065–1073.

Lerner, R., Brennan, A. L., Noh, E. R., & Wilson, C. (1998). *The parenting of adolescents and adolescents as parents: A developmental contextual perspective.* Retrieved from http://parenthood.library.wisc.edu/Lerner/Lerner.html

Lerner, R. M. (1982). Children and adolescents as producers of their own development. *Developmental Review, 2,* 342–370.

Lerner, R. M. (2002). *Concepts and theories of human development* (3rd ed.). Mahwah, NJ: Erlbaum.

Lerner, R. M., Brentano, C., Dowling, E. M., & Anderson, P. M. (2002). Positive youth development: Thriving as the basis of personhood and civil society. *New Directions in Youth Development, 95,* 11–33.

Lescano, C. M., Vazquez, E. A., Brown, L. K., Litvin, E. B., & Pugatch, D. (2006). Condom use with "casual" and "main" partners: What's in a name? *Journal of Adolescent Health, 39*(3), e1–e7.

Leslie, M. (2000). The vexing legacy of Lewis Terman. *Stanford Magazine.* Retrieved from http://www.stanfordalumni.org/news/magazine/2000/julaug/articles/terman.html

Lester, D. (2001). Conscientiousness in childhood and later suicide. *Crisis, 22*(4), 143.

Leventhal, J. M. (2003). Test of time: "The battered child syndrome" 40 years later. *Clinical Child Psychology and Psychiatry, 8*(4), 543–545.

Levine, L. E. (1983). Mine: Self-definition in 2-year-old boys. *Developmental Psychology, 19*(4), 544–549.

Levine, L. E. (2002). Kohlberg, Lawrence (1927–1987). In N. J. Salkind (Ed.), *Child development* (pp. 225–226). New York, NY: Macmillan Reference USA.

Levine, L. E. (2003). Mr. Rogers: The nature of the man. *Clio's Psyche, 10,* 24.

Levine, L. E., & Waite, B. M. (2000). Television viewing and attentional abilities in fourth and fifth grade children. *Journal of Applied Developmental Psychology, 21*(6), 667–679.

Levine, L. E., & Waite, B. M. (2002). Television and the American child. *Clio's Psyche, 9*(1), 24–26.

LeVine, R. A., Dixon, S., LeVine, S., Richman, A., Leiderman, P. H., Keefer, C. H., & Brazelton, T. B. (1994). *Child care and culture: Lessons from Africa.* Cambridge, England: Cambridge University Press.

Lewinsohn, P. M., Gotlib, I. H., Lewinsohn, M., Seeley, J. R., & Allen, N. B. (1998). Gender differences in anxiety disorders and anxiety symptoms in adolescents. *Journal of Abnormal Psychology, 107*(1), 109–117.

Lewis, C., & Carpendale, J. (2002). Social cognition. In P. K. Smith & C. H. Hart (Eds.), *Blackwell handbook of childhood social development* (pp. 375–393). Malden, MA: Blackwell.

Lewis, C., & Lamb, M. E. (2003). Fathers' influences on children's development: The evidence from two-parent families. *European Journal of Psychology of Education, 18*(2), 211–228.

Lewis, M., & Rosenblum, L. A. (1974). *The effect of the infant on its caregiver.* New York, NY: Wiley.

Lewis, T. E., & Phillipsen, L. C. (1998). Interactions on an elementary school playground: Variations by age, gender, race, group size, and playground area. *Child Study Journal, 28*(4), 309–320.

Li, R., Darling, N., Maurice, E., Barker, L., & Grummer-Strawn, L. M. (2005). Breastfeeding rates in the United States by characteristics of the child, mother, or family: The 2002 National Immunization Survey. *Pediatrics, 115*(1), e31–e37.

Li, Q. (2006). Cyberbullying in schools: A research of gender differences. *School Psychology International, 27*(2), 157–170.

Light, K. C., Smith, T. E., Johns, J. M., Brownley, K. A., Hofheimer, J. A., & Amico, J. A. (2000). Oxytocin responsivity in mothers of infants: A preliminary study of relationships with blood pressure during laboratory stress and normal ambulatory activity. *Health Psychology, 19*(6), 560–567.

Lilienfeld, S. O., Wood, J. M., & Garb, H. N. (2000). The scientific status of projective techniques. *Psychological Science in the Public Interest, 1*(2), 27–66.

Lillard, A. (1998). Ethnopsychologies: Cultural variations in theories of mind. *Psychological Bulletin, 123*(1), 3–32.

Lim, M. M., Wang, Z., Olazábal, D. E., Ren, X., Terwilliger, E. F., & Young, L. J. (2004). Enhanced partner preference in a promiscuous species by manipulating the expression of a single gene. *Nature, 429,* 754–757.

Lim, M. M., & Young, L. J. (2006). Neuropeptidergic regulation of affiliative *behavior* and social bonding in animals. *Hormones and Behavior, 50*(4), 506–517.

Limosin, F., Rouillon, F., Payan, C., Cohen, J. M., & Strub, N. (2003). Prenatal exposure to influenza as a risk factor for adult schizophrenia. *Acta Psychiatrica Scandinavica, 107*(5), 331–335.

Linares-Scott, T. J., & Feeny, N. C. (2006). Relapse prevention techniques in the treatment of childhood anxiety disorders: A case example. *Journal of Contemporary Psychotherapy, 36*(4), 151–157.

Lindholm-Leary, K. (2000). *Biliteracy for a global society: An idea book on dual language education.* Washington, DC: National Clearinghouse for Bilingual Education.

Lindsey, E. W., & Colwell, M. J. (2003). Preschoolers' emotional competence: Links to pretend and physical play. *Child Study Journal, 33*(1), 39–52.

Lindsey, E. W., & Mize, J. (2000). Parent-child physical and pretense play: Links to children's social competence. *Merrill-Palmer Quarterly, 46*(4), 565–591.

Lips, H. (2008). *Sex and gender* (6th ed.) Boston, MA: McGraw-Hill.

Lips, H. M. (2006). *A new psychology of women* (3rd ed.). New York, NY: McGraw-Hill.

Loeber, R., & Hay, D. (1997). Key issues in the development of aggression and violence from childhood to early adulthood. *Annual Review of Psychology, 48,* 371–410.

Loeber, R., Keenan, K., Lahey, B. B., & Green, S. M. (1993). Evidence for developmentally based diagnoses of oppositional defiant disorder and conduct disorder. *Journal of Abnormal Child Psychology, 21*(4), 377–410.

Loeber, R., & Stouthamer-Loeber, M. (1998). Development of juvenile aggression and violence: Some common misconceptions and controversies. *American Psychologist, 53*(2), 242–259.

Loehlin, J. C., Horn, J. M., & Willerman, L. (1997). Heredity, environment and IQ in the Texas Adoption Project. In R. J. Sternberg & E. L. Grigorenko (Eds.), *Intelligence, heredity, and environment* (pp. 105–125). New York, NY: Cambridge University Press.

Logsdon, M. C., Wisner, K., & Shanahan, B. (2007). Evidence on postpartum depression: 10 publications to guide nursing practice. *Issues in Mental Health Nursing, 28,* 445–451.

London, B., Downey, G., Bonica, C., & Paltin, I. (2007). Social causes and consequences of rejection sensitivity. *Journal of Research on Adolescence, 17*(3), 481–506.

London, K., Bruck, M., Wright, D. B., & Ceci, S. J. (2008). Review of the contemporary literature on how children report sexual abuse to others: Findings, methodological issues, and implications for forensic interviewers. *Memory, 16*(1), 29–47.

López, F., Menez, M., & Hernández-Guzmán, L. (2005). Sustained attention during learning activities: An observational study with pre-school children. *Early Child Development and Care, 175*(2), 131–138.

Lorence, J., & Dworkin, A. G. (2006). Elementary grade retention in Texas and reading achievement among racial groups: 1994–2002. *Review of Policy Research, 23*(5), 999–1033.

Lorenz, K. (1988). *Here am I—Where are you? The behavior of the graylag goose.* New York, NY: Harcourt Brace Jovanovich.

Lou, Y., Abrami, P. C., Spence, J. C., Poulsen, C., Chambers, B., & d'Appolonia, S. (1996). Within-class grouping: A meta-analysis. *Review of Educational Research, 66*(4), 423–458.

Lovas, G. S. (2005). Gender and patterns of emotional availability in mother-toddler and father-toddler dyads. *Infant Mental Health Journal, 26*(4), 327–353.

Lovering, D. (2007). Smiley emoticon 25 years old? :-O. *The Hartford Courant,* p. E2.

Lowe, W. (2007). "I finally got real parents, and now they are gonna die"—A case study of an adolescent with two HIV-positive parents. *Families, Systems, and Health, 25*(2), 227–233.

Lucas, S. R. (1999). *Tracking inequality. Stratification and mobility in American high schools.* New York, NY: Teachers College Press.

Luckey, A. J., & Fabes, R. A. (2005). Understanding nonsocial play in early childhood. *Early Childhood Education Journal, 33*(2), 67–72.

Lydon-Rochelle, M. T., Cárdenas, V., Nelson, J. C., Holt, V. L., Gardella, C., & Easterling, T. R. (2007). Induction of labor in the absence of standard medical indications: Incidence and correlates. *Medical Care, 45*(6), 505–512.

Lykken, D. T., McGue, M., Tellegen, A., & Bouchard, T. J. (1992). Emergenesis: Genetic traits that may not run in families. *American Psychologist, 47*(12), 1565–1577.

Lyman, R. D., & Barry, C. T. (2006). The continuum of residential treatment care for conduct-disordered youth. In W. M. Nelson, III, A. J. Finch, Jr., & K. J. Hart (Eds.), *Conduct disorders: A practitioner's guide to comparative treatments* (pp. 259–297). New York, NY: Spring.

Lynch, S. J. (1994). *Should gifted students be grade-advanced?* ERIC EC Digest #E526.

Lyte, G., Milnes, L., & Keating, P. (2007). Review management for children with asthma in primary care: A qualitative case study. *Journal of Clinical Nursing, 16,* 123–132.

Lytton, H., & Romney, D. M. (1991). Parents' differential socialization of boys and girls: A meta-analysis. *Psychological Bulletin, 109*(2), 267–296.

Ma, H., Unger, J. B., Chou, C., Sun, P., Palmer, P. H., Zhou, Y., . . . Johnson, C. A. (2008). Risk factors for adolescent smoking in urban and rural China: Findings from the China seven cities study. *Addictive Behaviors, 33*(8), 1081–1085.

Maanzo, E. (2005). Why do Kenyans dominate marathons? *BBC News*. Retrieved from http://news.bbc.co.uk/2/hi/africa/4405082.stm

MacBeth, T. M. (1996). Indirect effects of television: Creativity, persistence, school achievement, and participation in other activities. In T. M. MacBeth (Ed.), *Tuning into young viewers* (pp. 149–219). Thousand Oaks, CA: Sage.

Maccoby, E. E. (1990). Gender and relationships: A developmental account. *American Psychologist, 45,* 513–520.

Maccoby, E. E. (1998). *The two sexes: Growing up apart, coming together.* Cambridge, MA: Belknap Press.

Maccoby, E. E. (2002). Gender and group process: A developmental perspective. *Current Directions in Psychological Science, 11*(2), 54–58.

Maccoby, E. E., & Martin, J. A. (1983). Socialization in the context of the family: Parent–child interaction. In P. H. Mussen (Ed.) & E. M. Hetherington (Vol. Ed.), *Handbook of child psychology: Vol. 4. Socialization, personality, and social development* (4th ed., pp. 1–101). New York, NY: Wiley.

MacFarlane, A. (1975). Olfaction in the development of social preferences in the human neonate. *Ciba Foundation Symposium, 33,* 103–117.

Mackey, M. C. (1990). Women's preparation for the childbirth experience. *Maternal-Child Nursing Journal, 19*(20), 143–173.

MacLean, K. (2003). The impact of institutionalization on child development. *Development and Psychopathology, 15*(4), 853–884.

MacLennan, A. (1999). A template for defining a causal relation between acute intrapartum events and cerebral palsy: International consensus statement. *British Medical Journal, 319*(7216),1054–1059.

MacMillan, R., McMorris, B. J., & Kruttschnitt, C. (2004). Linked lives: Stability and change in maternal circumstances and trajectories of antisocial behavior in children. *Child Development, 75*(1), 205–220.

MacNeil, G. A., & Newell, J. M. (2004). School bullying: Who, why, and what to do. *Prevention Researcher, 11*(3), 15–17.

Mahler, M. S., Bergman, A., & Pine, F. (2000). *The psychological birth of the human infant: Symbiosis and individuation.* New York, NY: Basic Books.

Mahler, M. S., Pine, F., & Bergman, A. (1975). *The psychological birth of the human infant.* New York, NY: Basic Books.

Mahoney, J. L., Harris, A. L., & Eccles, J. S. (2006). Organized activity participation, positive youth development, and the over-scheduling hypothesis. *Society for Research in Child Development Social Policy Report, 20*(4), 3–30.

Mahoney, J. L., Stattin, H., & Lord, H. (2004). Unstructured youth recreation centre participation and antisocial behaviour development: Selection influences and the moderating role of antisocial peers. *International Journal of Behavioral Development, 28*(6), 553–560.

Main, M., & Solomon, J. (1990). Procedures for identifying infants as disorganized/disoriented during the Ainsworth Strange Situation. In M. T. Greenberg, D. Cicchetti, & E. M. Cummings (Eds.), *Attachment in the preschool years: Theory, research, and intervention* (pp. 121–160). Chicago, IL: University of Chicago Press.

Malanga, C. J., & Kosofsky, B. E. (2003). Does drug abuse beget drug abuse? Behavioral analysis of addiction liability in animal models of prenatal drug exposure. *Developmental Brain Research, 147*(1–2), 47–57.

Malina, R. M., Bouchard, C., & Oded, B. (2004). *Growth, maturation, and physical activity.* Champaign, IL: Human Kinetics.

Mampe, B., Friederici, A. D., Christophe, A., & Wermke, K. (2009). Newborns' cry melody is shaped by their native language. *Current Biology, 19*(23), 1994–1997.

Mandel, S., & Sharlin, S. A. (2006). The non-custodial father: His involvement in his children's lives and the connection between his role and the ex-wife's, child's and father's perception of that role. *Journal of Divorce & Remarriage, 45*(1/2), 79–95.

Mandela, N. (1994). *Long walk to freedom.* Boston, MA: Little, Brown.

Mantzicopoulos, P. Y., & Oh-Hwang, Y. (1998). The relationship of psychosocial maturity to parenting quality and intellectual ability for American and Korean adolescents. *Contemporary Educational Psychology, 23*(2), 195–206.

March of Dimes. (2008). *Genetic counseling.* Retrieved from http://www.marchofdimes.com/pnhec/4439_15008.asp

March of Dimes Perinatal Data Center. (2002). *Adequacy of prenatal care by state, 2000.* Retrieved from http://www.marchofdimes.com/aboutus/1537.asp

Marcia, J. E. (1966). Development and validation of ego-identity status. *Journal of Personality and Social Psychology, 3*(5), 551–558.

Marcia, J. E. (1976). Identity six years after: A follow-up study. *Journal of Youth and Adolescence, 5*(2), 145–160.

Mareschal, D., & Shultz, T. R. (1999). Development of children's seriation: A connectionist approach. *Connection Science, 11*(2), 149–186.

Margosein, C. M., Pascarella, E. T., & Pflaum, S. W. (1982). The effects of instruction using semantic mapping on vocabulary and comprehension. *Journal of Early Adolescence, 2*(2), 185–194.

Markman, E. M. (1990). Constraints children place on word meanings. *Cognitive Science, 14*(1), 57–77.

Markovits, H., Benenson, J., & Dolenszky, E. (2001). Evidence that children and adolescents have internal models of peer interactions that are gender differentiated. *Child Development, 72*(3), 879–886.

Marks, A. K., Szalacha, L. A., Lamarre, M., Boyd, M. J., & Coll, C. G. (2007). Emerging ethnic identity and interethnic group social preferences in middle childhood: Findings from the Children of Immigrants Development in Context (CIDC) study. *International Journal of Behavioral Development, 31*(5), 501–513.

Markstrom-Adams, C. (1989). Androgyny and its relation to adolescent psychosocial well-being: A review of the literature. *Sex Roles, 21*(5–6), 325–340.

Marlier, L., Schaal, B., & Soussignan, R. (1998). Neonatal responsiveness to the odor of amniotic and lacteal fluids: A test of perinatal chemosensory continuity. *Child Development, 69*(3), 611–623.

Marsh, H. W., Seaton, M., Trautwein, R., Ludtke, O., Hau, K. T., O'Mara, A. J., & Craven, R. G. (2008). The big-fish-little-pond-effect stands up to critical scrutiny: Implications for theory, methodology, and future research. *Educational Psychology Review, 20*(3), 319–350.

Martin, C. L. (1990). Attitudes and expectations about children with nontraditional and traditional gender roles. *Sex Roles, 22*(3–4), 151–165.

Martin, M. T., Emery, R. E., & Peris, T. S. (2004). Single-parent families—Risk, resilience and change. In M. Coleman & L. H. Ganong (Eds.), *Handbook of contemporary families* (pp. 282–301). Thousand Oaks, CA: Sage.

Martinez, C. R., & Forgatch, M. S. (2002). Adjusting to change: Linking family structure transitions with parenting and boys' adjustment. *Journal of Family Psychology, 16,* 107–117.

Martinez, I., & Garcia, J. F. (2008). Internalization of values and self-esteem among Brazilian teenagers from authoritative, indulgent, authoritarian, and neglectful homes. *Family Therapy, 35*(1), 43–59.

Martino, S. C., Elliott, M. N., Collins, R. L., Kanouse, D. E., & Berry, S. H. (2008). Virginity pledges among the willing: Delays in first intercourse and consistency of condom use. *Journal of Adolescent Health, 43*(4), 341–348.

Martino, W., & Kehler, M. (2006). Male teachers and the "boy problem": An issue of recuperative masculinity politics. *McGill Journal of Education, 41*(2), 113–131.

Martins, C., & Gaffan, E. A. (2000). Effects of early maternal depression on patterns of infant-mother attachment: A meta-analytic investigation. *Journal of Child Psychology and Psychiatry, 41*(6), 737–746.

Maryland Committee for Children. (2006). *Staff turnover in child care centers: Maryland 2006.* Retrieved from http://www.mdchild-care.org/mdcfc/pdfs/staff_turnover06.pdf

Mash, E. J., & Hunsley, J. (2007). Assessment of child and family disturbance. In E. J. Mash & R. A. Barkley (Eds.), *Assessment of childhood disorders* (pp. 3–50). New York, NY: Guilford.

Masoni, M. A., Trimarchi, G., dePunzio, C., & Fioretti, P. (1994). The couvade syndrome. *Journal of Psychosomatic Obstetrics and Gynaecology, 15*(3), 125–131.

Massaro, D. W., & Cowan, N. (1993). Information-processing models: Microscopes of the mind. *Annual Review of Psychology, 44,* 383–425.

Masten, A. S. (2001). Ordinary magic: Resilience process in development. *American Psychologist, 56*(3), 227–238.

Masuda, T., & Nisbett, R. E. (2001). Attending holistically versus analytically: Comparing the context sensitivity of Japanese and Americans. *Journal of Personality and Social Psychology, 81*(5), 922–934.

Mathematical Association of America. (1998). *Birthday surprises.* Retrieved from http://www.maa.org/mathland/math-trek_11_23_98.html

Matsumoto, D. (1992). American-Japanese cultural differences in the recognition of universal facial expressions. *Journal of Cross-Cultural Psychology, 23*(1), 72–84.

Matsumoto, D. (2006). Are cultural differences in emotion regulation mediated by personality traits? *Journal of Cross-Cultural Psychology, 37*(4), 421–437.

Matsumoto, D., & Assar, M. (1992). The effects of language on judgments of universal facial expressions of emotion. *Journal of Nonverbal Behavior, 16*(2), 85–99.

Matsumoto, D., Consolacion, T., & Yamada, H. (2002). American-Japanese cultural differences in judgments of emotional expressions of different intensities. *Cognition and Emotion, 16*(6), 721–747.

Matsumoto, D., & Juang, L. (2004). *Culture and psychology* (3rd ed.). Belmont, CA: Wadsworth/Thomson.

Matsumoto, D., Yoo, S. H., Fontaine, J., & 56 members of the Multinational Study of Cultural Display Rules. (2009). Hypocrisy or maturity? Culture and context differentiation. *European Journal of Personality, 23,* 251–264.

Maurer, D., & Maurer, C. (1988). *The world of the newborn.* New York, NY: Basic Books.

Mayer, S. J. (2005). The early evolution of Jean Piaget's clinical method. *History of Psychology, 8*(4), 362–382.

Maynard, A. E. (2008). What we thought we knew and how we came to know it: Four decades of cross-cultural research

from a Piagetian point of view. *Human Development, 51,* 56–65.

Maynard, A. E., & Greenfield, P. M. (2003). Implicit cognitive development in cultural tools and children: Lessons from Maya Mexico. *Cognitive Development, 18*(4), 489–510.

Mayo Clinic. (2008). *Children's illness: Top 5 causes of missed school.* Retrieved from http://www.mayoclinic.com/print/childrens-conditions/CC00059/METHOD=print

Mayo Clinic. (2009a). *Reye's syndrome.* Retrieved from http://www.mayoclinic.com/health/reyes-syndrome/DS00142

Mayo Clinic. (2009b). *Sudden infant death syndrome (SIDS).* Retrieved from http://www.mayoclinic.com/print/sudden-infant-death-syndrome/DS00145/DSECTION=all&METHOD=print

Mayo Clinic. (2010). *Childhood asthma.* Retrieved from http://www.mayoclinic.com/health/childhood-asthma/DS00849

McCabe, L. A., & Brooks-Gunn, J. (2007). With a little help from my friends? Self-regulation in groups of young children. *Infant Mental Health Journal, 28*(6), 584–605.

McClelland, J. L., & Patterson, K. (2003). Differentiation and integration in human language: Reply. *Trends in Cognitive Sciences, 7*(2), 63–64.

McClun, L. A., & Merrell, K. W. (1998). Relationship of perceived parenting styles, locus of control orientation, and self-concept among junior high age students. *Psychology in the Schools, 35*(4), 381–390.

McClure, M. M., & Fitch, R. H. (2005). Hormones. In N. J. Salkind (Ed.), *Encyclopedia of human development* (pp. 646–649). Thousand Oaks, CA: Sage.

McCormick, T. W. (1988). *Theories of reading in dialogue: An interdisciplinary study.* New York, NY: University Press of America.

McCoy, K., Cummings, E. M., & Davies, P. T. (2009). Constructive and destructive marital conflict, emotional security and children's prosocial behavior. *Journal of Child Psychology and Psychiatry, 50*(3), 270–279.

McDonell, M. G., & McClellan, J. M. (2007). Early-onset schizophrenia. In E. J. Mash & R. A. Barkley (Eds.), *Assessment of childhood disorders* (pp. 526–550). New York, NY: Guilford.

McElwain, N. L., Booth-LaForce, C., Lansford, J. E., Wu, X., & Dyer, W. J. (2008). A process model of attachment-friend linkages: Hostile attribution biases, language ability, and mother-child affective mutuality as intervening mechanisms. *Child Development, 79*(6), 1891–1906.

McFeatters, A. (2002). Fred Rogers gets Presidential Medal of Freedom. *Post-Gazette.* Retrieved from http://www.post-gazette.com/ae/20020710fredrogersp1.asp

McGhee, P. E. (1979). *Humor: Its origin and development.* San Francisco, CA: Freeman.

McGue, M., Elkins, I., Walden, B., & Iacono, W. G. (2005). Perceptions of the parent-adolescent relationship: A longitudinal investigation. *Developmental Psychology, 41*(6), 972–984.

McGuffin, P., Riley, B., & Plomin, R. (2001). Genomics and behavior: Toward behavioral genomics. *Science, 291*(5507), 1232–1249.

McHale, S. M., Crouter, A. C., McGuire, S. A., & Updegraff, K. A. (1995). Congruence between mothers' and fathers' differential treatment of siblings: Links with family relations and children's well being. *Child Development, 66,* 116–128.

McHale, S. M., & Pawletko, T. M. (1992). Differential treatment of siblings in two family contexts. *Child Development, 63,* 68–81.

McHale, S. M., Whiteman, S. D., Kim, J., & Crouter, A. C. (2007). Characteristics and correlates of sibling relationships in two-parent African American families. *Journal of Family Psychology, 21*(2), 227–235.

McKeachie, W., & Sims, B. (2004). Review of *Educational Psychology: A century of contributions* [A project of Division 15 (Educational Psychology) of the American Psychological Association]. *Educational Psychology Review, 16*(3), 283–298.

McKim, M. K., Cramer, K. M., Stuart, B., & O'Connor, D. L. (1999). Infant care decisions and attachment security: The Canadian Transition to Child Care Study. *Canadian Journal of Behavioural Science, 31*(2), 92–106.

McKown, D., & Weinstein, R. S. (2008). Teacher expectations, classroom context, and the achievement gap. *Journal of School Psychology, 46*(3), 235–261.

McLanahan, S., & Carlson, M. S. (2004). Fathers in fragile families. In M. E. Lamb (Ed.), *The role of the father in child development* (4th ed., pp. 368–396). Hoboken, NJ: Wiley.

McLane, J. B., & McNamee, G. D. (1990). *Early literacy.* Cambridge, MA: Harvard University Press.

McLoyd, V. C. (1998). Socioeconomic disadvantage and child development. *American Psychologist, 53*(2), 185–204.

McLoyd, V. C. (2000). Childhood poverty. In A. E. Kazdin (Ed.), *Encyclopedia of psychology* (pp. 251–257). New York, NY: Oxford University Press.

McLoyd, V. C., Hill, N. E., & Dodge, K. A. (2005). Ecological and cultural diversity in African American family life. In V. C. McLoyd, N. E. Hill, & K. A. Dodge (Eds.), *African American family life* (pp. 3–20). New York, NY: Guilford

McMahon, R. J., & Kotler, J. S. (2006). Conduct problems. In D. A. Wolfe & E. J. Mash (Eds.), *Behavioral and emotional disorders in adolescents* (pp. 153–225). New York, NY: Guilford.

McMahon, R. J., Wells, K. C., & Kotler, J. S. (2006). Conduct problems. In E. J. Mash &

R. A. Barkley (Eds.), *Treatment of childhood disorders* (3rd ed., pp. 137–268). New York, NY: Guilford.

McPherson, F. (2001). *Elaborating the information for better remembering.* Retrieved from http://www.memory-key.com/improving/strategies/study/elaborating

Mead, S. (2006). Evidence suggests otherwise: The truth about boys and girls. *Education Sector.* Retrieved from http://www.educationsector.org/usr_doc/ESO_BoysAndGirls.pdf

Meadows, S. (2006). *The child as thinker: The development and acquisition of cognition in childhood* (2nd ed.). London, England: Routledge.

Meaney, M. J. (2004). The nature of nurture: Maternal effects and chromatin remodeling. In J. T. Cacioppo & G. G. Bentson (Eds.), *Essays in social neuroscience* (pp. 1–14). Cambridge, MA: MIT Press.

Mecca, A. M., Smelser, N. J., & Vasconcellos, J. (1989). *The social importance of self-esteem.* Berkeley: University of California Press.

Meisels, S. J., & Liaw, F. (1993). Failure in grade: Do retained children catch up? *Journal of Educational Research, 87*(2), 69–77.

Mellman, M., Lazarus, E., & Rivlin, A. (1990). Family time, family values. In D. G. Blankerhorn, S. Bayme, J. B. Elshtain, & J. Bethke (Eds.), *Rebuilding the nest: A new commitment to the American family* (pp. 79–92). Milwaukee, WI: Family Service America.

Meltzoff, A. N., & Moore, M. K. (1997). Explaining facial imitation: A theoretical model. *Early Development and Parenting, 6*(3–4), 179–192.

Mendola, K. (1999). *Natural childbirth options.* Retrieved from http://www.webmd.com/baby/guide/natural-childbirth-options

Menéndez, R. (Director). (1988). Stand and deliver [Motion picture]. United States: American Playhouse.

Menn, L., & Stoel-Gammon, C. (2005). Phonological development: Learning sounds and sound patterns. In J. B. Gleason (Ed.), *The development of language* (6th ed., pp. 39–61). Boston, MA: Pearson.

Mennella, J. A., Griffin, C. E., & Beauchamp, G. K. (2004). Flavor programming during infancy. *Pediatrics, 113*(4), 840–845.

Menzies, R. G., & Clarke, J. C. (1993). The etiology of childhood water phobia. *Behaviour Research and Therapy, 31*(5), 499–501.

Merck Manual. (2008). *Function and dysfunction of the cerebral lobes.* Retrieved from http://www.merck.com/mmpe/sec16/ch210/ch210a.html#sec16-ch210-ch210a-313

Merriam-Webster. (2010). *Heteronomous.* Retrieved from http://www.merriam-webster.com/dictionary/heteronomous

Mielke, K. W. (2001). A review of research on the educational and social impact of *Sesame Street.* In S. M. Fisch & R. T. Truglio (Eds.), *"G" is for growing—Thirty years of research on children and* Sesame Street (pp. 83–96). Mahwah, NJ: Erlbaum.

Miller, A. M., & Harwood, R. L. (2002). The cultural organization of parenting: Change and stability of behavior patterns during feeding and social play across the first year of life. *Parenting: Science and Practice, 2*(3), 241–272.

Miller, N. B., Cowan, P. A., Cowan, C. P., Hetherington, E. M., & Clingempeel, W. G. (1993). Externalizing in preschoolers and early adolescents: A cross-study replication of a family model. *Developmental Psychology, 29*(1), 3–18.

Miller, P. (2006). Commentary on: Constructing and deconstructing development. *New Ideas in Psychology, 23*(3), 207–211.

Miller, P. H., Slawinski Blessing, J., & Schwartz, S. (2006). Gender differences in high school students' views about science. *International Journal of Science Education, 28*(4), 363–381.

Miller, P. J., Fung, H., & Mintz, J. (1996). Self-construction through narrative practices: A Chinese and American comparison of early socialization. *Ethos, 24*(2), 237–280.

Miller, R. B., & Wright, D. W. (1995). Detecting and correcting attrition bias in longitudinal family research. *Journal of Marriage and Family, 57*(4), 921–919.

Miller-Perrin, C. L., & Perrin, R. D. (1999). *Child maltreatment: An introduction.* Thousand Oaks, CA: Sage.

Miniño, A. M., Heron, M. P., Murphy, S. L., & Kochanek, K. D. (2007). Deaths: Final data for 2004. *National Vital Statistics Report, 55*(19). Hyattsville, MD: National Center for Health Statistics.

Mischel, W., & Ayduk, O. (2004). Willpower in a cognitive-affective processing system: The dynamics of delay of gratification. In R. F. Baumeister & K. D. Vohs (Eds.), *Handbook of self-regulation: Research, theory, and applications* (pp. 99–129). New York, NY: Guilford.

Mitchell, A. W. (2005). *Stair steps to quality: A guide for states and communities developing quality rating systems for early care and education.* Fairfax, VA: National Child Care Information Center.

Mitchell, J. E., Peterson, C. B., Myers, T., & Wonderlich, S. (2001). Combining pharmacotherapy and psychotherapy in the treatment of patients with eating disorders. *Psychiatric Clinics of North America, 24*(2), 315–323.

Mitchell, M. (2007). *Doctors to treat PTSD with virtual reality.* Retrieved from http://today.msnbc.msn.com/id/20109659/

Mitchell, R. (2009, February 18). *Tuition to rise 3.5 percent at Harvard for 2009-10.* Retrieved from http://www.fas.harvard.edu/home/news-and-notices/news/press-releases/tuition-02182009.shtml

Miyake, K., & Yamazaki, K. (1995). Self-conscious emotions, child rearing, and child psychopathology in Japanese culture. In J. P. Tangney & K. W. Fischer (Eds.), *Self-conscious emotions: The psychology of shame, guilt, embarrassment, and pride* (pp. 488–504). New York, NY: Guilford.

Moffitt, T. E., & Caspi, A. (2001). Childhood predictors differentiate life-course persistent and adolescence-limited antisocial pathways among males and females. *Development and Psychopathology, 13*(2), 355–375.

Mohn, J. K., Tingle, L. R., & Finger, R. (2002). An analysis of the causes of the decline in non-marital birth and pregnancy rates for teens from 1991 to 1995. *Adolescent and Family Health, 3*(1), 39–47.

Montemayor, R. (1983). Parents and adolescents in conflict: All families some of the time and some families most of the time. *Journal of Early Adolescence, 3*(1–2), 83–103.

Montgomery, M. J. (2005). Psychosocial intimacy and identity: From early adolescence to emerging adulthood. *Journal of Adolescent Research, 20*(3), 346–374.

Moore, K. A. (2009). *Teen births: Examining the recent increase.* Child Trends Research Brief, Publication 2009–08. Washington, DC: Child Trends.

Moore, K. L., & Persaud, T. V. N. (2003). *The developing human: Clinically oriented embryology* (7th ed.). Philadelphia, PA: W. B. Saunders.

Moran, E. (2000). *Dick and Jane readers.* In S. Pendergast & T. Pendergast (Eds.), *St. James encyclopedia of popular culture* (Vol. 1, pp. 700–701). Detroit, MI: St. James Press.

Moreno, S., Marques, C., Santos, A., Santos, M., Castro, S. L., & Besson, M. (2009). Musical training influences linguistic abilities in 8-year-old children: More evidence for brain plasticity. *Cerebral Cortex, 19*(3), 712–723.

Morgane, P. J., Austin-LaFrance, R., Brozino, J. D., Tonkiss, J., Diaz-Cintra, S., Cintra, L., . . . Galler, J. R. (1993). Prenatal malnutrition and development of the brain. *Neuroscience and Biobehavioral Reviews, 17*(1), 91–128.

Moriarty, P. H., & Wagner, L. D. (2004). Family rituals that provide meaning for single-parent families. *Journal of Family Nursing, 10*(2), 190–210.

Morison, S. J., & Ellwood, A. (2000). Resiliency in the aftermath of deprivation: A second look at the development of Romanian orphanage children. *Merrill-Palmer Quarterly, 46*(4), 717–737.

Morris-Lindsey, T. (2006). *Earning by Learning of Dallas: About us.* Retrieved from http://www.eblofdallas.org/aboutus.html

Moss, E., Cyr, C., Bureau, J., Tarabulsy, G. M., & Dubois-Comtois, K. (2005). Stability of attachment during the preschool period. *Developmental Psychology, 41*(5), 773–783.

Mounts, N. S., & Steinberg, L. (1995). An ecological analysis of peer influence on adolescent grade point average and drug use. *Developmental Psychology, 31*(6), 915–922.

Moustafa, M. (2001). Contemporary reading instruction. In T. Loveless (Ed.), *The great curriculum debate* (pp. 247–267). Washington, DC: The Brookings Institution Press.

Müller, U., Dick, A. S., Gela, K., Overton, W. F., & Zelazo, P. D. (2006). The role of negative priming in preschoolers' flexible rule use on the dimensional change card sort task. *Child Development, 77*(2), 395–412.

Mundy, P. (2003). The neural basis of social impairments in autism: The role of the dorsal medial-frontal cortex and anterior cingulate system. *Journal of Child Psychology and Psychiatry, 44*(6), 793–809.

Munhall, P. L. (2007). *Nursing research: A qualitative perspective* (4th ed.). Sudbury, MA: Jones & Bartlett.

Munroe, R. L., & Romney, A. K. (2006). Gender and age differences in same-sex aggregation and social behavior: A four-culture study. *Journal of Cross-Cultural Psychology, 37*, 3–19.

Munsch, J., & Blyth, D. A. (1993). An analysis of the functional nature of adolescents' supportive relationships. *Journal of Early Adolescence, 13*(2), 132–153.

Munsch, J., Woodward, J., & Darling, N. (1995). Children's perceptions of their relationships with coresiding and non-custodial fathers. *Journal of Divorce and Remarriage, 23*(1–2), 39–54.

Murch, S. H., Anthony, A., Casson, D. H., Malik, M., Berelowitz, M., Dhillon, A. P., ... Walker-Smith, J. A. (2004). Retraction of an interpretation. *Lancet, 363*(9411), 750.

Muris, P., Merckelbach, H., Gadet, B., & Moulaert, V. (2000). Fears, worries and scary dreams in 4- to 12-year-old children: Their content, developmental pattern, and origins. *Journal of Clinical Child Psychology, 29*(1), 43–52.

Murphy, J. J., & Boggess, S. (1998). Increased condom use among teenage males, 1988–1995: The role of attitudes. *Family Planning Perspectives, 30*(6), 276–280, 303.

Mussen, P. H., & Jones, M. C. (1957). Self-conceptions, motivations, and interpersonal attitudes of late- and early-maturing boys. *Child Development, 28*, 243–256.

Muzzatti, B., & Agnoli, F. (2007). Gender and mathematics: Attitudes and stereotype threat susceptibility in Italian children. *Developmental Psychology, 43*(3), 747–759.

Myers, B. J. (1984). Mother-infant bonding: Rejoinder to Kennell and Klaus. *Developmental Review, 4*(3), 283–288.

Nakagawa, M., Lamb, M. E., & Miyaki, K. (1992). Antecedents and correlates of the Strange Situation behavior of Japanese infants. *Journal of Cross-Cultural Psychology, 23*(3), 300–310.

Nagin, D., & Tremblay, R. E. (1999). Trajectories of boys' physical aggression, opposition, and hyperactivity on the path to physically violent and nonviolent juvenile delinquency. *Child Development, 70*(5), 1181–1196.

Naigles, L. R., Hoff, E., Vear, D., Tomasello, M., Brandt, S., Waxman, S. R., & Childers, J. B. (2009). Flexibility in early verb use: Evidence from a multiple-N dairy study:

VII. General discussion. *Monographs of the Society for Research in Child Development, 74*(2), 91–104.

Nansel, T. R., Overpeck, M., Pilla, R. S., Ruan, W. J., Simons-Morton, B., & Scheidt, P. (2001). Bullying behaviors among U.S. youth: Prevalence and association with psychosocial adjustment. *Journal of the American Medical Association, 285*(16), 2094–2100, 2141–2142.

Nathan, R. (2005). *My freshman year*. Ithaca, NY: Cornell University Press.

Nathanson, A. I. (1999). Identifying and explaining the relationship between parental mediation and children's aggression. *Communication Research, 26*, 124–143.

National Association for the Education of Young Children. (2000). *STILL unacceptable trends in kindergarten entry and placement.* Retrieved from http://www.naeyc.org/files/naeyc/file/positions/Psunacc.pdf

National Cancer Institute Fact Sheet. (2006). *Gene therapy for cancer: Questions and answers.* Retrieved from http://www.cancer.gov/cancertopics/factsheet/Therapy/gene

National Center for Chronic Disease Prevention and Health Promotion. (2009). *Chronic diseases: The power to prevent, the call to control.* Retrieved from http://www.cdc.gov/chronicdisease/resources/publications/AAG/pdf/chronic.pdf

National Center for Education Statistics. (2004). *Trends in educational equity for girls and women: 2004* [NCES 2000–021]. U.S. Department of Education. Washington, DC: U.S. Government Printing Office.

National Center for Learning Disabilities. (2010). *LD explained.* Retrieved from http://www.ncld.org/ld-basics/ld-explained

National Children's Study. (2003). *The social environment and children's health and development.* Retrieved from http://www.nationalchildrensstudy.gov/about/organization/advisorycommittee/2003Sep/Pages/social-environment-Document-1.pdf

National Clearinghouse for English Language Acquisition and Language Instruction Educational Programs. (2006). *What is an English language learner (ELL)?* Retrieved from http://www.ncela.gwu.edu/about/lieps/2_ELL.html **[AQ: This URL generates an error message—please update if possible.]**

National Commission on Writing. (2004). *Writing: A ticket to work . . . or a ticket out.* Retrieved from http://www.writingcommission.org/prod_downloads/writingcom/writing-ticket-to-work.pdf

National Dissemination Center for Children with Disabilities. (2009a). *Categories of disabilities under IDEA.* Retrieved from http://www.nichcy.org/InformationResources/Documents/NICHCY%20PUBS/gr3.pdf

National Dissemination Center for Children with Disabilities. (2009b). *Intellectual disability (formerly mental retardation).*

Retrieved from http://www.nichcy.org/InformationResources/Documents/NICHCY%20PUBS/fs8.pdf

National Endowment for the Arts. (2007). *To read or not to read: A question of national consequence.* Research Report No. 47. Washington, DC: Author.

National Heart, Lung and Blood Institute. (2007). *What is sickle-cell anemia?* Retrieved from http://www.nhlbi.nih.gov/health/dci/Diseases/Sca/SCA_WhatIs.html

National Human Genome Research Institute. (2007a). *Chromosome abnormalities.* Retrieved from http://www.genome.gov/11508982#6

National Human Genome Research Institute. (2007b). *Frequently asked questions about genetic disorders.* Retrieved from http://www.genome.gov/19016930

National Human Genome Research Institute. (2007c). *Learning about Down syndrome.* Retrieved from http://www.genome.gov/19517824

National Human Genome Research Institute. (2009). *An overview of the human genome project.* Retrieved from http://www.genome.gov/12011239

National Institute of Child Health and Human Development. (2006). *Phenylketonuria (PKU).* Retrieved from http://www.nichd.nih.gov/health/topics/phenylketonuria.cfm

National Institute of Child Health and Human Development. (2007). *NICHD and other NIH institutes aim to prevent obesity and overweight in children.* Retrieved from http://www.nichd.nih.gov/news/resources/spotlight/042407_wecan.cfm

National Institute of Child Health and Human Development. (2008). *Division of Intramural Research.* Retrieved from http://dir.nichd.nih.gov/dirweb/home.html

National Institute of Child Health and Human Development. (2010). *Back to Sleep public education campaign.* Retrieved from http://www.nichd.nih.gov/sids/

National Institute of Mental Health. (1993). *Learning disabilities* (NIH Publication 93–3611). Washington, DC: U.S. Government Printing Office.

National Institute of Mental Health. (2009a). *Bipolar disorder in children and teens: A parent's guide.* NIH Publication No. 08–6380. Washington, DC: Author.

National Institute of Mental Health. (2009b). *The diagnosis of autism spectrum disorders.* Retrieved from http://www.nimh.nih.gov/health/publications/autism/complete-index.shtml#pub3

National Institute of Neurological Disorders and Stroke. (2007). *NINDS learning disabilities information page.* Retrieved from http://www.ninds.nih.gov/disorders/learningdisabilities/learningdisabilities.htm?css=print

National Institute of Neurological Disorders and Stroke. (2008). *Autism fact sheet.*

Retrieved from http://www.ninds.nih.gov/disorders/autism/detail_autism.htm

National Institute on Deafness and Other Communication Disorders. (2008). *Autism and communication.* Retrieved from http://www.nidcd.nih.gov/health/voice/autism.asp#3

National Institute on Drug Abuse. (1997). National pregnancy and health survey—Drug use among women delivering live births: 1992. NCADI Publication No. BKD192.

National Institutes of Health. (2009). *Infant-newborn development.* Retrieved from http://www.nlm.nih.gov/MEDLINEPLUS/ency/article/002004.htm

National Park Service. (n.d.). *Rosie the Riveter—World War II Home Front National Historical Park.* Retrieved from http://www.nps.gov/history/nr/travel/wwIIbayarea/ros.htm

National Reading Panel. (2000). Alphabetics Part II: Phonics instruction. In *Report of the National Reading Panel: Teaching children to read: An evidence-based assessment of the scientific research literature on reading and its implications for reading instruction: Reports of the subgroups.* Rockville, MD: NICHD Clearinghouse.

National Research Council, Commission on Behavioral and Social Sciences and Education. (1997, January 14). *Political debate interferes with research on educating children with limited English proficiency.* Retrieved from http://www8.nationalacademies.org/onpinews/newsitem.aspx?RecordID=5286

National Research Council and Institute of Medicine. (2004). *Community programs to promote youth development.* Retrieved from http://www7.nationalacademies.org/bocyf/youth_development_brief.pdf

National Youth Violence Prevention Resource Center. (2007). *Intimate partner and family violence fact sheet.* Retrieved from http://www.safeyouth.org/scripts/facts/intimate.asp#dating

National Youth Violence Prevention Resource Center. (2008). *School violence fact sheet.* Retrieved from http://www.safeyouth.org/scripts/facts/school.asp

Natsuaki, M. N., Biehl, M. C., & Ge, X. (2009). Trajectories of depressed mood from early adolescence to young adulthood: The effects of pubertal timing and adolescent dating. *Journal of Research on Adolescence, 19*(1), 47–74.

Neber, H., Finsterwald, M., & Urban, N. (2001). Cooperative learning with gifted and high-achieving students: A review and meta-analyses of 12 studies. *High Ability Studies, 12*(2), 199–214.

Neiderhiser, J. M., Reiss, D., Hetherington, E. M., & Plomin, R. (1999). Relationships between parenting and adolescent adjustment over time: Genetic and environmental contributions. *Developmental Psychology, 35,* 680–692.

Neisser, U., Boodoo, G., Bouchard, T. J., Boykin, A. W., Brody, N., Ceci, S. J., . . . Urbina, S. (1996). Intelligence: Knowns and unknowns. *American Psychologist, 51*(2), 77–101.

Nelms, B. C. (2005). Giving children a great gift: Family traditions. *Journal of Pediatric Health Care, 19*(6), 345–346.

Nelson, C. (1999). How important are the first 3 years of life? *Applied Developmental Science, 3*(4), 235–238.

Nemours Foundation. (1995–2009). *Tips for divorcing parents.* Retrieved from http://kidshealth.org/parent/emotions/feelings/divorce.html?tracking=P_RelatedArticle#

Nemours Foundation. (2004). *Your child's growth.* Retrieved from http://kidshealth.org/parent/growth/growing/childs_growth.html

Nemours Foundation. (2007). *Stress.* Retrieved from http://kidshealth.org/teen/your_mind/emotions/stress.html

Neonatology on the Web. (2007, April 29). *Incubators for infants.* Retrieved from http://www.neonatology.org/classics/portroyal.html

Neumark-Sztainer, D. (2008). Family meals in adolescents: Findings from Project EAT. *Society for Research in Child Development Social Policy Reports, 22*(4), 11.

Neumark-Sztainer, D., Eisenberg, M. E., Fulkerson, J. A., Story, M., & Larson, N. I. (2008). Family meals and disorder eating in adolescents: Longitudinal findings from Project EAT. *Archives of Pediatric Adolescent Medicine, 162*(1), 17–22.

Newcombe, N. S., Sluzenski, J., & Huttenlocher, J. (2005). Preexisting knowledge versus on-line learning: What do young infants really know about spatial location? *Psychological Science, 16*(3), 222–227.

Newman, B. M., & Newman, P. R. (2007). *Theories of human development.* Mahwah, NJ: Erlbaum.

Newman, J., Bidjerano, T., Özdogru, A. A., Kao, C., Özköse-Biyik, C., & Johnson, J. J. (2007). What do they usually do after school? A comparative analysis of fourth-grade children in Bulgaria, Taiwan, and the United States. *Journal of Early Adolescence, 27,* 431–456.

NICHD Early Child Care Research Network. (1997). The effects of infant child care on infant-mother attachment security: Results of the NICHD study of early child care. *Child Development, 68*(5), 860–879.

NICHD Early Child Care Research Network. (2004). Trajectories of physical aggression from toddlerhood to middle childhood. *Monographs of the Society for Research in Child Development, 69*(4).

Nichols, H. (2008). *Outcomes for one-child families: The positive and negative effects of being an only child.* Retrieved from http://inter chil drelationships.suite101.com/article.cfm/only_children

Nield, L. S., Cakan, N., & Kamat, D. (2007). A practical approach to precocious puberty. *Clinical Pediatrics, 46*(4), 299–306.

Nijhof, K. S., & Engels, R. C. M. E. (2007). Parenting styles, coping strategies, and the expression of homesickness. *Journal of Adolescence, 30*(5), 709–720.

Nikkel, C. (2009). Women, children and air-bags: The basic facts and how to stay safe. *Road and Travel Magazine.* Retrieved from http://www.roadandtravel.com/carcare/airbags.htm

Nolan, M., & Carr, A. (2000). Attention deficit hyperactivity disorder. In A. Carr (Ed.), *What works with children and adolescents? A critical review of psychological interventions with children, adolescents and their families* (pp. 65–101). New York, NY: Routledge.

Nolen-Hoeksema, S. (1987). Sex differences in unipolar depression: Evidence and theory. *Psychological Bulletin, 101,* 259–282.

Nolin, M. J., Chaney, B., & Chapman, C. (1997). *Student participation in community service activity.* National Household Education Survey. National Center for Education Statistics. Retrieved from http://nces.ed.gov/pubs97/97331.pdf

Nomaguchi, K. M., & Milkie, M. A. (2003). Costs and rewards of children: The effect of becoming a parent on adults' lives. *Journal of Marriage and Family, 65*(2), 356–374.

Nsamenang, A. B., & Lo-oh, J. L. (2010). Afrique noir. In M. H. Bornstein (Ed.), *Handbook of cultural developmental science* (pp. 383–407). New York, NY: Psychology Press.

Nucci, L. (2004). Reflections on the moral self construct. In D. K. Lapsley & D. Narvaez (Eds.), *Moral development, self, and identity* (pp. 111–132). Mahwah, NJ: Erlbaum.

O'Connor, T. G., Bredenkamp, D., Rutter, M., & The English and Romanian Adoptees (ERA) Study Team. (1999). Attachment disturbances and disorders in children exposed to early severe deprivation. *Infant Mental Health Journal, 20*(1), 10–29.

Oatley, K., Keltner, D., & Jenkins, J. M. (2006). *Understanding emotions* (2nd ed.). Malden, MA: Blackwell.

Ocampo, K. A., Knight, G. P., & Bernal, M. E. (1997). The development of cognitive abilities and social identities in children: The case of ethnic identity. *International Journal of Behavioral Development, 21*(3), 479–500.

Offer, D., & Schonert-Reichl, K. A. (1992). Debunking the myths of adolescence: Findings from recent research. *Journal of the American Academy of Child & Adolescent Psychiatry, 31*(6), 1003–1014.

Ohene, S., Ireland, M., McNeely, C., & Borowsky, I. W. (2006). Parental expectations, physical punishment, and violence among adolescents who score positive on a psychosocial screening test in primary care. *Pediatrics, 117,* 441–447.

Olds, S. B., London, M. L., & Ladewig, P. A. (2002). *Maternal-newborn nursing: A family and community-based approach* (6th ed.) Upper Saddle River, NJ: Prentice Hall.

Olson, S. L., Bates, J. E., Sandy, J. M., & Lanthier, R. (2000). Early developmental precursors of externalizing behavior in middle childhood and adolescence. *Journal of Abnormal Child Psychology, 28*(2), 119–133.

Olweus, D. (1993). *Bullying at school: What we know and what we can do.* Cambridge, MA: Blackwell.

Olweus, D. (2003). A profile of bullying at school. *Educational Leadership, 60*(6), 12–17.

Organisation for Economic Co-operation and Development. (2009). *Equally prepared for life? How 15-year-old boys and girls perform in school.* Washington, DC: Author.

Osborne, C., & McLanahan, S. (2007). Partnership instability and child well-being. *Journal of Marriage and Family, 69,* 1065–1083.

Osgood, D. W., Anderson, A. L., & Shaffer, J. N. (2005). Unstructured leisure in the after-school hours. In J. L. Mahoney, R. W. Larson, & J. S. Eccles (Eds.), *Organized activities as contexts of development* (pp. 45–64). Mahwah, NJ: Erlbaum.

Osgood, D. W., Wilson, J. K., O'Malley, P. M., Bachman, J. G., & Johnston, L. D. (1996). Routine activities and individual deviant behavior. *American Sociological Review, 61*(4), 635–655.

Ostrov, J. M., Gentile, D. A., & Crick, N. R. (2006). Media exposure, aggression and prosocial behavior during early childhood: A longitudinal study. *Social Development, 15*(4), 612–627.

Ouellette, G., & Senechal, M. (2008). Pathways to literacy: A study of invented spelling and its role in learning to read. *Child Development, 79*(4), 899–913.

Ovando, C. J., & McLaren, P. (2000). *The politics of multiculturalism and bilingual education: Students and teachers caught in the crossfire.* Boston, MA: McGraw-Hill.

Oyserman, D., Coon, H. M., & Kemmelmeier, M. (2002). Rethinking individualism and collectivism: Evaluations of theoretical assumptions and meta-analyses. *Psychological Bulletin, 128*(1), 3–72.

Pagan, J. L., Rose, R. J., Viken, R. J., Pulkkinen, L., Kaprio, J., & Dick, D. M. (2006). Genetic and environmental influences on stages of alcohol use across adolescence and into young adulthood. *Behavior Genetics, 36*(4), 483–497.

Pajares, F. (2002). *Overview of social cognitive theory and of self-efficacy.* Retrieved from http://www.emory.edu/EDUCATION/mfp/eff.html

Pajares, F. (2005). Self-efficacy during childhood and adolescence. In F. Pajares, & T. C. Urdan (Eds.), *Self-efficacy beliefs of adolescents* (pp. 339–367). Charlotte, NC: Information Age.

Pajares, F., & Schunk, D. H. (2002). Self and self-belief in psychology and education: An historical perspective. In J. Aronson (Ed.), *Improving academic achievement* (pp. 5–21). New York, NY: Academic Press.

Pakkenberg, B., & Gundersen, H. J. G. (1997). Neocortical neuron number in humans: Effect of sex and age. *Journal of Comparative Neurology, 384,* 312–320.

Palusci, V. J., Crum, P., Bliss, R., & Bavolek, S. J. (2008). Changes in parenting attitudes and knowledge among inmates and other at-risk populations after a family nurturing program. *Children and Youth Services Review, 30*(1), 79–89.

Pan, B. A. (2005). Semantic development. In J. B. Gleason (Ed.), *The development of language* (6th ed., pp. 112–147). Boston, MA: Pearson.

Pandolfi, E., Chiaradia, G., Moncada, M., Rava, L., & Tozzi, A. E. (2009). Prevention of congenital rubella and congenital varicella in Europe. *Euro Surveillance, 14*(9), 16–20.

Papert, S. (1999). Jean Piaget. *Time.* Retrieved from http://205.188.238.181/time/time100/scientist/profile/piaget.html

Parasuraman, R. (1998). The attentive brain: Issues and prospects. In R. Parasuraman (Ed.), *The attentive brain* (pp. 3–15). Cambridge, MA: MIT Press.

Parent, A. S., Teilmann, G., Juul, A., Skakkebaek, N. E., Toppari, J., & Bourguignon, J. P. (2003). The timing of normal puberty and the age limits of sexual precocity: Variations around the world, secular trends, and changes after migration. *Endocrine Reviews, 24*(5), 668–693.

Parent Teacher Association. (2006). *Progress for American Children—2006 National PTA Annual Report.* Retrieved from http://www.pta.org/2006_Annual_Report.pdf

Parten, M. (1932). Social participation among pre-school children. *Journal of Abnormal and Social Psychology, 27*(3), 243–269.

Pasley, K., & Moorefield, B. S. (2004). Stepfamilies changes and challenges. In M. Coleman & L. H. Ganong (Eds.), *Handbook of contemporary families* (pp. 317–330). Thousand Oaks, CA: Sage.

Pass, S. (2007). When constructivists Jean Piaget and Lev Vygotsky were pedagogical collaborators: A viewpoint from a study of their communications. *Journal of Constructivist Psychology, 20*(3), 277–282.

Patterson, C. J. (2006). Children of lesbian and gay parents. *Current Directions in Psychological Science, 15*(5), 241–244.

Patterson, C. J. (2009). Children of lesbian and gay parents: Psychology, law and policy. *American Psychologist, 64*(8), 722–736.

Patterson, G. R. (1982). *Coercive family processes.* Eugene, OR: Castilia Press.

Patterson, G. R., Dishion, T. J., & Yoerger, K. (2000). Adolescent growth in new forms of problem behavior: Macro- and micro-peer dynamics. *Prevention Science, 1*(1), 3–13.

Patterson, G. R., Reid, J. B., & Dishion, T. (1992). *Antisocial boys.* Eugene, OR: Castalia Press.

Patterson, G. R., & Yoerger, K. (2002). A developmental model for early- and late-onset delinquency. In J. B. Reid, G. R. Patterson, & J. Snyder (Eds.), *Antisocial behavior in children and adolescents: A developmental analysis and model for intervention* (pp. 147–172). Washington, DC: American Psychological Association.

Pauli-Pott, U., Becker, K., Mertesacker, T., & Beckmann, D. (2000). Infants with "colic"—Mothers' perspectives on the crying problem. *Journal of Psychosomatic Research, 48*(2), 125–132.

Paulsen, K., & Johnson, M. (1983). Sex role attitudes and mathematical ability in 4th-, 8th-, and 11th-grade students from a high socioeconomic area. *Developmental Psychology, 19*(2), 210–214.

Paulson, A., & Teicher, S. A. (2006). Move to single-sex classes fans debate. *Christian Science Monitor.* Retrieved from http://www.csmonitor.com/2006/1026/p02s01-legn.html

Paus, T., Zijdenbos, A., Worsley, K., Collings, D. L., Blumenthal, J., Giedd, J. N., . . . Evans, A. C. (1999). Structural maturation of neural pathways in children and adolescents: In vivo study. *Science, 283*(5409), 1908–1911.

Pavlov, I. P. (1927). *Conditioned reflexes: An investigation of the physiological activity of the cerebral cortex.* Retrieved from http://www.ivanpavlov.com/lectures/ivan_pavlov-lecture_002.htm

PDR Network. (2009a). *Herbals, supplements & alternative therapies.* Retrieved from http://www.pdrhealth.com/drugs/otc/otc-a-z.aspx

PDR Network. (2009b). *Over the counter drugs A–Z.* Retrieved from http://pdrhealth.com/drugs/otc/otc-a-z.aspx

PDR Network. (2010). *Physicians' desk reference* (64th ed.). Available from http://www.pdrhealth.com/drugs/rx/rx-a-z.aspx

PDR Staff. (2010a). *Physicians' desk reference* (64th ed.). PDR Network, LLC.

PDR Staff. (2010b). *Physicians' desk reference for nonprescription drugs, dietary supplements, and herbs* (31st ed.). PDR Network, LLC.

Pearson, P. D. (2004). The reading wars. *Educational Policy, 18*(1), 216–252.

Pedersen, S., & Seidman, E. (2005). Contexts and correlates of out-of-school activity participation among low-income urban adolescents. In J. L. Mahoney, R. W. Larson, & J. S. Eccles (Eds.), *Organized activities as contexts of development* (pp. 85–110). Mahwah, NJ: Erlbaum.

Pellegrini, A. D. (1987). Rough-and-tumble play: Developmental and educational significance. *Educational Psychologist, 22*(1), 23–43.

Pellegrini, A. D. (2003). Perceptions and functions of play and real fighting in early adolescence. *Child Development, 74*(5), 1522–1533.

Pellegrini, A. D. (2005). *Recess—Its role in education and development.* Mahwah, NJ: Erlbaum.

Pelligrini, A. D. (2002). Rough-and-tumble play from childhood through adolescence: Development and possible functions. In P. K. Smith & C. Hart (Eds.), *Blackwell handbook of childhood social development* (pp. 438–453). Malden, MA: Blackwell.

Pereda, N., Guilera, G., Forns, M., & Gómez-Benito, J. (2009). The international epidemiology of child sexual abuse: A continuation of Finkelhor (1994). *Child Abuse & Neglect, 33*(6), 331–342.

Perrin, J. M., Bloom, S. R., & Gortmaker, S. L. (2007). The increase of childhood chronic conditions in the United States. *Journal of the American Medical Association, 297*(24), 2755–2759.

Perrone, V. (1991). *Association for Childhood Education International position paper on standardized testing.* Retrieved from http://www.udel.edu/bateman/acei/onstandard.htm#history

Peterson, S. E., DeGracie, J. S., & Ayabe, C. R. (1987). A longitudinal study of the effects of retention/promotion on academic achievement. *American Educational Research Journal, 24*(1), 107–118.

Petitto, L. A., Katerelos, M., Levy, B. G., Gauna, K., Tétreault, K., & Ferraro, V. (2001). Bilingual signed and spoken language acquisition from birth: Implications for the mechanisms underlying early bilingual language acquisition. *Journal of Child Language, 28*(2), 453–496.

Pett, M. A., Wampold, B. E., Turner, C. W., & Vaughan-Cole, B. (1999). Paths of influence of divorce on preschool children's psychosocial adjustment. *Journal of Family Psychology, 13*(2), 145–164.

Petterson, S. M., & Albers, A. B. (2001). Effects of poverty and maternal depression on early childhood development. *Child Development, 72*(6), 1794–1813.

Pfeifer, J. H., Brown, C. S., & Juvonen, J. (2007). Prejudice reduction in schools—Teaching tolerance in schools: Lessons learned since *Brown v. Board of Education* about the development and reduction of children's prejudice. *SRCD Social Policy Report, 21*(2), 3–13, 16–17, 20–23.

Philipp, B. L., Merewood, A., & O'Brien, S. (2001). Commentary: Physicians and breastfeeding promotion in the United States: A call for action. *Pediatrics, 107*(3), 584–587.

Phinney, J. S. (1989). Stages of ethnic identity development in minority group adolescents. *Journal of Early Adolescence, 9*(1–2), 34–49.

Phinney, J. S., Cantu, C. L., & Kurtz, D. A. (1997). Ethnic and American identity as predictors of self-esteem among African American, Latino, and White adolescents. *Journal of Youth and Adolescence, 26*(2), 165–185.

Phinney, J. S., Kim-Jo, T., Osorio, S., & Vilhjalmsdottir, P. (2005). Autonomy and relatedness in adolescent-parent disagreements: Ethnic and developmental factors. *Journal of Adolescent Research, 20*(1), 8–39.

Piaget, J. (1926). *The language and thought of the child.* New York, NY: Harcourt, Brace.

Piaget, J. (1952). *The origins of intelligence in children.* New York, NY: Norton.

Piaget, J. (1954). *The construction of reality in the child.* New York, NY: Basic Books.

Piaget, J. (1955). *The language and thought of the child.* New York, NY: Meridian Books.

Piaget, J. (1962). *Play, dreams and imitation in childhood.* New York, NY: Norton.

Piaget, J. (1963). *The origins of intelligence in children.* New York, NY: Norton.

Piaget, J. (1965). *The moral judgment of the child.* New York, NY: Free Press.

Piaget, J. (1969). *The child's conception of the world.* Totowa, NJ: Littlefield, Adams.

Piaget, J. (1973). *The language and thought of the child.* New York, NY: Meridian World.

Piaget, J. (1999). The stages of intellectual development in the child. In A. Slater & D. Muir (Eds.), *Blackwell reader in developmental psychology* (pp. 35–42). Malden, MA: Blackwell.

Piaget, J., & Inhelder, B. (1956). *The child's conception of space.* London, England: Routledge.

Pierce, J. L., Kostova, T., & Dirks, K. T. (2003). The state of psychological ownership: Integrating and extending a century of research. *Review of General Psychology, 7*(1), 84–107.

Pietromonaco, P. R., & Barrett, L. F. (2000). The internal working models concept: What do we really know about the self in relation to others? *Review of General Psychology, 4*(2), 155–175.

Pinheiro, P. S. (2006). *World report on violence against children.* Geneva, Switzerland: United Nations.

Pinker, S. (1984). *Language learnability and language development.* Cambridge, MA: Harvard University Press.

Pinker, S. (1999). *Words and rules: The ingredients of language.* New York, NY: Basic Books.

Planty, M., Provasnik, S., & Daniel, B. (2007). *High school coursetaking: Findings from the condition of education 2007* [NCES 2007–065]. U.S. Department of Education. Washington, DC: National Center for Education Statistics.

Plomin, R., Asbury, K., & Dunn, J. (2001). Why are children in the same family so different? Non-shared environment a decade later. *Canadian Journal of Psychiatry, 46,* 225–233.

Plomin, R., Chipuer, H. M., & Neiderhiser, J. M. (1994). Behavioral genetic evidence for the importance of nonshared environment. In E. M. Hetherington, D. Reiss, & R. Plomin (Eds.), *Separate social worlds of siblings: The impact of nonshared environment on development* (pp. 1–31). Hillsdale, NJ: Erlbaum.

Plomin, R., DeFries, J. C., Craig, I. W., & McGuffin, P. (2003a). Behavioral genetics. In R. Plomin, J. C. DeFries, I. W. Craig, & P. McGuffin (Eds.), *Behavioral genetics in the postgenomic era* (pp. 3–15). Washington, DC: American Psychological Association.

Plomin, R., DeFries, J. C., Craig, I. W., & McGuffin, P. (2003b). Behavioral genomics. In R. Plomin, J. C. DeFries, I. W. Craig, & P. McGuffin (Eds.), *Behavioral genetics in the postgenomic era* (pp. 531–540). Washington, DC: American Psychological Association.

Plomin, R., & Petrill, S. A. (1997). Genetics and intelligence: What's new? *Intelligence, 24*(1), 53–77.

Plous, S., & Neptune, D. (1997). Racial and gender biases in magazine advertising: A content-analytic study. *Psychology of Women Quarterly, 21*(4), 627–644.

Pollet, T. V. (2007). Genetic relatedness and sibling relationship characteristics in a modern society. *Evolution and Human Behavior, 28*(3), 176–185.

Polman, H., de Castro, B. O., & van Aken, M. A. G. (2008). Experimental study of the differential effects of playing versus watching violent video games on children's aggressive behavior. *Aggressive Behavior, 34*(3), 256–264.

Pool, M. M., Koolstra, C. M., & van der Voort, T. H. A. (2003). Distraction effects of background soap operas on homework performance: An experimental study enriched with observational data. *Educational Psychology, 23*(4), 361–380.

Pope, K. S. (1996). Memory, abuse, and science: Questioning claims about the False Memory Syndrome epidemic. *American Psychologist, 51*(9), 957–974.

Porcu, E., Venturoli, S., Fabbri, R., Paradisi, R., Longhi, M., Sganga, E., & Flamigni, C. (1994). Skeletal maturation and hormonal levels after the menarche. *Archives of Gynecology and Obstetrics, 255*(1), 43–46.

Posada, G., Jacobs, A., Richmond, M. K., Carbonell, O. A., Alzate, G., Bustamante, M. R., & Quiceno, J. (2002). Maternal caregiving and infant security in two cultures. *Developmental Psychology, 38*(1), 67–78.

Posner, M. I., Rothbart, M. K., & Sheese, B. E. (2007). Attention genes. *Developmental Science, 10*(1), 24–29.

Posner, R. B. (2006). Early menarche: A review of research on trends in timing racial differences, etiology and psychosocial consequences. *Sex Roles, 54*(5/6), 315–322.

Potter, A. E., & Williams, D. E. (1991). Development of a measure examining children's roles in alcoholic families. *Journal of Studies on Alcohol, 52*(1), 70–77.

Preissler, M. A., & Bloom, P. (2007). Two-year-olds appreciate the dual nature of pictures. *Psychological Science, 18*(1), 1–2.

Provost, M. A., & LaFreniere, P. J. (1991). Social participation and peer competence in preschool children: Evidence for discriminant and convergent validity. *Child Study Journal, 21*(1), 57–72.

Ptacek, J. T., Smith, R. E., & Dodge, K. L. (1994). Gender differences in coping with stress: When stressor and appraisals do not differ. *Personality and Social Psychology Bulletin, 20,* 421–430.

Public Broadcasting Service. (2005). *P.O.V. The Hobart Shakespeareans.* Retrieved from http://www.pbs.org/pov/hobart/film_description.php

Public Broadcasting Service. (2001). *Timeline: The bilingual education controversy.* Retrieved from http://www.pbs.org/kcet/publicschool/roots_in_history/bilingual.html

Public Health Agency of Canada. (2003). *Infant attachment: What professionals need to know.* Retrieved from http://www.phac-aspc.gc.ca/mh-sm/mhp-psm/pub/fc-pc/prof_know-eng.php

Pulakos, J. (1987). The effect of birth order on perceived family roles. *Individual Psychology, 43*(3), 319–328.

Putnam, F. W. (2003). Ten-year research update review: Child sexual abuse. *Journal of the American Academy of Child and Adolescent Psychiatry, 42*(3), 269–278.

Quigley, M. A., Kelly, Y. J., & Sacker, A. (2007). Breastfeeding and hospitalization for diarrheal and respiratory infection in the United Kingdom Millennium Cohort Study. *Pediatrics, 119*(4), e837–842.

Quinn, B. (2007). *Bipolar disorder.* Hoboken, NJ: Wiley.

Quiroga, T., Lemos-Britton, Z., Mostafapour, E., Abbott, R. D., & Berninger, V. W. (2002). Phonological awareness and beginning reading in Spanish-speaking ESL first graders: Research into practice. *Journal of School Psychology, 40*(1), 85–111.

Radziszewska, B., Richardson, J. L., Dent, C. W., & Flay, B. R. (1996). Parenting style and adolescent depressive symptoms, smoking, and academic achievement: Ethnic, gender, and SES differences. *Journal of Behavioral Medicine, 19*(3), 289–305.

Raeff, C. (2004). Within culture complexities: Multifaceted and interrelated autonomy and connectedness characteristics in late adolescent selves. In M. F. Mascolo & J. Li (Eds.), Culture and developing selves: Beyond dichotomization. *New Directions for Child and Adolescent Development, 104,* 61–78. San Francisco, CA: Jossey-Bass.

Raja, S. N., McGee, R., & Stanton, W. R. (1992). Perceived attachments to parents and peers and psychological well-being in adolescence. *Journal of Youth and Adolescence, 21*(4), 471–485.

Ramsey-Rennels, J. L., & Langlois, J. H. (2007). How infants perceive and process faces. In A. Slater & M. Lewis (Eds.), *Introduction to infant development* (pp. 191–215). New York, NY: Oxford University Press.

Rampage, C., Eovaldi, M., Ma, C., & Weigel-Foy, C. (2003). Adoptive families. In F. Walsh (Ed.), *Normal family processes* (3rd ed., pp. 210–232). New York, NY: Guilford.

The RAND Corporation. (2009). *RAND at a glance.* Retrieved from http://www.rand.org/about/glance.html

Rangel, M. C., Gavin, L., Reed, C., Fowler, M. G., & Lee, L. M. (2006). Epidemiology of HIV and AIDS among adolescents and young adults in the United States. *Journal of Adolescent Health, 39*(2), 156–163.

Raphel, S. (2008). Kinship care and the situation for grandparents. *Journal of Child and Adolescent Psychiatric Nursing, 21,* 118–120.

Raskind, M. H., Gerber, P. J., Goldberg, R. J., Higgins, E. L., & Herman, K. L. (1998). Longitudinal research in learning disabilities: Report on an international symposium. *Journal of Learning Disabilities, 31*(3), 266–277.

Ratjen, F., & Döring, G. (2003). Cystic fibrosis. *Lancet, 361*(9358), 681–689.

Raudenbush, S. W. (1984). Magnitude of teacher expectancy effects on pupil IQ as a function of the credibility of expectancy induction: A synthesis of findings from 18 experiments. *Journal of Educational Psychology, 76,* 85–97.

Rauh, V. A., Whyatt, R. M., Garfinkel, R., Andrews, H., Hoepner, L., Reyes, A., . . . Perera, F. P. (2004). Developmental effects of exposure to environmental tobacco smoke and material hardship among inner-city children. *Neurotoxicology and Teratology, 26*(3), 373–385.

Reed, R. K. (2005). *Birthing fathers: The transformation of men in American rites of birth.* New Brunswick, NJ: Rutgers University Press.

Reef, S., & Redd, S. (2008). Congenital rubella syndrome. In Centers for Disease Control and Prevention (Ed.), *Manual for the surveillance of vaccine-preventable diseases* (4th ed.). Retrieved from http://www.cdc.gov/vaccines/pubs/surv-manual/chpt15-crs.htm

Reeves, J. (2006). Recklessness, rescue and responsibility: Young men tell their stories of the transition to fatherhood. *Practice, 18*(2), 79–90.

Reif, A., Rosler, M., Freitag, C. M., Schneider, M., Eujen, A., Kissling, C., . . . Retz, W. (2007). Nature and nurture predispose to violent behavior: Serotonergic genes and adverse childhood environment. *Neuropsychopharmacology, 32*(11), 2375–2383.

Reis, S. M. (2004). Series introduction. In R. J. Sternberg (Ed.), *Definitions and conceptions of giftedness* (pp. ix–xxi). Thousand Oaks, CA: Corwin Press.

Reiss, D. (2001). Genetic influences on human behavior and development. *Lifelines, 5.* Retrieved from http://www.brown.edu/Departments/Human_Development_Center/pubs/l5respns.html

Reiss, D., Hetherington, E. M., Plomin, R., Howe, G. W., Simmens, S. J., Henderson, S. H., . . . Law, T. (1995). Genetic questions for environmental studies: Differential parenting and psychopathology in adolescence. *Archives of General Psychiatry, 52,* 925–936.

Repacholi, B. M., & Gopnik, A. (1997). Early reasoning about desires: Evidence from 14- and 18-month-olds. *Developmental Psychology, 33*(1), 12–21.

Reynolds, A. J., Temple, J., & McCoy, A. (1997, September 17). Grade retention doesn't work. *Education Week,* 36.

Rhodes, J. E., Contreras, J. M., & Mangelsdorf, S. C. (1994). Natural mentor relationships among Latina adolescent mothers: Psychological adjustment, moderating processes, and the role of early parental acceptance. *American Journal of Community Psychology, 22*(2), 211–227.

Rhodes, J. E., Ebert, L., & Fischer, K. (1992). Natural mentors: An overlooked resource in the social networks of young, African American mothers. *American Journal of Community Psychology, 20*(4), 445–461.

Ricard, M., Girouard, P. C., & Gouin Decairie, T. (1999). Personal pronouns and perspective taking in toddlers. *Journal of Child Language, 26*(3), 681–697.

Richmond, M. K., Stocker, C. M., & Rienks, S. L. (2005). Longitudinal associations between sibling relationship quality, parental differential treatment, and children's adjustment. *Journal of Family Psychology, 19*(4), 550–559.

Rideout, V., Foehr, U. G., & Roberts, D. F. (2010). *Generation M²: Media in the lives of 8- to 18-year-olds.* A Kaiser Family Foundation Study. Retrieved from http://www.kff.org/entmedia/upload/8010.pdf

Rideout, V., Roberts, D. F., & Foehr, U. G. (2005). *Executive summary: Generation M: Media in the lives of 8–18 year-olds.* Retrieved from http://www.kff.org/entmedia/7250.cfm

Rideout, V. J., Foehr, U. G., Roberts, D. F., & Brodie, M. (1999). *Kids & media @ the new millennium.* Henry J. Kaiser Family Foundation. Retrieved from http://www.kff.org/entmedia/upload/Kids-Media-The-New-Millennium-Executive-Summary.pdf

Rideout, V. J., & Hamel, E. (2006). *The media family: Electronic media in the lives of infants, toddlers, preschoolers and their parents.* Retrieved from http://www.kff.org/entmedia/upload/7500.pdf

Rieg, S. A., & Paquette, K. R. (2009). Using drama and movement to enhance English language learners' literacy development. *Journal of Instructional Psychology, 36*(2), 148–154.

Ringelhann, B., Hathorn, M. K., Jilly, P., Grant, F., & Parniczky, G. (1976). A new look at the protection of hemoglobin AS and AC genotypes against plasmodium falciparum infection: A census tract approach. *American Journal of Human Genetics, 28*(3), 270–279.

Rishel, C. W., Cottrell, L., Cottrell, S., Stanton, B., Gibson, C., & Bougher, K. (2007). Exploring adolescents' relationships with non-parental adults using the Non-Parental Adult Inventory (N.P.A.I.). *Child & Adolescent Social Work Journal, 24*(5), 495–508.

Ritchey, K. D., & Speece, D. L. (2006). From letter names to word reading: The nascent role of sublexical fluency. *Contemporary Educational Psychology, 31*(3), 301–327.

Rittle-Johnson, B., & Siegler, R. S. (1999). Learning to spell: Variability, choice, and change in children's strategy use. *Child Development, 70*(2) 332–348.

Rivadeneyra, R., Ward, L. M., & Gordon, M. (2007). Distorted reflections: Media exposure and Latino adolescents' conceptions of self. *Media Psychology, 9*(2), 261–290.

Rivera, R. (2007, April 25). In Mexican Town, maybe a way to reduce poverty in New York. *The New York Times.* Retrieved from http://www.nytimes .com/2007/04/25/nyregion/25antipoverty .html?pagewanted=1

Roberts, C., Bishop, B., & Rooney, R. (2008). Depression and bipolar disorder in childhood. In T. P. Gullotta & G. M. Blau (Eds.), *Handbook of childhood behavioral issues* (pp. 239–271). New York, NY: Routledge.

Roberts, D. (2002). *Shattered bonds: The color of child welfare.* New York, NY: Basic Civitas Books.

Roberts, D. F., & Foehr, U. G. (2008). Trends in media use. *The Future of Children, 18*(1), 11–37.

Roberts, M. W., Joe, V. C., & Rowe-Hallbert, A. (1992). Oppositional child behavior and parental locus of control. *Journal of Clinical Child Psychology, 21*(2), 170–177.

Roberts, R. E., Roberts, C. R., & Chen, Y. R. (1997). Ethnocultural differences in prevalence of adolescent depression. *American Journal of Community Psychology, 25*(1), 95–110.

Robins, R. W., Trzesniewski, K. H., Tracy, J. L., Gosling, S. D., & Potter, J. (2002). Global self-esteem across the lifespan. *Psychology and Aging, 17*, 423–434.

Robinson, J. L., Zahn-Waxler, C., & Emde, R. N. (1994). Patterns of development in early empathic behavior: Environmental and child constitutional influences. *Social Development, 3*(2), 125–145.

Robinson-Riegler, G., & Robinson-Riegler, B. (2008). *Cognitive psychology: Applying the science of the mind.* Boston, MA: Pearson/ Allyn & Bacon.

Rochat, P. (2001). Origins of self-concept. In G. Bremner & A. Fogel (Eds.), *Blackwell handbook of infant development* (pp. 191–212). Malden, MA: Blackwell.

Roche, A. F. (Ed.). (1979). Secular trends: Human growth, maturation, and development. *Monographs of the Society for Research in Child Development, 44*(179).

Roche, K. M., Ensminger, M. E., & Cherlin, A. J. (2007). Variations in parenting and adolescent outcomes among African American and Latino families living in low-income, urban areas. *Journal of Family Issues, 28,* 882–909.

Rochlin, M. (2008). *Heterosexual questionnaire— Handout: A lesson plan from Creating Safe Space for GLBTQ Youth: A Toolkit.* Adapted for use by Advocates for Youth. Retrieved from http://www.advocatesfo ryouth.org/index.php?option=com_con tent&task=view&id=223&Itemid=129 (Original work published in 1977)

Roderick, M., & Nagaoka, J. (2005). Retention under Chicago's high-stakes testing program: Helpful, harmful or harmless? *Education Evaluation and Policy Analysis, 27*(4), 309–340.

Rodkin, P. C., Farmer, T. W., Pearl, R., & Van Acker, R. (2000). Heterogeneity of popular boys: Antisocial and prosocial configurations. *Developmental Psychology, 36*(1), 14–24.

Roeser, R. W., & Peck, S. C. (2003). Patterns and pathways of educational achievement across adolescence: A holistic-developmental perspective. In W. Damon, S. C. Peck, & R. W. Roeser (Eds.), *New directions for child and adolescent development: Vol. 101. Person-centered approaches to studying human development in context* (pp. 39–62). San Francisco, CA: Jossey-Bass.

Rogers, J. M. (2009). Tobacco and pregnancy. *Reproductive Toxicology, 28*(2), 152–160.

Rose, A. J., & Montemayor, R. (1994). The relationship between gender role orientation and perceived self-competency in male and female adolescents. *Sex Roles, 31*(9–10), 579–595.

Rose, E. R. (1999). *A mother's job: The history of day care, 1890–1960.* New York, NY: Oxford University Press.

Rose, S. A., Feldman, J. F., & Wallace, I. F. (1992). Infant information processing in relation to six-year cognitive outcomes. *Child Development, 63*(5), 1126–1141.

Rose, S. A., Feldman, J. F., Wallace, I. F., & Cohen, P. (1992). Language: A partial link between infant attention and later intelligence. *Developmental Psychology, 27*(5), 798–805.

Rosenstein, D., & Oster, H. (2005). Differential facial responses to four basic tastes in newborns. In P. Ekman & E. L. Rosenberg (Eds.), *What the face reveals: Basic and applied studies of spontaneous expression using the facial action coding system (FACS)* (2nd ed., pp. 302–327). New York, NY: Oxford University Press.

Rosenthal, R., & Jacobson, L. (1968). *Pygmalion in the classroom: Teacher expectation and pupils' intellectual development.* New York, NY: Rinehart & Winston.

Rosenzweig, M. R., Breedlove, S. M., & Watson, N. V. (2005). *Biological psychology* (4th ed.). Sunderland, MA: Sinauer.

Ross, H., Tesla, C., Kenyon, B., & Lollis, S. (1990). Maternal intervention in toddler peer conflict: The socialization of principles of justice. *Developmental Psychology, 26*(6), 994–1003.

Ross, H. S., Recchia, H. E., & Carpendale, J. I. M. (2005). Making sense of divergent interpretations of conflict and developing an interpretive understanding of mind. *Journal of Cognition and Development, 6*(4), 571–592.

Rothbart, M. K., Derryberry, D., & Hershey, K. (2000). Stability of temperament in childhood: Laboratory infant assessment to parent report at seven years. In V. J. Molfese & D. L. Molfese (Eds.), *Temperament and personality development across the life span* (pp. 85–119). Mahwah, NJ: Erlbaum.

Rothbaum, R., Kakinuma, M., Nagaoka, R., & Azuma, H. (2007). Attachment and amae: Parent-child closeness in the United States and Japan. *Journal of Cross-Cultural Psychology, 38,* 465–486.

Rotheram-Borus, M. J., & Langabeer, K. A. (2001). Developmental trajectories of gay, lesbian and bisexual youth. In A. R. D'Augelli & C. J. Patterson (Eds.), *Lesbian, gay and bisexual identities and youth: Psychological perspectives* (pp. 97–128). New York, NY: Oxford University Press.

Rovee-Collier, C. (1999). The development of infant memory. *Current Directions in Psychological Science, 8*(3), 80–85.

Rowe, D. C. (2003). Assessing genotype-environment interactions and correlations in the postgenomic era. In R. Plomin, J. C. DeFries, I. W. Craig, & P. McGuffin (Eds.), *Behavioral genetics in the postgenomic era* (pp. 71–86). Washington, DC: American Psychological Association.

Rowe, M. L. (2008). Child-directed speech: Relation to socioeconomic status, knowledge of child development and child vocabulary skill. *Journal of Child Language, 35*(1), 185–205.

Rowe, M. L., & Goldin-Meadow, S. (2009). Differences in early gesture explain SES disparities in child vocabulary size at school entry. *Science, 323*(5916), 951–953.

Rubin, K. H., Lynch, D., Coplan, R., Rose-Krasnor, L., & Booth, C. L. (1994). "Birds of a feather . . .": Behavioral concordances and preferential personal attraction in children. *Child Development, 65*(6), 1778–1785.

Ruble, D. N., Taylor, L. J., Cyphers, L., Greulich, F. K., Lurye, L. E., & Shrout, P. E. (2007). The role of gender constancy in early gender development. *Child Development, 78*(4), 1121–1136.

Rudy, D., & Grusec, J. E. (2006). Authoritarian parenting in individualist and collectivist groups: Associations with maternal emotion and cognition and children's self-esteem. *Journal of Family Psychology, 20*(1), 68–78.

Ruffman, T., Perner, J., Naito, M., Parkin, L., & Clements, W. A. (1998). Older (but not younger) siblings facilitate false belief understanding. *Developmental Psychology, 34*(1), 161–174.

Ruffman, T., Perner, J., & Parkin, L. (1999). How parenting style affects false belief understanding. *Social Development, 8*(3), 395–411.

Runco, M. A., & Albert, R. S. (1986). The threshold theory regarding creativity and intelligence: An empirical test with gifted and nongifted children. *Creative Child and Adult Quarterly, 11,* 212–218.

Russell, A., Hart, C. H., Robinson, C. C., & Olsen, S. F. (2003). Children's sociable and aggressive behavior with peers: A comparison of the US and Australia, and contributions of temperament and parenting styles. *International Journal of Behavioral Development, 27*(1), 74–86.

Russell, A., & Saebel, J. (1997). Mother-son, mother-daughter, father-son, and father-daughter: Are they distinct relationships? *Developmental Review, 17*(2), 111–147.

Russell, J. A. (1994). Is there universal recognition of emotion from facial expressions? A review of the cross-cultural studies. *Psychological Bulletin, 115*(1), 102–141.

Ryan, R. M., Fauth, R. C., & Brooks-Gunn, J. (2006). Childhood poverty: Implications for school readiness and early childhood education. In B. Spodek & O. Saracho (Eds.), *Handbook of research on the education of young children* (2nd ed., pp. 323–346). Mahwah, NJ: Erlbaum.

Rymer, R. (1993). *Genie: An abused child's flight from silence.* New York, NY: Harper.

Sachs, J. (2005). Communication development in infancy. In J. B. Gleason (Ed.), *The development of language* (6th ed., pp. 39–61). Boston, MA: Pearson.

Safe Kids Worldwide. (2007). *Childhood injury trends fact sheet.* Washington, DC: Author.

Saffran, J. R., Johnson, E. K., Aslin, R. N., & Newport, E. L. (1999). Statistical learning of tone sequences by human infants and adults. *Cognition, 70*(1), 27–52.

Saffran, J. R., Newport, E. L., Aslin, R. N., Tunick, R. A., & Barrueco, S. (1997). Incidental language learning: Listening (and learning) out of the corner of your ear. *Psychological Science, 8*(2), 101–105.

Sagi, A., & Hoffman, M. L. (1976). Empathic distress in the newborn. *Developmental Psychology, 12*(2), 175–176.

Sagi, A., van IJzendoorn, M. H., & Koren-Karie, N. (1991). Primary appraisal of the Strange Situation: A cross-cultural analysis of preseparation episodes. *Developmental Psychology, 27*(4), 587–596.

Sales, J. M., & Fivush, R. (2005). Social and emotional functions of mother-child reminiscing about stressful events. *Social Cognition, 23*(1), 70–90.

Salkind, N. J. (2005a). Bayley Scales of Infant Development. In *Encyclopedia of human development.* Thousand Oaks, CA: Sage. Retrieved from http://www.sage-ereference .com/humandevelopment/Article_n81.html

Salkind, N. J. (2005b). Puberty. In *Encyclopedia of human development.* Thousand Oaks, CA: Sage. Retrieved from http://www .sage-ereference.com/humandevelopment/ Article_n507.html

Sammons, W. A. H., & Lewis, J. M. (1985). *Premature babies: A different beginning.* St. Louis, MO: Mosby.

Sandnabba, N. K., & Ahlberg, C. (1999). Parents' attitudes and expectations about children's cross-gender behavior. *Sex Roles, 40*(3–4), 249–263.

Sandstrom, M. J., & Zakriski, A. L. (2004). Understanding the experience of peer rejection. In J. B. Kupersmidt & K. A. Dodge (Eds.), *Children's peer relations: From development to intervention* (pp. 101–118). Washington, DC: American Psychological Association.

Sann, C., & Streri, A. (2007). Perception of object shape and texture in human newborns: Evidence from cross-modal transfer tasks. *Developmental Science, 10*(3), 399–410.

Sargent, J. D., Tickle, J. J., Beach, M. L., Dalton, M. A., Ahrens, M. B., & Heatherton, T. F. (2001). Brand appearances in contemporary cinema films and contribution to global marketing of cigarettes. *Lancet, 357*(9249), 29–32.

Sassu, K. A., Elinoff, M. J., Bray, M. A., & Kehle, T. J. (2004). *Bullies and victims: Information for parents.* Retrieved from http://www .nasponline.org/resources/handouts/ revisedPDFs/bulliesvictims.pdf

Sato, Y., Sogabe, Y., & Mazuka, R. (2010). Discrimination of phonemic vowel length by Japanese infants. *Developmental Psychology, 46*(1), 106–119.

Saul, R. A., & Tarleton, J. C. (1998). FMR1-related disorders. *Gene Reviews.* Retrieved from http://www.ncbi.nlm.nih.gov/book shelf/br.fcgi?book=gene&part=fragilex

Savin-Williams, R., & Berndt, T. J. (1993). Friendships and peer relations. In S. S. Feldman & G. R. Elliott (Eds.), *At the threshold: The developing adolescent* (pp. 227–307). Cambridge, MA: Harvard University Press.

Savin-Williams, R. C. (2006). *The new gay teenager.* Cambridge, MA: Harvard University Press.

Savin-Williams, R. C., & Diamond, L. M. (1999). Sexual orientation. In W. K. Silverman (Ed.), *Development issues in the clinical treatment of children* (pp. 241–258). Needham Heights, MA: Allyn & Bacon.

Savin-Williams, R. C., & Ream, G. L. (2003). Sex variations in the disclosure to parents of same-sex attractions. *Journal of Family Psychology, 17*(3), 429–438.

Sax, L. (2007). The boy problem: Many boys think school is stupid and reading stinks—Is there a remedy? *School Library Journal, 53*(9), 40–43.

Saxbe, D. E., & Repetti, R. L. (2009). Brief report: Fathers' and mothers' marital relationship predicts daughters' pubertal development two years later. *Journal of Adolescence, 32*(2), 415–423.

Saxe, G. B., & Moylan, T. (1982). The development of measurement operations among the Oksapmin of Papua New Guinea. *Child Development, 53*(5), 1242–1248.

Sayger, T. V., Bowersox, M. P., & Steinberg, E. B. (1996). Family therapy and the treatment

of chronic illness in a multidisciplinary world. *Family Journal, 4*(1), 12–21.

Sayler, M. F., & Brookshire, W. K. (2004). Social, emotional and behavior adjustment of accelerated students, students in gifted classes, and regular students in eighth grade. In S. M. Moon (Ed.), *Social/emotional issues, underachievement, and counseling of gifted and talented students* (pp. 9–19). Thousand Oaks, CA: Corwin Press.

Scarborough, A. A., Hebbeler, K. M., Spiker, D., & Simeonsson, R. J. (2007). Dimensions of behavior of toddlers entering early intervention: Child and family correlates. *Infant Behavior & Development, 30*(3), 466–478.

Scarlett, W. G., Naudeau, S., Salonius-Pasternak, D., & Ponte, I. (2005). *Children's play.* Thousand Oaks, CA: Sage.

Scarr, S. (1992). Developmental theories for the 1990s: Development and individual differences. *Child Development, 63,* 1–19.

Scarr, S., & McCartney, K. (1983). How people make their own environments: A theory of genotype → environment effects. *Child Development, 54*(2), 424–435.

Scarr, S., & Weinberg, R. A. (1986). The early childhood enterprise: Care and education of the young. *American Psychologist, 41*(10), 1140–1146.

Schaeberle, C. (2007). Fetal membranes. In *McGraw-Hill encyclopedia of science & technology* (Vol. 7, 10th ed., p. 101). New York, NY: McGraw-Hill.

Schalet, A. (2007). Adolescent sexuality viewed through two different cultural lenses. In M. S. Tepper & A. F. Owens (Eds.), *Sexual health: Moral and cultural foundations* (Vol. 3, pp. 365–387). Westport, CT: Praeger.

Schiffer, M. (Writer), & Avildsen, J. G. (Director). (1989). *Lean on me* [Motion picture]. United States: Warner Bros.

Schmidt, L. A., & Tasker, S. L. (2000). Childhood shyness: Determinants, development and "depathology." In W. R. Crozier (Ed.), *Shyness: Development, consolidation and change* (pp. 30–46). New York, NY: Routledge.

Schmidt, M. E., & Anderson, D. R. (2007). The impact of television on cognitive development and educational achievement. In N. Pecora, J. P. Murray, & E. A. Wartella (Eds.), *Children and television: Fifty years of research* (pp. 65–84). Mahwah, NJ: Erlbaum.

Schmidt, M. E., Pempek, T. A., Kirkorian, H. L., Lund, A. F., & Anderson, D. R. (2008). The effects of background television on the toy play behavior of very young children. *Child Development, 79*(4), 1137–1151.

Schmitt, N., Keeney, J., Oswald, F. L., Pleskac, T. J., Billington, A. Q., Sinha, R., & Zorzie, M. (2009). Prediction of 4-year college student performance using cognitive and noncognitive predictors and the impact on demographic status of admitted students. *Journal of Applied Psychology, 94*(6), 1479–1497.

Schneider, J. S., Stone, M. K., Wynne-Edwards, K. E., Horton, T. H., Lydon, J., O'Malley, B.,

& Levine, J. E. (2003). Progesterone receptors mediate male aggression toward infants. *Proceedings of the National Academy of Sciences, 100*(5), 2951–2956.

Schneider, W., & Bjorklund, D. F. (1992). Expertise, aptitude and strategic remembering. *Child Development, 63*(2), 461–473.

Schneider Rosen, K., & Burke, P. B. (1999). Multiple attachment relationships within families: Mothers and fathers with two young children. *Developmental Psychology, 35*(2), 436–441.

Scholte, R. H. J., Engels, R. C. M. E., de Kemp, R. A. T., Harakeh, Z., & Overbeek, G. (2007). Differential parental treatment, sibling relationships and delinquency in adolescence. *Journal of Youth and Adolescence, 36*(5), 661–671.

Schoppe-Sullivan, S. J., Diener, M. L., Mangelsdorf, S. C., Brown, G. L., McHale, J. L., & Frosch, C. A. (2006). Attachment and sensitivity in family context: The roles of parent and infant gender. *Infant and Child Development, 15*(4), 367–385.

Schuetze, P., Zeskind, P. S., & Eiden, R. D. (2003). The perceptions of infant distress signals varying in pitch by cocaine-using mothers. *Infancy, 4*(1), 65–83.

Schuntermann, P. (2007). The sibling experience: Growing up with a child who has pervasive developmental disorder or mental retardation. *Harvard Review of Psychiatry, 15*(3), 93–108.

Schwartzberg, B. (2004). "Lots of them did that": Desertion, bigamy, and marital fluidity in late-nineteenth-century America. *Journal of Social History, 37*(3), 573–600.

Scriver, C. R. (2007). The PAH gene, phenylketonuria, and a paradigm shift. *Human Mutation, 28*(9), 831–845.

Search Institute. (n.d.). *What kids need: Developmental assets.* Retrieved from http://www.search-institute.org/developmental-assets

Segal, M. (2004). The roots and fruits of pretending. In E. F. Zigler, D. G. Singer, & S. J. Bishop-Josef (Eds.), *Children's play—The roots of reading* (pp. 33–48). Washington, DC: Zero to Three Press.

Segui-Gomez, M. (2000). Drive air bag effectiveness by severity of the crash. *American Journal of Public Health, 90*(10), 1575–1581.

Sellers, R. M., Copeland-Linder, N., Martin, P. P., & Lewis, L. (2006). Racial identity matters: The relationship between racial discrimination and psychological functioning in African-American adolescents. *Journal of Research on Adolescence, 16*(2), 187–216.

Seo, Y., Abbott, R. D., & Hawkins, J. D. (2008). Outcome status of students with learning disabilities at ages 21 and 14. *Journal of Learning Disabilities, 41*(4), 300–314.

Sesma, A., Jr., Mannes, M., & Scales, P. C. (2005). Positive adaptation, resilience, and the developmental asset framework. In S. Goldstein & R. B. Brooks (Eds.), *Handbook of resilience in children* (pp. 281–296). New York, NY: Springer.

Sexuality Information and Education Council of the United States. (2005). *The truth about adolescent sexuality.* Retrieved from http://www.education.com/reference/article/Ref_Truth_About/

Shamir-Essakow, G., Ungerer, J. A., & Rapee, R. M. (2005). Attachment, behavioral inhibition, and anxiety in preschool children. *Journal of Abnormal Child Psychology, 33*(2), 131–143.

Shanahan, T. (2004). Critiques of the National Reading Panel report. In P. McCardle & V. Chhabra (Eds.), *The voice of evidence in reading research* (pp. 235–265). Baltimore, MD: Brooks.

Shapiro, L. R., Hurry, J., Masterson, J., Wydell, T. N., & Doctor, E. (2009). Classroom implications of recent research into literacy development: From predictors to assessment. *Dyslexia, 15*(1), 1–22.

Shaughnessy, J. J., & Zechmeister, E. B. (1994). *Research methods in psychology* (3rd ed.). New York, NY: McGraw-Hill.

Shaw, D. S., Owens, E. B., & Giovannelli, J. (2001). Infant and toddler pathways leading to early externalizing disorders. *Journal of the American Academy of Child and Adolescent Psychiatry, 40*(1), 36–43.

Shaywitz, B. A., Shaywitz, S. E., Pugh, K. R., Constable, R. T., Skudlarski, P., Fulbright, R. K., . . . Gores, J. C. (1995). Sex differences in the functional organization of the brain for language. *Nature, 373*(6515), 607–609.

She, H. C. (2000). The interplay of a biology teacher's beliefs, teaching practices and gender-based student–teacher classroom interaction. *Educational Research, 42*(1), 100–111.

Shea, A. K., & Steiner, M. (2008). Cigarette smoking during pregnancy. *Nicotine and Tobacco Research, 10*(2), 267–278.

Shearer, C. L., Crouter, A. C., & McHale, S. (2005). Parents' perceptions of changes in mother-child and father-child relationships during adolescence. *Journal of Adolescent Research, 20*(6), 662–684.

Shearer, W. T., Quinn, T. C., LaRussa, P., Lew, J. F., Mofenson, L., Almy, S., . . . The Women and Infants Transmission Study Group. (1997). Viral load and disease progression in infants infected with human immunodeficiency virus Type 1. *New England Journal of Medicine, 366,* 1337–1341.

Shelov, S. P., & Altmann, T. R. (2009). *Caring for your baby and young child* (5th ed.). Elk Grove, IL: American Academy of Pediatrics.

Shepard, S., & Metzler, D. (1988). Mental rotation: Effects of dimensionality of objects and type of task. *Journal of Experimental Psychology: Human Perception and Performance, 14*(1), 3–11. (Images come from their original 1971 research)

Sherrod, L. (2009). A nation in transition: Opportunities for using developmental research to promote the best interests of children, youth, and families. *SRCD Developments, 52*(1), 11–12.

Shin, N. (2004). Exploring pathways from television viewing to academic achievement in school age children. *Journal of Genetic Psychology, 165*(4), 367–381.

Shoda, Y., Mischel, W., & Peake, P. K. (1990). Predicting adolescent cognitive and self-regulatory competencies from preschool delay of gratification: Identifying diagnostic conditions. *Developmental Psychology, 26*(6), 978–986.

Shonkoff, J. P., & Phillips, D. A. (2000). *From neurons to neighborhoods: The science of early childhood development.* Washington, DC: National Academy Press.

Shultz, K. S., Hoffman, C. C., & Reiter-Polman, R. (2005). Using archival data for I-O research: Advantages, pitfalls, sources and examples. *The Industrial-Organizational Psychologist, 42,* 31–37.

Sidorowicz, L. S., & Lunney, G. S. (1980). Baby X revisited. *Sex Roles, 6*(1), 67–73.

Siegler, R., & Crowley, K. (1991). The microgenetic method: A direct means for studying cognitive development. *American Psychologist, 46*(6), 606–620.

Silberglitt, B., Appleton, J. J., Burns, M. K., & Jimerson, S. R. (2006). Examining the effects of grade retention on student reading performance: A longitudinal study. *Journal of School Psychology, 44*(4), 255–270.

Silverman, W. A. (1979). Incubator—Baby side shows. *Pediatrics, 64*(2), 127–141.

Silvia, P. J. (1965). Creativity and intelligence revisited: A latent variable analysis of Wallach and Kogan. *Creativity Research Journal, 20*(1), 34–39.

Simcock, G., & Hayne, H. (2002). Breaking the barrier? Children fail to translate their preverbal memories into language. *Psychological Science, 13*(3), 225–231.

Simmons, R. G., & Blyth, D. A. (1987). *Moving into adolescence: The impact of pubertal change and school context.* New York, NY: Aldine de Gruyter.

Simmons, S. (2010). Guillain-Barré syndrome: A nursing nightmare that usually ends well. *Nursing, 40*(1), 24–30.

Simpson, J. L. (2007). Causes of fetal wastage. *Clinical Obstetrics and Gynecology, 50*(1), 10–30.

Singer, D. G., & Revenson, T. A. (1996). *A Piaget primer* (Rev. ed.). New York, NY: Penguin Books.

Skinner, B. F. (1953). *Science and human behavior.* New York, NY: Macmillan.

Skinner, B. F. (1991). *Verbal behavior.* Acton, MA: Copley. (Original work published in 1957)

Slaby, R. G., & Frey, K. S. (1975). Development of gender constancy and selective attention to same-sex models. *Child Development, 46,* 849–856.

Slate, J. R., & Charlesworth, J. R. (1988). *Information processing theory: Classroom applications* (ERIC Document Reproduction Service No. 293792). Retrieved from ERIC database.

Slate, J. R., & Jones, C. H. (1998). Fourth and fifth grade students' attitudes toward science: Science motivation and science importance as a function of grade level, gender, and race. *Research in the Schools, 5*(1), 27–32.

Slater, A., Field, T., & Hernandez-Reif, M. (2007). The development of the senses. In A. Slater & M. Lewis (Eds.), *Introduction to infant development.* New York, NY: Oxford University Press.

Slotkin, T. A. (2008). If nicotine is a developmental neurotoxicant in animal studies, dare we recommend nicotine replacement therapy in pregnant women and adolescents? *Neurotoxicology and Teratology, 30*(1), 1–19.

Smetana, J. G. (1988). Concepts of self and social convention: Adolescents' and parents' reasoning about hypothetical and actual family conflicts. In M. R. Gunnar & W. A. Collins (Eds.), *Development during the transition to adolescence* (pp. 79–122). Hillsdale, NJ: Erlbaum.

Smetana, J. G., Metzger, A., & Campione-Barr, N. (2004). African American late adolescents' relationships with parents: Developmental transitions and longitudinal patterns. *Child Development, 75*(3), 932–947.

Smilansky, S. (1968). *The effects of sociodramatic play on disadvantaged preschool children.* New York, NY: Wiley.

Smith, D. H. (2007). Controversies in childhood bipolar disorders. *The Canadian Journal of Psychiatry/La Revue canadienne de psychiatrie, 52*(7), 407–408.

Smith, P. K. (2010). *Children and play.* Malden, MA: Wiley-Blackwell.

Smith, T. E. (1988). Parental control techniques: Relative frequencies and relationships with situational factors. *Journal of Family Issues, 9*(2), 155–176.

Smotherman, W. P., & Robinson, S. R. (1996). The development of behavior before birth. *Developmental Psychology, 32*(3), 425–434.

Snedeker, J., Geren, J., & Shafto, C. L. (2007). Starting over: International adoption as a natural experiment in language development. *Psychological Science, 18*(1), 79–87.

Snow, R. E. (1995). Pygmalion and intelligence? *Current Directions in Psychological Sciences, 4*(6), 169–171.

Snow, R. F. (1981, June/July). Martin Couney. *American Heritage Magazine, 32*(4). Retrieved from http://www.american heritage.com/articles/magazine/ah/1981/4/1981_4 90.shtml

Sobralske, M. C., & Gruber, M. E. (2009). Risks and benefits of parent/child bed sharing. *Journal of the American Academy of Nurse Practitioners, 21,* 474–479.

Society for Neuroscience. (2007a). Adult neurogenesis. *Brain Briefings.* Retrieved from http://www.sfn.org/index .aspx?pagename=brainBriefings_adult_ neurogenesis

Society for Neuroscience. (2007b). The adolescent brain. *Brain Briefings.* Retrieved from http://www.sfn.org/ index.aspx?pagename=brainBriefings_ Adolescent_brain

Society for Neuroscience. (2008). *Brain development.* Retrieved from http://www.sfn .org/skins/main/pdf/brainfacts/2008/brain_ development.pdf

Society for Research in Child Development. (2007). *Ethical standards for research with children.* Retrieved from http://www.srcd .org/index.php?option=com_content&task =view&id=68&Itemid=499

Society for the Confluence of Festivals in India. (n.d.). *Mother in different languages.* Retrieved from http://www.mothersday-celebration.com/mother-in-different-languages.html

Solomon, S., & Knafo, A. (2007). Value similarity in adolescent friendships. In T. C. Rhodes (Ed.), *Focus on adolescent behavior research* (pp 133–155). Hauppauge, NY: Nova Science.

Sorace, A. (2006). The more, the merrier: Facts and beliefs about the bilingual mind. In S. Della Sala (Ed.), *Tall tales about the mind and brain: Separating fact from fiction* (pp. 193–203). Oxford, England: Oxford University Press.

Sorsoli, L., Kia-Keating, M., & Grossman, F. K. (2008). "I keep that hush-hush": Male survivors of sexual abuse and the challenges of disclosure. *Journal of Counseling Psychology, 55*(3), 333–345.

Southam-Gerow, M. A., & Chorpita, B. F. (2007). Anxiety in children and adolescents. In E. J. Mash & R. A. Barkley (Eds.), *Assessment of childhood disorders* (pp. 347–397). New York, NY: Guilford.

Southern, W. T., Jones, E. D., & Fiscus, E. D. (1989). Practitioner objections to the academic acceleration of gifted children. *Gifted Child Quarterly, 33*(1), 29–35.

Southern Regional Education Board. (2001). *Finding alternatives to failure: Can states end social promotion and reduce retention rates?* Atlanta, GA: Author.

Spagnola, M., & Fiese, B. H. (2007). Family routines and rituals: A context for development in the lives of young children. *Infants & Young Children, 20*(4), 284–299.

Spelke, E. S. (2000). Core knowledge. *American Psychologist, 55*(11), 1233–1243.

Spelke, E. S., & Kinzler, K. D. (2007). Core knowledge. *Developmental Science 10*(1), 89–96.

Spencer, G. (2005) Studies expand understanding of X chromosome. *Medical News Today.* Retrieved from http://www.medi calnewstoday.com/articles/21399.php

Spencer, J. P., Clearfield, M., Corbetta, D., Ulrich, B., Buchanan, P., & Schoner, G. (2006). Moving toward a grand theory of development: In memory of Esther Thelen. *Child Development, 77*(6), 1521–1538.

Spencer, S. J., Steele, C. M., & Quinn, D. M. (1999). Stereotype threat and women's math performance. *Journal of Experimental Social Psychology, 35*(1), 4–28.

Spielberg, S. (Director). (1982). E.T.: The extra-terrestrial [Motion picture]. United States: Universal.

Spillius, A. (2007). Identical twins reunited after 35 years. *Telegraph.* Retrieved from http://www.telegraph.co.uk/news/world-news/1567542/Identical-twins-reunited-after-35-years.html

Spitzer, R. L. (1981). The diagnostic status of homosexuality in DSM-III: A reformulation of the issues. *American Journal of Psychiatry, 138,* 210–215.

Sroufe, L. A. (1997). *Emotional development.* Cambridge, England: Cambridge University Press.

Sroufe, L. A. (2005). Attachment and development: A prospective, longitudinal study from birth to adulthood. *Attachment and Human Development, 7*(4), 349–367.

Sroufe, L. A., Carlson, E., & Shulman, S. (1993). Individuals in relationships: Development from infancy through adolescence. In D. C. Funder, R. D. Parke, C. Tomlinson-Keasey, & K. Widaman (Eds.), *Studying lives through time* (pp. 315–342). Washington, DC: American Psychological Association.

Sroufe, L. A., Egeland, B., Carlson, E., & Collins, W. A. (2005a). *The development of the person.* New York, NY: Guilford.

Sroufe, L. A., Egeland, B., Carlson, E., & Collins, W. A. (2005b). Placing early attachment experiences in developmental context. In K. E. Grossmann, K. Grossmann, & E. Waters (Eds.), *Attachment from infancy to adulthood* (pp. 48–70). New York, NY: Guilford.

St. James-Roberts, I. (2007). Helping parents to manage infant crying and sleeping: A review of the evidence and its implications for services. *Child Abuse Review, 16*(1), 47–69.

St. Louis, G. R., & Liem, J. H. (2005). Ego identity, ethnic identity, and the psychosocial well-being of ethnic minority and majority college students. *Identity: An International Journal of Theory and Research, 5*(3), 227–246.

St. Rose, A. (2010). Why so few? Women in science, technology, engineering, and mathematics. *Outlook, 104*(1), 8–11.

Stacey, J., & Biblarz, T. J. (2001). (How) does the sexual orientation of parents matter? *American Sociological Review, 66,* 159–183.

Stallings, J., Fleming, A. S., Corter, C., Worthman, C., & Steiner, M (2001). The effects of infant cries and odors on sympathy, cortisol and autonomic responses in new mothers and nonpostpartum women. *Parenting: Science and Practice, 1,* 71–100.

Starko, A. J. (1990). Life and death of a gifted program: Lessons not yet learned. *Roeper Review, 13*(1), 33–38.

Stattin, H., & Magnusson, D. (1990). *Pubertal maturation in female development.* Hillsdale, NJ: Erlbaum.

Stebbins, L. F. (2001). *Work and family in America: A reference handbook.* Santa Barbara, CA: ABC-CLIO.

Steinberg, L. (1993). Autonomy, conflict, and harmony in the family relationship. In S. S. Feldman & G. R. Elliott (Eds.), *At the threshold: The developing adolescent* (pp. 255–276). Cambridge, MA: Harvard University Press.

Steinberg, L. (2001). We know some things: Adolescent-parent relationships in retrospect and prospect. *Journal of Research on Adolescence, 11,* 1–19.

Steinberg, L., Mounts, N. S., Lamborn, S. D., & Dornbusch, S. M. (1991). Authoritative parenting and adolescent adjustment across varied ecological niches. *Journal of Research on Adolescence, 1*(1), 19–36.

Steinberg, L., & Silk, J. S. (2002). Parenting adolescents. In M. H. Bornstein (Ed.), *Handbook of parenting* (2nd ed., pp. 103–133). Mahwah, NJ: Erlbaum.

Steinberg, L. D., Catalano, R., & Dooley, D. (1981). Economic antecedents of child abuse and neglect. *Child Development, 52*(3), 975–985.

Steinem, G. (1995). What if Freud were Phyllis? In G. Steinem (Ed.), *Moving beyond words: Age, rage, sex, power, money, muscles: Breaking boundaries of gender* (pp. 32–92). New York, NY: Simon & Schuster.

Steiner, G., & Smith, J. A. (1999). *Learning: Nineteen scenarios from everyday life.* Cambridge, England: Cambridge University Press.

Stern, M., & Karraker, K. H. (1989). Sex stereotyping of infants: A review of gender labeling studies. *Sex Roles, 20*(9–10), 501–522.

Stern, M., Karraker, K., McIntosh, B., Moritzen, S., & Olexa, M. (2006). Prematurity stereotyping and mothers' interaction with their premature and full-term infants during the first year. *Journal of Pediatric Psychology, 31*(6), 597–607.

Sternberg, R. B. (2003). Creative thinking in the classroom. *Scandinavian Journal of Educational Research, 47*(3), 325–338.

Sternberg, R. J. (2002a). Beyond g: The theory of successful intelligence. In R. J. Sternberg & E. L. Grigorenko (Eds.), *The general factor of intelligence: How general is it?* (pp. 447–479). Mahwah, NJ: Erlbaum.

Sternberg, R. J. (2002b). Individual differences in cognitive development. In U. Goswami (Ed.), *Blackwell handbook of childhood cognitive development* (pp. 600–619). Malden, MA: Blackwell.

Sternberg, R. J. (2002c). Raising the achievement of all students: Teaching for successful intelligence. *Educational Psychology Review, 14*(4), 383–393.

Sternberg, R. J. (2004). Introduction to definitions and conceptions of giftedness. In R. J. Sternberg (Ed.), *Definitions and conceptions of giftedness* (pp. xxiii–xxv). Thousand Oaks, CA: Corwin Press.

Sternberg, R. J., Castejón, J. L., Prieto, M. D., Hautamäki, J., & Grigorenko, E. L. (2001). Confirmatory factor analysis of the Sternberg Triarchic Abilities Test in three international samples: An empirical test of the triarchic theory of intelligence. *European Journal of Psychological Assessment, 17*(1), 1–16.

Sternberg, R. J., & Detterman, D. K. (Eds.). (1986). *What is intelligence? Contemporary viewpoints on its nature and definition.* Norwood, NJ: Ablex.

Sternberg, R. J., & Zhang, I. (1995). What do we mean by giftedness? A pentagonal implicit theory. *Gifted Child Quarterly, 39*(2), 88–94.

Stevenson, H. W., Lee, S., & Chen, C. (1990). Contexts of achievement: A study of American, Chinese, and Japanese children. *Monographs of the Society for Research in Child Development, 55*(1–2).

Stewart, P. K., & Steele, R. G. (2005). Wechsler Intelligence Scale for Children (WISC). In *Encyclopedia of human development.* Thousand Oaks, CA: Sage. Retrieved from http://www.sage-ereference.com/humandevelopment/Article_n637.html

Stice, E., Marti, C. N., Shaw, H., & Jaconis, M. (2009). An 8-year longitudinal study of the natural history of threshold, subthreshold, and partial eating disorders from a community sample of adolescents. *Journal of Abnormal Psychology, 118*(3), 587–597.

Stice, E., & Shaw, H. (2004). Eating disorder prevention programs: A meta-analytic review. *Psychological Bulletin, 130*(2), 206–227.

Stiefel Laboratories. (2008). *Contraception counseling referral program.* Retrieved from http://www.soriatane.com/media/ContraceptCounseling.pdf

Stipek, D., Gralinski, H., & Kopp, C. B. (1990). Self-concept development in the toddler years. *Developmental Psychology, 26*(6), 972–977.

Stipek, D., Milburn, S., Clements, D., & Daniels, D. H. (1992). Parents' beliefs about appropriate education for young children. *Journal of Applied Developmental Psychology, 13*(3), 293–310.

Stockhorst, U., Klosterhalfen, S., Klosterhalfen, W., Winkelmann, M., & Steingrueber, H. (1993). Anticipatory nausea in cancer patients receiving chemotherapy: Classical conditioning etiology and therapeutical implications. *Integrative Physiological & Behavioral Science, 28*(2), 177–181.

Stoicheva, M. (1999). *Balanced reading instruction.* ERIC Clearinghouse on Reading, English, and Communication, Digest #144. ERIC Document EDO-CS-99-05.

Stop Bullying Now! (2009). All about bullying: State laws on bullying. Retrieved from http://stopbullyingnow.hrsa.gov/adults/state-laws.aspx

Storey, A. E., Walsh, C. J., Quinton, R. L., & Wynne-Edwards, K. E. (2000). Hormonal correlates of paternal responsiveness in new and expectant fathers. *Evolution and Human Behavior, 21*(2), 79–95.

Story, M., Kaphingst, K. M., & French, S. (2006). The role of schools in obesity prevention. *The Future of Children, 16*(1), 109–142.

Strelau, J. (1998). *Temperament: A psychological perspective.* New York, NY: Plenum.

Strenger, C., & Burak, J. (2005). The Leonardo effect: Why entrepreneurs become their own fathers. *International Journal of Applied Psychoanalytic Studies, 2*(2), 103–128.

Stuart, M. (Director). (2005). *The Hobart Shakespeareans* [Documentary film]. United States: Warner Bros.

Sturm, L. (2004). Temperament in early childhood: A primer for the perplexed. In *Zero to Three.* Retrieved from http://www.zerotothree.org/site/DocServer/v0124-4a.pdf?docID=1761&AddInterest=1158

Suarez, E. C. (2004). C-reactive protein is associated with psychological risk factors of cardiovascular disease in apparently healthy adults. *Psychosomatic Medicine, 66,* 684–691.

Subrahmanyam, K., & Greenfield, P. (2008). Online communication and adolescent relationships. *The Future of Children, 18*(1), 119–146.

Substance Abuse and Mental Health Services Administration, Office of Applied Studies. (2007). *The NSDUH Report: Youth activities, substance use, and family income.* Rockville, MD: Author.

Sullivan, R. M., & Toubas, P. (1998). Clinical usefulness of maternal odor in newborns: Soothing and feeding preparatory responses. *Biology of the Neonate, 74*(6), 402–408.

Sullivan, O., & Coltrane, S. (2008). *Men's changing contribution to housework and child care.* Paper presented at the 11th Annual Conference of the Council on Contemporary Families, Chicago, IL, April 25–28.

Sulloway, F. J. (1997). *Born to rebel: Birth order, family dynamics, and creative lives.* New York, NY: Vintage.

Sumter, S. R., Bokhorst, C. L., Steinberg, L., & Westenberg, P. M. (2009). The developmental pattern of resistance to peer influence in adolescence: Will the teenager ever be able to resist? *Journal of Adolescence, 32*(4), 1009–1021.

Super, C. M. (1976). Environmental effects on motor development: The case of African infant precocity. *Developmental Medicine & Child Neurology, 18*(5), 561–567.

Surkan, P. J., Zhang, A., Trachtenberg, F., Daniel, D. B., McKinlay, S., & Bellinger, D. C. (2007). Neuropsychological function in children with blood lead levels <10 µg/dL. *NeuroToxicology, 28*(6), 1170–1177.

Susman-Stillman, A., Kalkose, M., Egeland, B., & Waldman, I. (1996). Infant temperament and maternal sensitivity as predictors of attachment security. *Infant Behavior & Development, 19*(1), 33–47.

Suzuki, L. K., & Beale, I. I. (2006). Personal Web home pages of adolescents with cancer: Self-presentation, information dissemination, and interpersonal connection. *Journal of Pediatric Oncology Nursing, 23*(3), 152–161.

Suzuki, L. K., & Calzo, J. P. (2004). The search for peer advice in cyberspace: An examination of online teen bulletin boards about health and sexuality. *Journal of Applied Developmental Psychology, 25*(6), 685–698.

Svanberg, P. O. G. (1998). Attachment, resilience and prevention. *Journal of Mental Health, 7*(6), 543–578.

Swartzwelder, J. (1994). *Itchy and Scratchy and Marge.* Retrieved from http://www.snpp .com/episodes/7F09.html

Sweet, J. A., & Bumpass, L. (1987). *American families and households.* New York, NY: Russell Sage Foundation.

Tamis-LeMonda, C. S., Bornstein, M. H., & Baumwell, L. (2001). Maternal responsiveness and children's achievement of language milestones. *Child Development, 72*(3), 748–767.

Tamis-LeMonda, C. S., Cristofaro, T. N., Rodriguez, E. T., & Bornstein, M. H. (2006). Early language development: Social influences in the first years of life. In L. Balter & C. S. Tamis-LeMonda (Eds.), *Child psychology: A handbook of contemporary issues* (2nd ed., pp. 79–108). New York, NY: Psychology Press.

Tardif, T., & Wellman, H. M. (2000). Acquisition of mental state language in Mandarin- and Cantonese-speaking children. *Developmental Psychology, 36*(1), 25–43.

Task Force on Sudden Infant Death Syndrome. (2005). The changing concept of sudden infant death syndrome: Diagnostic coding shifts, controversies regarding the sleeping environment, and new variables to consider in reducing risk. *Pediatrics, 116*(5), 1245–1255.

Tatum, B. D. (1997). Racial identity development and relational theory: The case of black women in white communities. In B. Jordan (Ed.), *Women's growth in diversity* (pp. 91–106). New York, NY: Guilford.

Taveras, E. M., Field, A. E., Berkey, C. S., Rifas-Shiman, S. L., Frazier, A. L., Colditz, G. A., & Gillman, M. W. (2007). Longitudinal relationship between television viewing and leisure-time physical activity during adolescence. *Pediatrics, 119*(2), 314–319.

Taylor, B. (2006). Vaccines and the changing epidemiology of autism. *Child Care, Health and Development, 32*(5), 511–519.

Taylor, M. J., & Carlson, S. M. (1997). The relation between individual differences in fantasy and theory of mind. *Child Development, 68,* 436–455.

Temple, E., Poldrack, R. A., Salidis, J., Deutsch, G. K., Tallal, P., Merzenich, M. M., & Gabrieli, J. D. E. (2001). Disrupted neural responses to phonological and orthographic processing in dyslexic children: An fMRI study. *NeuroReport: For Rapid Communication of Neuroscience Research, 12*(2), 299–307.

Terlecki, M. S., Newcombe, N. S., & Little, M. (2008). Durable and generalized effects of spatial experience on mental rotation: Gender differences in growth patterns. *Applied Cognitive Psychology, 22*(7), 996–1013.

Texas Education Agency. (2004). *Foundations of reading: Effective phonological awareness instruction and progress monitoring.* Retrieved from http://www.meadowscenter .org/vgc/downloads/primary/guides/PA_ Guide.pdf

The Free Dictionary. (2009). *Galant reflex.* Retrieved from http://medical-dictionary .thefreedictionary.com/Galant+reflex

Thelen, E. (1989). Self-organization in developmental processes: Can systems approaches work? In M. R. Gunnar & E. Thelen (Eds.), *Systems and development: The Minnesota symposia on child psychology* (pp. 77–117). Hillsdale, NJ: Erlbaum.

Thelen, E., Corbetta, D., Kamm, K., Spencer, J. P., Schneider, K., & Zernicke, R. F. (1993). The transition to reaching: Mapping intention and intrinsic dynamics. *Child Development, 64*(4), 1058–1098.

Thelen, E., Fisher, D. M., & Ridley-Johnson, R. (2002). The relationship between physical growth and a newborn reflex. *Infant Behavior & Development, 25*(1), 72–85.

Tinbergen, N. (1963). On aims and methods of ethology. *Zeitschrift für Tierpsychologie, 20,* 410–433.

Thomas, A., & Chess, S. (1977). *Temperament and development.* New York, NY: Brunner/ Mazel.

Thompson, J. K., & Heinberg, L. J. (1999). The media's influence on body image disturbance and eating disorders: We've reviled them, now we rehabilitate them? *Journal of Social Issues, 55*(2), 339–353.

Thompson, L. A., Fagan, J. F., & Fulker, D. W. (1991). Longitudinal prediction of specific cognitive abilities from infant novelty preference. *Child Development, 62,* 530–538.

Thomson, M. (1996). *Developmental dyslexia: Studies in disorders of communication.* London, England: Whurr.

Thorne, B. (1994). *Gender play—Girls and boys in school.* New Brunswick, NJ: Rutgers University Press.

Tiedemann, J. (2000). Parents' gender stereotypes and teachers' beliefs as predictors of children's concept of their mathematical ability in elementary school. *Journal of Educational Psychology, 92*(1), 144–151.

Tillman, K. H. (2007). Family structure pathways and academic disadvantage among adolescents in stepfamilies. *Sociological Inquiry, 77,* 383–424.

Tincoff, R., & Jusczyk, P. W. (1999). Some beginnings of word comprehension in 6-month-olds. *Psychological Science, 10*(2), 172–175.

Tither, J. M., & Ellis, B. J. (2008). Impact of fathers on daughters' age at menarche: A genetically and environmentally controlled sibling study. *Developmental Psychology, 44*(5), 1409–1420.

Tizard, B., & Rees, J. (1975). The effect of early institutional rearing on the behavior problems and affectional relationships of four-year-old children. *Journal of Child Psychology, Psychiatry, and Allied Disciplines, 27,* 61–73.

Tobin-Richards, M. H., Boxer, A. M., McNeill-Kavrell, S. A., & Petersen, A. C. (1984). Puberty and its psychological and social significance. In R. M. Lerner & N. L. Galambos (Eds.), *Experiencing adolescents: A sourcebook for parents, teachers, and teens* (pp. 17–50). New York, NY: Teachers College.

Torff, B. (1996). How are you smart? Multiple intelligences and classroom practices. *The NAMTA Journal, 21*(2), 31–43.

Torff, B., & Gardner, H. (1999). The vertical mind—The case for multiple intelligences. In M. Anderson (Ed.), *The development of intelligence* (pp. 139–159). Hove, East Sussex, UK: Psychology Press.

Tracy, J. L., & Robins, R. W. (2006). Appraisal antecedents of shame and guilt: Support for a theoretical model. *Personality and Social Psychology Bulletin, 32,* 1339–1351.

Tracy, J. L., & Robins, R. W. (2008). The nonverbal expression of pride: Evidence for cross-cultural recognition. *Journal of Personality and Social Psychology, 94*(3), 516–530.

Tracy, J. L., Robins, R. W., & Lagattuta, K. H. (2005). Can children recognize pride? *Emotion, 5*(3), 251–257.

Tram, J. M., & Cole, D. A. (2006). A multi-method examination of the stability of depressive symptoms in childhood and adolescence. *Journal of Abnormal Psychology, 115*(4), 674–686.

Trautwein, U., Ludtke, O., Marsh, H. W., Koller, O., & Baumert, J. (2006). Tracking, grading, and student motivation: Using group composition and status to predict self-concept and interest in ninth-grade mathematics. *Journal of Educational Psychology, 98*(4), 788–806.

Trevarthen, C. (1991). Reviewed work(s): *Developmental Psychology in the Soviet Union by Jaan Valsiner. Soviet Studies, 43*(1), 183–187.

Tschann, J. M., Adler, N. E., Irwin, C. E., Millstein, S. G., Turner, R. A., & Kegeles, S. (1994). Initiation of substance use in early adolescence: The roles of pubertal timing and emotional distress. *Health Psychology, 13*(4), 326–333.

Tu, M. T., Lupien, S. J., & Walker, C. (2005). Measuring stress responses in postpartum mothers: Perspectives from studies in human and animal populations. *Stress: The International Journal on the Biology of Stress, 8*(1), 19–34.

Turkheimer, E., & Waldron, M. (2000). Nonshared environment: A theoretical, methodological, and quantitative review. *Psychological Bulletin, 126*(1), 78–108.

Turkington, C. A. (2002). Infertility therapies. In J. L. Longe & D. S. Blanchfield (Eds.), *Gale encyclopedia of medicine* (Vol. 2, 2nd ed., pp. 1831–1833). Detroit, MI: Gale.

Twenge, J. M. (2000). The age of anxiety? The birth cohort change in anxiety and neuroticism, 1952–1993. *Journal of Personality and Social Psychology, 79*(6), 1007–1021.

Twenge, J. M. (2006). *Generation me: Why today's young Americans are more confident, assertive, entitled—and more miserable than ever before.* New York, NY: Free Press.

Twenge, J. M., Campbell, W. K., & Foster, C. A. (2003). Parenthood and marital satisfaction: A meta-analytic review. *Journal of Marriage and Family, 65,* 574–583.

Tyrka, A. R., Graber, J. A., & Brooks-Gunn, J. (2000). The development of disordered eating: Correlates and predictors of eating problems in the context of adolescence. In A. J. Sameroff, M. Lewis, & S. Miller (Eds.), *Handbook of developmental psychopathology* (2nd ed., pp. 607–624). New York, NY: Plenum Press.

Tyrrell, M. (2005). School phobia. *Journal of School Nursing, 21*(3), 147–151.

Tyson, J. E., Nehal, A. P., Langer, J., Green, C., & Higgins, R. D. (2008). Intensive care for extreme prematurity—Moving beyond gestational age. *New England Journal of Medicine, 358,* 1672–1681.

Ullman, S. E., & Filipas, H. H. (2005). Gender differences in social reactions to abuse disclosures, post-abuse coping, and PTSD of child sexual abuse survivors. *Child Abuse and Neglect, 29,* 767–782.

Ungerer, J. A., & Sigman, M. (1984). The relation of play and sensorimotor behavior to language in the second year. *Child Development, 55*(4), 1448–1455.

UNICEF. (2005). *Report Card No. 6: Child poverty in rich countries 2005.* Retrieved from http://unicef-icdc.org/publications/pdf/repcard6e.pdf

UNICEF. (2007). *The state of the world's children 2007.* Retrieved from http://www.unicef.org/sowc07/docs/sowc07.pdf

United Cerebral Palsy. (2007). *Vocabulary tips: Cerebral palsy—Facts & figures.* Retrieved from http://www.ucp.org/ucp_generaldoc.cfm/1/9/37/37–37/447

United Nations Committee on the Rights of the Child (CRC). (1999). *Report of the UN Committee on the Rights of the Child, Twentieth Session (Geneva, 11–29 January 1999).* Retrieved from http://www.unhcr.org/refworld/docid/3f4780674.html

Urberg, K. A., Degirmencioglu, S. M., & Tolson, J. M. (1998). Adolescent friendship selection and termination: The role of similarity. *Journal of Social and Personal Relationships, 15*(5), 703–710.

U.S. Census Bureau. (2006). *Grandparents day 2006: Sept. 10.* Retrieved from http://www.census.gov/newsroom/releases/archives/facts_for_features_special_editions/cb06-ff13.html

U.S. Census Bureau. (2007). *Current population survey—POV02: People in families by family structure, age, and sex, iterated by income-to-poverty ratio and race: 2007 below 100% of poverty—All races.* Retrieved from http://pubdb3.census.gov/macro/032008/pov/new02_100_01.htm

U.S. Census Bureau. (2008a). *Current population survey (CPS)—Definitions and explanations.* Retrieved from http://www.census.gov/population/www/cps/cpsdef.html

U.S. Census Bureau. (2008b). *Father's day: June 15, 2008.* Retrieved from http://www.census.gov/newsroom/releases/pdf/cb08-ff09.pdf

U.S. Census Bureau. (2008c). *Poverty.* Retrieved from http://www.census.gov/hhes/www/poverty/histpov/perindex.html

U.S. Census Bureau. (2008d). *Who's minding the kids? Child care arrangements: Spring 2005 detailed tables.* Retrieved from http://www.census.gov/population/www/socdemo/child/ppl-2005.html

U.S. Department of Agriculture. (2009a). *Dietary guidelines.* Retrieved from http://www.mypyramid.gov/guidelines/index.html

U.S. Department of Agriculture. (2009b). *Inside the pyramid.* Retrieved from http://www.mypyramid.gov/pyramid/index.html

U.S. Department of Commerce, Census Bureau, Current Population Survey (CPS), October (1972–2007). Dropout and completion rates in the United States: 2007. Retrieved from http://nces.ed.gov/pubs2009/dropout07/figures/figure_01.asp

U.S. Department of Education. (2006). *Secretary Spellings announces more choices in single sex education.* Retrieved from http://www.ed.gov/news/pressreleases/2006/10/10242006.html

U.S. Department of Education. (2007, February 12). *IDEA 2004 News, Information and Resources.* Retrieved from http://www.ed.gov/policy/speced/guid/idea/idea2004.html

U.S. Department of Energy Genome Programs. (2003). *Genomics and its impact on science and society: The human genome project and beyond (2008).* Retrieved from http://www.ornl.gov/sci/techresources/Human_Genome/publicat/primer/index.shtml

U.S. Department of Health and Human Services. (1999). *Mental health: A report of the Surgeon General.* Rockville, MD: National Institutes of Mental Health.

U.S. Department of Health and Human Services. (2005a). *Code of federal regulations.* Retrieved from http://www.hhs.gov/ohrp/humansubjects/guidance/45cfr46.htm

U.S. Department of Health and Human Services. (2005b). *U.S. Surgeon General releases advisory on alcohol use in pregnancy.* Health and Human Services Press Release. Retrieved from http://www.surgeongeneral.gov/pressreleases/sg02222005.html

U.S. Department of Health and Human Services. (2006). *Child maltreatment 2006.* Washington, DC: U.S. Government Printing Office.

U.S. Department of Health and Human Services. (2007, November 5). *Fact sheet: Positive youth development.* Retrieved from http://www.acf.hhs.gov/programs/fysb/content/positiveyouth/factsheet.htm

U.S. Department of Health and Human Services. (2008a). *Child maltreatment 2008.* Washington, DC: U.S. Government Printing Office.

U.S. Department of Health and Human Services. (2008b). *National survey on drug use and health: Alcohol use among pregnant women and recent mothers, 2002–2007.* Retrieved from http://www.oas.samhsa.gov/2k8/pregnantAlc/pregnantAlc.htm

U.S. Department of Health and Human Services. (2008c). *Protective factors.* Retrieved from http://www.childwelfare.gov/can/factors/protective.cfm

U.S. Department of Health and Human Services. (2008d). *State requirements for child-staff ratios and maximum group sizes for child care centers in 2007.* Retrieved from http://nccic.acf.hhs.gov/pubs/cclicensingreq/ratios.html

U.S. Department of Health and Human Services. (2009). *Sexually transmitted infections: Overview.* Retrieved from http://www.womenshealth.gov/faq/sexually-transmitted-infections.cfm

U.S. Department of Health and Human Services. (n.d.a). *A healthy start: Begin before baby's born.* Retrieved from http://mchb.hrsa.gov/programs/womeninfants/prenatal.htm

U.S. Department of Health and Human Services. (n.d.b). *Panel study of income dynamics child development supplement (PSID-CDS).* Retrieved from http://www.acf.hhs.gov/programs/opre/other_resrch/eval_data/reports/common_constructs/com_appb_incdyn.html

U.S. Department of Health and Human Services, Health Resources and Services Administration, Maternal and Child Health Bureau. (2004). *Child Health USA 2004: International infant mortality rates.* Rockville, MD: Author. Available from http://mchb.hrsa.gov/mchirc/chusa_04/pages/0405iimr.htm

U.S. Department of Health and Human Services, Health Resources and Services Administration, Maternal and Child Health Bureau. (2008–2009). *Child Health USA 2008–2009.* Rockville, MD: Author.

U.S. Department of Labor. (2010). *Fact Sheet #28: The Family and Medical Leave Act of 1993.* Retrieved from http://www.dol.gov/whd/regs/compliance/whdfs28.htm

U.S. Environmental Protection Agency. (2008). *Measure D5: Cancer incidence and mortality.* Retrieved from http://www.epa.gov/

economics/children/child_illness/d5-sources .html

U.S. Environmental Protection Agency. (2009a). *Children's health protection.* Retrieved from http://yosemite.epa.gov/ochp/ochpweb.nsf/content/homepage.htm

U.S. Environmental Protection Agency. (2009b). *Measure E5: Environmental tobacco smoke: Smoking in the home.* Retrieved from http://www.epa.gov/opeedweb/children/contaminants/e5-graph.html

U.S. Food and Drug Administration. (2008a). *A parent's guide to kids' vaccines.* Retrieved from http://www.fda.gov/ForConsumers/ConsumerUpdates/ucm048750.htm

U.S. Food and Drug Administration. (2008b). *FDA releases recommendations regarding use of over-the-counter cough and cold products.* Retrieved from http://www.fda.gov/NewsEvents/Newsroom/PressAnnouncements/2008/ucm116839.htm

U.S. National Library of Medicine. (2007). *Mental retardation.* Retrieved from http://www.nlm.nih.gov/medlineplus/ency/article/001523.htm

U.S. National Library of Medicine. (n.d.). *DNA structure.* Retrieved from http://medpediamedia.com/u/Dnastructure.jpg/Dnastructure.jpg

van der Veer, R. (2007). *Lev Vygotsky.* New York, NY: Continuum.

van Deutekom, J. C., Janson, A. A., Ginjaar, I. B., Frankhuizen, W. S., Aartsma-Rus, A., Bremmer-Bout, M., . . . van Ommen, G. -J. B. (2007). **New** *England Journal of Medicine,* 357(26), 2677–2686.

Van Evra, J. (2004). *Television and child development* (3rd ed.). Mahwah, NJ: Erlbaum.

Van Gelder, B. M., Tijhuis, M. A. R., Kalmijn, S., Giampaoli, S., Nissinen, A., & Kromhout, D. (2004). Physical activity in relation to cognitive decline in elderly men: The FINE Study. *Neurology, 63*(12), 2316–2321.

van Jaarsveld, C. H. M., Fidler, J. A., Simon, A. E., & Wardle, J. (2007). Persistent impact of pubertal timing on trends in smoking, food choice, activity, and stress in adolescence. *Psychosomatic Medicine, 69*(8), 798–806.

van Wel, F. (1994). "I count my parents among my best friends": Youths' bonds with parents and friends in the Netherlands. *Journal of Marriage and Family, 56*(4), 835–843.

Vaillancourt, T., Miller, J. L., Fagbemi, J., Cote, S., & Tremblay, R. E. (2007). Trajectories and predictors of indirect aggression: Results from a nationally representative longitudinal study of Canadian children aged 2–10. *Aggressive Behavior, 33*(4), 314–316.

Valkenburg, P. M., & Peter, J. (2007). Online communication and adolescent well-being: Testing the stimulation versus the displacement hypothesis. *Journal of Computer-Mediated Communication, 12*(4), 1169–1182.

Vance, E. (2007). Cuteness: We know it when we see it. *Observer, 20*(6), 8.

Vander Ven, T. M., Cullen, F. T., Carrozza, M. A., & Wright, J. P. (2001). Home alone: The impact of maternal employment on delinquency. *Social Problems, 48*(2), 236–257.

VanderBerg, K. A. (2007). Individualized developmental care for high risk newborns in the NICU: A practice guideline. *Early Human Development, 83*(7), 433–442.

Vandewater, E. A., Rideout, V. J., Wartella, E. A., Huang, X., Lee, J. H., & Shim, M. (2007). Digital childhood: Electronic media and technology use among infants, toddlers, and preschoolers. *Pediatrics, 119,* e1006–e1015.

Vandivere, S., Malm, K., & Radel, L. (2009). *Adoption USA: A chartbook based on the 2007 National Survey of Adoptive Parents.* Washington, DC: U.S. Department of Health and Human Services, Office of the Assistant Secretary for Planning and Evaluation. Retrieved from http://aspe.hhs.gov/hsp/09/NSAP/chartbook/index.pdf

Vargas, J. S. (2005). *A brief biography of B.F. Skinner.* Retrieved from http://www.bfskinner.org/BFSkinner/AboutSkinner.html

Vasilyeva, M., Waterfall, H., & Huttenlocher, J. (2008). Emergence of syntax: Commonalities and differences across children. *Developmental Science, 11*(1), 84–97.

Ventura, S. J. (2009). *NCHS data brief: Changing patterns of nonmaternal childbearing in the United States.* Centers for Disease Control and Prevention, National Center for Health Statistics. Retrieved from http://www.cdc.gov/nchs/data/databriefs/db18.htm

Vereijken, C. M. J. L., Riksen-Walraven, J. M., & Van Lieshout, C. F. M. (1997). Mother–infant relationships in Japan: Attachment, dependency, and amae. *Journal of Cross-Cultural Psychology, 28*(4), 442–462.

Vialle, W., Ashton, T., Carlon, G., & Rankin, F. (2001). Acceleration: A coat of many colours. *Roeper Review, 24*(1), 14–19.

Vickers, B. (2005). Cognitive model of the maintenance and treatment of post-traumatic stress. *Clinical Child Psychology and Psychiatry, 10*(2), 217–234.

Vinden, P. G. (1999). Children's understanding of mind and emotion: A multi-culture study. *Cognition and Emotion, 13*(1), 19–48.

Vinden, P. G. (2001). Parenting attitudes and children's understanding of mind: A comparison of Korean American and Anglo-American families. *Cognitive Development, 16,* 793–809.

Volk, A. A., Lukjanczuk, J. M., & Quinsey, V. L. (2005). Influence of infant and child facial cues of low body weight on adults' ratings of adoption preference, cuteness, and health. *Infant Mental Health Journal, 26*(5), 459–469.

Volkmar, F. R., & Tsatsanis, K. (2002). Psychosis and psychotic conditions in childhood and adolescence. In D. T. Marsh & M. A. Fristad (Eds.), *Handbook of serious emotional disturbance* (pp. 266–283). New York, NY: Wiley.

Volterra, V., Caselli, M. C., Capirci, O., & Pizzuto, E. (2005). Gesture and the emergence and development of language. In M. Tomasello & D. I. Slobin (Eds.), *Beyond nature-nurture* (pp. 3–40). Mahwah, NJ: Erlbaum.

Von Drehle, D. (2007). The myth about boys. *Time, 170*(6). Retrieved from http://www.time.com/time/magazine/article/0,9171,1647452,00.html

von Kries, R., Koletzko, B., Sauerwald, T., von Mutius, E., Barnert, D., Grunert, V., & von Voss, H. (1999). Breast feeding and obesity: Cross-sectional study. *British Medical Journal, 319,* 147–150.

Voyer, D., Voyer, S., & Bryden, M. P. (1995). Magnitude of sex differences in spatial abilities: A meta-analysis and consideration of critical variables. *Psychological Bulletin, 117*(2), 250–270.

Vygotsky, L. S. (1962). *Thought and language.* Cambridge, MA: MIT Press. (Original work published in 1934)

Vygotsky, L. S. (1978a). Interaction between learning and development. In M. Cole, V. John-Steiner, & E. Souberman (Eds.), *Mind in society: The development of higher psychological processes* (pp. 79–91). Cambridge, MA: Harvard University Press.

Vygotsky, L. S. (1978b). *Mind in society.* Cambridge, MA: Harvard University Press.

Vygotsky, L. S. (1986). *Thought and language.* Cambridge, MA: MIT Press.

Waddington, C. H. (1942). Canalization of development and the inheritance of acquired characters. *Nature, 150,* 563–564.

Wadhwa, P. D. (2005). Psychoneuroendocrine processes in human pregnancy influence fetal development and health. *Psychoneuroendocrinology, 30*(8), 724–743.

Wadsworth, B. J. (1996). *Piaget's theory of cognitive and affective development.* White Plains, NY: Longman.

Wakefield, A. J., Murch, S. H., Anthony, A., Linnell, J., Casson, D. M., Malik, M., . . . Walker-Smith, J. A. (1998). Ileal-lymphoid-nodular hyperplasia, non-specific colitis, and pervasive developmental disorder in children. *Lancet, 351*(9103), 637–641.

Walcott, D. D., Pratt, H. D., & Patel, D. R. (2003). Adolescents and eating disorders: Gender, racial ethnic, sociocultural and socioeconomic issues. *Journal of Adolescent Research, 18*(3), 223–243.

Walker, L. J. (1984). Sex differences in the development of moral reasoning: A critical review. *Child Development, 55*(3), 677–691.

Walker, S. K. (2005). Use of parenting newsletter series and other child-rearing information sources by mothers of infants. *Family and Consumer Sciences Research Journal, 34*(2), 153–172.

Wallach, M. A., & Kogan, N. (1965). *Modes of thinking in young children: A study of the creativity-intelligence distinction.* New York, NY: Holt, Rinehart & Winston.

Wallis, A. L., Cody, B. E., & Mickalide, A. D. (2003). Report to the nation: Trends in unintentional childhood injury mortality, 1987–2000. Washington, DC: National SAFE KIDS Campaign.

Walsh, W. B., & Betz, N. E. (1995). *Tests and assessment* (3rd ed.). Englewood Cliffs, NJ: Prentice Hall.

Walum, H., Westberg, L., Henningsson, S., Neiderhiser, J. M., Reiss, D., Igl, W., . . . Lichtenstein, P. (2008). Genetic variation in the vasopressin receptor 1a gene (AVPR1A) associates with pair-bonding behavior in humans. *Proceedings of the National Academy of Sciences, 105*(37), 14153–14156.

Wang, C. T, & Holton, J. (2007). *Total estimated cost of child abuse and neglect in the United States.* Retrieved from http://www.preventchildabuse.org/about_us/media_releases/pcaa_pew_economic_impact_study_final.pdf

Wang, J., Iannotti, R. J., & Nansel, T. R. (2009). School bullying among adolescents in the United States: Physical, verbal, relational, and cyber. *Journal of Adolescent Health, 45*(4), 368–375.

Wang, Q. (2004). The emergence of cultural self-constructs: Autobiographical memory and self-description in European American and Chinese children. *Developmental Psychology, 40*(1), 3–15.

Wang, Q. (2006). Culture and the development of self-knowledge. *Current Directions in Psychological Science, 15*(4), 182–187.

Wappner, R., Cho, S., Kronmal, R. A., Schuett, V., & Seashore, M. R. (1999). Management of phenylketonuria for optimal outcome: A review of guidelines for phenylketonuria management and a report of surveys of parents, patients, and clinic directors. *Pediatrics, 104*(6), e68.

Ward, L. M. (2004). Wading through the stereotypes: Positive and negative associations between media use and black adolescents' conception of self. *Developmental Psychology, 40*(2), 284–294.

Ward, L. M., & Friedman, K. (2006). Using TV as a guide: Associations between television viewing and adolescents' sexual attitudes and behavior. *Journal of Research on Adolescence, 16*(1), 133–156.

Wargo, E. (2007). Vive la difference (not la deficit). *APS Observer, 20*(7). Retrieved from http://www.psychologicalscience.org/observer/getArticle.cfm?id=2189

Wasden, L. (n.d.). *ProtecTeens: Family contract for Internet safety.* Office of the Attorney General. Retrieved from http://www2.state .id.us/ag/protecteens/Family_Internet_Contract.pdf

Wassenberg, R., Hendriksen, J. G. M., Hurks, P. P. M., Feron, F. J. M., Keulers, E. H. H., Vles, J. S. H., & Jolles, J. (2008). Development of inattention, impulsivity, and processing speed as measured by the d2 Test: Results of a large cross-sectional study in children aged 7–13. *Child Neuropsychology, 14*(3), 195–210.

Waterhouse, L. (2006). Multiple intelligences, the Mozart effect, and emotional intelligence: A critical review. *Educational Psychologist, 41*(4), 207–225.

Waters, H. S., Rodrigues, L. M., & Ridgeway, D. (1998). Cognitive underpinnings of narrative attachment assessment. *Journal of Experimental Child Psychology, 71*, 211–234.

Waters, H. S., & Waters, E. (2006). The attachment working models concept: Among other things, we build script-like representations of secure base experiences. *Attachment & Human Development, 8*, 185–198.

Watson, J. B. (1928). *Psychological care of infant and child.* New York, NY: Norton.

Watson, J. B. (1930). *Behaviorism.* New York, NY: Norton.

Watson, J. B. (1994). Psychology as the behaviorist views it. *Psychological Review, 101*(2), 248–253. (Original work published in 1913)

Watson, J. B., & Rayner, R. (1920). Conditioned emotional reactions. *Journal of Experimental Psychology, 3*(1), 1–14.

Watson, J. D. (2003). *DNA: The secret of life.* New York, NY: Knopf.

Watson, M. W., & Fischer, K. W. (1977). A developmental sequence of agent use in late infancy. *Child Development, 48*, 828–836.

Watson, M. W., & Fischer, K. W. (1980). Development of social roles in elicited and spontaneous behavior during the preschool years. *Developmental Psychology, 16*(5), 483–494.

Wauterickx, N., Gouwy, A., & Bracke, P. (2006). Parental divorce and depression: Long-term effects on adult children. *Journal of Divorce & Remarriage, 45*(3–4), 43–68.

Waxman, S. R., & Kosowski, T. D. (1990). Nouns mark category relations: Toddlers' and preschoolers' word-learning biases. *Child Development, 61*(5), 1461–1473.

Wechsler, D. (2003). *Wechsler intelligence scale for children* (4th ed.). San Antonio, TX: Pearson.

Wechsler, H., Lee, J. E., Kuo, M., Seibring, M., Nelson, T. F., & Lee, H. (2002). Trends in college binge drinking during a period of increased prevention efforts. *Journal of American College Health, 50*(5), 203–217.

Weems, C. F. (2008). Developmental trajectories of childhood anxiety: Identifying continuity and change in anxious emotion. *Developmental Review, 28*(4), 488–502.

Weimer, J. (2001). *The economic benefits of breastfeeding: A review and analysis* [Food Assistance and Nutrition Research Report No. 13]. Washington, DC: U.S. Department of Agriculture Economic Research Service.

Weinfield, N. S., Whaley, G. J. L., & Egeland, B. (2004). Continuity, discontinuity, and coherence in attachment from infancy to late adolescence: Sequelae of organization and disorganization. *Attachment and Human Development, 6*(1), 73–97.

Weinstock, H., Berman, S., & Cates, W., Jr. (2004). Sexually transmitted diseases among American youth: Incidence and prevalence estimates, 2000. *Perspectives on Sexual and Reproductive Health, 36*(1), 6–10.

Weir, K. N. (2007). Using integrative play therapy with adoptive families to treat reactive attachment disorder: A case example. *Journal of Family Psychotherapy, 18*(4), 1–16.

Wellman, H. (1990). *The child's theory of mind.* Cambridge, MA: MIT Press.

Wellman, H. M., Cross, D., & Watson, J. (2001). Meta-analysis of theory-of-mind development: The truth about false belief. *Child Development, 72*(3), 655–684.

Weltzin, T. E., Weisensel, N., Franczyk, D., Burnett, K., Klitz, C., & Bean, P. (2005). Eating disorders in men: Update. *Journal of Men's Health and Gender, 2*(2), 186–193.

Wenger, A., & Fowers, B. J. (2008). Positive illusion in parenting: Every child is above average. *Journal of Applied Social Psychology, 38*(3), 611–634.

Wenning, R., Herdman, P. A., & Smith, N. (2003). *No child left behind: Testing, reporting and accountability.* ERIC Document (ED480994).

Wenning, R., Herdman, P. A., Smith, N., McMahon, N., & Washington, K. (2003). *No child left behind: Testing, reporting and accountability* (ED480994). Available from ERIC at http://www.eric.ed.gov/ERICDocs/data/ericdocs2sql/content_storage_01/0000019b/80/1b/6d/0f.pdf

Werebe, M. G., & Baudonniere, P. (1991). Social pretend play among friends and familiar preschoolers. *International Journal of Behavioral Development, 14*(4), 411–428.

Werner, D., Sanders, D., & Brelsford, A. (1997). *Questioning the solution: The politics of primary health care.* Palo Alto, CA: Healthwrights.

Werner, E. E. (1992). The children of Kauai: Resiliency and recovery in adolescence and adulthood. *Journal of Adolescent Health, 13*(4), 262–268.

Werner, E. E. (2005). What can we learn about resilience from large-scale longitudinal studies? In S. Goldstein & R. B. Brooks (Eds.), *Handbook of resilience in children* (pp. 91–106). New York, NY: Springer.

Werner, E. E., & Smith, R. S. (1985). *Vulnerable but invincible: A study of resilient children.* New York, NY: McGraw-Hill.

Wertsch, J. V. (1985). *Vygotsky and the social formation of mind.* Cambridge, MA: Harvard University Press.

Westling, E., Andrews, J. A., Hampson, S. E., & Peterson, M. (2008). Pubertal timing and substance use: The effects of gender, parental monitoring and deviant peers. *Journal of Adolescent Health, 42*(6), 555–563.

Wetzels, C. (2001). *Squeezing birth into working life: Household data panel analyses comparing Germany, Great Britain, Sweden and the Netherlands.* Aldershot, UK: Ashgate.

Whitehurst, G. J. (1992). *Dialogic reading: An effective way to read to preschoolers.* Retrieved from http://www.readingrockets.org/arti cle/400

Whitehurst, G. J., Falco, F. L., Lonigan, C. J., Fischel, J. E., DeBaryshe, B. D.,

Valdez-Menchaca, M. C., & Caulfield, M. (1988). Accelerating language development through picture book reading. *Developmental Psychology, 24*(4), 552–559.

Whiteside, M. F., & Becker, B. J. (2000). Parental factors and the young child's post-divorce adjustment: A meta-analysis with implications for parenting arrangements. *Journal of Family Psychology, 14,* 5–26.

Whiting, B., & Edwards, C. P. (1973). A cross-cultural analysis of sex differences in the behavior of children aged three through 11. *Journal of Social Psychology, 91*(2), 171–188.

Whitley, B. E. (1983). Sex role orientation and self-esteem: A critical meta-analytic review. *Journal of Personality and Social Psychology, 44*(4), 765–778.

Whitman, A. (1980). Jean Piaget dies in Geneva at 84. *The New York Times.* Retrieved from http://www.nytimes.com/learning/general/onthisday/bday/0809.html

Wickrama, K. A. T., Wickrama, K. A. S., & Bryant, C. M. (2006). Community influence on adolescent obesity: Race/ethnic differences. *Journal of Youth and Adolescence, 35*(4), 641–651.

Wiederman, M. W., & Allgeier, E. R. (1992). Gender differences in mate selection criteria: Sociobiological or socioeconomic explanation? *Ethology & Sociobiology, 13*(2), 115–124.

Wier, L., Miller, A., & Steiner, C. (2009). *Sports injuries in children requiring hospital emergency care, 2006.* HCUP Statistical Brief #75. Rockville, MD: Agency for Healthcare Research and Quality. Available from www.hcup-us.ahrq.gov/reports/statbriefs/sb75.jsp

Wierzbicka, A. (1986). Human emotions: Universal or culture-specific? *American Anthropologist, 88*(3), 584–594.

Wiesner, M., & Ittel, A. (2002). Relation of pubertal timing and depressive symptoms to substance use in early adolescence. *Journal of Early Adolescence, 22*(1), 5–23.

Wigfield, A., Eccles, J. S., Yoon, K. S., Harold, R. D., Abreton, A. J. A., Freedman-Doan, C., & Blumenfeld, P. C. (1997). Change in children's competence beliefs and subjective task values across the elementary school years: A 3-year study. *Journal of Educational Psychology, 89*(3), 451–469.

Wilkins, J. S. (1998). What's in a meme? Reflections from the perspective of the history and philosophy of evolutionary biology. *Journal of Memetics—Evolutionary Models of Information Transmission, 2.* Retrieved from http://cfpm.org/jom-emit/1998/vol2/wilkins_js.html

Williams, K., & Umberson, D. (1999). Medical technology and childbirth: Experiences of expectant mothers and fathers. *Sex Roles, 21*(3–4), 147–168.

Williams-Rautiolla, S. (2008). *Cooney, Joan Ganz.* The Museum of Broadcast Communications. Retrieved from http://www.museum.tv/archives/etv/C/htmlC/cooneyjoan/cooneyjoan.htm

Williamson, D. M., Abe, K., Bean, C., Ferré, C., Henderson, Z., & Lackritz, E. (2008). Current research in preterm birth. *Journal of Women's Health, 17*(10), 1545–1549.

Wills, T. A., Sargent J. D., Stoolmiller, M., Gibbons, F. X., & Gerrard, M. (2008). Movie smoking exposure and smoking onset: A longitudinal study of mediation processes in a representative sample of U.S. adolescents. *Psychology of Addictive Behaviors, 22*(2), 269–277.

Wilson, E. O. (1975). *Sociobiology: The new synthesis.* Cambridge, MA: Harvard University Press.

Wineburg, S. S. (1987a). Does research count in the lives of social scientists? *Educational Researcher, 26,* 42–44.

Wineburg, S. S. (1987b). The self-fulfillment of the self-fulfilling prophecy. *Educational Researcher, 16,* 28–37.

Winerman, L. (2005). The mind's mirror. *Monitor on Psychology, 36*(9).

Winn, W. (2004). Cognitive perspectives in psychology. In D. H. Jonassen (Ed.), *Handbook of research for educational communications and technology* (2nd ed., pp. 79–112). New York, NY: Simon & Schuster.

Winsler, A., Madigan, A. L., & Aquilino, S. A. (2005). Correspondence between maternal and paternal parenting styles in early childhood. *Early Childhood Research Quarterly, 20*(1), 1–12.

Winsler, A., & Naglieri, J. (2003). Overt and covert verbal problem-solving strategies: Developmental trends in use, awareness, and relations with task performance in children aged 5 to 17. *Child Development, 74*(3), 659–678.

Wolak, J., Finkelhor, D., Mitchell, K. J., & Ybarra, M. L. (2008). Online "predators" and their victims: Myths, realities and implications for prevention treatment. *American Psychologist, 63*(2), 111–128.

Wolfe, D. A., & Mash, E. J. (Eds.). (2006). *Behavioral and emotional disorders in adolescents: Nature, assessment, and treatment.* New York, NY: Guilford.

Wolters Kluwer Health. (2009). *Professional guide to diseases* (9th ed.). Philadelphia, PA: Lippincott, Williams & Wilkins.

Wong, C. A., Eccles, J. S., & Sameroff, A. (2003). The influence of ethnic discrimination and ethnic identification on African American adolescents' school and socioemotional adjustment. *Journal of Personality, 71*(6), 1197–1232.

Woodward, A. L. (2009). Infants' grasp of others' intentions. *Current Directions in Psychological Science, 18*(1), 53–57.

Woodward, A. L., Markman, E. M., & Fitzsimmons, C. M. (1994). Rapid word learning in 13- and 18-month-olds. *Developmental Psychology, 30*(4), 553–566.

Wright, J. C., Huston, A. C., Scantlin, R., & Kotler, J. (2001). The Early Window Project: *Sesame Street* prepares children for school. In S. M. Fisch & R. T. Truglio (Eds.), *"G" is for growing—Thirty years of research on children and* Sesame Street (pp. 97–114). Mahwah, NJ: Erlbaum.

Wynn, K. (1992). Addition and subtraction by human infants. *Nature, 358*(6389), 749–750.

Yates, A. (1991). Childhood sexuality. In M. Lewis (Ed.), *Child and adolescent psychiatry* (pp. 195–215). Baltimore, MD: Williams & Wilkins.

Yatvin, J. (2002). Babes in the woods: The wanderings of the National Reading Panel. *Phi Delta Kappan, 83*(5), 364–369.

Yonkers, K. A., & Gurguis, G. (1995). Gender differences in the prevalence and expression of anxiety disorders. In M. V. Seeman (Ed.), *Gender and psychopathology* (pp. 113–130). Washington, DC: American Psychiatric Press.

Youngstrom, E. (2007). Pediatric bipolar disorder. In E. J. Mash & R. A. Barkley (Eds.), *Assessment of childhood disorders* (pp. 253–304). New York, NY: Guilford.

Yurgelun-Todd, D. (2007). Emotional and cognitive changes during adolescence. *Current Opinion in Neurobiology, 17*(2), 251–257.

Zadok-Levitan, O., & Bronz, R. (2004). Adults with learning disabilities who are successful at work. *Man and Work, 13*(1–2), 44–60, 69–70.

Zakriski, A. L., Wright, J. C., & Underwood, M. K. (2005). Gender similarities and differences in children's social behavior: Finding personality in contextualized patterns of adaptation. *Journal of Personality and Social Psychology, 88*(5), 844–855.

Zarbatany, L., McDougall, P., & Hymel, S. (2000). Gender-differentiated experience in the peer culture: Links to intimacy in preadolescence. *Social Development, 9*(1), 62–79.

Zeanah, C. H., Smyke, A. T., Koga, S. F., Carlson, E., & Bucharest Early Intervention Project Core Group. (2005). Attachment in institutionalized and community children in Romania. *Child Development, 76*(5), 1015–1028.

Zelazo, N. A., Zelazo, P. R., Cohen, K. M., & Zelazo, P. D. (1993). Specificity of practice effects on elementary neuromotor patterns. *Developmental Psychology, 29*(4), 686–691.

Zettergren, P. (2005). Childhood peer status as predictor of midadolescence peer situation and social adjustment. *Psychology in the Schools, 42*(7), 745–757.

Zhang, H. (1988). Psychological measurement in China. *International Journal of Psychology, 23,* 101–117.

Zhang, T., & Meaney, M. J. (2010). Epigenetics and the environmental regulation of the genome and its function. *Annual Review of Psychology, 61,* 439–466.

Zhou, Q., Hofer, C., Eisenberg, N., Reiser, M., Spinrad, T. L., & Fabes, R. A. (2007). The developmental trajectories of attention focusing, attentional and behavioral persistence, and externalizing problems during school-age years. *Developmental Psychology, 43*(2), 369–385.

Zigler, E., & Bishop-Josef, S. J. (2006). The cognitive child versus the whole child: Lessons from 40 years of Head Start. In D. G. Singer, R. M. Golinkoff, & K. Hirsh-Pasek (Eds.), *Play=learning* (pp. 15–35). New York, NY: Oxford University Press.

Zimmerman, F. J., & Christakis, D. A. (2007). Associations between content types of early media exposure and subsequent attentional problems. *Pediatrics, 120*(5), 986–992.

Zimmerman, F. J., Christakis, D. A., & Meltzoff, A. N. (2007). Associations between media viewing and language development in children under age two years. *Journal of Pediatrics, 151,* 364–368.

Zimmerman, L., & Reef, S. E. (2001). Incidence of congenital rubella syndrome at a hospital serving a predominantly Hispanic population, El Paso, Texas. *Pediatrics, 107*(3), e40.

Zimmerman, M. A., Bingenheimer, J. B., & Notaro, P. C. (2002). Natural mentors and adolescent resiliency: A study with urban youth. *American Journal of Community Psychology, 30*(2), 221–243.

Zook, R. (2010). *Why Computer Engineer Barbie is good for women in tech.* Retrieved from http://mashable.com/2010/03/09/computer-engineer-barbie/

Author Index

Subject Index

Supporting researchers for more than 40 years

Research methods have always been at the core of SAGE's publishing program. Founder Sara Miller McCune published SAGE's first methods book, *Public Policy Evaluation*, in 1970. Soon after, she launched the *Quantitative Applications in the Social Sciences* series—affectionately known as the "little green books."

Always at the forefront of developing and supporting new approaches in methods, SAGE published early groundbreaking texts and journals in the fields of qualitative methods and evaluation.

Today, more than 40 years and two million little green books later, SAGE continues to push the boundaries with a growing list of more than 1,200 research methods books, journals, and reference works across the social, behavioral, and health sciences. Its imprints—Pine Forge Press, home of innovative textbooks in sociology, and Corwin, publisher of PreK–12 resources for teachers and administrators—broaden SAGE's range of offerings in methods. SAGE further extended its impact in 2008 when it acquired CQ Press and its best-selling and highly respected political science research methods list.

From qualitative, quantitative, and mixed methods to evaluation, SAGE is the essential resource for academics and practitioners looking for the latest methods by leading scholars.

For more information, visit **www.sagepub.com**.